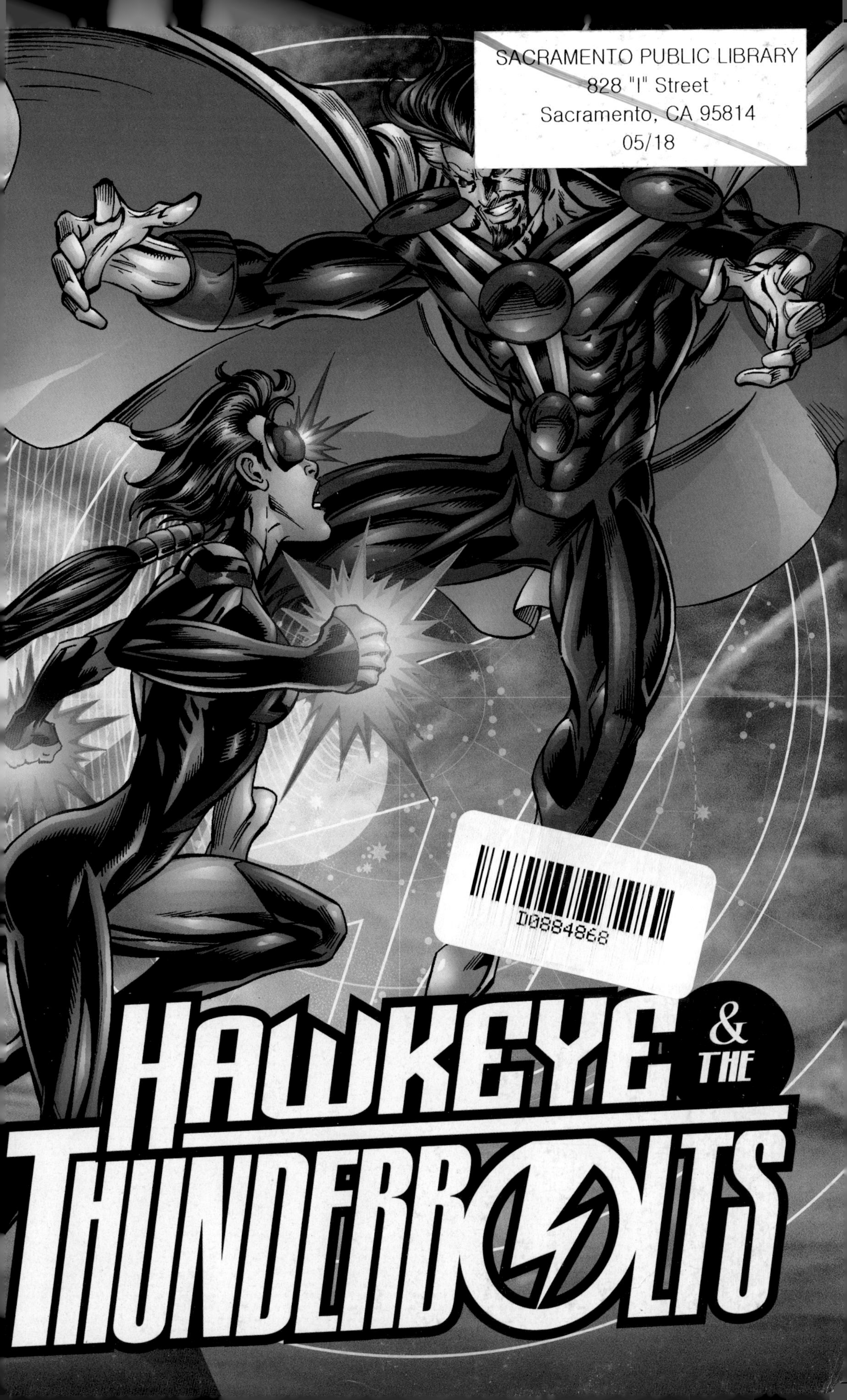
HAWKEYE & THE THUNDERBOLTS

MARVEL'S MOST WANTED: HAWKEYE & THE THUNDERBOLTS

WRITERS: KURT BUSIEK, JOE CASEY & FABIAN NICIEZA

PENCILERS: MARK BAGLEY, LEONARDO MANCO & NORM BREYFOGLE WITH RICHARD HOWELL

INKERS: SCOTT HANNA, BOB WIACEK, AL VEY, LEONARDO MANCO, GREG ADAMS & NORM BREYFOGLE WITH RICHARD HOWELL

COLORISTS: JOE ROSAS & TOM SMITH

LETTERERS: RICHARD STARKINGS & COMICRAFT WITH SAIDA TEMOFONTE, TROY PETERI, JASON LEVINE & OSCAR GONGORA

ASSISTANT EDITOR: GREGG SCHIGIEL

EDITOR: TOM BREVOORT

FRONT COVER ARTISTS: MARK BAGLEY, SCOTT HANNA AND TANYA & RICHARD HORIE
BACK COVER ARTISTS: MARK BAGLEY & SCOTT HANNA

COLLECTION EDITOR: MARK D. BEAZLEY
ASSOCIATE EDITOR: SARAH BRUNSTAD
ASSOCIATE MANAGING EDITOR, DIGITAL ASSETS: JOE HOCHSTEIN
ASSOCIATE MANAGING EDITOR: ALEX STARBUCK
EDITOR, SPECIAL PROJECTS: JENNIFER GRÜNWALD
VP, PRODUCTION & SPECIAL PROJECTS: JEFF YOUNGQUIST
RESEARCH: JOHN RHETT THOMAS
LAYOUT: JEPH YORK
PRODUCTION: RYAN DEVALL
BOOK DESIGNER: RODOLFO MURAGUCHI
SVP PRINT, SALES & MARKETING: DAVID GABRIEL
EDITOR IN CHIEF: AXEL ALONSO
CHIEF CREATIVE OFFICER: JOE QUESADA
PUBLISHER: DAN BUCKLEY
EXECUTIVE PRODUCER: ALAN FINE

HAWKEYE & THE THUNDERBOLTS VOL. 1. Contains material originally published in magazine form as THUNDERBOLTS #23-37 and ANNUAL 2000, and AVENGERS ANNUAL 2000. First printing 2016. ISBN# 978-0-7851-9528-3. Published by MARVEL WORLDWIDE, INC., a subsidiary of MARVEL ENTERTAINMENT, LLC. OFFICE OF PUBLICATION: 135 West 50th Street, New York, NY 10020. Copyright © 2016 MARVEL No similarity between any of the names, characters, persons, and/or institutions in this magazine with those of any living or dead person or institution is intended, and any such similarity which may exist is purely coincidental. **Printed in the U.S.A.** ALAN FINE, President, Marvel Entertainment; DAN BUCKLEY, President, TV, Publishing & Brand Management; JOE QUESADA, Chief Creative Officer; TOM BREVOORT, SVP of Publishing; DAVID BOGART, SVP of Business Affairs & Operations, Publishing & Partnership; C.B. CEBULSKI, VP of Brand Management & Development, Asia; DAVID GABRIEL, SVP of Sales & Marketing, Publishing; JEFF YOUNGQUIST, VP of Production & Special Projects; DAN CARR, Executive Director of Publishing Technology; ALEX MORALES, Director of Publishing Operations; SUSAN CRESPI, Production Manager; STAN LEE, Chairman Emeritus. For information regarding advertising in Marvel Comics or on Marvel.com, please contact Vit DeBellis, Integrated Sales Manager, at vdebellis@marvel.com. Marvel subscription inquiries, please call 888-511-5480. **Manufactured between 2/26/2016 and 4/4/2016 by R.R. DONNELLEY, INC., SALEM, VA, USA.**

10 9 8 7 6 5 4 3 2 1

PREVIOUSLY...

Months ago, the Avengers and Fantastic Four vanished, seemingly killed in battle against the villainous Onslaught. For the world, this was a tragedy — but for Baron Zemo and his newest Masters of Evil, it was an opportunity. Zemo invented new identities to disguise his team: The Fixer became Techno. Moonstone became Meteorite. Goliath became Atlas. The Beetle became MACH-1. Screaming Mimi became Songbird. And Zemo took on the identity of WWII hero Citizen V. Given new faces and costumes by Techno, the team went public — introducing themselves as the heroic Thunderbolts!

The public adored these new heroes, who filled the void left by the Avengers and Fantastic Four. The city of New York gave the Thunderbolts the FF's old headquarters, and assigned them a mayoral liaison named Dallas Riordan, who Atlas quickly developed feelings for. Meanwhile, MACH-1 and Songbird fell in love as well. The Thunderbolts began to relish their new lifestyle, and took on the idealistic new member Jolt — a teenaged girl orphaned during Onslaught's attack, who had been experimented on and empowered by Arnim Zola. But the team's heroic acts were part of Zemo's scheme to gather the power and resources needed to take over the world.

Months after their "deaths," the Avengers and Fantastic Four returned — and Zemo responded by publicly unveiling the Thunderbolts' true identities, blowing up the FF's headquarters, and mentally enslaving the planet using technology the team had amassed. Zemo had won — but most of the Thunderbolts, realizing that they truly wanted to reform, betrayed and defeated him. Zemo fled with Techno, and although the rest of the team had saved the planet, they were branded as outlaws.

The Thunderbolts relocated to the Midwest and continued fighting crime, trying in vain to restore their public image. They battled Graviton, whom the manipulative Moonstone defeated psychologically; and saved the town of Burton Canyon, Colorado from a takeover by the Imperial Forces of America and their mutated muscle Charcoal. Jolt stayed with them, believing in their intent to reform — though the public did not. When a new Masters of Evil team, led by the mysterious Crimson Cowl, tried to recruit the Thunderbolts, some members of the team began to waver. Meanwhile, Zemo and Techno were stalked by a new Citizen V, who claimed she was the descendant of the original WWII hero.

The Avengers' Hawkeye, who was originally a villain before reforming, saw something of himself in the Thunderbolts' public struggle for redemption. He left the Avengers, tracked down the Thunderbolts and offered them a second chance. He claimed that he had met with the government's Commission on Superhuman Activities and suggested a deal. If the team allowed him to lead them, and stayed on the straight and narrow, they would receive a full pardon.

However, Hawkeye was lying. The CSA had rejected his suggestion, and even threatened to jail him if he joined the Thunderbolts. But Hawkeye was determined, and willing to put himself on the line to help the team redeem themselves — even if that meant deceiving them.

The Thunderbolts talked things over and agreed to Hawkeye's offer, but there was one caveat: In order to show the public that they were serious about reforming, the only known murderer on the team — MACH-1, who had killed a corrupt doctor while leading the Sinister Syndicate as the Beetle — must turn himself in and go to jail!

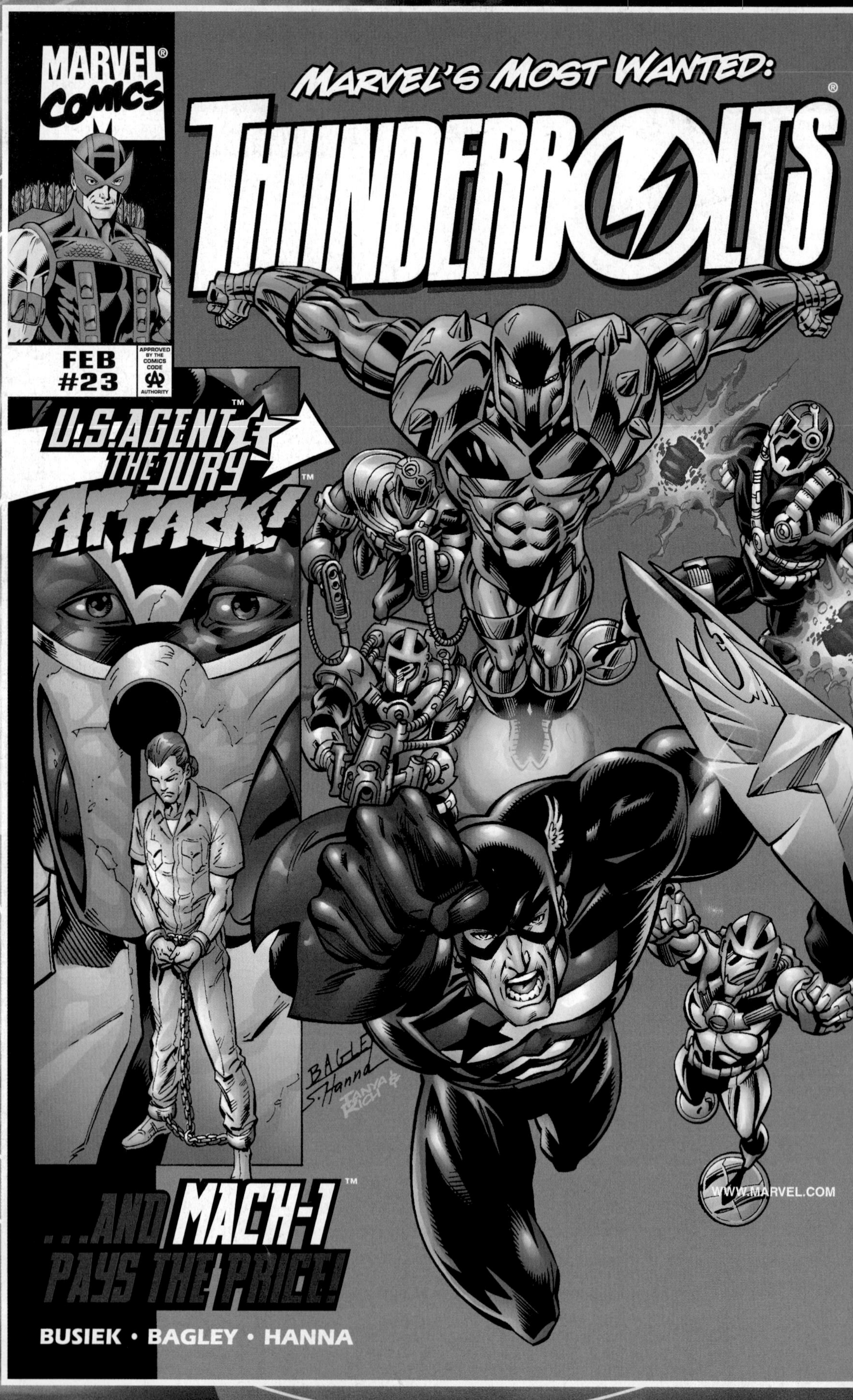
MARVEL® COMICS
MARVEL'S MOST WANTED:
THUNDERBOLTS®
FEB #23
APPROVED BY THE COMICS CODE AUTHORITY
U.S. AGENT™ & THE JURY™ ATTACK!
...AND MACH-1™ PAYS THE PRICE!
BUSIEK • BAGLEY • HANNA
WWW.MARVEL.COM

YOU **READY**?

NO.

BUT I'M NOT GOING TO GET ANY **READIER.**

YOU'LL BE OKAY, ABE, YOU CAN TAKE IT. THAT MUCH I'M **SURE** OF. OKAY --

-- LET'S **DO** IT.

HE DOESN'T **SAY** ANYTHING IN RESPONSE TO THAT. HE JUST **NODS,** TIGHTLY, CLENCHING HIS TEETH A LITTLE HARDER.

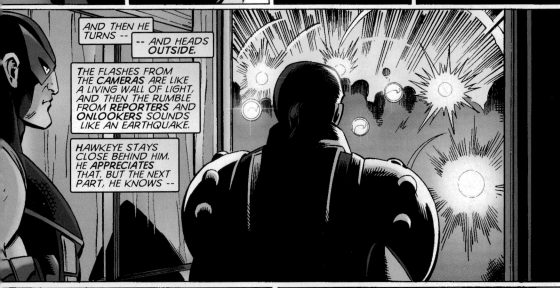

AND THEN HE TURNS --

-- AND HEADS **OUTSIDE.**

THE FLASHES FROM THE **CAMERAS** ARE LIKE A LIVING WALL OF LIGHT, AND THEN THE RUMBLE FROM **REPORTERS** AND **ONLOOKERS** SOUNDS LIKE AN EARTHQUAKE.

HAWKEYE STAYS CLOSE BEHIND HIM. HE **APPRECIATES** THAT. BUT THE NEXT PART, HE KNOWS --

-- HE'LL BE DOING **ALONE.**

CLK CLTCH

ABNER RONALD JENKINS -- A.K.A. **MACH-1,** A.K.A. THE **BEETLE** --

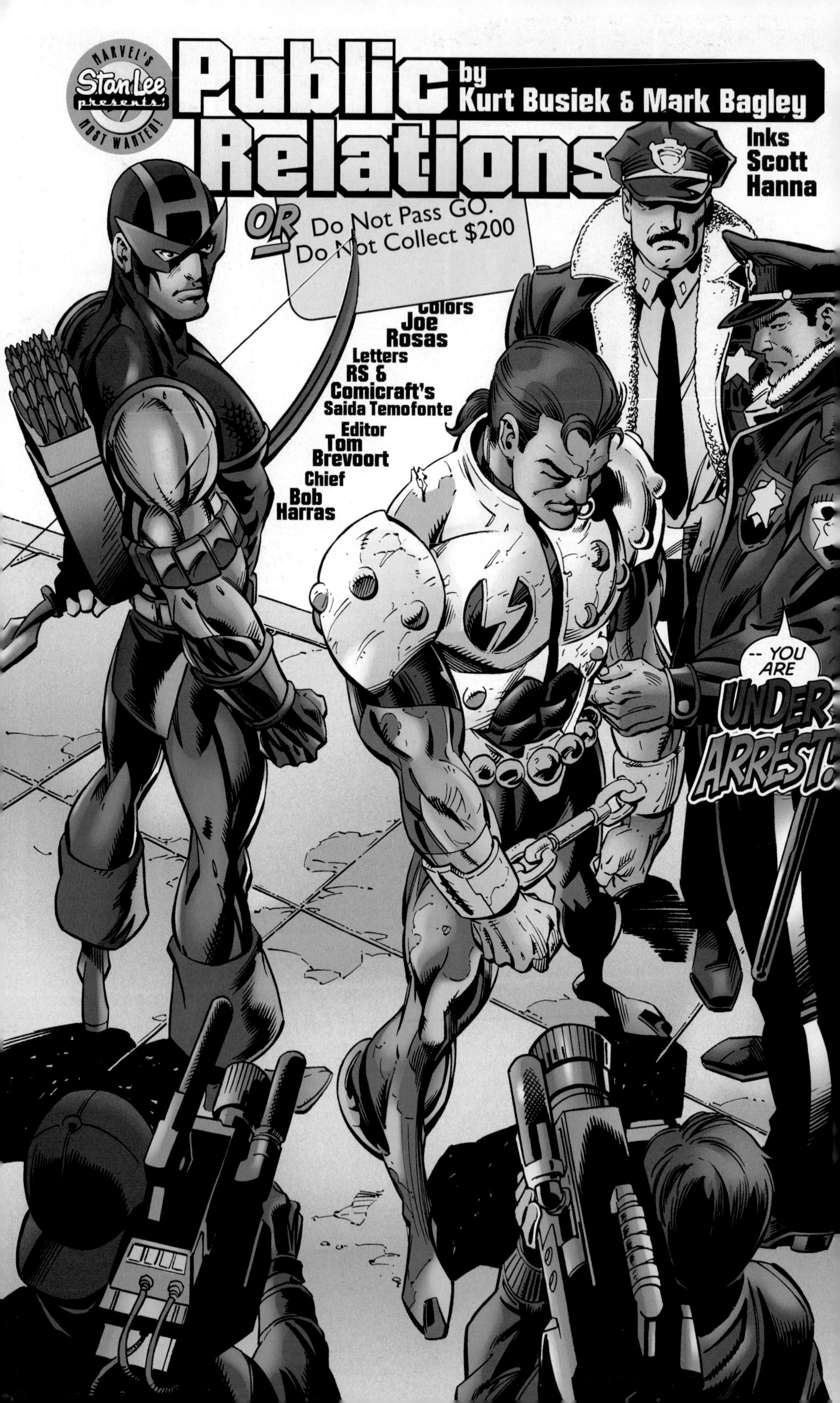

MARVEL'S Stan Lee presents! MOST WANTED!
Public Relations
by Kurt Busiek & Mark Bagley
Inks Scott Hanna
OR Do Not Pass GO. Do Not Collect $200
Colors Joe Rosas
Letters RS & Comicraft's Saida Temofonte
Editor Tom Brevoort
Chief Bob Harras
-- YOU ARE UNDER ARREST!

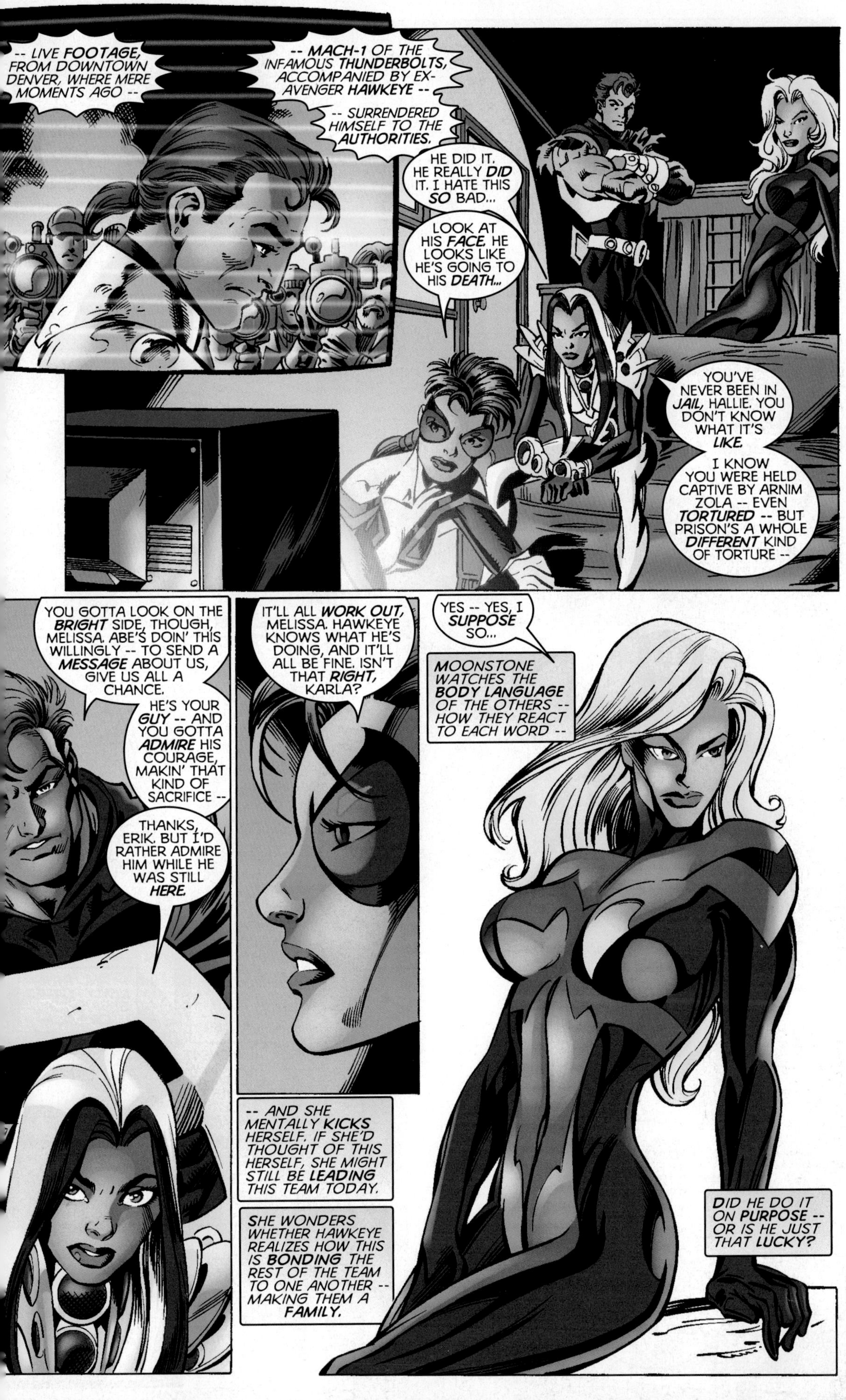
-- LIVE FOOTAGE, FROM DOWNTOWN DENVER, WHERE MERE MOMENTS AGO --
-- MACH-1 OF THE INFAMOUS THUNDERBOLTS, ACCOMPANIED BY EX-AVENGER HAWKEYE --
-- SURRENDERED HIMSELF TO THE AUTHORITIES.
HE DID IT. HE REALLY DID IT. I HATE THIS SO BAD...
LOOK AT HIS FACE. HE LOOKS LIKE HE'S GOING TO HIS DEATH...
YOU'VE NEVER BEEN IN JAIL, HALLIE. YOU DON'T KNOW WHAT IT'S LIKE.
I KNOW YOU WERE HELD CAPTIVE BY ARNIM ZOLA -- EVEN TORTURED -- BUT PRISON'S A WHOLE DIFFERENT KIND OF TORTURE --
YOU GOTTA LOOK ON THE BRIGHT SIDE, THOUGH, MELISSA. ABE'S DOIN' THIS WILLINGLY -- TO SEND A MESSAGE ABOUT US, GIVE US ALL A CHANCE.
HE'S YOUR GUY -- AND YOU GOTTA ADMIRE HIS COURAGE, MAKIN' THAT KIND OF SACRIFICE --
THANKS, ERIK. BUT I'D RATHER ADMIRE HIM WHILE HE WAS STILL HERE.
IT'LL ALL WORK OUT, MELISSA. HAWKEYE KNOWS WHAT HE'S DOING, AND IT'LL ALL BE FINE. ISN'T THAT RIGHT, KARLA?
-- AND SHE MENTALLY KICKS HERSELF. IF SHE'D THOUGHT OF THIS HERSELF, SHE MIGHT STILL BE LEADING THIS TEAM TODAY.
SHE WONDERS WHETHER HAWKEYE REALIZES HOW THIS IS BONDING THE REST OF THE TEAM TO ONE ANOTHER -- MAKING THEM A FAMILY.
YES -- YES, I SUPPOSE SO...
MOONSTONE WATCHES THE BODY LANGUAGE OF THE OTHERS -- HOW THEY REACT TO EACH WORD --
DID HE DO IT ON PURPOSE -- OR IS HE JUST THAT LUCKY?

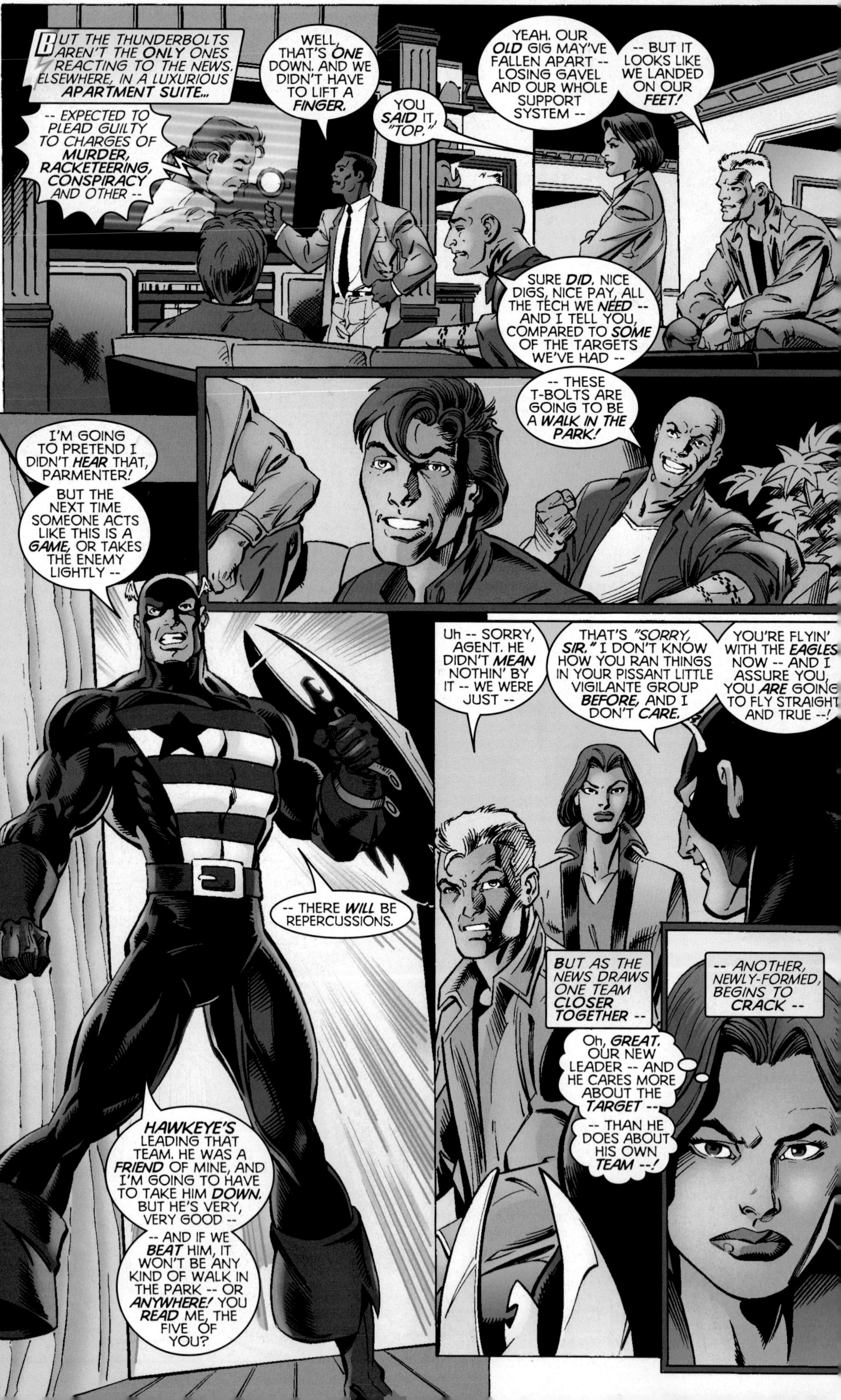
BUT THE THUNDERBOLTS AREN'T THE ONLY ONES REACTING TO THE NEWS. ELSEWHERE, IN A LUXURIOUS APARTMENT SUITE...
-- EXPECTED TO PLEAD GUILTY TO CHARGES OF MURDER, RACKETEERING, CONSPIRACY AND OTHER --
WELL, THAT'S ONE DOWN. AND WE DIDN'T HAVE TO LIFT A FINGER.
YOU SAID IT, "TOP."
YEAH. OUR OLD GIG MAY'VE FALLEN APART -- LOSING GAVEL AND OUR WHOLE SUPPORT SYSTEM --
-- BUT IT LOOKS LIKE WE LANDED ON OUR FEET!
SURE DID. NICE DIGS, NICE PAY, ALL THE TECH WE NEED -- AND I TELL YOU, COMPARED TO SOME OF THE TARGETS WE'VE HAD --
-- THESE T-BOLTS ARE GOING TO BE A WALK IN THE PARK!
I'M GOING TO PRETEND I DIDN'T HEAR THAT, PARMENTER!
BUT THE NEXT TIME SOMEONE ACTS LIKE THIS IS A GAME, OR TAKES THE ENEMY LIGHTLY --
-- THERE WILL BE REPERCUSSIONS.
HAWKEYE'S LEADING THAT TEAM. HE WAS A FRIEND OF MINE, AND I'M GOING TO HAVE TO TAKE HIM DOWN. BUT HE'S VERY, VERY GOOD --
-- AND IF WE BEAT HIM, IT WON'T BE ANY KIND OF WALK IN THE PARK -- OR ANYWHERE! YOU READ ME, THE FIVE OF YOU?
Uh -- SORRY, AGENT. HE DIDN'T MEAN NOTHIN' BY IT -- WE WERE JUST --
THAT'S "SORRY, SIR." I DON'T KNOW HOW YOU RAN THINGS IN YOUR PISSANT LITTLE VIGILANTE GROUP BEFORE, AND I DON'T CARE.
YOU'RE FLYIN' WITH THE EAGLES NOW -- AND I ASSURE YOU, YOU ARE GOING TO FLY STRAIGHT AND TRUE --!
BUT AS THE NEWS DRAWS ONE TEAM CLOSER TOGETHER --
-- ANOTHER, NEWLY-FORMED, BEGINS TO CRACK --
Oh, GREAT. OUR NEW LEADER -- AND HE CARES MORE ABOUT THE TARGET --
-- THAN HE DOES ABOUT HIS OWN TEAM --!

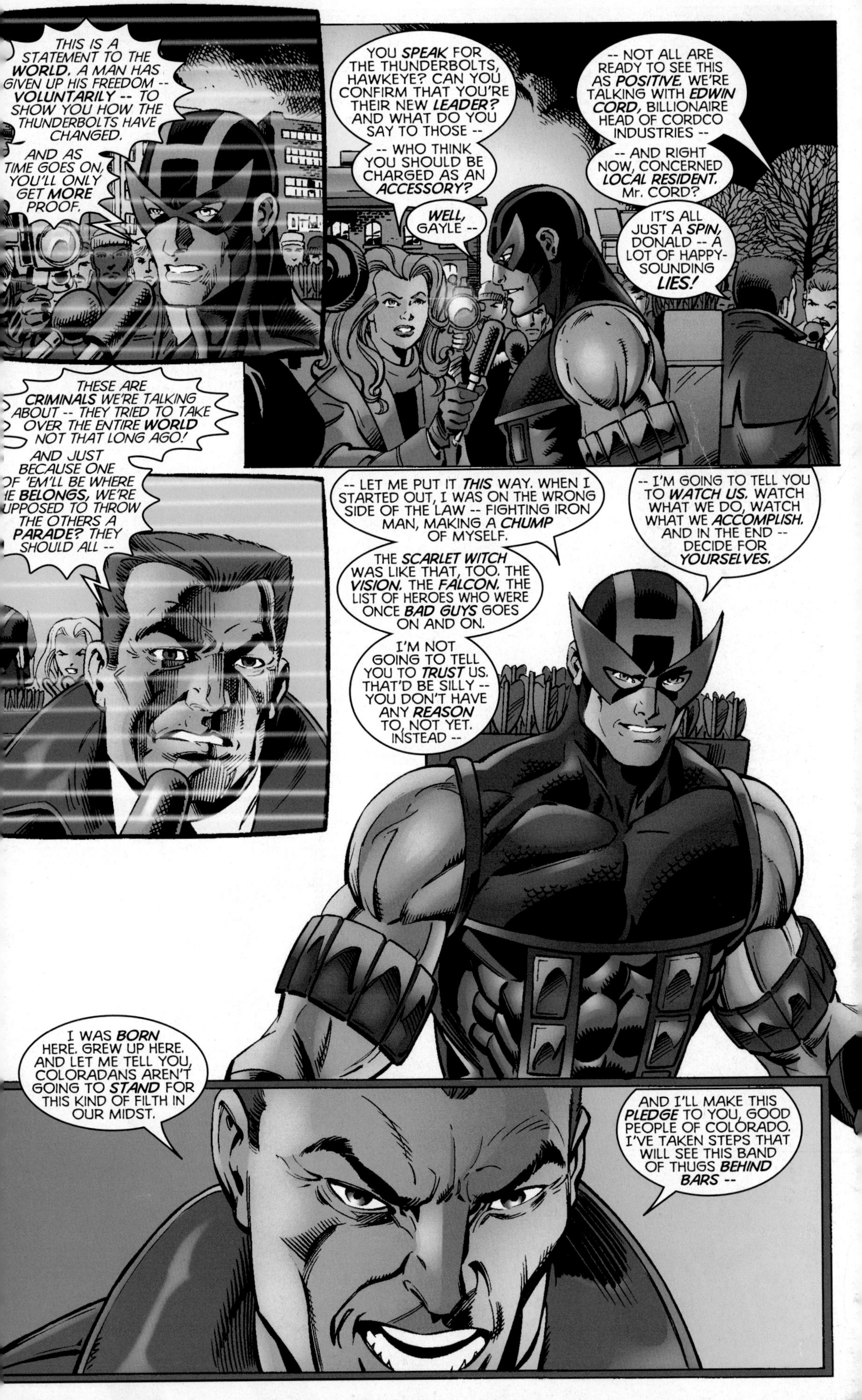

THIS IS A STATEMENT TO THE WORLD. A MAN HAS GIVEN UP HIS FREEDOM -- VOLUNTARILY -- TO SHOW YOU HOW THE THUNDERBOLTS HAVE CHANGED.
AND AS TIME GOES ON, YOU'LL ONLY GET MORE PROOF.
YOU SPEAK FOR THE THUNDERBOLTS, HAWKEYE? CAN YOU CONFIRM THAT YOU'RE THEIR NEW LEADER? AND WHAT DO YOU SAY TO THOSE --
-- WHO THINK YOU SHOULD BE CHARGED AS AN ACCESSORY?
WELL, GAYLE --
-- NOT ALL ARE READY TO SEE THIS AS POSITIVE. WE'RE TALKING WITH EDWIN CORD, BILLIONAIRE HEAD OF CORDCO INDUSTRIES --
-- AND RIGHT NOW, CONCERNED LOCAL RESIDENT. Mr. CORD?
IT'S ALL JUST A SPIN, DONALD -- A LOT OF HAPPY-SOUNDING LIES!
THESE ARE CRIMINALS WE'RE TALKING ABOUT -- THEY TRIED TO TAKE OVER THE ENTIRE WORLD NOT THAT LONG AGO!
AND JUST BECAUSE ONE OF 'EM'LL BE WHERE HE BELONGS, WE'RE SUPPOSED TO THROW THE OTHERS A PARADE? THEY SHOULD ALL --
-- LET ME PUT IT THIS WAY. WHEN I STARTED OUT, I WAS ON THE WRONG SIDE OF THE LAW -- FIGHTING IRON MAN, MAKING A CHUMP OF MYSELF.
THE SCARLET WITCH WAS LIKE THAT, TOO. THE VISION. THE FALCON. THE LIST OF HEROES WHO WERE ONCE BAD GUYS GOES ON AND ON.
I'M NOT GOING TO TELL YOU TO TRUST US. THAT'D BE SILLY -- YOU DON'T HAVE ANY REASON TO, NOT YET. INSTEAD --
-- I'M GOING TO TELL YOU TO WATCH US. WATCH WHAT WE DO, WATCH WHAT WE ACCOMPLISH. AND IN THE END -- DECIDE FOR YOURSELVES.
I WAS BORN HERE. GREW UP HERE. AND LET ME TELL YOU, COLORADANS AREN'T GOING TO STAND FOR THIS KIND OF FILTH IN OUR MIDST.
AND I'LL MAKE THIS PLEDGE TO YOU, GOOD PEOPLE OF COLORADO. I'VE TAKEN STEPS THAT WILL SEE THIS BAND OF THUGS BEHIND BARS --

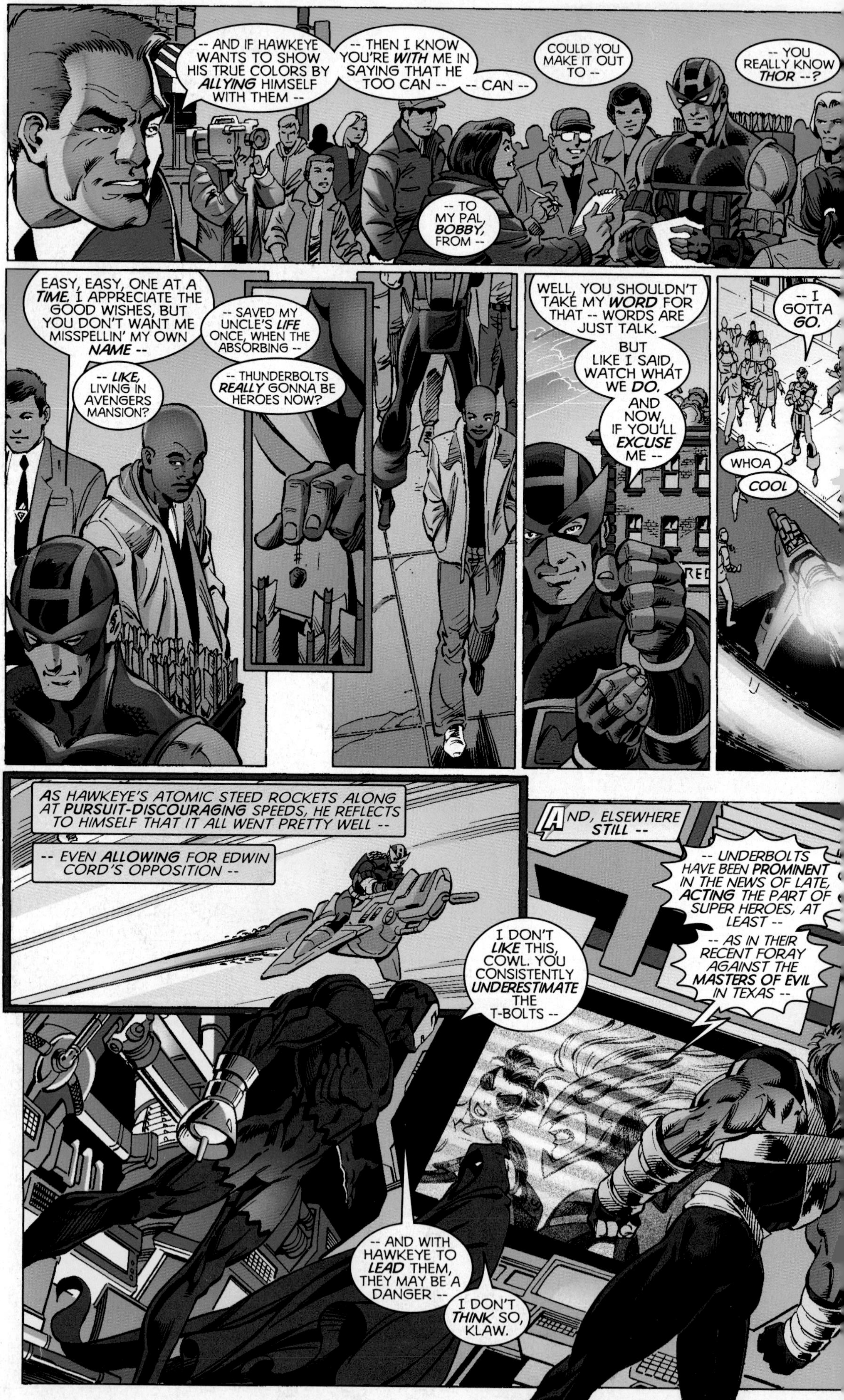
-- AND IF HAWKEYE WANTS TO SHOW HIS TRUE COLORS BY ALLYING HIMSELF WITH THEM --
-- THEN I KNOW YOU'RE WITH ME IN SAYING THAT HE TOO CAN --
-- CAN --
COULD YOU MAKE IT OUT TO --
-- YOU REALLY KNOW THOR --?
-- TO MY PAL, BOBBY, FROM --
EASY, EASY, ONE AT A TIME. I APPRECIATE THE GOOD WISHES, BUT YOU DON'T WANT ME MISSPELLIN' MY OWN NAME --
-- LIKE, LIVING IN AVENGERS MANSION?
-- SAVED MY UNCLE'S LIFE ONCE, WHEN THE ABSORBING --
-- THUNDERBOLTS REALLY GONNA BE HEROES NOW?
WELL, YOU SHOULDN'T TAKE MY WORD FOR THAT -- WORDS ARE JUST TALK.
BUT LIKE I SAID, WATCH WHAT WE DO.
AND NOW, IF YOU'LL EXCUSE ME --
-- I GOTTA GO.
WHOA
COOL
AS HAWKEYE'S ATOMIC STEED ROCKETS ALONG AT PURSUIT-DISCOURAGING SPEEDS, HE REFLECTS TO HIMSELF THAT IT ALL WENT PRETTY WELL --
-- EVEN ALLOWING FOR EDWIN CORD'S OPPOSITION --
AND, ELSEWHERE STILL --
-- UNDERBOLTS HAVE BEEN PROMINENT IN THE NEWS OF LATE, ACTING THE PART OF SUPER HEROES, AT LEAST --
-- AS IN THEIR RECENT FORAY AGAINST THE MASTERS OF EVIL IN TEXAS --
I DON'T LIKE THIS, COWL. YOU CONSISTENTLY UNDERESTIMATE THE T-BOLTS --
-- AND WITH HAWKEYE TO LEAD THEM, THEY MAY BE A DANGER --
I DON'T THINK SO, KLAW.

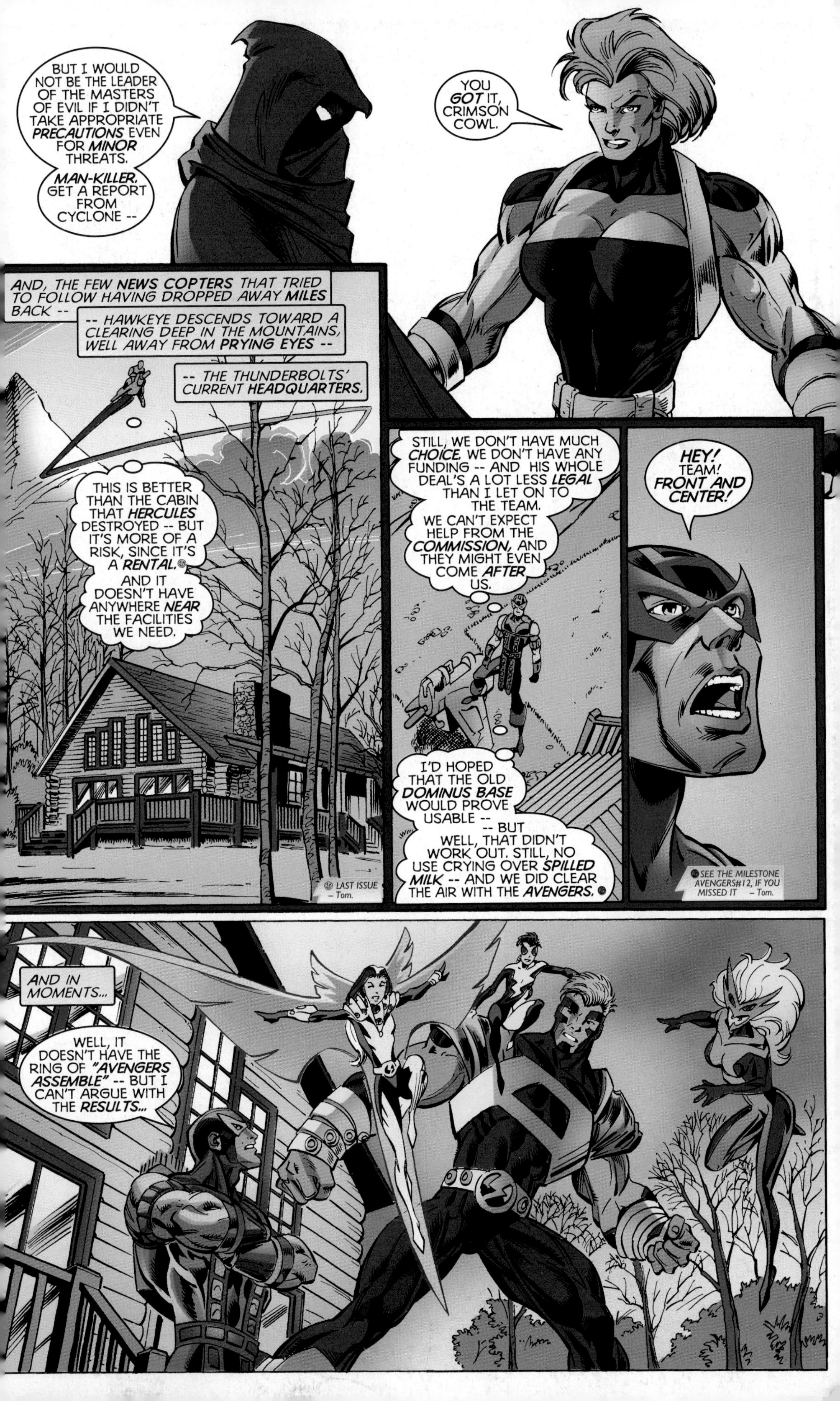
BUT I WOULD NOT BE THE LEADER OF THE MASTERS OF EVIL IF I DIDN'T TAKE APPROPRIATE PRECAUTIONS EVEN FOR MINOR THREATS.
MAN-KILLER. GET A REPORT FROM CYCLONE --
YOU GOT IT, CRIMSON COWL.
AND, THE FEW NEWS COPTERS THAT TRIED TO FOLLOW HAVING DROPPED AWAY MILES BACK --
-- HAWKEYE DESCENDS TOWARD A CLEARING DEEP IN THE MOUNTAINS, WELL AWAY FROM PRYING EYES --
-- THE THUNDERBOLTS' CURRENT HEADQUARTERS.
THIS IS BETTER THAN THE CABIN THAT HERCULES DESTROYED -- BUT IT'S MORE OF A RISK, SINCE IT'S A RENTAL.
AND IT DOESN'T HAVE ANYWHERE NEAR THE FACILITIES WE NEED.
LAST ISSUE – Tom.
STILL, WE DON'T HAVE MUCH CHOICE. WE DON'T HAVE ANY FUNDING -- AND HIS WHOLE DEAL'S A LOT LESS LEGAL THAN I LET ON TO THE TEAM.
WE CAN'T EXPECT HELP FROM THE COMMISSION, AND THEY MIGHT EVEN COME AFTER US.
I'D HOPED THAT THE OLD DOMINUS BASE WOULD PROVE USABLE --
-- BUT WELL, THAT DIDN'T WORK OUT. STILL, NO USE CRYING OVER SPILLED MILK -- AND WE DID CLEAR THE AIR WITH THE AVENGERS.
HEY! TEAM! FRONT AND CENTER!
SEE THE MILESTONE AVENGERS#12, IF YOU MISSED IT – Tom.
AND IN MOMENTS...
WELL, IT DOESN'T HAVE THE RING OF "AVENGERS ASSEMBLE" -- BUT I CAN'T ARGUE WITH THE RESULTS...

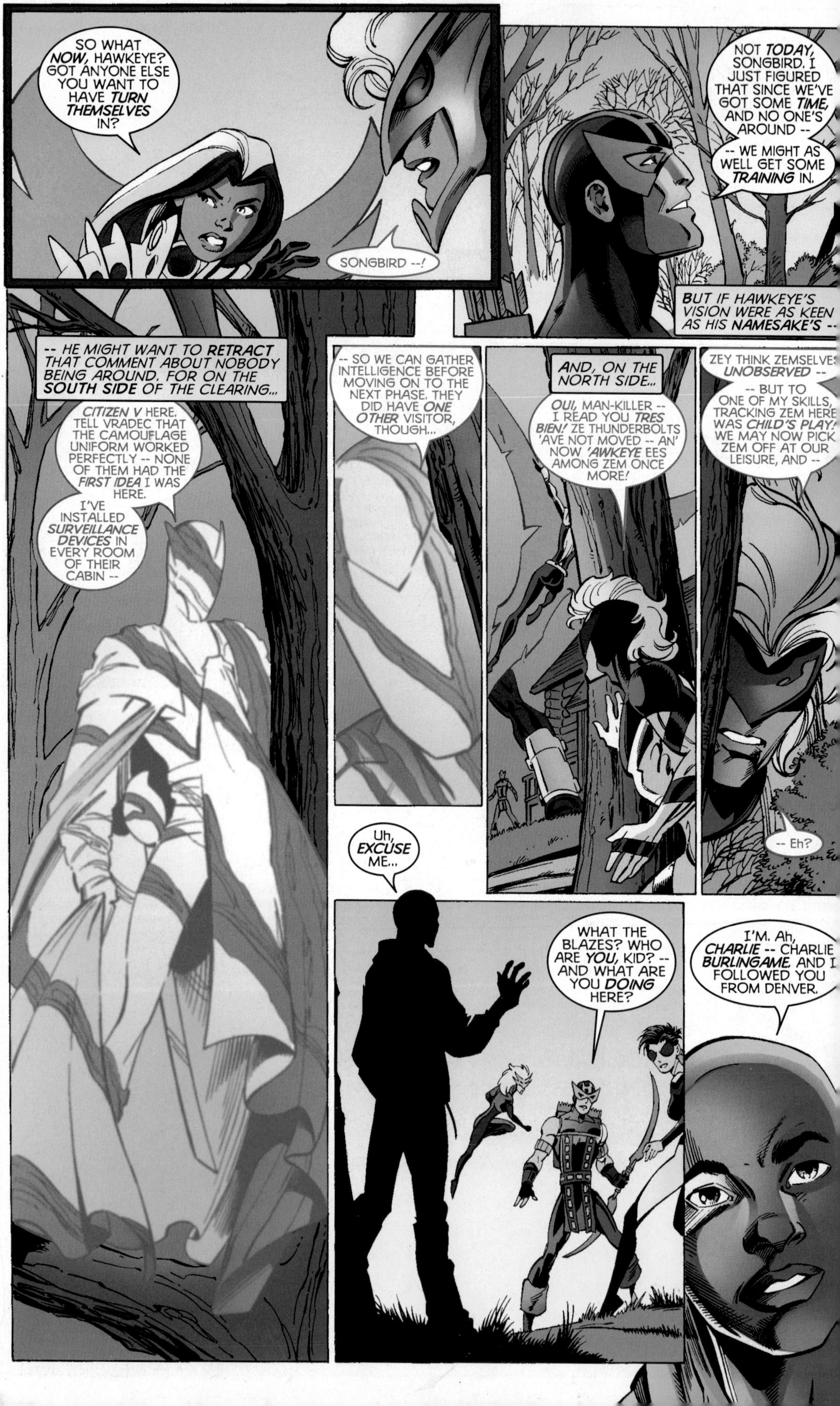

SO WHAT NOW, HAWKEYE? GOT ANYONE ELSE YOU WANT TO HAVE TURN THEMSELVES IN?
SONGBIRD --!
NOT TODAY, SONGBIRD. I JUST FIGURED THAT SINCE WE'VE GOT SOME TIME, AND NO ONE'S AROUND --
-- WE MIGHT AS WELL GET SOME TRAINING IN.
BUT IF HAWKEYE'S VISION WERE AS KEEN AS HIS NAMESAKE'S --
-- HE MIGHT WANT TO RETRACT THAT COMMENT ABOUT NOBODY BEING AROUND. FOR ON THE SOUTH SIDE OF THE CLEARING...
CITIZEN V HERE. TELL VRADEC THAT THE CAMOUFLAGE UNIFORM WORKED PERFECTLY -- NONE OF THEM HAD THE FIRST IDEA I WAS HERE.
I'VE INSTALLED SURVEILLANCE DEVICES IN EVERY ROOM OF THEIR CABIN --
-- SO WE CAN GATHER INTELLIGENCE BEFORE MOVING ON TO THE NEXT PHASE. THEY DID HAVE ONE OTHER VISITOR, THOUGH...
AND, ON THE NORTH SIDE...
OUI, MAN-KILLER -- I READ YOU TRES BIEN! ZE THUNDERBOLTS 'AVE NOT MOVED -- AN' NOW 'AWKEYE EES AMONG ZEM ONCE MORE!
ZEY THINK ZEMSELVES UNOBSERVED --
-- BUT TO ONE OF MY SKILLS, TRACKING ZEM HERE WAS CHILD'S PLAY! WE MAY NOW PICK ZEM OFF AT OUR LEISURE, AND --
-- Eh?
Uh, EXCUSE ME...
WHAT THE BLAZES? WHO ARE YOU, KID? -- AND WHAT ARE YOU DOING HERE?
I'M. Ah, CHARLIE -- CHARLIE BURLINGAME. AND I FOLLOWED YOU FROM DENVER.

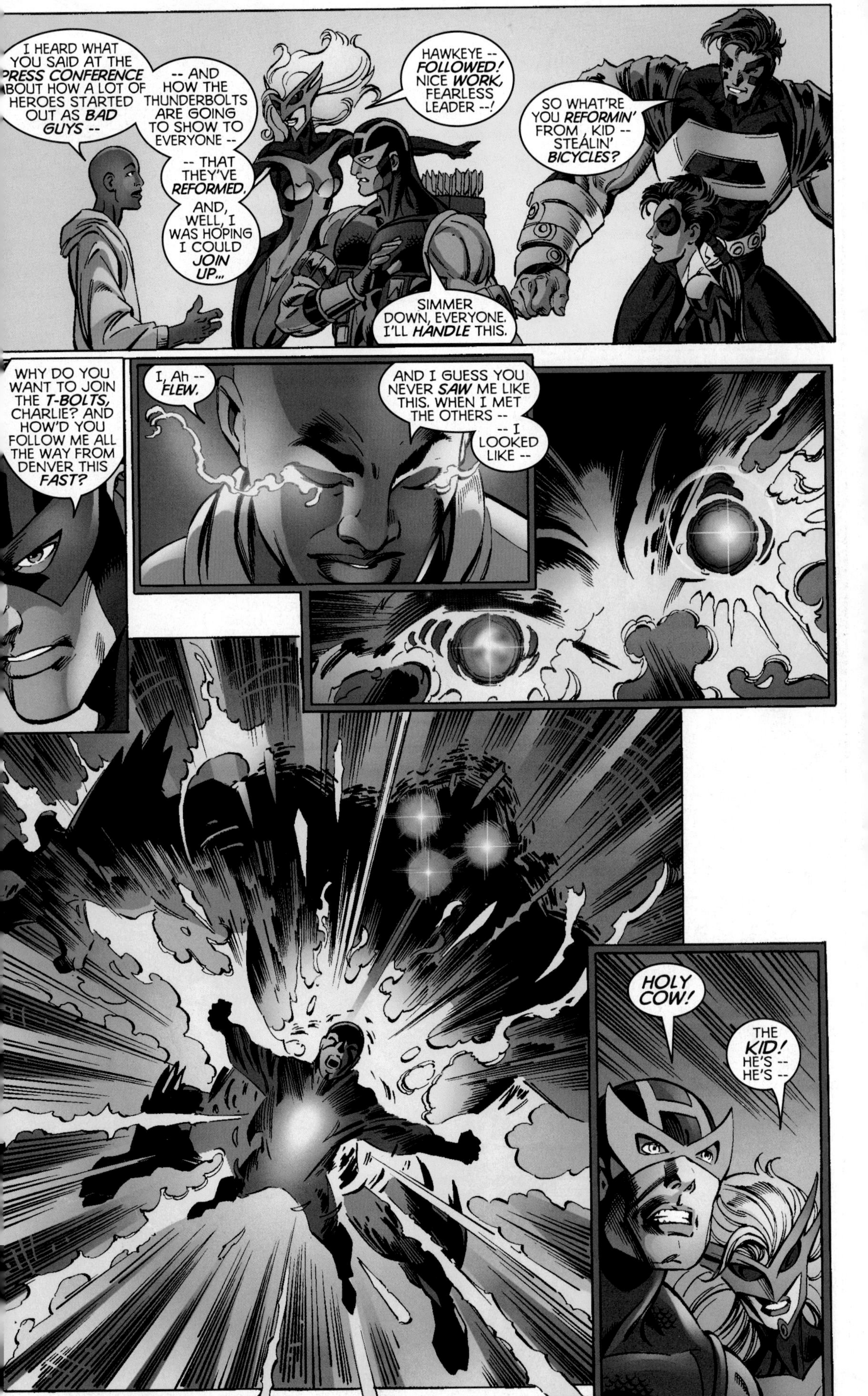
I HEARD WHAT YOU SAID AT THE PRESS CONFERENCE 'BOUT HOW A LOT OF HEROES STARTED OUT AS BAD GUYS --
-- AND HOW THE THUNDERBOLTS ARE GOING TO SHOW TO EVERYONE --
-- THAT THEY'VE REFORMED.
AND, WELL, I WAS HOPING I COULD JOIN UP...
HAWKEYE -- FOLLOWED! NICE WORK, FEARLESS LEADER --!
SIMMER DOWN, EVERYONE. I'LL HANDLE THIS.
SO WHAT'RE YOU REFORMIN' FROM, KID -- STEALIN' BICYCLES?
WHY DO YOU WANT TO JOIN THE T-BOLTS, CHARLIE? AND HOW'D YOU FOLLOW ME ALL THE WAY FROM DENVER THIS FAST?
I, Ah -- FLEW.
AND I GUESS YOU NEVER SAW ME LIKE THIS. WHEN I MET THE OTHERS --
-- I LOOKED LIKE --
HOLY COW!
THE KID! HE'S -- HE'S --

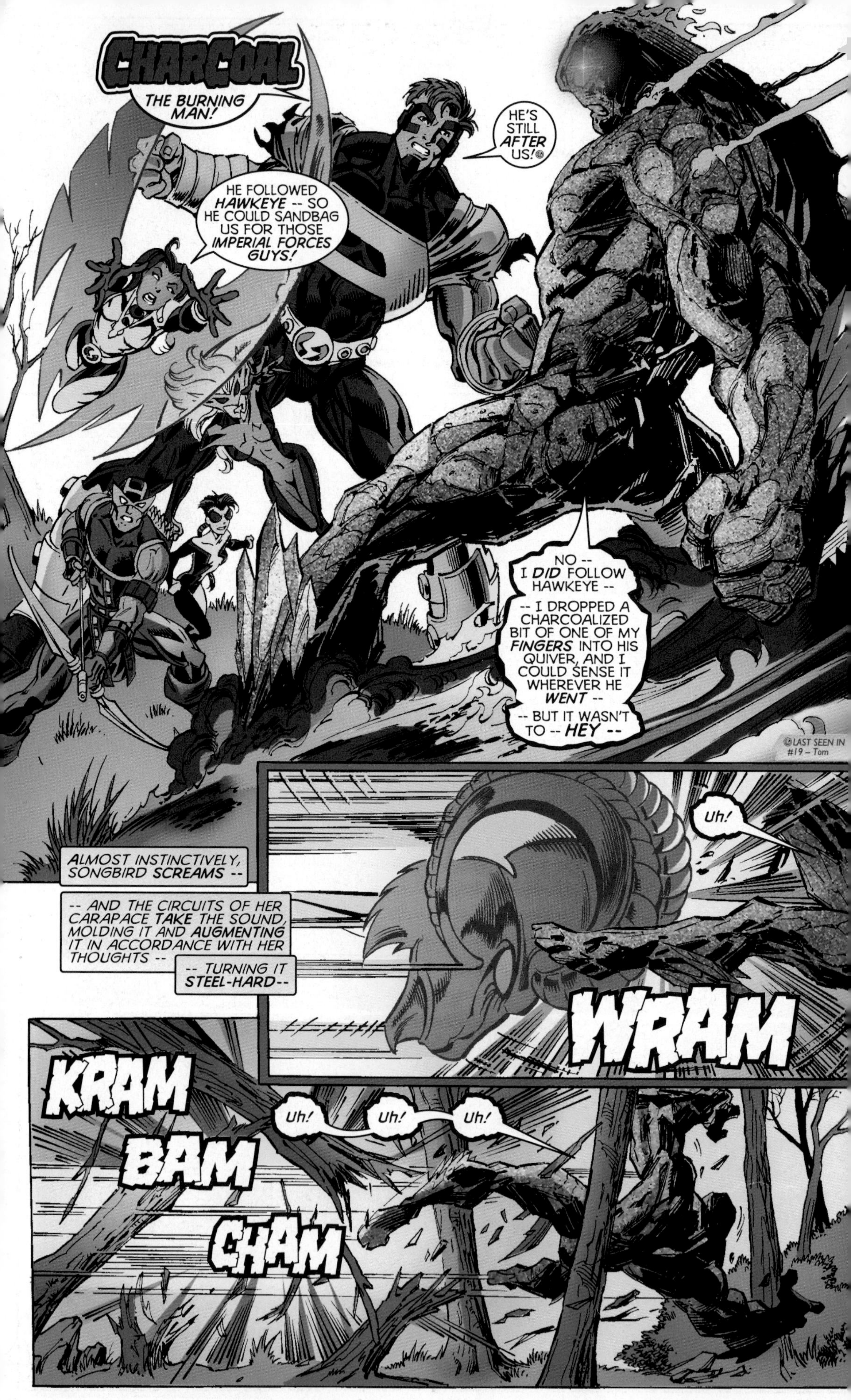
CHARCOAL
THE BURNING MAN!
HE'S STILL AFTER US!©
HE FOLLOWED HAWKEYE -- SO HE COULD SANDBAG US FOR THOSE IMPERIAL FORCES GUYS!
NO -- I DID FOLLOW HAWKEYE --
-- I DROPPED A CHARCOALIZED BIT OF ONE OF MY FINGERS INTO HIS QUIVER, AND I COULD SENSE IT WHEREVER HE WENT --
-- BUT IT WASN'T TO -- HEY --
©LAST SEEN IN #19 – Tom
ALMOST INSTINCTIVELY, SONGBIRD SCREAMS --
-- AND THE CIRCUITS OF HER CARAPACE TAKE THE SOUND, MOLDING IT AND AUGMENTING IT IN ACCORDANCE WITH HER THOUGHTS --
-- TURNING IT STEEL-HARD--
Uh!
WRAM
KRAM
Uh!
Uh!
Uh!
BAM
CHAM

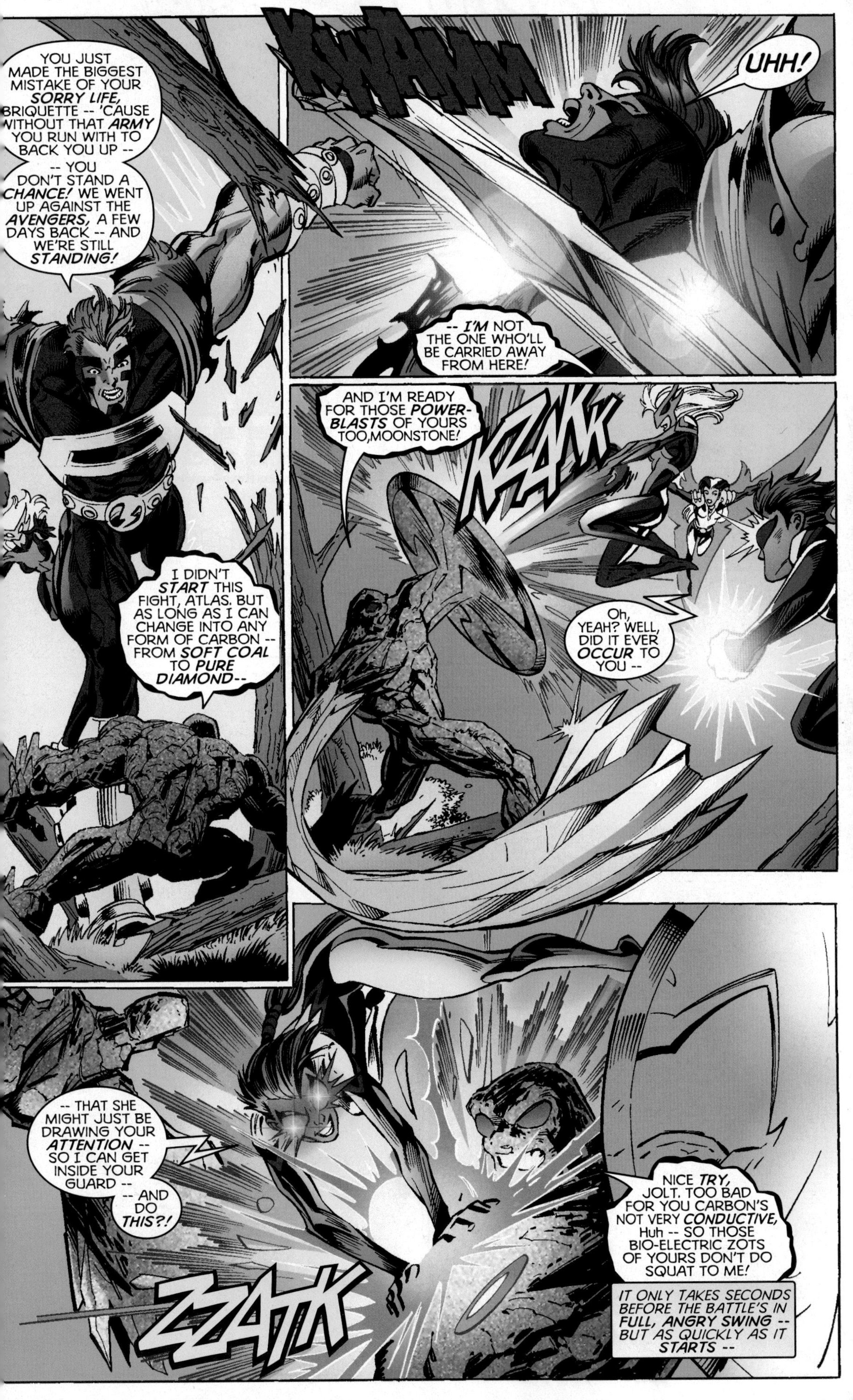
YOU JUST MADE THE BIGGEST MISTAKE OF YOUR SORRY LIFE, BRIQUETTE -- 'CAUSE WITHOUT THAT ARMY YOU RUN WITH TO BACK YOU UP --
-- YOU DON'T STAND A CHANCE! WE WENT UP AGAINST THE AVENGERS, A FEW DAYS BACK -- AND WE'RE STILL STANDING!
I DIDN'T START THIS FIGHT, ATLAS. BUT AS LONG AS I CAN CHANGE INTO ANY FORM OF CARBON -- FROM SOFT COAL TO PURE DIAMOND--
KWAMM
UHH!
-- I'M NOT THE ONE WHO'LL BE CARRIED AWAY FROM HERE!
AND I'M READY FOR THOSE POWER-BLASTS OF YOURS TOO,MOONSTONE!
KZAKK
Oh, YEAH? WELL, DID IT EVER OCCUR TO YOU --
-- THAT SHE MIGHT JUST BE DRAWING YOUR ATTENTION -- SO I CAN GET INSIDE YOUR GUARD --
-- AND DO THIS?!
ZZATK
NICE TRY, JOLT. TOO BAD FOR YOU CARBON'S NOT VERY CONDUCTIVE, Huh -- SO THOSE BIO-ELECTRIC ZOTS OF YOURS DON'T DO SQUAT TO ME!
IT ONLY TAKES SECONDS BEFORE THE BATTLE'S IN FULL, ANGRY SWING -- BUT AS QUICKLY AS IT STARTS --

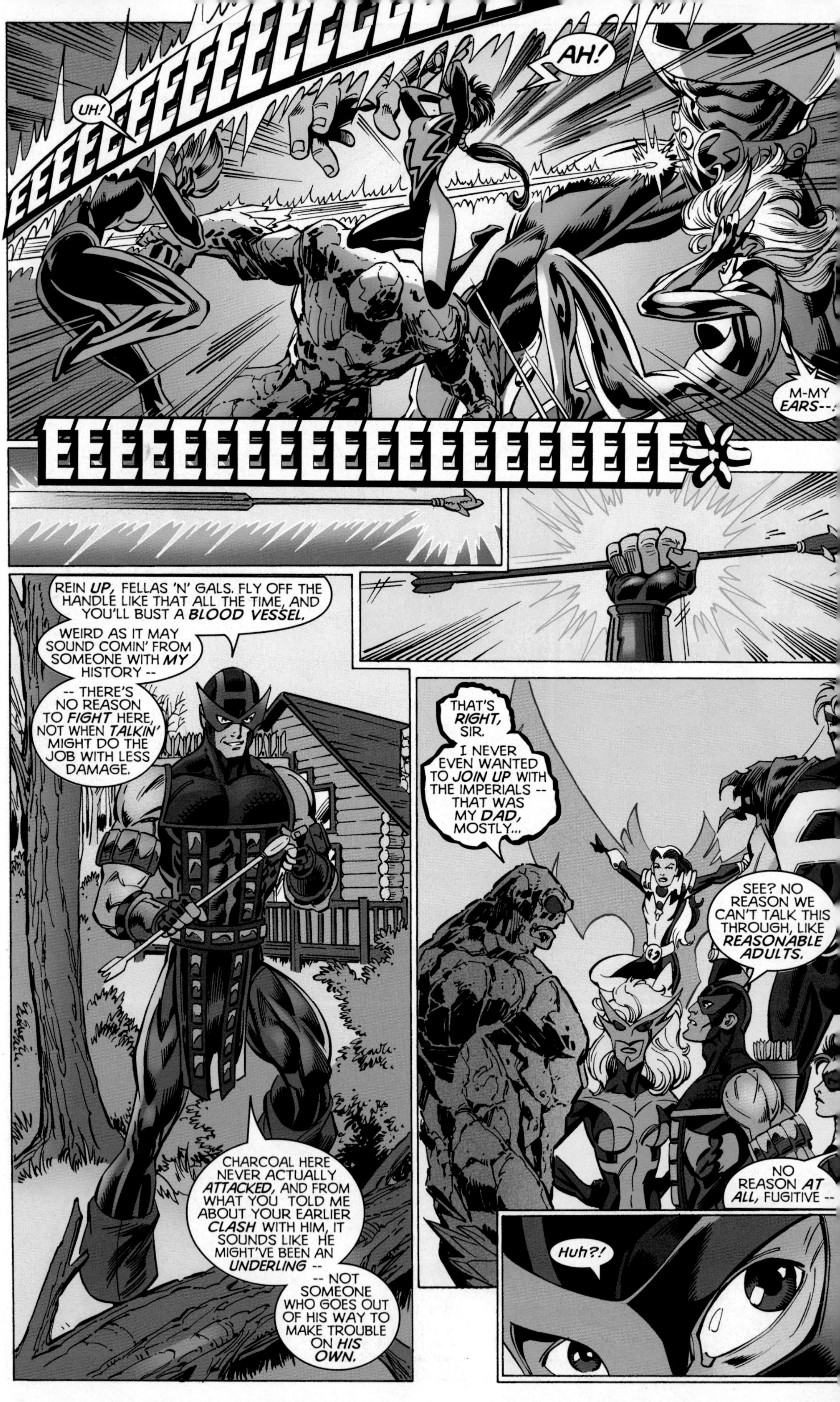
EEEEEEEEEEEEEEEEE
UH!
AH!
M-MY EARS--!
EEEEEEEEEEEEEEEEEEEEEEEE
REIN UP, FELLAS 'N' GALS. FLY OFF THE HANDLE LIKE THAT ALL THE TIME, AND YOU'LL BUST A BLOOD VESSEL.
WEIRD AS IT MAY SOUND COMIN' FROM SOMEONE WITH MY HISTORY --
-- THERE'S NO REASON TO FIGHT HERE, NOT WHEN TALKIN' MIGHT DO THE JOB WITH LESS DAMAGE.
CHARCOAL HERE NEVER ACTUALLY ATTACKED, AND FROM WHAT YOU TOLD ME ABOUT YOUR EARLIER CLASH WITH HIM, IT SOUNDS LIKE HE MIGHT'VE BEEN AN UNDERLING --
-- NOT SOMEONE WHO GOES OUT OF HIS WAY TO MAKE TROUBLE ON HIS OWN.
THAT'S RIGHT, SIR.
I NEVER EVEN WANTED TO JOIN UP WITH THE IMPERIALS -- THAT WAS MY DAD, MOSTLY...
SEE? NO REASON WE CAN'T TALK THIS THROUGH, LIKE REASONABLE ADULTS.
NO REASON AT ALL, FUGITIVE --
Huh?!

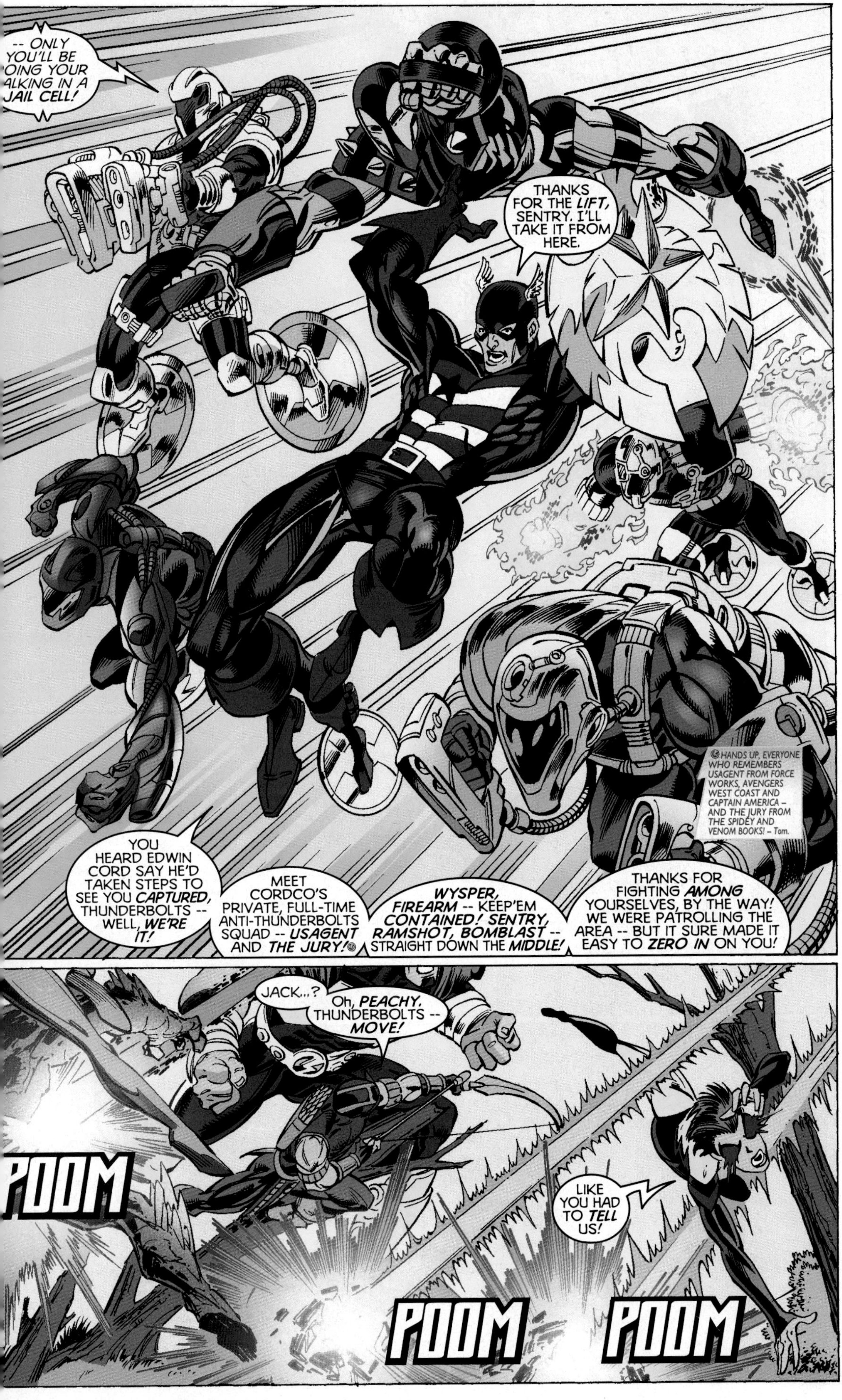
-- ONLY YOU'LL BE OING YOUR ALKING IN A JAIL CELL!
THANKS FOR THE LIFT, SENTRY. I'LL TAKE IT FROM HERE.
HANDS UP, EVERYONE WHO REMEMBERS USAGENT FROM FORCE WORKS, AVENGERS WEST COAST AND CAPTAIN AMERICA – AND THE JURY FROM THE SPIDEY AND VENOM BOOKS! – Tom.
YOU HEARD EDWIN CORD SAY HE'D TAKEN STEPS TO SEE YOU CAPTURED, THUNDERBOLTS -- WELL, WE'RE IT!
MEET CORDCO'S PRIVATE, FULL-TIME ANTI-THUNDERBOLTS SQUAD -- USAGENT AND THE JURY!
WYSPER, FIREARM -- KEEP'EM CONTAINED! SENTRY, RAMSHOT, BOMBLAST -- STRAIGHT DOWN THE MIDDLE!
THANKS FOR FIGHTING AMONG YOURSELVES, BY THE WAY! WE WERE PATROLLING THE AREA -- BUT IT SURE MADE IT EASY TO ZERO IN ON YOU!
JACK...?
Oh, PEACHY. THUNDERBOLTS -- MOVE!
POOM
LIKE YOU HAD TO TELL US!
POOM
POOM

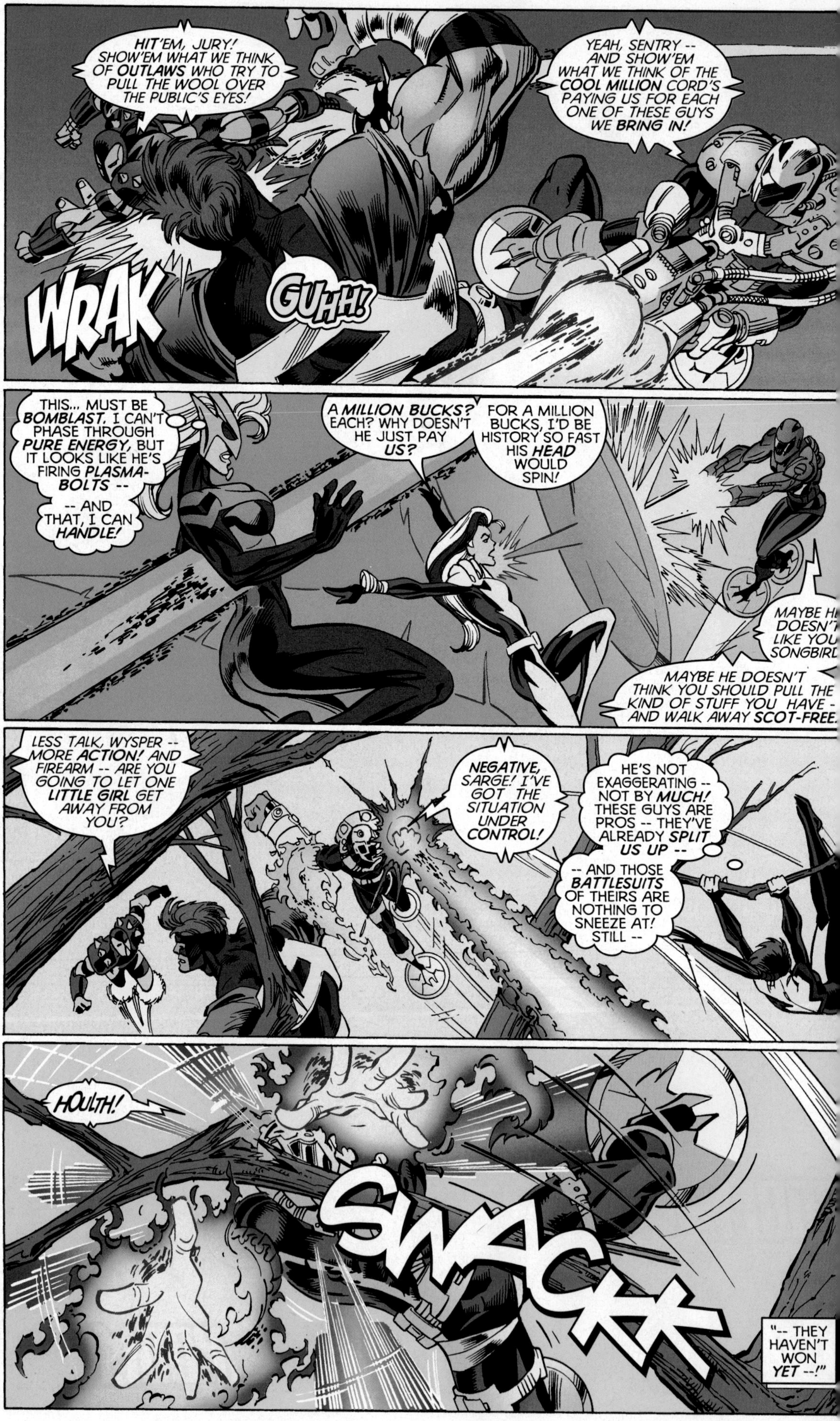
HIT'EM, JURY! SHOW'EM WHAT WE THINK OF OUTLAWS WHO TRY TO PULL THE WOOL OVER THE PUBLIC'S EYES!
YEAH, SENTRY -- AND SHOW'EM WHAT WE THINK OF THE COOL MILLION CORD'S PAYING US FOR EACH ONE OF THESE GUYS WE BRING IN!
WRAK
GUHH!
THIS... MUST BE BOMBLAST. I CAN'T PHASE THROUGH PURE ENERGY, BUT IT LOOKS LIKE HE'S FIRING PLASMA-BOLTS --
-- AND THAT, I CAN HANDLE!
A MILLION BUCKS? EACH? WHY DOESN'T HE JUST PAY US?
FOR A MILLION BUCKS, I'D BE HISTORY SO FAST HIS HEAD WOULD SPIN!
MAYBE HE DOESN'T LIKE YOU SONGBIRD
MAYBE HE DOESN'T THINK YOU SHOULD PULL THE KIND OF STUFF YOU HAVE -- AND WALK AWAY SCOT-FREE.
LESS TALK, WYSPER -- MORE ACTION! AND FIREARM -- ARE YOU GOING TO LET ONE LITTLE GIRL GET AWAY FROM YOU?
NEGATIVE, SARGE! I'VE GOT THE SITUATION UNDER CONTROL!
HE'S NOT EXAGGERATING -- NOT BY MUCH! THESE GUYS ARE PROS -- THEY'VE ALREADY SPLIT US UP --
-- AND THOSE BATTLESUITS OF THEIRS ARE NOTHING TO SNEEZE AT! STILL --
HOULTH!
SWACKK
"-- THEY HAVEN'T WON YET --!"

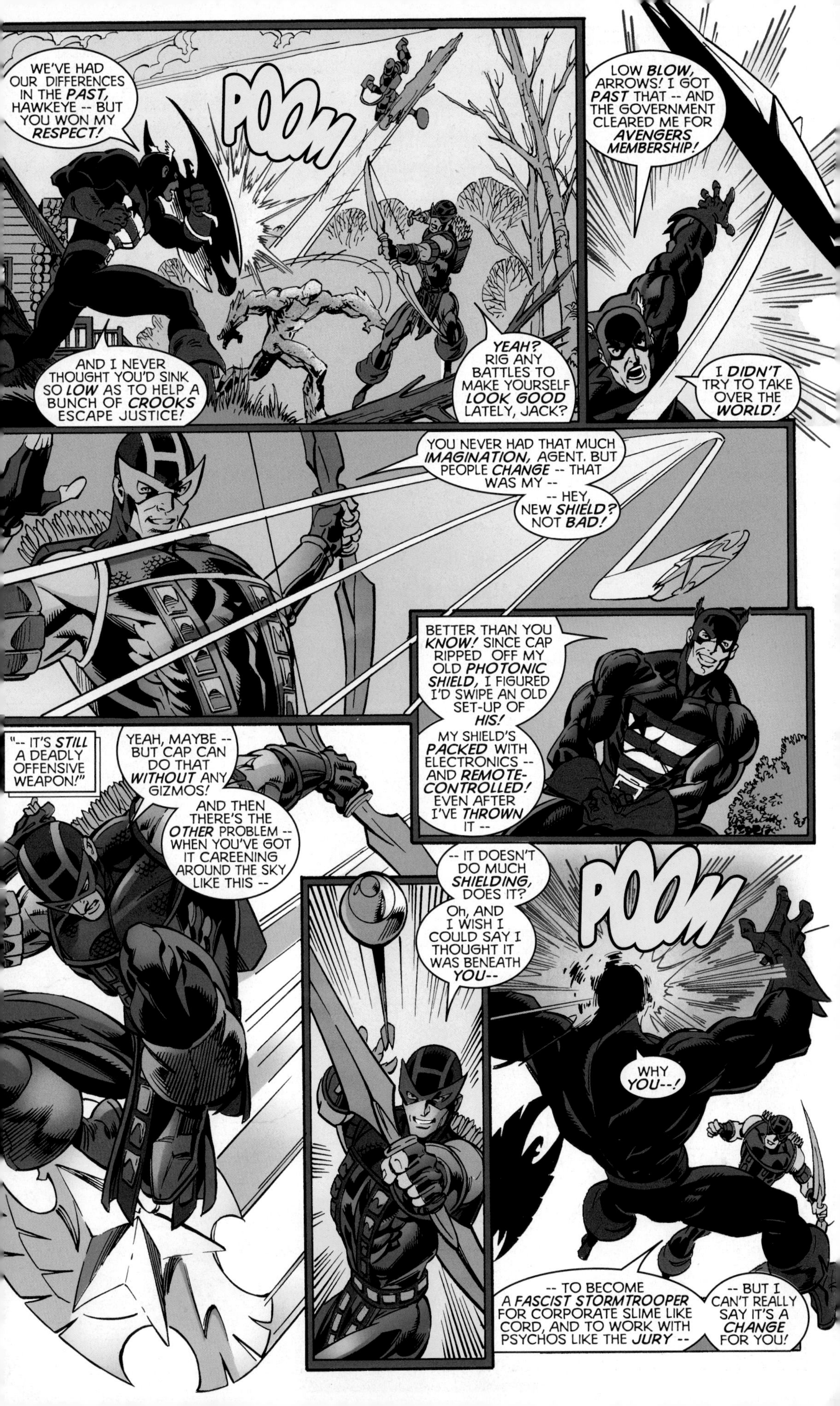
WE'VE HAD OUR DIFFERENCES IN THE PAST, HAWKEYE -- BUT YOU WON MY RESPECT!
POOM
AND I NEVER THOUGHT YOU'D SINK SO LOW AS TO HELP A BUNCH OF CROOKS ESCAPE JUSTICE!
YEAH? RIG ANY BATTLES TO MAKE YOURSELF LOOK GOOD LATELY, JACK?
LOW BLOW, ARROWS! I GOT PAST THAT -- AND THE GOVERNMENT CLEARED ME FOR AVENGERS MEMBERSHIP!
I DIDN'T TRY TO TAKE OVER THE WORLD!
YOU NEVER HAD THAT MUCH IMAGINATION, AGENT. BUT PEOPLE CHANGE -- THAT WAS MY --
-- HEY, NEW SHIELD? NOT BAD!
BETTER THAN YOU KNOW! SINCE CAP RIPPED OFF MY OLD PHOTONIC SHIELD, I FIGURED I'D SWIPE AN OLD SET-UP OF HIS!
MY SHIELD'S PACKED WITH ELECTRONICS -- AND REMOTE-CONTROLLED! EVEN AFTER I'VE THROWN IT --
"-- IT'S STILL A DEADLY OFFENSIVE WEAPON!"
YEAH, MAYBE -- BUT CAP CAN DO THAT WITHOUT ANY GIZMOS!
AND THEN THERE'S THE OTHER PROBLEM -- WHEN YOU'VE GOT IT CAREENING AROUND THE SKY LIKE THIS --
-- IT DOESN'T DO MUCH SHIELDING, DOES IT?
Oh, AND I WISH I COULD SAY I THOUGHT IT WAS BENEATH YOU--
-- TO BECOME A FASCIST STORMTROOPER FOR CORPORATE SLIME LIKE CORD, AND TO WORK WITH PSYCHOS LIKE THE JURY --
POOM
WHY YOU--!
-- BUT I CAN'T REALLY SAY IT'S A CHANGE FOR YOU!

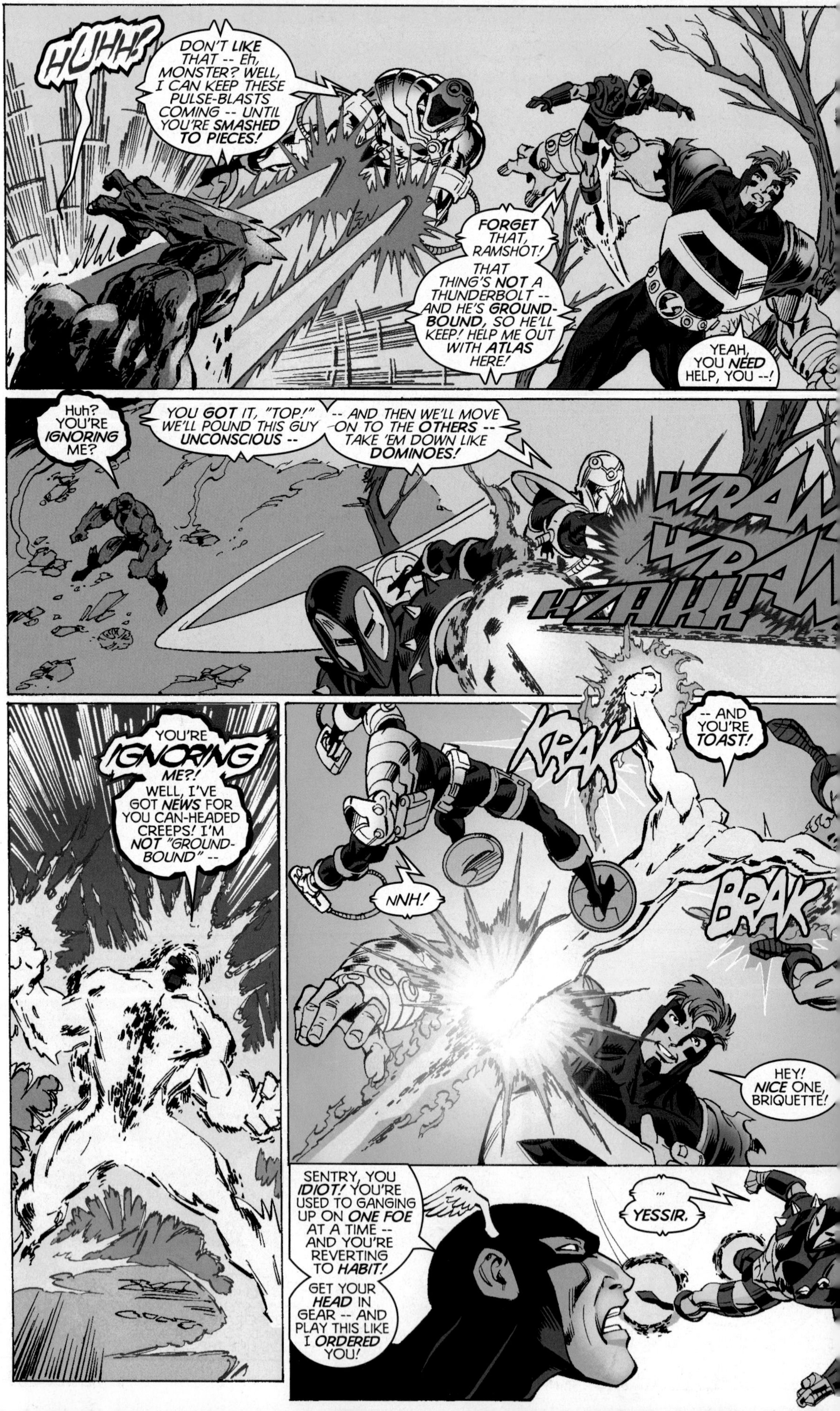
HUHH!
DON'T LIKE THAT -- Eh, MONSTER? WELL, I CAN KEEP THESE PULSE-BLASTS COMING -- UNTIL YOU'RE SMASHED TO PIECES!
FORGET THAT, RAMSHOT!
THAT THING'S NOT A THUNDERBOLT -- AND HE'S GROUND-BOUND, SO HE'LL KEEP! HELP ME OUT WITH ATLAS HERE!
YEAH, YOU NEED HELP, YOU --!
Huh? YOU'RE IGNORING ME?
YOU GOT IT, "TOP!" WE'LL POUND THIS GUY UNCONSCIOUS --
-- AND THEN WE'LL MOVE ON TO THE OTHERS -- TAKE 'EM DOWN LIKE DOMINOES!
HZAKK
YOU'RE IGNORING ME?! WELL, I'VE GOT NEWS FOR YOU CAN-HEADED CREEPS! I'M NOT "GROUND-BOUND" --
KRAK
-- AND YOU'RE TOAST!
NNH!
BRAK
HEY! NICE ONE, BRIQUETTE!
SENTRY, YOU IDIOT! YOU'RE USED TO GANGING UP ON ONE FOE AT A TIME -- AND YOU'RE REVERTING TO HABIT!
GET YOUR HEAD IN GEAR -- AND PLAY THIS LIKE I ORDERED YOU!
...
YESSIR.

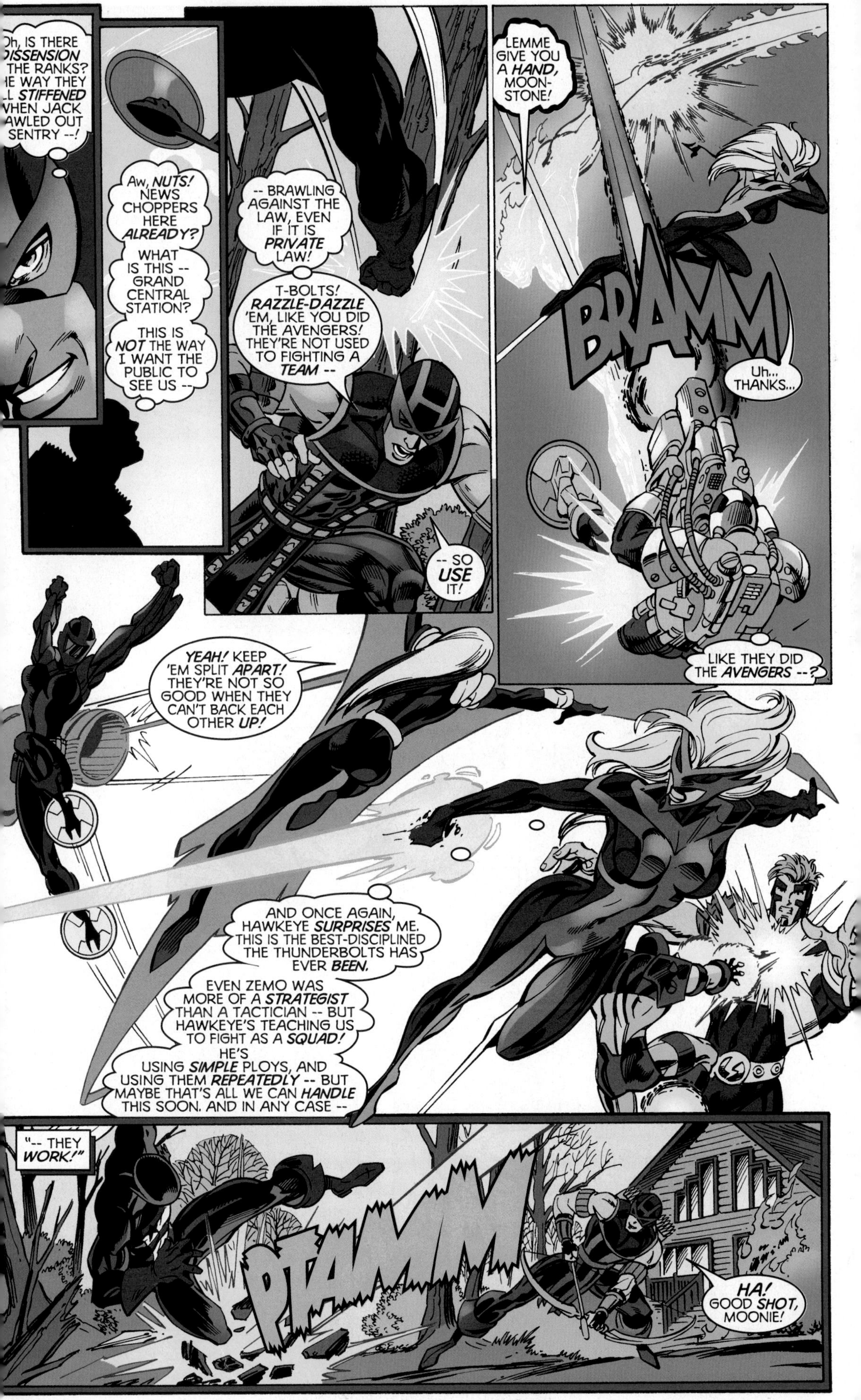
Oh, IS THERE DISSENSION IN THE RANKS? THE WAY THEY ALL STIFFENED WHEN JACK BAWLED OUT SENTRY --!
Aw, NUTS! NEWS CHOPPERS HERE ALREADY?
WHAT IS THIS -- GRAND CENTRAL STATION?
THIS IS NOT THE WAY I WANT THE PUBLIC TO SEE US --
-- BRAWLING AGAINST THE LAW, EVEN IF IT IS PRIVATE LAW!
T-BOLTS! RAZZLE-DAZZLE 'EM, LIKE YOU DID THE AVENGERS! THEY'RE NOT USED TO FIGHTING A TEAM --
-- SO USE IT!
LEMME GIVE YOU A HAND, MOON-STONE!
BRAMM
Uh... THANKS...
LIKE THEY DID THE AVENGERS --?
YEAH! KEEP 'EM SPLIT APART! THEY'RE NOT SO GOOD WHEN THEY CAN'T BACK EACH OTHER UP!
AND ONCE AGAIN, HAWKEYE SURPRISES ME. THIS IS THE BEST-DISCIPLINED THE THUNDERBOLTS HAS EVER BEEN.
EVEN ZEMO WAS MORE OF A STRATEGIST THAN A TACTICIAN -- BUT HAWKEYE'S TEACHING US TO FIGHT AS A SQUAD!
HE'S USING SIMPLE PLOYS, AND USING THEM REPEATEDLY -- BUT MAYBE THAT'S ALL WE CAN HANDLE THIS SOON. AND IN ANY CASE --
"-- THEY WORK!"
PTAMM
HA! GOOD SHOT, MOONIE!

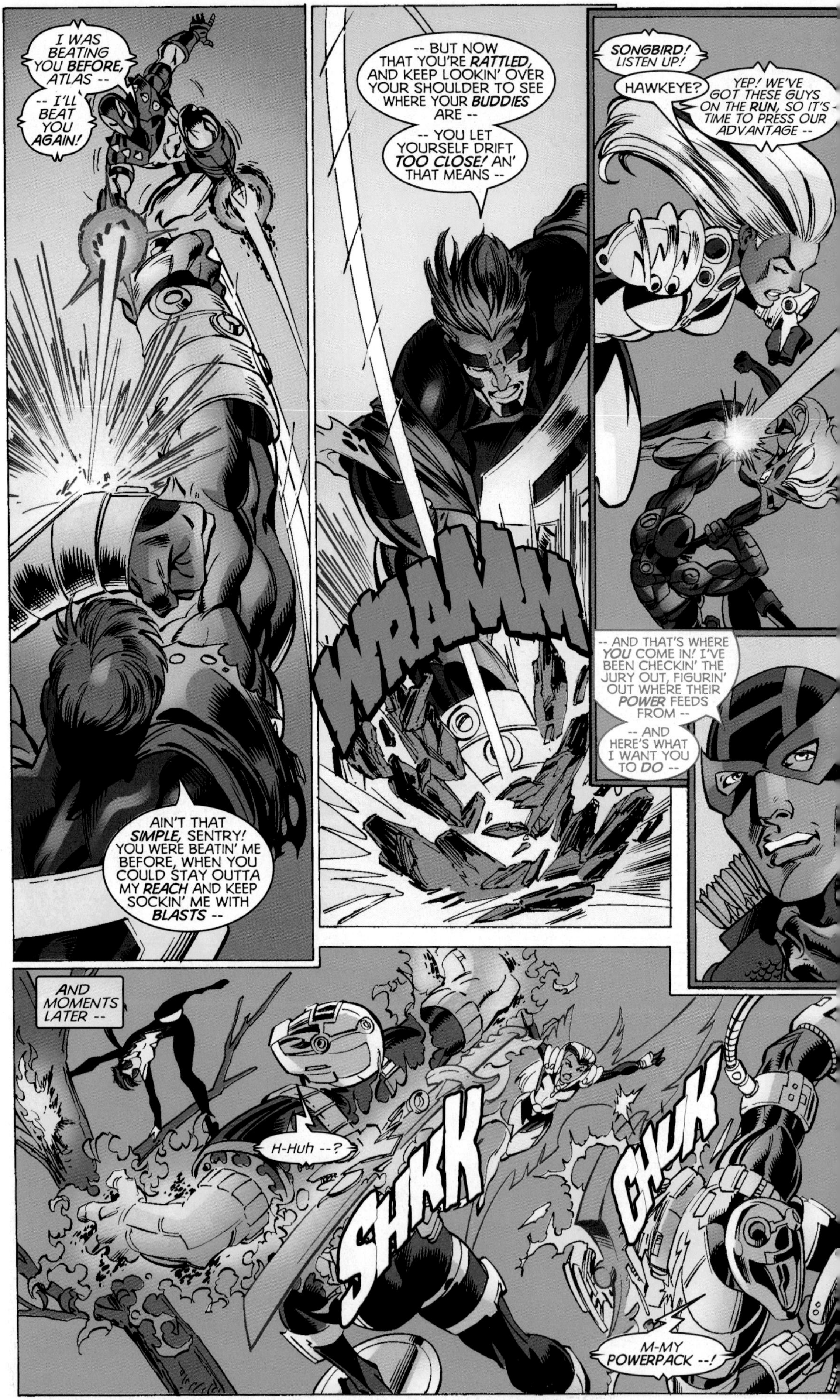
I WAS BEATING YOU BEFORE, ATLAS --
-- I'LL BEAT YOU AGAIN!
AIN'T THAT SIMPLE, SENTRY! YOU WERE BEATIN' ME BEFORE, WHEN YOU COULD STAY OUTTA MY REACH AND KEEP SOCKIN' ME WITH BLASTS --
-- BUT NOW THAT YOU'RE RATTLED, AND KEEP LOOKIN' OVER YOUR SHOULDER TO SEE WHERE YOUR BUDDIES ARE --
-- YOU LET YOURSELF DRIFT TOO CLOSE! AN' THAT MEANS --
WRAMM
SONGBIRD! LISTEN UP!
HAWKEYE?
YEP! WE'VE GOT THESE GUYS ON THE RUN, SO IT'S TIME TO PRESS OUR ADVANTAGE --
-- AND THAT'S WHERE YOU COME IN! I'VE BEEN CHECKIN' THE JURY OUT, FIGURIN' OUT WHERE THEIR POWER FEEDS FROM --
-- AND HERE'S WHAT I WANT YOU TO DO --
AND MOMENTS LATER --
H-Huh --?
SHKK
CHUK
M-MY POWERPACK --!

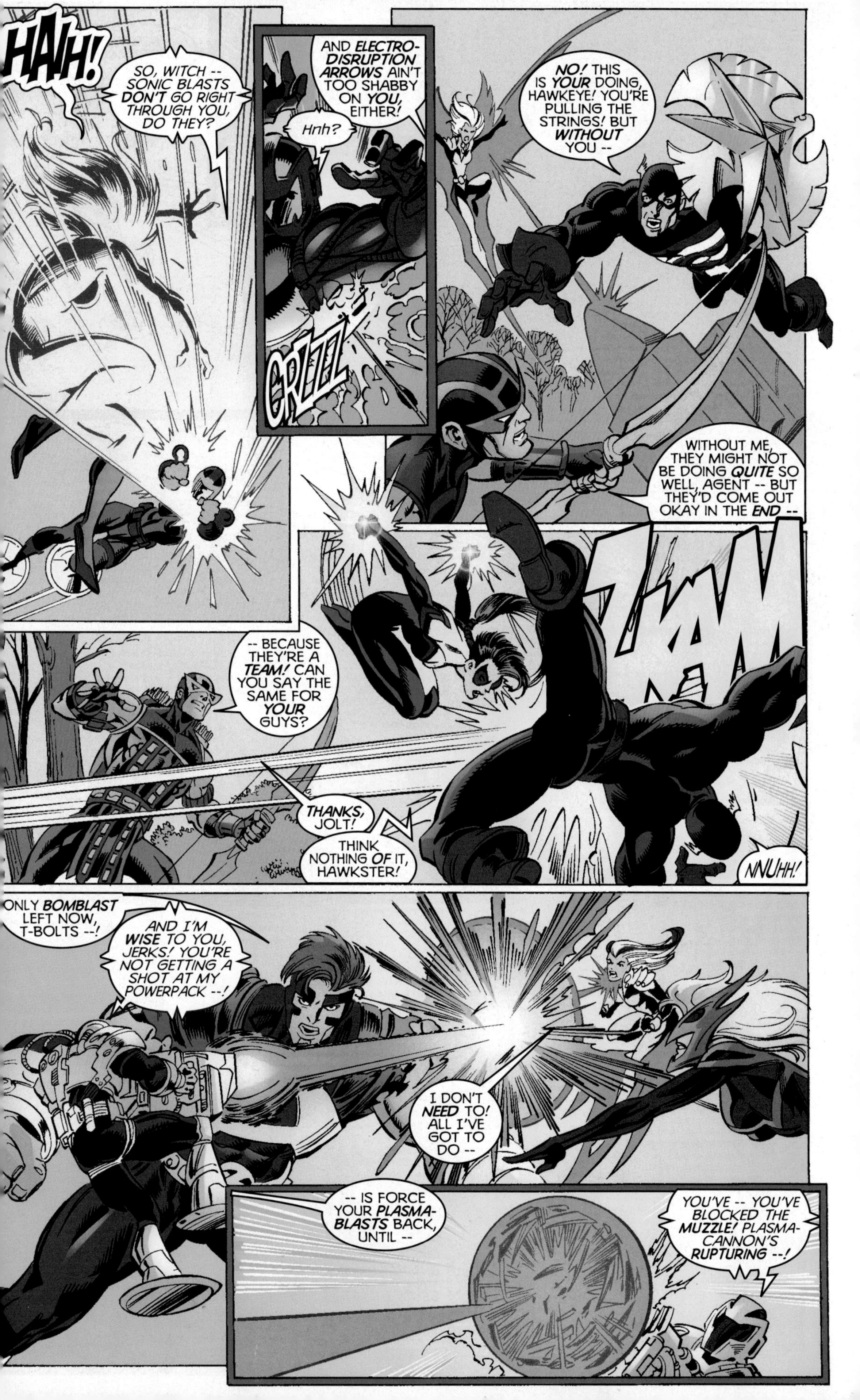
HAIH!
SO, WITCH -- SONIC BLASTS DON'T GO RIGHT THROUGH YOU, DO THEY?
AND ELECTRO-DISRUPTION ARROWS AIN'T TOO SHABBY ON YOU, EITHER!
Hnh?
CRZZZ
NO! THIS IS YOUR DOING, HAWKEYE! YOU'RE PULLING THE STRINGS! BUT WITHOUT YOU --
WITHOUT ME, THEY MIGHT NOT BE DOING QUITE SO WELL, AGENT -- BUT THEY'D COME OUT OKAY IN THE END --
-- BECAUSE THEY'RE A TEAM! CAN YOU SAY THE SAME FOR YOUR GUYS?
ZZAM
THANKS, JOLT!
THINK NOTHING OF IT, HAWKSTER!
NNUHH!
ONLY BOMBLAST LEFT NOW, T-BOLTS --!
AND I'M WISE TO YOU, JERKS! YOU'RE NOT GETTING A SHOT AT MY POWERPACK --!
I DON'T NEED TO! ALL I'VE GOT TO DO --
-- IS FORCE YOUR PLASMA-BLASTS BACK, UNTIL --
YOU'VE -- YOU'VE BLOCKED THE MUZZLE! PLASMA-CANNON'S RUPTURING --!

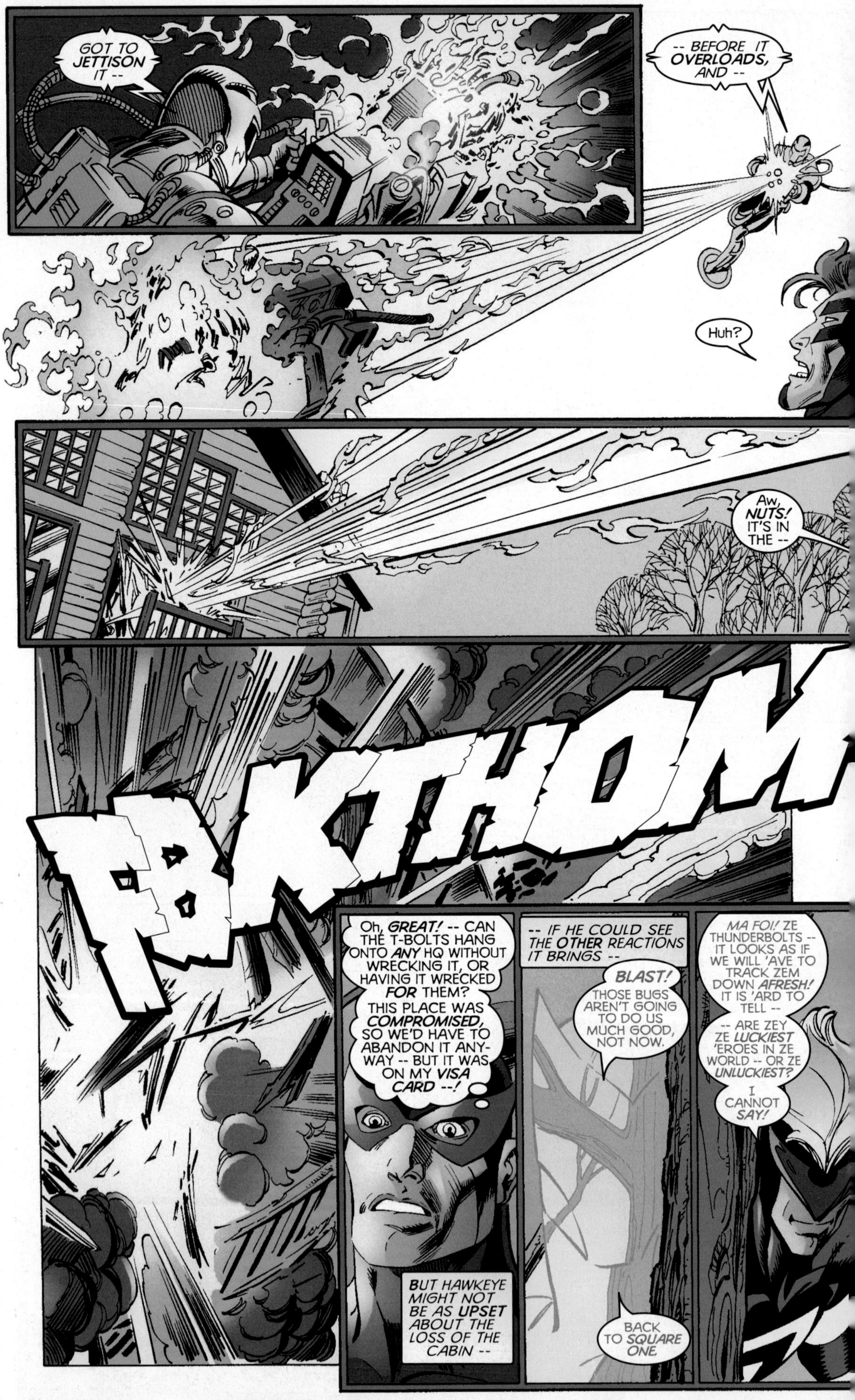
GOT TO JETTISON IT --
-- BEFORE IT OVERLOADS, AND --
Huh?
Aw, NUTS! IT'S IN THE --
BKTHOM
Oh, GREAT! -- CAN THE T-BOLTS HANG ONTO ANY HQ WITHOUT WRECKING IT, OR HAVING IT WRECKED FOR THEM? THIS PLACE WAS COMPROMISED, SO WE'D HAVE TO ABANDON IT ANY-WAY -- BUT IT WAS ON MY VISA CARD --!
BUT HAWKEYE MIGHT NOT BE AS UPSET ABOUT THE LOSS OF THE CABIN --
-- IF HE COULD SEE THE OTHER REACTIONS IT BRINGS --
BLAST! THOSE BUGS AREN'T GOING TO DO US MUCH GOOD, NOT NOW.
BACK TO SQUARE ONE.
MA FOI! ZE THUNDERBOLTS -- IT LOOKS AS IF WE WILL 'AVE TO TRACK ZEM DOWN AFRESH! IT IS 'ARD TO TELL --
-- ARE ZEY ZE LUCKIEST 'EROES IN ZE WORLD -- OR ZE UNLUCKIEST?
I CANNOT SAY!

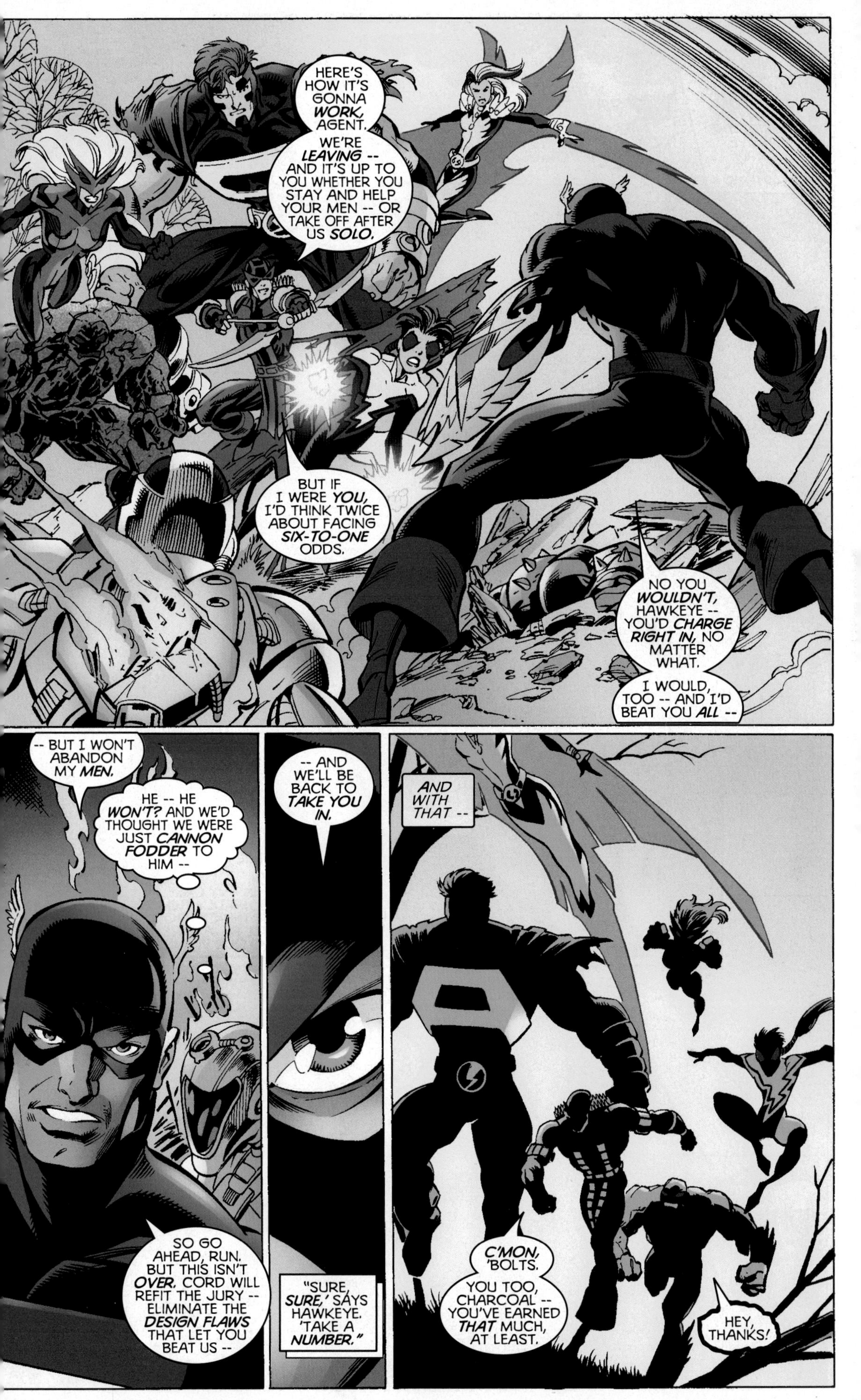
HERE'S HOW IT'S GONNA WORK, AGENT.
WE'RE LEAVING -- AND IT'S UP TO YOU WHETHER YOU STAY AND HELP YOUR MEN -- OR TAKE OFF AFTER US SOLO.
BUT IF I WERE YOU, I'D THINK TWICE ABOUT FACING SIX-TO-ONE ODDS.
NO YOU WOULDN'T, HAWKEYE -- YOU'D CHARGE RIGHT IN, NO MATTER WHAT.
I WOULD, TOO -- AND I'D BEAT YOU ALL --
-- BUT I WON'T ABANDON MY MEN.
HE -- HE WON'T? AND WE'D THOUGHT WE WERE JUST CANNON FODDER TO HIM --
SO GO AHEAD, RUN. BUT THIS ISN'T OVER. CORD WILL REFIT THE JURY -- ELIMINATE THE DESIGN FLAWS THAT LET YOU BEAT US --
-- AND WE'LL BE BACK TO TAKE YOU IN.
"SURE, SURE,' SAYS HAWKEYE. 'TAKE A NUMBER."
AND WITH THAT --
C'MON, 'BOLTS.
YOU TOO, CHARCOAL -- YOU'VE EARNED THAT MUCH, AT LEAST.
HEY, THANKS!

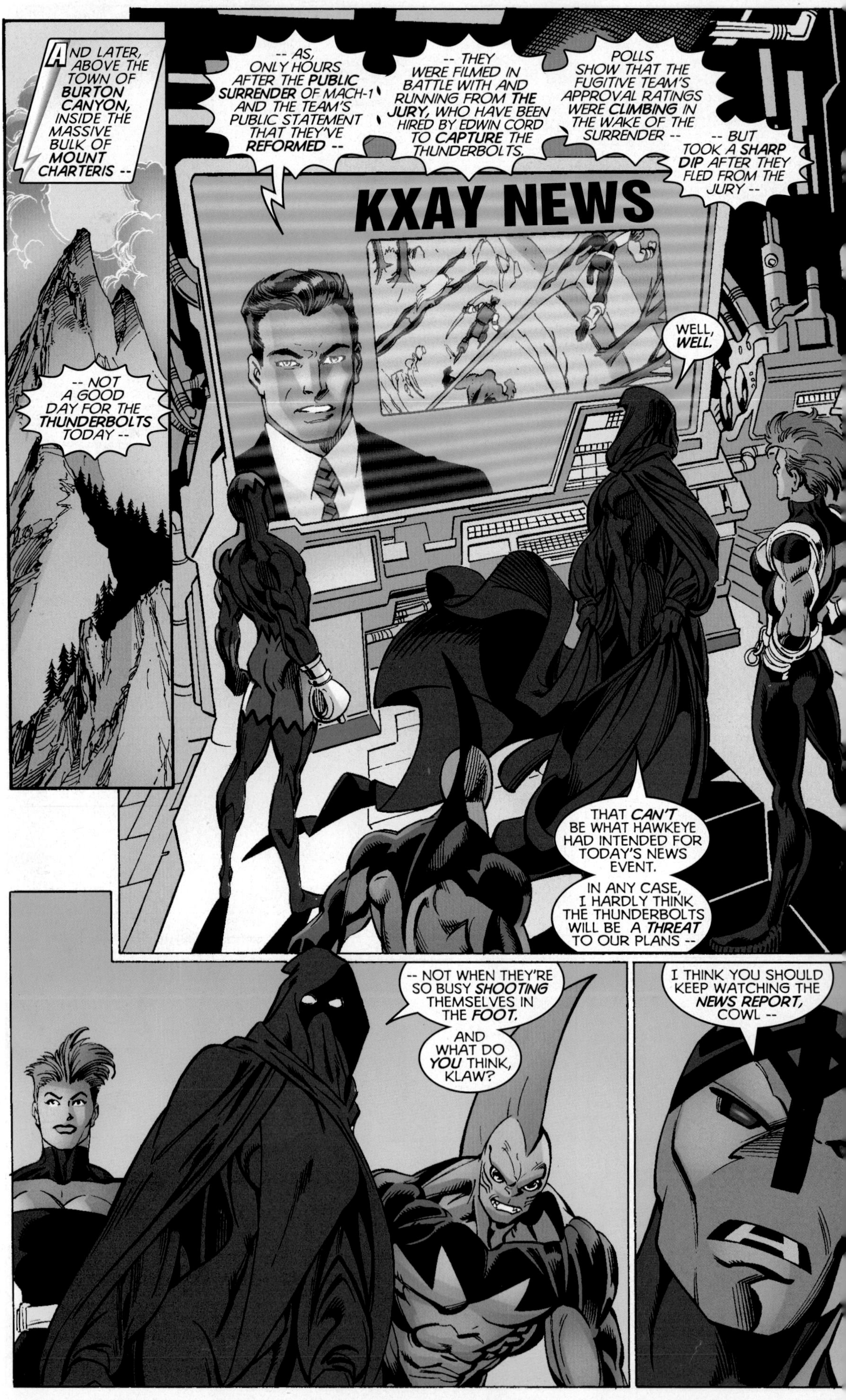
AND LATER, ABOVE THE TOWN OF BURTON CANYON, INSIDE THE MASSIVE BULK OF MOUNT CHARTERIS --
-- NOT A GOOD DAY FOR THE THUNDERBOLTS TODAY --
-- AS, ONLY HOURS AFTER THE PUBLIC SURRENDER OF MACH-1 AND THE TEAM'S PUBLIC STATEMENT THAT THEY'VE REFORMED --
-- THEY WERE FILMED IN BATTLE WITH AND RUNNING FROM THE JURY, WHO HAVE BEEN HIRED BY EDWIN CORD TO CAPTURE THE THUNDERBOLTS.
POLLS SHOW THAT THE FUGITIVE TEAM'S APPROVAL RATINGS WERE CLIMBING IN THE WAKE OF THE SURRENDER --
-- BUT TOOK A SHARP DIP AFTER THEY FLED FROM THE JURY --
KXAY NEWS
WELL, WELL.
THAT CAN'T BE WHAT HAWKEYE HAD INTENDED FOR TODAY'S NEWS EVENT.
IN ANY CASE, I HARDLY THINK THE THUNDERBOLTS WILL BE A THREAT TO OUR PLANS --
-- NOT WHEN THEY'RE SO BUSY SHOOTING THEMSELVES IN THE FOOT.
AND WHAT DO YOU THINK, KLAW?
I THINK YOU SHOULD KEEP WATCHING THE NEWS REPORT, COWL --

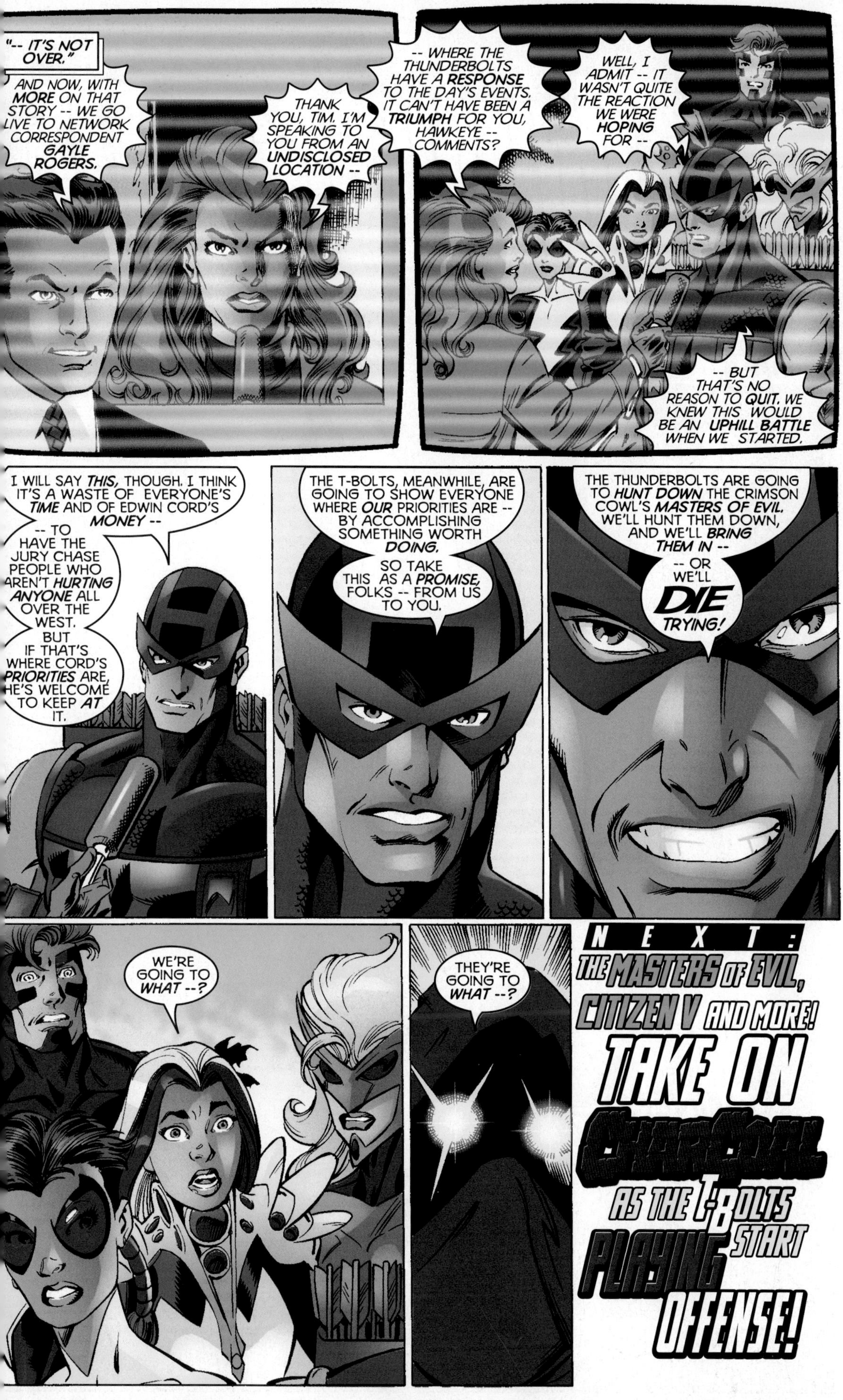
"-- IT'S NOT OVER."
AND NOW, WITH MORE ON THAT STORY -- WE GO LIVE TO NETWORK CORRESPONDENT GAYLE ROGERS.
THANK YOU, TIM. I'M SPEAKING TO YOU FROM AN UNDISCLOSED LOCATION --
-- WHERE THE THUNDERBOLTS HAVE A RESPONSE TO THE DAY'S EVENTS. IT CAN'T HAVE BEEN A TRIUMPH FOR YOU, HAWKEYE -- COMMENTS?
WELL, I ADMIT -- IT WASN'T QUITE THE REACTION WE WERE HOPING FOR --
-- BUT THAT'S NO REASON TO QUIT. WE KNEW THIS WOULD BE AN UPHILL BATTLE WHEN WE STARTED.
I WILL SAY THIS, THOUGH. I THINK IT'S A WASTE OF EVERYONE'S TIME AND OF EDWIN CORD'S MONEY --
-- TO HAVE THE JURY CHASE PEOPLE WHO AREN'T HURTING ANYONE ALL OVER THE WEST. BUT IF THAT'S WHERE CORD'S PRIORITIES ARE, HE'S WELCOME TO KEEP AT IT.
THE T-BOLTS, MEANWHILE, ARE GOING TO SHOW EVERYONE WHERE OUR PRIORITIES ARE -- BY ACCOMPLISHING SOMETHING WORTH DOING.
SO TAKE THIS AS A PROMISE, FOLKS -- FROM US TO YOU.
THE THUNDERBOLTS ARE GOING TO HUNT DOWN THE CRIMSON COWL'S MASTERS OF EVIL. WE'LL HUNT THEM DOWN, AND WE'LL BRING THEM IN --
-- OR WE'LL DIE TRYING!
WE'RE GOING TO WHAT --?
THEY'RE GOING TO WHAT --?
NEXT:
THE MASTERS OF EVIL, CITIZEN V AND MORE!
TAKE ON
AS THE T-BOLTS START PLAYING OFFENSE!

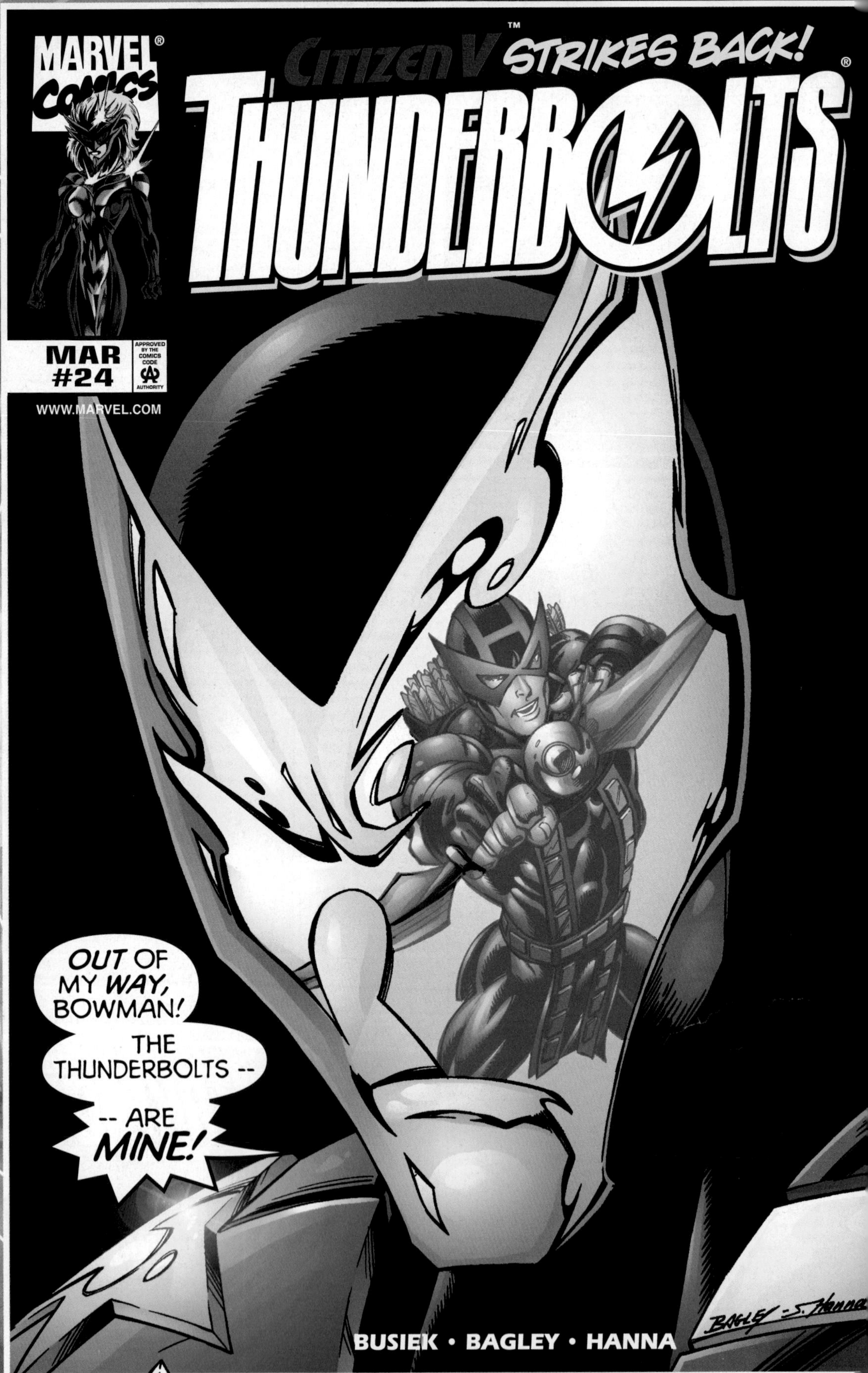
MARVEL® COMICS
CITIZEN V™ STRIKES BACK!
THUNDERBOLTS®
MAR #24
APPROVED BY THE COMICS CODE AUTHORITY
WWW.MARVEL.COM
OUT OF MY WAY, BOWMAN!
THE THUNDERBOLTS --
-- ARE MINE!
BAGLEY - S. HANNA
BUSIEK • BAGLEY • HANNA

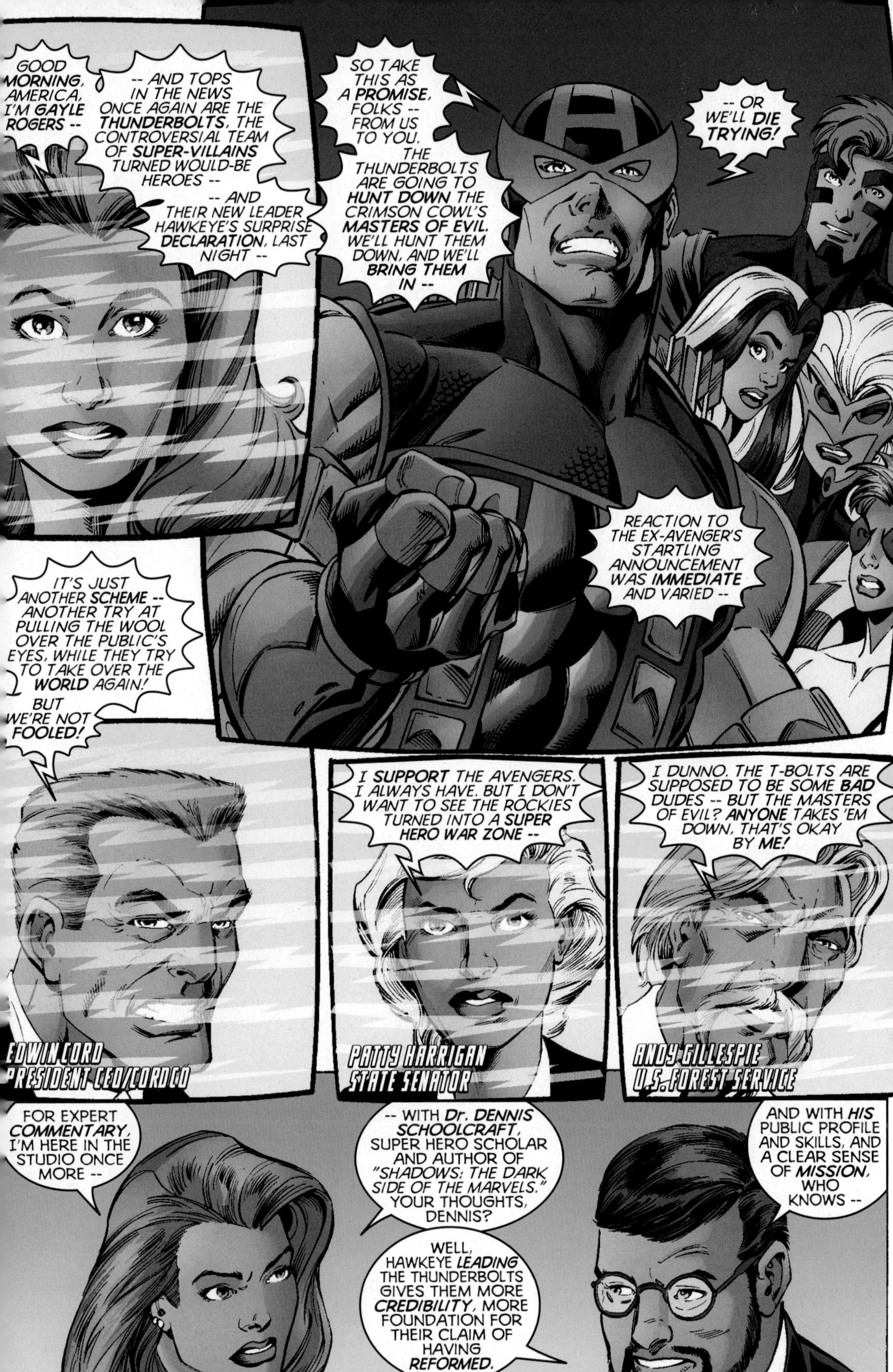
GOOD MORNING, AMERICA, I'M GAYLE ROGERS --
-- AND TOPS IN THE NEWS ONCE AGAIN ARE THE THUNDERBOLTS, THE CONTROVERSIAL TEAM OF SUPER-VILLAINS TURNED WOULD-BE HEROES --
-- AND THEIR NEW LEADER HAWKEYE'S SURPRISE DECLARATION, LAST NIGHT --
SO TAKE THIS AS A PROMISE, FOLKS -- FROM US TO YOU. THE THUNDERBOLTS ARE GOING TO HUNT DOWN THE CRIMSON COWL'S MASTERS OF EVIL. WE'LL HUNT THEM DOWN, AND WE'LL BRING THEM IN --
-- OR WE'LL DIE TRYING!
REACTION TO THE EX-AVENGER'S STARTLING ANNOUNCEMENT WAS IMMEDIATE AND VARIED --
IT'S JUST ANOTHER SCHEME -- ANOTHER TRY AT PULLING THE WOOL OVER THE PUBLIC'S EYES, WHILE THEY TRY TO TAKE OVER THE WORLD AGAIN!
BUT WE'RE NOT FOOLED!
EDWIN CORD
PRESIDENT CEO/CORDCO
I SUPPORT THE AVENGERS. I ALWAYS HAVE. BUT I DON'T WANT TO SEE THE ROCKIES TURNED INTO A SUPER HERO WAR ZONE --
PATTY HARRIGAN
STATE SENATOR
I DUNNO. THE T-BOLTS ARE SUPPOSED TO BE SOME BAD DUDES -- BUT THE MASTERS OF EVIL? ANYONE TAKES 'EM DOWN, THAT'S OKAY BY ME!
ANDY GILLESPIE
U.S. FOREST SERVICE
FOR EXPERT COMMENTARY, I'M HERE IN THE STUDIO ONCE MORE --
-- WITH Dr. DENNIS SCHOOLCRAFT, SUPER HERO SCHOLAR AND AUTHOR OF "SHADOWS: THE DARK SIDE OF THE MARVELS." YOUR THOUGHTS, DENNIS?
WELL, HAWKEYE LEADING THE THUNDERBOLTS GIVES THEM MORE CREDIBILITY, MORE FOUNDATION FOR THEIR CLAIM OF HAVING REFORMED.
AND WITH HIS PUBLIC PROFILE AND SKILLS, AND A CLEAR SENSE OF MISSION, WHO KNOWS --

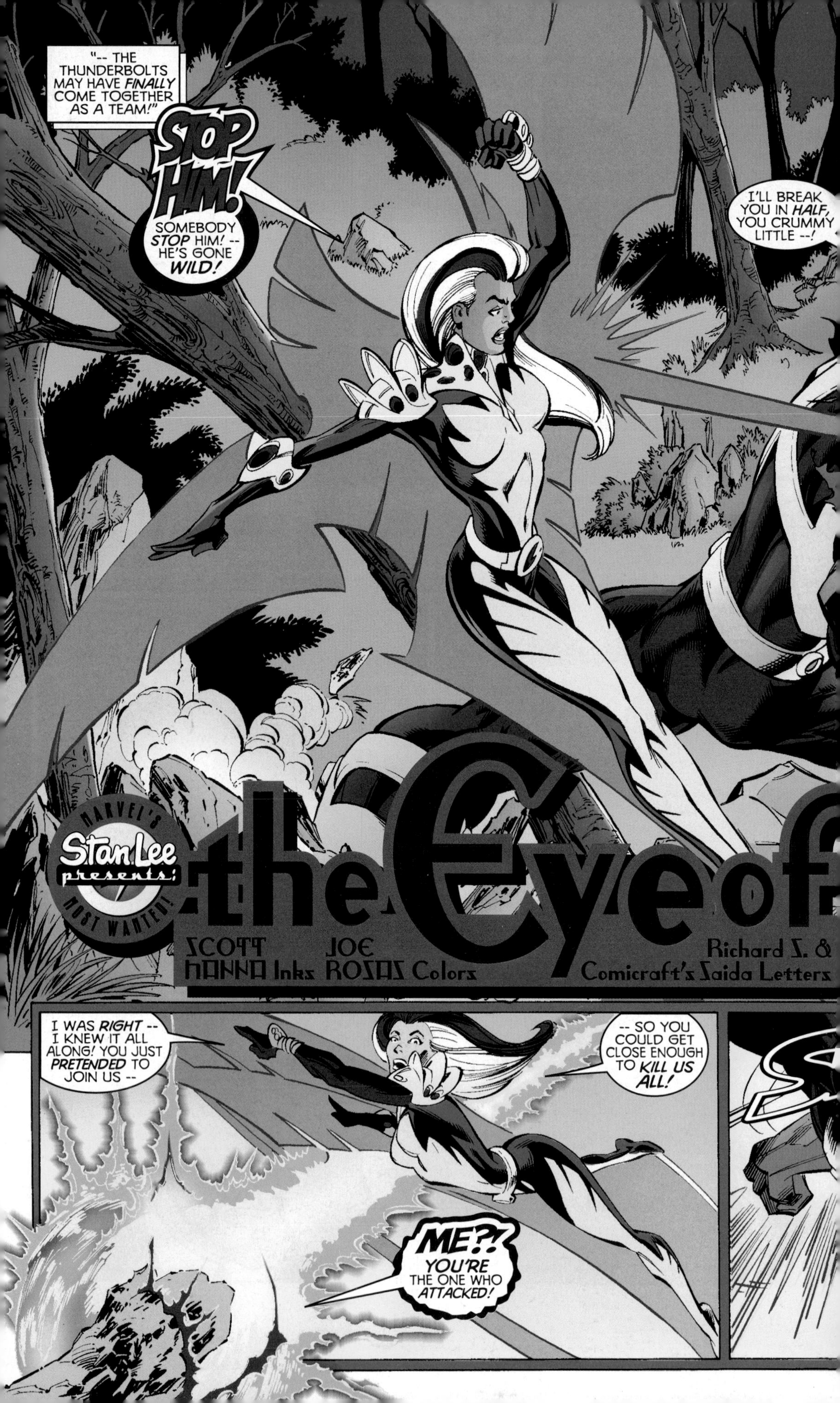
"-- THE THUNDERBOLTS MAY HAVE FINALLY COME TOGETHER AS A TEAM!"
STOP HIM! SOMEBODY STOP HIM! -- HE'S GONE WILD!
I'LL BREAK YOU IN HALF, YOU CRUMMY LITTLE --!
MARVEL'S MOST WANTED! Stan Lee presents:
the Eye of
SCOTT HANNA Inks
JOE ROSAS Colors
Richard S. &
Comicraft's Saida Letters
I WAS RIGHT -- I KNEW IT ALL ALONG! YOU JUST PRETENDED TO JOIN US --
-- SO YOU COULD GET CLOSE ENOUGH TO KILL US ALL!
ME?! YOU'RE THE ONE WHO ATTACKED!

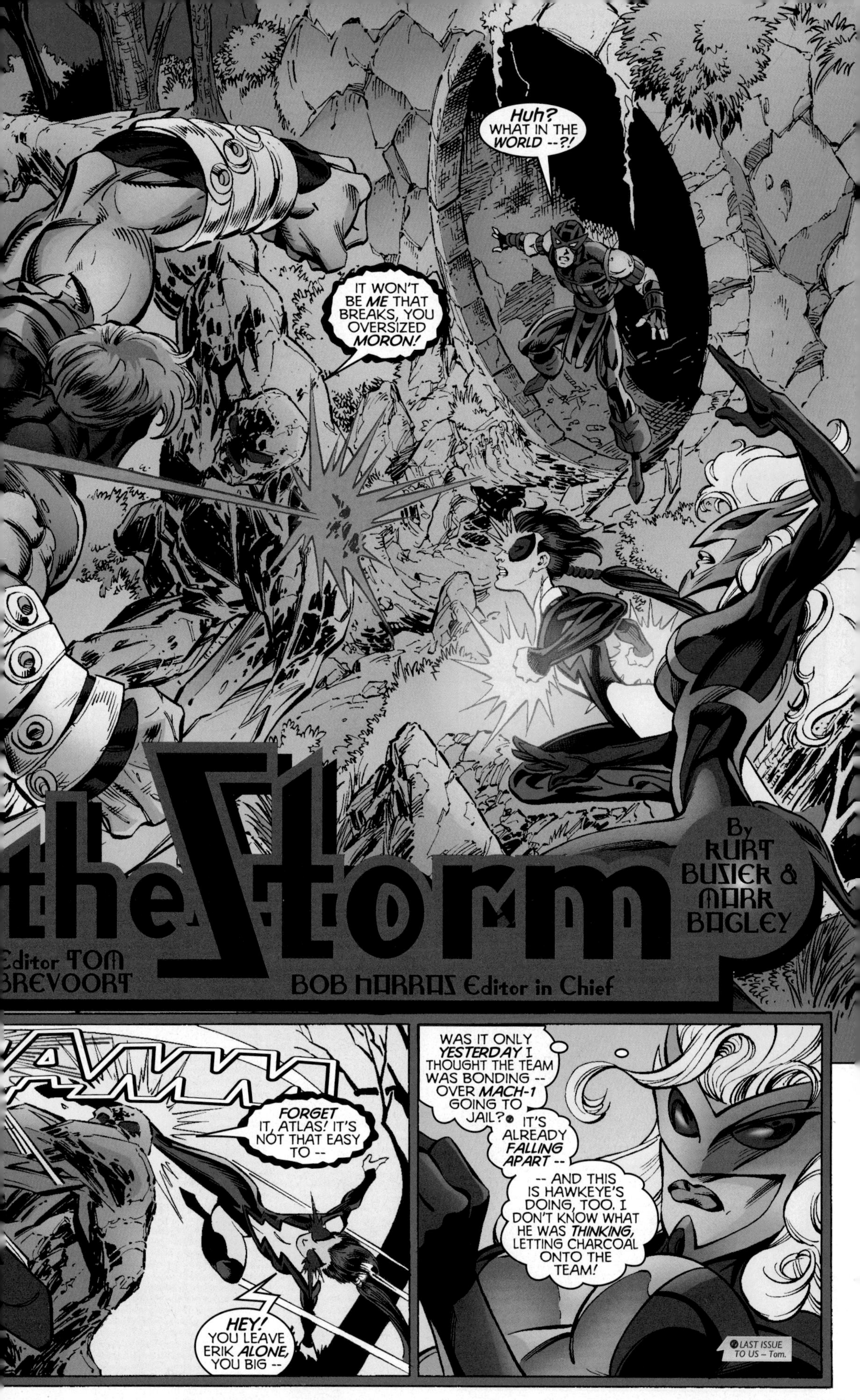
Huh? WHAT IN THE WORLD --?!
IT WON'T BE ME THAT BREAKS, YOU OVERSIZED MORON!
the Storm
By KURT BUSIEK & MARK BAGLEY
Editor TOM BREVOORT
BOB HARRAS Editor in Chief
FORGET IT, ATLAS! IT'S NOT THAT EASY TO --
HEY! YOU LEAVE ERIK ALONE, YOU BIG --
WAS IT ONLY YESTERDAY I THOUGHT THE TEAM WAS BONDING -- OVER MACH-1 GOING TO JAIL?* IT'S ALREADY FALLING APART --
-- AND THIS IS HAWKEYE'S DOING, TOO. I DON'T KNOW WHAT HE WAS THINKING, LETTING CHARCOAL ONTO THE TEAM!
* LAST ISSUE TO US – Tom.

ALL RIGHT, EVERYONE *STAND DOWN* -- NOW! AND I MEAN --

NOW!

Huh --?

WHAT?

?

THANK YOU. THAT'S VERY CONSIDERATE OF YOU, ON A MORNING WHERE THERE'S NO COFFEE IN *SIGHT*. NOW -- DOES ANYONE WANT TO TAKE A *CRACK* AT TELLING ME WHAT THE HECK'S *GOING ON* HERE?

CHARCOAL ATTACKED *MELISSA* --

I WASN'T ATTACKING *ANYONE!*

I *WOKE UP*, AND THERE HE WAS, LOOMING OVER ME, ABOUT TO *CRUSH* ME -- SO I *DEFENDED* MYSELF!

I WAS JUST TRYING TO GET *PAST* HER -- SO I COULD GO OFF INTO THE WOODS AND GO TO THE *BATHROOM*, FOR PETE'S SAKE!

HE WAS IN HIS *MONSTER* FORM!

MY *MONSTER* FORM?

IN CASE ANYONE HADN'T NOTICED, IT'S *COLD* OUT HERE! M CHARCOAL FORM IS *WARMER*, THAT'S ALL!

WHAT, SHE WANTS ME TO *FREEZE* --?

REEL BIG FISH

⌐SIGH⌐ WHAT AM I GONNA *DO* WITH THIS BUNCH OF *YAHOOS* --?

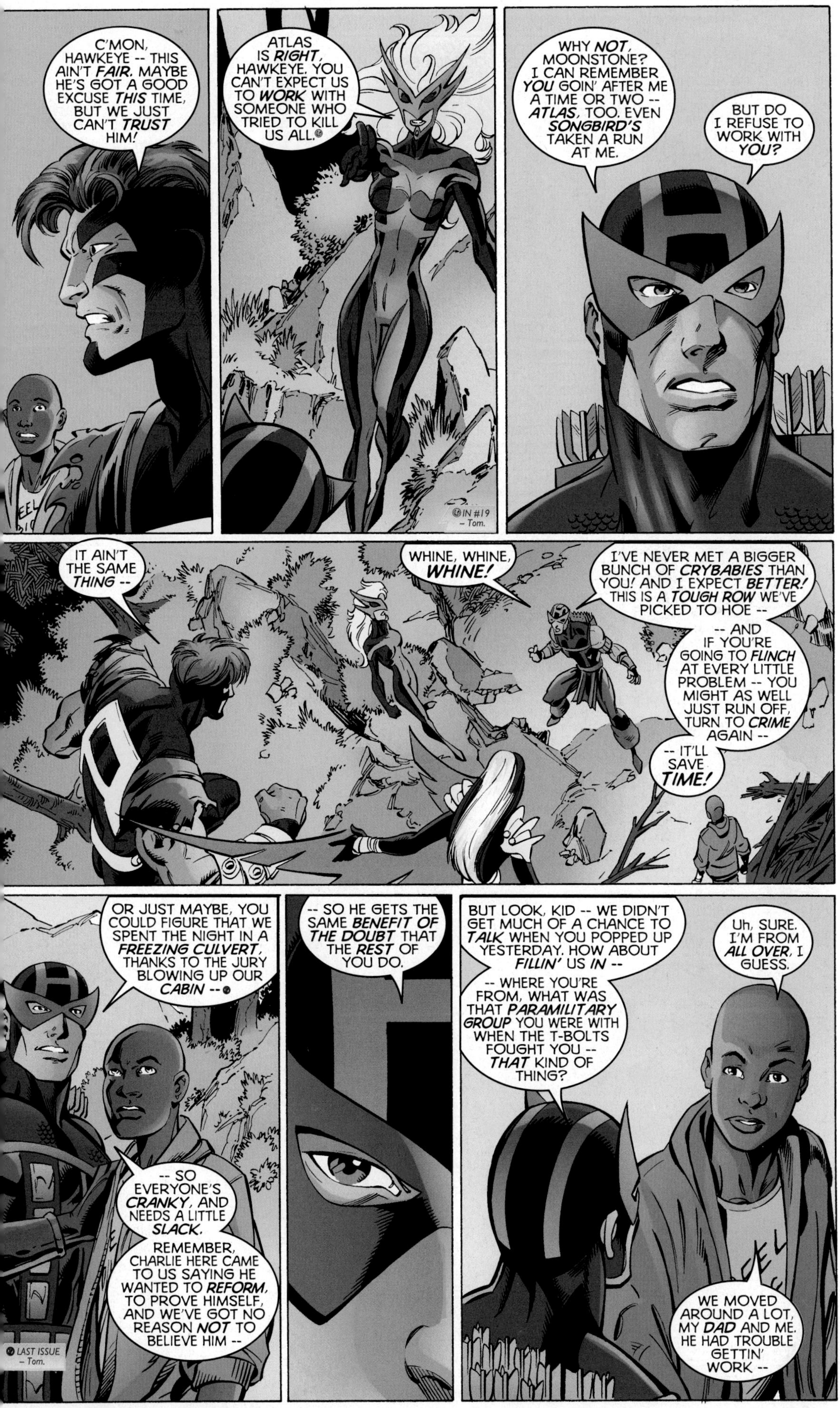
C'MON, HAWKEYE -- THIS AIN'T FAIR. MAYBE HE'S GOT A GOOD EXCUSE THIS TIME, BUT WE JUST CAN'T TRUST HIM!
ATLAS IS RIGHT, HAWKEYE. YOU CAN'T EXPECT US TO WORK WITH SOMEONE WHO TRIED TO KILL US ALL.
IN #19 – Tom.
WHY NOT, MOONSTONE? I CAN REMEMBER YOU GOIN' AFTER ME A TIME OR TWO -- ATLAS, TOO. EVEN SONGBIRD'S TAKEN A RUN AT ME.
BUT DO I REFUSE TO WORK WITH YOU?
IT AIN'T THE SAME THING --
WHINE, WHINE, WHINE!
I'VE NEVER MET A BIGGER BUNCH OF CRYBABIES THAN YOU! AND I EXPECT BETTER! THIS IS A TOUGH ROW WE'VE PICKED TO HOE --
-- AND IF YOU'RE GOING TO FLINCH AT EVERY LITTLE PROBLEM -- YOU MIGHT AS WELL JUST RUN OFF, TURN TO CRIME AGAIN --
-- IT'LL SAVE TIME!
OR JUST MAYBE, YOU COULD FIGURE THAT WE SPENT THE NIGHT IN A FREEZING CULVERT, THANKS TO THE JURY BLOWING UP OUR CABIN --
-- SO EVERYONE'S CRANKY, AND NEEDS A LITTLE SLACK.
REMEMBER, CHARLIE HERE CAME TO US SAYING HE WANTED TO REFORM, TO PROVE HIMSELF, AND WE'VE GOT NO REASON NOT TO BELIEVE HIM --
LAST ISSUE – Tom.
-- SO HE GETS THE SAME BENEFIT OF THE DOUBT THAT THE REST OF YOU DO.
BUT LOOK, KID -- WE DIDN'T GET MUCH OF A CHANCE TO TALK WHEN YOU POPPED UP YESTERDAY. HOW ABOUT FILLIN' US IN --
-- WHERE YOU'RE FROM, WHAT WAS THAT PARAMILITARY GROUP YOU WERE WITH WHEN THE T-BOLTS FOUGHT YOU -- THAT KIND OF THING?
Uh, SURE. I'M FROM ALL OVER, I GUESS.
WE MOVED AROUND A LOT, MY DAD AND ME. HE HAD TROUBLE GETTIN' WORK --

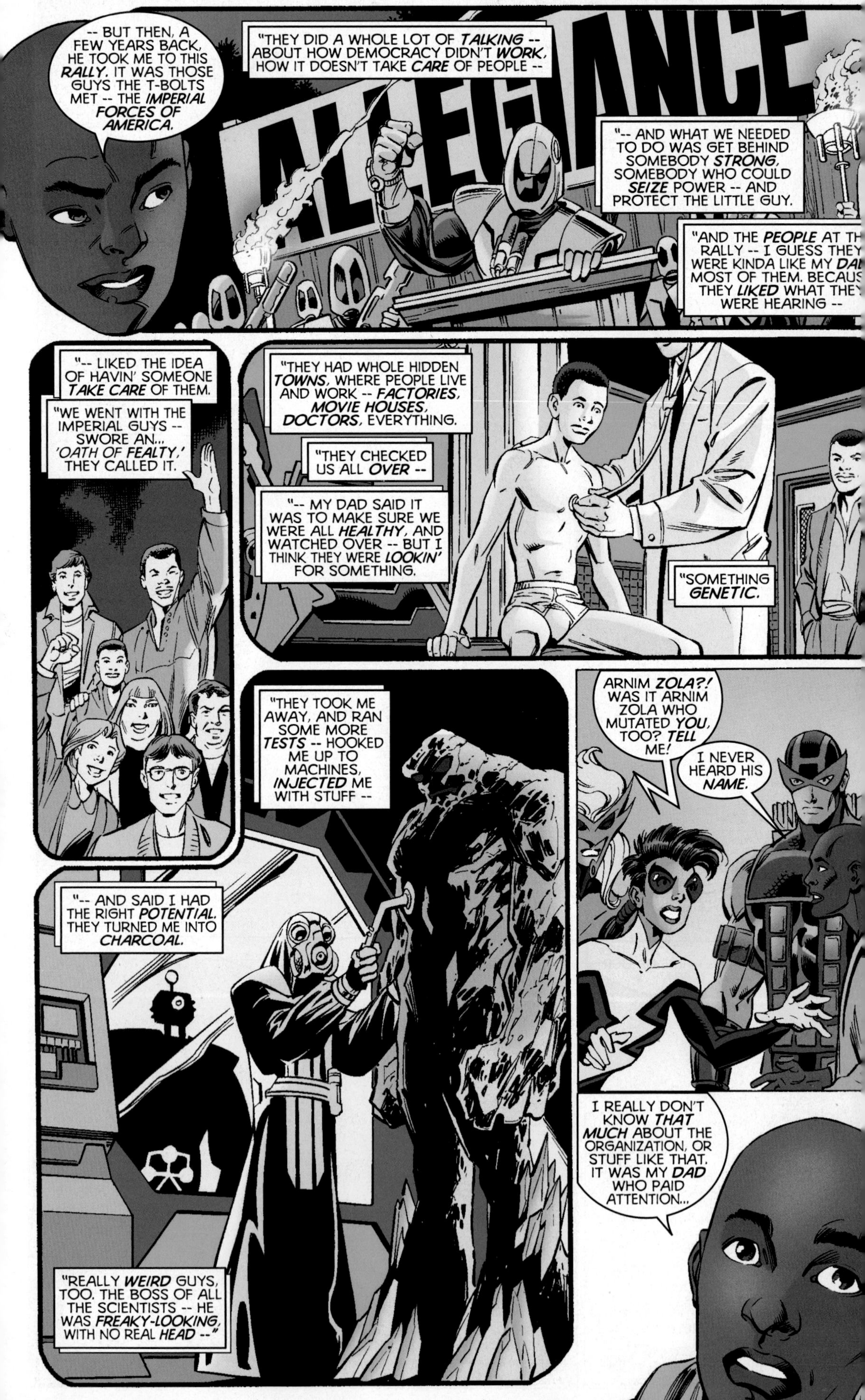
-- BUT THEN, A FEW YEARS BACK, HE TOOK ME TO THIS RALLY. IT WAS THOSE GUYS THE T-BOLTS MET -- THE IMPERIAL FORCES OF AMERICA.
"THEY DID A WHOLE LOT OF TALKING -- ABOUT HOW DEMOCRACY DIDN'T WORK, HOW IT DOESN'T TAKE CARE OF PEOPLE --
ALLEGIANCE
"-- AND WHAT WE NEEDED TO DO WAS GET BEHIND SOMEBODY STRONG, SOMEBODY WHO COULD SEIZE POWER -- AND PROTECT THE LITTLE GUY.
"AND THE PEOPLE AT THE RALLY -- I GUESS THEY WERE KINDA LIKE MY DAD MOST OF THEM. BECAUSE THEY LIKED WHAT THEY WERE HEARING --
"-- LIKED THE IDEA OF HAVIN' SOMEONE TAKE CARE OF THEM.
"WE WENT WITH THE IMPERIAL GUYS -- SWORE AN... 'OATH OF FEALTY,' THEY CALLED IT.
"THEY HAD WHOLE HIDDEN TOWNS, WHERE PEOPLE LIVE AND WORK -- FACTORIES, MOVIE HOUSES, DOCTORS, EVERYTHING.
"THEY CHECKED US ALL OVER --
"-- MY DAD SAID IT WAS TO MAKE SURE WE WERE ALL HEALTHY, AND WATCHED OVER -- BUT I THINK THEY WERE LOOKIN' FOR SOMETHING.
"SOMETHING GENETIC.
"THEY TOOK ME AWAY, AND RAN SOME MORE TESTS -- HOOKED ME UP TO MACHINES, INJECTED ME WITH STUFF --
"-- AND SAID I HAD THE RIGHT POTENTIAL. THEY TURNED ME INTO CHARCOAL.
"REALLY WEIRD GUYS, TOO. THE BOSS OF ALL THE SCIENTISTS -- HE WAS FREAKY-LOOKING, WITH NO REAL HEAD --"
ARNIM ZOLA?! WAS IT ARNIM ZOLA WHO MUTATED YOU, TOO? TELL ME!
I NEVER HEARD HIS NAME.
I REALLY DON'T KNOW THAT MUCH ABOUT THE ORGANIZATION, OR STUFF LIKE THAT. IT WAS MY DAD WHO PAID ATTENTION...

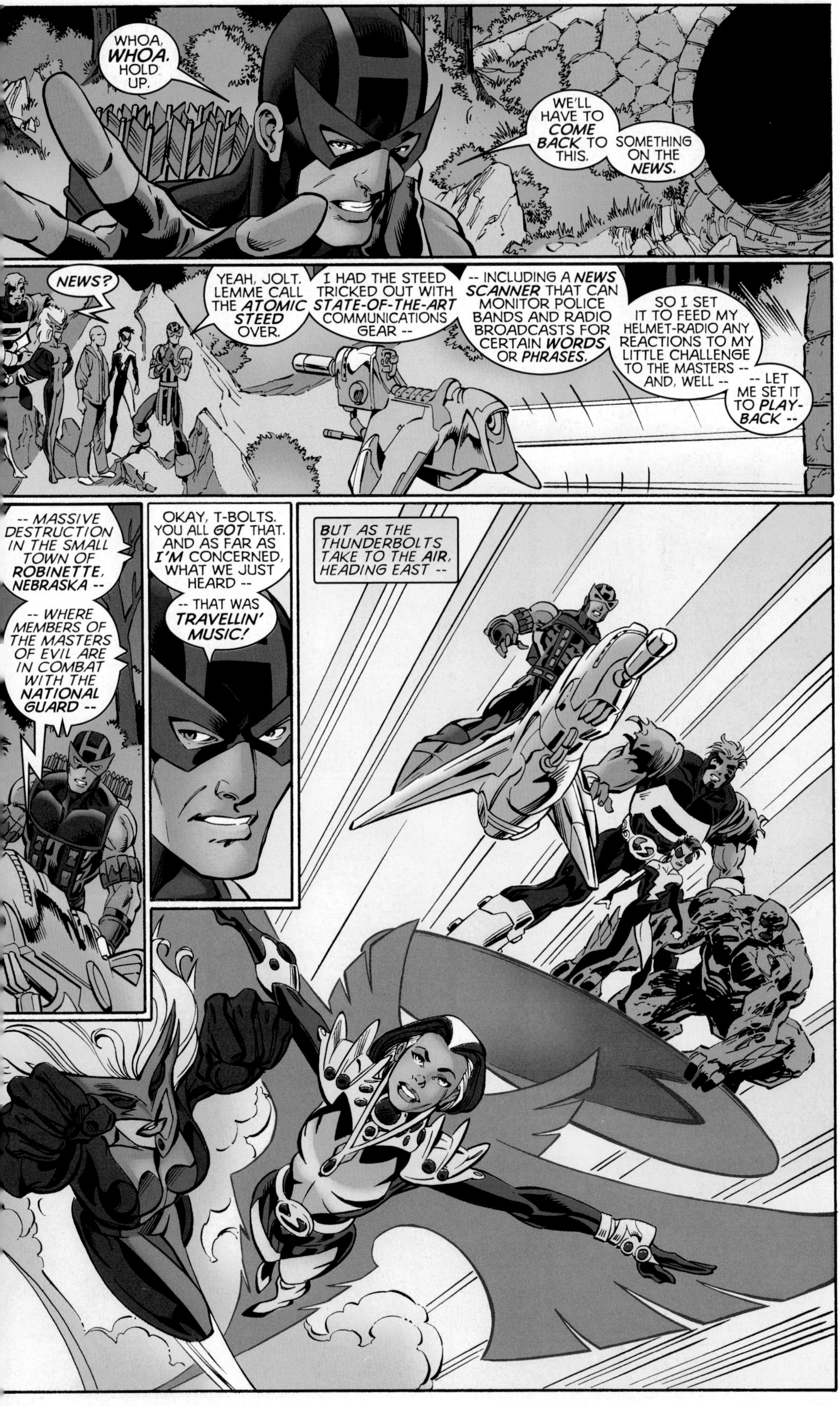
WHOA, WHOA. HOLD UP.
WE'LL HAVE TO COME BACK TO THIS.
SOMETHING ON THE NEWS.
NEWS?
YEAH, JOLT. LEMME CALL THE ATOMIC STEED OVER.
I HAD THE STEED TRICKED OUT WITH STATE-OF-THE-ART COMMUNICATIONS GEAR --
-- INCLUDING A NEWS SCANNER THAT CAN MONITOR POLICE BANDS AND RADIO BROADCASTS FOR CERTAIN WORDS OR PHRASES.
SO I SET IT TO FEED MY HELMET-RADIO ANY REACTIONS TO MY LITTLE CHALLENGE TO THE MASTERS -- AND, WELL --
-- LET ME SET IT TO PLAYBACK --
-- MASSIVE DESTRUCTION IN THE SMALL TOWN OF ROBINETTE, NEBRASKA --
-- WHERE MEMBERS OF THE MASTERS OF EVIL ARE IN COMBAT WITH THE NATIONAL GUARD --
OKAY, T-BOLTS. YOU ALL GOT THAT. AND AS FAR AS I'M CONCERNED, WHAT WE JUST HEARD --
-- THAT WAS TRAVELLIN' MUSIC!
BUT AS THE THUNDERBOLTS TAKE TO THE AIR, HEADING EAST --

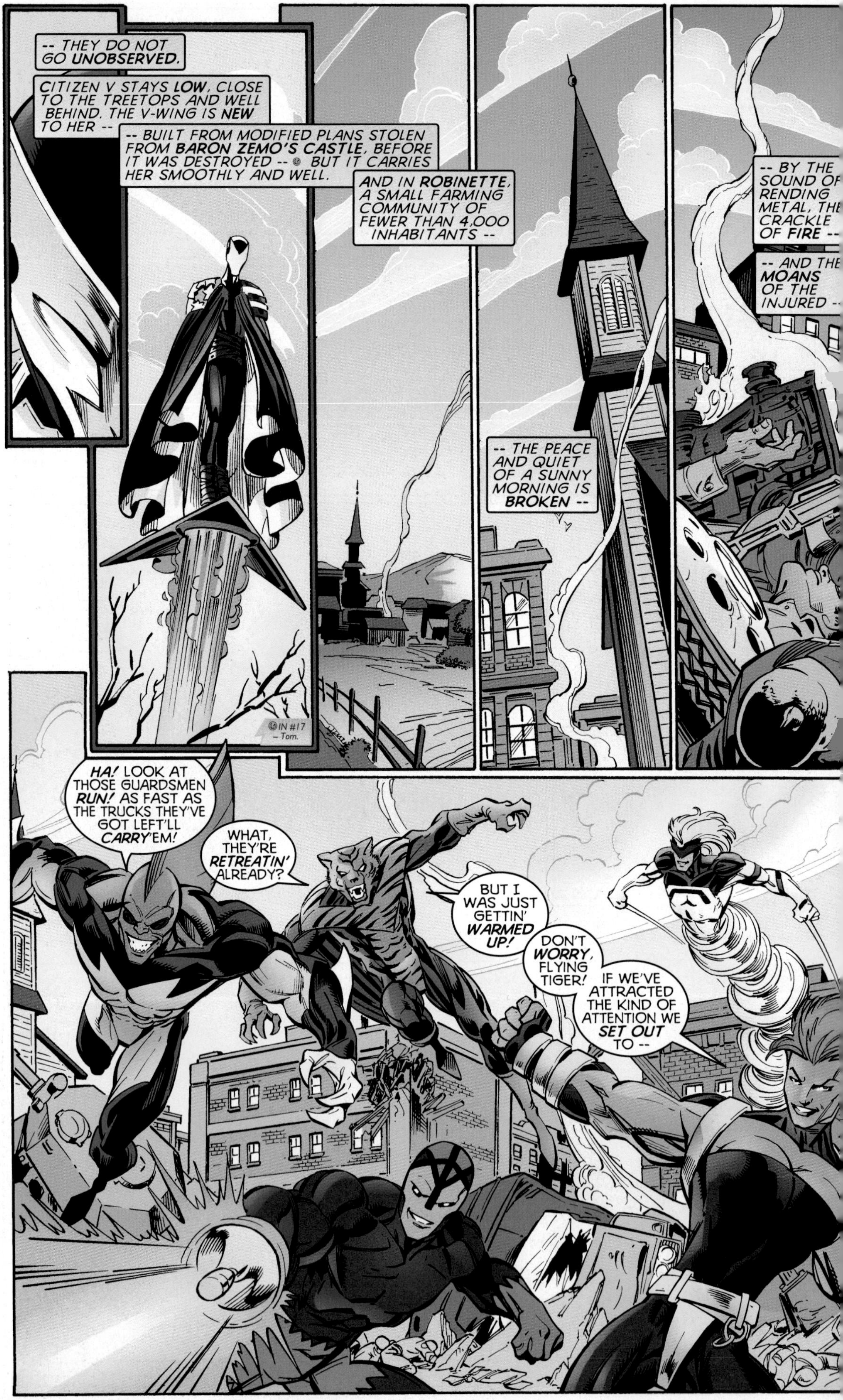

-- THEY DO NOT GO UNOBSERVED.
CITIZEN V STAYS LOW, CLOSE TO THE TREETOPS AND WELL BEHIND. THE V-WING IS NEW TO HER --
-- BUILT FROM MODIFIED PLANS STOLEN FROM BARON ZEMO'S CASTLE, BEFORE IT WAS DESTROYED -- BUT IT CARRIES HER SMOOTHLY AND WELL.
IN #17 – Tom.
AND IN ROBINETTE, A SMALL FARMING COMMUNITY OF FEWER THAN 4,000 INHABITANTS --
-- THE PEACE AND QUIET OF A SUNNY MORNING IS BROKEN --
-- BY THE SOUND OF RENDING METAL, THE CRACKLE OF FIRE --
-- AND THE MOANS OF THE INJURED --
HA! LOOK AT THOSE GUARDSMEN RUN! AS FAST AS THE TRUCKS THEY'VE GOT LEFT'LL CARRY'EM!
WHAT, THEY'RE RETREATIN' ALREADY?
BUT I WAS JUST GETTIN' WARMED UP!
DON'T WORRY, FLYING TIGER!
IF WE'VE ATTRACTED THE KIND OF ATTENTION WE SET OUT TO --

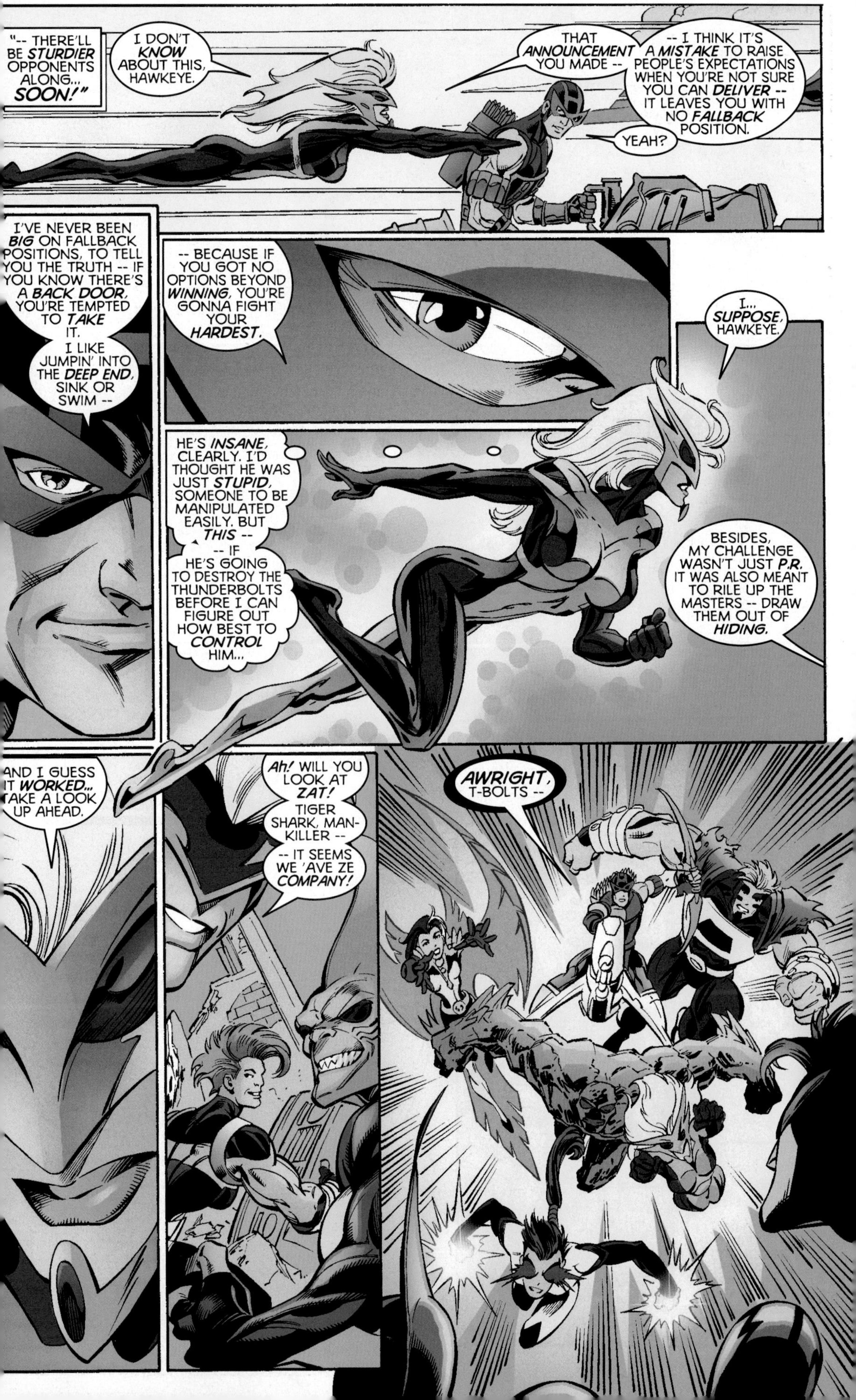
"-- THERE'LL BE STURDIER OPPONENTS ALONG... SOON!"
I DON'T KNOW ABOUT THIS, HAWKEYE.
THAT ANNOUNCEMENT YOU MADE --
-- I THINK IT'S A MISTAKE TO RAISE PEOPLE'S EXPECTATIONS WHEN YOU'RE NOT SURE YOU CAN DELIVER -- IT LEAVES YOU WITH NO FALLBACK POSITION.
YEAH?
I'VE NEVER BEEN BIG ON FALLBACK POSITIONS, TO TELL YOU THE TRUTH -- IF YOU KNOW THERE'S A BACK DOOR, YOU'RE TEMPTED TO TAKE IT.
I LIKE JUMPIN' INTO THE DEEP END, SINK OR SWIM --
-- BECAUSE IF YOU GOT NO OPTIONS BEYOND WINNING, YOU'RE GONNA FIGHT YOUR HARDEST.
I... SUPPOSE, HAWKEYE.
HE'S INSANE, CLEARLY. I'D THOUGHT HE WAS JUST STUPID, SOMEONE TO BE MANIPULATED EASILY. BUT THIS --
-- IF HE'S GOING TO DESTROY THE THUNDERBOLTS BEFORE I CAN FIGURE OUT HOW BEST TO CONTROL HIM...
BESIDES, MY CHALLENGE WASN'T JUST P.R. IT WAS ALSO MEANT TO RILE UP THE MASTERS -- DRAW THEM OUT OF HIDING.
AND I GUESS IT WORKED... TAKE A LOOK UP AHEAD.
Ah! WILL YOU LOOK AT ZAT!
TIGER SHARK, MAN-KILLER --
-- IT SEEMS WE 'AVE ZE COMPANY!
AWRIGHT, T-BOLTS --

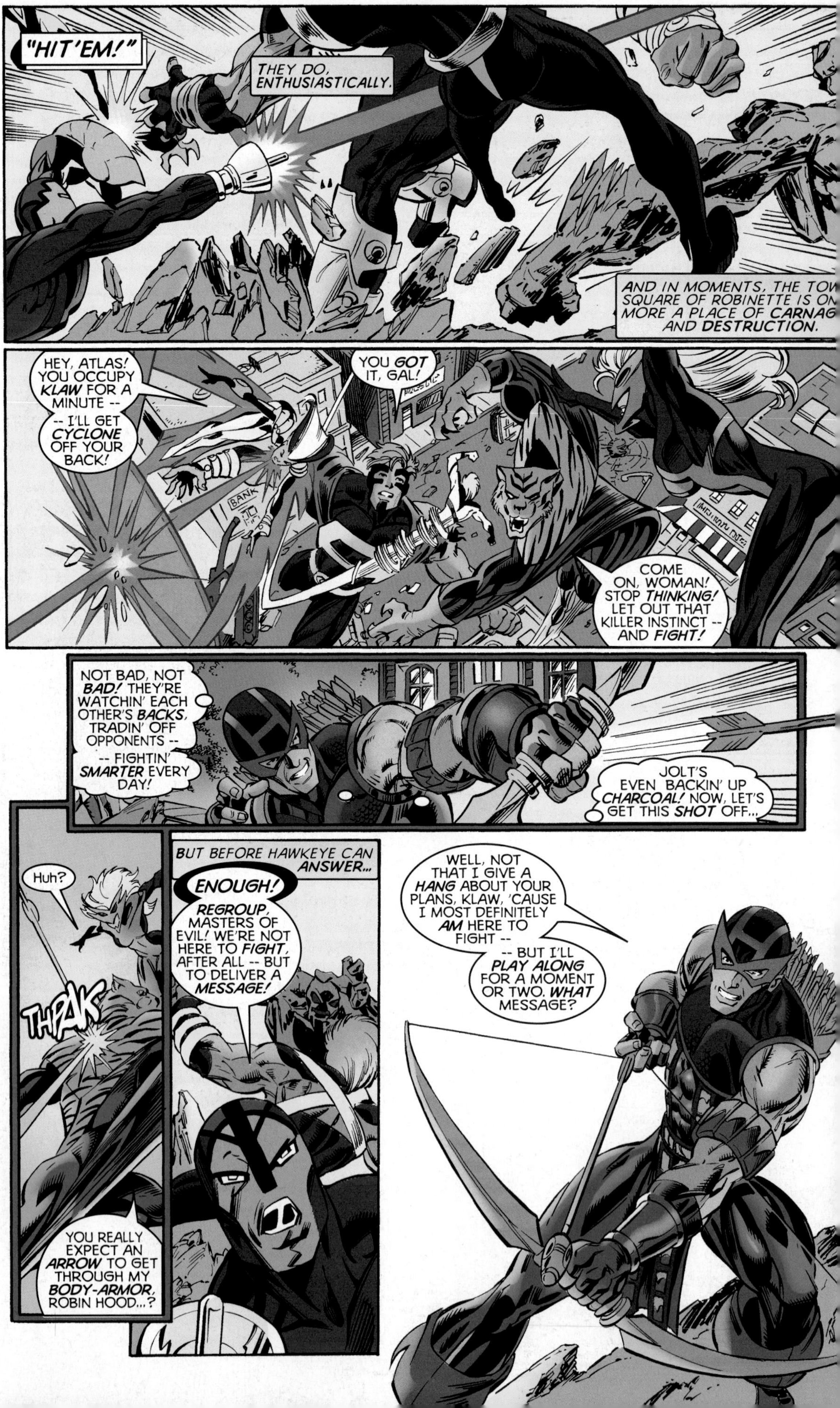
"HIT 'EM!"
THEY DO, ENTHUSIASTICALLY.
AND IN MOMENTS, THE TOW SQUARE OF ROBINETTE IS ON MORE A PLACE OF CARNAG AND DESTRUCTION.
HEY, ATLAS! YOU OCCUPY KLAW FOR A MINUTE --
-- I'LL GET CYCLONE OFF YOUR BACK!
YOU GOT IT, GAL!
BANK
COME ON, WOMAN! STOP THINKING! LET OUT THAT KILLER INSTINCT -- AND FIGHT!
NOT BAD, NOT BAD! THEY'RE WATCHIN' EACH OTHER'S BACKS, TRADIN' OFF OPPONENTS --
-- FIGHTIN' SMARTER EVERY DAY!
JOLT'S EVEN BACKIN' UP CHARCOAL! NOW, LET'S GET THIS SHOT OFF...
Huh?
THPAK
YOU REALLY EXPECT AN ARROW TO GET THROUGH MY BODY-ARMOR, ROBIN HOOD...?
BUT BEFORE HAWKEYE CAN ANSWER...
ENOUGH!
REGROUP, MASTERS OF EVIL! WE'RE NOT HERE TO FIGHT, AFTER ALL -- BUT TO DELIVER A MESSAGE!
WELL, NOT THAT I GIVE A HANG ABOUT YOUR PLANS, KLAW, 'CAUSE I MOST DEFINITELY AM HERE TO FIGHT --
-- BUT I'LL PLAY ALONG FOR A MOMENT OR TWO. WHAT MESSAGE?

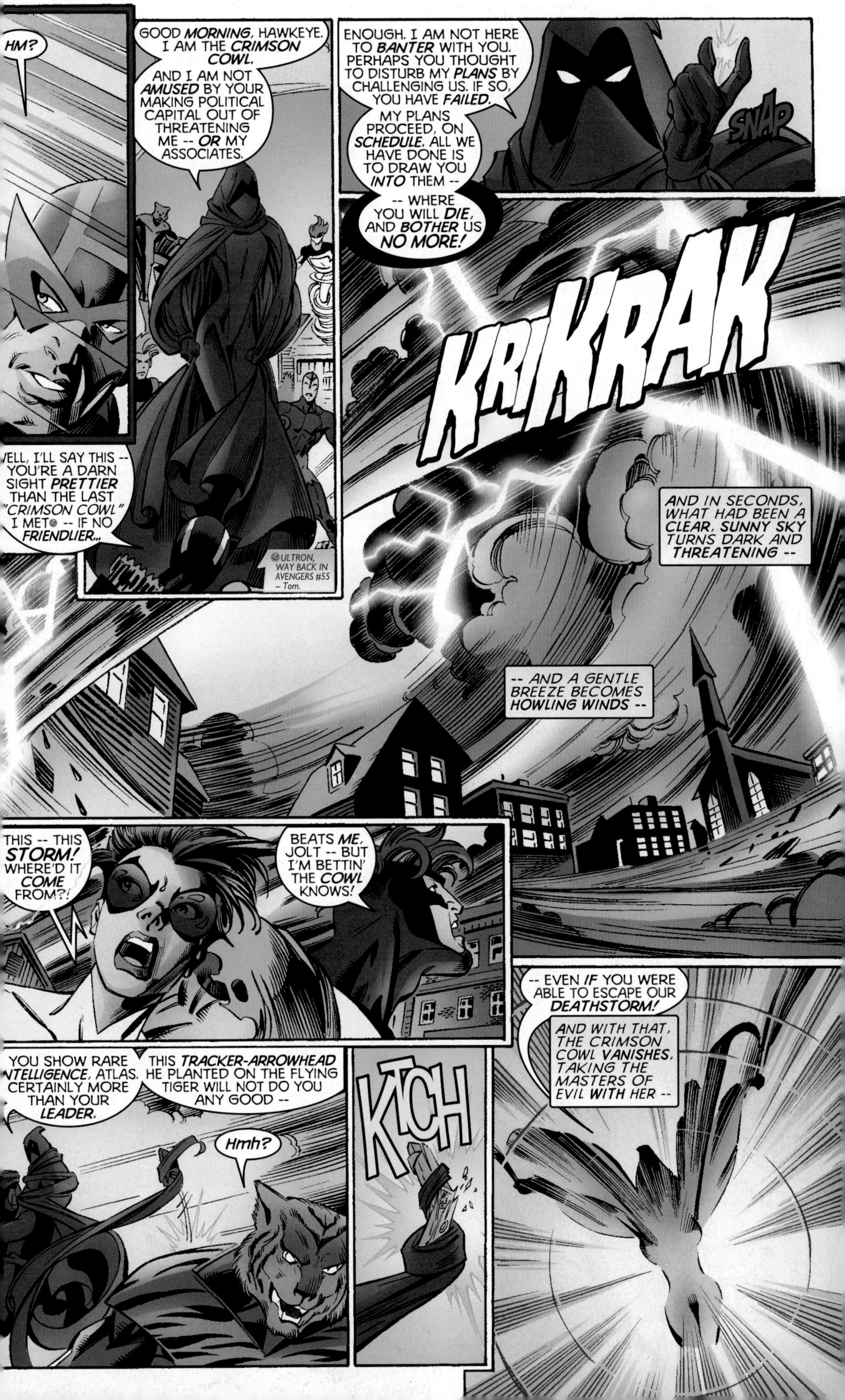
HM?
GOOD MORNING, HAWKEYE. I AM THE CRIMSON COWL.
AND I AM NOT AMUSED BY YOUR MAKING POLITICAL CAPITAL OUT OF THREATENING ME -- OR MY ASSOCIATES.
WELL, I'LL SAY THIS -- YOU'RE A DARN SIGHT PRETTIER THAN THE LAST "CRIMSON COWL" I MET -- IF NO FRIENDLIER...
ULTRON, WAY BACK IN AVENGERS #55 – Tom.
ENOUGH. I AM NOT HERE TO BANTER WITH YOU. PERHAPS YOU THOUGHT TO DISTURB MY PLANS BY CHALLENGING US. IF SO, YOU HAVE FAILED.
MY PLANS PROCEED, ON SCHEDULE. ALL WE HAVE DONE IS TO DRAW YOU INTO THEM --
SNAP
-- WHERE YOU WILL DIE, AND BOTHER US NO MORE!
KRIKRAK
AND IN SECONDS, WHAT HAD BEEN A CLEAR, SUNNY SKY TURNS DARK AND THREATENING --
-- AND A GENTLE BREEZE BECOMES HOWLING WINDS --
THIS -- THIS STORM! WHERE'D IT COME FROM?!
BEATS ME, JOLT -- BUT I'M BETTIN' THE COWL KNOWS!
YOU SHOW RARE INTELLIGENCE, ATLAS. CERTAINLY MORE THAN YOUR LEADER.
THIS TRACKER-ARROWHEAD HE PLANTED ON THE FLYING TIGER WILL NOT DO YOU ANY GOOD --
Hmh?
KTCH
-- EVEN IF YOU WERE ABLE TO ESCAPE OUR DEATHSTORM!
AND WITH THAT, THE CRIMSON COWL VANISHES, TAKING THE MASTERS OF EVIL WITH HER --

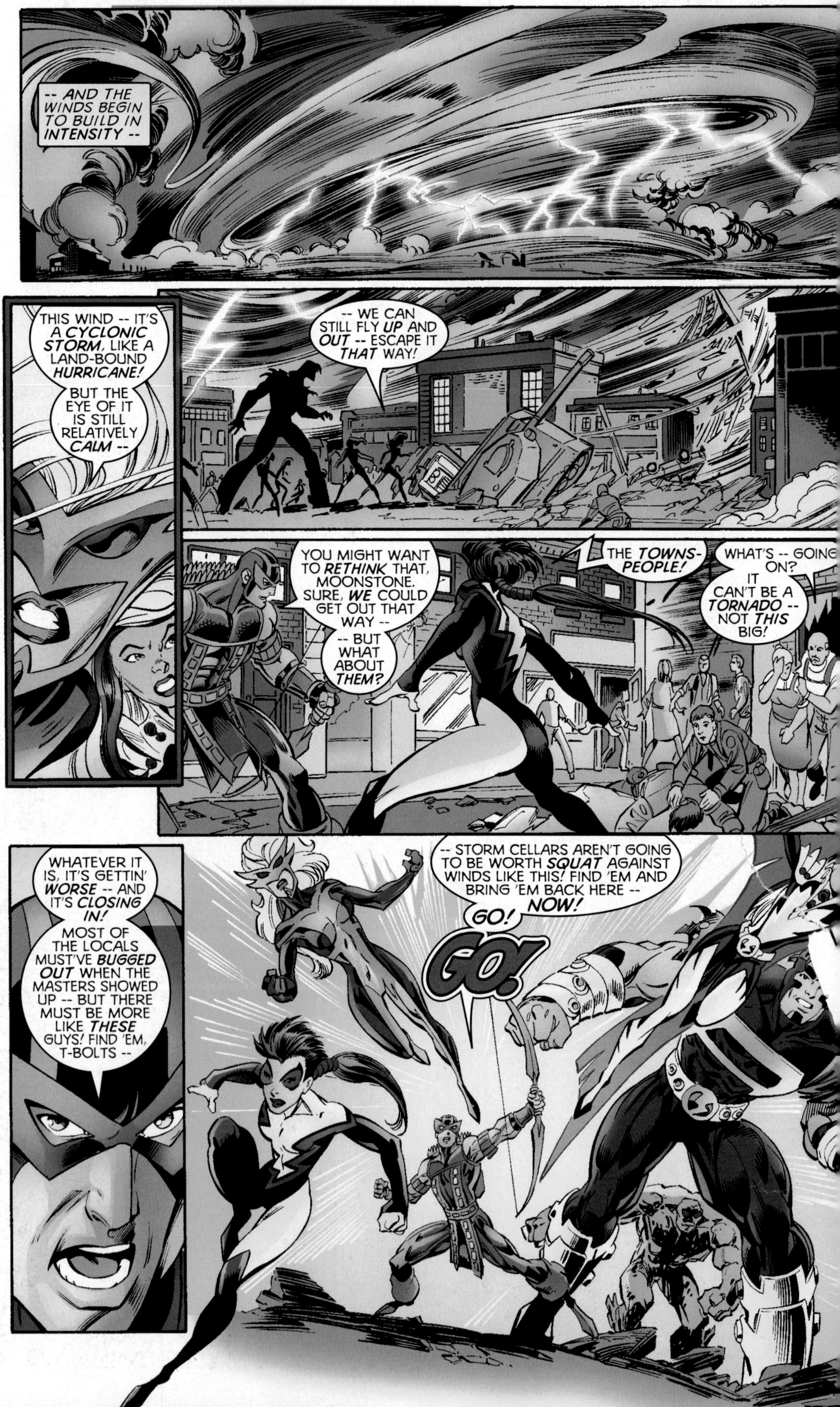

-- AND THE WINDS BEGIN TO BUILD IN INTENSITY --
THIS WIND -- IT'S A CYCLONIC STORM, LIKE A LAND-BOUND HURRICANE!
BUT THE EYE OF IT IS STILL RELATIVELY CALM --
-- WE CAN STILL FLY UP AND OUT -- ESCAPE IT THAT WAY!
YOU MIGHT WANT TO RETHINK THAT, MOONSTONE. SURE, WE COULD GET OUT THAT WAY --
-- BUT WHAT ABOUT THEM?
THE TOWNS-PEOPLE!
WHAT'S -- GOING ON?
IT CAN'T BE A TORNADO -- NOT THIS BIG!
WHATEVER IT IS, IT'S GETTIN' WORSE -- AND IT'S CLOSING IN!
MOST OF THE LOCALS MUST'VE BUGGED OUT WHEN THE MASTERS SHOWED UP -- BUT THERE MUST BE MORE LIKE THESE GUYS! FIND 'EM, T-BOLTS --
-- STORM CELLARS AREN'T GOING TO BE WORTH SQUAT AGAINST WINDS LIKE THIS! FIND 'EM AND BRING 'EM BACK HERE -- NOW!
GO!
GO!

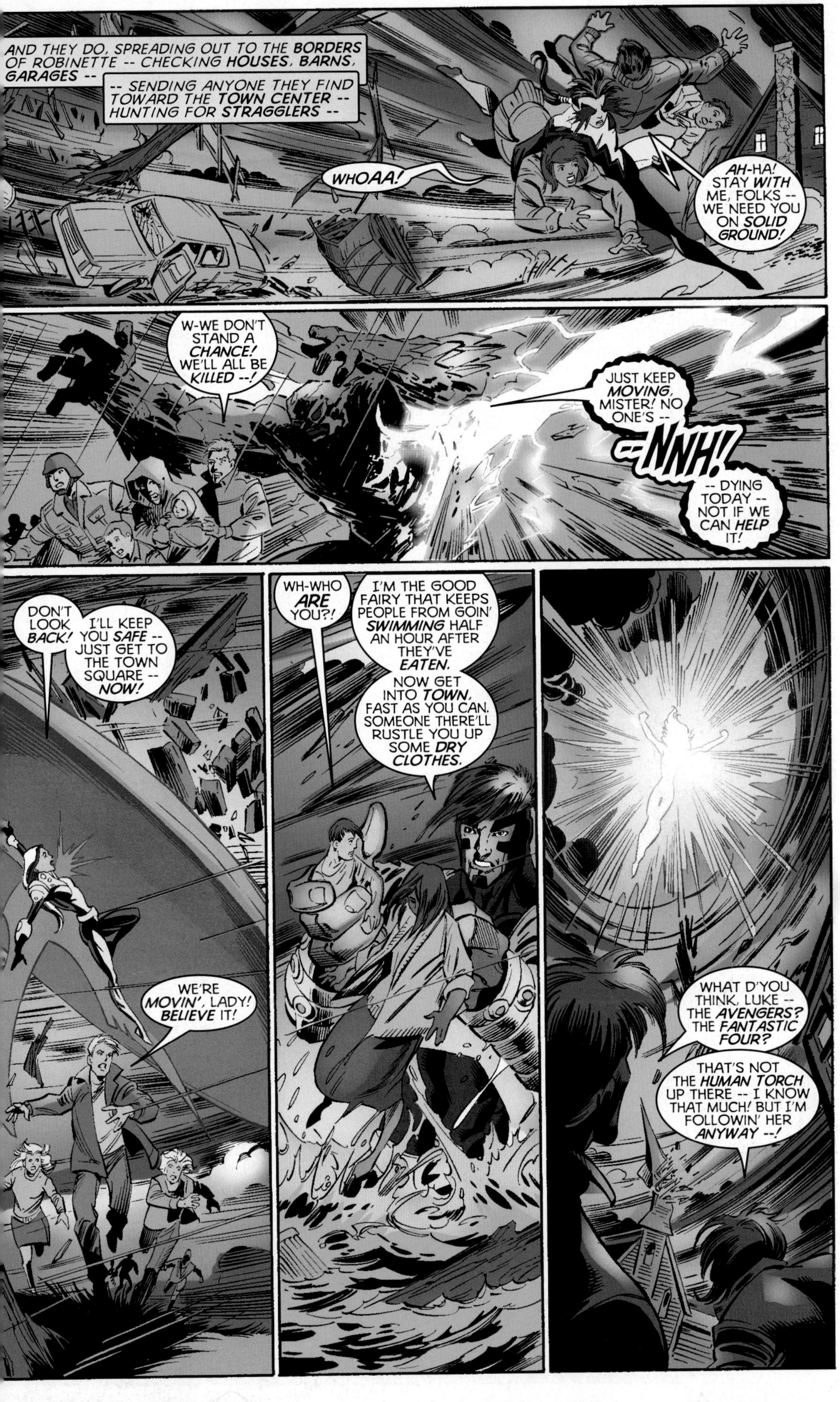
AND THEY DO, SPREADING OUT TO THE BORDERS OF ROBINETTE -- CHECKING HOUSES, BARNS, GARAGES --
-- SENDING ANYONE THEY FIND TOWARD THE TOWN CENTER -- HUNTING FOR STRAGGLERS --
WHOAA!
AH-HA! STAY WITH ME, FOLKS -- WE NEED YOU ON SOLID GROUND!
W-WE DON'T STAND A CHANCE! WE'LL ALL BE KILLED --!
JUST KEEP MOVING, MISTER! NO ONE'S --
--NNH!
-- DYING TODAY -- NOT IF WE CAN HELP IT!
DON'T LOOK BACK!
I'LL KEEP YOU SAFE -- JUST GET TO THE TOWN SQUARE -- NOW!
WE'RE MOVIN', LADY! BELIEVE IT!
WH-WHO ARE YOU?!
I'M THE GOOD FAIRY THAT KEEPS PEOPLE FROM GOIN' SWIMMING HALF AN HOUR AFTER THEY'VE EATEN.
NOW GET INTO TOWN, FAST AS YOU CAN. SOMEONE THERE'LL RUSTLE YOU UP SOME DRY CLOTHES.
WHAT D'YOU THINK, LUKE -- THE AVENGERS? THE FANTASTIC FOUR?
THAT'S NOT THE HUMAN TORCH UP THERE -- I KNOW THAT MUCH! BUT I'M FOLLOWIN' HER ANYWAY --!

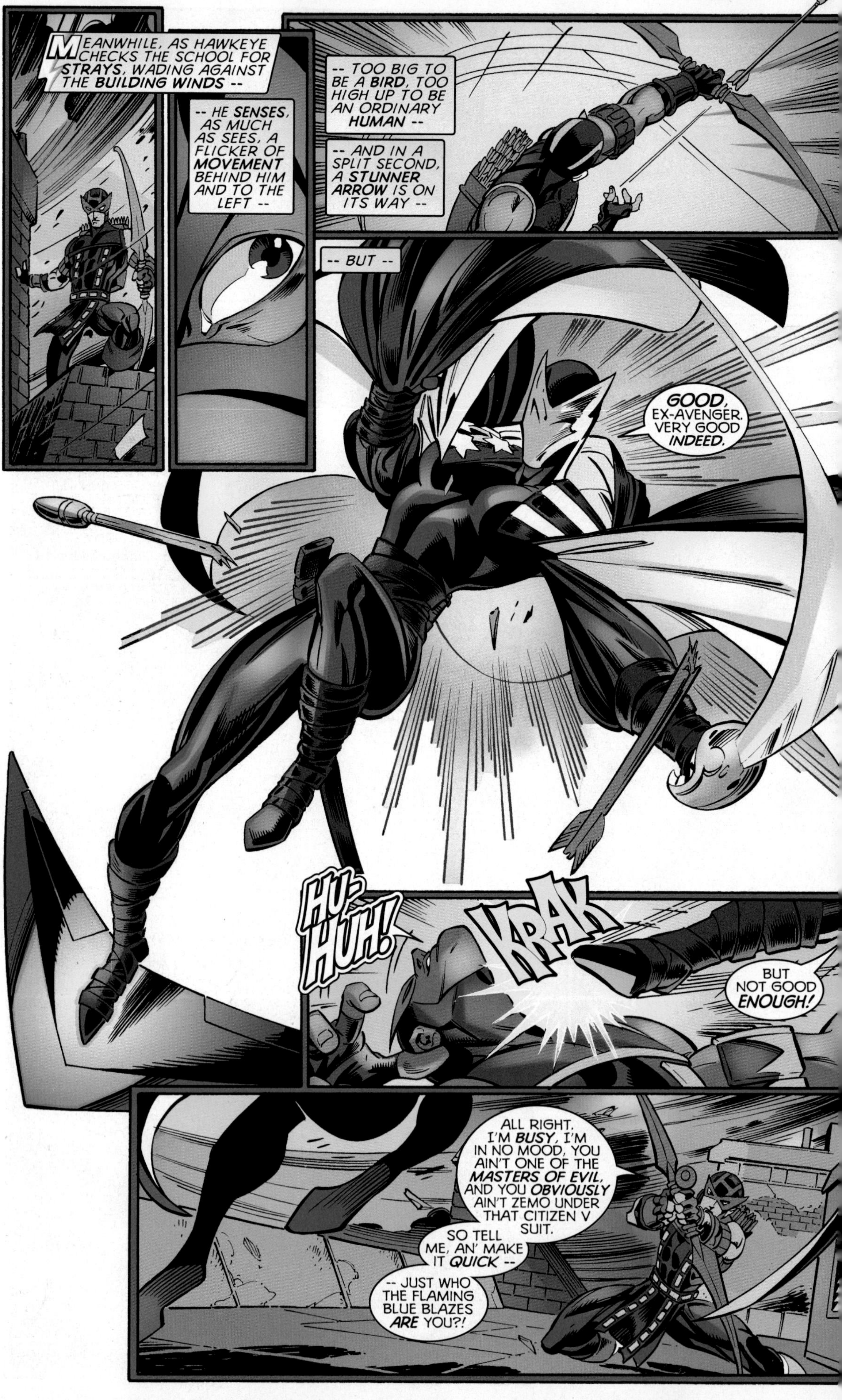
MEANWHILE, AS HAWKEYE CHECKS THE SCHOOL FOR STRAYS, WADING AGAINST THE BUILDING WINDS --
-- HE SENSES, AS MUCH AS SEES, A FLICKER OF MOVEMENT BEHIND HIM AND TO THE LEFT --
-- TOO BIG TO BE A BIRD, TOO HIGH UP TO BE AN ORDINARY HUMAN --
-- AND IN A SPLIT SECOND, A STUNNER ARROW IS ON ITS WAY --
-- BUT --
GOOD, EX-AVENGER. VERY GOOD INDEED.
HU-HUH!
KRAK
BUT NOT GOOD ENOUGH!
ALL RIGHT. I'M BUSY, I'M IN NO MOOD, YOU AIN'T ONE OF THE MASTERS OF EVIL, AND YOU OBVIOUSLY AIN'T ZEMO UNDER THAT CITIZEN V SUIT.
SO TELL ME, AN' MAKE IT QUICK --
-- JUST WHO THE FLAMING BLUE BLAZES ARE YOU?!

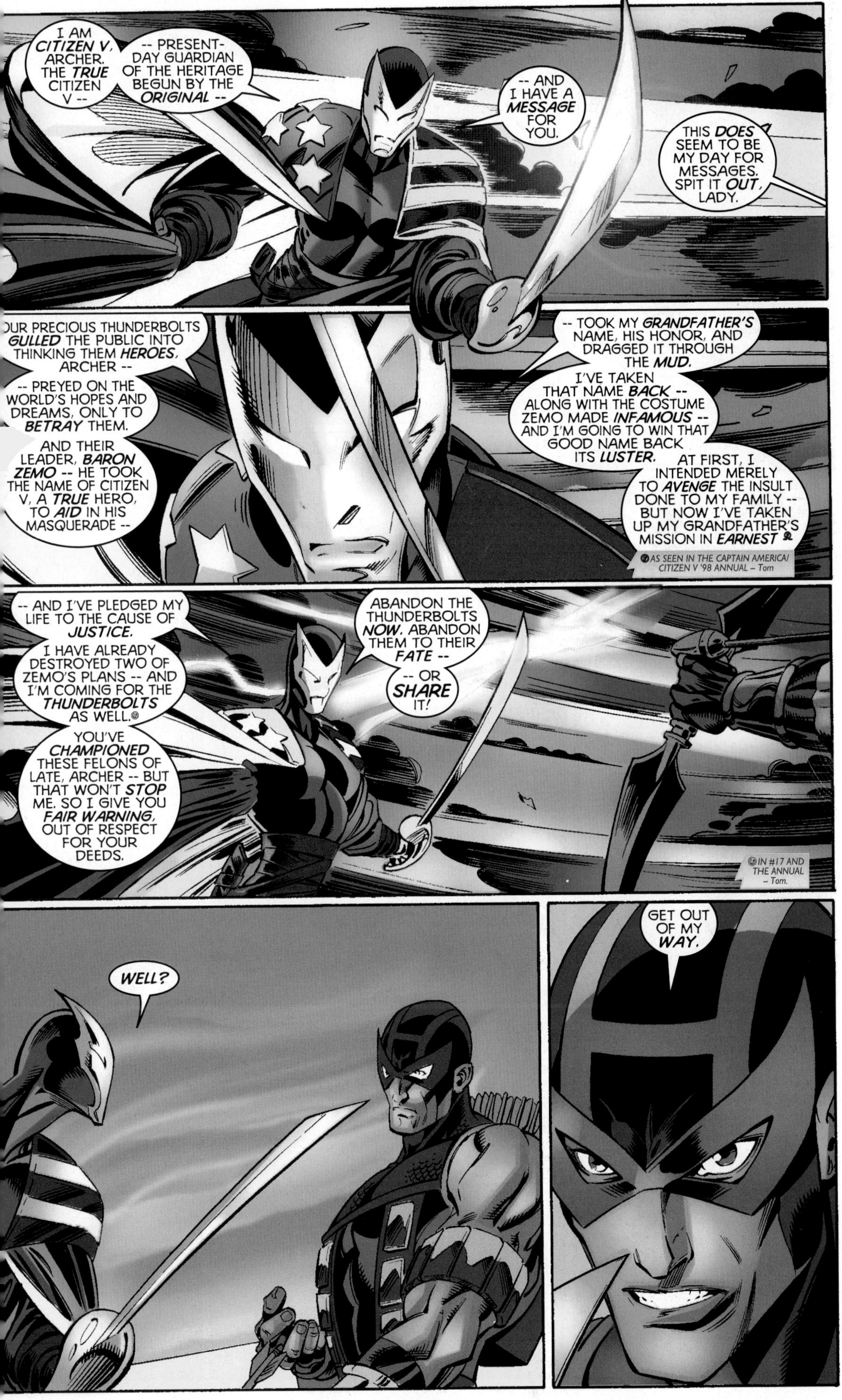
I AM CITIZEN V, ARCHER. THE TRUE CITIZEN V --
-- PRESENT-DAY GUARDIAN OF THE HERITAGE BEGUN BY THE ORIGINAL --
-- AND I HAVE A MESSAGE FOR YOU.
THIS DOES SEEM TO BE MY DAY FOR MESSAGES. SPIT IT OUT, LADY.
OUR PRECIOUS THUNDERBOLTS GULLED THE PUBLIC INTO THINKING THEM HEROES, ARCHER --
-- PREYED ON THE WORLD'S HOPES AND DREAMS, ONLY TO BETRAY THEM.
AND THEIR LEADER, BARON ZEMO -- HE TOOK THE NAME OF CITIZEN V, A TRUE HERO, TO AID IN HIS MASQUERADE --
-- TOOK MY GRANDFATHER'S NAME, HIS HONOR, AND DRAGGED IT THROUGH THE MUD.
I'VE TAKEN THAT NAME BACK -- ALONG WITH THE COSTUME ZEMO MADE INFAMOUS -- AND I'M GOING TO WIN THAT GOOD NAME BACK ITS LUSTER.
AT FIRST, I INTENDED MERELY TO AVENGE THE INSULT DONE TO MY FAMILY -- BUT NOW I'VE TAKEN UP MY GRANDFATHER'S MISSION IN EARNEST.
AS SEEN IN THE CAPTAIN AMERICA/CITIZEN V '98 ANNUAL – Tom
-- AND I'VE PLEDGED MY LIFE TO THE CAUSE OF JUSTICE.
I HAVE ALREADY DESTROYED TWO OF ZEMO'S PLANS -- AND I'M COMING FOR THE THUNDERBOLTS AS WELL.
YOU'VE CHAMPIONED THESE FELONS OF LATE, ARCHER -- BUT THAT WON'T STOP ME. SO I GIVE YOU FAIR WARNING, OUT OF RESPECT FOR YOUR DEEDS.
ABANDON THE THUNDERBOLTS NOW. ABANDON THEM TO THEIR FATE --
-- OR SHARE IT!
IN #17 AND THE ANNUAL – Tom.
WELL?
GET OUT OF MY WAY.

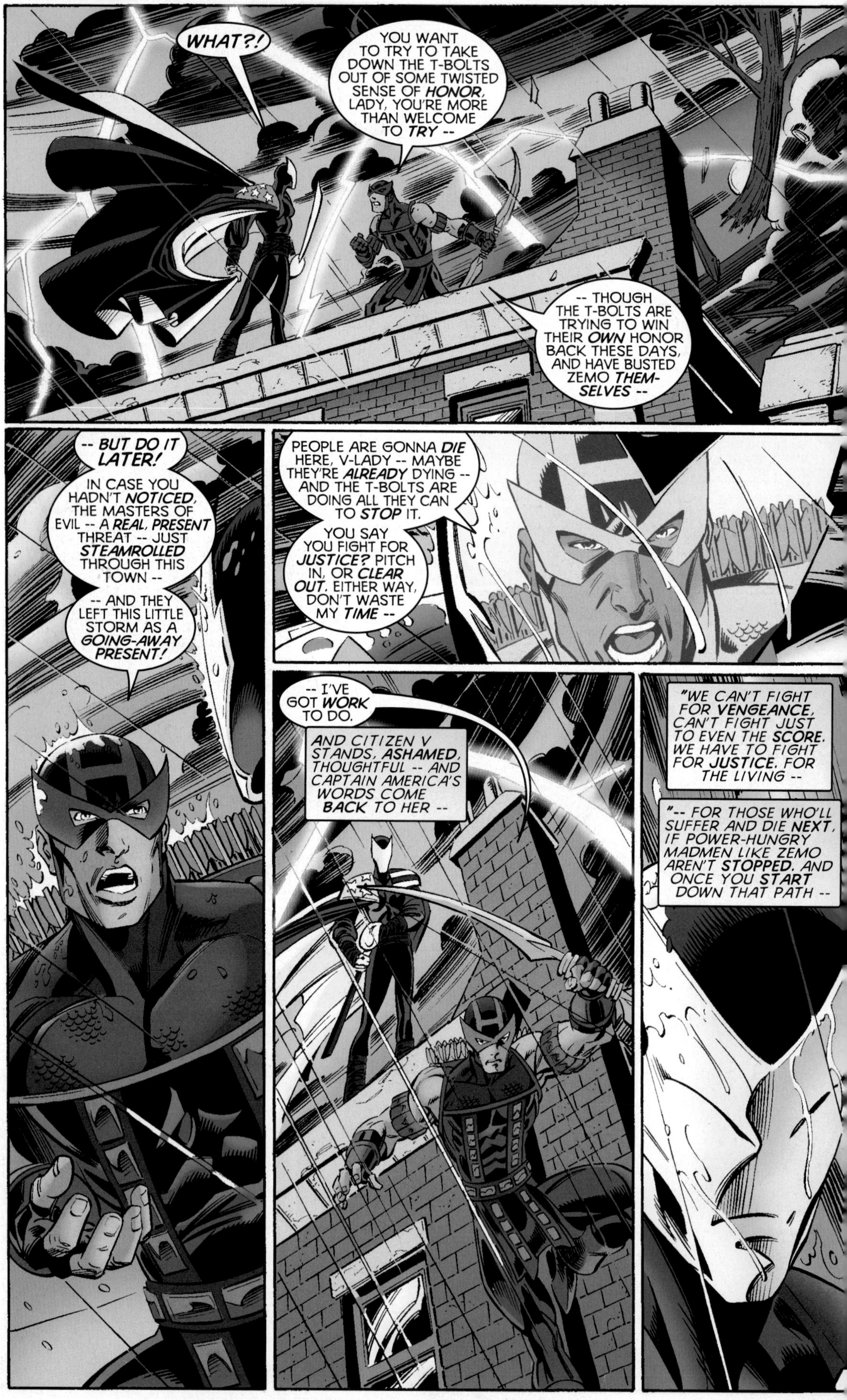
WHAT?!
YOU WANT TO TRY TO TAKE DOWN THE T-BOLTS OUT OF SOME TWISTED SENSE OF HONOR, LADY, YOU'RE MORE THAN WELCOME TO TRY --
-- THOUGH THE T-BOLTS ARE TRYING TO WIN THEIR OWN HONOR BACK THESE DAYS, AND HAVE BUSTED ZEMO THEMSELVES --
-- BUT DO IT LATER!
IN CASE YOU HADN'T NOTICED, THE MASTERS OF EVIL -- A REAL, PRESENT THREAT -- JUST STEAMROLLED THROUGH THIS TOWN --
-- AND THEY LEFT THIS LITTLE STORM AS A GOING-AWAY PRESENT!
PEOPLE ARE GONNA DIE HERE, V-LADY -- MAYBE THEY'RE ALREADY DYING -- AND THE T-BOLTS ARE DOING ALL THEY CAN TO STOP IT.
YOU SAY YOU FIGHT FOR JUSTICE? PITCH IN, OR CLEAR OUT. EITHER WAY, DON'T WASTE MY TIME --
-- I'VE GOT WORK TO DO.
AND CITIZEN V STANDS, ASHAMED, THOUGHTFUL -- AND CAPTAIN AMERICA'S WORDS COME BACK TO HER --
"WE CAN'T FIGHT FOR VENGEANCE, CAN'T FIGHT JUST TO EVEN THE SCORE. WE HAVE TO FIGHT FOR JUSTICE. FOR THE LIVING --
"-- FOR THOSE WHO'LL SUFFER AND DIE NEXT, IF POWER-HUNGRY MADMEN LIKE ZEMO AREN'T STOPPED. AND ONCE YOU START DOWN THAT PATH --

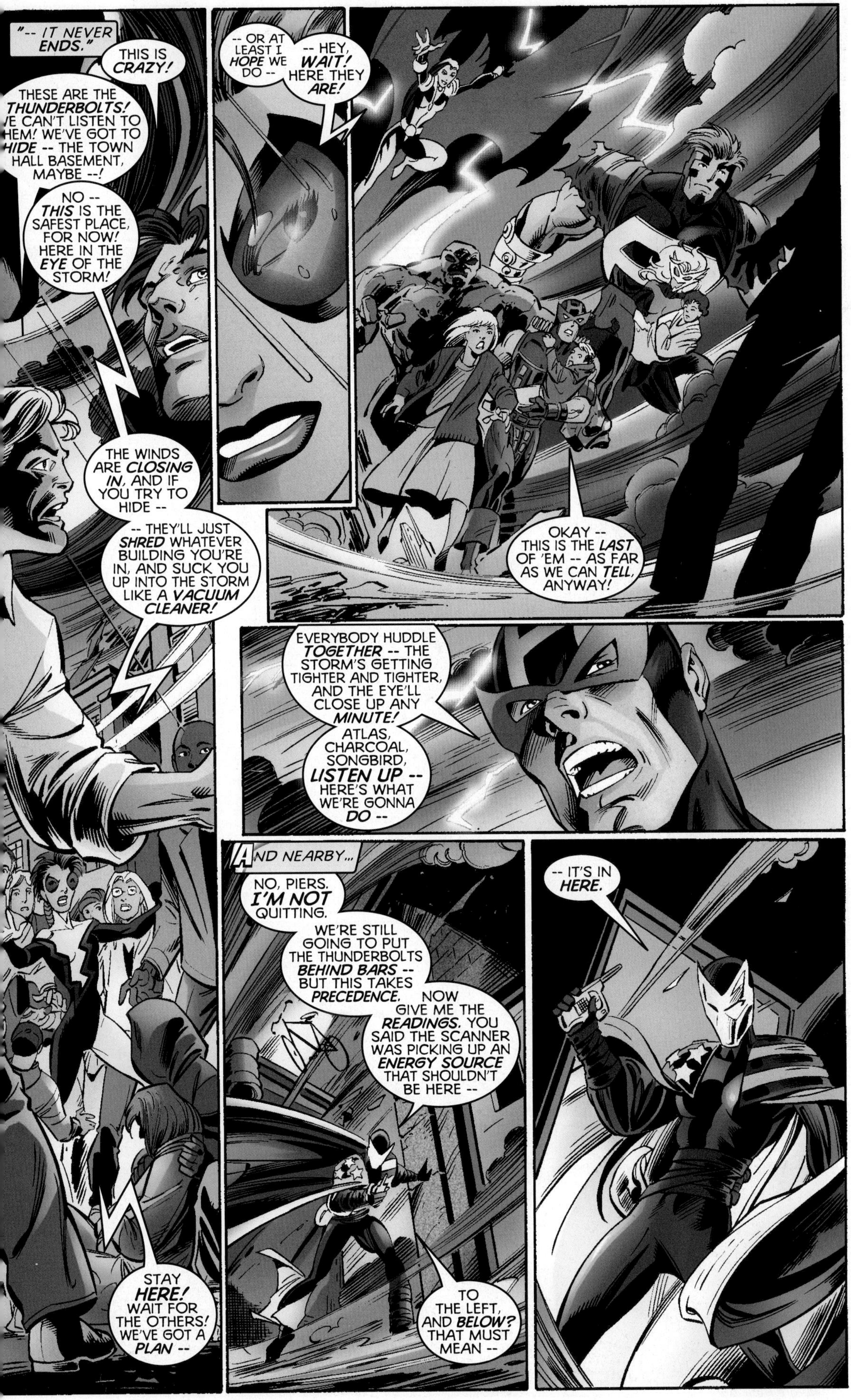
"-- IT NEVER ENDS."
THIS IS CRAZY!
THESE ARE THE THUNDERBOLTS! E CAN'T LISTEN TO HEM! WE'VE GOT TO HIDE -- THE TOWN HALL BASEMENT, MAYBE --!
NO -- THIS IS THE SAFEST PLACE, FOR NOW! HERE IN THE EYE OF THE STORM!
THE WINDS ARE CLOSING IN, AND IF YOU TRY TO HIDE --
-- THEY'LL JUST SHRED WHATEVER BUILDING YOU'RE IN, AND SUCK YOU UP INTO THE STORM LIKE A VACUUM CLEANER!
STAY HERE! WAIT FOR THE OTHERS! WE'VE GOT A PLAN --
-- OR AT LEAST I HOPE WE DO --
-- HEY, WAIT! HERE THEY ARE!
OKAY -- THIS IS THE LAST OF 'EM -- AS FAR AS WE CAN TELL, ANYWAY!
EVERYBODY HUDDLE TOGETHER -- THE STORM'S GETTING TIGHTER AND TIGHTER, AND THE EYE'LL CLOSE UP ANY MINUTE!
ATLAS, CHARCOAL, SONGBIRD, LISTEN UP -- HERE'S WHAT WE'RE GONNA DO --
AND NEARBY...
NO, PIERS. I'M NOT QUITTING.
WE'RE STILL GOING TO PUT THE THUNDERBOLTS BEHIND BARS -- BUT THIS TAKES PRECEDENCE.
NOW GIVE ME THE READINGS. YOU SAID THE SCANNER WAS PICKING UP AN ENERGY SOURCE THAT SHOULDN'T BE HERE --
TO THE LEFT, AND BELOW? THAT MUST MEAN --
-- IT'S IN HERE.

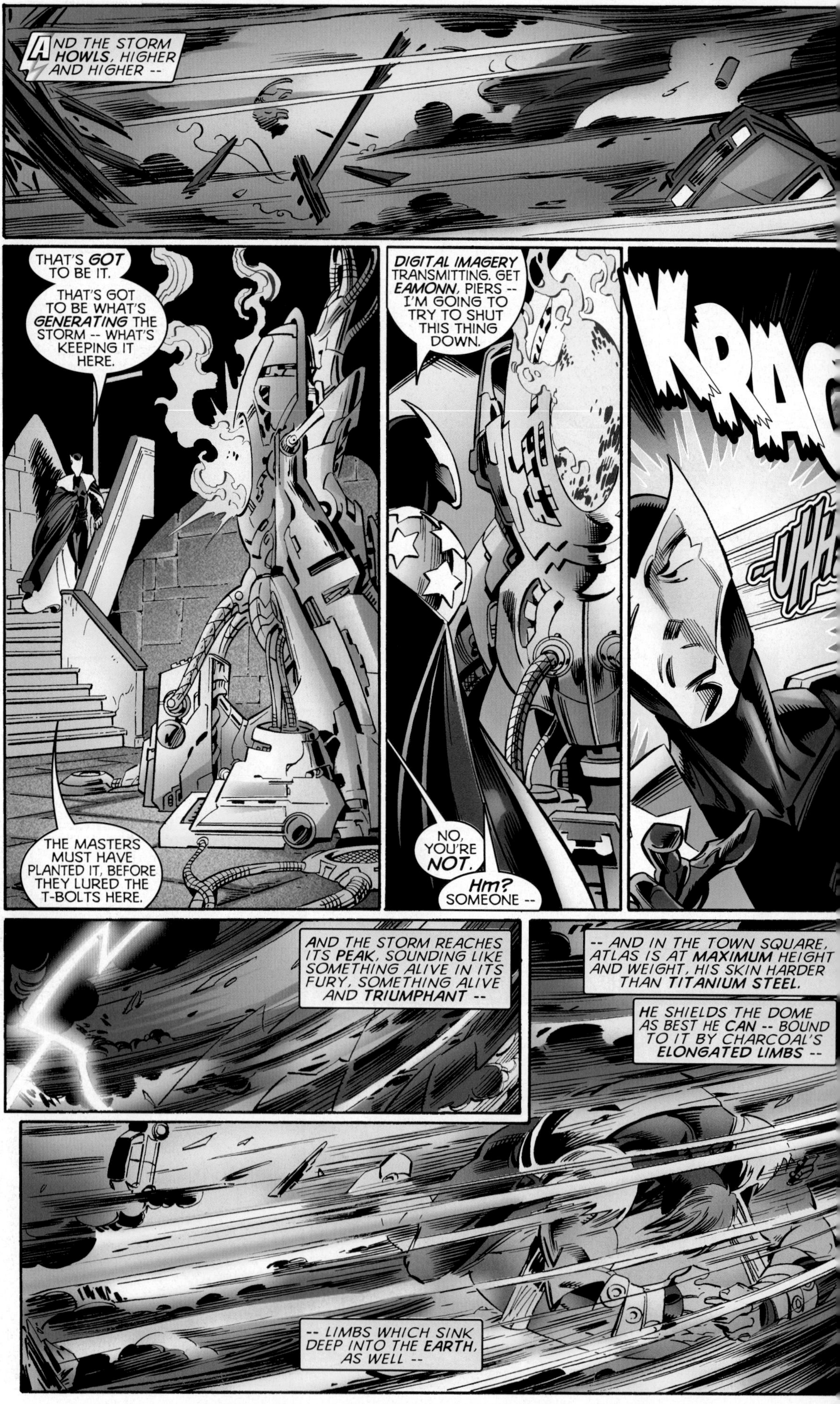
AND THE STORM HOWLS, HIGHER AND HIGHER --
THAT'S GOT TO BE IT.
THAT'S GOT TO BE WHAT'S GENERATING THE STORM -- WHAT'S KEEPING IT HERE.
THE MASTERS MUST HAVE PLANTED IT, BEFORE THEY LURED THE T-BOLTS HERE.
DIGITAL IMAGERY TRANSMITTING. GET EAMONN, PIERS -- I'M GOING TO TRY TO SHUT THIS THING DOWN.
NO, YOU'RE NOT.
Hm? SOMEONE --
KRAC
AND THE STORM REACHES ITS PEAK, SOUNDING LIKE SOMETHING ALIVE IN ITS FURY, SOMETHING ALIVE AND TRIUMPHANT --
-- AND IN THE TOWN SQUARE, ATLAS IS AT MAXIMUM HEIGHT AND WEIGHT, HIS SKIN HARDER THAN TITANIUM STEEL.
HE SHIELDS THE DOME AS BEST HE CAN -- BOUND TO IT BY CHARCOAL'S ELONGATED LIMBS --
-- LIMBS WHICH SINK DEEP INTO THE EARTH, AS WELL --

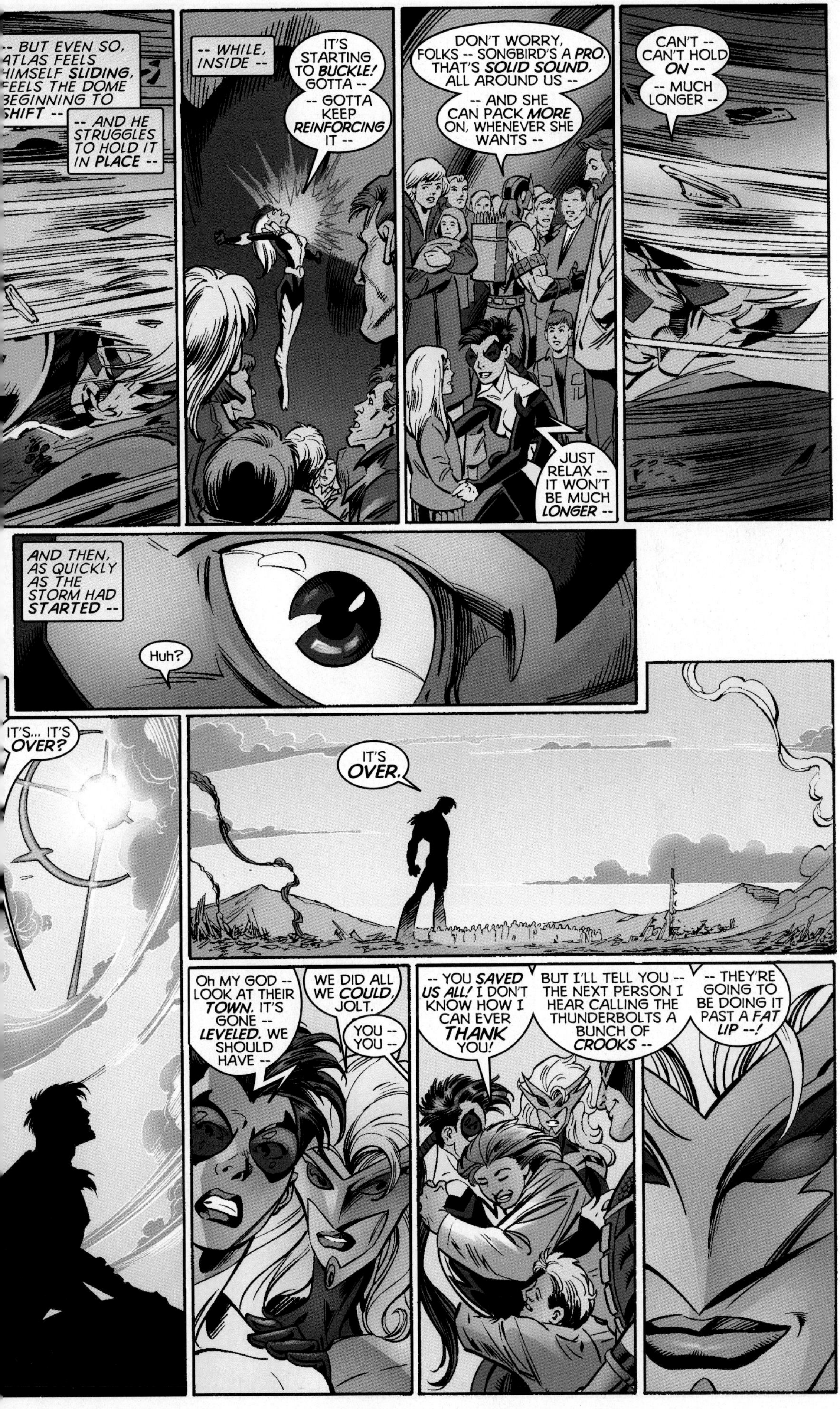
-- BUT EVEN SO, ATLAS FEELS HIMSELF SLIDING, FEELS THE DOME BEGINNING TO SHIFT --
-- AND HE STRUGGLES TO HOLD IT IN PLACE --
-- WHILE, INSIDE --
IT'S STARTING TO BUCKLE! GOTTA --
-- GOTTA KEEP REINFORCING IT --
DON'T WORRY, FOLKS -- SONGBIRD'S A PRO. THAT'S SOLID SOUND, ALL AROUND US --
-- AND SHE CAN PACK MORE ON, WHENEVER SHE WANTS --
JUST RELAX -- IT WON'T BE MUCH LONGER --
CAN'T -- CAN'T HOLD ON --
-- MUCH LONGER --
AND THEN, AS QUICKLY AS THE STORM HAD STARTED --
Huh?
IT'S... IT'S OVER?
IT'S OVER.
Oh MY GOD -- LOOK AT THEIR TOWN. IT'S GONE -- LEVELED. WE SHOULD HAVE --
WE DID ALL WE COULD, JOLT.
YOU -- YOU --
-- YOU SAVED US ALL! I DON'T KNOW HOW I CAN EVER THANK YOU!
BUT I'LL TELL YOU -- THE NEXT PERSON I HEAR CALLING THE THUNDERBOLTS A BUNCH OF CROOKS --
-- THEY'RE GOING TO BE DOING IT PAST A FAT LIP --!

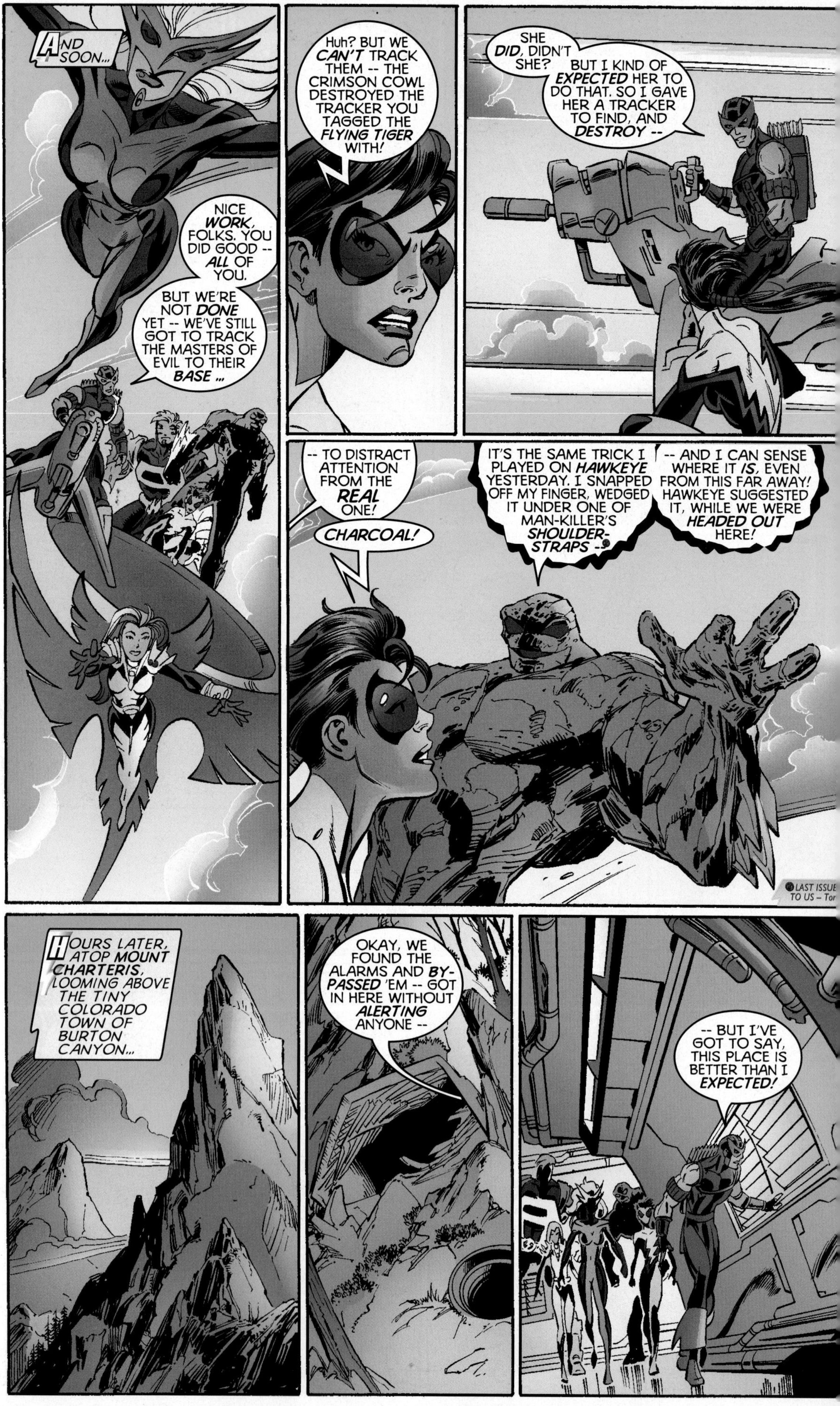
AND SOON...
NICE WORK, FOLKS. YOU DID GOOD -- ALL OF YOU.
BUT WE'RE NOT DONE YET -- WE'VE STILL GOT TO TRACK THE MASTERS OF EVIL TO THEIR BASE ...
Huh? BUT WE CAN'T TRACK THEM -- THE CRIMSON COWL DESTROYED THE TRACKER YOU TAGGED THE FLYING TIGER WITH!
SHE DID, DIDN'T SHE?
BUT I KIND OF EXPECTED HER TO DO THAT. SO I GAVE HER A TRACKER TO FIND, AND DESTROY --
-- TO DISTRACT ATTENTION FROM THE REAL ONE!
CHARCOAL!
IT'S THE SAME TRICK I PLAYED ON HAWKEYE YESTERDAY. I SNAPPED OFF MY FINGER, WEDGED IT UNDER ONE OF MAN-KILLER'S SHOULDER-STRAPS --
-- AND I CAN SENSE WHERE IT IS, EVEN FROM THIS FAR AWAY! HAWKEYE SUGGESTED IT, WHILE WE WERE HEADED OUT HERE!
LAST ISSUE
TO US –
HOURS LATER, ATOP MOUNT CHARTERIS, LOOMING ABOVE THE TINY COLORADO TOWN OF BURTON CANYON...
OKAY, WE FOUND THE ALARMS AND BY-PASSED 'EM -- GOT IN HERE WITHOUT ALERTING ANYONE --
-- BUT I'VE GOT TO SAY, THIS PLACE IS BETTER THAN I EXPECTED!

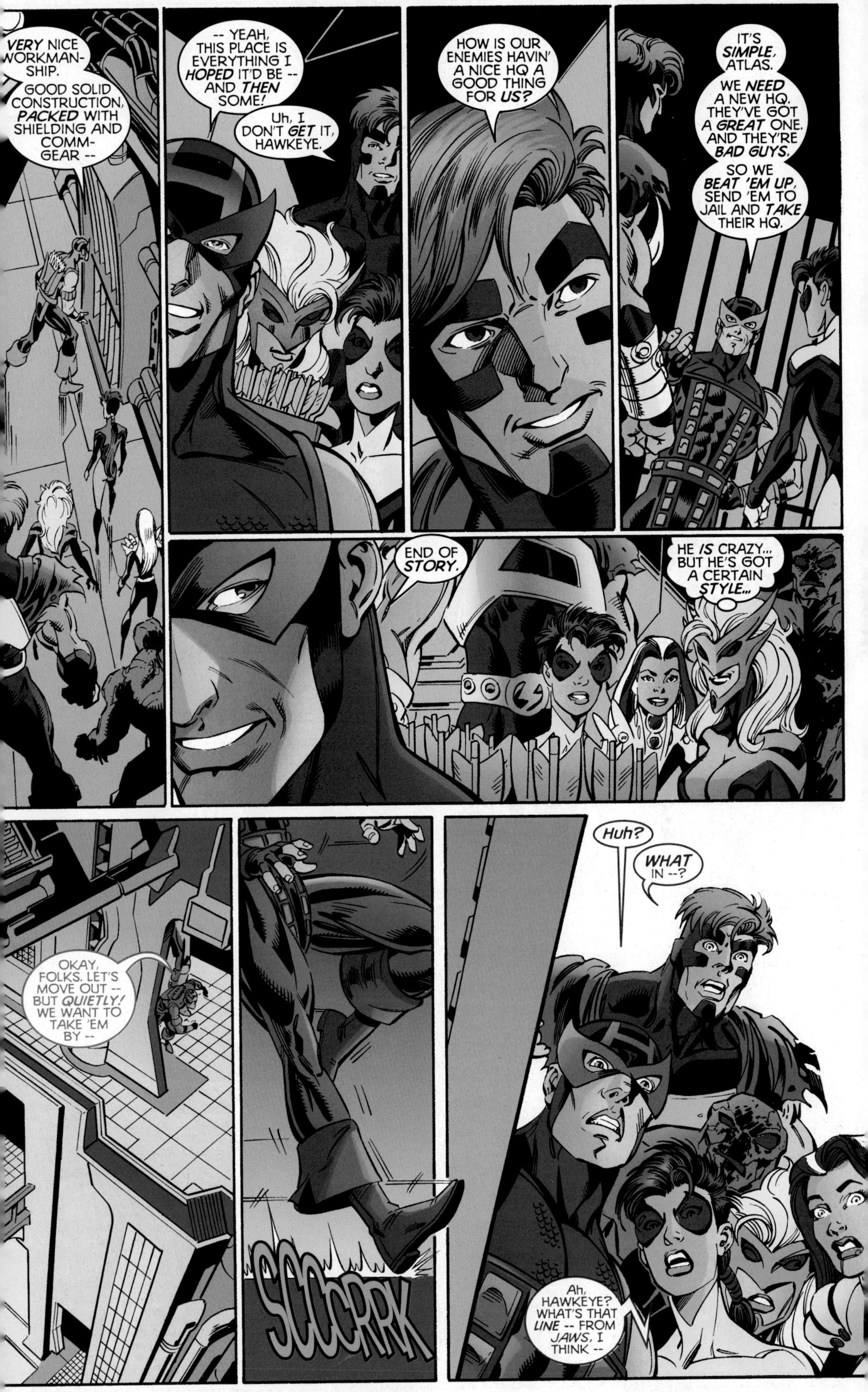
VERY NICE WORKMANSHIP. GOOD SOLID CONSTRUCTION, PACKED WITH SHIELDING AND COMM-GEAR --
-- YEAH, THIS PLACE IS EVERYTHING I HOPED IT'D BE -- AND THEN SOME!
Uh, I DON'T GET IT, HAWKEYE.
HOW IS OUR ENEMIES HAVIN' A NICE HQ A GOOD THING FOR US?
IT'S SIMPLE, ATLAS.
WE NEED A NEW HQ. THEY'VE GOT A GREAT ONE. AND THEY'RE BAD GUYS.
SO WE BEAT 'EM UP, SEND 'EM TO JAIL AND TAKE THEIR HQ.
END OF STORY.
HE IS CRAZY... BUT HE'S GOT A CERTAIN STYLE...
OKAY, FOLKS. LET'S MOVE OUT -- BUT QUIETLY! WE WANT TO TAKE 'EM BY --
SCCCRRK
Huh?
WHAT IN --?
Ah, HAWKEYE? WHAT'S THAT LINE -- FROM JAWS, I THINK --

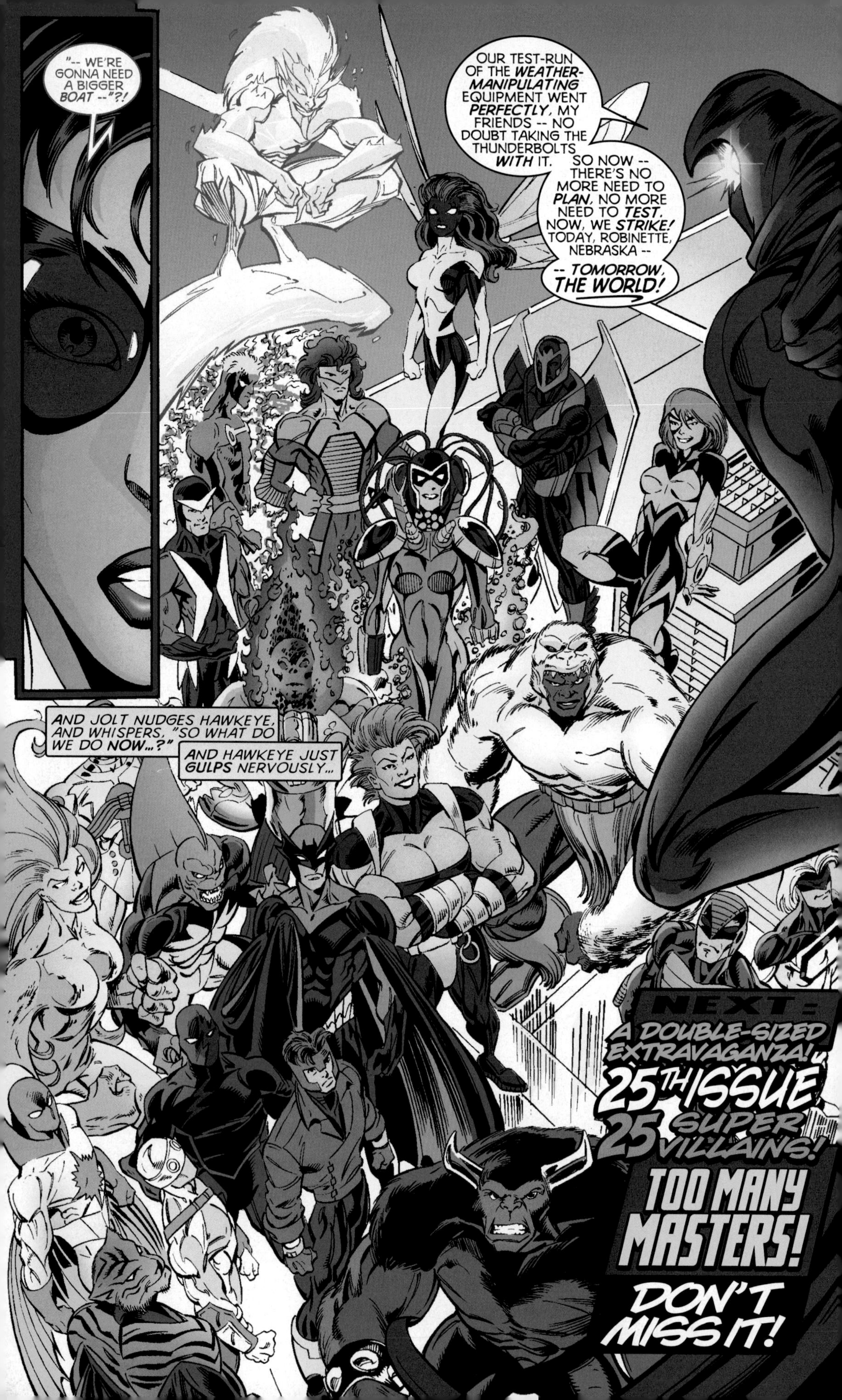
"-- WE'RE GONNA NEED A BIGGER BOAT --"?!
OUR TEST-RUN OF THE WEATHER-MANIPULATING EQUIPMENT WENT PERFECTLY, MY FRIENDS -- NO DOUBT TAKING THE THUNDERBOLTS WITH IT.
SO NOW -- THERE'S NO MORE NEED TO PLAN, NO MORE NEED TO TEST. NOW, WE STRIKE! TODAY, ROBINETTE, NEBRASKA --
-- TOMORROW, THE WORLD!
AND JOLT NUDGES HAWKEYE, AND WHISPERS, "SO WHAT DO WE DO NOW...?"
AND HAWKEYE JUST GULPS NERVOUSLY...
NEXT:
A DOUBLE-SIZED EXTRAVAGANZA!
25TH ISSUE, 25 SUPER VILLAINS!
TOO MANY MASTERS!
DON'T MISS IT!

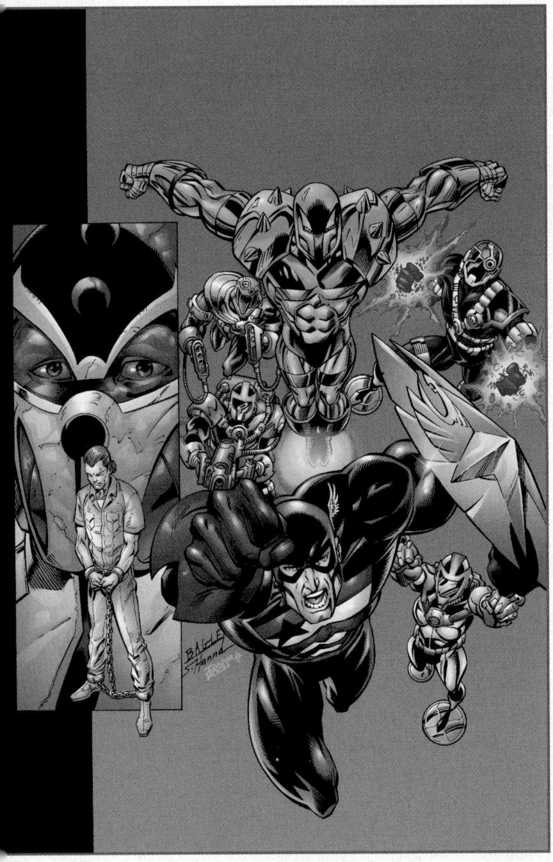

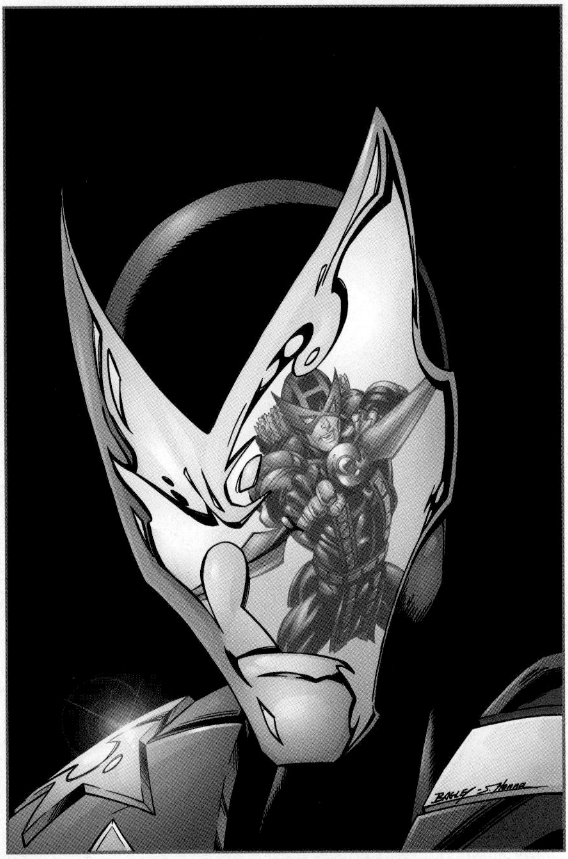
BAGLEY -S. Hanna

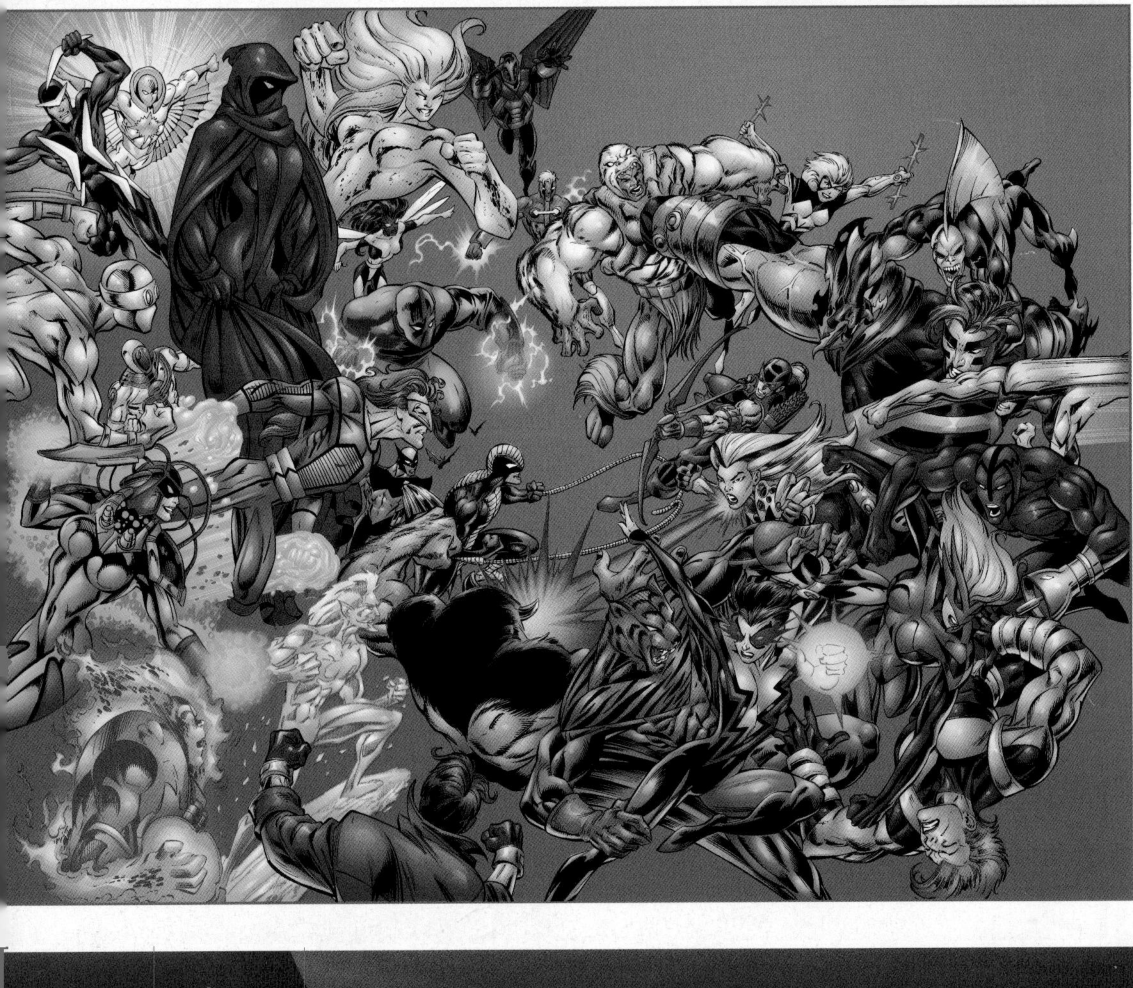

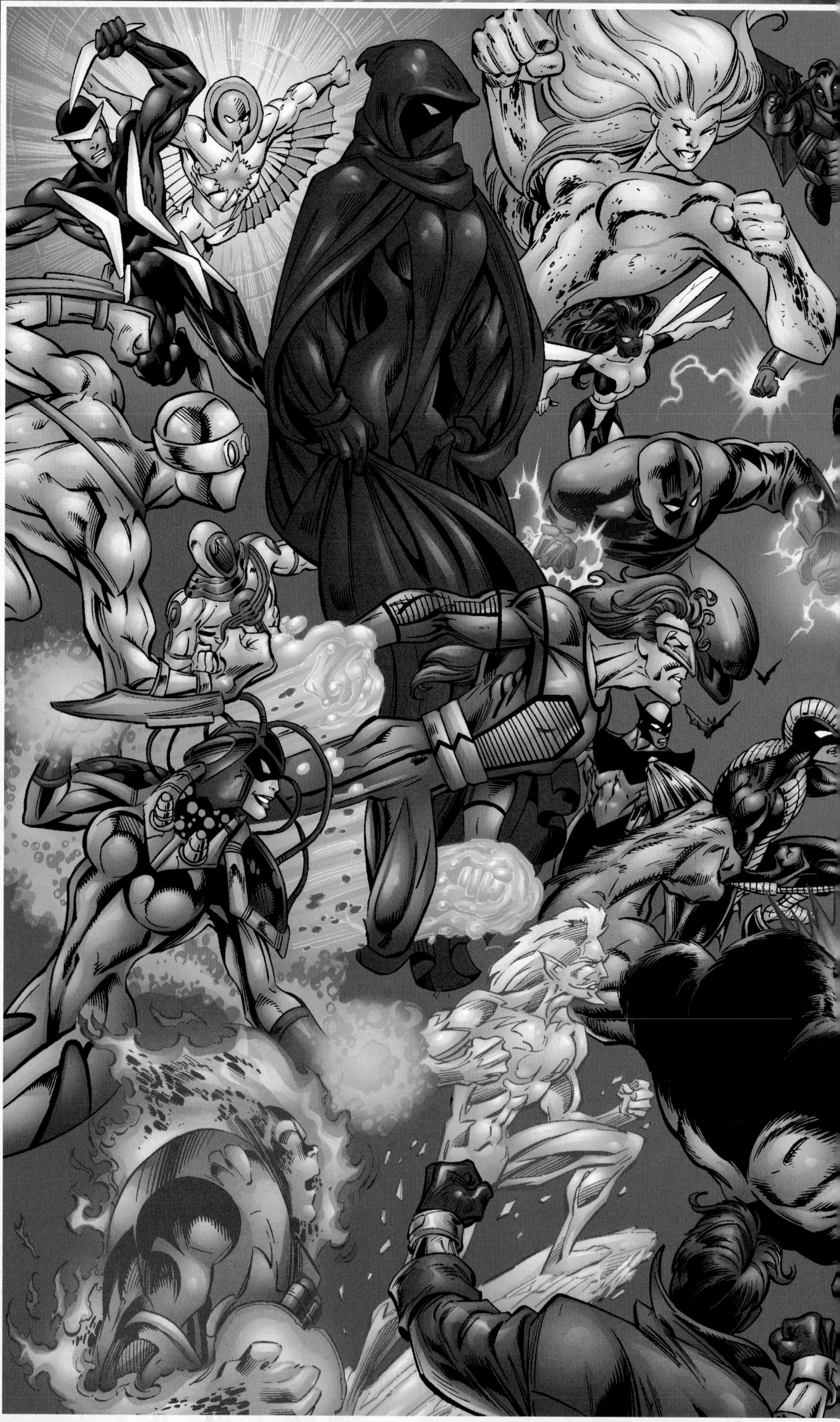

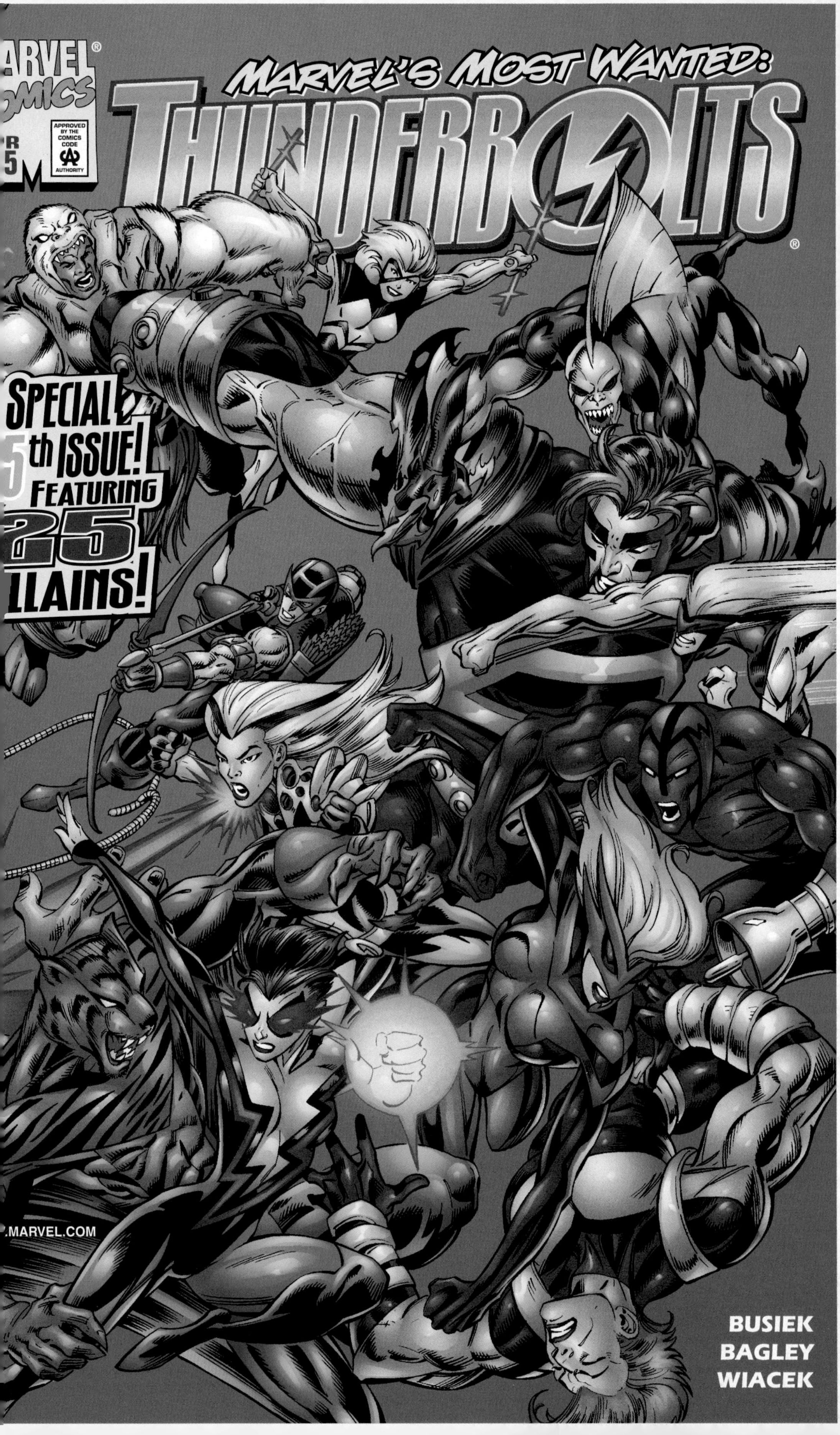

MARVEL COMICS
APPROVED BY THE COMICS CODE AUTHORITY
R 5
MARVEL'S MOST WANTED:
THUNDERBOLTS
SPECIAL 5th ISSUE! FEATURING 25 VILLAINS!
.MARVEL.COM
BUSIEK
BAGLEY
WIACEK

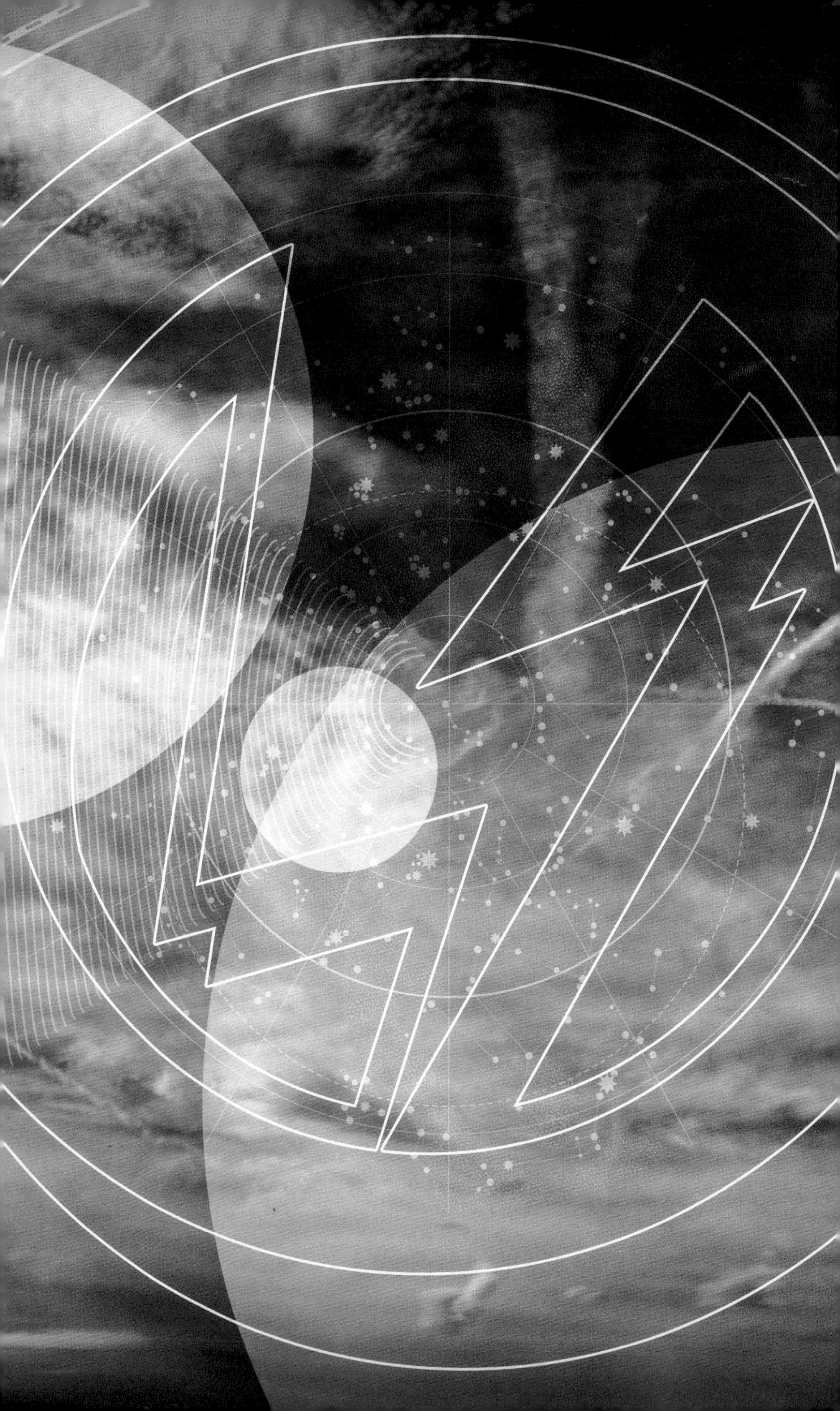

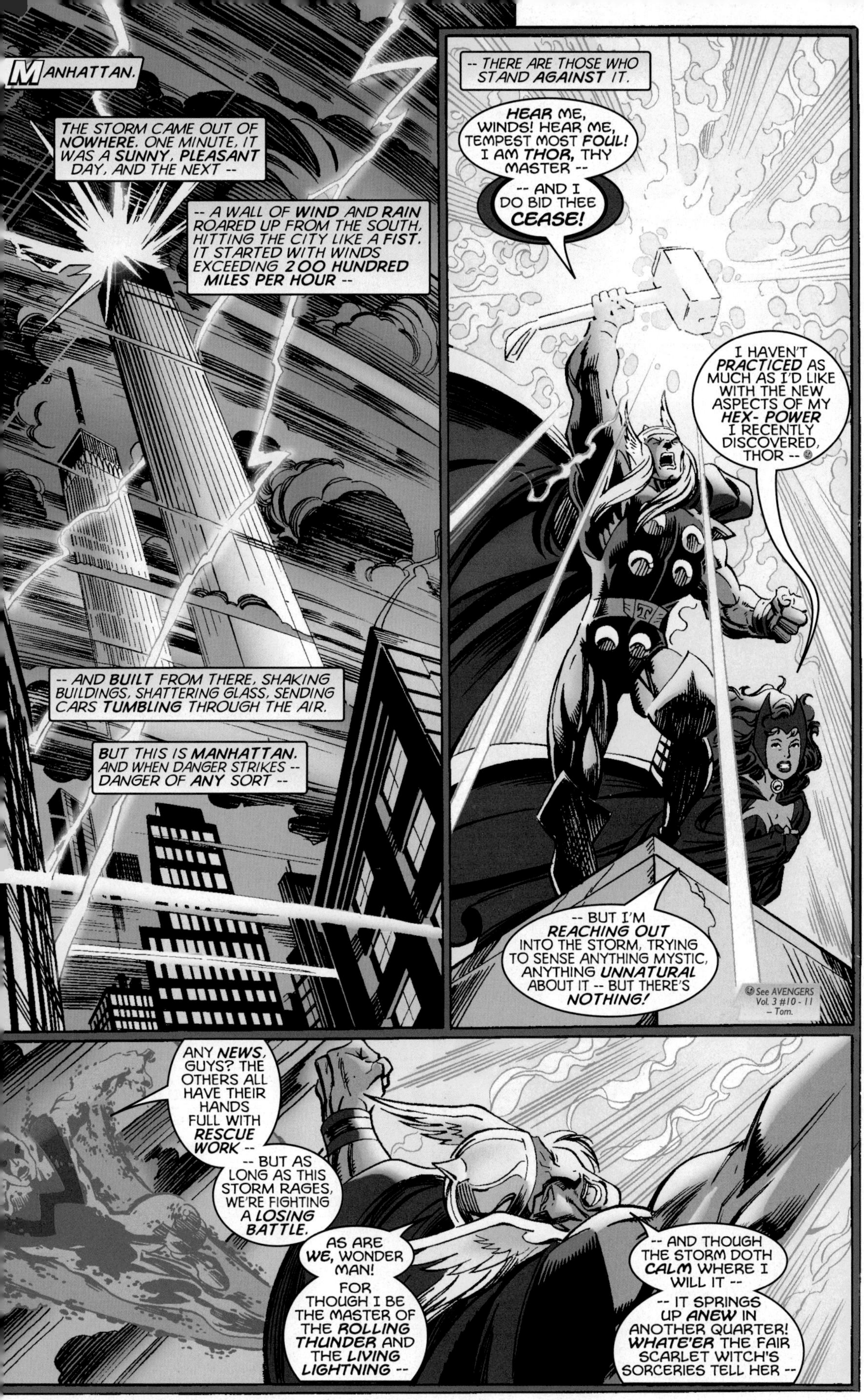
MANHATTAN.
THE STORM CAME OUT OF NOWHERE. ONE MINUTE, IT WAS A SUNNY, PLEASANT DAY, AND THE NEXT --
-- A WALL OF WIND AND RAIN ROARED UP FROM THE SOUTH, HITTING THE CITY LIKE A FIST. IT STARTED WITH WINDS EXCEEDING 200 HUNDRED MILES PER HOUR --
-- AND BUILT FROM THERE, SHAKING BUILDINGS, SHATTERING GLASS, SENDING CARS TUMBLING THROUGH THE AIR.
BUT THIS IS MANHATTAN. AND WHEN DANGER STRIKES -- DANGER OF ANY SORT --
-- THERE ARE THOSE WHO STAND AGAINST IT.
HEAR ME, WINDS! HEAR ME, TEMPEST MOST FOUL! I AM THOR, THY MASTER --
-- AND I DO BID THEE CEASE!
I HAVEN'T PRACTICED AS MUCH AS I'D LIKE WITH THE NEW ASPECTS OF MY HEX- POWER I RECENTLY DISCOVERED, THOR --
-- BUT I'M REACHING OUT INTO THE STORM, TRYING TO SENSE ANYTHING MYSTIC, ANYTHING UNNATURAL ABOUT IT -- BUT THERE'S NOTHING!
See AVENGERS Vol. 3 #10-11 – Tom.
ANY NEWS, GUYS? THE OTHERS ALL HAVE THEIR HANDS FULL WITH RESCUE WORK --
-- BUT AS LONG AS THIS STORM RAGES, WE'RE FIGHTING A LOSING BATTLE.
AS ARE WE, WONDER MAN!
FOR THOUGH I BE THE MASTER OF THE ROLLING THUNDER AND THE LIVING LIGHTNING --
-- AND THOUGH THE STORM DOTH CALM WHERE I WILL IT --
-- IT SPRINGS UP ANEW IN ANOTHER QUARTER! WHATE'ER THE FAIR SCARLET WITCH'S SORCERIES TELL HER --

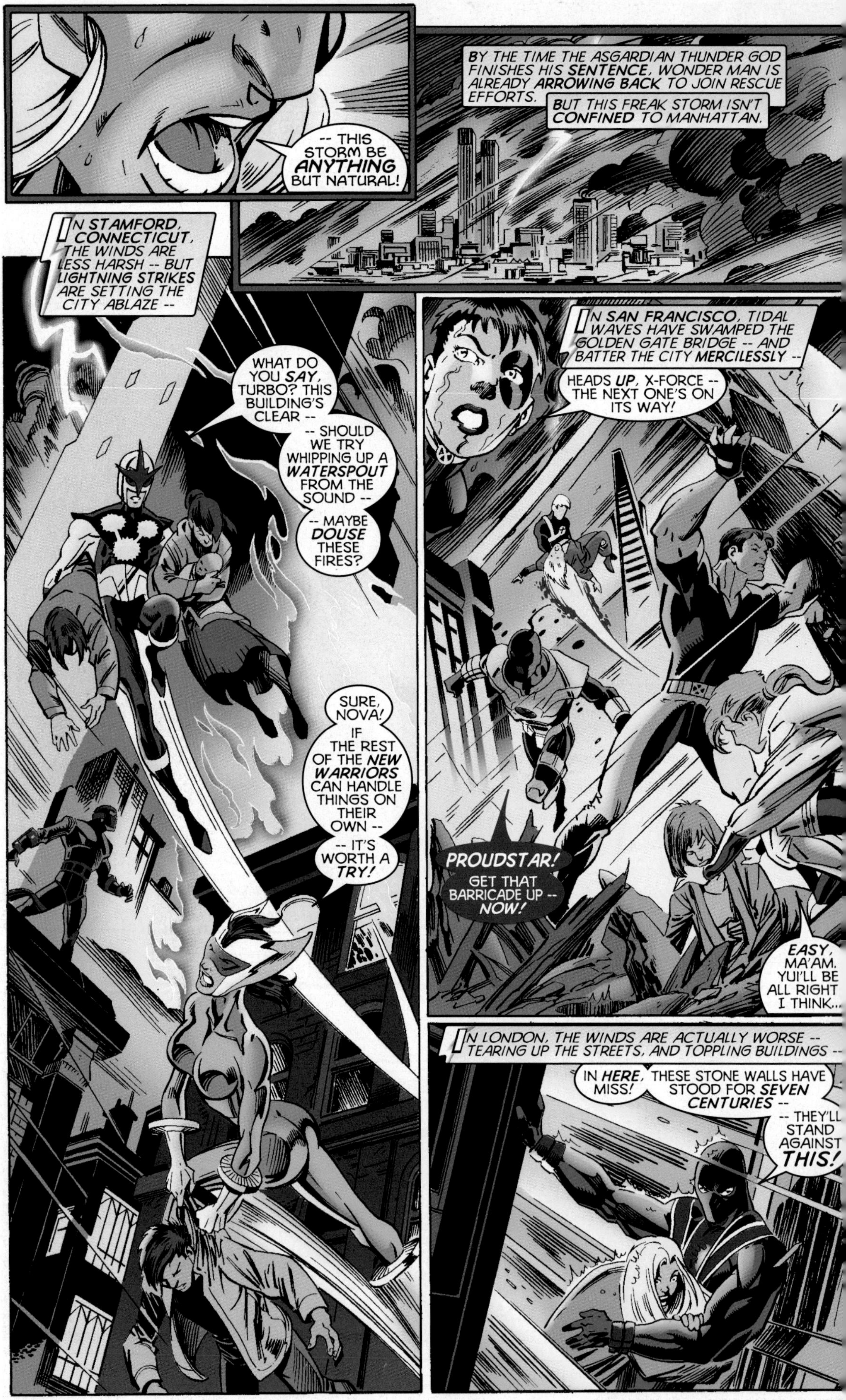
-- THIS STORM BE ANYTHING BUT NATURAL!
BY THE TIME THE ASGARDIAN THUNDER GOD FINISHES HIS SENTENCE, WONDER MAN IS ALREADY ARROWING BACK TO JOIN RESCUE EFFORTS.
BUT THIS FREAK STORM ISN'T CONFINED TO MANHATTAN.
IN STAMFORD, CONNECTICUT, THE WINDS ARE LESS HARSH -- BUT LIGHTNING STRIKES ARE SETTING THE CITY ABLAZE --
WHAT DO YOU SAY, TURBO? THIS BUILDING'S CLEAR --
-- SHOULD WE TRY WHIPPING UP A WATERSPOUT FROM THE SOUND --
-- MAYBE DOUSE THESE FIRES?
SURE, NOVA! IF THE REST OF THE NEW WARRIORS CAN HANDLE THINGS ON THEIR OWN --
-- IT'S WORTH A TRY!
IN SAN FRANCISCO, TIDAL WAVES HAVE SWAMPED THE GOLDEN GATE BRIDGE -- AND BATTER THE CITY MERCILESSLY --
HEADS UP, X-FORCE -- THE NEXT ONE'S ON ITS WAY!
PROUDSTAR! GET THAT BARRICADE UP -- NOW!
EASY, MA'AM. YUI'LL BE ALL RIGHT I THINK...
IN LONDON, THE WINDS ARE ACTUALLY WORSE -- TEARING UP THE STREETS, AND TOPPLING BUILDINGS --
IN HERE, MISS!
THESE STONE WALLS HAVE STOOD FOR SEVEN CENTURIES --
-- THEY'LL STAND AGAINST THIS!

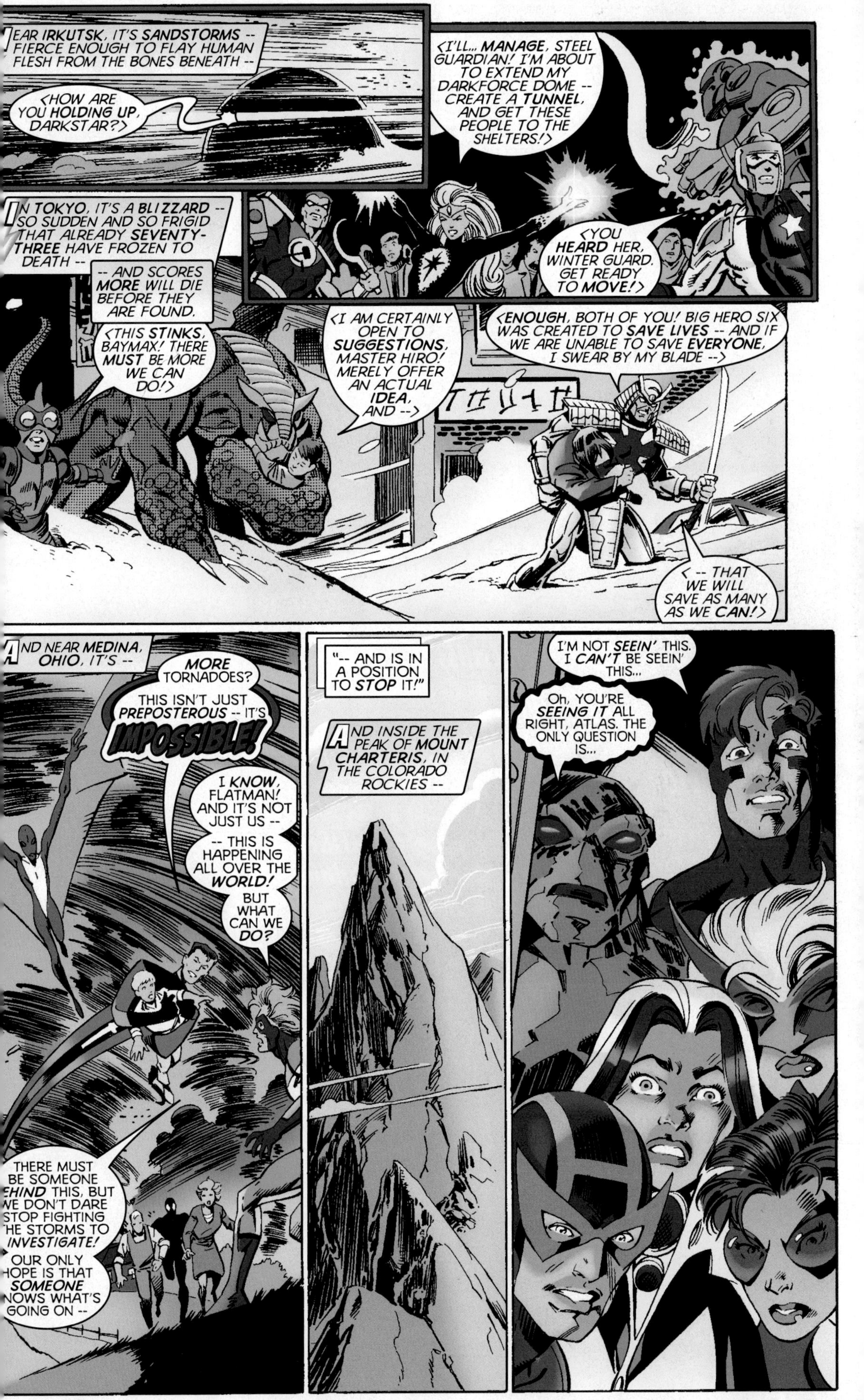
NEAR IRKUTSK, IT'S SANDSTORMS -- FIERCE ENOUGH TO FLAY HUMAN FLESH FROM THE BONES BENEATH --
<HOW ARE YOU HOLDING UP, DARKSTAR?>
<I'LL... MANAGE, STEEL GUARDIAN! I'M ABOUT TO EXTEND MY DARKFORCE DOME -- CREATE A TUNNEL, AND GET THESE PEOPLE TO THE SHELTERS!>
<YOU HEARD HER, WINTER GUARD. GET READY TO MOVE!>
IN TOKYO, IT'S A BLIZZARD -- SO SUDDEN AND SO FRIGID THAT ALREADY SEVENTY-THREE HAVE FROZEN TO DEATH --
-- AND SCORES MORE WILL DIE BEFORE THEY ARE FOUND.
<THIS STINKS, BAYMAX! THERE MUST BE MORE WE CAN DO!>
<I AM CERTAINLY OPEN TO SUGGESTIONS, MASTER HIRO! MERELY OFFER AN ACTUAL IDEA, AND -->
<ENOUGH, BOTH OF YOU! BIG HERO SIX WAS CREATED TO SAVE LIVES -- AND IF WE ARE UNABLE TO SAVE EVERYONE, I SWEAR BY MY BLADE -->
< -- THAT WE WILL SAVE AS MANY AS WE CAN!>
AND NEAR MEDINA, OHIO, IT'S --
MORE TORNADOES? THIS ISN'T JUST PREPOSTEROUS -- IT'S IMPOSSIBLE!
I KNOW, FLATMAN! AND IT'S NOT JUST US --
-- THIS IS HAPPENING ALL OVER THE WORLD! BUT WHAT CAN WE DO?
THERE MUST BE SOMEONE EHIND THIS, BUT VE DON'T DARE STOP FIGHTING HE STORMS TO INVESTIGATE!
OUR ONLY HOPE IS THAT SOMEONE NOWS WHAT'S GOING ON --
"-- AND IS IN A POSITION TO STOP IT!"
AND INSIDE THE PEAK OF MOUNT CHARTERIS, IN THE COLORADO ROCKIES --
I'M NOT SEEIN' THIS. I CAN'T BE SEEIN' THIS...
Oh, YOU'RE SEEING IT ALL RIGHT, ATLAS. THE ONLY QUESTION IS...

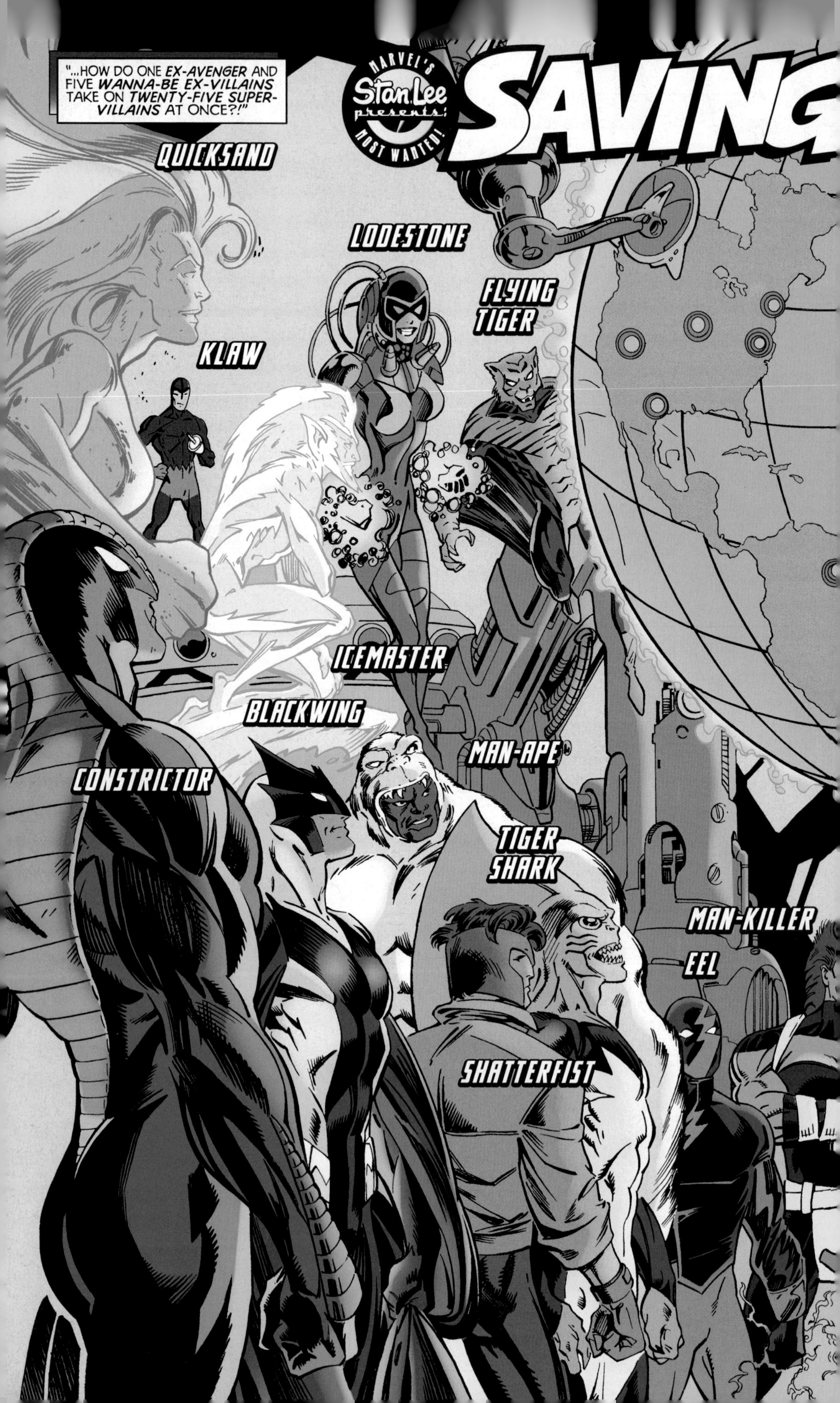
"...HOW DO ONE EX-AVENGER AND FIVE WANNA-BE EX-VILLAINS TAKE ON TWENTY-FIVE SUPER-VILLAINS AT ONCE?!"
MARVEL'S Stan Lee presents! MOST WANTED!
SAVING
QUICKSAND
LODESTONE
FLYING TIGER
KLAW
ICEMASTER
BLACKWING
MAN-APE
CONSTRICTOR
TIGER SHARK
MAN-KILLER
EEL
SHATTERFIST

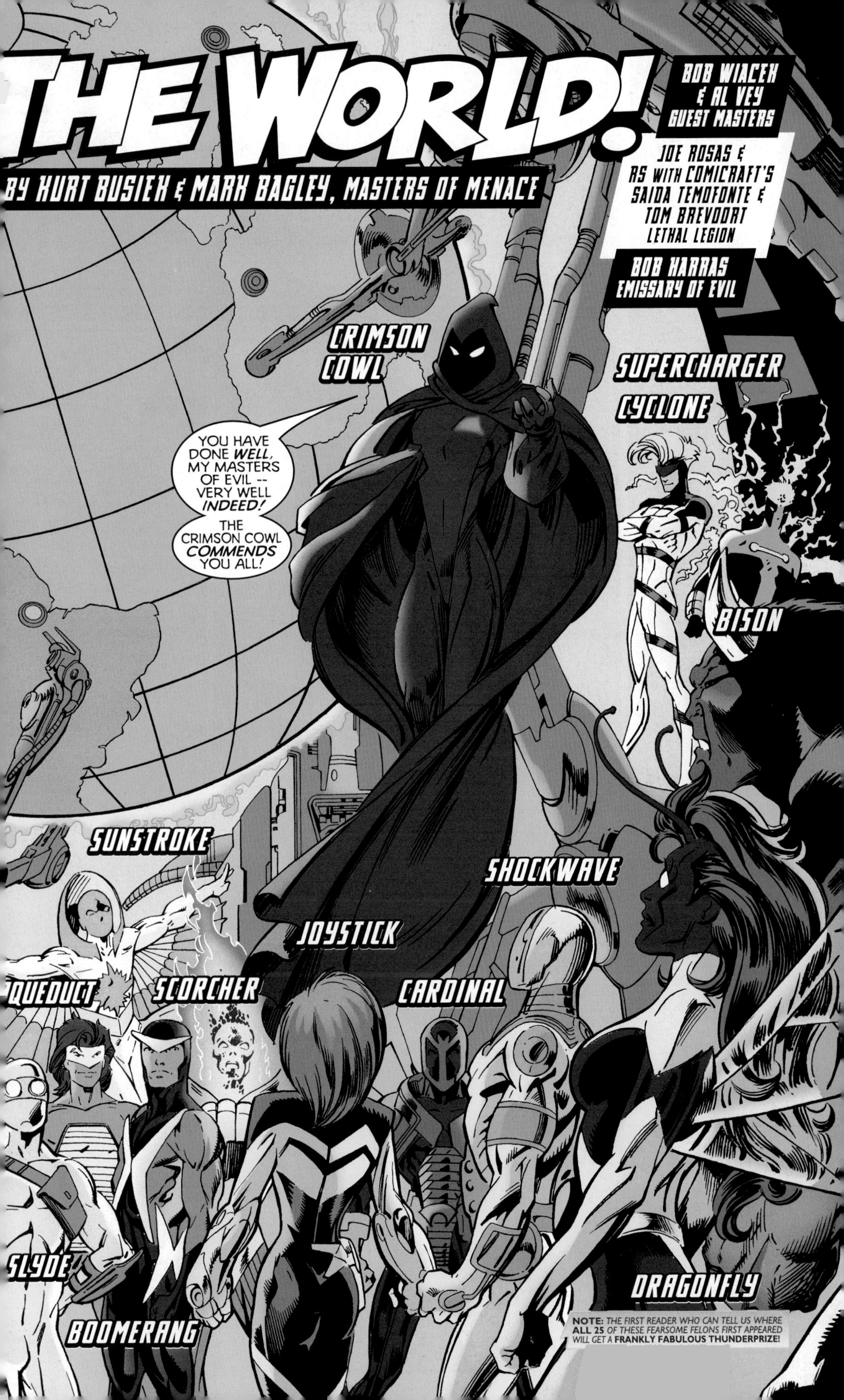
THE WORLD!
BY KURT BUSIEK & MARK BAGLEY, MASTERS OF MENACE
BOB WIACEK & AL VEY GUEST MASTERS
JOE ROSAS & RS WITH COMICRAFT'S SAIDA TEMOFONTE & TOM BREVOORT LETHAL LEGION
BOB HARRAS EMISSARY OF EVIL
CRIMSON COWL
SUPERCHARGER
CYCLONE
YOU HAVE DONE WELL, MY MASTERS OF EVIL -- VERY WELL INDEED!
THE CRIMSON COWL COMMENDS YOU ALL!
BISON
SUNSTROKE
SHOCKWAVE
JOYSTICK
QUEDUCT
SCORCHER
CARDINAL
SLYDE
DRAGONFLY
BOOMERANG
NOTE: THE FIRST READER WHO CAN TELL US WHERE ALL 25 OF THESE FEARSOME FELONS FIRST APPEARED WILL GET A FRANKLY FABULOUS THUNDERPRIZE!

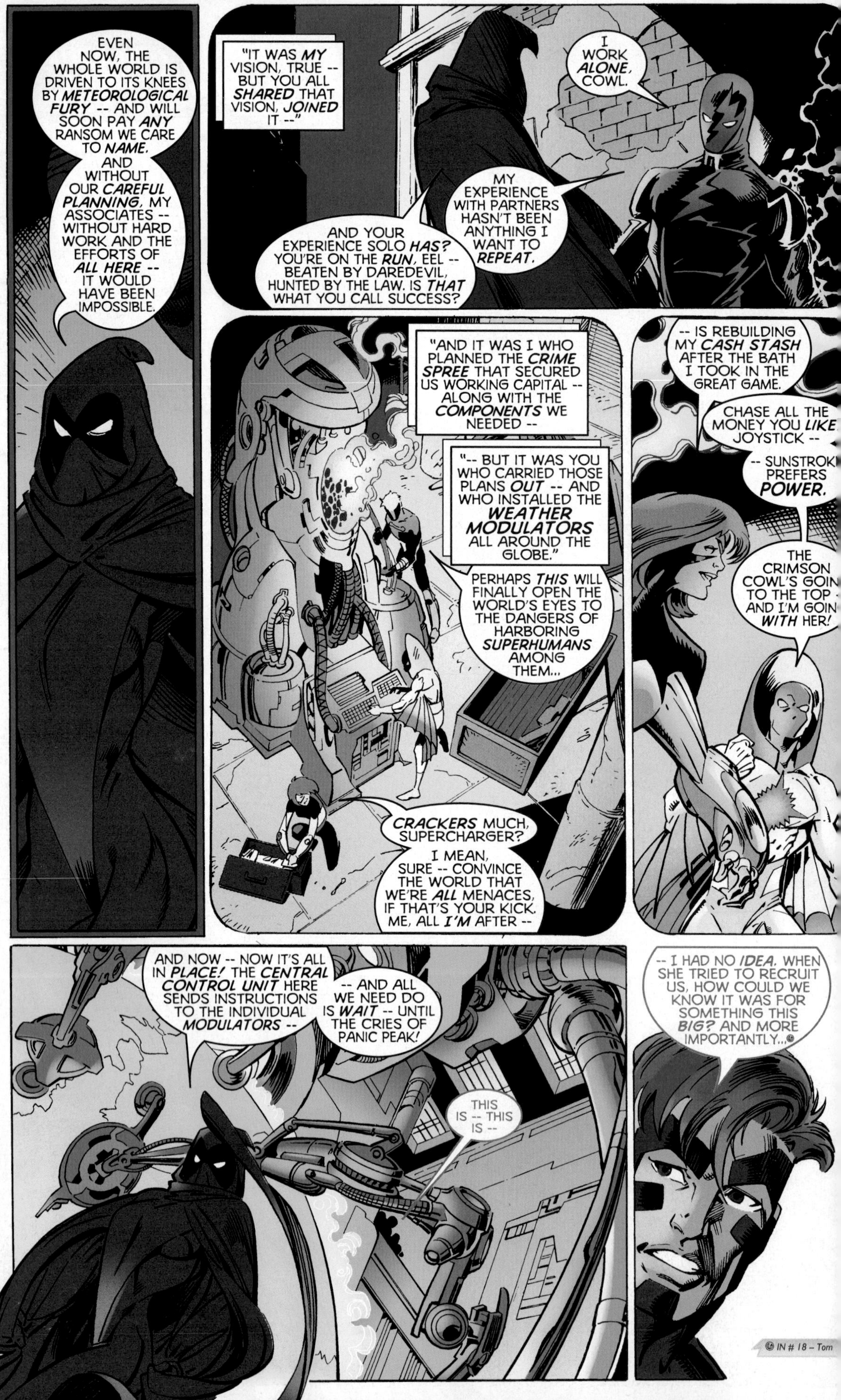
EVEN NOW, THE WHOLE WORLD IS DRIVEN TO ITS KNEES BY METEOROLOGICAL FURY -- AND WILL SOON PAY ANY RANSOM WE CARE TO NAME.
AND WITHOUT OUR CAREFUL PLANNING, MY ASSOCIATES -- WITHOUT HARD WORK AND THE EFFORTS OF ALL HERE -- IT WOULD HAVE BEEN IMPOSSIBLE.
"IT WAS MY VISION, TRUE -- BUT YOU ALL SHARED THAT VISION, JOINED IT --"
I WORK ALONE, COWL.
MY EXPERIENCE WITH PARTNERS HASN'T BEEN ANYTHING I WANT TO REPEAT.
AND YOUR EXPERIENCE SOLO HAS? YOU'RE ON THE RUN, EEL -- BEATEN BY DAREDEVIL, HUNTED BY THE LAW. IS THAT WHAT YOU CALL SUCCESS?
"AND IT WAS I WHO PLANNED THE CRIME SPREE THAT SECURED US WORKING CAPITAL -- ALONG WITH THE COMPONENTS WE NEEDED --
"-- BUT IT WAS YOU WHO CARRIED THOSE PLANS OUT -- AND WHO INSTALLED THE WEATHER MODULATORS ALL AROUND THE GLOBE."
PERHAPS THIS WILL FINALLY OPEN THE WORLD'S EYES TO THE DANGERS OF HARBORING SUPERHUMANS AMONG THEM...
CRACKERS MUCH, SUPERCHARGER?
I MEAN, SURE -- CONVINCE THE WORLD THAT WE'RE ALL MENACES, IF THAT'S YOUR KICK. ME, ALL I'M AFTER --
-- IS REBUILDING MY CASH STASH AFTER THE BATH I TOOK IN THE GREAT GAME.
CHASE ALL THE MONEY YOU LIKE JOYSTICK --
-- SUNSTROK PREFERS POWER.
THE CRIMSON COWL'S GOIN TO THE TOP -- AND I'M GOIN WITH HER!
AND NOW -- NOW IT'S ALL IN PLACE! THE CENTRAL CONTROL UNIT HERE SENDS INSTRUCTIONS TO THE INDIVIDUAL MODULATORS --
-- AND ALL WE NEED DO IS WAIT -- UNTIL THE CRIES OF PANIC PEAK!
THIS IS -- THIS IS --
-- I HAD NO IDEA. WHEN SHE TRIED TO RECRUIT US, HOW COULD WE KNOW IT WAS FOR SOMETHING THIS BIG? AND MORE IMPORTANTLY...©
© IN # 18 – Tom

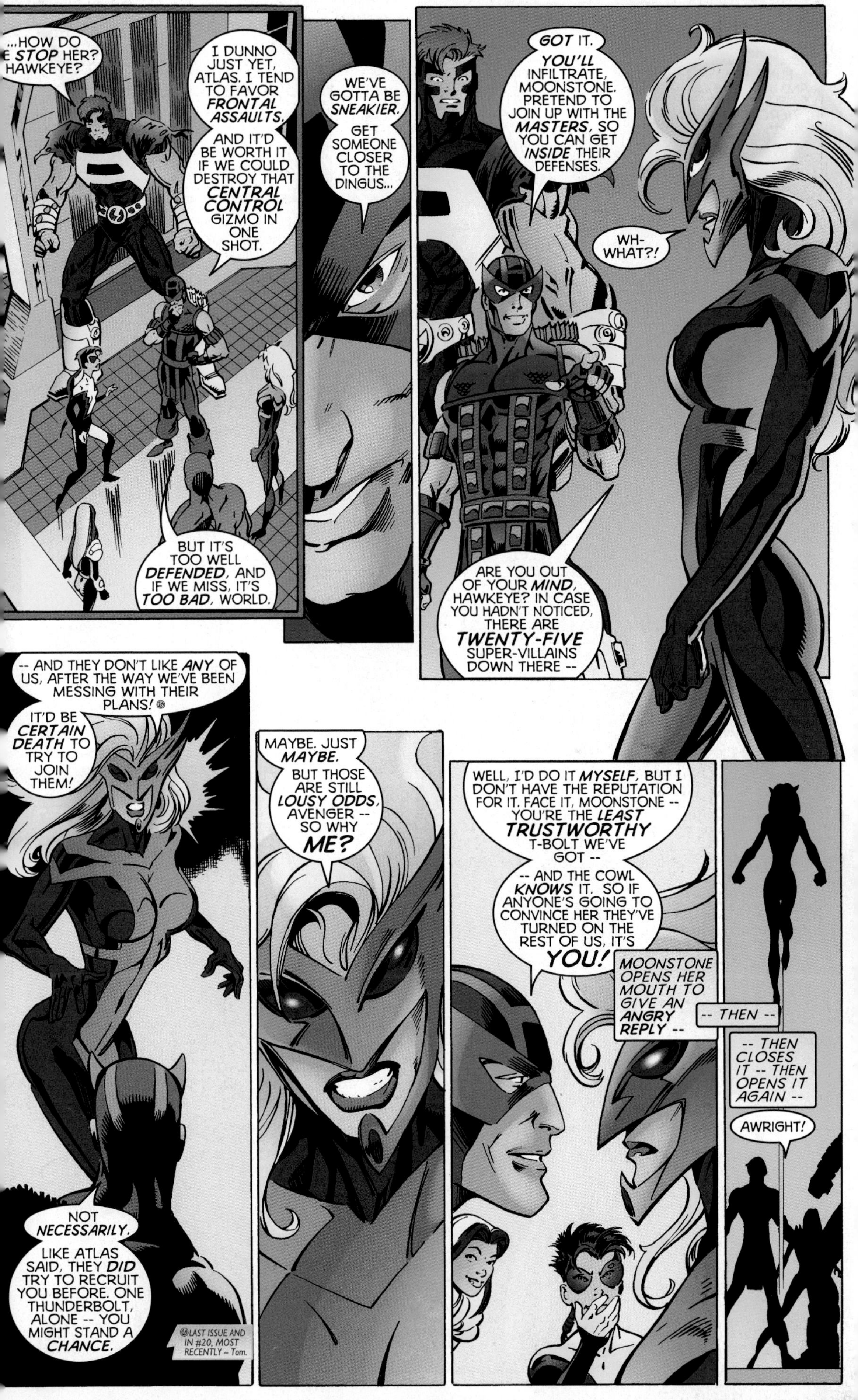
...HOW DO E STOP HER? HAWKEYE?
I DUNNO JUST YET, ATLAS. I TEND TO FAVOR FRONTAL ASSAULTS.
AND IT'D BE WORTH IT IF WE COULD DESTROY THAT CENTRAL CONTROL GIZMO IN ONE SHOT.
BUT IT'S TOO WELL DEFENDED, AND IF WE MISS, IT'S TOO BAD, WORLD.
WE'VE GOTTA BE SNEAKIER.
GET SOMEONE CLOSER TO THE DINGUS...
GOT IT.
YOU'LL INFILTRATE, MOONSTONE. PRETEND TO JOIN UP WITH THE MASTERS, SO YOU CAN GET INSIDE THEIR DEFENSES.
WH-WHAT?!
ARE YOU OUT OF YOUR MIND, HAWKEYE? IN CASE YOU HADN'T NOTICED, THERE ARE TWENTY-FIVE SUPER-VILLAINS DOWN THERE --
-- AND THEY DON'T LIKE ANY OF US, AFTER THE WAY WE'VE BEEN MESSING WITH THEIR PLANS!
IT'D BE CERTAIN DEATH TO TRY TO JOIN THEM!
NOT NECESSARILY.
LIKE ATLAS SAID, THEY DID TRY TO RECRUIT YOU BEFORE. ONE THUNDERBOLT, ALONE -- YOU MIGHT STAND A CHANCE.
LAST ISSUE AND IN #20, MOST RECENTLY – Tom.
MAYBE. JUST MAYBE.
BUT THOSE ARE STILL LOUSY ODDS, AVENGER -- SO WHY ME?
WELL, I'D DO IT MYSELF, BUT I DON'T HAVE THE REPUTATION FOR IT. FACE IT, MOONSTONE -- YOU'RE THE LEAST TRUSTWORTHY T-BOLT WE'VE GOT --
-- AND THE COWL KNOWS IT. SO IF ANYONE'S GOING TO CONVINCE HER THEY'VE TURNED ON THE REST OF US, IT'S YOU!
MOONSTONE OPENS HER MOUTH TO GIVE AN ANGRY REPLY --
-- THEN --
-- THEN CLOSES IT -- THEN OPENS IT AGAIN --
AWRIGHT!

BLAST HIM!

BLAST HIM AND HIS **SMUG,** SIMPLE-MINDED **HEROISM!**

IT'S ALMOST AS IF HE'S **DARING** ME TO LIVE DOWN TO HIS **EXPECTATIONS** OF ME!

AND HOW DID WE GET **INTO** THIS POSITION ANYWAY? SAVING THE **WORLD?**

WHEN THE **THUNDERBOLTS** DECIDED TO TRY TO PROVE WE'D **REFORMED,** I IMAGINED FIGHTING **BANK ROBBERS** -- SAVING **LIVES!**

BUT PUTTING **OUR** LIVES ON THE LINE TO SAVE THE WORLD? THAT'S NOT **ME.** IT NEVER **HAS** BEEN -- NOT FROM THE VERY **START...**

AND SHE FINDS HERSELF THINKING BACK TO HER **CHILDHOOD** --

-- BACK TO THAT SUMPTUOUS, **MILLION-DOLLAR** MANSION IN THE HOLLYWOOD HILLS.

BEING WAITED ON **HAND** AND **FOOT,** THROWING PARTIES ATTENDED BY DOZENS OF MOVIE AND TV STARS, **ROLLING** IN MONEY....

QUITE A LIFE, FOR **CHARLES STOCKBRIDGE,** THE MULTIPLE OSCAR-WINNING PRODUCER WHOSE HOME IT WAS.

BUT JUST AN ARDUOUS, NEVER-ENDING JOB FOR HIS **BUTLER** --

-- AND FOR THE BUTLER'S DAUGHTER, IT WAS ALL A **PARADE** -- OF ALL THE THINGS SHE **WANTED,** BUT COULDN'T HAVE --

KARLA?

BUT, **MA** -- I WAS ONLY --

YES, I KNOW -- AND **YOU** KNOW YOU SHOULD BE IN YOUR **ROOM!**

HOW MANY **TIMES** HAVE I TOLD YOU NOT TO BOTHER THE **BOSS** AND HIS **FRIENDS,** Hm?

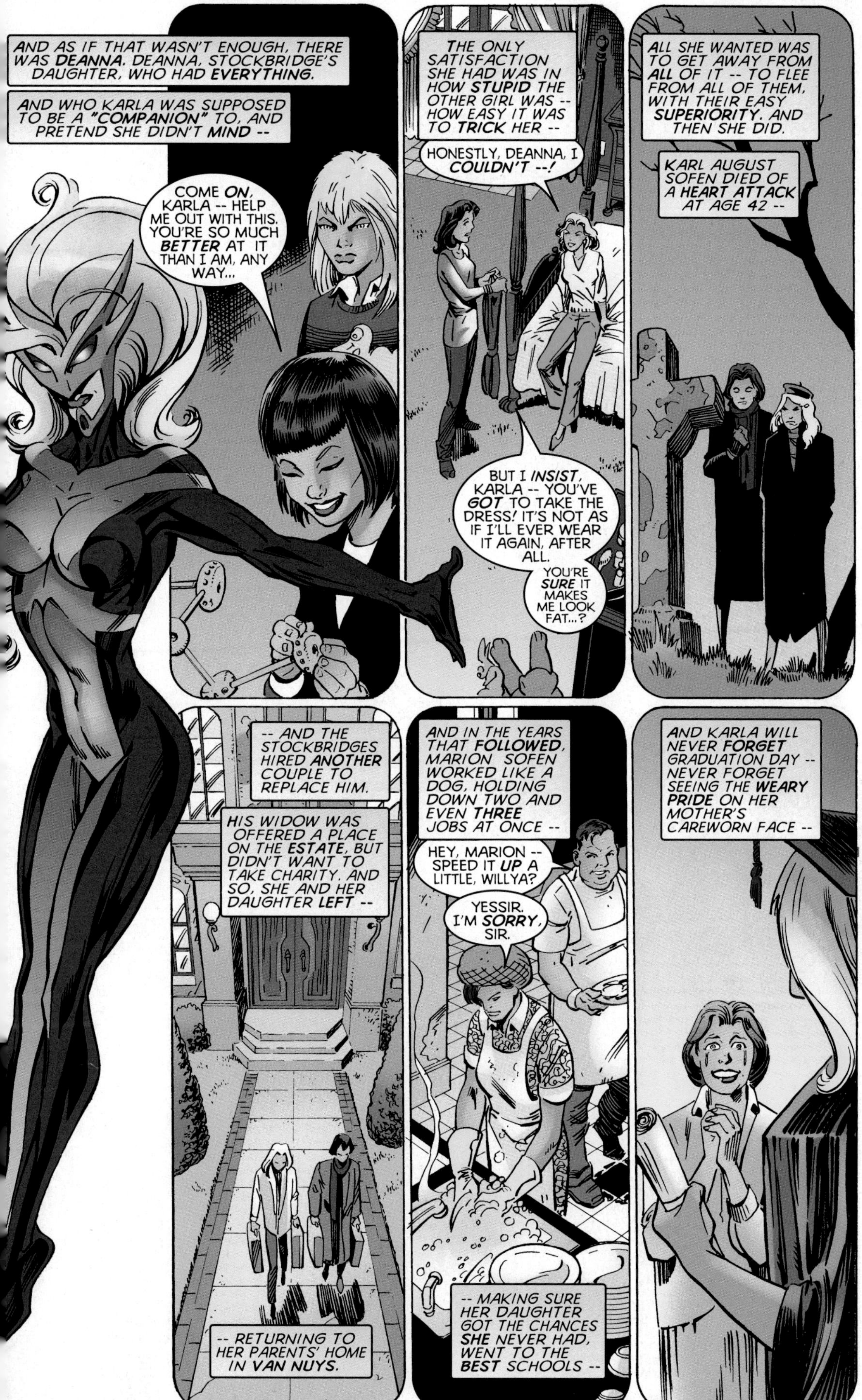
AND AS IF THAT WASN'T ENOUGH, THERE WAS DEANNA. DEANNA, STOCKBRIDGE'S DAUGHTER, WHO HAD EVERYTHING.
AND WHO KARLA WAS SUPPOSED TO BE A "COMPANION" TO, AND PRETEND SHE DIDN'T MIND --
COME ON, KARLA -- HELP ME OUT WITH THIS. YOU'RE SO MUCH BETTER AT IT THAN I AM, ANY WAY...
THE ONLY SATISFACTION SHE HAD WAS IN HOW STUPID THE OTHER GIRL WAS -- HOW EASY IT WAS TO TRICK HER --
HONESTLY, DEANNA, I COULDN'T --!
BUT I INSIST, KARLA -- YOU'VE GOT TO TAKE THE DRESS! IT'S NOT AS IF I'LL EVER WEAR IT AGAIN, AFTER ALL.
YOU'RE SURE IT MAKES ME LOOK FAT...?
ALL SHE WANTED WAS TO GET AWAY FROM ALL OF IT -- TO FLEE FROM ALL OF THEM, WITH THEIR EASY SUPERIORITY. AND THEN SHE DID.
KARL AUGUST SOFEN DIED OF A HEART ATTACK AT AGE 42 --
-- AND THE STOCKBRIDGES HIRED ANOTHER COUPLE TO REPLACE HIM.
HIS WIDOW WAS OFFERED A PLACE ON THE ESTATE, BUT DIDN'T WANT TO TAKE CHARITY. AND SO, SHE AND HER DAUGHTER LEFT --
-- RETURNING TO HER PARENTS' HOME IN VAN NUYS.
AND IN THE YEARS THAT FOLLOWED, MARION SOFEN WORKED LIKE A DOG, HOLDING DOWN TWO AND EVEN THREE JOBS AT ONCE --
HEY, MARION -- SPEED IT UP A LITTLE, WILLYA?
YESSIR. I'M SORRY, SIR.
-- MAKING SURE HER DAUGHTER GOT THE CHANCES SHE NEVER HAD, WENT TO THE BEST SCHOOLS --
AND KARLA WILL NEVER FORGET GRADUATION DAY -- NEVER FORGET SEEING THE WEARY PRIDE ON HER MOTHER'S CAREWORN FACE --

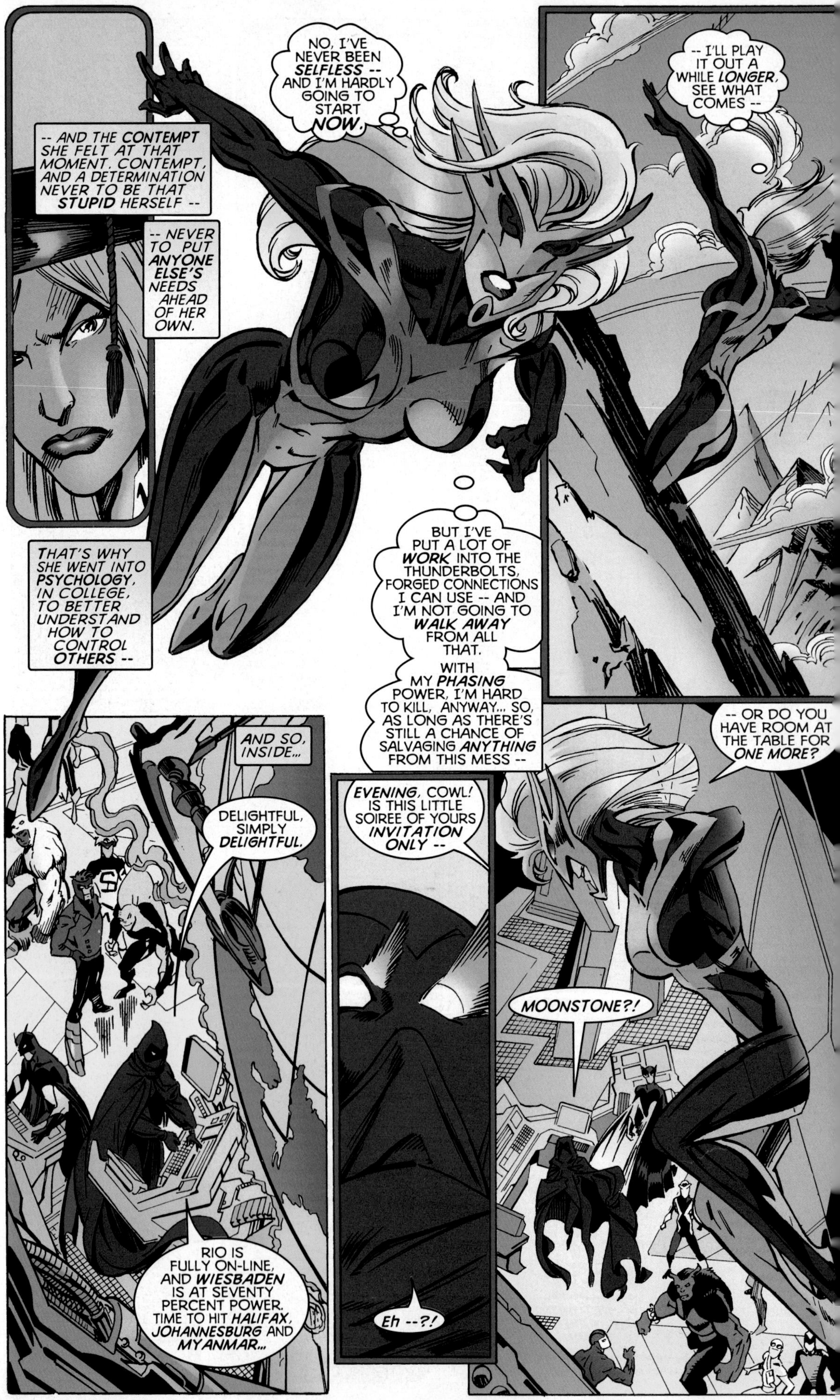
-- AND THE CONTEMPT SHE FELT AT THAT MOMENT. CONTEMPT, AND A DETERMINATION NEVER TO BE THAT STUPID HERSELF --
-- NEVER TO PUT ANYONE ELSE'S NEEDS AHEAD OF HER OWN.
NO, I'VE NEVER BEEN SELFLESS -- AND I'M HARDLY GOING TO START NOW.
THAT'S WHY SHE WENT INTO PSYCHOLOGY, IN COLLEGE, TO BETTER UNDERSTAND HOW TO CONTROL OTHERS --
BUT I'VE PUT A LOT OF WORK INTO THE THUNDERBOLTS, FORGED CONNECTIONS I CAN USE -- AND I'M NOT GOING TO WALK AWAY FROM ALL THAT.
WITH MY PHASING POWER, I'M HARD TO KILL, ANYWAY... SO, AS LONG AS THERE'S STILL A CHANCE OF SALVAGING ANYTHING FROM THIS MESS --
-- I'LL PLAY IT OUT A WHILE LONGER, SEE WHAT COMES --
AND SO, INSIDE...
DELIGHTFUL, SIMPLY DELIGHTFUL.
RIO IS FULLY ON-LINE, AND WIESBADEN IS AT SEVENTY PERCENT POWER. TIME TO HIT HALIFAX, JOHANNESBURG AND MYANMAR...
EVENING, COWL! IS THIS LITTLE SOIREE OF YOURS INVITATION ONLY --
Eh --?!
-- OR DO YOU HAVE ROOM AT THE TABLE FOR ONE MORE?
MOONSTONE?!

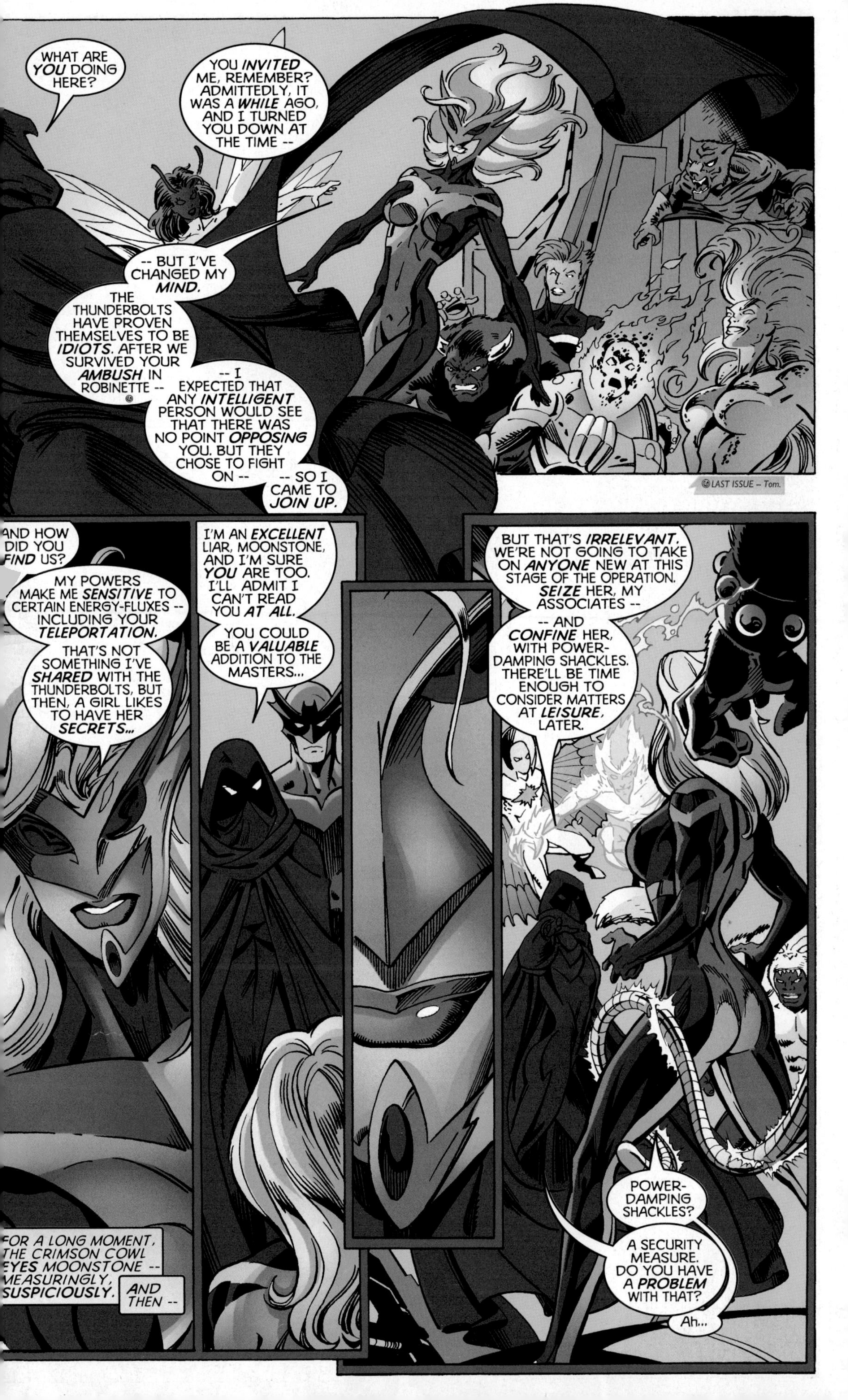
WHAT ARE YOU DOING HERE?
YOU INVITED ME, REMEMBER? ADMITTEDLY, IT WAS A WHILE AGO, AND I TURNED YOU DOWN AT THE TIME --
-- BUT I'VE CHANGED MY MIND.
THE THUNDERBOLTS HAVE PROVEN THEMSELVES TO BE IDIOTS. AFTER WE SURVIVED YOUR AMBUSH IN ROBINETTE --
-- I EXPECTED THAT ANY INTELLIGENT PERSON WOULD SEE THAT THERE WAS NO POINT OPPOSING YOU. BUT THEY CHOSE TO FIGHT ON --
-- SO I CAME TO JOIN UP.
LAST ISSUE – Tom.
AND HOW DID YOU FIND US?
MY POWERS MAKE ME SENSITIVE TO CERTAIN ENERGY-FLUXES -- INCLUDING YOUR TELEPORTATION.
THAT'S NOT SOMETHING I'VE SHARED WITH THE THUNDERBOLTS, BUT THEN, A GIRL LIKES TO HAVE HER SECRETS...
FOR A LONG MOMENT, THE CRIMSON COWL EYES MOONSTONE -- MEASURINGLY, SUSPICIOUSLY.
AND THEN --
I'M AN EXCELLENT LIAR, MOONSTONE, AND I'M SURE YOU ARE TOO. I'LL ADMIT I CAN'T READ YOU AT ALL.
YOU COULD BE A VALUABLE ADDITION TO THE MASTERS...
BUT THAT'S IRRELEVANT. WE'RE NOT GOING TO TAKE ON ANYONE NEW AT THIS STAGE OF THE OPERATION. SEIZE HER, MY ASSOCIATES --
-- AND CONFINE HER, WITH POWER-DAMPING SHACKLES. THERE'LL BE TIME ENOUGH TO CONSIDER MATTERS AT LEISURE, LATER.
POWER-DAMPING SHACKLES?
A SECURITY MEASURE. DO YOU HAVE A PROBLEM WITH THAT?
Ah...

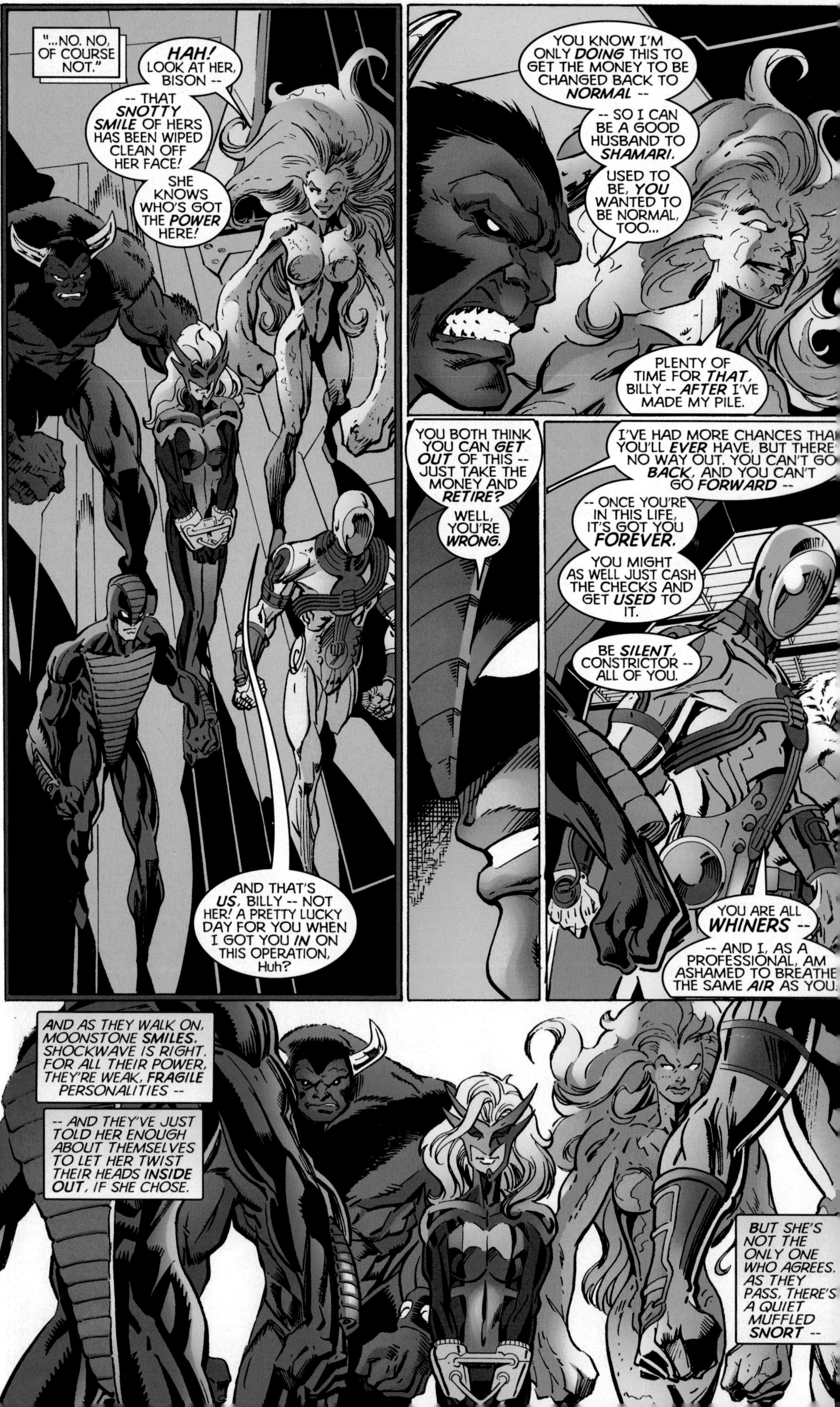
"...NO. NO, OF COURSE NOT."
HAH! LOOK AT HER, BISON --
-- THAT SNOTTY SMILE OF HERS HAS BEEN WIPED CLEAN OFF HER FACE!
SHE KNOWS WHO'S GOT THE POWER HERE!
AND THAT'S US, BILLY -- NOT HER! A PRETTY LUCKY DAY FOR YOU WHEN I GOT YOU IN ON THIS OPERATION, Huh?
YOU KNOW I'M ONLY DOING THIS TO GET THE MONEY TO BE CHANGED BACK TO NORMAL --
-- SO I CAN BE A GOOD HUSBAND TO SHAMARI.
USED TO BE, YOU WANTED TO BE NORMAL, TOO...
PLENTY OF TIME FOR THAT, BILLY -- AFTER I'VE MADE MY PILE.
YOU BOTH THINK YOU CAN GET OUT OF THIS -- JUST TAKE THE MONEY AND RETIRE?
WELL, YOU'RE WRONG.
I'VE HAD MORE CHANCES THA YOU'LL EVER HAVE, BUT THERE' NO WAY OUT. YOU CAN'T GO BACK, AND YOU CAN'T GO FORWARD --
-- ONCE YOU'RE IN THIS LIFE, IT'S GOT YOU FOREVER.
YOU MIGHT AS WELL JUST CASH THE CHECKS AND GET USED TO IT.
BE SILENT, CONSTRICTOR -- ALL OF YOU.
YOU ARE ALL WHINERS --
-- AND I, AS A PROFESSIONAL, AM ASHAMED TO BREATHE THE SAME AIR AS YOU.
AND AS THEY WALK ON, MOONSTONE SMILES. SHOCKWAVE IS RIGHT. FOR ALL THEIR POWER, THEY'RE WEAK, FRAGILE PERSONALITIES --
-- AND THEY'VE JUST TOLD HER ENOUGH ABOUT THEMSELVES TO LET HER TWIST THEIR HEADS INSIDE OUT, IF SHE CHOSE.
BUT SHE'S NOT THE ONLY ONE WHO AGREES. AS THEY PASS, THERE'S A QUIET MUFFLED SNORT --

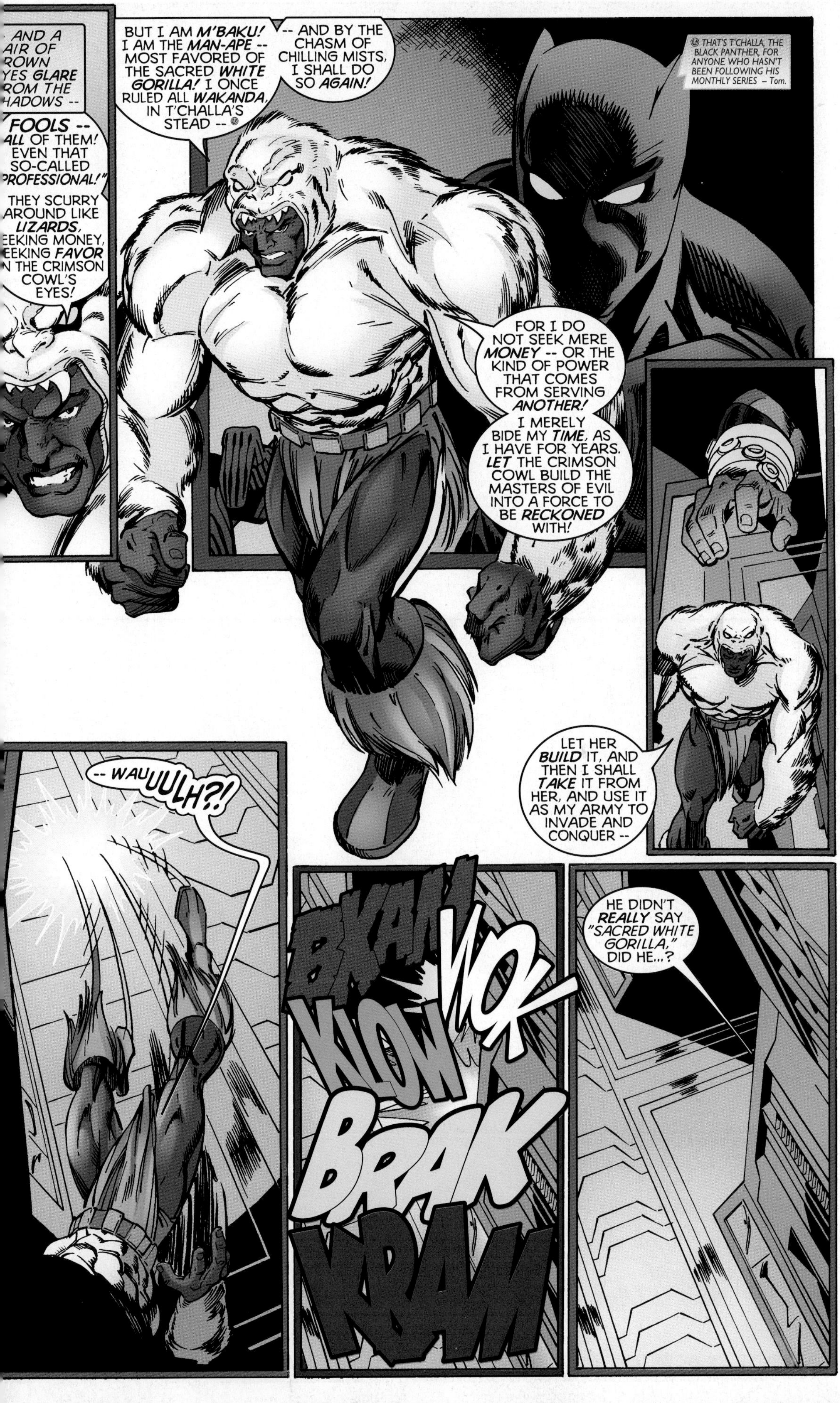

AND A
AIR OF
ROWN
YES GLARE
ROM THE
HADOWS --
"FOOLS -- ALL OF THEM! EVEN THAT SO-CALLED PROFESSIONAL!"
THEY SCURRY AROUND LIKE LIZARDS, SEEKING MONEY, SEEKING FAVOR IN THE CRIMSON COWL'S EYES!
BUT I AM M'BAKU! I AM THE MAN-APE -- MOST FAVORED OF THE SACRED WHITE GORILLA! I ONCE RULED ALL WAKANDA, IN T'CHALLA'S STEAD --
-- AND BY THE CHASM OF CHILLING MISTS, I SHALL DO SO AGAIN!
THAT'S T'CHALLA, THE BLACK PANTHER, FOR ANYONE WHO HASN'T BEEN FOLLOWING HIS MONTHLY SERIES – Tom.
FOR I DO NOT SEEK MERE MONEY -- OR THE KIND OF POWER THAT COMES FROM SERVING ANOTHER!
I MERELY BIDE MY TIME, AS I HAVE FOR YEARS. LET THE CRIMSON COWL BUILD THE MASTERS OF EVIL INTO A FORCE TO BE RECKONED WITH!
LET HER BUILD IT, AND THEN I SHALL TAKE IT FROM HER, AND USE IT AS MY ARMY TO INVADE AND CONQUER --
-- WAUUULH?!
BKAM
VOK
KLOW
BRAK
KRAM
HE DIDN'T REALLY SAY "SACRED WHITE GORILLA," DID HE...?

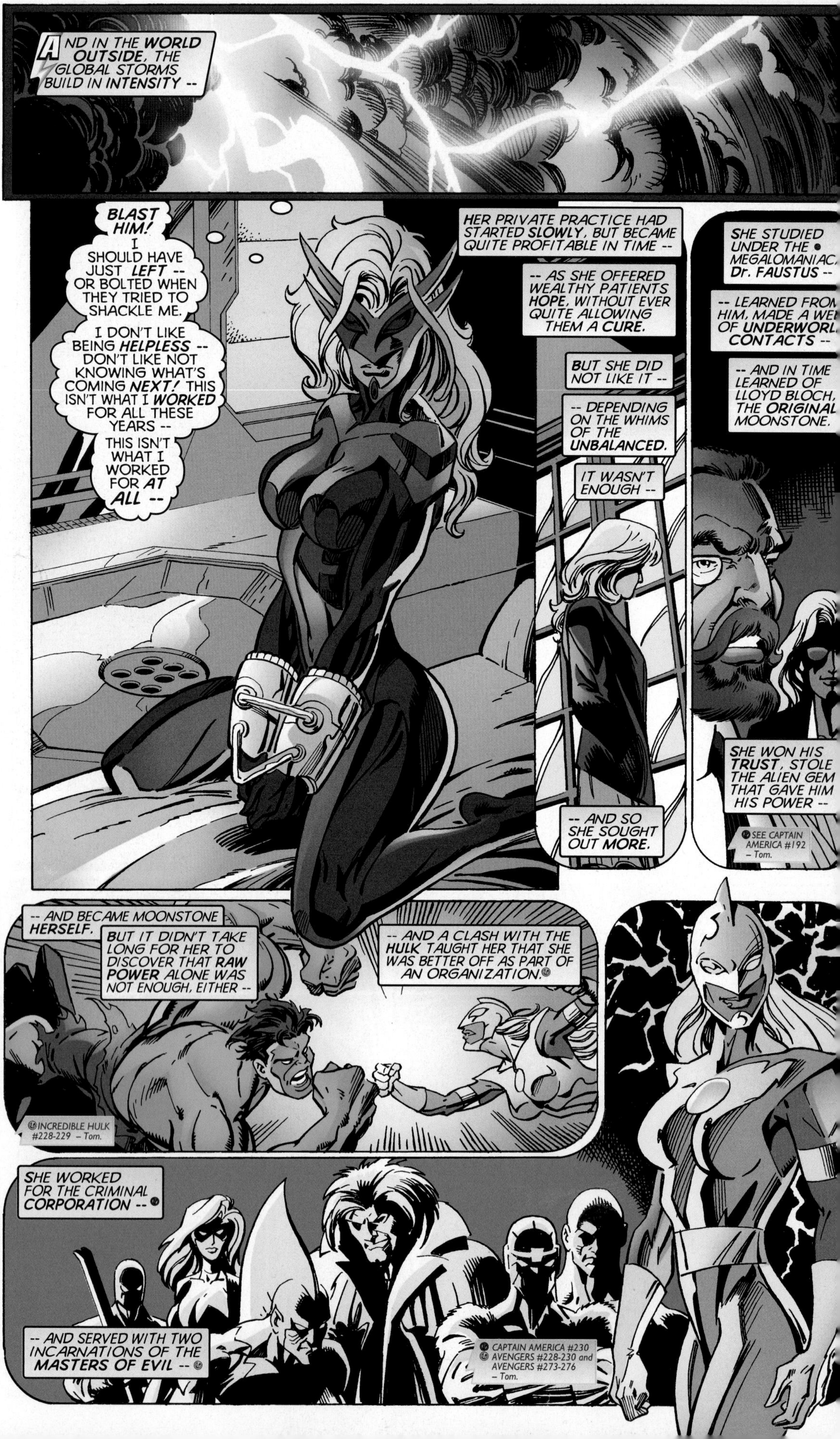
AND IN THE WORLD OUTSIDE, THE GLOBAL STORMS BUILD IN INTENSITY --
BLAST HIM! I SHOULD HAVE JUST LEFT -- OR BOLTED WHEN THEY TRIED TO SHACKLE ME.
I DON'T LIKE BEING HELPLESS -- DON'T LIKE NOT KNOWING WHAT'S COMING NEXT! THIS ISN'T WHAT I WORKED FOR ALL THESE YEARS --
THIS ISN'T WHAT I WORKED FOR AT ALL --
HER PRIVATE PRACTICE HAD STARTED SLOWLY, BUT BECAME QUITE PROFITABLE IN TIME --
-- AS SHE OFFERED WEALTHY PATIENTS HOPE, WITHOUT EVER QUITE ALLOWING THEM A CURE.
BUT SHE DID NOT LIKE IT --
-- DEPENDING ON THE WHIMS OF THE UNBALANCED.
IT WASN'T ENOUGH --
-- AND SO SHE SOUGHT OUT MORE.
SHE STUDIED UNDER THE MEGALOMANIAC Dr. FAUSTUS --
-- LEARNED FROM HIM, MADE A WE OF UNDERWORL CONTACTS --
-- AND IN TIME LEARNED OF LLOYD BLOCH, THE ORIGINAL MOONSTONE.
SHE WON HIS TRUST, STOLE THE ALIEN GEM THAT GAVE HIM HIS POWER --
SEE CAPTAIN AMERICA #192 – Tom.
-- AND BECAME MOONSTONE HERSELF.
BUT IT DIDN'T TAKE LONG FOR HER TO DISCOVER THAT RAW POWER ALONE WAS NOT ENOUGH, EITHER --
-- AND A CLASH WITH THE HULK TAUGHT HER THAT SHE WAS BETTER OFF AS PART OF AN ORGANIZATION.
INCREDIBLE HULK #228-229 – Tom.
SHE WORKED FOR THE CRIMINAL CORPORATION --
-- AND SERVED WITH TWO INCARNATIONS OF THE MASTERS OF EVIL --
CAPTAIN AMERICA #230
AVENGERS #228-230 and AVENGERS #273-276 – Tom.

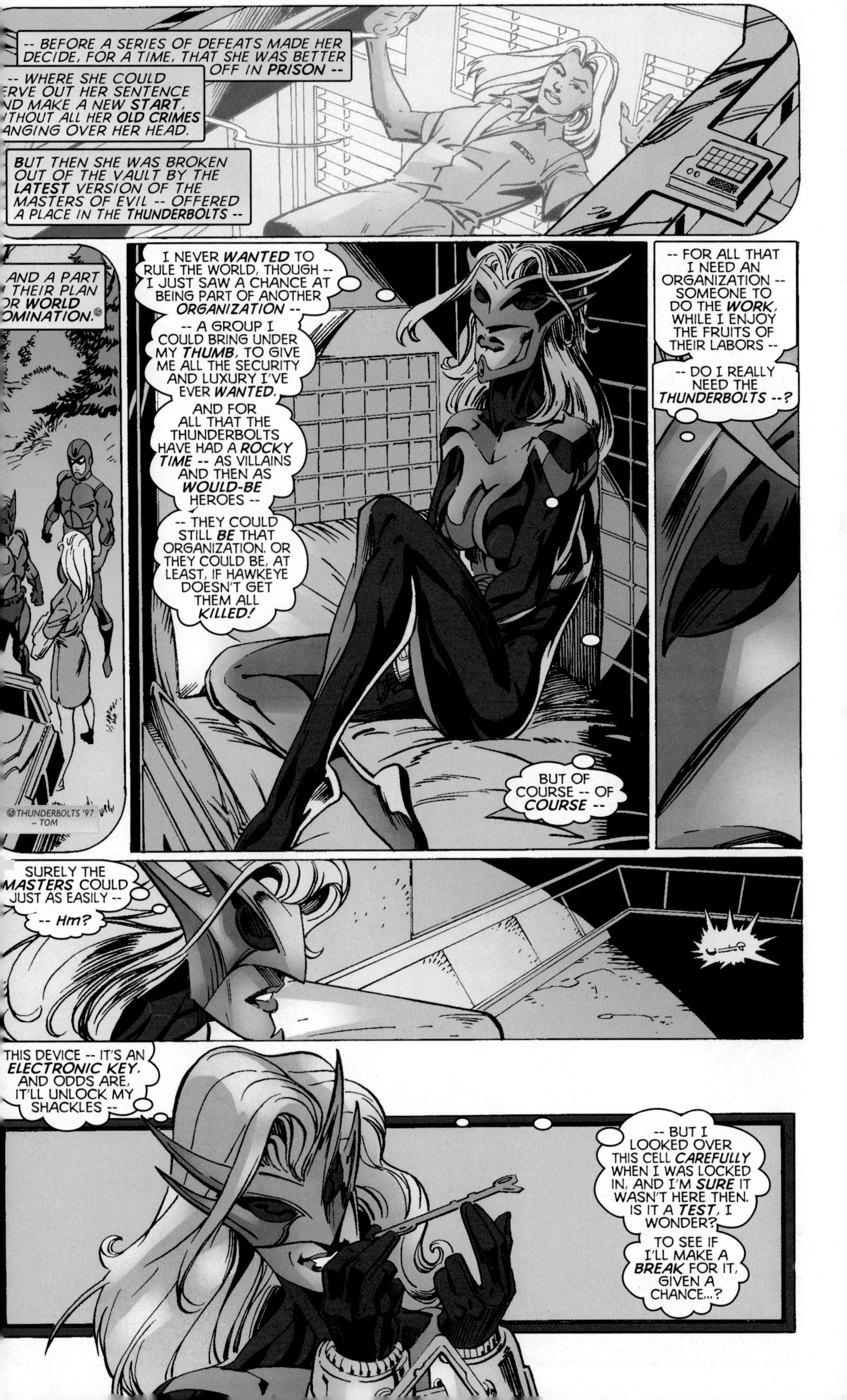

-- BEFORE A SERIES OF DEFEATS MADE HER DECIDE, FOR A TIME, THAT SHE WAS BETTER OFF IN PRISON --
-- WHERE SHE COULD ERVE OUT HER SENTENCE ND MAKE A NEW START, ITHOUT ALL HER OLD CRIMES ANGING OVER HER HEAD.
BUT THEN SHE WAS BROKEN OUT OF THE VAULT BY THE LATEST VERSION OF THE MASTERS OF EVIL -- OFFERED A PLACE IN THE THUNDERBOLTS --
AND A PART THEIR PLAN OR WORLD OMINATION.
THUNDERBOLTS '97 – TOM
I NEVER WANTED TO RULE THE WORLD, THOUGH -- I JUST SAW A CHANCE AT BEING PART OF ANOTHER ORGANIZATION --
-- A GROUP I COULD BRING UNDER MY THUMB, TO GIVE ME ALL THE SECURITY AND LUXURY I'VE EVER WANTED.
AND FOR ALL THAT THE THUNDERBOLTS HAVE HAD A ROCKY TIME -- AS VILLAINS AND THEN AS WOULD-BE HEROES --
-- THEY COULD STILL BE THAT ORGANIZATION. OR THEY COULD BE, AT LEAST, IF HAWKEYE DOESN'T GET THEM ALL KILLED!
BUT OF COURSE -- OF COURSE --
-- FOR ALL THAT I NEED AN ORGANIZATION -- SOMEONE TO DO THE WORK, WHILE I ENJOY THE FRUITS OF THEIR LABORS --
-- DO I REALLY NEED THE THUNDERBOLTS --?
SURELY THE MASTERS COULD JUST AS EASILY --
-- Hm?
THIS DEVICE -- IT'S AN ELECTRONIC KEY. AND ODDS ARE, IT'LL UNLOCK MY SHACKLES --
-- BUT I LOOKED OVER THIS CELL CAREFULLY WHEN I WAS LOCKED IN, AND I'M SURE IT WASN'T HERE THEN. IS IT A TEST, I WONDER?
TO SEE IF I'LL MAKE A BREAK FOR IT, GIVEN A CHANCE...?

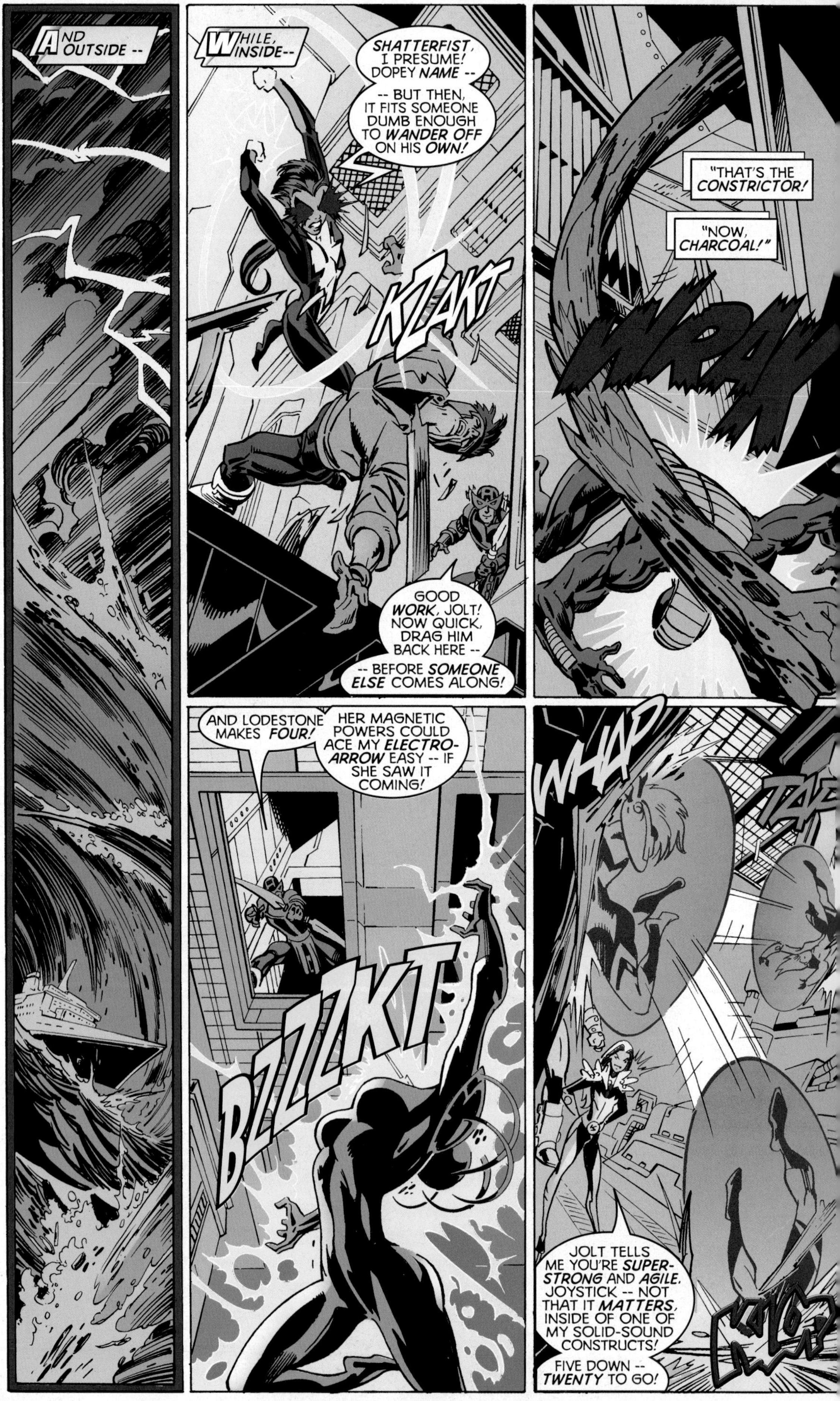

AND OUTSIDE --
WHILE, INSIDE--
SHATTERFIST, I PRESUME! DOPEY NAME --
-- BUT THEN, IT FITS SOMEONE DUMB ENOUGH TO WANDER OFF ON HIS OWN!
KZAKT
GOOD WORK, JOLT! NOW QUICK, DRAG HIM BACK HERE --
-- BEFORE SOMEONE ELSE COMES ALONG!
"THAT'S THE CONSTRICTOR!
"NOW, CHARCOAL!"
WRAK
AND LODESTONE MAKES FOUR!
HER MAGNETIC POWERS COULD ACE MY ELECTRO-ARROW EASY -- IF SHE SAW IT COMING!
BZZZKT
WHAP
JOLT TELLS ME YOU'RE SUPER-STRONG AND AGILE, JOYSTICK -- NOT THAT IT MATTERS, INSIDE OF ONE OF MY SOLID-SOUND CONSTRUCTS!
FIVE DOWN -- TWENTY TO GO!

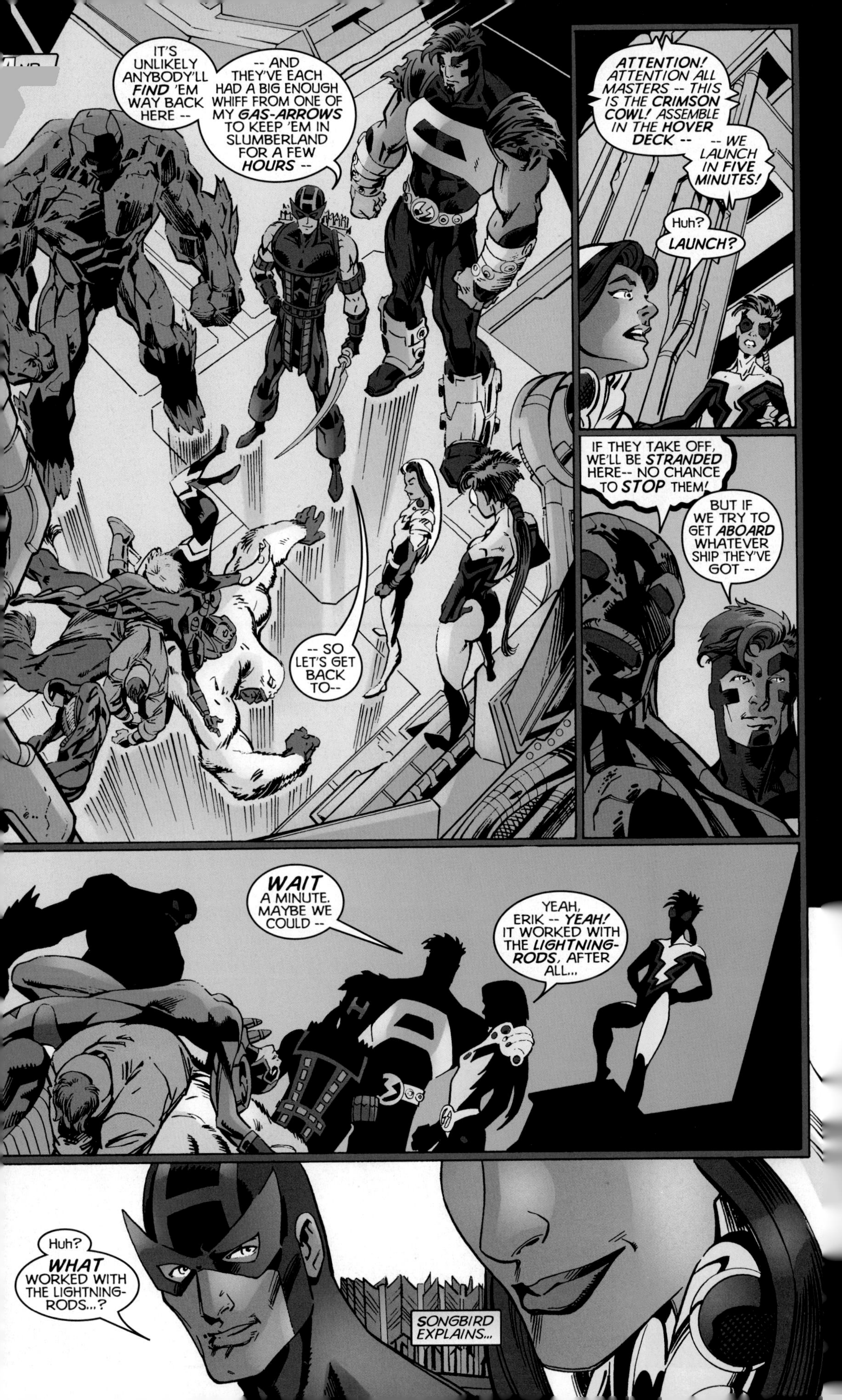

IT'S UNLIKELY ANYBODY'LL FIND 'EM WAY BACK HERE --
-- AND THEY'VE EACH HAD A BIG ENOUGH WHIFF FROM ONE OF MY GAS-ARROWS TO KEEP 'EM IN SLUMBERLAND FOR A FEW HOURS --
-- SO LET'S GET BACK TO--
ATTENTION! ATTENTION ALL MASTERS -- THIS IS THE CRIMSON COWL! ASSEMBLE IN THE HOVER DECK --
-- WE LAUNCH IN FIVE MINUTES!
Huh?
LAUNCH?
IF THEY TAKE OFF, WE'LL BE STRANDED HERE-- NO CHANCE TO STOP THEM!
BUT IF WE TRY TO GET ABOARD WHATEVER SHIP THEY'VE GOT --
WAIT A MINUTE. MAYBE WE COULD --
YEAH, ERIK -- YEAH! IT WORKED WITH THE LIGHTNING-RODS, AFTER ALL...
Huh? WHAT WORKED WITH THE LIGHTNING-RODS...?
SONGBIRD EXPLAINS...

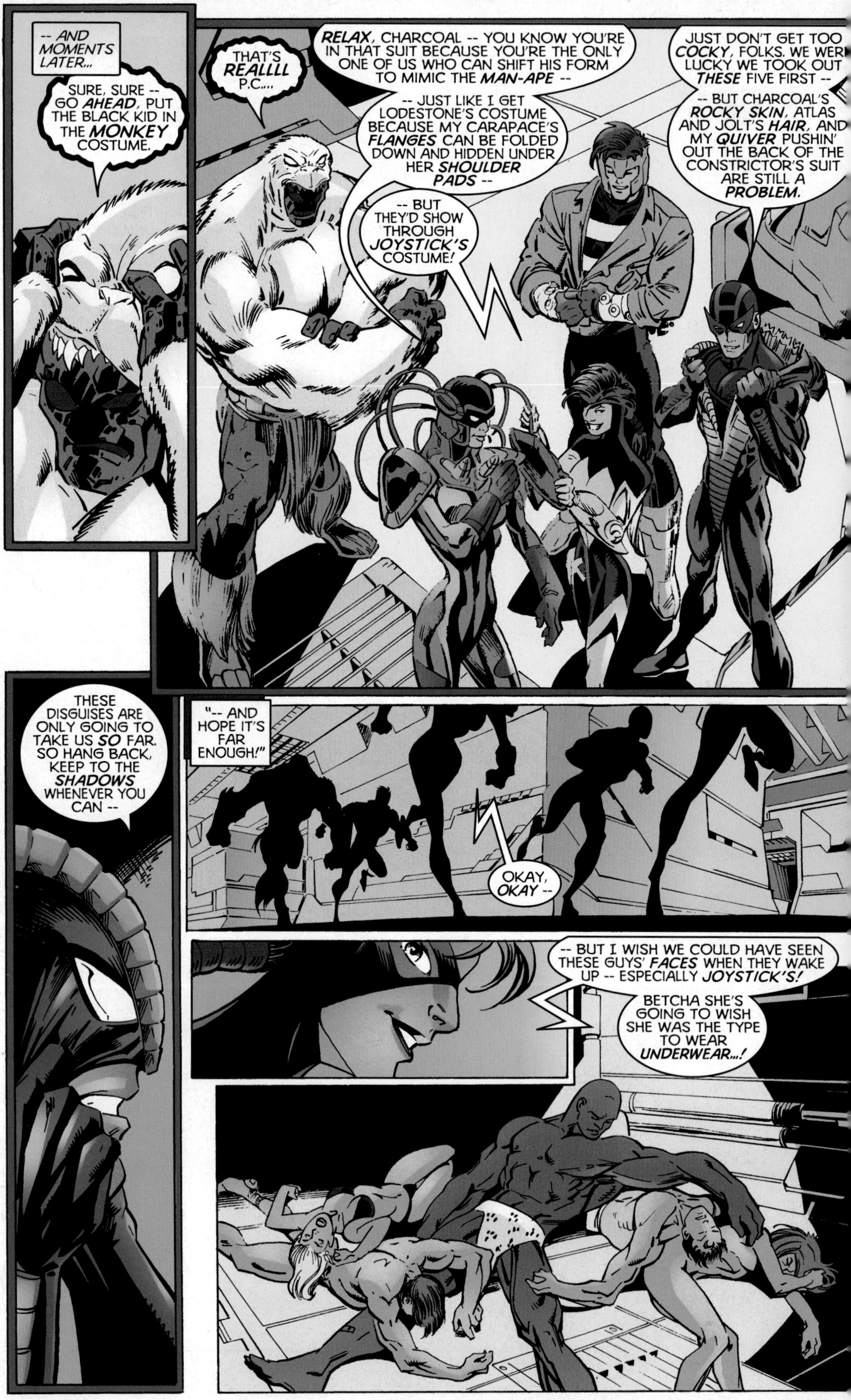

-- AND MOMENTS LATER...
SURE, SURE -- GO AHEAD, PUT THE BLACK KID IN THE MONKEY COSTUME.
THAT'S REALLLL P.C....
RELAX, CHARCOAL -- YOU KNOW YOU'RE IN THAT SUIT BECAUSE YOU'RE THE ONLY ONE OF US WHO CAN SHIFT HIS FORM TO MIMIC THE MAN-APE --
-- JUST LIKE I GET LODESTONE'S COSTUME BECAUSE MY CARAPACE'S FLANGES CAN BE FOLDED DOWN AND HIDDEN UNDER HER SHOULDER PADS --
-- BUT THEY'D SHOW THROUGH JOYSTICK'S COSTUME!
JUST DON'T GET TOO COCKY, FOLKS. WE WER LUCKY WE TOOK OUT THESE FIVE FIRST --
-- BUT CHARCOAL'S ROCKY SKIN, ATLAS AND JOLT'S HAIR, AND MY QUIVER PUSHIN' OUT THE BACK OF THE CONSTRICTOR'S SUIT ARE STILL A PROBLEM.
THESE DISGUISES ARE ONLY GOING TO TAKE US SO FAR. SO HANG BACK, KEEP TO THE SHADOWS WHENEVER YOU CAN --
"-- AND HOPE IT'S FAR ENOUGH!"
OKAY, OKAY --
-- BUT I WISH WE COULD HAVE SEEN THESE GUYS' FACES WHEN THEY WAKE UP -- ESPECIALLY JOYSTICK'S!
BETCHA SHE'S GOING TO WISH SHE WAS THE TYPE TO WEAR UNDERWEAR...!

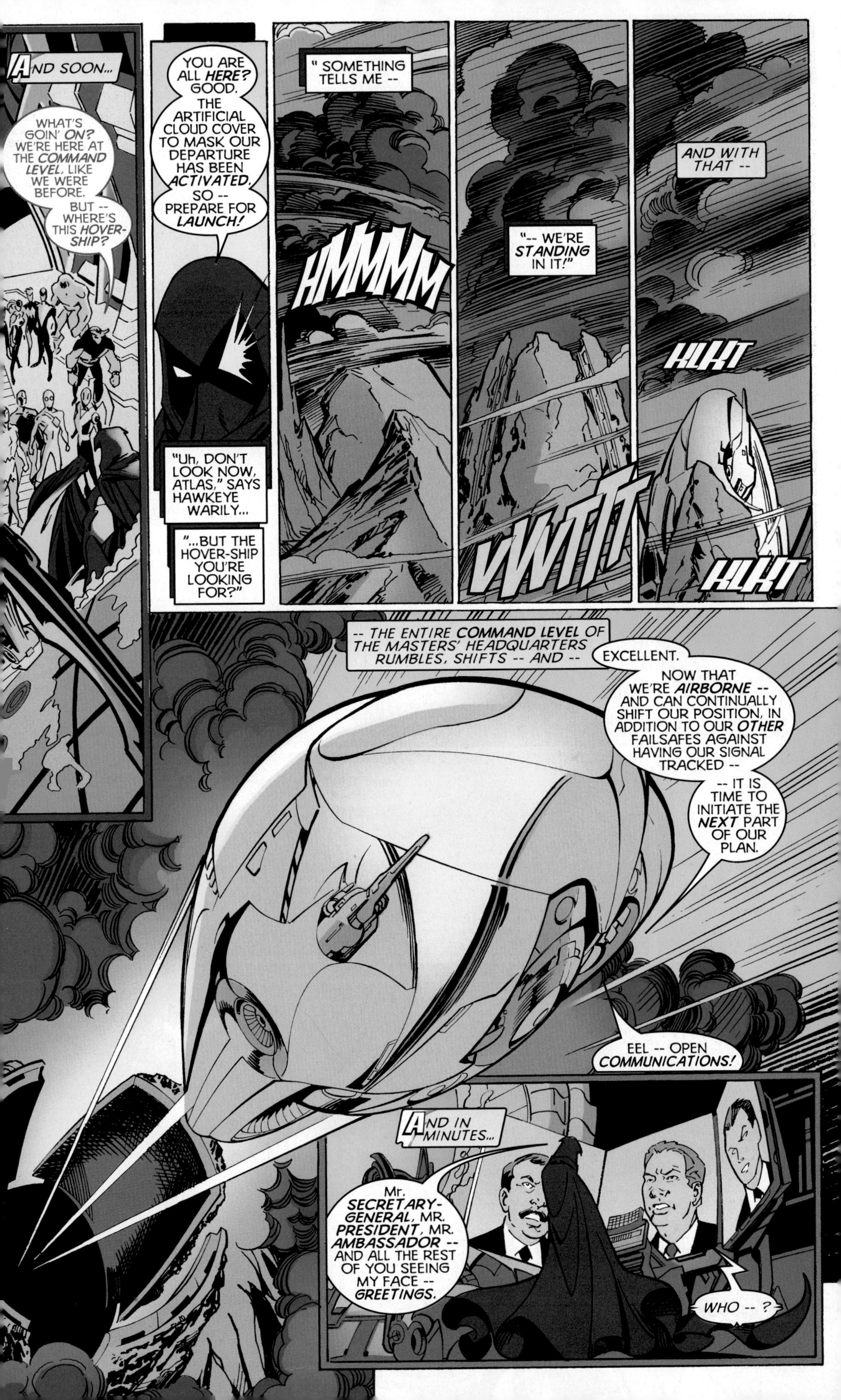
AND SOON...
WHAT'S GOIN' ON? WE'RE HERE AT THE COMMAND LEVEL, LIKE WE WERE BEFORE.
BUT -- WHERE'S THIS HOVER-SHIP?
YOU ARE ALL HERE? GOOD. THE ARTIFICIAL CLOUD COVER TO MASK OUR DEPARTURE HAS BEEN ACTIVATED. SO -- PREPARE FOR LAUNCH!
"Uh, DON'T LOOK NOW, ATLAS," SAYS HAWKEYE WARILY...
"...BUT THE HOVER-SHIP YOU'RE LOOKING FOR?"
" SOMETHING TELLS ME --
HMMMM
"-- WE'RE STANDING IN IT!"
VVVTTTT
AND WITH THAT --
KLKT
KLKT
-- THE ENTIRE COMMAND LEVEL OF THE MASTERS' HEADQUARTERS RUMBLES, SHIFTS -- AND --
EXCELLENT.
NOW THAT WE'RE AIRBORNE -- AND CAN CONTINUALLY SHIFT OUR POSITION, IN ADDITION TO OUR OTHER FAILSAFES AGAINST HAVING OUR SIGNAL TRACKED --
-- IT IS TIME TO INITIATE THE NEXT PART OF OUR PLAN.
EEL -- OPEN COMMUNICATIONS!
AND IN MINUTES...
Mr. SECRETARY-GENERAL, MR. PRESIDENT, MR. AMBASSADOR -- AND ALL THE REST OF YOU SEEING MY FACE -- GREETINGS.
WHO -- ?

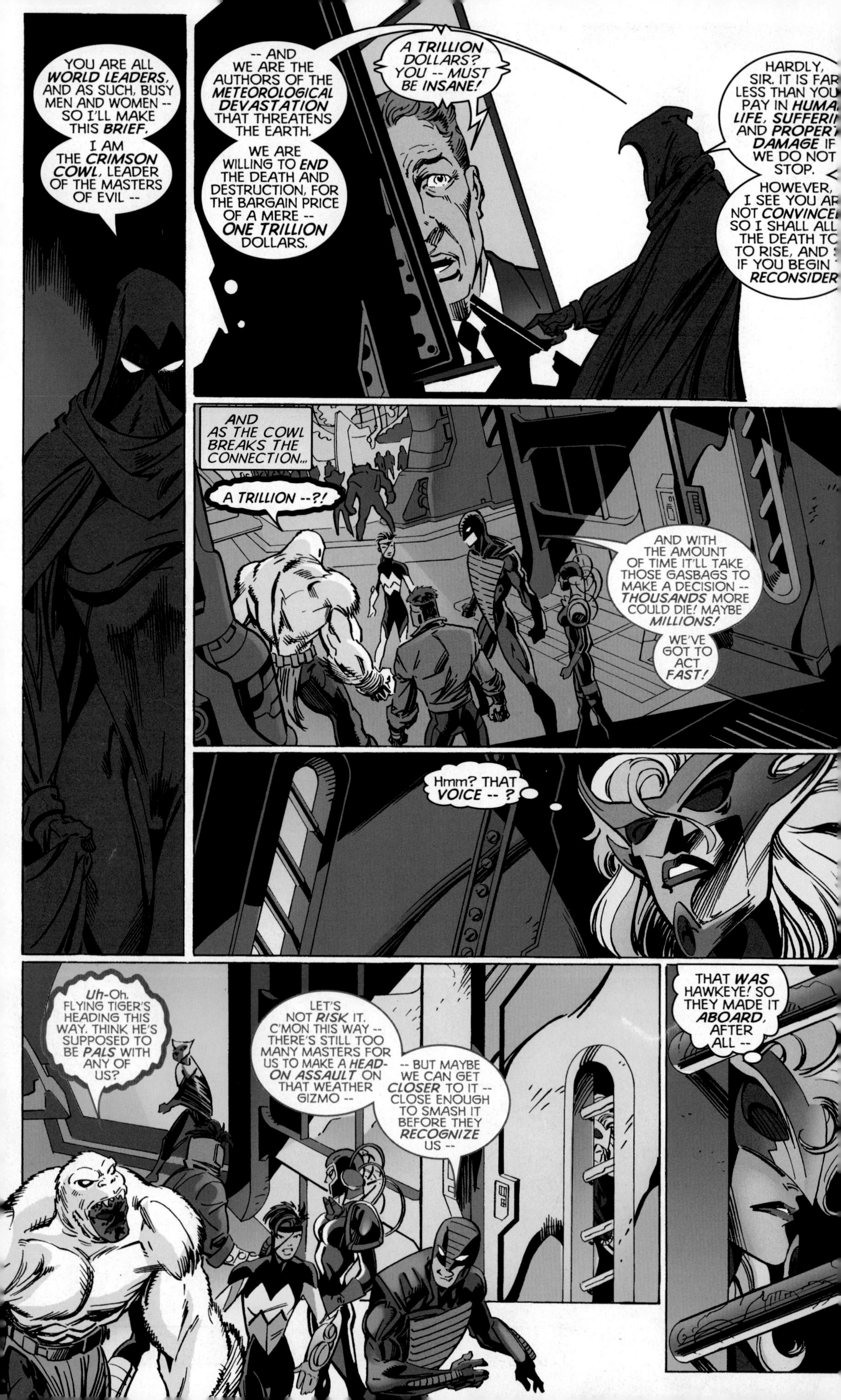

YOU ARE ALL WORLD LEADERS, AND AS SUCH, BUSY MEN AND WOMEN -- SO I'LL MAKE THIS BRIEF.
I AM THE CRIMSON COWL, LEADER OF THE MASTERS OF EVIL --
-- AND WE ARE THE AUTHORS OF THE METEOROLOGICAL DEVASTATION THAT THREATENS THE EARTH.
WE ARE WILLING TO END THE DEATH AND DESTRUCTION, FOR THE BARGAIN PRICE OF A MERE -- ONE TRILLION DOLLARS.
A TRILLION DOLLARS? YOU -- MUST BE INSANE!
HARDLY, SIR. IT IS FAR LESS THAN YOU PAY IN HUMA LIFE, SUFFERI AND PROPER DAMAGE IF WE DO NOT STOP.
HOWEVER, I SEE YOU A NOT CONVINCE SO I SHALL ALL THE DEATH T TO RISE, AND IF YOU BEGIN RECONSIDER
AND AS THE COWL BREAKS THE CONNECTION...
A TRILLION --?!
AND WITH THE AMOUNT OF TIME IT'LL TAKE THOSE GASBAGS TO MAKE A DECISION -- THOUSANDS MORE COULD DIE! MAYBE MILLIONS!
WE'VE GOT TO ACT FAST!
Hmm? THAT VOICE -- ?
Uh-Oh. FLYING TIGER'S HEADING THIS WAY. THINK HE'S SUPPOSED TO BE PALS WITH ANY OF US?
LET'S NOT RISK IT. C'MON THIS WAY -- THERE'S STILL TOO MANY MASTERS FOR US TO MAKE A HEAD-ON ASSAULT ON THAT WEATHER GIZMO --
-- BUT MAYBE WE CAN GET CLOSER TO IT -- CLOSE ENOUGH TO SMASH IT BEFORE THEY RECOGNIZE US --
THAT WAS HAWKEYE! SO THEY MADE IT ABOARD, AFTER ALL --

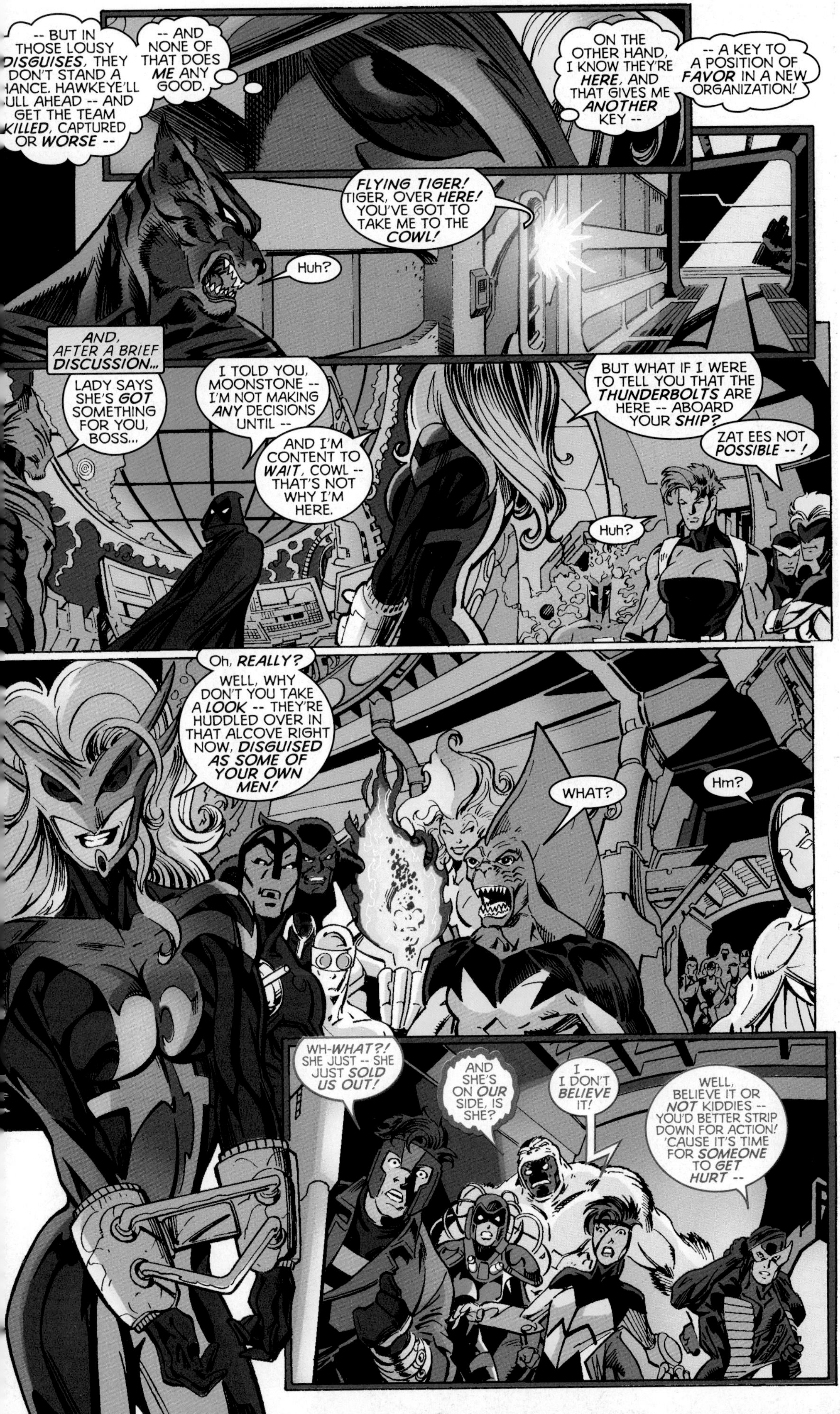
-- BUT IN THOSE LOUSY DISGUISES, THEY DON'T STAND A HANCE. HAWKEYE'LL ULL AHEAD -- AND GET THE TEAM KILLED, CAPTURED OR WORSE --
-- AND NONE OF THAT DOES ME ANY GOOD.
ON THE OTHER HAND, I KNOW THEY'RE HERE, AND THAT GIVES ME ANOTHER KEY --
-- A KEY TO A POSITION OF FAVOR IN A NEW ORGANIZATION!
FLYING TIGER! TIGER, OVER HERE! YOU'VE GOT TO TAKE ME TO THE COWL!
Huh?
AND, AFTER A BRIEF DISCUSSION...
LADY SAYS SHE'S GOT SOMETHING FOR YOU, BOSS...
I TOLD YOU, MOONSTONE -- I'M NOT MAKING ANY DECISIONS UNTIL --
AND I'M CONTENT TO WAIT, COWL -- THAT'S NOT WHY I'M HERE.
BUT WHAT IF I WERE TO TELL YOU THAT THE THUNDERBOLTS ARE HERE -- ABOARD YOUR SHIP?
ZAT EES NOT POSSIBLE -- !
Huh?
Oh, REALLY? WELL, WHY DON'T YOU TAKE A LOOK -- THEY'RE HUDDLED OVER IN THAT ALCOVE RIGHT NOW, DISGUISED AS SOME OF YOUR OWN MEN!
WHAT?
Hm?
WH-WHAT?! SHE JUST -- SHE JUST SOLD US OUT!
AND SHE'S ON OUR SIDE, IS SHE?
I -- I DON'T BELIEVE IT!
WELL, BELIEVE IT OR NOT KIDDIES -- YOU'D BETTER STRIP DOWN FOR ACTION! 'CAUSE IT'S TIME FOR SOMEONE TO GET HURT --

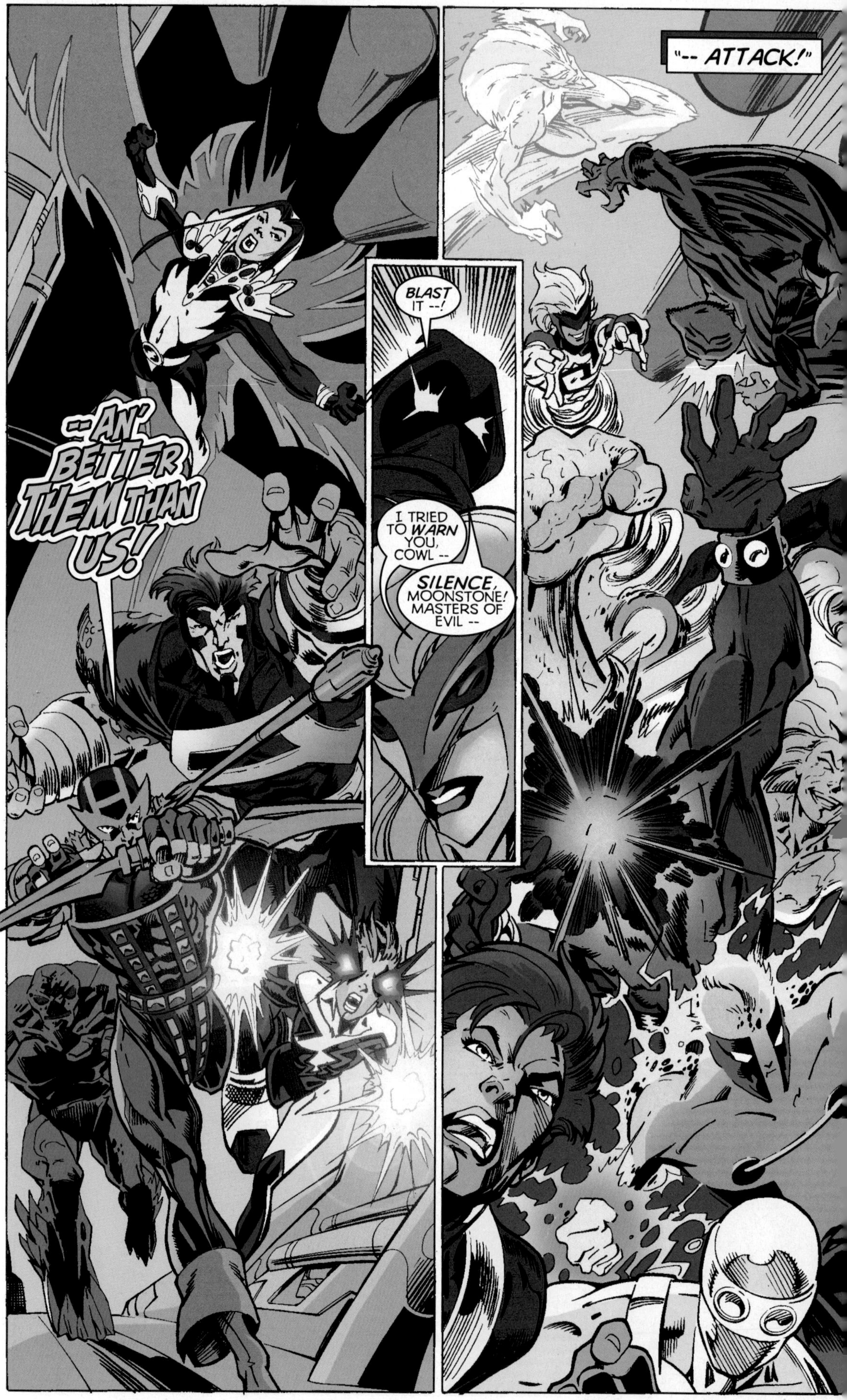
-- AN' BETTER THEM THAN US!
BLAST IT --!
I TRIED TO WARN YOU, COWL --
SILENCE, MOONSTONE! MASTERS OF EVIL --
"-- ATTACK!"

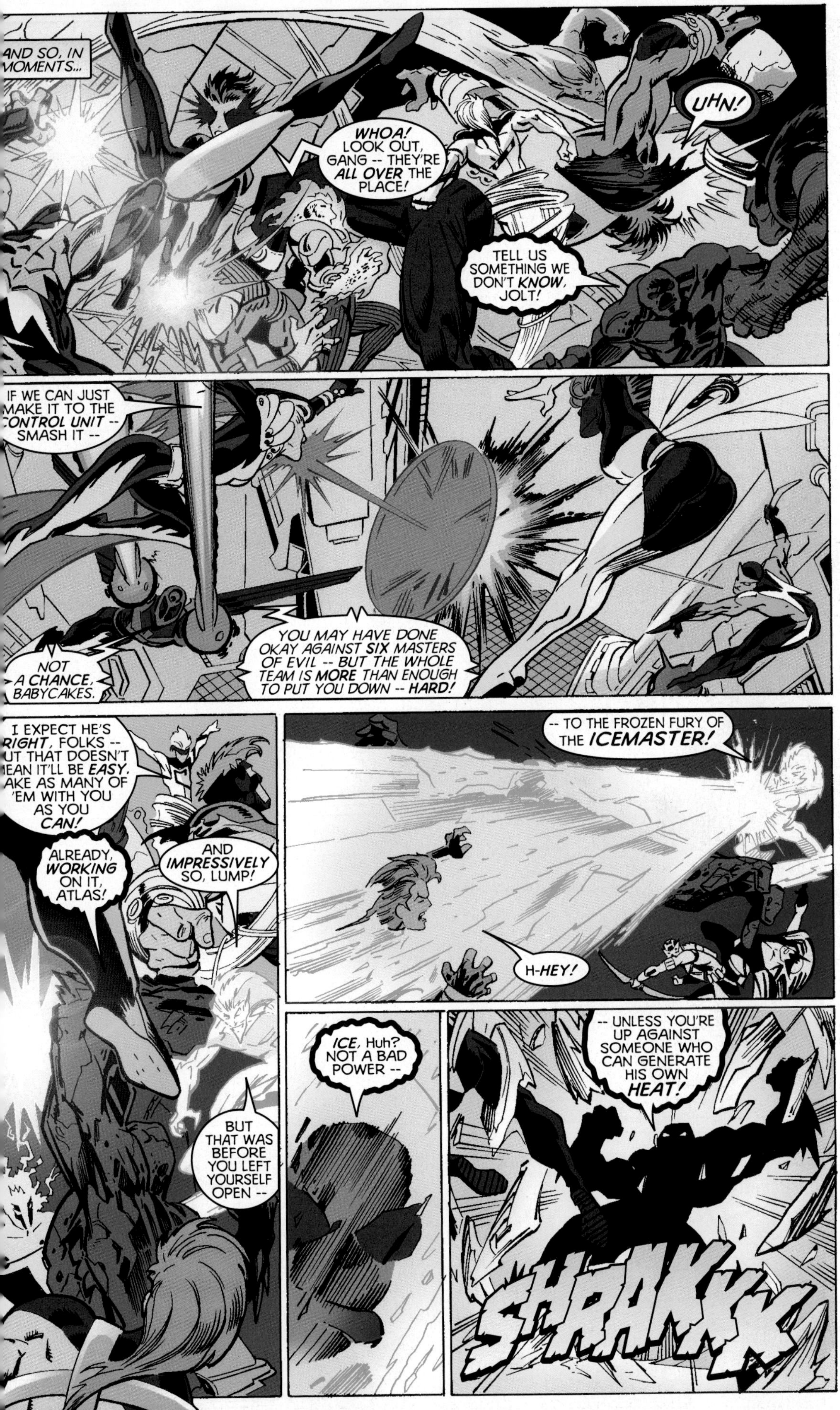
AND SO, IN MOMENTS...
WHOA! LOOK OUT, GANG -- THEY'RE ALL OVER THE PLACE!
UHN!
TELL US SOMETHING WE DON'T KNOW, JOLT!
IF WE CAN JUST MAKE IT TO THE CONTROL UNIT -- SMASH IT --
NOT A CHANCE, BABYCAKES.
YOU MAY HAVE DONE OKAY AGAINST SIX MASTERS OF EVIL -- BUT THE WHOLE TEAM IS MORE THAN ENOUGH TO PUT YOU DOWN -- HARD!
I EXPECT HE'S RIGHT, FOLKS -- UT THAT DOESN'T EAN IT'LL BE EASY. AKE AS MANY OF 'EM WITH YOU AS YOU CAN!
ALREADY WORKING ON IT, ATLAS!
AND IMPRESSIVELY SO, LUMP!
BUT THAT WAS BEFORE YOU LEFT YOURSELF OPEN --
-- TO THE FROZEN FURY OF THE ICEMASTER!
H-HEY!
ICE, Huh? NOT A BAD POWER --
-- UNLESS YOU'RE UP AGAINST SOMEONE WHO CAN GENERATE HIS OWN HEAT!
SHRAKKK

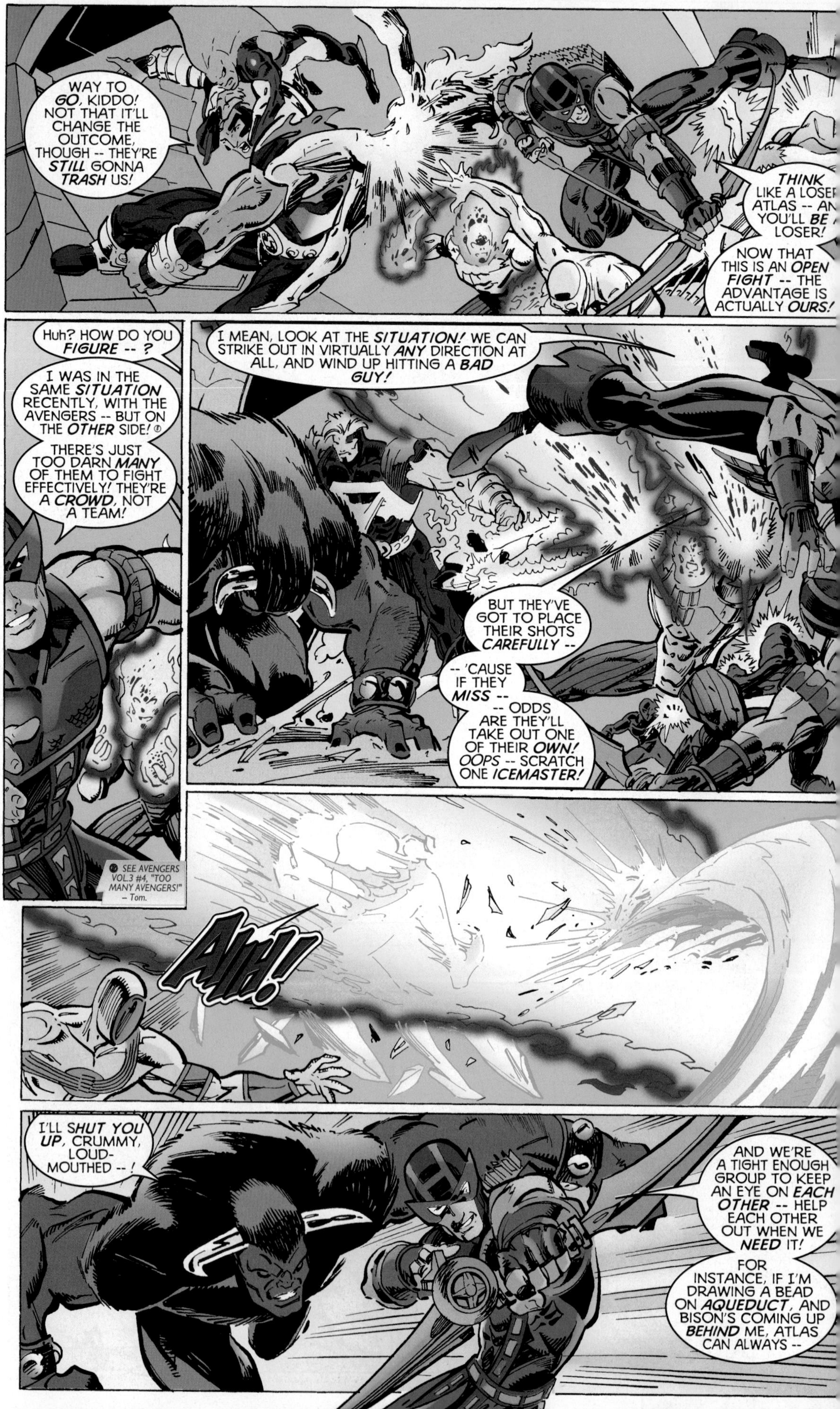
WAY TO GO, KIDDO! NOT THAT IT'LL CHANGE THE OUTCOME, THOUGH -- THEY'RE STILL GONNA TRASH US!
THINK LIKE A LOSER ATLAS -- AN YOU'LL BE A LOSER!
NOW THAT THIS IS AN OPEN FIGHT -- THE ADVANTAGE IS ACTUALLY OURS!
Huh? HOW DO YOU FIGURE -- ?
I WAS IN THE SAME SITUATION RECENTLY, WITH THE AVENGERS -- BUT ON THE OTHER SIDE!
THERE'S JUST TOO DARN MANY OF THEM TO FIGHT EFFECTIVELY! THEY'RE A CROWD, NOT A TEAM!
SEE AVENGERS VOL.3 #4, "TOO MANY AVENGERS!" – Tom.
I MEAN, LOOK AT THE SITUATION! WE CAN STRIKE OUT IN VIRTUALLY ANY DIRECTION AT ALL, AND WIND UP HITTING A BAD GUY!
BUT THEY'VE GOT TO PLACE THEIR SHOTS CAREFULLY --
-- 'CAUSE IF THEY MISS --
-- ODDS ARE THEY'LL TAKE OUT ONE OF THEIR OWN! OOPS -- SCRATCH ONE ICEMASTER!
AIIH!
I'LL SHUT YOU UP, CRUMMY, LOUD-MOUTHED -- !
AND WE'RE A TIGHT ENOUGH GROUP TO KEEP AN EYE ON EACH OTHER -- HELP EACH OTHER OUT WHEN WE NEED IT!
FOR INSTANCE, IF I'M DRAWING A BEAD ON AQUEDUCT, AND BISON'S COMING UP BEHIND ME, ATLAS CAN ALWAYS --

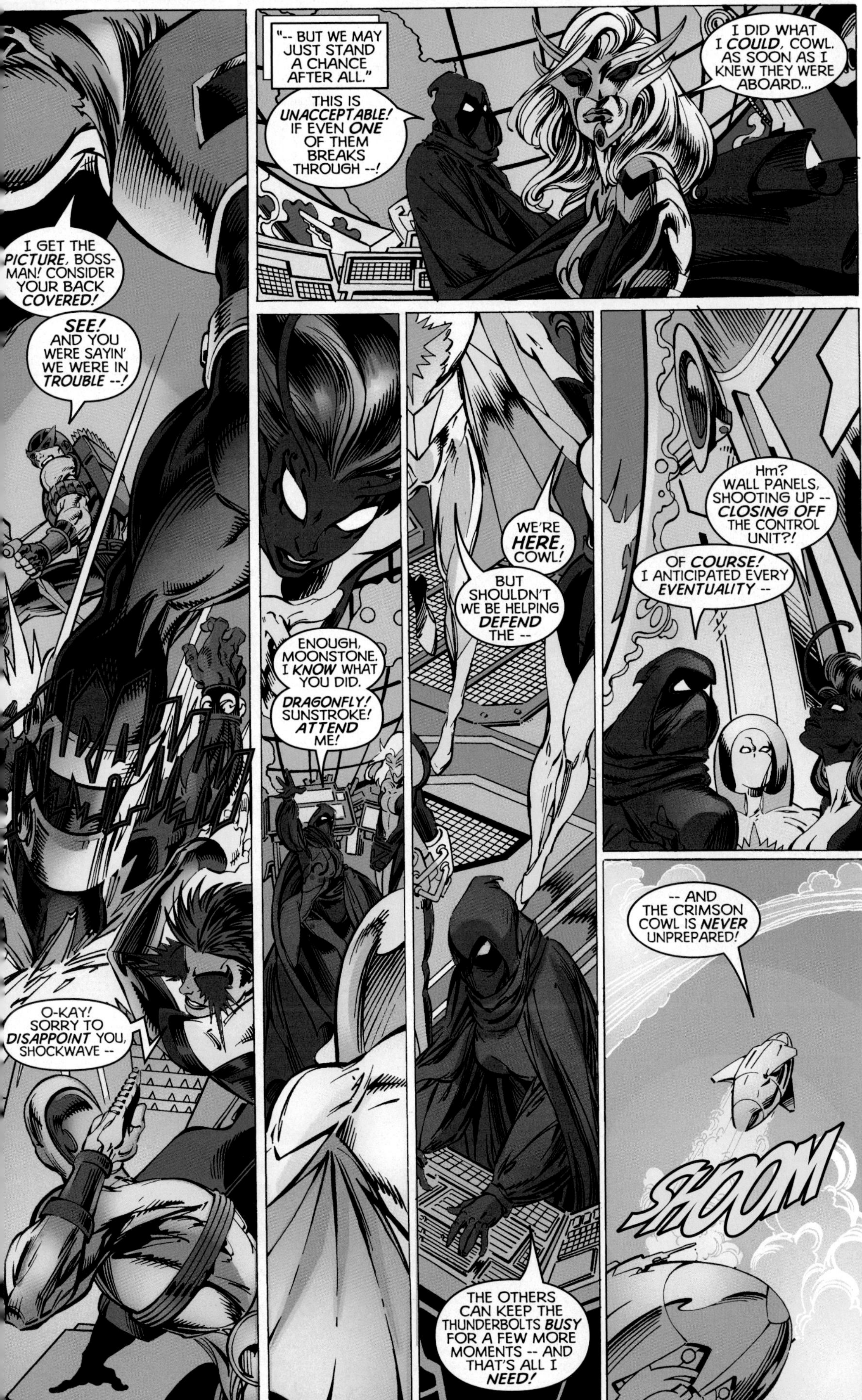
I GET THE *PICTURE*, BOSS-MAN! CONSIDER YOUR BACK *COVERED!*
SEE! AND YOU WERE SAYIN' WE WERE IN *TROUBLE* --!
O-KAY! SORRY TO *DISAPPOINT* YOU, SHOCKWAVE --
"-- BUT WE MAY JUST STAND A CHANCE AFTER ALL."
THIS IS *UNACCEPTABLE!* IF EVEN *ONE* OF THEM BREAKS THROUGH --!
I DID WHAT I *COULD*, COWL. AS SOON AS I KNEW THEY WERE ABOARD...
ENOUGH, MOONSTONE. I *KNOW* WHAT YOU DID. *DRAGONFLY!* SUNSTROKE! *ATTEND* ME!
WE'RE *HERE*, COWL!
BUT SHOULDN'T WE BE HELPING *DEFEND* THE --
THE OTHERS CAN KEEP THE THUNDERBOLTS *BUSY* FOR A FEW MORE MOMENTS -- AND THAT'S ALL I *NEED!*
Hm? WALL PANELS, SHOOTING UP -- *CLOSING OFF* THE CONTROL UNIT?!
OF *COURSE!* I ANTICIPATED EVERY *EVENTUALITY* --
-- AND THE CRIMSON COWL IS *NEVER* UNPREPARED!
SHOOOM

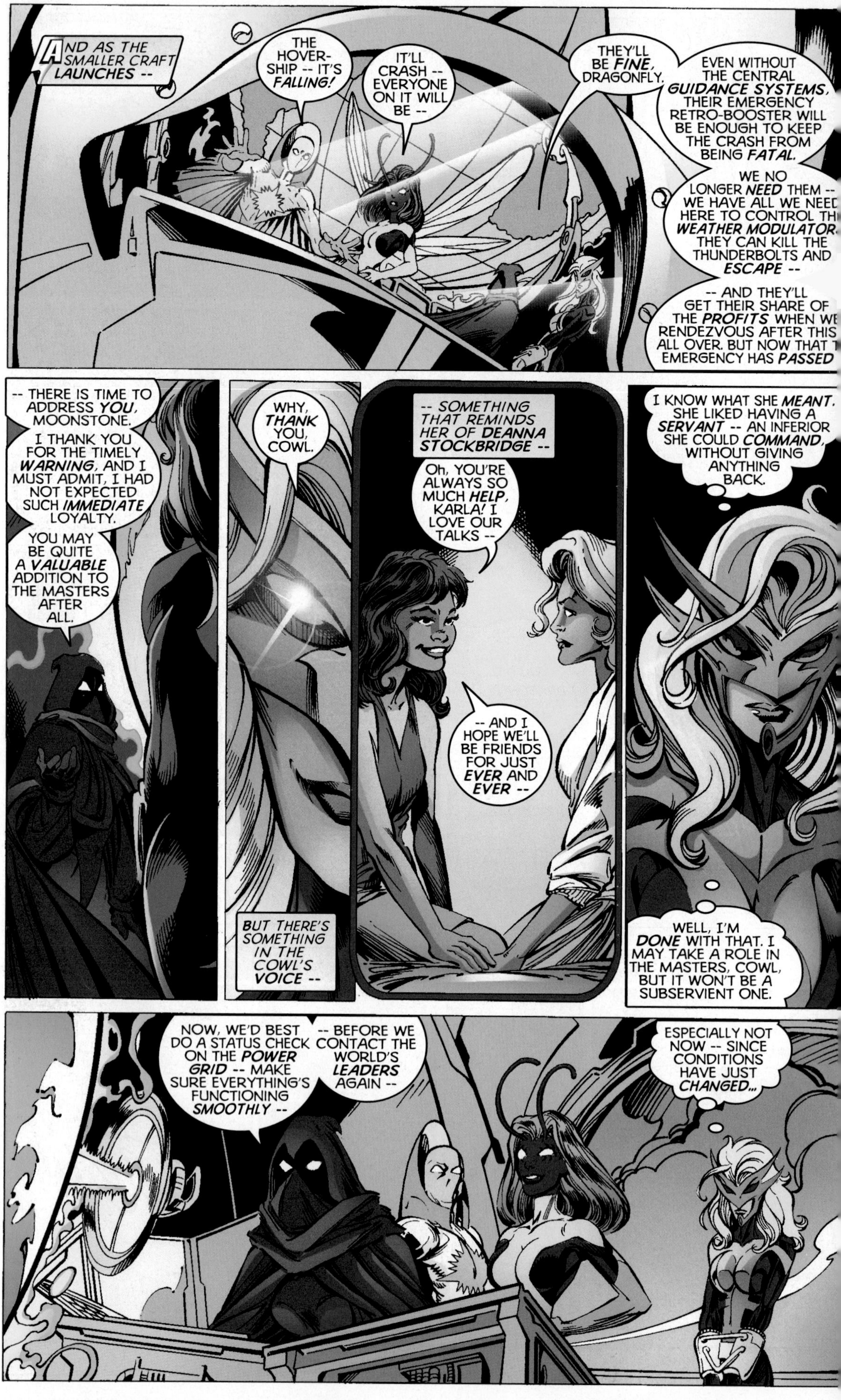

AND AS THE SMALLER CRAFT LAUNCHES --
THE HOVER-SHIP -- IT'S FALLING!
IT'LL CRASH -- EVERYONE ON IT WILL BE --
THEY'LL BE FINE, DRAGONFLY.
EVEN WITHOUT THE CENTRAL GUIDANCE SYSTEMS, THEIR EMERGENCY RETRO-BOOSTER WILL BE ENOUGH TO KEEP THE CRASH FROM BEING FATAL.
WE NO LONGER NEED THEM -- WE HAVE ALL WE NEE HERE TO CONTROL TH WEATHER MODULATOR THEY CAN KILL THE THUNDERBOLTS AND ESCAPE --
-- AND THEY'LL GET THEIR SHARE OF THE PROFITS WHEN WE RENDEZVOUS AFTER THIS ALL OVER. BUT NOW THAT EMERGENCY HAS PASSED
-- THERE IS TIME TO ADDRESS YOU, MOONSTONE.
I THANK YOU FOR THE TIMELY WARNING, AND I MUST ADMIT, I HAD NOT EXPECTED SUCH IMMEDIATE LOYALTY.
YOU MAY BE QUITE A VALUABLE ADDITION TO THE MASTERS AFTER ALL.
WHY, THANK YOU, COWL.
BUT THERE'S SOMETHING IN THE COWL'S VOICE --
-- SOMETHING THAT REMINDS HER OF DEANNA STOCKBRIDGE --
Oh, YOU'RE ALWAYS SO MUCH HELP, KARLA! I LOVE OUR TALKS --
-- AND I HOPE WE'LL BE FRIENDS FOR JUST EVER AND EVER --
I KNOW WHAT SHE MEANT. SHE LIKED HAVING A SERVANT -- AN INFERIOR SHE COULD COMMAND, WITHOUT GIVING ANYTHING BACK.
WELL, I'M DONE WITH THAT. I MAY TAKE A ROLE IN THE MASTERS, COWL, BUT IT WON'T BE A SUBSERVIENT ONE.
NOW, WE'D BEST DO A STATUS CHECK ON THE POWER GRID -- MAKE SURE EVERYTHING'S FUNCTIONING SMOOTHLY --
-- BEFORE WE CONTACT THE WORLD'S LEADERS AGAIN --
ESPECIALLY NOT NOW -- SINCE CONDITIONS HAVE JUST CHANGED...

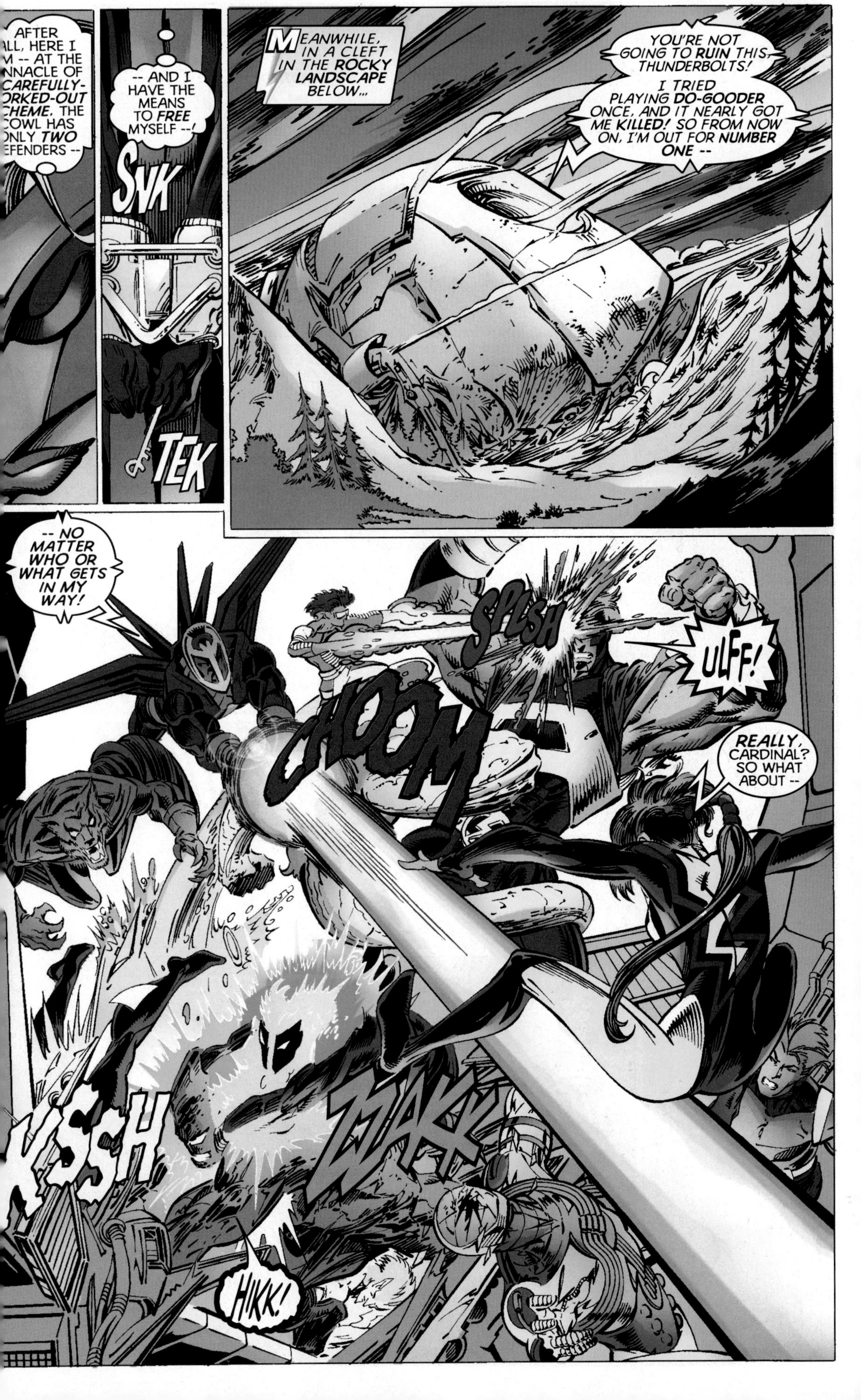
AFTER ALL, HERE I AM -- AT THE PINNACLE OF A CAREFULLY-WORKED-OUT SCHEME. THE COWL HAS ONLY TWO DEFENDERS --
-- AND I HAVE THE MEANS TO FREE MYSELF --!
SNK
TEK
MEANWHILE, IN A CLEFT IN THE ROCKY LANDSCAPE BELOW...
YOU'RE NOT GOING TO RUIN THIS, THUNDERBOLTS!
I TRIED PLAYING DO-GOODER ONCE, AND IT NEARLY GOT ME KILLED! SO FROM NOW ON, I'M OUT FOR NUMBER ONE --
-- NO MATTER WHO OR WHAT GETS IN MY WAY!
SPLSH
ULFF!
CHOOM
REALLY, CARDINAL? SO WHAT ABOUT --
KSSH
ZAKK
HIKK!

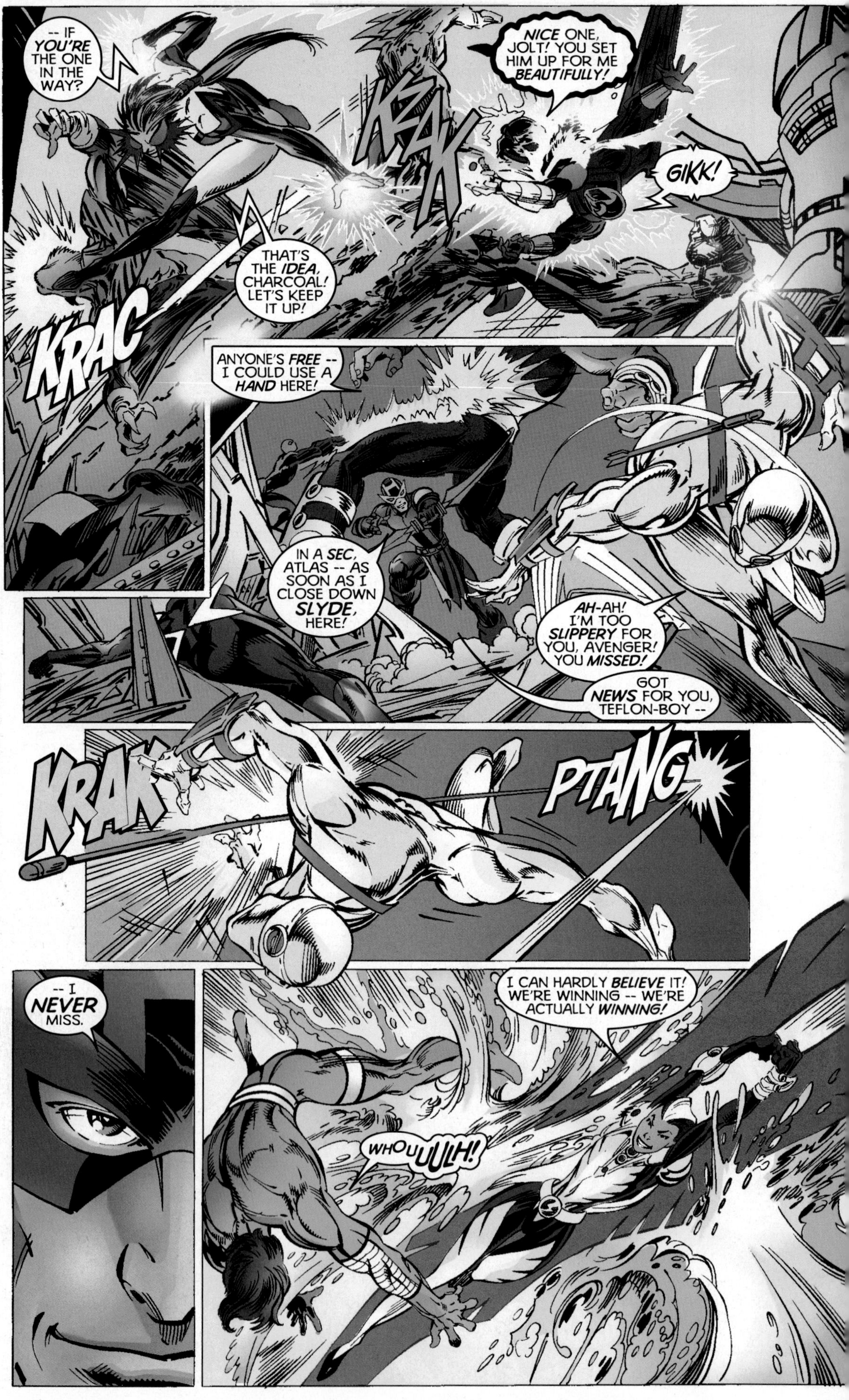
-- IF YOU'RE THE ONE IN THE WAY?
KRAK
NICE ONE, JOLT! YOU SET HIM UP FOR ME BEAUTIFULLY!
GIKK!
THAT'S THE IDEA, CHARCOAL! LET'S KEEP IT UP!
KRAC
ANYONE'S FREE -- I COULD USE A HAND HERE!
IN A SEC, ATLAS -- AS SOON AS I CLOSE DOWN SLYDE, HERE!
AH-AH! I'M TOO SLIPPERY FOR YOU, AVENGER! YOU MISSED!
GOT NEWS FOR YOU, TEFLON-BOY --
KRAK
PTANG
-- I NEVER MISS.
I CAN HARDLY BELIEVE IT! WE'RE WINNING -- WE'RE ACTUALLY WINNING!
WHOUUULH!

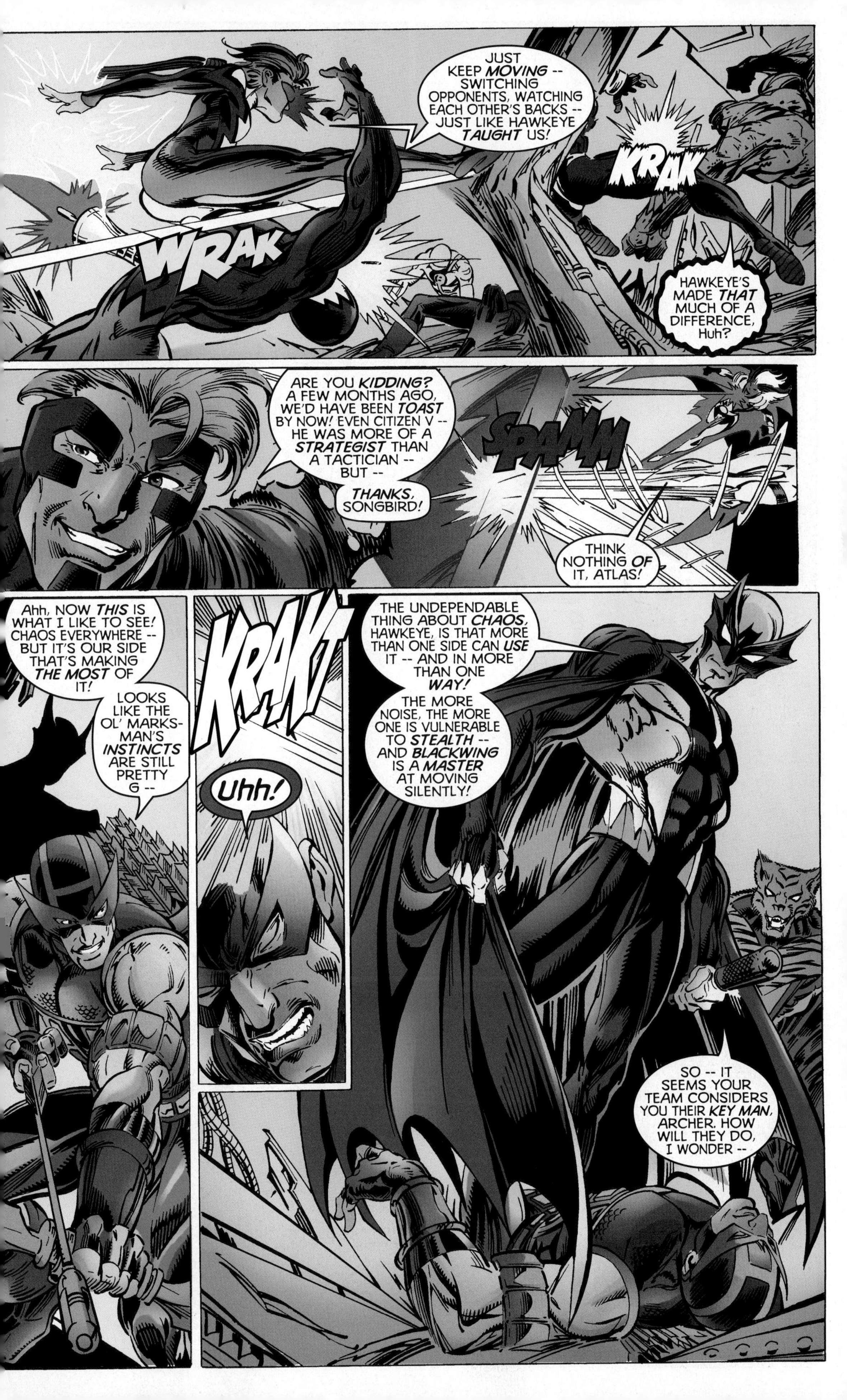
JUST KEEP MOVING -- SWITCHING OPPONENTS, WATCHING EACH OTHER'S BACKS -- JUST LIKE HAWKEYE TAUGHT US!
KRAK
WRAK
HAWKEYE'S MADE THAT MUCH OF A DIFFERENCE, Huh?
ARE YOU KIDDING? A FEW MONTHS AGO, WE'D HAVE BEEN TOAST BY NOW! EVEN CITIZEN V -- HE WAS MORE OF A STRATEGIST THAN A TACTICIAN -- BUT --
THANKS, SONGBIRD!
SPAMM
THINK NOTHING OF IT, ATLAS!
Ahh, NOW THIS IS WHAT I LIKE TO SEE! CHAOS EVERYWHERE -- BUT IT'S OUR SIDE THAT'S MAKING THE MOST OF IT!
LOOKS LIKE THE OL' MARKS-MAN'S INSTINCTS ARE STILL PRETTY G --
KRANT
Uhh!
THE UNDEPENDABLE THING ABOUT CHAOS, HAWKEYE, IS THAT MORE THAN ONE SIDE CAN USE IT -- AND IN MORE THAN ONE WAY!
THE MORE NOISE, THE MORE ONE IS VULNERABLE TO STEALTH -- AND BLACKWING IS A MASTER AT MOVING SILENTLY!
SO -- IT SEEMS YOUR TEAM CONSIDERS YOU THEIR KEY MAN, ARCHER. HOW WILL THEY DO, I WONDER --

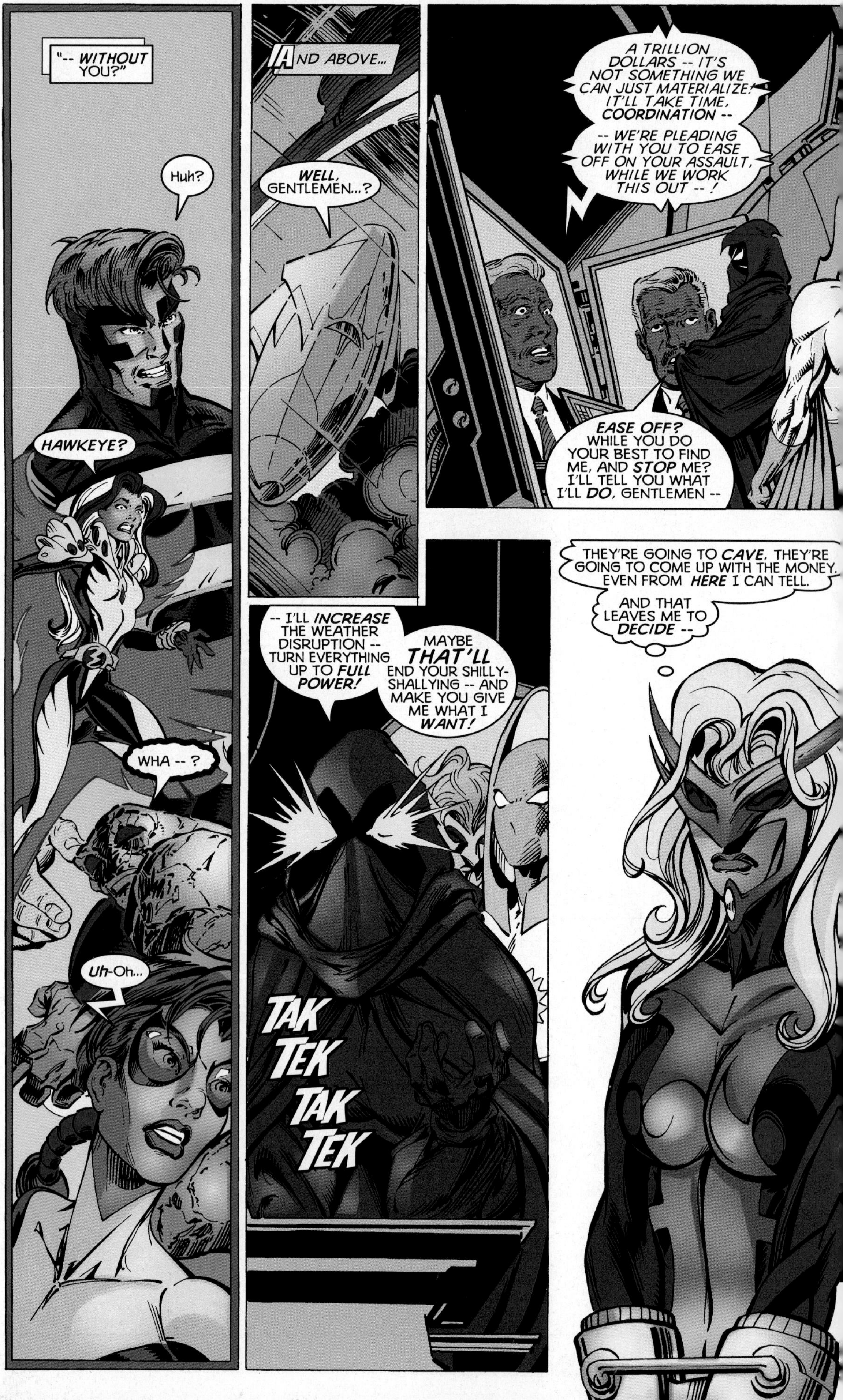
"-- WITHOUT YOU?"
Huh?
HAWKEYE?
WHA -- ?
Uh-Oh...
AND ABOVE...
WELL, GENTLEMEN...?
A TRILLION DOLLARS -- IT'S NOT SOMETHING WE CAN JUST MATERIALIZE! IT'LL TAKE TIME, COORDINATION --
-- WE'RE PLEADING WITH YOU TO EASE OFF ON YOUR ASSAULT, WHILE WE WORK THIS OUT -- !
EASE OFF? WHILE YOU DO YOUR BEST TO FIND ME, AND STOP ME? I'LL TELL YOU WHAT I'LL DO, GENTLEMEN --
-- I'LL INCREASE THE WEATHER DISRUPTION -- TURN EVERYTHING UP TO FULL POWER!
MAYBE THAT'LL END YOUR SHILLY-SHALLYING -- AND MAKE YOU GIVE ME WHAT I WANT!
TAK TEK TAK TEK
THEY'RE GOING TO CAVE. THEY'RE GOING TO COME UP WITH THE MONEY. EVEN FROM HERE I CAN TELL.
AND THAT LEAVES ME TO DECIDE --

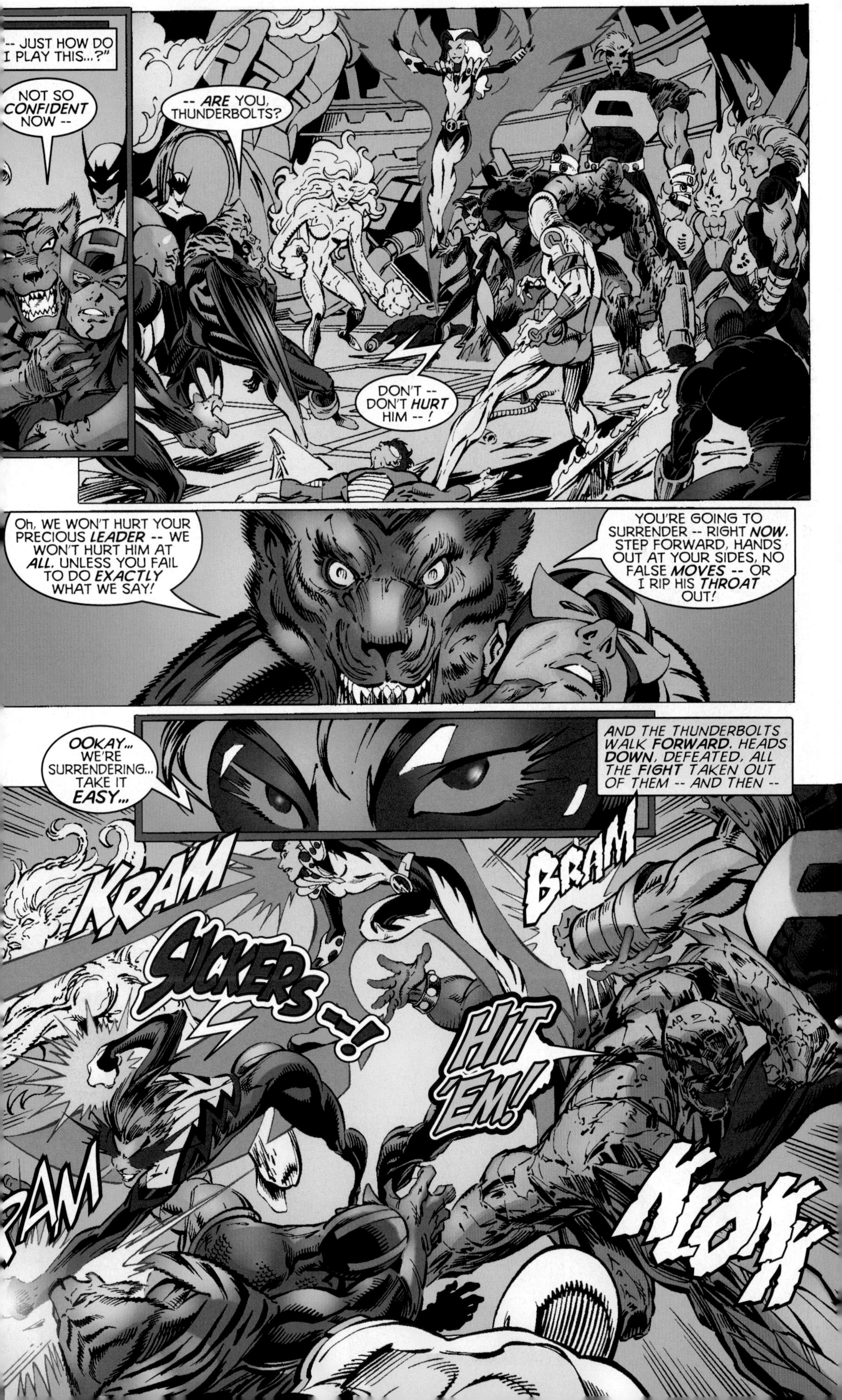

-- JUST HOW DO I PLAY THIS...?"
NOT SO **CONFIDENT** NOW --
-- **ARE** YOU, THUNDERBOLTS?
DON'T -- DON'T **HURT** HIM -- !
Oh, WE WON'T HURT YOUR PRECIOUS **LEADER** -- WE WON'T HURT HIM AT **ALL**, UNLESS YOU FAIL TO DO **EXACTLY** WHAT WE SAY!
YOU'RE GOING TO SURRENDER -- RIGHT **NOW**. STEP FORWARD, HANDS OUT AT YOUR SIDES, NO FALSE **MOVES** -- OR I RIP HIS **THROAT** OUT!
OOKAY... WE'RE SURRENDERING... TAKE IT **EASY...**
AND THE THUNDERBOLTS WALK **FORWARD**, HEADS **DOWN**, DEFEATED, ALL THE **FIGHT** TAKEN OUT OF THEM -- AND THEN --
KRAM
BRAM
SUCKERS --!
HIT 'EM!
PAM
KLOK

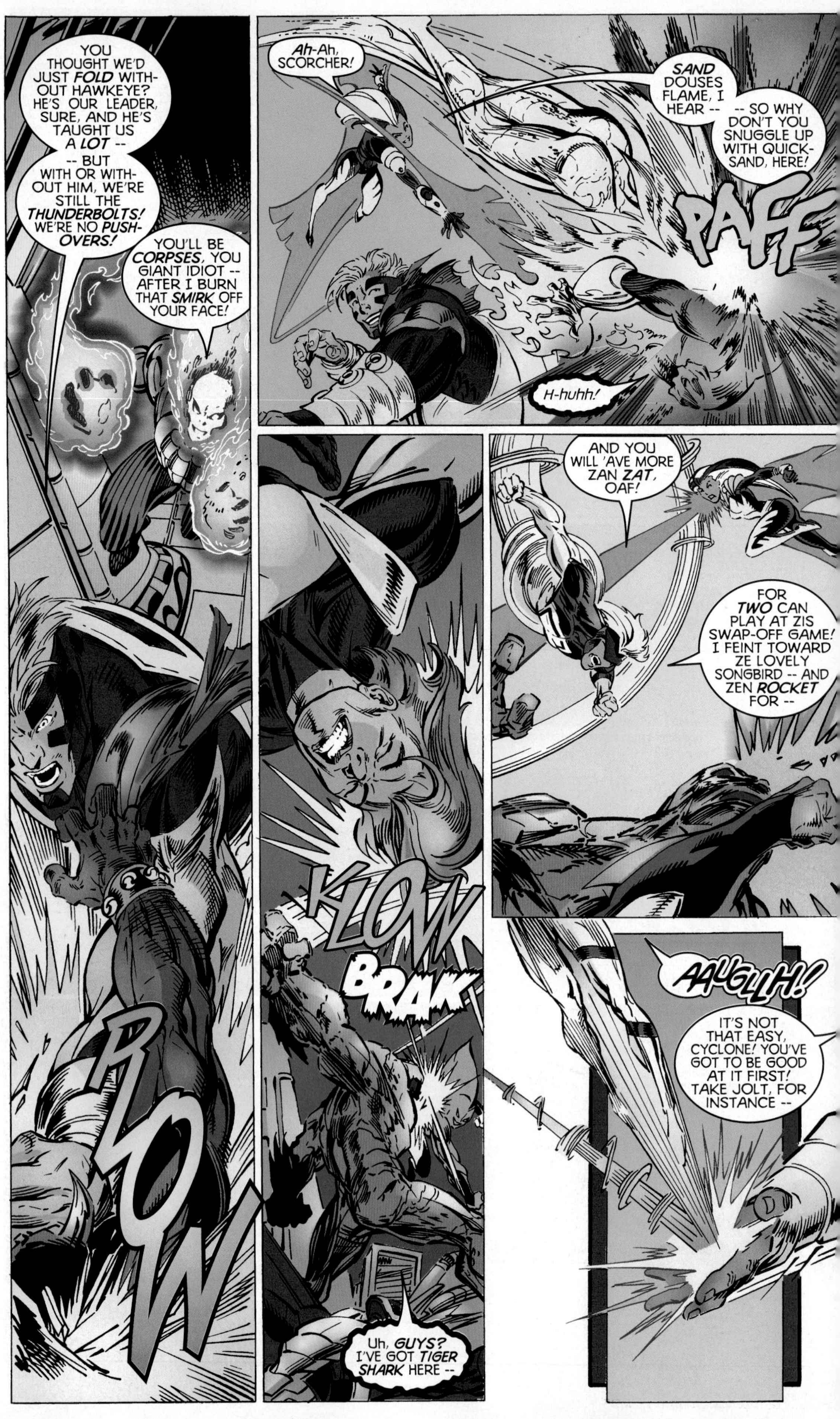
YOU THOUGHT WE'D JUST *FOLD* WITH-OUT HAWKEYE? HE'S OUR LEADER, SURE, AND HE'S TAUGHT US *A LOT* --
-- BUT WITH OR WITH-OUT HIM, WE'RE STILL THE *THUNDERBOLTS!* WE'RE NO *PUSH-OVERS!*
YOU'LL BE *CORPSES*, YOU GIANT IDIOT -- AFTER I BURN THAT *SMIRK* OFF YOUR FACE!
RROW
Ah-Ah, SCORCHER!
SAND DOUSES FLAME, I HEAR --
-- SO WHY DON'T YOU SNUGGLE UP WITH QUICK-SAND, HERE!
PAFF
H-huhh!
KLOW
BRAK
Uh, *GUYS?* I'VE GOT *TIGER SHARK* HERE --
AND YOU WILL 'AVE MORE ZAN *ZAT*, OAF!
FOR *TWO* CAN PLAY AT ZIS SWAP-OFF GAME! I FEINT TOWARD ZE LOVELY SONGBIRD -- AND ZEN *ROCKET* FOR --
AAUGLLH!
IT'S NOT THAT EASY, CYCLONE! YOU'VE GOT TO BE GOOD AT IT FIRST! TAKE JOLT, FOR INSTANCE --

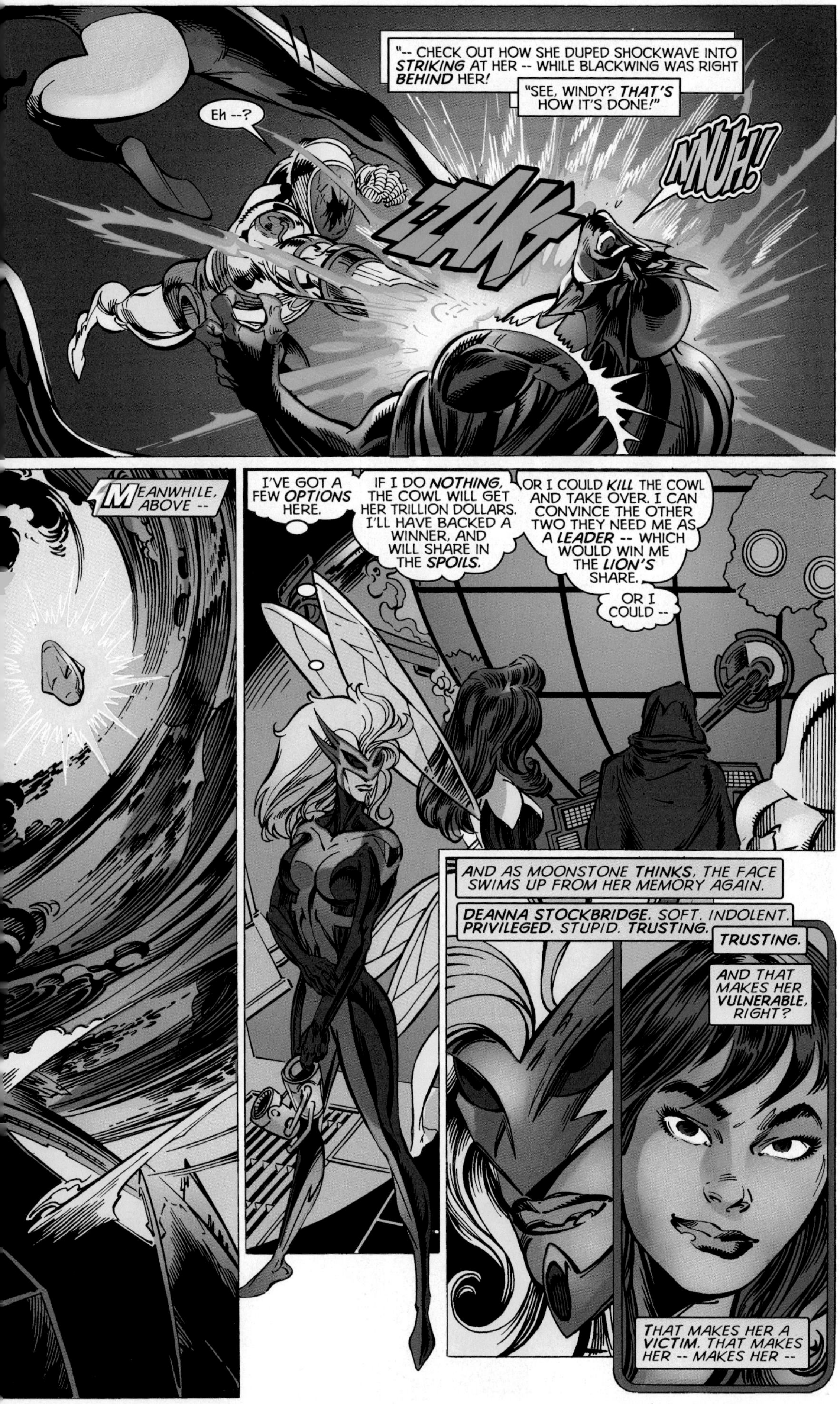
"-- CHECK OUT HOW SHE DUPED SHOCKWAVE INTO STRIKING AT HER -- WHILE BLACKWING WAS RIGHT BEHIND HER!
"SEE, WINDY? THAT'S HOW IT'S DONE!"
Eh --?
ZZAK
NNUH!
MEANWHILE, ABOVE --
I'VE GOT A FEW OPTIONS HERE.
IF I DO NOTHING, THE COWL WILL GET HER TRILLION DOLLARS. I'LL HAVE BACKED A WINNER, AND WILL SHARE IN THE SPOILS.
OR I COULD KILL THE COWL AND TAKE OVER. I CAN CONVINCE THE OTHER TWO THEY NEED ME AS A LEADER -- WHICH WOULD WIN ME THE LION'S SHARE.
OR I COULD --
AND AS MOONSTONE THINKS, THE FACE SWIMS UP FROM HER MEMORY AGAIN.
DEANNA STOCKBRIDGE. SOFT. INDOLENT. PRIVILEGED. STUPID. TRUSTING.
TRUSTING.
AND THAT MAKES HER VULNERABLE, RIGHT?
THAT MAKES HER A VICTIM. THAT MAKES HER -- MAKES HER --

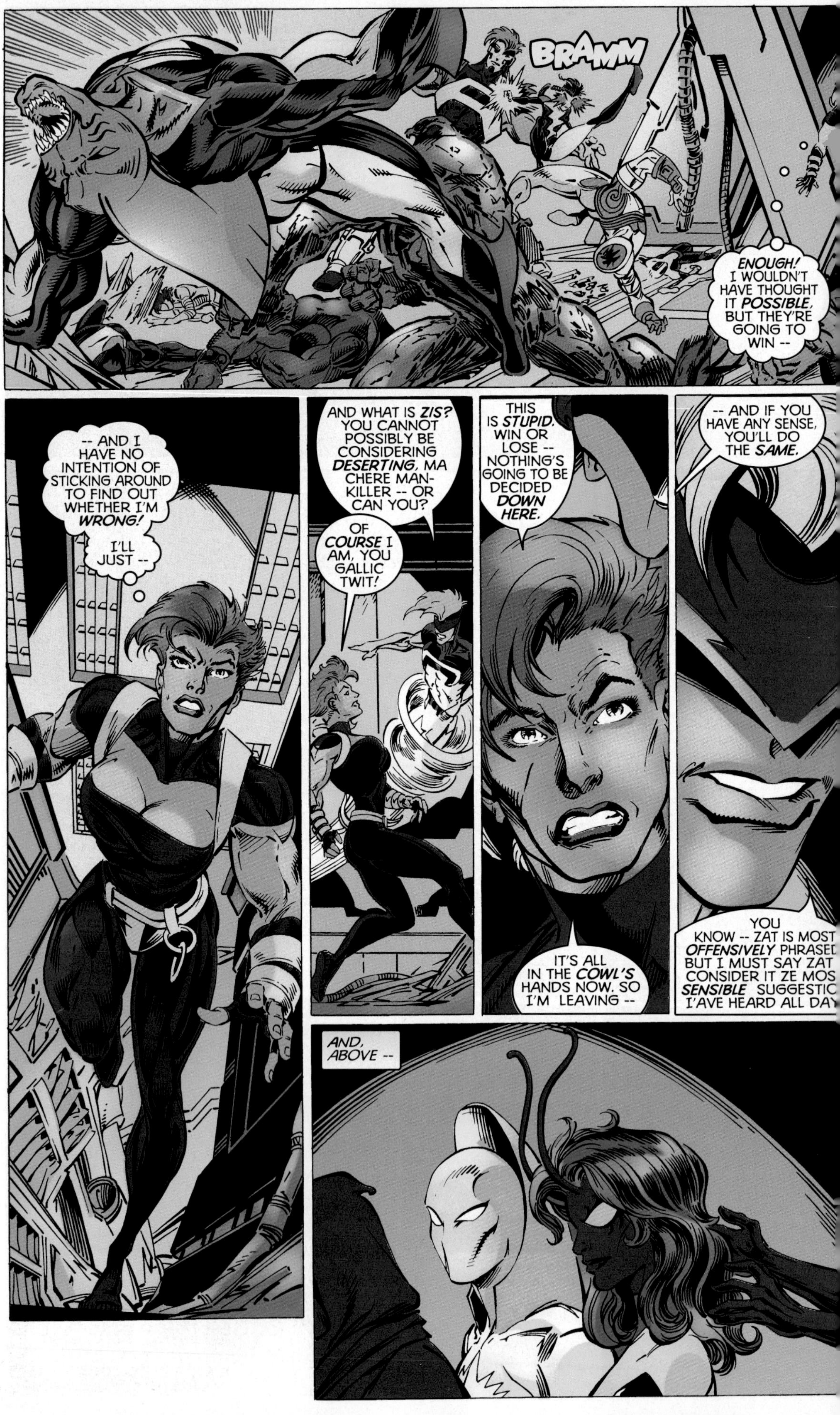
BRAMM
ENOUGH! I WOULDN'T HAVE THOUGHT IT POSSIBLE, BUT THEY'RE GOING TO WIN --
-- AND I HAVE NO INTENTION OF STICKING AROUND TO FIND OUT WHETHER I'M WRONG!
I'LL JUST --
AND WHAT IS ZIS? YOU CANNOT POSSIBLY BE CONSIDERING DESERTING, MA CHERE MAN-KILLER -- OR CAN YOU?
OF COURSE I AM, YOU GALLIC TWIT!
THIS IS STUPID. WIN OR LOSE -- NOTHING'S GOING TO BE DECIDED DOWN HERE.
IT'S ALL IN THE COWL'S HANDS NOW. SO I'M LEAVING --
-- AND IF YOU HAVE ANY SENSE, YOU'LL DO THE SAME.
YOU KNOW -- ZAT IS MOST OFFENSIVELY PHRASED BUT I MUST SAY ZAT I CONSIDER IT ZE MOST SENSIBLE SUGGESTION I'AVE HEARD ALL DAY
AND, ABOVE --

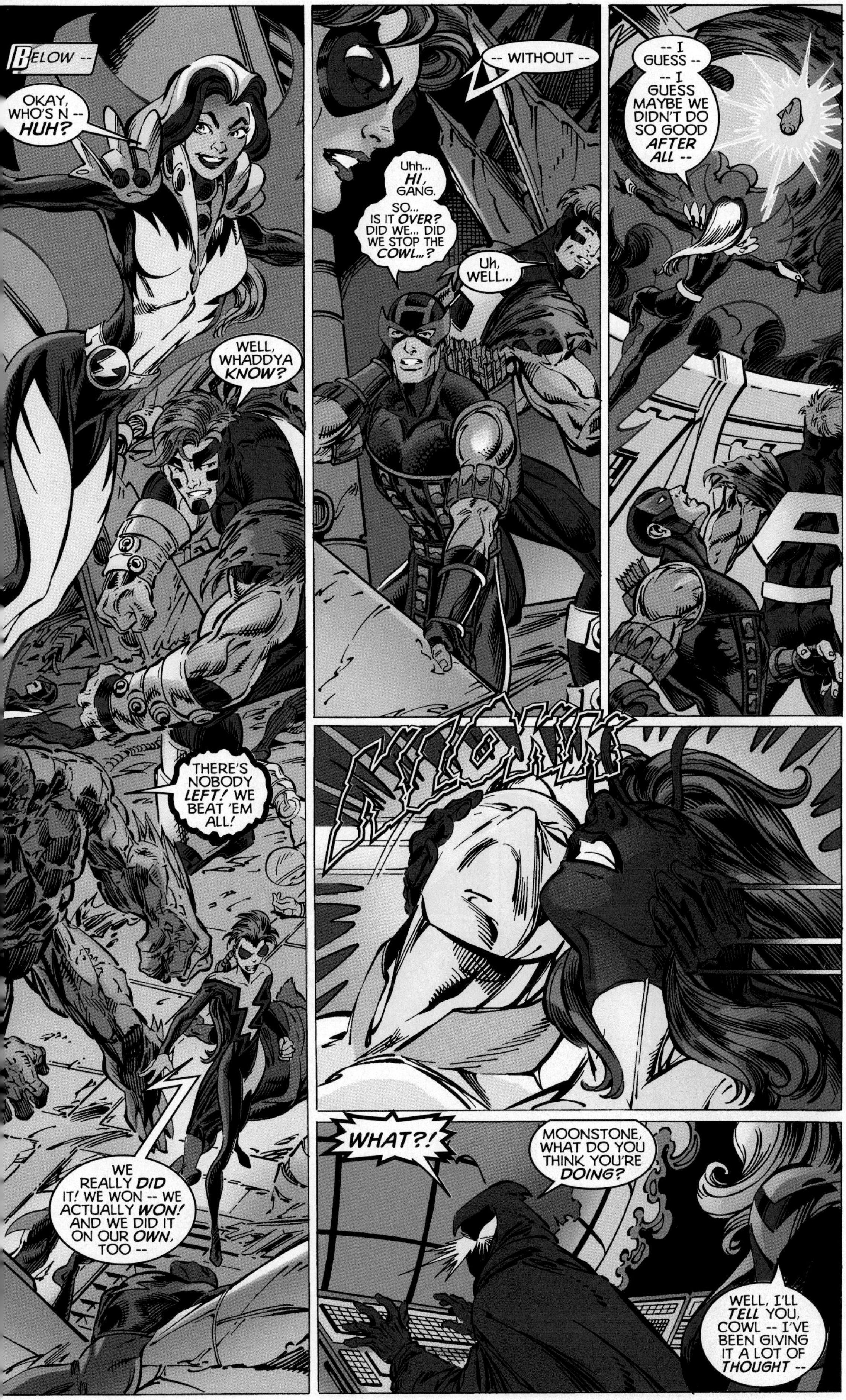
BELOW --
OKAY, WHO'S N -- HUH?
WELL, WHADDYA KNOW?
THERE'S NOBODY LEFT! WE BEAT 'EM ALL!
WE REALLY DID IT! WE WON -- WE ACTUALLY WON! AND WE DID IT ON OUR OWN, TOO --
-- WITHOUT --
Uhh... HI, GANG. SO... IS IT OVER? DID WE... DID WE STOP THE COWL...?
Uh, WELL...
-- I GUESS --
-- I GUESS MAYBE WE DIDN'T DO SO GOOD AFTER ALL --
KLONKK
WHAT?!
MOONSTONE, WHAT DO YOU THINK YOU'RE DOING?
WELL, I'LL TELL YOU, COWL -- I'VE BEEN GIVING IT A LOT OF THOUGHT --

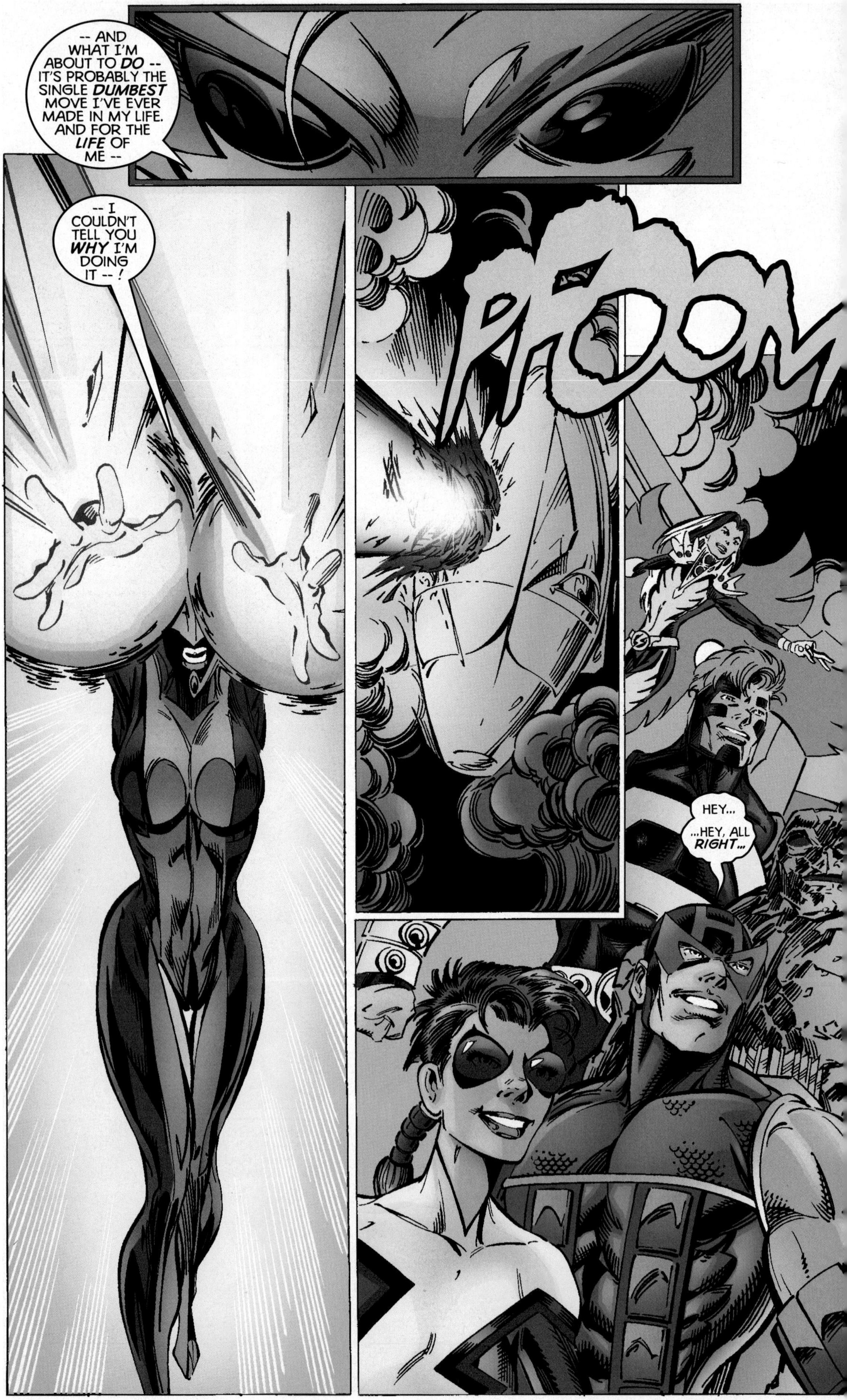
-- AND WHAT I'M ABOUT TO DO -- IT'S PROBABLY THE SINGLE DUMBEST MOVE I'VE EVER MADE IN MY LIFE. AND FOR THE LIFE OF ME --
-- I COULDN'T TELL YOU WHY I'M DOING IT -- !
PFOOM
HEY... ...HEY, ALL RIGHT...

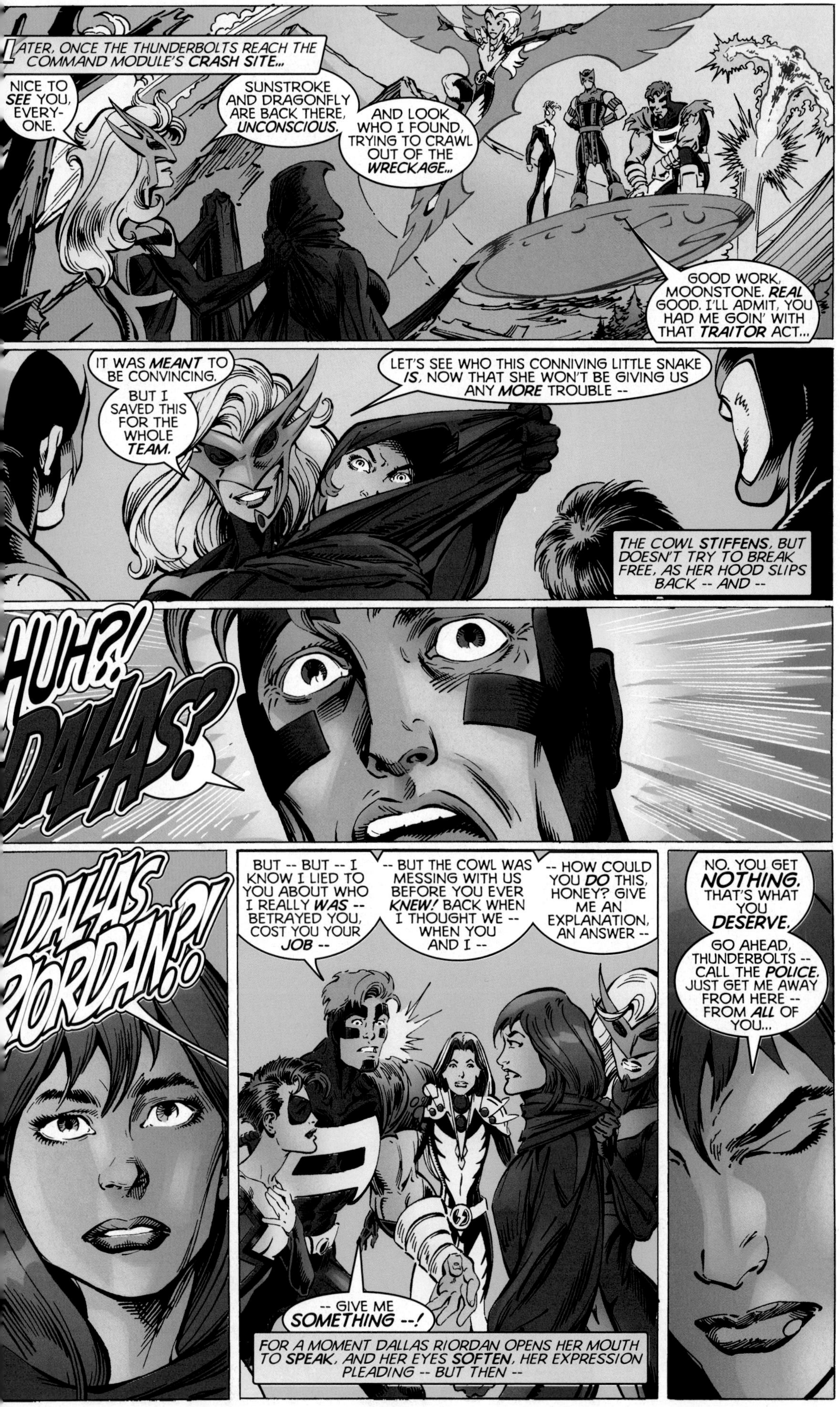
LATER, ONCE THE THUNDERBOLTS REACH THE COMMAND MODULE'S CRASH SITE...
NICE TO SEE YOU, EVERY-ONE.
SUNSTROKE AND DRAGONFLY ARE BACK THERE, UNCONSCIOUS.
AND LOOK WHO I FOUND, TRYING TO CRAWL OUT OF THE WRECKAGE...
GOOD WORK, MOONSTONE. REAL GOOD. I'LL ADMIT, YOU HAD ME GOIN' WITH THAT TRAITOR ACT...
IT WAS MEANT TO BE CONVINCING.
BUT I SAVED THIS FOR THE WHOLE TEAM.
LET'S SEE WHO THIS CONNIVING LITTLE SNAKE IS, NOW THAT SHE WON'T BE GIVING US ANY MORE TROUBLE --
THE COWL STIFFENS, BUT DOESN'T TRY TO BREAK FREE, AS HER HOOD SLIPS BACK -- AND --
HUH?! DALLAS?!
DALLAS RIORDAN?!
BUT -- BUT -- I KNOW I LIED TO YOU ABOUT WHO I REALLY WAS -- BETRAYED YOU, COST YOU YOUR JOB --
-- BUT THE COWL WAS MESSING WITH US BEFORE YOU EVER KNEW! BACK WHEN I THOUGHT WE -- WHEN YOU AND I --
-- HOW COULD YOU DO THIS, HONEY? GIVE ME AN EXPLANATION, AN ANSWER --
-- GIVE ME SOMETHING --!
FOR A MOMENT DALLAS RIORDAN OPENS HER MOUTH TO SPEAK, AND HER EYES SOFTEN, HER EXPRESSION PLEADING -- BUT THEN --
NO, YOU GET NOTHING. THAT'S WHAT YOU DESERVE.
GO AHEAD, THUNDERBOLTS -- CALL THE POLICE. JUST GET ME AWAY FROM HERE -- FROM ALL OF YOU...

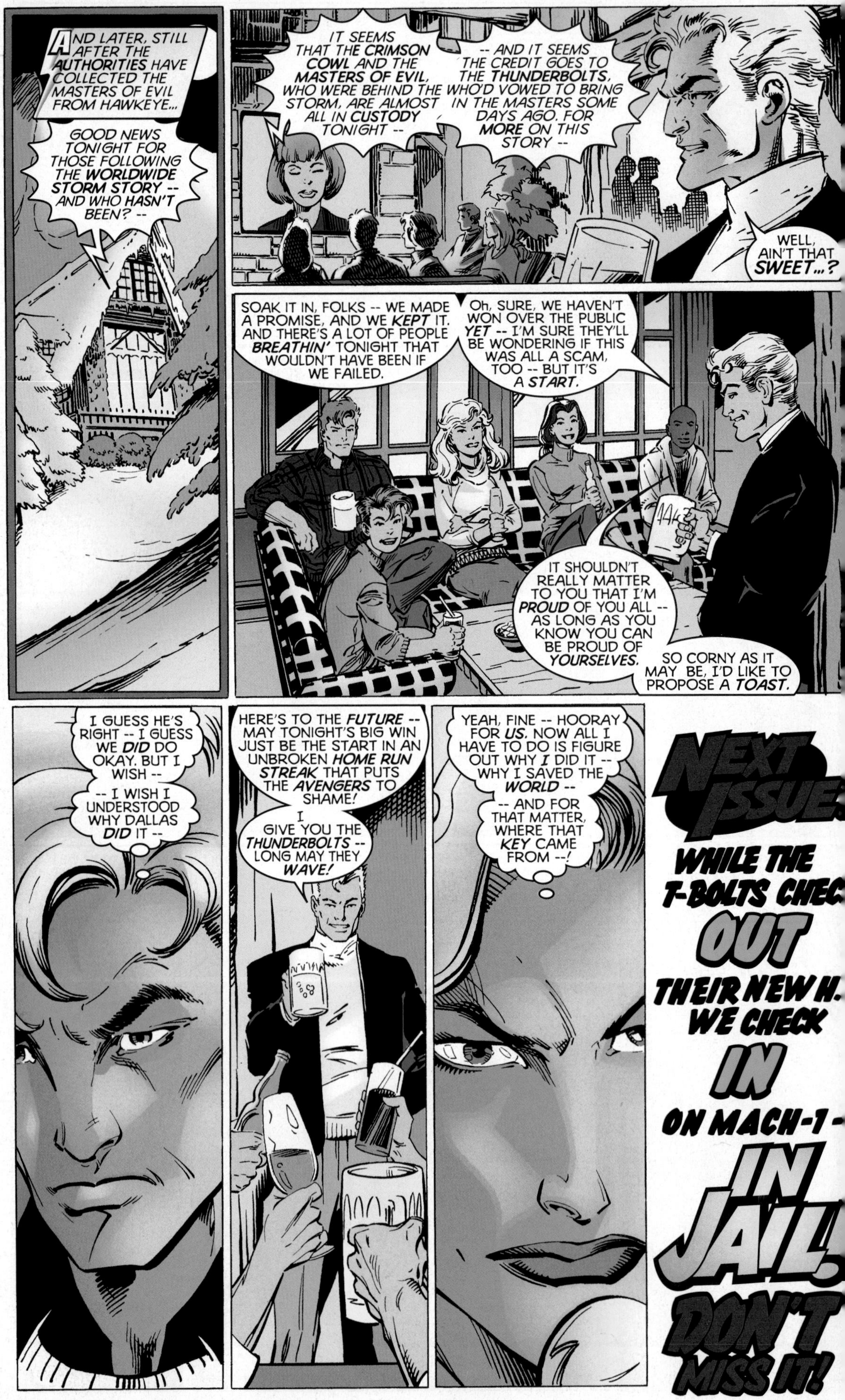
AND LATER, STILL AFTER THE AUTHORITIES HAVE COLLECTED THE MASTERS OF EVIL FROM HAWKEYE...
GOOD NEWS TONIGHT FOR THOSE FOLLOWING THE WORLDWIDE STORM STORY -- AND WHO HASN'T BEEN? --
IT SEEMS THAT THE CRIMSON COWL AND THE MASTERS OF EVIL, WHO WERE BEHIND THE STORM, ARE ALMOST ALL IN CUSTODY TONIGHT --
-- AND IT SEEMS THE CREDIT GOES TO THE THUNDERBOLTS, WHO'D VOWED TO BRING IN THE MASTERS SOME DAYS AGO. FOR MORE ON THIS STORY --
WELL, AIN'T THAT SWEET...?
SOAK IT IN, FOLKS -- WE MADE A PROMISE, AND WE KEPT IT. AND THERE'S A LOT OF PEOPLE BREATHIN' TONIGHT THAT WOULDN'T HAVE BEEN IF WE FAILED.
Oh, SURE, WE HAVEN'T WON OVER THE PUBLIC YET -- I'M SURE THEY'LL BE WONDERING IF THIS WAS ALL A SCAM, TOO -- BUT IT'S A START.
IT SHOULDN'T REALLY MATTER TO YOU THAT I'M PROUD OF YOU ALL -- AS LONG AS YOU KNOW YOU CAN BE PROUD OF YOURSELVES.
SO CORNY AS IT MAY BE, I'D LIKE TO PROPOSE A TOAST.
I GUESS HE'S RIGHT -- I GUESS WE DID DO OKAY. BUT I WISH --
-- I WISH I UNDERSTOOD WHY DALLAS DID IT --
HERE'S TO THE FUTURE -- MAY TONIGHT'S BIG WIN JUST BE THE START IN AN UNBROKEN HOME RUN STREAK THAT PUTS THE AVENGERS TO SHAME!
I GIVE YOU THE THUNDERBOLTS -- LONG MAY THEY WAVE!
YEAH, FINE -- HOORAY FOR US. NOW ALL I HAVE TO DO IS FIGURE OUT WHY I DID IT -- WHY I SAVED THE WORLD --
-- AND FOR THAT MATTER, WHERE THAT KEY CAME FROM --!
NEXT ISSUE:
WHILE THE T-BOLTS CHEC
OUT
THEIR NEW H.
WE CHECK
IN
ON MACH-1 -
IN JAIL!
DON'T MISS IT!

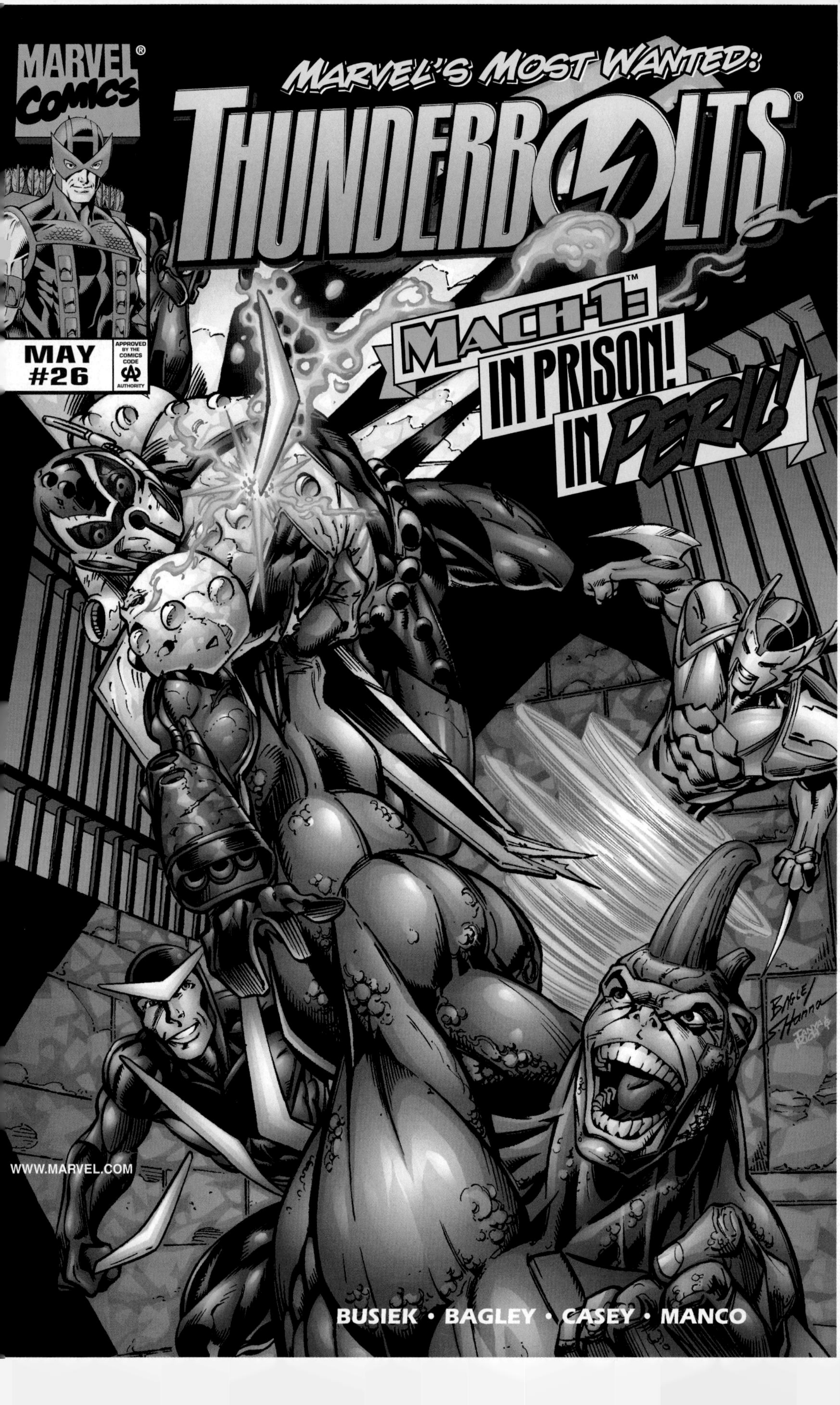

MARVEL® COMICS
MARVEL'S MOST WANTED:
THUNDERBOLTS®
MAY #26
APPROVED BY THE COMICS CODE AUTHORITY
MACH-1™: IN PRISON! IN PERIL!
WWW.MARVEL.COM
BUSIEK • BAGLEY • CASEY • MANCO

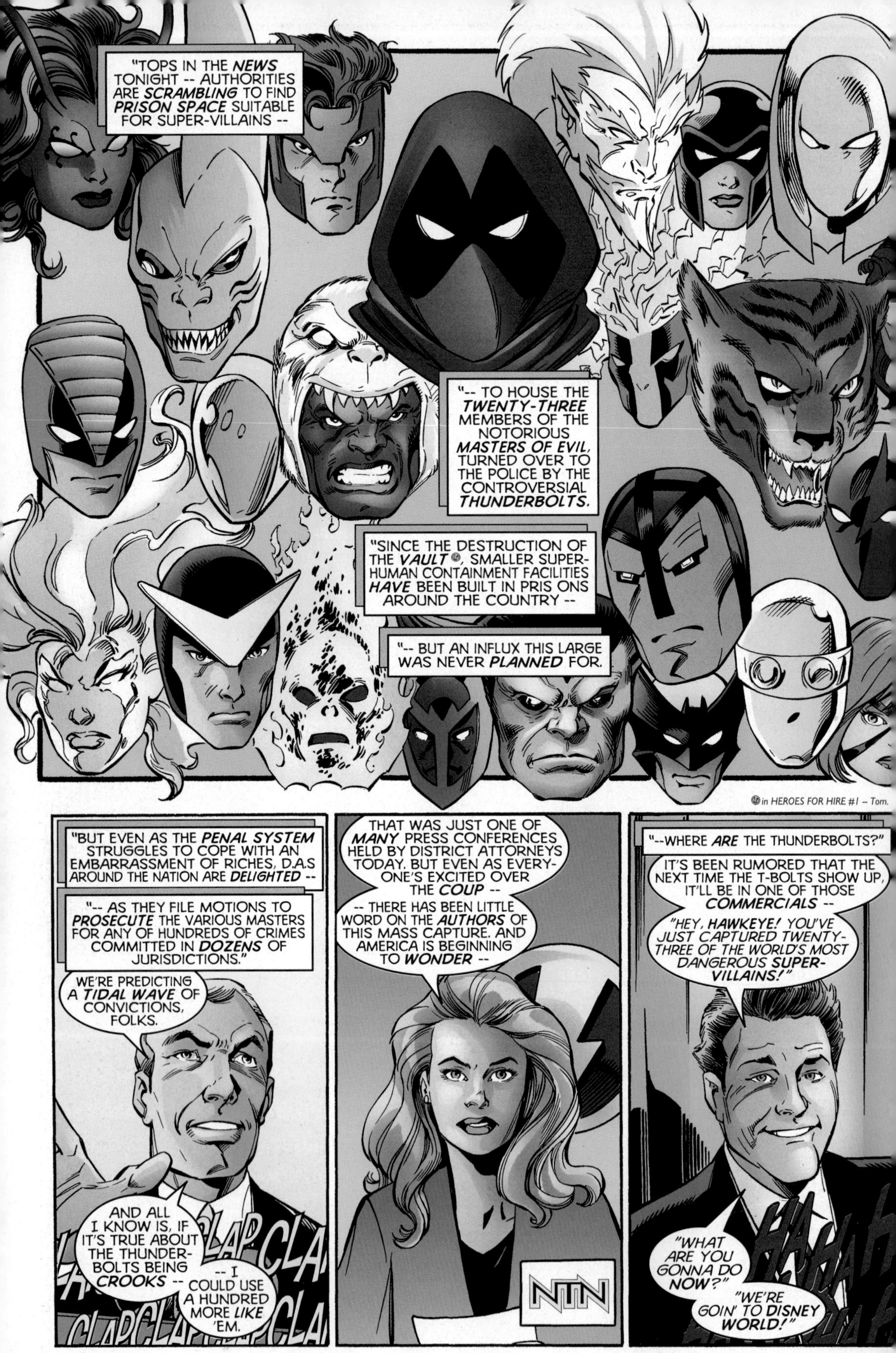
"TOPS IN THE NEWS TONIGHT -- AUTHORITIES ARE SCRAMBLING TO FIND PRISON SPACE SUITABLE FOR SUPER-VILLAINS --
"-- TO HOUSE THE TWENTY-THREE MEMBERS OF THE NOTORIOUS MASTERS OF EVIL, TURNED OVER TO THE POLICE BY THE CONTROVERSIAL THUNDERBOLTS.
"SINCE THE DESTRUCTION OF THE VAULT, SMALLER SUPER-HUMAN CONTAINMENT FACILITIES HAVE BEEN BUILT IN PRIS ONS AROUND THE COUNTRY --
"-- BUT AN INFLUX THIS LARGE WAS NEVER PLANNED FOR.
in HEROES FOR HIRE #1 – Tom.
"BUT EVEN AS THE PENAL SYSTEM STRUGGLES TO COPE WITH AN EMBARRASSMENT OF RICHES, D.A.S AROUND THE NATION ARE DELIGHTED --
"-- AS THEY FILE MOTIONS TO PROSECUTE THE VARIOUS MASTERS FOR ANY OF HUNDREDS OF CRIMES COMMITTED IN DOZENS OF JURISDICTIONS."
WE'RE PREDICTING A TIDAL WAVE OF CONVICTIONS, FOLKS.
AND ALL I KNOW IS, IF IT'S TRUE ABOUT THE THUNDER-BOLTS BEING CROOKS --
-- I COULD USE A HUNDRED MORE LIKE 'EM.
CLAP CLAP CLAPCLAP
THAT WAS JUST ONE OF MANY PRESS CONFERENCES HELD BY DISTRICT ATTORNEYS TODAY. BUT EVEN AS EVERY-ONE'S EXCITED OVER THE COUP --
-- THERE HAS BEEN LITTLE WORD ON THE AUTHORS OF THIS MASS CAPTURE. AND AMERICA IS BEGINNING TO WONDER --
NTN
"--WHERE ARE THE THUNDERBOLTS?"
IT'S BEEN RUMORED THAT THE NEXT TIME THE T-BOLTS SHOW UP, IT'LL BE IN ONE OF THOSE COMMERCIALS --
"HEY, HAWKEYE! YOU'VE JUST CAPTURED TWENTY-THREE OF THE WORLD'S MOST DANGEROUS SUPER-VILLAINS!"
"WHAT ARE YOU GONNA DO NOW?"
"WE'RE GOIN' TO DISNEY WORLD!"
HAHAH

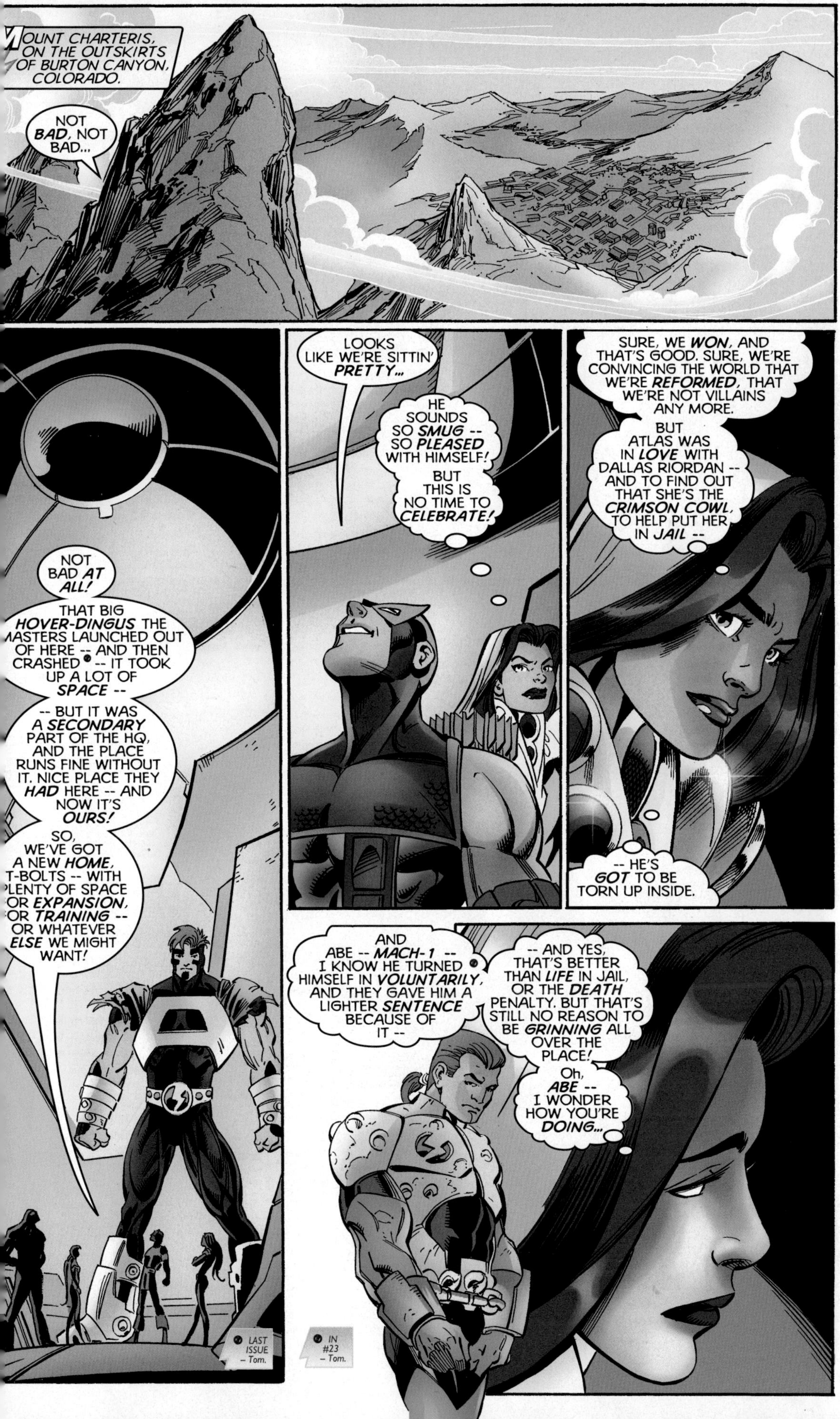
MOUNT CHARTERIS, ON THE OUTSKIRTS OF BURTON CANYON, COLORADO.
NOT BAD, NOT BAD...
NOT BAD AT ALL!
THAT BIG HOVER-DINGUS THE MASTERS LAUNCHED OUT OF HERE -- AND THEN CRASHED -- IT TOOK UP A LOT OF SPACE --
-- BUT IT WAS A SECONDARY PART OF THE HQ, AND THE PLACE RUNS FINE WITHOUT IT. NICE PLACE THEY HAD HERE -- AND NOW IT'S OURS!
SO, WE'VE GOT A NEW HOME, T-BOLTS -- WITH PLENTY OF SPACE FOR EXPANSION, FOR TRAINING -- OR WHATEVER ELSE WE MIGHT WANT!
LAST ISSUE – Tom.
LOOKS LIKE WE'RE SITTIN' PRETTY...
HE SOUNDS SO SMUG -- SO PLEASED WITH HIMSELF!
BUT THIS IS NO TIME TO CELEBRATE!
SURE, WE WON, AND THAT'S GOOD. SURE, WE'RE CONVINCING THE WORLD THAT WE'RE REFORMED, THAT WE'RE NOT VILLAINS ANY MORE.
BUT ATLAS WAS IN LOVE WITH DALLAS RIORDAN -- AND TO FIND OUT THAT SHE'S THE CRIMSON COWL, TO HELP PUT HER IN JAIL --
-- HE'S GOT TO BE TORN UP INSIDE.
AND ABE -- MACH-1 -- I KNOW HE TURNED HIMSELF IN VOLUNTARILY, AND THEY GAVE HIM A LIGHTER SENTENCE BECAUSE OF IT --
-- AND YES, THAT'S BETTER THAN LIFE IN JAIL, OR THE DEATH PENALTY. BUT THAT'S STILL NO REASON TO BE GRINNING ALL OVER THE PLACE!
Oh, ABE -- I WONDER HOW YOU'RE DOING...
IN #23 – Tom.

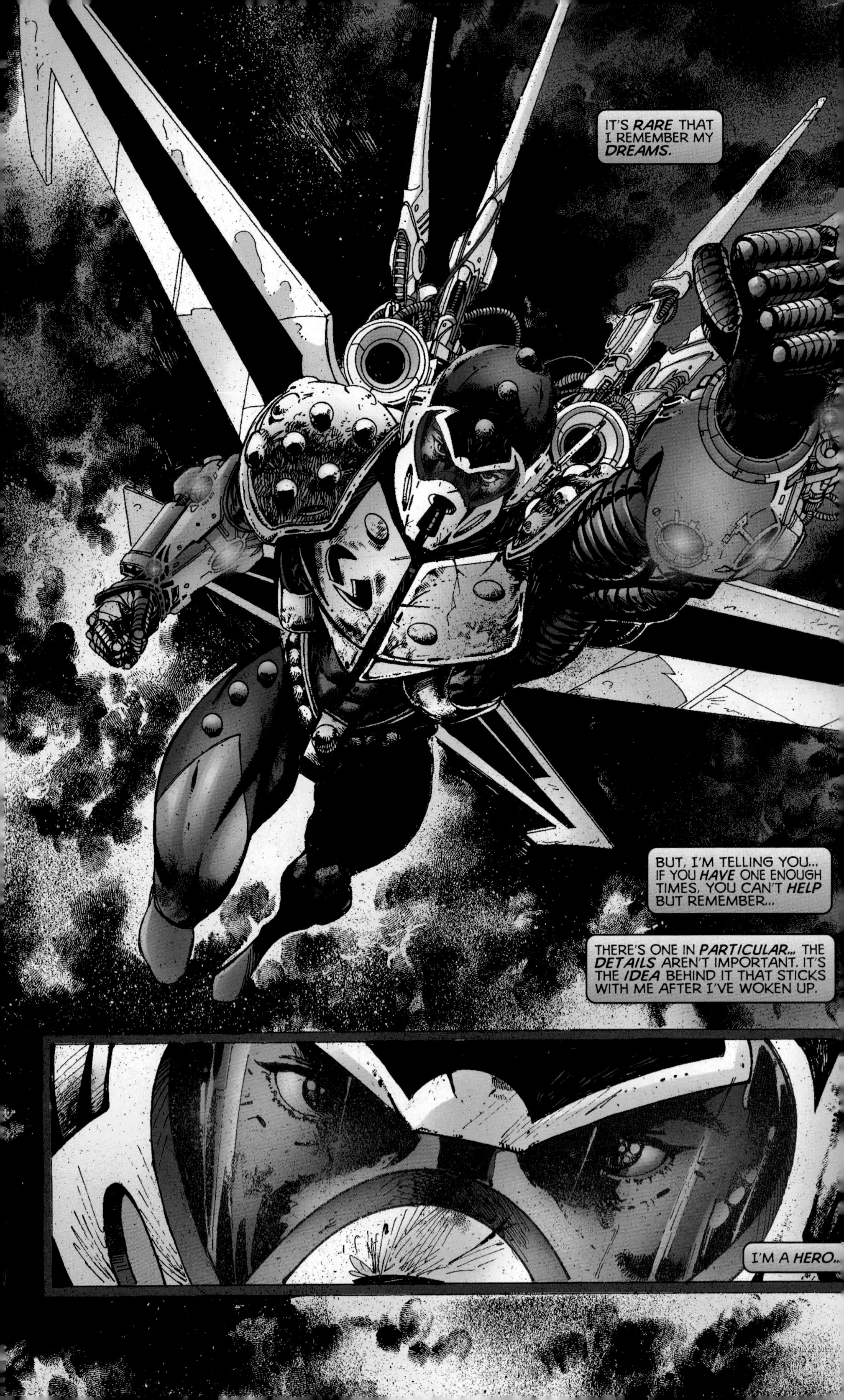
IT'S *RARE* THAT I REMEMBER MY *DREAMS.*
BUT, I'M TELLING YOU... IF YOU *HAVE* ONE ENOUGH TIMES, YOU CAN'T *HELP* BUT REMEMBER...
THERE'S ONE IN *PARTICULAR...* THE *DETAILS* AREN'T IMPORTANT. IT'S THE *IDEA* BEHIND IT THAT STICKS WITH ME AFTER I'VE WOKEN UP.
I'M A *HERO...*

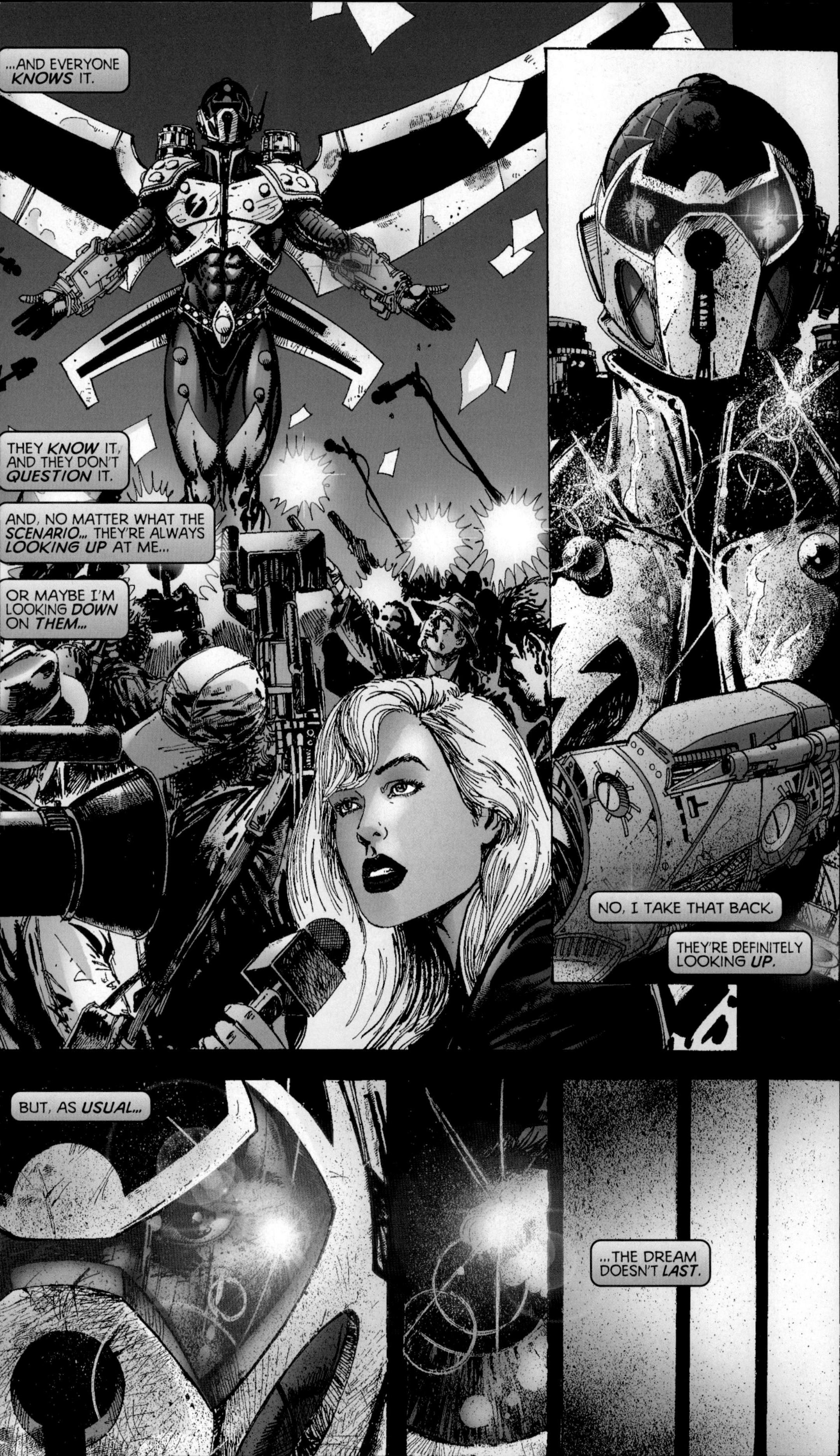
...AND EVERYONE KNOWS IT.
THEY KNOW IT, AND THEY DON'T QUESTION IT.
AND, NO MATTER WHAT THE SCENARIO... THEY'RE ALWAYS LOOKING UP AT ME...
OR MAYBE I'M LOOKING DOWN ON THEM...
NO, I TAKE THAT BACK.
THEY'RE DEFINITELY LOOKING UP.
BUT, AS USUAL...
...THE DREAM DOESN'T LAST.

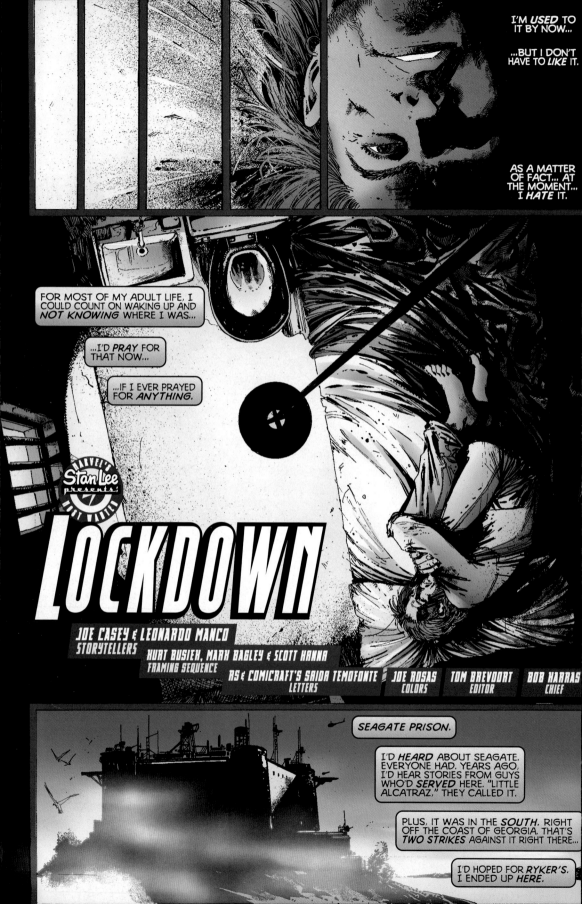

I'M *USED* TO IT BY NOW...

...BUT I DON'T HAVE TO *LIKE* IT.

AS A MATTER OF FACT... AT THE MOMENT... I *HATE* IT.

FOR MOST OF MY ADULT LIFE, I COULD COUNT ON WAKING UP AND *NOT KNOWING* WHERE I WAS...

...I'D *PRAY* FOR THAT NOW...

...IF I EVER PRAYED FOR *ANYTHING*.

MARVEL'S Stan Lee presents:

LOCKDOWN

JOE CASEY & LEONARDO MANCO
STORYTELLERS

KURT BUSIEK, MARK BAGLEY & SCOTT HANNA
FRAMING SEQUENCE

RS & COMICRAFT'S SAIDA TEMOFONTE
LETTERS

JOE ROSAS
COLORS

TOM BREVOORT
EDITOR

BOB HARRAS
CHIEF

SEAGATE PRISON.

I'D *HEARD* ABOUT SEAGATE. EVERYONE HAD. YEARS AGO, I'D HEAR STORIES FROM GUYS WHO'D *SERVED* HERE. "LITTLE ALCATRAZ," THEY CALLED IT.

PLUS, IT WAS IN THE *SOUTH*. RIGHT OFF THE COAST OF GEORGIA. THAT'S *TWO STRIKES* AGAINST IT RIGHT THERE...

I'D HOPED FOR *RYKER'S*. I ENDED UP *HERE*.

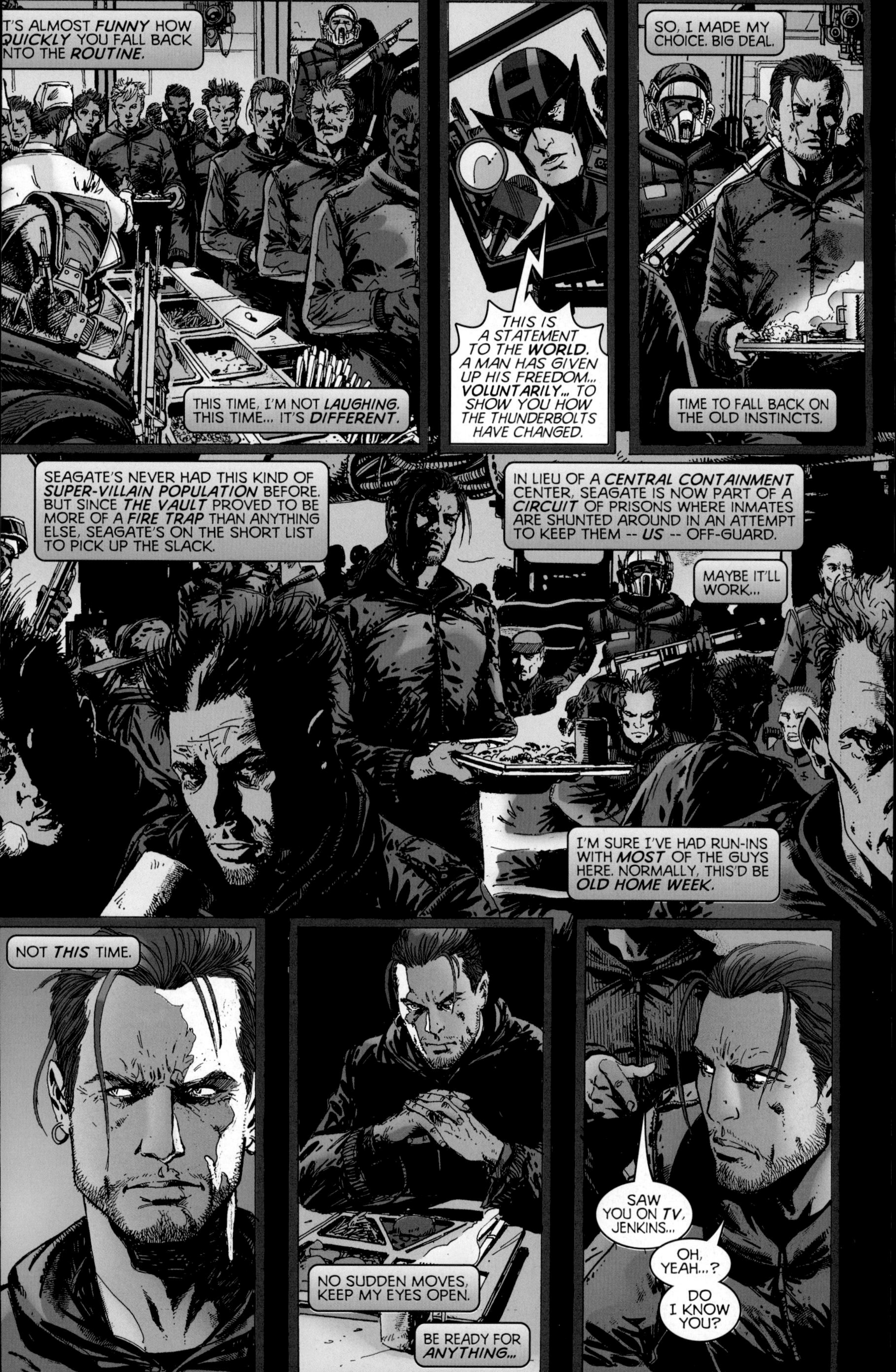
IT'S ALMOST FUNNY HOW QUICKLY YOU FALL BACK INTO THE ROUTINE.
THIS TIME, I'M NOT LAUGHING. THIS TIME... IT'S DIFFERENT.
THIS IS A STATEMENT TO THE WORLD. A MAN HAS GIVEN UP HIS FREEDOM... VOLUNTARILY... TO SHOW YOU HOW THE THUNDERBOLTS HAVE CHANGED.
SO, I MADE MY CHOICE. BIG DEAL.
TIME TO FALL BACK ON THE OLD INSTINCTS.
SEAGATE'S NEVER HAD THIS KIND OF SUPER-VILLAIN POPULATION BEFORE. BUT SINCE THE VAULT PROVED TO BE MORE OF A FIRE TRAP THAN ANYTHING ELSE, SEAGATE'S ON THE SHORT LIST TO PICK UP THE SLACK.
IN LIEU OF A CENTRAL CONTAINMENT CENTER, SEAGATE IS NOW PART OF A CIRCUIT OF PRISONS WHERE INMATES ARE SHUNTED AROUND IN AN ATTEMPT TO KEEP THEM -- US -- OFF-GUARD.
MAYBE IT'LL WORK...
I'M SURE I'VE HAD RUN-INS WITH MOST OF THE GUYS HERE. NORMALLY, THIS'D BE OLD HOME WEEK.
NOT THIS TIME.
NO SUDDEN MOVES, KEEP MY EYES OPEN.
BE READY FOR ANYTHING...
SAW YOU ON TV, JENKINS...
OH, YEAH...?
DO I KNOW YOU?

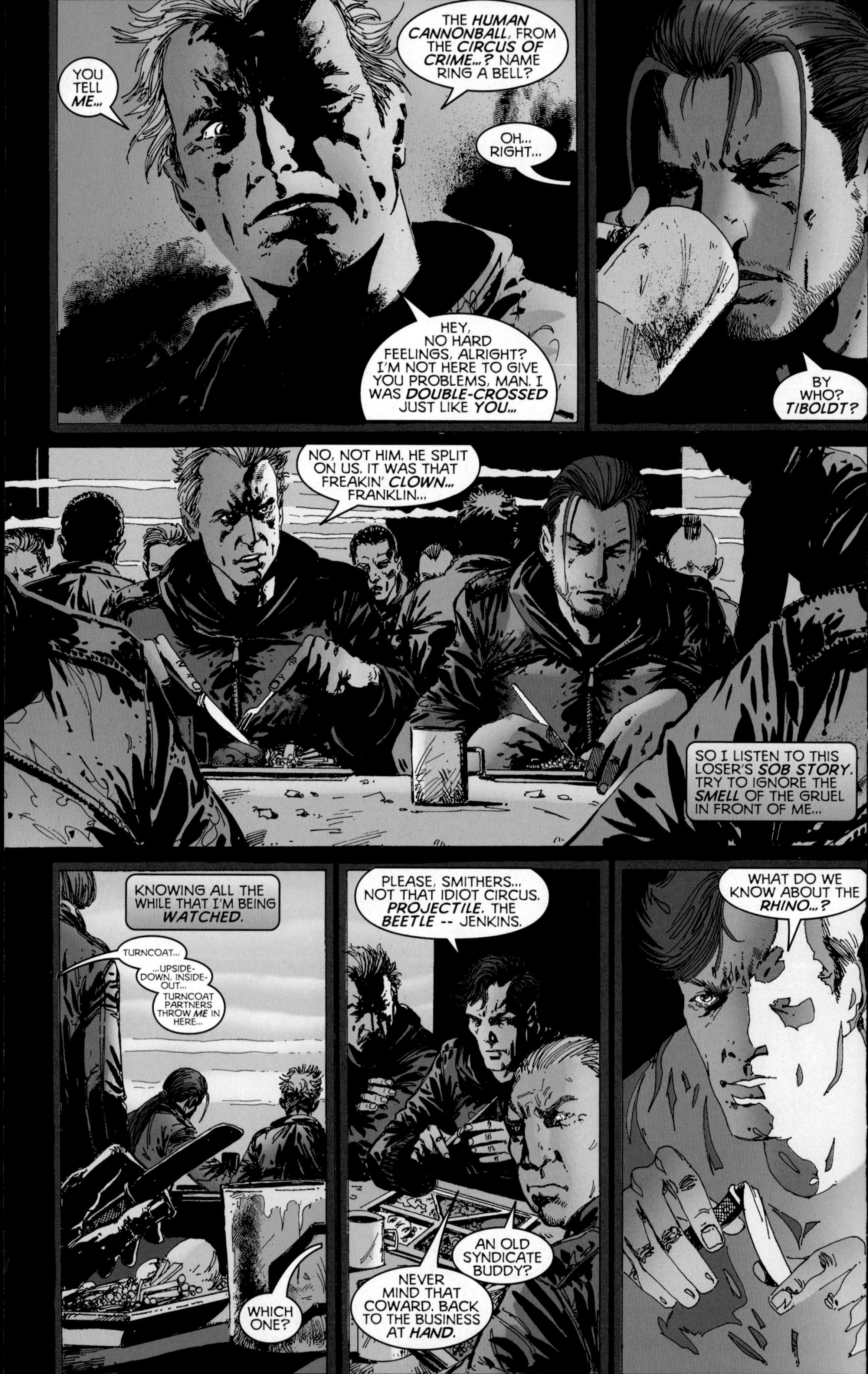
YOU TELL ME...
THE HUMAN CANNONBALL, FROM THE CIRCUS OF CRIME...? NAME RING A BELL?
OH... RIGHT...
HEY, NO HARD FEELINGS, ALRIGHT? I'M NOT HERE TO GIVE YOU PROBLEMS, MAN. I WAS DOUBLE-CROSSED JUST LIKE YOU...
BY WHO? TIBOLDT?
NO, NOT HIM. HE SPLIT ON US. IT WAS THAT FREAKIN' CLOWN... FRANKLIN...
SO I LISTEN TO THIS LOSER'S SOB STORY. TRY TO IGNORE THE SMELL OF THE GRUEL IN FRONT OF ME...
KNOWING ALL THE WHILE THAT I'M BEING WATCHED.
TURNCOAT...
...UPSIDE-DOWN, INSIDE-OUT...
TURNCOAT PARTNERS THROW ME IN HERE...
WHICH ONE?
PLEASE, SMITHERS... NOT THAT IDIOT CIRCUS. PROJECTILE. THE BEETLE -- JENKINS.
AN OLD SYNDICATE BUDDY?
NEVER MIND THAT COWARD. BACK TO THE BUSINESS AT HAND.
WHAT DO WE KNOW ABOUT THE RHINO...?

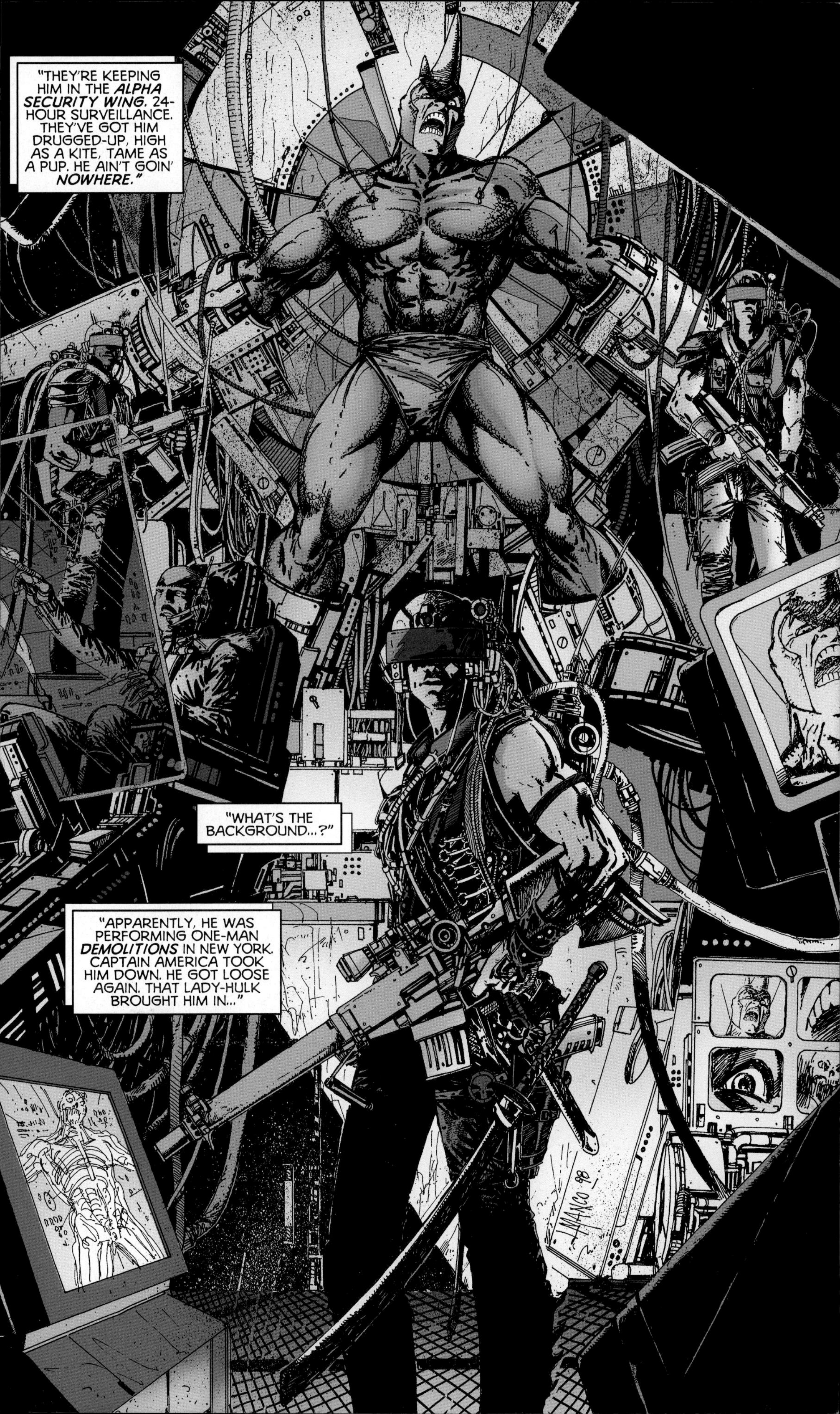
"THEY'RE KEEPING HIM IN THE *ALPHA SECURITY WING.* 24-HOUR SURVEILLANCE. THEY'VE GOT HIM DRUGGED-UP, HIGH AS A KITE, TAME AS A PUP. HE AIN'T GOIN' ***NOWHERE."***
"WHAT'S THE BACKGROUND...?"
"APPARENTLY, HE WAS PERFORMING ONE-MAN *DEMOLITIONS* IN NEW YORK. CAPTAIN AMERICA TOOK HIM DOWN. HE GOT LOOSE AGAIN. THAT LADY-HULK BROUGHT HIM IN..."

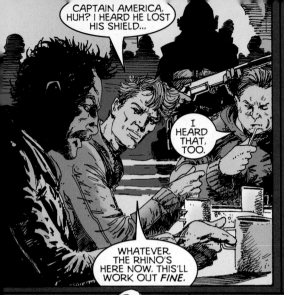

CAPTAIN AMERICA, HUH? I HEARD HE LOST HIS SHIELD...

I HEARD THAT, TOO.

WHATEVER. THE RHINO'S HERE NOW. THIS'LL WORK OUT *FINE*.

ALL RIGHT, *MYERS*... WHAT'S WITH THE WHISPERING OVER HERE?

THE NAME'S *BOOMERANG*.

YOU AIN'T A *NAME*...

...YOU'RE A *NUMBER*.

IS THAT A *FACT*, ROSCOE...?

LEMME TELL YA. IF I EVER SEE THAT *BOZO-LOOKIN'* FREAK AGAIN, I'M GONNA TAKE THAT *UNICYCLE* AND STICK IT UP HIS --

FAP

WEAPON!

DROP IT, JENKINS!

KRASH

I DON'T OFFER ANY *RESISTANCE*.

WHAT'S THE POINT?

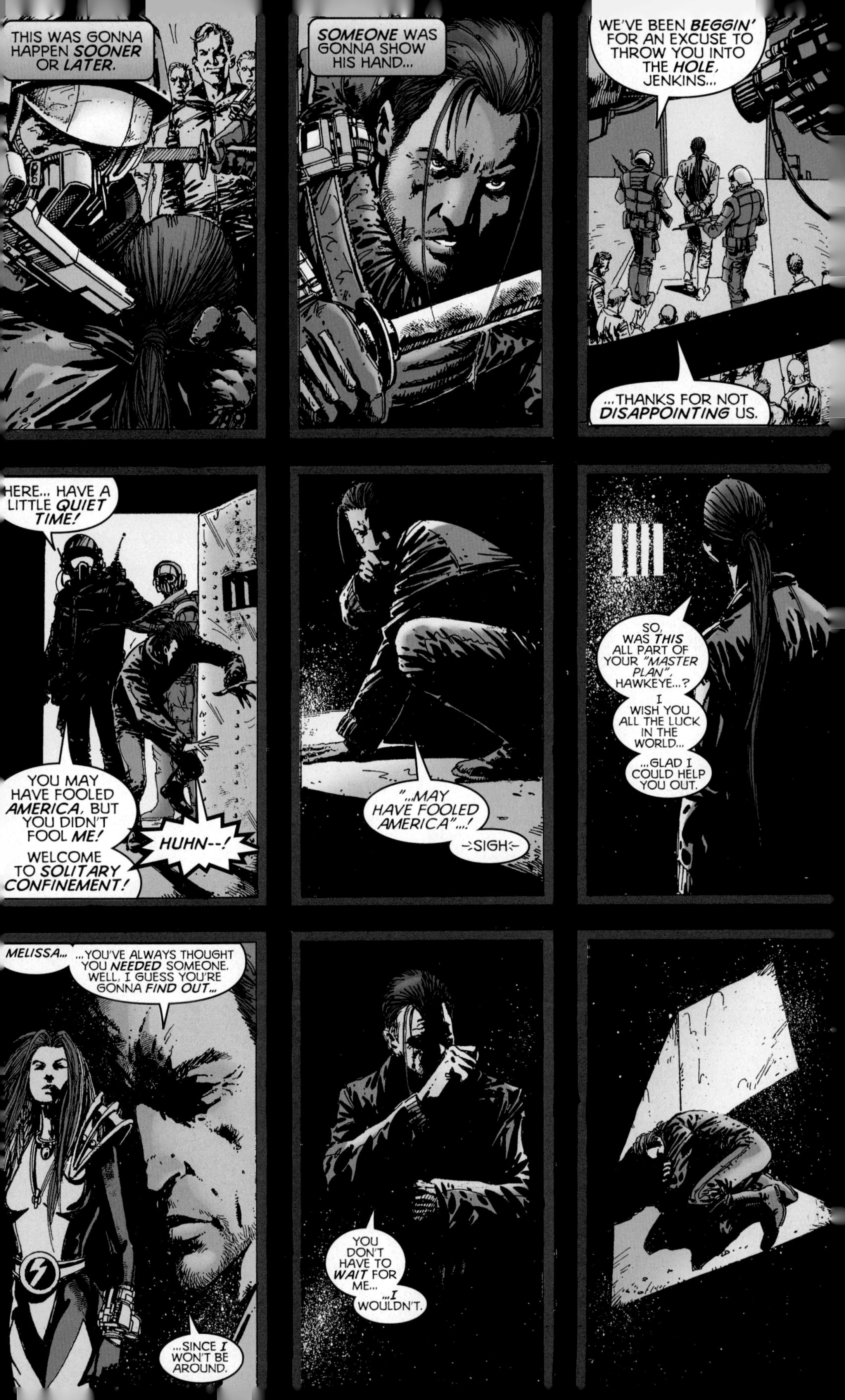
THIS WAS GONNA HAPPEN *SOONER* OR *LATER.*
SOMEONE WAS GONNA SHOW HIS HAND...
WE'VE BEEN *BEGGIN'* FOR AN EXCUSE TO THROW YOU INTO THE *HOLE,* JENKINS...
...THANKS FOR NOT *DISAPPOINTING* US.
HERE... HAVE A LITTLE *QUIET TIME!*
YOU MAY HAVE FOOLED *AMERICA,* BUT YOU DIDN'T FOOL *ME!*
WELCOME TO *SOLITARY CONFINEMENT!*
HUHN--!
"...MAY HAVE FOOLED AMERICA"...!
-SIGH-
SO, WAS *THIS* ALL PART OF YOUR *"MASTER PLAN",* HAWKEYE...?
I WISH YOU ALL THE LUCK IN THE WORLD...
...GLAD I COULD HELP YOU OUT.
MELISSA...
...YOU'VE ALWAYS THOUGHT YOU *NEEDED* SOMEONE. WELL, I GUESS YOU'RE GONNA *FIND OUT...*
...SINCE *I* WON'T BE AROUND.
YOU DON'T HAVE TO *WAIT* FOR ME...
...*I* WOULDN'T.

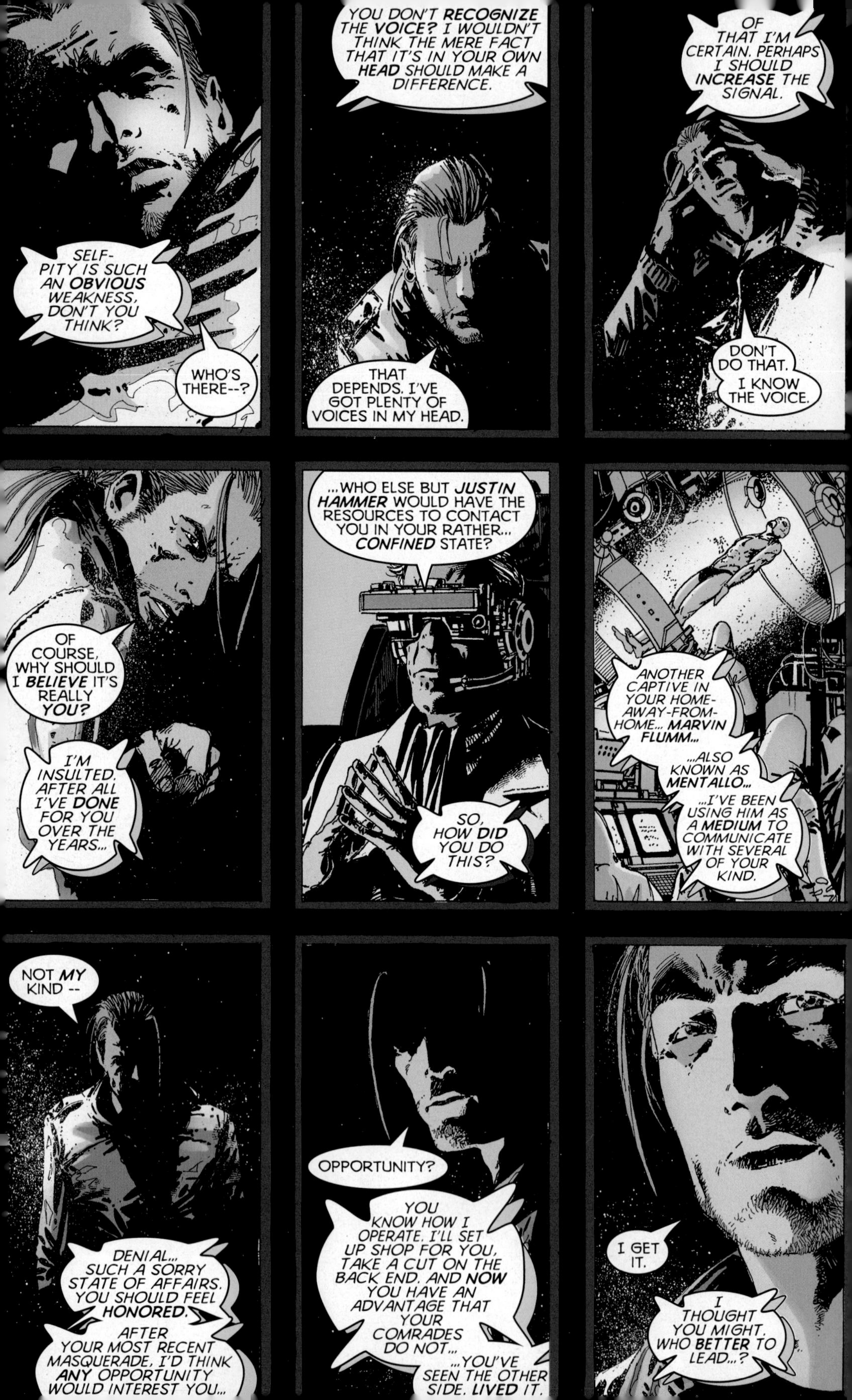
SELF-PITY IS SUCH AN OBVIOUS WEAKNESS, DON'T YOU THINK?
WHO'S THERE--?
YOU DON'T RECOGNIZE THE VOICE? I WOULDN'T THINK THE MERE FACT THAT IT'S IN YOUR OWN HEAD SHOULD MAKE A DIFFERENCE.
THAT DEPENDS. I'VE GOT PLENTY OF VOICES IN MY HEAD.
OF THAT I'M CERTAIN. PERHAPS I SHOULD INCREASE THE SIGNAL.
DON'T DO THAT.
I KNOW THE VOICE.
OF COURSE, WHY SHOULD I BELIEVE IT'S REALLY YOU?
I'M INSULTED. AFTER ALL I'VE DONE FOR YOU OVER THE YEARS...
...WHO ELSE BUT JUSTIN HAMMER WOULD HAVE THE RESOURCES TO CONTACT YOU IN YOUR RATHER... CONFINED STATE?
SO, HOW DID YOU DO THIS?
ANOTHER CAPTIVE IN YOUR HOME-AWAY-FROM-HOME... MARVIN FLUMM...
...ALSO KNOWN AS MENTALLO...
...I'VE BEEN USING HIM AS A MEDIUM TO COMMUNICATE WITH SEVERAL OF YOUR KIND.
NOT MY KIND --
DENIAL... SUCH A SORRY STATE OF AFFAIRS. YOU SHOULD FEEL HONORED.
AFTER YOUR MOST RECENT MASQUERADE, I'D THINK ANY OPPORTUNITY WOULD INTEREST YOU...
OPPORTUNITY?
YOU KNOW HOW I OPERATE. I'LL SET UP SHOP FOR YOU, TAKE A CUT ON THE BACK END. AND NOW YOU HAVE AN ADVANTAGE THAT YOUR COMRADES DO NOT...
...YOU'VE SEEN THE OTHER SIDE. LIVED IT.
I GET IT.
I THOUGHT YOU MIGHT. WHO BETTER TO LEAD...?

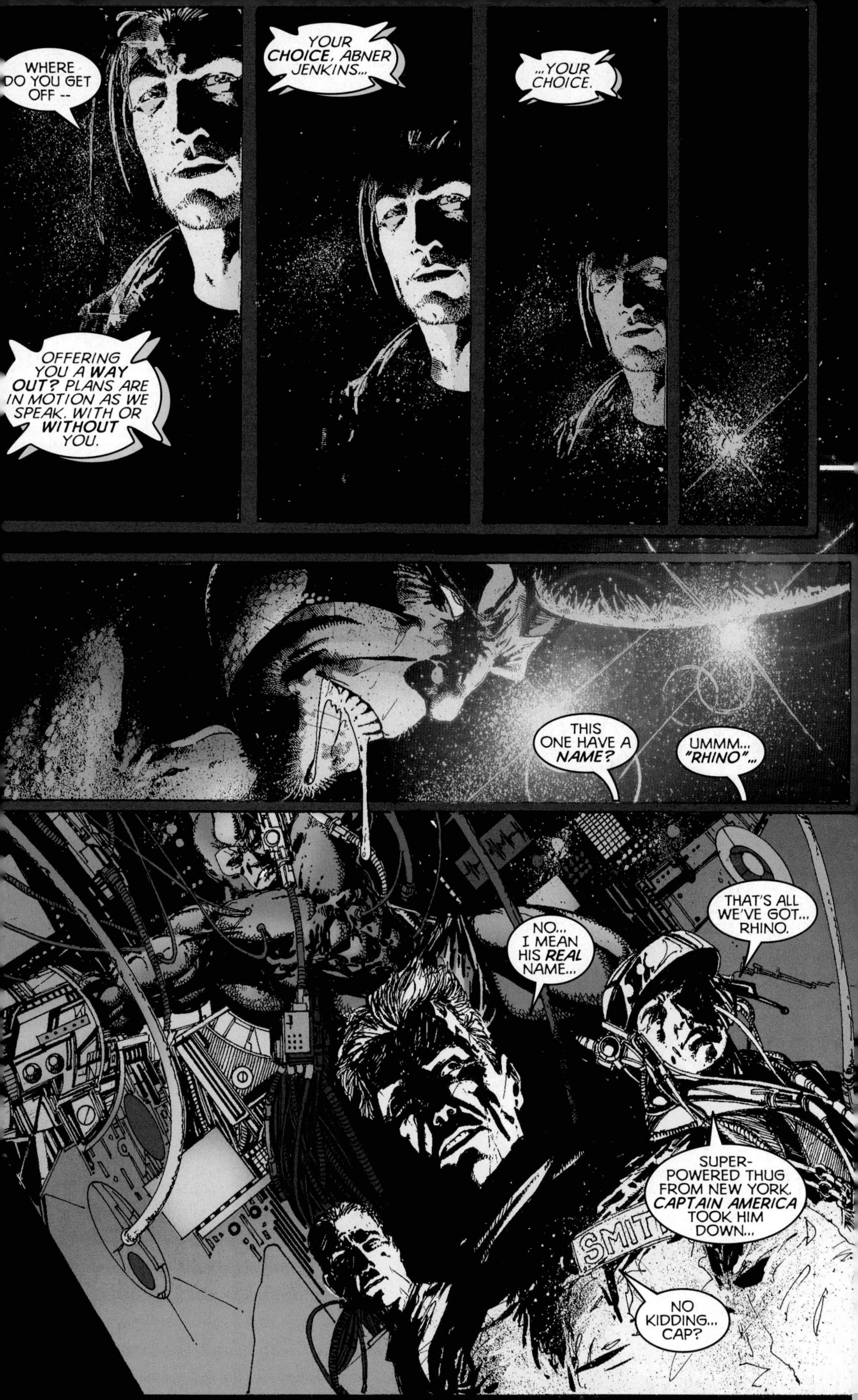
WHERE DO YOU GET OFF --
OFFERING YOU A **WAY OUT?** PLANS ARE IN MOTION AS WE SPEAK. WITH OR **WITHOUT** YOU.
YOUR **CHOICE**, ABNER JENKINS...
...YOUR CHOICE.
THIS ONE HAVE A **NAME?**
UMMM... **"RHINO"**...
NO... I MEAN HIS **REAL** NAME...
THAT'S ALL WE'VE GOT... RHINO.
SUPER-POWERED THUG FROM NEW YORK. **CAPTAIN AMERICA** TOOK HIM DOWN...
NO KIDDING... CAP?

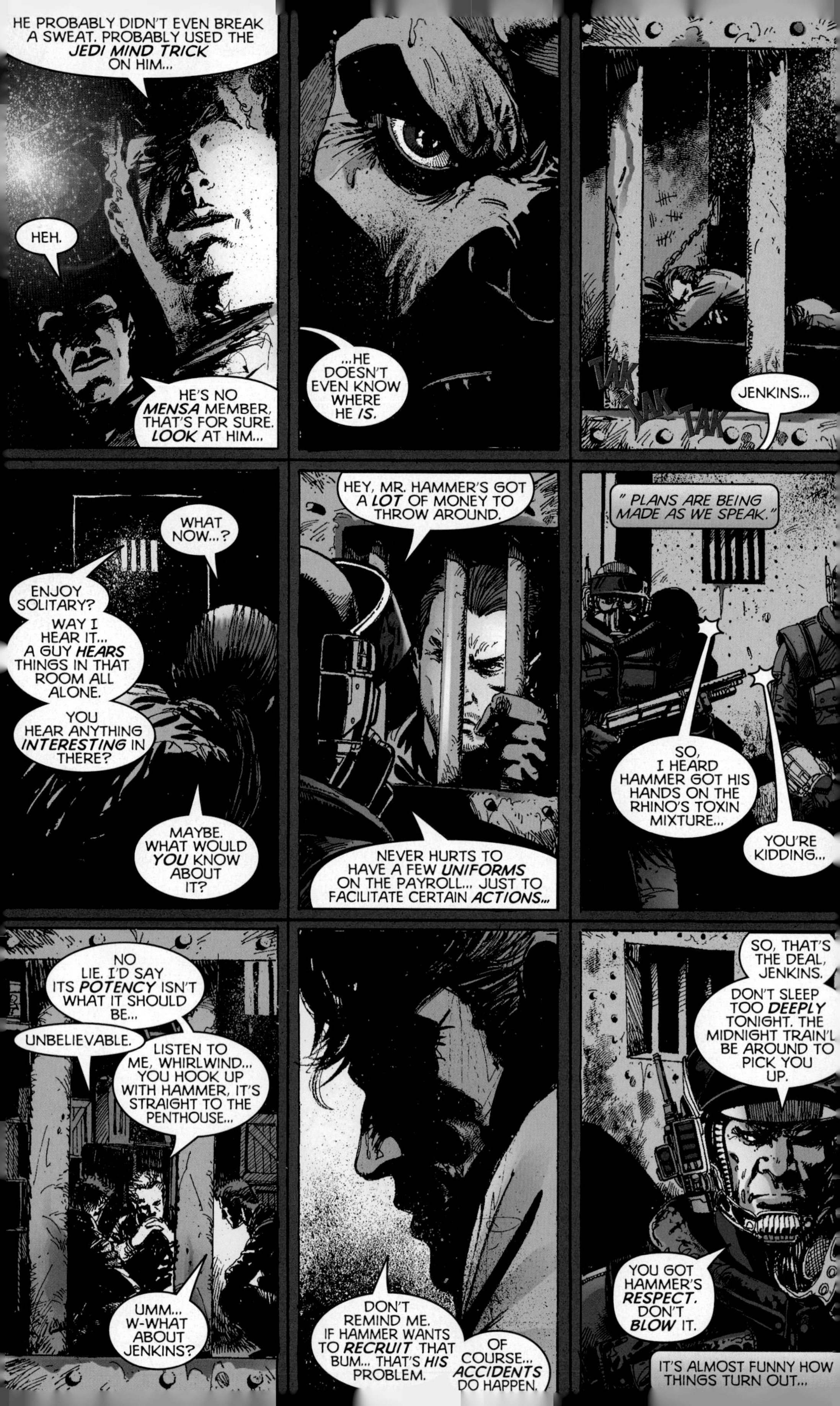
HE PROBABLY DIDN'T EVEN BREAK A SWEAT. PROBABLY USED THE *JEDI MIND TRICK* ON HIM...
HEH.
HE'S NO *MENSA* MEMBER, THAT'S FOR SURE. *LOOK* AT HIM...
...HE DOESN'T EVEN KNOW WHERE HE *IS*.
TAK
TAK
TAK
JENKINS...
WHAT NOW...?
ENJOY SOLITARY?
WAY I HEAR IT... A GUY *HEARS* THINGS IN THAT ROOM ALL ALONE.
YOU HEAR ANYTHING *INTERESTING* IN THERE?
MAYBE. WHAT WOULD *YOU* KNOW ABOUT IT?
HEY, MR. HAMMER'S GOT A *LOT* OF MONEY TO THROW AROUND.
NEVER HURTS TO HAVE A FEW *UNIFORMS* ON THE PAYROLL... JUST TO FACILITATE CERTAIN *ACTIONS*...
"PLANS ARE BEING MADE AS WE SPEAK."
SO, I HEARD HAMMER GOT HIS HANDS ON THE RHINO'S TOXIN MIXTURE...
YOU'RE KIDDING...
NO LIE. I'D SAY ITS *POTENCY* ISN'T WHAT IT SHOULD BE...
UNBELIEVABLE.
LISTEN TO ME, WHIRLWIND... YOU HOOK UP WITH HAMMER, IT'S STRAIGHT TO THE PENTHOUSE...
UMM... W-WHAT ABOUT JENKINS?
DON'T REMIND ME. IF HAMMER WANTS TO *RECRUIT* THAT BUM... THAT'S *HIS* PROBLEM.
OF COURSE... *ACCIDENTS* DO HAPPEN.
SO, THAT'S THE DEAL, JENKINS.
DON'T SLEEP TOO *DEEPLY* TONIGHT. THE MIDNIGHT TRAIN'L BE AROUND TO PICK YOU UP.
YOU GOT HAMMER'S *RESPECT*. DON'T *BLOW* IT.
IT'S ALMOST FUNNY HOW THINGS TURN OUT...

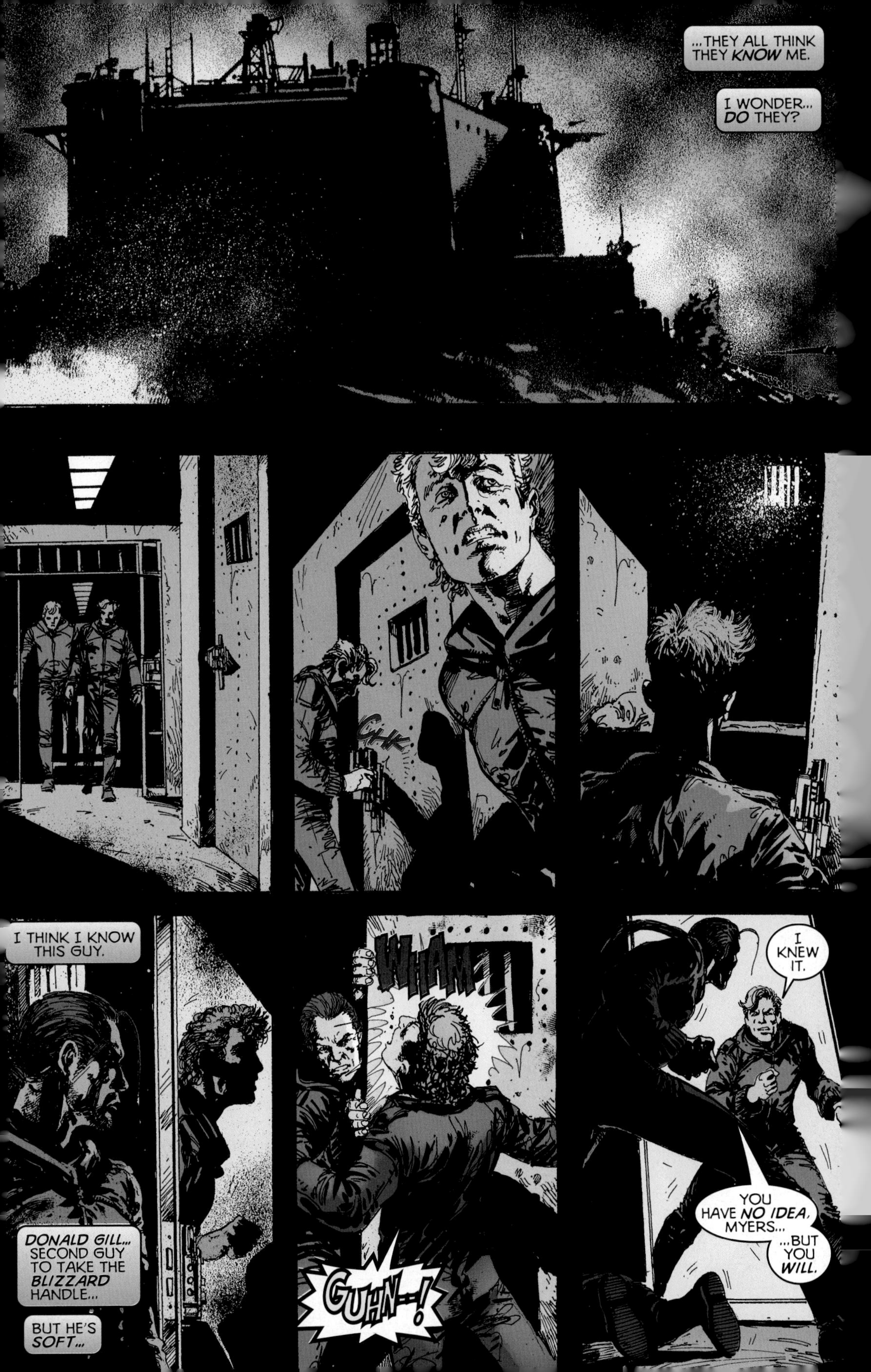
...THEY ALL THINK THEY *KNOW* ME.
I WONDER... *DO* THEY?
CHK
I THINK I KNOW THIS GUY.
DONALD GILL... SECOND GUY TO TAKE THE *BLIZZARD* HANDLE...
BUT HE'S *SOFT*...
WHAM!!
GUHN--!
I KNEW IT.
YOU HAVE *NO IDEA*, MYERS...
...BUT YOU *WILL*.

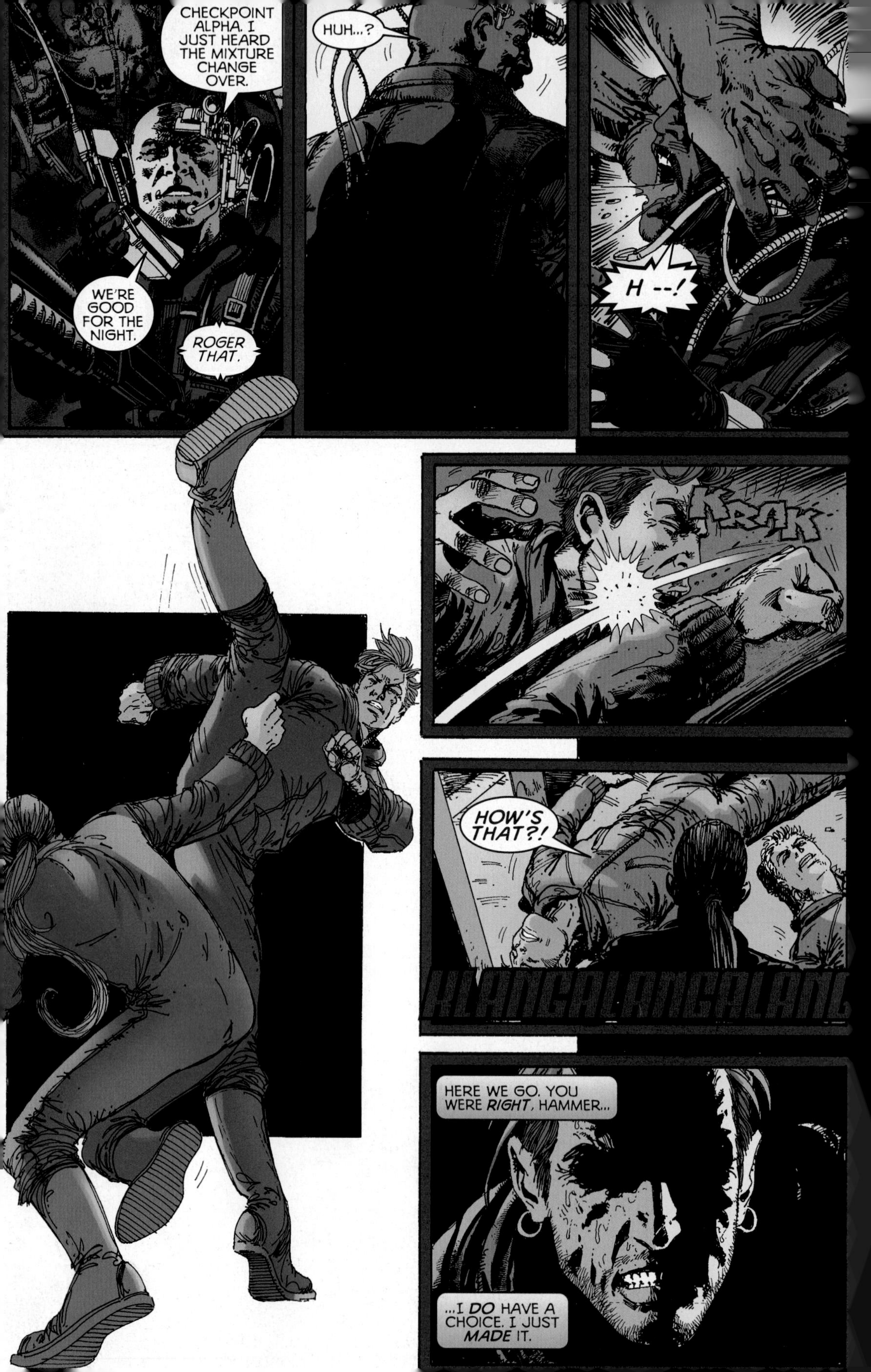

CHECKPOINT ALPHA. I JUST HEARD THE MIXTURE CHANGE OVER.
WE'RE GOOD FOR THE NIGHT.
ROGER THAT.
HUH...?
H --!
KRAK
HOW'S THAT?!
KLANGALANGALANG
HERE WE GO. YOU WERE RIGHT, HAMMER...
...I DO HAVE A CHOICE. I JUST MADE IT.

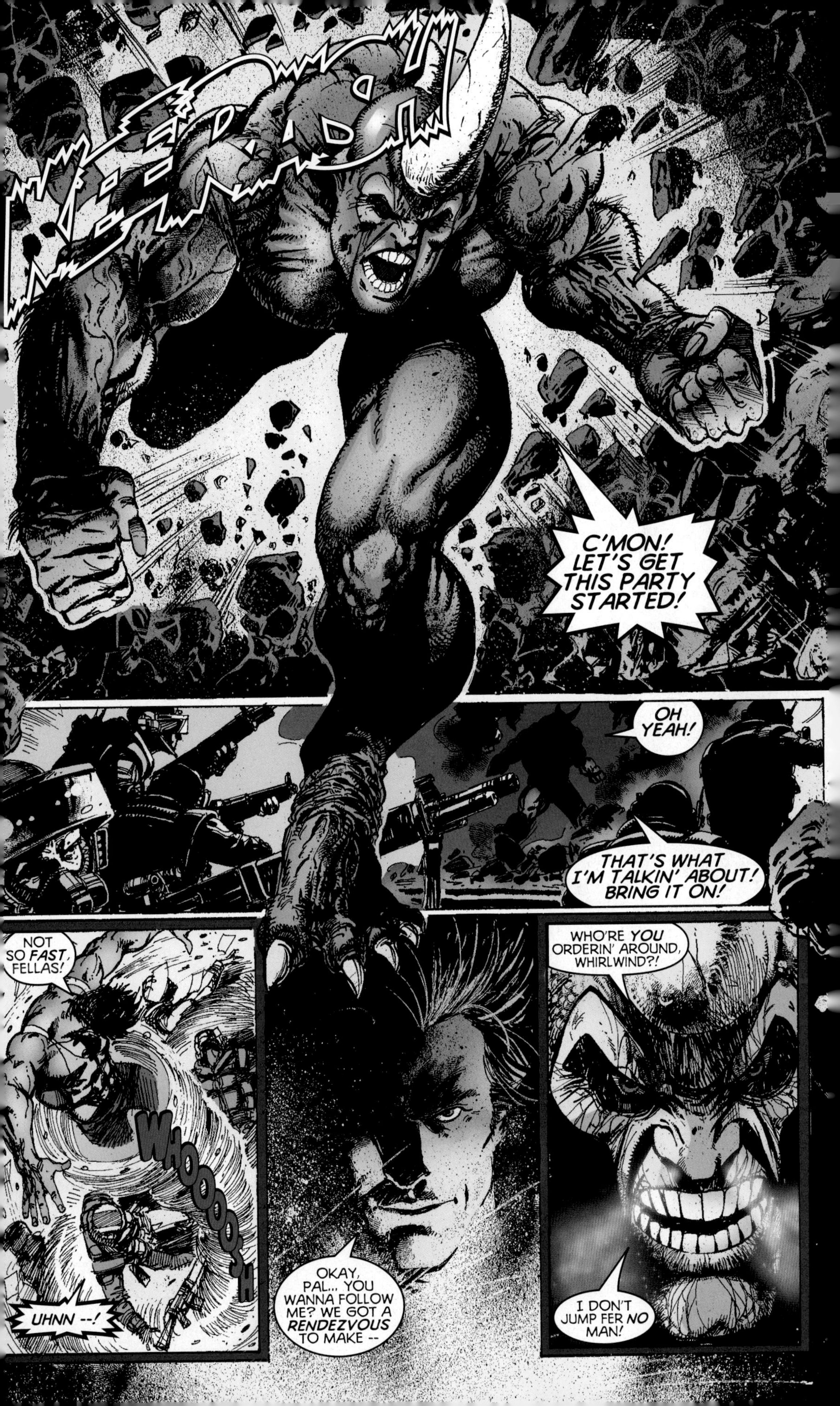
C'MON! LET'S GET THIS PARTY STARTED!
OH YEAH!
THAT'S WHAT I'M TALKIN' ABOUT! BRING IT ON!
NOT SO *FAST*, FELLAS!
WHOOOOSH
UHNN --!
OKAY, PAL... YOU WANNA FOLLOW ME? WE GOT A *RENDEZVOUS* TO MAKE --
WHO'RE *YOU* ORDERIN' AROUND, WHIRLWIND?!
I DON'T JUMP FER *NO* MAN!

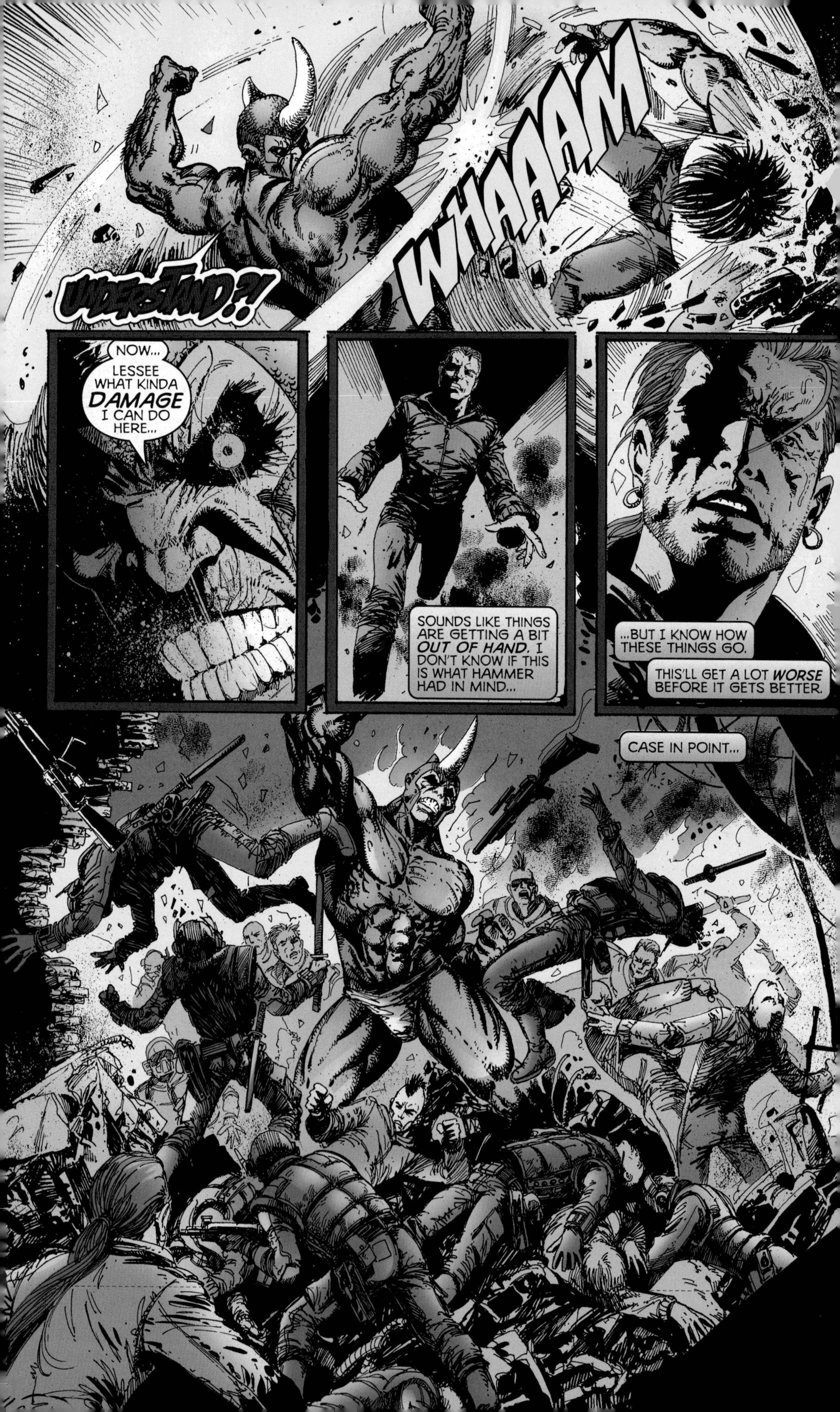
UNDERSTAND?!
WHAAAAM
NOW... LESSEE WHAT KINDA DAMAGE I CAN DO HERE...
SOUNDS LIKE THINGS ARE GETTING A BIT OUT OF HAND. I DON'T KNOW IF THIS IS WHAT HAMMER HAD IN MIND...
...BUT I KNOW HOW THESE THINGS GO.
THIS'LL GET A LOT WORSE BEFORE IT GETS BETTER.
CASE IN POINT...

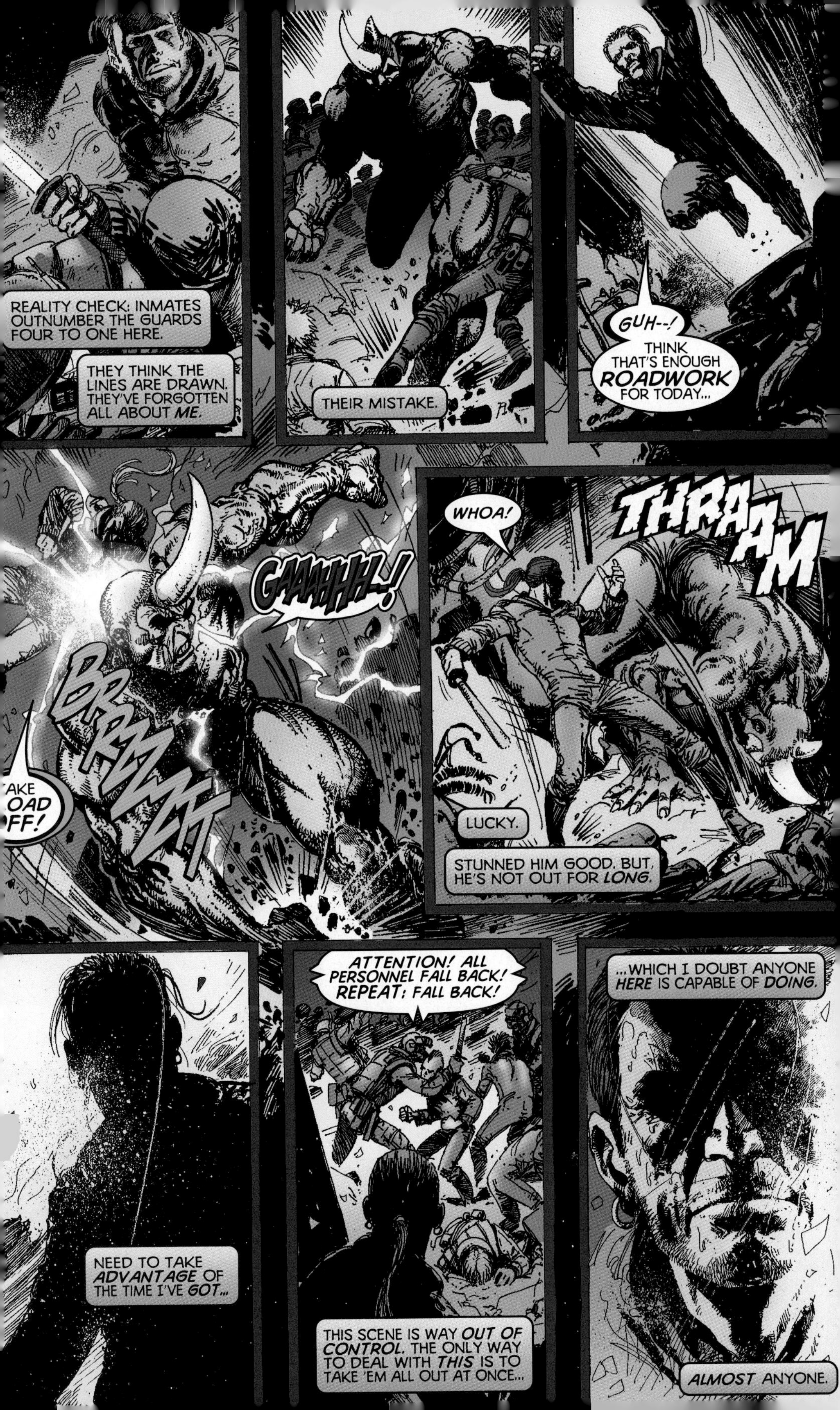

REALITY CHECK: INMATES OUTNUMBER THE GUARDS FOUR TO ONE HERE.
THEY THINK THE LINES ARE DRAWN. THEY'VE FORGOTTEN ALL ABOUT *ME.*
THEIR MISTAKE.
GUH--!
THINK THAT'S ENOUGH **ROADWORK** FOR TODAY...
GAAAHHH--!
BRRMMK
AKE OAD FF!
WHOA!
THRAAAM
LUCKY.
STUNNED HIM GOOD. BUT, HE'S NOT OUT FOR *LONG.*
NEED TO TAKE *ADVANTAGE* OF THE TIME I'VE *GOT...*
ATTENTION! ALL PERSONNEL FALL BACK! REPEAT: FALL BACK!
THIS SCENE IS WAY *OUT OF CONTROL.* THE ONLY WAY TO DEAL WITH *THIS* IS TO TAKE 'EM ALL OUT AT ONCE...
...WHICH I DOUBT ANYONE *HERE* IS CAPABLE OF *DOING.*
ALMOST ANYONE.

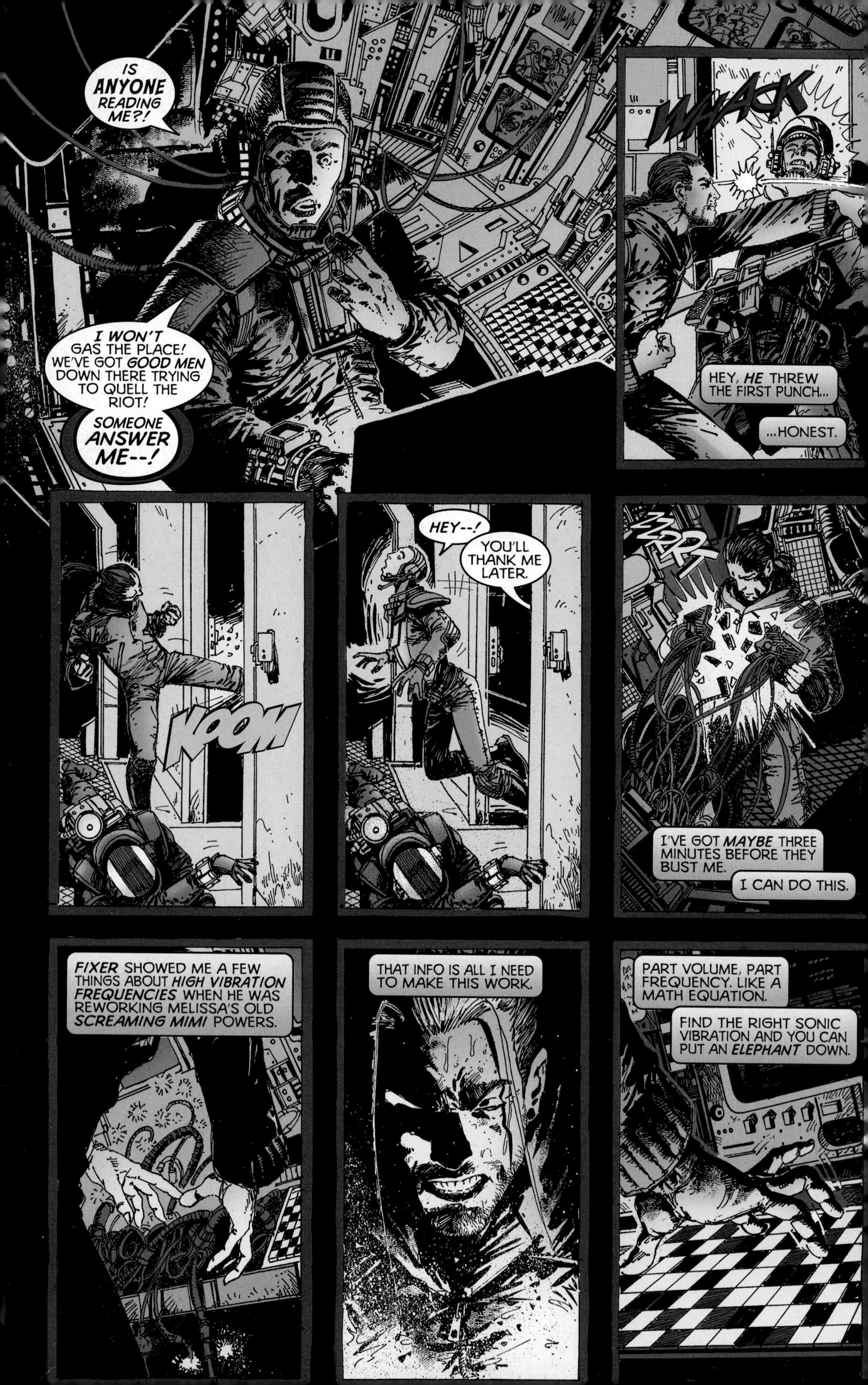
IS ANYONE READING ME?!
I WON'T GAS THE PLACE! WE'VE GOT GOOD MEN DOWN THERE TRYING TO QUELL THE RIOT!
SOMEONE ANSWER ME--!
WHACK
HEY, HE THREW THE FIRST PUNCH...
...HONEST.
KOOM
HEY--!
YOU'LL THANK ME LATER.
I'VE GOT MAYBE THREE MINUTES BEFORE THEY BUST ME.
I CAN DO THIS.
FIXER SHOWED ME A FEW THINGS ABOUT HIGH VIBRATION FREQUENCIES WHEN HE WAS REWORKING MELISSA'S OLD SCREAMING MIMI POWERS.
THAT INFO IS ALL I NEED TO MAKE THIS WORK.
PART VOLUME, PART FREQUENCY. LIKE A MATH EQUATION.
FIND THE RIGHT SONIC VIBRATION AND YOU CAN PUT AN ELEPHANT DOWN.

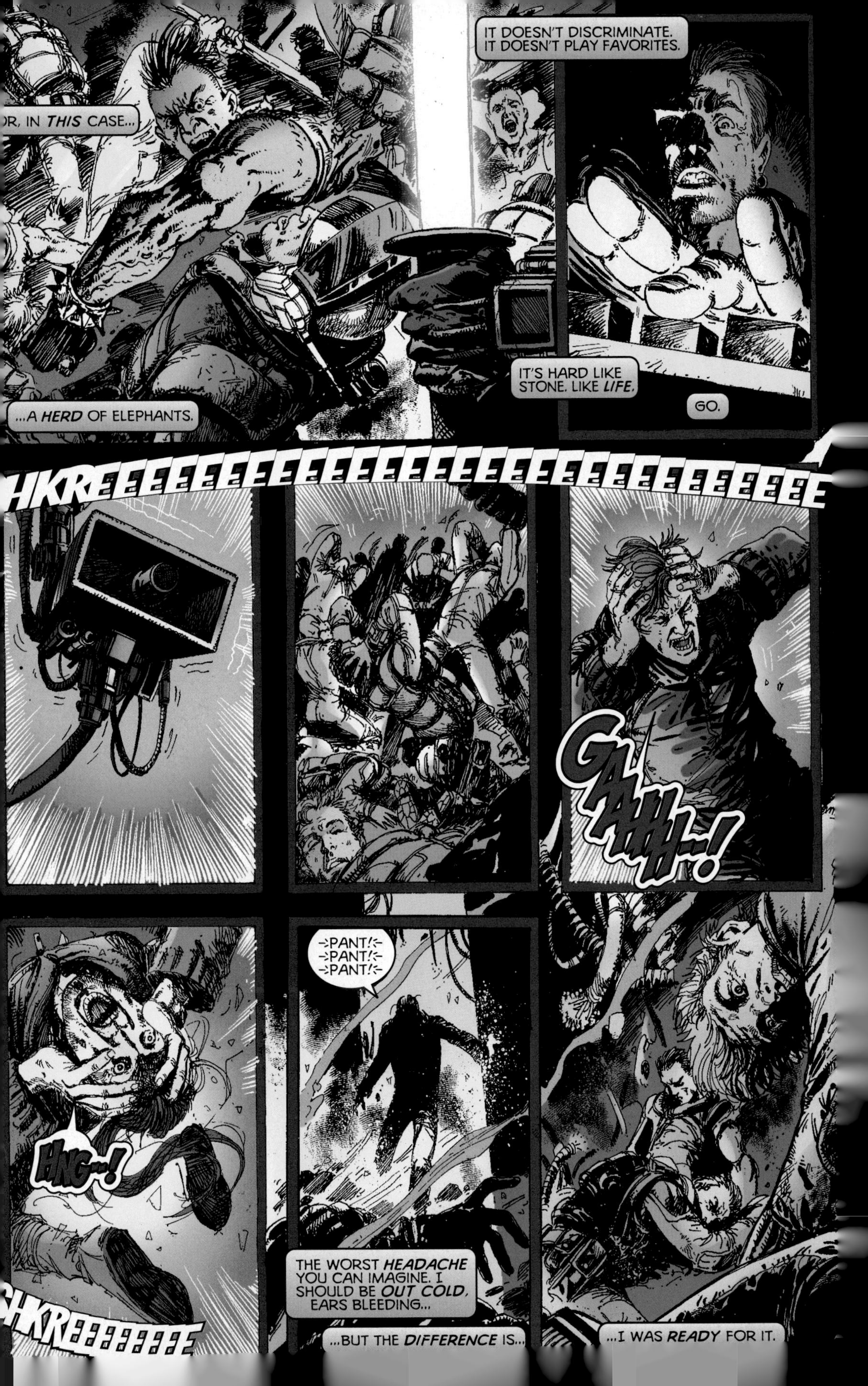
OR, IN THIS CASE...
...A HERD OF ELEPHANTS.
IT DOESN'T DISCRIMINATE. IT DOESN'T PLAY FAVORITES.
IT'S HARD LIKE STONE. LIKE LIFE.
GO.
HKREEEEEEEEEEEEEEEEEEEEEEEEEEEEE
GAAHH--!
HNG--!
SHKREEEEEEEEEE
-PANT!- -PANT!- -PANT!-
THE WORST HEADACHE YOU CAN IMAGINE. I SHOULD BE OUT COLD, EARS BLEEDING...
...BUT THE DIFFERENCE IS...
...I WAS READY FOR IT.

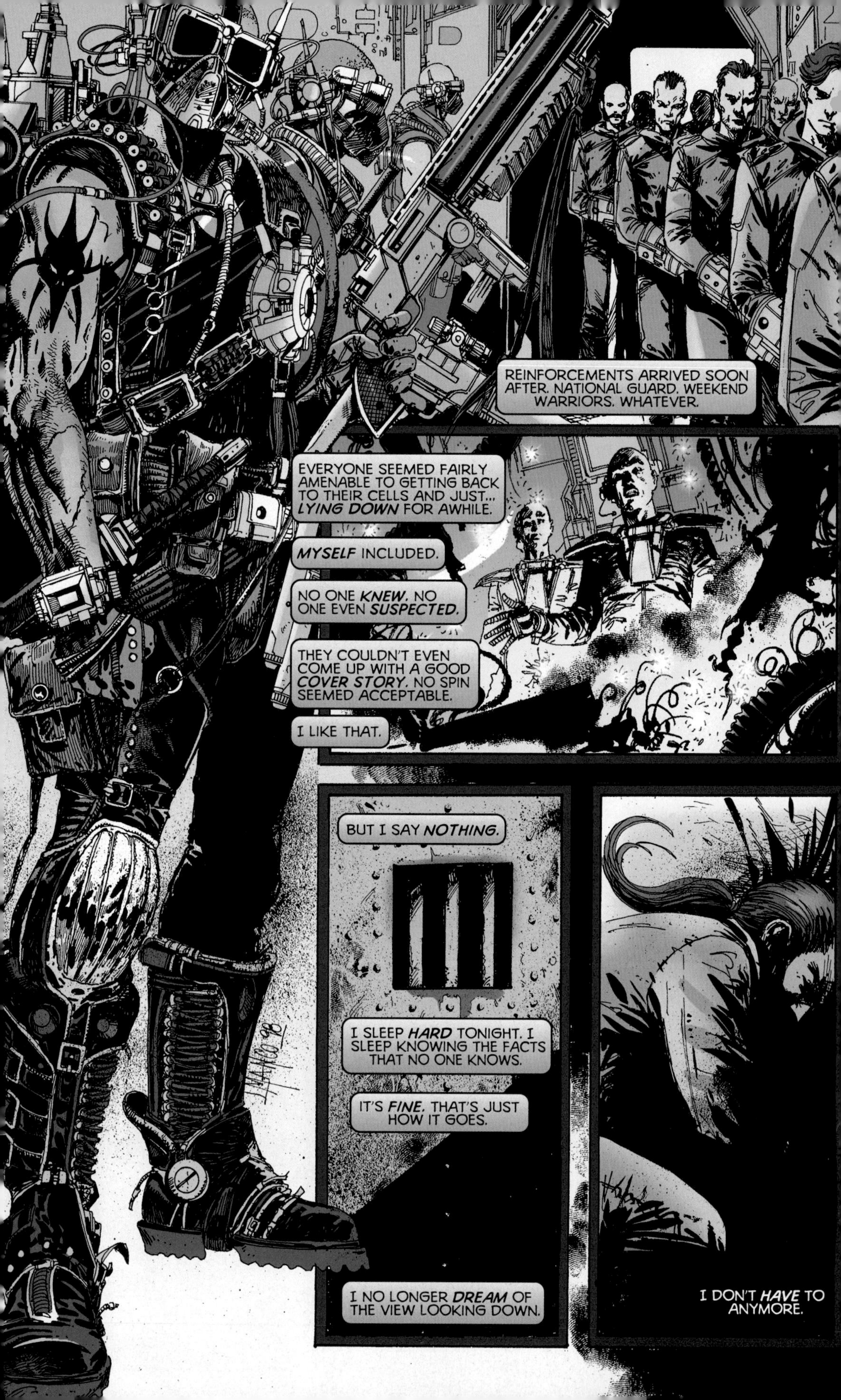
REINFORCEMENTS ARRIVED SOON AFTER. NATIONAL GUARD. WEEKEND WARRIORS. WHATEVER.
EVERYONE SEEMED FAIRLY AMENABLE TO GETTING BACK TO THEIR CELLS AND JUST... *LYING DOWN* FOR AWHILE.
MYSELF INCLUDED.
NO ONE *KNEW.* NO ONE EVEN *SUSPECTED.*
THEY COULDN'T EVEN COME UP WITH A GOOD *COVER STORY.* NO SPIN SEEMED ACCEPTABLE.
I LIKE THAT.
BUT I SAY *NOTHING.*
I SLEEP *HARD* TONIGHT. I SLEEP KNOWING THE FACTS THAT NO ONE KNOWS.
IT'S *FINE.* THAT'S JUST HOW IT GOES.
I NO LONGER *DREAM* OF THE VIEW LOOKING DOWN.
I DON'T *HAVE* TO ANYMORE.

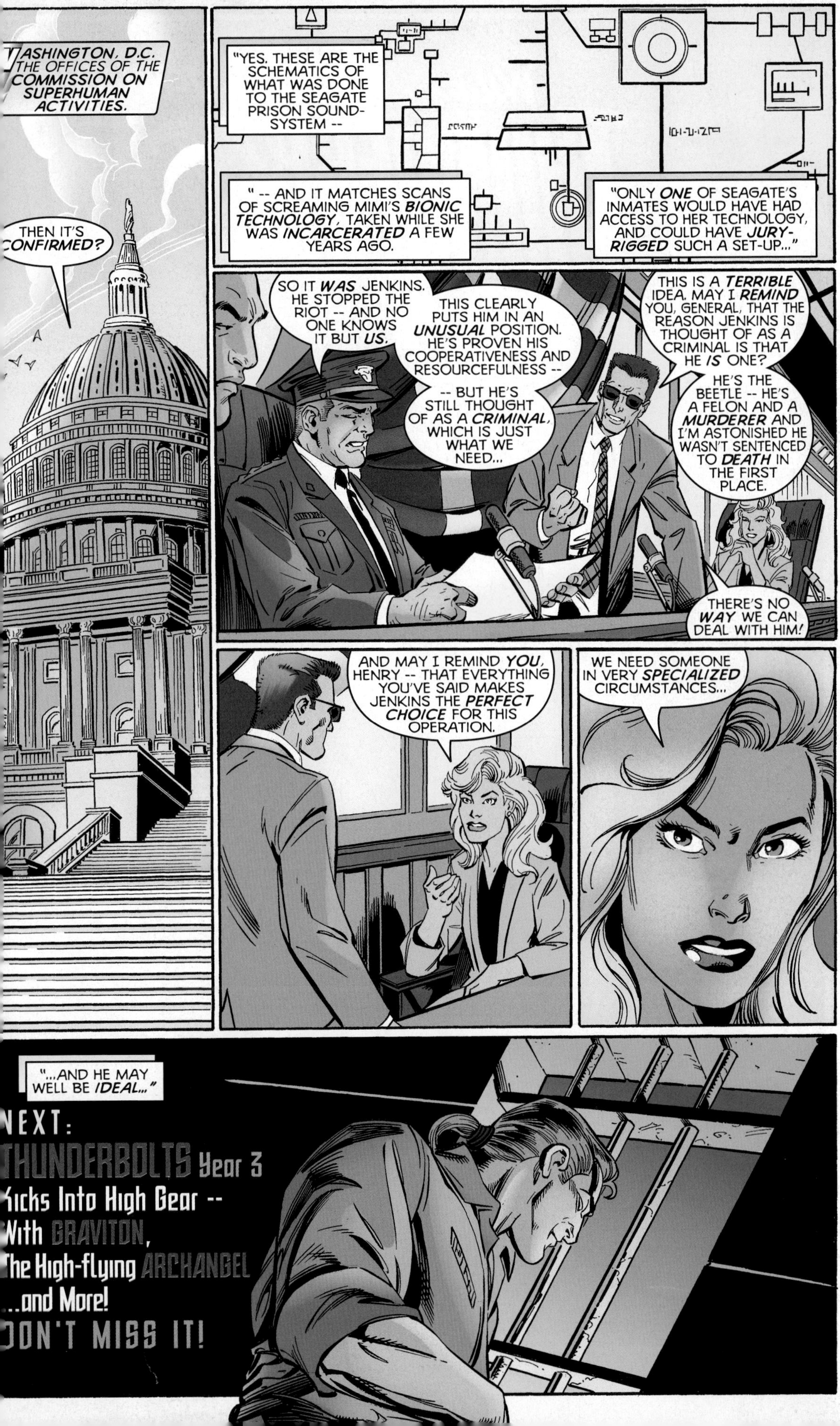

WASHINGTON, D.C. THE OFFICES OF THE COMMISSION ON SUPERHUMAN ACTIVITIES.
THEN IT'S CONFIRMED?
"YES. THESE ARE THE SCHEMATICS OF WHAT WAS DONE TO THE SEAGATE PRISON SOUND-SYSTEM --
" -- AND IT MATCHES SCANS OF SCREAMING MIMI'S BIONIC TECHNOLOGY, TAKEN WHILE SHE WAS INCARCERATED A FEW YEARS AGO.
"ONLY ONE OF SEAGATE'S INMATES WOULD HAVE HAD ACCESS TO HER TECHNOLOGY, AND COULD HAVE JURY-RIGGED SUCH A SET-UP..."
SO IT WAS JENKINS. HE STOPPED THE RIOT -- AND NO ONE KNOWS IT BUT US.
THIS CLEARLY PUTS HIM IN AN UNUSUAL POSITION. HE'S PROVEN HIS COOPERATIVENESS AND RESOURCEFULNESS --
-- BUT HE'S STILL THOUGHT OF AS A CRIMINAL, WHICH IS JUST WHAT WE NEED...
THIS IS A TERRIBLE IDEA. MAY I REMIND YOU, GENERAL, THAT THE REASON JENKINS IS THOUGHT OF AS A CRIMINAL IS THAT HE IS ONE?
HE'S THE BEETLE -- HE'S A FELON AND A MURDERER AND I'M ASTONISHED HE WASN'T SENTENCED TO DEATH IN THE FIRST PLACE.
THERE'S NO WAY WE CAN DEAL WITH HIM!
AND MAY I REMIND YOU, HENRY -- THAT EVERYTHING YOU'VE SAID MAKES JENKINS THE PERFECT CHOICE FOR THIS OPERATION.
WE NEED SOMEONE IN VERY SPECIALIZED CIRCUMSTANCES...
"...AND HE MAY WELL BE IDEAL..."
NEXT:
THUNDERBOLTS Year 3
Kicks Into High Gear --
With GRAVITON,
The High-flying ARCHANGEL
...and More!
DON'T MISS IT!

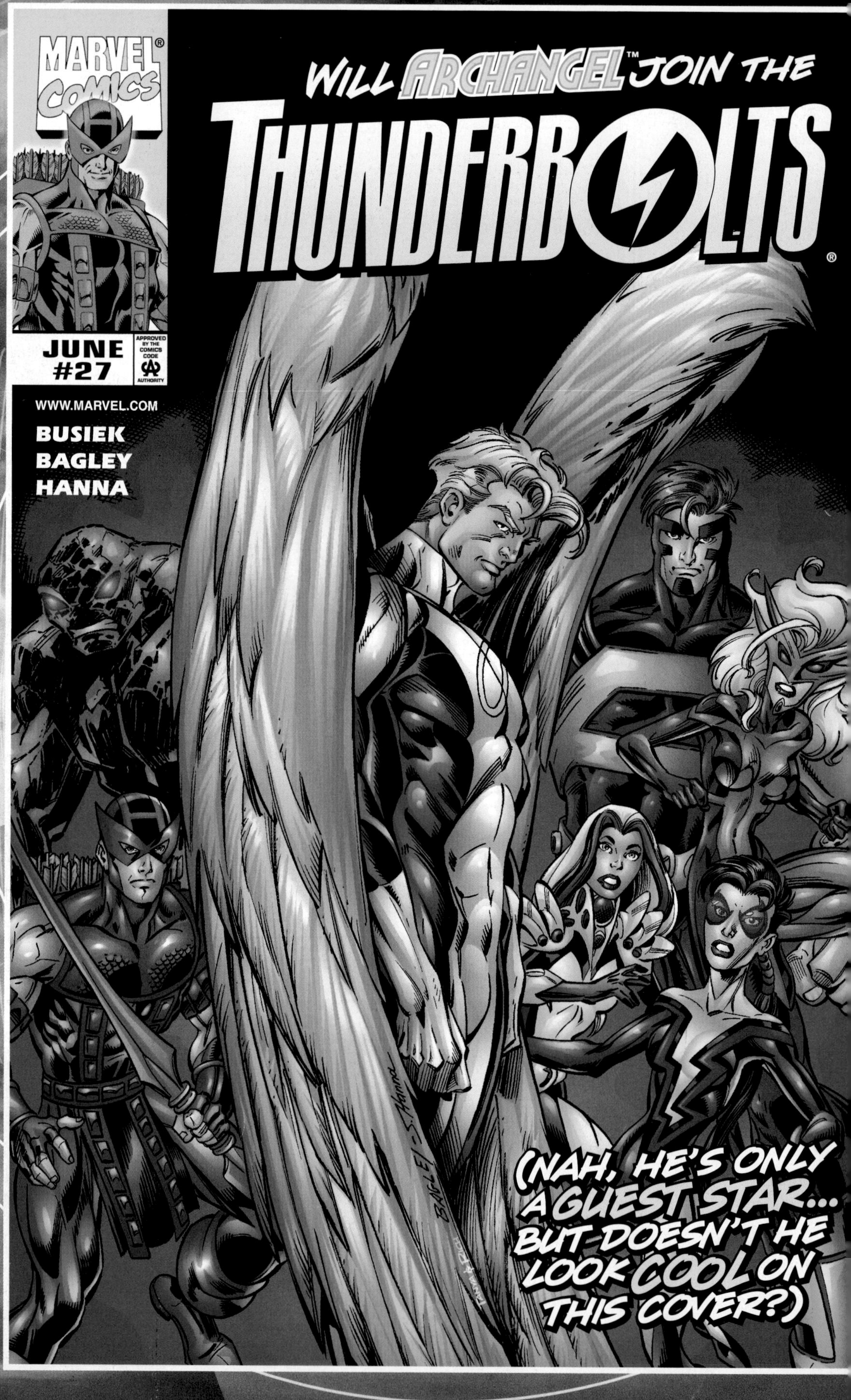
MARVEL® COMICS
WILL ARCHANGEL™ JOIN THE
THUNDERBOLTS®
JUNE #27
APPROVED BY THE COMICS CODE AUTHORITY
WWW.MARVEL.COM
BUSIEK
BAGLEY
HANNA
(NAH, HE'S ONLY A GUEST STAR... BUT DOESN'T HE LOOK COOL ON THIS COVER?)

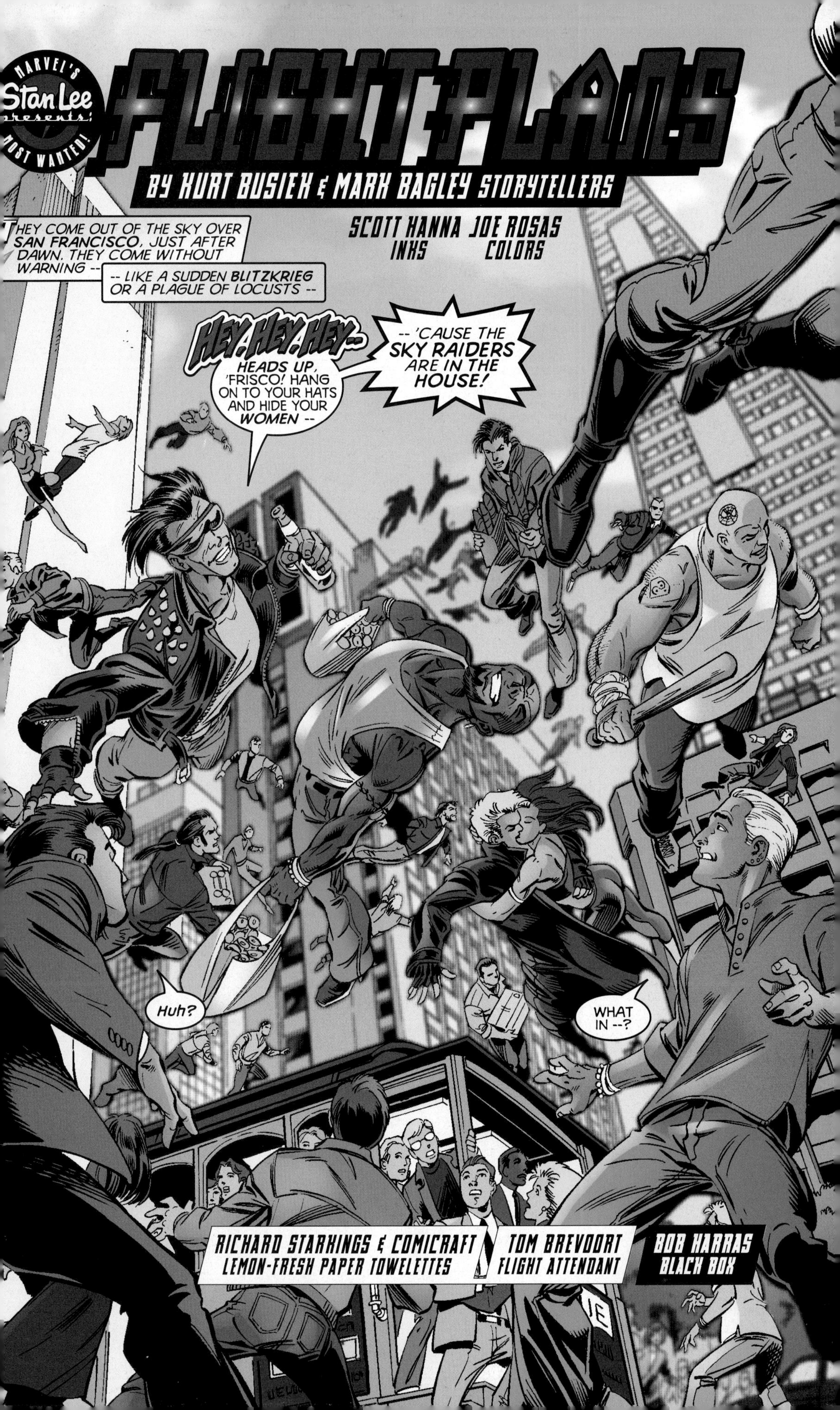
MARVEL'S Stan Lee presents: MOST WANTED!
FLIGHTPLANS
BY KURT BUSIEK & MARK BAGLEY STORYTELLERS
SCOTT HANNA INKS
JOE ROSAS COLORS
THEY COME OUT OF THE SKY OVER SAN FRANCISCO, JUST AFTER DAWN. THEY COME WITHOUT WARNING --
-- LIKE A SUDDEN BLITZKRIEG OR A PLAGUE OF LOCUSTS --
HEY. HEY. HEY--
HEADS UP, 'FRISCO! HANG ON TO YOUR HATS AND HIDE YOUR WOMEN --
-- 'CAUSE THE SKY RAIDERS ARE IN THE HOUSE!
Huh?
WHAT IN --?
RICHARD STARKINGS & COMICRAFT LEMON-FRESH PAPER TOWELETTES
TOM BREVOORT FLIGHT ATTENDANT
BOB HARRAS BLACK BOX

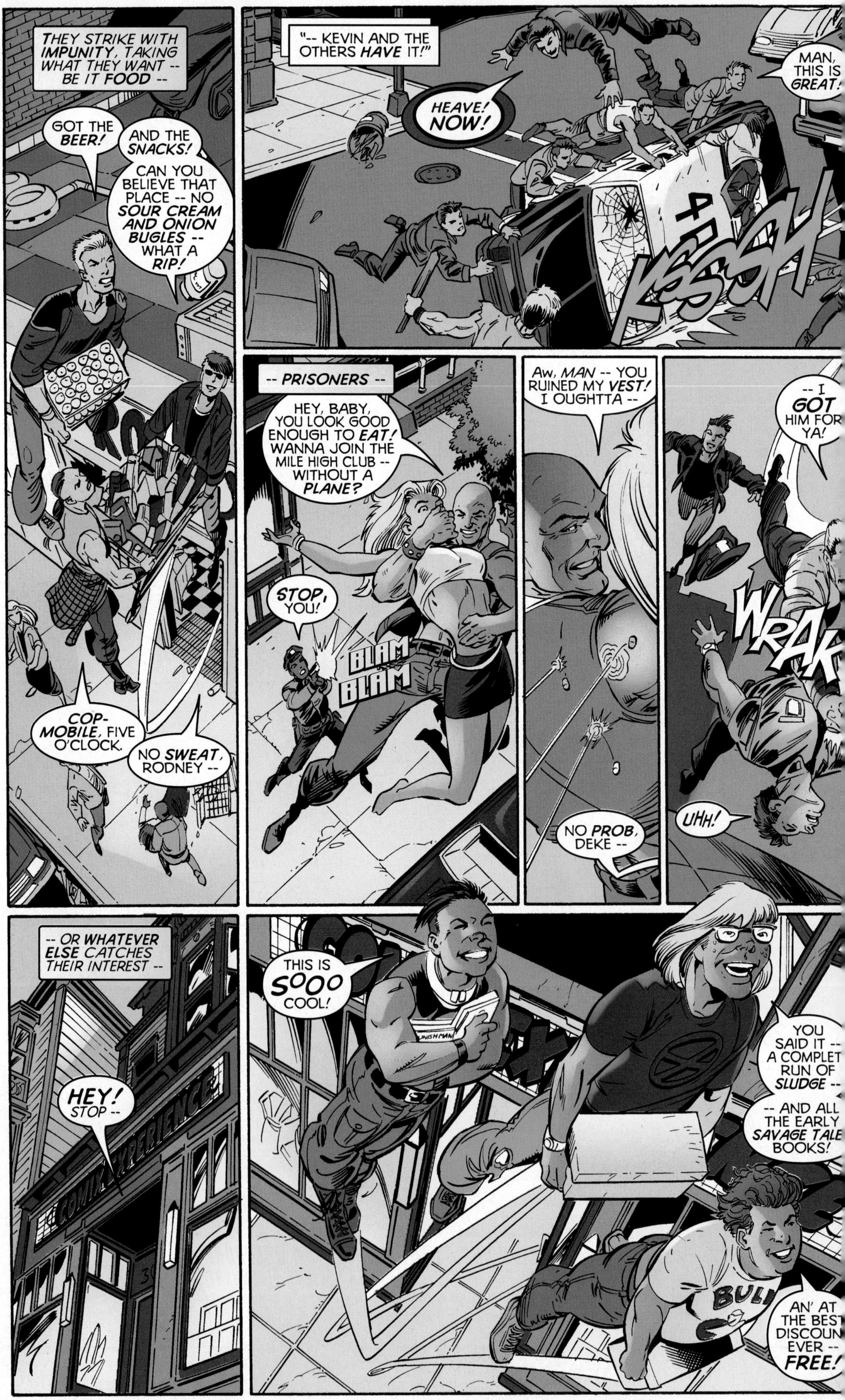
THEY STRIKE WITH IMPUNITY, TAKING WHAT THEY WANT -- BE IT FOOD --
GOT THE BEER!
AND THE SNACKS!
CAN YOU BELIEVE THAT PLACE -- NO SOUR CREAM AND ONION BUGLES -- WHAT A RIP!
COP-MOBILE, FIVE O'CLOCK.
NO SWEAT, RODNEY --
"-- KEVIN AND THE OTHERS HAVE IT!"
HEAVE! NOW!
MAN, THIS IS GREAT!
-- PRISONERS --
HEY, BABY, YOU LOOK GOOD ENOUGH TO EAT! WANNA JOIN THE MILE HIGH CLUB -- WITHOUT A PLANE?
STOP, YOU!
BLAM BLAM
AW, MAN -- YOU RUINED MY VEST! I OUGHTTA --
NO PROB, DEKE --
-- I GOT HIM FOR YA!
WRAK
UHH!
-- OR WHATEVER ELSE CATCHES THEIR INTEREST --
HEY! STOP --
COMIC EXPERIENCE
THIS IS SOOO COOL!
YOU SAID IT -- A COMPLET RUN OF SLUDGE --
-- AND ALL THE EARLY SAVAGE TALE BOOKS!
AN' AT THE BEST DISCOUN EVER -- FREE!

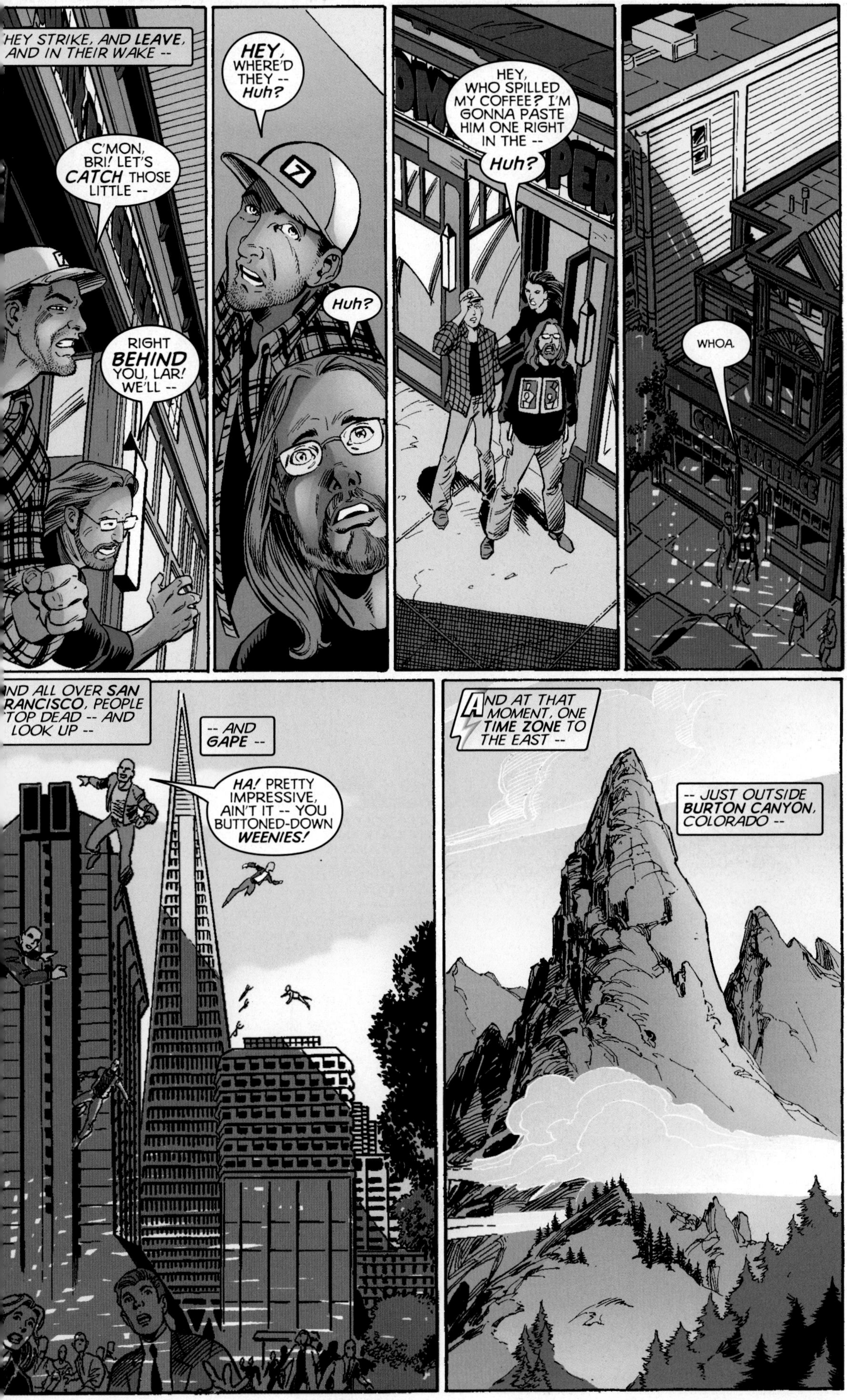

THEY STRIKE, AND LEAVE, AND IN THEIR WAKE --
C'MON, BRI! LET'S CATCH THOSE LITTLE --
RIGHT BEHIND YOU, LAR! WE'LL --
HEY, WHERE'D THEY -- Huh?
Huh?
HEY, WHO SPILLED MY COFFEE? I'M GONNA PASTE HIM ONE RIGHT IN THE --
Huh?
WHOA.
COMIC EXPERIENCE
ND ALL OVER SAN RANCISCO, PEOPLE TOP DEAD -- AND LOOK UP --
-- AND GAPE --
HA! PRETTY IMPRESSIVE, AIN'T IT -- YOU BUTTONED-DOWN WEENIES!
AND AT THAT MOMENT, ONE TIME ZONE TO THE EAST --
-- JUST OUTSIDE BURTON CANYON, COLORADO --

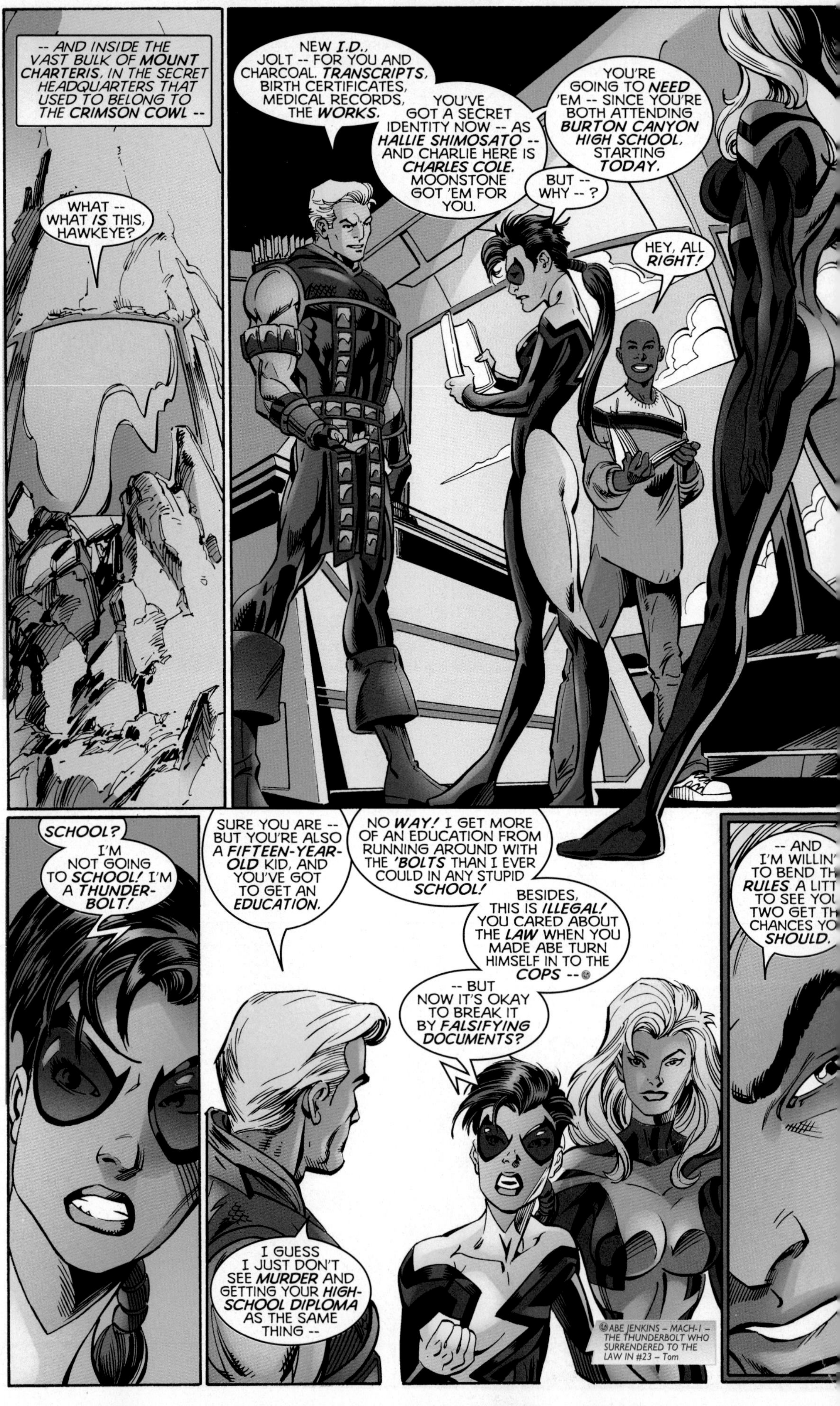
-- AND INSIDE THE VAST BULK OF MOUNT CHARTERIS, IN THE SECRET HEADQUARTERS THAT USED TO BELONG TO THE CRIMSON COWL --
WHAT -- WHAT IS THIS, HAWKEYE?
NEW I.D., JOLT -- FOR YOU AND CHARCOAL. TRANSCRIPTS, BIRTH CERTIFICATES, MEDICAL RECORDS, THE WORKS.
YOU'VE GOT A SECRET IDENTITY NOW -- AS HALLIE SHIMOSATO -- AND CHARLIE HERE IS CHARLES COLE. MOONSTONE GOT 'EM FOR YOU.
BUT -- WHY -- ?
YOU'RE GOING TO NEED 'EM -- SINCE YOU'RE BOTH ATTENDING BURTON CANYON HIGH SCHOOL, STARTING TODAY.
HEY, ALL RIGHT!
SCHOOL? I'M NOT GOING TO SCHOOL! I'M A THUNDER-BOLT!
SURE YOU ARE -- BUT YOU'RE ALSO A FIFTEEN-YEAR-OLD KID, AND YOU'VE GOT TO GET AN EDUCATION.
NO WAY! I GET MORE OF AN EDUCATION FROM RUNNING AROUND WITH THE 'BOLTS THAN I EVER COULD IN ANY STUPID SCHOOL!
BESIDES, THIS IS ILLEGAL! YOU CARED ABOUT THE LAW WHEN YOU MADE ABE TURN HIMSELF IN TO THE COPS --
-- BUT NOW IT'S OKAY TO BREAK IT BY FALSIFYING DOCUMENTS?
I GUESS I JUST DON'T SEE MURDER AND GETTING YOUR HIGH-SCHOOL DIPLOMA AS THE SAME THING --
ABE JENKINS – MACH-I – THE THUNDERBOLT WHO SURRENDERED TO THE LAW IN #23 – Tom
-- AND I'M WILLIN' TO BEND TH RULES A LITT TO SEE YOU TWO GET TH CHANCES YO SHOULD.

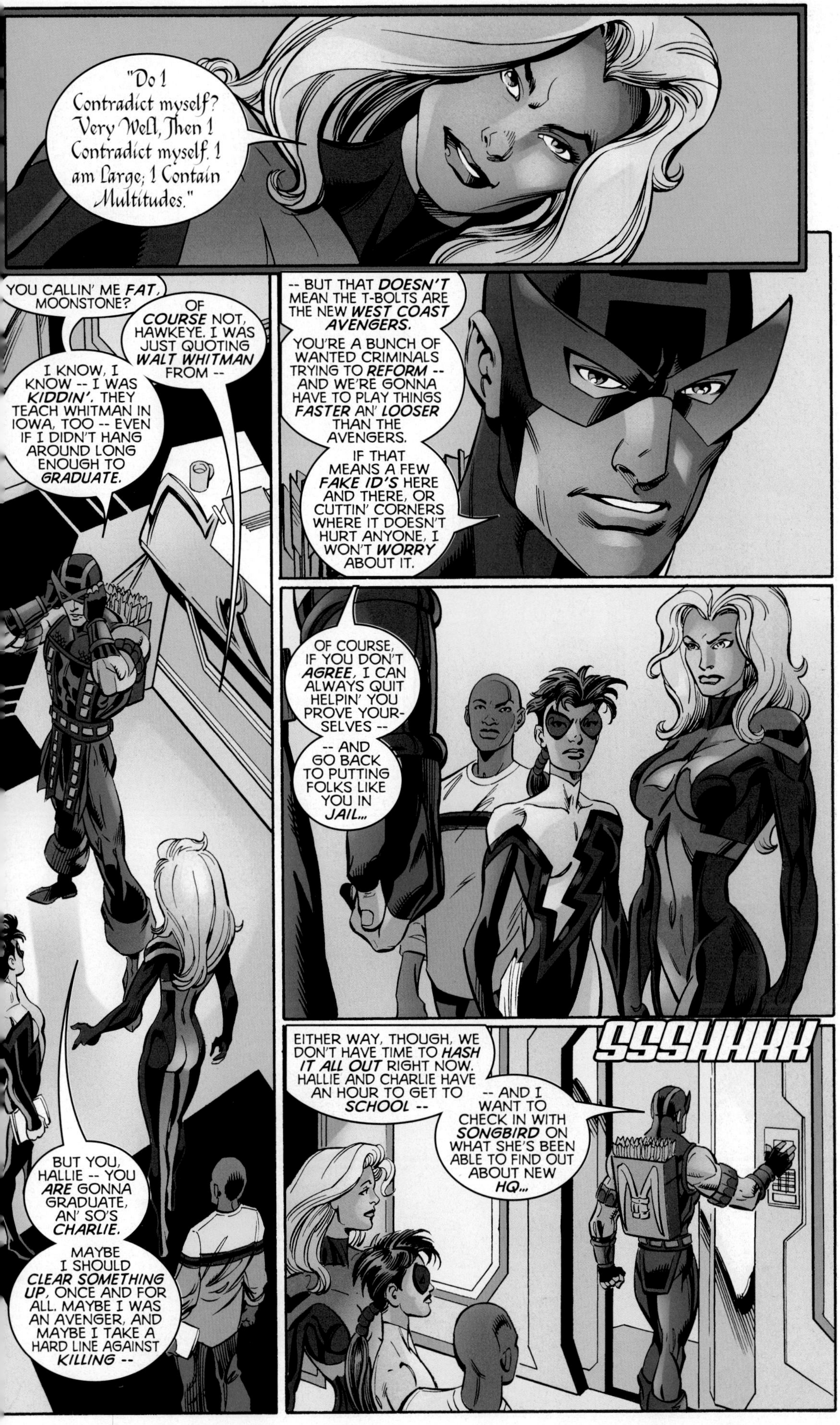
"Do I Contradict myself? Very Well, Then I Contradict myself. I am Large; I Contain Multitudes."
YOU CALLIN' ME FAT, MOONSTONE?
OF COURSE NOT, HAWKEYE. I WAS JUST QUOTING WALT WHITMAN FROM --
I KNOW, I KNOW -- I WAS KIDDIN'. THEY TEACH WHITMAN IN IOWA, TOO -- EVEN IF I DIDN'T HANG AROUND LONG ENOUGH TO GRADUATE.
BUT YOU, HALLIE -- YOU ARE GONNA GRADUATE, AN' SO'S CHARLIE.
MAYBE I SHOULD CLEAR SOMETHING UP, ONCE AND FOR ALL. MAYBE I WAS AN AVENGER, AND MAYBE I TAKE A HARD LINE AGAINST KILLING --
-- BUT THAT DOESN'T MEAN THE T-BOLTS ARE THE NEW WEST COAST AVENGERS.
YOU'RE A BUNCH OF WANTED CRIMINALS TRYING TO REFORM -- AND WE'RE GONNA HAVE TO PLAY THINGS FASTER AN' LOOSER THAN THE AVENGERS.
IF THAT MEANS A FEW FAKE ID'S HERE AND THERE, OR CUTTIN' CORNERS WHERE IT DOESN'T HURT ANYONE, I WON'T WORRY ABOUT IT.
OF COURSE, IF YOU DON'T AGREE, I CAN ALWAYS QUIT HELPIN' YOU PROVE YOURSELVES --
-- AND GO BACK TO PUTTING FOLKS LIKE YOU IN JAIL...
SSSHHKK
EITHER WAY, THOUGH, WE DON'T HAVE TIME TO HASH IT ALL OUT RIGHT NOW. HALLIE AND CHARLIE HAVE AN HOUR TO GET TO SCHOOL --
-- AND I WANT TO CHECK IN WITH SONGBIRD ON WHAT SHE'S BEEN ABLE TO FIND OUT ABOUT NEW HQ...

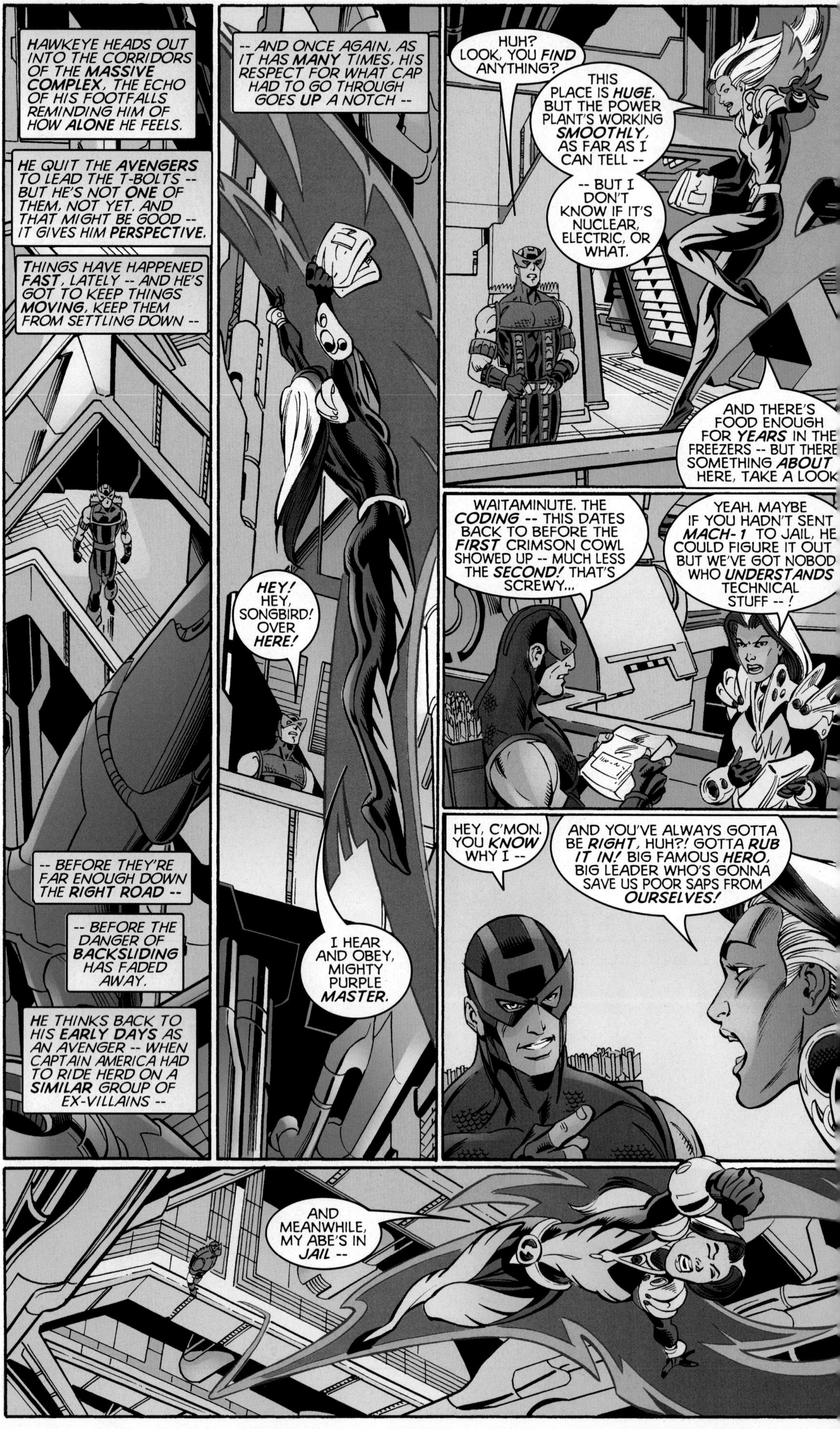
HAWKEYE HEADS OUT INTO THE CORRIDORS OF THE MASSIVE COMPLEX, THE ECHO OF HIS FOOTFALLS REMINDING HIM OF HOW ALONE HE FEELS.
HE QUIT THE AVENGERS TO LEAD THE T-BOLTS -- BUT HE'S NOT ONE OF THEM, NOT YET. AND THAT MIGHT BE GOOD -- IT GIVES HIM PERSPECTIVE.
THINGS HAVE HAPPENED FAST, LATELY -- AND HE'S GOT TO KEEP THINGS MOVING, KEEP THEM FROM SETTLING DOWN --
-- BEFORE THEY'RE FAR ENOUGH DOWN THE RIGHT ROAD --
-- BEFORE THE DANGER OF BACKSLIDING HAS FADED AWAY.
HE THINKS BACK TO HIS EARLY DAYS AS AN AVENGER -- WHEN CAPTAIN AMERICA HAD TO RIDE HERD ON A SIMILAR GROUP OF EX-VILLAINS --
-- AND ONCE AGAIN, AS IT HAS MANY TIMES, HIS RESPECT FOR WHAT CAP HAD TO GO THROUGH GOES UP A NOTCH --
HEY! HEY, SONGBIRD! OVER HERE!
I HEAR AND OBEY, MIGHTY PURPLE MASTER.
HUH? LOOK, YOU FIND ANYTHING?
THIS PLACE IS HUGE, BUT THE POWER PLANT'S WORKING SMOOTHLY, AS FAR AS I CAN TELL --
-- BUT I DON'T KNOW IF IT'S NUCLEAR, ELECTRIC, OR WHAT.
AND THERE'S FOOD ENOUGH FOR YEARS IN THE FREEZERS -- BUT THERE SOMETHING ABOUT HERE, TAKE A LOOK
WAITAMINUTE. THE CODING -- THIS DATES BACK TO BEFORE THE FIRST CRIMSON COWL SHOWED UP -- MUCH LESS THE SECOND! THAT'S SCREWY...
YEAH. MAYBE IF YOU HADN'T SENT MACH-1 TO JAIL, HE COULD FIGURE IT OUT BUT WE'VE GOT NOBOD WHO UNDERSTANDS TECHNICAL STUFF -- !
HEY, C'MON. YOU KNOW WHY I --
AND YOU'VE ALWAYS GOTTA BE RIGHT, HUH?! GOTTA RUB IT IN! BIG FAMOUS HERO, BIG LEADER WHO'S GONNA SAVE US POOR SAPS FROM OURSELVES!
AND MEANWHILE, MY ABE'S IN JAIL --

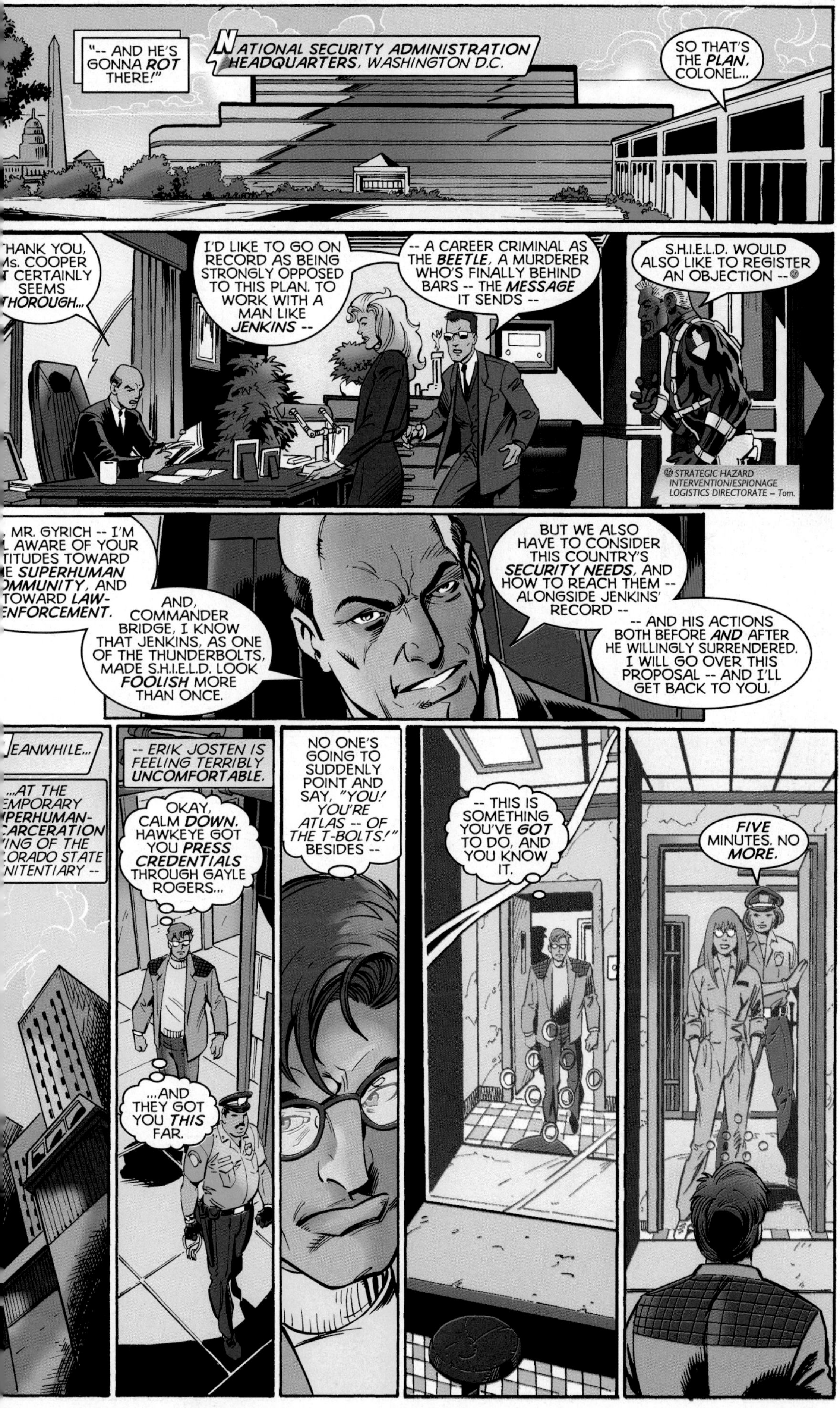
"-- AND HE'S GONNA ROT THERE!"
NATIONAL SECURITY ADMINISTRATION HEADQUARTERS, WASHINGTON D.C.
SO THAT'S THE PLAN, COLONEL...
HANK YOU, Ms. COOPER T CERTAINLY SEEMS THOROUGH...
I'D LIKE TO GO ON RECORD AS BEING STRONGLY OPPOSED TO THIS PLAN. TO WORK WITH A MAN LIKE JENKINS --
-- A CAREER CRIMINAL AS THE BEETLE, A MURDERER WHO'S FINALLY BEHIND BARS -- THE MESSAGE IT SENDS --
S.H.I.E.L.D. WOULD ALSO LIKE TO REGISTER AN OBJECTION --
STRATEGIC HAZARD INTERVENTION/ESPIONAGE LOGISTICS DIRECTORATE – Tom.
MR. GYRICH -- I'M AWARE OF YOUR TITUDES TOWARD E SUPERHUMAN MMUNITY, AND TOWARD LAW-ENFORCEMENT.
AND, COMMANDER BRIDGE, I KNOW THAT JENKINS, AS ONE OF THE THUNDERBOLTS, MADE S.H.I.E.L.D. LOOK FOOLISH MORE THAN ONCE.
BUT WE ALSO HAVE TO CONSIDER THIS COUNTRY'S SECURITY NEEDS, AND HOW TO REACH THEM -- ALONGSIDE JENKINS' RECORD --
-- AND HIS ACTIONS BOTH BEFORE AND AFTER HE WILLINGLY SURRENDERED. I WILL GO OVER THIS PROPOSAL -- AND I'LL GET BACK TO YOU.
EANWHILE...
...AT THE EMPORARY UPERHUMAN-CARCERATION ING OF THE ORADO STATE NITENTIARY --
-- ERIK JOSTEN IS FEELING TERRIBLY UNCOMFORTABLE.
OKAY, CALM DOWN. HAWKEYE GOT YOU PRESS CREDENTIALS THROUGH GAYLE ROGERS...
...AND THEY GOT YOU THIS FAR.
NO ONE'S GOING TO SUDDENLY POINT AND SAY, "YOU! YOU'RE ATLAS -- OF THE T-BOLTS!" BESIDES --
-- THIS IS SOMETHING YOU'VE GOT TO DO, AND YOU KNOW IT.
FIVE MINUTES. NO MORE.

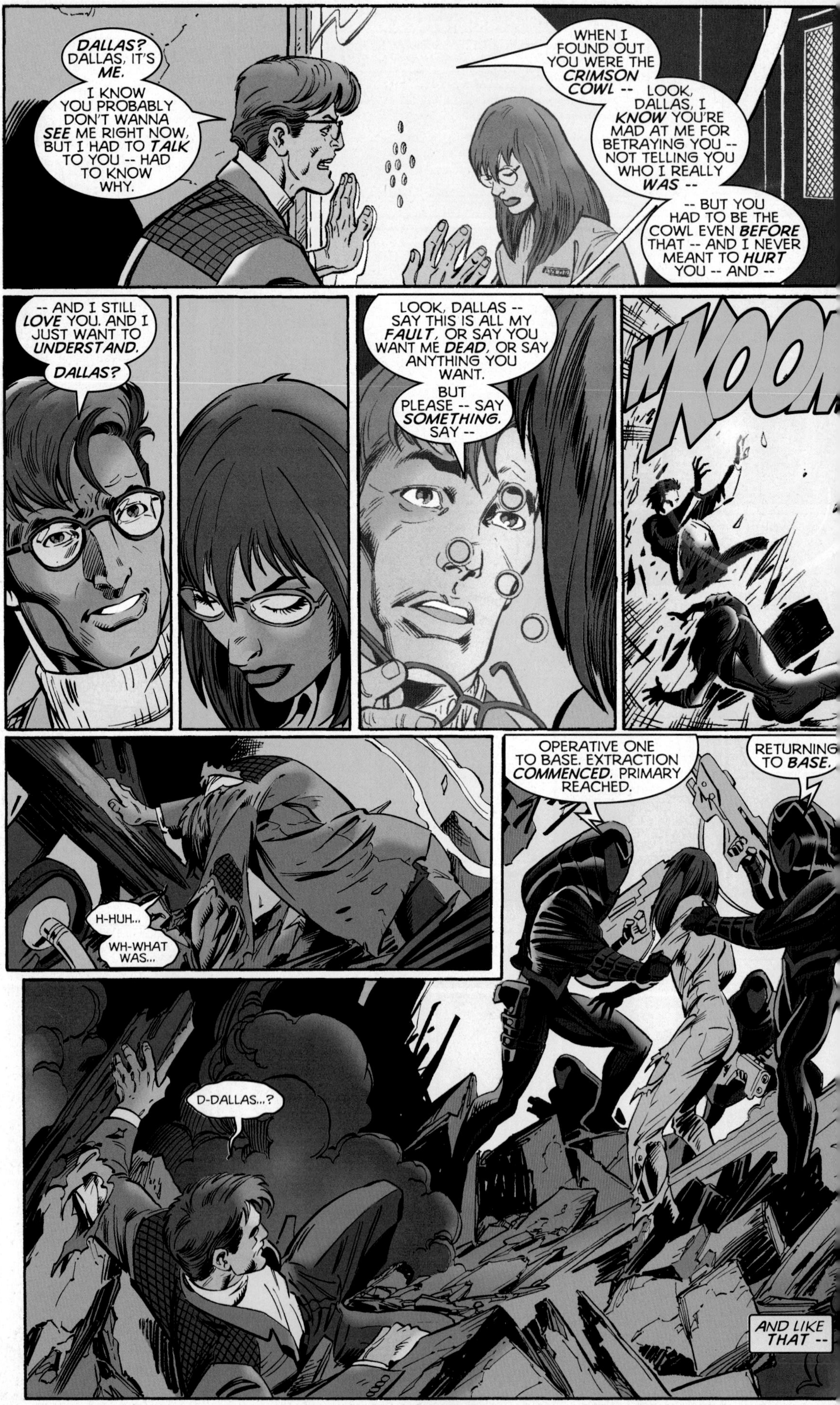
DALLAS? DALLAS, IT'S ME.
I KNOW YOU PROBABLY DON'T WANNA SEE ME RIGHT NOW, BUT I HAD TO TALK TO YOU -- HAD TO KNOW WHY.
WHEN I FOUND OUT YOU WERE THE CRIMSON COWL --
LOOK, DALLAS, I KNOW YOU'RE MAD AT ME FOR BETRAYING YOU -- NOT TELLING YOU WHO I REALLY WAS --
-- BUT YOU HAD TO BE THE COWL EVEN BEFORE THAT -- AND I NEVER MEANT TO HURT YOU -- AND --
-- AND I STILL LOVE YOU. AND I JUST WANT TO UNDERSTAND.
DALLAS?
LOOK, DALLAS -- SAY THIS IS ALL MY FAULT, OR SAY YOU WANT ME DEAD, OR SAY ANYTHING YOU WANT.
BUT PLEASE -- SAY SOMETHING. SAY --
WKOOM
H-HUH...
WH-WHAT WAS...
OPERATIVE ONE TO BASE. EXTRACTION COMMENCED. PRIMARY REACHED.
RETURNING TO BASE.
D-DALLAS...?
AND LIKE THAT --

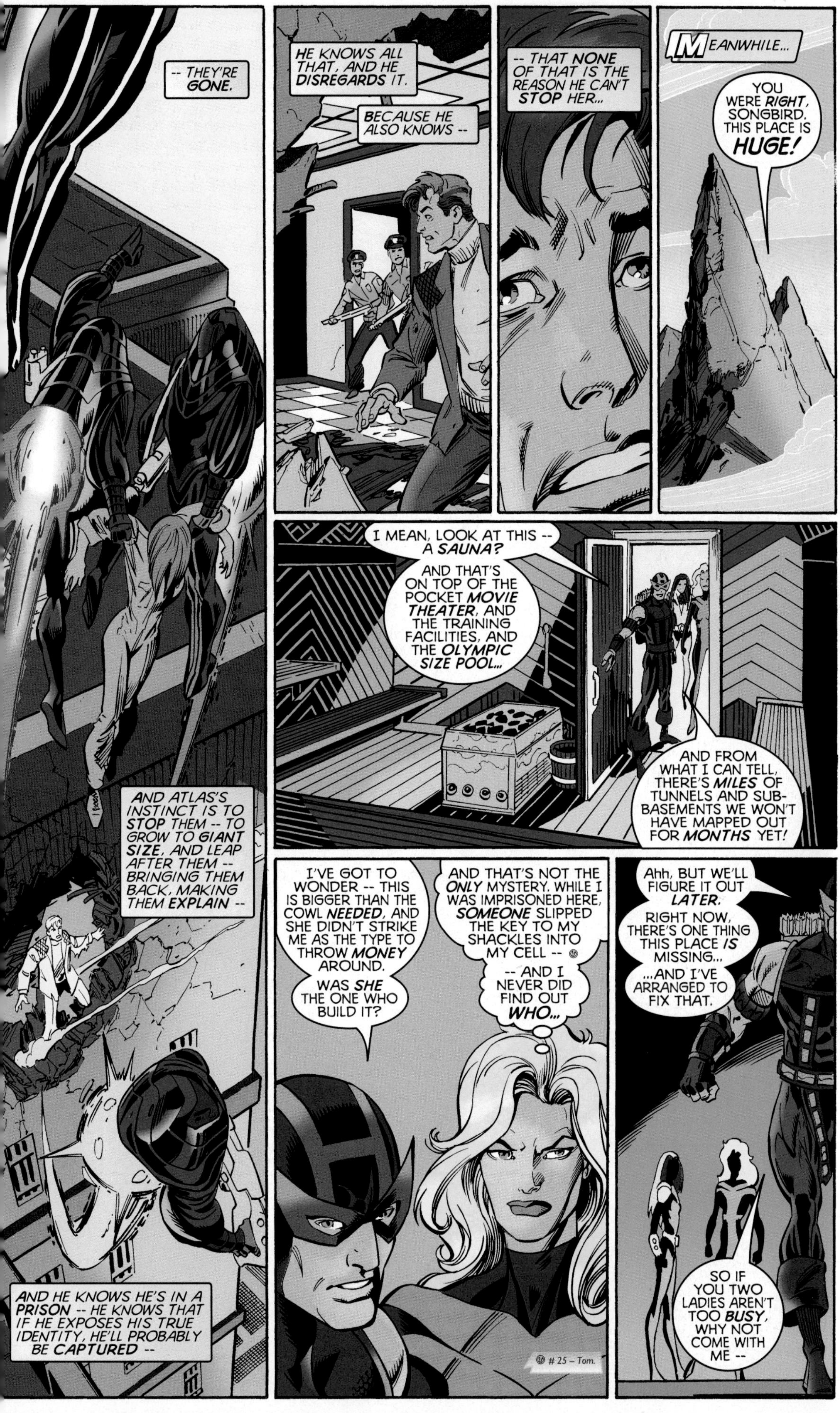

-- THEY'RE GONE.
AND ATLAS'S INSTINCT IS TO STOP THEM -- TO GROW TO GIANT SIZE, AND LEAP AFTER THEM -- BRINGING THEM BACK, MAKING THEM EXPLAIN --
AND HE KNOWS HE'S IN A PRISON -- HE KNOWS THAT IF HE EXPOSES HIS TRUE IDENTITY, HE'LL PROBABLY BE CAPTURED --
HE KNOWS ALL THAT, AND HE DISREGARDS IT.
BECAUSE HE ALSO KNOWS --
-- THAT NONE OF THAT IS THE REASON HE CAN'T STOP HER...
MEANWHILE...
YOU WERE RIGHT, SONGBIRD. THIS PLACE IS HUGE!
I MEAN, LOOK AT THIS -- A SAUNA?
AND THAT'S ON TOP OF THE POCKET MOVIE THEATER, AND THE TRAINING FACILITIES, AND THE OLYMPIC SIZE POOL...
AND FROM WHAT I CAN TELL, THERE'S MILES OF TUNNELS AND SUB-BASEMENTS WE WON'T HAVE MAPPED OUT FOR MONTHS YET!
I'VE GOT TO WONDER -- THIS IS BIGGER THAN THE COWL NEEDED, AND SHE DIDN'T STRIKE ME AS THE TYPE TO THROW MONEY AROUND.
WAS SHE THE ONE WHO BUILD IT?
AND THAT'S NOT THE ONLY MYSTERY. WHILE I WAS IMPRISONED HERE, SOMEONE SLIPPED THE KEY TO MY SHACKLES INTO MY CELL --
-- AND I NEVER DID FIND OUT WHO...
25 – Tom.
Ahh, BUT WE'LL FIGURE IT OUT LATER.
RIGHT NOW, THERE'S ONE THING THIS PLACE IS MISSING...
...AND I'VE ARRANGED TO FIX THAT.
SO IF YOU TWO LADIES AREN'T TOO BUSY, WHY NOT COME WITH ME --

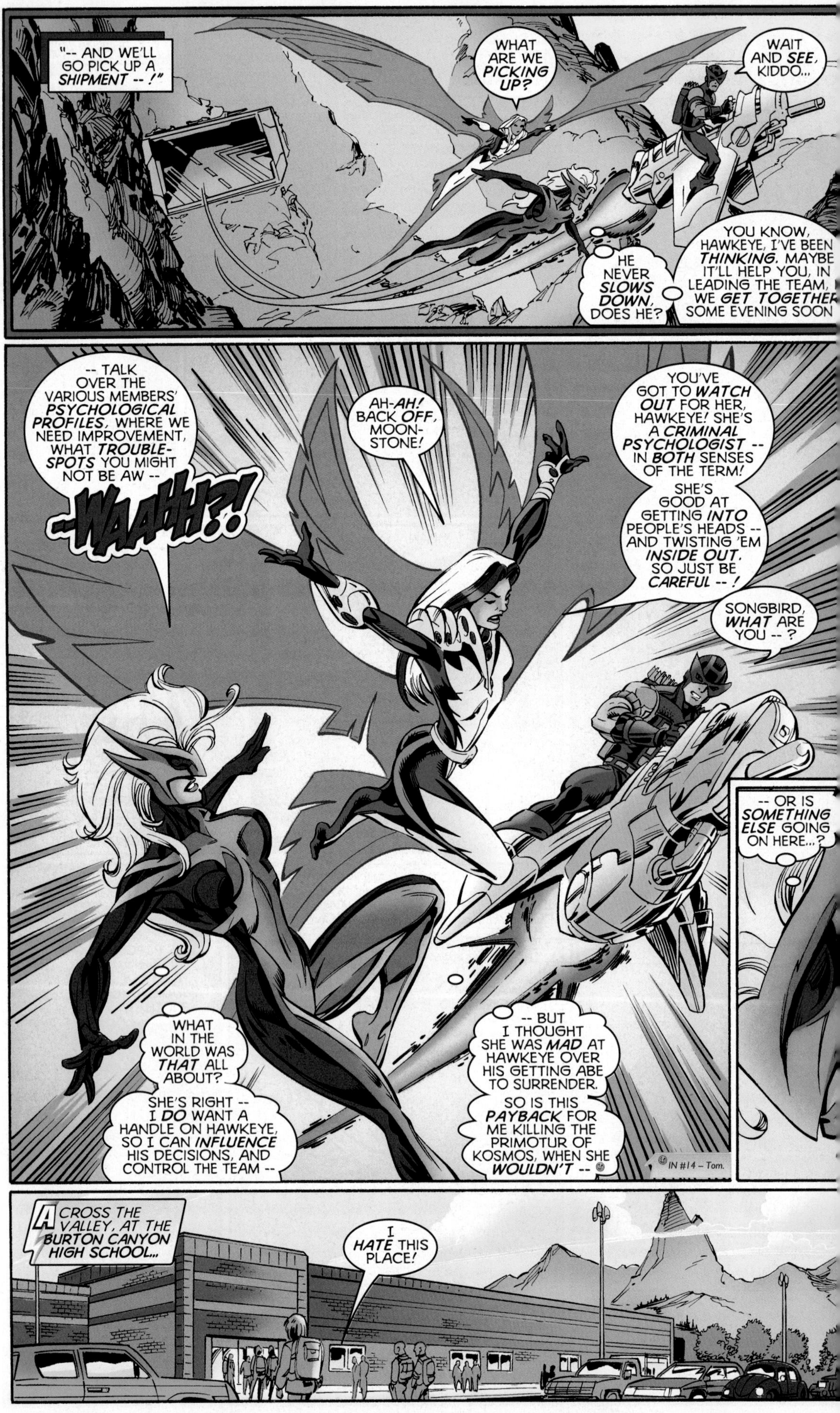
"-- AND WE'LL GO PICK UP A *SHIPMENT* -- !"
WHAT ARE WE *PICKING UP?*
WAIT AND *SEE,* KIDDO...
HE NEVER *SLOWS DOWN,* DOES HE?
YOU KNOW, HAWKEYE, I'VE BEEN *THINKING.* MAYBE IT'LL HELP YOU, IN LEADING THE TEAM, IF WE *GET TOGETHER* SOME EVENING SOON
-- TALK OVER THE VARIOUS MEMBERS' *PSYCHOLOGICAL PROFILES,* WHERE WE NEED IMPROVEMENT, WHAT *TROUBLE-SPOTS* YOU MIGHT NOT BE AW --
-WAAHH?!
AH-*AH!* BACK *OFF,* MOONSTONE!
YOU'VE GOT TO *WATCH OUT* FOR HER, HAWKEYE! SHE'S A *CRIMINAL PSYCHOLOGIST* -- IN *BOTH* SENSES OF THE TERM!
SHE'S GOOD AT GETTING *INTO* PEOPLE'S HEADS -- AND TWISTING 'EM *INSIDE OUT.* SO JUST BE *CAREFUL* -- !
SONGBIRD, *WHAT* ARE YOU -- ?
WHAT IN THE WORLD WAS *THAT* ALL ABOUT?
SHE'S RIGHT -- I *DO* WANT A HANDLE ON HAWKEYE, SO I CAN *INFLUENCE* HIS DECISIONS, AND CONTROL THE TEAM --
-- BUT I THOUGHT SHE WAS *MAD* AT HAWKEYE OVER HIS GETTING ABE TO SURRENDER.
SO IS THIS *PAYBACK* FOR ME KILLING THE PRIMOTUR OF KOSMOS, WHEN SHE *WOULDN'T* --
IN #14 – Tom.
-- OR IS *SOMETHING ELSE* GOING ON HERE...?
ACROSS THE VALLEY, AT THE BURTON CANYON HIGH SCHOOL...
I *HATE* THIS PLACE!

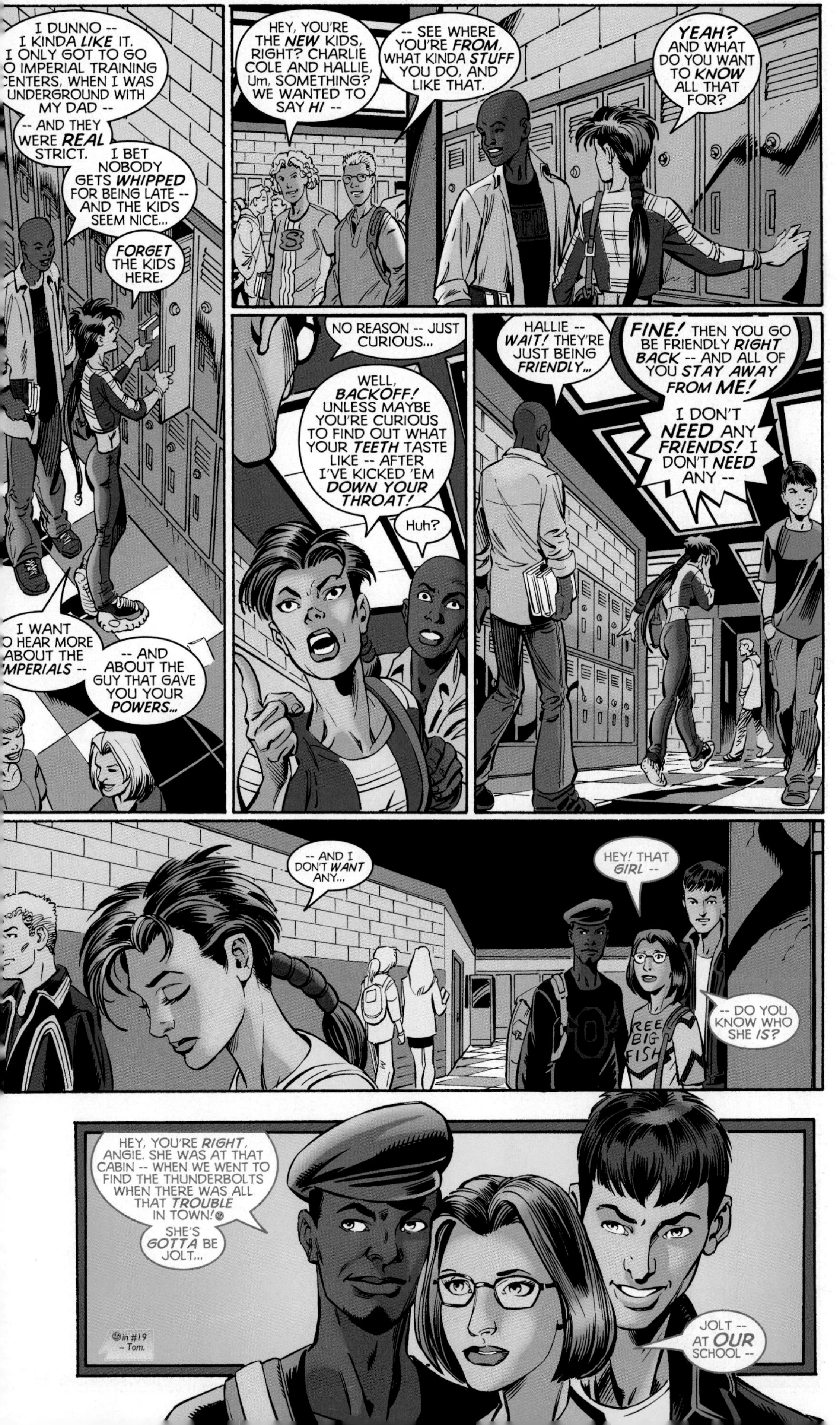
I DUNNO -- I KINDA *LIKE* IT. I ONLY GOT TO GO O IMPERIAL TRAINING CENTERS, WHEN I WAS UNDERGROUND WITH MY DAD --
-- AND THEY WERE *REAL* STRICT.
I BET NOBODY GETS *WHIPPED* FOR BEING LATE -- AND THE KIDS SEEM NICE...
FORGET THE KIDS HERE.
I WANT O HEAR MORE ABOUT THE MPERIALS --
-- AND ABOUT THE GUY THAT GAVE YOU YOUR *POWERS...*
HEY, YOU'RE THE *NEW* KIDS, RIGHT? CHARLIE COLE AND HALLIE, Um, SOMETHING? WE WANTED TO SAY *HI* --
-- SEE WHERE YOU'RE *FROM*, WHAT KINDA *STUFF* YOU DO, AND LIKE THAT.
YEAH? AND WHAT DO YOU WANT TO *KNOW* ALL THAT FOR?
NO REASON -- JUST CURIOUS...
WELL, *BACKOFF!* UNLESS MAYBE YOU'RE CURIOUS TO FIND OUT WHAT YOUR *TEETH* TASTE LIKE -- AFTER I'VE KICKED 'EM *DOWN YOUR THROAT!*
Huh?
HALLIE -- *WAIT!* THEY'RE JUST BEING *FRIENDLY...*
FINE! THEN YOU GO BE FRIENDLY *RIGHT BACK* -- AND ALL OF YOU *STAY AWAY FROM ME!*
I DON'T *NEED* ANY *FRIENDS!* I DON'T *NEED* ANY --
-- AND I DON'T *WANT* ANY...
HEY! THAT *GIRL* --
-- DO YOU KNOW WHO SHE *IS?*
HEY, YOU'RE *RIGHT*, ANGIE. SHE WAS AT THAT CABIN -- WHEN WE WENT TO FIND THE THUNDERBOLTS WHEN THERE WAS ALL THAT *TROUBLE* IN TOWN!
SHE'S *GOTTA* BE JOLT...
JOLT -- AT *OUR* SCHOOL --
in #19 – Tom.

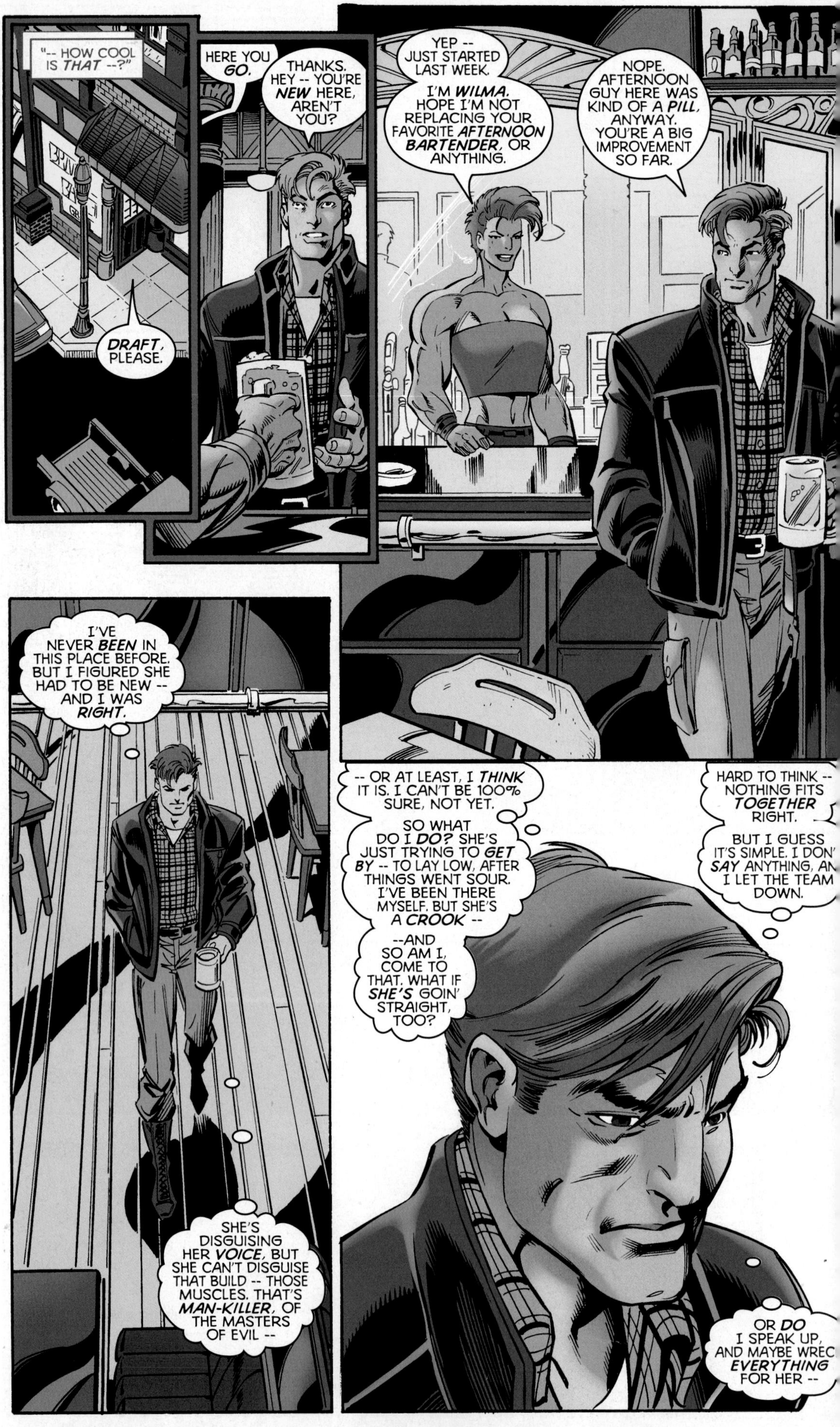

"-- HOW COOL IS *THAT* --?"
DRAFT, PLEASE.
HERE YOU *GO.*
THANKS. HEY -- YOU'RE *NEW* HERE, AREN'T YOU?
YEP -- JUST STARTED LAST WEEK.
I'M *WILMA.* HOPE I'M NOT REPLACING YOUR FAVORITE *AFTERNOON BARTENDER*, OR ANYTHING.
NOPE. AFTERNOON GUY HERE WAS KIND OF A *PILL*, ANYWAY. YOU'RE A BIG IMPROVEMENT SO FAR.
I'VE NEVER *BEEN* IN THIS PLACE BEFORE. BUT I FIGURED SHE HAD TO BE NEW -- AND I WAS *RIGHT*.
SHE'S DISGUISING HER *VOICE*, BUT SHE CAN'T DISGUISE THAT BUILD -- THOSE MUSCLES. THAT'S *MAN-KILLER*, OF THE MASTERS OF EVIL --
-- OR AT LEAST, I *THINK* IT IS. I CAN'T BE 100% SURE, NOT YET.
SO WHAT DO I *DO?* SHE'S JUST TRYING TO *GET BY* -- TO LAY LOW, AFTER THINGS WENT SOUR. I'VE BEEN THERE MYSELF. BUT SHE'S A *CROOK* --
--AND SO AM I, COME TO THAT. WHAT IF *SHE'S* GOIN' STRAIGHT, TOO?
HARD TO THINK -- NOTHING FITS *TOGETHER* RIGHT.
BUT I GUESS IT'S SIMPLE. I DON' *SAY* ANYTHING, AN I LET THE TEAM DOWN.
OR *DO* I SPEAK UP, AND MAYBE WREC *EVERYTHING* FOR HER --

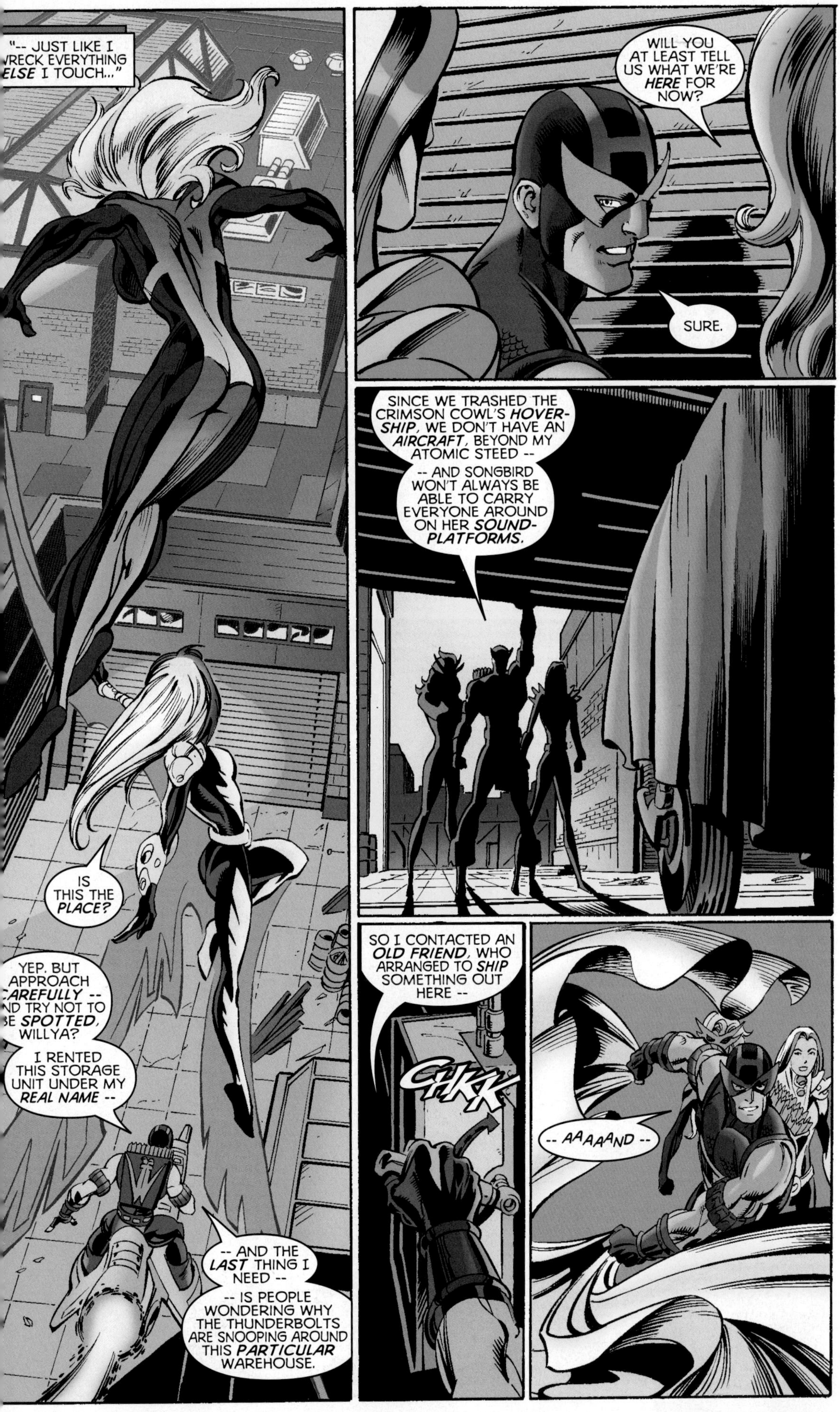
"-- JUST LIKE I WRECK EVERYTHING ELSE I TOUCH..."
IS THIS THE PLACE?
YEP. BUT APPROACH CAREFULLY -- AND TRY NOT TO BE SPOTTED, WILLYA?
I RENTED THIS STORAGE UNIT UNDER MY REAL NAME --
-- AND THE LAST THING I NEED --
-- IS PEOPLE WONDERING WHY THE THUNDERBOLTS ARE SNOOPING AROUND THIS PARTICULAR WAREHOUSE.
WILL YOU AT LEAST TELL US WHAT WE'RE HERE FOR NOW?
SURE.
SINCE WE TRASHED THE CRIMSON COWL'S HOVER-SHIP, WE DON'T HAVE AN AIRCRAFT, BEYOND MY ATOMIC STEED --
-- AND SONGBIRD WON'T ALWAYS BE ABLE TO CARRY EVERYONE AROUND ON HER SOUND-PLATFORMS.
SO I CONTACTED AN OLD FRIEND, WHO ARRANGED TO SHIP SOMETHING OUT HERE --
CHKK
-- AAAAAND --

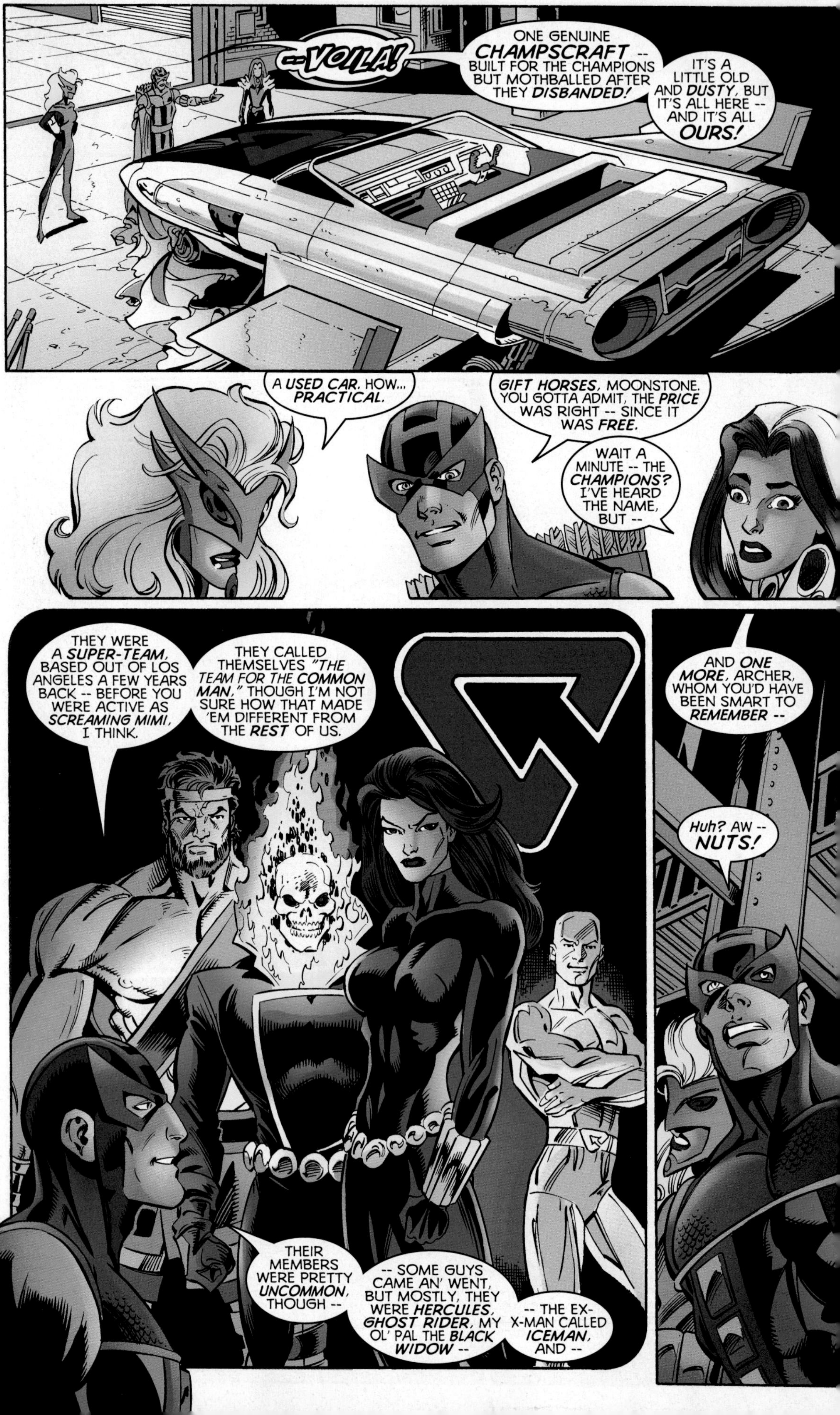
--VOILA!
ONE GENUINE CHAMPSCRAFT -- BUILT FOR THE CHAMPIONS BUT MOTHBALLED AFTER THEY DISBANDED!
IT'S A LITTLE OLD AND DUSTY, BUT IT'S ALL HERE -- AND IT'S ALL OURS!
A USED CAR. HOW... PRACTICAL.
GIFT HORSES, MOONSTONE. YOU GOTTA ADMIT, THE PRICE WAS RIGHT -- SINCE IT WAS FREE.
WAIT A MINUTE -- THE CHAMPIONS? I'VE HEARD THE NAME, BUT --
THEY WERE A SUPER-TEAM, BASED OUT OF LOS ANGELES A FEW YEARS BACK -- BEFORE YOU WERE ACTIVE AS SCREAMING MIMI, I THINK.
THEY CALLED THEMSELVES "THE TEAM FOR THE COMMON MAN," THOUGH I'M NOT SURE HOW THAT MADE 'EM DIFFERENT FROM THE REST OF US.
THEIR MEMBERS WERE PRETTY UNCOMMON, THOUGH --
-- SOME GUYS CAME AN' WENT, BUT MOSTLY, THEY WERE HERCULES, GHOST RIDER, MY OL' PAL THE BLACK WIDOW --
-- THE EX-X-MAN CALLED ICEMAN, AND --
AND ONE MORE, ARCHER, WHOM YOU'D HAVE BEEN SMART TO REMEMBER --
Huh? AW -- NUTS!

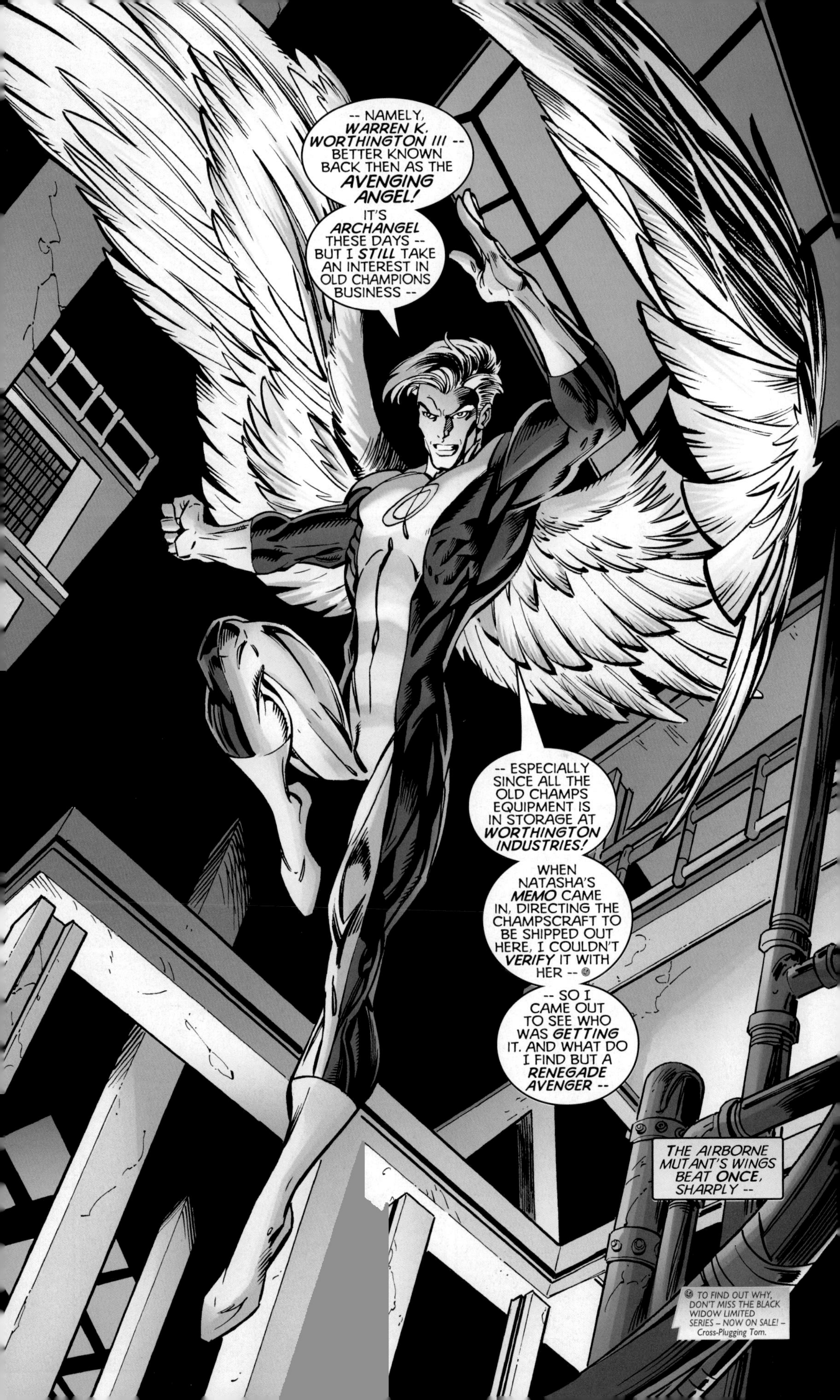

-- NAMELY, WARREN K. WORTHINGTON III -- BETTER KNOWN BACK THEN AS THE AVENGING ANGEL!
IT'S ARCHANGEL THESE DAYS -- BUT I STILL TAKE AN INTEREST IN OLD CHAMPIONS BUSINESS --
-- ESPECIALLY SINCE ALL THE OLD CHAMPS EQUIPMENT IS IN STORAGE AT WORTHINGTON INDUSTRIES!
WHEN NATASHA'S MEMO CAME IN, DIRECTING THE CHAMPSCRAFT TO BE SHIPPED OUT HERE, I COULDN'T VERIFY IT WITH HER --
-- SO I CAME OUT TO SEE WHO WAS GETTING IT. AND WHAT DO I FIND BUT A RENEGADE AVENGER --
THE AIRBORNE MUTANT'S WINGS BEAT ONCE, SHARPLY --
TO FIND OUT WHY, DON'T MISS THE BLACK WIDOW LIMITED SERIES – NOW ON SALE! – Cross-Plugging Tom.

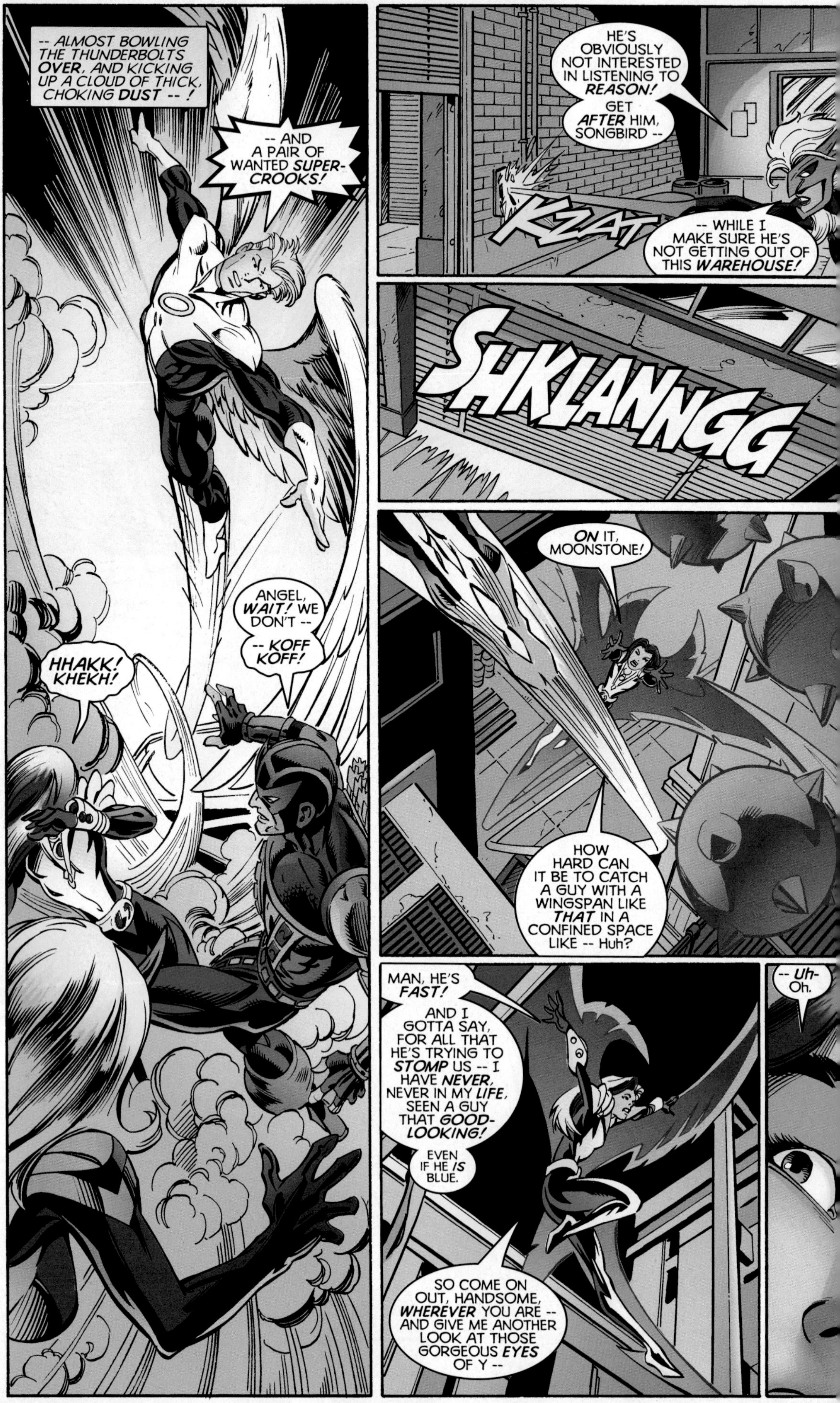
-- ALMOST BOWLING THE THUNDERBOLTS OVER, AND KICKING UP A CLOUD OF THICK, CHOKING DUST -- !
-- AND A PAIR OF WANTED SUPER-CROOKS!
ANGEL, WAIT! WE DON'T --
-- KOFF KOFF!
HHAKK! KHEKH!
HE'S OBVIOUSLY NOT INTERESTED IN LISTENING TO REASON!
GET AFTER HIM, SONGBIRD --
KZZAT
-- WHILE I MAKE SURE HE'S NOT GETTING OUT OF THIS WAREHOUSE!
SHKLANNGG
ON IT, MOONSTONE!
HOW HARD CAN IT BE TO CATCH A GUY WITH A WINGSPAN LIKE THAT IN A CONFINED SPACE LIKE -- Huh?
MAN, HE'S FAST!
AND I GOTTA SAY, FOR ALL THAT HE'S TRYING TO STOMP US -- I HAVE NEVER, NEVER IN MY LIFE, SEEN A GUY THAT GOOD-LOOKING!
EVEN IF HE IS BLUE.
SO COME ON OUT, HANDSOME, WHEREVER YOU ARE -- AND GIVE ME ANOTHER LOOK AT THOSE GORGEOUS EYES OF Y --
-- Uh-Oh.

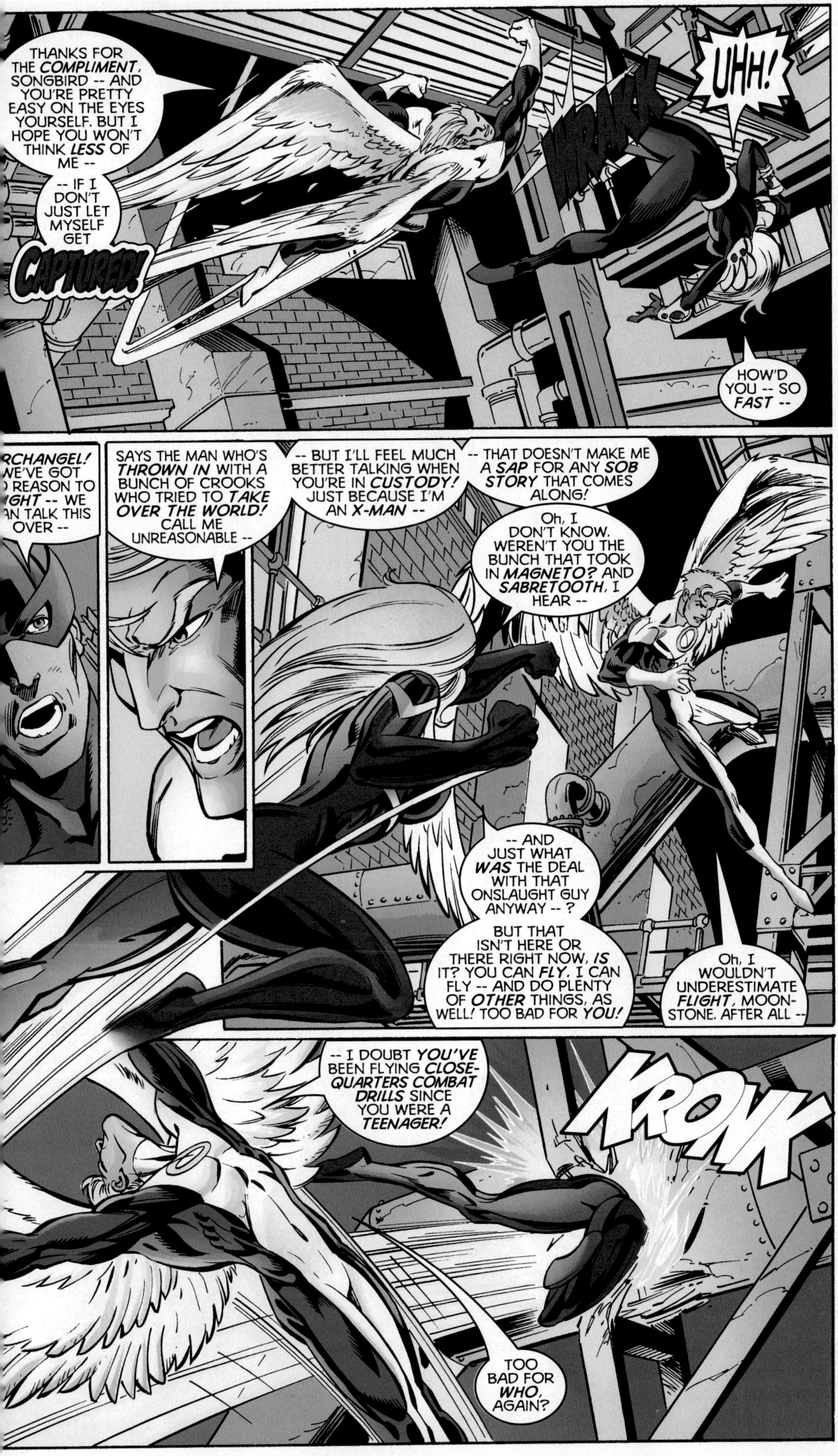
THANKS FOR THE COMPLIMENT, SONGBIRD -- AND YOU'RE PRETTY EASY ON THE EYES YOURSELF. BUT I HOPE YOU WON'T THINK LESS OF ME --
-- IF I DON'T JUST LET MYSELF GET CAPTURED!
WRAKK
UHH!
HOW'D YOU -- SO FAST --
RCHANGEL! WE'VE GOT REASON TO IGHT -- WE AN TALK THIS OVER --
SAYS THE MAN WHO'S THROWN IN WITH A BUNCH OF CROOKS WHO TRIED TO TAKE OVER THE WORLD! CALL ME UNREASONABLE --
-- BUT I'LL FEEL MUCH BETTER TALKING WHEN YOU'RE IN CUSTODY! JUST BECAUSE I'M AN X-MAN --
-- THAT DOESN'T MAKE ME A SAP FOR ANY SOB STORY THAT COMES ALONG!
Oh, I DON'T KNOW. WEREN'T YOU THE BUNCH THAT TOOK IN MAGNETO? AND SABRETOOTH, I HEAR --
-- AND JUST WHAT WAS THE DEAL WITH THAT ONSLAUGHT GUY ANYWAY -- ?
BUT THAT ISN'T HERE OR THERE RIGHT NOW, IS IT? YOU CAN FLY. I CAN FLY -- AND DO PLENTY OF OTHER THINGS, AS WELL! TOO BAD FOR YOU!
Oh, I WOULDN'T UNDERESTIMATE FLIGHT, MOONSTONE. AFTER ALL --
-- I DOUBT YOU'VE BEEN FLYING CLOSE-QUARTERS COMBAT DRILLS SINCE YOU WERE A TEENAGER!
KRONK
TOO BAD FOR WHO, AGAIN?

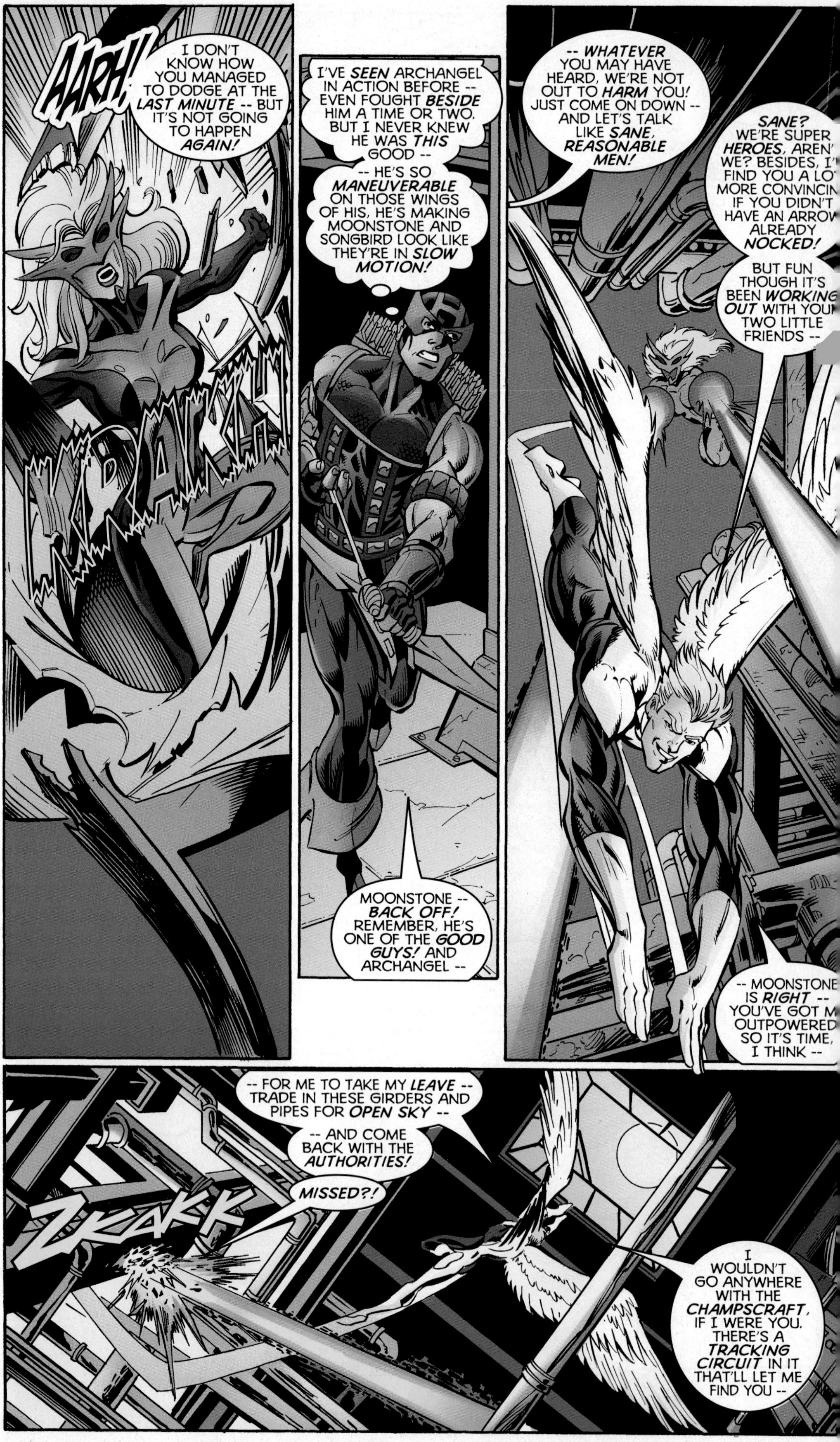
AARH!
I DON'T KNOW HOW YOU MANAGED TO DODGE AT THE LAST MINUTE -- BUT IT'S NOT GOING TO HAPPEN AGAIN!
I'VE SEEN ARCHANGEL IN ACTION BEFORE -- EVEN FOUGHT BESIDE HIM A TIME OR TWO. BUT I NEVER KNEW HE WAS THIS GOOD --
-- HE'S SO MANEUVERABLE ON THOSE WINGS OF HIS, HE'S MAKING MOONSTONE AND SONGBIRD LOOK LIKE THEY'RE IN SLOW MOTION!
MOONSTONE -- BACK OFF! REMEMBER, HE'S ONE OF THE GOOD GUYS! AND ARCHANGEL --
-- WHATEVER YOU MAY HAVE HEARD, WE'RE NOT OUT TO HARM YOU! JUST COME ON DOWN -- AND LET'S TALK LIKE SANE, REASONABLE MEN!
SANE? WE'RE SUPER HEROES, AREN' WE? BESIDES, I' FIND YOU A LO MORE CONVINCIN IF YOU DIDN'T HAVE AN ARROW ALREADY NOCKED!
BUT FUN THOUGH IT'S BEEN WORKING OUT WITH YOU TWO LITTLE FRIENDS --
-- MOONSTONE IS RIGHT -- YOU'VE GOT M OUTPOWERED SO IT'S TIME, I THINK --
-- FOR ME TO TAKE MY LEAVE -- TRADE IN THESE GIRDERS AND PIPES FOR OPEN SKY --
-- AND COME BACK WITH THE AUTHORITIES!
MISSED?!
ZRAKK
I WOULDN'T GO ANYWHERE WITH THE CHAMPSCRAFT, IF I WERE YOU. THERE'S A TRACKING CIRCUIT IN IT THAT'LL LET ME FIND YOU --

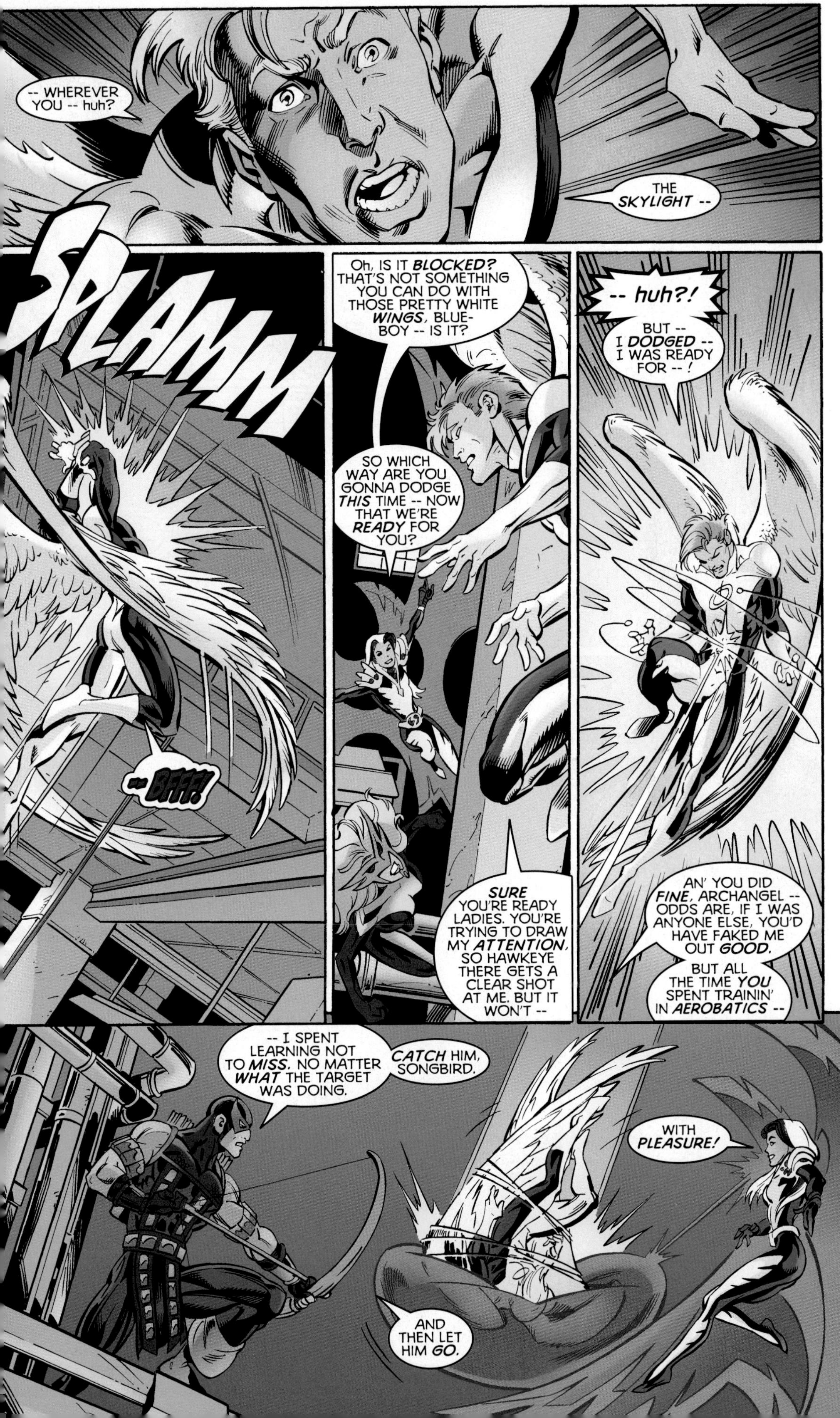
-- WHEREVER YOU -- huh?
THE SKYLIGHT --
SPLAMM
--BFFF!
Oh, IS IT BLOCKED? THAT'S NOT SOMETHING YOU CAN DO WITH THOSE PRETTY WHITE WINGS, BLUE-BOY -- IS IT?
SO WHICH WAY ARE YOU GONNA DODGE THIS TIME -- NOW THAT WE'RE READY FOR YOU?
SURE YOU'RE READY LADIES. YOU'RE TRYING TO DRAW MY ATTENTION, SO HAWKEYE THERE GETS A CLEAR SHOT AT ME. BUT IT WON'T --
-- huh?!
BUT -- I DODGED -- I WAS READY FOR -- !
AN' YOU DID FINE, ARCHANGEL -- ODDS ARE, IF I WAS ANYONE ELSE, YOU'D HAVE FAKED ME OUT GOOD.
BUT ALL THE TIME YOU SPENT TRAININ' IN AEROBATICS --
-- I SPENT LEARNING NOT TO MISS, NO MATTER WHAT THE TARGET WAS DOING.
CATCH HIM, SONGBIRD.
AND THEN LET HIM GO.
WITH PLEASURE!

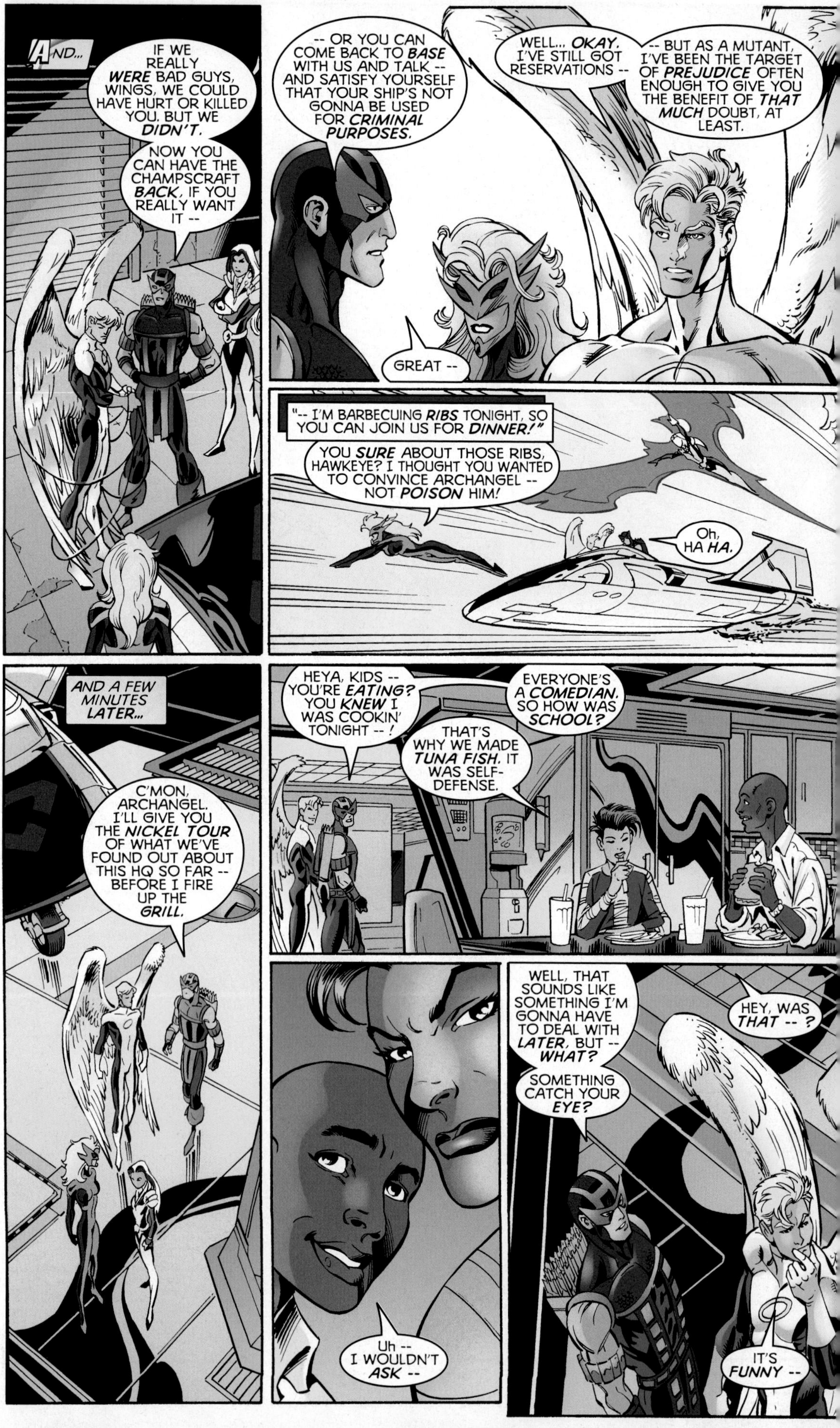
AND...
IF WE REALLY WERE BAD GUYS, WINGS, WE COULD HAVE HURT OR KILLED YOU. BUT WE DIDN'T.
NOW YOU CAN HAVE THE CHAMPSCRAFT BACK, IF YOU REALLY WANT IT --
-- OR YOU CAN COME BACK TO BASE WITH US AND TALK -- AND SATISFY YOURSELF THAT YOUR SHIP'S NOT GONNA BE USED FOR CRIMINAL PURPOSES.
GREAT --
WELL... OKAY. I'VE STILL GOT RESERVATIONS --
-- BUT AS A MUTANT, I'VE BEEN THE TARGET OF PREJUDICE OFTEN ENOUGH TO GIVE YOU THE BENEFIT OF THAT MUCH DOUBT, AT LEAST.
"-- I'M BARBECUING RIBS TONIGHT, SO YOU CAN JOIN US FOR DINNER!"
YOU SURE ABOUT THOSE RIBS, HAWKEYE? I THOUGHT YOU WANTED TO CONVINCE ARCHANGEL -- NOT POISON HIM!
Oh, HA HA.
AND A FEW MINUTES LATER...
C'MON, ARCHANGEL. I'LL GIVE YOU THE NICKEL TOUR OF WHAT WE'VE FOUND OUT ABOUT THIS HQ SO FAR -- BEFORE I FIRE UP THE GRILL.
HEYA, KIDS -- YOU'RE EATING? YOU KNEW I WAS COOKIN' TONIGHT -- !
THAT'S WHY WE MADE TUNA FISH. IT WAS SELF-DEFENSE.
EVERYONE'S A COMEDIAN. SO HOW WAS SCHOOL?
Uh -- I WOULDN'T ASK --
WELL, THAT SOUNDS LIKE SOMETHING I'M GONNA HAVE TO DEAL WITH LATER, BUT -- WHAT?
SOMETHING CATCH YOUR EYE?
HEY, WAS THAT -- ?
IT'S FUNNY --

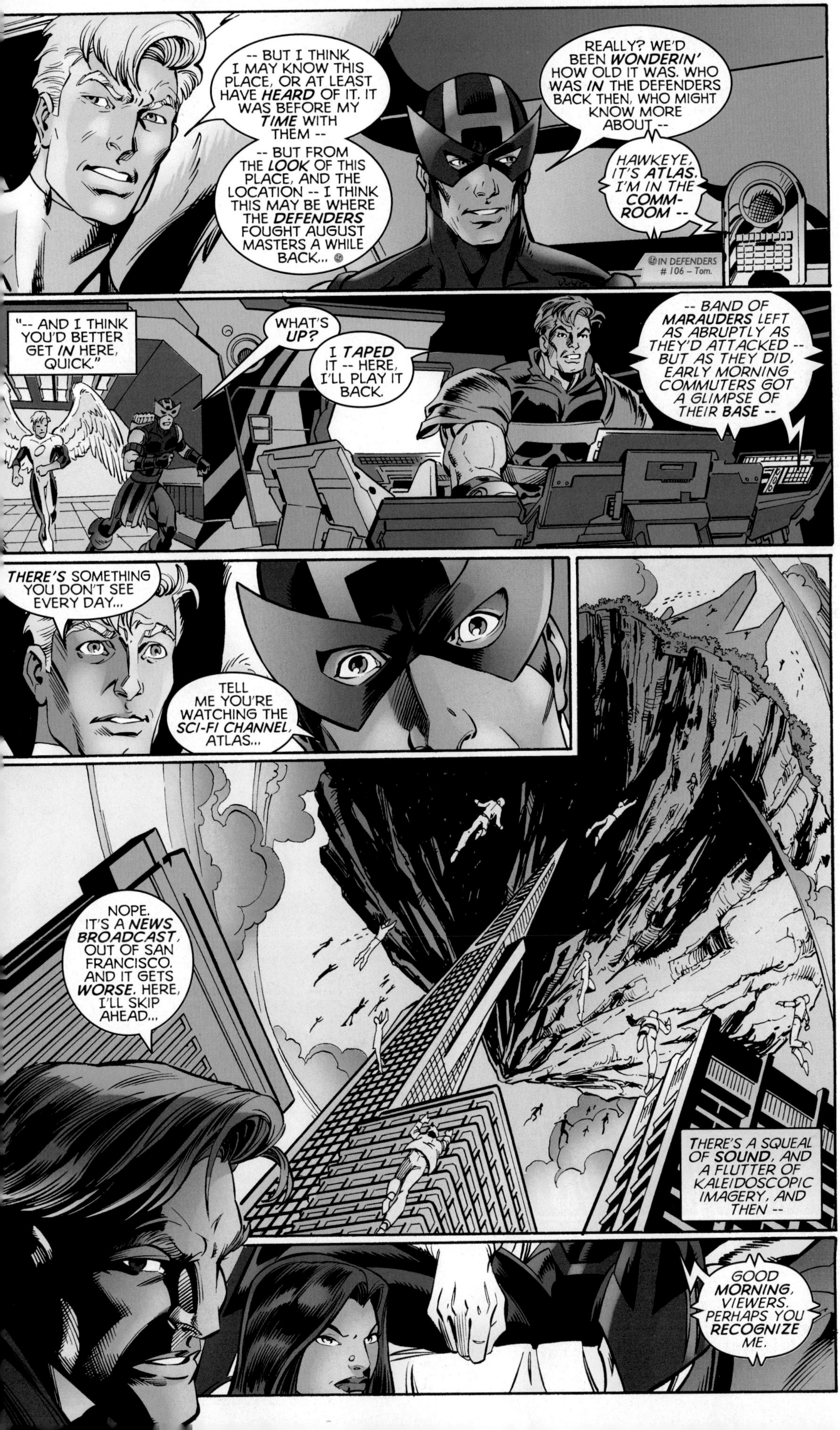
-- BUT I THINK I MAY KNOW THIS PLACE, OR AT LEAST HAVE HEARD OF IT. IT WAS BEFORE MY TIME WITH THEM --
-- BUT FROM THE LOOK OF THIS PLACE, AND THE LOCATION -- I THINK THIS MAY BE WHERE THE DEFENDERS FOUGHT AUGUST MASTERS A WHILE BACK...
REALLY? WE'D BEEN WONDERIN' HOW OLD IT WAS. WHO WAS IN THE DEFENDERS BACK THEN, WHO MIGHT KNOW MORE ABOUT --
HAWKEYE, IT'S ATLAS. I'M IN THE COMM-ROOM --
IN DEFENDERS # 106 – Tom.
"-- AND I THINK YOU'D BETTER GET IN HERE, QUICK."
WHAT'S UP?
I TAPED IT -- HERE, I'LL PLAY IT BACK.
-- BAND OF MARAUDERS LEFT AS ABRUPTLY AS THEY'D ATTACKED -- BUT AS THEY DID, EARLY MORNING COMMUTERS GOT A GLIMPSE OF THEIR BASE --
THERE'S SOMETHING YOU DON'T SEE EVERY DAY...
TELL ME YOU'RE WATCHING THE SCI-FI CHANNEL, ATLAS...
NOPE. IT'S A NEWS BROADCAST, OUT OF SAN FRANCISCO. AND IT GETS WORSE. HERE, I'LL SKIP AHEAD...
THERE'S A SQUEAL OF SOUND, AND A FLUTTER OF KALEIDOSCOPIC IMAGERY, AND THEN --
GOOD MORNING, VIEWERS. PERHAPS YOU RECOGNIZE ME.

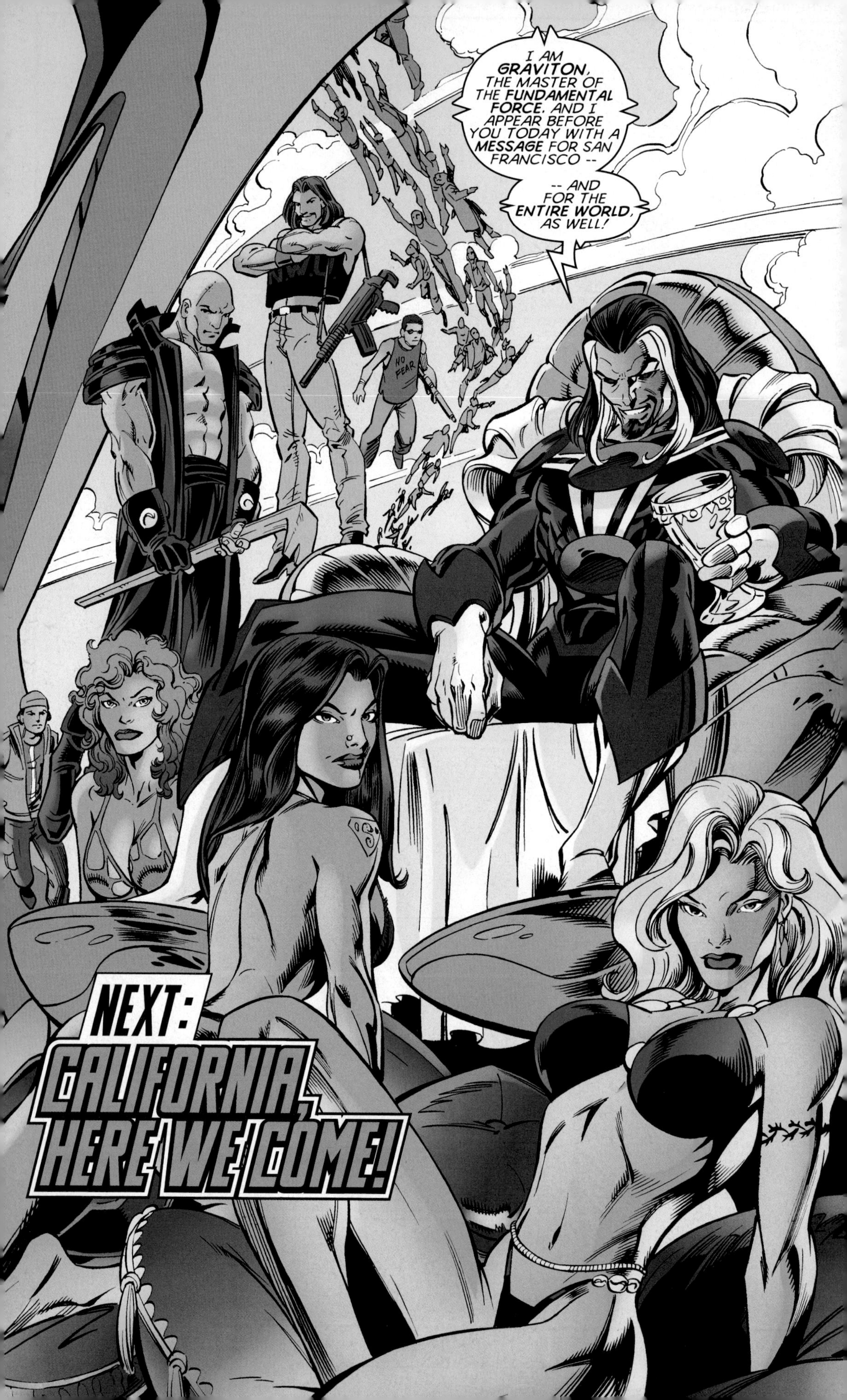
I AM GRAVITON, THE MASTER OF THE FUNDAMENTAL FORCE. AND I APPEAR BEFORE YOU TODAY WITH A MESSAGE FOR SAN FRANCISCO --
-- AND FOR THE ENTIRE WORLD, AS WELL!
N.W.O.
NO FEAR
NEXT:
CALIFORNIA, HERE WE COME!

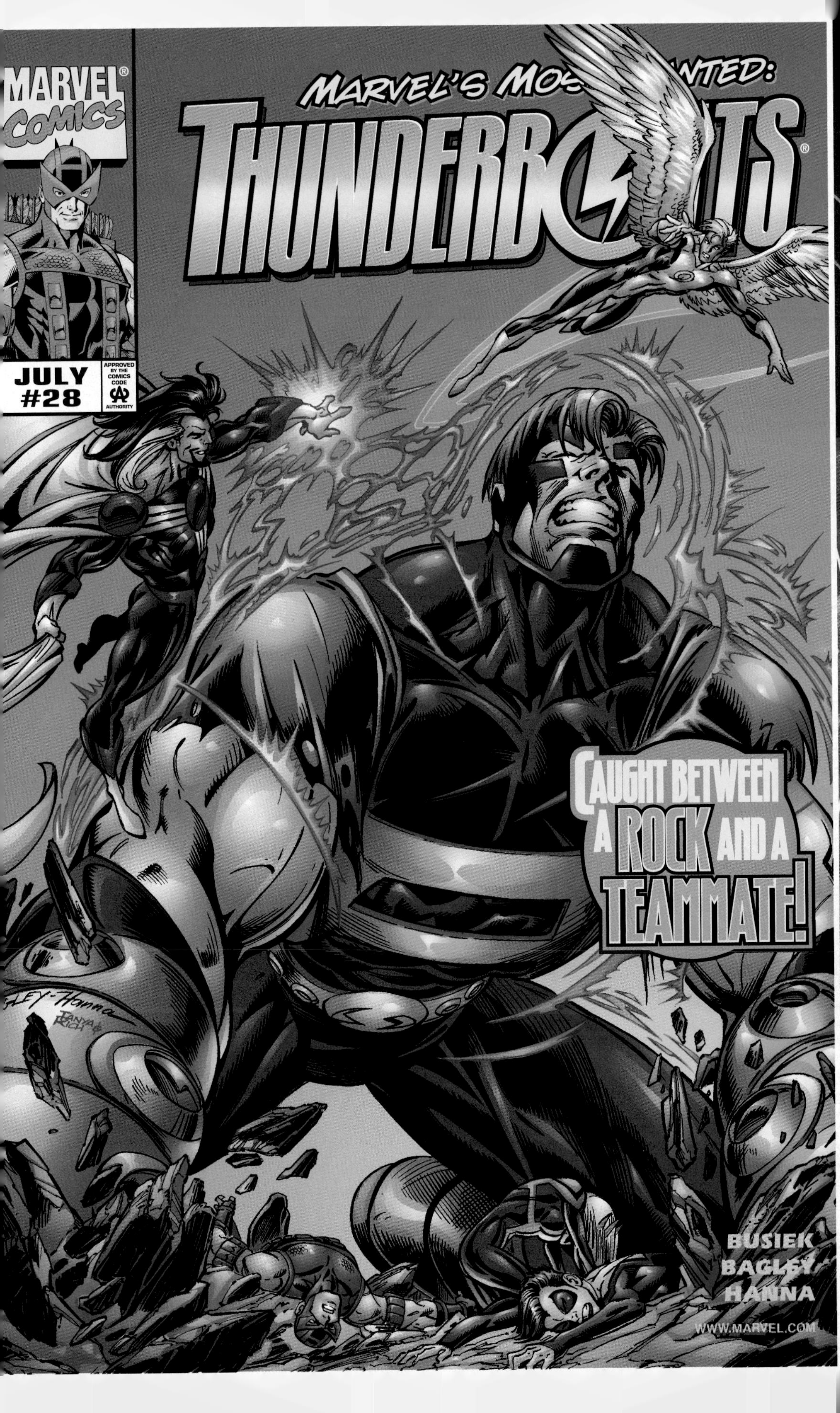
MARVEL COMICS
MARVEL'S MOS NTED:
THUNDERBOLTS
JULY #28
APPROVED BY THE COMICS CODE AUTHORITY
CAUGHT BETWEEN A ROCK AND A TEAMMATE!
BUSIEK
BAGLEY
HANNA
WWW.MARVEL.COM

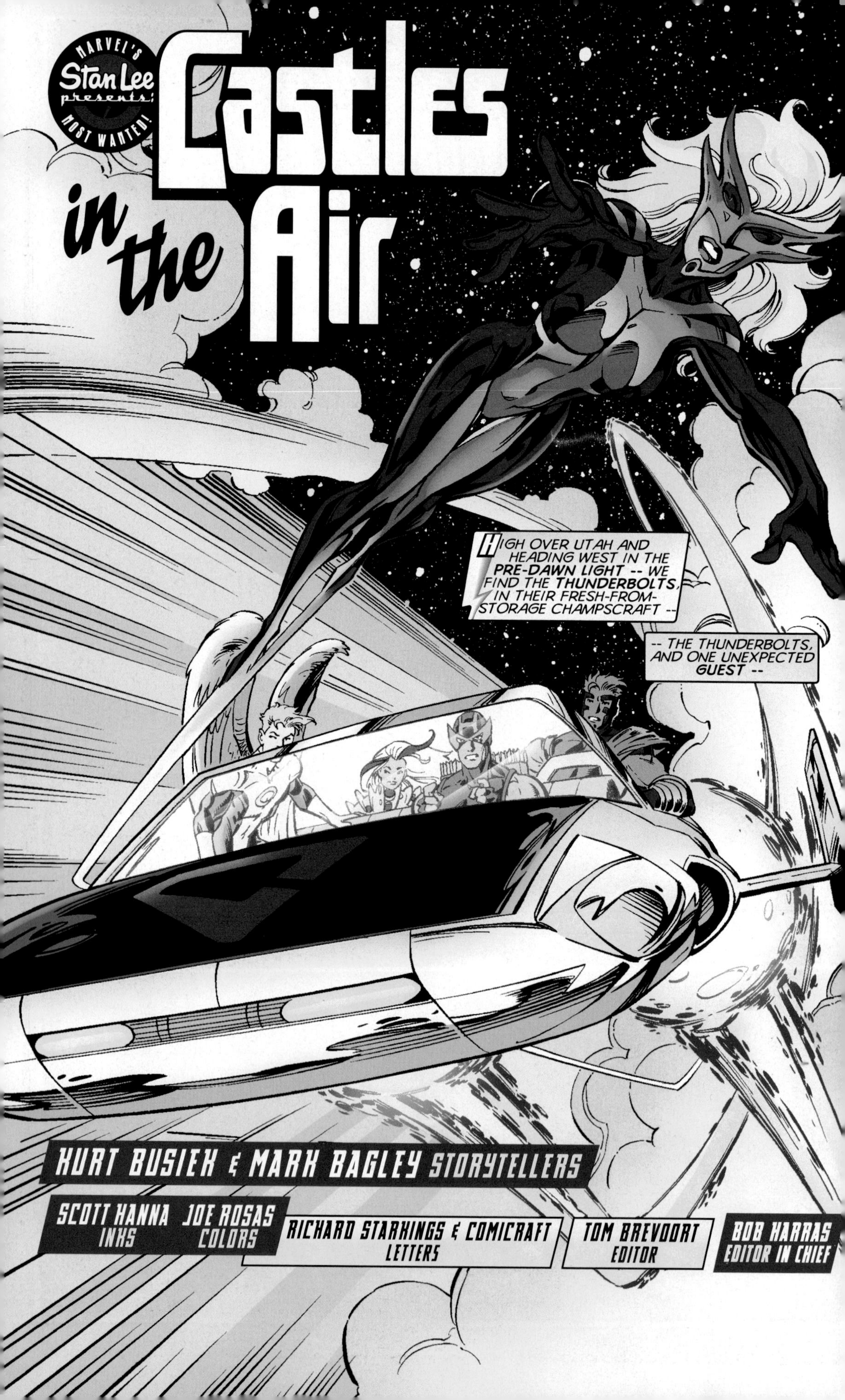
MARVEL'S Stan Lee presents: MOST WANTED!
Castles in the Air
HIGH OVER UTAH AND HEADING WEST IN THE PRE-DAWN LIGHT -- WE FIND THE THUNDERBOLTS, IN THEIR FRESH-FROM-STORAGE CHAMPSCRAFT --
-- THE THUNDERBOLTS, AND ONE UNEXPECTED GUEST --
KURT BUSIEK & MARK BAGLEY STORYTELLERS
SCOTT HANNA INKS
JOE ROSAS COLORS
RICHARD STARKINGS & COMICRAFT LETTERS
TOM BREVOORT EDITOR
BOB HARRAS EDITOR IN CHIEF

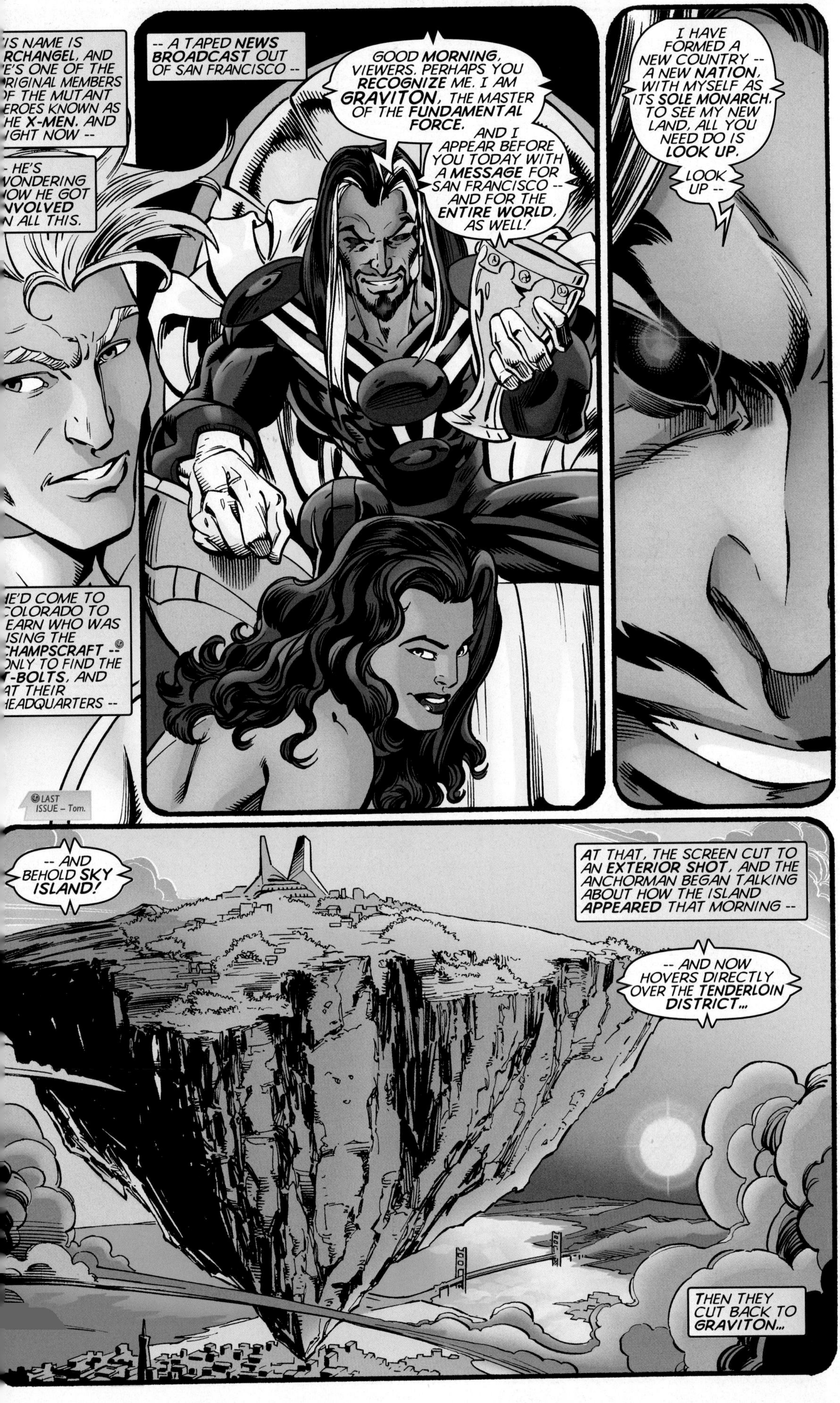

IS NAME IS RCHANGEL, AND E'S ONE OF THE RIGINAL MEMBERS F THE MUTANT EROES KNOWN AS HE X-MEN. AND IGHT NOW --
- HE'S VONDERING OW HE GOT NVOLVED N ALL THIS.
IE'D COME TO COLORADO TO EARN WHO WAS ISING THE CHAMPSCRAFT -- ONLY TO FIND THE T-BOLTS, AND AT THEIR HEADQUARTERS --
LAST ISSUE – Tom.
-- A TAPED NEWS BROADCAST OUT OF SAN FRANCISCO --
GOOD MORNING, VIEWERS. PERHAPS YOU RECOGNIZE ME. I AM GRAVITON, THE MASTER OF THE FUNDAMENTAL FORCE.
AND I APPEAR BEFORE YOU TODAY WITH A MESSAGE FOR SAN FRANCISCO -- AND FOR THE ENTIRE WORLD, AS WELL!
I HAVE FORMED A NEW COUNTRY -- A NEW NATION, WITH MYSELF AS ITS SOLE MONARCH. TO SEE MY NEW LAND, ALL YOU NEED DO IS LOOK UP.
LOOK UP --
-- AND BEHOLD SKY ISLAND!
AT THAT, THE SCREEN CUT TO AN EXTERIOR SHOT, AND THE ANCHORMAN BEGAN TALKING ABOUT HOW THE ISLAND APPEARED THAT MORNING --
-- AND NOW HOVERS DIRECTLY OVER THE TENDERLOIN DISTRICT...
THEN THEY CUT BACK TO GRAVITON...

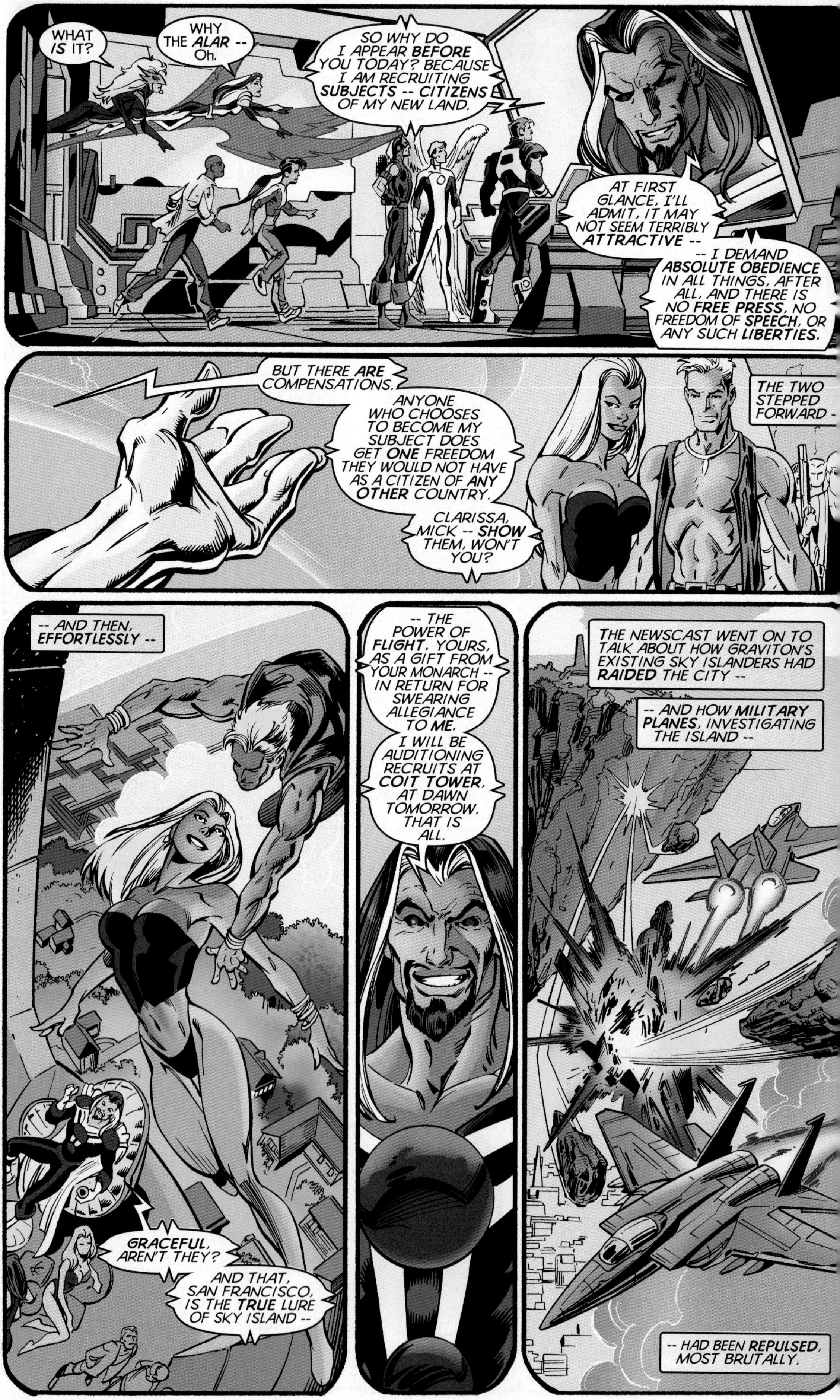

WHAT IS IT?
WHY THE ALAR -- Oh.
SO WHY DO I APPEAR BEFORE YOU TODAY? BECAUSE I AM RECRUITING SUBJECTS -- CITIZENS OF MY NEW LAND.
AT FIRST GLANCE, I'LL ADMIT, IT MAY NOT SEEM TERRIBLY ATTRACTIVE --
-- I DEMAND ABSOLUTE OBEDIENCE IN ALL THINGS, AFTER ALL, AND THERE IS NO FREE PRESS, NO FREEDOM OF SPEECH, OR ANY SUCH LIBERTIES.
BUT THERE ARE COMPENSATIONS.
ANYONE WHO CHOOSES TO BECOME MY SUBJECT DOES GET ONE FREEDOM THEY WOULD NOT HAVE AS A CITIZEN OF ANY OTHER COUNTRY.
CLARISSA, MICK -- SHOW THEM, WON'T YOU?
THE TWO STEPPED FORWARD --
-- AND THEN, EFFORTLESSLY --
GRACEFUL, AREN'T THEY?
AND THAT, SAN FRANCISCO, IS THE TRUE LURE OF SKY ISLAND --
-- THE POWER OF FLIGHT. YOURS, AS A GIFT FROM YOUR MONARCH -- IN RETURN FOR SWEARING ALLEGIANCE TO ME.
I WILL BE AUDITIONING RECRUITS AT COIT TOWER, AT DAWN TOMORROW. THAT IS ALL.
THE NEWSCAST WENT ON TO TALK ABOUT HOW GRAVITON'S EXISTING SKY ISLANDERS HAD RAIDED THE CITY --
-- AND HOW MILITARY PLANES, INVESTIGATING THE ISLAND --
-- HAD BEEN REPULSED, MOST BRUTALLY.

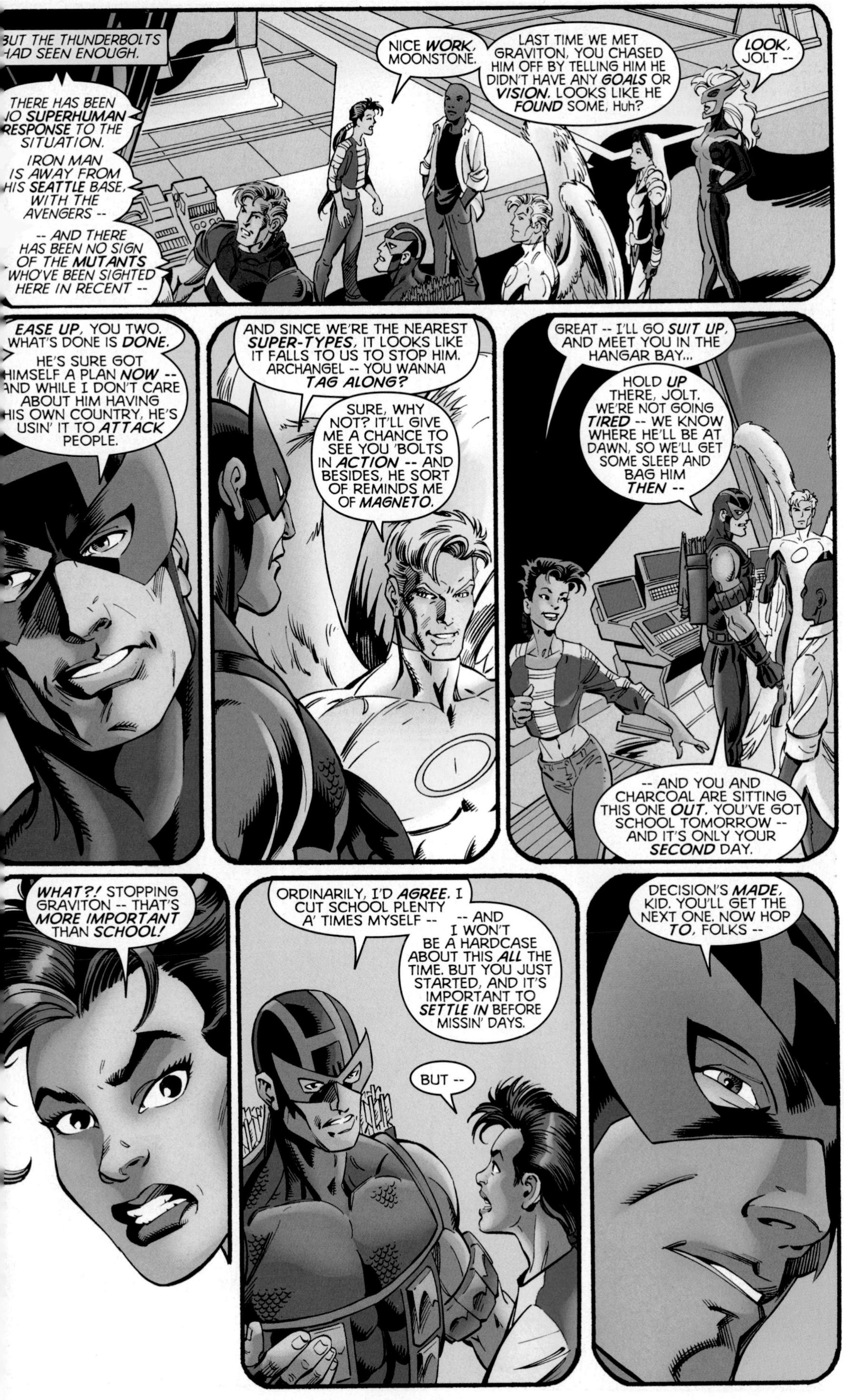
BUT THE THUNDERBOLTS HAD SEEN ENOUGH.
THERE HAS BEEN NO SUPERHUMAN RESPONSE TO THE SITUATION.
IRON MAN IS AWAY FROM HIS SEATTLE BASE, WITH THE AVENGERS --
-- AND THERE HAS BEEN NO SIGN OF THE MUTANTS WHO'VE BEEN SIGHTED HERE IN RECENT --
NICE WORK, MOONSTONE.
LAST TIME WE MET GRAVITON, YOU CHASED HIM OFF BY TELLING HIM HE DIDN'T HAVE ANY GOALS OR VISION. LOOKS LIKE HE FOUND SOME, Huh?
LOOK, JOLT --
EASE UP, YOU TWO. WHAT'S DONE IS DONE.
HE'S SURE GOT HIMSELF A PLAN NOW -- AND WHILE I DON'T CARE ABOUT HIM HAVING HIS OWN COUNTRY, HE'S USIN' IT TO ATTACK PEOPLE.
AND SINCE WE'RE THE NEAREST SUPER-TYPES, IT LOOKS LIKE IT FALLS TO US TO STOP HIM. ARCHANGEL -- YOU WANNA TAG ALONG?
SURE, WHY NOT? IT'LL GIVE ME A CHANCE TO SEE YOU 'BOLTS IN ACTION -- AND BESIDES, HE SORT OF REMINDS ME OF MAGNETO.
GREAT -- I'LL GO SUIT UP, AND MEET YOU IN THE HANGAR BAY...
HOLD UP THERE, JOLT. WE'RE NOT GOING TIRED -- WE KNOW WHERE HE'LL BE AT DAWN, SO WE'LL GET SOME SLEEP AND BAG HIM THEN --
-- AND YOU AND CHARCOAL ARE SITTING THIS ONE OUT. YOU'VE GOT SCHOOL TOMORROW -- AND IT'S ONLY YOUR SECOND DAY.
WHAT?! STOPPING GRAVITON -- THAT'S MORE IMPORTANT THAN SCHOOL!
ORDINARILY, I'D AGREE. I CUT SCHOOL PLENTY A' TIMES MYSELF --
-- AND I WON'T BE A HARDCASE ABOUT THIS ALL THE TIME. BUT YOU JUST STARTED, AND IT'S IMPORTANT TO SETTLE IN BEFORE MISSIN' DAYS.
BUT --
DECISION'S MADE, KID. YOU'LL GET THE NEXT ONE. NOW HOP TO, FOLKS --

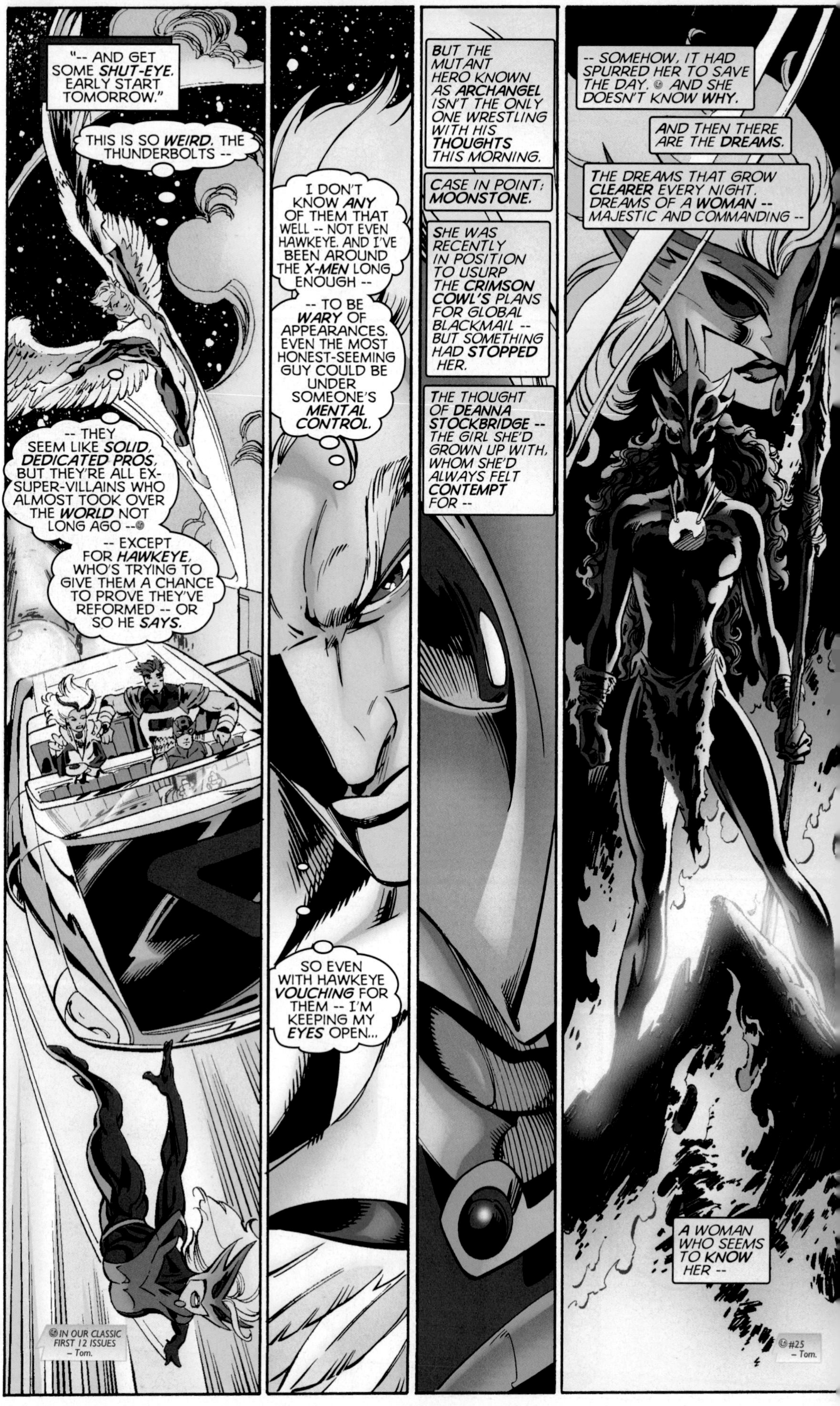
"-- AND GET SOME SHUT-EYE. EARLY START TOMORROW."
THIS IS SO WEIRD. THE THUNDERBOLTS --
-- THEY SEEM LIKE SOLID, DEDICATED PROS, BUT THEY'RE ALL EX-SUPER-VILLAINS WHO ALMOST TOOK OVER THE WORLD NOT LONG AGO --
-- EXCEPT FOR HAWKEYE, WHO'S TRYING TO GIVE THEM A CHANCE TO PROVE THEY'VE REFORMED -- OR SO HE SAYS.
IN OUR CLASSIC FIRST 12 ISSUES – Tom.
I DON'T KNOW ANY OF THEM THAT WELL -- NOT EVEN HAWKEYE. AND I'VE BEEN AROUND THE X-MEN LONG ENOUGH --
-- TO BE WARY OF APPEARANCES. EVEN THE MOST HONEST-SEEMING GUY COULD BE UNDER SOMEONE'S MENTAL CONTROL.
SO EVEN WITH HAWKEYE VOUCHING FOR THEM -- I'M KEEPING MY EYES OPEN...
BUT THE MUTANT HERO KNOWN AS ARCHANGEL ISN'T THE ONLY ONE WRESTLING WITH HIS THOUGHTS THIS MORNING.
CASE IN POINT: MOONSTONE.
SHE WAS RECENTLY IN POSITION TO USURP THE CRIMSON COWL'S PLANS FOR GLOBAL BLACKMAIL -- BUT SOMETHING HAD STOPPED HER.
THE THOUGHT OF DEANNA STOCKBRIDGE -- THE GIRL SHE'D GROWN UP WITH, WHOM SHE'D ALWAYS FELT CONTEMPT FOR --
-- SOMEHOW, IT HAD SPURRED HER TO SAVE THE DAY. AND SHE DOESN'T KNOW WHY.
AND THEN THERE ARE THE DREAMS.
THE DREAMS THAT GROW CLEARER EVERY NIGHT. DREAMS OF A WOMAN -- MAJESTIC AND COMMANDING --
A WOMAN WHO SEEMS TO KNOW HER --
#25 – Tom.

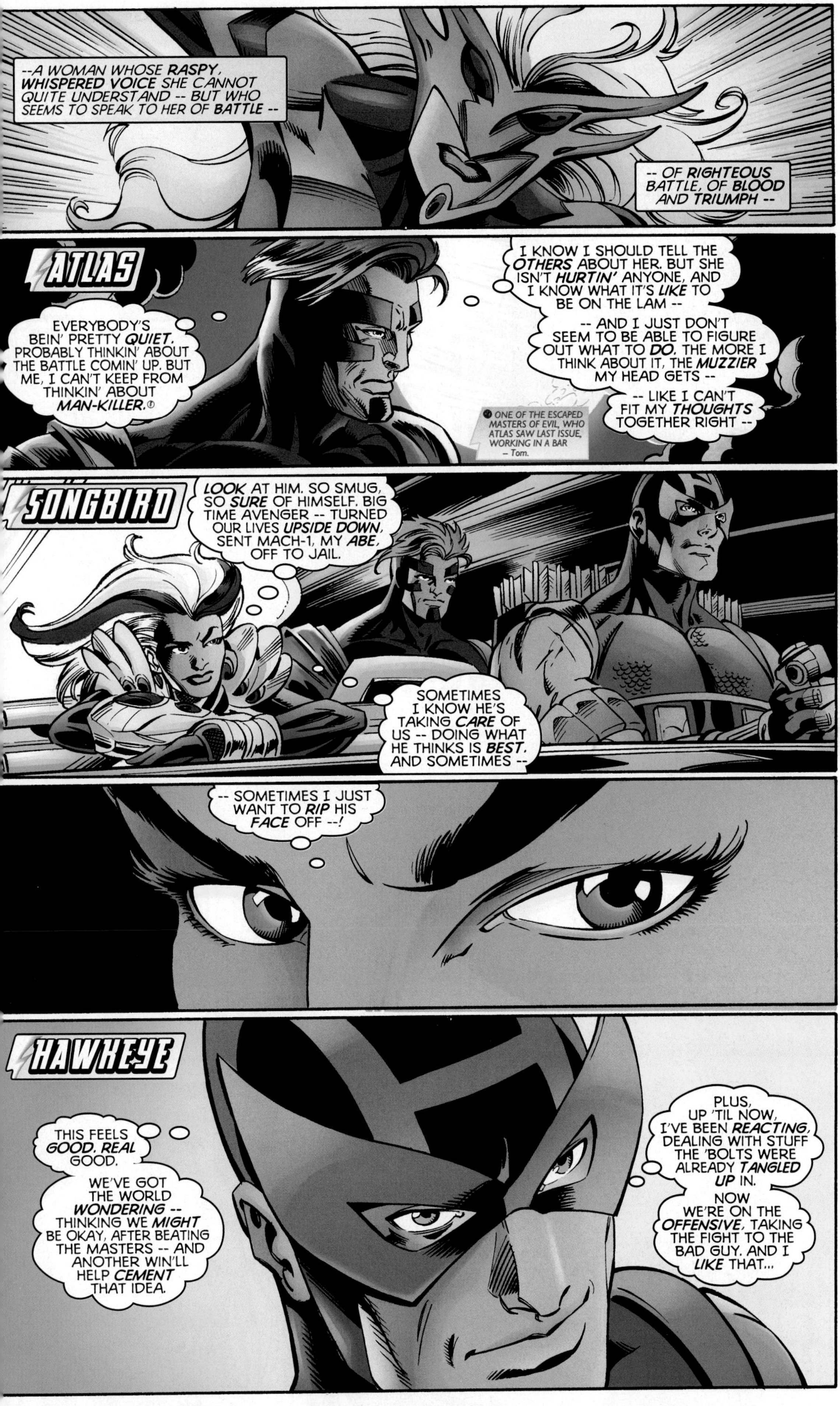
--A WOMAN WHOSE RASPY, WHISPERED VOICE SHE CANNOT QUITE UNDERSTAND -- BUT WHO SEEMS TO SPEAK TO HER OF BATTLE --
-- OF RIGHTEOUS BATTLE, OF BLOOD AND TRIUMPH --
ATLAS
EVERYBODY'S BEIN' PRETTY QUIET. PROBABLY THINKIN' ABOUT THE BATTLE COMIN' UP. BUT ME, I CAN'T KEEP FROM THINKIN' ABOUT MAN-KILLER.
ONE OF THE ESCAPED MASTERS OF EVIL, WHO ATLAS SAW LAST ISSUE, WORKING IN A BAR -- Tom.
I KNOW I SHOULD TELL THE OTHERS ABOUT HER. BUT SHE ISN'T HURTIN' ANYONE, AND I KNOW WHAT IT'S LIKE TO BE ON THE LAM --
-- AND I JUST DON'T SEEM TO BE ABLE TO FIGURE OUT WHAT TO DO. THE MORE I THINK ABOUT IT, THE MUZZIER MY HEAD GETS --
-- LIKE I CAN'T FIT MY THOUGHTS TOGETHER RIGHT --
SONGBIRD
LOOK AT HIM. SO SMUG, SO SURE OF HIMSELF. BIG TIME AVENGER -- TURNED OUR LIVES UPSIDE DOWN, SENT MACH-1, MY ABE, OFF TO JAIL.
SOMETIMES I KNOW HE'S TAKING CARE OF US -- DOING WHAT HE THINKS IS BEST. AND SOMETIMES --
-- SOMETIMES I JUST WANT TO RIP HIS FACE OFF --!
HAWKEYE
THIS FEELS GOOD. REAL GOOD.
WE'VE GOT THE WORLD WONDERING -- THINKING WE MIGHT BE OKAY, AFTER BEATING THE MASTERS -- AND ANOTHER WIN'LL HELP CEMENT THAT IDEA.
PLUS, UP 'TIL NOW, I'VE BEEN REACTING, DEALING WITH STUFF THE 'BOLTS WERE ALREADY TANGLED UP IN.
NOW WE'RE ON THE OFFENSIVE, TAKING THE FIGHT TO THE BAD GUY. AND I LIKE THAT...

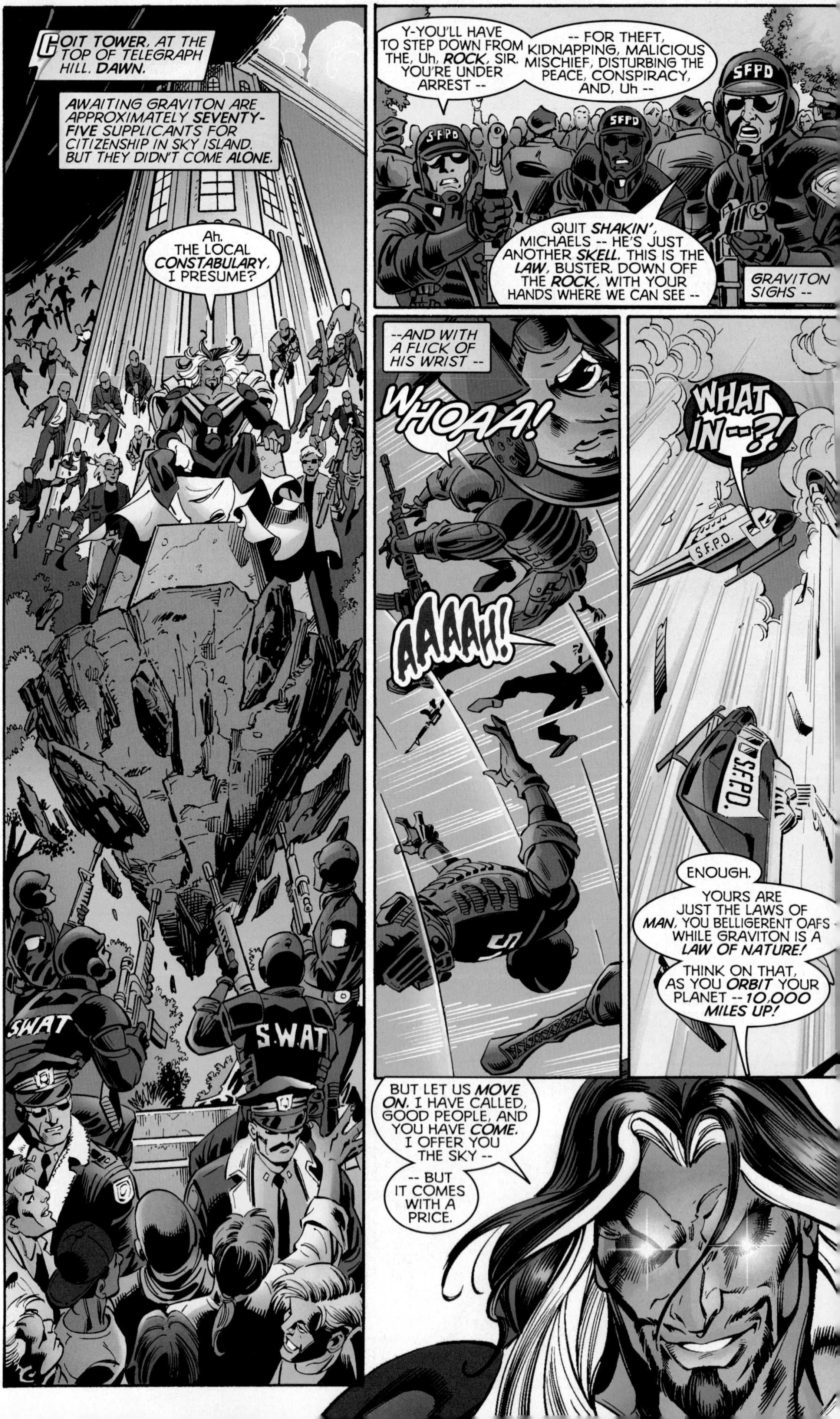

COIT TOWER, AT THE TOP OF TELEGRAPH HILL. DAWN.
AWAITING GRAVITON ARE APPROXIMATELY SEVENTY-FIVE SUPPLICANTS FOR CITIZENSHIP IN SKY ISLAND. BUT THEY DIDN'T COME ALONE.
Ah. THE LOCAL CONSTABULARY, I PRESUME?
SWAT
S.W.A.T
Y-YOU'LL HAVE TO STEP DOWN FROM THE, Uh, ROCK, SIR. YOU'RE UNDER ARREST --
-- FOR THEFT, KIDNAPPING, MALICIOUS MISCHIEF, DISTURBING THE PEACE, CONSPIRACY, AND, Uh --
SFPD
QUIT SHAKIN', MICHAELS -- HE'S JUST ANOTHER SKELL. THIS IS THE LAW, BUSTER. DOWN OFF THE ROCK, WITH YOUR HANDS WHERE WE CAN SEE --
GRAVITON SIGHS --
--AND WITH A FLICK OF HIS WRIST --
WHOAA!
AAAAH!
WHAT IN--?!
S.F.P.D.
S.F.P.D.
ENOUGH.
YOURS ARE JUST THE LAWS OF MAN, YOU BELLIGERENT OAFS WHILE GRAVITON IS A LAW OF NATURE!
THINK ON THAT, AS YOU ORBIT YOUR PLANET -- 10,000 MILES UP!
BUT LET US MOVE ON. I HAVE CALLED, GOOD PEOPLE, AND YOU HAVE COME. I OFFER YOU THE SKY --
-- BUT IT COMES WITH A PRICE.

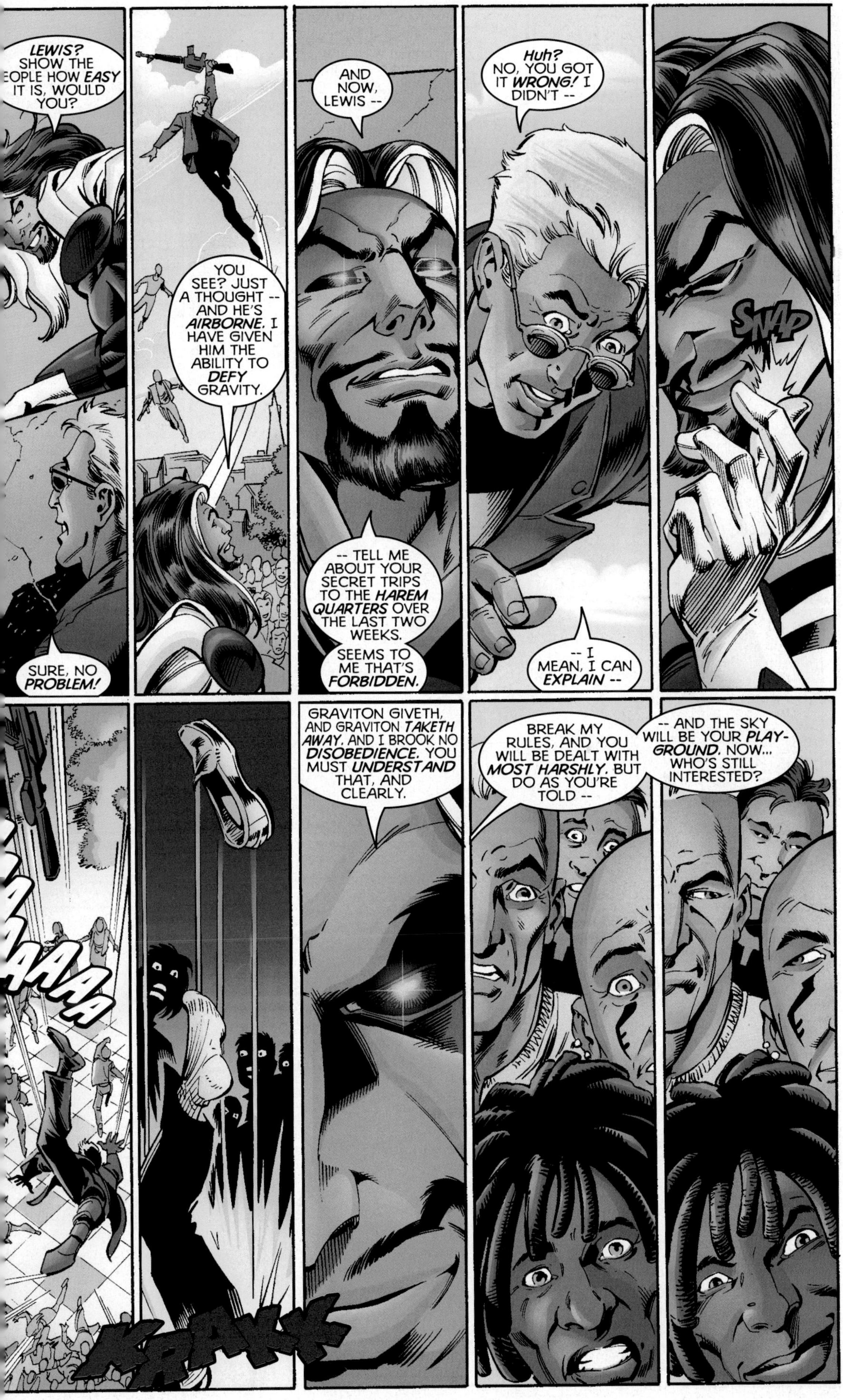
LEWIS? SHOW THE EOPLE HOW EASY IT IS, WOULD YOU?
SURE, NO PROBLEM!
YOU SEE? JUST A THOUGHT -- AND HE'S AIRBORNE. I HAVE GIVEN HIM THE ABILITY TO DEFY GRAVITY.
AND NOW, LEWIS --
-- TELL ME ABOUT YOUR SECRET TRIPS TO THE HAREM QUARTERS OVER THE LAST TWO WEEKS.
SEEMS TO ME THAT'S FORBIDDEN.
Huh? NO, YOU GOT IT WRONG! I DIDN'T --
-- I MEAN, I CAN EXPLAIN --
SNAP
AAAAAAA
KRAKK
GRAVITON GIVETH, AND GRAVITON TAKETH AWAY. AND I BROOK NO DISOBEDIENCE. YOU MUST UNDERSTAND THAT, AND CLEARLY.
BREAK MY RULES, AND YOU WILL BE DEALT WITH MOST HARSHLY. BUT DO AS YOU'RE TOLD --
-- AND THE SKY WILL BE YOUR PLAY-GROUND. NOW... WHO'S STILL INTERESTED?

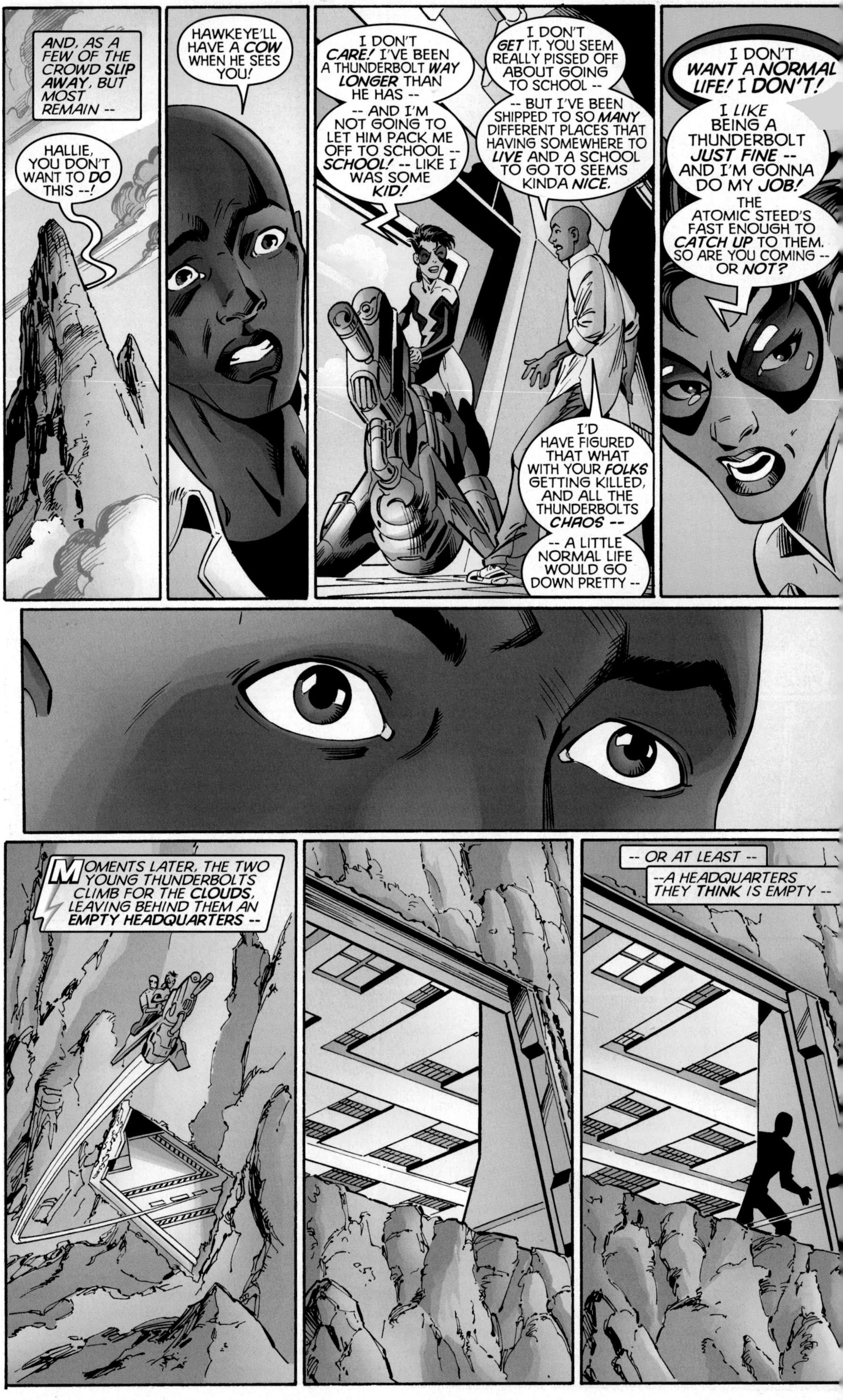
AND, AS A FEW OF THE CROWD SLIP AWAY, BUT MOST REMAIN --
HALLIE, YOU DON'T WANT TO DO THIS --!
HAWKEYE'LL HAVE A COW WHEN HE SEES YOU!
I DON'T CARE! I'VE BEEN A THUNDERBOLT WAY LONGER THAN HE HAS --
-- AND I'M NOT GOING TO LET HIM PACK ME OFF TO SCHOOL -- SCHOOL! -- LIKE I WAS SOME KID!
I DON'T GET IT. YOU SEEM REALLY PISSED OFF ABOUT GOING TO SCHOOL --
-- BUT I'VE BEEN SHIPPED TO SO MANY DIFFERENT PLACES THAT HAVING SOMEWHERE TO LIVE AND A SCHOOL TO GO TO SEEMS KINDA NICE.
I'D HAVE FIGURED THAT WHAT WITH YOUR FOLKS GETTING KILLED, AND ALL THE THUNDERBOLTS CHAOS --
-- A LITTLE NORMAL LIFE WOULD GO DOWN PRETTY --
I DON'T WANT A NORMAL LIFE! I DON'T!
I LIKE BEING A THUNDERBOLT JUST FINE -- AND I'M GONNA DO MY JOB!
THE ATOMIC STEED'S FAST ENOUGH TO CATCH UP TO THEM. SO ARE YOU COMING -- OR NOT?
MOMENTS LATER, THE TWO YOUNG THUNDERBOLTS CLIMB FOR THE CLOUDS, LEAVING BEHIND THEM AN EMPTY HEADQUARTERS --
-- OR AT LEAST --
--A HEADQUARTERS THEY THINK IS EMPTY --

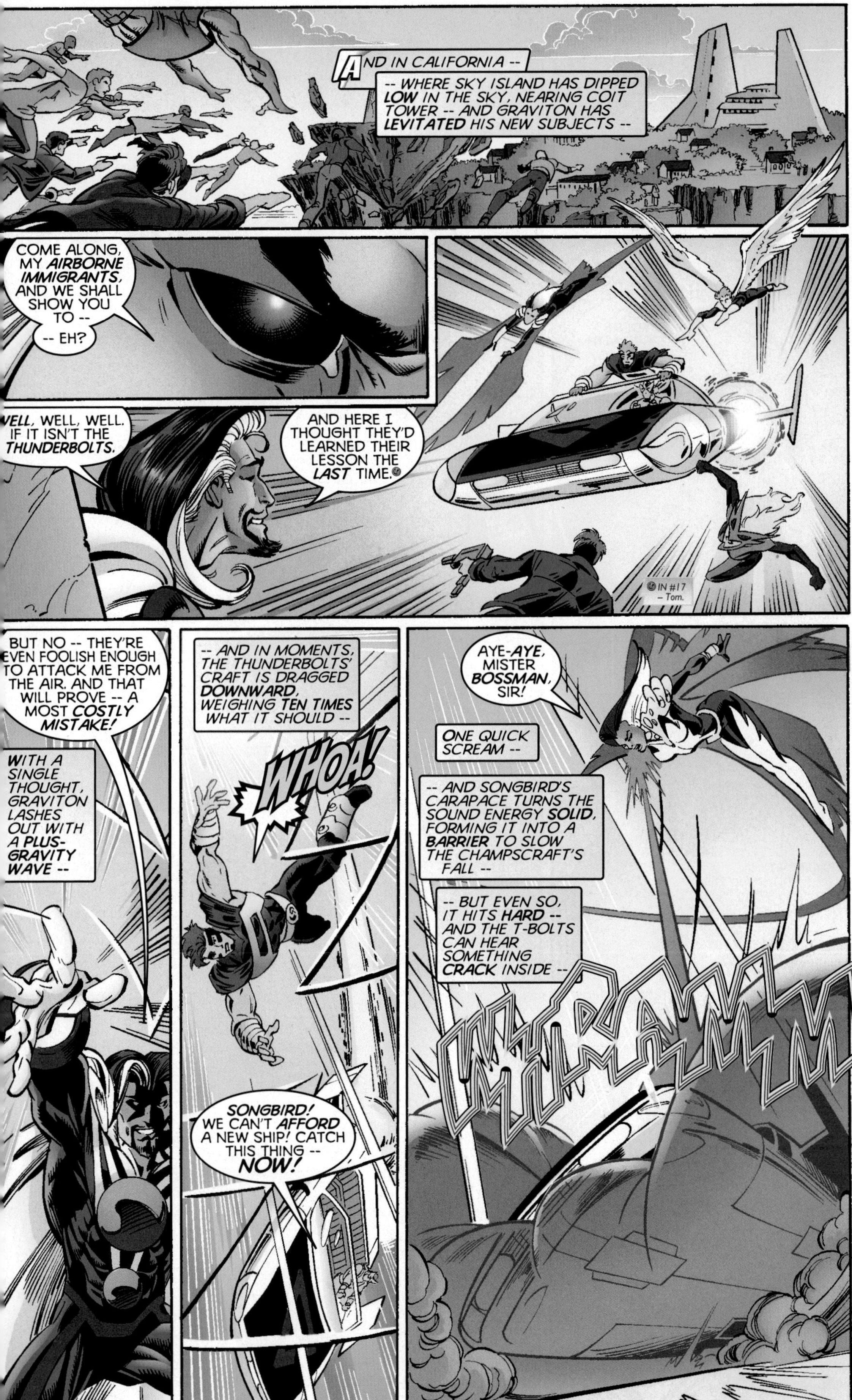
AND IN CALIFORNIA --
-- WHERE SKY ISLAND HAS DIPPED LOW IN THE SKY, NEARING COIT TOWER -- AND GRAVITON HAS LEVITATED HIS NEW SUBJECTS --
COME ALONG, MY AIRBORNE IMMIGRANTS, AND WE SHALL SHOW YOU TO --
-- EH?
WELL, WELL, WELL. IF IT ISN'T THE THUNDERBOLTS.
AND HERE I THOUGHT THEY'D LEARNED THEIR LESSON THE LAST TIME.
IN #17 – Tom.
BUT NO -- THEY'RE EVEN FOOLISH ENOUGH TO ATTACK ME FROM THE AIR. AND THAT WILL PROVE -- A MOST COSTLY MISTAKE!
WITH A SINGLE THOUGHT, GRAVITON LASHES OUT WITH A PLUS-GRAVITY WAVE --
-- AND IN MOMENTS, THE THUNDERBOLTS' CRAFT IS DRAGGED DOWNWARD, WEIGHING TEN TIMES WHAT IT SHOULD --
WHOA!
SONGBIRD! WE CAN'T AFFORD A NEW SHIP! CATCH THIS THING -- NOW!
AYE-AYE, MISTER BOSSMAN, SIR!
ONE QUICK SCREAM --
-- AND SONGBIRD'S CARAPACE TURNS THE SOUND ENERGY SOLID, FORMING IT INTO A BARRIER TO SLOW THE CHAMPSCRAFT'S FALL --
-- BUT EVEN SO, IT HITS HARD -- AND THE T-BOLTS CAN HEAR SOMETHING CRACK INSIDE --

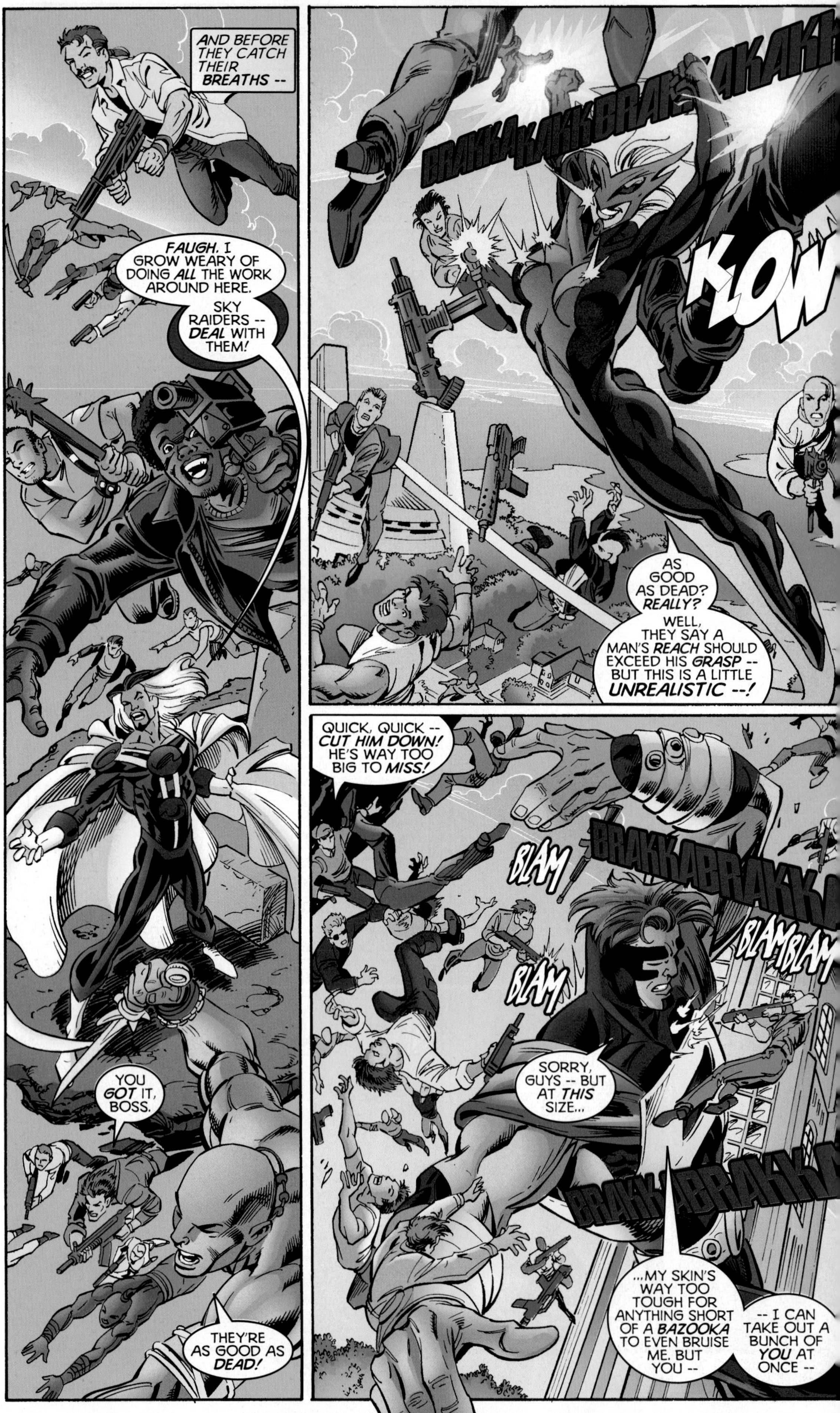
AND BEFORE THEY CATCH THEIR BREATHS --
FAUGH. I GROW WEARY OF DOING ALL THE WORK AROUND HERE.
SKY RAIDERS -- DEAL WITH THEM!
YOU GOT IT, BOSS.
THEY'RE AS GOOD AS DEAD!
BRAKKAKAKKBRAKKAKAKK
KLOW
AS GOOD AS DEAD? REALLY?
WELL, THEY SAY A MAN'S REACH SHOULD EXCEED HIS GRASP -- BUT THIS IS A LITTLE UNREALISTIC --!
QUICK, QUICK -- CUT HIM DOWN! HE'S WAY TOO BIG TO MISS!
BLAM
BRAKKABRAKKA
BLAMBLAM
BLAM
SORRY, GUYS -- BUT AT THIS SIZE...
BRAKKABRAKK
...MY SKIN'S WAY TOO TOUGH FOR ANYTHING SHORT OF A BAZOOKA TO EVEN BRUISE ME. BUT YOU --
-- I CAN TAKE OUT A BUNCH OF YOU AT ONCE --

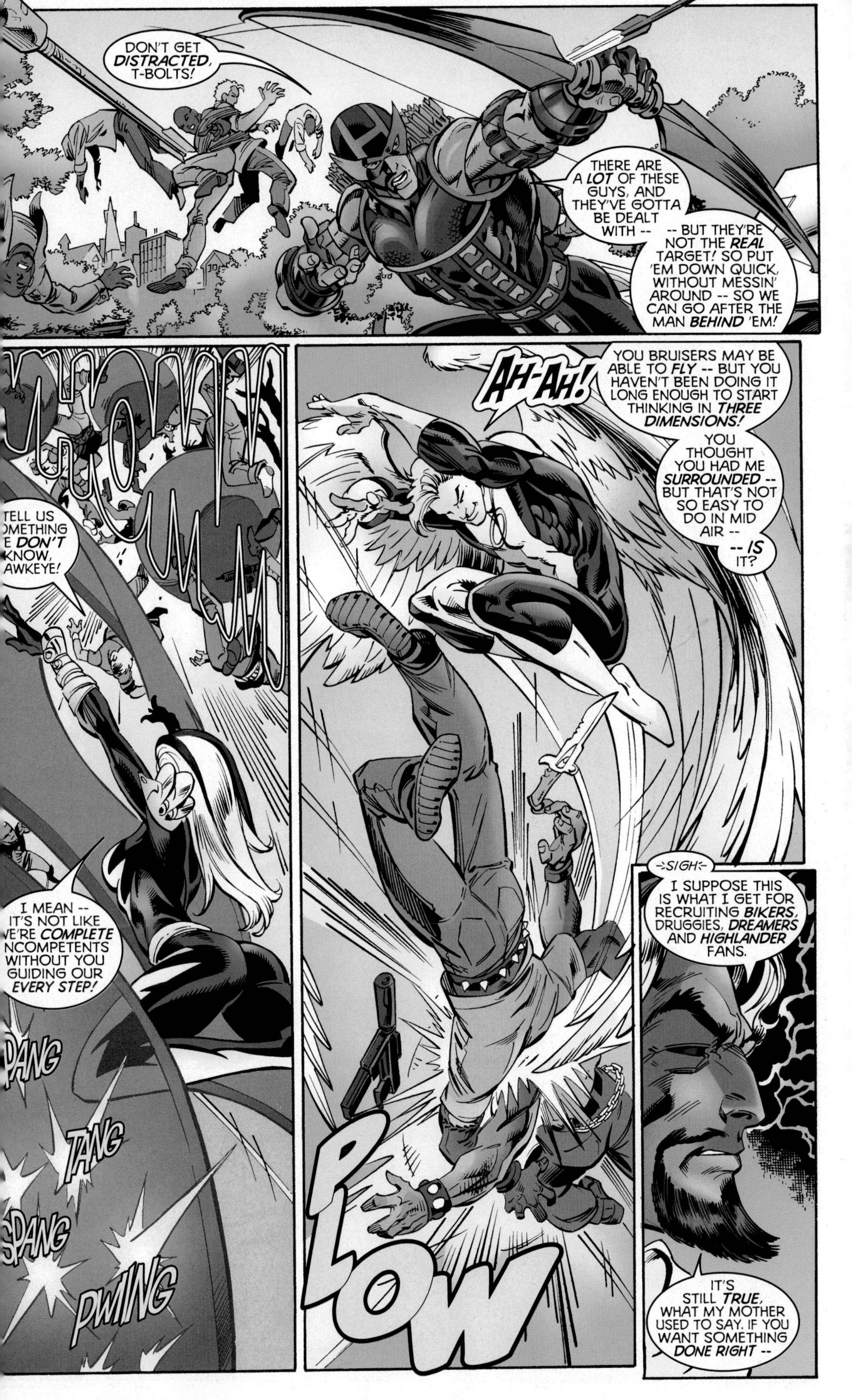

DON'T GET *DISTRACTED*, T-BOLTS!
THERE ARE A *LOT* OF THESE GUYS, AND THEY'VE GOTTA BE DEALT WITH --
-- BUT THEY'RE NOT THE *REAL* TARGET! SO PUT 'EM DOWN QUICK, WITHOUT MESSIN' AROUND -- SO WE CAN GO AFTER THE MAN *BEHIND* 'EM!
TELL US OMETHING E *DON'T* KNOW, AWKEYE!
I MEAN -- IT'S NOT LIKE E'RE *COMPLETE* NCOMPETENTS WITHOUT YOU UIDING OUR *EVERY STEP!*
PANG
TANG
SPANG
PWING
AH-AH!
YOU BRUISERS MAY BE ABLE TO *FLY* -- BUT YOU HAVEN'T BEEN DOING IT LONG ENOUGH TO START THINKING IN *THREE DIMENSIONS!*
YOU THOUGHT YOU HAD ME *SURROUNDED* -- BUT THAT'S NOT SO EASY TO DO IN MID AIR --
-- *IS* IT?
PLOW
-SIGH-
I SUPPOSE THIS IS WHAT I GET FOR RECRUITING *BIKERS*, DRUGGIES, *DREAMERS* AND *HIGHLANDER* FANS.
IT'S STILL *TRUE*, WHAT MY MOTHER USED TO SAY. IF YOU WANT SOMETHING *DONE RIGHT* --

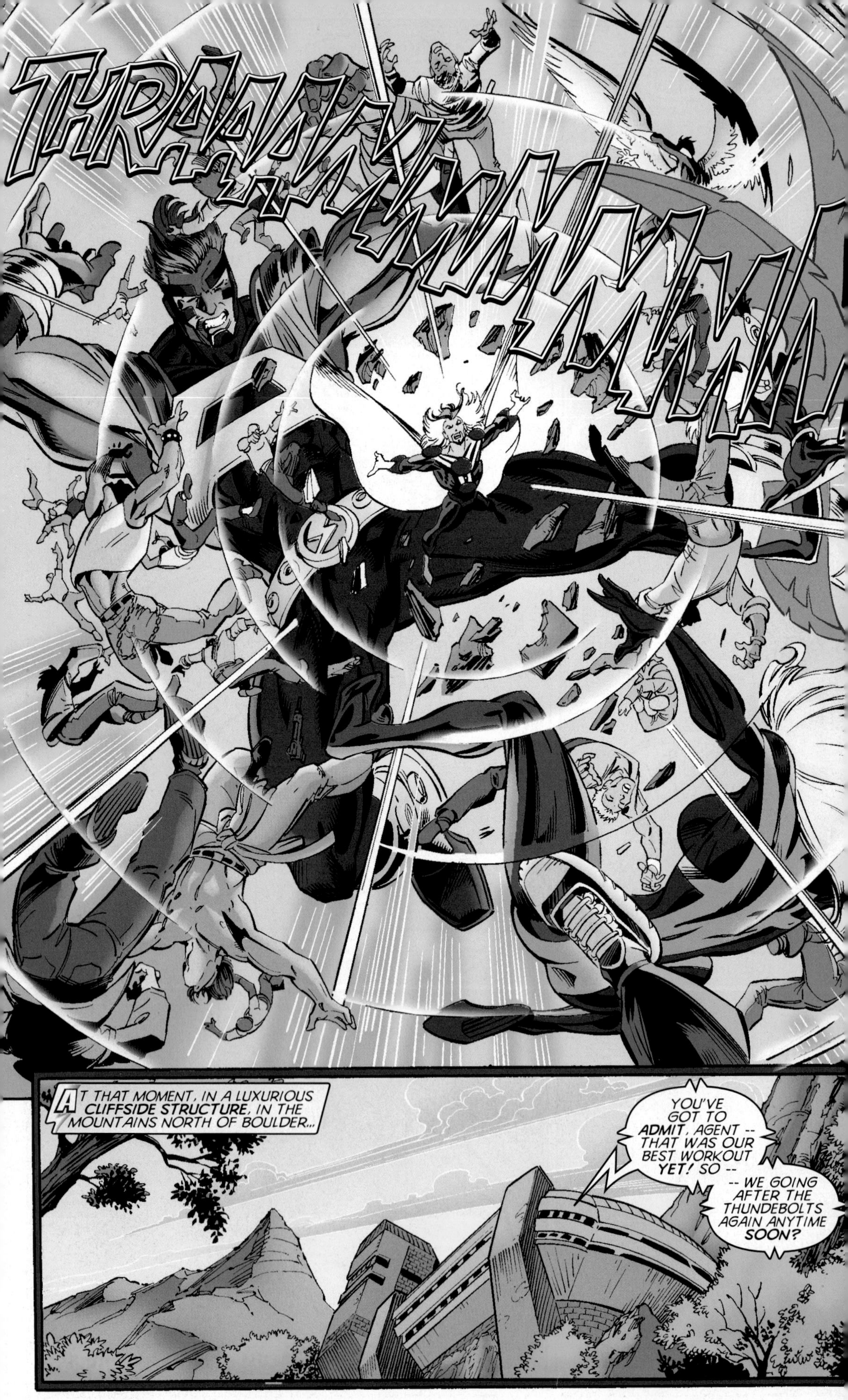
THRAAAAMMMMMMM
AT THAT MOMENT, IN A LUXURIOUS CLIFFSIDE STRUCTURE, IN THE MOUNTAINS NORTH OF BOULDER...
YOU'VE GOT TO ADMIT, AGENT -- THAT WAS OUR BEST WORKOUT YET! SO --
-- WE GOING AFTER THE THUNDEBOLTS AGAIN ANYTIME SOON?

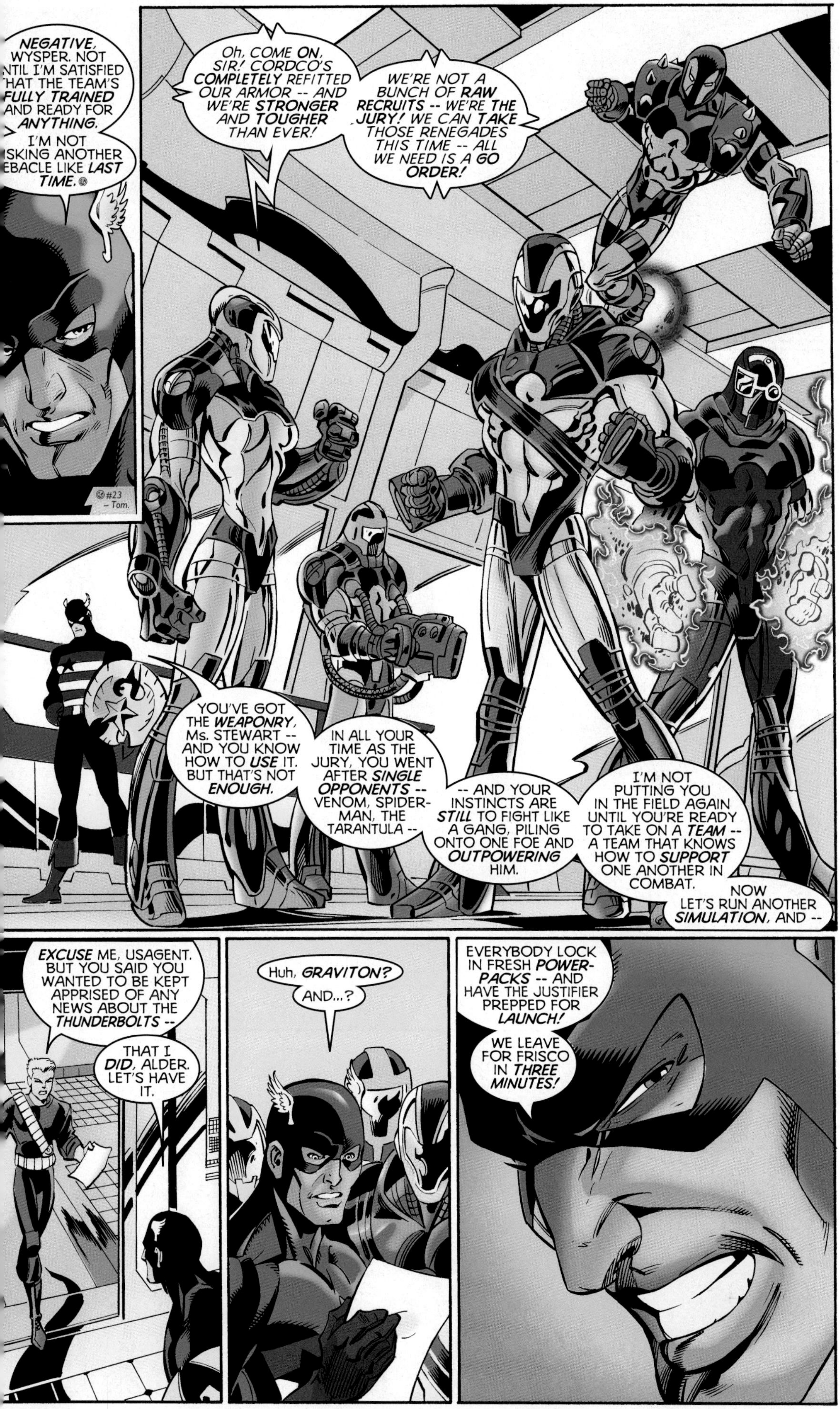
NEGATIVE, WYSPER. NOT NTIL I'M SATISFIED HAT THE TEAM'S FULLY TRAINED AND READY FOR ANYTHING.
I'M NOT ISKING ANOTHER EBACLE LIKE LAST TIME.
#23 – Tom.
Oh, COME ON, SIR! CORDCO'S COMPLETELY REFITTED OUR ARMOR -- AND WE'RE STRONGER AND TOUGHER THAN EVER!
WE'RE NOT A BUNCH OF RAW RECRUITS -- WE'RE THE JURY! WE CAN TAKE THOSE RENEGADES THIS TIME -- ALL WE NEED IS A GO ORDER!
YOU'VE GOT THE WEAPONRY, Ms. STEWART -- AND YOU KNOW HOW TO USE IT. BUT THAT'S NOT ENOUGH.
IN ALL YOUR TIME AS THE JURY, YOU WENT AFTER SINGLE OPPONENTS -- VENOM, SPIDER-MAN, THE TARANTULA --
-- AND YOUR INSTINCTS ARE STILL TO FIGHT LIKE A GANG, PILING ONTO ONE FOE AND OUTPOWERING HIM.
I'M NOT PUTTING YOU IN THE FIELD AGAIN UNTIL YOU'RE READY TO TAKE ON A TEAM -- A TEAM THAT KNOWS HOW TO SUPPORT ONE ANOTHER IN COMBAT.
NOW LET'S RUN ANOTHER SIMULATION, AND --
EXCUSE ME, USAGENT. BUT YOU SAID YOU WANTED TO BE KEPT APPRISED OF ANY NEWS ABOUT THE THUNDERBOLTS --
THAT I DID, ALDER. LET'S HAVE IT.
Huh, GRAVITON?
AND...?
EVERYBODY LOCK IN FRESH POWER-PACKS -- AND HAVE THE JUSTIFIER PREPPED FOR LAUNCH!
WE LEAVE FOR FRISCO IN THREE MINUTES!

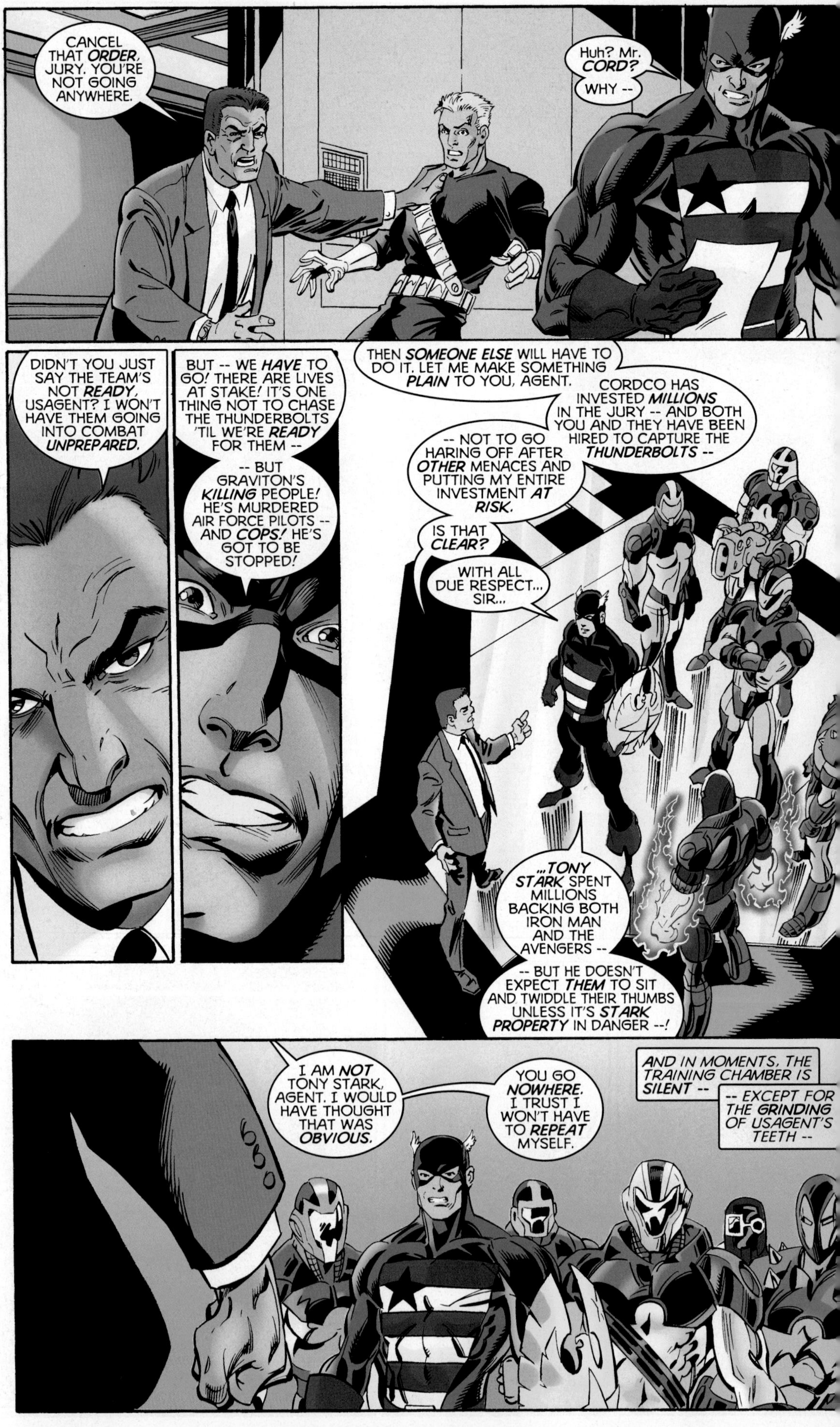
CANCEL THAT ORDER, JURY. YOU'RE NOT GOING ANYWHERE.
Huh? Mr. CORD?
WHY --
DIDN'T YOU JUST SAY THE TEAM'S NOT READY, USAGENT? I WON'T HAVE THEM GOING INTO COMBAT UNPREPARED.
BUT -- WE HAVE TO GO! THERE ARE LIVES AT STAKE! IT'S ONE THING NOT TO CHASE THE THUNDERBOLTS 'TIL WE'RE READY FOR THEM --
-- BUT GRAVITON'S KILLING PEOPLE! HE'S MURDERED AIR FORCE PILOTS -- AND COPS! HE'S GOT TO BE STOPPED!
THEN SOMEONE ELSE WILL HAVE TO DO IT. LET ME MAKE SOMETHING PLAIN TO YOU, AGENT.
CORDCO HAS INVESTED MILLIONS IN THE JURY -- AND BOTH YOU AND THEY HAVE BEEN HIRED TO CAPTURE THE THUNDERBOLTS --
-- NOT TO GO HARING OFF AFTER OTHER MENACES AND PUTTING MY ENTIRE INVESTMENT AT RISK.
IS THAT CLEAR?
WITH ALL DUE RESPECT... SIR...
...TONY STARK SPENT MILLIONS BACKING BOTH IRON MAN AND THE AVENGERS --
-- BUT HE DOESN'T EXPECT THEM TO SIT AND TWIDDLE THEIR THUMBS UNLESS IT'S STARK PROPERTY IN DANGER --!
I AM NOT TONY STARK, AGENT. I WOULD HAVE THOUGHT THAT WAS OBVIOUS.
YOU GO NOWHERE. I TRUST I WON'T HAVE TO REPEAT MYSELF.
AND IN MOMENTS, THE TRAINING CHAMBER IS SILENT --
-- EXCEPT FOR THE GRINDING OF USAGENT'S TEETH --

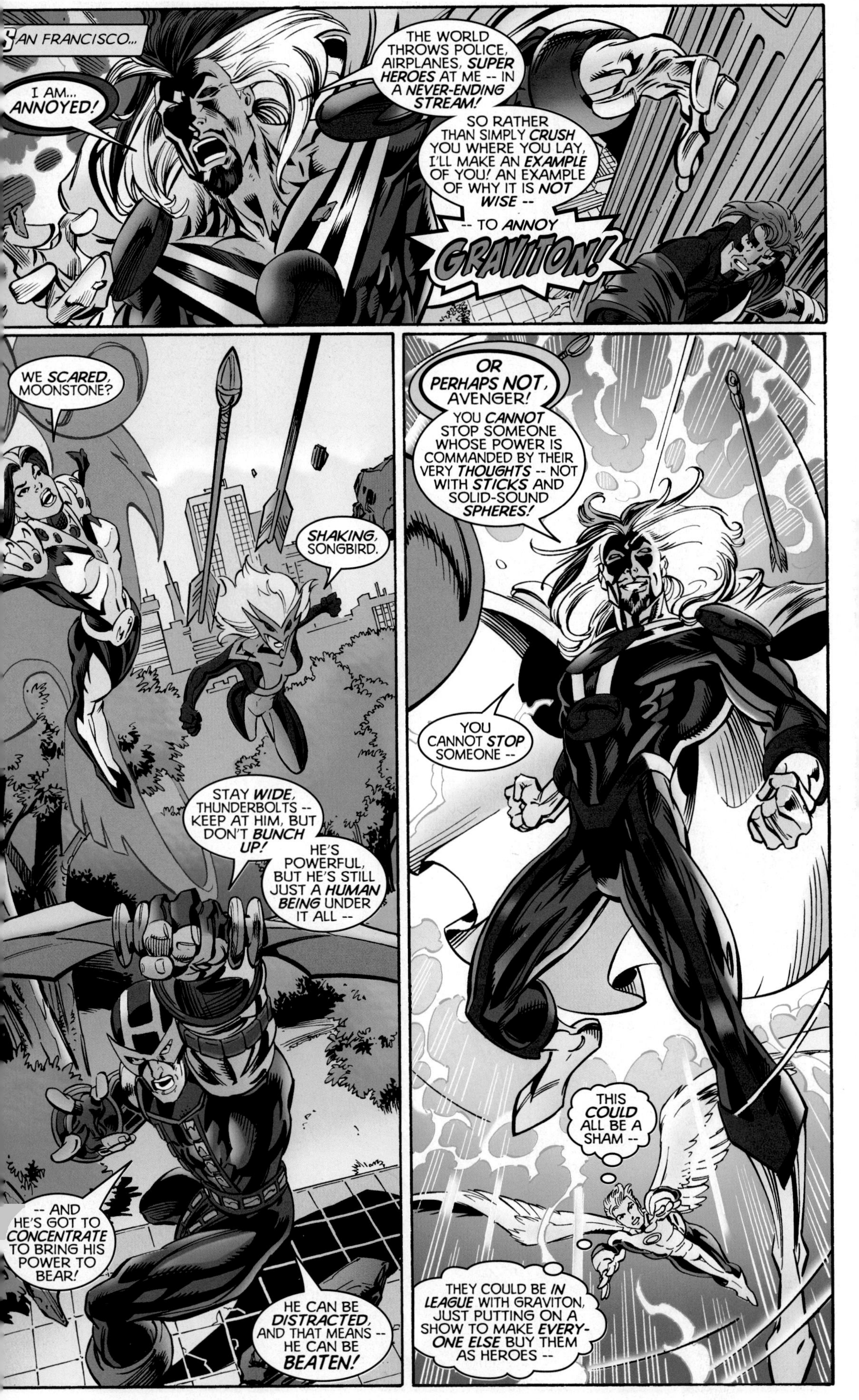
SAN FRANCISCO...
I AM... ANNOYED!
THE WORLD THROWS POLICE, AIRPLANES, SUPER HEROES AT ME -- IN A NEVER-ENDING STREAM!
SO RATHER THAN SIMPLY CRUSH YOU WHERE YOU LAY, I'LL MAKE AN EXAMPLE OF YOU! AN EXAMPLE OF WHY IT IS NOT WISE --
-- TO ANNOY
GRAVITON!
WE SCARED, MOONSTONE?
SHAKING, SONGBIRD.
STAY WIDE, THUNDERBOLTS -- KEEP AT HIM, BUT DON'T BUNCH UP!
HE'S POWERFUL, BUT HE'S STILL JUST A HUMAN BEING UNDER IT ALL --
-- AND HE'S GOT TO CONCENTRATE TO BRING HIS POWER TO BEAR!
HE CAN BE DISTRACTED, AND THAT MEANS -- HE CAN BE BEATEN!
OR PERHAPS NOT, AVENGER!
YOU CANNOT STOP SOMEONE WHOSE POWER IS COMMANDED BY THEIR VERY THOUGHTS -- NOT WITH STICKS AND SOLID-SOUND SPHERES!
YOU CANNOT STOP SOMEONE --
THIS COULD ALL BE A SHAM --
THEY COULD BE IN LEAGUE WITH GRAVITON, JUST PUTTING ON A SHOW TO MAKE EVERY-ONE ELSE BUY THEM AS HEROES --

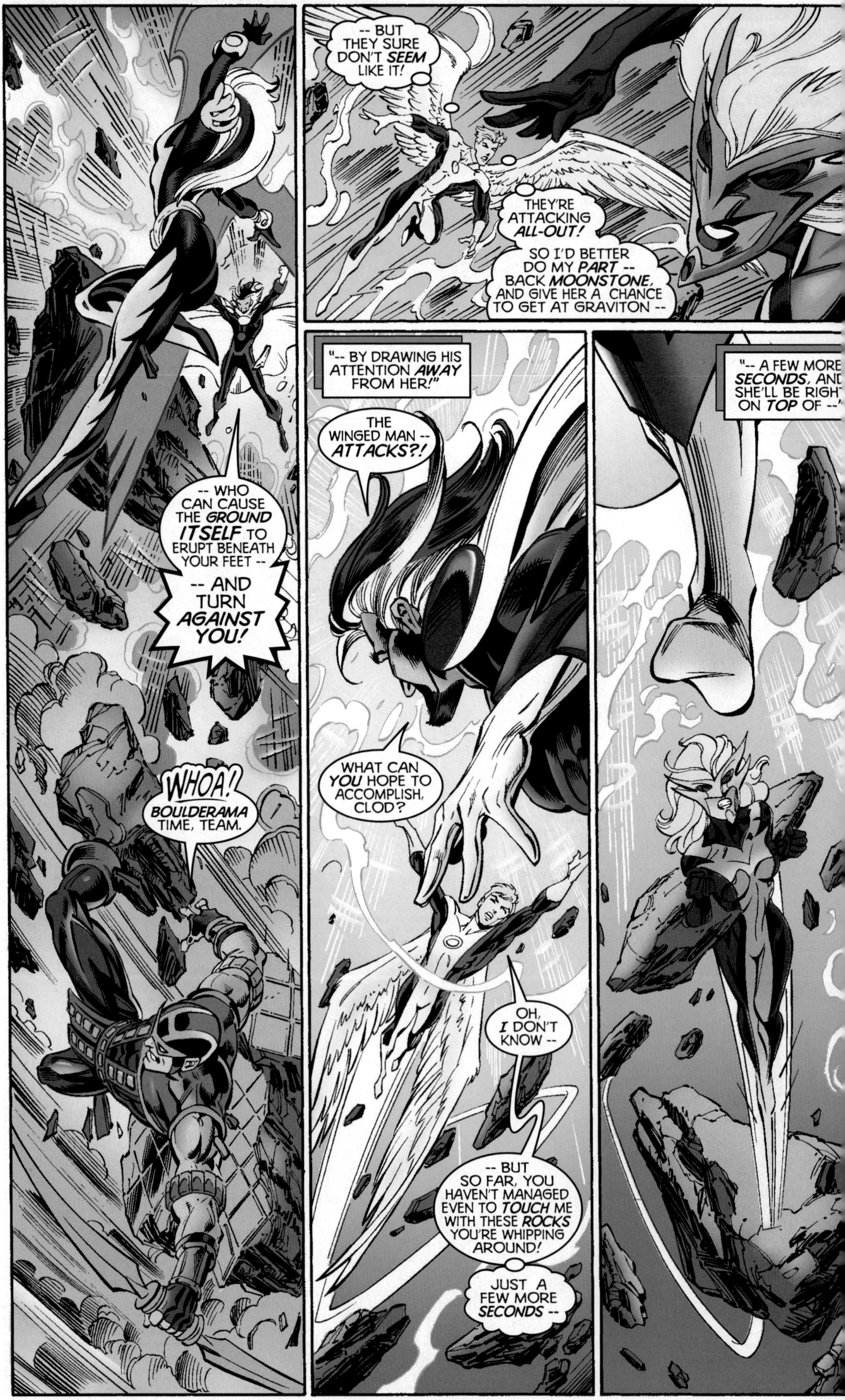
-- WHO CAN CAUSE THE GROUND ITSELF TO ERUPT BENEATH YOUR FEET --
-- AND TURN AGAINST YOU!
WHOA! BOULDERAMA TIME, TEAM.
-- BUT THEY SURE DON'T SEEM LIKE IT!
THEY'RE ATTACKING ALL-OUT!
SO I'D BETTER DO MY PART -- BACK MOONSTONE, AND GIVE HER A CHANCE TO GET AT GRAVITON --
"-- BY DRAWING HIS ATTENTION AWAY FROM HER!"
THE WINGED MAN -- ATTACKS?!
WHAT CAN YOU HOPE TO ACCOMPLISH, CLOD?
OH, I DON'T KNOW --
-- BUT SO FAR, YOU HAVEN'T MANAGED EVEN TO TOUCH ME WITH THESE ROCKS YOU'RE WHIPPING AROUND!
JUST A FEW MORE SECONDS --
"-- A FEW MORE SECONDS, AND SHE'LL BE RIGHT ON TOP OF --"

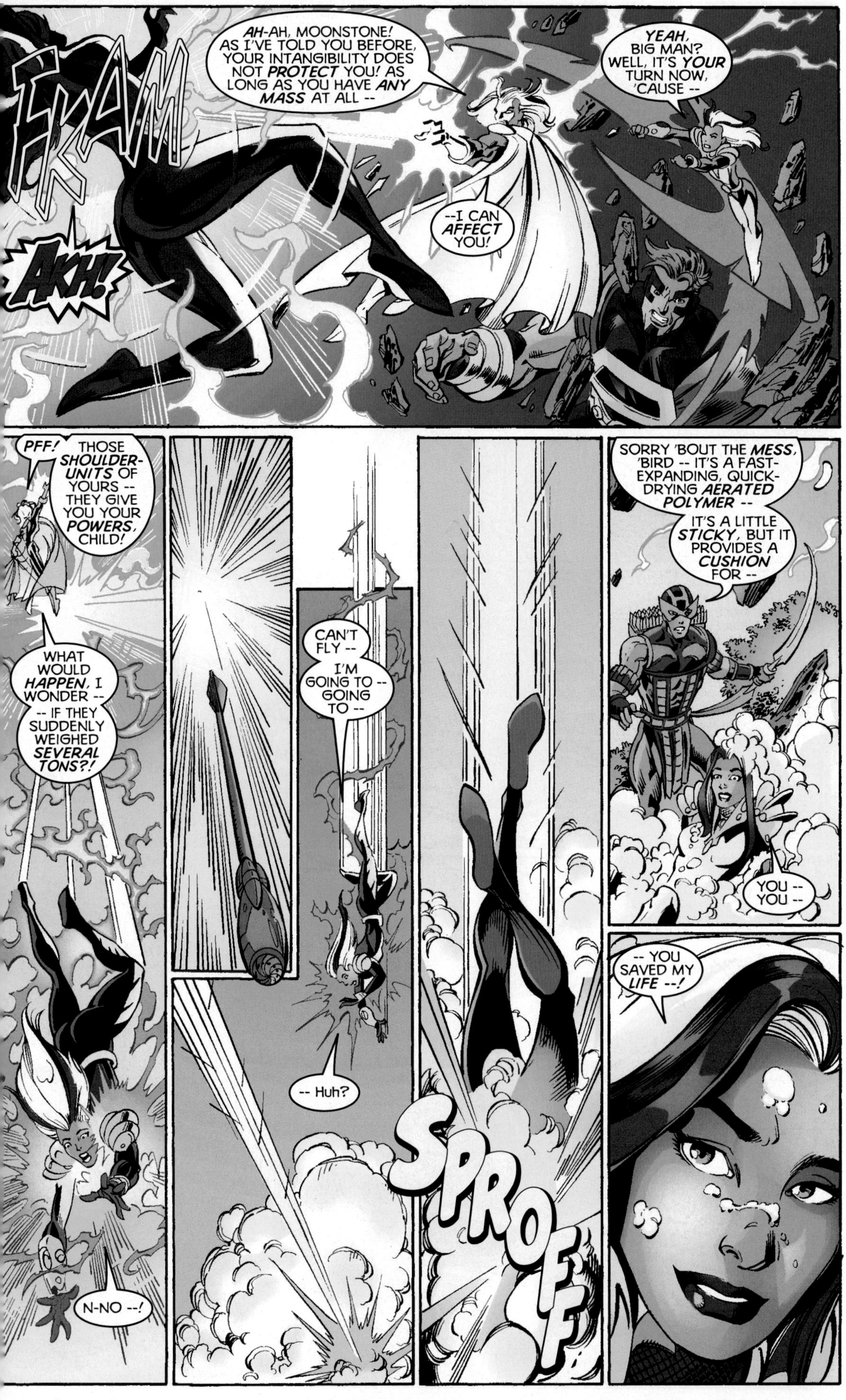
FZAM
AKH!
AH-AH, MOONSTONE! AS I'VE TOLD YOU BEFORE, YOUR INTANGIBILITY DOES NOT PROTECT YOU! AS LONG AS YOU HAVE ANY MASS AT ALL --
--I CAN AFFECT YOU!
YEAH, BIG MAN? WELL, IT'S YOUR TURN NOW, 'CAUSE --
PFF!
THOSE SHOULDER-UNITS OF YOURS -- THEY GIVE YOU YOUR POWERS, CHILD!
WHAT WOULD HAPPEN, I WONDER --
-- IF THEY SUDDENLY WEIGHED SEVERAL TONS?!
N-NO --!
CAN'T FLY --
I'M GOING TO -- GOING TO --
-- Huh?
SPROFF
SORRY 'BOUT THE MESS, 'BIRD -- IT'S A FAST-EXPANDING, QUICK-DRYING AERATED POLYMER --
IT'S A LITTLE STICKY, BUT IT PROVIDES A CUSHION FOR --
YOU -- YOU --
-- YOU SAVED MY LIFE --!

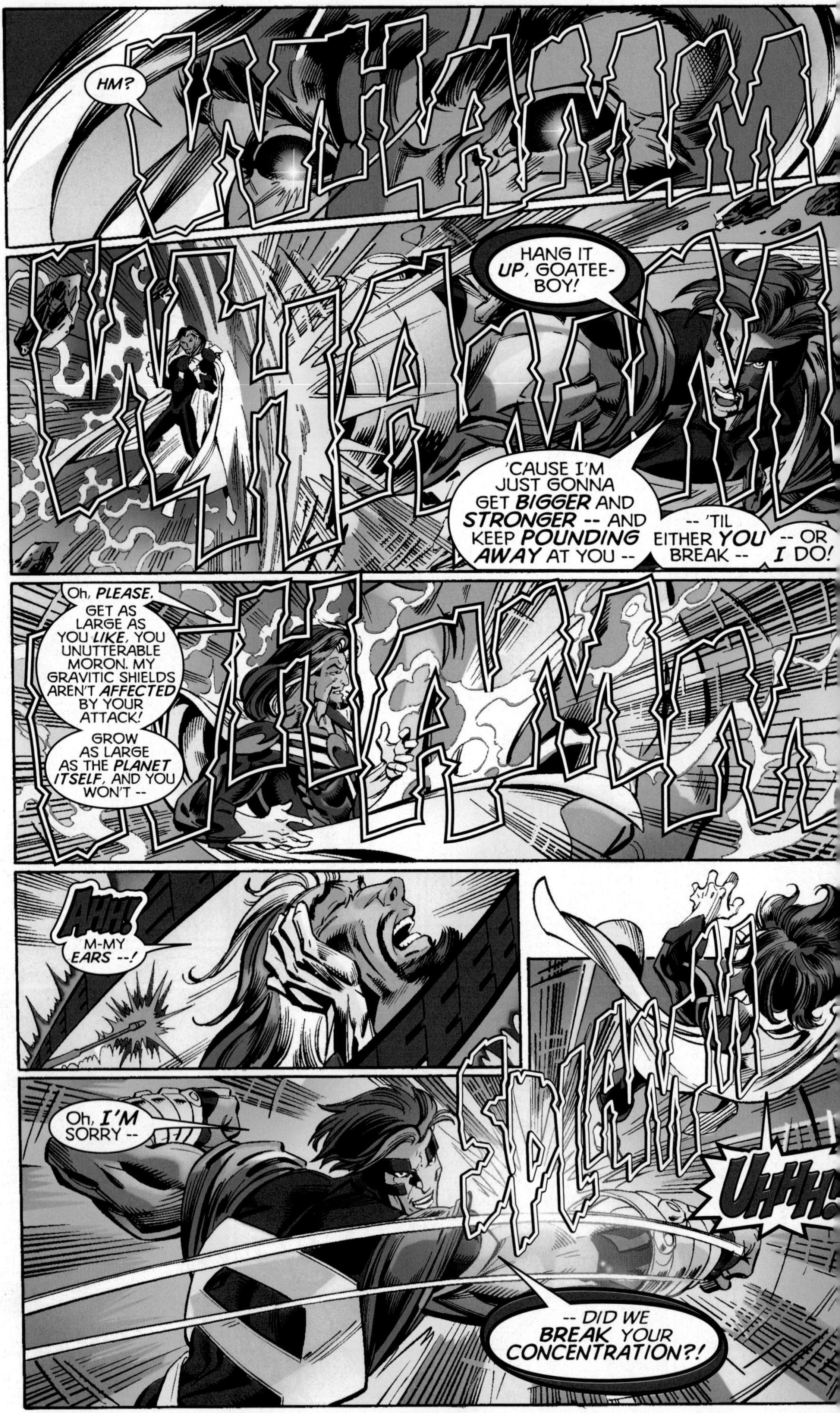
HM?
HANG IT UP, GOATEE-BOY!
'CAUSE I'M JUST GONNA GET BIGGER AND STRONGER -- AND KEEP POUNDING AWAY AT YOU --
-- 'TIL EITHER YOU BREAK --
-- OR I DO!
Oh, PLEASE. GET AS LARGE AS YOU LIKE, YOU UNUTTERABLE MORON. MY GRAVITIC SHIELDS AREN'T AFFECTED BY YOUR ATTACK!
GROW AS LARGE AS THE PLANET ITSELF, AND YOU WON'T --
AHH!
M-MY EARS --!
Oh, I'M SORRY --
UHHH!
-- DID WE BREAK YOUR CONCENTRATION?!

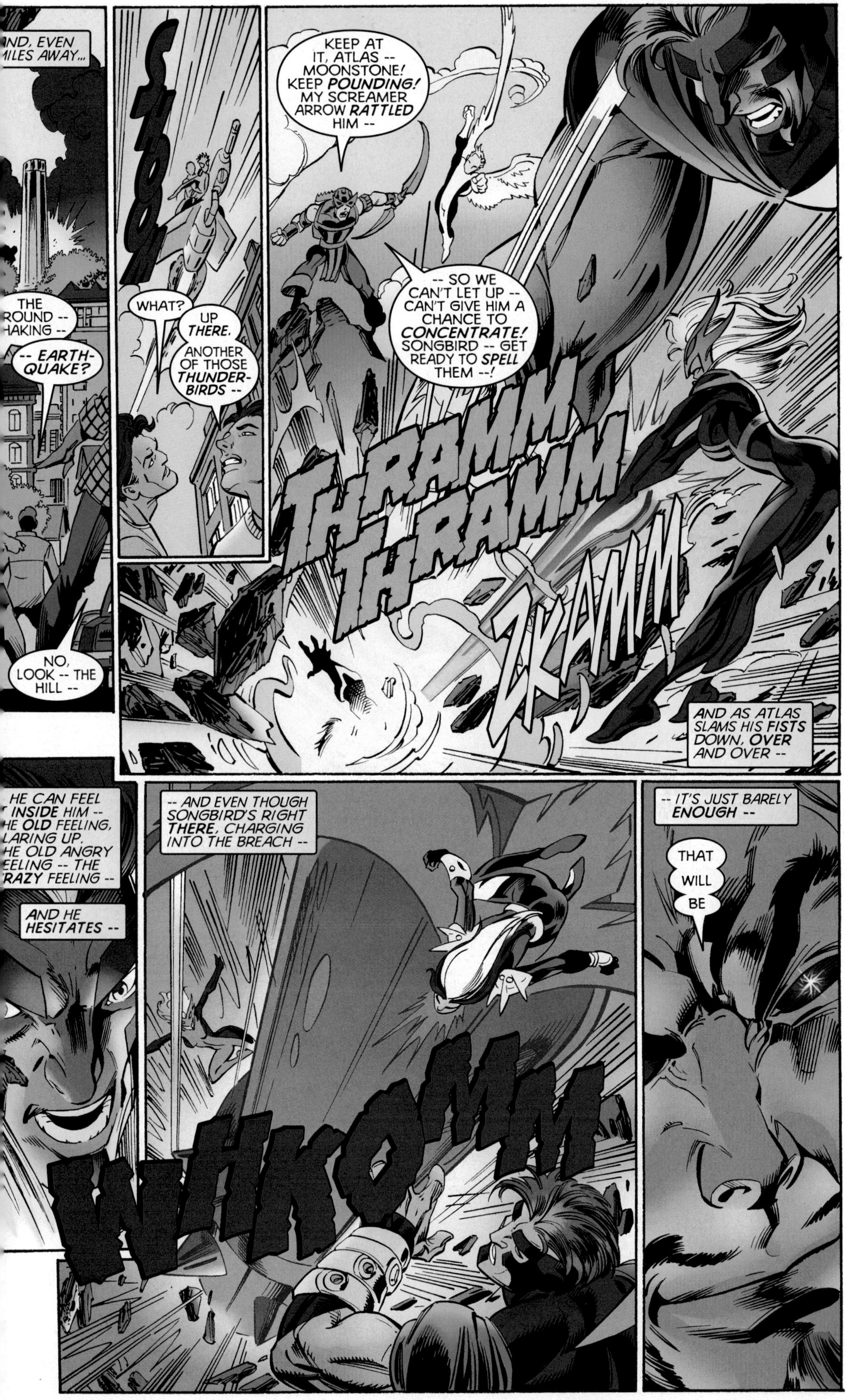
ND, EVEN MILES AWAY...
THE ROUND -- HAKING --
-- EARTH-QUAKE?
NO, LOOK -- THE HILL --
SHOOOM
WHAT?
UP THERE. ANOTHER OF THOSE THUNDER-BIRDS --
KEEP AT IT, ATLAS -- MOONSTONE! KEEP POUNDING! MY SCREAMER ARROW RATTLED HIM --
-- SO WE CAN'T LET UP -- CAN'T GIVE HIM A CHANCE TO CONCENTRATE! SONGBIRD -- GET READY TO SPELL THEM --!
THRAMM THRAMM THRAMM
ZKAMM
AND AS ATLAS SLAMS HIS FISTS DOWN, OVER AND OVER --
HE CAN FEEL INSIDE HIM -- HE OLD FEELING, LARING UP. HE OLD ANGRY EELING -- THE RAZY FEELING --
AND HE HESITATES --
-- AND EVEN THOUGH SONGBIRD'S RIGHT THERE, CHARGING INTO THE BREACH --
WHKOMM
-- IT'S JUST BARELY ENOUGH --
THAT WILL BE

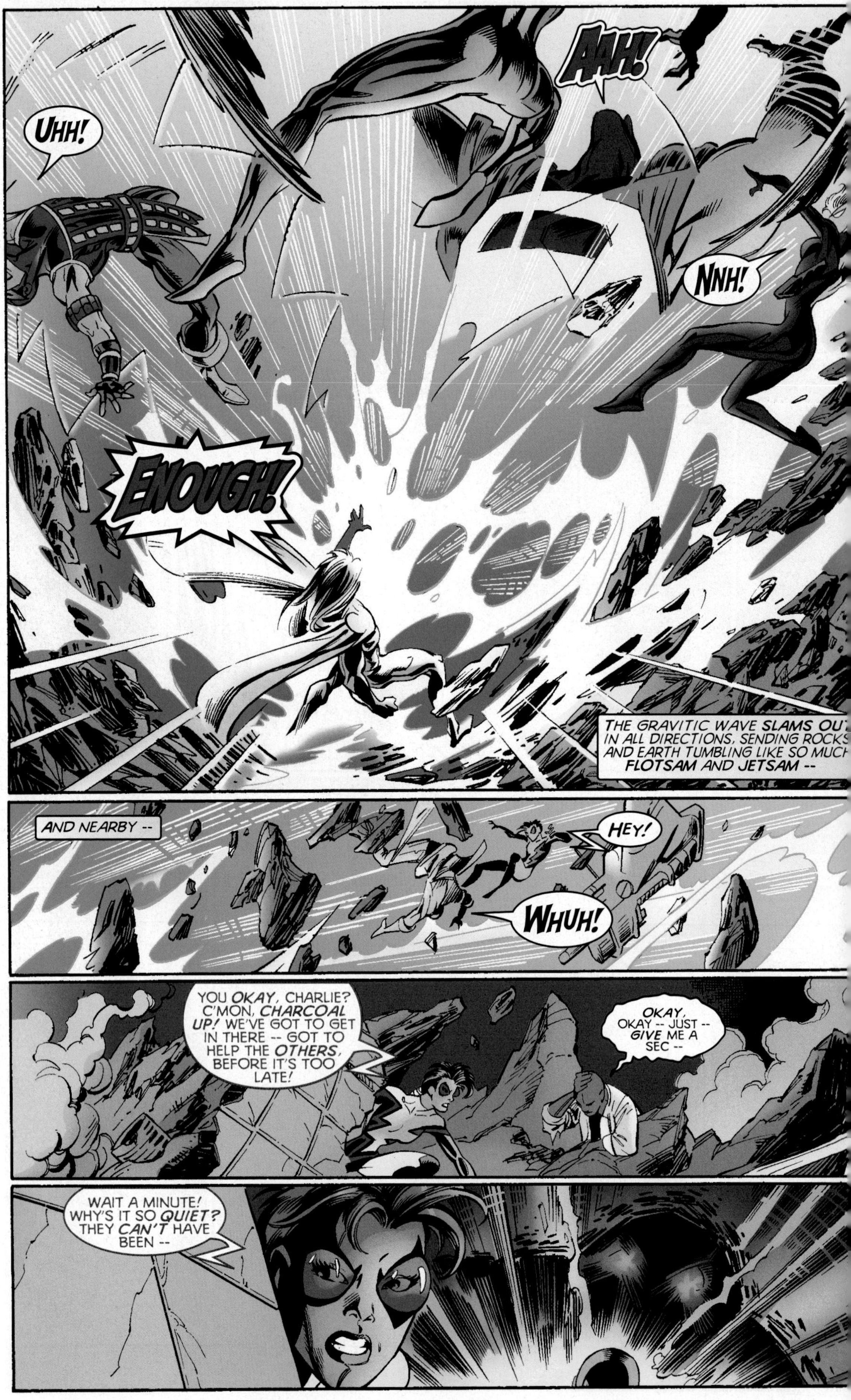
UHH!
AAH!
NNH!
ENOUGH!
THE GRAVITIC WAVE SLAMS OUT IN ALL DIRECTIONS, SENDING ROCKS AND EARTH TUMBLING LIKE SO MUCH FLOTSAM AND JETSAM --
AND NEARBY --
HEY!
WHUH!
YOU OKAY, CHARLIE? C'MON, CHARCOAL UP! WE'VE GOT TO GET IN THERE -- GOT TO HELP THE OTHERS, BEFORE IT'S TOO LATE!
OKAY, OKAY -- JUST -- GIVE ME A SEC --
WAIT A MINUTE! WHY'S IT SO QUIET? THEY CAN'T HAVE BEEN --

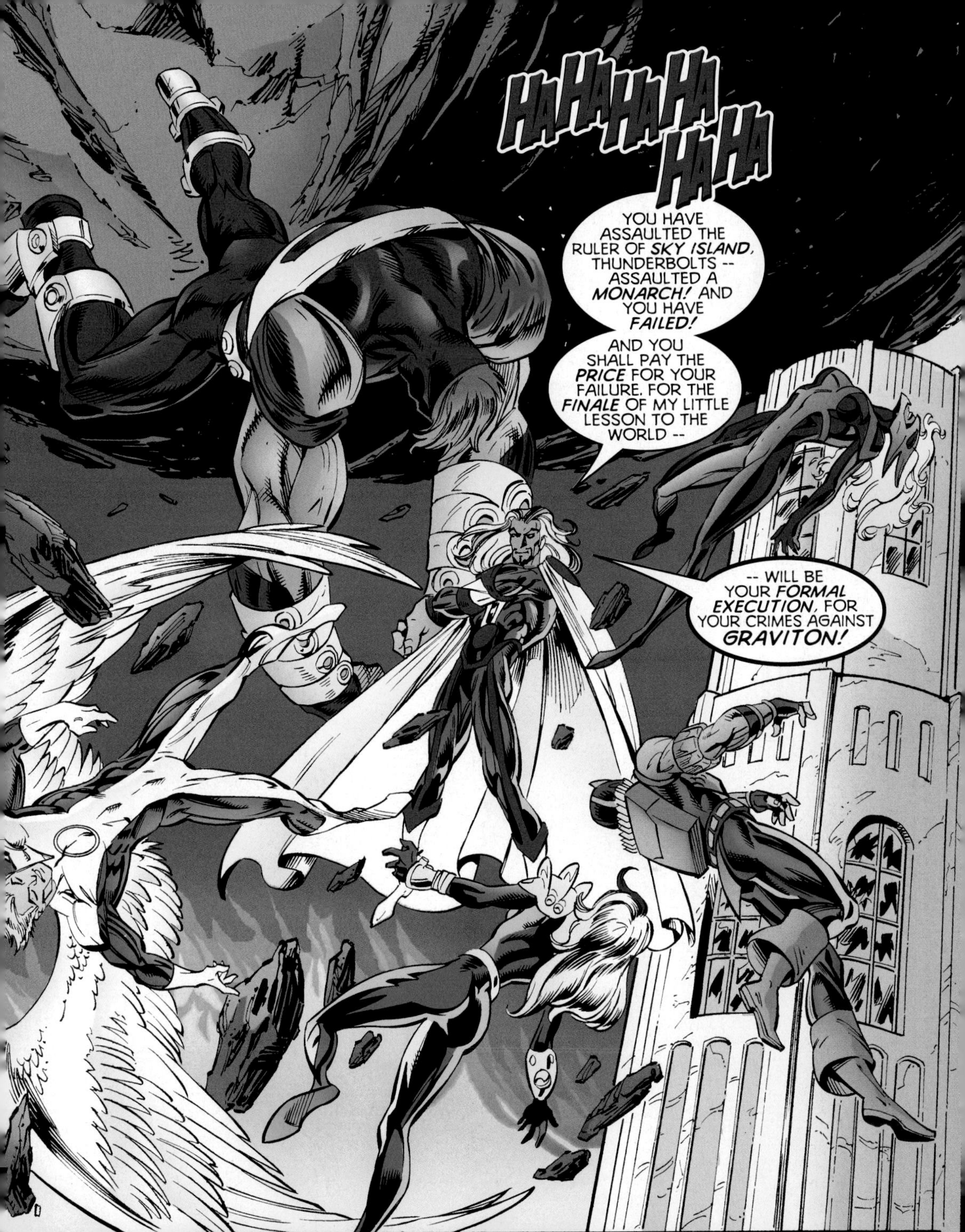
HA HA HA HA HA HA HA
YOU HAVE ASSAULTED THE RULER OF SKY ISLAND, THUNDERBOLTS -- ASSAULTED A MONARCH! AND YOU HAVE FAILED!
AND YOU SHALL PAY THE PRICE FOR YOUR FAILURE. FOR THE FINALE OF MY LITTLE LESSON TO THE WORLD --
-- WILL BE YOUR FORMAL EXECUTION, FOR YOUR CRIMES AGAINST GRAVITON!
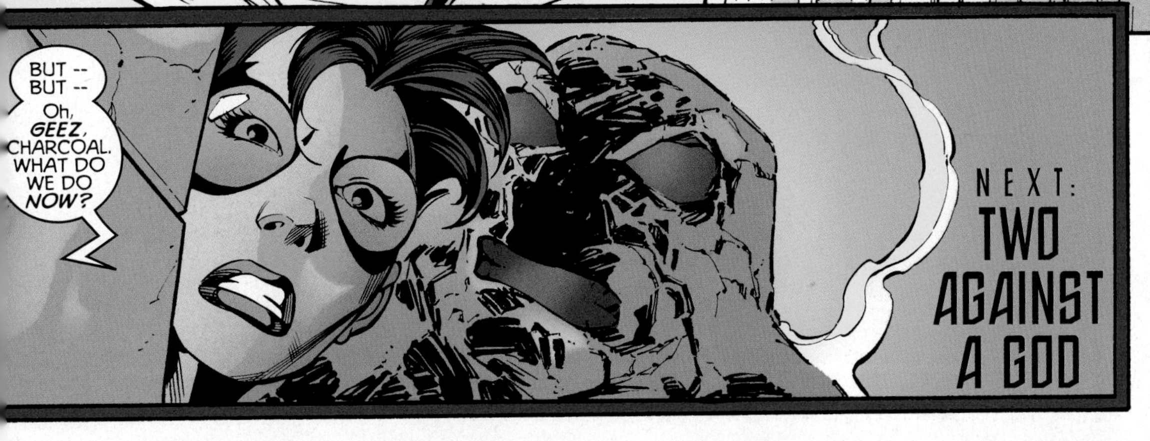
BUT -- BUT -- Oh, GEEZ, CHARCOAL. WHAT DO WE DO NOW?
NEXT: TWO AGAINST A GOD

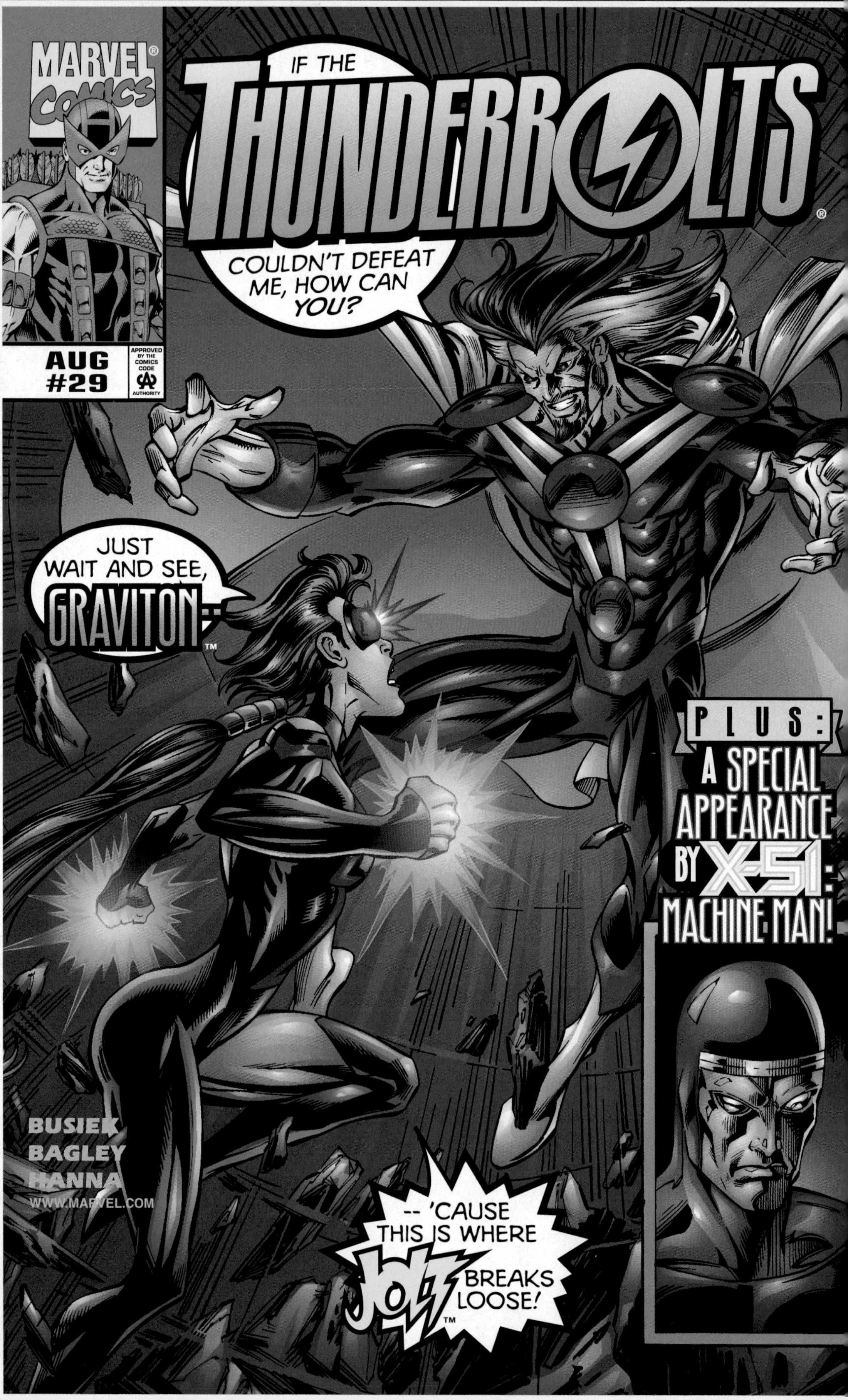
MARVEL COMICS
IF THE
THUNDERBOLTS
COULDN'T DEFEAT ME, HOW CAN YOU?
AUG #29
APPROVED BY THE COMICS CODE AUTHORITY
JUST WAIT AND SEE, GRAVITON--
PLUS: A SPECIAL APPEARANCE BY X-51: MACHINE MAN!
BUSIEK
BAGLEY
HANNA
WWW.MARVEL.COM
-- 'CAUSE THIS IS WHERE JOLT BREAKS LOOSE!

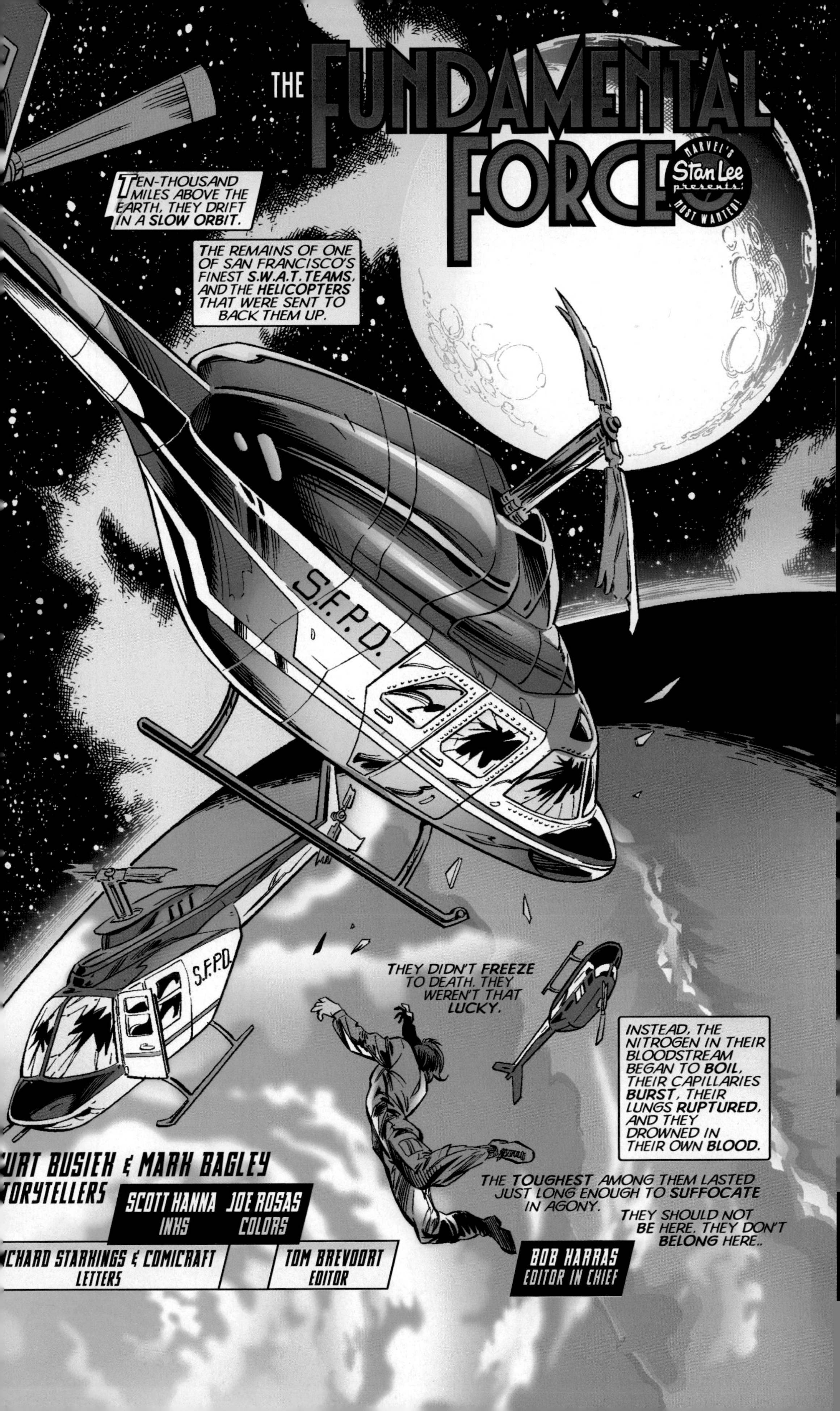
THE FUNDAMENTAL FORCE
MARVEL'S Stan Lee presents! MOST WANTED!
TEN-THOUSAND MILES ABOVE THE EARTH, THEY DRIFT IN A SLOW ORBIT.
THE REMAINS OF ONE OF SAN FRANCISCO'S FINEST S.W.A.T. TEAMS, AND THE HELICOPTERS THAT WERE SENT TO BACK THEM UP.
S.F.P.D.
S.F.P.D.
THEY DIDN'T FREEZE TO DEATH. THEY WEREN'T THAT LUCKY.
INSTEAD, THE NITROGEN IN THEIR BLOODSTREAM BEGAN TO BOIL, THEIR CAPILLARIES BURST, THEIR LUNGS RUPTURED, AND THEY DROWNED IN THEIR OWN BLOOD.
THE TOUGHEST AMONG THEM LASTED JUST LONG ENOUGH TO SUFFOCATE IN AGONY.
THEY SHOULD NOT BE HERE. THEY DON'T BELONG HERE..
URT BUSIEK & MARK BAGLEY
TORYTELLERS
SCOTT HANNA INKS
JOE ROSAS COLORS
ICHARD STARKINGS & COMICRAFT LETTERS
TOM BREVOORT EDITOR
BOB HARRAS EDITOR IN CHIEF

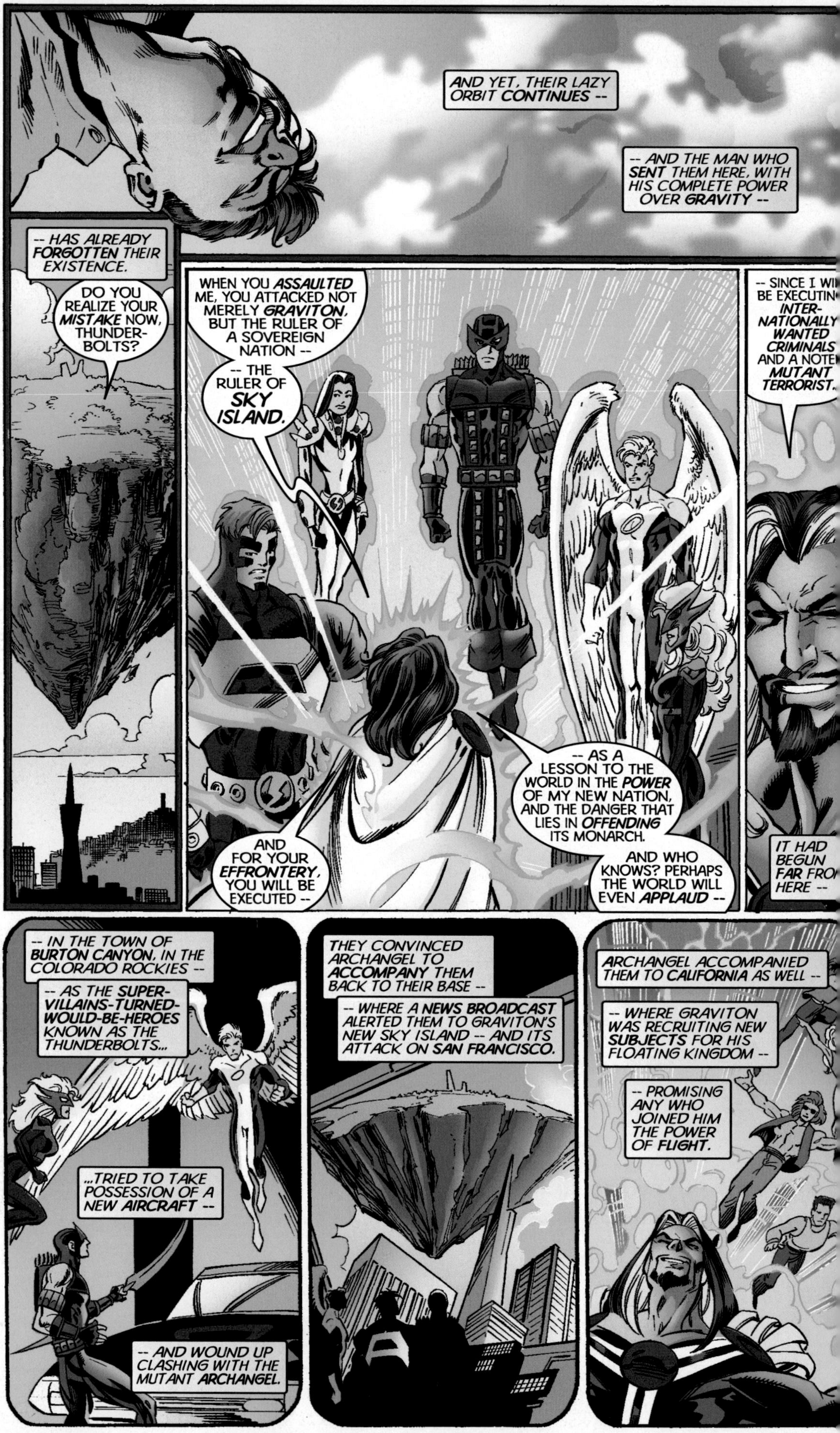
AND YET, THEIR LAZY ORBIT CONTINUES --
-- AND THE MAN WHO SENT THEM HERE, WITH HIS COMPLETE POWER OVER GRAVITY --
-- HAS ALREADY FORGOTTEN THEIR EXISTENCE.
DO YOU REALIZE YOUR MISTAKE NOW, THUNDERBOLTS?
WHEN YOU ASSAULTED ME, YOU ATTACKED NOT MERELY GRAVITON, BUT THE RULER OF A SOVEREIGN NATION --
-- THE RULER OF SKY ISLAND.
AND FOR YOUR EFFRONTERY, YOU WILL BE EXECUTED --
-- AS A LESSON TO THE WORLD IN THE POWER OF MY NEW NATION, AND THE DANGER THAT LIES IN OFFENDING ITS MONARCH.
AND WHO KNOWS? PERHAPS THE WORLD WILL EVEN APPLAUD --
-- SINCE I WI BE EXECUTIN INTER-NATIONALLY WANTED CRIMINALS AND A NOTE MUTANT TERRORIST.
IT HAD BEGUN FAR FRO HERE --
-- IN THE TOWN OF BURTON CANYON, IN THE COLORADO ROCKIES --
-- AS THE SUPER-VILLAINS-TURNED-WOULD-BE-HEROES KNOWN AS THE THUNDERBOLTS...
...TRIED TO TAKE POSSESSION OF A NEW AIRCRAFT --
-- AND WOUND UP CLASHING WITH THE MUTANT ARCHANGEL.
THEY CONVINCED ARCHANGEL TO ACCOMPANY THEM BACK TO THEIR BASE --
-- WHERE A NEWS BROADCAST ALERTED THEM TO GRAVITON'S NEW SKY ISLAND -- AND ITS ATTACK ON SAN FRANCISCO.
ARCHANGEL ACCOMPANIED THEM TO CALIFORNIA AS WELL --
-- WHERE GRAVITON WAS RECRUITING NEW SUBJECTS FOR HIS FLOATING KINGDOM --
-- PROMISING ANY WHO JOINED HIM THE POWER OF FLIGHT.

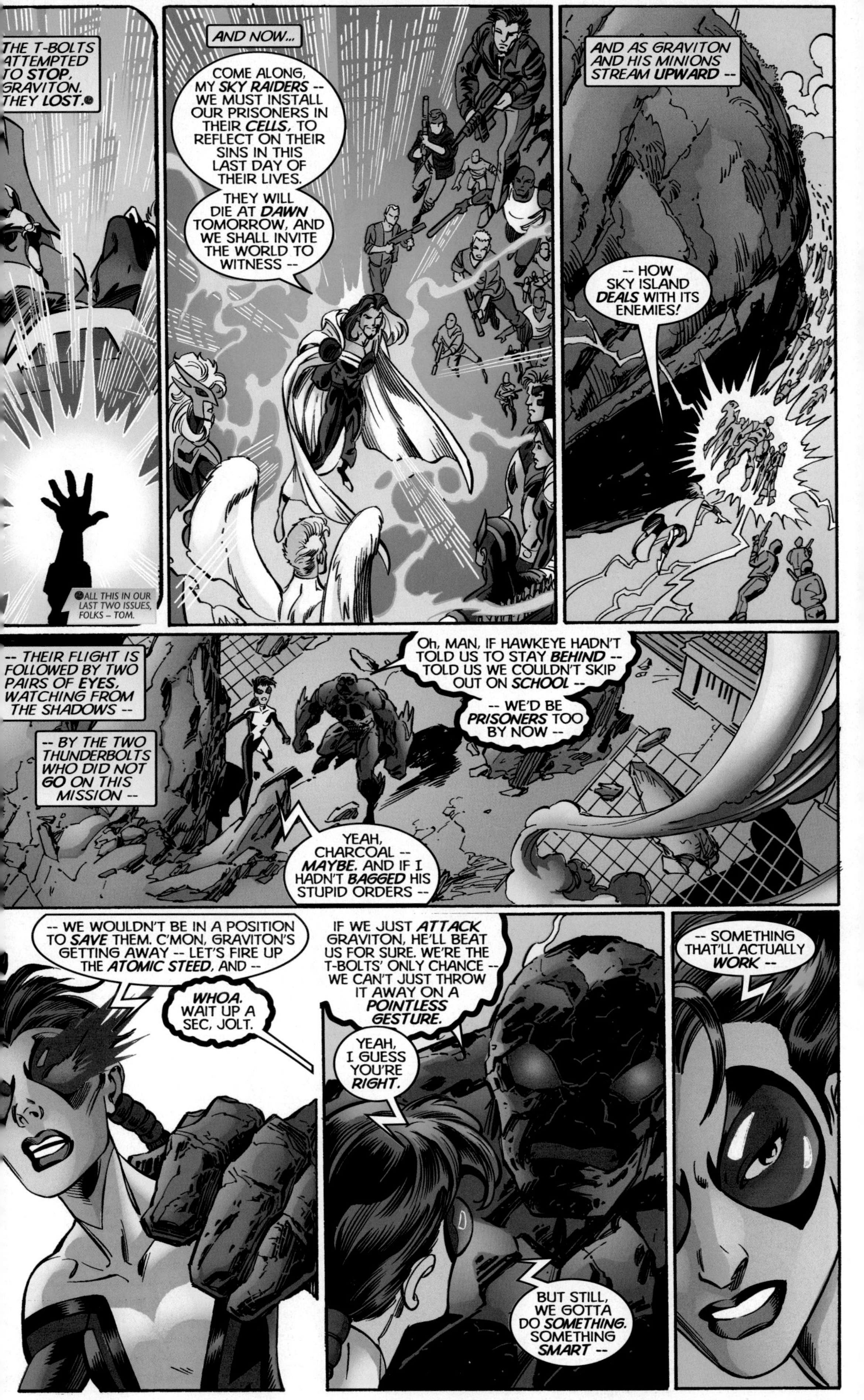
THE T-BOLTS ATTEMPTED TO STOP GRAVITON. THEY LOST.
ALL THIS IN OUR LAST TWO ISSUES, FOLKS – TOM.
AND NOW...
COME ALONG, MY SKY RAIDERS -- WE MUST INSTALL OUR PRISONERS IN THEIR CELLS, TO REFLECT ON THEIR SINS IN THIS LAST DAY OF THEIR LIVES.
THEY WILL DIE AT DAWN TOMORROW, AND WE SHALL INVITE THE WORLD TO WITNESS --
AND AS GRAVITON AND HIS MINIONS STREAM UPWARD --
-- HOW SKY ISLAND DEALS WITH ITS ENEMIES!
-- THEIR FLIGHT IS FOLLOWED BY TWO PAIRS OF EYES, WATCHING FROM THE SHADOWS --
-- BY THE TWO THUNDERBOLTS WHO DID NOT GO ON THIS MISSION --
Oh, MAN, IF HAWKEYE HADN'T TOLD US TO STAY BEHIND -- TOLD US WE COULDN'T SKIP OUT ON SCHOOL --
-- WE'D BE PRISONERS TOO BY NOW --
YEAH, CHARCOAL -- MAYBE. AND IF I HADN'T BAGGED HIS STUPID ORDERS --
-- WE WOULDN'T BE IN A POSITION TO SAVE THEM. C'MON, GRAVITON'S GETTING AWAY -- LET'S FIRE UP THE ATOMIC STEED, AND --
WHOA. WAIT UP A SEC, JOLT.
IF WE JUST ATTACK GRAVITON, HE'LL BEAT US FOR SURE. WE'RE THE T-BOLTS' ONLY CHANCE -- WE CAN'T JUST THROW IT AWAY ON A POINTLESS GESTURE.
YEAH, I GUESS YOU'RE RIGHT.
BUT STILL, WE GOTTA DO SOMETHING. SOMETHING SMART --
-- SOMETHING THAT'LL ACTUALLY WORK --

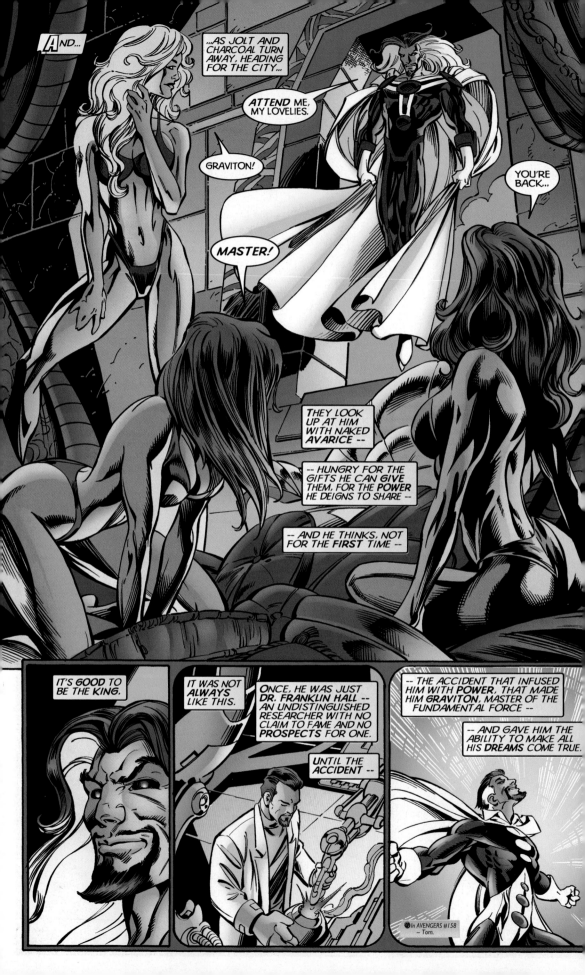

AND...

...AS JOLT AND CHARCOAL TURN AWAY, HEADING FOR THE CITY...

ATTEND ME, MY LOVELIES.

GRAVITON!

YOU'RE BACK...

MASTER!

THEY LOOK UP AT HIM WITH NAKED *AVARICE* --

-- HUNGRY FOR THE *GIFTS* HE CAN *GIVE* THEM, FOR THE *POWER* HE DEIGNS TO SHARE --

-- AND HE THINKS, NOT FOR THE *FIRST* TIME --

IT'S GOOD TO BE THE KING.

IT WAS NOT *ALWAYS* LIKE THIS.

ONCE, HE WAS JUST DR. *FRANKLIN HALL* -- AN UNDISTINGUISHED RESEARCHER WITH NO CLAIM TO FAME AND NO PROSPECTS FOR ONE.

UNTIL THE *ACCIDENT* --

-- THE *ACCIDENT* THAT INFUSED HIM WITH *POWER*, THAT MADE HIM *GRAVITON*, MASTER OF THE FUNDAMENTAL FORCE --

-- AND GAVE HIM THE ABILITY TO MAKE ALL HIS *DREAMS* COME TRUE.

*In AVENGERS #158 -- Tom.

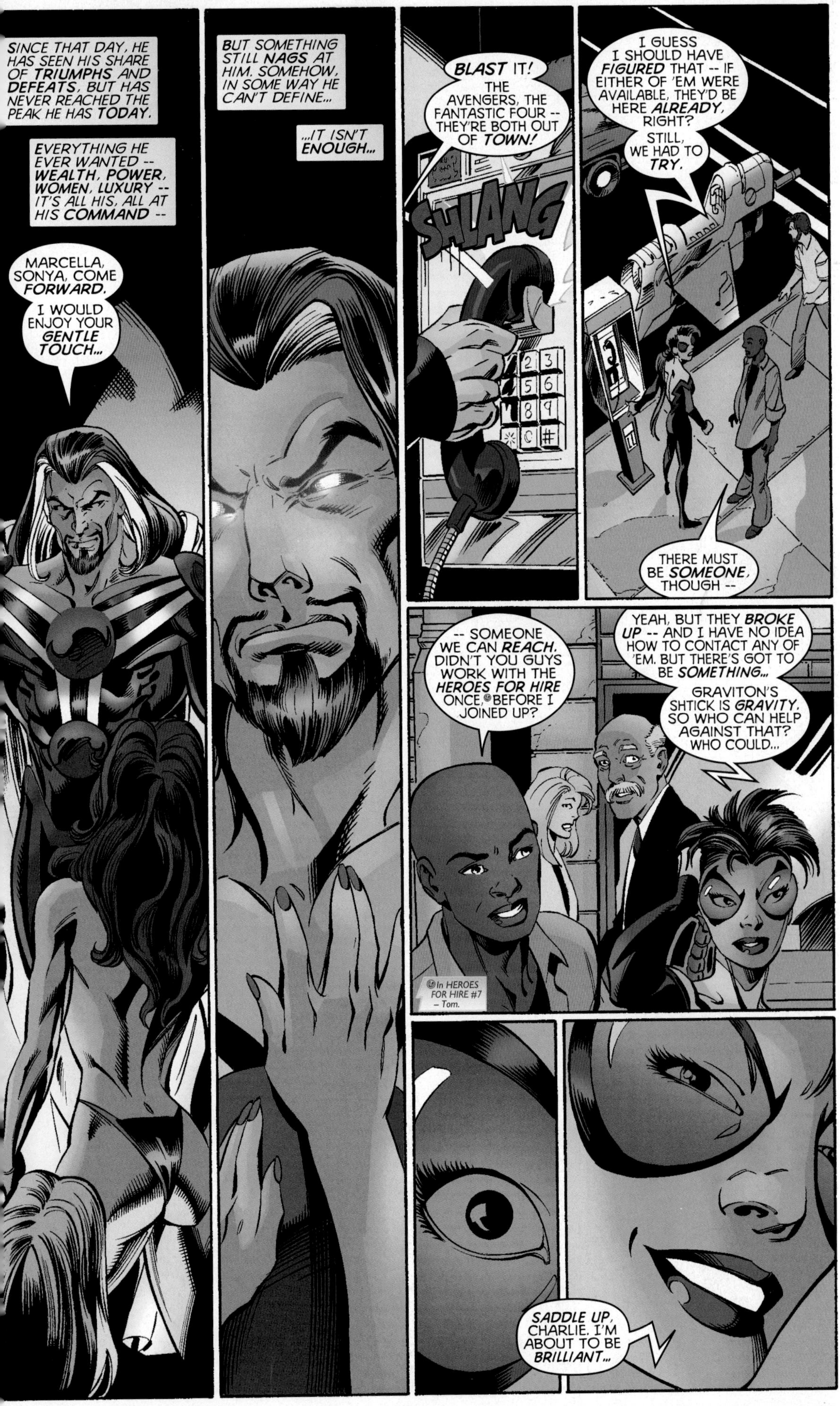
SINCE THAT DAY, HE HAS SEEN HIS SHARE OF TRIUMPHS AND DEFEATS, BUT HAS NEVER REACHED THE PEAK HE HAS TODAY.
EVERYTHING HE EVER WANTED -- WEALTH, POWER, WOMEN, LUXURY -- IT'S ALL HIS, ALL AT HIS COMMAND --
MARCELLA, SONYA, COME FORWARD.
I WOULD ENJOY YOUR GENTLE TOUCH...
BUT SOMETHING STILL NAGS AT HIM. SOMEHOW, IN SOME WAY HE CAN'T DEFINE...
...IT ISN'T ENOUGH...
BLAST IT!
THE AVENGERS, THE FANTASTIC FOUR -- THEY'RE BOTH OUT OF TOWN!
SHLANG
I GUESS I SHOULD HAVE FIGURED THAT -- IF EITHER OF 'EM WERE AVAILABLE, THEY'D BE HERE ALREADY, RIGHT?
STILL, WE HAD TO TRY.
THERE MUST BE SOMEONE, THOUGH --
-- SOMEONE WE CAN REACH. DIDN'T YOU GUYS WORK WITH THE HEROES FOR HIRE ONCE, BEFORE I JOINED UP?
YEAH, BUT THEY BROKE UP -- AND I HAVE NO IDEA HOW TO CONTACT ANY OF 'EM. BUT THERE'S GOT TO BE SOMETHING...
GRAVITON'S SHTICK IS GRAVITY, SO WHO CAN HELP AGAINST THAT? WHO COULD...
In HEROES FOR HIRE #7 – Tom.
SADDLE UP, CHARLIE. I'M ABOUT TO BE BRILLIANT...

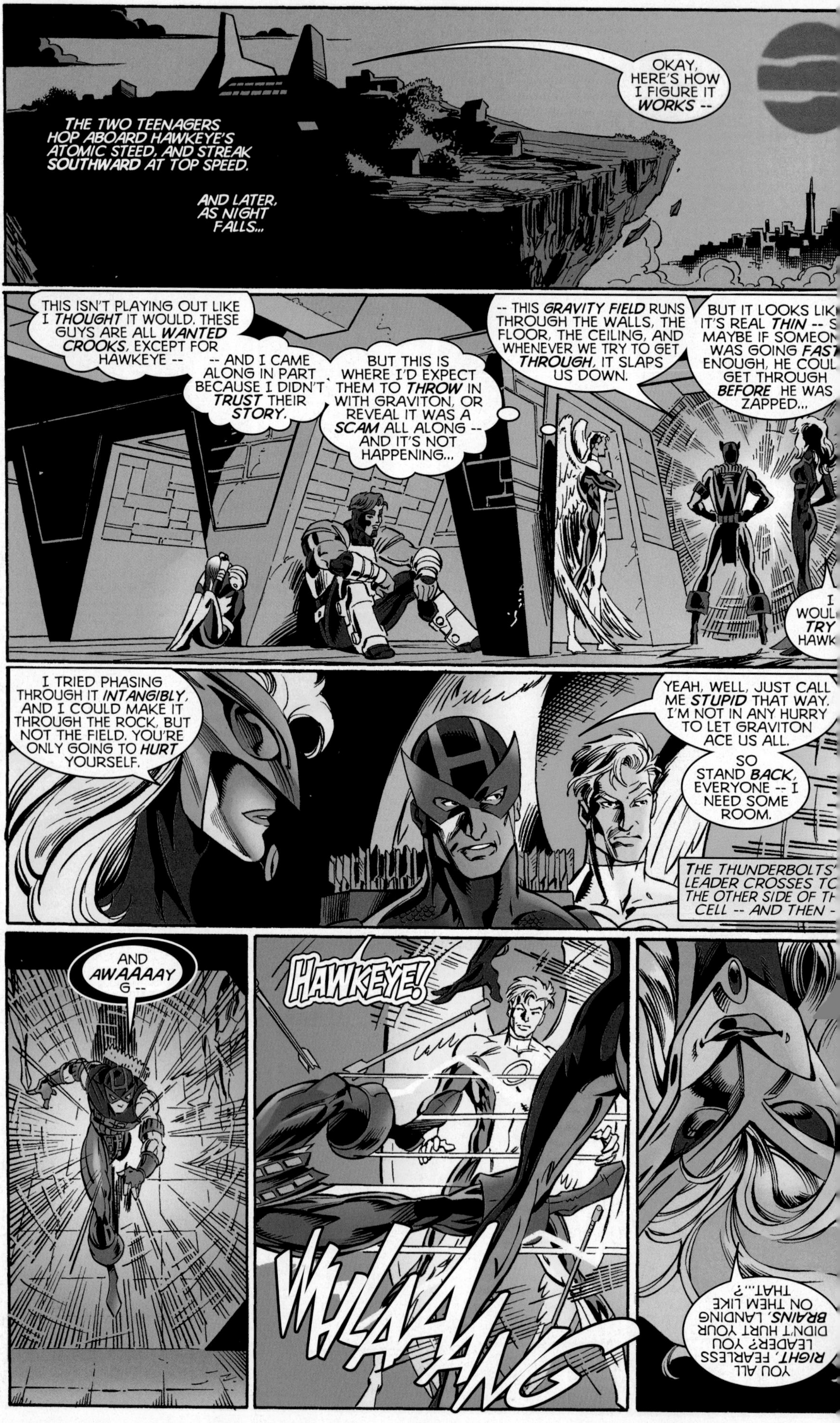
OKAY, HERE'S HOW I FIGURE IT WORKS --
THE TWO TEENAGERS HOP ABOARD HAWKEYE'S ATOMIC STEED, AND STREAK SOUTHWARD AT TOP SPEED.
AND LATER, AS NIGHT FALLS...
THIS ISN'T PLAYING OUT LIKE I THOUGHT IT WOULD. THESE GUYS ARE ALL WANTED CROOKS, EXCEPT FOR HAWKEYE --
-- AND I CAME ALONG IN PART BECAUSE I DIDN'T TRUST THEIR STORY.
BUT THIS IS WHERE I'D EXPECT THEM TO THROW IN WITH GRAVITON, OR REVEAL IT WAS A SCAM ALL ALONG -- AND IT'S NOT HAPPENING...
-- THIS GRAVITY FIELD RUNS THROUGH THE WALLS, THE FLOOR, THE CEILING, AND WHENEVER WE TRY TO GET THROUGH, IT SLAPS US DOWN.
BUT IT LOOKS LIK IT'S REAL THIN -- S MAYBE IF SOMEON WAS GOING FAST ENOUGH, HE COUL GET THROUGH BEFORE HE WAS ZAPPED...
I WOUL TRY HAWK
I TRIED PHASING THROUGH IT INTANGIBLY, AND I COULD MAKE IT THROUGH THE ROCK, BUT NOT THE FIELD. YOU'RE ONLY GOING TO HURT YOURSELF.
YEAH, WELL, JUST CALL ME STUPID THAT WAY. I'M NOT IN ANY HURRY TO LET GRAVITON ACE US ALL.
SO STAND BACK, EVERYONE -- I NEED SOME ROOM.
THE THUNDERBOLTS' LEADER CROSSES TO THE OTHER SIDE OF TH CELL -- AND THEN -
AND AWAAAAY G --
HAWKEYE!
WHLAAANG
YOU ALL RIGHT, FEARLESS LEADER? YOU DIDN'T HURT YOUR BRAINS, LANDING ON THEM LIKE THAT...?

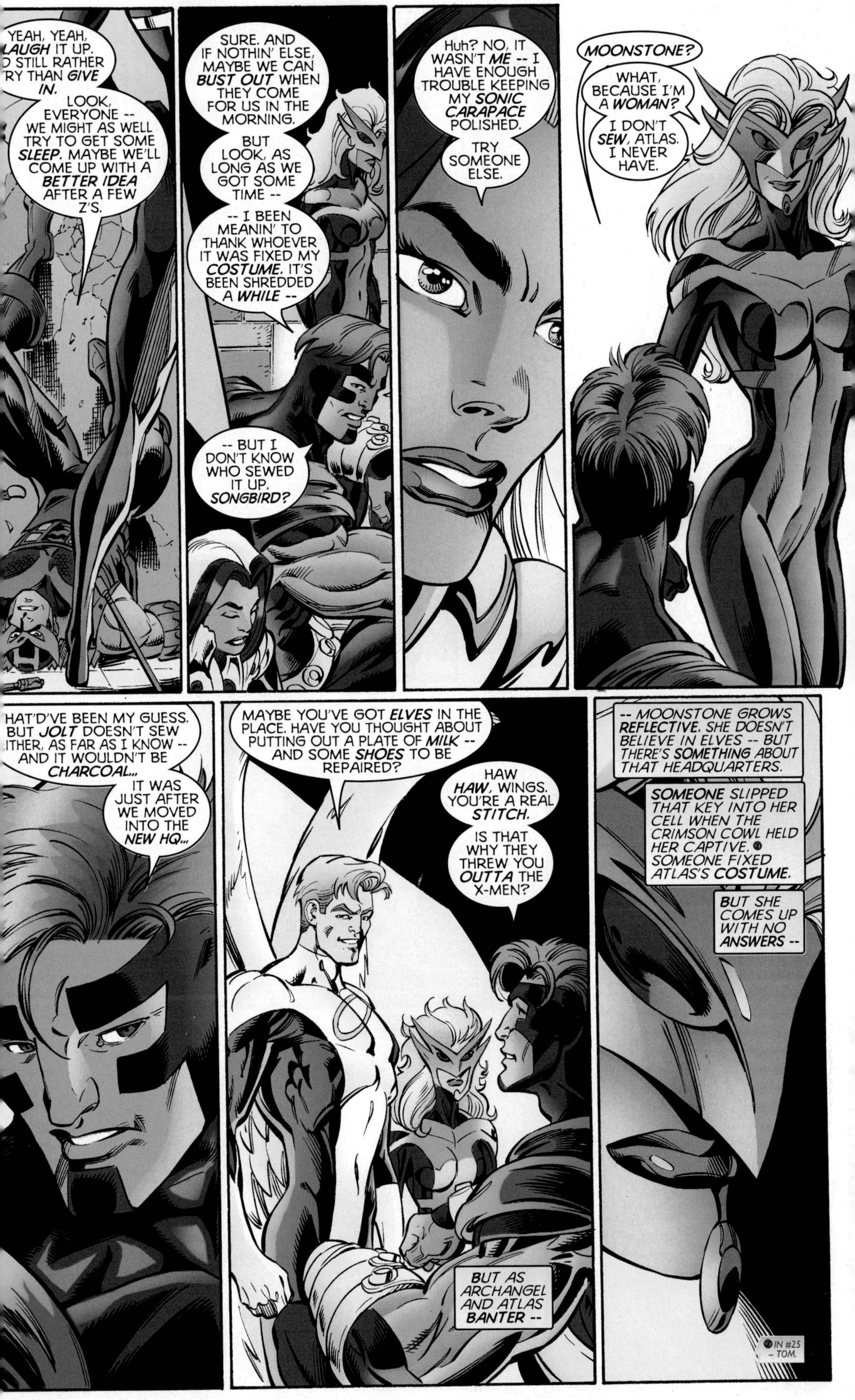

YEAH, YEAH, LAUGH IT UP. 'D STILL RATHER TRY THAN GIVE IN.
LOOK, EVERYONE -- WE MIGHT AS WELL TRY TO GET SOME SLEEP. MAYBE WE'LL COME UP WITH A BETTER IDEA AFTER A FEW Z'S.
SURE. AND IF NOTHIN' ELSE, MAYBE WE CAN BUST OUT WHEN THEY COME FOR US IN THE MORNING.
BUT LOOK, AS LONG AS WE GOT SOME TIME --
-- I BEEN MEANIN' TO THANK WHOEVER IT WAS FIXED MY COSTUME. IT'S BEEN SHREDDED A WHILE --
-- BUT I DON'T KNOW WHO SEWED IT UP. SONGBIRD?
Huh? NO, IT WASN'T ME -- I HAVE ENOUGH TROUBLE KEEPING MY SONIC CARAPACE POLISHED.
TRY SOMEONE ELSE.
MOONSTONE?
WHAT, BECAUSE I'M A WOMAN?
I DON'T SEW, ATLAS. I NEVER HAVE.
HAT'D'VE BEEN MY GUESS. BUT JOLT DOESN'T SEW EITHER, AS FAR AS I KNOW -- AND IT WOULDN'T BE CHARCOAL...
IT WAS JUST AFTER WE MOVED INTO THE NEW HQ...
MAYBE YOU'VE GOT ELVES IN THE PLACE. HAVE YOU THOUGHT ABOUT PUTTING OUT A PLATE OF MILK -- AND SOME SHOES TO BE REPAIRED?
HAW HAW, WINGS. YOU'RE A REAL STITCH.
IS THAT WHY THEY THREW YOU OUTTA THE X-MEN?
BUT AS ARCHANGEL AND ATLAS BANTER --
-- MOONSTONE GROWS REFLECTIVE. SHE DOESN'T BELIEVE IN ELVES -- BUT THERE'S SOMETHING ABOUT THAT HEADQUARTERS.
SOMEONE SLIPPED THAT KEY INTO HER CELL WHEN THE CRIMSON COWL HELD HER CAPTIVE. SOMEONE FIXED ATLAS'S COSTUME.
BUT SHE COMES UP WITH NO ANSWERS --
IN #25 – TOM.

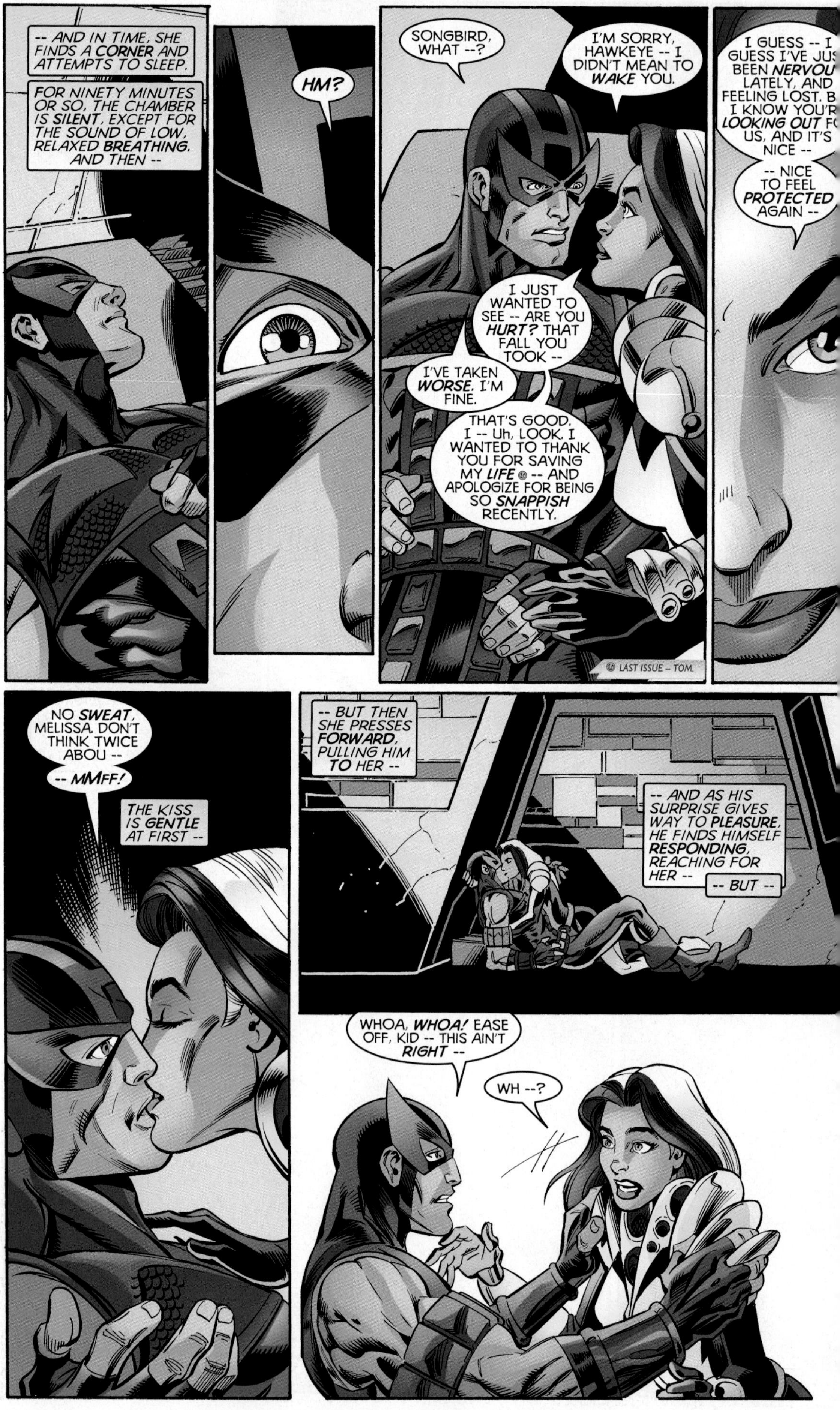
-- AND IN TIME, SHE FINDS A CORNER AND ATTEMPTS TO SLEEP.
FOR NINETY MINUTES OR SO, THE CHAMBER IS SILENT, EXCEPT FOR THE SOUND OF LOW, RELAXED BREATHING. AND THEN --
HM?
SONGBIRD, WHAT --?
I'M SORRY, HAWKEYE -- I DIDN'T MEAN TO WAKE YOU.
I JUST WANTED TO SEE -- ARE YOU HURT? THAT FALL YOU TOOK --
I'VE TAKEN WORSE. I'M FINE.
THAT'S GOOD. I -- Uh, LOOK. I WANTED TO THANK YOU FOR SAVING MY LIFE -- AND APOLOGIZE FOR BEING SO SNAPPISH RECENTLY.
LAST ISSUE – TOM.
I GUESS -- I GUESS I'VE JUS BEEN NERVOU LATELY, AND FEELING LOST. B I KNOW YOU'R LOOKING OUT F US, AND IT'S NICE --
-- NICE TO FEEL PROTECTED AGAIN --
NO SWEAT, MELISSA. DON'T THINK TWICE ABOU --
-- MMFF!
THE KISS IS GENTLE AT FIRST --
-- BUT THEN SHE PRESSES FORWARD, PULLING HIM TO HER --
-- AND AS HIS SURPRISE GIVES WAY TO PLEASURE, HE FINDS HIMSELF RESPONDING, REACHING FOR HER --
-- BUT --
WHOA, WHOA! EASE OFF, KID -- THIS AIN'T RIGHT --
WH --?

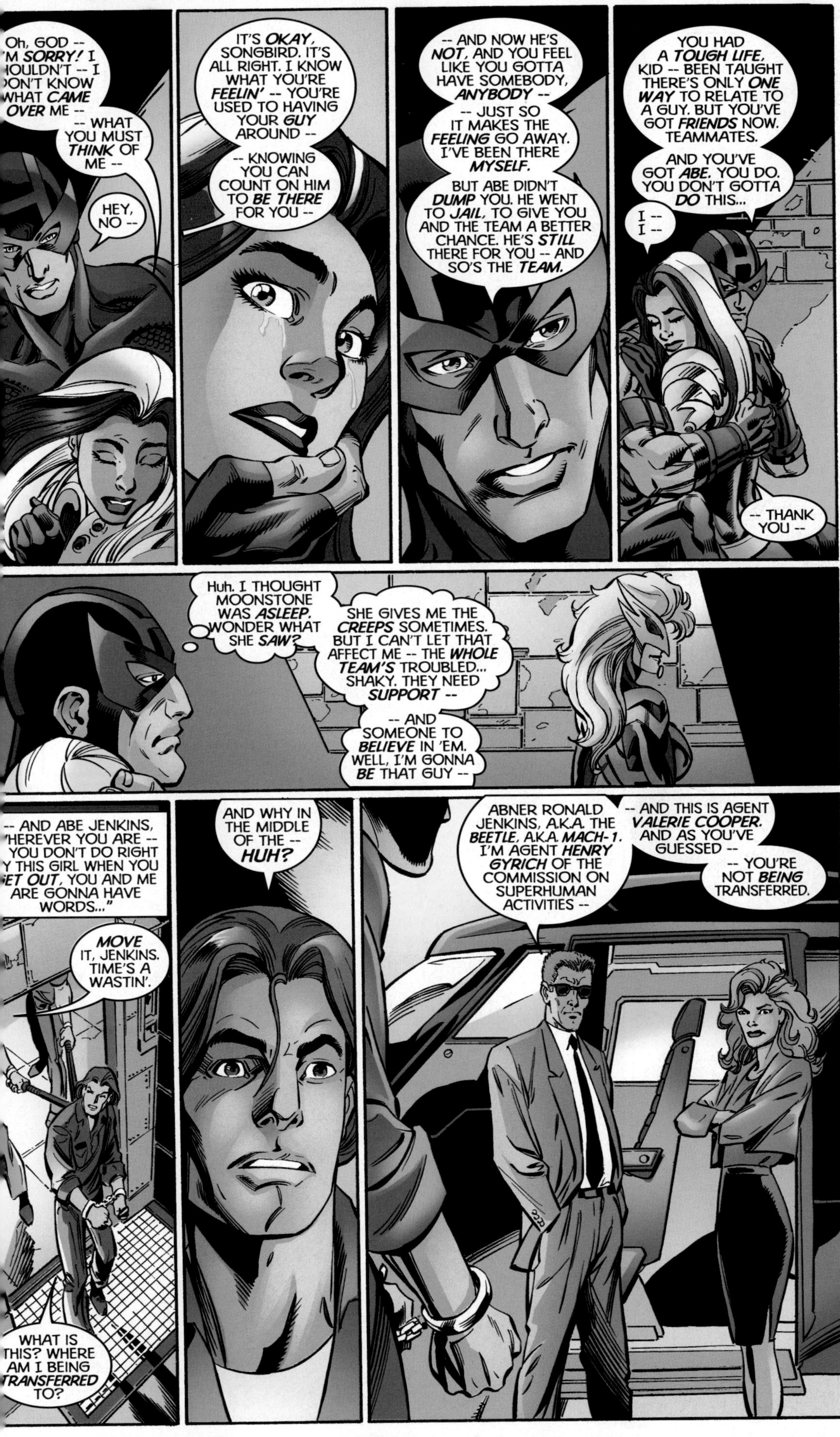
Oh, GOD -- 'M SORRY! I HOULDN'T -- I DON'T KNOW WHAT CAME OVER ME --
-- WHAT YOU MUST THINK OF ME --
HEY, NO --
IT'S OKAY, SONGBIRD. IT'S ALL RIGHT. I KNOW WHAT YOU'RE FEELIN' -- YOU'RE USED TO HAVING YOUR GUY AROUND --
-- KNOWING YOU CAN COUNT ON HIM TO BE THERE FOR YOU --
-- AND NOW HE'S NOT, AND YOU FEEL LIKE YOU GOTTA HAVE SOMEBODY, ANYBODY --
-- JUST SO IT MAKES THE FEELING GO AWAY. I'VE BEEN THERE MYSELF.
BUT ABE DIDN'T DUMP YOU. HE WENT TO JAIL, TO GIVE YOU AND THE TEAM A BETTER CHANCE. HE'S STILL THERE FOR YOU -- AND SO'S THE TEAM.
YOU HAD A TOUGH LIFE, KID -- BEEN TAUGHT THERE'S ONLY ONE WAY TO RELATE TO A GUY. BUT YOU'VE GOT FRIENDS NOW. TEAMMATES.
AND YOU'VE GOT ABE. YOU DO. YOU DON'T GOTTA DO THIS...
I -- I --
-- THANK YOU --
Huh. I THOUGHT MOONSTONE WAS ASLEEP. WONDER WHAT SHE SAW?
SHE GIVES ME THE CREEPS SOMETIMES. BUT I CAN'T LET THAT AFFECT ME -- THE WHOLE TEAM'S TROUBLED... SHAKY. THEY NEED SUPPORT --
-- AND SOMEONE TO BELIEVE IN 'EM. WELL, I'M GONNA BE THAT GUY --
-- AND ABE JENKINS, 'HEREVER YOU ARE -- YOU DON'T DO RIGHT Y THIS GIRL WHEN YOU ET OUT, YOU AND ME ARE GONNA HAVE WORDS..."
MOVE IT, JENKINS. TIME'S A WASTIN'.
WHAT IS THIS? WHERE AM I BEING TRANSFERRED TO?
AND WHY IN THE MIDDLE OF THE -- HUH?
ABNER RONALD JENKINS, A.K.A. THE BEETLE, A.K.A. MACH-1. I'M AGENT HENRY GYRICH OF THE COMMISSION ON SUPERHUMAN ACTIVITIES --
-- AND THIS IS AGENT VALERIE COOPER. AND AS YOU'VE GUESSED --
-- YOU'RE NOT BEING TRANSFERRED.

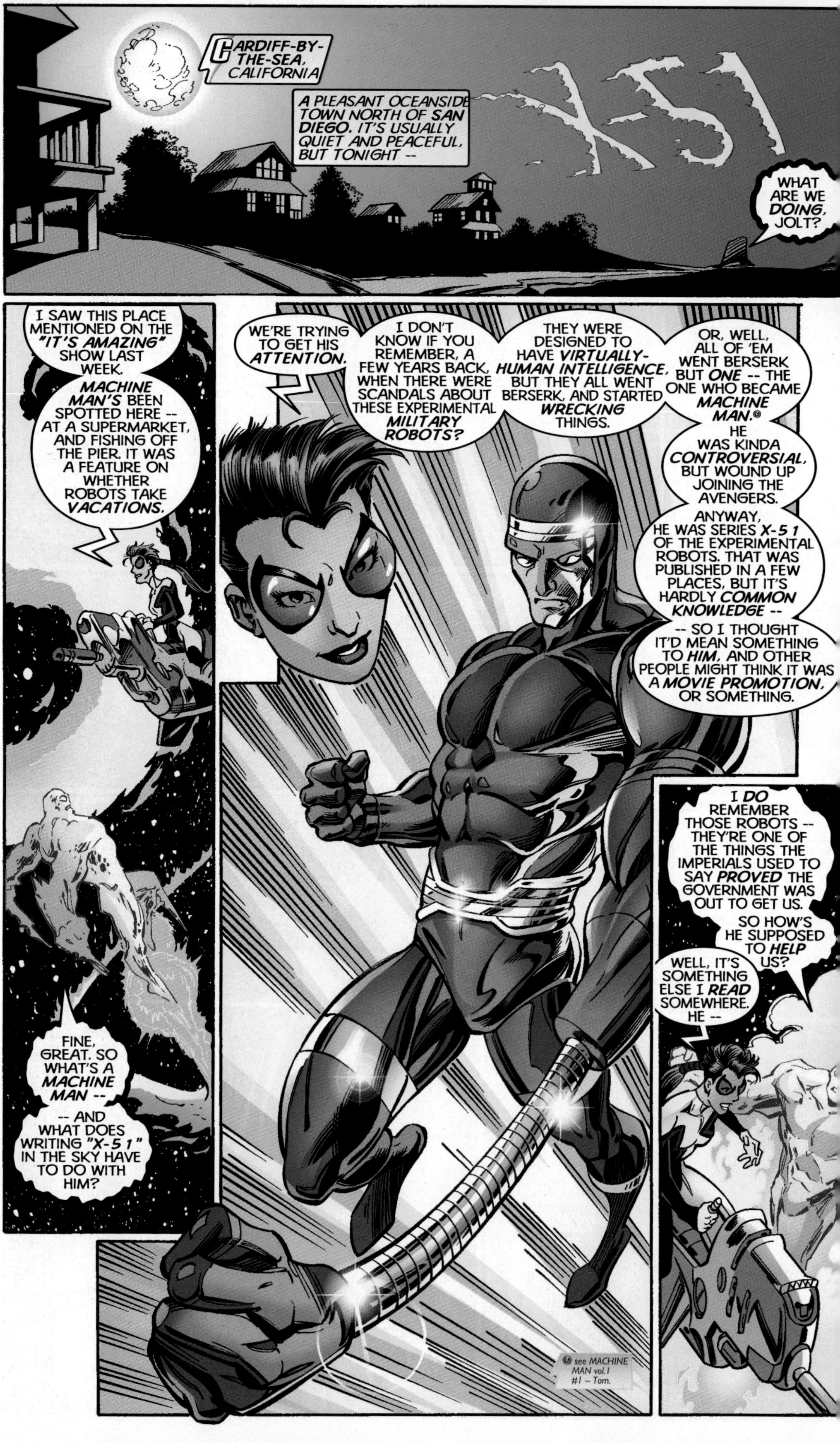
CARDIFF-BY-THE-SEA, CALIFORNIA
A PLEASANT OCEANSIDE TOWN NORTH OF SAN DIEGO. IT'S USUALLY QUIET AND PEACEFUL, BUT TONIGHT --
X-51
WHAT ARE WE DOING, JOLT?
I SAW THIS PLACE MENTIONED ON THE "IT'S AMAZING" SHOW LAST WEEK.
MACHINE MAN'S BEEN SPOTTED HERE -- AT A SUPERMARKET, AND FISHING OFF THE PIER. IT WAS A FEATURE ON WHETHER ROBOTS TAKE VACATIONS.
FINE, GREAT. SO WHAT'S A MACHINE MAN --
-- AND WHAT DOES WRITING "X-5 1" IN THE SKY HAVE TO DO WITH HIM?
WE'RE TRYING TO GET HIS ATTENTION.
I DON'T KNOW IF YOU REMEMBER, A FEW YEARS BACK, WHEN THERE WERE SCANDALS ABOUT THESE EXPERIMENTAL MILITARY ROBOTS?
THEY WERE DESIGNED TO HAVE VIRTUALLY-HUMAN INTELLIGENCE, BUT THEY ALL WENT BERSERK, AND STARTED WRECKING THINGS.
OR, WELL, ALL OF 'EM WENT BERSERK BUT ONE -- THE ONE WHO BECAME MACHINE MAN.
HE WAS KINDA CONTROVERSIAL, BUT WOUND UP JOINING THE AVENGERS.
ANYWAY, HE WAS SERIES X-5 1 OF THE EXPERIMENTAL ROBOTS. THAT WAS PUBLISHED IN A FEW PLACES, BUT IT'S HARDLY COMMON KNOWLEDGE --
-- SO I THOUGHT IT'D MEAN SOMETHING TO HIM, AND OTHER PEOPLE MIGHT THINK IT WAS A MOVIE PROMOTION, OR SOMETHING.
I DO REMEMBER THOSE ROBOTS -- THEY'RE ONE OF THE THINGS THE IMPERIALS USED TO SAY PROVED THE GOVERNMENT WAS OUT TO GET US.
SO HOW'S HE SUPPOSED TO HELP US?
WELL, IT'S SOMETHING ELSE I READ SOMEWHERE. HE --
see MACHINE MAN vol.1 #1 – Tom.

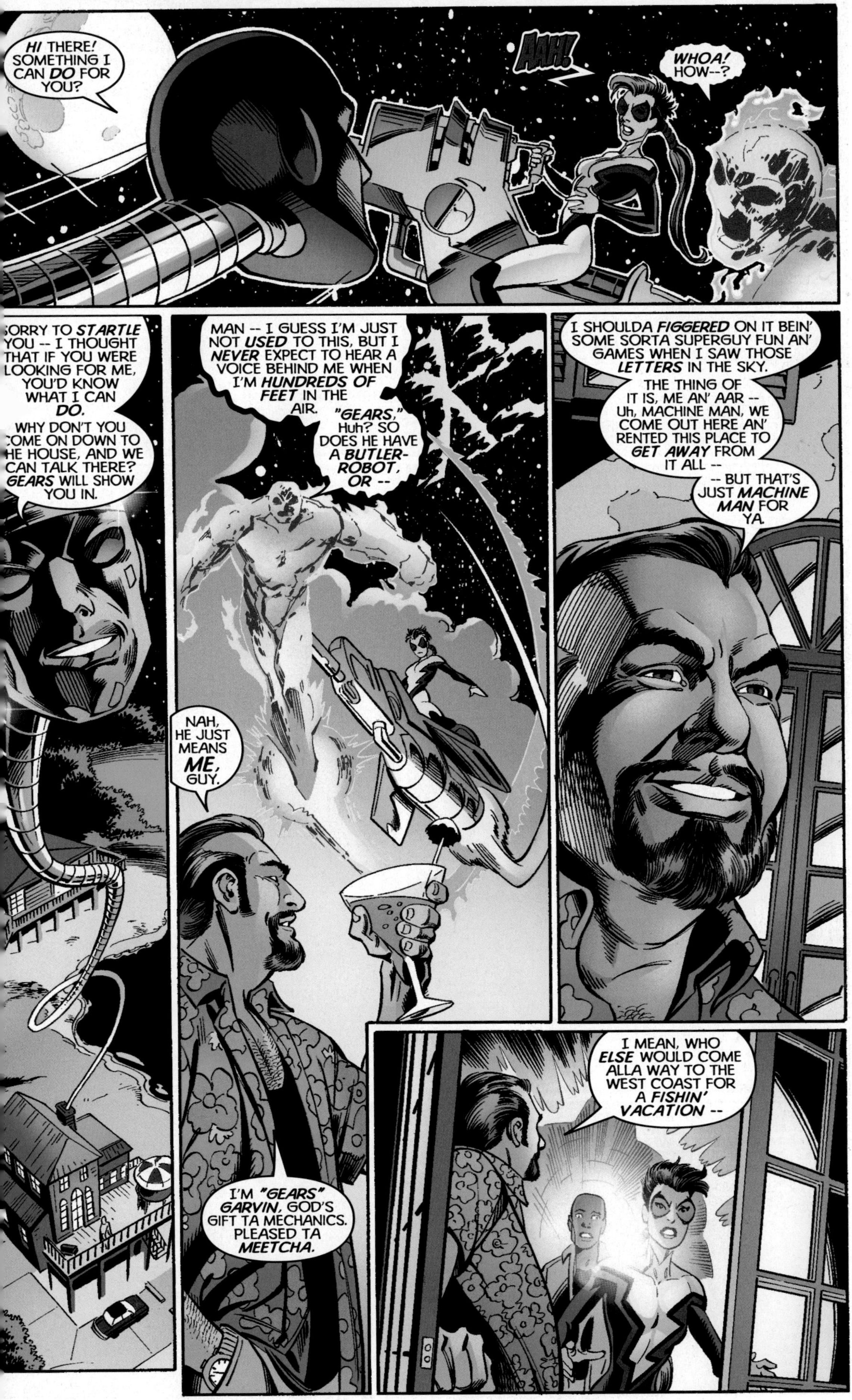
HI THERE! SOMETHING I CAN DO FOR YOU?
AAH!
WHOA! HOW--?
SORRY TO STARTLE YOU -- I THOUGHT THAT IF YOU WERE LOOKING FOR ME, YOU'D KNOW WHAT I CAN DO.
WHY DON'T YOU COME ON DOWN TO THE HOUSE, AND WE CAN TALK THERE? GEARS WILL SHOW YOU IN.
MAN -- I GUESS I'M JUST NOT USED TO THIS, BUT I NEVER EXPECT TO HEAR A VOICE BEHIND ME WHEN I'M HUNDREDS OF FEET IN THE AIR.
"GEARS," Huh? SO DOES HE HAVE A BUTLER-ROBOT, OR --
NAH, HE JUST MEANS ME, GUY.
I'M "GEARS" GARVIN, GOD'S GIFT TA MECHANICS. PLEASED TA MEETCHA.
I SHOULDA FIGGERED ON IT BEIN' SOME SORTA SUPERGUY FUN AN' GAMES WHEN I SAW THOSE LETTERS IN THE SKY.
THE THING OF IT IS, ME AN' AAR -- Uh, MACHINE MAN, WE COME OUT HERE AN' RENTED THIS PLACE TO GET AWAY FROM IT ALL --
-- BUT THAT'S JUST MACHINE MAN FOR YA.
I MEAN, WHO ELSE WOULD COME ALLA WAY TO THE WEST COAST FOR A FISHIN' VACATION --

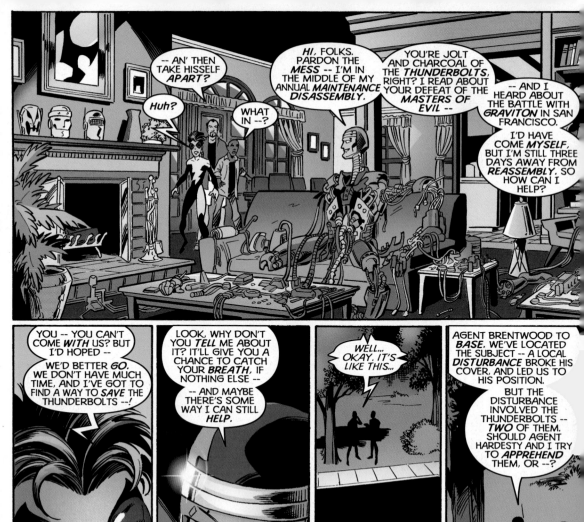

AN' THEN TAKE HISSELF *APART*?

Huh?

WHAT IN --?

HI, FOLKS. PARDON THE *MESS* -- I'M IN THE MIDDLE OF MY ANNUAL *MAINTENANCE DISASSEMBLY*.

YOU'RE JOLT AND CHARCOAL OF THE *THUNDERBOLTS*, RIGHT? I READ ABOUT YOUR DEFEAT OF THE *MASTERS OF EVIL* --

-- AND I HEARD ABOUT THE BATTLE WITH *GRAVITON* IN SAN FRANCISCO.

I'D HAVE COME *MYSELF*, BUT I'M STILL THREE DAYS AWAY FROM *REASSEMBLY*. SO HOW CAN I HELP?

YOU -- YOU CAN'T COME *WITH* US? BUT I'D HOPED --

WE'D BETTER *GO*. WE DON'T HAVE MUCH TIME, AND I'VE GOT TO FIND A WAY TO *SAVE* THE THUNDERBOLTS --!

LOOK, WHY DON'T YOU *TELL* ME ABOUT IT? IT'LL GIVE YOU A CHANCE TO CATCH YOUR *BREATH*, IF NOTHING ELSE --

-- AND MAYBE THERE'S SOME WAY I CAN STILL *HELP*.

WELL... OKAY. IT'S LIKE THIS...

AGENT BRENTWOOD TO *BASE*. WE'VE LOCATED THE SUBJECT -- A LOCAL *DISTURBANCE* BROKE HIS COVER, AND LED US TO HIS POSITION.

BUT THE DISTURBANCE INVOLVED THE THUNDERBOLTS -- *TWO* OF THEM. SHOULD AGENT HARDESTY AND I TRY TO *APPREHEND* THEM, OR --?

UNDERSTOOD, BASE. THE X-51 UNIT IS THE *PRIME TARGET*. WE'LL MAINTAIN OUR PRESENT POSITION-- -- AND AWAIT *REINFORCEMENTS*.

SO -- WE LET *THEM* GO AND STAY ON *HIM*? FIGURES.

AND WHAT ARE S.H.I.E.L.D. AGENTS DOING SPYING ON MACHINE MAN?

THE ANSWER TO THAT WILL HAVE TO WAIT FOR UNCANNY X-MEN #371 TO BE REVEALED -- BUT IN THE MEANTIME --

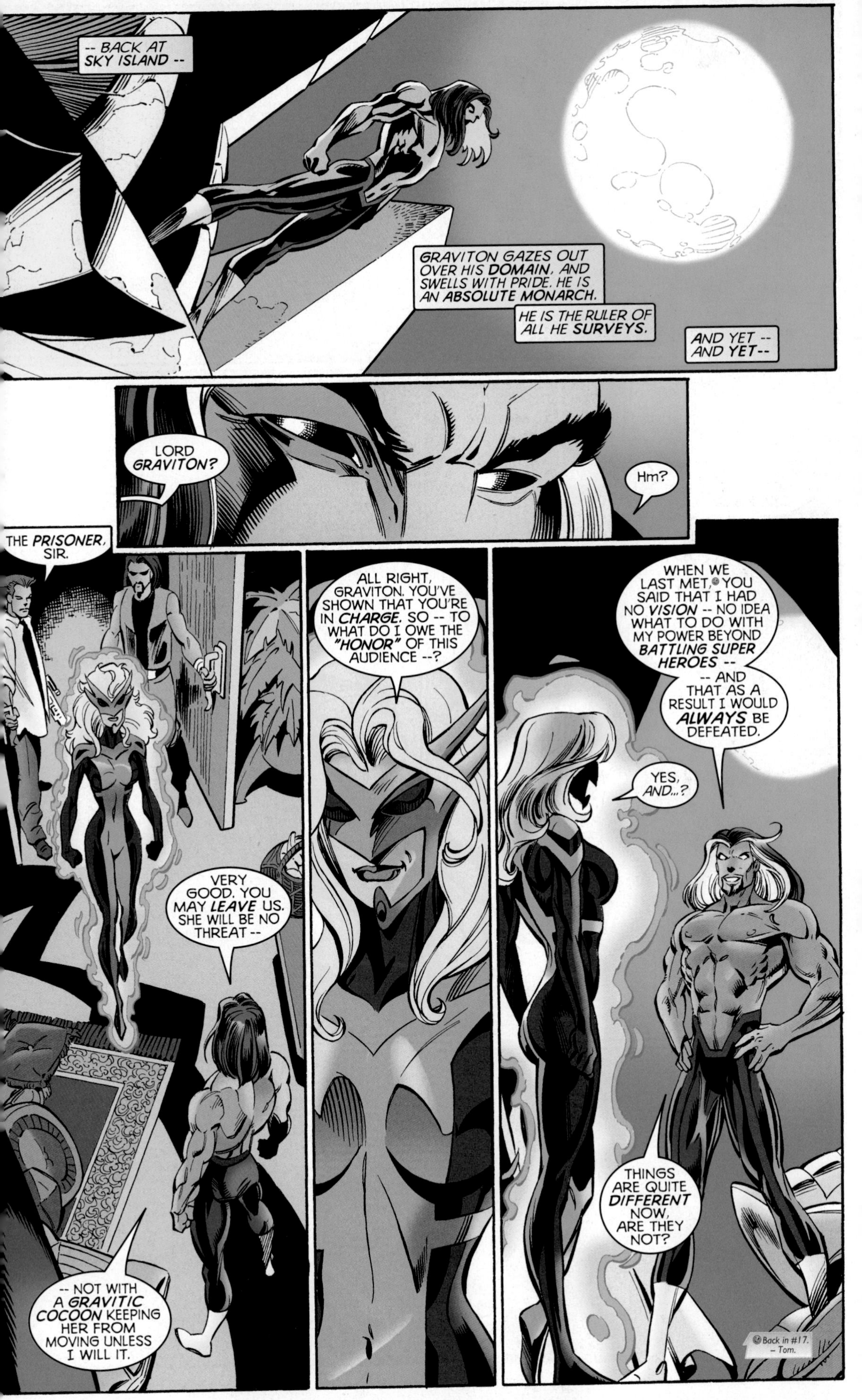
-- BACK AT SKY ISLAND --
GRAVITON GAZES OUT OVER HIS DOMAIN, AND SWELLS WITH PRIDE. HE IS AN ABSOLUTE MONARCH.
HE IS THE RULER OF ALL HE SURVEYS.
AND YET -- AND YET--
LORD GRAVITON?
Hm?
THE PRISONER, SIR.
VERY GOOD. YOU MAY LEAVE US. SHE WILL BE NO THREAT --
-- NOT WITH A GRAVITIC COCOON KEEPING HER FROM MOVING UNLESS I WILL IT.
ALL RIGHT, GRAVITON. YOU'VE SHOWN THAT YOU'RE IN CHARGE. SO -- TO WHAT DO I OWE THE "HONOR" OF THIS AUDIENCE --?
WHEN WE LAST MET, YOU SAID THAT I HAD NO VISION -- NO IDEA WHAT TO DO WITH MY POWER BEYOND BATTLING SUPER HEROES --
-- AND THAT AS A RESULT I WOULD ALWAYS BE DEFEATED.
YES, AND...?
THINGS ARE QUITE DIFFERENT NOW, ARE THEY NOT?
Back in #17. – Tom.

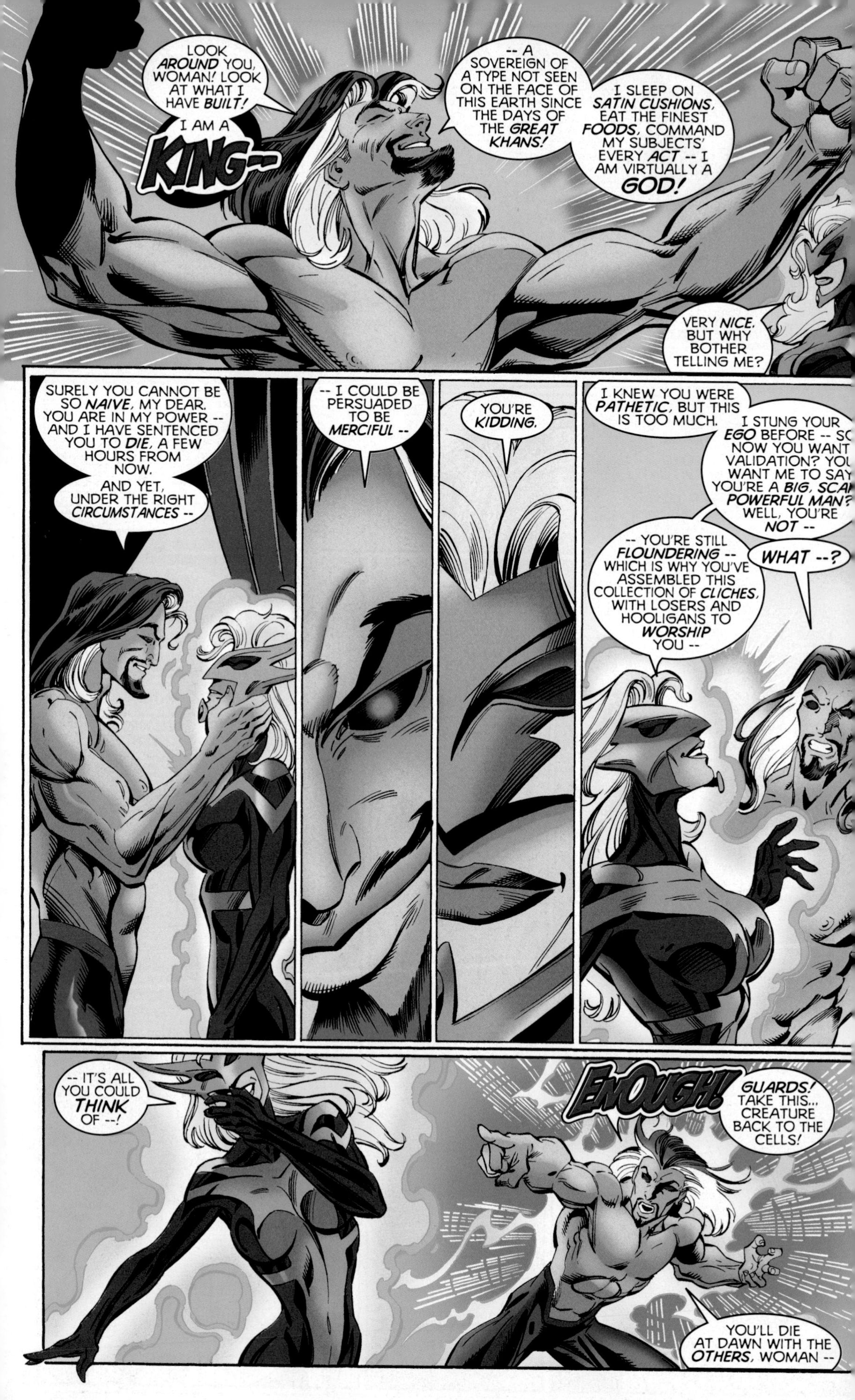
LOOK AROUND YOU, WOMAN! LOOK AT WHAT I HAVE BUILT!
I AM A KING--
-- A SOVEREIGN OF A TYPE NOT SEEN ON THE FACE OF THIS EARTH SINCE THE DAYS OF THE GREAT KHANS!
I SLEEP ON SATIN CUSHIONS, EAT THE FINEST FOODS, COMMAND MY SUBJECTS' EVERY ACT -- I AM VIRTUALLY A GOD!
VERY NICE, BUT WHY BOTHER TELLING ME?
SURELY YOU CANNOT BE SO NAIVE, MY DEAR. YOU ARE IN MY POWER -- AND I HAVE SENTENCED YOU TO DIE, A FEW HOURS FROM NOW.
AND YET, UNDER THE RIGHT CIRCUMSTANCES --
-- I COULD BE PERSUADED TO BE MERCIFUL --
YOU'RE KIDDING.
I KNEW YOU WERE PATHETIC, BUT THIS IS TOO MUCH.
WHAT --?
-- YOU'RE STILL FLOUNDERING -- WHICH IS WHY YOU'VE ASSEMBLED THIS COLLECTION OF CLICHES, WITH LOSERS AND HOOLIGANS TO WORSHIP YOU --
-- IT'S ALL YOU COULD THINK OF --!
ENOUGH!
GUARDS! TAKE THIS... CREATURE BACK TO THE CELLS!
YOU'LL DIE AT DAWN WITH THE OTHERS, WOMAN --

"-- YOU'LL DIE!"

MOONSTONE IS ROUGHLY DRAGGED BACK TO THE PRISON CHAMBER --

-- AND THE GRAVITIC FIELD IS DROPPED JUST LONG ENOUGH TO SHOVE HER IN.

AND LATER, AS THE SUN RISES OVER OAKLAND AND THE BAY --

-- THE GUARDS COME ONCE AGAIN FOR THE THUNDERBOLTS.

THIS TIME, WHEN THE FIELD IS DROPPED, THEY'RE READY --

-- CHARGING FORWARD, STRIKING AT THE GUARDS WITHOUT WARNING.

BUT IT DOES NO GOOD. THEY DOWN TEN OF THE SKY RAIDERS BEFORE THE ELEMENT OF SURPRISE FAILS THEM --

-- AND THEY'RE CRUSHED TO THE FLAGSTONES BY GRAVITON'S POWER.

AND SOON...

THE CRIMINALS BEFORE ME HAVE OFFENDED THE PERSONAGE OF GRAVITON THE FIRST, EMPEROR OF SKY ISLAND -- AND THE PENALTY IS DEATH.

BEGIN THE VIDEO TRANSMISSION, AND LET THE WORLD WATCH.

BUT GRAVITON IS A JUST MAN. A FAIR MAN -- AND WILL THEREFORE OFFER THEM ONE MORE CHANCE TO ESCAPE DEATH --

-- AND LIVE OUT THEIR LIVES AS PRISONERS --

-- BY HUMBLY BEGGING FOR MERCY --

SO BE IT. BREATHE DEEPLY, THUNDERBOLTS.

FOR I ASSURE YOU, IT IS THE LAST BREATH YOU SHALL EVER --

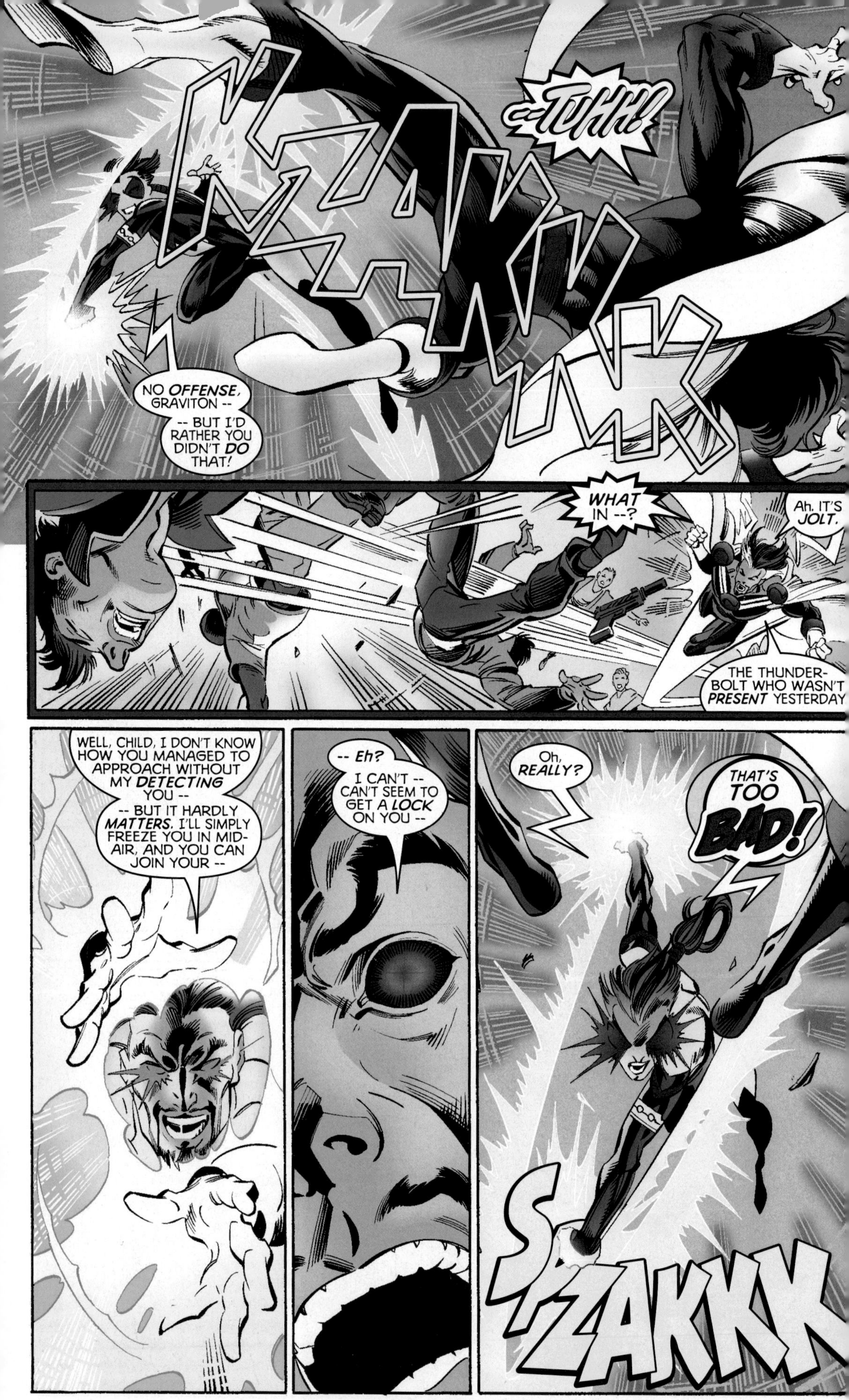

KLANNNNK
-TUHH!
NO OFFENSE, GRAVITON --
-- BUT I'D RATHER YOU DIDN'T DO THAT!
WHAT IN --?
Ah. IT'S JOLT.
THE THUNDER-BOLT WHO WASN'T PRESENT YESTERDAY
WELL, CHILD, I DON'T KNOW HOW YOU MANAGED TO APPROACH WITHOUT MY DETECTING YOU --
-- BUT IT HARDLY MATTERS. I'LL SIMPLY FREEZE YOU IN MID-AIR, AND YOU CAN JOIN YOUR --
-- Eh?
I CAN'T -- CAN'T SEEM TO GET A LOCK ON YOU --
Oh, REALLY?
THAT'S TOO BAD!
SZAKKK

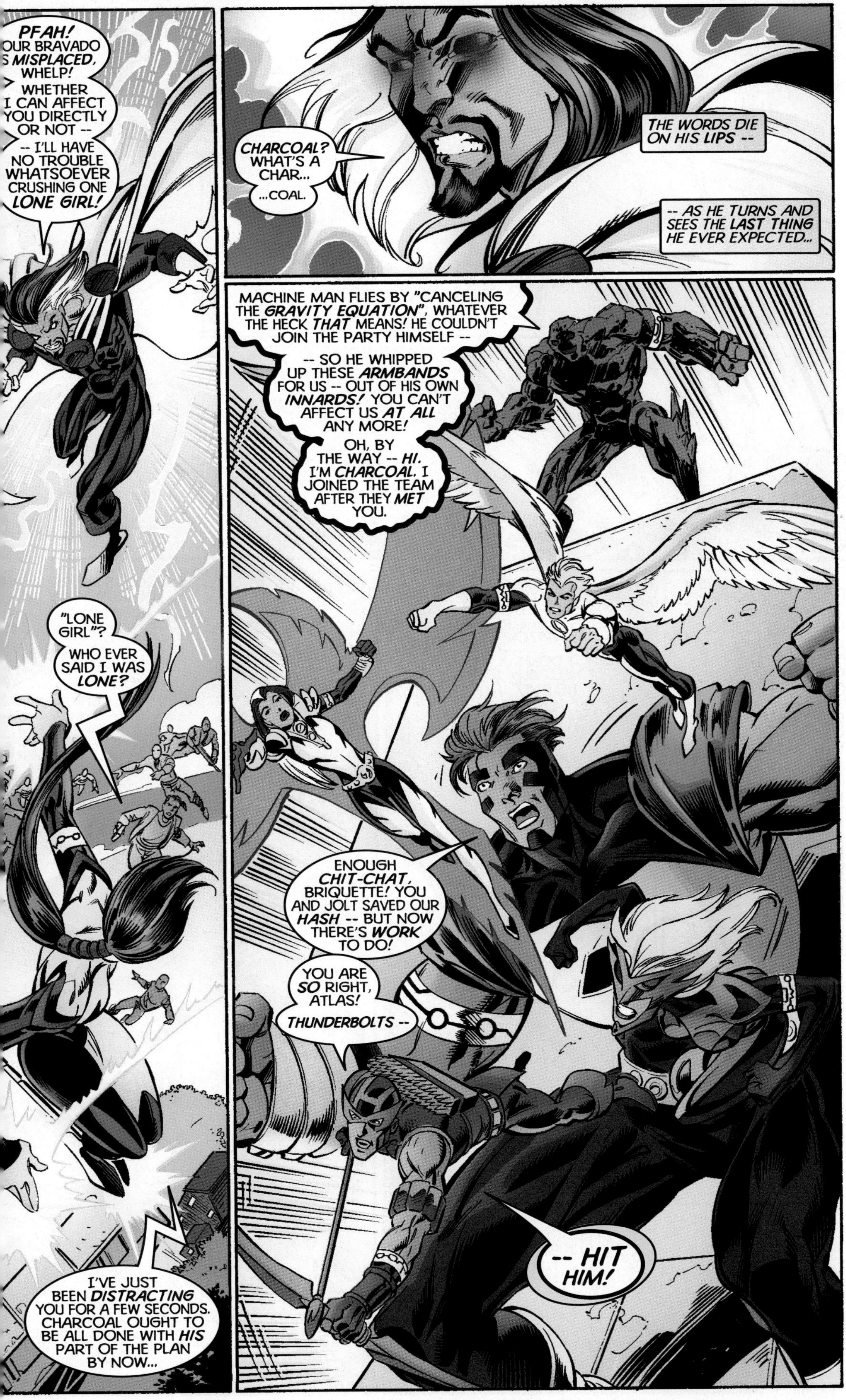
PFAH! OUR BRAVADO S MISPLACED, WHELP!
WHETHER I CAN AFFECT YOU DIRECTLY OR NOT --
-- I'LL HAVE NO TROUBLE WHATSOEVER CRUSHING ONE LONE GIRL!
"LONE GIRL"? WHO EVER SAID I WAS LONE?
I'VE JUST BEEN DISTRACTING YOU FOR A FEW SECONDS. CHARCOAL OUGHT TO BE ALL DONE WITH HIS PART OF THE PLAN BY NOW...
CHARCOAL? WHAT'S A CHAR...
...COAL.
THE WORDS DIE ON HIS LIPS --
-- AS HE TURNS AND SEES THE LAST THING HE EVER EXPECTED...
MACHINE MAN FLIES BY "CANCELING THE GRAVITY EQUATION", WHATEVER THE HECK THAT MEANS! HE COULDN'T JOIN THE PARTY HIMSELF --
-- SO HE WHIPPED UP THESE ARMBANDS FOR US -- OUT OF HIS OWN INNARDS! YOU CAN'T AFFECT US AT ALL ANY MORE!
OH, BY THE WAY -- HI. I'M CHARCOAL. I JOINED THE TEAM AFTER THEY MET YOU.
ENOUGH CHIT-CHAT, BRIQUETTE! YOU AND JOLT SAVED OUR HASH -- BUT NOW THERE'S WORK TO DO!
YOU ARE SO RIGHT, ATLAS!
THUNDERBOLTS --
-- HIT HIM!

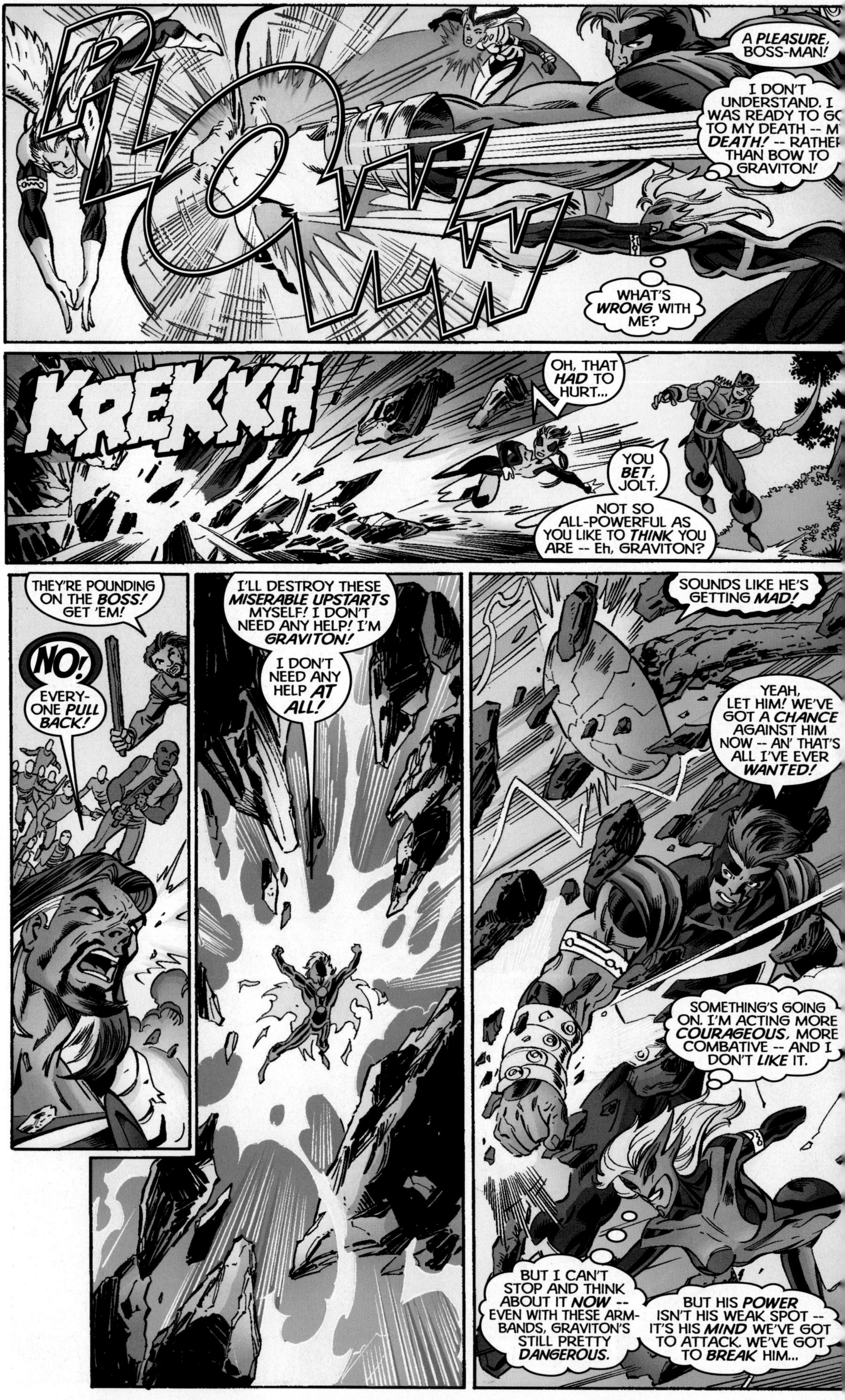
BLOOWW
A PLEASURE, BOSS-MAN!
I DON'T UNDERSTAND. I WAS READY TO GO TO MY DEATH -- MY DEATH! -- RATHER THAN BOW TO GRAVITON!
WHAT'S WRONG WITH ME?
KREKKH
OH, THAT HAD TO HURT...
YOU BET, JOLT.
NOT SO ALL-POWERFUL AS YOU LIKE TO THINK YOU ARE -- Eh, GRAVITON?
THEY'RE POUNDING ON THE BOSS! GET 'EM!
NO! EVERY-ONE PULL BACK!
I'LL DESTROY THESE MISERABLE UPSTARTS MYSELF! I DON'T NEED ANY HELP! I'M GRAVITON!
I DON'T NEED ANY HELP AT ALL!
SOUNDS LIKE HE'S GETTING MAD!
YEAH, LET HIM! WE'VE GOT A CHANCE AGAINST HIM NOW -- AN' THAT'S ALL I'VE EVER WANTED!
SOMETHING'S GOING ON. I'M ACTING MORE COURAGEOUS, MORE COMBATIVE -- AND I DON'T LIKE IT.
BUT I CAN'T STOP AND THINK ABOUT IT NOW -- EVEN WITH THESE ARM-BANDS, GRAVITON'S STILL PRETTY DANGEROUS.
BUT HIS POWER ISN'T HIS WEAK SPOT -- IT'S HIS MIND WE'VE GOT TO ATTACK. WE'VE GOT TO BREAK HIM...

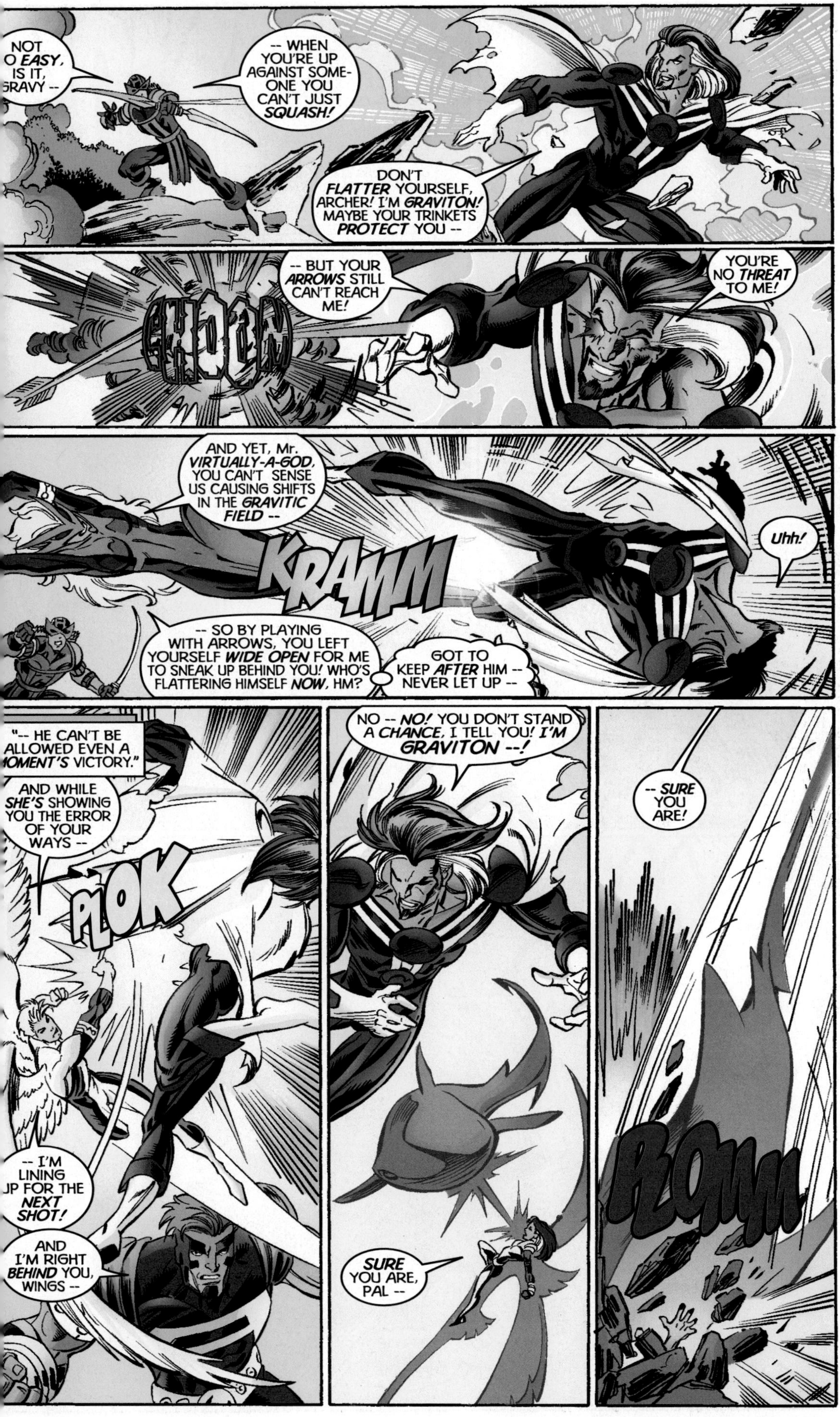

NOT SO *EASY,* IS IT, GRAVY --
-- WHEN YOU'RE UP AGAINST SOME-ONE YOU CAN'T JUST *SQUASH!*
DON'T *FLATTER* YOURSELF, ARCHER! I'M *GRAVITON!* MAYBE YOUR TRINKETS *PROTECT* YOU --
-- BUT YOUR *ARROWS* STILL CAN'T REACH ME!
YOU'RE NO *THREAT* TO ME!
AND YET, Mr. *VIRTUALLY-A-GOD,* YOU CAN'T SENSE US CAUSING SHIFTS IN THE *GRAVITIC FIELD* --
KRAMM
Uhh!
-- SO BY PLAYING WITH ARROWS, YOU LEFT YOURSELF *WIDE OPEN* FOR ME TO SNEAK UP BEHIND YOU! WHO'S FLATTERING HIMSELF *NOW,* HM?
GOT TO KEEP *AFTER* HIM -- NEVER LET UP --
"-- HE CAN'T BE ALLOWED EVEN A MOMENT'S VICTORY."
AND WHILE *SHE'S* SHOWING YOU THE ERROR OF YOUR WAYS --
PLOK
-- I'M LINING UP FOR THE *NEXT SHOT!*
AND I'M RIGHT *BEHIND* YOU, WINGS --
NO -- *NO!* YOU DON'T STAND A *CHANCE,* I TELL YOU! *I'M GRAVITON --!*
SURE YOU ARE, PAL --
-- *SURE* YOU ARE!

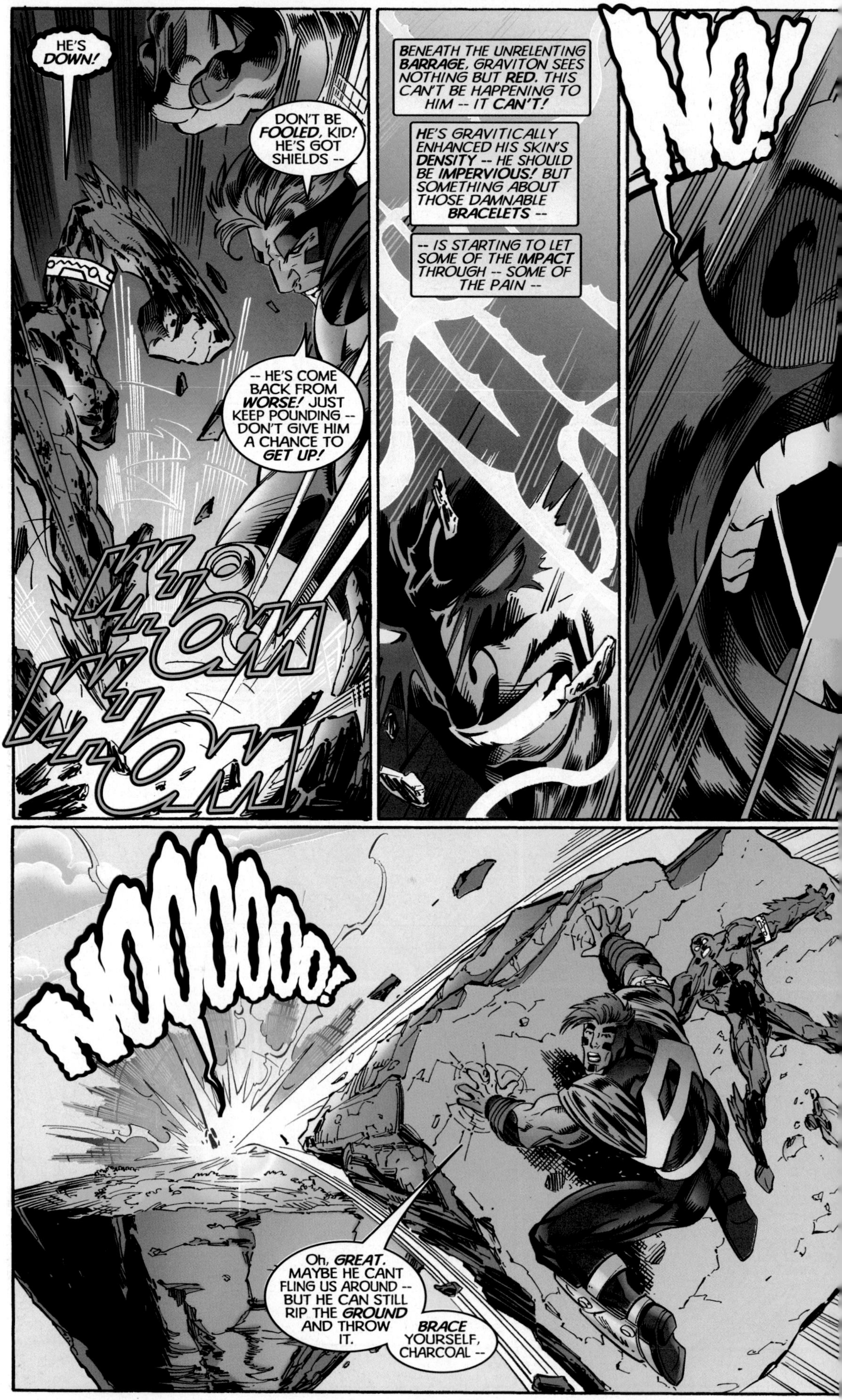
HE'S DOWN!
DON'T BE FOOLED, KID! HE'S GOT SHIELDS --
-- HE'S COME BACK FROM WORSE! JUST KEEP POUNDING -- DON'T GIVE HIM A CHANCE TO GET UP!
WHOM WHOM WHOM
BENEATH THE UNRELENTING BARRAGE, GRAVITON SEES NOTHING BUT RED. THIS CAN'T BE HAPPENING TO HIM -- IT CAN'T!
HE'S GRAVITICALLY ENHANCED HIS SKIN'S DENSITY -- HE SHOULD BE IMPERVIOUS! BUT SOMETHING ABOUT THOSE DAMNABLE BRACELETS --
-- IS STARTING TO LET SOME OF THE IMPACT THROUGH -- SOME OF THE PAIN --
NO!
NOOOOOO!
Oh, GREAT. MAYBE HE CANT FLING US AROUND -- BUT HE CAN STILL RIP THE GROUND AND THROW IT.
BRACE YOURSELF, CHARCOAL --

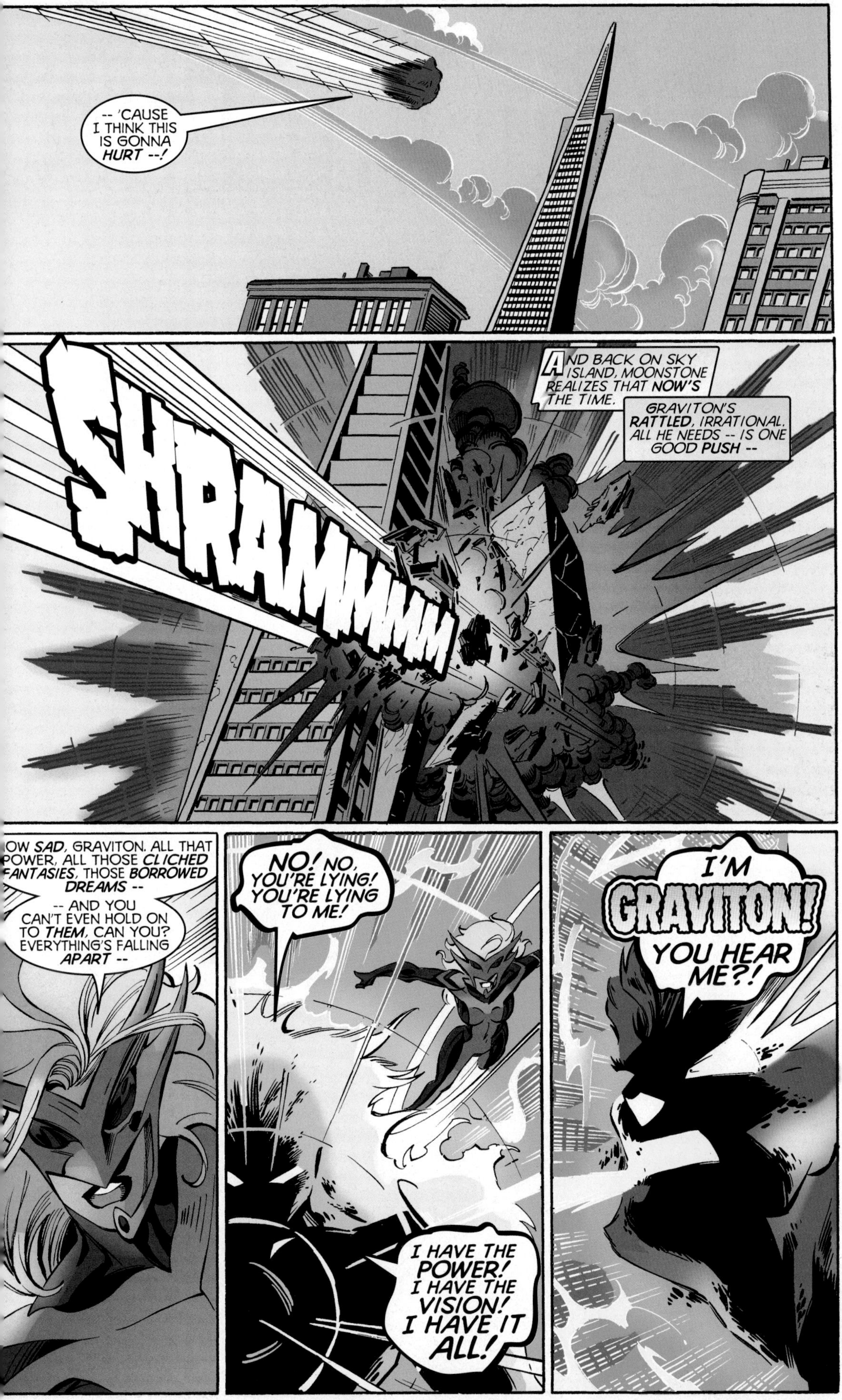
-- 'CAUSE I THINK THIS IS GONNA HURT --!
SHRAMMMMM
AND BACK ON SKY ISLAND, MOONSTONE REALIZES THAT NOW'S THE TIME.
GRAVITON'S RATTLED, IRRATIONAL. ALL HE NEEDS -- IS ONE GOOD PUSH --
OW SAD, GRAVITON. ALL THAT POWER, ALL THOSE CLICHED FANTASIES, THOSE BORROWED DREAMS --
-- AND YOU CAN'T EVEN HOLD ON TO THEM, CAN YOU? EVERYTHING'S FALLING APART --
NO! NO, YOU'RE LYING! YOU'RE LYING TO ME!
I HAVE THE POWER! I HAVE THE VISION! I HAVE IT ALL!
I'M GRAVITON! YOU HEAR ME?!

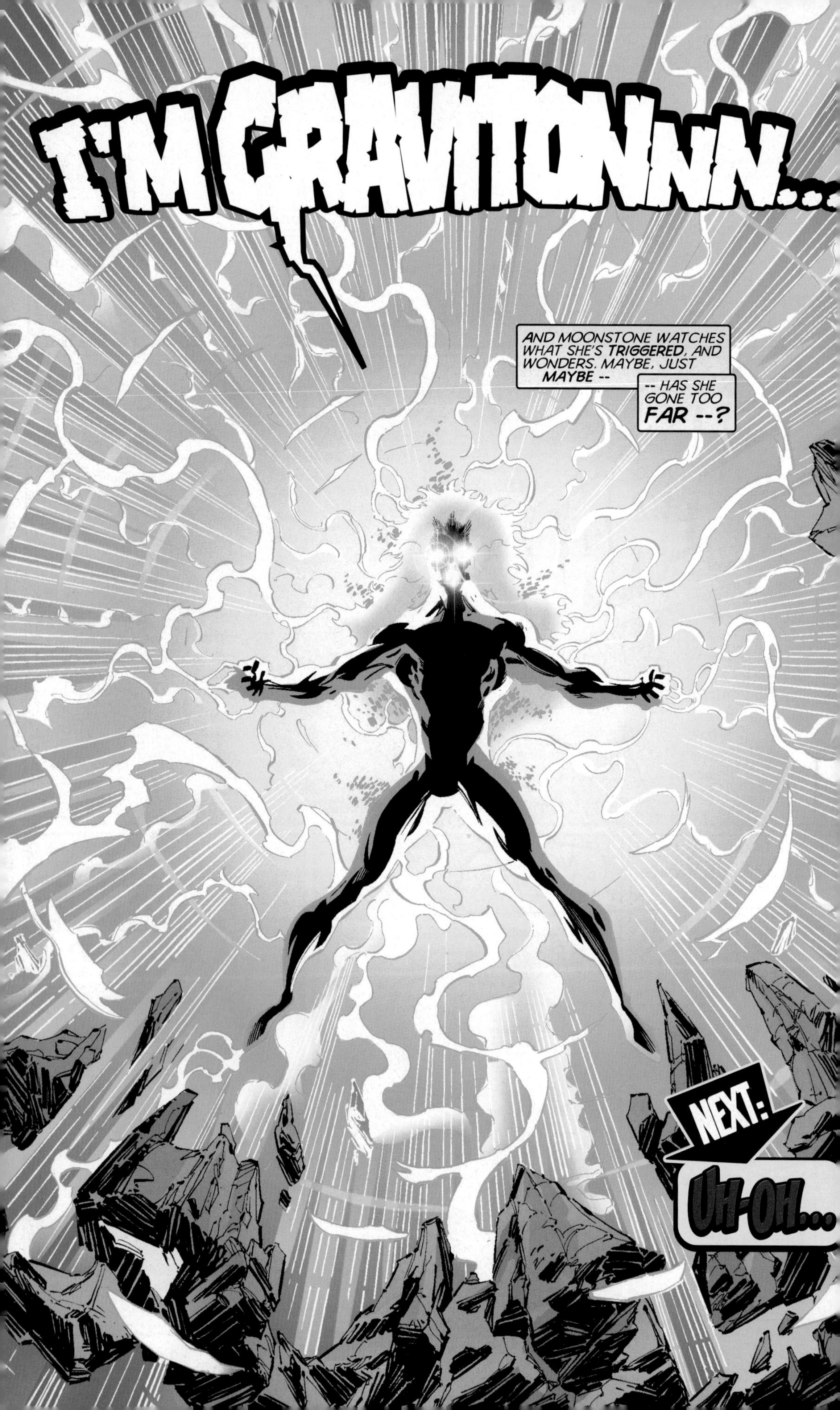
I'M GRAVITONNNN...
AND MOONSTONE WATCHES WHAT SHE'S TRIGGERED, AND WONDERS. MAYBE, JUST MAYBE --
-- HAS SHE GONE TOO FAR --?
NEXT:
UH-OH...

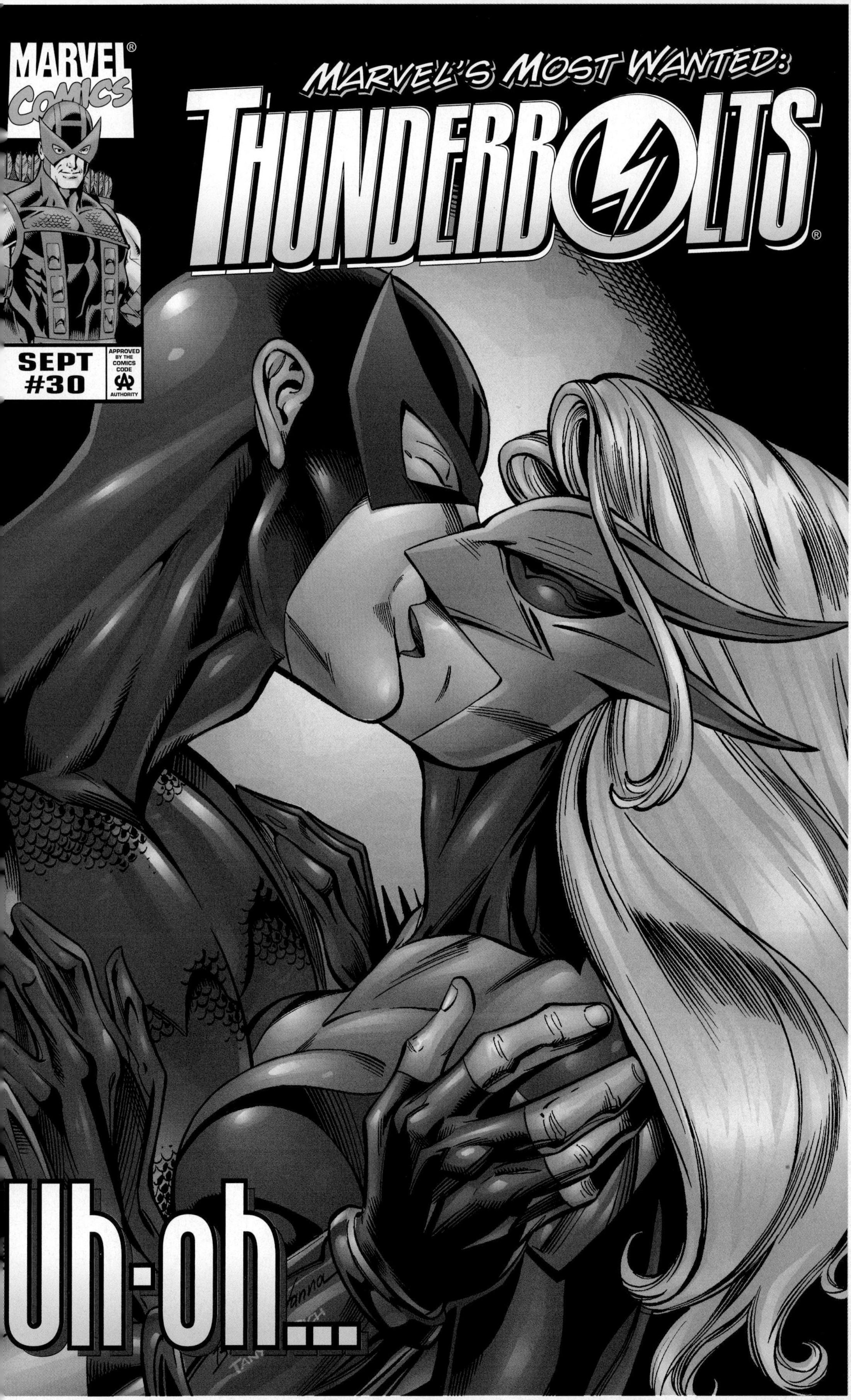
MARVEL® COMICS
MARVEL'S MOST WANTED:
THUNDERBOLTS®
SEPT #30
APPROVED BY THE COMICS CODE AUTHORITY
Uh-oh...

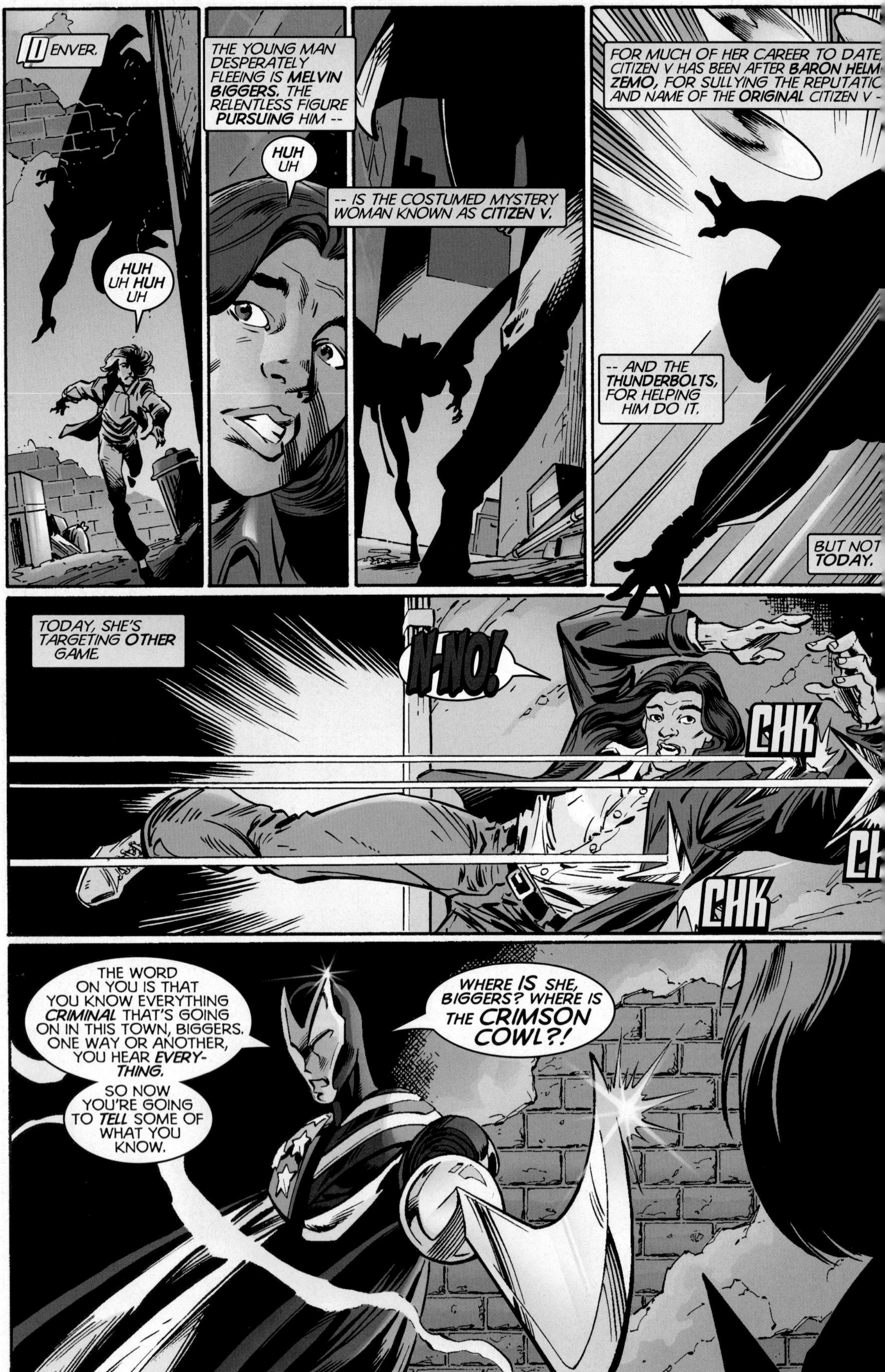
DENVER.
HUH UH HUH UH
THE YOUNG MAN DESPERATELY FLEEING IS MELVIN BIGGERS. THE RELENTLESS FIGURE PURSUING HIM --
HUH UH
-- IS THE COSTUMED MYSTERY WOMAN KNOWN AS CITIZEN V.
FOR MUCH OF HER CAREER TO DATE, CITIZEN V HAS BEEN AFTER BARON HELM ZEMO, FOR SULLYING THE REPUTATIC AND NAME OF THE ORIGINAL CITIZEN V --
-- AND THE THUNDERBOLTS, FOR HELPING HIM DO IT.
BUT NOT TODAY.
TODAY, SHE'S TARGETING OTHER GAME.
N-NO!
CHK
CHK
THE WORD ON YOU IS THAT YOU KNOW EVERYTHING CRIMINAL THAT'S GOING ON IN THIS TOWN, BIGGERS. ONE WAY OR ANOTHER, YOU HEAR EVERY-THING.
SO NOW YOU'RE GOING TO TELL SOME OF WHAT YOU KNOW.
WHERE IS SHE, BIGGERS? WHERE IS THE CRIMSON COWL?!

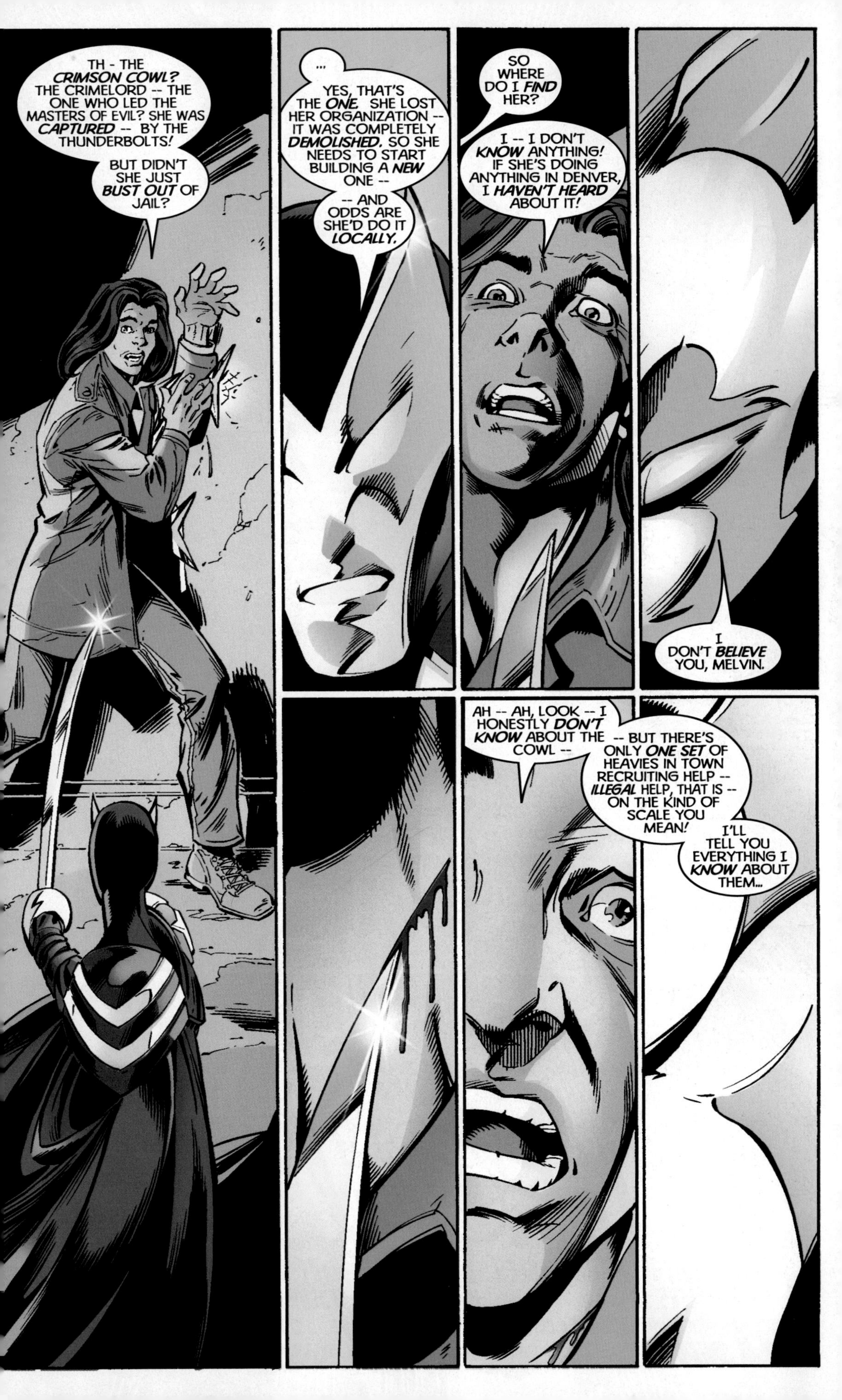
TH - THE CRIMSON COWL? THE CRIMELORD -- THE ONE WHO LED THE MASTERS OF EVIL? SHE WAS CAPTURED -- BY THE THUNDERBOLTS!
BUT DIDN'T SHE JUST BUST OUT OF JAIL?
...
YES, THAT'S THE ONE. SHE LOST HER ORGANIZATION -- IT WAS COMPLETELY DEMOLISHED. SO SHE NEEDS TO START BUILDING A NEW ONE --
-- AND ODDS ARE SHE'D DO IT LOCALLY.
SO WHERE DO I FIND HER?
I -- I DON'T KNOW ANYTHING! IF SHE'S DOING ANYTHING IN DENVER, I HAVEN'T HEARD ABOUT IT!
I DON'T BELIEVE YOU, MELVIN.
AH -- AH, LOOK -- I HONESTLY DON'T KNOW ABOUT THE COWL --
-- BUT THERE'S ONLY ONE SET OF HEAVIES IN TOWN RECRUITING HELP -- ILLEGAL HELP, THAT IS -- ON THE KIND OF SCALE YOU MEAN!
I'LL TELL YOU EVERYTHING I KNOW ABOUT THEM...

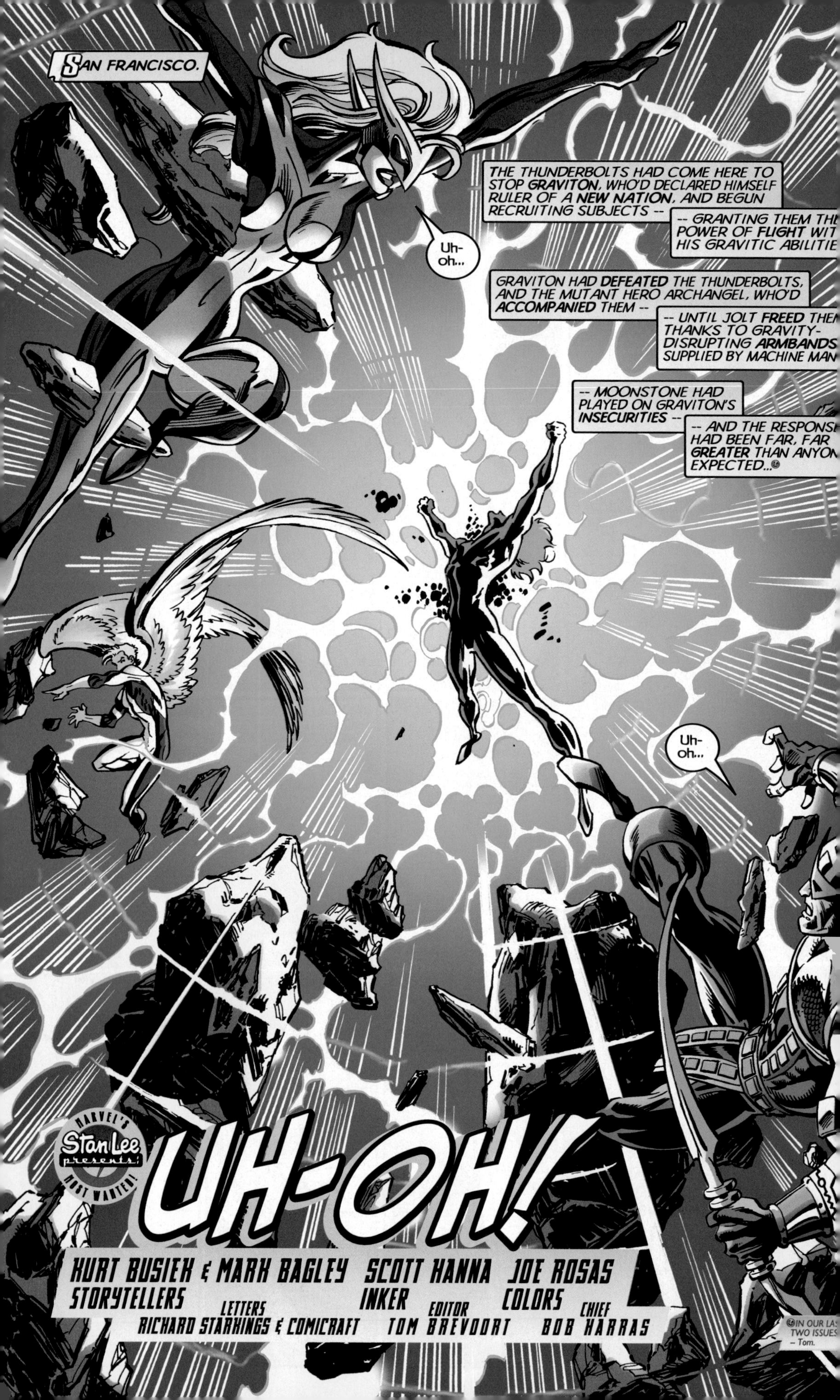
SAN FRANCISCO.
THE THUNDERBOLTS HAD COME HERE TO STOP GRAVITON, WHO'D DECLARED HIMSELF RULER OF A NEW NATION, AND BEGUN RECRUITING SUBJECTS --
-- GRANTING THEM TH POWER OF FLIGHT WIT HIS GRAVITIC ABILITIE
Uh-oh...
GRAVITON HAD DEFEATED THE THUNDERBOLTS, AND THE MUTANT HERO ARCHANGEL, WHO'D ACCOMPANIED THEM --
-- UNTIL JOLT FREED THEM THANKS TO GRAVITY-DISRUPTING ARMBANDS SUPPLIED BY MACHINE MAN
-- MOONSTONE HAD PLAYED ON GRAVITON'S INSECURITIES --
-- AND THE RESPONS HAD BEEN FAR, FAR GREATER THAN ANYON EXPECTED...
Uh-oh...
MARVEL'S Stan Lee presents! MOST WANTED!
UH-OH!
KURT BUSIEK & MARK BAGLEY STORYTELLERS
SCOTT HANNA INKER
JOE ROSAS COLORS
LETTERS RICHARD STARKINGS & COMICRAFT
EDITOR TOM BREVOORT
CHIEF BOB HARRAS
IN OUR LA TWO ISSUES – Tom.

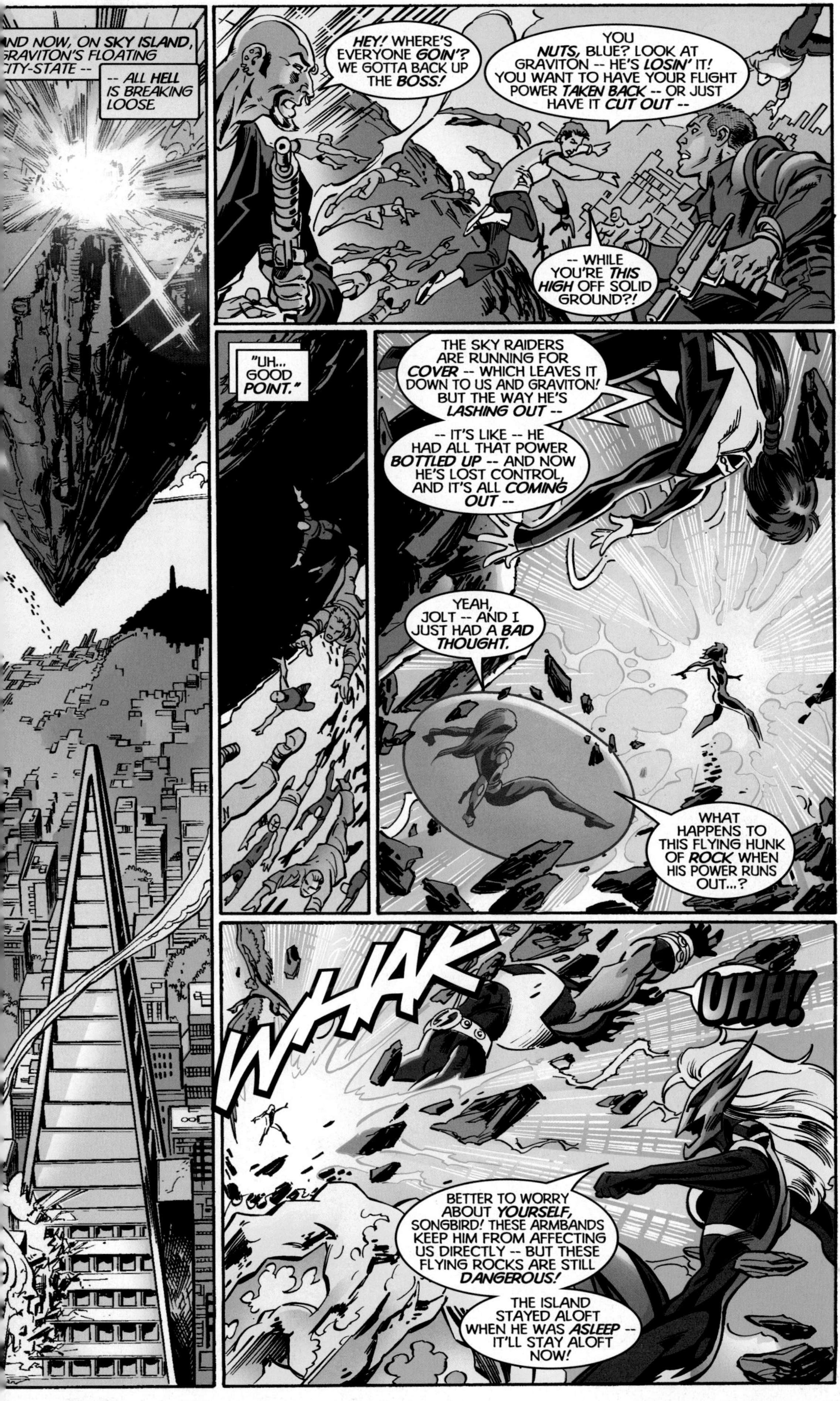

ND NOW, ON SKY ISLAND, GRAVITON'S FLOATING CITY-STATE --
-- ALL HELL IS BREAKING LOOSE.
HEY! WHERE'S EVERYONE GOIN'? WE GOTTA BACK UP THE BOSS!
YOU NUTS, BLUE? LOOK AT GRAVITON -- HE'S LOSIN' IT! YOU WANT TO HAVE YOUR FLIGHT POWER TAKEN BACK -- OR JUST HAVE IT CUT OUT --
-- WHILE YOU'RE THIS HIGH OFF SOLID GROUND?!
"UH... GOOD POINT."
THE SKY RAIDERS ARE RUNNING FOR COVER -- WHICH LEAVES IT DOWN TO US AND GRAVITON! BUT THE WAY HE'S LASHING OUT --
-- IT'S LIKE -- HE HAD ALL THAT POWER BOTTLED UP -- AND NOW HE'S LOST CONTROL, AND IT'S ALL COMING OUT --
YEAH, JOLT -- AND I JUST HAD A BAD THOUGHT.
WHAT HAPPENS TO THIS FLYING HUNK OF ROCK WHEN HIS POWER RUNS OUT...?
WHAK
UHH!
BETTER TO WORRY ABOUT YOURSELF, SONGBIRD! THESE ARMBANDS KEEP HIM FROM AFFECTING US DIRECTLY -- BUT THESE FLYING ROCKS ARE STILL DANGEROUS!
THE ISLAND STAYED ALOFT WHEN HE WAS ASLEEP -- IT'LL STAY ALOFT NOW!

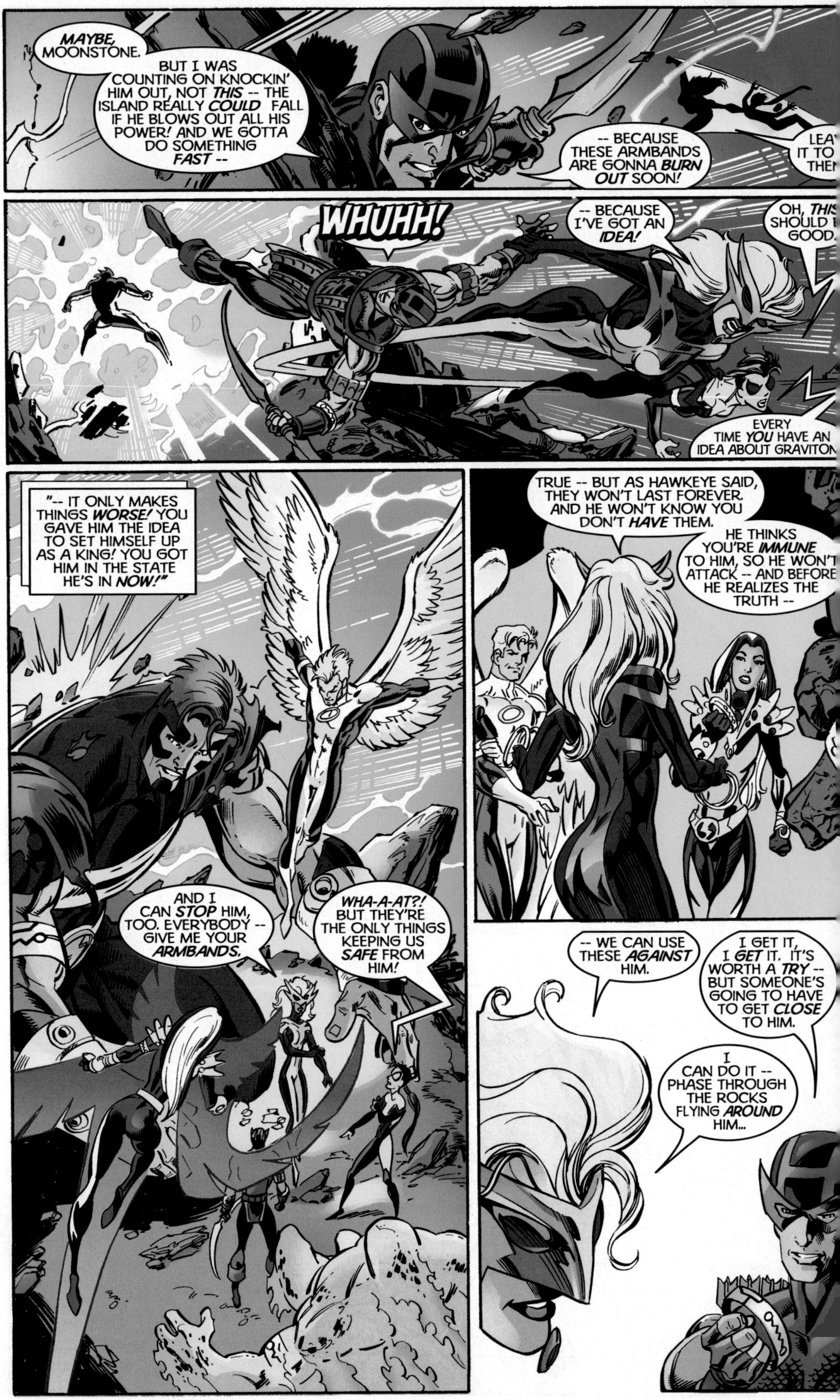
MAYBE, MOONSTONE.
BUT I WAS COUNTING ON KNOCKIN' HIM OUT, NOT THIS -- THE ISLAND REALLY COULD FALL IF HE BLOWS OUT ALL HIS POWER! AND WE GOTTA DO SOMETHING FAST --
-- BECAUSE THESE ARMBANDS ARE GONNA BURN OUT SOON!
WHUHH!
-- BECAUSE I'VE GOT AN IDEA!
EVERY TIME YOU HAVE AN IDEA ABOUT GRAVITON
"-- IT ONLY MAKES THINGS WORSE! YOU GAVE HIM THE IDEA TO SET HIMSELF UP AS A KING! YOU GOT HIM IN THE STATE HE'S IN NOW!"
AND I CAN STOP HIM, TOO. EVERYBODY -- GIVE ME YOUR ARMBANDS.
WHA-A-AT?! BUT THEY'RE THE ONLY THINGS KEEPING US SAFE FROM HIM!
TRUE -- BUT AS HAWKEYE SAID, THEY WON'T LAST FOREVER. AND HE WON'T KNOW YOU DON'T HAVE THEM.
HE THINKS YOU'RE IMMUNE TO HIM, SO HE WON'T ATTACK -- AND BEFORE HE REALIZES THE TRUTH --
-- WE CAN USE THESE AGAINST HIM.
I GET IT, I GET IT. IT'S WORTH A TRY -- BUT SOMEONE'S GOING TO HAVE TO GET CLOSE TO HIM.
I CAN DO IT -- PHASE THROUGH THE ROCKS FLYING AROUND HIM...

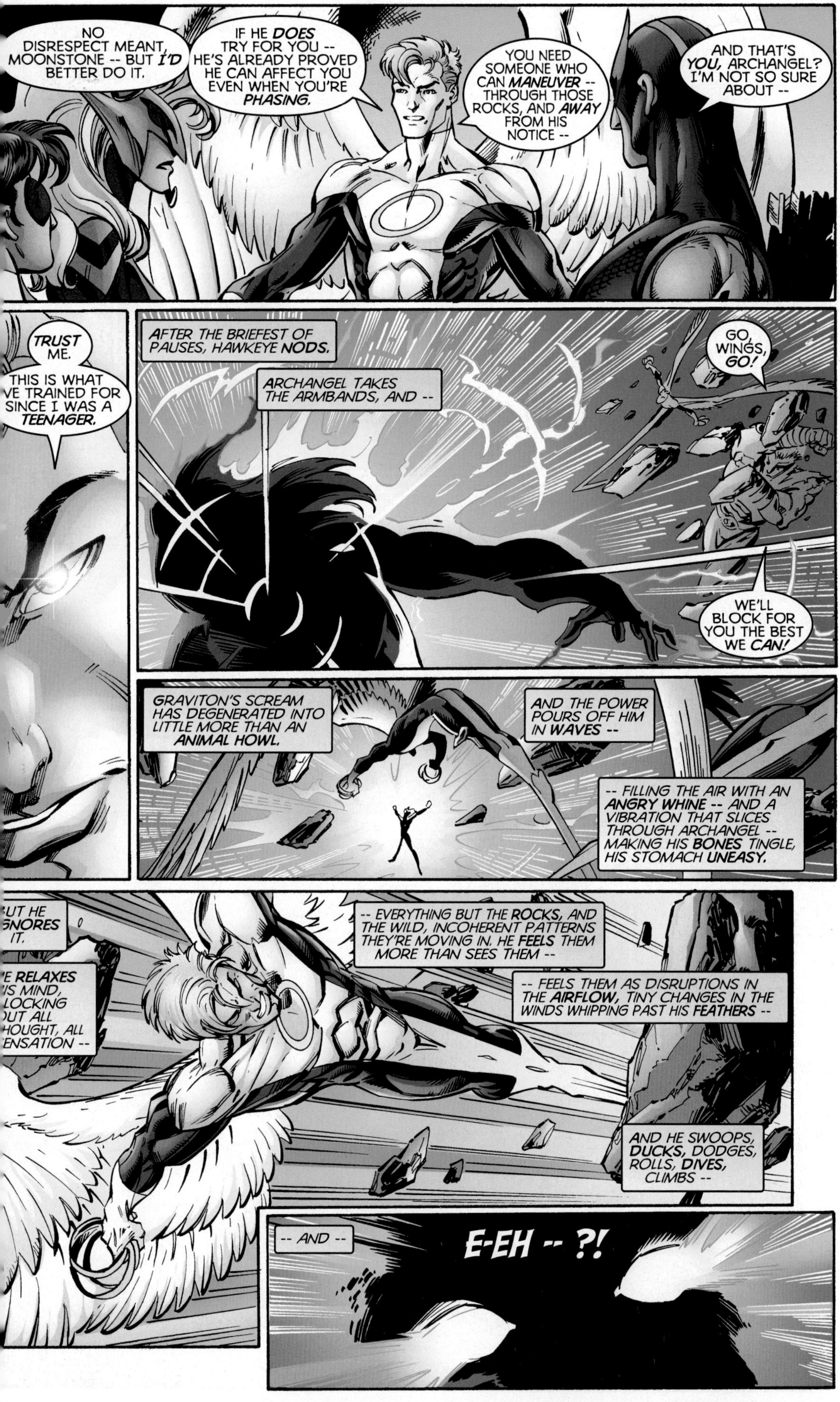
NO DISRESPECT MEANT, MOONSTONE -- BUT I'D BETTER DO IT.
IF HE DOES TRY FOR YOU -- HE'S ALREADY PROVED HE CAN AFFECT YOU EVEN WHEN YOU'RE PHASING.
YOU NEED SOMEONE WHO CAN MANEUVER -- THROUGH THOSE ROCKS, AND AWAY FROM HIS NOTICE --
AND THAT'S YOU, ARCHANGEL? I'M NOT SO SURE ABOUT --
TRUST ME.
THIS IS WHAT VE TRAINED FOR SINCE I WAS A TEENAGER.
AFTER THE BRIEFEST OF PAUSES, HAWKEYE NODS.
ARCHANGEL TAKES THE ARMBANDS, AND --
GO, WINGS, GO!
WE'LL BLOCK FOR YOU THE BEST WE CAN!
GRAVITON'S SCREAM HAS DEGENERATED INTO LITTLE MORE THAN AN ANIMAL HOWL.
AND THE POWER POURS OFF HIM IN WAVES --
-- FILLING THE AIR WITH AN ANGRY WHINE -- AND A VIBRATION THAT SLICES THROUGH ARCHANGEL -- MAKING HIS BONES TINGLE, HIS STOMACH UNEASY.
UT HE GNORES IT.
E RELAXES IS MIND, LOCKING OUT ALL HOUGHT, ALL ENSATION --
-- EVERYTHING BUT THE ROCKS, AND THE WILD, INCOHERENT PATTERNS THEY'RE MOVING IN. HE FEELS THEM MORE THAN SEES THEM --
-- FEELS THEM AS DISRUPTIONS IN THE AIRFLOW, TINY CHANGES IN THE WINDS WHIPPING PAST HIS FEATHERS --
AND HE SWOOPS, DUCKS, DODGES, ROLLS, DIVES, CLIMBS --
-- AND --
E-EH -- ?!

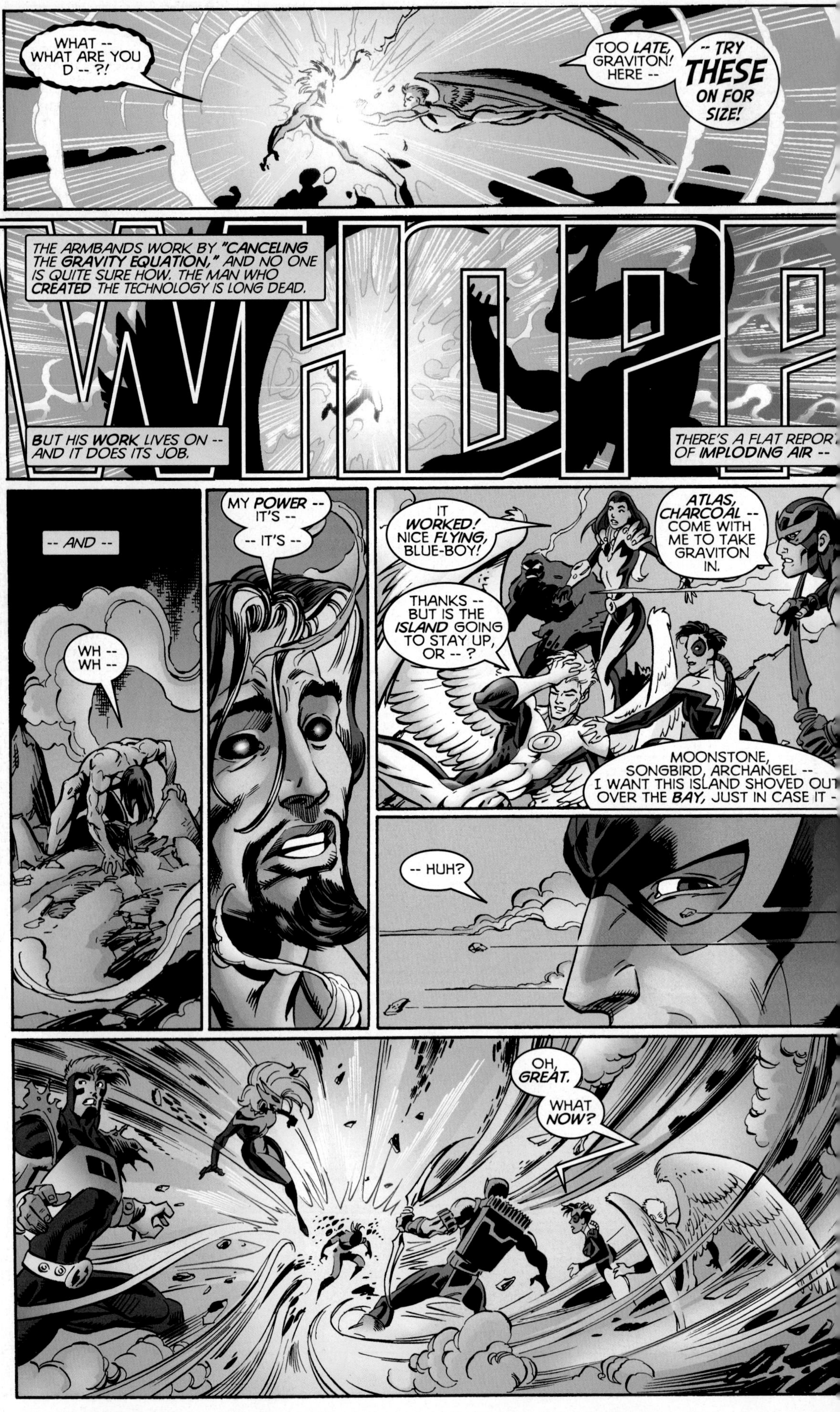
WHAT -- WHAT ARE YOU D -- ?!
TOO LATE, GRAVITON! HERE --
-- TRY THESE ON FOR SIZE!
THE ARMBANDS WORK BY "CANCELING THE GRAVITY EQUATION," AND NO ONE IS QUITE SURE HOW. THE MAN WHO CREATED THE TECHNOLOGY IS LONG DEAD.
WHOP
BUT HIS WORK LIVES ON -- AND IT DOES ITS JOB.
THERE'S A FLAT REPORT OF IMPLODING AIR --
-- AND --
WH -- WH --
MY POWER -- IT'S --
-- IT'S --
IT WORKED! NICE FLYING, BLUE-BOY!
ATLAS, CHARCOAL -- COME WITH ME TO TAKE GRAVITON IN.
THANKS -- BUT IS THE ISLAND GOING TO STAY UP, OR -- ?
MOONSTONE, SONGBIRD, ARCHANGEL -- I WANT THIS ISLAND SHOVED OUT OVER THE BAY, JUST IN CASE IT --
-- HUH?
OH, GREAT.
WHAT NOW?

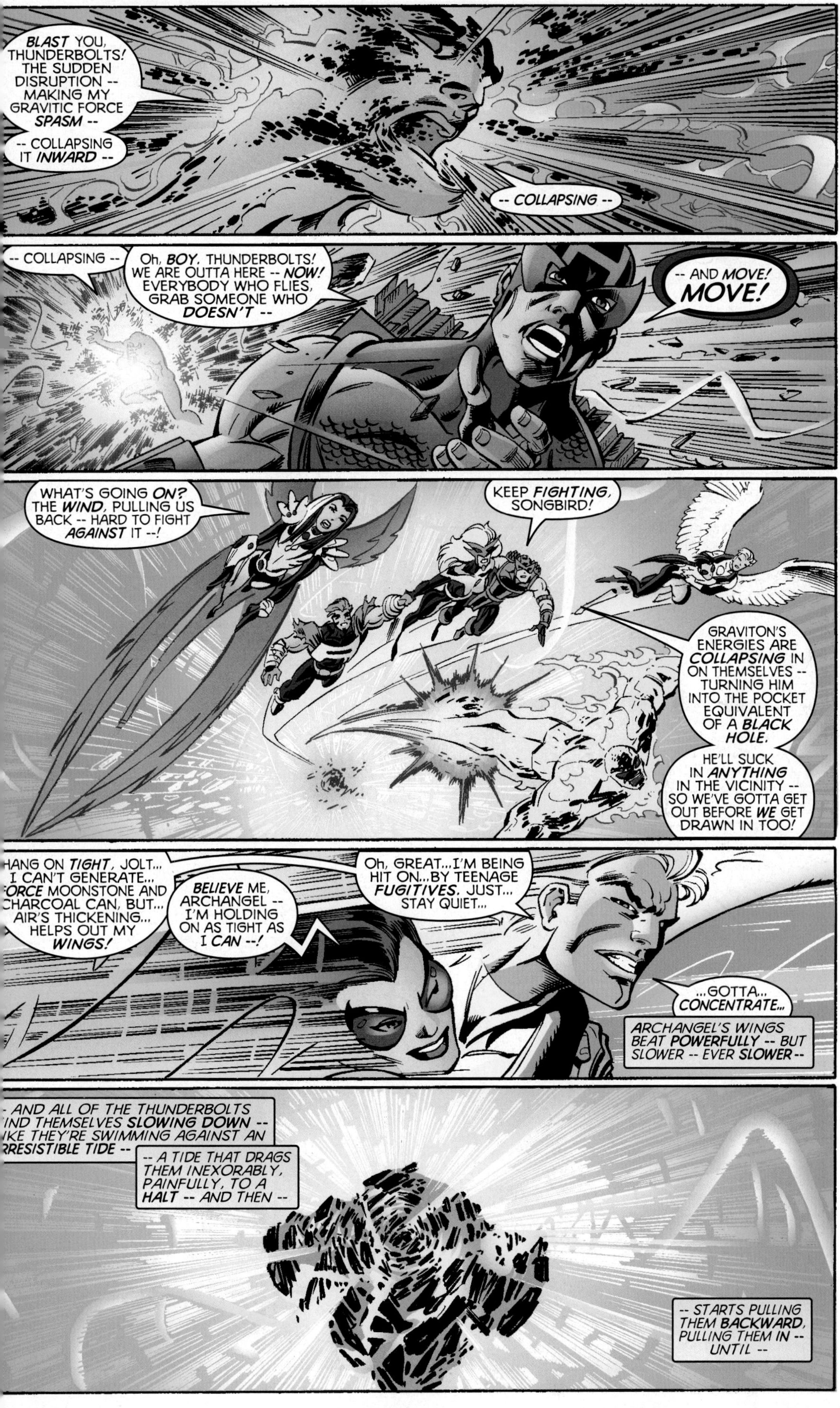
BLAST YOU, THUNDERBOLTS! THE SUDDEN DISRUPTION -- MAKING MY GRAVITIC FORCE SPASM --
-- COLLAPSING IT INWARD --
-- COLLAPSING --
-- COLLAPSING --
Oh, BOY. THUNDERBOLTS! WE ARE OUTTA HERE -- NOW! EVERYBODY WHO FLIES, GRAB SOMEONE WHO DOESN'T --
-- AND MOVE! MOVE!
WHAT'S GOING ON? THE WIND, PULLING US BACK -- HARD TO FIGHT AGAINST IT --!
KEEP FIGHTING, SONGBIRD!
GRAVITON'S ENERGIES ARE COLLAPSING IN ON THEMSELVES -- TURNING HIM INTO THE POCKET EQUIVALENT OF A BLACK HOLE.
HE'LL SUCK IN ANYTHING IN THE VICINITY -- SO WE'VE GOTTA GET OUT BEFORE WE GET DRAWN IN TOO!
HANG ON TIGHT, JOLT... I CAN'T GENERATE... FORCE MOONSTONE AND CHARCOAL CAN, BUT... AIR'S THICKENING... HELPS OUT MY WINGS!
BELIEVE ME, ARCHANGEL -- I'M HOLDING ON AS TIGHT AS I CAN --!
Oh, GREAT...I'M BEING HIT ON...BY TEENAGE FUGITIVES. JUST... STAY QUIET...
...GOTTA... CONCENTRATE...
ARCHANGEL'S WINGS BEAT POWERFULLY -- BUT SLOWER -- EVER SLOWER --
-- AND ALL OF THE THUNDERBOLTS FIND THEMSELVES SLOWING DOWN -- LIKE THEY'RE SWIMMING AGAINST AN IRRESISTIBLE TIDE --
-- A TIDE THAT DRAGS THEM INEXORABLY, PAINFULLY, TO A HALT -- AND THEN --
-- STARTS PULLING THEM BACKWARD, PULLING THEM IN -- UNTIL --

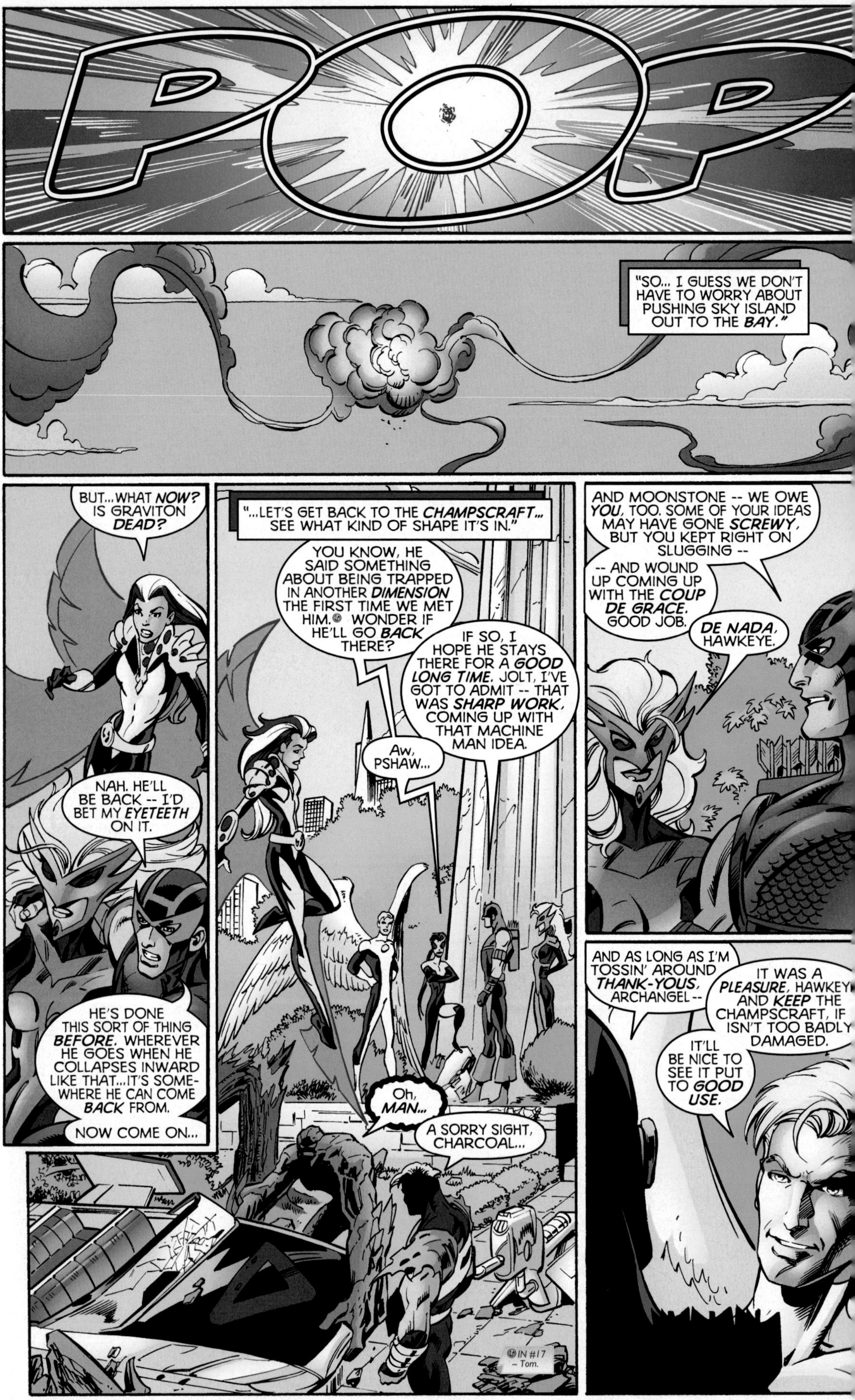
POP
"SO... I GUESS WE DON'T HAVE TO WORRY ABOUT PUSHING SKY ISLAND OUT TO THE *BAY.*"
BUT...WHAT *NOW?* IS GRAVITON *DEAD?*
NAH. HE'LL BE BACK -- I'D BET MY *EYETEETH* ON IT.
HE'S DONE THIS SORT OF THING *BEFORE.* WHEREVER HE GOES WHEN HE COLLAPSES INWARD LIKE THAT...IT'S SOMEWHERE HE CAN COME *BACK* FROM.
NOW COME ON...
"...LET'S GET BACK TO THE *CHAMPSCRAFT*... SEE WHAT KIND OF SHAPE IT'S IN."
YOU KNOW, HE SAID SOMETHING ABOUT BEING TRAPPED IN ANOTHER *DIMENSION* THE FIRST TIME WE MET HIM. WONDER IF HE'LL GO *BACK* THERE?
IF SO, I HOPE HE STAYS THERE FOR A *GOOD LONG TIME.* JOLT, I'VE GOT TO ADMIT -- THAT WAS *SHARP WORK,* COMING UP WITH THAT MACHINE MAN IDEA.
Aw, PSHAW...
AND MOONSTONE -- WE OWE *YOU*, TOO. SOME OF YOUR IDEAS MAY HAVE GONE *SCREWY*, BUT YOU KEPT RIGHT ON SLUGGING --
-- AND WOUND UP COMING UP WITH THE *COUP DE GRACE.* GOOD JOB.
DE NADA, HAWKEYE.
Oh, *MAN*...
A SORRY SIGHT, CHARCOAL...
IN #17 – Tom.
AND AS LONG AS I'M TOSSIN' AROUND *THANK-YOUS,* ARCHANGEL --
IT WAS A *PLEASURE,* HAWKEY AND *KEEP* THE CHAMPSCRAFT, IF ISN'T TOO BADLY DAMAGED.
IT'LL BE NICE TO SEE IT PUT TO *GOOD USE.*

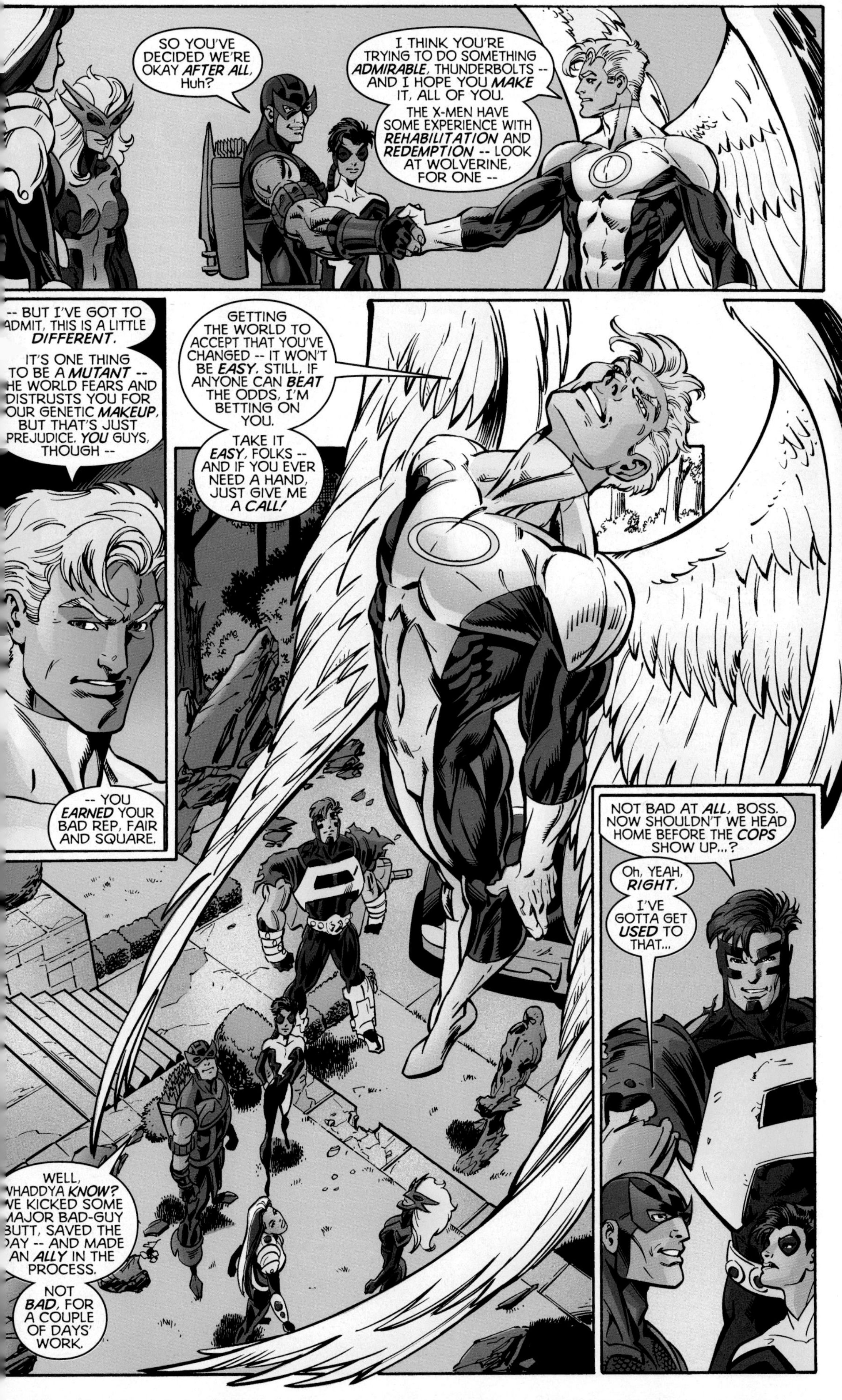
SO YOU'VE DECIDED WE'RE OKAY *AFTER ALL*, Huh?
I THINK YOU'RE TRYING TO DO SOMETHING *ADMIRABLE*, THUNDERBOLTS -- AND I HOPE YOU *MAKE* IT, ALL OF YOU.
THE X-MEN HAVE SOME EXPERIENCE WITH *REHABILITATION* AND *REDEMPTION* -- LOOK AT WOLVERINE, FOR ONE --
-- BUT I'VE GOT TO ADMIT, THIS IS A LITTLE *DIFFERENT*.
IT'S ONE THING TO BE A *MUTANT* -- HE WORLD FEARS AND DISTRUSTS YOU FOR OUR GENETIC *MAKEUP*, BUT THAT'S JUST PREJUDICE. *YOU* GUYS, THOUGH --
-- YOU *EARNED* YOUR BAD REP, FAIR AND SQUARE.
GETTING THE WORLD TO ACCEPT THAT YOU'VE CHANGED -- IT WON'T BE *EASY*. STILL, IF ANYONE CAN *BEAT* THE ODDS, I'M BETTING ON YOU.
TAKE IT *EASY*, FOLKS -- AND IF YOU EVER NEED A HAND, JUST GIVE ME A *CALL!*
WELL, VHADDYA *KNOW?* VE KICKED SOME MAJOR BAD-GUY BUTT, SAVED THE DAY -- AND MADE AN *ALLY* IN THE PROCESS.
NOT *BAD*, FOR A COUPLE OF DAYS' WORK.
NOT BAD AT *ALL*, BOSS. NOW SHOULDN'T WE HEAD HOME BEFORE THE *COPS* SHOW UP...?
Oh, YEAH, *RIGHT*.
I'VE GOTTA GET *USED* TO THAT...

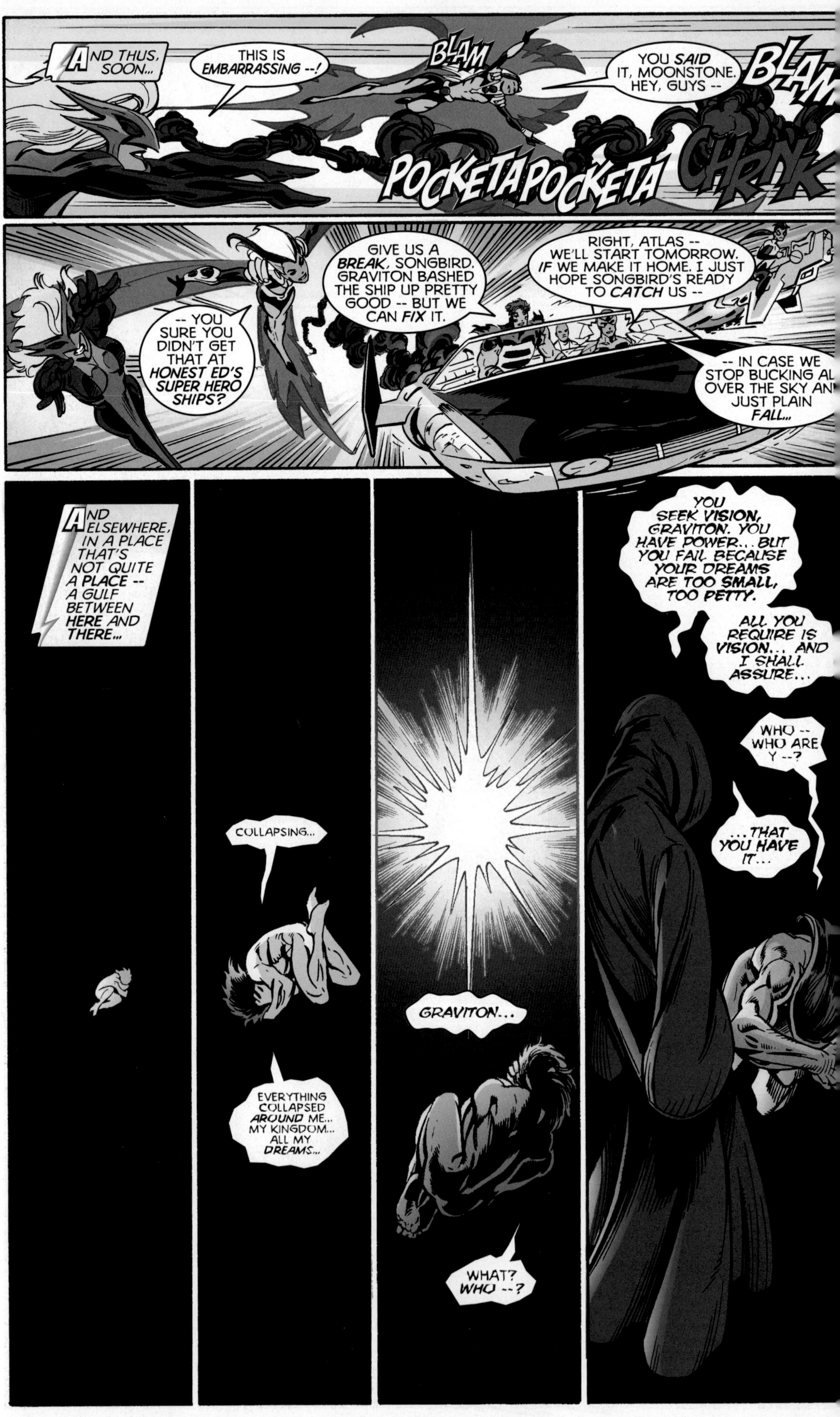
AND THUS, SOON...
THIS IS EMBARRASSING --!
BLAM
YOU SAID IT, MOONSTONE. HEY, GUYS --
BLAM
POCKETAPOCKETA
CHRNK
-- YOU SURE YOU DIDN'T GET THAT AT HONEST ED'S SUPER HERO SHIPS?
GIVE US A BREAK, SONGBIRD. GRAVITON BASHED THE SHIP UP PRETTY GOOD -- BUT WE CAN FIX IT.
RIGHT, ATLAS -- WE'LL START TOMORROW. IF WE MAKE IT HOME. I JUST HOPE SONGBIRD'S READY TO CATCH US --
-- IN CASE WE STOP BUCKING AL OVER THE SKY AN JUST PLAIN FALL...
AND ELSEWHERE, IN A PLACE THAT'S NOT QUITE A PLACE -- A GULF BETWEEN HERE AND THERE...
COLLAPSING...
EVERYTHING COLLAPSED AROUND ME... MY KINGDOM... ALL MY DREAMS...
GRAVITON...
WHAT? WHO --?
YOU SEEK VISION, GRAVITON. YOU HAVE POWER... BUT YOU FAIL BECAUSE YOUR DREAMS ARE TOO SMALL, TOO PETTY.
ALL YOU REQUIRE IS VISION... AND I SHALL ASSURE...
WHO -- WHO ARE Y --?
...THAT YOU HAVE IT...

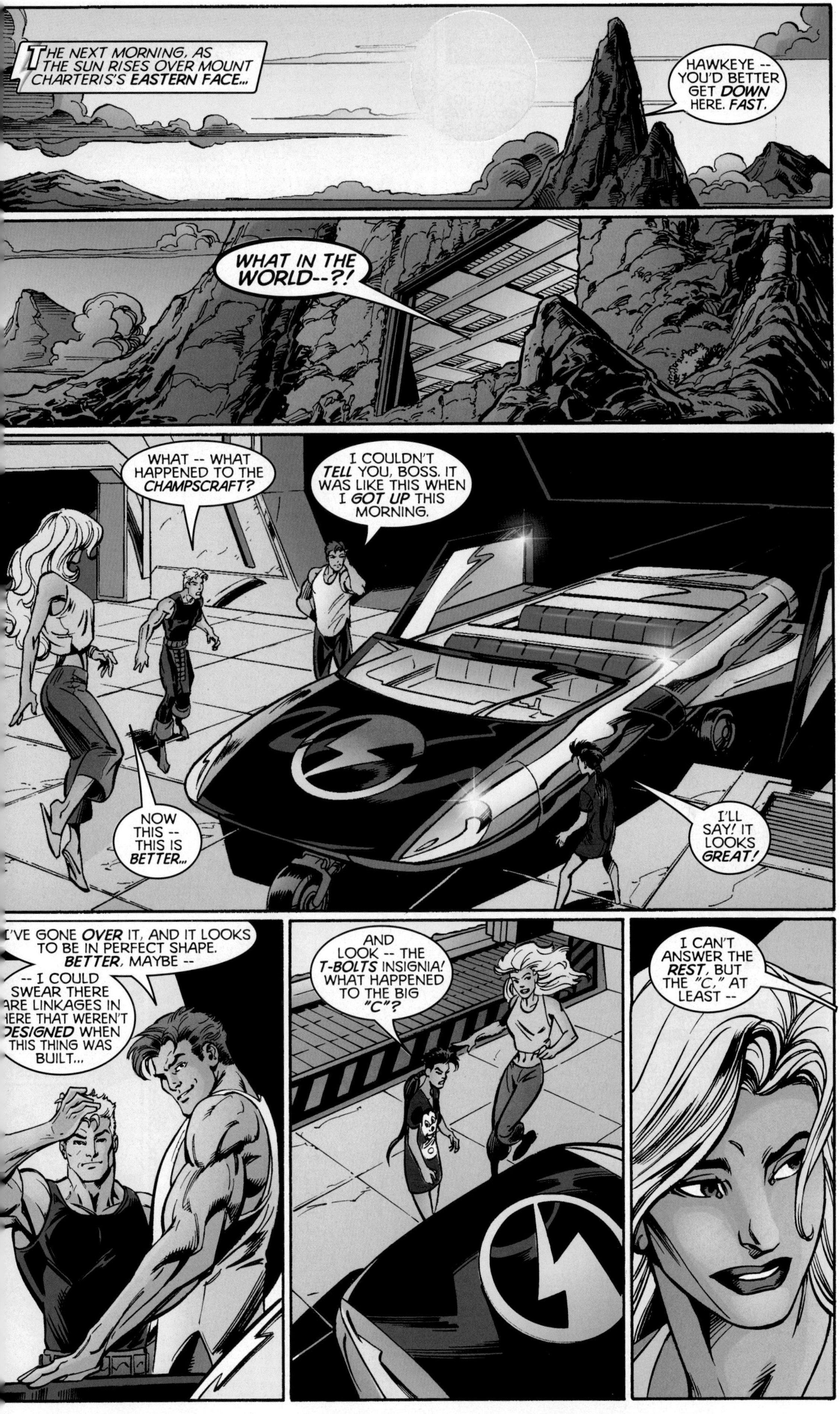

THE NEXT MORNING, AS THE SUN RISES OVER MOUNT CHARTERIS'S EASTERN FACE...
HAWKEYE -- YOU'D BETTER GET DOWN HERE. FAST.
WHAT IN THE WORLD--?!
WHAT -- WHAT HAPPENED TO THE CHAMPSCRAFT?
I COULDN'T TELL YOU, BOSS. IT WAS LIKE THIS WHEN I GOT UP THIS MORNING.
NOW THIS -- THIS IS BETTER...
I'LL SAY! IT LOOKS GREAT!
I'VE GONE OVER IT, AND IT LOOKS TO BE IN PERFECT SHAPE. BETTER, MAYBE --
-- I COULD SWEAR THERE ARE LINKAGES IN HERE THAT WEREN'T DESIGNED WHEN THIS THING WAS BUILT...
AND LOOK -- THE T-BOLTS INSIGNIA! WHAT HAPPENED TO THE BIG "C"?
I CAN'T ANSWER THE REST, BUT THE "C," AT LEAST --

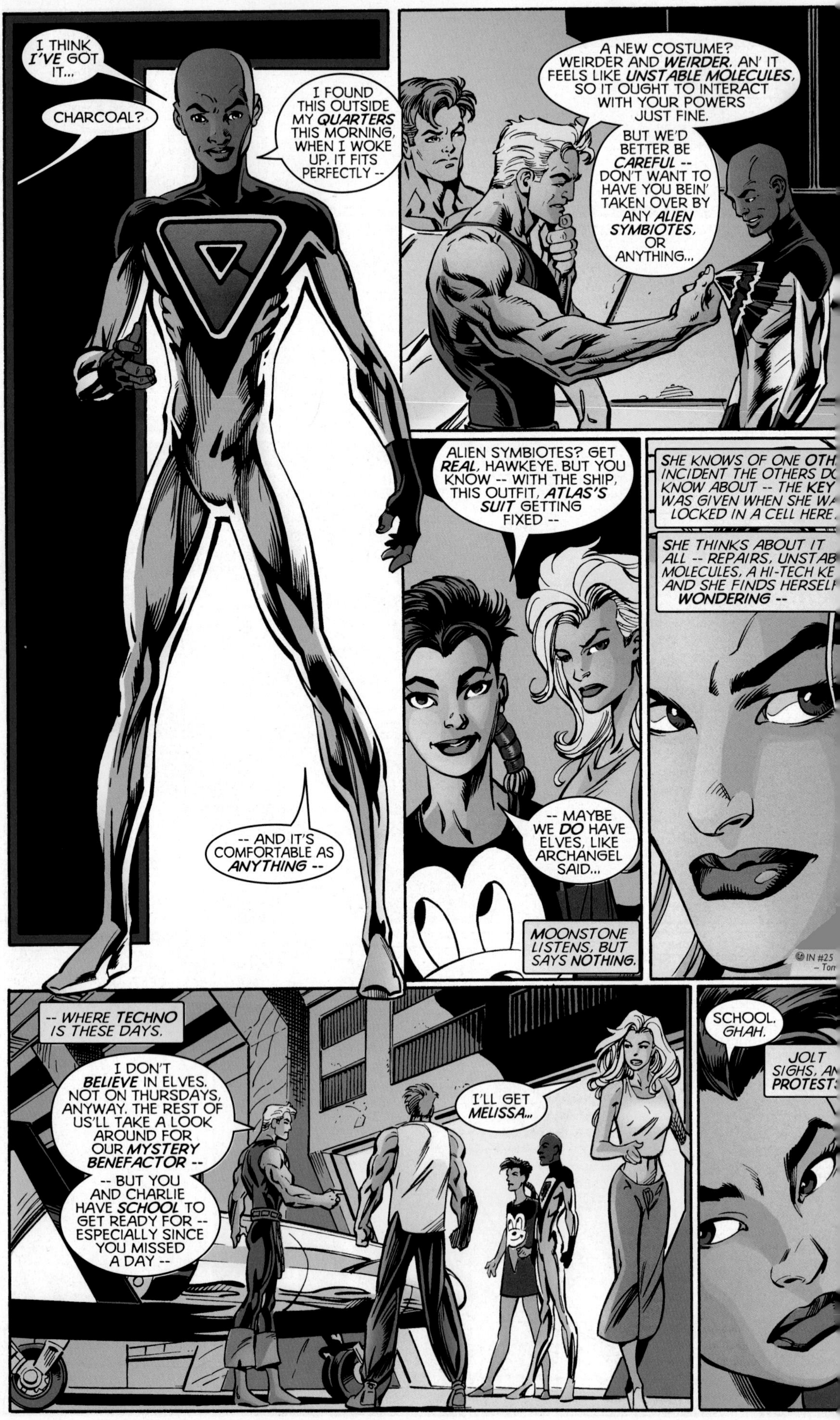

I THINK *I'VE* GOT IT...
CHARCOAL?
I FOUND THIS OUTSIDE MY *QUARTERS* THIS MORNING, WHEN I WOKE UP. IT FITS PERFECTLY --
-- AND IT'S COMFORTABLE AS *ANYTHING* --
A NEW COSTUME? WEIRDER AND *WEIRDER*. AN' IT FEELS LIKE *UNSTABLE MOLECULES*, SO IT OUGHT TO INTERACT WITH YOUR POWERS JUST FINE.
BUT WE'D BETTER BE *CAREFUL* -- DON'T WANT TO HAVE YOU BEIN' TAKEN OVER BY ANY *ALIEN SYMBIOTES*, OR ANYTHING...
ALIEN SYMBIOTES? GET *REAL*, HAWKEYE. BUT YOU KNOW -- WITH THE SHIP, THIS OUTFIT, *ATLAS'S SUIT* GETTING FIXED --
-- MAYBE WE *DO* HAVE ELVES, LIKE ARCHANGEL SAID...
MOONSTONE LISTENS, BUT SAYS NOTHING.
SHE KNOWS OF ONE OTH INCIDENT THE OTHERS DO KNOW ABOUT -- THE KEY WAS GIVEN WHEN SHE WA LOCKED IN A CELL HERE.
SHE THINKS ABOUT IT ALL -- REPAIRS, UNSTAB MOLECULES, A HI-TECH KE AND SHE FINDS HERSELF WONDERING --
IN #25 – Tom
-- WHERE TECHNO IS THESE DAYS.
I DON'T *BELIEVE* IN ELVES. NOT ON THURSDAYS, ANYWAY. THE REST OF US'LL TAKE A LOOK AROUND FOR OUR *MYSTERY BENEFACTOR* --
-- BUT YOU AND CHARLIE HAVE *SCHOOL* TO GET READY FOR -- ESPECIALLY SINCE YOU MISSED A DAY --
I'LL GET *MELISSA*...
SCHOOL. *GHAH.*
JOLT SIGHS, AN PROTEST:

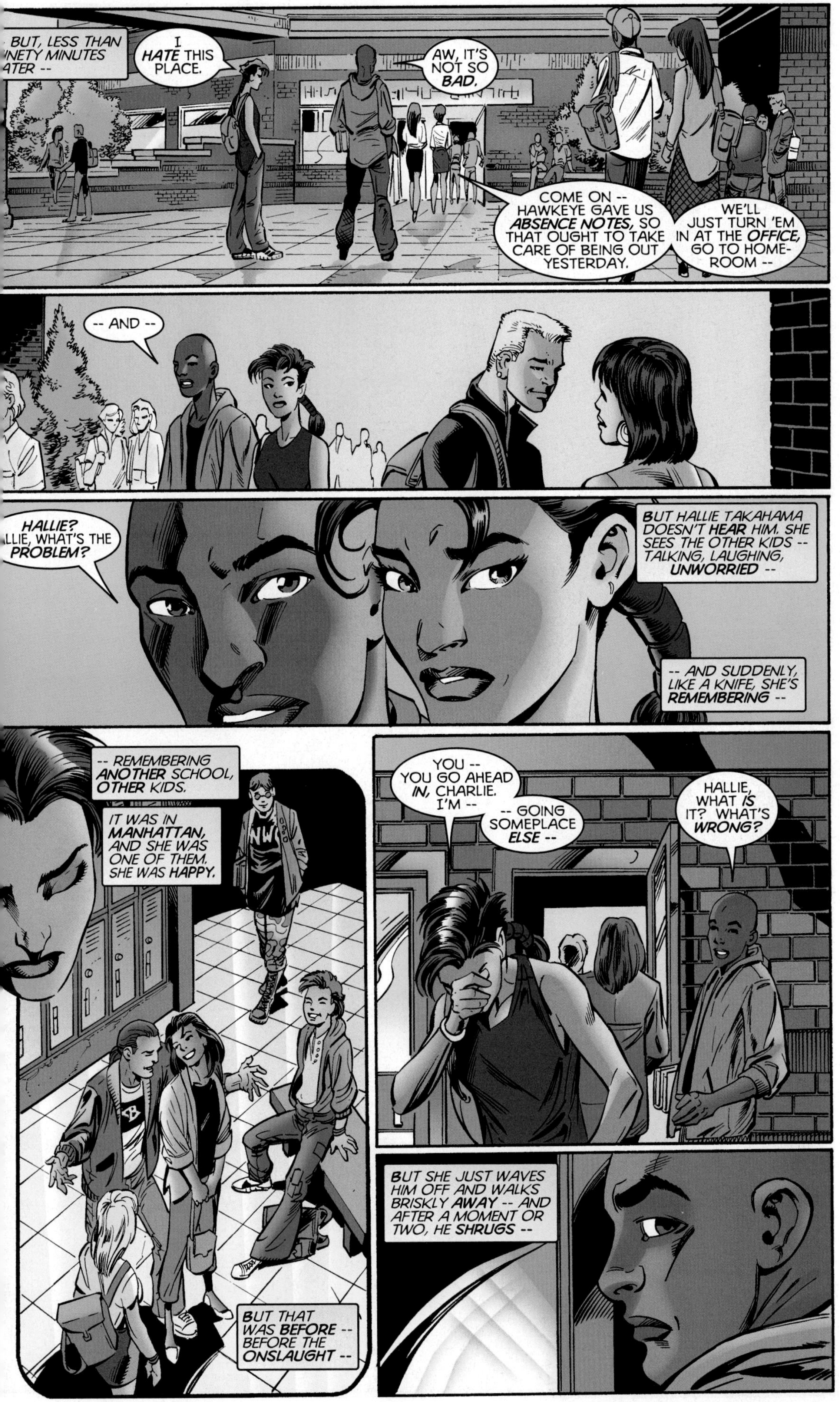
BUT, LESS THAN NINETY MINUTES LATER --
I HATE THIS PLACE.
AW, IT'S NOT SO BAD.
COME ON -- HAWKEYE GAVE US ABSENCE NOTES, SO THAT OUGHT TO TAKE CARE OF BEING OUT YESTERDAY.
WE'LL JUST TURN 'EM IN AT THE OFFICE, GO TO HOME-ROOM --
-- AND --
HALLIE? HALLIE, WHAT'S THE PROBLEM?
BUT HALLIE TAKAHAMA DOESN'T HEAR HIM. SHE SEES THE OTHER KIDS -- TALKING, LAUGHING, UNWORRIED --
-- AND SUDDENLY, LIKE A KNIFE, SHE'S REMEMBERING --
-- REMEMBERING ANOTHER SCHOOL, OTHER KIDS.
IT WAS IN MANHATTAN, AND SHE WAS ONE OF THEM. SHE WAS HAPPY.
BUT THAT WAS BEFORE -- BEFORE THE ONSLAUGHT --
YOU -- YOU GO AHEAD IN, CHARLIE. I'M --
-- GOING SOMEPLACE ELSE --
HALLIE, WHAT IS IT? WHAT'S WRONG?
BUT SHE JUST WAVES HIM OFF AND WALKS BRISKLY AWAY -- AND AFTER A MOMENT OR TWO, HE SHRUGS --

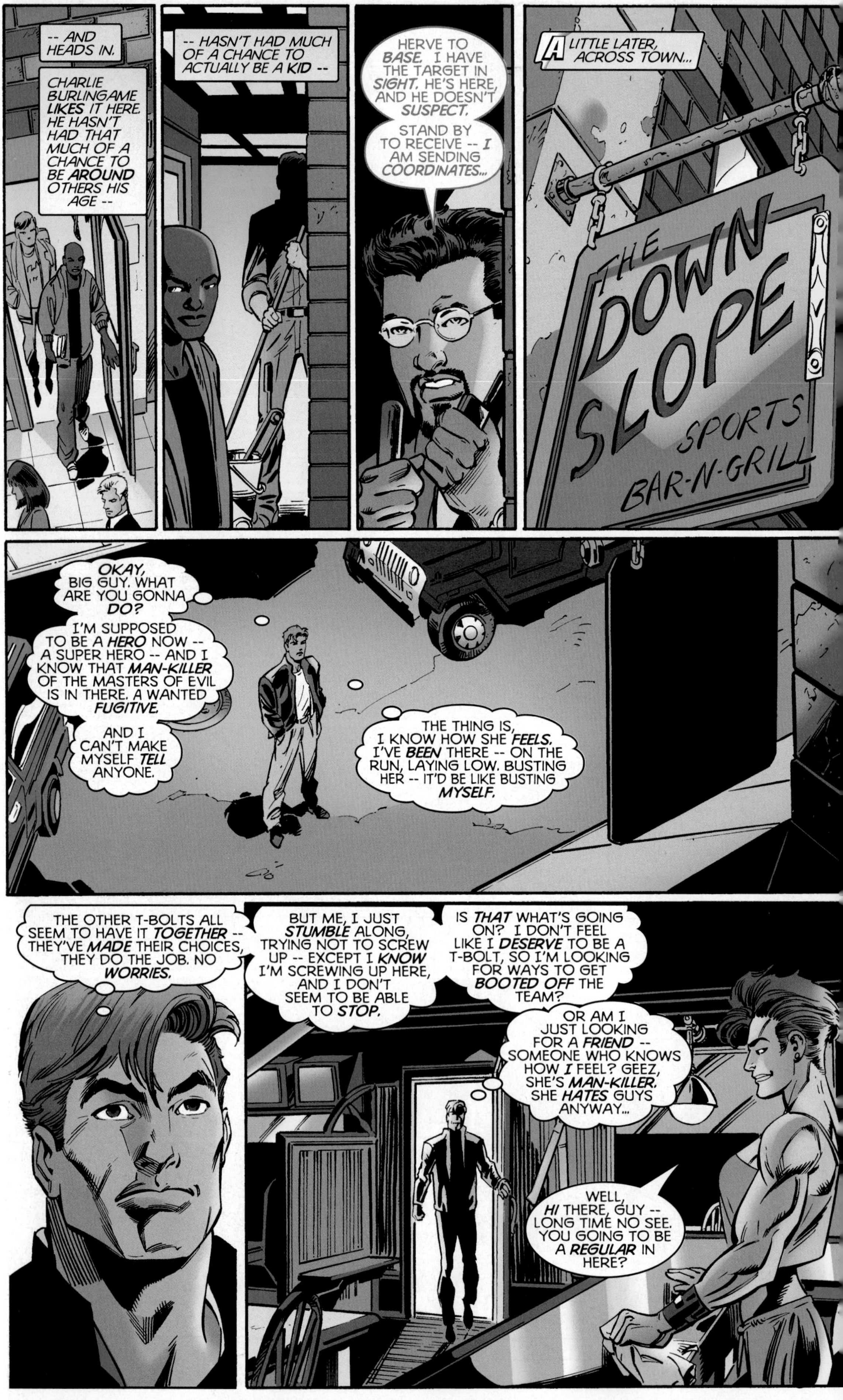
-- AND HEADS IN.
CHARLIE BURLINGAME LIKES IT HERE. HE HASN'T HAD THAT MUCH OF A CHANCE TO BE AROUND OTHERS HIS AGE --
-- HASN'T HAD MUCH OF A CHANCE TO ACTUALLY BE A KID --
HERVE TO BASE. I HAVE THE TARGET IN SIGHT. HE'S HERE, AND HE DOESN'T SUSPECT.
STAND BY TO RECEIVE -- I AM SENDING COORDINATES...
A LITTLE LATER, ACROSS TOWN...
THE DOWN SLOPE SPORTS BAR-N-GRILL
OKAY, BIG GUY. WHAT ARE YOU GONNA DO?
I'M SUPPOSED TO BE A HERO NOW -- A SUPER HERO -- AND I KNOW THAT MAN-KILLER OF THE MASTERS OF EVIL IS IN THERE. A WANTED FUGITIVE.
AND I CAN'T MAKE MYSELF TELL ANYONE.
THE THING IS, I KNOW HOW SHE FEELS. I'VE BEEN THERE -- ON THE RUN, LAYING LOW. BUSTING HER -- IT'D BE LIKE BUSTING MYSELF.
THE OTHER T-BOLTS ALL SEEM TO HAVE IT TOGETHER -- THEY'VE MADE THEIR CHOICES, THEY DO THE JOB. NO WORRIES.
BUT ME, I JUST STUMBLE ALONG, TRYING NOT TO SCREW UP -- EXCEPT I KNOW I'M SCREWING UP HERE, AND I DON'T SEEM TO BE ABLE TO STOP.
IS THAT WHAT'S GOING ON? I DON'T FEEL LIKE I DESERVE TO BE A T-BOLT, SO I'M LOOKING FOR WAYS TO GET BOOTED OFF THE TEAM?
OR AM I JUST LOOKING FOR A FRIEND -- SOMEONE WHO KNOWS HOW I FEEL? GEEZ, SHE'S MAN-KILLER. SHE HATES GUYS ANYWAY...
WELL, HI THERE, GUY -- LONG TIME NO SEE. YOU GOING TO BE A REGULAR IN HERE?

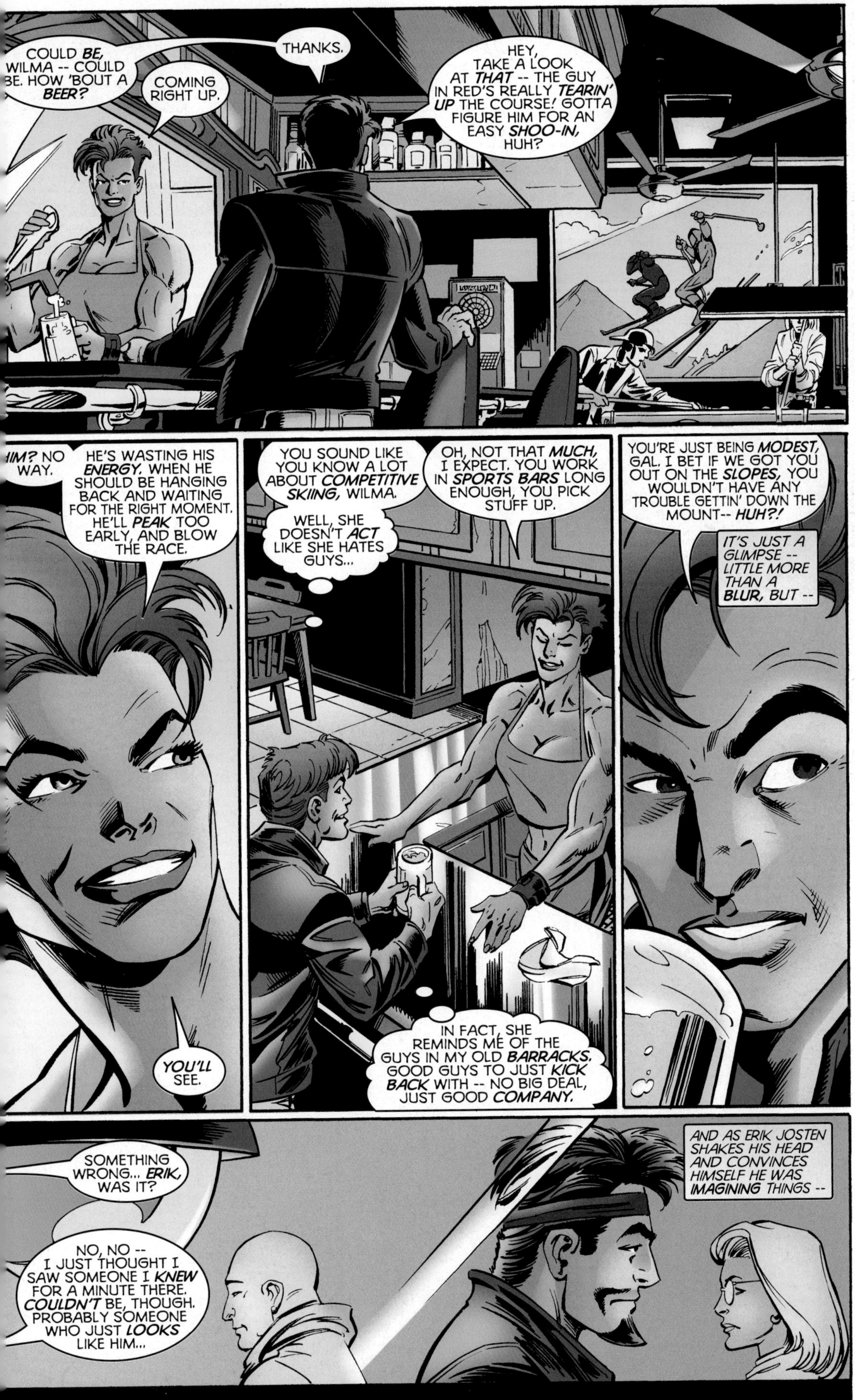

COULD BE, WILMA -- COULD BE. HOW 'BOUT A BEER?
COMING RIGHT UP.
THANKS.
HEY, TAKE A LOOK AT THAT -- THE GUY IN RED'S REALLY TEARIN' UP THE COURSE! GOTTA FIGURE HIM FOR AN EASY SHOO-IN, HUH?
HIM? NO WAY.
HE'S WASTING HIS ENERGY, WHEN HE SHOULD BE HANGING BACK AND WAITING FOR THE RIGHT MOMENT. HE'LL PEAK TOO EARLY, AND BLOW THE RACE.
YOU'LL SEE.
YOU SOUND LIKE YOU KNOW A LOT ABOUT COMPETITIVE SKIING, WILMA.
WELL, SHE DOESN'T ACT LIKE SHE HATES GUYS...
OH, NOT THAT MUCH, I EXPECT. YOU WORK IN SPORTS BARS LONG ENOUGH, YOU PICK STUFF UP.
IN FACT, SHE REMINDS ME OF THE GUYS IN MY OLD BARRACKS. GOOD GUYS TO JUST KICK BACK WITH -- NO BIG DEAL, JUST GOOD COMPANY.
YOU'RE JUST BEING MODEST, GAL. I BET IF WE GOT YOU OUT ON THE SLOPES, YOU WOULDN'T HAVE ANY TROUBLE GETTIN' DOWN THE MOUNT-- HUH?!
IT'S JUST A GLIMPSE -- LITTLE MORE THAN A BLUR, BUT --
SOMETHING WRONG... ERIK, WAS IT?
NO, NO -- I JUST THOUGHT I SAW SOMEONE I KNEW FOR A MINUTE THERE. COULDN'T BE, THOUGH. PROBABLY SOMEONE WHO JUST LOOKS LIKE HIM...
AND AS ERIK JOSTEN SHAKES HIS HEAD AND CONVINCES HIMSELF HE WAS IMAGINING THINGS --

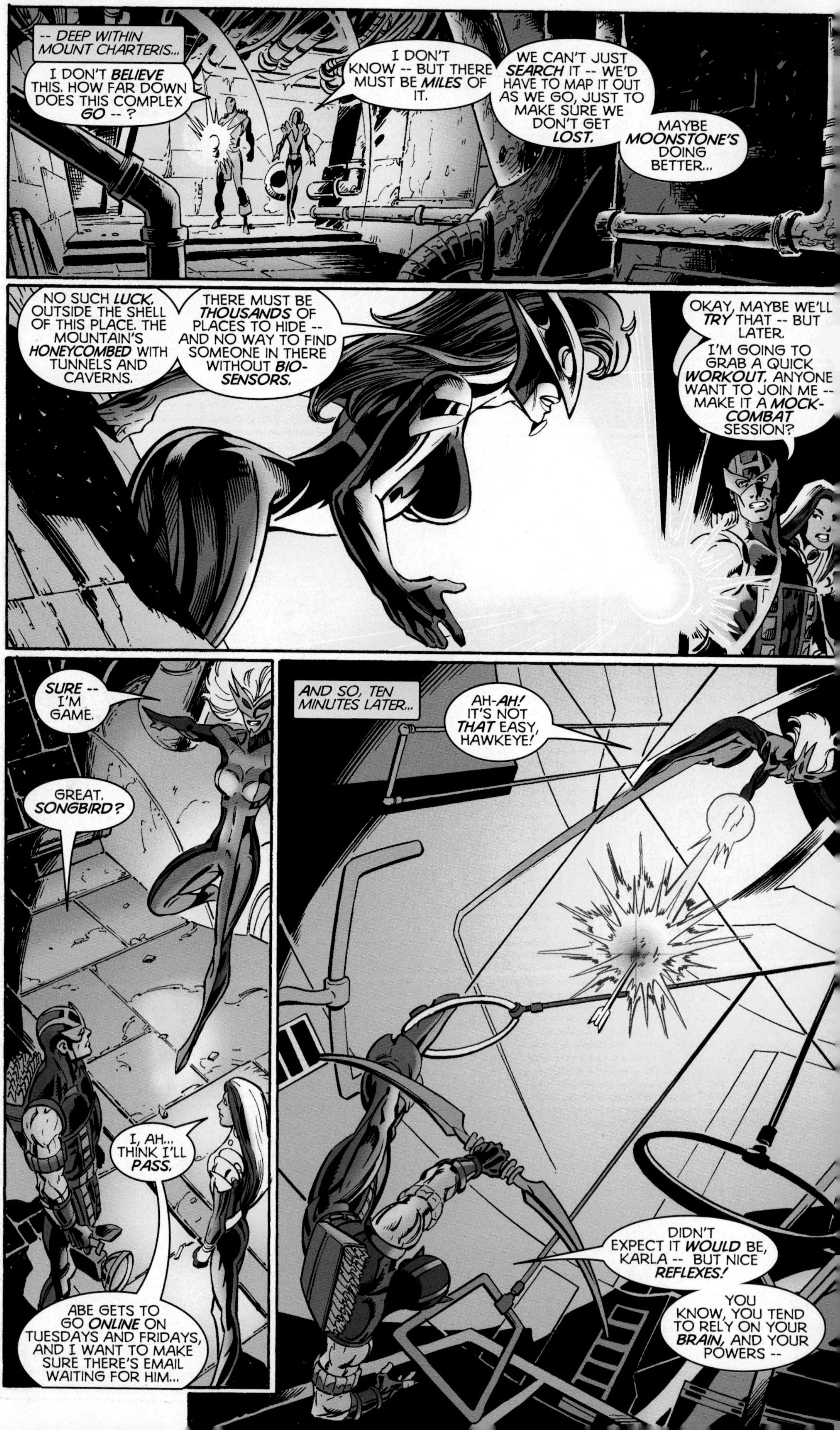
-- DEEP WITHIN MOUNT CHARTERIS...
I DON'T BELIEVE THIS. HOW FAR DOWN DOES THIS COMPLEX GO -- ?
I DON'T KNOW -- BUT THERE MUST BE MILES OF IT.
WE CAN'T JUST SEARCH IT -- WE'D HAVE TO MAP IT OUT AS WE GO, JUST TO MAKE SURE WE DON'T GET LOST.
MAYBE MOONSTONE'S DOING BETTER...
NO SUCH LUCK. OUTSIDE THE SHELL OF THIS PLACE. THE MOUNTAIN'S HONEYCOMBED WITH TUNNELS AND CAVERNS.
THERE MUST BE THOUSANDS OF PLACES TO HIDE -- AND NO WAY TO FIND SOMEONE IN THERE WITHOUT BIO-SENSORS.
OKAY, MAYBE WE'LL TRY THAT -- BUT LATER.
I'M GOING TO GRAB A QUICK WORKOUT. ANYONE WANT TO JOIN ME -- MAKE IT A MOCK-COMBAT SESSION?
SURE -- I'M GAME.
GREAT. SONGBIRD?
I, AH... THINK I'LL PASS.
ABE GETS TO GO ONLINE ON TUESDAYS AND FRIDAYS, AND I WANT TO MAKE SURE THERE'S EMAIL WAITING FOR HIM...
AND SO, TEN MINUTES LATER...
AH-AH! IT'S NOT THAT EASY, HAWKEYE!
DIDN'T EXPECT IT WOULD BE, KARLA -- BUT NICE REFLEXES!
YOU KNOW, YOU TEND TO RELY ON YOUR BRAIN, AND YOUR POWERS --

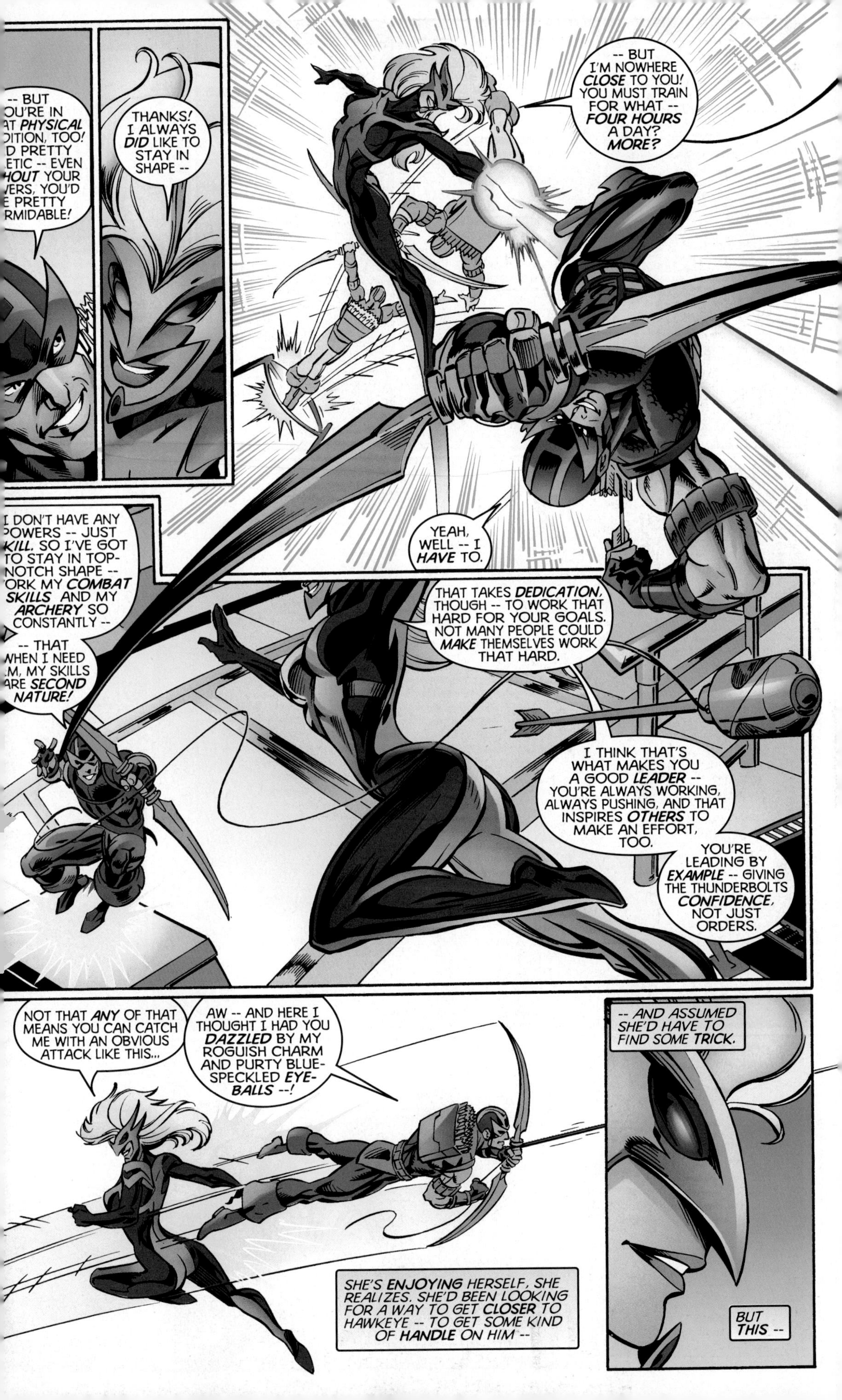

-- BUT OU'RE IN AT PHYSICAL DITION, TOO! D PRETTY ETIC -- EVEN HOUT YOUR VERS, YOU'D E PRETTY RMIDABLE!
THANKS! I ALWAYS DID LIKE TO STAY IN SHAPE --
-- BUT I'M NOWHERE CLOSE TO YOU! YOU MUST TRAIN FOR WHAT -- FOUR HOURS A DAY? MORE?
YEAH, WELL -- I HAVE TO.
I DON'T HAVE ANY POWERS -- JUST KILL, SO I'VE GOT TO STAY IN TOP-NOTCH SHAPE -- ORK MY COMBAT SKILLS AND MY ARCHERY SO CONSTANTLY --
-- THAT WHEN I NEED EM, MY SKILLS ARE SECOND NATURE!
THAT TAKES DEDICATION, THOUGH -- TO WORK THAT HARD FOR YOUR GOALS. NOT MANY PEOPLE COULD MAKE THEMSELVES WORK THAT HARD.
I THINK THAT'S WHAT MAKES YOU A GOOD LEADER -- YOU'RE ALWAYS WORKING, ALWAYS PUSHING, AND THAT INSPIRES OTHERS TO MAKE AN EFFORT, TOO.
YOU'RE LEADING BY EXAMPLE -- GIVING THE THUNDERBOLTS CONFIDENCE, NOT JUST ORDERS.
NOT THAT ANY OF THAT MEANS YOU CAN CATCH ME WITH AN OBVIOUS ATTACK LIKE THIS...
AW -- AND HERE I THOUGHT I HAD YOU DAZZLED BY MY ROGUISH CHARM AND PURTY BLUE-SPECKLED EYE-BALLS --!
SHE'S ENJOYING HERSELF, SHE REALIZES. SHE'D BEEN LOOKING FOR A WAY TO GET CLOSER TO HAWKEYE -- TO GET SOME KIND OF HANDLE ON HIM --
-- AND ASSUMED SHE'D HAVE TO FIND SOME TRICK.
BUT THIS --

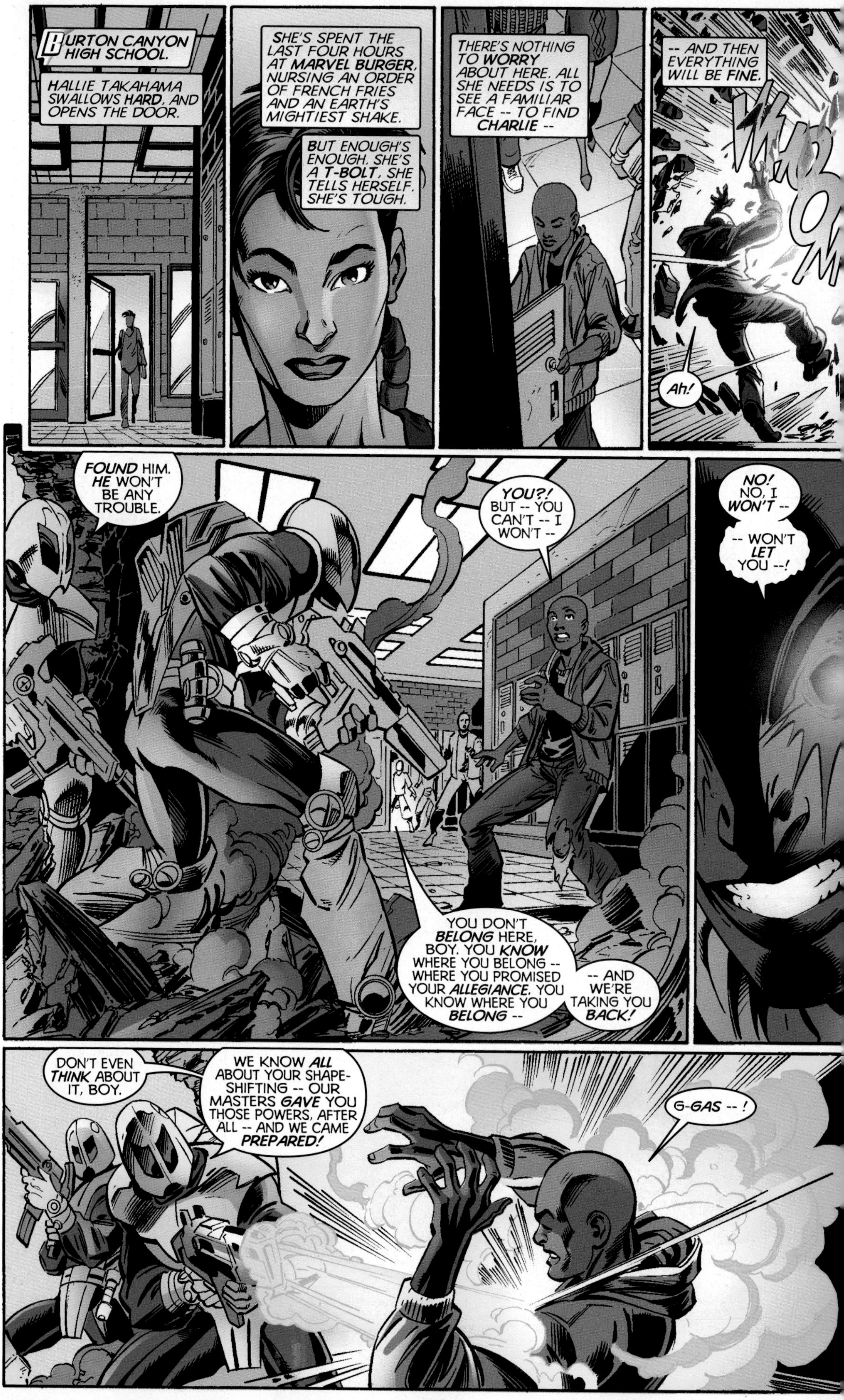
BURTON CANYON HIGH SCHOOL.
HALLIE TAKAHAMA SWALLOWS HARD, AND OPENS THE DOOR.
SHE'S SPENT THE LAST FOUR HOURS AT MARVEL BURGER, NURSING AN ORDER OF FRENCH FRIES AND AN EARTH'S MIGHTIEST SHAKE.
BUT ENOUGH'S ENOUGH. SHE'S A T-BOLT, SHE TELLS HERSELF. SHE'S TOUGH.
THERE'S NOTHING TO WORRY ABOUT HERE. ALL SHE NEEDS IS TO SEE A FAMILIAR FACE -- TO FIND CHARLIE --
-- AND THEN EVERYTHING WILL BE FINE.
Ah!
FOUND HIM. HE WON'T BE ANY TROUBLE.
YOU?! BUT -- YOU CAN'T -- I WON'T --
YOU DON'T BELONG HERE, BOY. YOU KNOW WHERE YOU BELONG -- WHERE YOU PROMISED YOUR ALLEGIANCE. YOU KNOW WHERE YOU BELONG --
-- AND WE'RE TAKING YOU BACK!
NO! NO, I WON'T --
-- WON'T LET YOU --!
DON'T EVEN THINK ABOUT IT, BOY.
WE KNOW ALL ABOUT YOUR SHAPE-SHIFTING -- OUR MASTERS GAVE YOU THOSE POWERS, AFTER ALL -- AND WE CAME PREPARED!
G-GAS -- !

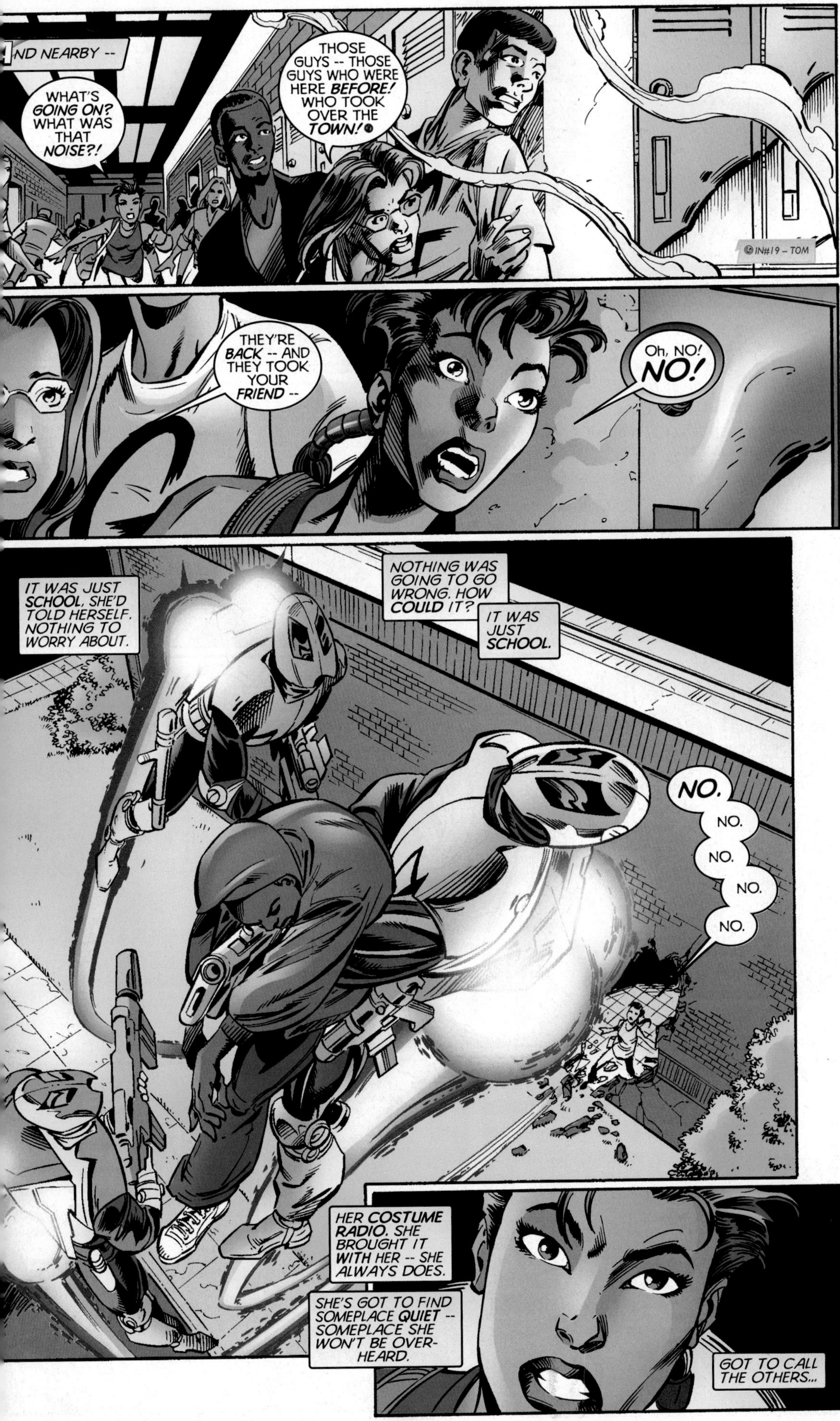
AND NEARBY --
WHAT'S *GOING ON?* WHAT WAS THAT *NOISE?!*
THOSE GUYS -- THOSE GUYS WHO WERE HERE *BEFORE!* WHO TOOK OVER THE *TOWN!*
IN#19 – TOM
THEY'RE *BACK* -- AND THEY TOOK YOUR *FRIEND* --
Oh, NO! **NO!**
IT WAS JUST **SCHOOL**, SHE'D TOLD HERSELF. NOTHING TO WORRY ABOUT.
NOTHING WAS GOING TO GO WRONG. HOW **COULD** IT?
IT WAS JUST **SCHOOL**.
NO.
NO.
NO.
NO.
NO.
HER **COSTUME RADIO**. SHE BROUGHT IT **WITH** HER -- SHE ALWAYS DOES.
SHE'S GOT TO FIND SOMEPLACE **QUIET** -- SOMEPLACE SHE WON'T BE OVER-HEARD.
GOT TO CALL THE OTHERS...

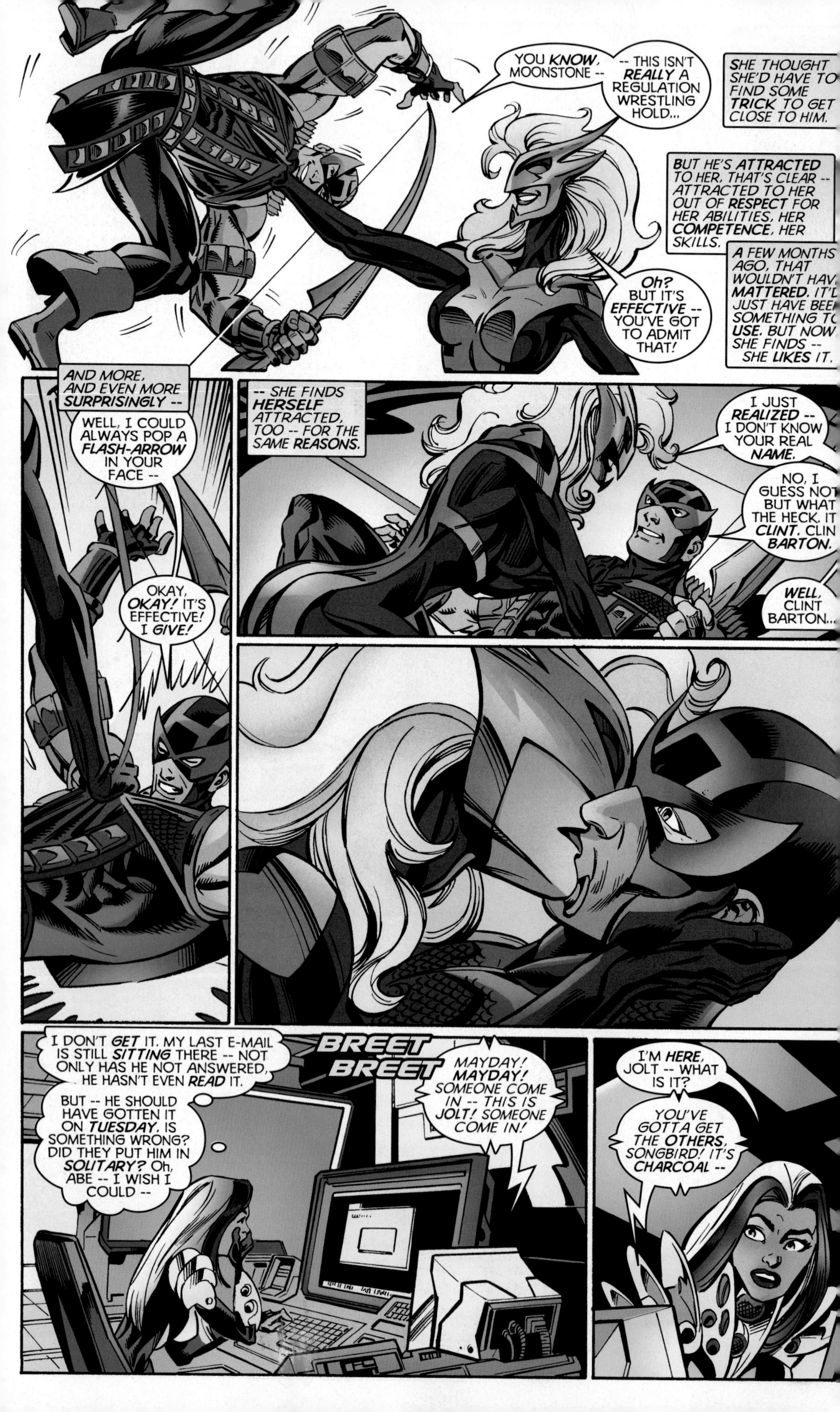

YOU KNOW, MOONSTONE --
-- THIS ISN'T REALLY A REGULATION WRESTLING HOLD...
SHE THOUGHT SHE'D HAVE TO FIND SOME TRICK TO GET CLOSE TO HIM.
BUT HE'S ATTRACTED TO HER, THAT'S CLEAR -- ATTRACTED TO HER OUT OF RESPECT FOR HER ABILITIES, HER COMPETENCE, HER SKILLS.
Oh? BUT IT'S EFFECTIVE -- YOU'VE GOT TO ADMIT THAT!
A FEW MONTHS AGO, THAT WOULDN'T HAV MATTERED. IT'D JUST HAVE BEE SOMETHING TO USE. BUT NOW SHE FINDS -- SHE LIKES IT.
AND MORE, AND EVEN MORE SURPRISINGLY --
WELL, I COULD ALWAYS POP A FLASH-ARROW IN YOUR FACE --
OKAY, OKAY! IT'S EFFECTIVE! I GIVE!
-- SHE FINDS HERSELF ATTRACTED, TOO -- FOR THE SAME REASONS.
I JUST REALIZED -- I DON'T KNOW YOUR REAL NAME.
NO, I GUESS NOT BUT WHAT THE HECK. IT CLINT. CLIN BARTON.
WELL, CLINT BARTON...
I DON'T GET IT. MY LAST E-MAIL IS STILL SITTING THERE -- NOT ONLY HAS HE NOT ANSWERED, HE HASN'T EVEN READ IT.
BUT -- HE SHOULD HAVE GOTTEN IT ON TUESDAY. IS SOMETHING WRONG? DID THEY PUT HIM IN SOLITARY? Oh, ABE -- I WISH I COULD --
BREET BREET
MAYDAY! MAYDAY! SOMEONE COME IN -- THIS IS JOLT! SOMEONE COME IN!
I'M HERE, JOLT -- WHAT IS IT?
YOU'VE GOTTA GET THE OTHERS, SONGBIRD! IT'S CHARCOAL --

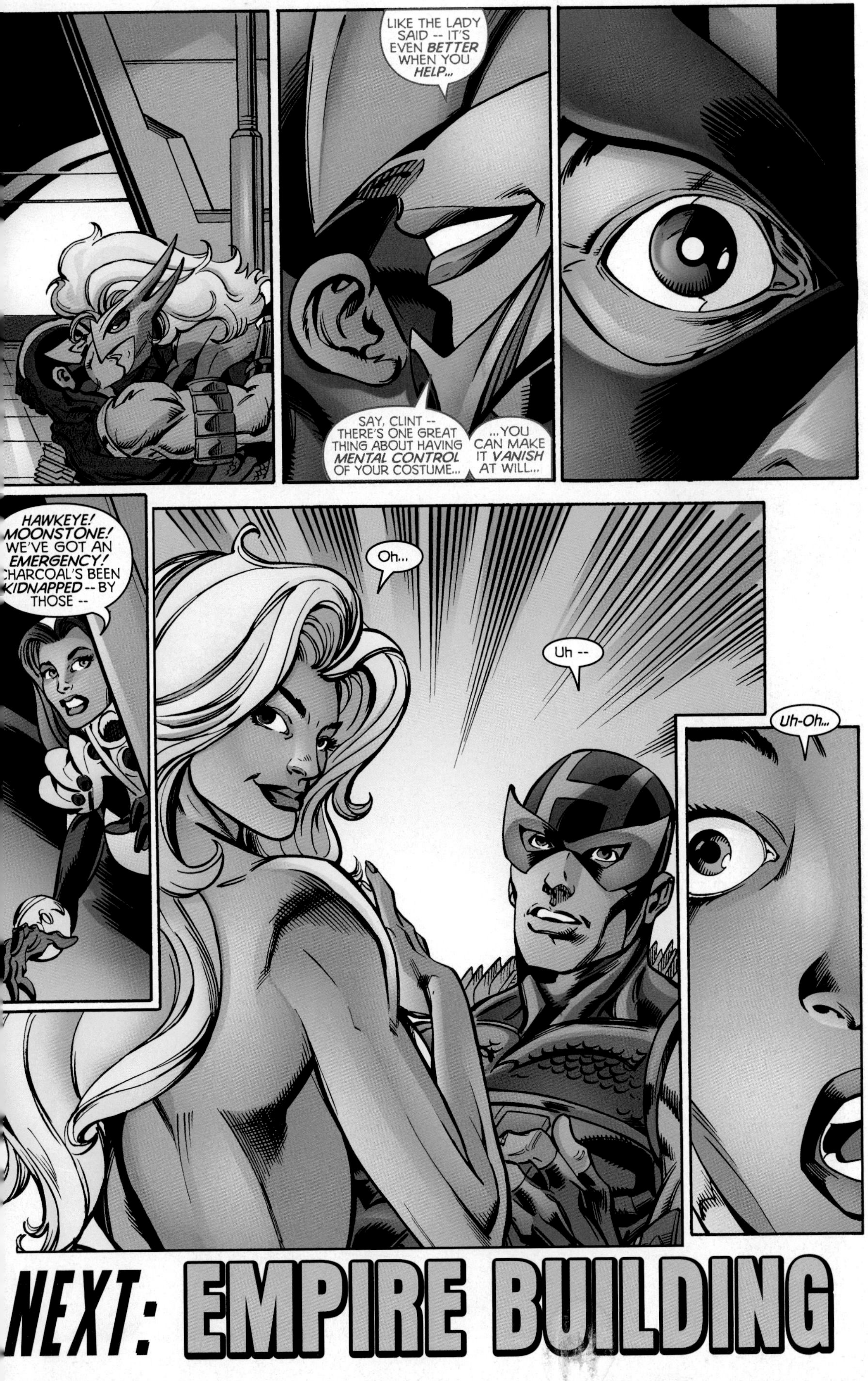
LIKE THE LADY SAID -- IT'S EVEN BETTER WHEN YOU HELP...
SAY, CLINT -- THERE'S ONE GREAT THING ABOUT HAVING MENTAL CONTROL OF YOUR COSTUME...
...YOU CAN MAKE IT VANISH AT WILL...
HAWKEYE! MOONSTONE! WE'VE GOT AN EMERGENCY! CHARCOAL'S BEEN KIDNAPPED -- BY THOSE --
Oh...
Uh --
Uh-Oh...
NEXT: EMPIRE BUILDING

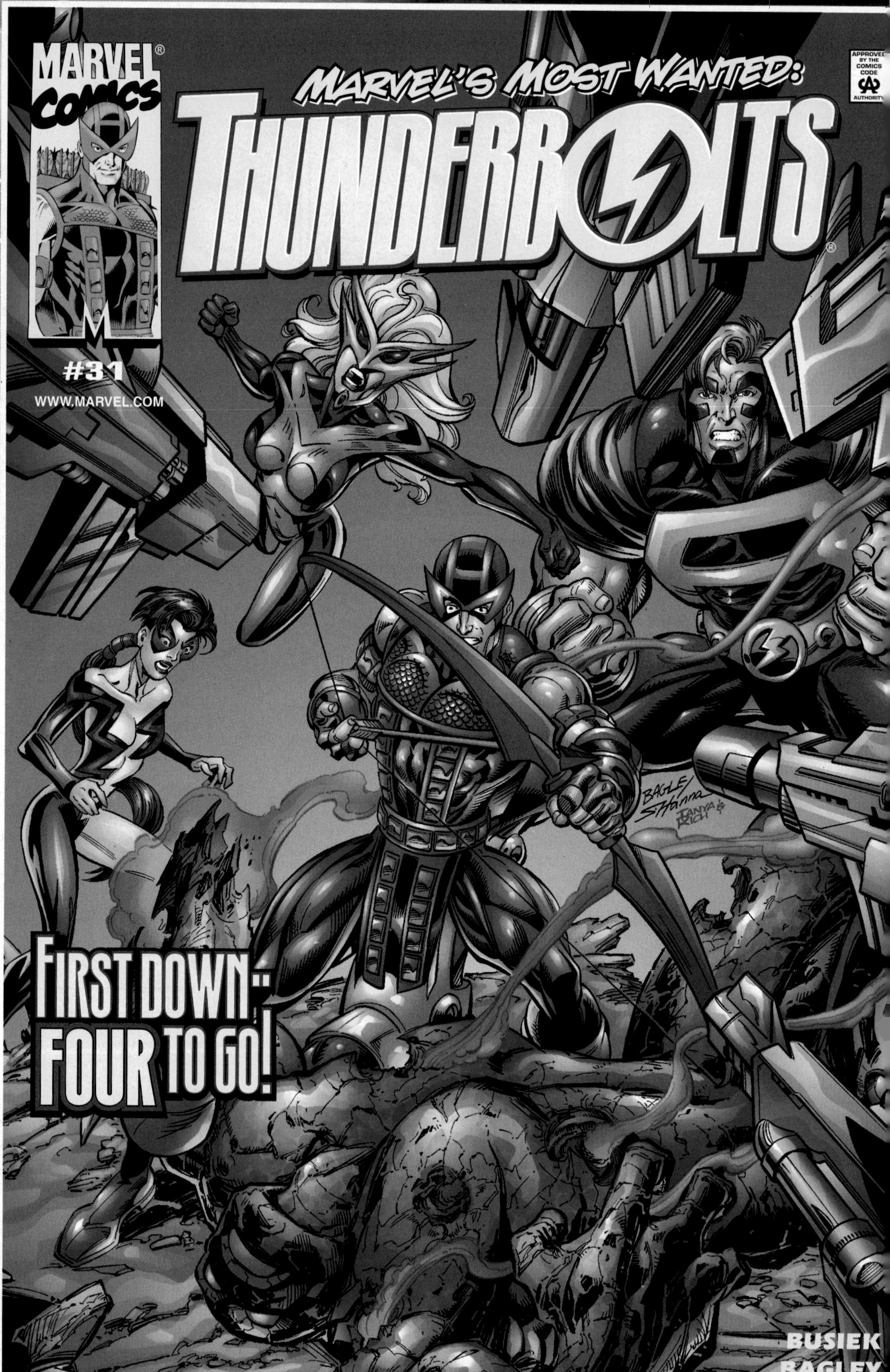
MARVEL COMICS
MARVEL'S MOST WANTED:
THUNDERBOLTS
APPROVED BY THE COMICS CODE AUTHORITY
#31
WWW.MARVEL.COM
FIRST DOWN--
FOUR TO GO!
BUSIEK
BAGLEY
HANNA

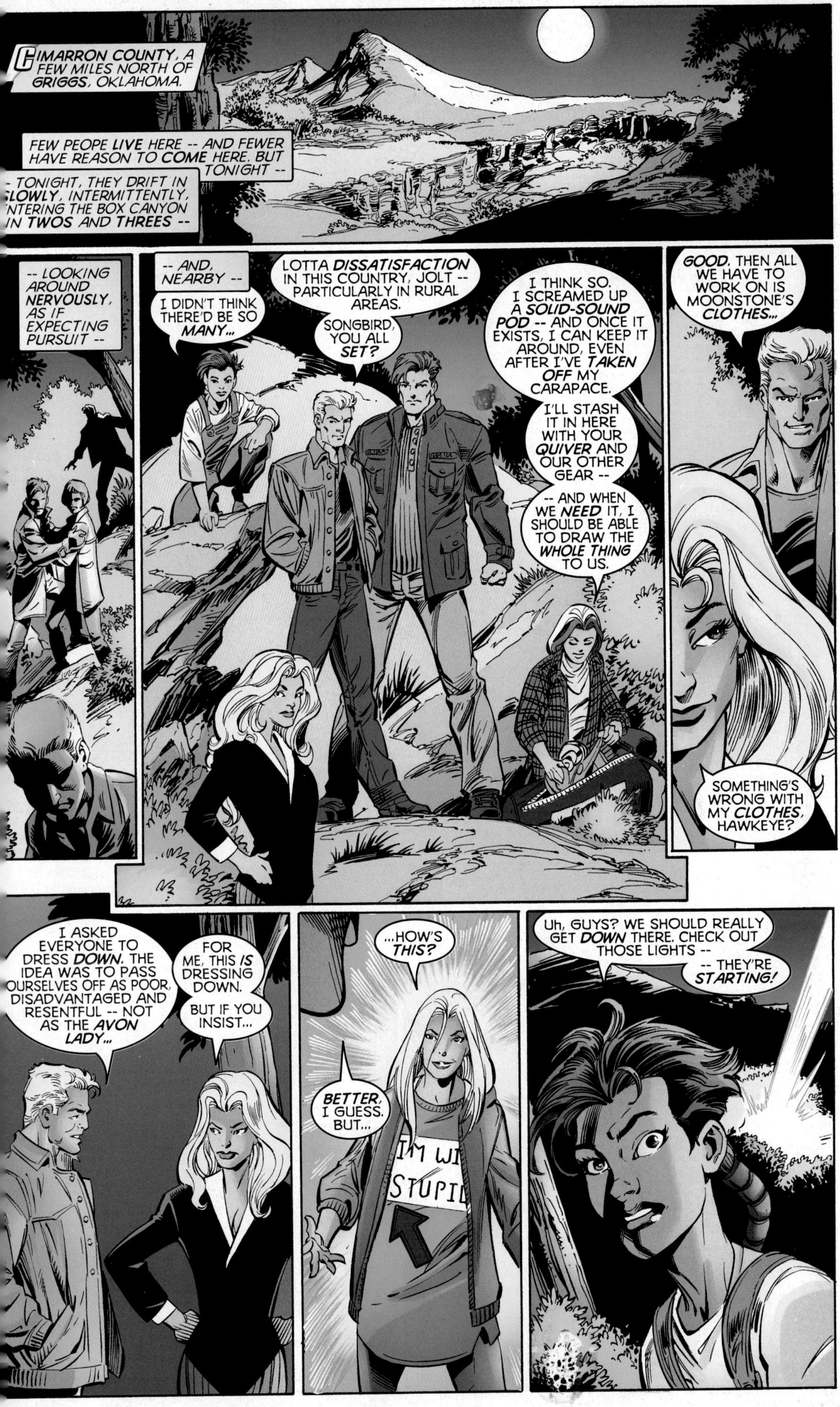
CIMARRON COUNTY, A FEW MILES NORTH OF GRIGGS, OKLAHOMA.
FEW PEOPE LIVE HERE -- AND FEWER HAVE REASON TO COME HERE. BUT TONIGHT --
- TONIGHT, THEY DRIFT IN SLOWLY, INTERMITTENTLY, ENTERING THE BOX CANYON IN TWOS AND THREES --
-- LOOKING AROUND NERVOUSLY, AS IF EXPECTING PURSUIT --
-- AND, NEARBY --
I DIDN'T THINK THERE'D BE SO MANY...
LOTTA DISSATISFACTION IN THIS COUNTRY, JOLT -- PARTICULARLY IN RURAL AREAS.
SONGBIRD, YOU ALL SET?
I THINK SO. I SCREAMED UP A SOLID-SOUND POD -- AND ONCE IT EXISTS, I CAN KEEP IT AROUND, EVEN AFTER I'VE TAKEN OFF MY CARAPACE.
I'LL STASH IT IN HERE WITH YOUR QUIVER AND OUR OTHER GEAR --
-- AND WHEN WE NEED IT, I SHOULD BE ABLE TO DRAW THE WHOLE THING TO US.
GOOD. THEN ALL WE HAVE TO WORK ON IS MOONSTONE'S CLOTHES...
SOMETHING'S WRONG WITH MY CLOTHES, HAWKEYE?
I ASKED EVERYONE TO DRESS DOWN. THE IDEA WAS TO PASS OURSELVES OFF AS POOR, DISADVANTAGED AND RESENTFUL -- NOT AS THE AVON LADY...
FOR ME, THIS IS DRESSING DOWN.
BUT IF YOU INSIST...
...HOW'S THIS?
BETTER, I GUESS. BUT...
Uh, GUYS? WE SHOULD REALLY GET DOWN THERE. CHECK OUT THOSE LIGHTS --
-- THEY'RE STARTING!

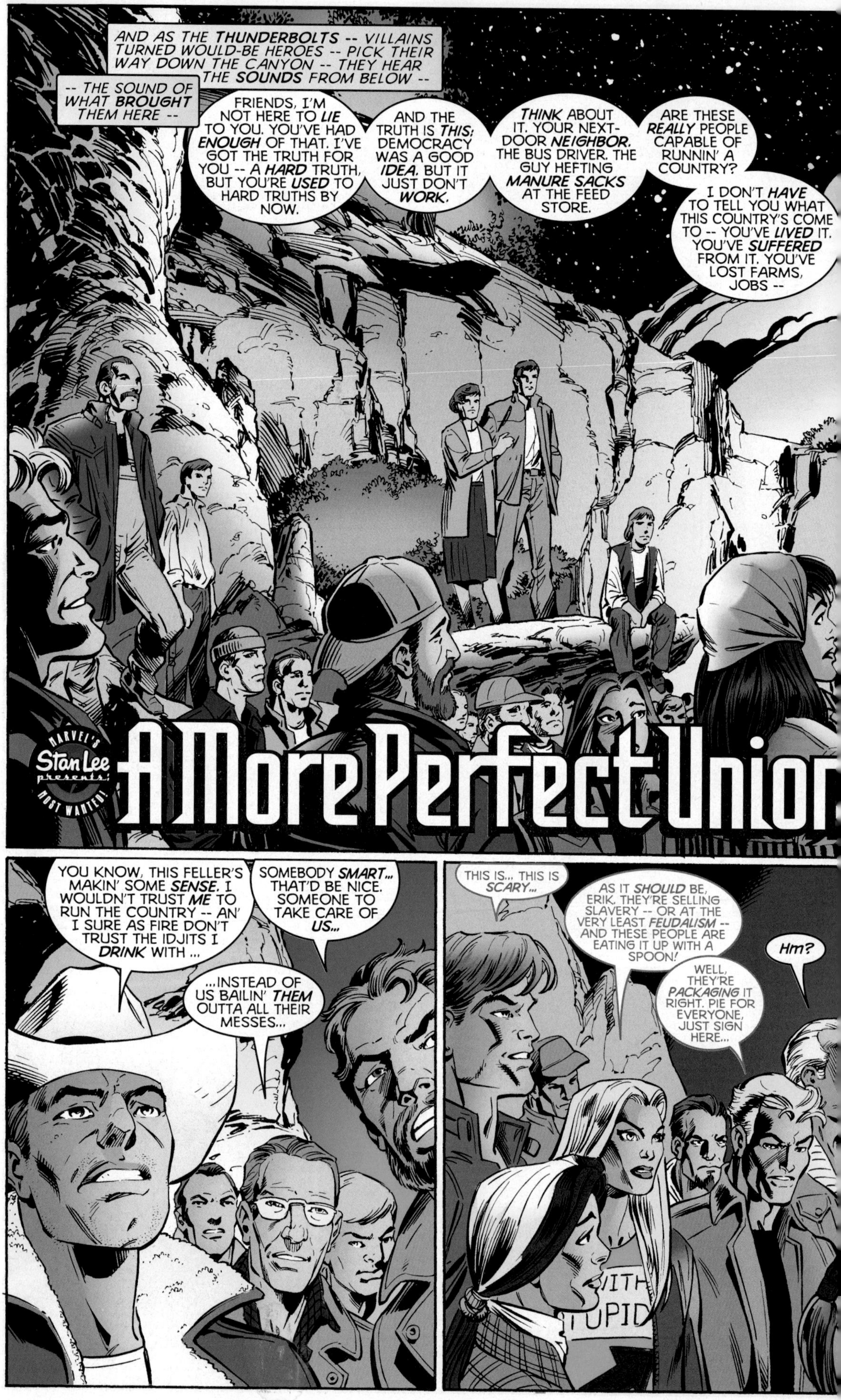
AND AS THE THUNDERBOLTS -- VILLAINS TURNED WOULD-BE HEROES -- PICK THEIR WAY DOWN THE CANYON -- THEY HEAR THE SOUNDS FROM BELOW --
-- THE SOUND OF WHAT BROUGHT THEM HERE --
FRIENDS, I'M NOT HERE TO LIE TO YOU. YOU'VE HAD ENOUGH OF THAT. I'VE GOT THE TRUTH FOR YOU -- A HARD TRUTH, BUT YOU'RE USED TO HARD TRUTHS BY NOW.
AND THE TRUTH IS THIS: DEMOCRACY WAS A GOOD IDEA, BUT IT JUST DON'T WORK.
THINK ABOUT IT. YOUR NEXT-DOOR NEIGHBOR. THE BUS DRIVER. THE GUY HEFTING MANURE SACKS AT THE FEED STORE.
ARE THESE REALLY PEOPLE CAPABLE OF RUNNIN' A COUNTRY?
I DON'T HAVE TO TELL YOU WHAT THIS COUNTRY'S COME TO -- YOU'VE LIVED IT. YOU'VE SUFFERED FROM IT. YOU'VE LOST FARMS, JOBS --
MARVEL'S Stan Lee presents! MOST WANTED!
A More Perfect Union
YOU KNOW, THIS FELLER'S MAKIN' SOME SENSE. I WOULDN'T TRUST ME TO RUN THE COUNTRY -- AN' I SURE AS FIRE DON'T TRUST THE IDJITS I DRINK WITH ...
SOMEBODY SMART... THAT'D BE NICE. SOMEONE TO TAKE CARE OF US...
...INSTEAD OF US BAILIN' THEM OUTTA ALL THEIR MESSES...
THIS IS... THIS IS SCARY...
AS IT SHOULD BE, ERIK. THEY'RE SELLING SLAVERY -- OR AT THE VERY LEAST FEUDALISM -- AND THESE PEOPLE ARE EATING IT UP WITH A SPOON!
Hm?
WELL, THEY'RE PACKAGING IT RIGHT. PIE FOR EVERYONE, JUST SIGN HERE...

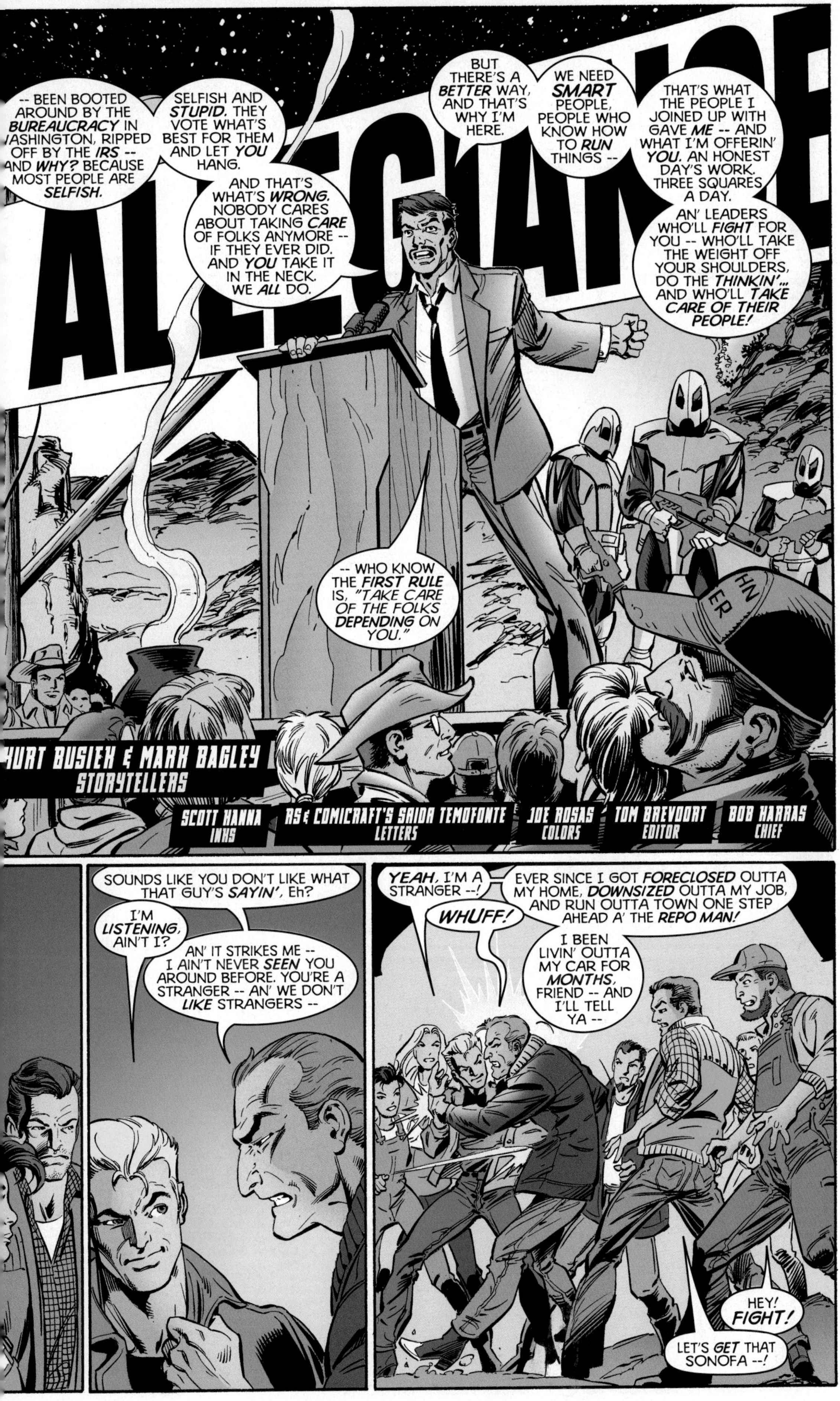
ALLEGIANCE
-- BEEN BOOTED AROUND BY THE BUREAUCRACY IN WASHINGTON, RIPPED OFF BY THE IRS -- AND WHY? BECAUSE MOST PEOPLE ARE SELFISH.
SELFISH AND STUPID. THEY VOTE WHAT'S BEST FOR THEM AND LET YOU HANG.
AND THAT'S WHAT'S WRONG. NOBODY CARES ABOUT TAKING CARE OF FOLKS ANYMORE -- IF THEY EVER DID. AND YOU TAKE IT IN THE NECK. WE ALL DO.
BUT THERE'S A BETTER WAY, AND THAT'S WHY I'M HERE.
WE NEED SMART PEOPLE, PEOPLE WHO KNOW HOW TO RUN THINGS --
-- WHO KNOW THE FIRST RULE IS, "TAKE CARE OF THE FOLKS DEPENDING ON YOU."
THAT'S WHAT THE PEOPLE I JOINED UP WITH GAVE ME -- AND WHAT I'M OFFERIN' YOU. AN HONEST DAY'S WORK. THREE SQUARES A DAY.
AN' LEADERS WHO'LL FIGHT FOR YOU -- WHO'LL TAKE THE WEIGHT OFF YOUR SHOULDERS, DO THE THINKIN'... AND WHO'LL TAKE CARE OF THEIR PEOPLE!
KURT BUSIEK & MARK BAGLEY STORYTELLERS
SCOTT HANNA INKS
RS & COMICRAFT'S SAIDA TEMOFONTE LETTERS
JOE ROSAS COLORS
TOM BREVOORT EDITOR
BOB HARRAS CHIEF
SOUNDS LIKE YOU DON'T LIKE WHAT THAT GUY'S SAYIN', Eh?
I'M LISTENING, AIN'T I?
AN' IT STRIKES ME -- I AIN'T NEVER SEEN YOU AROUND BEFORE. YOU'RE A STRANGER -- AN' WE DON'T LIKE STRANGERS --
YEAH, I'M A STRANGER --!
WHUFF!
EVER SINCE I GOT FORECLOSED OUTTA MY HOME, DOWNSIZED OUTTA MY JOB, AND RUN OUTTA TOWN ONE STEP AHEAD A' THE REPO MAN!
I BEEN LIVIN' OUTTA MY CAR FOR MONTHS, FRIEND -- AND I'LL TELL YA --
HEY! FIGHT!
LET'S GET THAT SONOFA --!

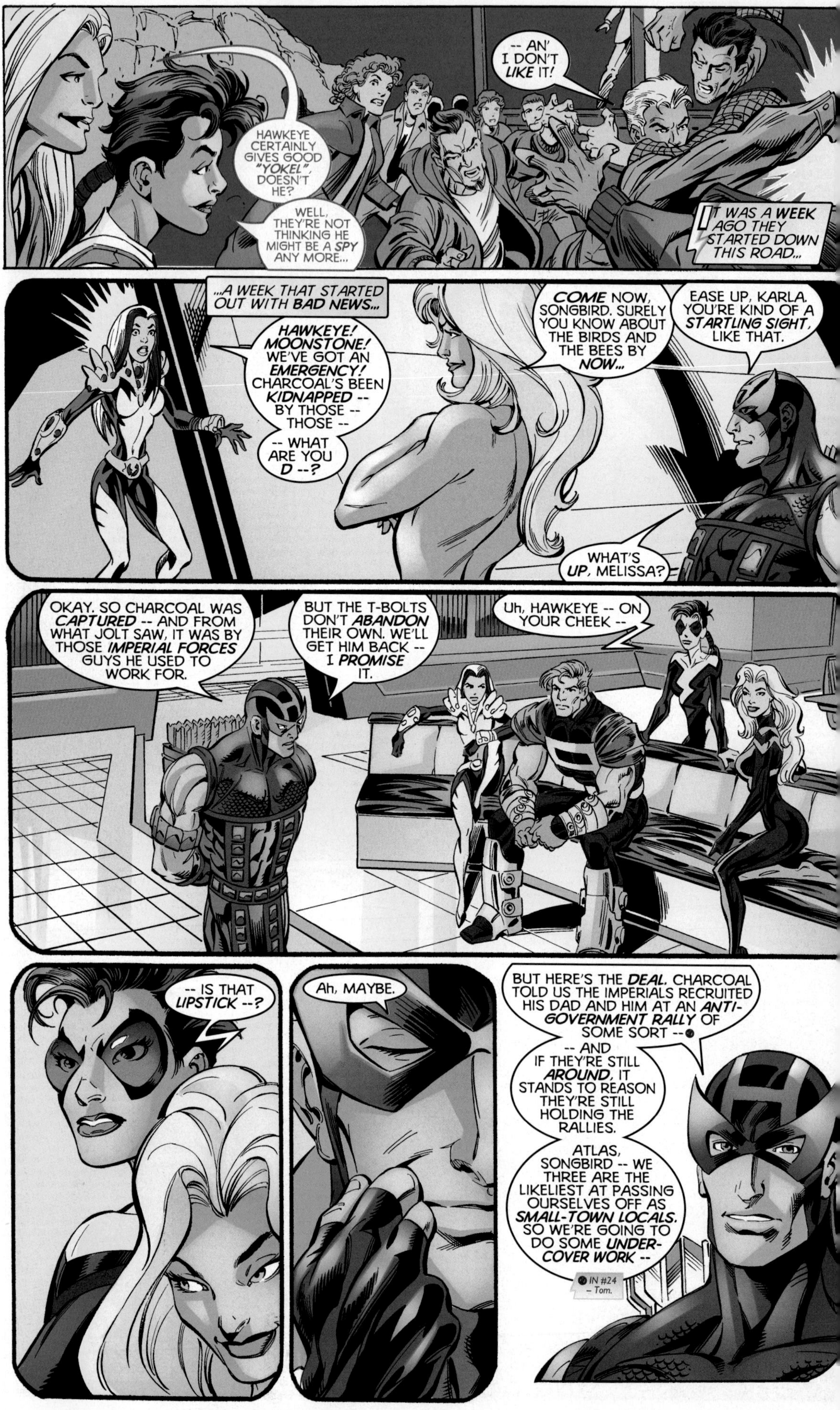
HAWKEYE CERTAINLY GIVES GOOD "YOKEL", DOESN'T HE?
WELL, THEY'RE NOT THINKING HE MIGHT BE A SPY ANY MORE...
-- AN' I DON'T LIKE IT!
IT WAS A WEEK AGO THEY STARTED DOWN THIS ROAD...
...A WEEK THAT STARTED OUT WITH BAD NEWS...
HAWKEYE! MOONSTONE! WE'VE GOT AN EMERGENCY! CHARCOAL'S BEEN KIDNAPPED -- BY THOSE -- THOSE --
-- WHAT ARE YOU D --?
COME NOW, SONGBIRD. SURELY YOU KNOW ABOUT THE BIRDS AND THE BEES BY NOW...
EASE UP, KARLA. YOU'RE KIND OF A STARTLING SIGHT, LIKE THAT.
WHAT'S UP, MELISSA?
OKAY. SO CHARCOAL WAS CAPTURED -- AND FROM WHAT JOLT SAW, IT WAS BY THOSE IMPERIAL FORCES GUYS HE USED TO WORK FOR.
BUT THE T-BOLTS DON'T ABANDON THEIR OWN. WE'LL GET HIM BACK -- I PROMISE IT.
Uh, HAWKEYE -- ON YOUR CHEEK --
-- IS THAT LIPSTICK --?
Ah, MAYBE.
BUT HERE'S THE DEAL. CHARCOAL TOLD US THE IMPERIALS RECRUITED HIS DAD AND HIM AT AN ANTI-GOVERNMENT RALLY OF SOME SORT --
-- AND IF THEY'RE STILL AROUND, IT STANDS TO REASON THEY'RE STILL HOLDING THE RALLIES.
ATLAS, SONGBIRD -- WE THREE ARE THE LIKELIEST AT PASSING OURSELVES OFF AS SMALL-TOWN LOCALS. SO WE'RE GOING TO DO SOME UNDER-COVER WORK --
IN #24 – Tom.

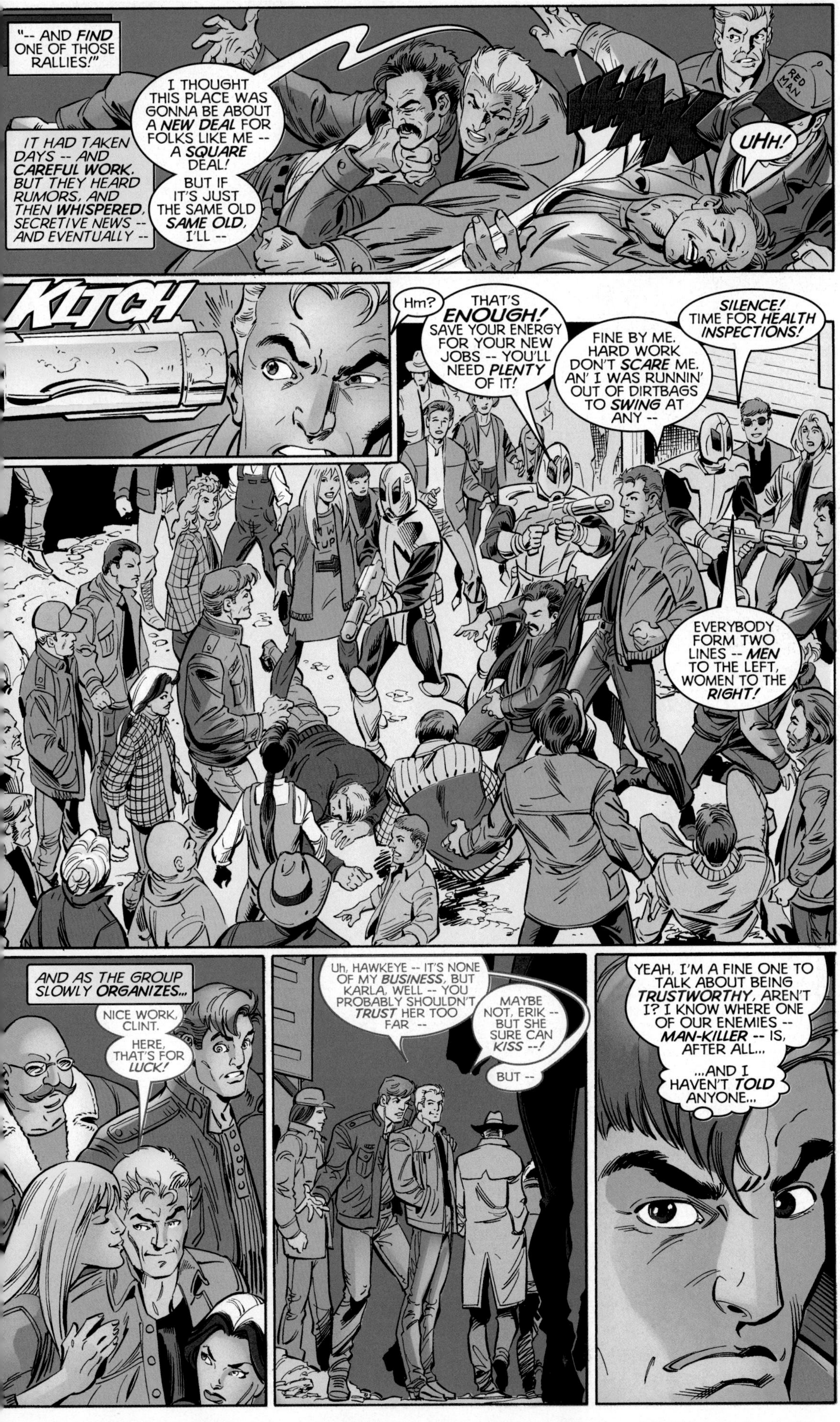
"-- AND FIND ONE OF THOSE RALLIES!"
IT HAD TAKEN DAYS -- AND CAREFUL WORK. BUT THEY HEARD RUMORS, AND THEN WHISPERED, SECRETIVE NEWS -- AND EVENTUALLY --
I THOUGHT THIS PLACE WAS GONNA BE ABOUT A NEW DEAL FOR FOLKS LIKE ME -- A SQUARE DEAL!
BUT IF IT'S JUST THE SAME OLD SAME OLD, I'LL --
RED MAN
UHH!
KLITCH
Hm?
THAT'S ENOUGH! SAVE YOUR ENERGY FOR YOUR NEW JOBS -- YOU'LL NEED PLENTY OF IT!
FINE BY ME. HARD WORK DON'T SCARE ME. AN' I WAS RUNNIN' OUT OF DIRTBAGS TO SWING AT ANY --
SILENCE! TIME FOR HEALTH INSPECTIONS!
EVERYBODY FORM TWO LINES -- MEN TO THE LEFT, WOMEN TO THE RIGHT!
AND AS THE GROUP SLOWLY ORGANIZES...
NICE WORK, CLINT.
HERE, THAT'S FOR LUCK!
Uh, HAWKEYE -- IT'S NONE OF MY BUSINESS, BUT KARLA, WELL -- YOU PROBABLY SHOULDN'T TRUST HER TOO FAR --
MAYBE NOT, ERIK -- BUT SHE SURE CAN KISS --!
BUT --
YEAH, I'M A FINE ONE TO TALK ABOUT BEING TRUSTWORTHY, AREN'T I? I KNOW WHERE ONE OF OUR ENEMIES -- MAN-KILLER -- IS, AFTER ALL...
...AND I HAVEN'T TOLD ANYONE...

AND AS ERIK JOSTEN FALLS INTO A TROUBLED SILENCE...

SO THIS IS YOUR *NEW PLAN*, MOONSTONE?

USING SEX TO GET HAWKEYE UNDER YOUR *THUMB*?

WHAT'S *REALLY* BOTHERING YOU, MELISSA...

...THAT I MIGHT BE *SEDUCING* HAWKEYE? OR THAT IT DIDN'T WORK WHEN *YOU* TRIED IT?

SEE #29 — Tom.

THAT'S *NOT* WHAT -- IT WASN'T WHAT I WAS --

KARLA SOFEN JUST *SMILES*. BUT SHE, TOO, IS THOUGHTFUL. SHE HAD INTENDED TO VAMP HAWKEYE, IT'S TRUE -- BUT NOW, FOR SOME REASON --

-- SOMETHING SHE CAN'T PUT HER FINGER ON, SHE FINDS HERSELF -- *LIKING* HIM.

AND SOON IT'S THEIR TURN IN THE *EXAMINATION* TENT...

OPEN. SAY "*AHHH*."

Ahhh...

ANY HISTORY OF *CANCER* IN YOUR FAMILY? ANY CHILDHOOD DISEASES? *MUMPS,* CHICKEN POX, *RUBELLA...*

NO, NO, YES, NO...

BUT AS THE EXAMINATION *CONTINUES* --

-- ON THE OTHER SIDE OF THE *WALL* --

INITIAL *BIO-SCANS* LOOK GOOD. DNA PROFILE EXCELLENT. AND --

-- HOLD IT, WHAT'S *THIS*?

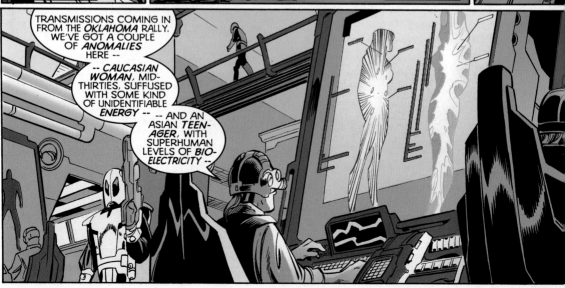

TRANSMISSIONS COMING IN FROM THE *OKLAHOMA* RALLY. WE'VE GOT A COUPLE OF *ANOMALIES* HERE --

-- *CAUCASIAN WOMAN,* MID-THIRTIES, SUFFUSED WITH SOME KIND OF UNIDENTIFIABLE *ENERGY* -- -- AND AN *ASIAN TEEN-AGER,* WITH SUPERHUMAN LEVELS OF *BIO-ELECTRICITY* --

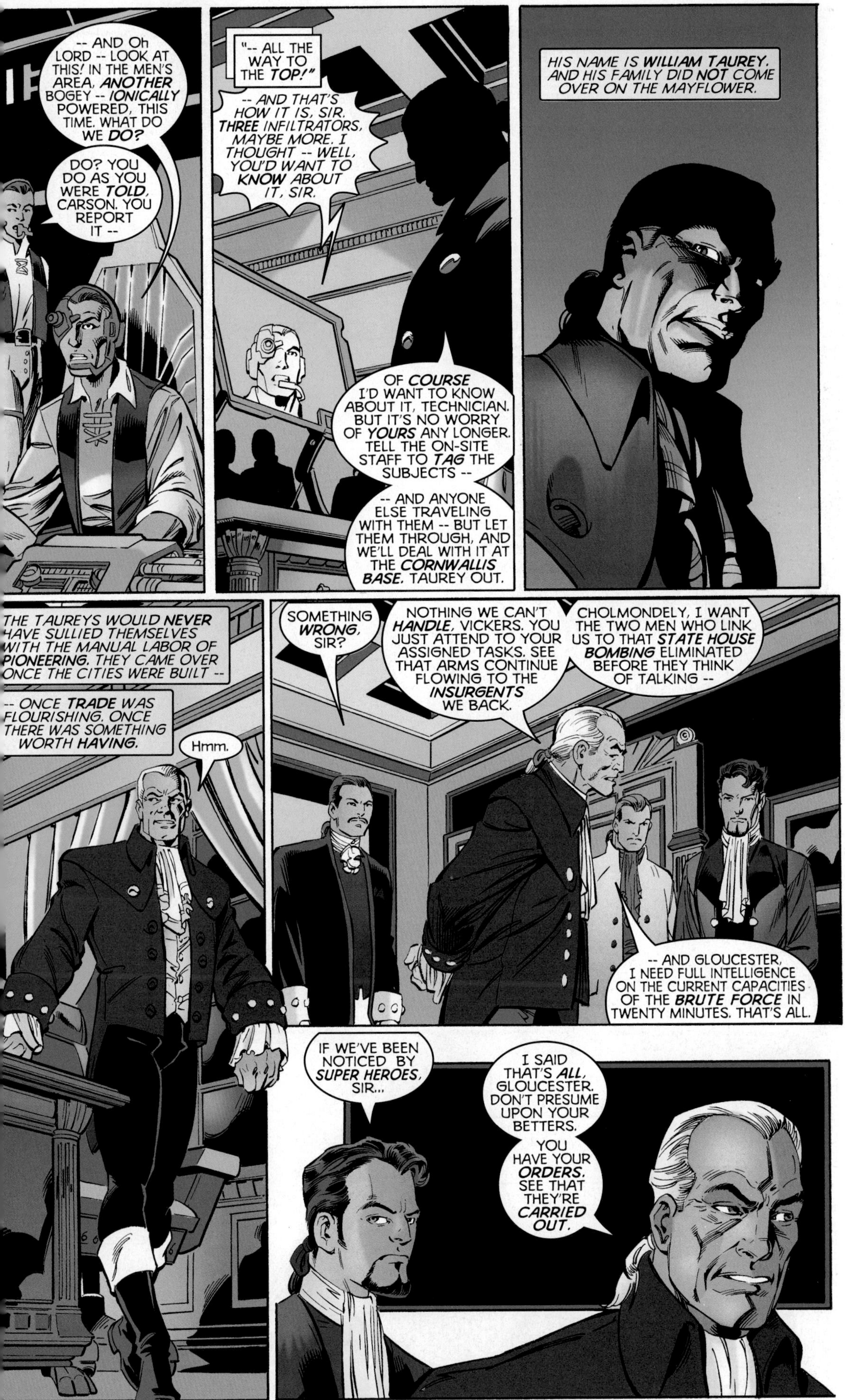
-- AND Oh LORD -- LOOK AT THIS! IN THE MEN'S AREA, ANOTHER BOGEY -- IONICALLY POWERED, THIS TIME. WHAT DO WE DO?
DO? YOU DO AS YOU WERE TOLD, CARSON. YOU REPORT IT --
"-- ALL THE WAY TO THE TOP!"
-- AND THAT'S HOW IT IS, SIR. THREE INFILTRATORS, MAYBE MORE. I THOUGHT -- WELL, YOU'D WANT TO KNOW ABOUT IT, SIR.
OF COURSE I'D WANT TO KNOW ABOUT IT, TECHNICIAN. BUT IT'S NO WORRY OF YOURS ANY LONGER. TELL THE ON-SITE STAFF TO TAG THE SUBJECTS --
-- AND ANYONE ELSE TRAVELING WITH THEM -- BUT LET THEM THROUGH, AND WE'LL DEAL WITH IT AT THE CORNWALLIS BASE. TAUREY OUT.
HIS NAME IS WILLIAM TAUREY. AND HIS FAMILY DID NOT COME OVER ON THE MAYFLOWER.
THE TAUREYS WOULD NEVER HAVE SULLIED THEMSELVES WITH THE MANUAL LABOR OF PIONEERING. THEY CAME OVER ONCE THE CITIES WERE BUILT --
-- ONCE TRADE WAS FLOURISHING. ONCE THERE WAS SOMETHING WORTH HAVING.
Hmm.
SOMETHING WRONG, SIR?
NOTHING WE CAN'T HANDLE, VICKERS. YOU JUST ATTEND TO YOUR ASSIGNED TASKS. SEE THAT ARMS CONTINUE FLOWING TO THE INSURGENTS WE BACK.
CHOLMONDELY, I WANT THE TWO MEN WHO LINK US TO THAT STATE HOUSE BOMBING ELIMINATED BEFORE THEY THINK OF TALKING --
-- AND GLOUCESTER, I NEED FULL INTELLIGENCE ON THE CURRENT CAPACITIES OF THE BRUTE FORCE IN TWENTY MINUTES. THAT'S ALL.
IF WE'VE BEEN NOTICED BY SUPER HEROES, SIR...
I SAID THAT'S ALL, GLOUCESTER. DON'T PRESUME UPON YOUR BETTERS.
YOU HAVE YOUR ORDERS. SEE THAT THEY'RE CARRIED OUT.

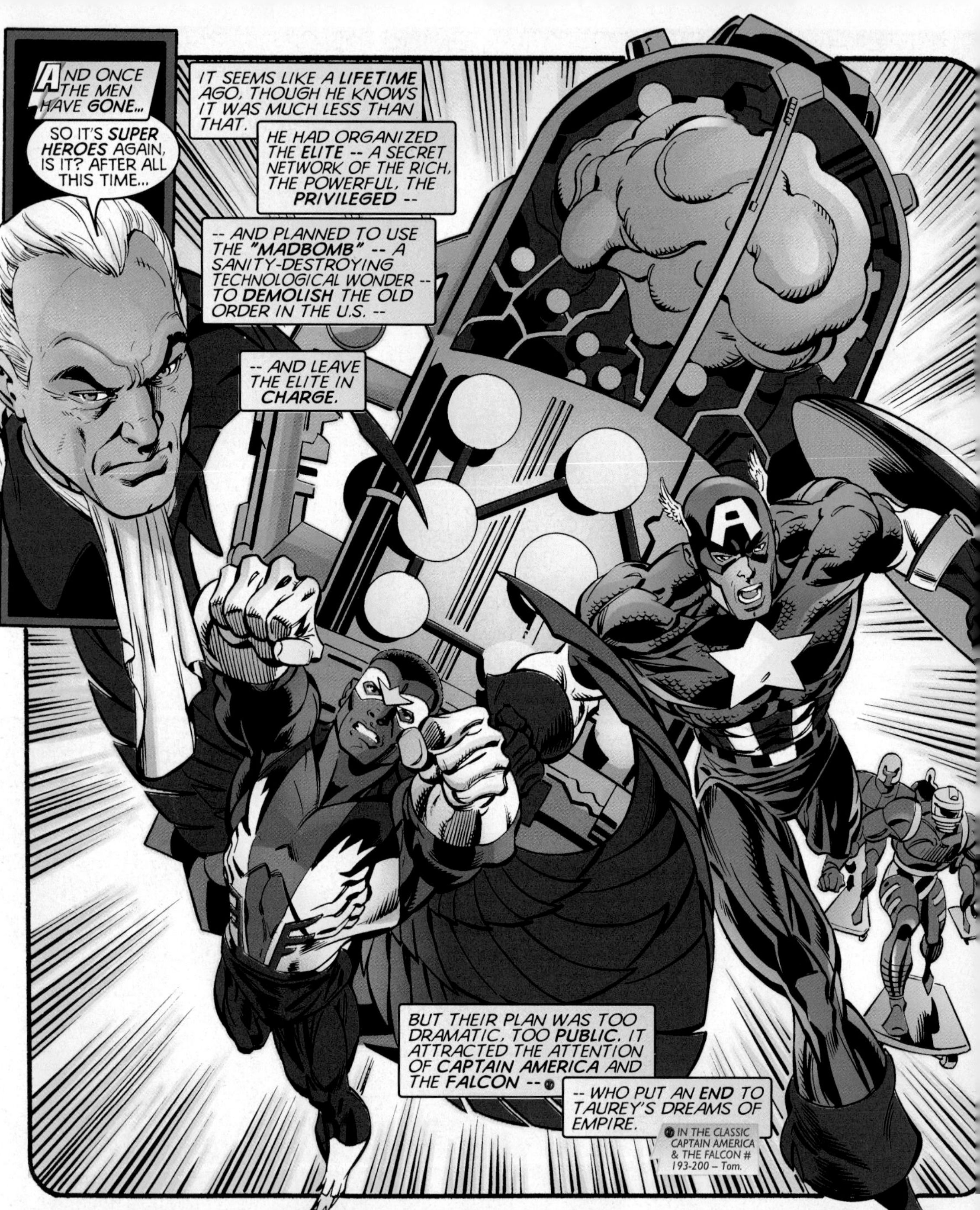

AND ONCE THE MEN HAVE GONE...
SO IT'S SUPER HEROES AGAIN, IS IT? AFTER ALL THIS TIME...
IT SEEMS LIKE A LIFETIME AGO, THOUGH HE KNOWS IT WAS MUCH LESS THAN THAT.
HE HAD ORGANIZED THE ELITE -- A SECRET NETWORK OF THE RICH, THE POWERFUL, THE PRIVILEGED --
-- AND PLANNED TO USE THE "MADBOMB" -- A SANITY-DESTROYING TECHNOLOGICAL WONDER -- TO DEMOLISH THE OLD ORDER IN THE U.S. --
-- AND LEAVE THE ELITE IN CHARGE.
BUT THEIR PLAN WAS TOO DRAMATIC, TOO PUBLIC. IT ATTRACTED THE ATTENTION OF CAPTAIN AMERICA AND THE FALCON --
-- WHO PUT AN END TO TAUREY'S DREAMS OF EMPIRE.
IN THE CLASSIC CAPTAIN AMERICA & THE FALCON # 193-200 – Tom.

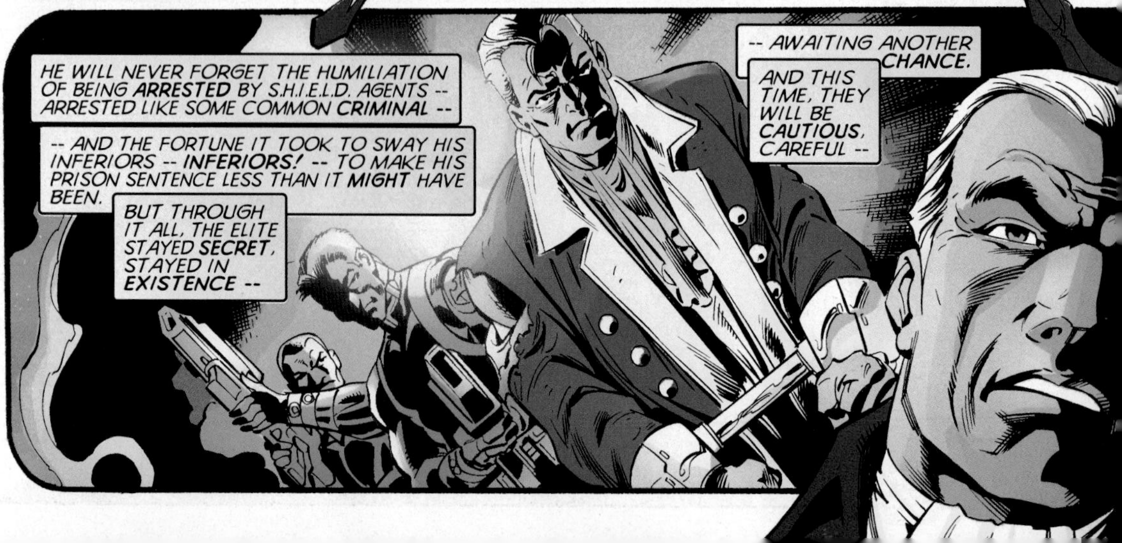

HE WILL NEVER FORGET THE HUMILIATION OF BEING ARRESTED BY S.H.I.E.L.D. AGENTS -- ARRESTED LIKE SOME COMMON CRIMINAL --
-- AND THE FORTUNE IT TOOK TO SWAY HIS INFERIORS -- INFERIORS! -- TO MAKE HIS PRISON SENTENCE LESS THAN IT MIGHT HAVE BEEN.
BUT THROUGH IT ALL, THE ELITE STAYED SECRET, STAYED IN EXISTENCE --
-- AWAITING ANOTHER CHANCE.
AND THIS TIME, THEY WILL BE CAUTIOUS, CAREFUL --

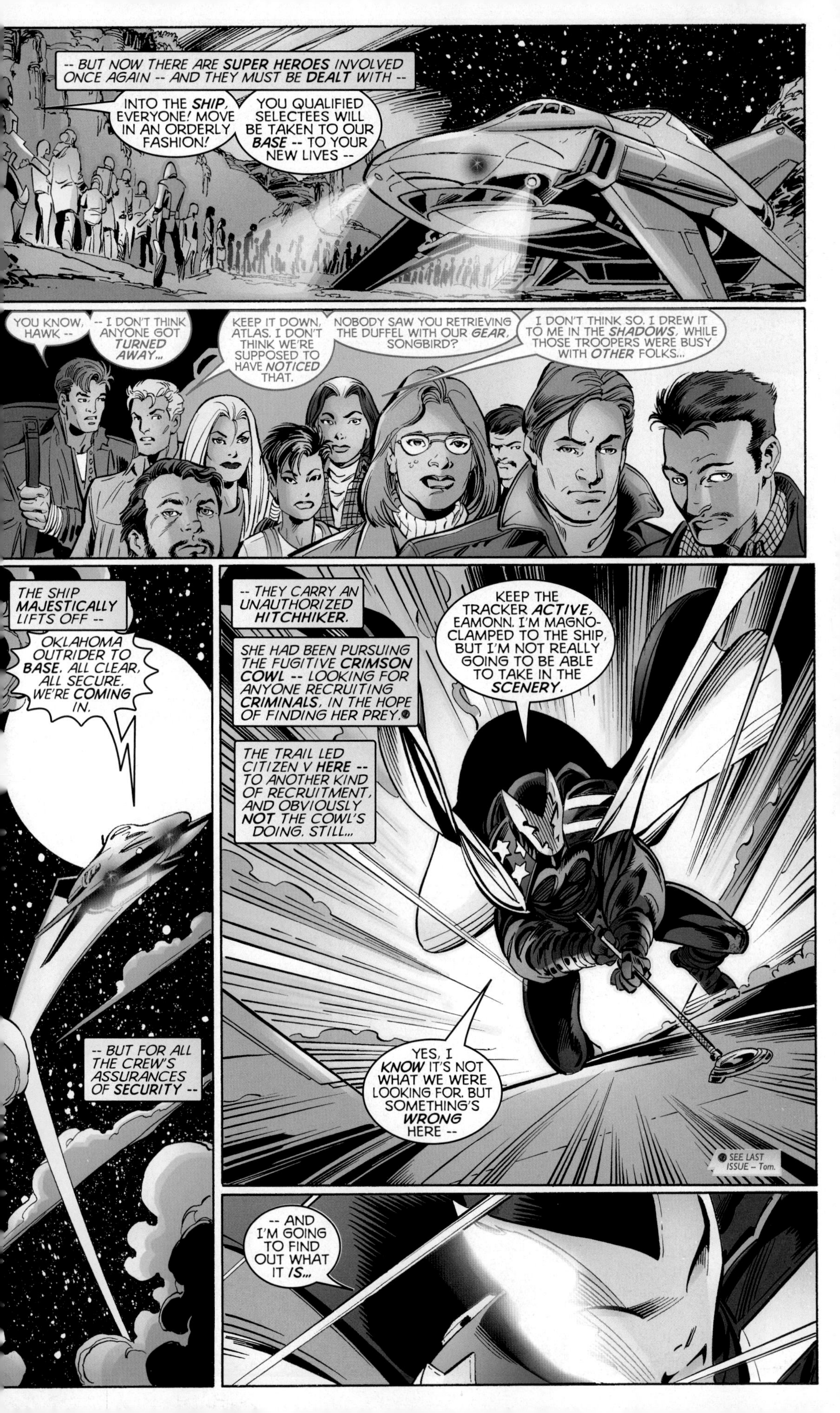
-- BUT NOW THERE ARE SUPER HEROES INVOLVED ONCE AGAIN -- AND THEY MUST BE DEALT WITH --
INTO THE SHIP, EVERYONE! MOVE IN AN ORDERLY FASHION!
YOU QUALIFIED SELECTEES WILL BE TAKEN TO OUR BASE -- TO YOUR NEW LIVES --
YOU KNOW, HAWK --
-- I DON'T THINK ANYONE GOT TURNED AWAY...
KEEP IT DOWN, ATLAS. I DON'T THINK WE'RE SUPPOSED TO HAVE NOTICED THAT.
NOBODY SAW YOU RETRIEVING THE DUFFEL WITH OUR GEAR, SONGBIRD?
I DON'T THINK SO. I DREW IT TO ME IN THE SHADOWS, WHILE THOSE TROOPERS WERE BUSY WITH OTHER FOLKS...
THE SHIP MAJESTICALLY LIFTS OFF --
OKLAHOMA OUTRIDER TO BASE. ALL CLEAR, ALL SECURE. WE'RE COMING IN.
-- BUT FOR ALL THE CREW'S ASSURANCES OF SECURITY --
-- THEY CARRY AN UNAUTHORIZED HITCHHIKER.
SHE HAD BEEN PURSUING THE FUGITIVE CRIMSON COWL -- LOOKING FOR ANYONE RECRUITING CRIMINALS, IN THE HOPE OF FINDING HER PREY.
THE TRAIL LED CITIZEN V HERE -- TO ANOTHER KIND OF RECRUITMENT, AND OBVIOUSLY NOT THE COWL'S DOING. STILL...
KEEP THE TRACKER ACTIVE, EAMONN. I'M MAGNO-CLAMPED TO THE SHIP, BUT I'M NOT REALLY GOING TO BE ABLE TO TAKE IN THE SCENERY.
YES, I KNOW IT'S NOT WHAT WE WERE LOOKING FOR. BUT SOMETHING'S WRONG HERE --
SEE LAST ISSUE – Tom.
-- AND I'M GOING TO FIND OUT WHAT IT IS...

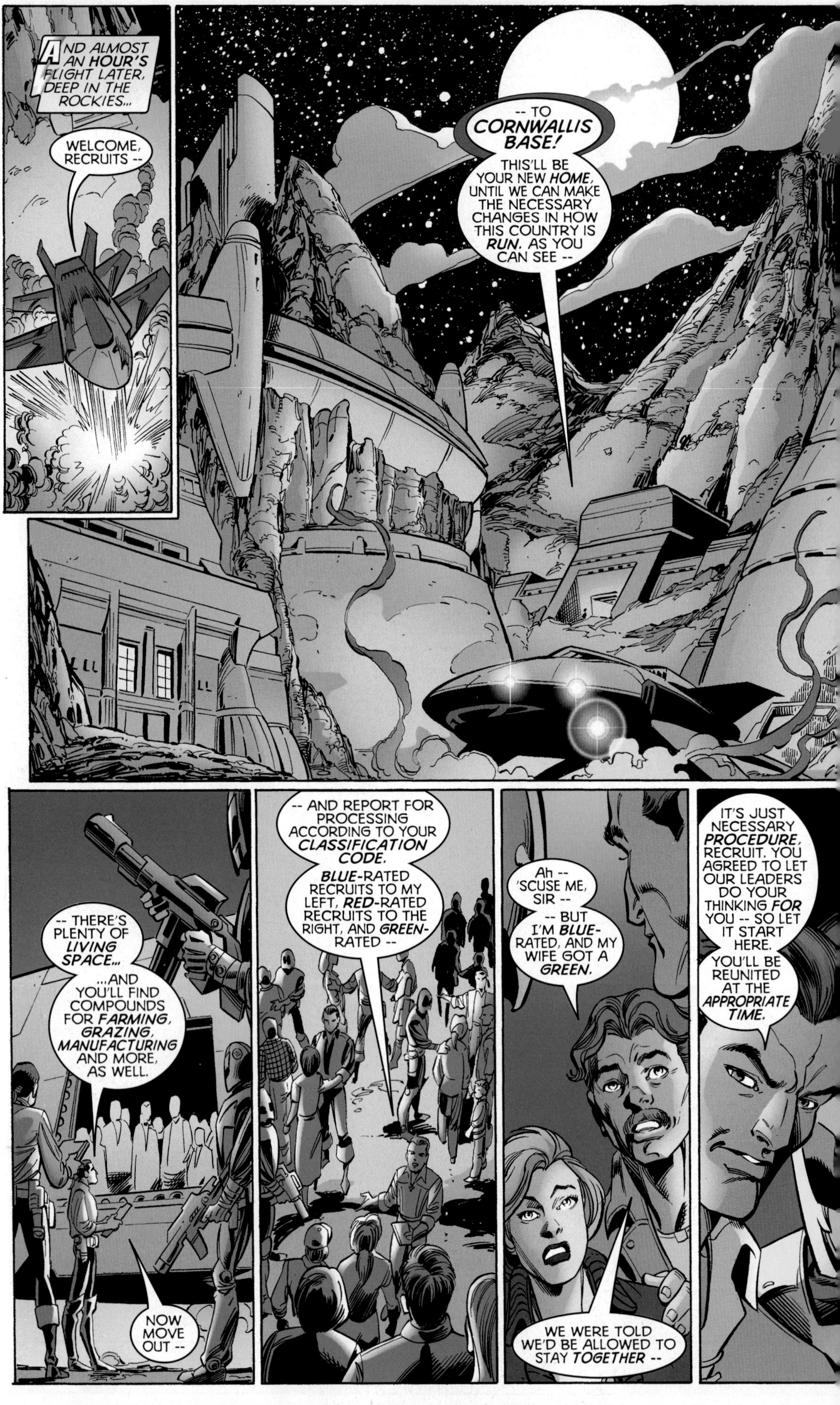
AND ALMOST AN HOUR'S FLIGHT LATER, DEEP IN THE ROCKIES...
WELCOME, RECRUITS --
-- TO CORNWALLIS BASE!
THIS'LL BE YOUR NEW HOME, UNTIL WE CAN MAKE THE NECESSARY CHANGES IN HOW THIS COUNTRY IS RUN. AS YOU CAN SEE --
-- THERE'S PLENTY OF LIVING SPACE...
...AND YOU'LL FIND COMPOUNDS FOR FARMING, GRAZING, MANUFACTURING AND MORE, AS WELL.
NOW MOVE OUT --
-- AND REPORT FOR PROCESSING ACCORDING TO YOUR CLASSIFICATION CODE.
BLUE-RATED RECRUITS TO MY LEFT, RED-RATED RECRUITS TO THE RIGHT, AND GREEN-RATED --
Ah -- 'SCUSE ME, SIR --
-- BUT I'M BLUE-RATED, AND MY WIFE GOT A GREEN.
WE WERE TOLD WE'D BE ALLOWED TO STAY TOGETHER --
IT'S JUST NECESSARY PROCEDURE, RECRUIT. YOU AGREED TO LET OUR LEADERS DO YOUR THINKING FOR YOU -- SO LET IT START HERE.
YOU'LL BE REUNITED AT THE APPROPRIATE TIME.

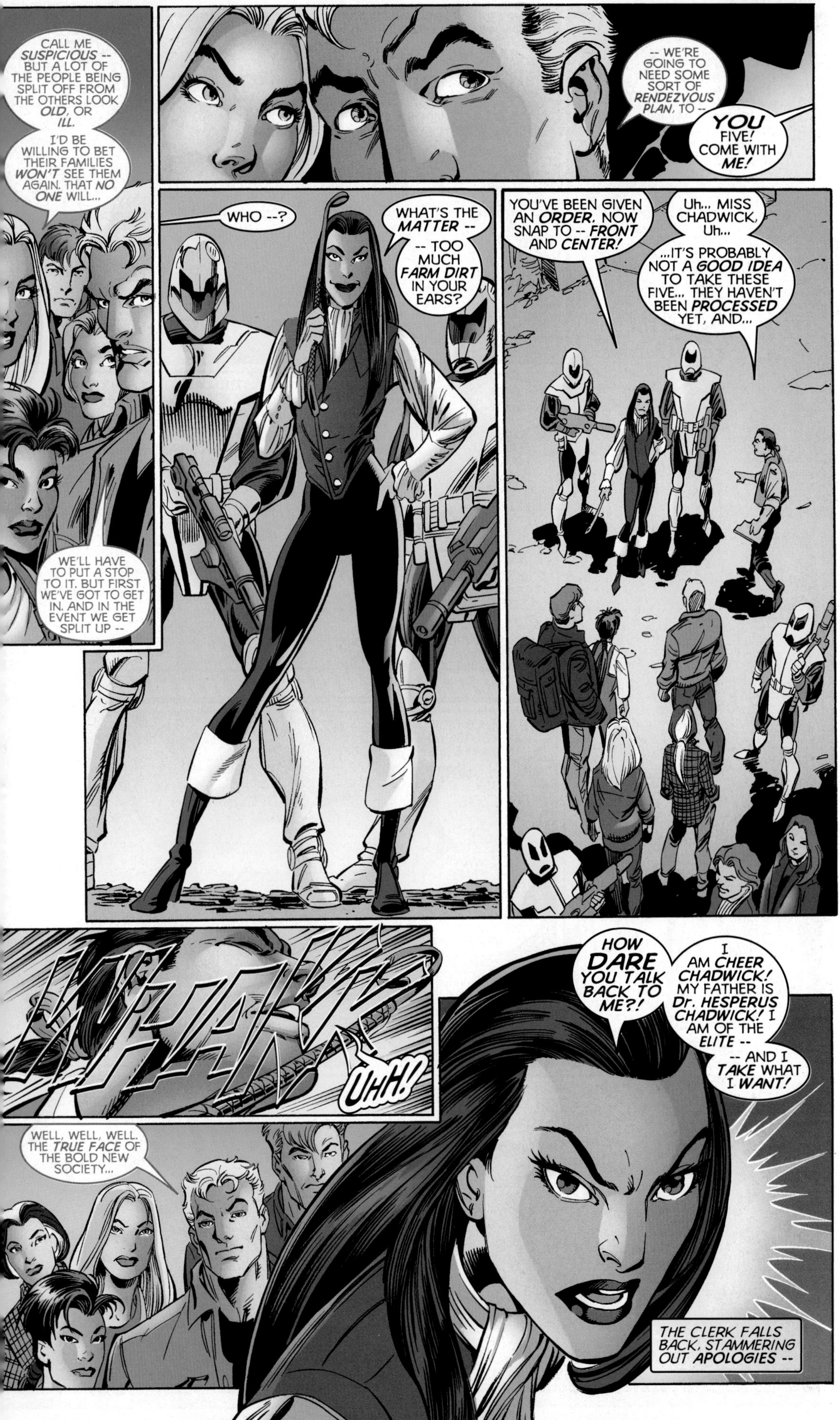
CALL ME SUSPICIOUS -- BUT A LOT OF THE PEOPLE BEING SPLIT OFF FROM THE OTHERS LOOK OLD, OR ILL.
I'D BE WILLING TO BET THEIR FAMILIES WON'T SEE THEM AGAIN. THAT NO ONE WILL...
WE'LL HAVE TO PUT A STOP TO IT. BUT FIRST WE'VE GOT TO GET IN. AND IN THE EVENT WE GET SPLIT UP --
-- WE'RE GOING TO NEED SOME SORT OF RENDEZVOUS PLAN, TO --
YOU FIVE! COME WITH ME!
WHO --?
WHAT'S THE MATTER --
-- TOO MUCH FARM DIRT IN YOUR EARS?
YOU'VE BEEN GIVEN AN ORDER. NOW SNAP TO -- FRONT AND CENTER!
Uh... MISS CHADWICK, Uh...
...IT'S PROBABLY NOT A GOOD IDEA TO TAKE THESE FIVE... THEY HAVEN'T BEEN PROCESSED YET, AND...
WHAK!
OHH!
HOW DARE YOU TALK BACK TO ME?!
I AM CHEER CHADWICK! MY FATHER IS Dr. HESPERUS CHADWICK! I AM OF THE ELITE --
-- AND I TAKE WHAT I WANT!
WELL, WELL, WELL. THE TRUE FACE OF THE BOLD NEW SOCIETY...
THE CLERK FALLS BACK, STAMMERING OUT APOLOGIES --

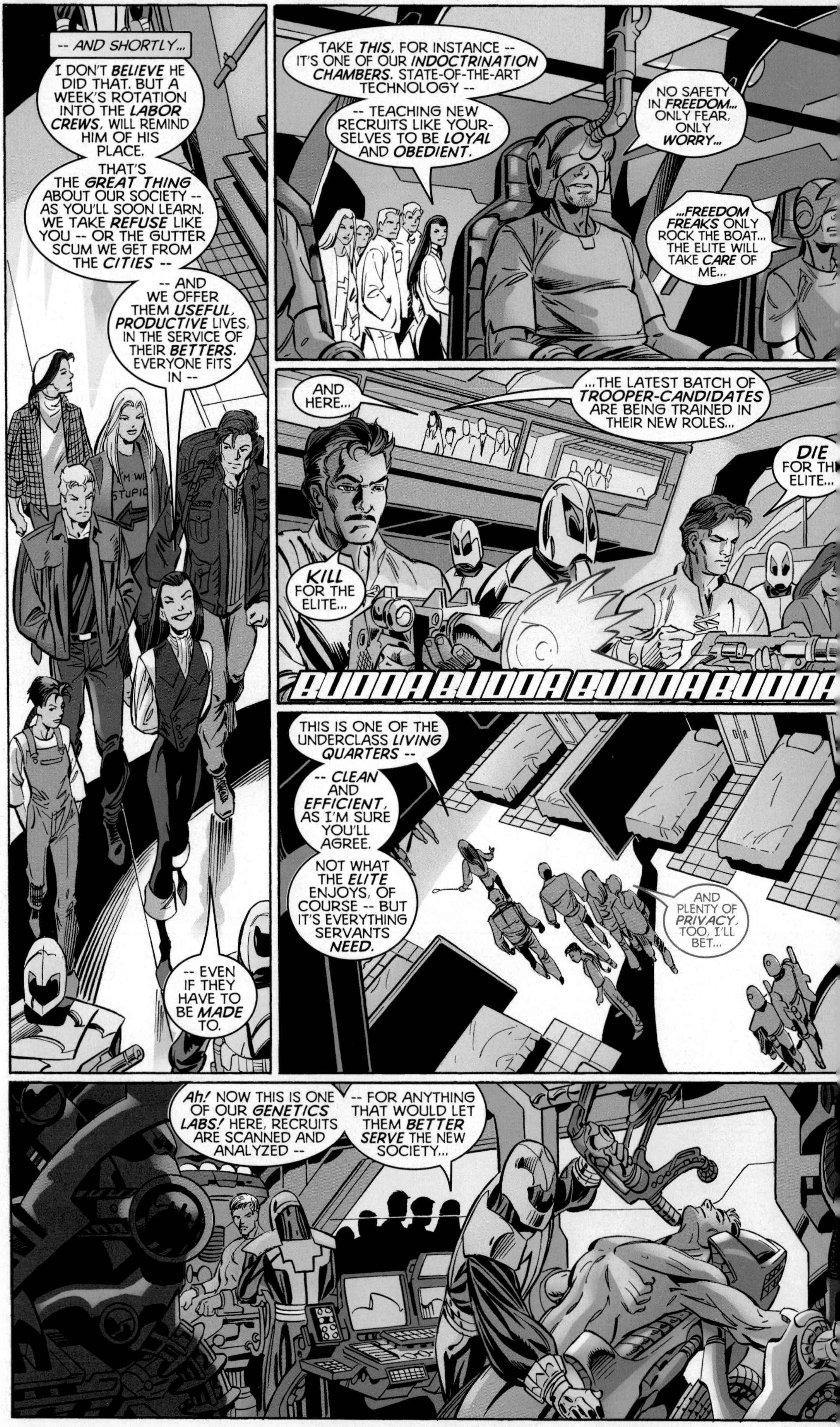

-- AND SHORTLY...
I DON'T BELIEVE HE DID THAT. BUT A WEEK'S ROTATION INTO THE LABOR CREWS, WILL REMIND HIM OF HIS PLACE.
THAT'S THE GREAT THING ABOUT OUR SOCIETY -- AS YOU'LL SOON LEARN. WE TAKE REFUSE LIKE YOU -- OR THE GUTTER SCUM WE GET FROM THE CITIES --
-- AND WE OFFER THEM USEFUL, PRODUCTIVE LIVES, IN THE SERVICE OF THEIR BETTERS. EVERYONE FITS IN --
-- EVEN IF THEY HAVE TO BE MADE TO.
TAKE THIS, FOR INSTANCE -- IT'S ONE OF OUR INDOCTRINATION CHAMBERS. STATE-OF-THE-ART TECHNOLOGY --
-- TEACHING NEW RECRUITS LIKE YOURSELVES TO BE LOYAL AND OBEDIENT.
NO SAFETY IN FREEDOM... ONLY FEAR, ONLY WORRY...
...FREEDOM FREAKS ONLY ROCK THE BOAT... THE ELITE WILL TAKE CARE OF ME...
AND HERE...
...THE LATEST BATCH OF TROOPER-CANDIDATES ARE BEING TRAINED IN THEIR NEW ROLES...
DIE FOR TH
ELITE...
KILL FOR THE ELITE...
BUDDA BUDDA BUDDA BUDDA
THIS IS ONE OF THE UNDERCLASS LIVING QUARTERS --
-- CLEAN AND EFFICIENT, AS I'M SURE YOU'LL AGREE.
NOT WHAT THE ELITE ENJOYS, OF COURSE -- BUT IT'S EVERYTHING SERVANTS NEED.
AND PLENTY OF PRIVACY, TOO, I'LL BET...
Ah! NOW THIS IS ONE OF OUR GENETICS LABS! HERE, RECRUITS ARE SCANNED AND ANALYZED --
-- FOR ANYTHING THAT WOULD LET THEM BETTER SERVE THE NEW SOCIETY...

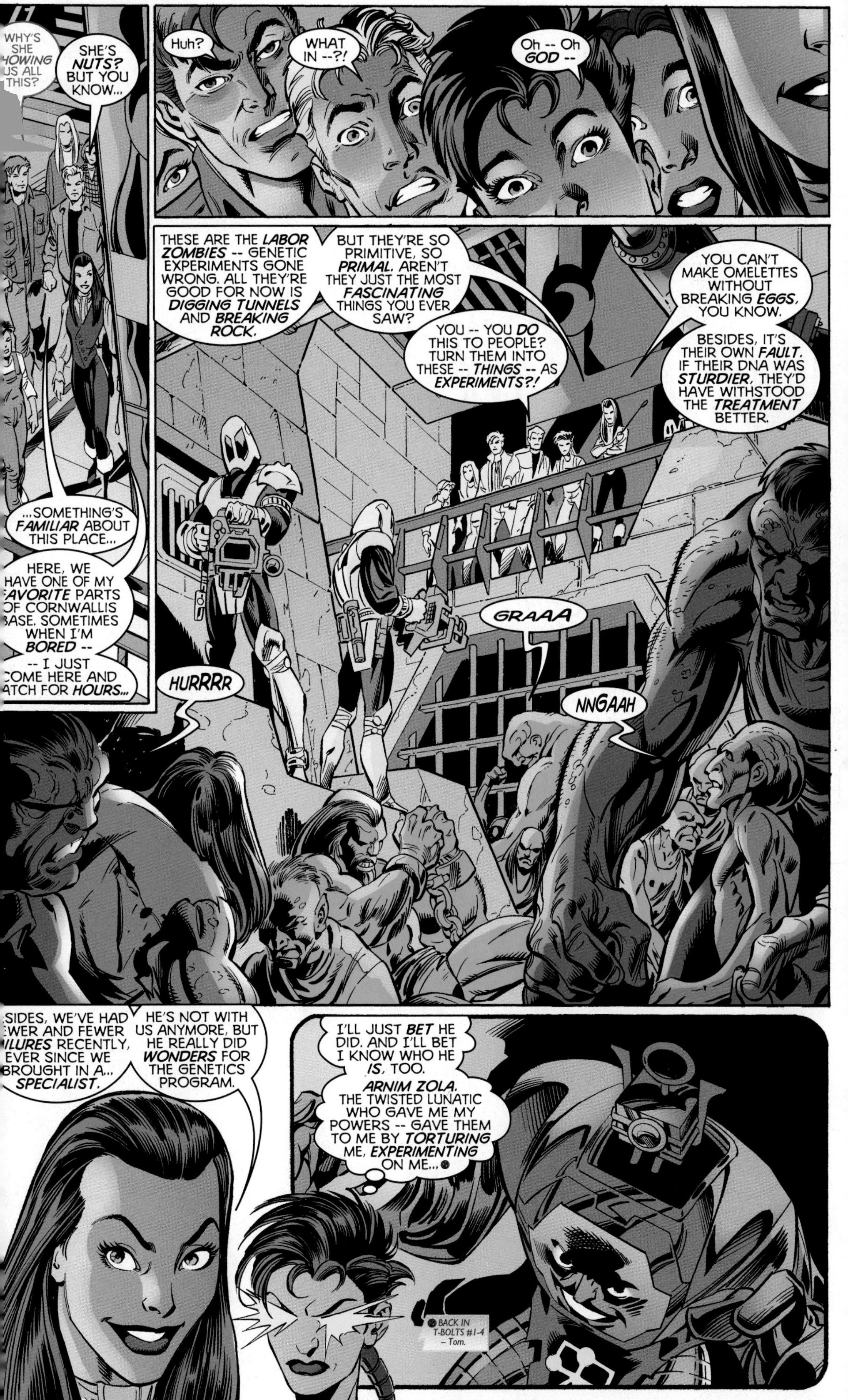

WHY'S SHE HOWING US ALL THIS?
SHE'S NUTS? BUT YOU KNOW...
...SOMETHING'S FAMILIAR ABOUT THIS PLACE...
HERE, WE HAVE ONE OF MY FAVORITE PARTS OF CORNWALLIS BASE. SOMETIMES WHEN I'M BORED --
-- I JUST COME HERE AND ATCH FOR HOURS...
Huh?
WHAT IN --?!
Oh -- Oh GOD --
THESE ARE THE LABOR ZOMBIES -- GENETIC EXPERIMENTS GONE WRONG. ALL THEY'RE GOOD FOR NOW IS DIGGING TUNNELS AND BREAKING ROCK.
BUT THEY'RE SO PRIMITIVE, SO PRIMAL. AREN'T THEY JUST THE MOST FASCINATING THINGS YOU EVER SAW?
YOU -- YOU DO THIS TO PEOPLE? TURN THEM INTO THESE -- THINGS -- AS EXPERIMENTS?!
YOU CAN'T MAKE OMELETTES WITHOUT BREAKING EGGS, YOU KNOW.
BESIDES, IT'S THEIR OWN FAULT. IF THEIR DNA WAS STURDIER, THEY'D HAVE WITHSTOOD THE TREATMENT BETTER.
HURRRR
GRAAA
NNGAAH
SIDES, WE'VE HAD EWER AND FEWER ILURES RECENTLY, EVER SINCE WE BROUGHT IN A... SPECIALIST.
HE'S NOT WITH US ANYMORE, BUT HE REALLY DID WONDERS FOR THE GENETICS PROGRAM.
I'LL JUST BET HE DID. AND I'LL BET I KNOW WHO HE IS, TOO.
ARNIM ZOLA. THE TWISTED LUNATIC WHO GAVE ME MY POWERS -- GAVE THEM TO ME BY TORTURING ME, EXPERIMENTING ON ME...
BACK IN T-BOLTS #1-4 – Tom.

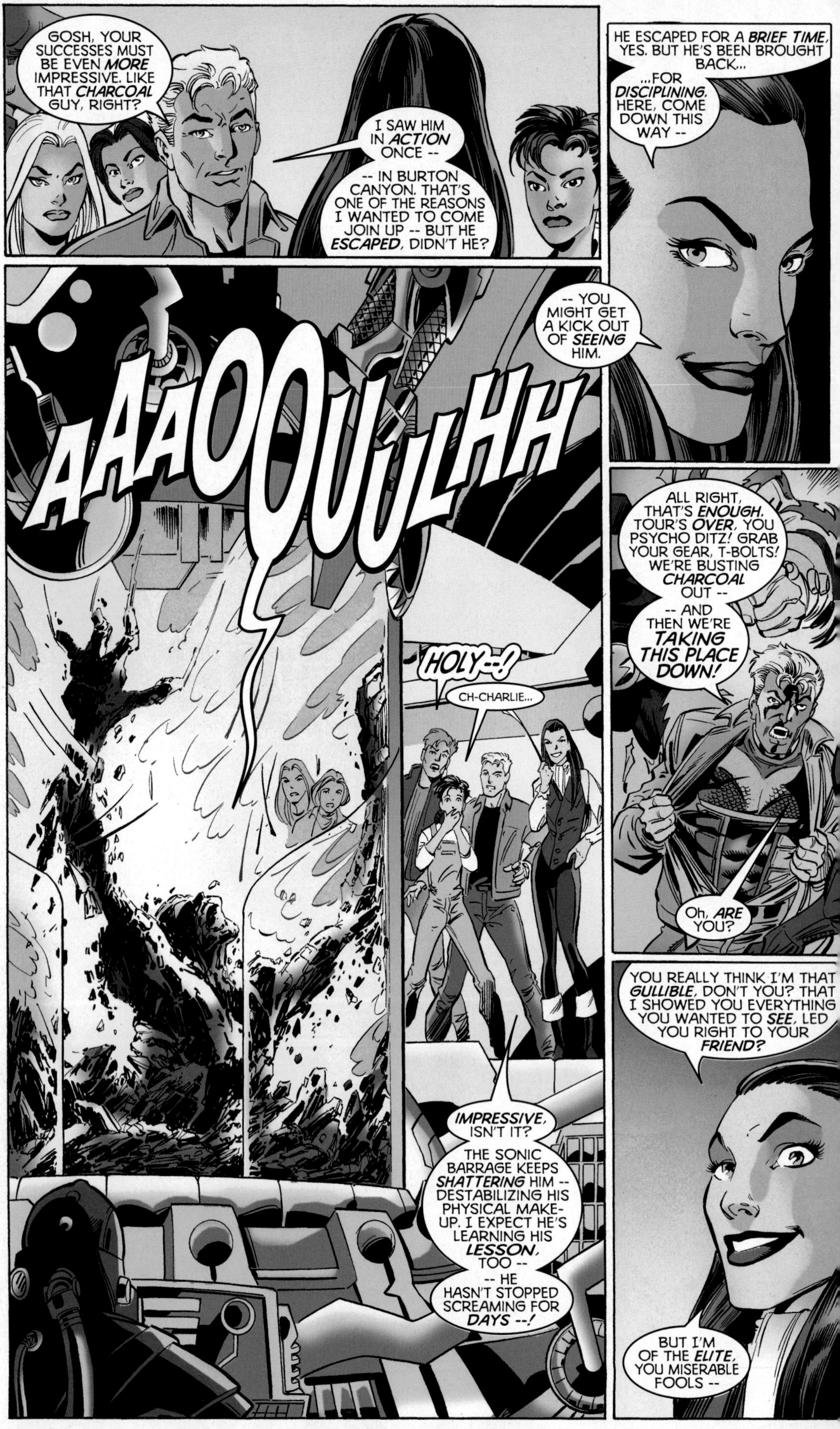
GOSH, YOUR SUCCESSES MUST BE EVEN MORE IMPRESSIVE. LIKE THAT CHARCOAL GUY, RIGHT?
I SAW HIM IN ACTION ONCE --
-- IN BURTON CANYON. THAT'S ONE OF THE REASONS I WANTED TO COME JOIN UP -- BUT HE ESCAPED, DIDN'T HE?
HE ESCAPED FOR A BRIEF TIME, YES. BUT HE'S BEEN BROUGHT BACK...
...FOR DISCIPLINING. HERE, COME DOWN THIS WAY --
-- YOU MIGHT GET A KICK OUT OF SEEING HIM.
AAAOOUULHH
HOLY--!
CH-CHARLIE...
IMPRESSIVE, ISN'T IT?
THE SONIC BARRAGE KEEPS SHATTERING HIM -- DESTABILIZING HIS PHYSICAL MAKE-UP. I EXPECT HE'S LEARNING HIS LESSON, TOO --
-- HE HASN'T STOPPED SCREAMING FOR DAYS --!
ALL RIGHT, THAT'S ENOUGH. TOUR'S OVER, YOU PSYCHO DITZ! GRAB YOUR GEAR, T-BOLTS! WE'RE BUSTING CHARCOAL OUT --
-- AND THEN WE'RE TAKING THIS PLACE DOWN!
Oh, ARE YOU?
YOU REALLY THINK I'M THAT GULLIBLE, DON'T YOU? THAT I SHOWED YOU EVERYTHING YOU WANTED TO SEE, LED YOU RIGHT TO YOUR FRIEND?
BUT I'M OF THE ELITE, YOU MISERABLE FOOLS --

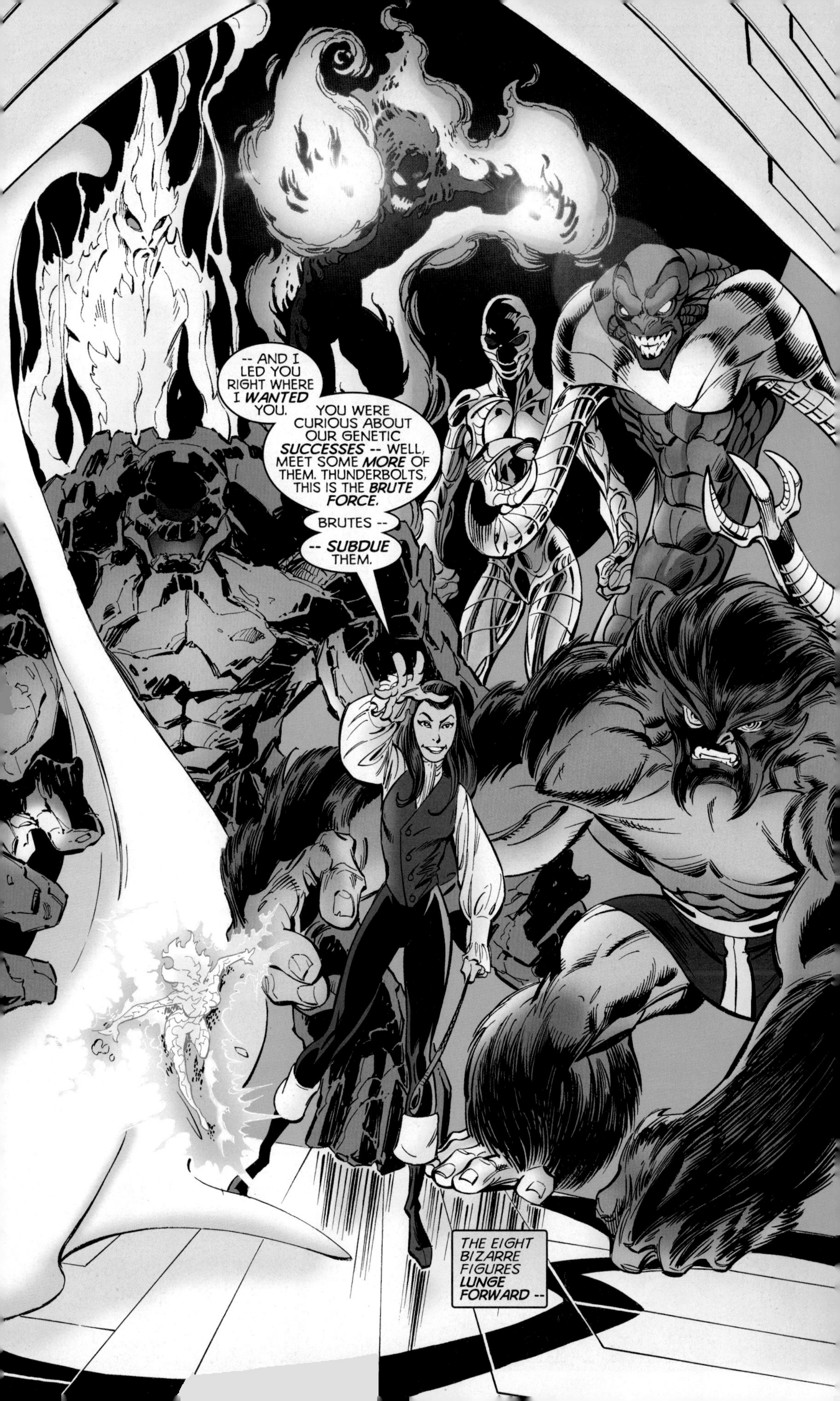
-- AND I LED YOU RIGHT WHERE I WANTED YOU.
YOU WERE CURIOUS ABOUT OUR GENETIC SUCCESSES -- WELL, MEET SOME MORE OF THEM. THUNDERBOLTS, THIS IS THE BRUTE FORCE.
BRUTES --
-- SUBDUE THEM.
THE EIGHT BIZARRE FIGURES LUNGE FORWARD --

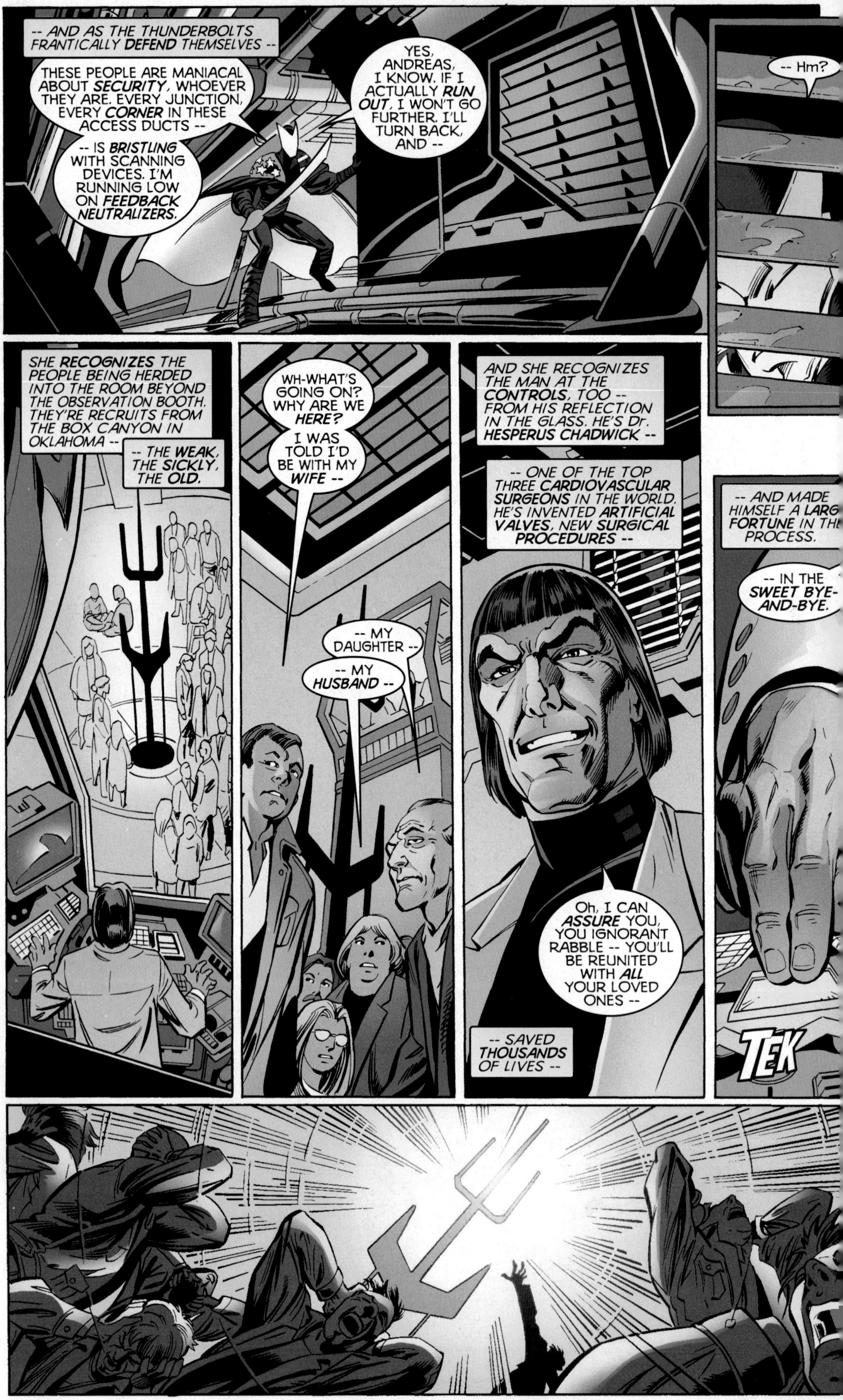

-- AND AS THE THUNDERBOLTS FRANTICALLY DEFEND THEMSELVES --
THESE PEOPLE ARE MANIACAL ABOUT SECURITY, WHOEVER THEY ARE. EVERY JUNCTION, EVERY CORNER IN THESE ACCESS DUCTS --
-- IS BRISTLING WITH SCANNING DEVICES. I'M RUNNING LOW ON FEEDBACK NEUTRALIZERS.
YES, ANDREAS, I KNOW. IF I ACTUALLY RUN OUT, I WON'T GO FURTHER. I'LL TURN BACK, AND --
-- Hm?
SHE RECOGNIZES THE PEOPLE BEING HERDED INTO THE ROOM BEYOND THE OBSERVATION BOOTH. THEY'RE RECRUITS FROM THE BOX CANYON IN OKLAHOMA --
-- THE WEAK, THE SICKLY, THE OLD.
WH-WHAT'S GOING ON? WHY ARE WE HERE?
I WAS TOLD I'D BE WITH MY WIFE --
-- MY DAUGHTER --
-- MY HUSBAND --
AND SHE RECOGNIZES THE MAN AT THE CONTROLS, TOO -- FROM HIS REFLECTION IN THE GLASS. HE'S Dr. HESPERUS CHADWICK --
-- ONE OF THE TOP THREE CARDIOVASCULAR SURGEONS IN THE WORLD. HE'S INVENTED ARTIFICIAL VALVES, NEW SURGICAL PROCEDURES --
Oh, I CAN ASSURE YOU, YOU IGNORANT RABBLE -- YOU'LL BE REUNITED WITH ALL YOUR LOVED ONES --
-- SAVED THOUSANDS OF LIVES --
-- AND MADE HIMSELF A LARG FORTUNE IN THE PROCESS.
-- IN THE SWEET BYE-AND-BYE.
TEK

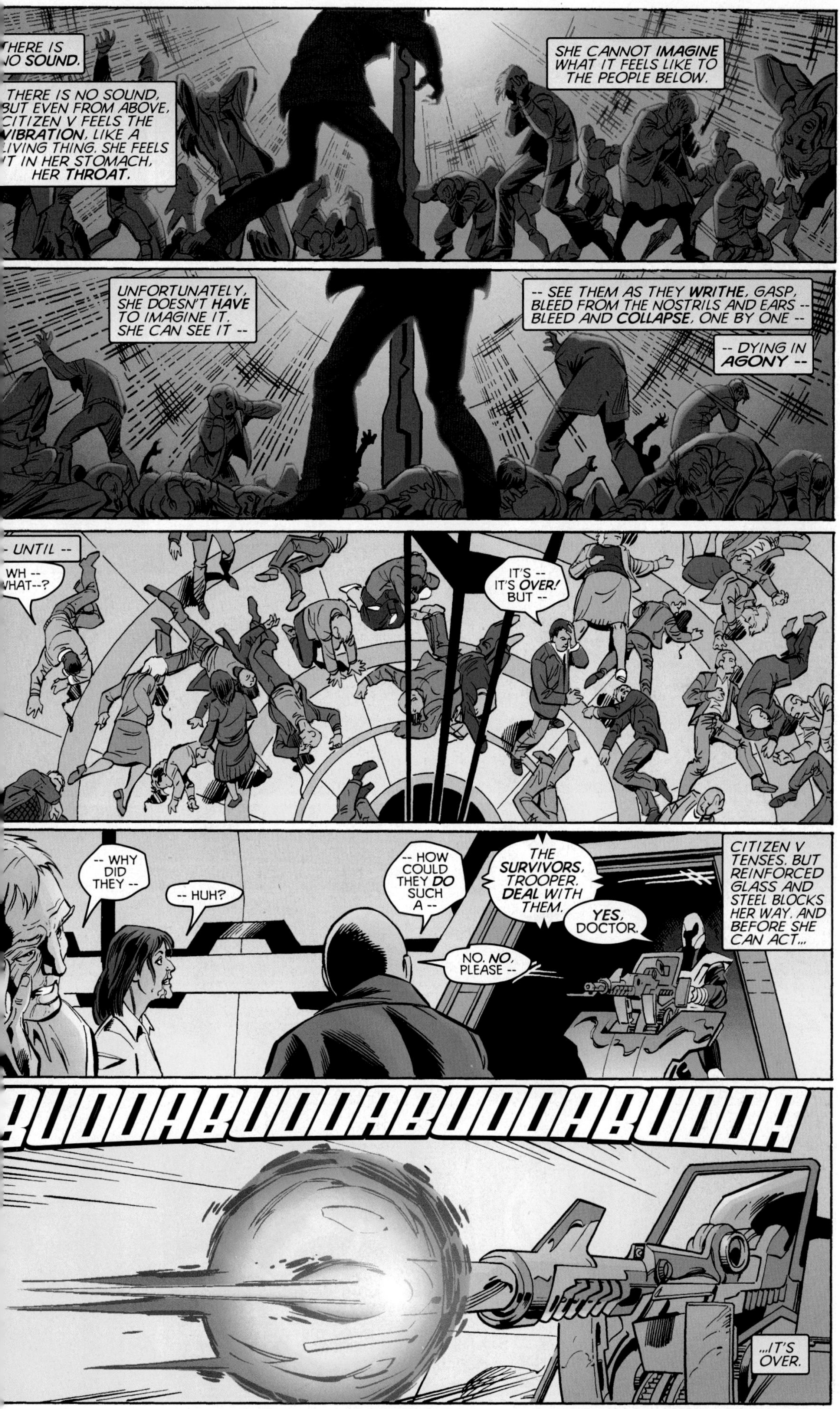
THERE IS NO SOUND.
THERE IS NO SOUND, BUT EVEN FROM ABOVE, CITIZEN V FEELS THE VIBRATION, LIKE A LIVING THING. SHE FEELS IT IN HER STOMACH, HER THROAT.
SHE CANNOT IMAGINE WHAT IT FEELS LIKE TO THE PEOPLE BELOW.
UNFORTUNATELY, SHE DOESN'T HAVE TO IMAGINE IT. SHE CAN SEE IT --
-- SEE THEM AS THEY WRITHE, GASP, BLEED FROM THE NOSTRILS AND EARS -- BLEED AND COLLAPSE, ONE BY ONE --
-- DYING IN AGONY --
-- UNTIL --
WH -- WHAT--?
IT'S -- IT'S OVER! BUT --
-- WHY DID THEY --
-- HUH?
-- HOW COULD THEY DO SUCH A --
THE SURVIVORS, TROOPER. DEAL WITH THEM.
YES, DOCTOR.
CITIZEN V TENSES, BUT REINFORCED GLASS AND STEEL BLOCKS HER WAY. AND BEFORE SHE CAN ACT...
NO. NO, PLEASE --
BUDDABUDDABUDDABUDDA
...IT'S OVER.

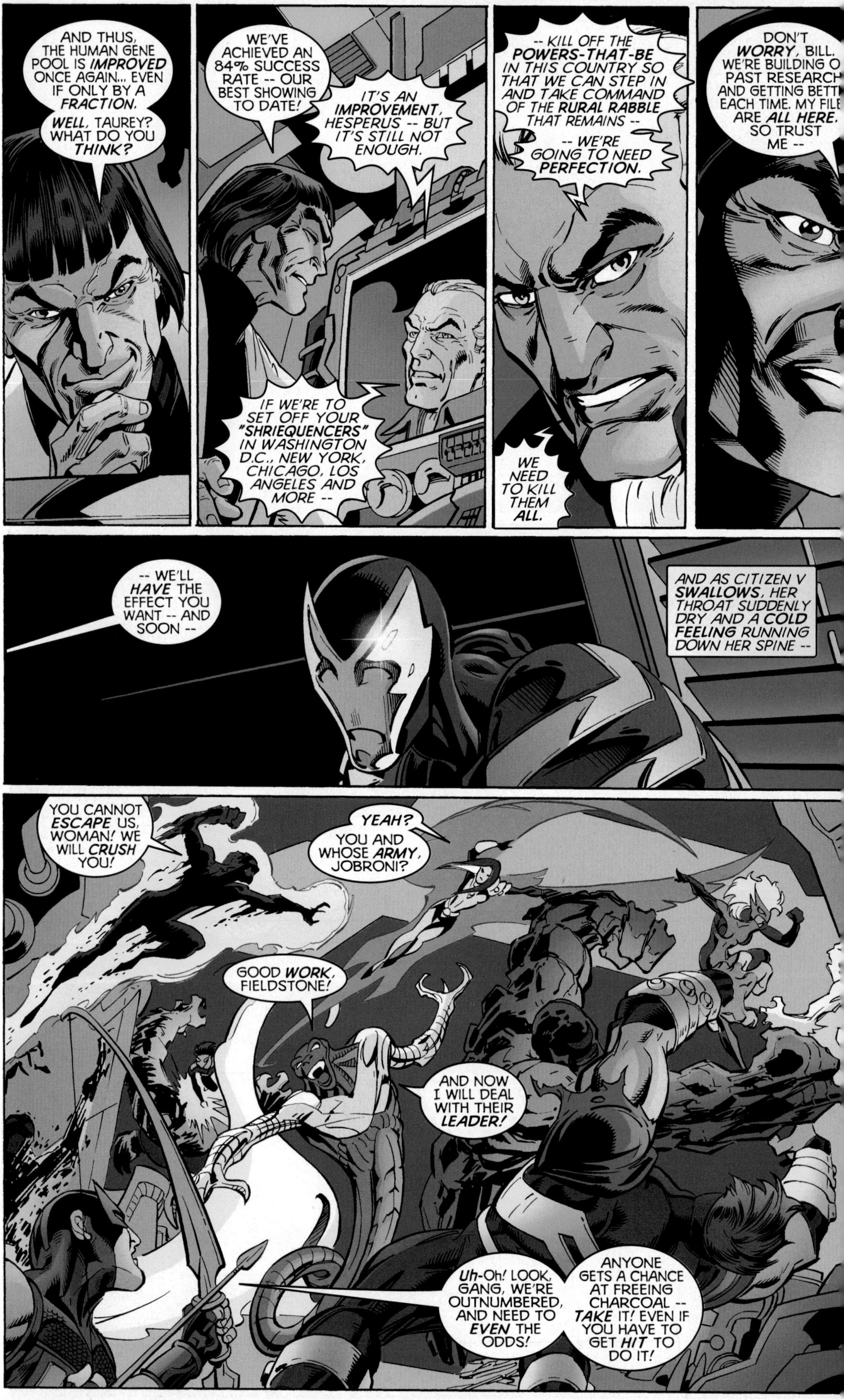
AND THUS, THE HUMAN GENE POOL IS IMPROVED ONCE AGAIN... EVEN IF ONLY BY A FRACTION.
WELL, TAUREY? WHAT DO YOU THINK?
WE'VE ACHIEVED AN 84% SUCCESS RATE -- OUR BEST SHOWING TO DATE!
IT'S AN IMPROVEMENT, HESPERUS -- BUT IT'S STILL NOT ENOUGH.
IF WE'RE TO SET OFF YOUR "SHRIEQUENCERS" IN WASHINGTON D.C., NEW YORK, CHICAGO, LOS ANGELES AND MORE --
-- KILL OFF THE POWERS-THAT-BE IN THIS COUNTRY SO THAT WE CAN STEP IN AND TAKE COMMAND OF THE RURAL RABBLE THAT REMAINS --
-- WE'RE GOING TO NEED PERFECTION.
WE NEED TO KILL THEM ALL.
DON'T WORRY, BILL. WE'RE BUILDING O PAST RESEARCH AND GETTING BETT EACH TIME. MY FILE ARE ALL HERE. SO TRUST ME --
-- WE'LL HAVE THE EFFECT YOU WANT -- AND SOON --
AND AS CITIZEN V SWALLOWS, HER THROAT SUDDENLY DRY AND A COLD FEELING RUNNING DOWN HER SPINE --
YOU CANNOT ESCAPE US, WOMAN! WE WILL CRUSH YOU!
YEAH? YOU AND WHOSE ARMY, JOBRONI?
GOOD WORK, FIELDSTONE!
AND NOW I WILL DEAL WITH THEIR LEADER!
Uh-Oh! LOOK, GANG, WE'RE OUTNUMBERED, AND NEED TO EVEN THE ODDS!
ANYONE GETS A CHANCE AT FREEING CHARCOAL -- TAKE IT! EVEN IF YOU HAVE TO GET HIT TO DO IT!

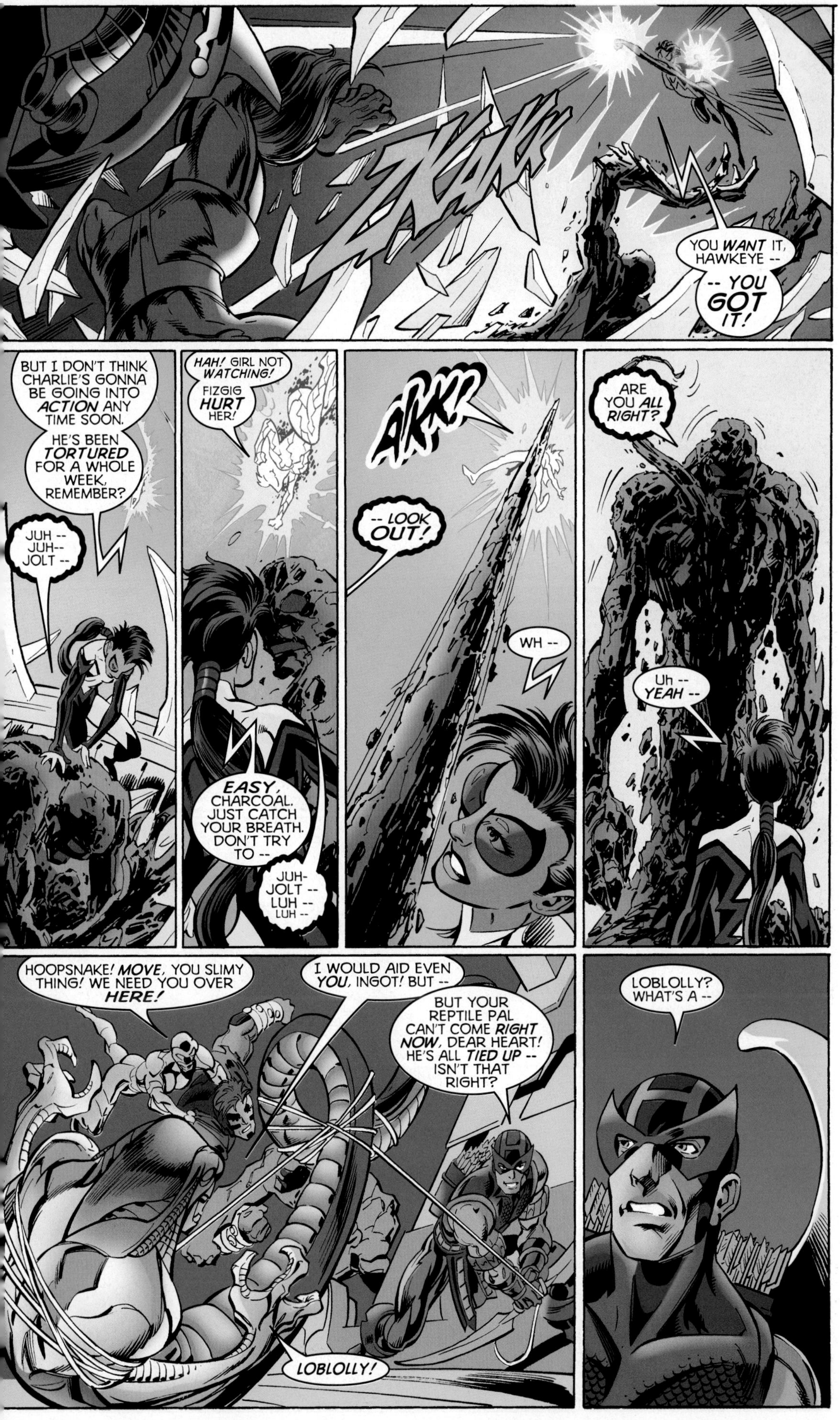

ZAKK!
YOU WANT IT, HAWKEYE --
-- YOU GOT IT!
BUT I DON'T THINK CHARLIE'S GONNA BE GOING INTO ACTION ANY TIME SOON.
HE'S BEEN TORTURED FOR A WHOLE WEEK, REMEMBER?
JUH -- JUH-- JOLT --
HAH! GIRL NOT WATCHING! FIZGIG HURT HER!
EASY, CHARCOAL. JUST CATCH YOUR BREATH. DON'T TRY TO --
JUH- JOLT -- LUH -- LUH --
AKK!
-- LOOK OUT!
WH --
ARE YOU ALL RIGHT?
Uh -- YEAH --
HOOPSNAKE! MOVE, YOU SLIMY THING! WE NEED YOU OVER HERE!
I WOULD AID EVEN YOU, INGOT! BUT --
BUT YOUR REPTILE PAL CAN'T COME RIGHT NOW, DEAR HEART! HE'S ALL TIED UP -- ISN'T THAT RIGHT?
LOBLOLLY!
LOBLOLLY? WHAT'S A --

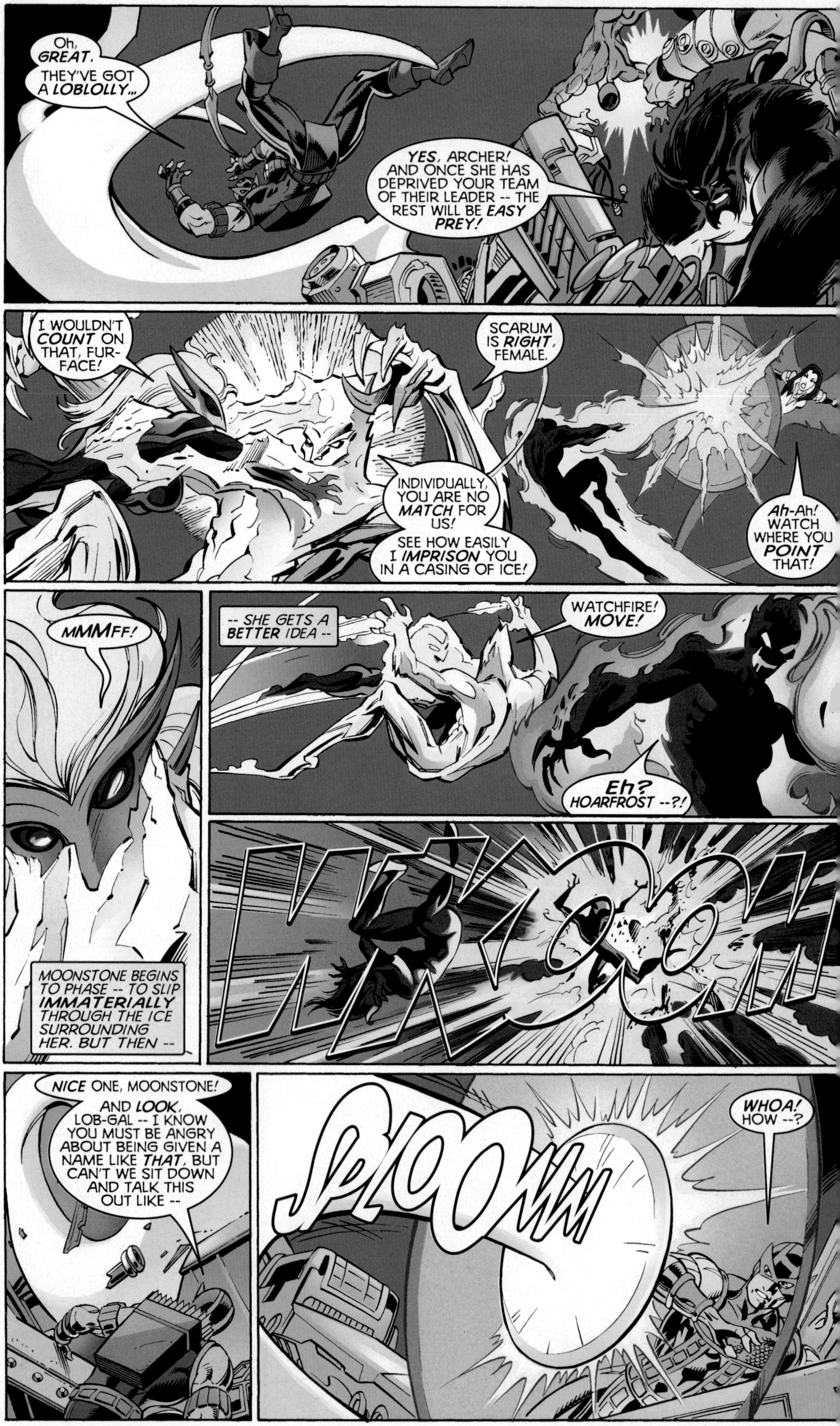
Oh, GREAT. THEY'VE GOT A LOBLOLLY...
YES, ARCHER! AND ONCE SHE HAS DEPRIVED YOUR TEAM OF THEIR LEADER -- THE REST WILL BE EASY PREY!
I WOULDN'T COUNT ON THAT, FUR-FACE!
SCARUM IS RIGHT, FEMALE.
INDIVIDUALLY, YOU ARE NO MATCH FOR US!
SEE HOW EASILY I IMPRISON YOU IN A CASING OF ICE!
Ah-Ah! WATCH WHERE YOU POINT THAT!
MMMFF!
MOONSTONE BEGINS TO PHASE -- TO SLIP IMMATERIALLY THROUGH THE ICE SURROUNDING HER. BUT THEN --
-- SHE GETS A BETTER IDEA --
WATCHFIRE! MOVE!
Eh? HOARFROST --?!
NICE ONE, MOONSTONE!
AND LOOK, LOB-GAL -- I KNOW YOU MUST BE ANGRY ABOUT BEING GIVEN A NAME LIKE THAT, BUT CAN'T WE SIT DOWN AND TALK THIS OUT LIKE --
WHOA! HOW --?

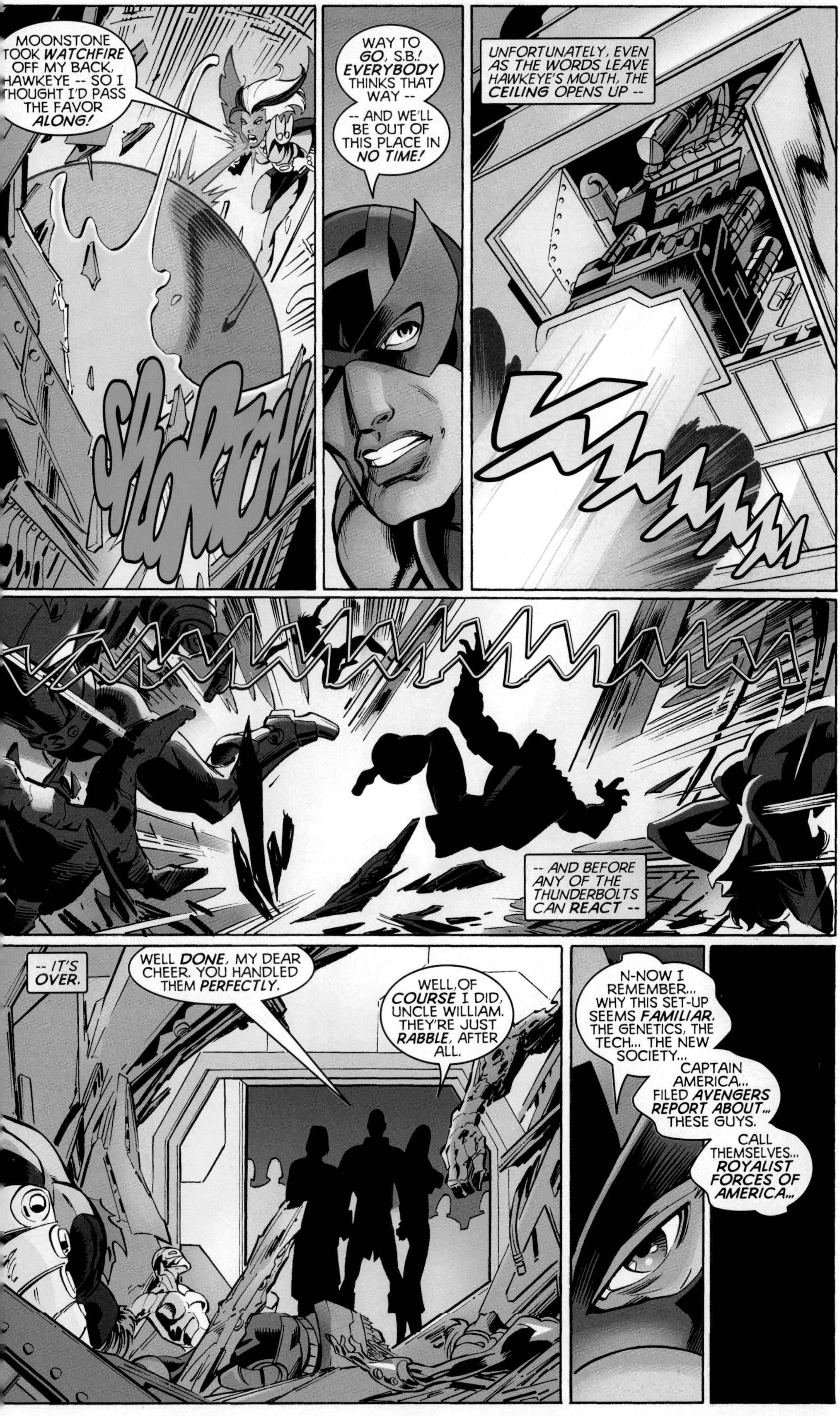
MOONSTONE TOOK WATCHFIRE OFF MY BACK, HAWKEYE -- SO I THOUGHT I'D PASS THE FAVOR ALONG!
SHKRTCH
WAY TO GO, S.B.! EVERYBODY THINKS THAT WAY --
-- AND WE'LL BE OUT OF THIS PLACE IN NO TIME!
UNFORTUNATELY, EVEN AS THE WORDS LEAVE HAWKEYE'S MOUTH, THE CEILING OPENS UP --
-- AND BEFORE ANY OF THE THUNDERBOLTS CAN REACT --
-- IT'S OVER.
WELL DONE, MY DEAR CHEER. YOU HANDLED THEM PERFECTLY.
WELL, OF COURSE I DID, UNCLE WILLIAM. THEY'RE JUST RABBLE, AFTER ALL.
N-NOW I REMEMBER... WHY THIS SET-UP SEEMS FAMILIAR. THE GENETICS, THE TECH... THE NEW SOCIETY...
CAPTAIN AMERICA... FILED AVENGERS REPORT ABOUT... THESE GUYS.
CALL THEMSELVES... ROYALIST FORCES OF AMERICA...

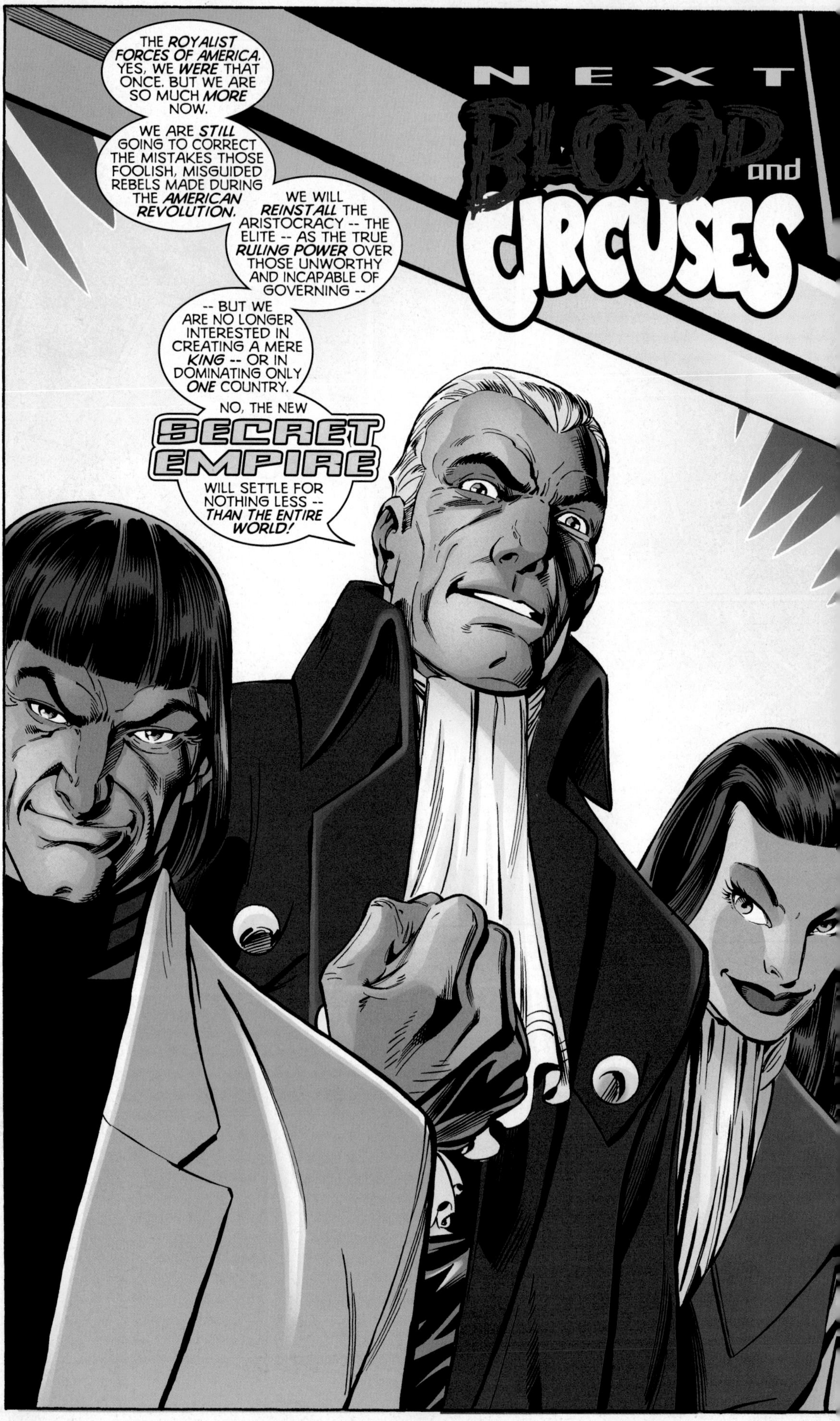
NEXT
BLOOD and CIRCUSES
THE ROYALIST FORCES OF AMERICA. YES, WE WERE THAT ONCE. BUT WE ARE SO MUCH MORE NOW.
WE ARE STILL GOING TO CORRECT THE MISTAKES THOSE FOOLISH, MISGUIDED REBELS MADE DURING THE AMERICAN REVOLUTION.
WE WILL REINSTALL THE ARISTOCRACY -- THE ELITE -- AS THE TRUE RULING POWER OVER THOSE UNWORTHY AND INCAPABLE OF GOVERNING --
-- BUT WE ARE NO LONGER INTERESTED IN CREATING A MERE KING -- OR IN DOMINATING ONLY ONE COUNTRY.
NO, THE NEW SECRET EMPIRE WILL SETTLE FOR NOTHING LESS -- THAN THE ENTIRE WORLD!

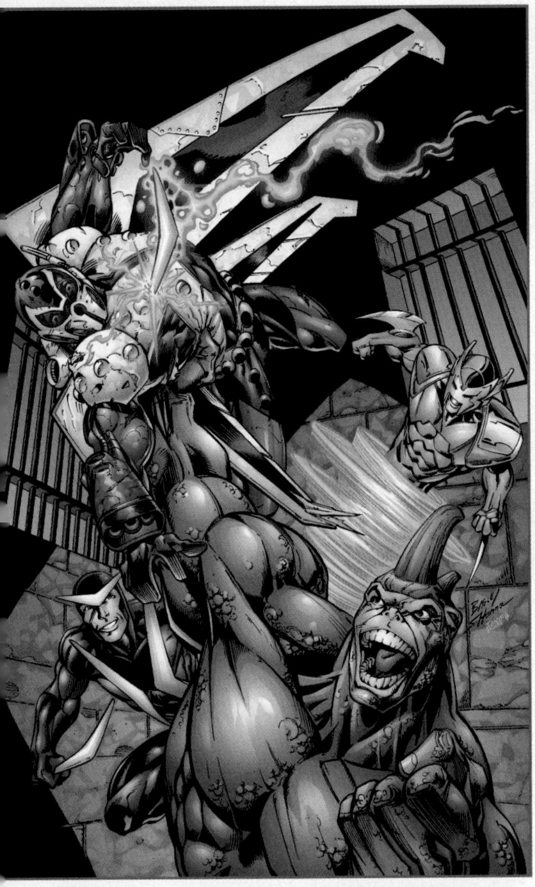
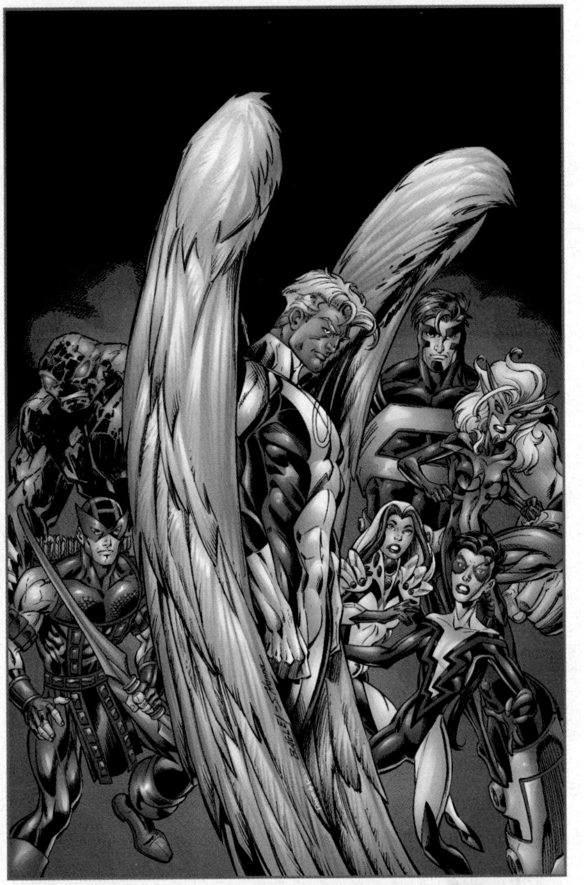
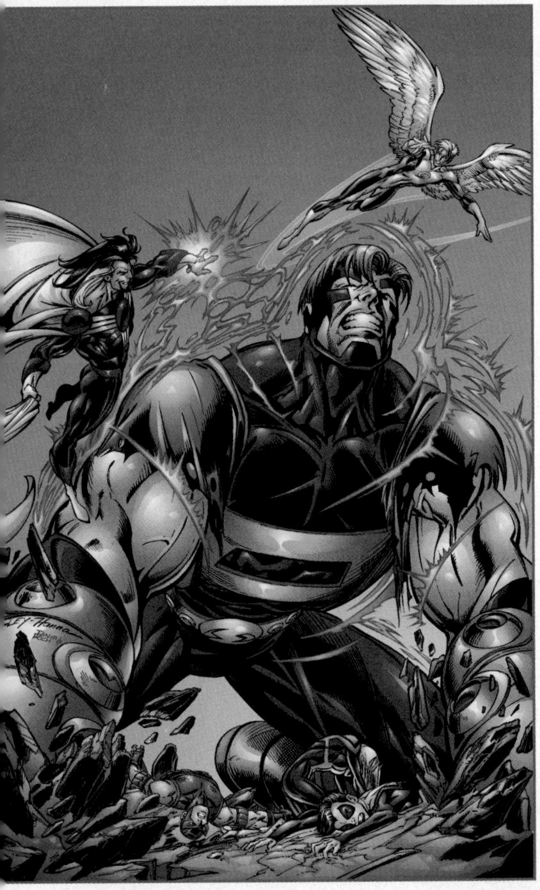
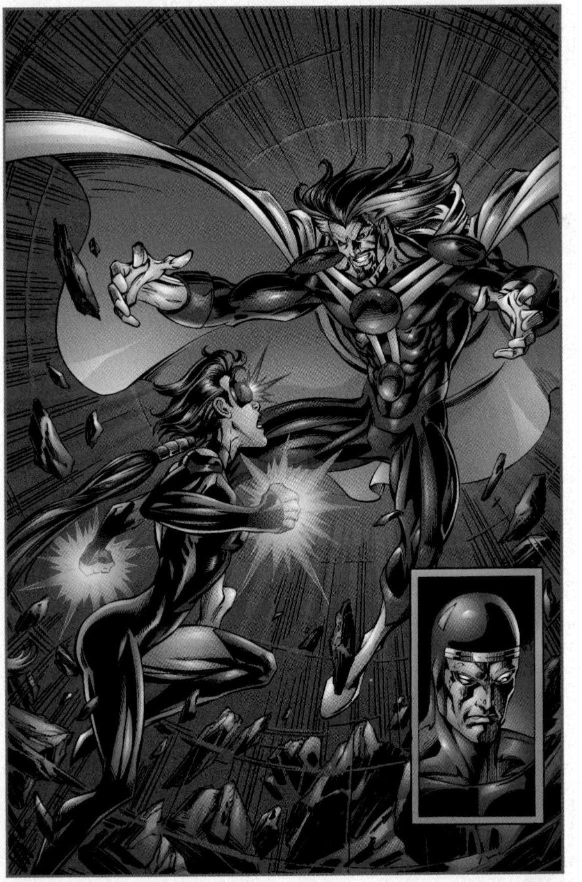

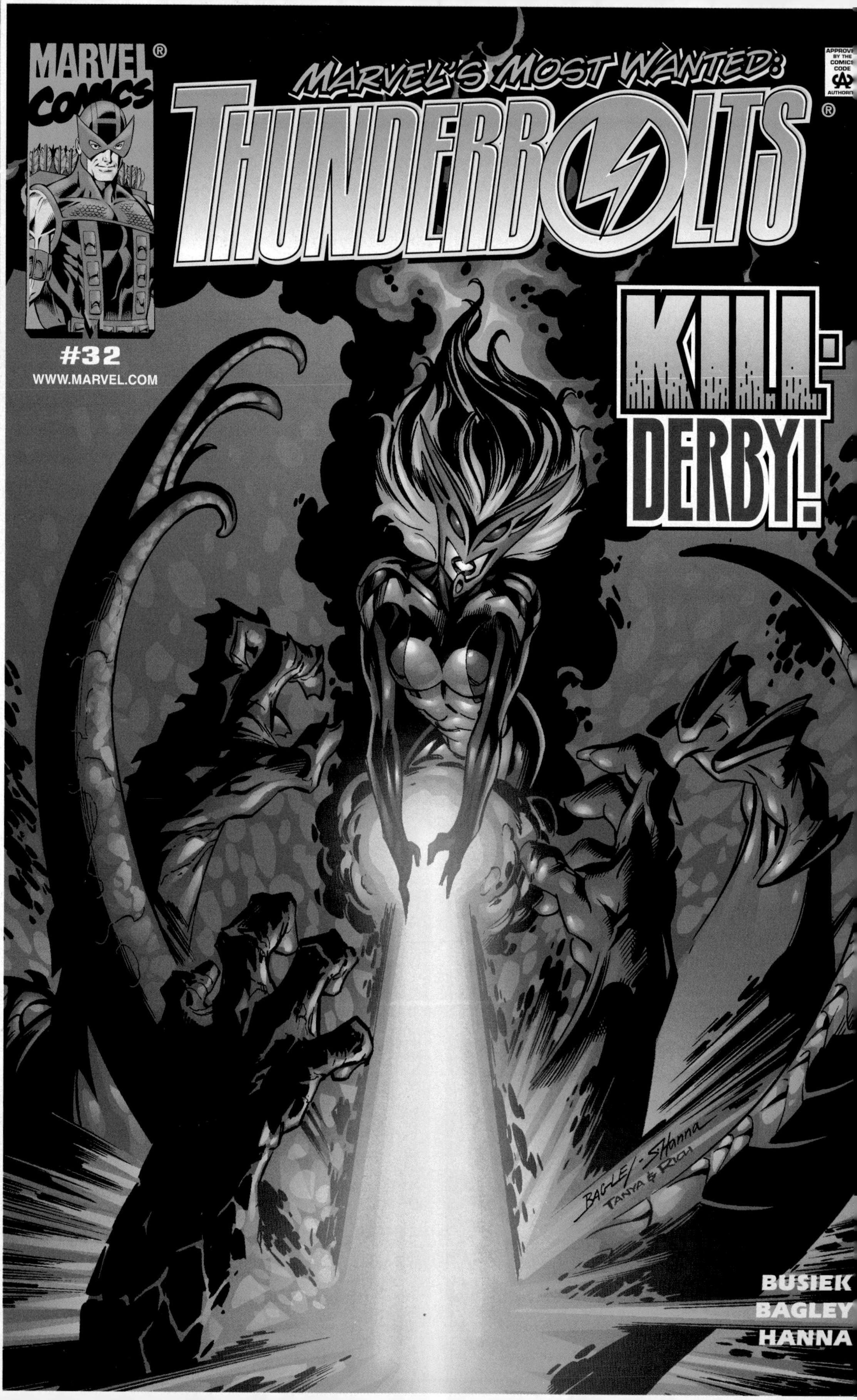
MARVEL COMICS
MARVEL'S MOST WANTED:
THUNDERBOLTS
#32
WWW.MARVEL.COM
KILL-DERBY!
BAGLEY-HANNA
TANYA & RICH
BUSIEK
BAGLEY
HANNA

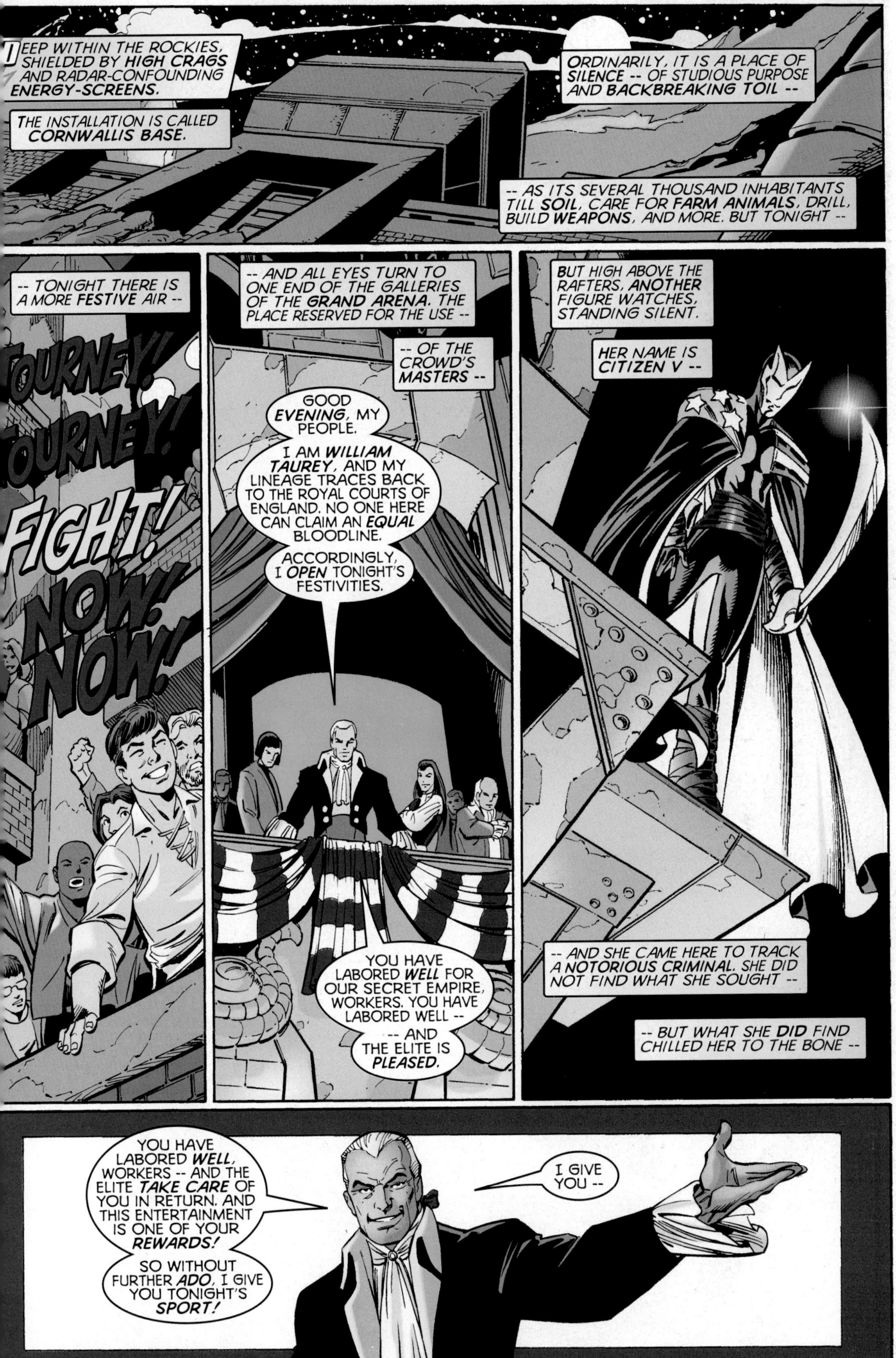
DEEP WITHIN THE ROCKIES, SHIELDED BY HIGH CRAGS AND RADAR-CONFOUNDING ENERGY-SCREENS.
THE INSTALLATION IS CALLED CORNWALLIS BASE.
ORDINARILY, IT IS A PLACE OF SILENCE -- OF STUDIOUS PURPOSE AND BACKBREAKING TOIL --
-- AS ITS SEVERAL THOUSAND INHABITANTS TILL SOIL, CARE FOR FARM ANIMALS, DRILL, BUILD WEAPONS, AND MORE. BUT TONIGHT --
-- TONIGHT THERE IS A MORE FESTIVE AIR --
TOURNEY! TOURNEY!
FIGHT! NOW! NOW!
-- AND ALL EYES TURN TO ONE END OF THE GALLERIES OF THE GRAND ARENA. THE PLACE RESERVED FOR THE USE --
-- OF THE CROWD'S MASTERS --
GOOD EVENING, MY PEOPLE.
I AM WILLIAM TAUREY, AND MY LINEAGE TRACES BACK TO THE ROYAL COURTS OF ENGLAND. NO ONE HERE CAN CLAIM AN EQUAL BLOODLINE.
ACCORDINGLY, I OPEN TONIGHT'S FESTIVITIES.
YOU HAVE LABORED WELL FOR OUR SECRET EMPIRE, WORKERS. YOU HAVE LABORED WELL --
-- AND THE ELITE IS PLEASED.
BUT HIGH ABOVE THE RAFTERS, ANOTHER FIGURE WATCHES, STANDING SILENT.
HER NAME IS CITIZEN V --
-- AND SHE CAME HERE TO TRACK A NOTORIOUS CRIMINAL. SHE DID NOT FIND WHAT SHE SOUGHT --
-- BUT WHAT SHE DID FIND CHILLED HER TO THE BONE --
YOU HAVE LABORED WELL, WORKERS -- AND THE ELITE TAKE CARE OF YOU IN RETURN. AND THIS ENTERTAINMENT IS ONE OF YOUR REWARDS!
SO WITHOUT FURTHER ADO, I GIVE YOU TONIGHT'S SPORT!
I GIVE YOU --

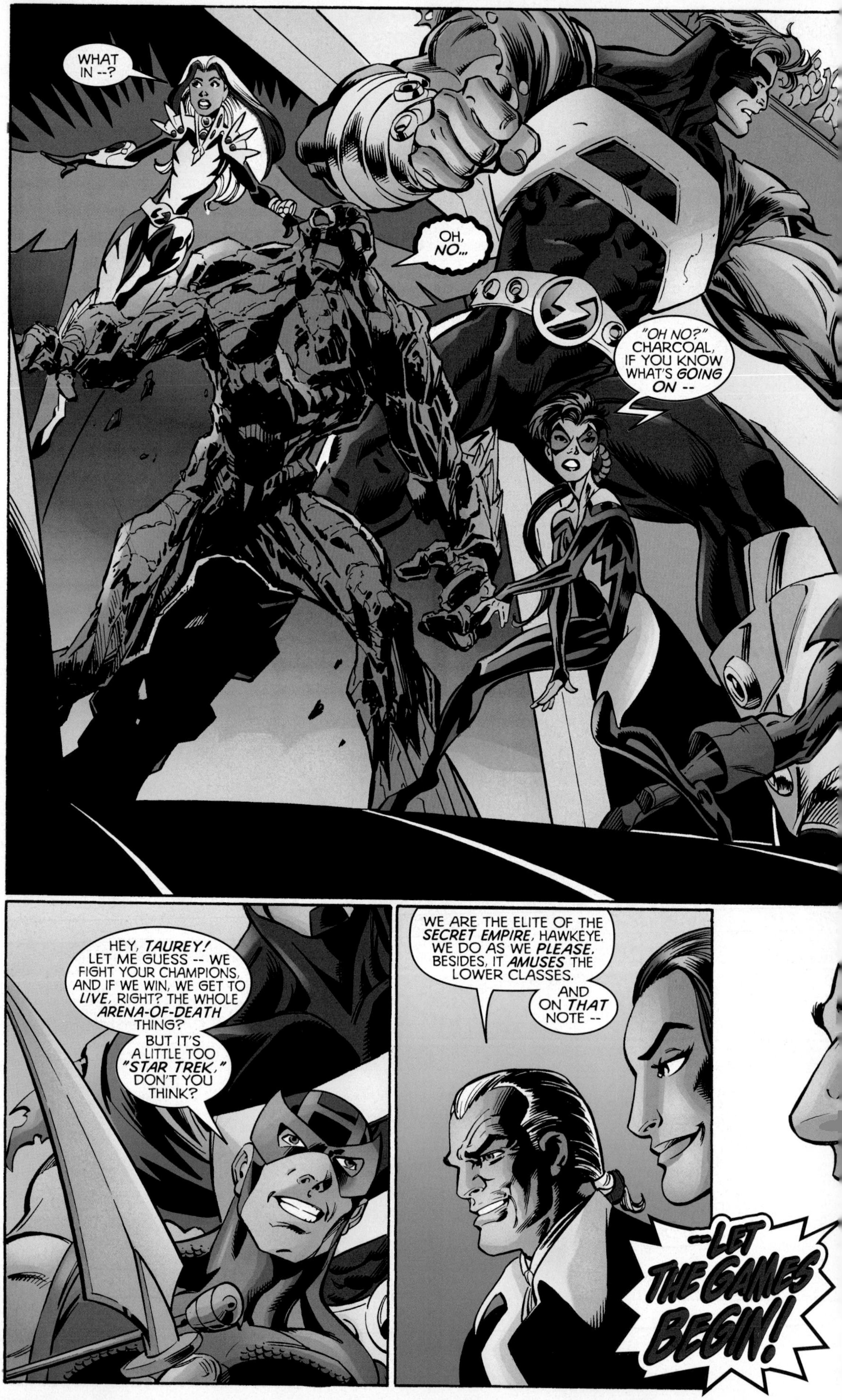
WHAT IN --?
OH, NO...
"OH NO?" CHARCOAL, IF YOU KNOW WHAT'S GOING ON --
HEY, TAUREY! LET ME GUESS -- WE FIGHT YOUR CHAMPIONS, AND IF WE WIN, WE GET TO LIVE, RIGHT? THE WHOLE ARENA-OF-DEATH THING?
BUT IT'S A LITTLE TOO "STAR TREK," DON'T YOU THINK?
WE ARE THE ELITE OF THE SECRET EMPIRE, HAWKEYE. WE DO AS WE PLEASE. BESIDES, IT AMUSES THE LOWER CLASSES.
AND ON THAT NOTE --
--LET THE GAMES BEGIN!

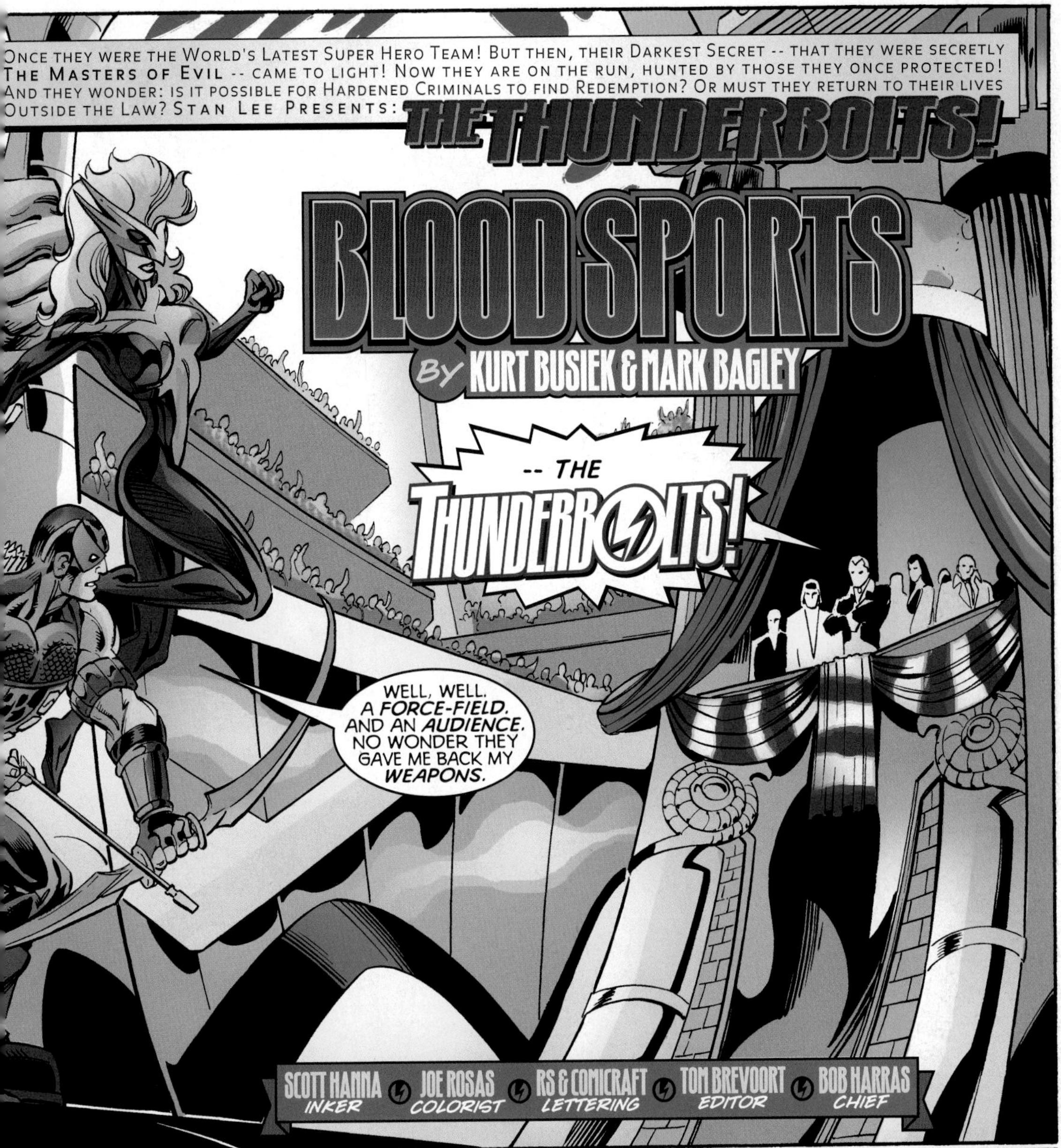

Once they were the World's Latest Super Hero Team! But then, their Darkest Secret -- that they were secretly The Masters of Evil -- came to light! Now they are on the run, hunted by those they once protected! And they wonder: is it possible for Hardened Criminals to find Redemption? Or must they return to their lives Outside the Law? Stan Lee Presents: THE THUNDERBOLTS!
BLOOD SPORTS
By KURT BUSIEK & MARK BAGLEY
-- THE THUNDERBOLTS!
WELL, WELL. A FORCE-FIELD. AND AN AUDIENCE. NO WONDER THEY GAVE ME BACK MY WEAPONS.
SCOTT HANNA INKER
JOE ROSAS COLORIST
RS & COMICRAFT LETTERING
TOM BREVOORT EDITOR
BOB HARRAS CHIEF

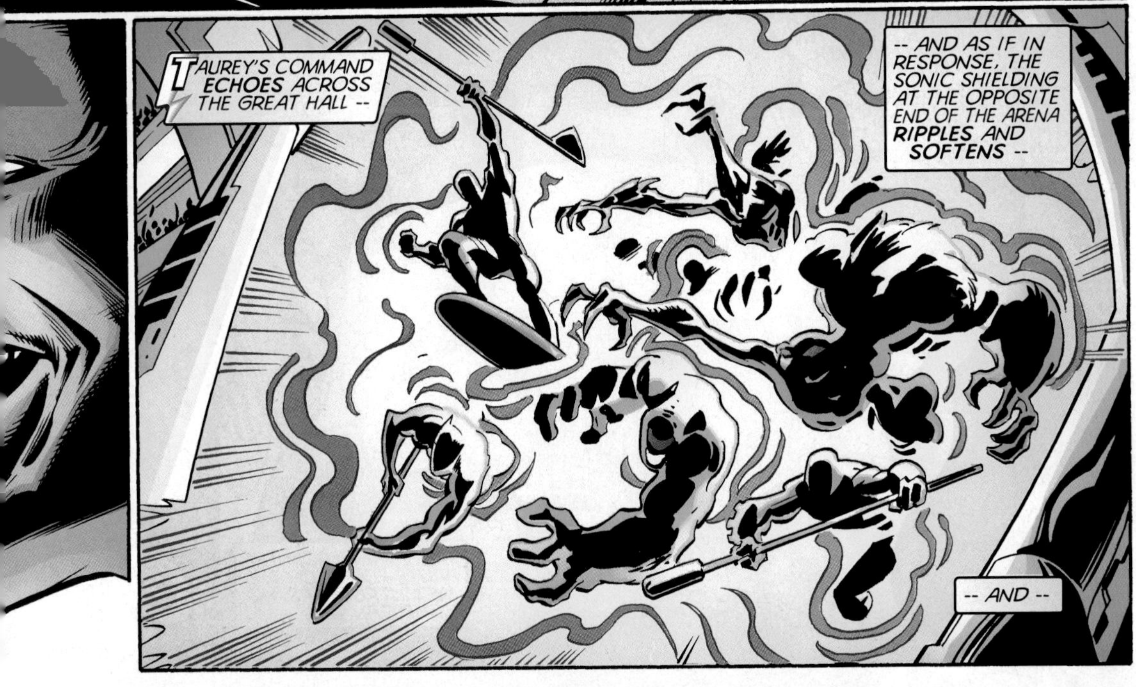

TAUREY'S COMMAND ECHOES ACROSS THE GREAT HALL --
-- AND AS IF IN RESPONSE, THE SONIC SHIELDING AT THE OPPOSITE END OF THE ARENA RIPPLES AND SOFTENS --
-- AND --

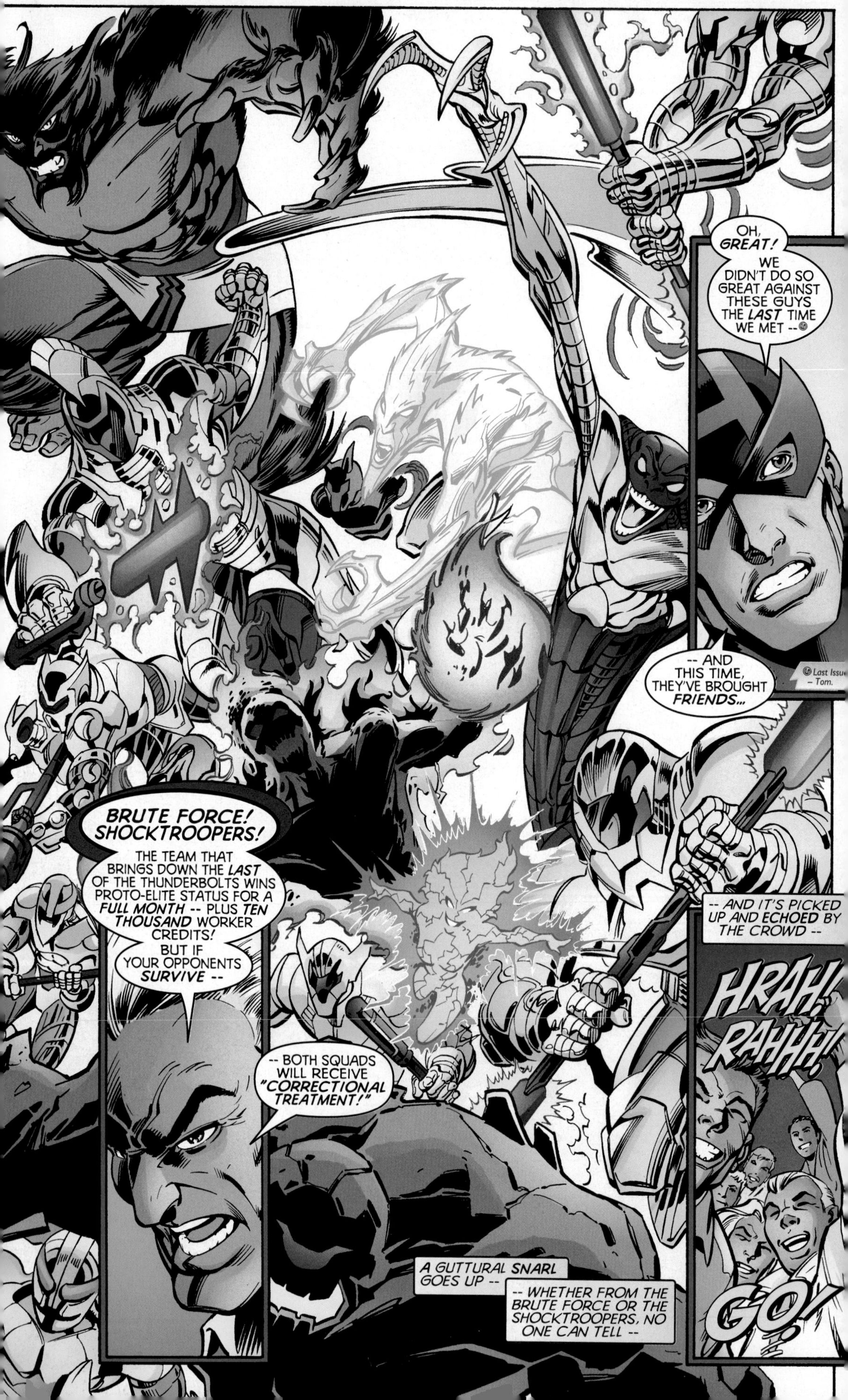
OH, GREAT! WE DIDN'T DO SO GREAT AGAINST THESE GUYS THE LAST TIME WE MET --
-- AND THIS TIME, THEY'VE BROUGHT FRIENDS...
Last Issue – Tom.
BRUTE FORCE! SHOCKTROOPERS!
THE TEAM THAT BRINGS DOWN THE LAST OF THE THUNDERBOLTS WINS PROTO-ELITE STATUS FOR A FULL MONTH -- PLUS TEN THOUSAND WORKER CREDITS! BUT IF YOUR OPPONENTS SURVIVE --
-- BOTH SQUADS WILL RECEIVE "CORRECTIONAL TREATMENT!"
A GUTTURAL SNARL GOES UP --
-- WHETHER FROM THE BRUTE FORCE OR THE SHOCKTROOPERS, NO ONE CAN TELL --
-- AND IT'S PICKED UP AND ECHOED BY THE CROWD --
HRAH! RAHH!
GO!

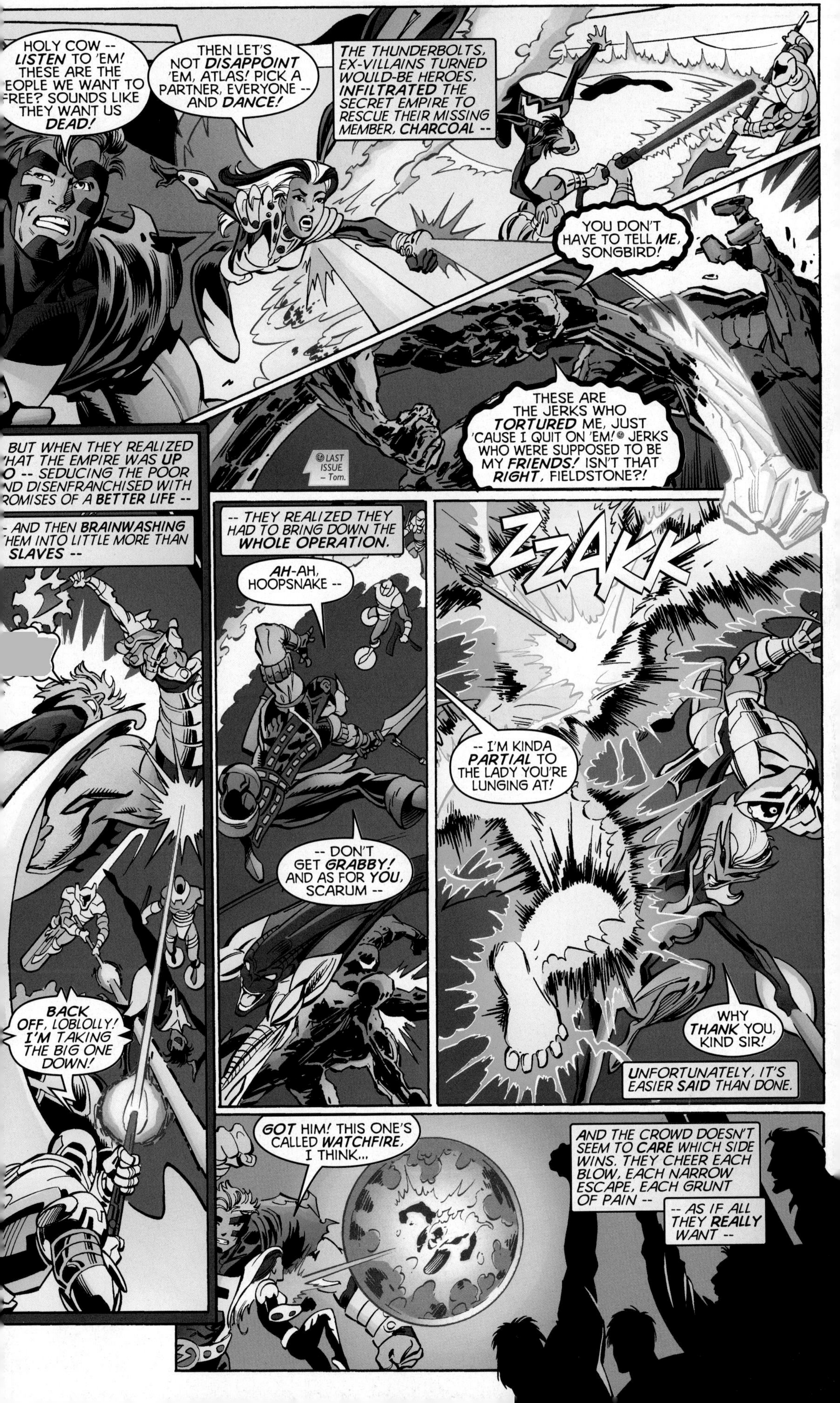
HOLY COW -- LISTEN TO 'EM! THESE ARE THE EOPLE WE WANT TO FREE? SOUNDS LIKE THEY WANT US DEAD!
THEN LET'S NOT DISAPPOINT 'EM, ATLAS! PICK A PARTNER, EVERYONE -- AND DANCE!
THE THUNDERBOLTS, EX-VILLAINS TURNED WOULD-BE HEROES, INFILTRATED THE SECRET EMPIRE TO RESCUE THEIR MISSING MEMBER, CHARCOAL --
YOU DON'T HAVE TO TELL ME, SONGBIRD!
THESE ARE THE JERKS WHO TORTURED ME, JUST 'CAUSE I QUIT ON 'EM! JERKS WHO WERE SUPPOSED TO BE MY FRIENDS! ISN'T THAT RIGHT, FIELDSTONE?!
LAST ISSUE -- Tom.
BUT WHEN THEY REALIZED HAT THE EMPIRE WAS UP O -- SEDUCING THE POOR ND DISENFRANCHISED WITH ROMISES OF A BETTER LIFE --
-- AND THEN BRAINWASHING THEM INTO LITTLE MORE THAN SLAVES --
BACK OFF, LOBLOLLY! I'M TAKING THE BIG ONE DOWN!
-- THEY REALIZED THEY HAD TO BRING DOWN THE WHOLE OPERATION.
AH-AH, HOOPSNAKE --
-- DON'T GET GRABBY! AND AS FOR YOU, SCARUM --
ZZAKK
-- I'M KINDA PARTIAL TO THE LADY YOU'RE LUNGING AT!
WHY THANK YOU, KIND SIR!
UNFORTUNATELY, IT'S EASIER SAID THAN DONE.
GOT HIM! THIS ONE'S CALLED WATCHFIRE, I THINK...
AND THE CROWD DOESN'T SEEM TO CARE WHICH SIDE WINS. THEY CHEER EACH BLOW, EACH NARROW ESCAPE, EACH GRUNT OF PAIN --
-- AS IF ALL THEY REALLY WANT --

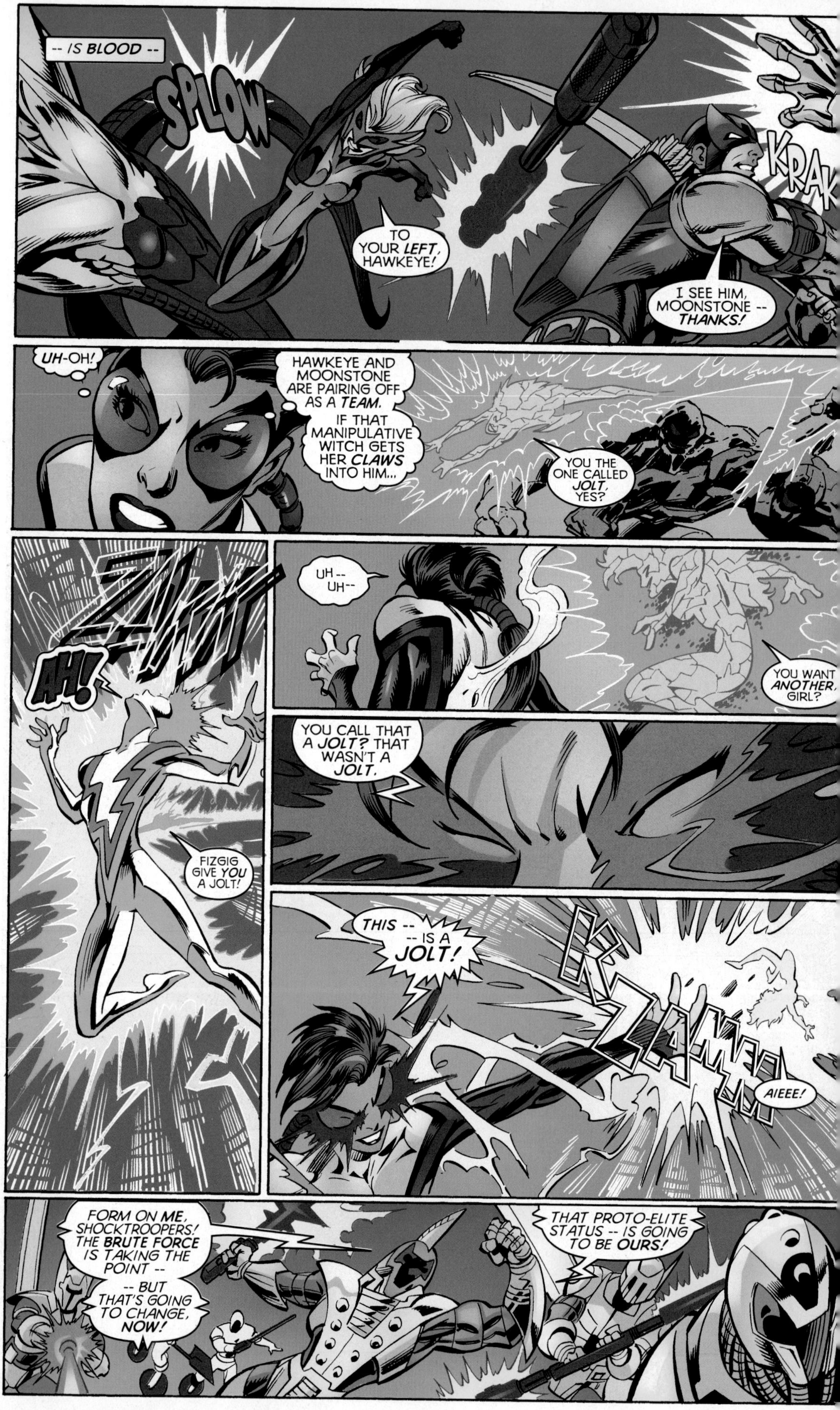

-- IS BLOOD --
SPLOW
TO YOUR LEFT, HAWKEYE!
KRAK
I SEE HIM, MOONSTONE -- THANKS!
UH-OH!
HAWKEYE AND MOONSTONE ARE PAIRING OFF AS A TEAM.
IF THAT MANIPULATIVE WITCH GETS HER CLAWS INTO HIM...
YOU THE ONE CALLED JOLT, YES?
ZAKT
AH!
FIZGIG GIVE YOU A JOLT!
UH -- UH--
YOU WANT ANOTHER, GIRL?
YOU CALL THAT A JOLT? THAT WASN'T A JOLT.
THIS --
-- IS A JOLT!
KRZAMM
AIEEE!
FORM ON ME, SHOCKTROOPERS! THE BRUTE FORCE IS TAKING THE POINT --
-- BUT THAT'S GOING TO CHANGE, NOW!
THAT PROTO-ELITE STATUS -- IS GOING TO BE OURS!

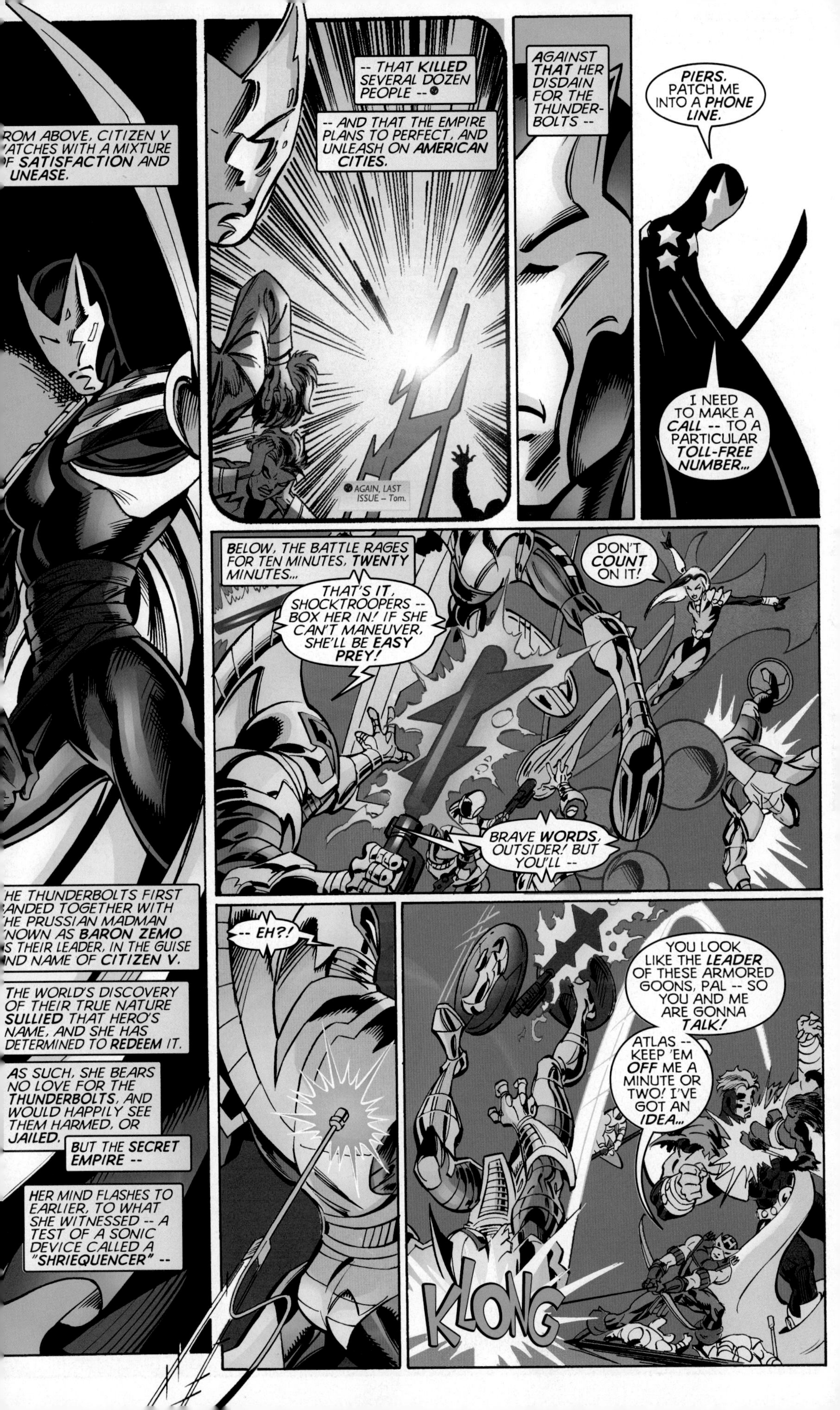
ROM ABOVE, CITIZEN V WATCHES WITH A MIXTURE OF SATISFACTION AND UNEASE.
HE THUNDERBOLTS FIRST BANDED TOGETHER WITH THE PRUSSIAN MADMAN KNOWN AS BARON ZEMO S THEIR LEADER, IN THE GUISE ND NAME OF CITIZEN V.
THE WORLD'S DISCOVERY OF THEIR TRUE NATURE SULLIED THAT HERO'S NAME, AND SHE HAS DETERMINED TO REDEEM IT.
AS SUCH, SHE BEARS NO LOVE FOR THE THUNDERBOLTS, AND WOULD HAPPILY SEE THEM HARMED, OR JAILED.
BUT THE SECRET EMPIRE --
HER MIND FLASHES TO EARLIER, TO WHAT SHE WITNESSED -- A TEST OF A SONIC DEVICE CALLED A "SHRIEQUENCER" --
-- THAT KILLED SEVERAL DOZEN PEOPLE --
-- AND THAT THE EMPIRE PLANS TO PERFECT, AND UNLEASH ON AMERICAN CITIES.
AGAIN, LAST ISSUE – Tom.
AGAINST THAT HER DISDAIN FOR THE THUNDERBOLTS --
PIERS. PATCH ME INTO A PHONE LINE.
I NEED TO MAKE A CALL -- TO A PARTICULAR TOLL-FREE NUMBER...
BELOW, THE BATTLE RAGES FOR TEN MINUTES, TWENTY MINUTES...
THAT'S IT, SHOCKTROOPERS -- BOX HER IN! IF SHE CAN'T MANEUVER, SHE'LL BE EASY PREY!
DON'T COUNT ON IT!
BRAVE WORDS, OUTSIDER! BUT YOU'LL --
-- EH?!
YOU LOOK LIKE THE LEADER OF THESE ARMORED GOONS, PAL -- SO YOU AND ME ARE GONNA TALK!
ATLAS -- KEEP 'EM OFF ME A MINUTE OR TWO! I'VE GOT AN IDEA...
KLONG

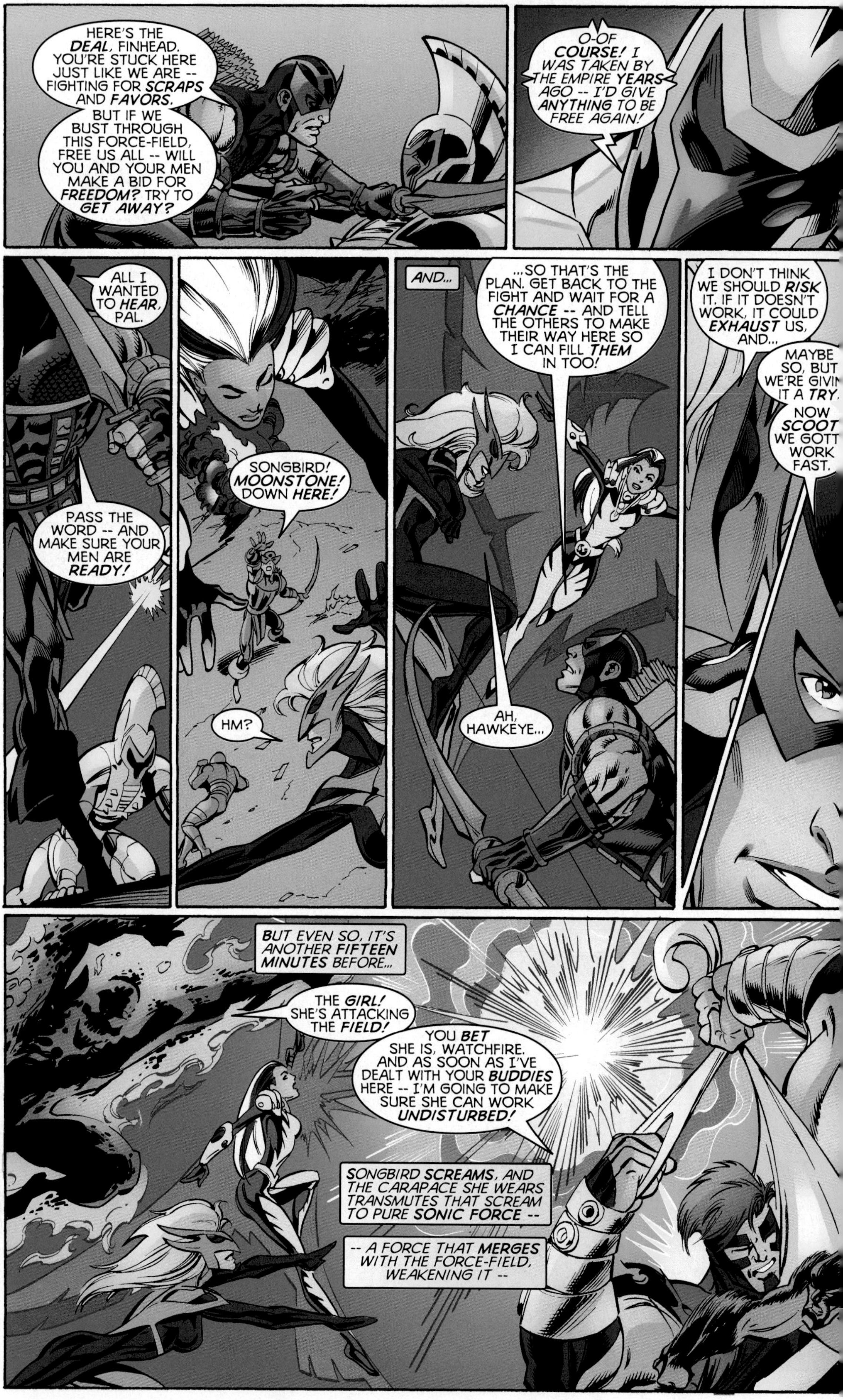
HERE'S THE DEAL, FINHEAD. YOU'RE STUCK HERE JUST LIKE WE ARE -- FIGHTING FOR SCRAPS AND FAVORS.
BUT IF WE BUST THROUGH THIS FORCE-FIELD, FREE US ALL -- WILL YOU AND YOUR MEN MAKE A BID FOR FREEDOM? TRY TO GET AWAY?
O-OF COURSE! I WAS TAKEN BY THE EMPIRE YEARS AGO -- I'D GIVE ANYTHING TO BE FREE AGAIN!
ALL I WANTED TO HEAR, PAL.
PASS THE WORD -- AND MAKE SURE YOUR MEN ARE READY!
SONGBIRD! MOONSTONE! DOWN HERE!
HM?
AND...
...SO THAT'S THE PLAN. GET BACK TO THE FIGHT AND WAIT FOR A CHANCE -- AND TELL THE OTHERS TO MAKE THEIR WAY HERE SO I CAN FILL THEM IN TOO!
AH, HAWKEYE...
I DON'T THINK WE SHOULD RISK IT. IF IT DOESN'T WORK, IT COULD EXHAUST US, AND...
MAYBE SO, BUT WE'RE GIVIN IT A TRY.
NOW SCOOT WE GOTT WORK FAST.
BUT EVEN SO, IT'S ANOTHER FIFTEEN MINUTES BEFORE...
THE GIRL! SHE'S ATTACKING THE FIELD!
YOU BET SHE IS, WATCHFIRE. AND AS SOON AS I'VE DEALT WITH YOUR BUDDIES HERE -- I'M GOING TO MAKE SURE SHE CAN WORK UNDISTURBED!
SONGBIRD SCREAMS, AND THE CARAPACE SHE WEARS TRANSMUTES THAT SCREAM TO PURE SONIC FORCE --
-- A FORCE THAT MERGES WITH THE FORCE-FIELD, WEAKENING IT --

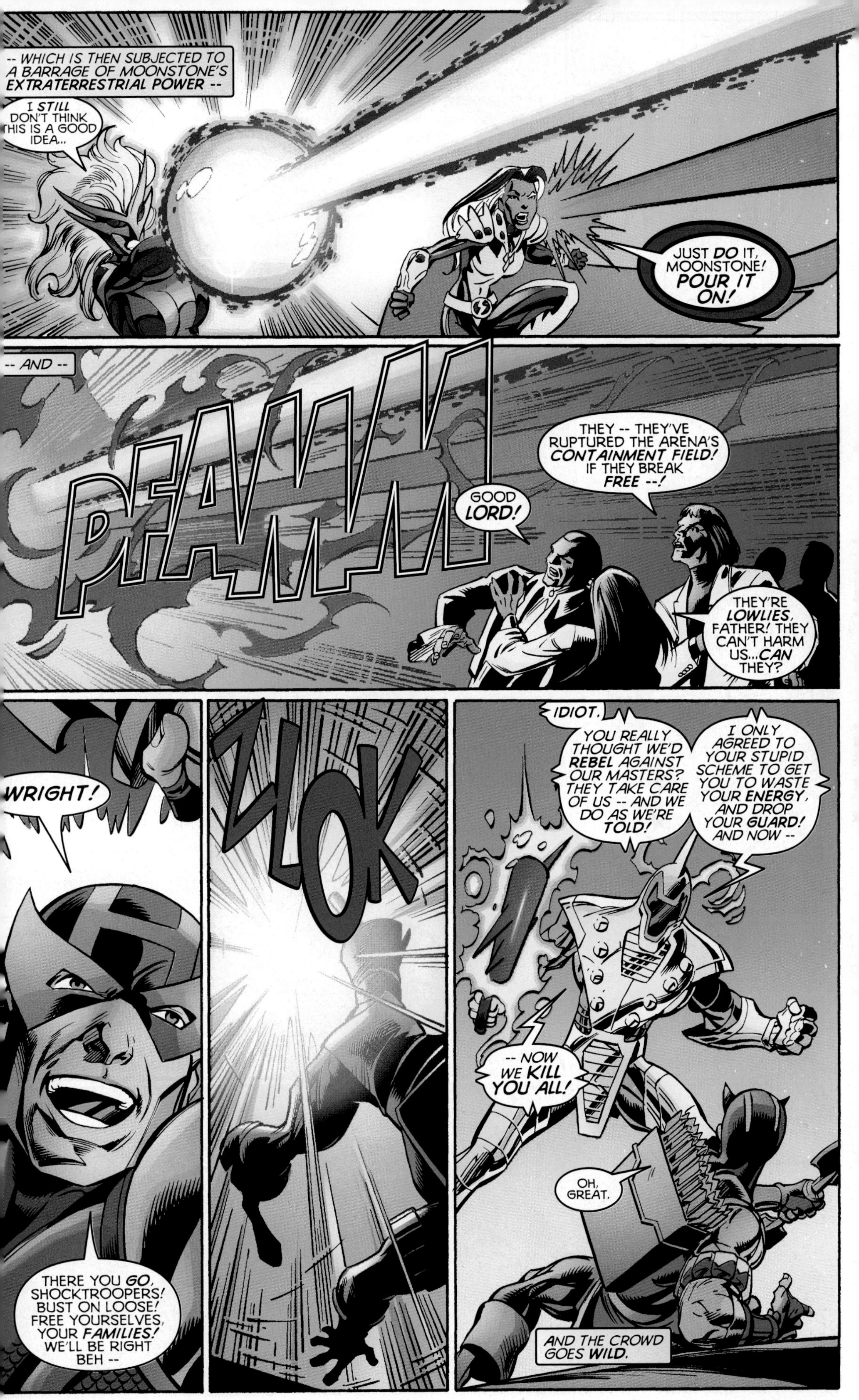

-- WHICH IS THEN SUBJECTED TO A BARRAGE OF MOONSTONE'S EXTRATERRESTRIAL POWER --
I STILL DON'T THINK THIS IS A GOOD IDEA...
JUST DO IT, MOONSTONE! POUR IT ON!
-- AND --
PFAVVV
THEY -- THEY'VE RUPTURED THE ARENA'S CONTAINMENT FIELD! IF THEY BREAK FREE --!
GOOD LORD!
THEY'RE LOWLIES, FATHER! THEY CAN'T HARM US...CAN THEY?
WRIGHT!
THERE YOU GO, SHOCKTROOPERS! BUST ON LOOSE! FREE YOURSELVES, YOUR FAMILIES! WE'LL BE RIGHT BEH --
ZLOK
IDIOT.
YOU REALLY THOUGHT WE'D REBEL AGAINST OUR MASTERS? THEY TAKE CARE OF US -- AND WE DO AS WE'RE TOLD!
I ONLY AGREED TO YOUR STUPID SCHEME TO GET YOU TO WASTE YOUR ENERGY, AND DROP YOUR GUARD! AND NOW --
-- NOW WE KILL YOU ALL!
OH, GREAT.
AND THE CROWD GOES WILD.

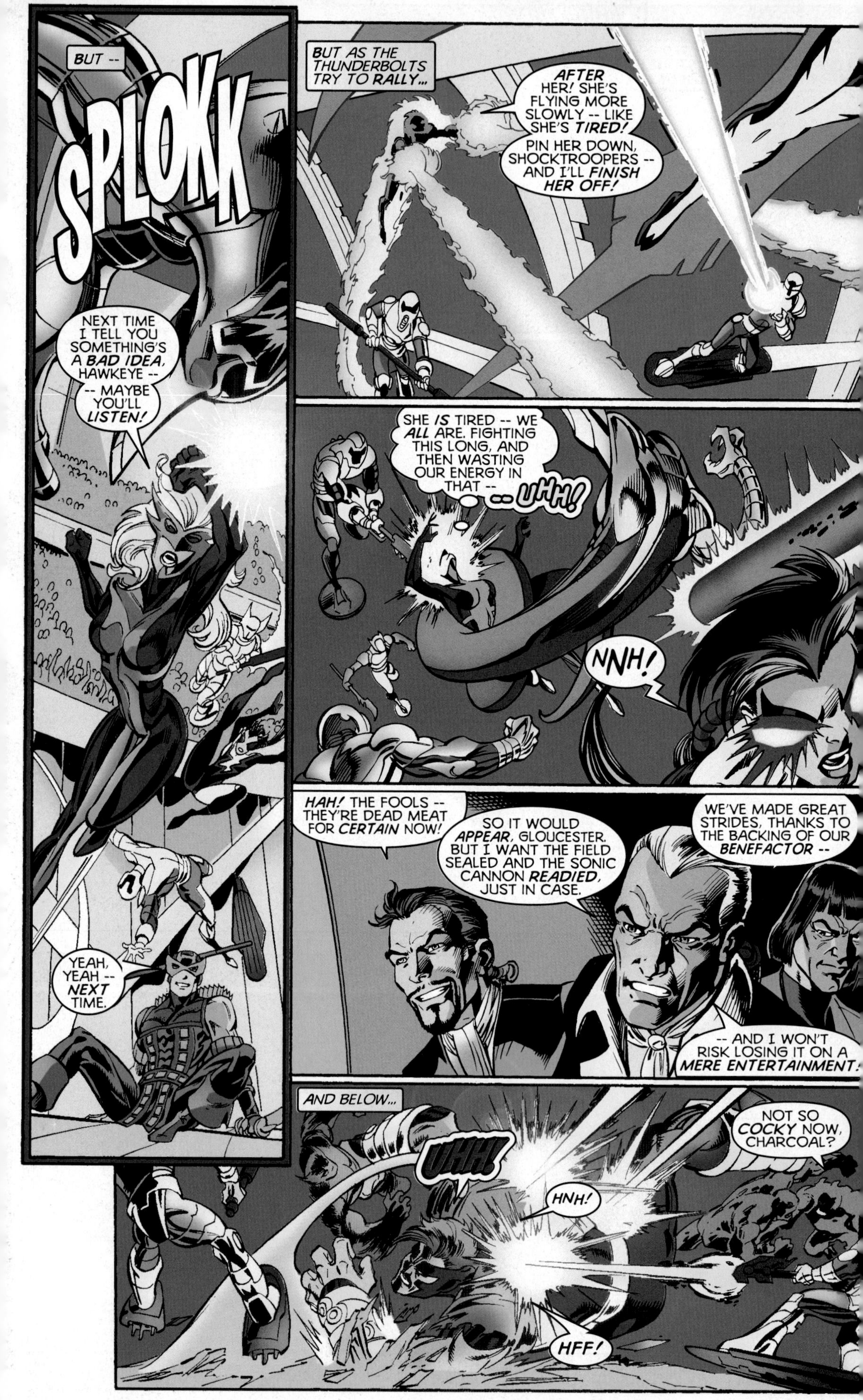
BUT --
SPLOKK
NEXT TIME I TELL YOU SOMETHING'S A BAD IDEA, HAWKEYE --
-- MAYBE YOU'LL LISTEN!
YEAH, YEAH -- NEXT TIME.
BUT AS THE THUNDERBOLTS TRY TO RALLY...
AFTER HER! SHE'S FLYING MORE SLOWLY -- LIKE SHE'S TIRED!
PIN HER DOWN, SHOCKTROOPERS -- AND I'LL FINISH HER OFF!
SHE IS TIRED -- WE ALL ARE. FIGHTING THIS LONG, AND THEN WASTING OUR ENERGY IN THAT --
-- UHH!
NNH!
HAH! THE FOOLS -- THEY'RE DEAD MEAT FOR CERTAIN NOW!
SO IT WOULD APPEAR, GLOUCESTER. BUT I WANT THE FIELD SEALED AND THE SONIC CANNON READIED, JUST IN CASE.
WE'VE MADE GREAT STRIDES, THANKS TO THE BACKING OF OUR BENEFACTOR --
-- AND I WON'T RISK LOSING IT ON A MERE ENTERTAINMENT.
AND BELOW...
UHH!
HNH!
NOT SO COCKY NOW, CHARCOAL?
HFF!

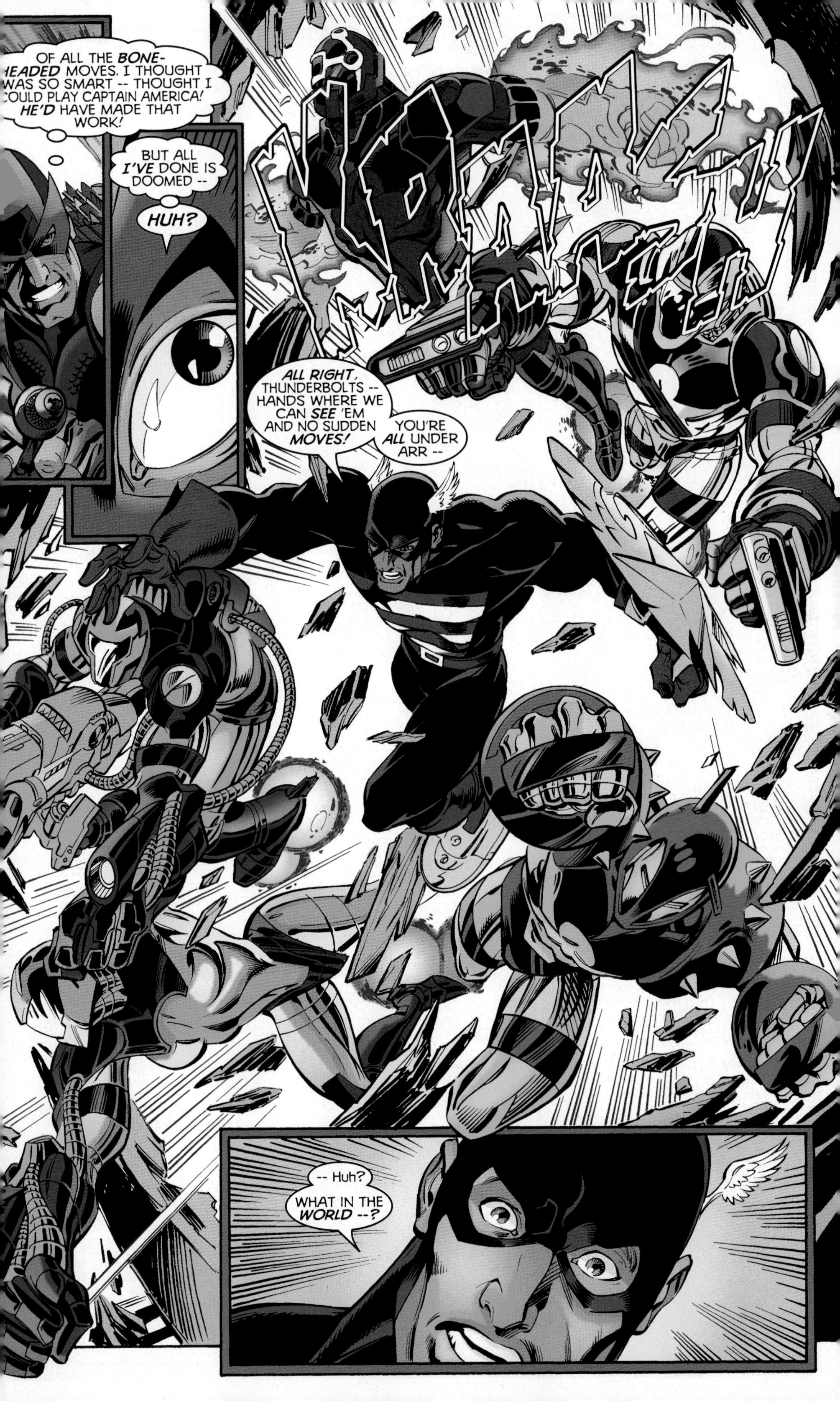
OF ALL THE BONE-HEADED MOVES. I THOUGHT I WAS SO SMART -- THOUGHT I COULD PLAY CAPTAIN AMERICA! HE'D HAVE MADE THAT WORK!
BUT ALL I'VE DONE IS DOOMED --
HUH?
ALL RIGHT, THUNDERBOLTS -- HANDS WHERE WE CAN SEE 'EM AND NO SUDDEN MOVES!
YOU'RE ALL UNDER ARR --
-- Huh?
WHAT IN THE WORLD --?

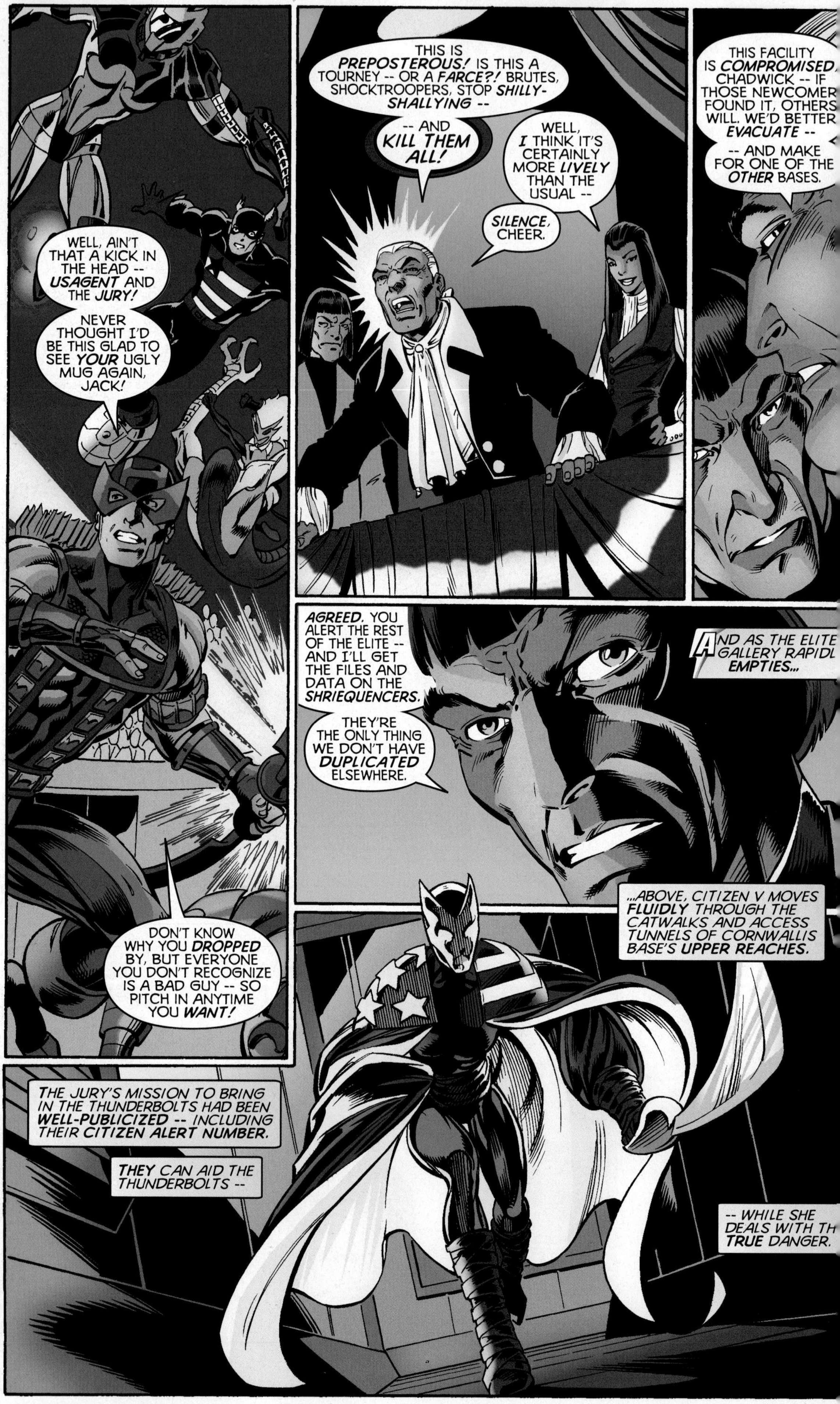

WELL, AIN'T THAT A KICK IN THE HEAD -- USAGENT AND THE JURY!
NEVER THOUGHT I'D BE THIS GLAD TO SEE YOUR UGLY MUG AGAIN, JACK!
DON'T KNOW WHY YOU DROPPED BY, BUT EVERYONE YOU DON'T RECOGNIZE IS A BAD GUY -- SO PITCH IN ANYTIME YOU WANT!
THIS IS PREPOSTEROUS! IS THIS A TOURNEY -- OR A FARCE?! BRUTES, SHOCKTROOPERS, STOP SHILLY-SHALLYING --
-- AND KILL THEM ALL!
WELL, I THINK IT'S CERTAINLY MORE LIVELY THAN THE USUAL --
SILENCE, CHEER.
THIS FACILITY IS COMPROMISED, CHADWICK -- IF THOSE NEWCOMER FOUND IT, OTHERS WILL. WE'D BETTER EVACUATE --
-- AND MAKE FOR ONE OF THE OTHER BASES.
AGREED. YOU ALERT THE REST OF THE ELITE -- AND I'LL GET THE FILES AND DATA ON THE SHRIEQUENCERS.
THEY'RE THE ONLY THING WE DON'T HAVE DUPLICATED ELSEWHERE.
AND AS THE ELITE GALLERY RAPIDL EMPTIES...
THE JURY'S MISSION TO BRING IN THE THUNDERBOLTS HAD BEEN WELL-PUBLICIZED -- INCLUDING THEIR CITIZEN ALERT NUMBER.
THEY CAN AID THE THUNDERBOLTS --
...ABOVE, CITIZEN V MOVES FLUIDLY THROUGH THE CATWALKS AND ACCESS TUNNELS OF CORNWALLIS BASE'S UPPER REACHES.
-- WHILE SHE DEALS WITH TH TRUE DANGER.

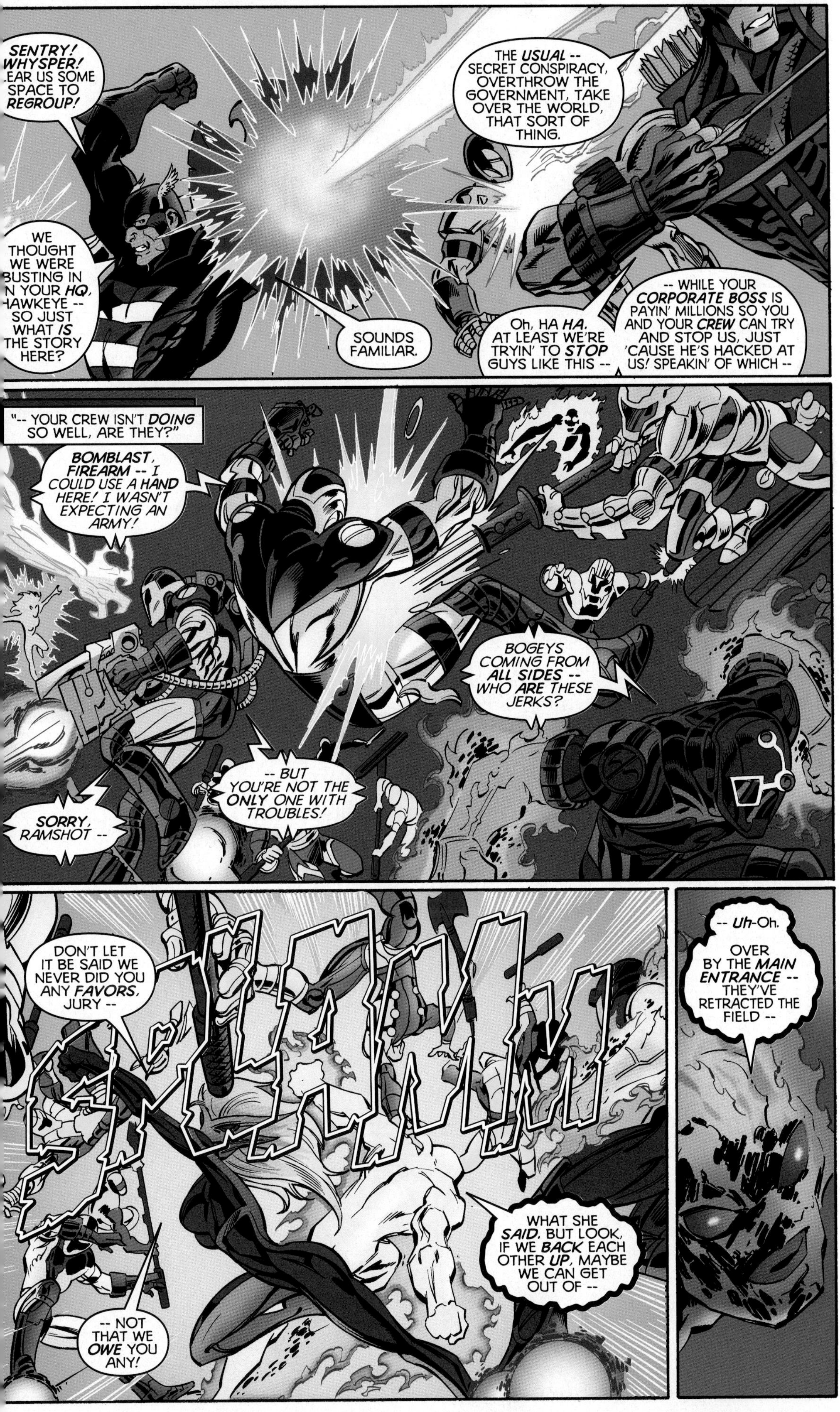

SENTRY! WHYSPER! ...EAR US SOME SPACE TO REGROUP!
THE USUAL -- SECRET CONSPIRACY, OVERTHROW THE GOVERNMENT, TAKE OVER THE WORLD, THAT SORT OF THING.
WE THOUGHT WE WERE BUSTING IN ...N YOUR HQ, ...AWKEYE -- SO JUST WHAT IS THE STORY HERE?
SOUNDS FAMILIAR.
Oh, HA HA. AT LEAST WE'RE TRYIN' TO STOP GUYS LIKE THIS --
-- WHILE YOUR CORPORATE BOSS IS PAYIN' MILLIONS SO YOU AND YOUR CREW CAN TRY AND STOP US, JUST 'CAUSE HE'S HACKED AT US! SPEAKIN' OF WHICH --
"-- YOUR CREW ISN'T DOING SO WELL, ARE THEY?"
BOMBLAST, FIREARM -- I COULD USE A HAND HERE! I WASN'T EXPECTING AN ARMY!
BOGEYS COMING FROM ALL SIDES -- WHO ARE THESE JERKS?
-- BUT YOU'RE NOT THE ONLY ONE WITH TROUBLES!
SORRY, RAMSHOT --
DON'T LET IT BE SAID WE NEVER DID YOU ANY FAVORS, JURY --
WHAT SHE SAID. BUT LOOK, IF WE BACK EACH OTHER UP, MAYBE WE CAN GET OUT OF --
-- NOT THAT WE OWE YOU ANY!
-- Uh-Oh.
OVER BY THE MAIN ENTRANCE -- THEY'VE RETRACTED THE FIELD --

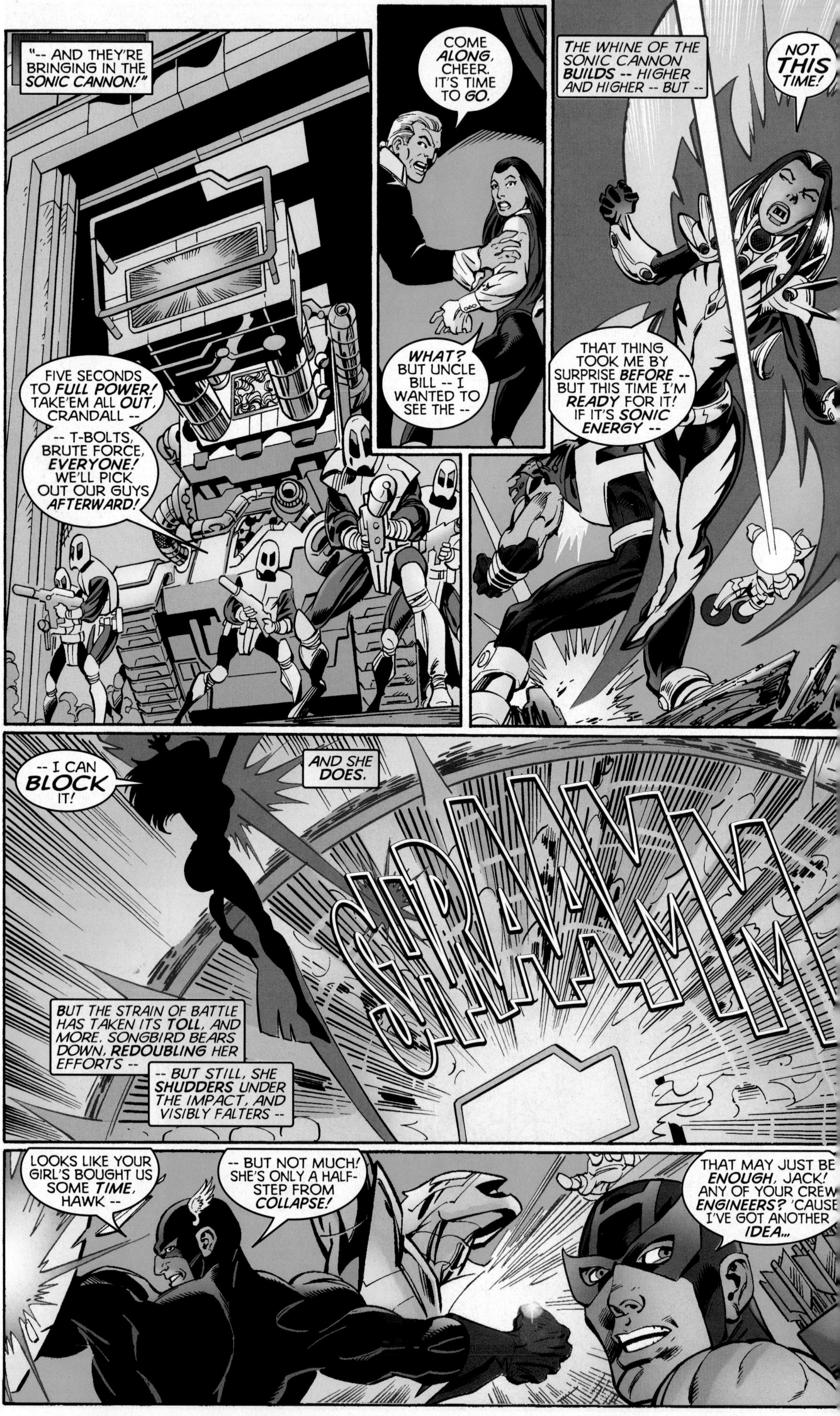
"-- AND THEY'RE BRINGING IN THE SONIC CANNON!"
FIVE SECONDS TO FULL POWER! TAKE'EM ALL OUT, CRANDALL --
-- T-BOLTS, BRUTE FORCE, EVERYONE! WE'LL PICK OUT OUR GUYS AFTERWARD!
COME ALONG, CHEER. IT'S TIME TO GO.
WHAT? BUT UNCLE BILL -- I WANTED TO SEE THE --
THE WHINE OF THE SONIC CANNON BUILDS -- HIGHER AND HIGHER -- BUT --
NOT THIS TIME!
THAT THING TOOK ME BY SURPRISE BEFORE -- BUT THIS TIME I'M READY FOR IT! IF IT'S SONIC ENERGY --
-- I CAN BLOCK IT!
AND SHE DOES.
SHRAAAMMM
BUT THE STRAIN OF BATTLE HAS TAKEN ITS TOLL, AND MORE. SONGBIRD BEARS DOWN, REDOUBLING HER EFFORTS --
-- BUT STILL, SHE SHUDDERS UNDER THE IMPACT, AND VISIBLY FALTERS --
LOOKS LIKE YOUR GIRL'S BOUGHT US SOME TIME, HAWK --
-- BUT NOT MUCH! SHE'S ONLY A HALF-STEP FROM COLLAPSE!
THAT MAY JUST BE ENOUGH, JACK! ANY OF YOUR CREW ENGINEERS? 'CAUSE I'VE GOT ANOTHER IDEA...

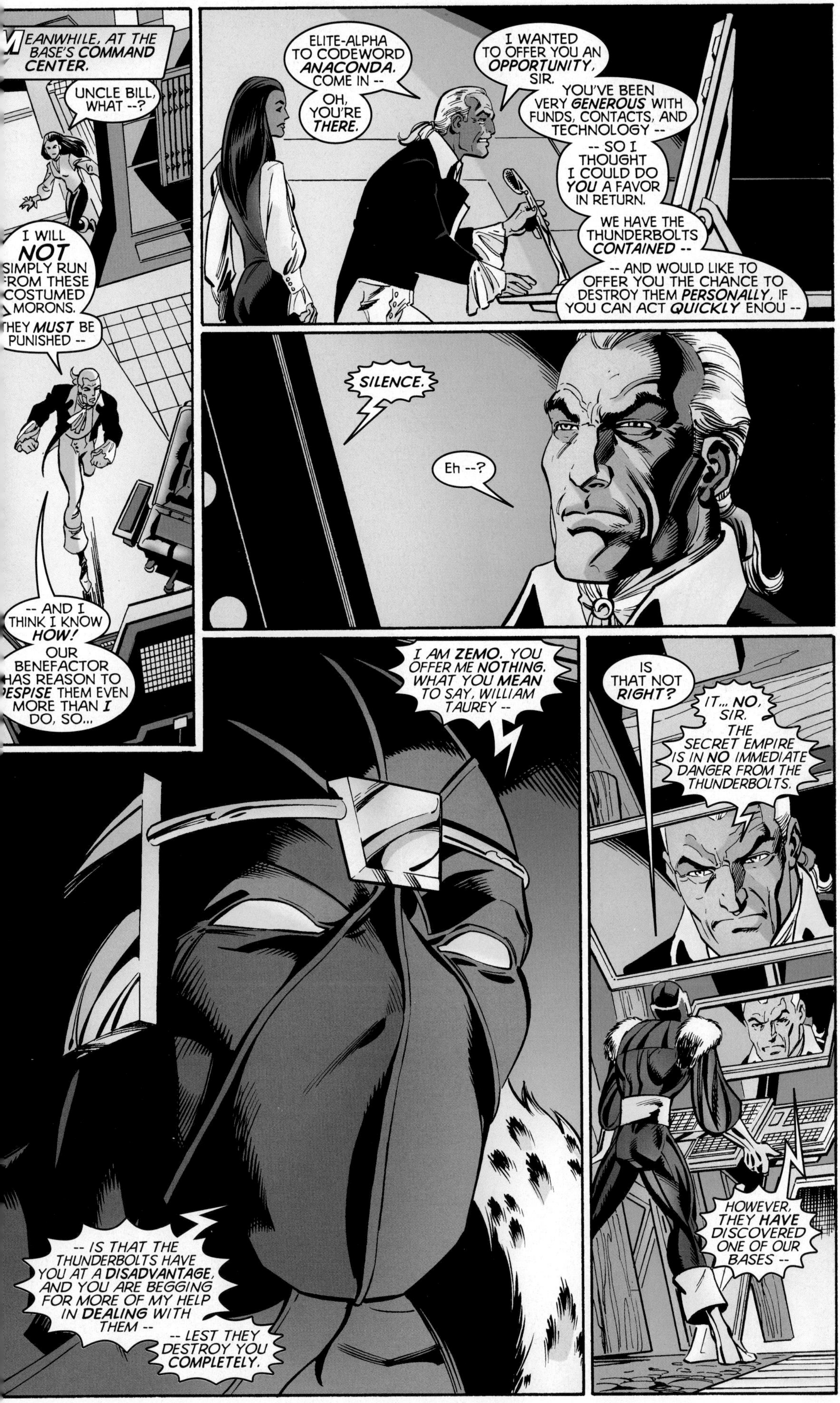
MEANWHILE, AT THE BASE'S COMMAND CENTER.
UNCLE BILL, WHAT --?
I WILL NOT SIMPLY RUN FROM THESE COSTUMED MORONS.
THEY MUST BE PUNISHED --
-- AND I THINK I KNOW HOW!
OUR BENEFACTOR HAS REASON TO DESPISE THEM EVEN MORE THAN I DO, SO...
ELITE-ALPHA TO CODEWORD ANACONDA. COME IN --
OH, YOU'RE THERE.
I WANTED TO OFFER YOU AN OPPORTUNITY, SIR.
YOU'VE BEEN VERY GENEROUS WITH FUNDS, CONTACTS, AND TECHNOLOGY --
-- SO I THOUGHT I COULD DO YOU A FAVOR IN RETURN.
WE HAVE THE THUNDERBOLTS CONTAINED --
-- AND WOULD LIKE TO OFFER YOU THE CHANCE TO DESTROY THEM PERSONALLY, IF YOU CAN ACT QUICKLY ENOU --
SILENCE.
Eh --?
I AM ZEMO. YOU OFFER ME NOTHING. WHAT YOU MEAN TO SAY, WILLIAM TAUREY --
-- IS THAT THE THUNDERBOLTS HAVE YOU AT A DISADVANTAGE, AND YOU ARE BEGGING FOR MORE OF MY HELP IN DEALING WITH THEM --
-- LEST THEY DESTROY YOU COMPLETELY.
IS THAT NOT RIGHT?
IT... NO, SIR.
THE SECRET EMPIRE IS IN NO IMMEDIATE DANGER FROM THE THUNDERBOLTS.
HOWEVER, THEY HAVE DISCOVERED ONE OF OUR BASES --

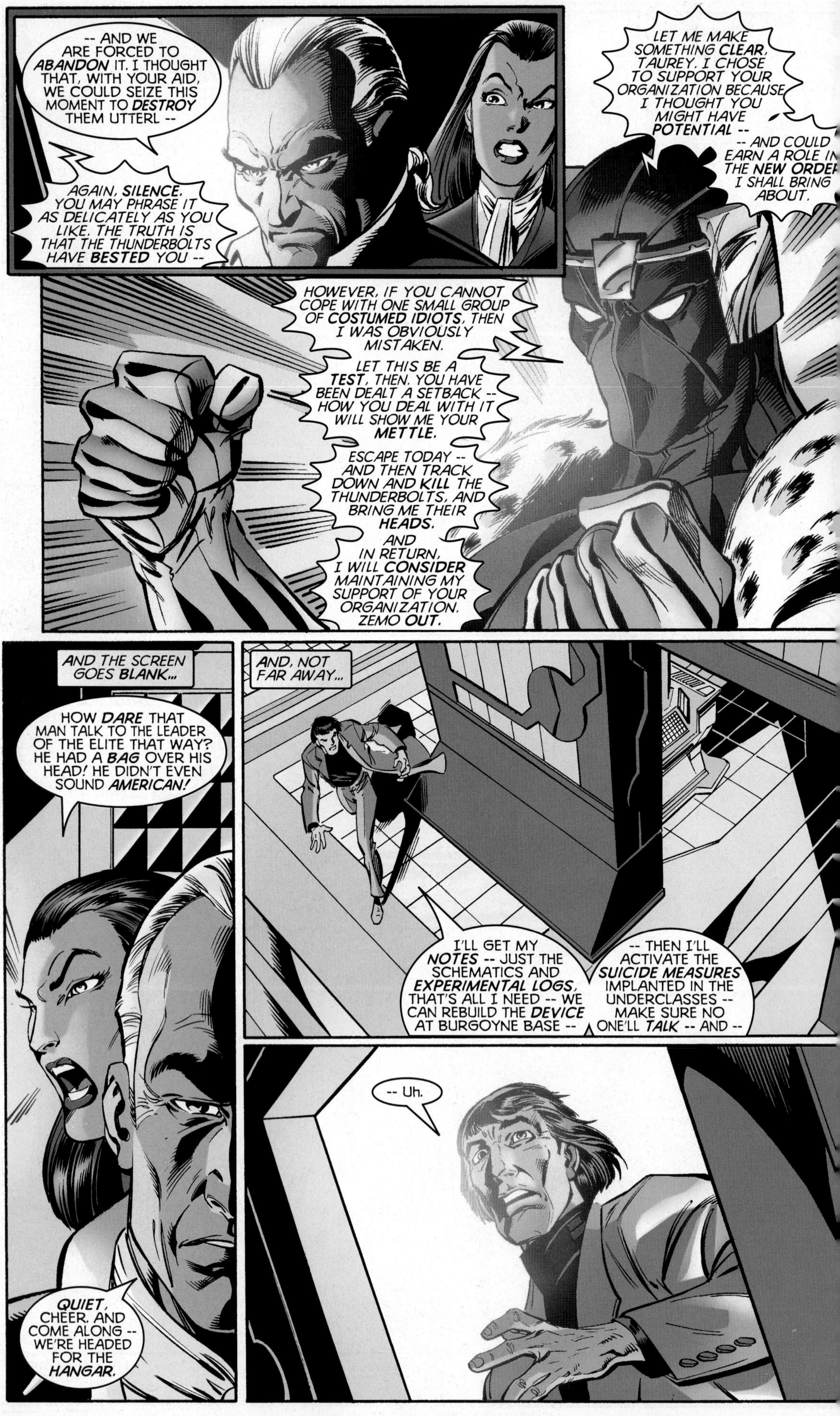
-- AND WE ARE FORCED TO ABANDON IT. I THOUGHT THAT, WITH YOUR AID, WE COULD SEIZE THIS MOMENT TO DESTROY THEM UTTERL --
AGAIN, SILENCE. YOU MAY PHRASE IT AS DELICATELY AS YOU LIKE. THE TRUTH IS THAT THE THUNDERBOLTS HAVE BESTED YOU --
LET ME MAKE SOMETHING CLEAR, TAUREY. I CHOSE TO SUPPORT YOUR ORGANIZATION BECAUSE I THOUGHT YOU MIGHT HAVE POTENTIAL --
-- AND COULD EARN A ROLE IN THE NEW ORDER I SHALL BRING ABOUT.
HOWEVER, IF YOU CANNOT COPE WITH ONE SMALL GROUP OF COSTUMED IDIOTS, THEN I WAS OBVIOUSLY MISTAKEN.
LET THIS BE A TEST, THEN. YOU HAVE BEEN DEALT A SETBACK -- HOW YOU DEAL WITH IT WILL SHOW ME YOUR METTLE.
ESCAPE TODAY -- AND THEN TRACK DOWN AND KILL THE THUNDERBOLTS, AND BRING ME THEIR HEADS.
AND IN RETURN, I WILL CONSIDER MAINTAINING MY SUPPORT OF YOUR ORGANIZATION. ZEMO OUT.
AND THE SCREEN GOES BLANK...
HOW DARE THAT MAN TALK TO THE LEADER OF THE ELITE THAT WAY? HE HAD A BAG OVER HIS HEAD! HE DIDN'T EVEN SOUND AMERICAN!
QUIET, CHEER, AND COME ALONG -- WE'RE HEADED FOR THE HANGAR.
AND, NOT FAR AWAY...
I'LL GET MY NOTES -- JUST THE SCHEMATICS AND EXPERIMENTAL LOGS, THAT'S ALL I NEED -- WE CAN REBUILD THE DEVICE AT BURGOYNE BASE --
-- THEN I'LL ACTIVATE THE SUICIDE MEASURES IMPLANTED IN THE UNDERCLASSES -- MAKE SURE NO ONE'LL TALK -- AND --
-- Uh.

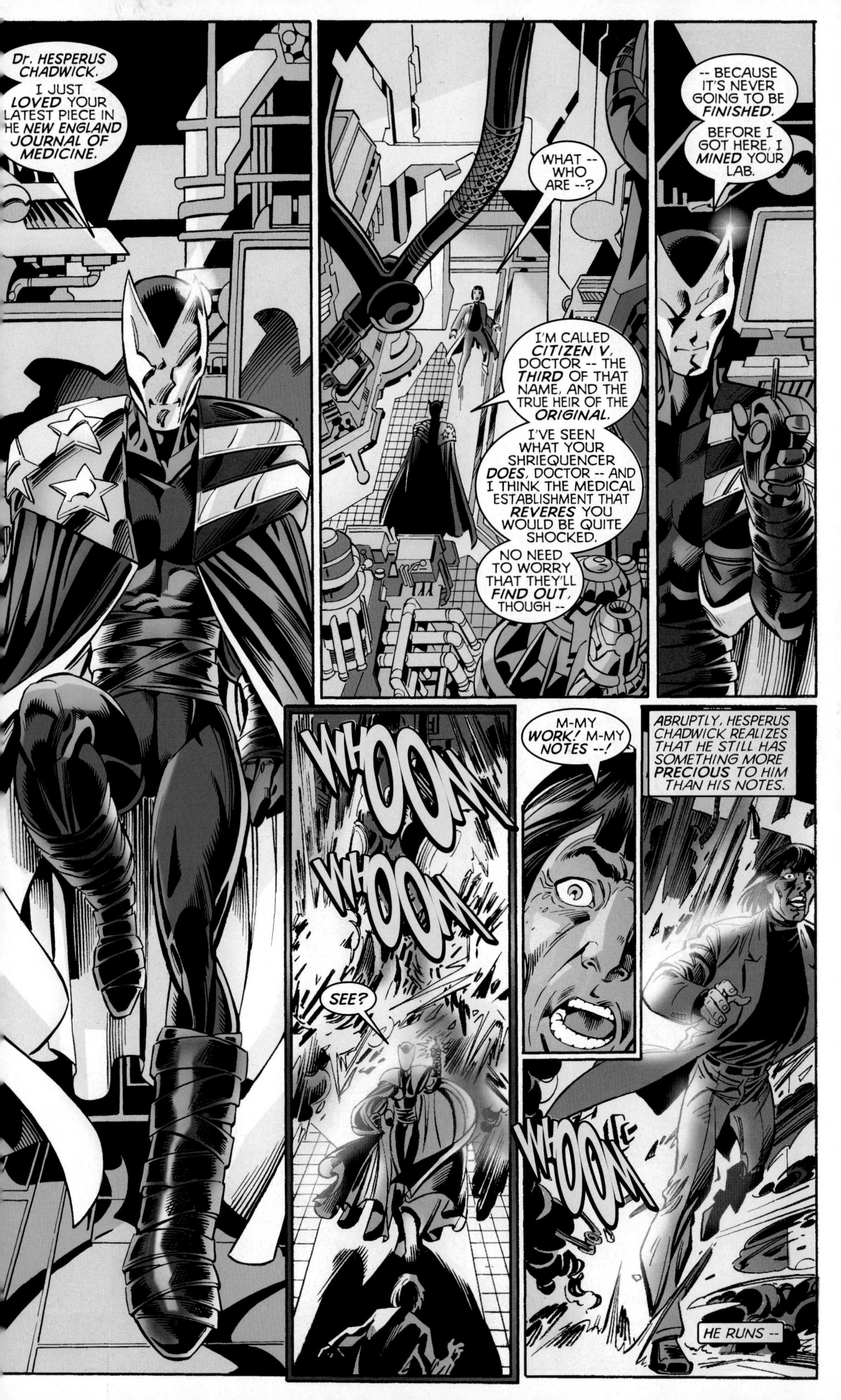

Dr. HESPERUS CHADWICK. I JUST LOVED YOUR LATEST PIECE IN HE NEW ENGLAND JOURNAL OF MEDICINE.
WHAT -- WHO ARE --?
I'M CALLED CITIZEN V, DOCTOR -- THE THIRD OF THAT NAME, AND THE TRUE HEIR OF THE ORIGINAL.
I'VE SEEN WHAT YOUR SHRIEQUENCER DOES, DOCTOR -- AND I THINK THE MEDICAL ESTABLISHMENT THAT REVERES YOU WOULD BE QUITE SHOCKED.
NO NEED TO WORRY THAT THEY'LL FIND OUT, THOUGH --
-- BECAUSE IT'S NEVER GOING TO BE FINISHED.
BEFORE I GOT HERE, I MINED YOUR LAB.
WHOOM
WHOOM
SEE?
M-MY WORK! M-MY NOTES --!
ABRUPTLY, HESPERUS CHADWICK REALIZES THAT HE STILL HAS SOMETHING MORE PRECIOUS TO HIM THAN HIS NOTES.
WHOOM
HE RUNS --

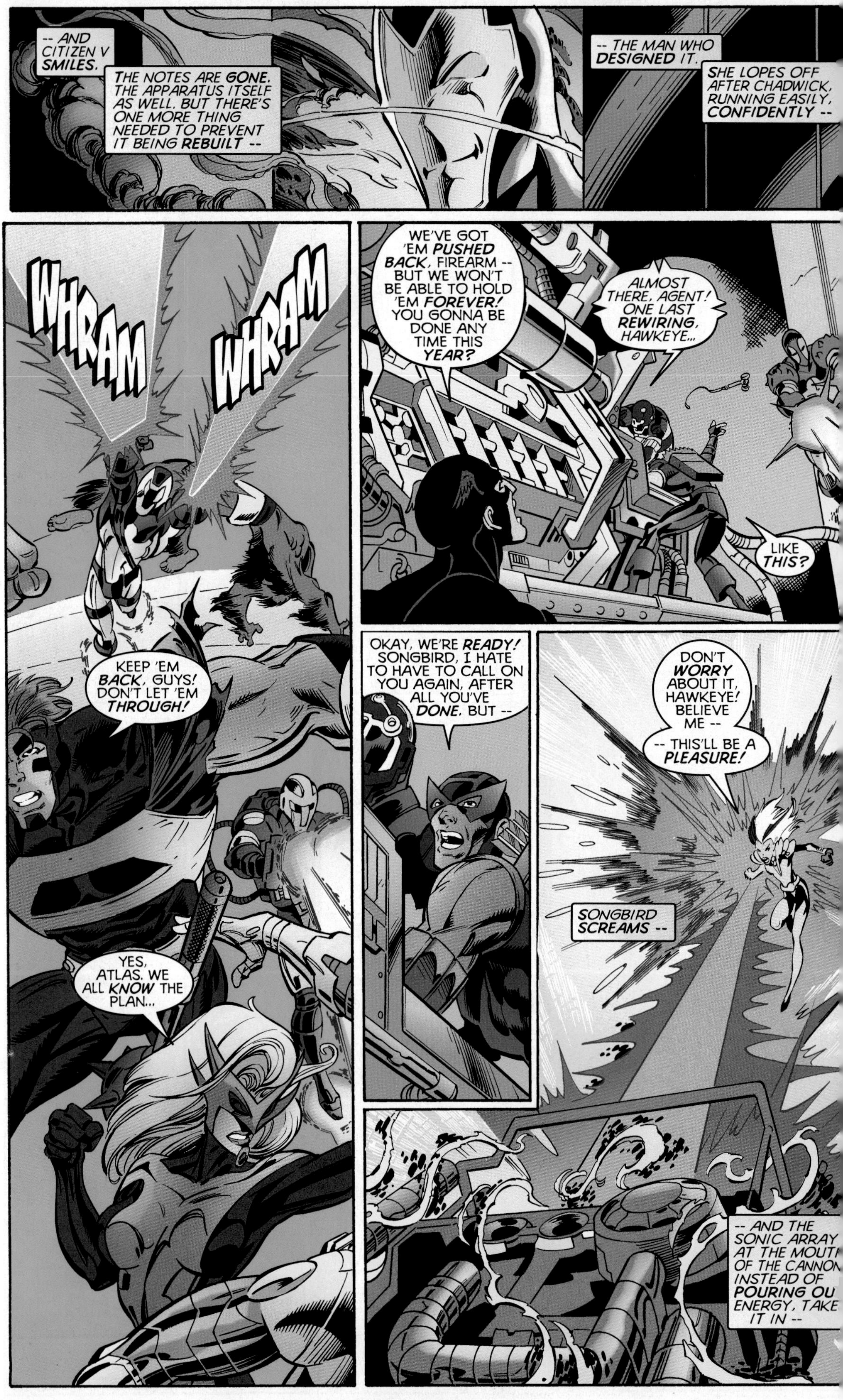
-- AND CITIZEN V SMILES.
THE NOTES ARE GONE. THE APPARATUS ITSELF AS WELL. BUT THERE'S ONE MORE THING NEEDED TO PREVENT IT BEING REBUILT --
-- THE MAN WHO DESIGNED IT.
SHE LOPES OFF AFTER CHADWICK, RUNNING EASILY, CONFIDENTLY --
WHRAM
WHRAM
KEEP 'EM BACK, GUYS! DON'T LET 'EM THROUGH!
YES, ATLAS. WE ALL KNOW THE PLAN...
WE'VE GOT 'EM PUSHED BACK, FIREARM -- BUT WE WON'T BE ABLE TO HOLD 'EM FOREVER! YOU GONNA BE DONE ANY TIME THIS YEAR?
ALMOST THERE, AGENT! ONE LAST REWIRING, HAWKEYE...
LIKE THIS?
OKAY, WE'RE READY! SONGBIRD, I HATE TO HAVE TO CALL ON YOU AGAIN, AFTER ALL YOU'VE DONE. BUT --
DON'T WORRY ABOUT IT, HAWKEYE! BELIEVE ME --
-- THIS'LL BE A PLEASURE!
SONGBIRD SCREAMS --
-- AND THE SONIC ARRAY AT THE MOUT OF THE CANNON INSTEAD OF POURING OU ENERGY, TAKE IT IN --

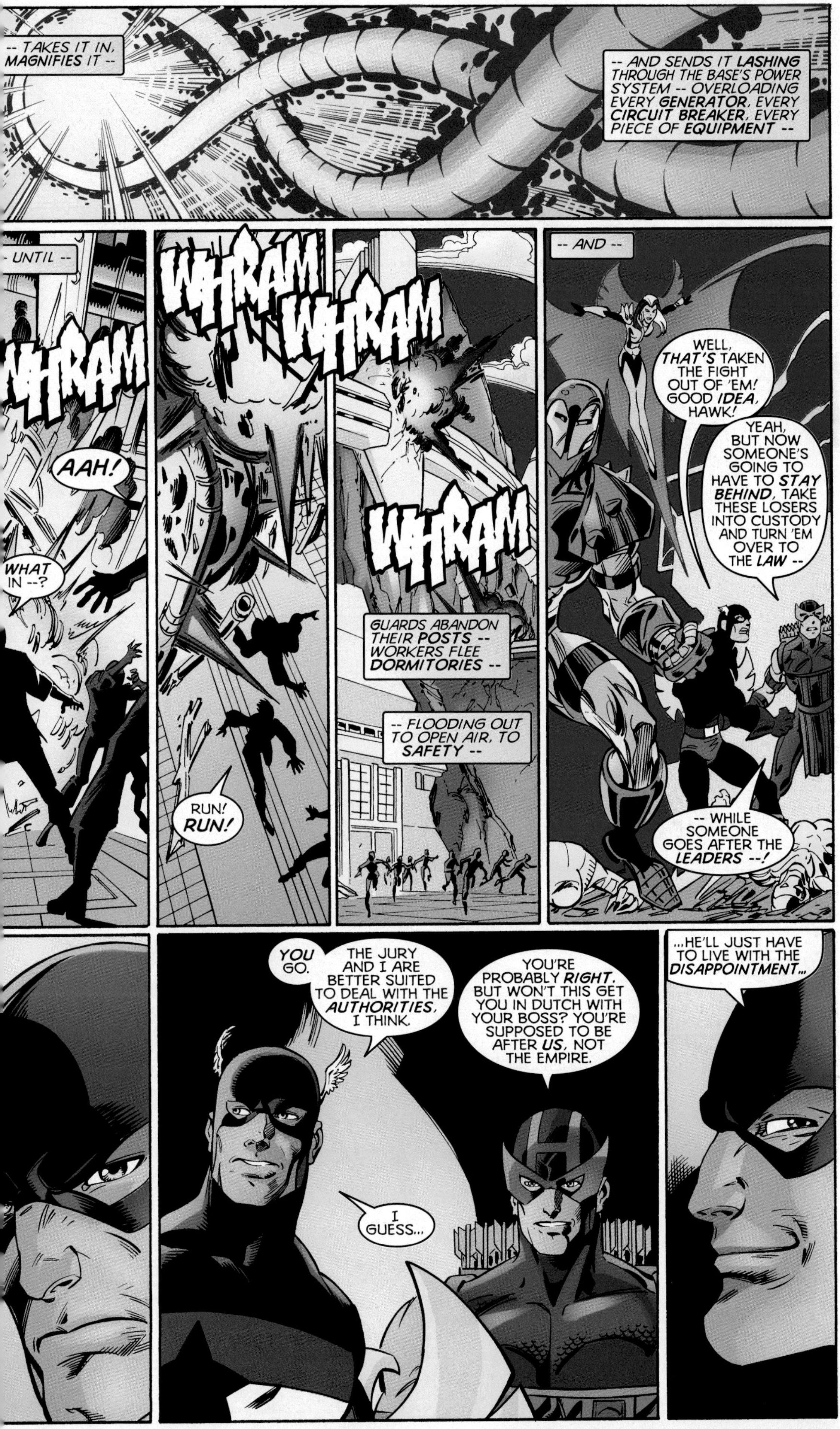
-- TAKES IT IN, MAGNIFIES IT --
-- AND SENDS IT LASHING THROUGH THE BASE'S POWER SYSTEM -- OVERLOADING EVERY GENERATOR, EVERY CIRCUIT BREAKER, EVERY PIECE OF EQUIPMENT --
- UNTIL --
WHRAM
AAH!
WHAT IN --?
WHRAM
WHRAM
RUN! RUN!
WHRAM
GUARDS ABANDON THEIR POSTS -- WORKERS FLEE DORMITORIES --
-- FLOODING OUT TO OPEN AIR, TO SAFETY --
-- AND --
WELL, THAT'S TAKEN THE FIGHT OUT OF 'EM! GOOD IDEA, HAWK!
YEAH, BUT NOW SOMEONE'S GOING TO HAVE TO STAY BEHIND, TAKE THESE LOSERS INTO CUSTODY AND TURN 'EM OVER TO THE LAW --
-- WHILE SOMEONE GOES AFTER THE LEADERS --!
YOU GO.
THE JURY AND I ARE BETTER SUITED TO DEAL WITH THE AUTHORITIES, I THINK.
YOU'RE PROBABLY RIGHT. BUT WON'T THIS GET YOU IN DUTCH WITH YOUR BOSS? YOU'RE SUPPOSED TO BE AFTER US, NOT THE EMPIRE.
I GUESS...
...HE'LL JUST HAVE TO LIVE WITH THE DISAPPOINTMENT...

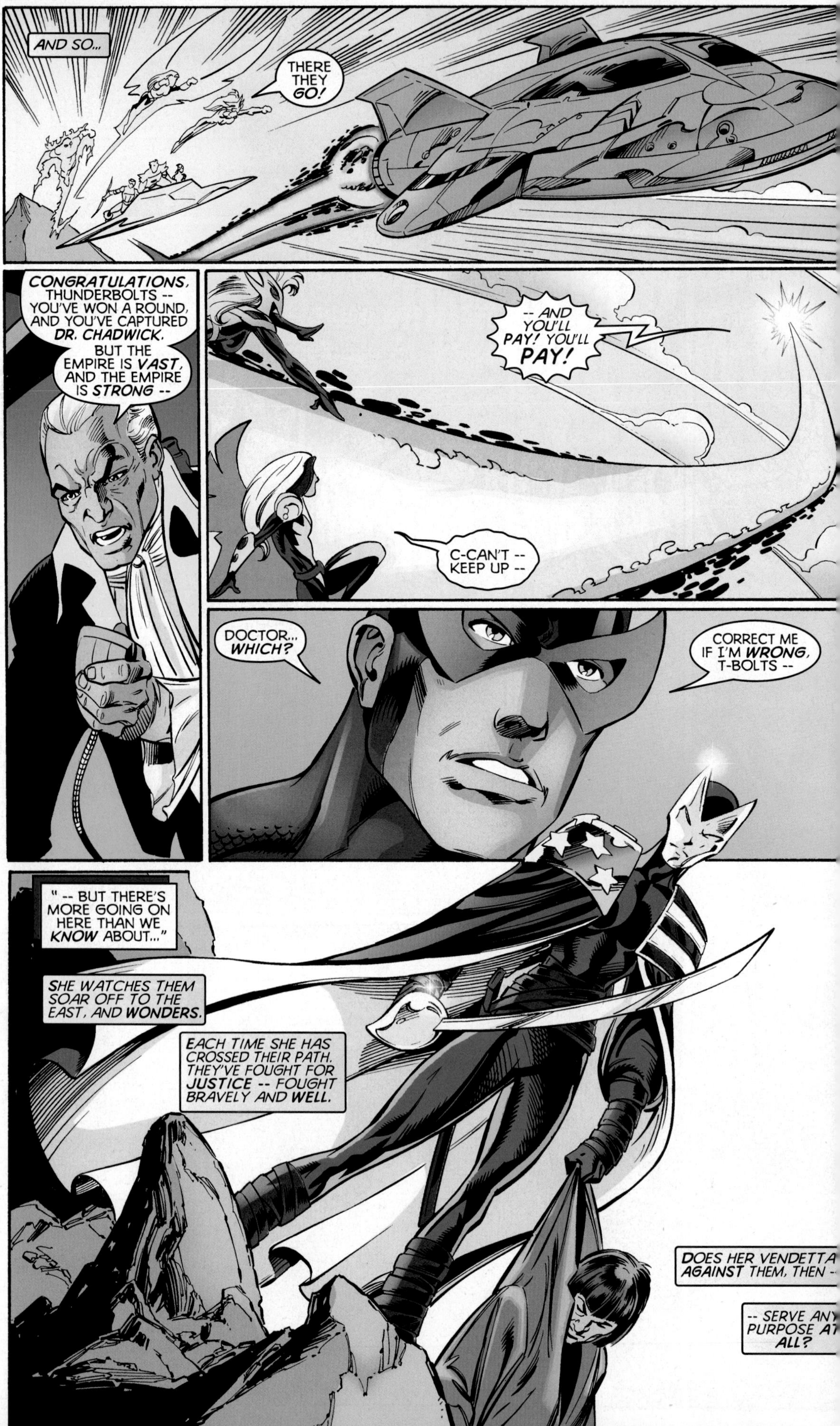
AND SO...
THERE THEY GO!
CONGRATULATIONS, THUNDERBOLTS -- YOU'VE WON A ROUND, AND YOU'VE CAPTURED DR. CHADWICK. BUT THE EMPIRE IS VAST, AND THE EMPIRE IS STRONG --
-- AND YOU'LL PAY! YOU'LL PAY!
C-CAN'T -- KEEP UP --
DOCTOR... WHICH?
CORRECT ME IF I'M WRONG, T-BOLTS --
" -- BUT THERE'S MORE GOING ON HERE THAN WE KNOW ABOUT..."
SHE WATCHES THEM SOAR OFF TO THE EAST, AND WONDERS.
EACH TIME SHE HAS CROSSED THEIR PATH, THEY'VE FOUGHT FOR JUSTICE -- FOUGHT BRAVELY AND WELL.
DOES HER VENDETTA AGAINST THEM, THEN --
-- SERVE ANY PURPOSE AT ALL?

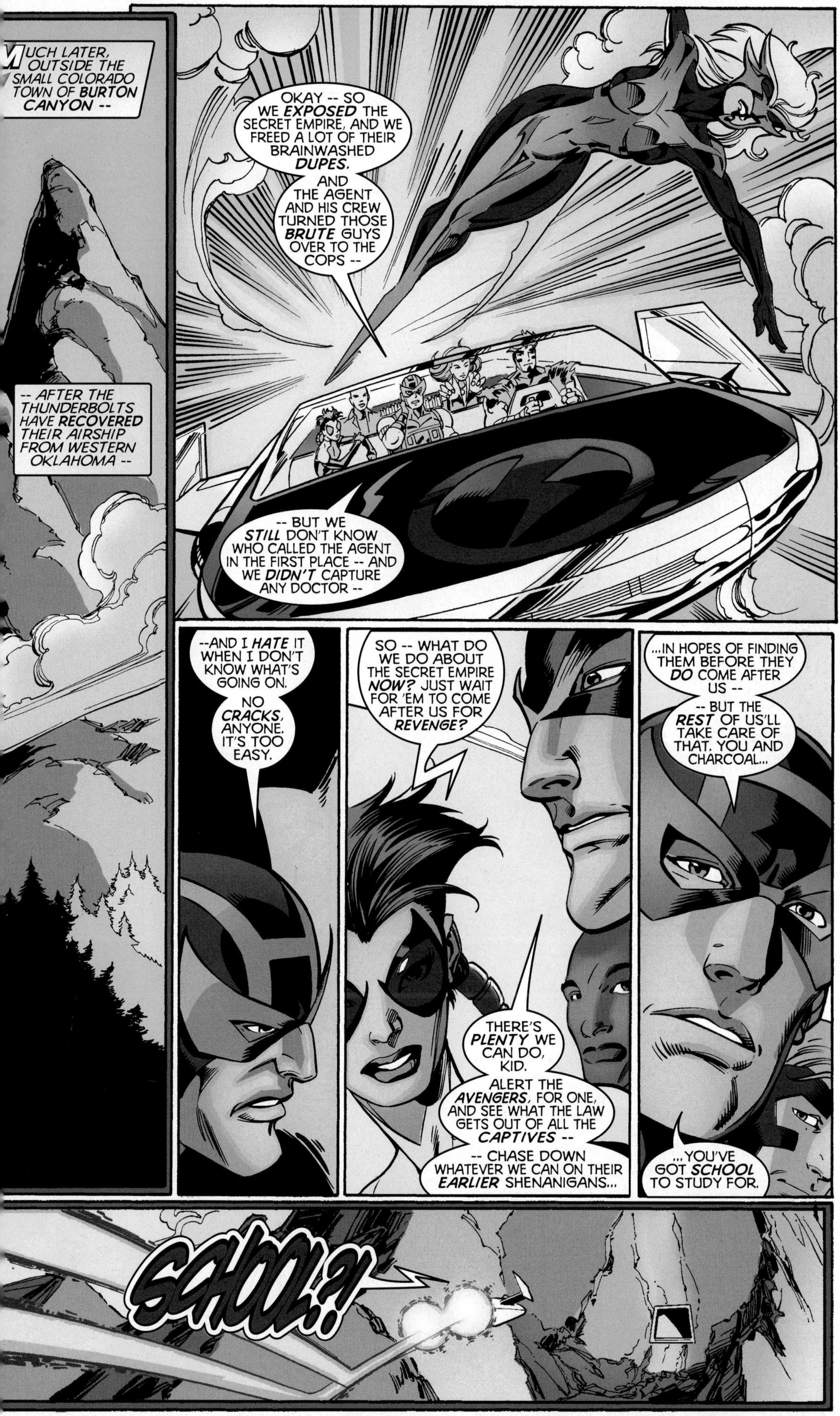
MUCH LATER, OUTSIDE THE SMALL COLORADO TOWN OF BURTON CANYON --
-- AFTER THE THUNDERBOLTS HAVE RECOVERED THEIR AIRSHIP FROM WESTERN OKLAHOMA --
OKAY -- SO WE EXPOSED THE SECRET EMPIRE, AND WE FREED A LOT OF THEIR BRAINWASHED DUPES.
AND THE AGENT AND HIS CREW TURNED THOSE BRUTE GUYS OVER TO THE COPS --
-- BUT WE STILL DON'T KNOW WHO CALLED THE AGENT IN THE FIRST PLACE -- AND WE DIDN'T CAPTURE ANY DOCTOR --
--AND I HATE IT WHEN I DON'T KNOW WHAT'S GOING ON.
NO CRACKS, ANYONE. IT'S TOO EASY.
SO -- WHAT DO WE DO ABOUT THE SECRET EMPIRE NOW? JUST WAIT FOR 'EM TO COME AFTER US FOR REVENGE?
THERE'S PLENTY WE CAN DO, KID.
ALERT THE AVENGERS, FOR ONE, AND SEE WHAT THE LAW GETS OUT OF ALL THE CAPTIVES --
-- CHASE DOWN WHATEVER WE CAN ON THEIR EARLIER SHENANIGANS...
...IN HOPES OF FINDING THEM BEFORE THEY DO COME AFTER US --
-- BUT THE REST OF US'LL TAKE CARE OF THAT. YOU AND CHARCOAL...
...YOU'VE GOT SCHOOL TO STUDY FOR.
SCHOOL?!

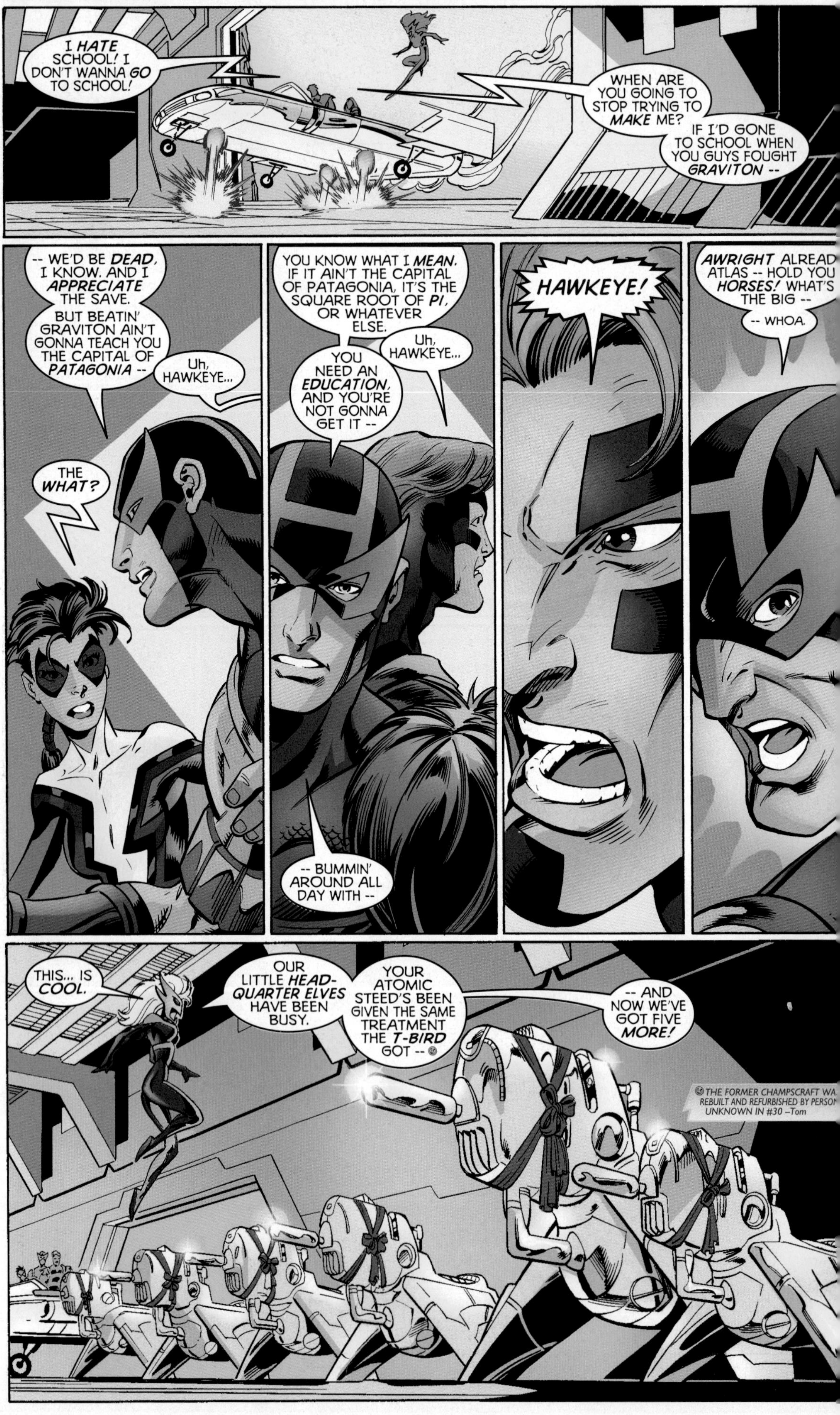

I HATE SCHOOL! I DON'T WANNA GO TO SCHOOL!
WHEN ARE YOU GOING TO STOP TRYING TO MAKE ME?
IF I'D GONE TO SCHOOL WHEN YOU GUYS FOUGHT GRAVITON --
-- WE'D BE DEAD, I KNOW. AND I APPRECIATE THE SAVE.
BUT BEATIN' GRAVITON AIN'T GONNA TEACH YOU THE CAPITAL OF PATAGONIA --
Uh, HAWKEYE...
THE WHAT?
YOU KNOW WHAT I MEAN. IF IT AIN'T THE CAPITAL OF PATAGONIA, IT'S THE SQUARE ROOT OF PI, OR WHATEVER ELSE.
Uh, HAWKEYE...
YOU NEED AN EDUCATION, AND YOU'RE NOT GONNA GET IT --
-- BUMMIN' AROUND ALL DAY WITH --
HAWKEYE!
AWRIGHT ALREAD ATLAS -- HOLD YOU HORSES! WHAT'S THE BIG --
-- WHOA.
THIS... IS COOL.
OUR LITTLE HEAD-QUARTER ELVES HAVE BEEN BUSY.
YOUR ATOMIC STEED'S BEEN GIVEN THE SAME TREATMENT THE T-BIRD GOT --
-- AND NOW WE'VE GOT FIVE MORE!
THE FORMER CHAMPSCRAFT WA REBUILT AND REFURBISHED BY PERSO UNKNOWN IN #30 –Tom

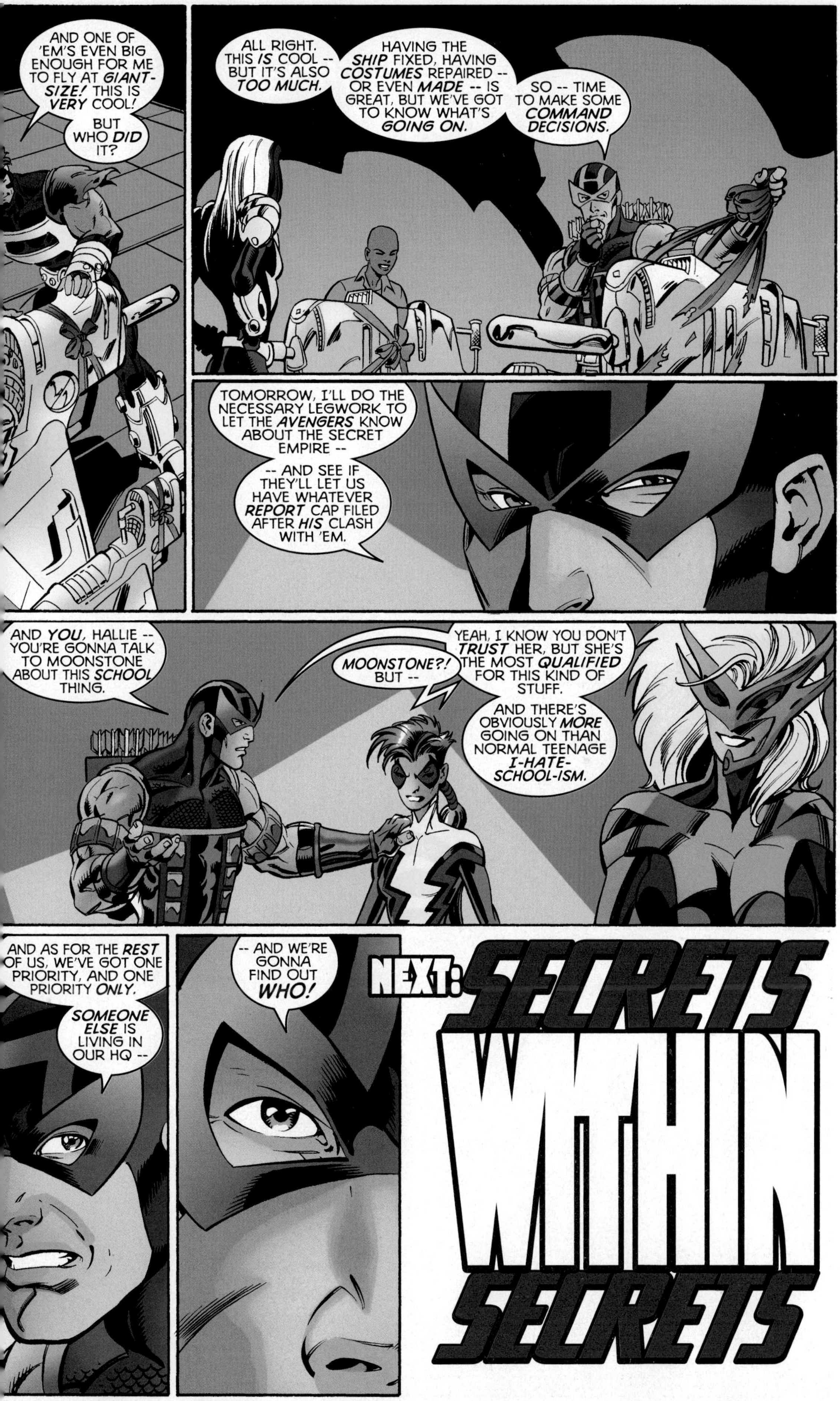
AND ONE OF 'EM'S EVEN BIG ENOUGH FOR ME TO FLY AT GIANT-SIZE! THIS IS VERY COOL!
BUT WHO DID IT?
ALL RIGHT. THIS IS COOL -- BUT IT'S ALSO TOO MUCH.
HAVING THE SHIP FIXED, HAVING COSTUMES REPAIRED -- OR EVEN MADE -- IS GREAT, BUT WE'VE GOT TO KNOW WHAT'S GOING ON.
SO -- TIME TO MAKE SOME COMMAND DECISIONS.
TOMORROW, I'LL DO THE NECESSARY LEGWORK TO LET THE AVENGERS KNOW ABOUT THE SECRET EMPIRE --
-- AND SEE IF THEY'LL LET US HAVE WHATEVER REPORT CAP FILED AFTER HIS CLASH WITH 'EM.
AND YOU, HALLIE -- YOU'RE GONNA TALK TO MOONSTONE ABOUT THIS SCHOOL THING.
MOONSTONE?! BUT --
YEAH, I KNOW YOU DON'T TRUST HER, BUT SHE'S THE MOST QUALIFIED FOR THIS KIND OF STUFF.
AND THERE'S OBVIOUSLY MORE GOING ON THAN NORMAL TEENAGE I-HATE-SCHOOL-ISM.
AND AS FOR THE REST OF US, WE'VE GOT ONE PRIORITY, AND ONE PRIORITY ONLY.
SOMEONE ELSE IS LIVING IN OUR HQ --
-- AND WE'RE GONNA FIND OUT WHO!
NEXT: SECRETS WITHIN SECRETS

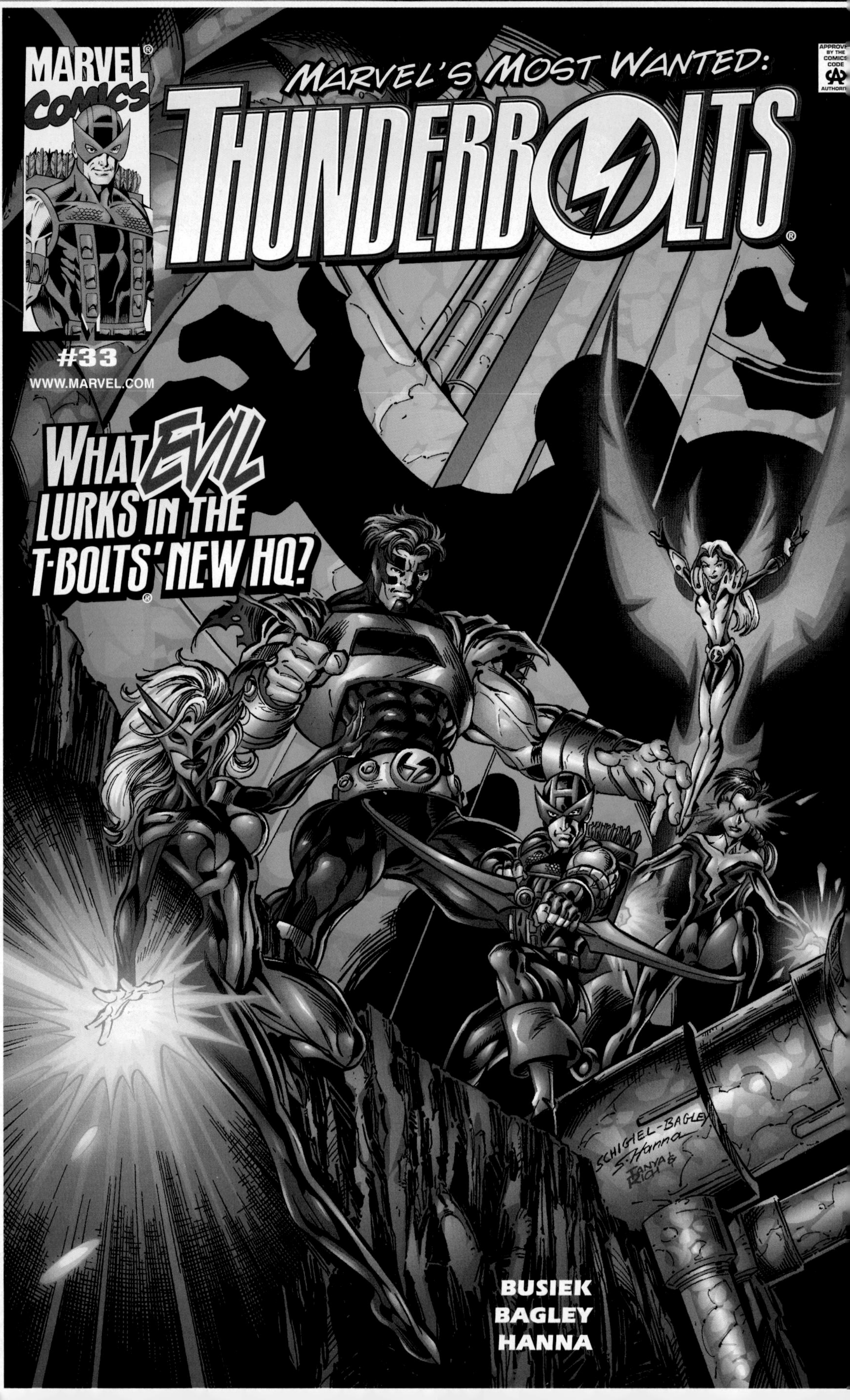
MARVEL COMICS
APPROVED BY THE COMICS CODE AUTHORITY
MARVEL'S MOST WANTED:
THUNDERBOLTS
#33
WWW.MARVEL.COM
WHAT EVIL LURKS IN THE T-BOLTS' NEW HQ?
SCHIGIEL-BAGLEY
S. HANNA
TANYA & RICH
BUSIEK
BAGLEY
HANNA

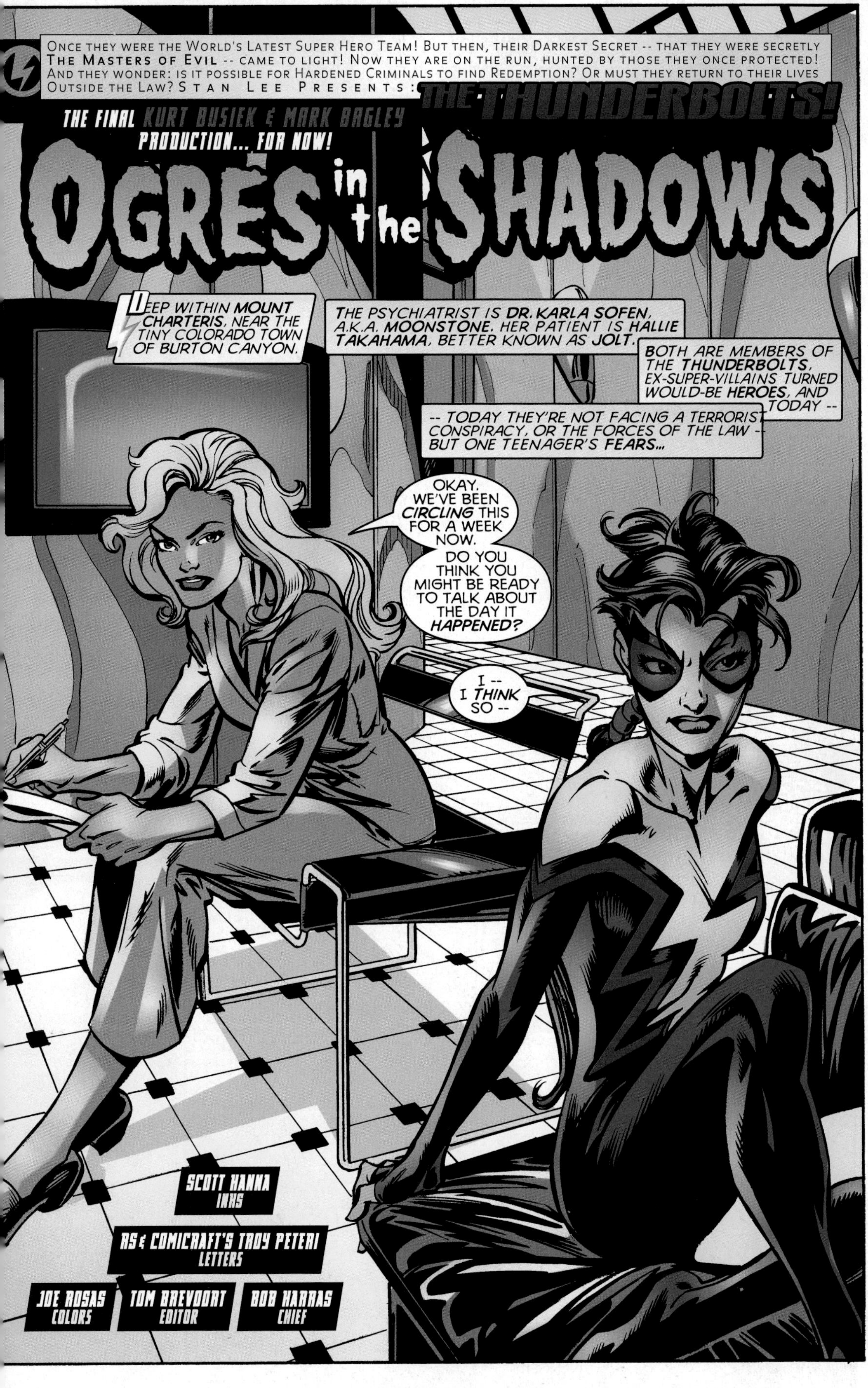

ONCE THEY WERE THE WORLD'S LATEST SUPER HERO TEAM! BUT THEN, THEIR DARKEST SECRET -- THAT THEY WERE SECRETLY THE MASTERS OF EVIL -- CAME TO LIGHT! NOW THEY ARE ON THE RUN, HUNTED BY THOSE THEY ONCE PROTECTED! AND THEY WONDER: IS IT POSSIBLE FOR HARDENED CRIMINALS TO FIND REDEMPTION? OR MUST THEY RETURN TO THEIR LIVES OUTSIDE THE LAW? STAN LEE PRESENTS: THE THUNDERBOLTS!
THE FINAL KURT BUSIEK & MARK BAGLEY PRODUCTION... FOR NOW!
OGRES in the SHADOWS
DEEP WITHIN MOUNT CHARTERIS, NEAR THE TINY COLORADO TOWN OF BURTON CANYON.
THE PSYCHIATRIST IS DR. KARLA SOFEN, A.K.A. MOONSTONE. HER PATIENT IS HALLIE TAKAHAMA, BETTER KNOWN AS JOLT.
BOTH ARE MEMBERS OF THE THUNDERBOLTS, EX-SUPER-VILLAINS TURNED WOULD-BE HEROES, AND TODAY --
-- TODAY THEY'RE NOT FACING A TERRORIST CONSPIRACY, OR THE FORCES OF THE LAW -- BUT ONE TEENAGER'S FEARS...
OKAY. WE'VE BEEN CIRCLING THIS FOR A WEEK NOW.
DO YOU THINK YOU MIGHT BE READY TO TALK ABOUT THE DAY IT HAPPENED?
I -- I THINK SO --
SCOTT HANNA INKS
RS & COMICRAFT'S TROY PETERI LETTERS
JOE ROSAS COLORS
TOM BREVOORT EDITOR
BOB HARRAS CHIEF

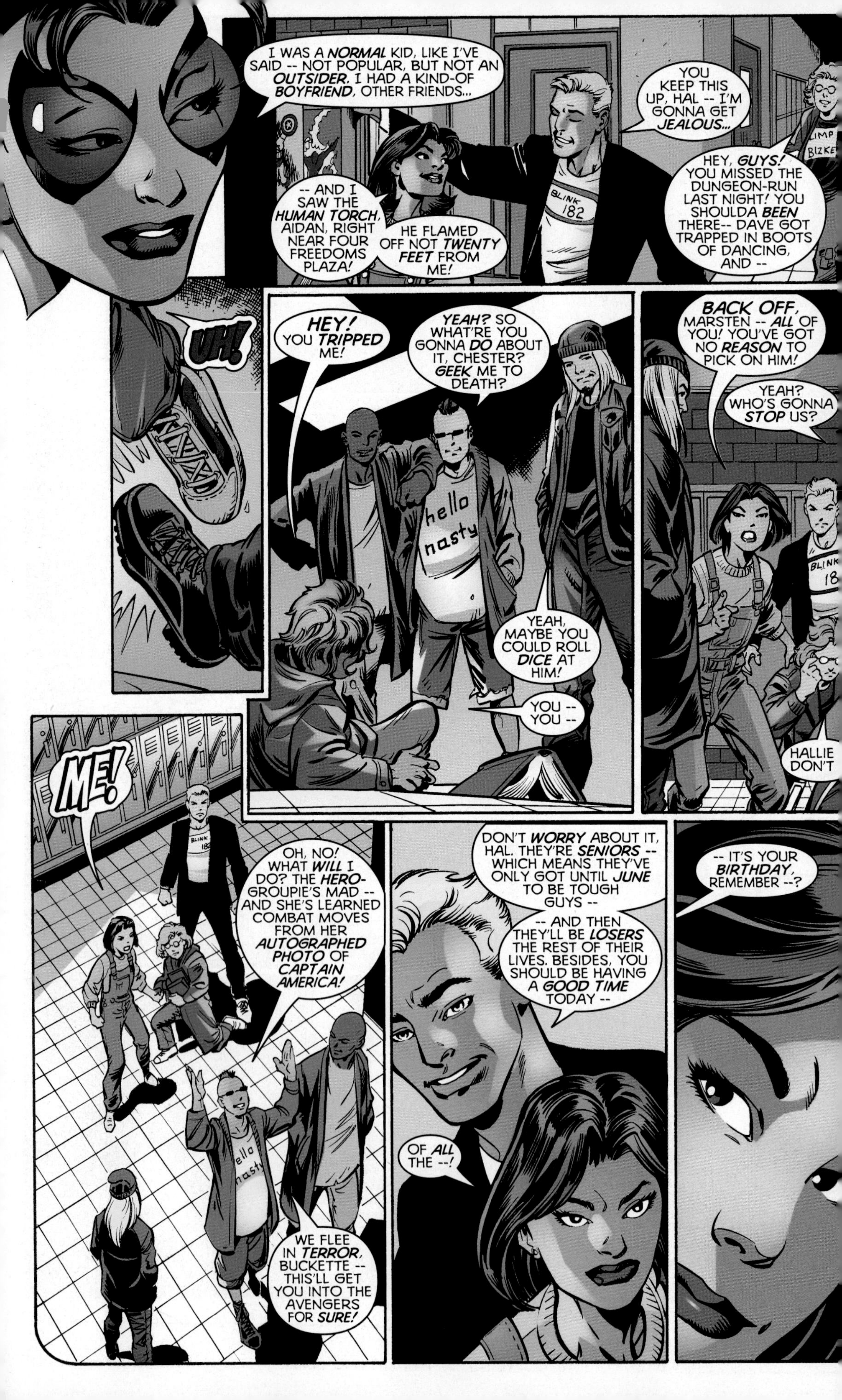
I WAS A NORMAL KID, LIKE I'VE SAID -- NOT POPULAR, BUT NOT AN OUTSIDER. I HAD A KIND-OF BOYFRIEND, OTHER FRIENDS...
-- AND I SAW THE HUMAN TORCH, AIDAN, RIGHT NEAR FOUR FREEDOMS PLAZA!
HE FLAMED OFF NOT TWENTY FEET FROM ME!
YOU KEEP THIS UP, HAL -- I'M GONNA GET JEALOUS...
HEY, GUYS! YOU MISSED THE DUNGEON-RUN LAST NIGHT! YOU SHOULDA BEEN THERE-- DAVE GOT TRAPPED IN BOOTS OF DANCING, AND --
UH!
HEY! YOU TRIPPED ME!
YEAH? SO WHAT'RE YOU GONNA DO ABOUT IT, CHESTER? GEEK ME TO DEATH?
YEAH, MAYBE YOU COULD ROLL DICE AT HIM!
YOU -- YOU --
BACK OFF, MARSTEN -- ALL OF YOU! YOU'VE GOT NO REASON TO PICK ON HIM!
YEAH? WHO'S GONNA STOP US?
HALLIE DON'T
ME!
OH, NO! WHAT WILL I DO? THE HERO-GROUPIE'S MAD -- AND SHE'S LEARNED COMBAT MOVES FROM HER AUTOGRAPHED PHOTO OF CAPTAIN AMERICA!
WE FLEE IN TERROR, BUCKETTE -- THIS'LL GET YOU INTO THE AVENGERS FOR SURE!
DON'T WORRY ABOUT IT, HAL. THEY'RE SENIORS -- WHICH MEANS THEY'VE ONLY GOT UNTIL JUNE TO BE TOUGH GUYS --
-- AND THEN THEY'LL BE LOSERS THE REST OF THEIR LIVES. BESIDES, YOU SHOULD BE HAVING A GOOD TIME TODAY --
OF ALL THE --!
-- IT'S YOUR BIRTHDAY, REMEMBER --?

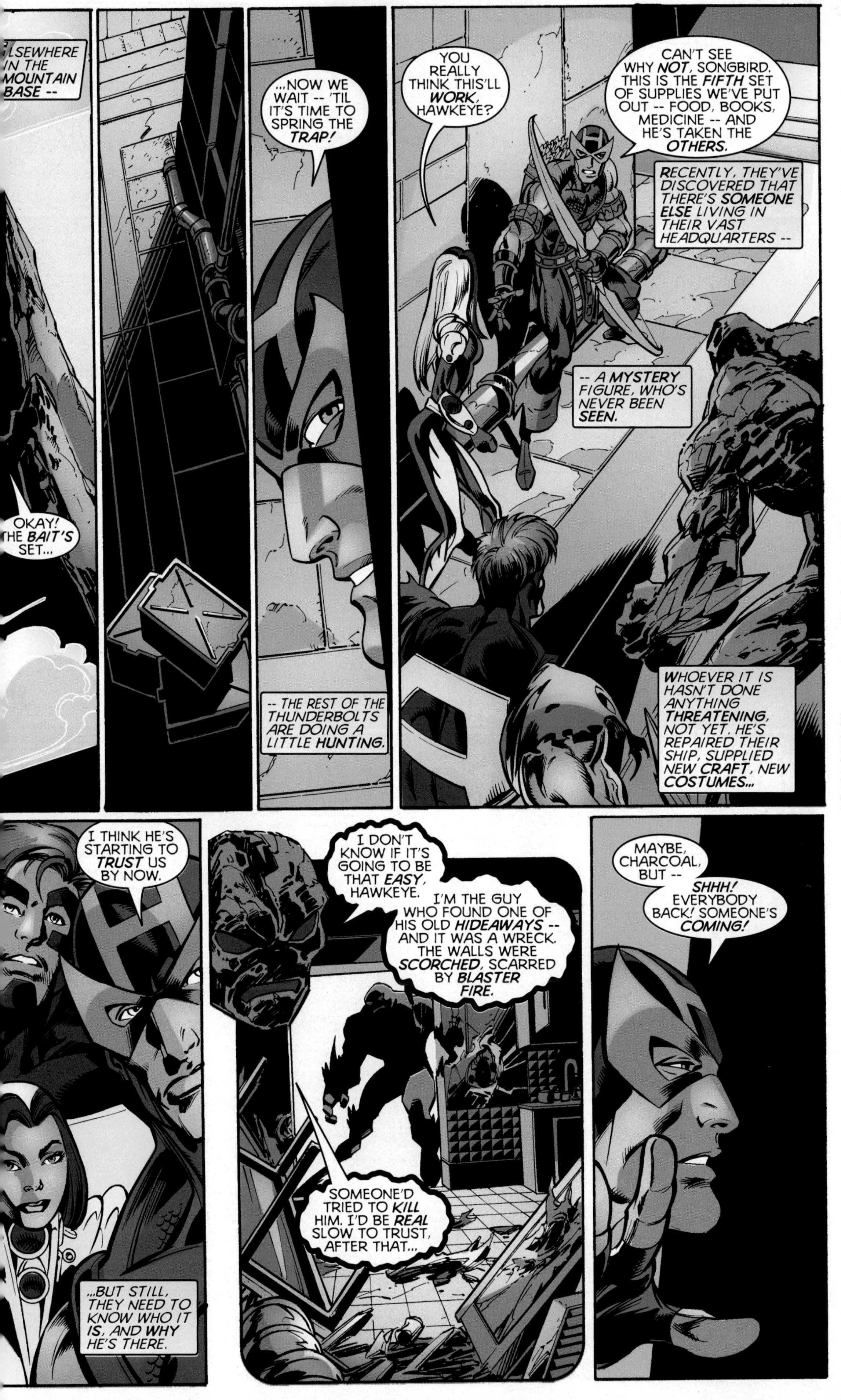
ELSEWHERE IN THE MOUNTAIN BASE --
OKAY! THE BAIT'S SET...
...NOW WE WAIT -- 'TIL IT'S TIME TO SPRING THE TRAP!
-- THE REST OF THE THUNDERBOLTS ARE DOING A LITTLE HUNTING.
YOU REALLY THINK THIS'LL WORK, HAWKEYE?
CAN'T SEE WHY NOT, SONGBIRD. THIS IS THE FIFTH SET OF SUPPLIES WE'VE PUT OUT -- FOOD, BOOKS, MEDICINE -- AND HE'S TAKEN THE OTHERS.
RECENTLY, THEY'VE DISCOVERED THAT THERE'S SOMEONE ELSE LIVING IN THEIR VAST HEADQUARTERS --
-- A MYSTERY FIGURE, WHO'S NEVER BEEN SEEN.
WHOEVER IT IS HASN'T DONE ANYTHING THREATENING, NOT YET. HE'S REPAIRED THEIR SHIP, SUPPLIED NEW CRAFT, NEW COSTUMES...
I THINK HE'S STARTING TO TRUST US BY NOW.
...BUT STILL, THEY NEED TO KNOW WHO IT IS, AND WHY HE'S THERE.
I DON'T KNOW IF IT'S GOING TO BE THAT EASY, HAWKEYE.
I'M THE GUY WHO FOUND ONE OF HIS OLD HIDEAWAYS -- AND IT WAS A WRECK. THE WALLS WERE SCORCHED, SCARRED BY BLASTER FIRE.
SOMEONE'D TRIED TO KILL HIM. I'D BE REAL SLOW TO TRUST, AFTER THAT...
MAYBE, CHARCOAL, BUT --
SHHH! EVERYBODY BACK! SOMEONE'S COMING!

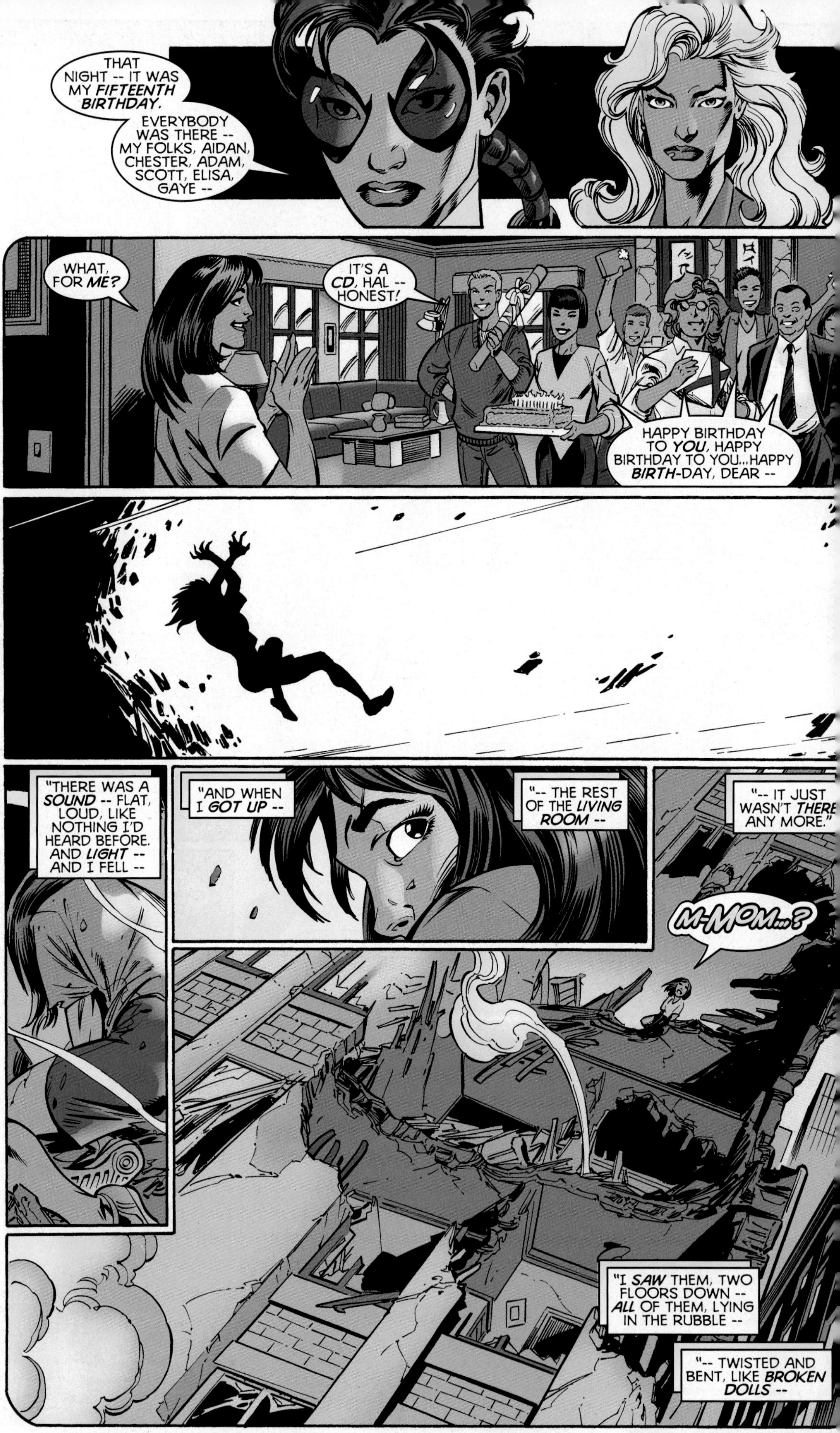
THAT NIGHT -- IT WAS MY *FIFTEENTH BIRTHDAY.*
EVERYBODY WAS THERE -- MY FOLKS, AIDAN, CHESTER, ADAM, SCOTT, ELISA, GAYE --
WHAT, FOR *ME?*
IT'S A *CD,* HAL -- HONEST!
HAPPY BIRTHDAY TO *YOU,* HAPPY BIRTHDAY TO YOU...HAPPY *BIRTH*-DAY, DEAR --
"THERE WAS A *SOUND* -- FLAT, LOUD, LIKE NOTHING I'D HEARD BEFORE. AND *LIGHT* -- AND I FELL --
"AND WHEN I *GOT UP* --
"-- THE REST OF THE *LIVING ROOM* --
"-- IT JUST WASN'T *THERE* ANY MORE."
M-MOM...?
"I *SAW* THEM, TWO FLOORS DOWN -- *ALL* OF THEM, LYING IN THE RUBBLE --
"-- TWISTED AND BENT, LIKE *BROKEN DOLLS* --

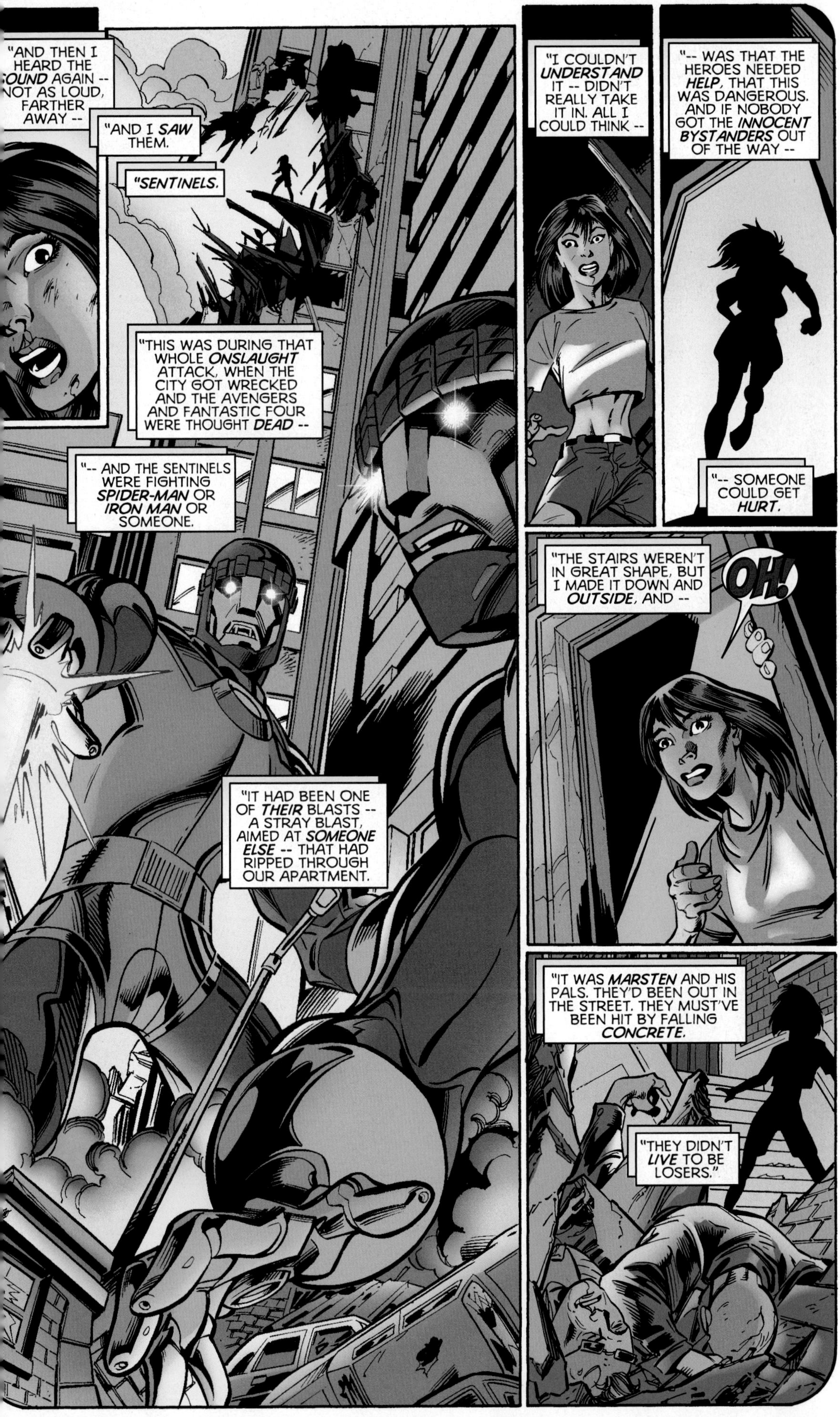
"AND THEN I HEARD THE SOUND AGAIN -- NOT AS LOUD, FARTHER AWAY --
"AND I SAW THEM.
"SENTINELS.
"THIS WAS DURING THAT WHOLE ONSLAUGHT ATTACK, WHEN THE CITY GOT WRECKED AND THE AVENGERS AND FANTASTIC FOUR WERE THOUGHT DEAD --
"-- AND THE SENTINELS WERE FIGHTING SPIDER-MAN OR IRON MAN OR SOMEONE.
"IT HAD BEEN ONE OF THEIR BLASTS -- A STRAY BLAST, AIMED AT SOMEONE ELSE -- THAT HAD RIPPED THROUGH OUR APARTMENT.
"I COULDN'T UNDERSTAND IT -- DIDN'T REALLY TAKE IT IN. ALL I COULD THINK --
"-- WAS THAT THE HEROES NEEDED HELP, THAT THIS WAS DANGEROUS. AND IF NOBODY GOT THE INNOCENT BYSTANDERS OUT OF THE WAY --
"-- SOMEONE COULD GET HURT.
"THE STAIRS WEREN'T IN GREAT SHAPE, BUT I MADE IT DOWN AND OUTSIDE, AND --
OH!
"IT WAS MARSTEN AND HIS PALS. THEY'D BEEN OUT IN THE STREET. THEY MUST'VE BEEN HIT BY FALLING CONCRETE.
"THEY DIDN'T LIVE TO BE LOSERS."

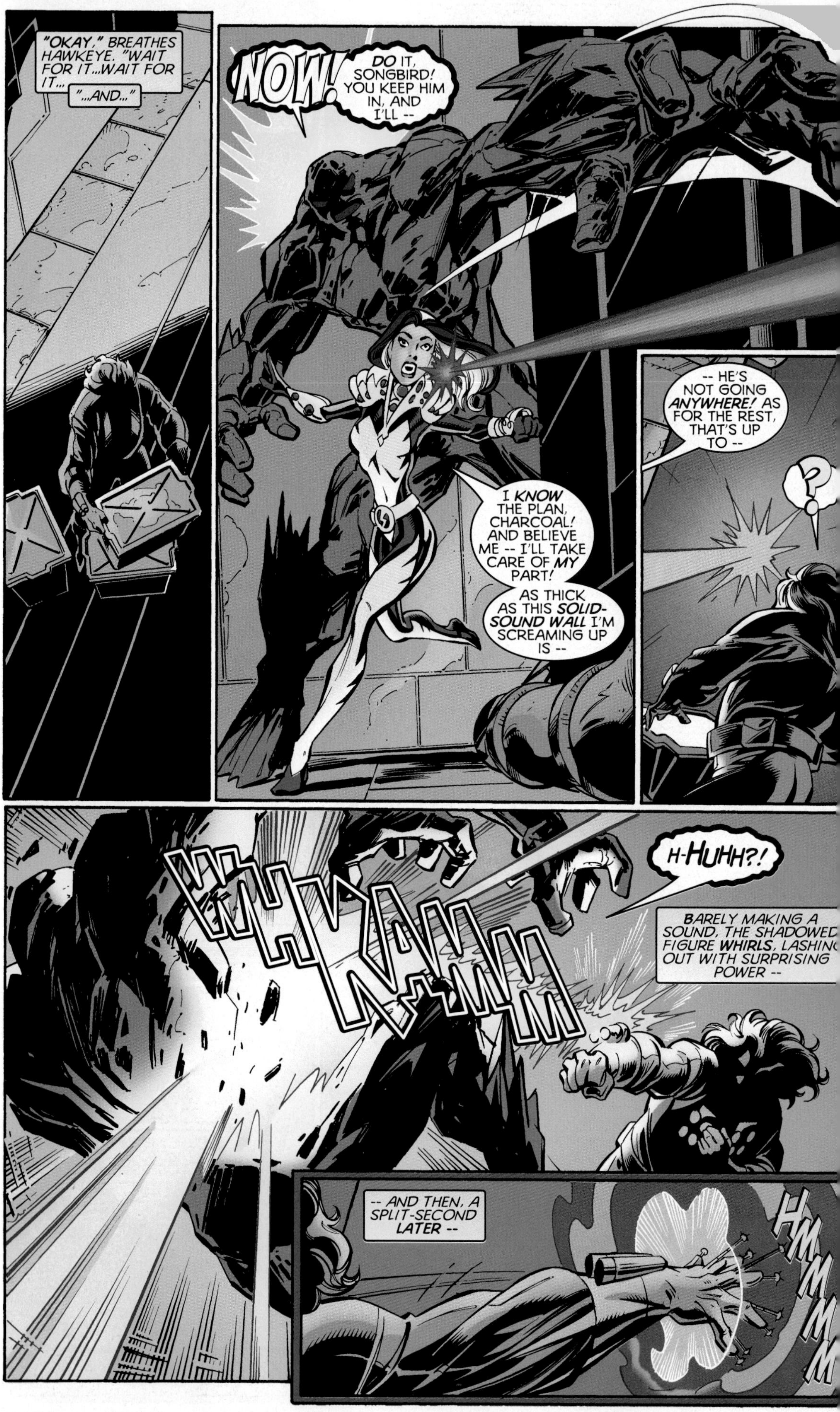
"OKAY," BREATHES HAWKEYE. "WAIT FOR IT...WAIT FOR IT..."
"...AND..."
NOW!
DO IT, SONGBIRD! YOU KEEP HIM IN, AND I'LL --
I KNOW THE PLAN, CHARCOAL! AND BELIEVE ME -- I'LL TAKE CARE OF MY PART!
AS THICK AS THIS SOLID-SOUND WALL I'M SCREAMING UP IS --
-- HE'S NOT GOING ANYWHERE! AS FOR THE REST, THAT'S UP TO --
?
WHAMM
H-HUHH?!
BARELY MAKING A SOUND, THE SHADOWED FIGURE WHIRLS, LASHING OUT WITH SURPRISING POWER --
-- AND THEN, A SPLIT-SECOND LATER --
HMMMMM

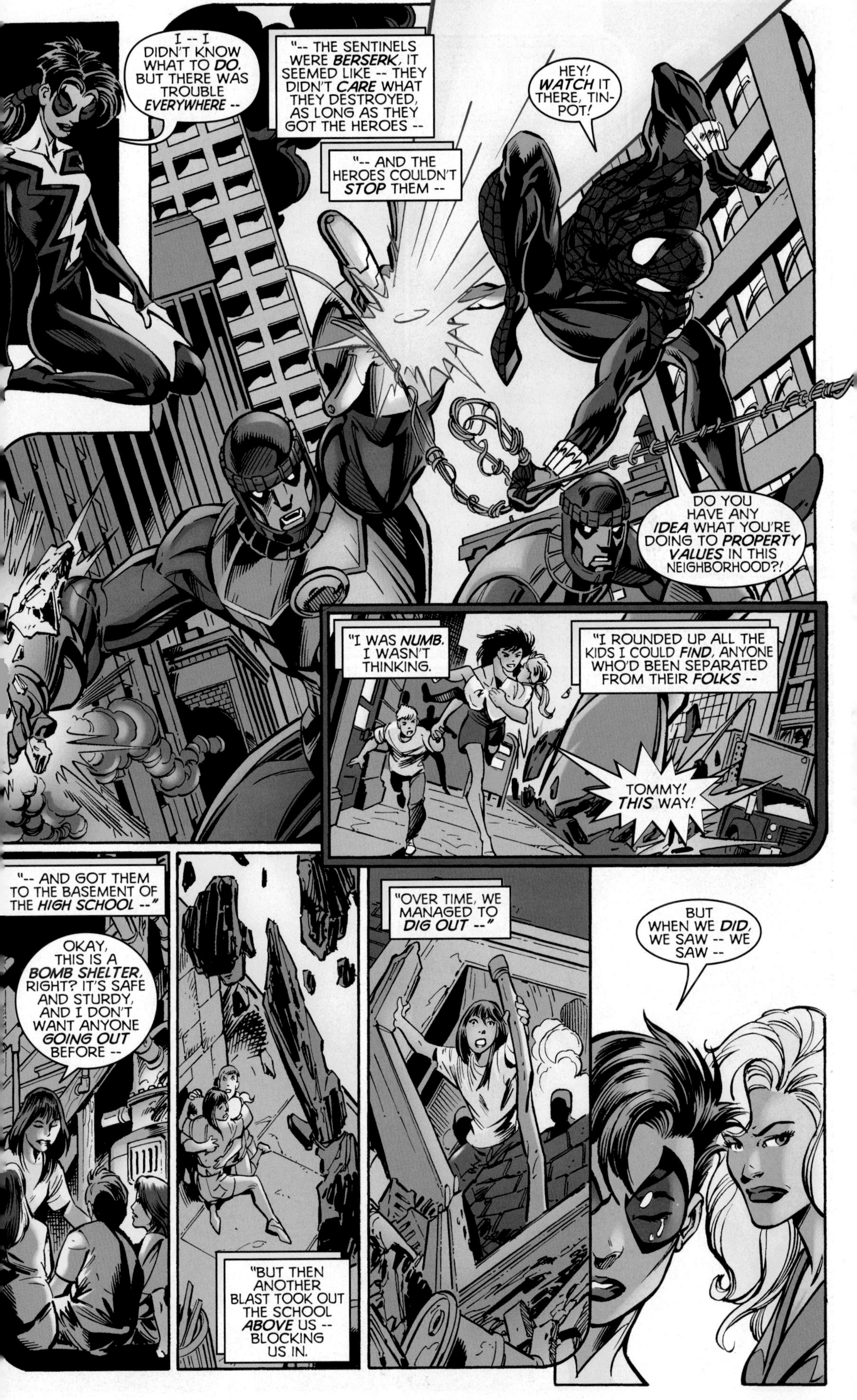
I -- I DIDN'T KNOW WHAT TO DO. BUT THERE WAS TROUBLE EVERYWHERE --
"-- THE SENTINELS WERE BERSERK, IT SEEMED LIKE -- THEY DIDN'T CARE WHAT THEY DESTROYED, AS LONG AS THEY GOT THE HEROES --
"-- AND THE HEROES COULDN'T STOP THEM --
HEY! WATCH IT THERE, TIN-POT!
DO YOU HAVE ANY IDEA WHAT YOU'RE DOING TO PROPERTY VALUES IN THIS NEIGHBORHOOD?!
"I WAS NUMB. I WASN'T THINKING.
"I ROUNDED UP ALL THE KIDS I COULD FIND, ANYONE WHO'D BEEN SEPARATED FROM THEIR FOLKS --
TOMMY! THIS WAY!
"-- AND GOT THEM TO THE BASEMENT OF THE HIGH SCHOOL --"
OKAY, THIS IS A BOMB SHELTER, RIGHT? IT'S SAFE AND STURDY, AND I DON'T WANT ANYONE GOING OUT BEFORE --
"BUT THEN ANOTHER BLAST TOOK OUT THE SCHOOL ABOVE US -- BLOCKING US IN.
"OVER TIME, WE MANAGED TO DIG OUT --"
BUT WHEN WE DID, WE SAW -- WE SAW --

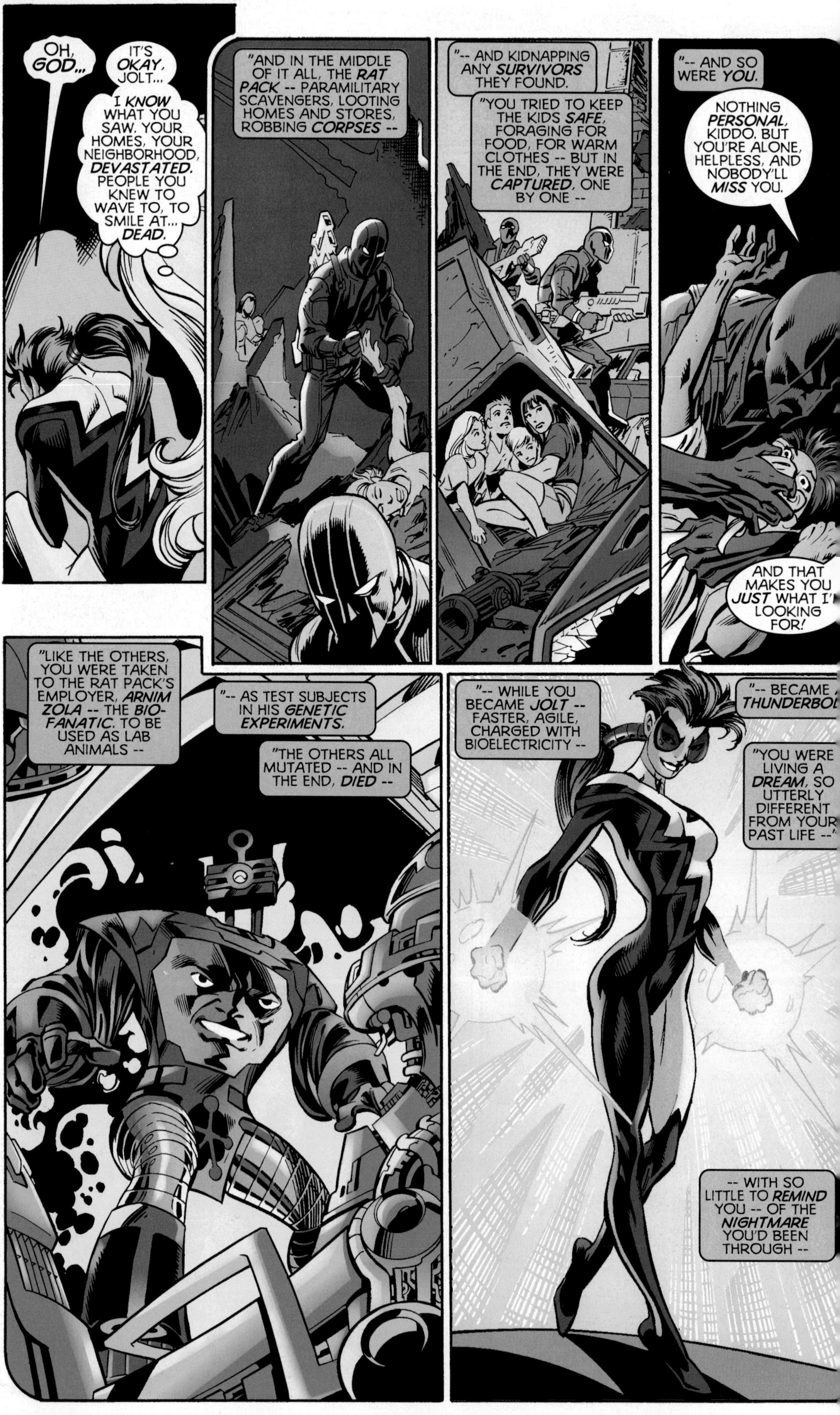
OH, GOD...
IT'S OKAY, JOLT... I KNOW WHAT YOU SAW. YOUR HOMES, YOUR NEIGHBORHOOD, DEVASTATED. PEOPLE YOU KNEW TO WAVE TO, TO SMILE AT... DEAD.
"AND IN THE MIDDLE OF IT ALL, THE RAT PACK -- PARAMILITARY SCAVENGERS, LOOTING HOMES AND STORES, ROBBING CORPSES --
"-- AND KIDNAPPING ANY SURVIVORS THEY FOUND.
"YOU TRIED TO KEEP THE KIDS SAFE, FORAGING FOR FOOD, FOR WARM CLOTHES -- BUT IN THE END, THEY WERE CAPTURED, ONE BY ONE --
"-- AND SO WERE YOU.
NOTHING PERSONAL, KIDDO. BUT YOU'RE ALONE, HELPLESS, AND NOBODY'LL MISS YOU.
AND THAT MAKES YOU JUST WHAT I' LOOKING FOR!
"LIKE THE OTHERS, YOU WERE TAKEN TO THE RAT PACK'S EMPLOYER, ARNIM ZOLA -- THE BIO-FANATIC. TO BE USED AS LAB ANIMALS --
"-- AS TEST SUBJECTS IN HIS GENETIC EXPERIMENTS.
"THE OTHERS ALL MUTATED -- AND IN THE END, DIED --
"-- WHILE YOU BECAME JOLT -- FASTER, AGILE, CHARGED WITH BIOELECTRICITY --
"-- BECAME THUNDERBOL
"YOU WERE LIVING A DREAM, SO UTTERLY DIFFERENT FROM YOUR PAST LIFE --"
-- WITH SO LITTLE TO REMIND YOU -- OF THE NIGHTMARE YOU'D BEEN THROUGH --

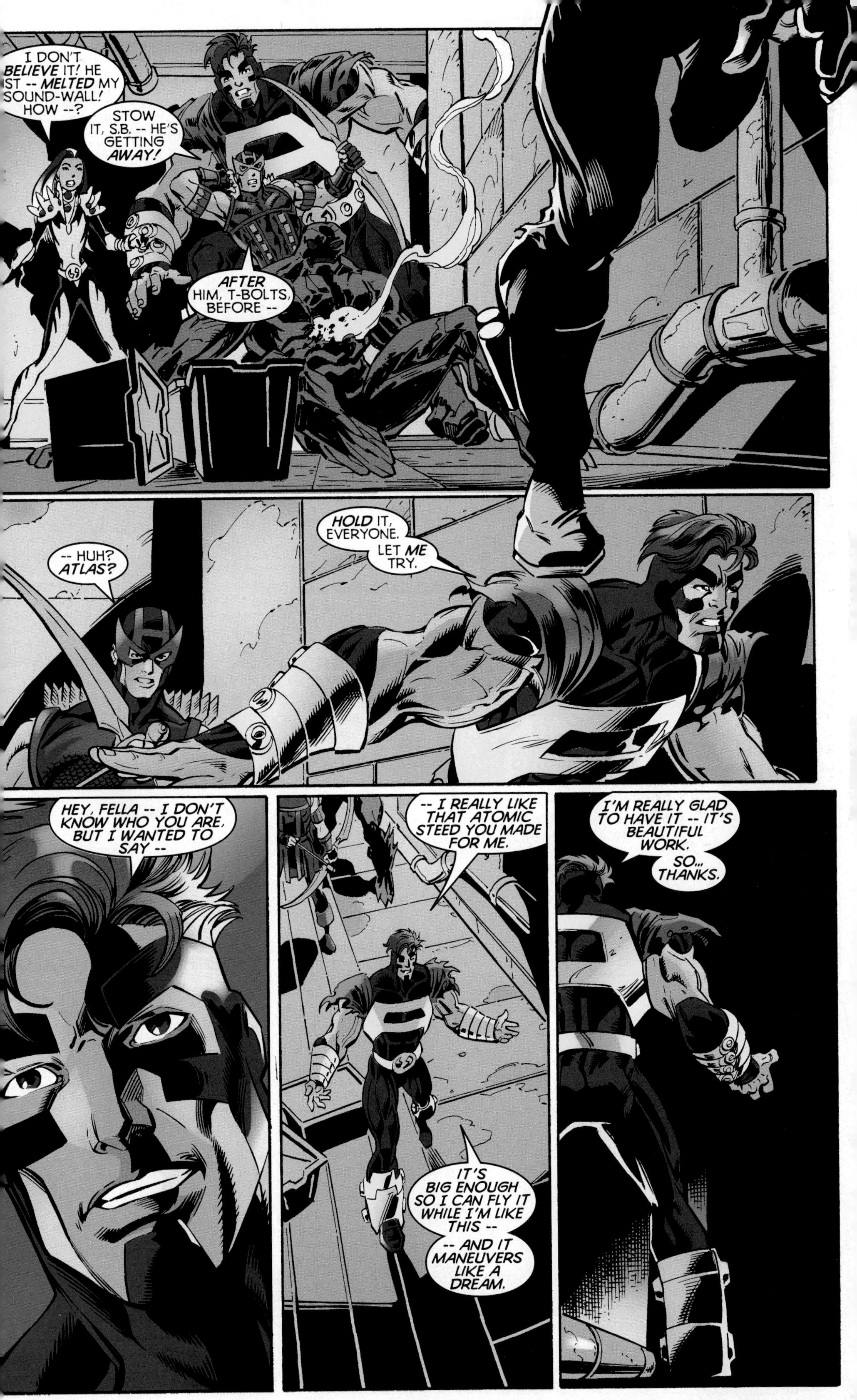
I DON'T BELIEVE IT! HE JUST -- MELTED MY SOUND-WALL! HOW --?
STOW IT, S.B. -- HE'S GETTING AWAY!
AFTER HIM, T-BOLTS, BEFORE --
-- HUH? ATLAS?
HOLD IT, EVERYONE. LET ME TRY.
HEY, FELLA -- I DON'T KNOW WHO YOU ARE, BUT I WANTED TO SAY --
-- I REALLY LIKE THAT ATOMIC STEED YOU MADE FOR ME.
IT'S BIG ENOUGH SO I CAN FLY IT WHILE I'M LIKE THIS --
-- AND IT MANEUVERS LIKE A DREAM.
I'M REALLY GLAD TO HAVE IT -- IT'S BEAUTIFUL WORK.
SO... THANKS.

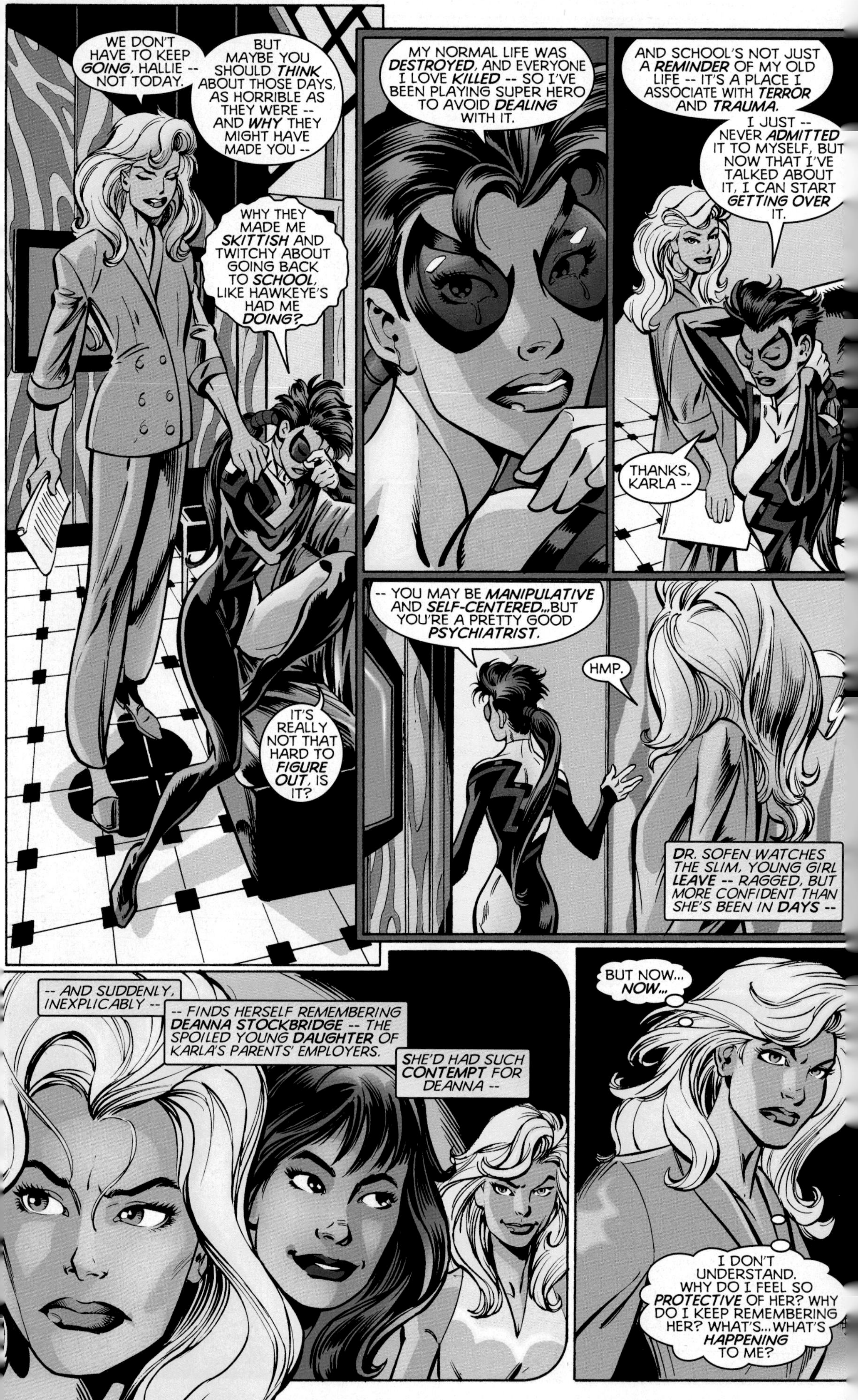

WE DON'T HAVE TO KEEP GOING, HALLIE -- NOT TODAY.
BUT MAYBE YOU SHOULD THINK ABOUT THOSE DAYS, AS HORRIBLE AS THEY WERE -- AND WHY THEY MIGHT HAVE MADE YOU --
WHY THEY MADE ME SKITTISH AND TWITCHY ABOUT GOING BACK TO SCHOOL, LIKE HAWKEYE'S HAD ME DOING?
IT'S REALLY NOT THAT HARD TO FIGURE OUT, IS IT?
MY NORMAL LIFE WAS DESTROYED, AND EVERYONE I LOVE KILLED -- SO I'VE BEEN PLAYING SUPER HERO TO AVOID DEALING WITH IT.
AND SCHOOL'S NOT JUST A REMINDER OF MY OLD LIFE -- IT'S A PLACE I ASSOCIATE WITH TERROR AND TRAUMA.
I JUST -- NEVER ADMITTED IT TO MYSELF, BUT NOW THAT I'VE TALKED ABOUT IT, I CAN START GETTING OVER IT.
THANKS, KARLA --
-- YOU MAY BE MANIPULATIVE AND SELF-CENTERED...BUT YOU'RE A PRETTY GOOD PSYCHIATRIST.
HMP.
DR. SOFEN WATCHES THE SLIM, YOUNG GIRL LEAVE -- RAGGED, BUT MORE CONFIDENT THAN SHE'S BEEN IN DAYS --
-- AND SUDDENLY, INEXPLICABLY --
-- FINDS HERSELF REMEMBERING DEANNA STOCKBRIDGE -- THE SPOILED YOUNG DAUGHTER OF KARLA'S PARENTS' EMPLOYERS.
SHE'D HAD SUCH CONTEMPT FOR DEANNA --
BUT NOW... NOW...
I DON'T UNDERSTAND. WHY DO I FEEL SO PROTECTIVE OF HER? WHY DO I KEEP REMEMBERING HER? WHAT'S...WHAT'S HAPPENING TO ME?

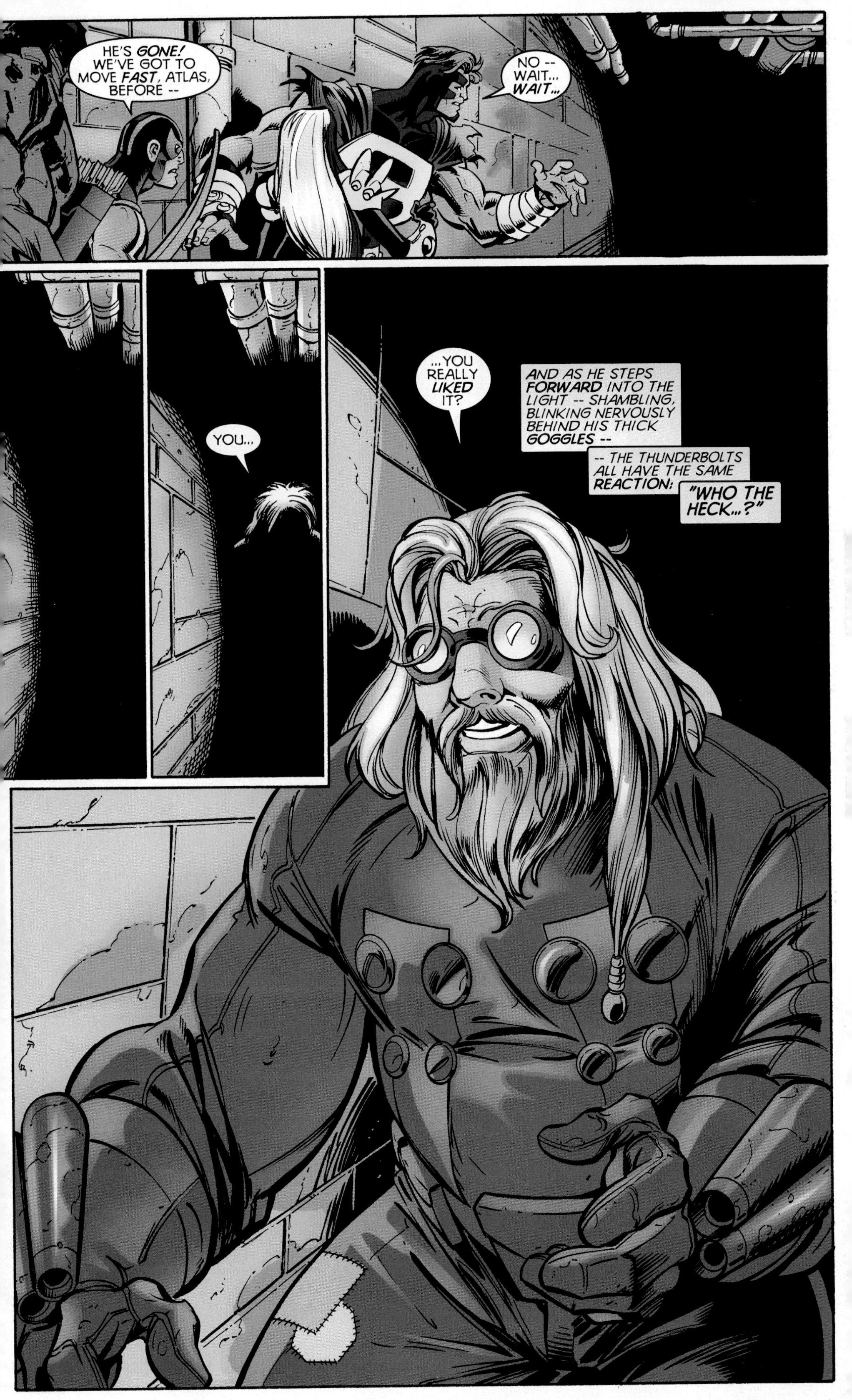
HE'S GONE! WE'VE GOT TO MOVE FAST, ATLAS, BEFORE --
NO -- WAIT... WAIT...
YOU...
...YOU REALLY LIKED IT?
AND AS HE STEPS FORWARD INTO THE LIGHT -- SHAMBLING, BLINKING NERVOUSLY BEHIND HIS THICK GOGGLES --
-- THE THUNDERBOLTS ALL HAVE THE SAME REACTION:
"WHO THE HECK...?"

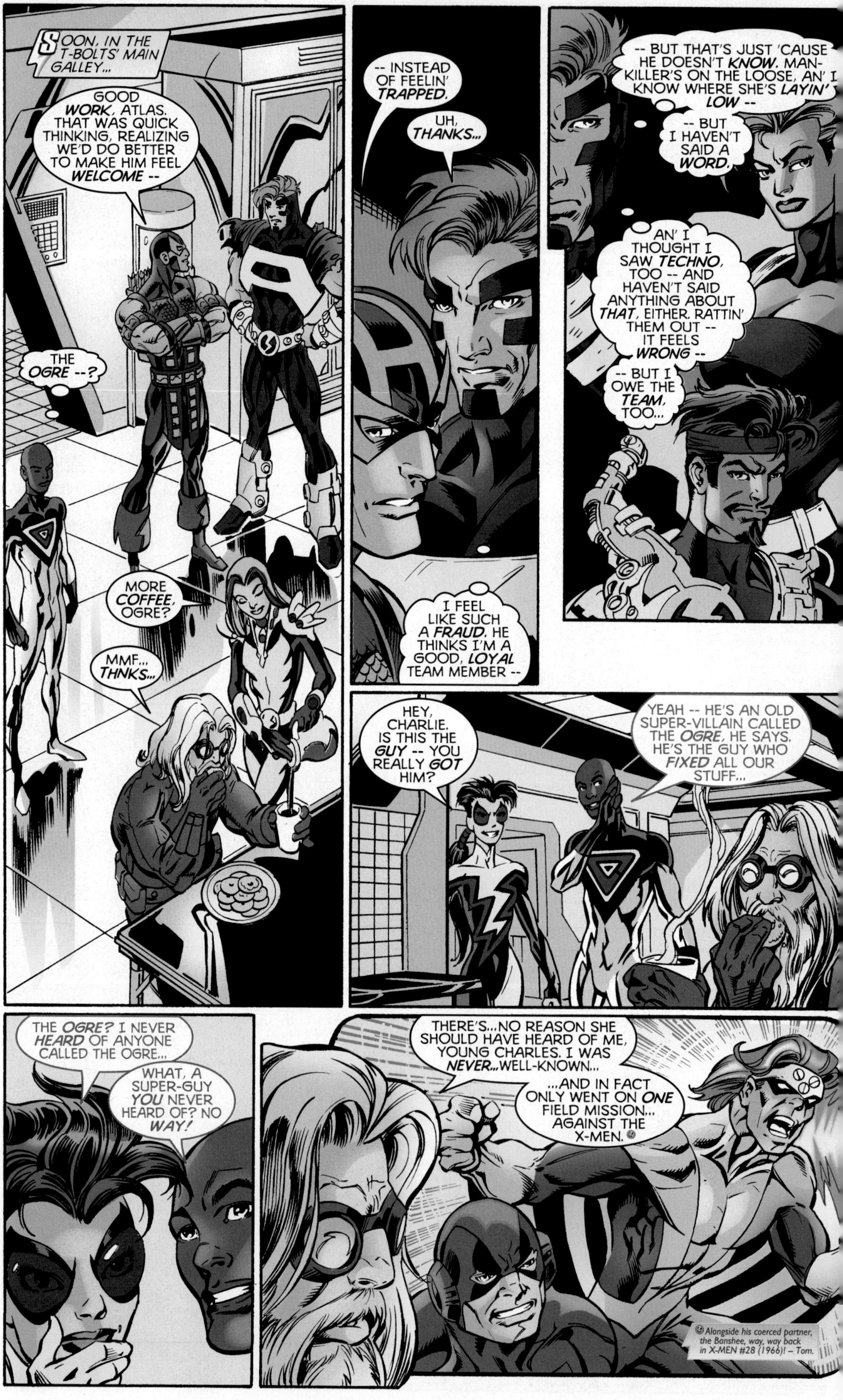
SOON, IN THE T-BOLTS' MAIN GALLEY...
GOOD WORK, ATLAS. THAT WAS QUICK THINKING, REALIZING WE'D DO BETTER TO MAKE HIM FEEL WELCOME --
THE OGRE --?
MORE COFFEE, OGRE?
MMF... THNKS...
-- INSTEAD OF FEELIN' TRAPPED.
UH, THANKS...
I FEEL LIKE SUCH A FRAUD. HE THINKS I'M A GOOD, LOYAL TEAM MEMBER --
-- BUT THAT'S JUST 'CAUSE HE DOESN'T KNOW. MAN-KILLER'S ON THE LOOSE, AN' I KNOW WHERE SHE'S LAYIN' LOW --
-- BUT I HAVEN'T SAID A WORD.
AN' I THOUGHT I SAW TECHNO, TOO -- AND HAVEN'T SAID ANYTHING ABOUT THAT, EITHER. RATTIN' THEM OUT -- IT FEELS WRONG --
-- BUT I OWE THE TEAM, TOO...
HEY, CHARLIE. IS THIS THE GUY -- YOU REALLY GOT HIM?
YEAH -- HE'S AN OLD SUPER-VILLAIN CALLED THE OGRE, HE SAYS. HE'S THE GUY WHO FIXED ALL OUR STUFF...
THE OGRE? I NEVER HEARD OF ANYONE CALLED THE OGRE...
WHAT, A SUPER-GUY YOU NEVER HEARD OF? NO WAY!
THERE'S...NO REASON SHE SHOULD HAVE HEARD OF ME, YOUNG CHARLES. I WAS NEVER...WELL-KNOWN...
...AND IN FACT ONLY WENT ON ONE FIELD MISSION... AGAINST THE X-MEN.
Alongside his coerced partner, the Banshee, way, way back in X-MEN #28 (1966)! – Tom.

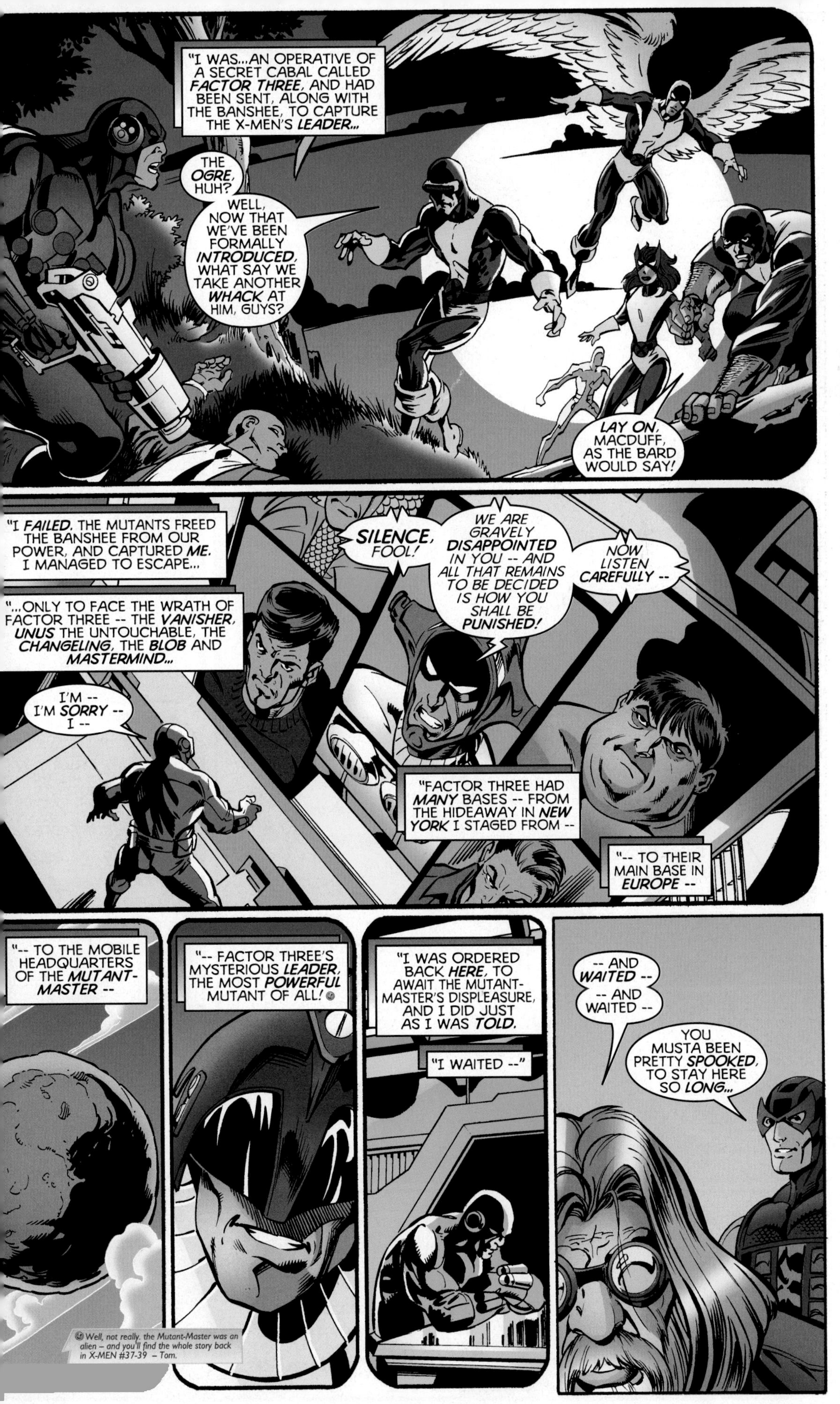
"I WAS...AN OPERATIVE OF A SECRET CABAL CALLED FACTOR THREE, AND HAD BEEN SENT, ALONG WITH THE BANSHEE, TO CAPTURE THE X-MEN'S LEADER...
THE OGRE, HUH?
WELL, NOW THAT WE'VE BEEN FORMALLY INTRODUCED, WHAT SAY WE TAKE ANOTHER WHACK AT HIM, GUYS?
LAY ON, MACDUFF, AS THE BARD WOULD SAY!
"I FAILED. THE MUTANTS FREED THE BANSHEE FROM OUR POWER, AND CAPTURED ME. I MANAGED TO ESCAPE...
"...ONLY TO FACE THE WRATH OF FACTOR THREE -- THE VANISHER, UNUS THE UNTOUCHABLE, THE CHANGELING, THE BLOB AND MASTERMIND...
I'M -- I'M SORRY -- I --
SILENCE, FOOL!
WE ARE GRAVELY DISAPPOINTED IN YOU -- AND ALL THAT REMAINS TO BE DECIDED IS HOW YOU SHALL BE PUNISHED!
NOW LISTEN CAREFULLY --
"FACTOR THREE HAD MANY BASES -- FROM THE HIDEAWAY IN NEW YORK I STAGED FROM --
"-- TO THEIR MAIN BASE IN EUROPE --
"-- TO THE MOBILE HEADQUARTERS OF THE MUTANT-MASTER --
Well, not really. the Mutant-Master was an alien – and you'll find the whole story back in X-MEN #37-39 – Tom.
"-- FACTOR THREE'S MYSTERIOUS LEADER, THE MOST POWERFUL MUTANT OF ALL!
"I WAS ORDERED BACK HERE, TO AWAIT THE MUTANT-MASTER'S DISPLEASURE, AND I DID JUST AS I WAS TOLD.
"I WAITED --"
-- AND WAITED --
-- AND WAITED --
YOU MUSTA BEEN PRETTY SPOOKED, TO STAY HERE SO LONG...

WELL...I'VE *NEVER* BEEN A TERRIBLY *ASSERTIVE* PERSON...

IN ANY CASE, IT WAS *YEARS* LATER THAT THEY RETURNED -- OR *MOST* OF THEM DID, ANYWAY...

YOU SHOULDA *SEEN* IT, VANISHER. THAT *"BEAST"* CHARACTER -- LIKE THE X-MEN'S BEAST, BUT HAIRY AND *SAVAGE* --

-- HE PLOWED THROUGH MASTERMIND'S ILLUSIONS LIKE THEY WEREN'T EVEN *THERE* -- LEFT HIM RAVING IN THE *GUTTER!*

HMMPH. AS I *RECALL*, UNUS, YOU AND THE BLOB HARDLY FARED ANY *BETTER*... ©

THANKS TO THE VANISHER TELEPORTIN' AND MASTERMI COVER-ILLUSIONS, WE G US A TAP ON THAT *CEREB COMPUTER* OF THE X-MEN'S.

INTERNAL SECURITY *BURNT IT OUT* REAL FAST --

© *They're talking about* AMAZING ADVENTURES #13 *(1972) -- Tom.*

YEAH, WELL, THAT AIN'T *IMPORTANT* NO MORE -- NOW THAT *FACTOR THREE* IS UP AN' RUNNIN' AGAIN!

"I DIDN'T KNOW WHERE THEY'D *BEEN*, OR WHY THEY WAITED SO LONG TO *REUNITE* --

-- BUT NOT BEFORE WE SECURED *INFORMATION* ON ALL THE MUTANTS XAVIER KNOWS OF BUT HASN'T *CONTACTED* YET! AND *WITH* THAT INFORMATION --

"-- I WAS JUST HAPPY TO FEEL *USEFUL* AGAIN.

"BUT AFTER A WEEK OR TWO, THEY *LEFT*, TELLING ME TO KEEP AN *EYE* ON THINGS...

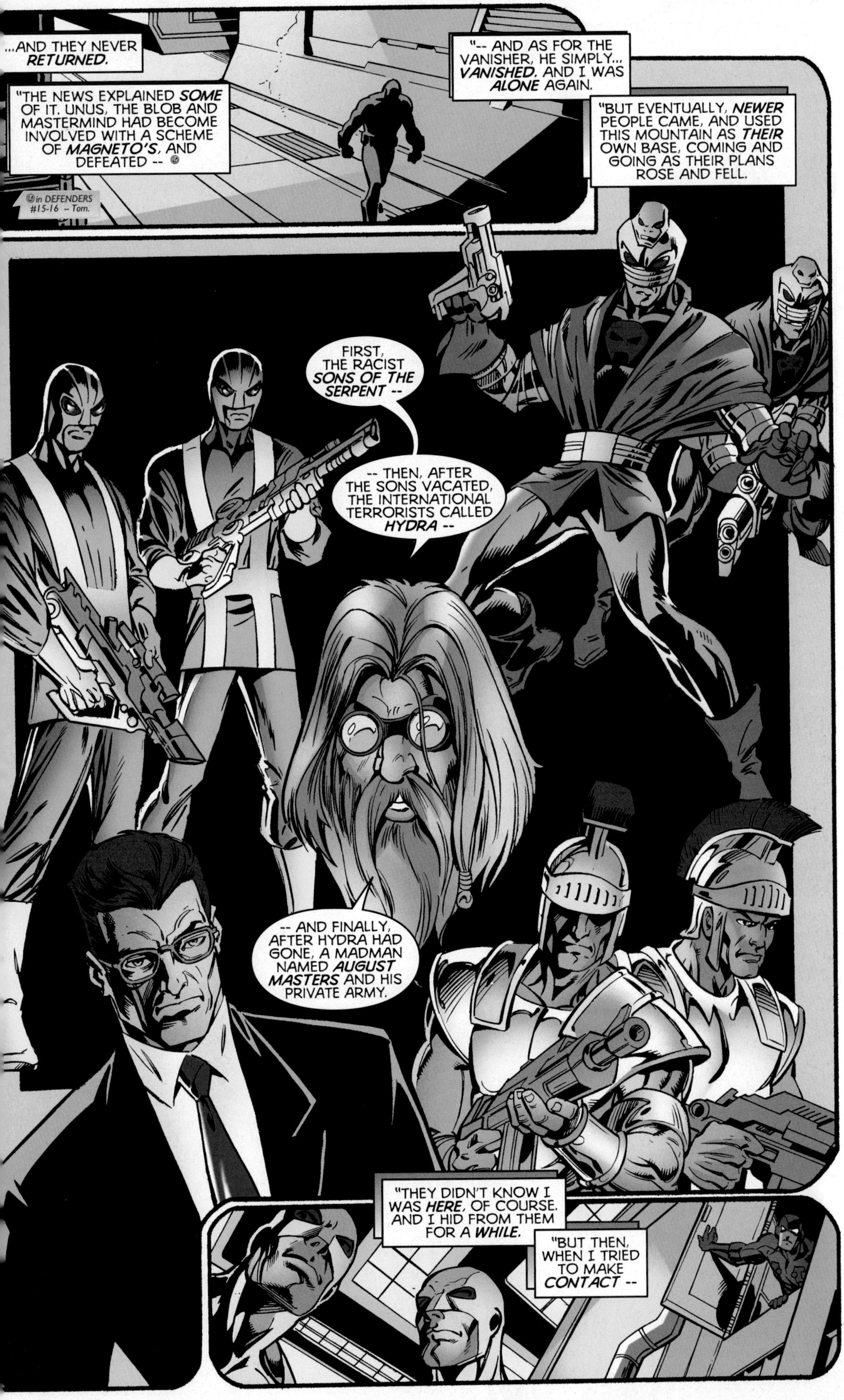

...AND THEY NEVER RETURNED.
"THE NEWS EXPLAINED SOME OF IT. UNUS, THE BLOB AND MASTERMIND HAD BECOME INVOLVED WITH A SCHEME OF MAGNETO'S, AND DEFEATED --
in DEFENDERS #15-16 – Tom.
"-- AND AS FOR THE VANISHER, HE SIMPLY... VANISHED. AND I WAS ALONE AGAIN.
"BUT EVENTUALLY, NEWER PEOPLE CAME, AND USED THIS MOUNTAIN AS THEIR OWN BASE, COMING AND GOING AS THEIR PLANS ROSE AND FELL.
FIRST, THE RACIST SONS OF THE SERPENT --
-- THEN, AFTER THE SONS VACATED, THE INTERNATIONAL TERRORISTS CALLED HYDRA --
-- AND FINALLY, AFTER HYDRA HAD GONE, A MADMAN NAMED AUGUST MASTERS AND HIS PRIVATE ARMY.
"THEY DIDN'T KNOW I WAS HERE, OF COURSE. AND I HID FROM THEM FOR A WHILE.
"BUT THEN, WHEN I TRIED TO MAKE CONTACT --

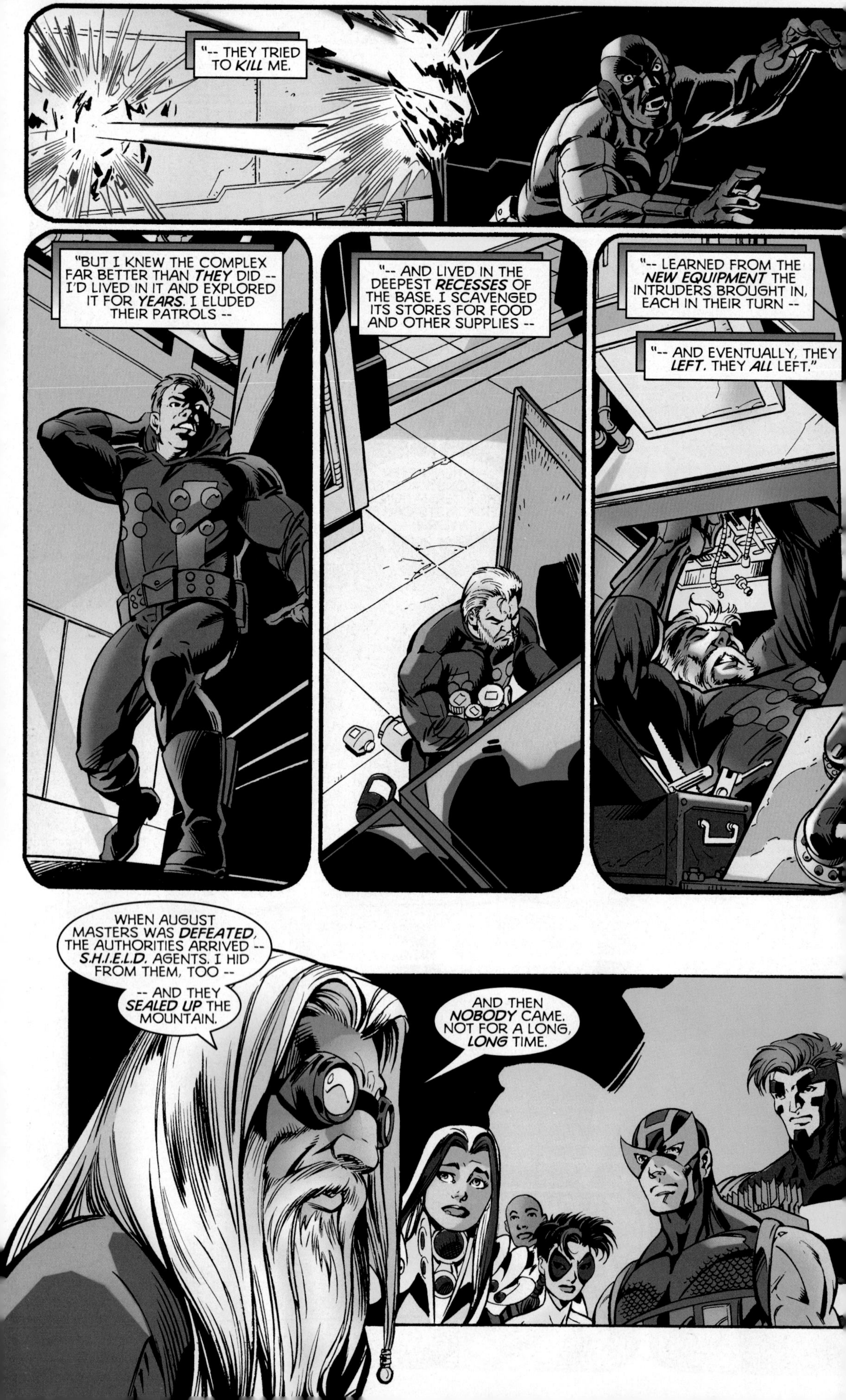
"-- THEY TRIED TO *KILL* ME.
"BUT I KNEW THE COMPLEX FAR BETTER THAN *THEY* DID -- I'D LIVED IN IT AND EXPLORED IT FOR *YEARS*. I ELUDED THEIR PATROLS --
"-- AND LIVED IN THE DEEPEST *RECESSES* OF THE BASE. I SCAVENGED ITS STORES FOR FOOD AND OTHER SUPPLIES --
"-- LEARNED FROM THE *NEW EQUIPMENT* THE INTRUDERS BROUGHT IN, EACH IN THEIR TURN --
"-- AND EVENTUALLY, THEY *LEFT*. THEY *ALL* LEFT."
WHEN AUGUST MASTERS WAS *DEFEATED*, THE AUTHORITIES ARRIVED -- *S.H.I.E.L.D.* AGENTS. I HID FROM THEM, TOO --
-- AND THEY *SEALED UP* THE MOUNTAIN.
AND THEN *NOBODY* CAME. NOT FOR A LONG, *LONG* TIME.

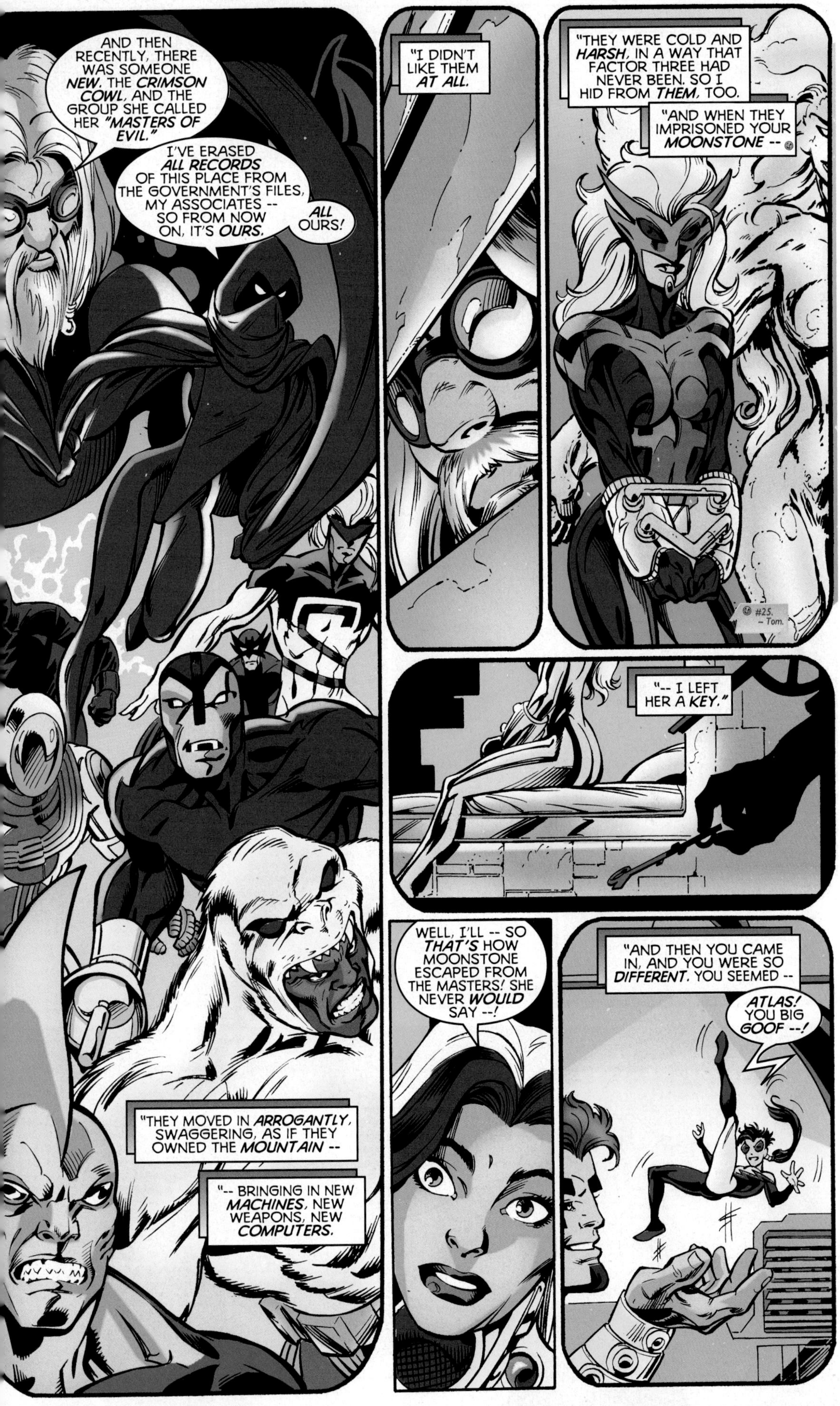
AND THEN RECENTLY, THERE WAS SOMEONE NEW. THE CRIMSON COWL, AND THE GROUP SHE CALLED HER "MASTERS OF EVIL."
I'VE ERASED ALL RECORDS OF THIS PLACE FROM THE GOVERNMENT'S FILES, MY ASSOCIATES -- SO FROM NOW ON, IT'S OURS.
ALL OURS!
"THEY MOVED IN ARROGANTLY, SWAGGERING, AS IF THEY OWNED THE MOUNTAIN --
"-- BRINGING IN NEW MACHINES, NEW WEAPONS, NEW COMPUTERS.
"I DIDN'T LIKE THEM AT ALL.
"THEY WERE COLD AND HARSH, IN A WAY THAT FACTOR THREE HAD NEVER BEEN. SO I HID FROM THEM, TOO.
"AND WHEN THEY IMPRISONED YOUR MOONSTONE --
#25. -- Tom.
"-- I LEFT HER A KEY."
WELL, I'LL -- SO THAT'S HOW MOONSTONE ESCAPED FROM THE MASTERS! SHE NEVER WOULD SAY --!
"AND THEN YOU CAME IN, AND YOU WERE SO DIFFERENT. YOU SEEMED --
ATLAS! YOU BIG GOOF --!

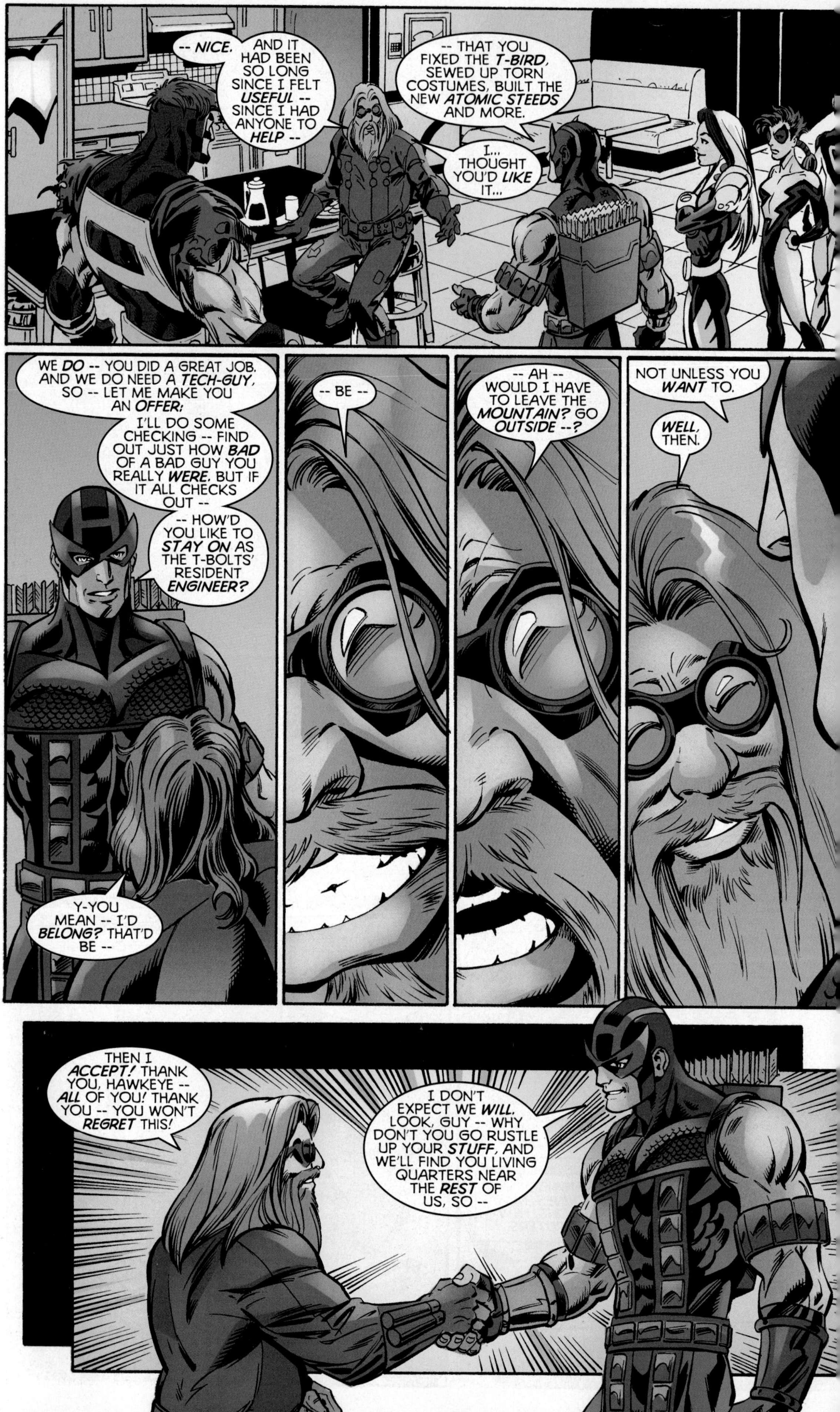
-- NICE.
AND IT HAD BEEN SO LONG SINCE I FELT USEFUL -- SINCE I HAD ANYONE TO HELP --
-- THAT YOU FIXED THE T-BIRD, SEWED UP TORN COSTUMES, BUILT THE NEW ATOMIC STEEDS AND MORE.
I... THOUGHT YOU'D LIKE IT...
WE DO -- YOU DID A GREAT JOB. AND WE DO NEED A TECH-GUY, SO -- LET ME MAKE YOU AN OFFER:
I'LL DO SOME CHECKING -- FIND OUT JUST HOW BAD OF A BAD GUY YOU REALLY WERE. BUT IF IT ALL CHECKS OUT --
-- HOW'D YOU LIKE TO STAY ON AS THE T-BOLTS' RESIDENT ENGINEER?
Y-YOU MEAN -- I'D BELONG? THAT'D BE --
-- BE --
-- AH -- WOULD I HAVE TO LEAVE THE MOUNTAIN? GO OUTSIDE --?
NOT UNLESS YOU WANT TO.
WELL, THEN.
THEN I ACCEPT! THANK YOU, HAWKEYE -- ALL OF YOU! THANK YOU -- YOU WON'T REGRET THIS!
I DON'T EXPECT WE WILL. LOOK, GUY -- WHY DON'T YOU GO RUSTLE UP YOUR STUFF, AND WE'LL FIND YOU LIVING QUARTERS NEAR THE REST OF US, SO --

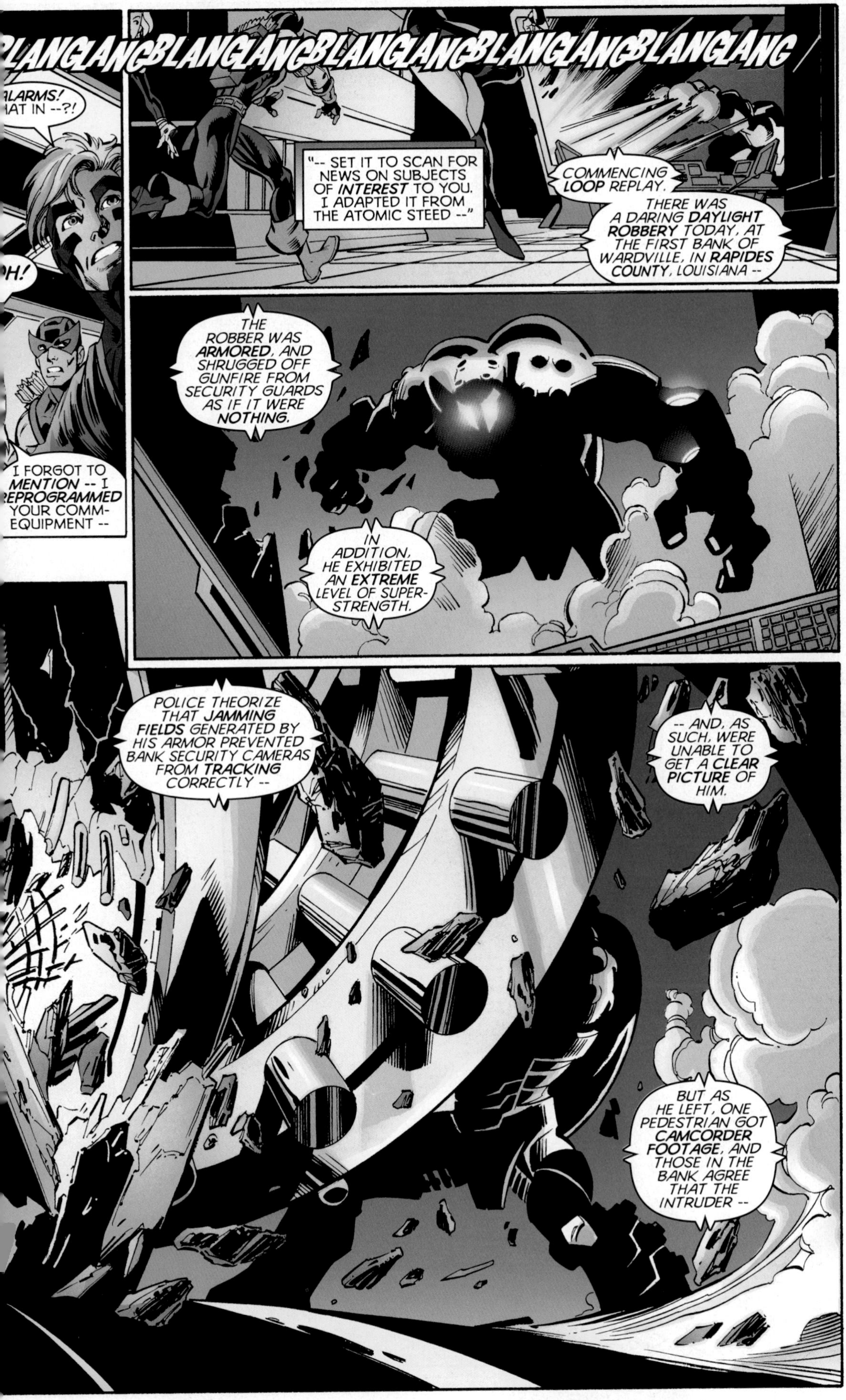
BLANGLANGBLANGLANGBLANGLANGBLANGLANGBLANGLANG
ALARMS! WHAT IN --?!
"-- SET IT TO SCAN FOR NEWS ON SUBJECTS OF INTEREST TO YOU. I ADAPTED IT FROM THE ATOMIC STEED --"
COMMENCING LOOP REPLAY.
THERE WAS A DARING DAYLIGHT ROBBERY TODAY, AT THE FIRST BANK OF WARDVILLE, IN RAPIDES COUNTY, LOUISIANA --
OH!
I FORGOT TO MENTION -- I REPROGRAMMED YOUR COMM-EQUIPMENT --
THE ROBBER WAS ARMORED, AND SHRUGGED OFF GUNFIRE FROM SECURITY GUARDS AS IF IT WERE NOTHING.
IN ADDITION, HE EXHIBITED AN EXTREME LEVEL OF SUPER-STRENGTH.
POLICE THEORIZE THAT JAMMING FIELDS GENERATED BY HIS ARMOR PREVENTED BANK SECURITY CAMERAS FROM TRACKING CORRECTLY --
-- AND, AS SUCH, WERE UNABLE TO GET A CLEAR PICTURE OF HIM.
BUT AS HE LEFT, ONE PEDESTRIAN GOT CAMCORDER FOOTAGE, AND THOSE IN THE BANK AGREE THAT THE INTRUDER --

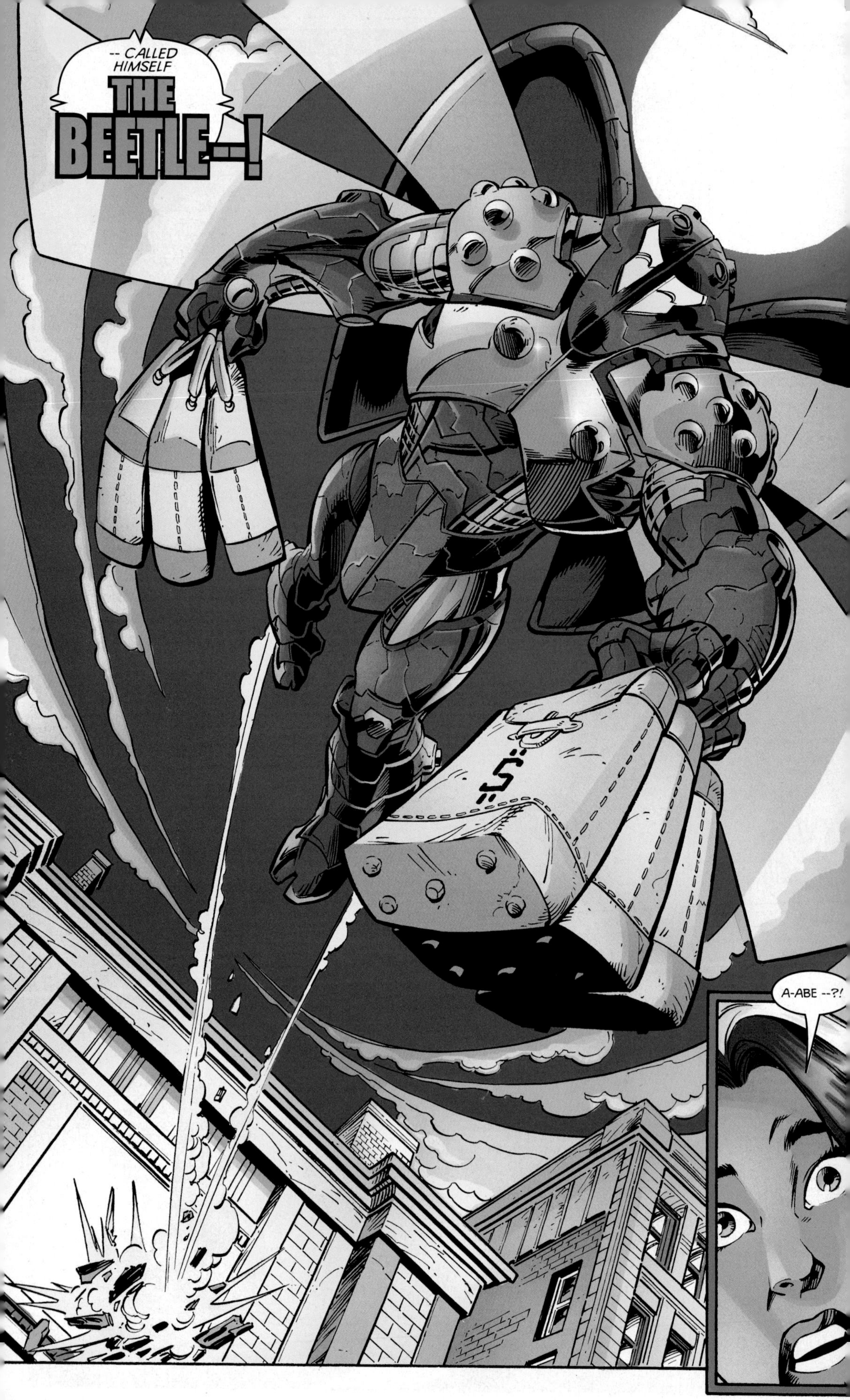
-- CALLED HIMSELF
THE BEETLE--!
A-ABE --?!

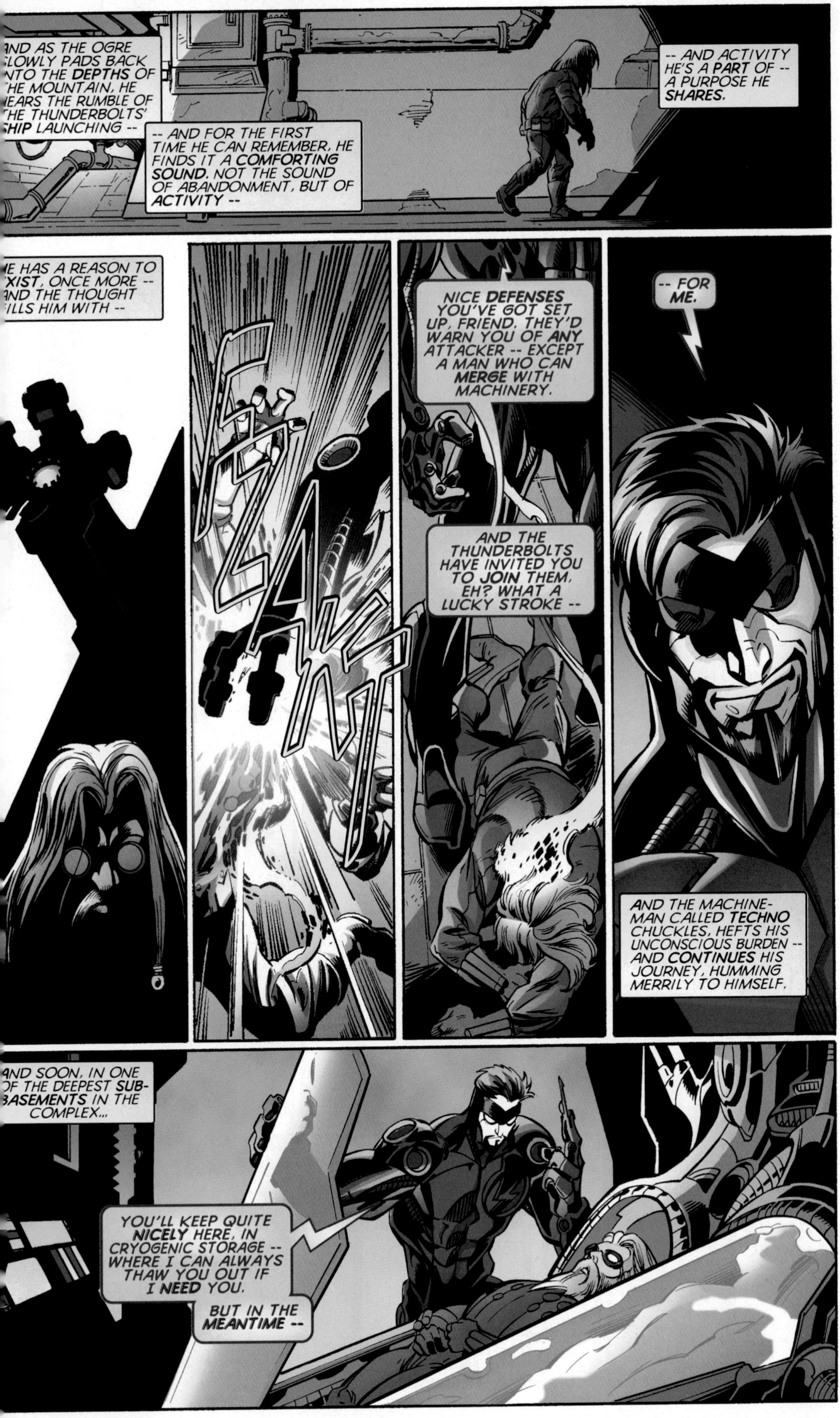

AND AS THE OGRE SLOWLY PADS BACK INTO THE DEPTHS OF THE MOUNTAIN, HE HEARS THE RUMBLE OF THE THUNDERBOLTS' SHIP LAUNCHING --
-- AND FOR THE FIRST TIME HE CAN REMEMBER, HE FINDS IT A COMFORTING SOUND. NOT THE SOUND OF ABANDONMENT, BUT OF ACTIVITY --
-- AND ACTIVITY HE'S A PART OF -- A PURPOSE HE SHARES.
HE HAS A REASON TO EXIST, ONCE MORE -- AND THE THOUGHT FILLS HIM WITH --
FZZAKT
NICE DEFENSES YOU'VE GOT SET UP, FRIEND. THEY'D WARN YOU OF ANY ATTACKER -- EXCEPT A MAN WHO CAN MERGE WITH MACHINERY.
AND THE THUNDERBOLTS HAVE INVITED YOU TO JOIN THEM, EH? WHAT A LUCKY STROKE --
-- FOR ME.
AND THE MACHINE-MAN CALLED TECHNO CHUCKLES, HEFTS HIS UNCONSCIOUS BURDEN -- AND CONTINUES HIS JOURNEY, HUMMING MERRILY TO HIMSELF.
AND SOON, IN ONE OF THE DEEPEST SUB-BASEMENTS IN THE COMPLEX...
YOU'LL KEEP QUITE NICELY HERE, IN CRYOGENIC STORAGE -- WHERE I CAN ALWAYS THAW YOU OUT IF I NEED YOU.
BUT IN THE MEANTIME --

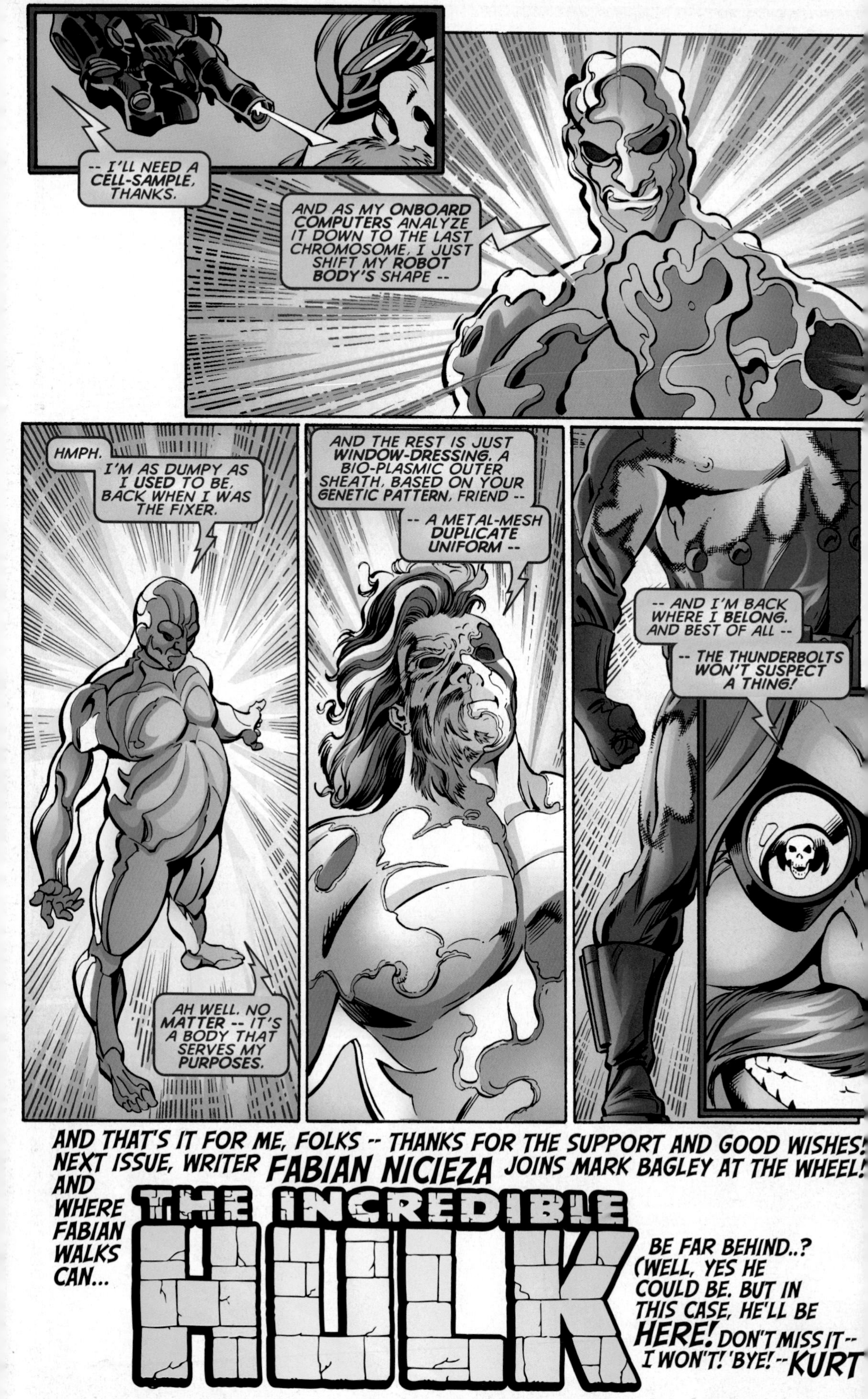
-- I'LL NEED A CELL-SAMPLE, THANKS.
AND AS MY ONBOARD COMPUTERS ANALYZE IT DOWN TO THE LAST CHROMOSOME, I JUST SHIFT MY ROBOT BODY'S SHAPE --
HMPH.
I'M AS DUMPY AS I USED TO BE, BACK WHEN I WAS THE FIXER.
AH WELL. NO MATTER -- IT'S A BODY THAT SERVES MY PURPOSES.
AND THE REST IS JUST WINDOW-DRESSING. A BIO-PLASMIC OUTER SHEATH, BASED ON YOUR GENETIC PATTERN, FRIEND
-- A METAL-MESH DUPLICATE UNIFORM --
-- AND I'M BACK WHERE I BELONG. AND BEST OF ALL --
-- THE THUNDERBOLTS WON'T SUSPECT A THING!

AND THAT'S IT FOR ME, FOLKS -- THANKS FOR THE SUPPORT AND GOOD WISHES! NEXT ISSUE, WRITER **FABIAN NICIEZA** JOINS MARK BAGLEY AT THE WHEEL! AND WHERE FABIAN WALKS CAN... **THE INCREDIBLE HULK** BE FAR BEHIND..? (WELL, YES HE COULD BE. BUT IN THIS CASE, HE'LL BE **HERE!** DON'T MISS IT-- I WON'T! 'BYE! --**KURT**

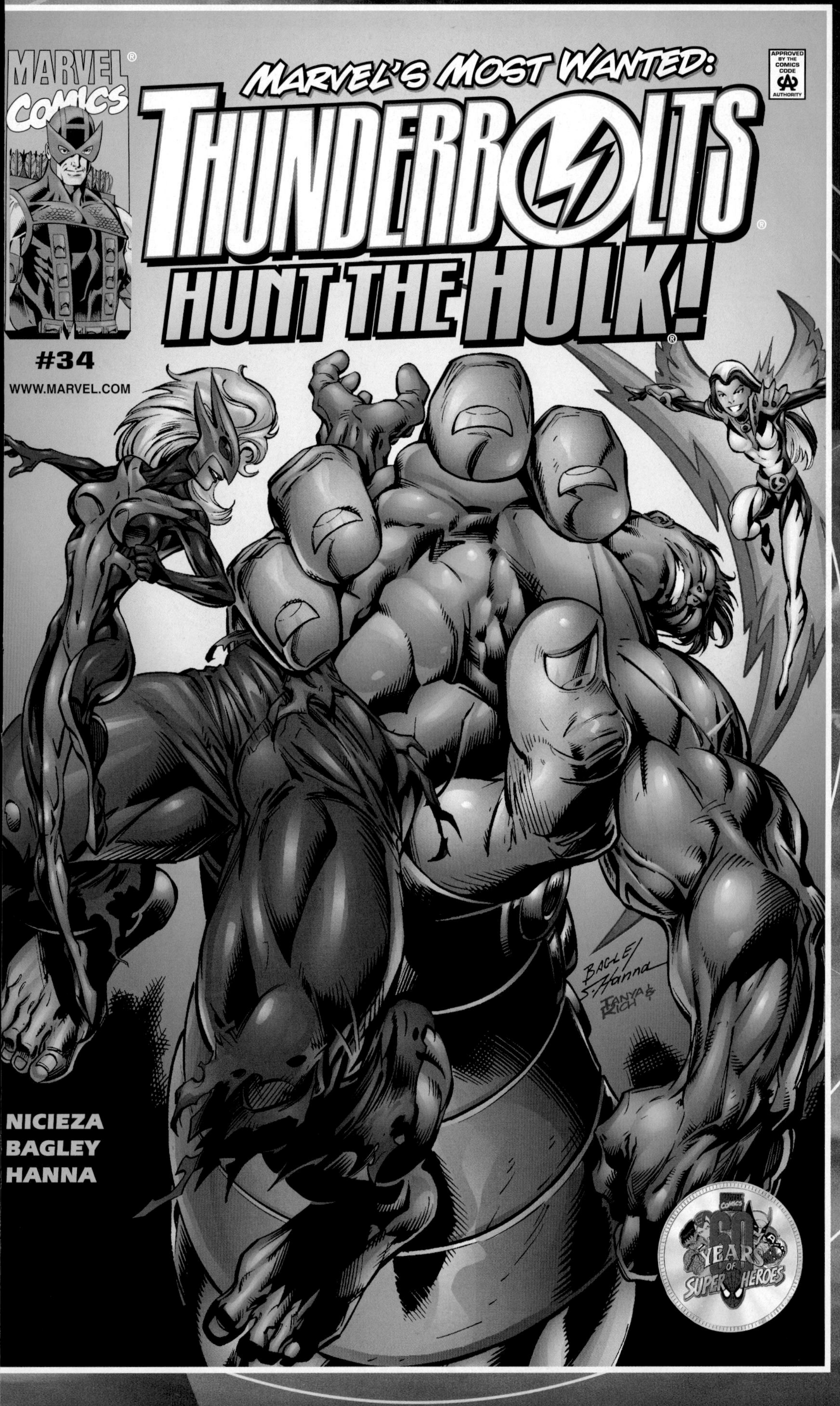
MARVEL COMICS
APPROVED BY THE COMICS CODE AUTHORITY
MARVEL'S MOST WANTED:
THUNDERBOLTS
HUNT THE HULK!
#34
WWW.MARVEL.COM
NICIEZA
BAGLEY
HANNA
60 YEARS OF SUPER HEROES

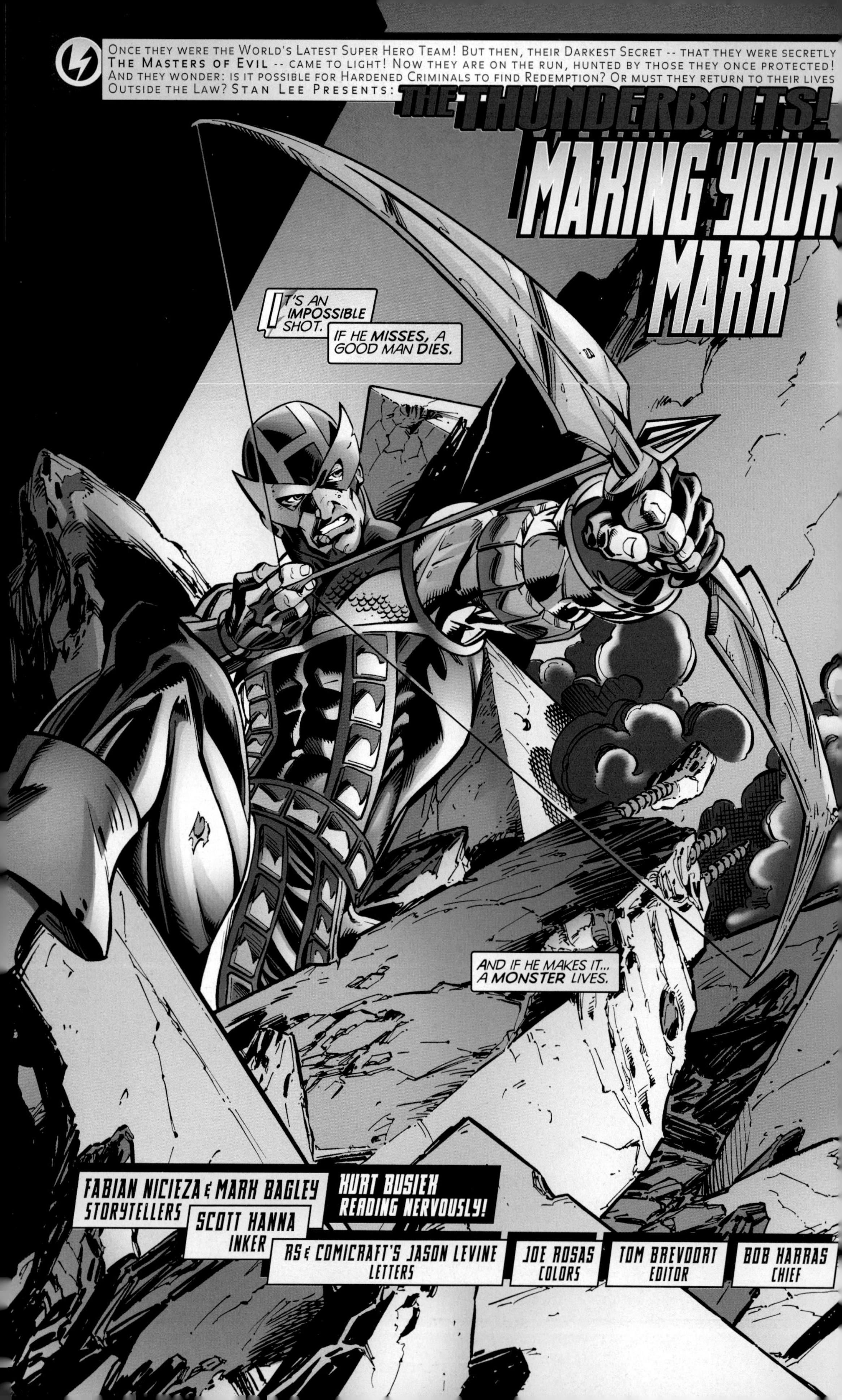
Once they were the World's Latest Super Hero Team! But then, their Darkest Secret -- that they were secretly The Masters of Evil -- came to light! Now they are on the run, hunted by those they once protected! And they wonder: is it possible for Hardened Criminals to find Redemption? Or must they return to their lives Outside the Law? Stan Lee Presents:
THE THUNDERBOLTS!
MAKING YOUR MARK
IT'S AN IMPOSSIBLE SHOT.
IF HE MISSES, A GOOD MAN DIES.
AND IF HE MAKES IT... A MONSTER LIVES.
FABIAN NICIEZA & MARK BAGLEY STORYTELLERS
KURT BUSIEK READING NERVOUSLY!
SCOTT HANNA INKER
RS & COMICRAFT'S JASON LEVINE LETTERS
JOE ROSAS COLORS
TOM BREVOORT EDITOR
BOB HARRAS CHIEF

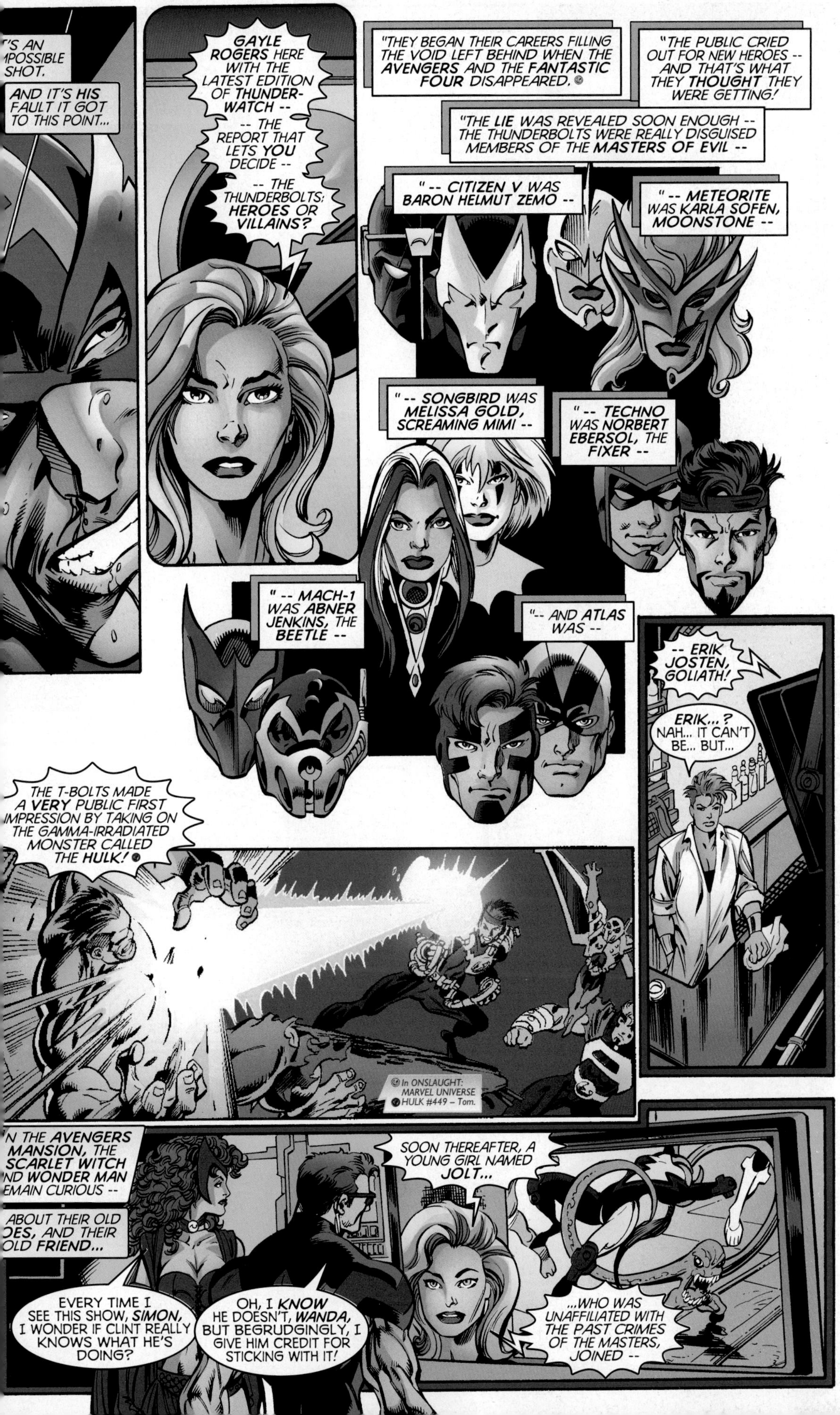

'S AN
MPOSSIBLE
SHOT.
AND IT'S HIS FAULT IT GOT TO THIS POINT...
GAYLE ROGERS HERE WITH THE LATEST EDITION OF THUNDER-WATCH --
-- THE REPORT THAT LETS YOU DECIDE --
-- THE THUNDERBOLTS: HEROES OR VILLAINS?
"THEY BEGAN THEIR CAREERS FILLING THE VOID LEFT BEHIND WHEN THE AVENGERS AND THE FANTASTIC FOUR DISAPPEARED.
"THE PUBLIC CRIED OUT FOR NEW HEROES -- AND THAT'S WHAT THEY THOUGHT THEY WERE GETTING!
"THE LIE WAS REVEALED SOON ENOUGH -- THE THUNDERBOLTS WERE REALLY DISGUISED MEMBERS OF THE MASTERS OF EVIL --
" -- CITIZEN V WAS BARON HELMUT ZEMO --
" -- METEORITE WAS KARLA SOFEN, MOONSTONE --
" -- SONGBIRD WAS MELISSA GOLD, SCREAMING MIMI --
" -- TECHNO WAS NORBERT EBERSOL, THE FIXER --
" -- MACH-1 WAS ABNER JENKINS, THE BEETLE --
"-- AND ATLAS WAS --
-- ERIK JOSTEN, GOLIATH!
ERIK...? NAH... IT CAN'T BE... BUT...
THE T-BOLTS MADE A VERY PUBLIC FIRST IMPRESSION BY TAKING ON THE GAMMA-IRRADIATED MONSTER CALLED THE HULK!
In ONSLAUGHT: MARVEL UNIVERSE
HULK #449 – Tom.
N THE AVENGERS MANSION, THE SCARLET WITCH ND WONDER MAN EMAIN CURIOUS --
ABOUT THEIR OLD OES, AND THEIR OLD FRIEND...
EVERY TIME I SEE THIS SHOW, SIMON, I WONDER IF CLINT REALLY KNOWS WHAT HE'S DOING?
OH, I KNOW HE DOESN'T, WANDA, BUT BEGRUDGINGLY, I GIVE HIM CREDIT FOR STICKING WITH IT!
SOON THEREAFTER, A YOUNG GIRL NAMED JOLT...
...WHO WAS UNAFFILIATED WITH THE PAST CRIMES OF THE MASTERS, JOINED --

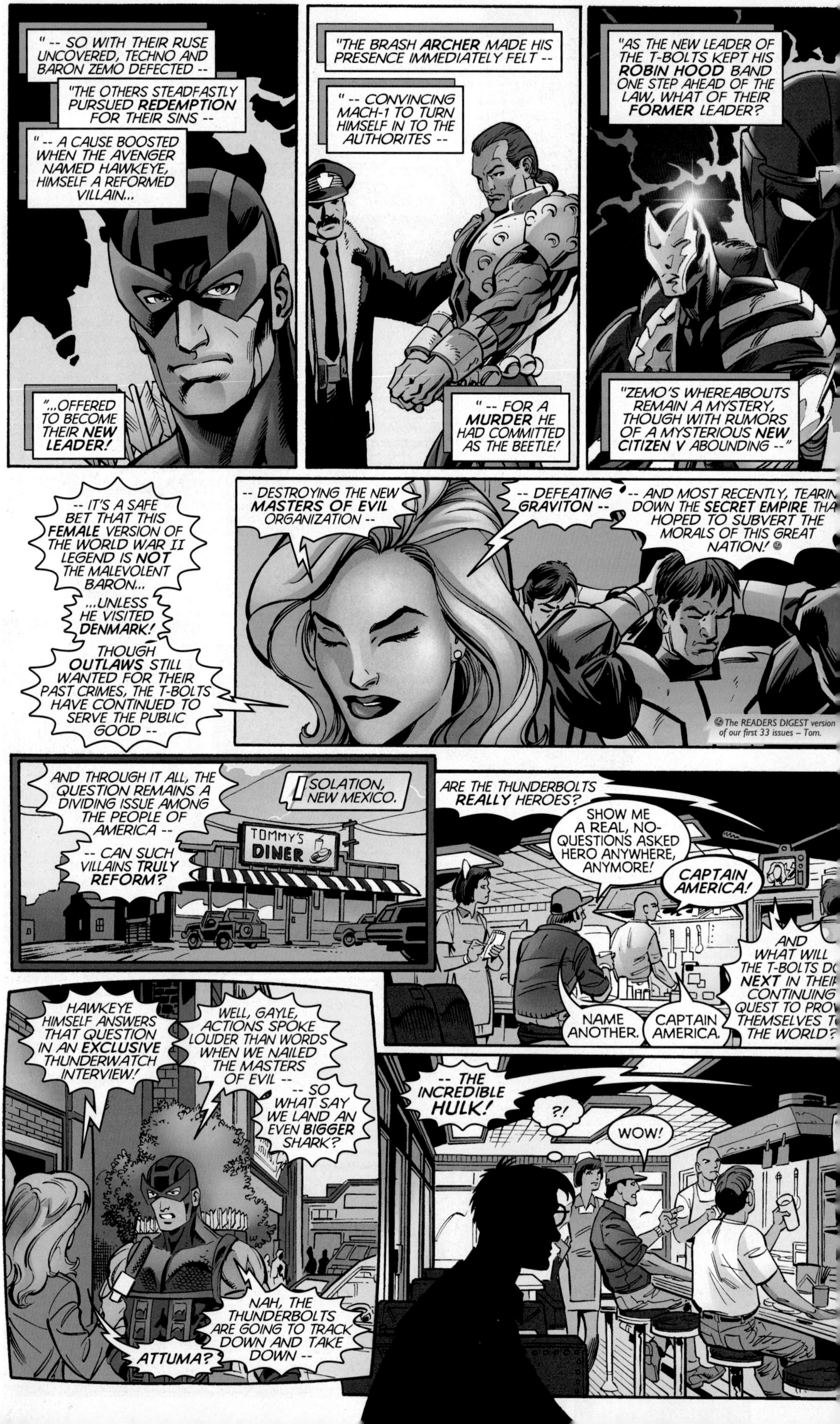
" -- SO WITH THEIR RUSE UNCOVERED, TECHNO AND BARON ZEMO DEFECTED --
"THE OTHERS STEADFASTLY PURSUED REDEMPTION FOR THEIR SINS --
" -- A CAUSE BOOSTED WHEN THE AVENGER NAMED HAWKEYE, HIMSELF A REFORMED VILLAIN...
"...OFFERED TO BECOME THEIR NEW LEADER!
"THE BRASH ARCHER MADE HIS PRESENCE IMMEDIATELY FELT --
" -- CONVINCING MACH-1 TO TURN HIMSELF IN TO THE AUTHORITES --
" -- FOR A MURDER HE HAD COMMITTED AS THE BEETLE!
"AS THE NEW LEADER OF THE T-BOLTS KEPT HIS ROBIN HOOD BAND ONE STEP AHEAD OF THE LAW, WHAT OF THEIR FORMER LEADER?
"ZEMO'S WHEREABOUTS REMAIN A MYSTERY, THOUGH WITH RUMORS OF A MYSTERIOUS NEW CITIZEN V ABOUNDING --"
-- IT'S A SAFE BET THAT THIS FEMALE VERSION OF THE WORLD WAR II LEGEND IS NOT THE MALEVOLENT BARON...
...UNLESS HE VISITED DENMARK!
THOUGH OUTLAWS STILL WANTED FOR THEIR PAST CRIMES, THE T-BOLTS HAVE CONTINUED TO SERVE THE PUBLIC GOOD --
-- DESTROYING THE NEW MASTERS OF EVIL ORGANIZATION --
-- DEFEATING GRAVITON --
-- AND MOST RECENTLY, TEARIN DOWN THE SECRET EMPIRE THA HOPED TO SUBVERT THE MORALS OF THIS GREAT NATION!
The READERS DIGEST version of our first 33 issues -- Tom.
AND THROUGH IT ALL, THE QUESTION REMAINS A DIVIDING ISSUE AMONG THE PEOPLE OF AMERICA --
-- CAN SUCH VILLAINS TRULY REFORM?
ISOLATION, NEW MEXICO.
TOMMY'S DINER
ARE THE THUNDERBOLTS REALLY HEROES?
SHOW ME A REAL, NO-QUESTIONS ASKED HERO ANYWHERE, ANYMORE!
CAPTAIN AMERICA!
NAME ANOTHER.
CAPTAIN AMERICA.
AND WHAT WILL THE T-BOLTS DO NEXT IN THEIR CONTINUING QUEST TO PROV THEMSELVES T THE WORLD?
HAWKEYE HIMSELF ANSWERS THAT QUESTION IN AN EXCLUSIVE THUNDERWATCH INTERVIEW!
WELL, GAYLE, ACTIONS SPOKE LOUDER THAN WORDS WHEN WE NAILED THE MASTERS OF EVIL --
-- SO WHAT SAY WE LAND AN EVEN BIGGER SHARK?
ATTUMA?
NAH, THE THUNDERBOLTS ARE GOING TO TRACK DOWN AND TAKE DOWN --
-- THE INCREDIBLE HULK!
?!
WOW!

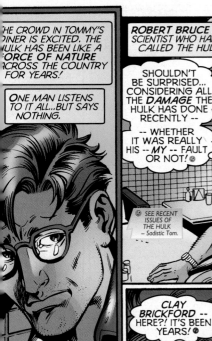

THE CROWD IN TOMMY'S DINER IS EXCITED. THE HULK HAS BEEN LIKE A FORCE OF NATURE ACROSS THE COUNTRY FOR YEARS!

ONE MAN LISTENS TO IT ALL...BUT SAYS NOTHING.

ROBERT BRUCE BANNER, A FRAIL SCIENTIST WHO HARBORS THE CREATURE CALLED THE HULK INSIDE HIM!

SHOULDN'T BE SURPRISED... CONSIDERING ALL THE DAMAGE THE HULK HAS DONE RECENTLY --

-- WHETHER IT WAS REALLY HIS -- MY -- FAULT OR NOT!

SEE RECENT ISSUES OF THE HULK – Sadistic Tom.

AFTER THAT AIRPLANE CRASH KILLED SO MANY PEOPLE, YA'D THINK SOMEONE WOULDA HAD THE STONES TO DO THIS BY NOW!

MORE POWER TO THE T-BOLTS IF THEY GET HIM!

GET WHO?

OH, HEY, CLAY, HOW'S IT GOIN' AT THE SITE?

CLAY BRICKFORD -- HERE?! IT'S BEEN YEARS!

SINCE HULK #179, TO BE PRECISE – Tom.

ROXXON BROKE GROUND AN' JUST LIKE THEY PROMISED --

-- RESIDENTS OF ISOLATION GET FIRST CRACK AT THE JOBS!

HOPE THERE'RE STILL JOBS LEFT AFTER THE HULK SHOWS UP!

THE HULK? HAS HE BEEN SEEN NEARBY?

THAT MONSTER WON'T RUIN MY LIFE AGAIN!

CLAY? HEY, HE WAS IN TEXAS, LAST ANYONE HEARD! I WAS JUST KIDDING --

MT. CHARTERIS OVERLOOKING BURTON CANYON, COLORADO --

THWUDD

-- WHOSE VAST INTERIOR SERVES AS THE SECRET HEADQUARTERS OF THE THUNDERBOLTS...

YOU SAID WE'D DO WHAT?!

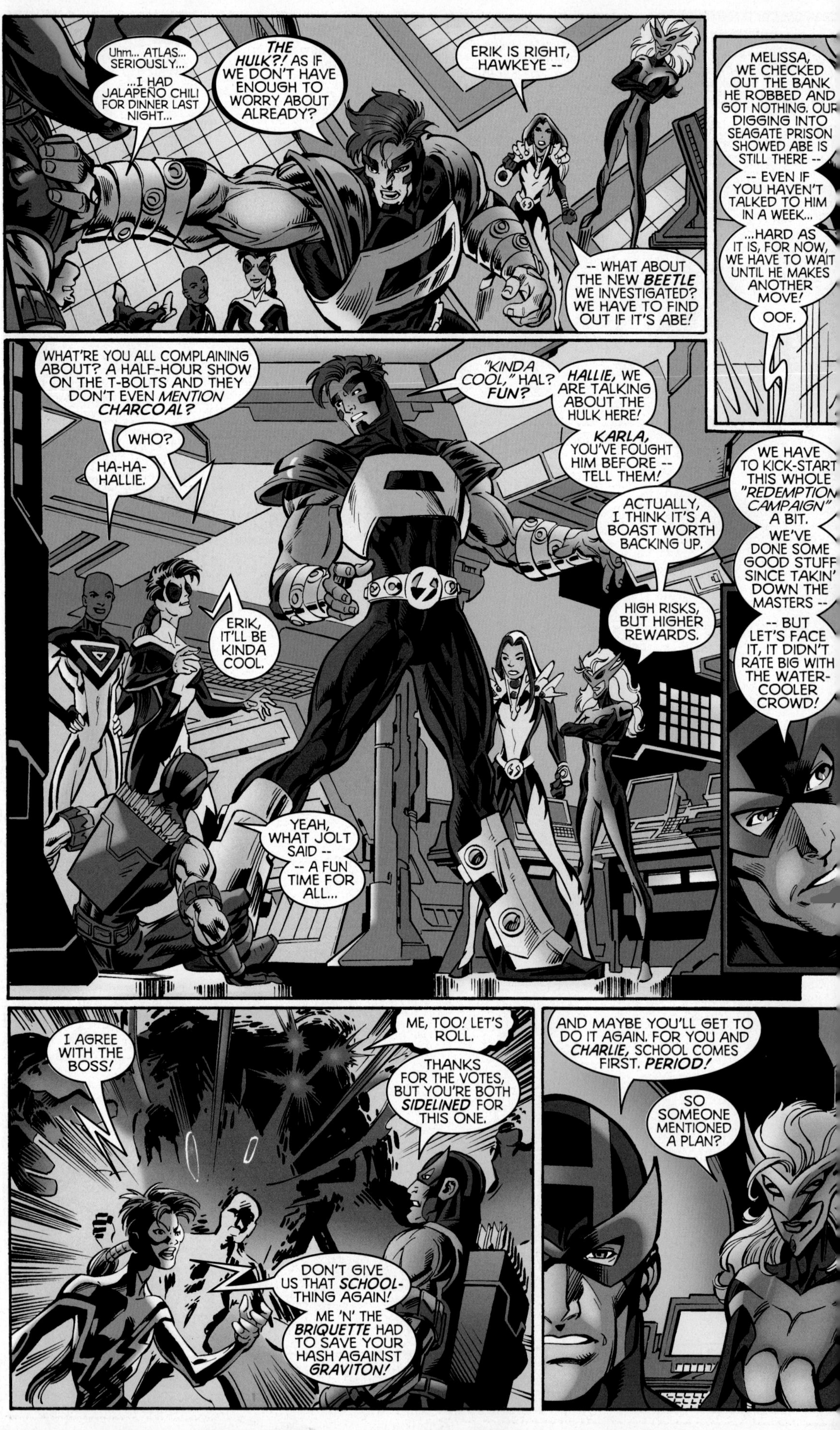

Uhm... ATLAS... SERIOUSLY... ...I HAD JALAPEÑO CHILI FOR DINNER LAST NIGHT...
THE HULK?! AS IF WE DON'T HAVE ENOUGH TO WORRY ABOUT ALREADY?
ERIK IS RIGHT, HAWKEYE --
-- WHAT ABOUT THE NEW BEETLE WE INVESTIGATED? WE HAVE TO FIND OUT IF IT'S ABE!
MELISSA, WE CHECKED OUT THE BANK HE ROBBED AND GOT NOTHING. OUR DIGGING INTO SEAGATE PRISON SHOWED ABE IS STILL THERE --
-- EVEN IF YOU HAVEN'T TALKED TO HIM IN A WEEK...
...HARD AS IT IS, FOR NOW, WE HAVE TO WAIT UNTIL HE MAKES ANOTHER MOVE!
OOF.
WHAT'RE YOU ALL COMPLAINING ABOUT? A HALF-HOUR SHOW ON THE T-BOLTS AND THEY DON'T EVEN MENTION CHARCOAL?
WHO?
HA-HA-HALLIE.
ERIK, IT'LL BE KINDA COOL.
"KINDA COOL," HAL? FUN?
HALLIE, WE ARE TALKING ABOUT THE HULK HERE!
KARLA, YOU'VE FOUGHT HIM BEFORE -- TELL THEM!
ACTUALLY, I THINK IT'S A BOAST WORTH BACKING UP.
HIGH RISKS, BUT HIGHER REWARDS.
YEAH, WHAT JOLT SAID -- -- A FUN TIME FOR ALL...
WE HAVE TO KICK-START THIS WHOLE "REDEMPTION CAMPAIGN" A BIT.
WE'VE DONE SOME GOOD STUFF SINCE TAKIN' DOWN THE MASTERS --
-- BUT LET'S FACE IT, IT DIDN'T RATE BIG WITH THE WATER-COOLER CROWD!
I AGREE WITH THE BOSS!
ME, TOO! LET'S ROLL.
THANKS FOR THE VOTES, BUT YOU'RE BOTH SIDELINED FOR THIS ONE.
DON'T GIVE US THAT SCHOOL-THING AGAIN!
ME 'N' THE BRIQUETTE HAD TO SAVE YOUR HASH AGAINST GRAVITON!
AND MAYBE YOU'LL GET TO DO IT AGAIN. FOR YOU AND CHARLIE, SCHOOL COMES FIRST. PERIOD!
SO SOMEONE MENTIONED A PLAN?

IT'S FLAWLESS! FAULTLESS! AND ANY OTHER WORDS THAT START WITH "F".

OOLHARDY?

"YE OF LITTLE FAITH! YOU'LL SEE, EVEN AS WE SPEAK, OUR RESIDENT MECHANIC, THE *OGRE* --

" -- IS INSTALLING A *GAMMA-RADIATION DETECTOR* IN THE T-BIRD!"

HE WORKS QUIETLY.

HAPPY TO HAVE SUCH A DAILY DIVERSITY OF TECHNOLOGICAL CHALLENGES.

HE'S ALWAYS BEEN GOOD AT FIXING THINGS.

SO TAKING THE OGRE'S PLACE WAS LOGICAL FOR THE FORMER T-BOLT NAMED *TECHNO.*

AND NO ONE HAS TO KNOW HE'S DONE IT... OR WHY...

..ESPECIALLY SINCE HE'S NOT SURE HIMSELF...

GIVE YOUR TEACHERS AN APPLE, KIDS. MAYBE IF YOU BUTTER 'EM UP, THEY'LL LET YOU WATCH *LIVE COVERAGE* OF THE T-BOLTS TAKING DOWN THE BIG GREEN GALOOT!

A MILE-LONG WALK TO SCHOOL LATER...

HOW CAN YOU BE SO COOL ABOUT THIS, CHARLIE?

HEY, BEING CHARCOAL IS A BLAST, HALLIE --

-- BUT AFTER EVERYTHING I'VE BEEN THROUGH WITH MY DAD AND THE *IMPERIAL FORCES* --

-- I APPRECIATE NORMAL STUFF LIKE SCHOOL A LOT.

I THOUGHT YOU WERE TALKING TO KARLA ABOUT YOUR PROBLEMS WITH SCHOOL?

THIS ISN'T ABOUT THAT -- IT'S ABOUT --

IXNAY ON THE ULKHAY.

MORNIN', CHUCK... HAL...

OH -- HEY, SPITZ, WHAT'S UP?

ANOTHER MORNING...

"...ANOTHER ORING DAY..."

3ARRY SPITZ DOESN'T HEAR THE *GRINDING* OF HALLIE TAKAHAMA'S TEETH.

ND NEITHER DO THE THERS, MILES AWAY V THE TEAM'S SUB- SONIC SKIMMER...

-- AND THAT'S WHAT I HAD IN MIND. WORKABLE?

SURPRISING IN ITS SIMPLICITY AND ITS POTENTIAL FOR SUCCESS.

WHAT MOONSTONE SAID, JUST SHORTENED TO: YEAH.

ATLAS --?

FIVE BUCKS SAYS *PLAN A* IS A BUST.

YOU'RE ON!

THEY ALL LAUGH. HIS SMILE THINS OUT. HE'S SENDING THEM AFTER **THE HULK!** AND THEY'RE **FOLLOWING** HIM!
THEY **TRUST** HIM. AND HIS INVOLVEMENT IS GROWING DEEPER THAN MATTERS OF **HONOR** OR **REDEMPTION.**
THEY ARE BECOMING HIS **FRIENDS...** AND MAYBE, IN THE CASE OF MOONSTONE, **MORE.** HOW DEEP SHOULD HE LET HIMSELF GET?
ATLAS WILL DO WHAT IS EXPECTED OF HIM.
BUT A GNAWING DOUBT GROWS WITHIN HIM: DOES HE ACT OUT OF LOYALTY OR **GUILT?**
HOW MUCH LONGER CAN HE HIDE THE TRUTH ABOUT **MAN-KILLER,** AN ESCAPED FELON HE KNOWS IS WORKING AT A BAR IN BURTON CANYON?
MOONSTONE WONDERS HOW COULD SHE HAVE BACKED HAWKEYE'S PLAN TO FIGHT THE HULK? WHAT IS **WRONG** WITH HER LATELY?
WAS IT TO FURTHER HER **MANIPULATIONS** OF THEIR LEADER -- OR TO IMPRESS HIM?
THE MOST ANGERING, LONELY AND ENTICING ASPECT OF IT IS...**SHE** DOESN'T KNOW THE ANSWER HERSELF...
SONGBIRD THINKS, IF THIS **IS A SUICIDE RUN** SHE WISHES THE MAN SHE LOVES COULD BE AT HER SIDE.
BUT SHE HASN'T HEAR BACK FROM ABE JENKIN IN A WEEK. CONFUSION TURNED TO ANGER AN NOW, TO **FEAR.**
WHAT IF SOMETHING'S HAPPENED TO HIM IN **PRISON?** AND IF HE'S OKAY...
...THEN WHY ISN'T HE ANSWERING?
IF MELISSA COULD SEE THE **ROXXON ENERGY** RESEARCH LAB OUTSIDE OF DENVER, COLORADO, SHE'D HAVE HER ANSWER...
...THOUGH SHE MIGHT NOT **LIKE** IT!
INSIDE, FACILITY COORDINATOR, **SAMUEL HIGGINS** PRESIDES OVER THE FINAL STAGES OF A VERY DELICATE EXPERIMENT...
HOW LATE?
Uhm... TWO DAYS?
MY **BONUS** GETS FLUSHED, I'LL TAKE YOURS DOWN WITH ME!
GRRMMM
DIDN'T WE FIX THE AIR-CONDITIONING --
THERE GOES THE QUARTERLY BUDGET...

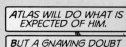

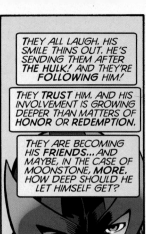

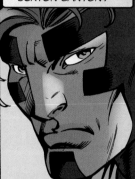

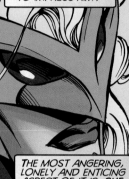

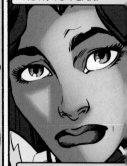

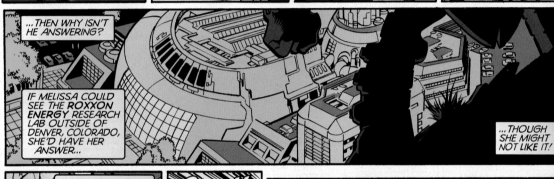

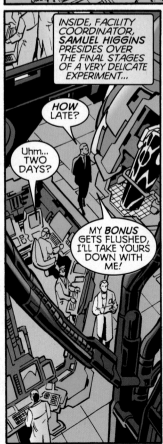

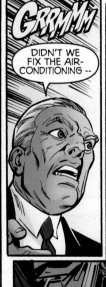

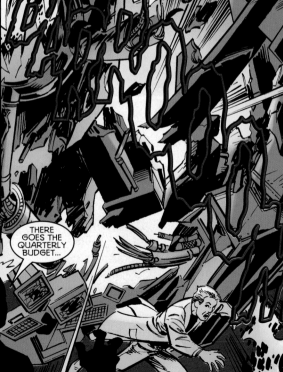

THE **INTRUDER** REMAINS SILENT, SAVE FOR THE SOFT WHIRRING OF HIS ARMORED COMPONENTS.

HE JUST TRUDGES FORWARD.

RELENTLESS.

UNSTOPPABLE.

WINGS COMPOSED OF MOLECULE-THIN **GRAVITONIC SPATIAL** DISTORTIONS CUT THROUGH THE FACILITY'S MECHANICAL DEFENSES.

SWEEEEEERR

ALARM KLAXONS DO THEIR BEST IMPERSONATION OF A **METALLICA** CONCERT.

SCIENTISTS AND TECHNICIANS DO THEIR BEST IMPERSONATION OF FRANCE IN WORLD WAR II.

THE **WALKING TANK** SPOTS ITS QUARRY.

NO...NOT THAT...

...WORKED TOO HARD TO CLIMB BACK UP THE LADDER AFTER THAT **HUDSON** FIASCO --*

* SEE ALPHA FLIGHT VOL 1, #87-90. – Tom.

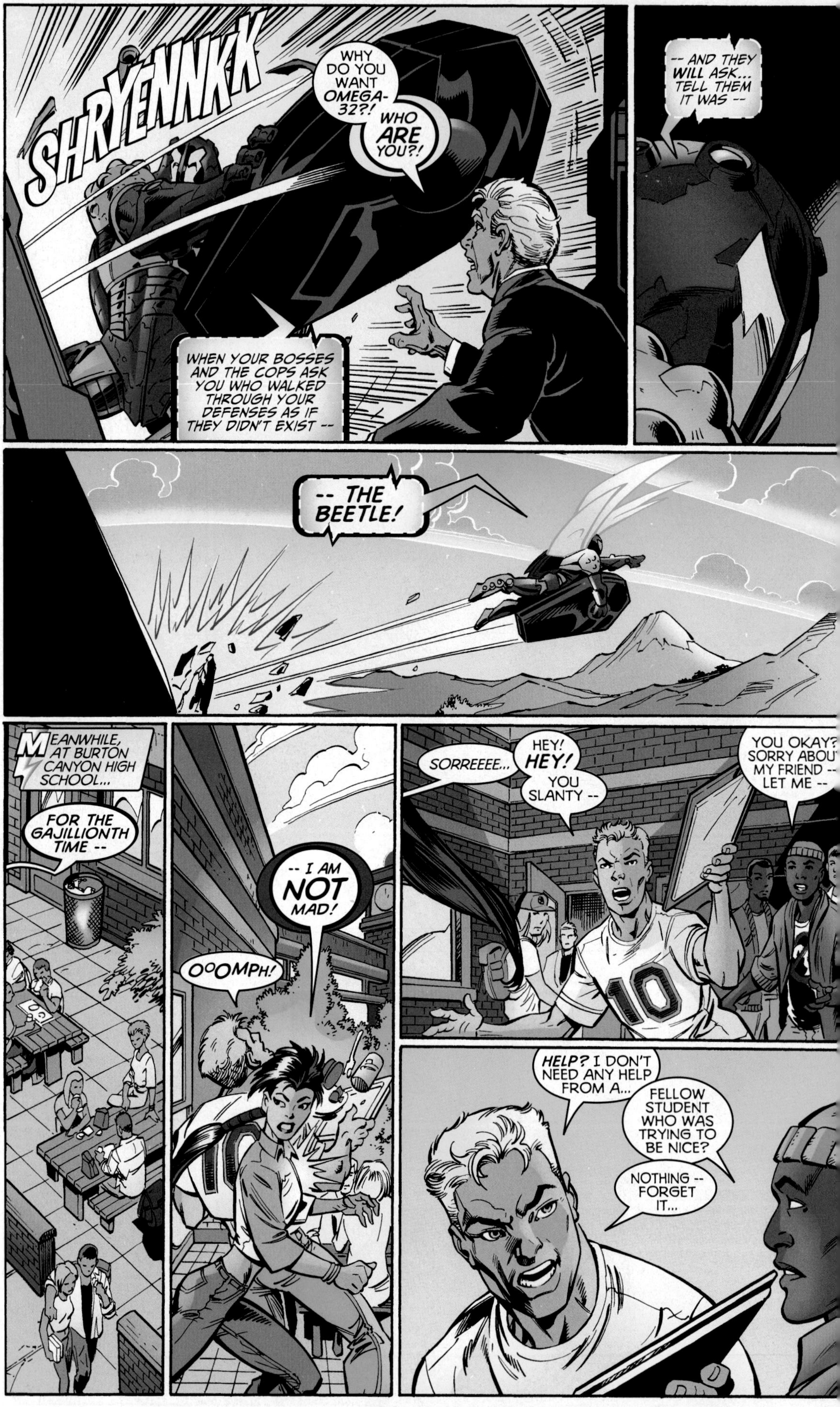
SHRYENNKK
WHY DO YOU WANT OMEGA-32?!
WHO ARE YOU?!
WHEN YOUR BOSSES AND THE COPS ASK YOU WHO WALKED THROUGH YOUR DEFENSES AS IF THEY DIDN'T EXIST --
-- AND THEY WILL ASK... TELL THEM IT WAS --
-- THE BEETLE!
MEANWHILE, AT BURTON CANYON HIGH SCHOOL...
FOR THE GAJILLIONTH TIME --
-- I AM NOT MAD!
OOOMPH!
SORREEEE...
HEY! HEY! YOU SLANTY --
YOU OKAY? SORRY ABOU MY FRIEND -- LET ME --
HELP? I DON'T NEED ANY HELP FROM A...
FELLOW STUDENT WHO WAS TRYING TO BE NICE?
NOTHING -- FORGET IT...

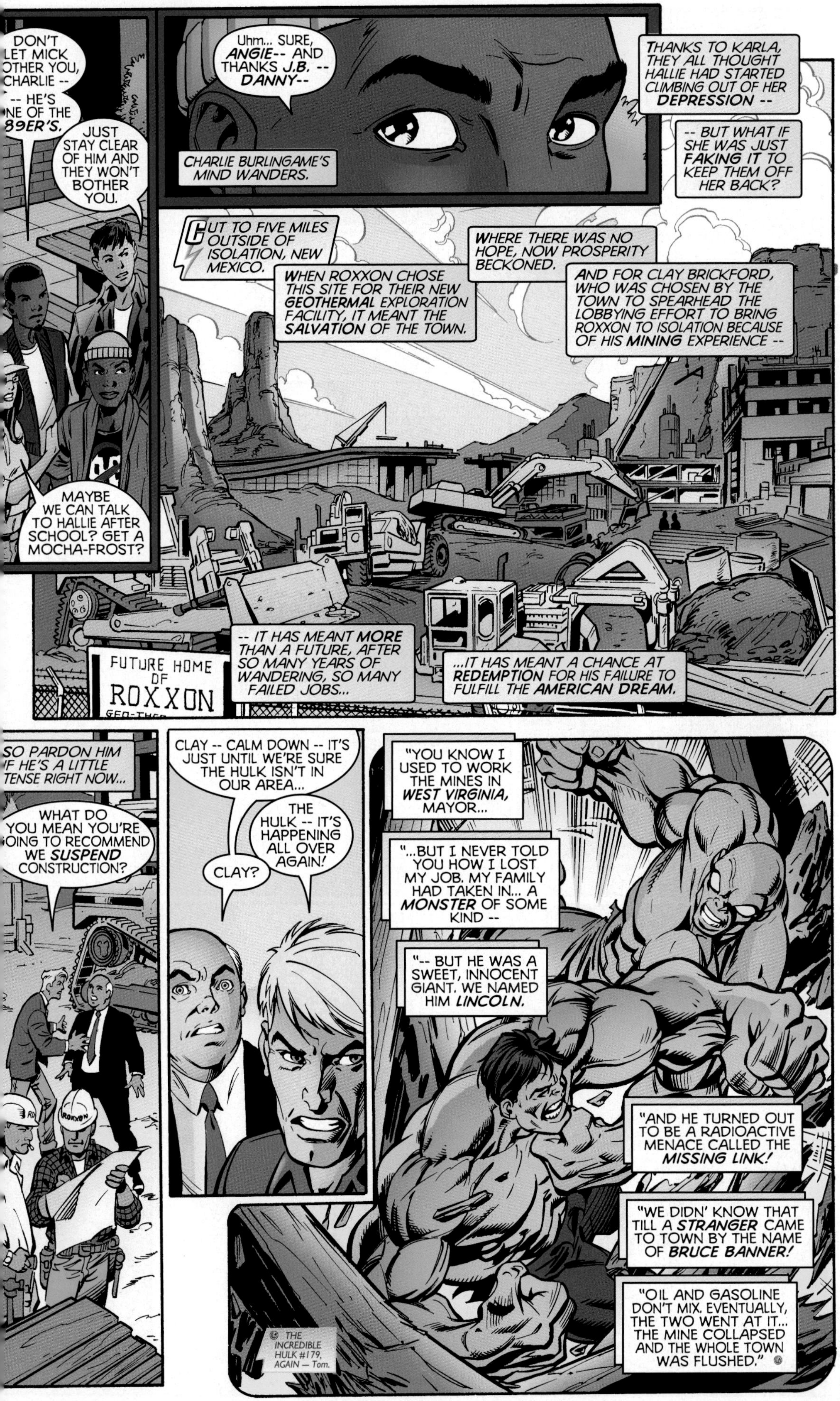
DON'T LET MICK OTHER YOU, CHARLIE -- -- HE'S NE OF THE 89ER'S.
JUST STAY CLEAR OF HIM AND THEY WON'T BOTHER YOU.
MAYBE WE CAN TALK TO HALLIE AFTER SCHOOL? GET A MOCHA-FROST?
Uhm... SURE, ANGIE-- AND THANKS J.B. -- DANNY--
CHARLIE BURLINGAME'S MIND WANDERS.
THANKS TO KARLA, THEY ALL THOUGHT HALLIE HAD STARTED CLIMBING OUT OF HER DEPRESSION --
-- BUT WHAT IF SHE WAS JUST FAKING IT TO KEEP THEM OFF HER BACK?
CUT TO FIVE MILES OUTSIDE OF ISOLATION, NEW MEXICO.
WHEN ROXXON CHOSE THIS SITE FOR THEIR NEW GEOTHERMAL EXPLORATION FACILITY, IT MEANT THE SALVATION OF THE TOWN.
WHERE THERE WAS NO HOPE, NOW PROSPERITY BECKONED.
AND FOR CLAY BRICKFORD, WHO WAS CHOSEN BY THE TOWN TO SPEARHEAD THE LOBBYING EFFORT TO BRING ROXXON TO ISOLATION BECAUSE OF HIS MINING EXPERIENCE --
FUTURE HOME OF ROXXON
-- IT HAS MEANT MORE THAN A FUTURE, AFTER SO MANY YEARS OF WANDERING, SO MANY FAILED JOBS...
...IT HAS MEANT A CHANCE AT REDEMPTION FOR HIS FAILURE TO FULFILL THE AMERICAN DREAM.
SO PARDON HIM IF HE'S A LITTLE TENSE RIGHT NOW...
WHAT DO YOU MEAN YOU'RE GOING TO RECOMMEND WE SUSPEND CONSTRUCTION?
ROXXON
CLAY -- CALM DOWN -- IT'S JUST UNTIL WE'RE SURE THE HULK ISN'T IN OUR AREA...
THE HULK -- IT'S HAPPENING ALL OVER AGAIN!
CLAY?
"YOU KNOW I USED TO WORK THE MINES IN WEST VIRGINIA, MAYOR...
"...BUT I NEVER TOLD YOU HOW I LOST MY JOB. MY FAMILY HAD TAKEN IN... A MONSTER OF SOME KIND --
"-- BUT HE WAS A SWEET, INNOCENT GIANT. WE NAMED HIM LINCOLN.
"AND HE TURNED OUT TO BE A RADIOACTIVE MENACE CALLED THE MISSING LINK!
"WE DIDN' KNOW THAT TILL A STRANGER CAME TO TOWN BY THE NAME OF BRUCE BANNER!
"OIL AND GASOLINE DON'T MIX. EVENTUALLY, THE TWO WENT AT IT... THE MINE COLLAPSED AND THE WHOLE TOWN WAS FLUSHED."
THE INCREDIBLE HULK #179, AGAIN — Tom.

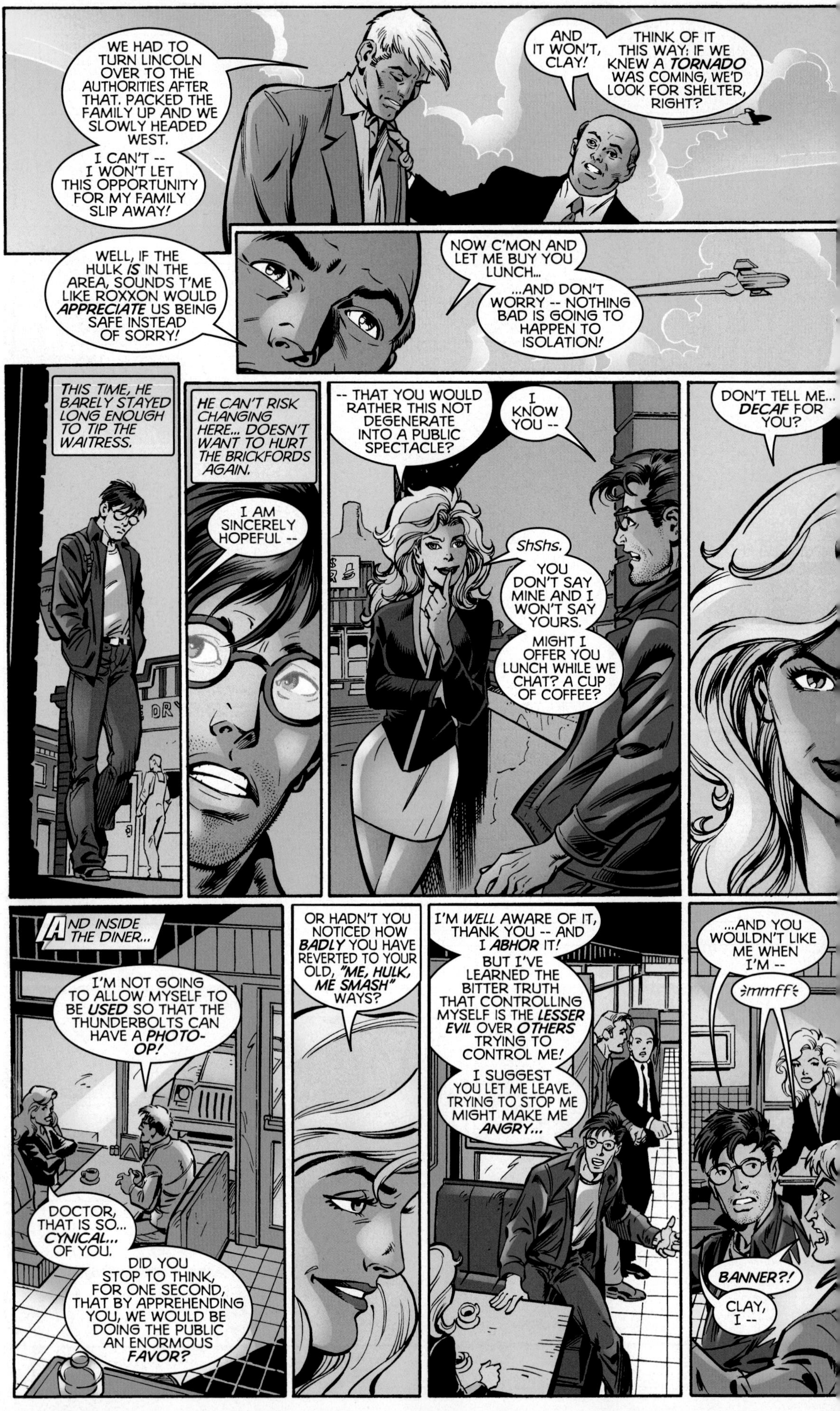
WE HAD TO TURN LINCOLN OVER TO THE AUTHORITIES AFTER THAT. PACKED THE FAMILY UP AND WE SLOWLY HEADED WEST.
I CAN'T -- I WON'T LET THIS OPPORTUNITY FOR MY FAMILY SLIP AWAY!
AND IT WON'T, CLAY!
THINK OF IT THIS WAY: IF WE KNEW A *TORNADO* WAS COMING, WE'D LOOK FOR SHELTER, RIGHT?
WELL, IF THE HULK *IS* IN THE AREA, SOUNDS T'ME LIKE ROXXON WOULD *APPRECIATE* US BEING SAFE INSTEAD OF SORRY!
NOW C'MON AND LET ME BUY YOU LUNCH...
...AND DON'T WORRY -- NOTHING BAD IS GOING TO HAPPEN TO ISOLATION!
THIS TIME, HE BARELY STAYED LONG ENOUGH TO TIP THE WAITRESS.
HE CAN'T RISK CHANGING HERE... DOESN'T WANT TO HURT THE BRICKFORDS AGAIN.
I AM SINCERELY HOPEFUL --
-- THAT YOU WOULD RATHER THIS NOT DEGENERATE INTO A PUBLIC SPECTACLE?
I KNOW YOU --
ShShs.
YOU DON'T SAY MINE AND I WON'T SAY YOURS.
MIGHT I OFFER YOU LUNCH WHILE WE CHAT? A CUP OF COFFEE?
DON'T TELL ME... *DECAF* FOR YOU?
AND INSIDE THE DINER...
I'M NOT GOING TO ALLOW MYSELF TO BE *USED* SO THAT THE THUNDERBOLTS CAN HAVE A *PHOTO-OP!*
DOCTOR, THAT IS SO... *CYNICAL...* OF YOU.
DID YOU STOP TO THINK, FOR ONE SECOND, THAT BY APPREHENDING YOU, WE WOULD BE DOING THE PUBLIC AN ENORMOUS *FAVOR?*
OR HADN'T YOU NOTICED HOW *BADLY* YOU HAVE REVERTED TO YOUR OLD, *"ME, HULK, ME SMASH"* WAYS?
I'M *WELL* AWARE OF IT, THANK YOU -- AND I *ABHOR* IT!
BUT I'VE LEARNED THE BITTER TRUTH THAT CONTROLLING MYSELF IS THE *LESSER EVIL* OVER *OTHERS* TRYING TO CONTROL ME!
I SUGGEST YOU LET ME LEAVE. TRYING TO STOP ME MIGHT MAKE ME *ANGRY...*
...AND YOU WOULDN'T LIKE ME WHEN I'M --
mmff
BANNER?!
CLAY, I --

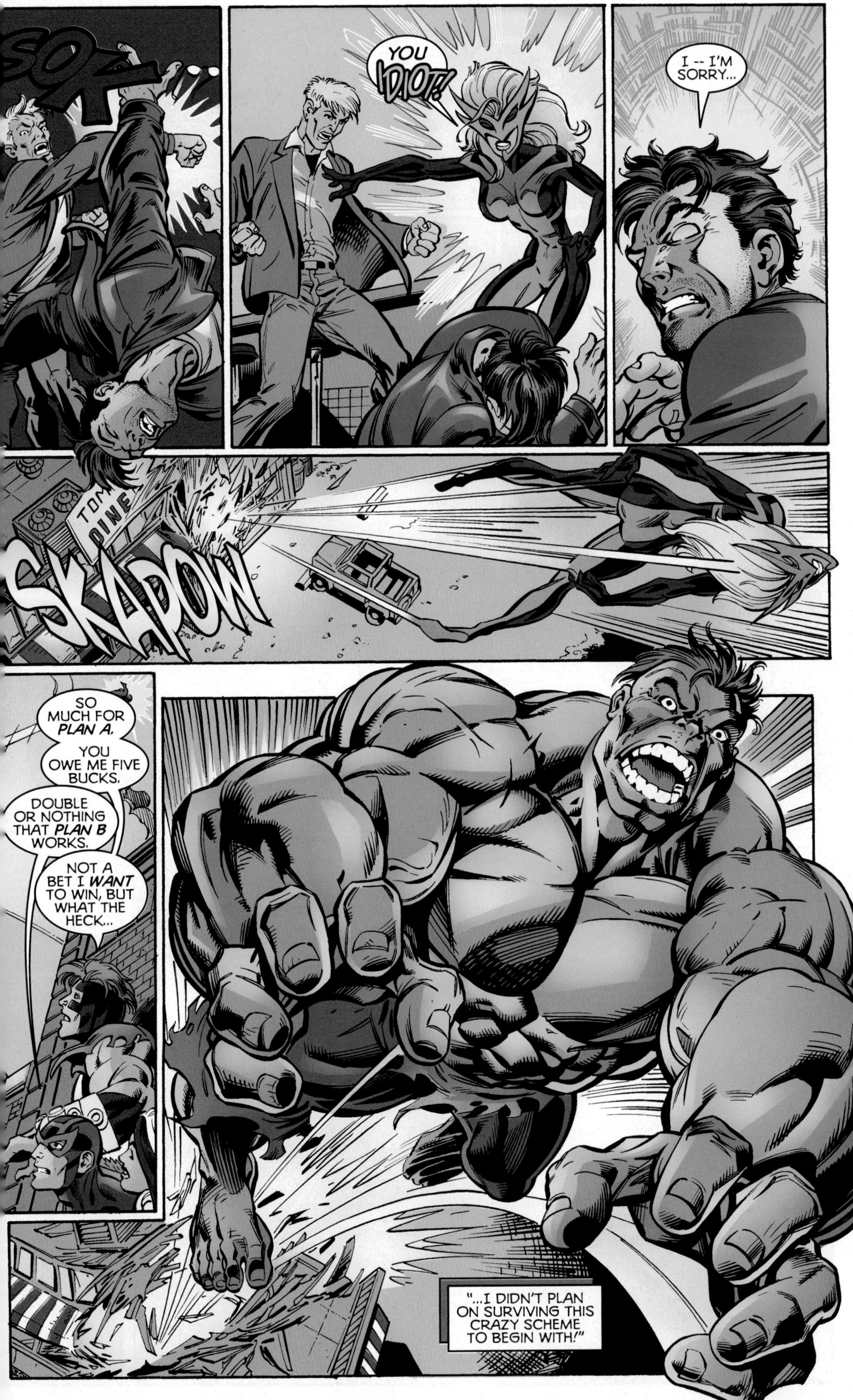
SOK
YOU IDIOT!
I -- I'M SORRY...
TOM DINE
SKADOW
SO MUCH FOR *PLAN A.*
YOU OWE ME FIVE BUCKS.
DOUBLE OR NOTHING THAT *PLAN B* WORKS.
NOT A BET I *WANT* TO WIN, BUT WHAT THE HECK...
"...I DIDN'T PLAN ON SURVIVING THIS CRAZY SCHEME TO BEGIN WITH!"

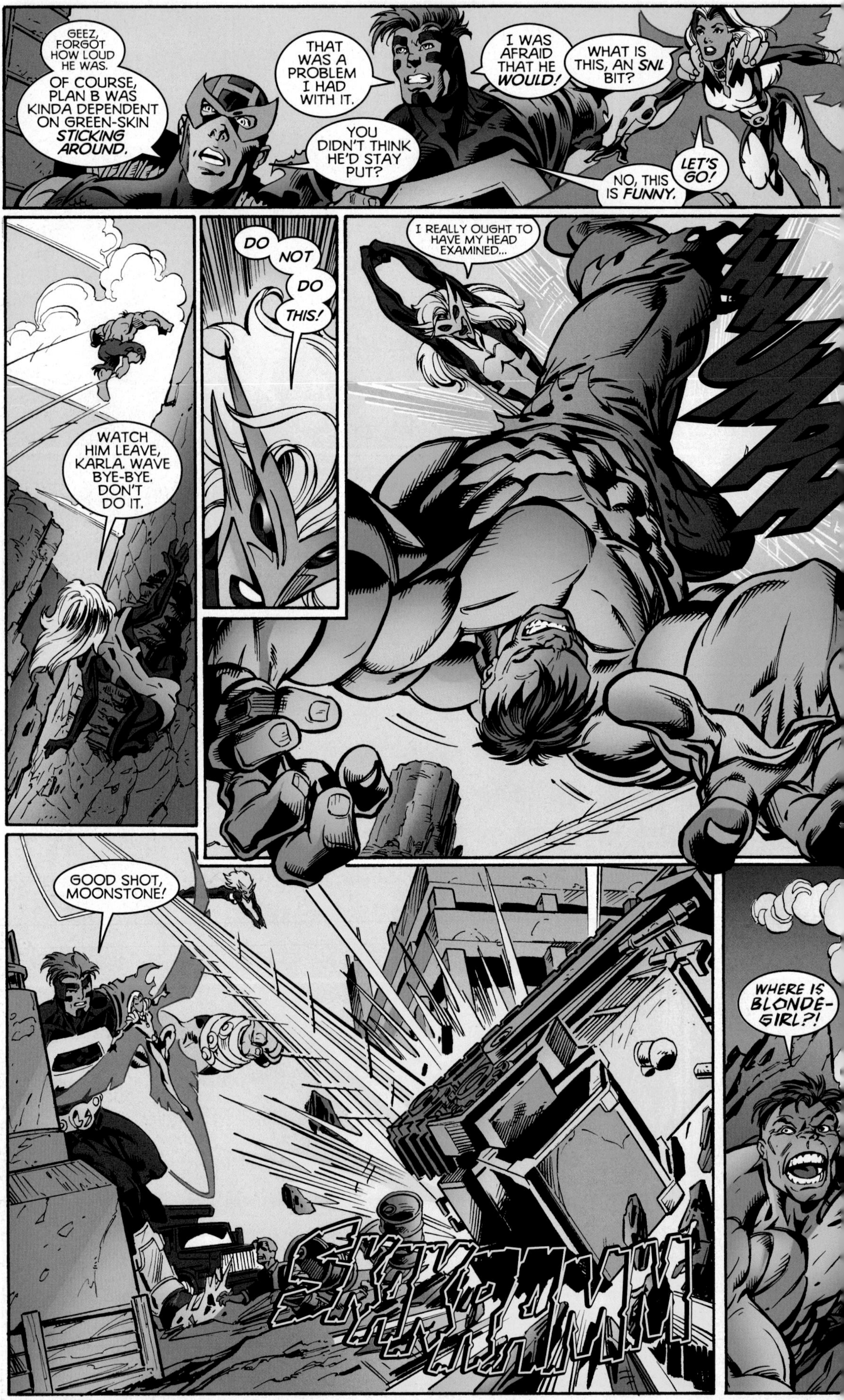
GEEZ, FORGOT HOW LOUD HE WAS.
OF COURSE, PLAN B WAS KINDA DEPENDENT ON GREEN-SKIN *STICKING AROUND.*
THAT WAS A PROBLEM I HAD WITH IT.
YOU DIDN'T THINK HE'D STAY PUT?
I WAS AFRAID THAT HE *WOULD!*
WHAT IS THIS, AN *SNL* BIT?
NO, THIS IS *FUNNY.*
LET'S GO!
WATCH HIM LEAVE, KARLA. WAVE BYE-BYE. DON'T DO IT.
DO NOT DO THIS!
I REALLY OUGHT TO HAVE MY HEAD EXAMINED...
GOOD SHOT, MOONSTONE!
WHERE IS BLONDE-GIRL?!

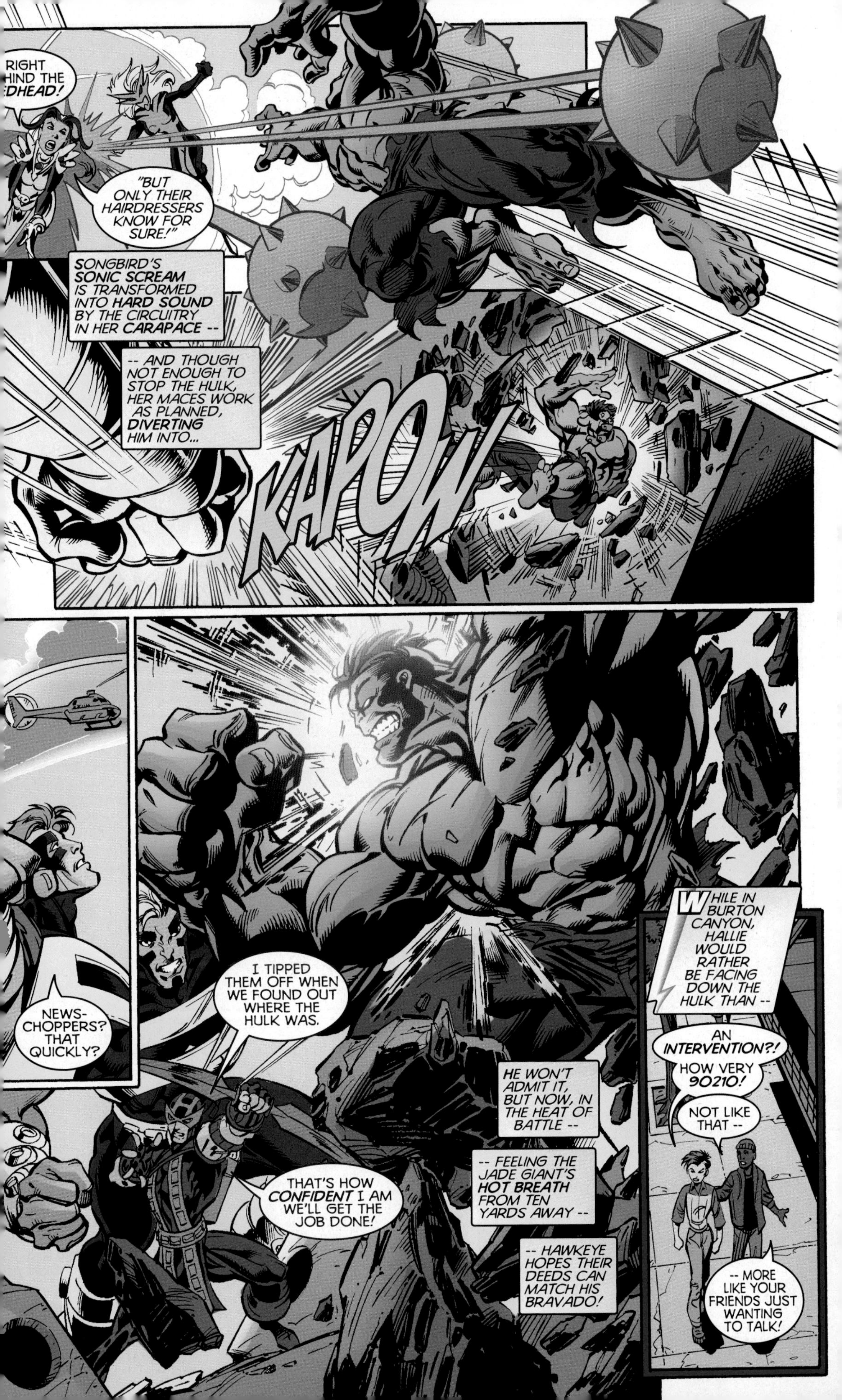
RIGHT
HIND THE
EDHEAD!
"BUT ONLY THEIR HAIRDRESSERS KNOW FOR SURE!"
SONGBIRD'S SONIC SCREAM IS TRANSFORMED INTO HARD SOUND BY THE CIRCUITRY IN HER CARAPACE --
-- AND THOUGH NOT ENOUGH TO STOP THE HULK, HER MACES WORK AS PLANNED, DIVERTING HIM INTO...
KAPOW
NEWS-CHOPPERS? THAT QUICKLY?
I TIPPED THEM OFF WHEN WE FOUND OUT WHERE THE HULK WAS.
THAT'S HOW CONFIDENT I AM WE'LL GET THE JOB DONE!
HE WON'T ADMIT IT, BUT NOW, IN THE HEAT OF BATTLE --
-- FEELING THE JADE GIANT'S HOT BREATH FROM TEN YARDS AWAY --
-- HAWKEYE HOPES THEIR DEEDS CAN MATCH HIS BRAVADO!
WHILE IN BURTON CANYON, HALLIE WOULD RATHER BE FACING DOWN THE HULK THAN --
AN INTERVENTION?! HOW VERY 90210!
NOT LIKE THAT --
-- MORE LIKE YOUR FRIENDS JUST WANTING TO TALK!

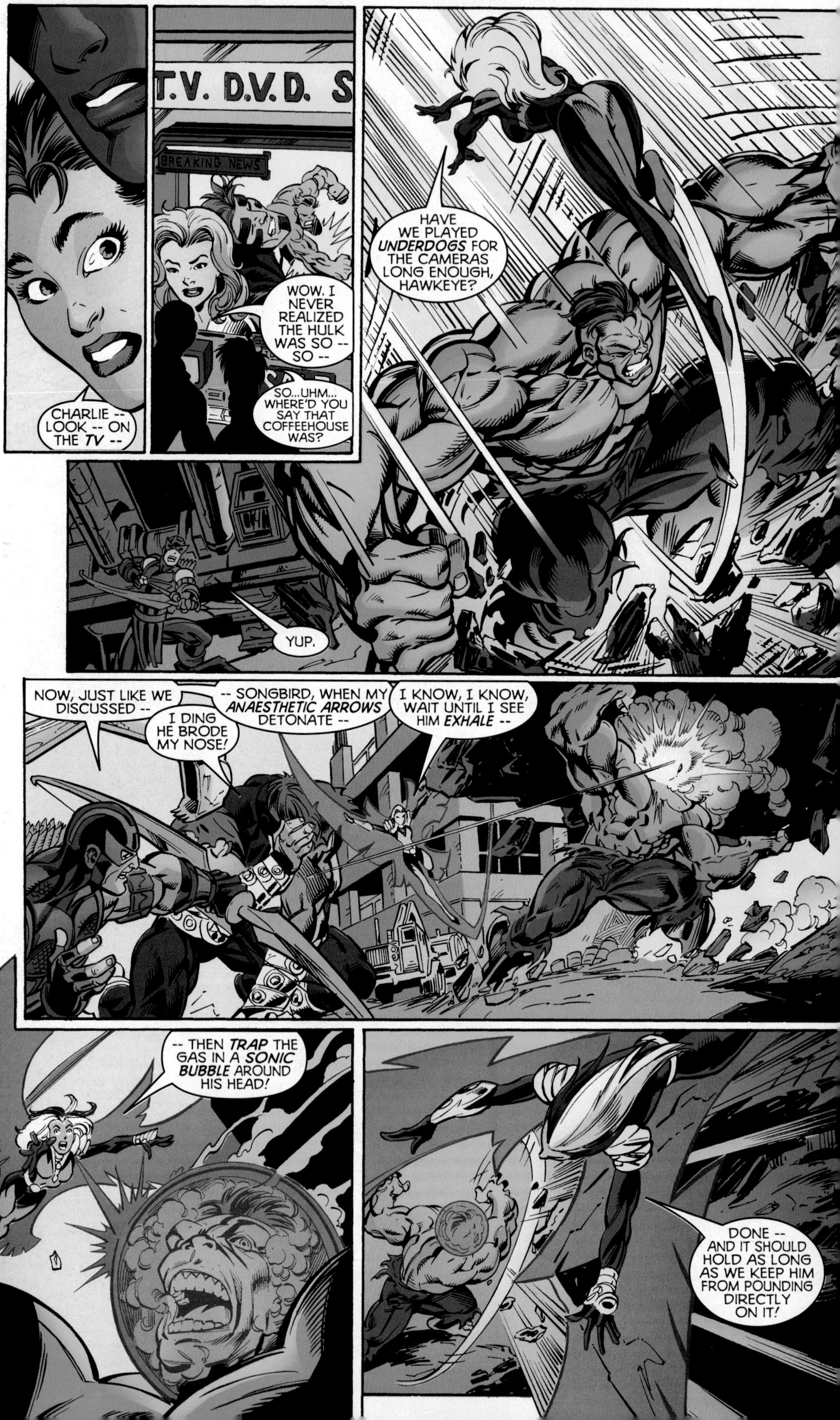

CHARLIE -- LOOK -- ON THE *TV* --
T.V. D.V.D. S
BREAKING NEWS
WOW. I NEVER REALIZED THE HULK WAS SO -- SO --
SO...UHM... WHERE'D YOU SAY THAT COFFEEHOUSE WAS?
HAVE WE PLAYED ***UNDERDOGS*** FOR THE CAMERAS LONG ENOUGH, HAWKEYE?
YUP.
NOW, JUST LIKE WE DISCUSSED --
I DING HE BRODE MY NOSE!
-- SONGBIRD, WHEN MY ***ANAESTHETIC ARROWS*** DETONATE --
I KNOW, I KNOW, WAIT UNTIL I SEE HIM ***EXHALE*** --
-- THEN ***TRAP*** THE GAS IN A ***SONIC BUBBLE*** AROUND HIS HEAD!
DONE -- AND IT SHOULD HOLD AS LONG AS WE KEEP HIM FROM POUNDING DIRECTLY ON IT!

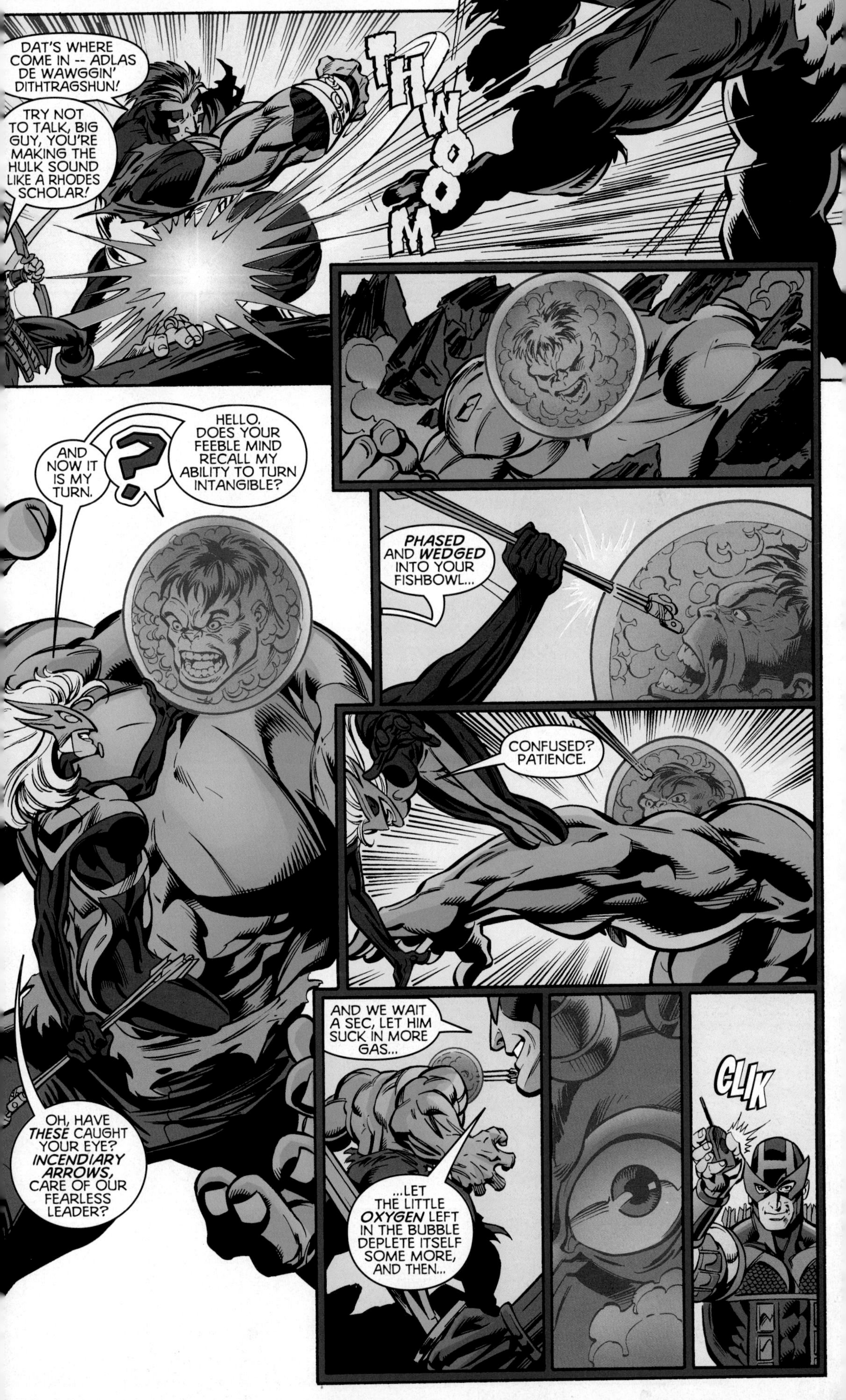
DAT'S WHERE COME IN -- ADLAS DE WAWGGIN' DITHTRAGSHUN!
TRY NOT TO TALK, BIG GUY, YOU'RE MAKING THE HULK SOUND LIKE A RHODES SCHOLAR!
THWOOM
AND NOW IT IS MY TURN.
?
HELLO. DOES YOUR FEEBLE MIND RECALL MY ABILITY TO TURN INTANGIBLE?
OH, HAVE *THESE* CAUGHT YOUR EYE? ***INCENDIARY ARROWS,*** CARE OF OUR FEARLESS LEADER?
PHASED AND ***WEDGED*** INTO YOUR FISHBOWL...
CONFUSED? PATIENCE.
AND WE WAIT A SEC, LET HIM SUCK IN MORE GAS...
...LET THE LITTLE ***OXYGEN*** LEFT IN THE BUBBLE DEPLETE ITSELF SOME MORE, AND THEN...
CLIK

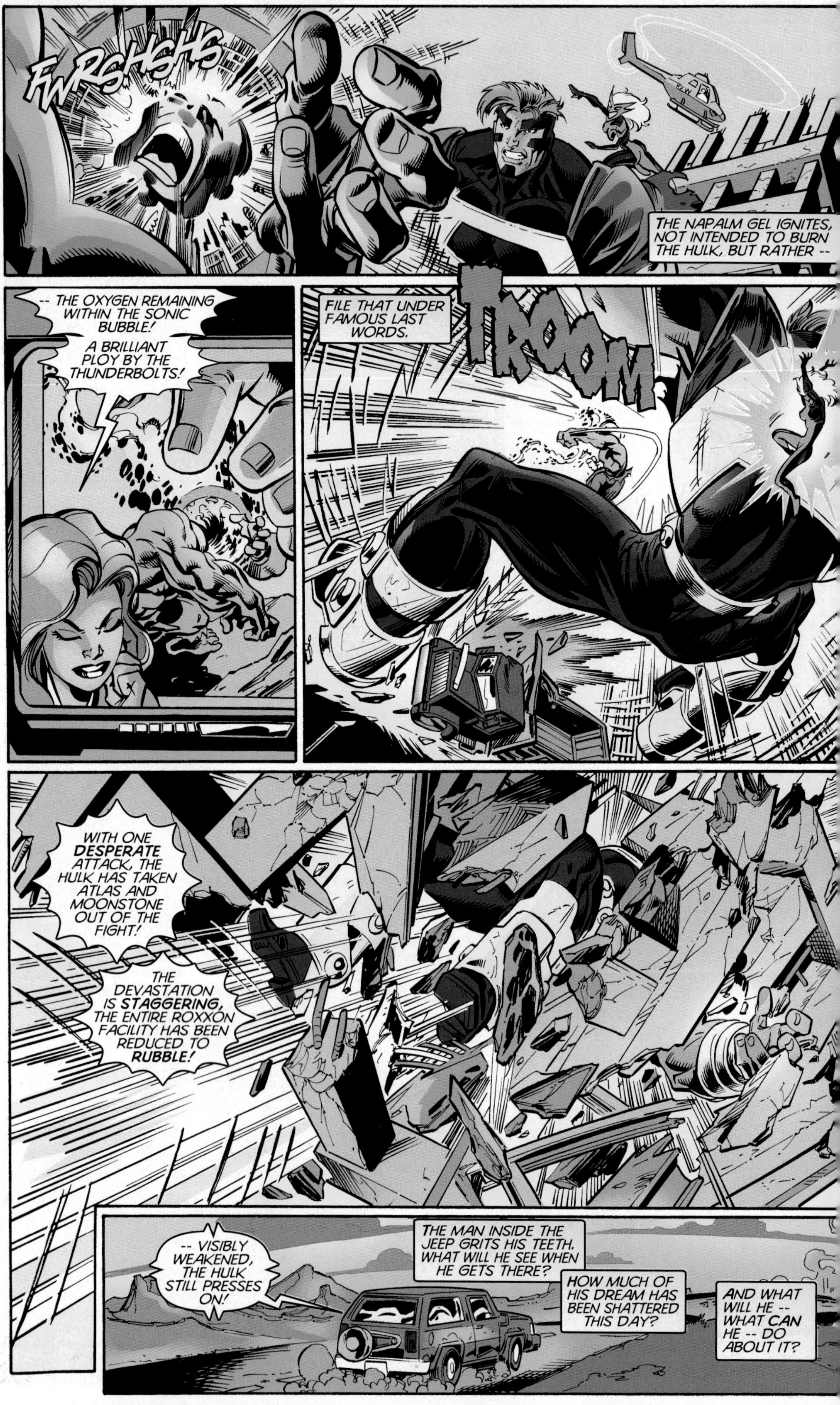
FWRSHSHS
THE NAPALM GEL IGNITES, NOT INTENDED TO BURN THE HULK, BUT RATHER --
-- THE OXYGEN REMAINING WITHIN THE SONIC BUBBLE!
A BRILLIANT PLOY BY THE THUNDERBOLTS!
FILE THAT UNDER FAMOUS LAST WORDS.
TROOM
WITH ONE DESPERATE ATTACK, THE HULK HAS TAKEN ATLAS AND MOONSTONE OUT OF THE FIGHT!
THE DEVASTATION IS STAGGERING, THE ENTIRE ROXXON FACILITY HAS BEEN REDUCED TO RUBBLE!
-- VISIBLY WEAKENED, THE HULK STILL PRESSES ON!
THE MAN INSIDE THE JEEP GRITS HIS TEETH. WHAT WILL HE SEE WHEN HE GETS THERE?
HOW MUCH OF HIS DREAM HAS BEEN SHATTERED THIS DAY?
AND WHAT WILL HE -- WHAT CAN HE -- DO ABOUT IT?

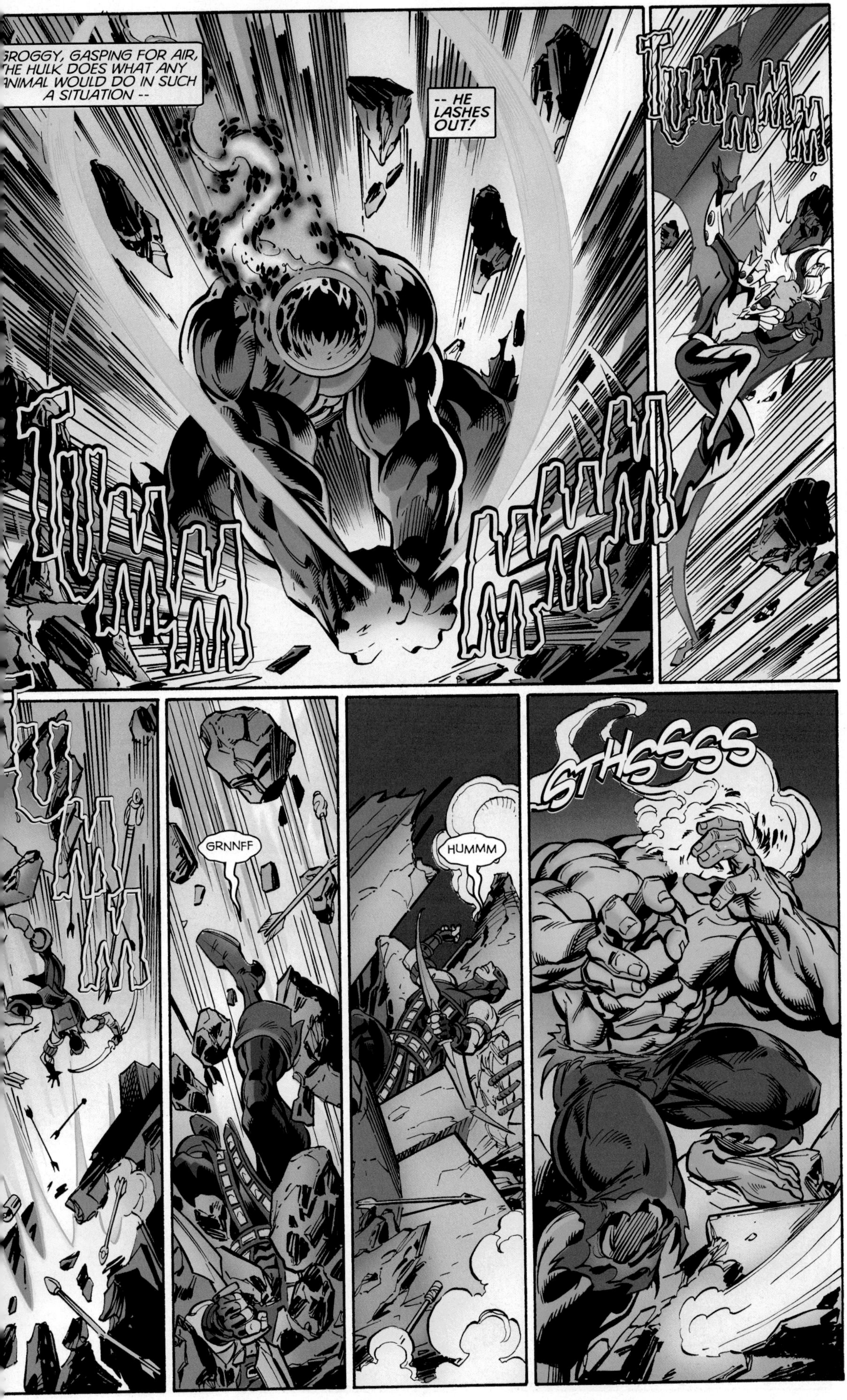
GROGGY, GASPING FOR AIR, THE HULK DOES WHAT ANY ANIMAL WOULD DO IN SUCH A SITUATION --
-- HE LASHES OUT!
GRNNFF
HUMMM
STHSSSS

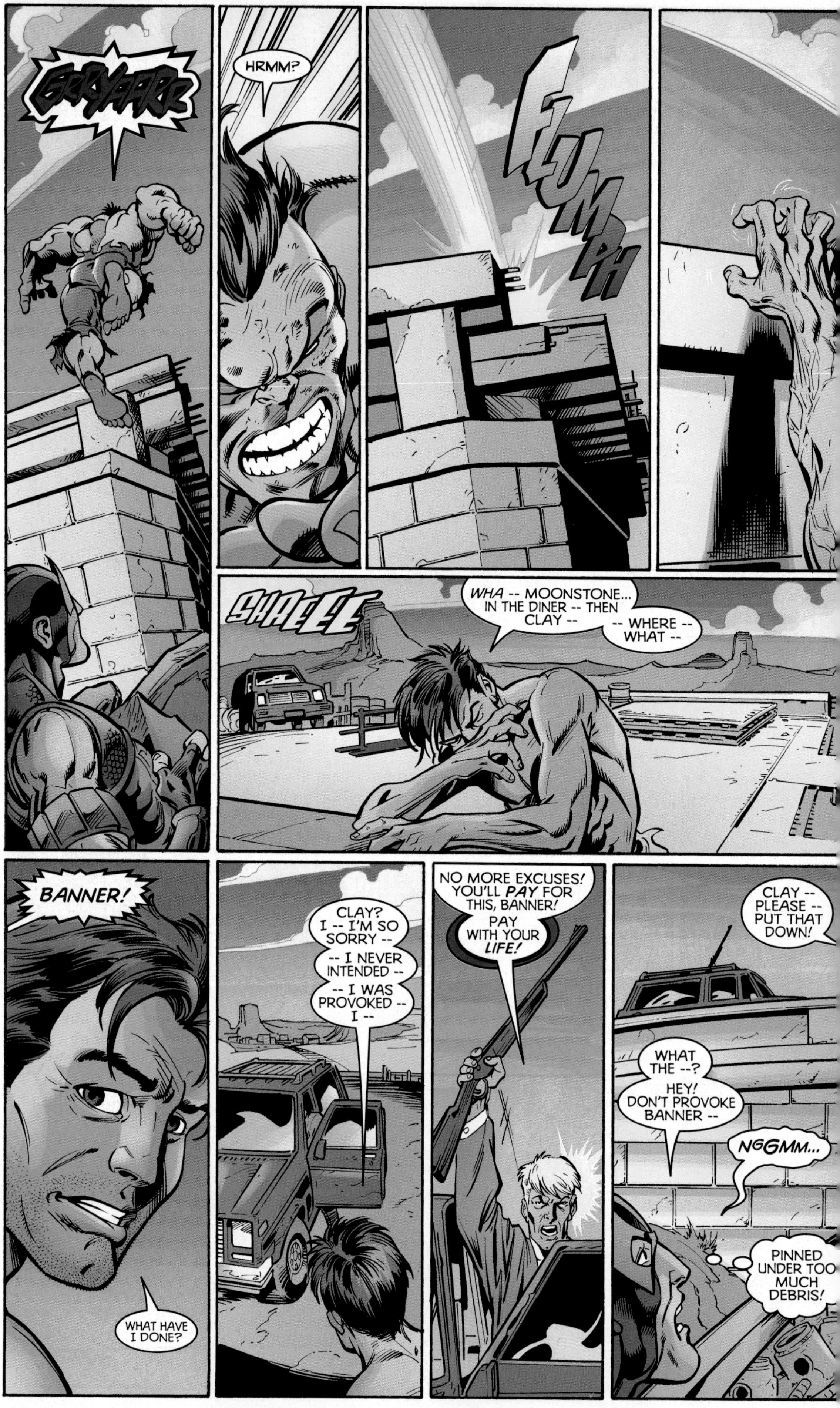
GRRYAARR
HRMM?
FLUMPH
SHREEE
WHA -- MOONSTONE... IN THE DINER -- THEN CLAY --
-- WHERE -- WHAT --
BANNER!
WHAT HAVE I DONE?
CLAY? I -- I'M SO SORRY --
-- I NEVER INTENDED --
-- I WAS PROVOKED -- I --
NO MORE EXCUSES! YOU'LL PAY FOR THIS, BANNER!
PAY WITH YOUR LIFE!
CLAY -- PLEASE -- PUT THAT DOWN!
WHAT THE --?
HEY! DON'T PROVOKE BANNER --
NGGMM...
PINNED UNDER TOO MUCH DEBRIS!

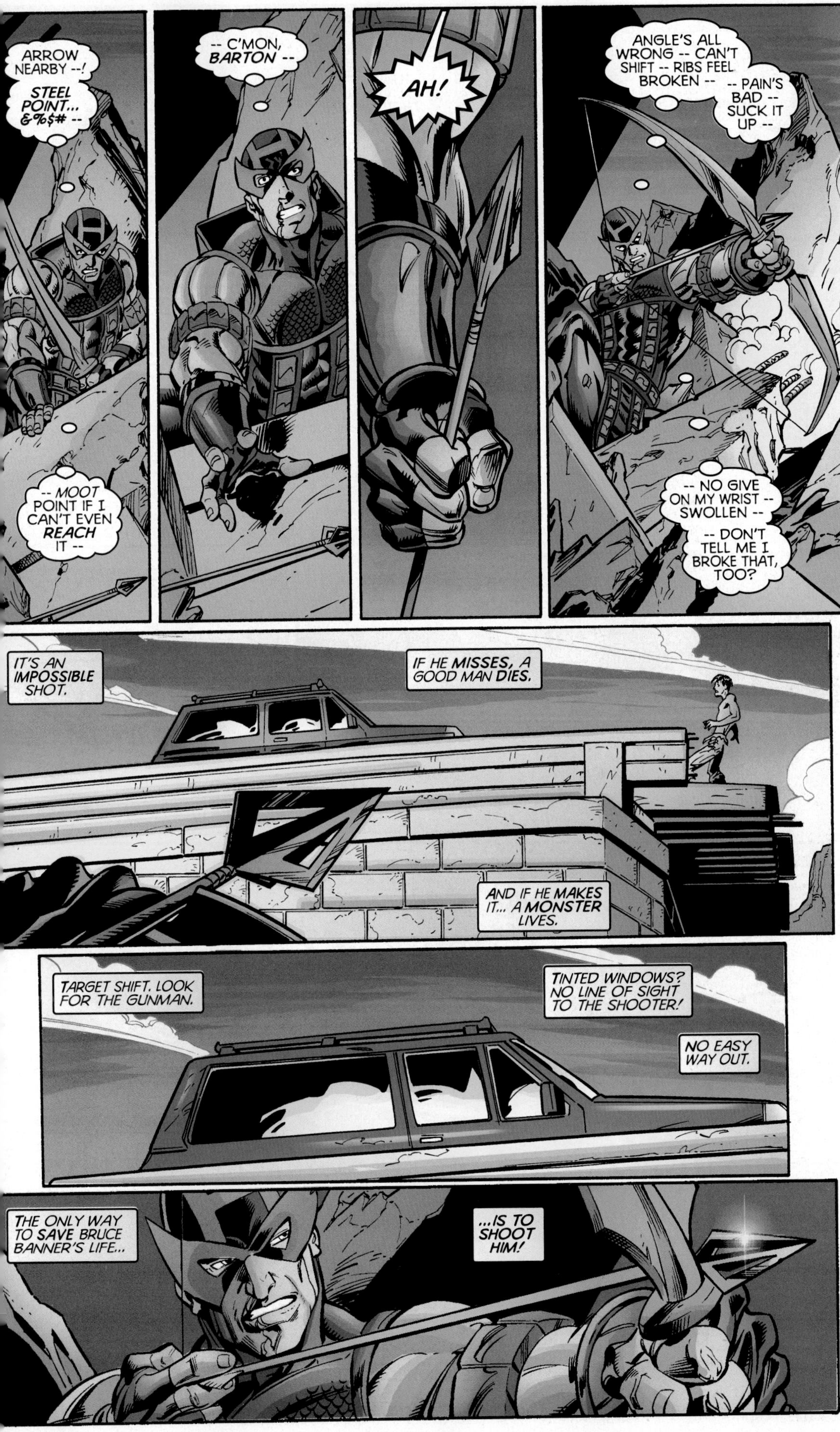
ARROW NEARBY --!
STEEL POINT... &%$# --
-- MOOT POINT IF I CAN'T EVEN REACH IT --
-- C'MON, BARTON --
AH!
ANGLE'S ALL WRONG -- CAN'T SHIFT -- RIBS FEEL BROKEN --
-- PAIN'S BAD -- SUCK IT UP --
-- NO GIVE ON MY WRIST -- SWOLLEN --
-- DON'T TELL ME I BROKE THAT, TOO?
IT'S AN IMPOSSIBLE SHOT.
IF HE MISSES, A GOOD MAN DIES.
AND IF HE MAKES IT... A MONSTER LIVES.
TARGET SHIFT. LOOK FOR THE GUNMAN.
TINTED WINDOWS? NO LINE OF SIGHT TO THE SHOOTER!
NO EASY WAY OUT.
THE ONLY WAY TO SAVE BRUCE BANNER'S LIFE...
...IS TO SHOOT HIM!

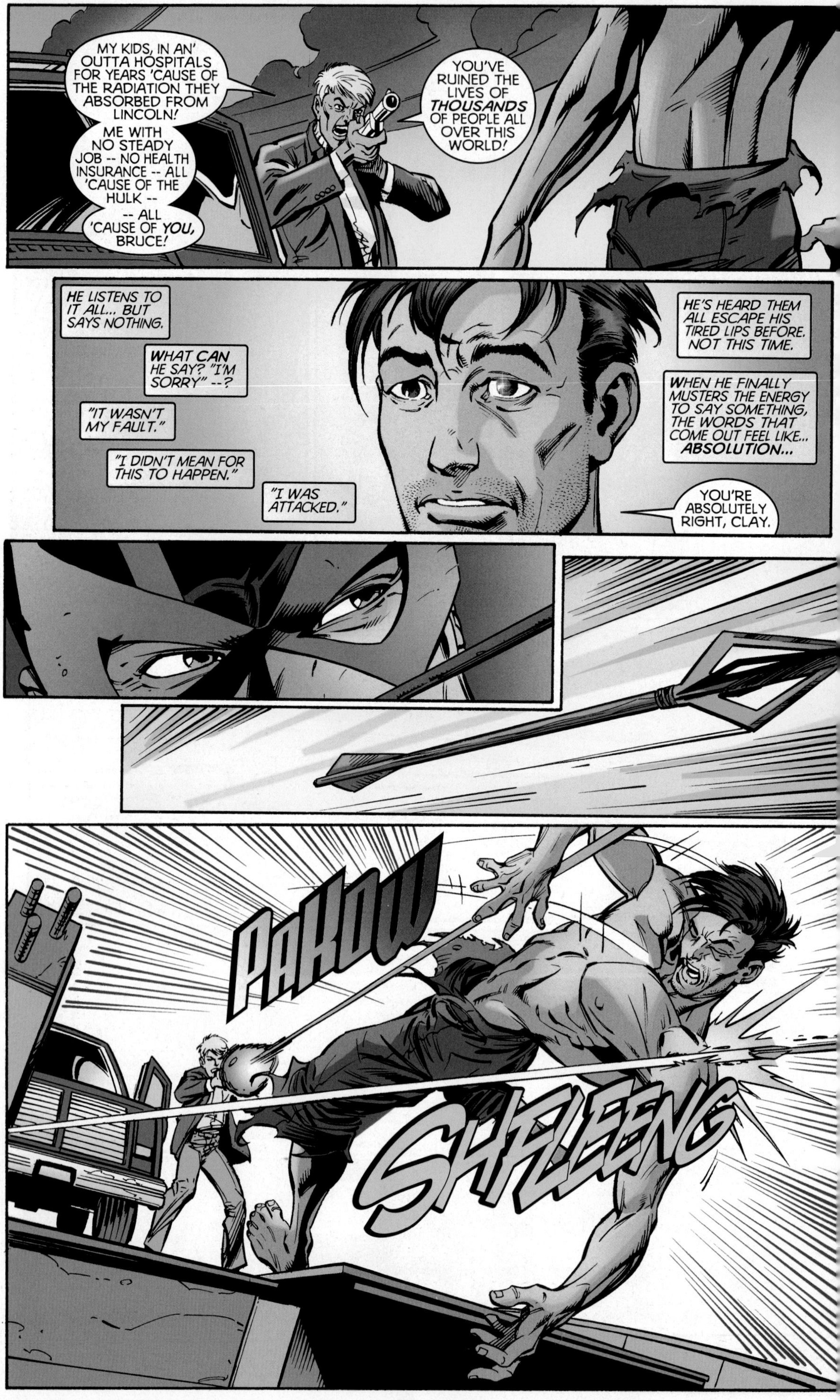
MY KIDS, IN AN' OUTTA HOSPITALS FOR YEARS 'CAUSE OF THE RADIATION THEY ABSORBED FROM LINCOLN!
ME WITH NO STEADY JOB -- NO HEALTH INSURANCE -- ALL 'CAUSE OF THE HULK --
-- ALL 'CAUSE OF *YOU*, BRUCE!
YOU'VE RUINED THE LIVES OF ***THOUSANDS*** OF PEOPLE ALL OVER THIS WORLD!
HE LISTENS TO IT ALL... BUT SAYS NOTHING.
WHAT CAN HE SAY? "I'M SORRY" --?
"IT WASN'T MY FAULT."
"I DIDN'T MEAN FOR THIS TO HAPPEN."
"I WAS ATTACKED."
HE'S HEARD THEM ALL ESCAPE HIS TIRED LIPS BEFORE. NOT THIS TIME.
*WHEN HE FINALLY MUSTERS THE ENERGY TO SAY SOMETHING, THE WORDS THAT COME OUT FEEL LIKE... **ABSOLUTION...***
YOU'RE ABSOLUTELY RIGHT, CLAY.
PAKOW
SHFLEENG

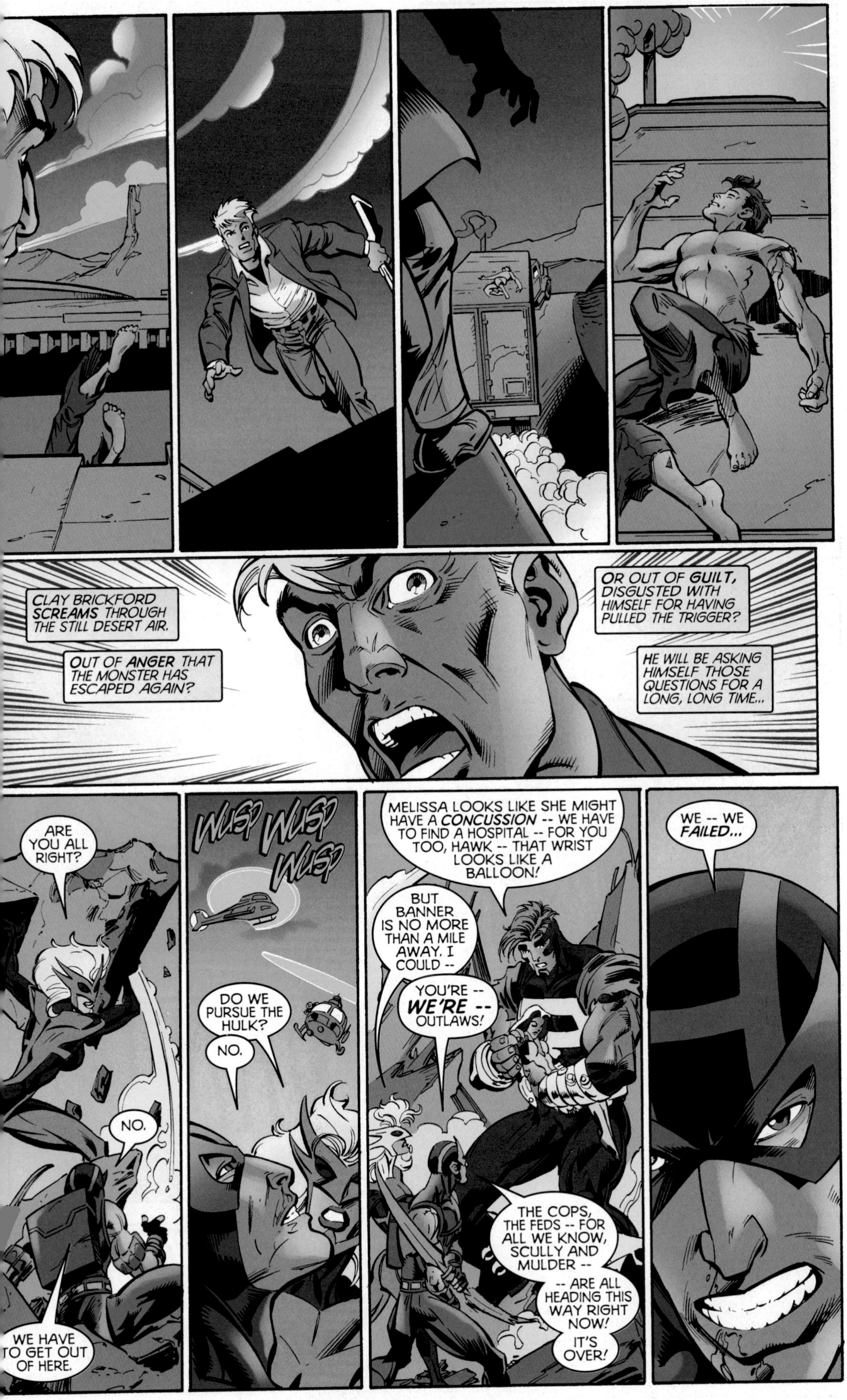
CLAY BRICKFORD SCREAMS THROUGH THE STILL DESERT AIR.
OUT OF ANGER THAT THE MONSTER HAS ESCAPED AGAIN?
OR OUT OF GUILT, DISGUSTED WITH HIMSELF FOR HAVING PULLED THE TRIGGER?
HE WILL BE ASKING HIMSELF THOSE QUESTIONS FOR A LONG, LONG TIME...
ARE YOU ALL RIGHT?
NO.
WE HAVE TO GET OUT OF HERE.
WUSP WUSP WUSP
DO WE PURSUE THE HULK?
NO.
MELISSA LOOKS LIKE SHE MIGHT HAVE A CONCUSSION -- WE HAVE TO FIND A HOSPITAL -- FOR YOU TOO, HAWK -- THAT WRIST LOOKS LIKE A BALLOON!
BUT BANNER IS NO MORE THAN A MILE AWAY. I COULD --
YOU'RE -- WE'RE -- OUTLAWS!
THE COPS, THE FEDS -- FOR ALL WE KNOW, SCULLY AND MULDER --
-- ARE ALL HEADING THIS WAY RIGHT NOW!
IT'S OVER!
WE -- WE FAILED...

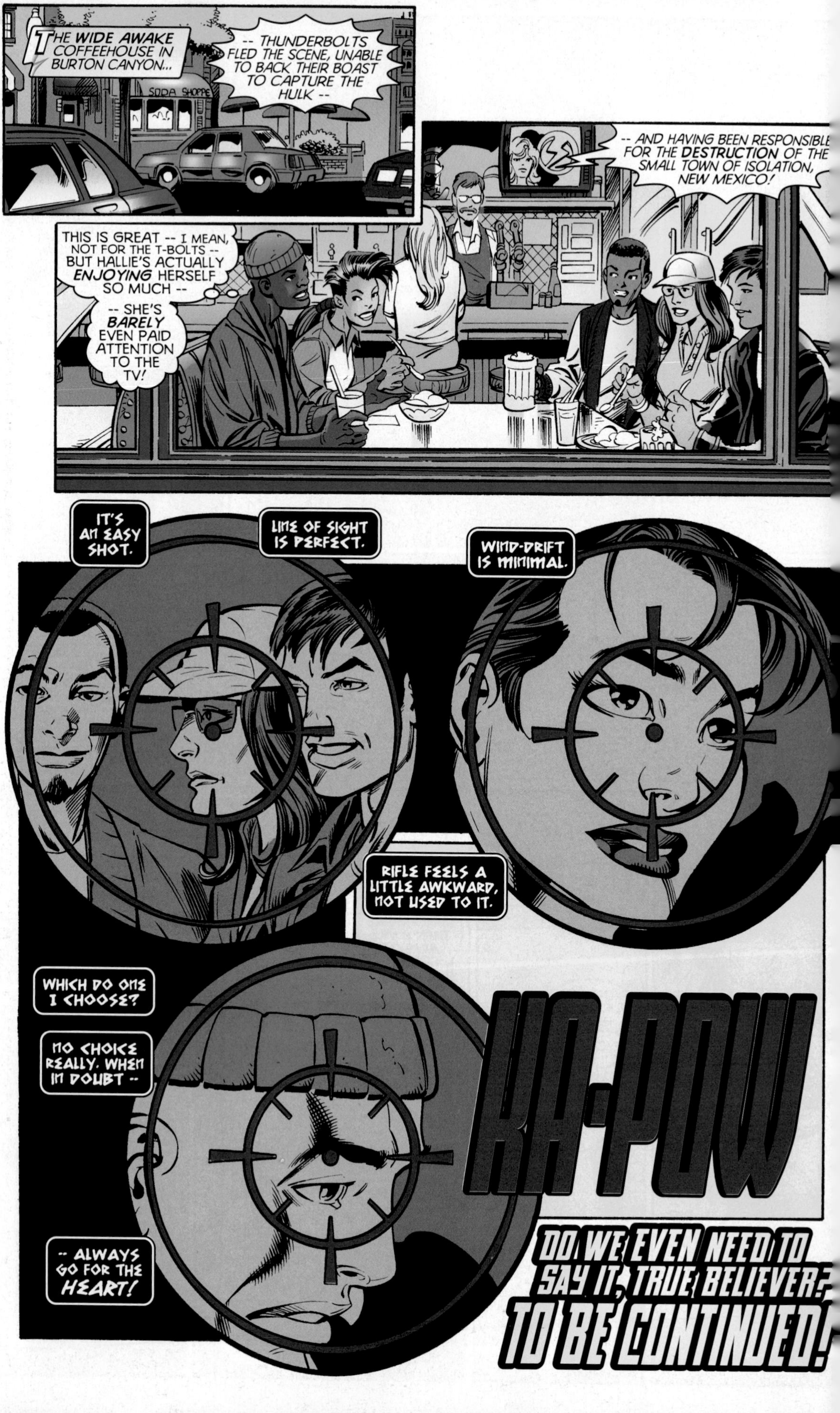
THE WIDE AWAKE COFFEEHOUSE IN BURTON CANYON...
-- THUNDERBOLTS FLED THE SCENE, UNABLE TO BACK THEIR BOAST TO CAPTURE THE HULK --
SODA SHOPPE
-- AND HAVING BEEN RESPONSIBLE FOR THE DESTRUCTION OF THE SMALL TOWN OF ISOLATION, NEW MEXICO!
THIS IS GREAT -- I MEAN, NOT FOR THE T-BOLTS -- BUT HALLIE'S ACTUALLY ENJOYING HERSELF SO MUCH --
-- SHE'S BARELY EVEN PAID ATTENTION TO THE TV!
IT'S AN EASY SHOT.
LINE OF SIGHT IS PERFECT.
WIND-DRIFT IS MINIMAL.
RIFLE FEELS A LITTLE AWKWARD, NOT USED TO IT.
WHICH DO ONE I CHOOSE?
NO CHOICE REALLY. WHEN IN DOUBT --
-- ALWAYS GO FOR THE HEART!
KA-POW
DO WE EVEN NEED TO SAY IT, TRUE BELIEVER?
TO BE CONTINUED!

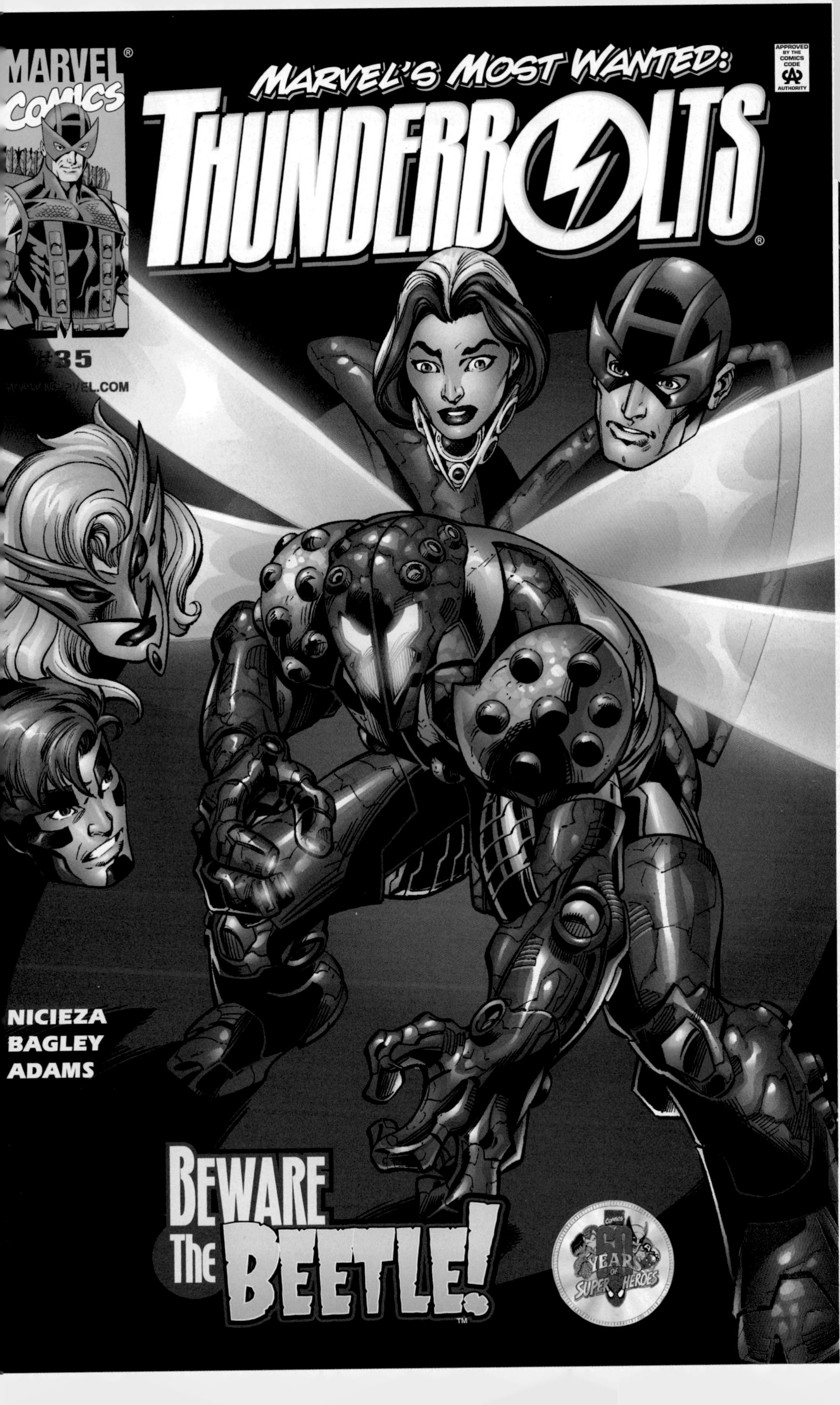

MARVEL COMICS
APPROVED BY THE COMICS CODE AUTHORITY
MARVEL'S MOST WANTED:
THUNDERBOLTS
#35
NICIEZA
BAGLEY
ADAMS
BEWARE The BEETLE!
60 YEARS OF SUPER HEROES

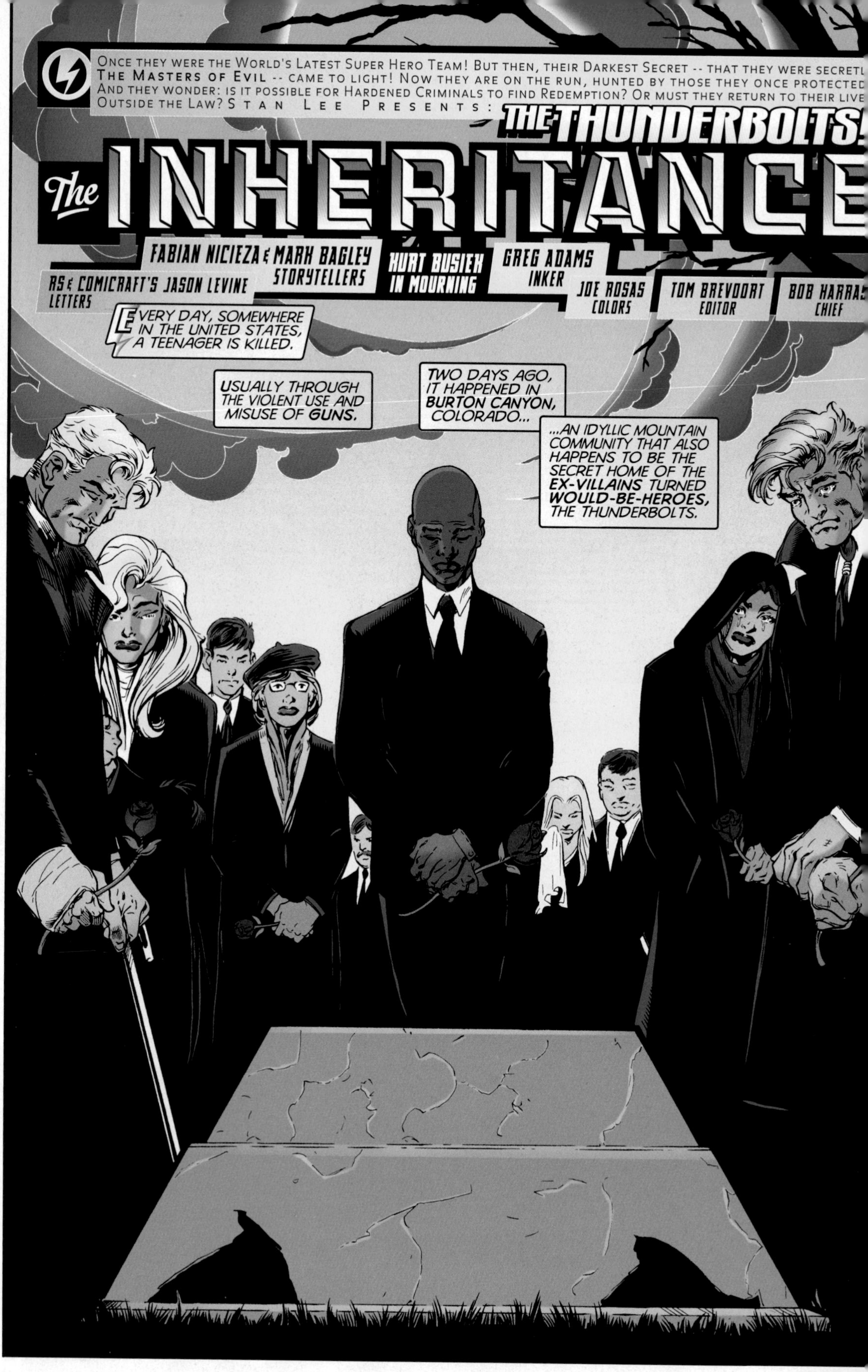

Once they were the World's Latest Super Hero Team! But then, their Darkest Secret -- that they were secretl The Masters of Evil -- came to light! Now they are on the run, hunted by those they once protected And they wonder: is it possible for Hardened Criminals to find Redemption? Or must they return to their live Outside the Law? Stan Lee Presents:
The Thunderbolts!
The Inheritance
Fabian Nicieza & Mark Bagley Storytellers
Kurt Busiek in Mourning
Greg Adams Inker
RS & Comicraft's Jason Levine Letters
Joe Rosas Colors
Tom Brevoort Editor
Bob Harras Chief
Every day, somewhere in the United States, a teenager is killed.
Usually through the violent use and misuse of guns.
Two days ago, it happened in Burton Canyon, Colorado...
...an idyllic mountain community that also happens to be the secret home of the ex-villains turned would-be-heroes, the Thunderbolts.

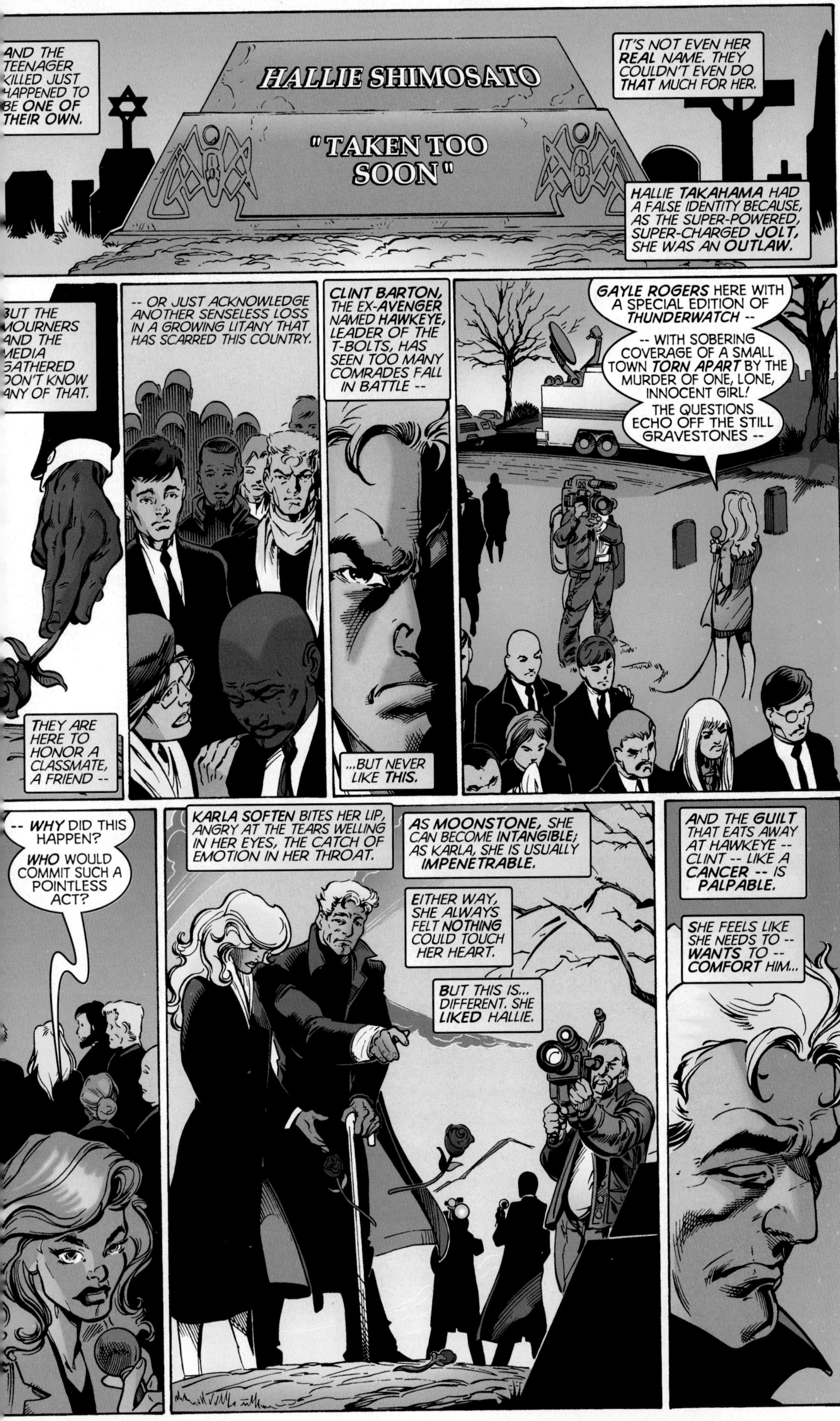
AND THE TEENAGER KILLED JUST HAPPENED TO BE ONE OF THEIR OWN.
HALLIE SHIMOSATO
"TAKEN TOO SOON"
IT'S NOT EVEN HER REAL NAME. THEY COULDN'T EVEN DO THAT MUCH FOR HER.
HALLIE TAKAHAMA HAD A FALSE IDENTITY BECAUSE, AS THE SUPER-POWERED, SUPER-CHARGED JOLT, SHE WAS AN OUTLAW.
BUT THE MOURNERS AND THE MEDIA GATHERED DON'T KNOW ANY OF THAT.
THEY ARE HERE TO HONOR A CLASSMATE, A FRIEND --
-- OR JUST ACKNOWLEDGE ANOTHER SENSELESS LOSS IN A GROWING LITANY THAT HAS SCARRED THIS COUNTRY.
CLINT BARTON, THE EX-AVENGER NAMED HAWKEYE, LEADER OF THE T-BOLTS, HAS SEEN TOO MANY COMRADES FALL IN BATTLE --
...BUT NEVER LIKE THIS.
GAYLE ROGERS HERE WITH A SPECIAL EDITION OF THUNDERWATCH --
-- WITH SOBERING COVERAGE OF A SMALL TOWN TORN APART BY THE MURDER OF ONE, LONE, INNOCENT GIRL! THE QUESTIONS ECHO OFF THE STILL GRAVESTONES --
-- WHY DID THIS HAPPEN? WHO WOULD COMMIT SUCH A POINTLESS ACT?
KARLA SOFTEN BITES HER LIP, ANGRY AT THE TEARS WELLING IN HER EYES, THE CATCH OF EMOTION IN HER THROAT.
AS MOONSTONE, SHE CAN BECOME INTANGIBLE; AS KARLA, SHE IS USUALLY IMPENETRABLE.
EITHER WAY, SHE ALWAYS FELT NOTHING COULD TOUCH HER HEART.
BUT THIS IS... DIFFERENT. SHE LIKED HALLIE.
AND THE GUILT THAT EATS AWAY AT HAWKEYE -- CLINT -- LIKE A CANCER -- IS PALPABLE.
SHE FEELS LIKE SHE NEEDS TO -- WANTS TO -- COMFORT HIM...

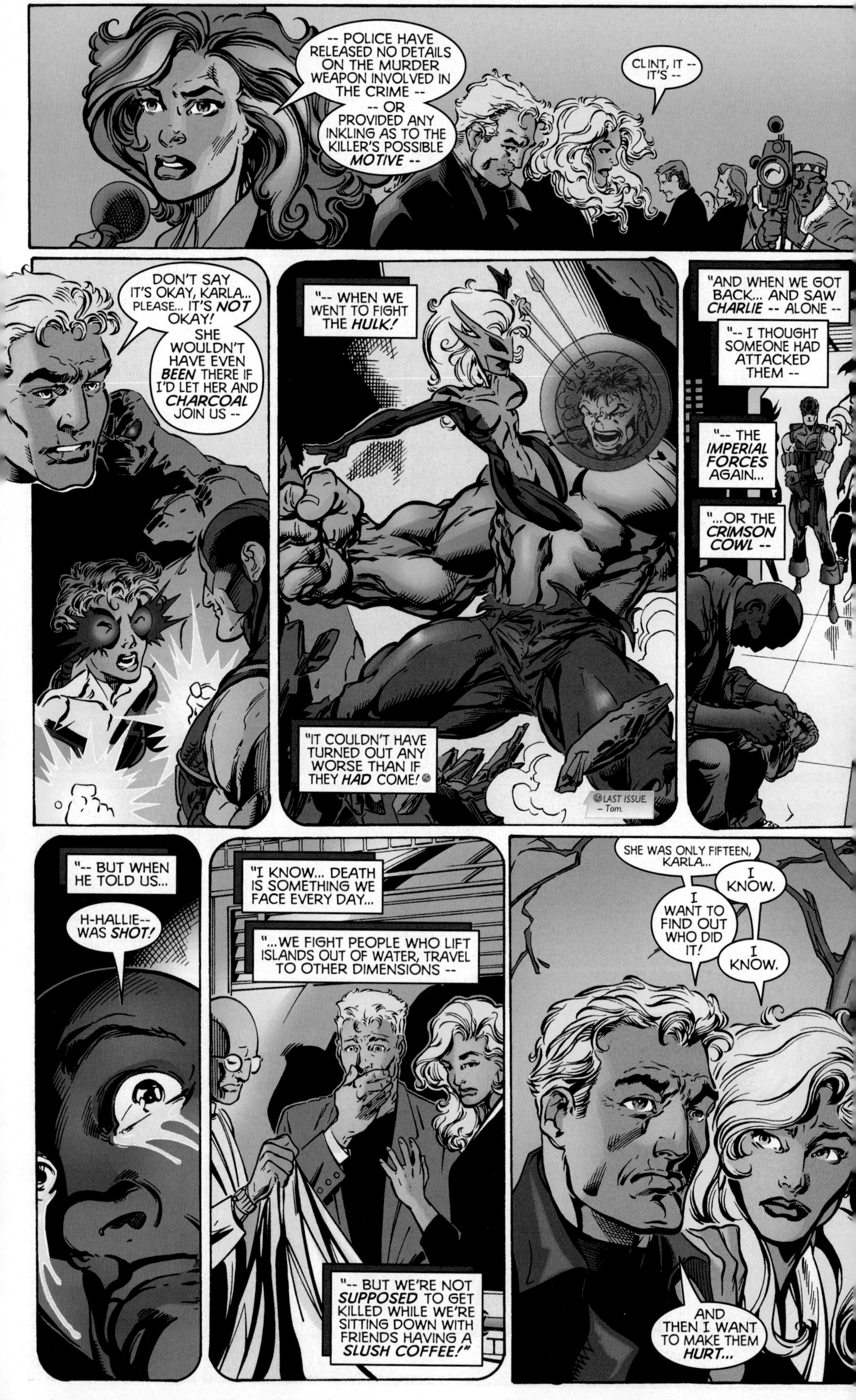
-- POLICE HAVE RELEASED NO DETAILS ON THE MURDER WEAPON INVOLVED IN THE CRIME --
-- OR PROVIDED ANY INKLING AS TO THE KILLER'S POSSIBLE MOTIVE --
CLINT, IT -- IT'S --
DON'T SAY IT'S OKAY, KARLA... PLEASE... IT'S NOT OKAY!
SHE WOULDN'T HAVE EVEN BEEN THERE IF I'D LET HER AND CHARCOAL JOIN US --
"-- WHEN WE WENT TO FIGHT THE HULK!
"IT COULDN'T HAVE TURNED OUT ANY WORSE THAN IF THEY HAD COME!
LAST ISSUE. – Tom.
"AND WHEN WE GOT BACK... AND SAW CHARLIE -- ALONE --
"-- I THOUGHT SOMEONE HAD ATTACKED THEM --
"-- THE IMPERIAL FORCES AGAIN...
"...OR THE CRIMSON COWL --
"-- BUT WHEN HE TOLD US...
H-HALLIE-- WAS SHOT!
"I KNOW... DEATH IS SOMETHING WE FACE EVERY DAY...
"...WE FIGHT PEOPLE WHO LIFT ISLANDS OUT OF WATER, TRAVEL TO OTHER DIMENSIONS --
"-- BUT WE'RE NOT SUPPOSED TO GET KILLED WHILE WE'RE SITTING DOWN WITH FRIENDS HAVING A SLUSH COFFEE!"
SHE WAS ONLY FIFTEEN, KARLA...
I KNOW.
I WANT TO FIND OUT WHO DID IT!
I KNOW.
AND THEN I WANT TO MAKE THEM HURT...

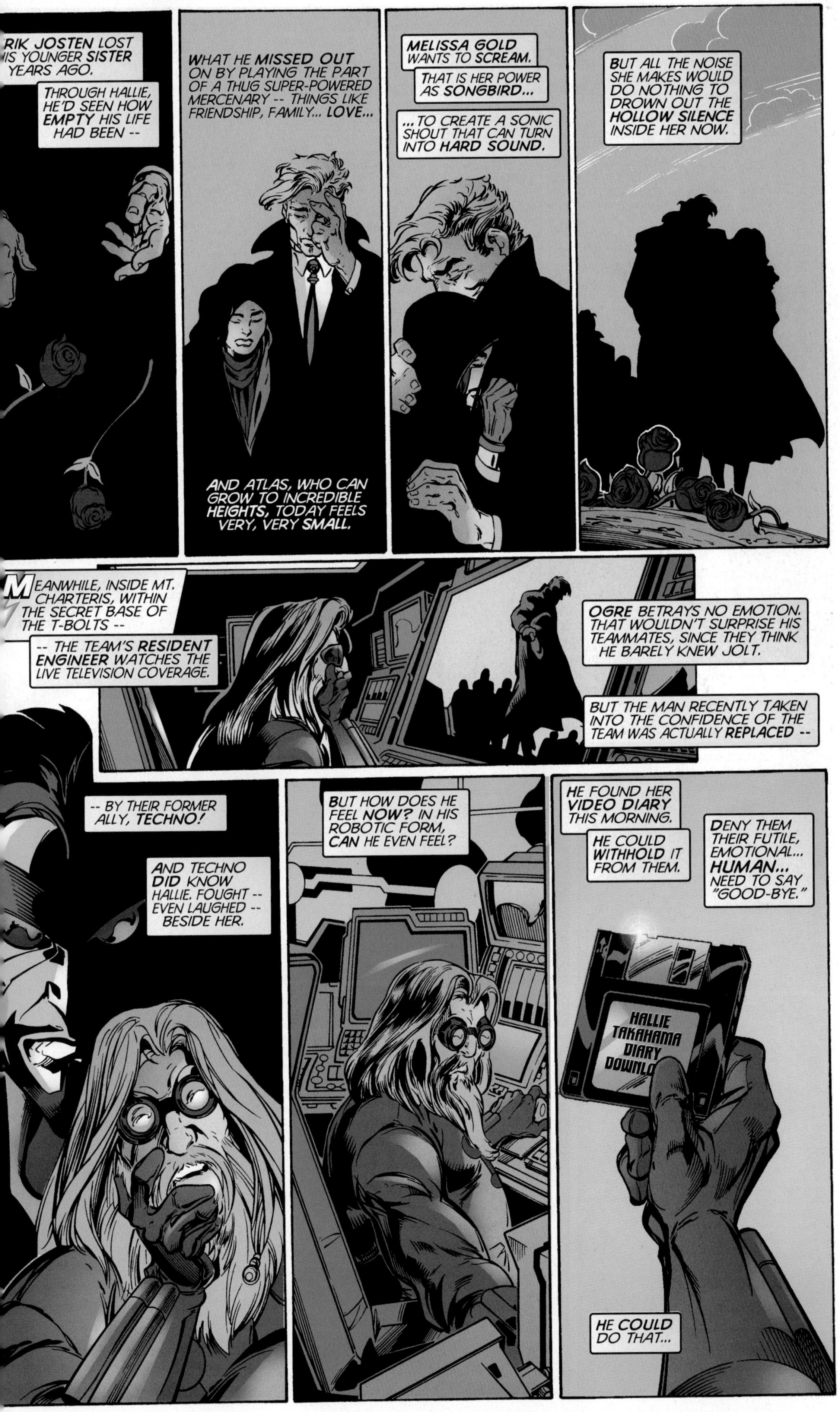
RIK JOSTEN LOST IS YOUNGER SISTER YEARS AGO.
THROUGH HALLIE, HE'D SEEN HOW EMPTY HIS LIFE HAD BEEN --
WHAT HE MISSED OUT ON BY PLAYING THE PART OF A THUG SUPER-POWERED MERCENARY -- THINGS LIKE FRIENDSHIP, FAMILY... LOVE...
AND ATLAS, WHO CAN GROW TO INCREDIBLE HEIGHTS, TODAY FEELS VERY, VERY SMALL.
MELISSA GOLD WANTS TO SCREAM.
THAT IS HER POWER AS SONGBIRD...
...TO CREATE A SONIC SHOUT THAT CAN TURN INTO HARD SOUND.
BUT ALL THE NOISE SHE MAKES WOULD DO NOTHING TO DROWN OUT THE HOLLOW SILENCE INSIDE HER NOW.
MEANWHILE, INSIDE MT. CHARTERIS, WITHIN THE SECRET BASE OF THE T-BOLTS --
-- THE TEAM'S RESIDENT ENGINEER WATCHES THE LIVE TELEVISION COVERAGE.
OGRE BETRAYS NO EMOTION. THAT WOULDN'T SURPRISE HIS TEAMMATES, SINCE THEY THINK HE BARELY KNEW JOLT.
BUT THE MAN RECENTLY TAKEN INTO THE CONFIDENCE OF THE TEAM WAS ACTUALLY REPLACED --
-- BY THEIR FORMER ALLY, TECHNO!
AND TECHNO DID KNOW HALLIE. FOUGHT -- EVEN LAUGHED -- BESIDE HER.
BUT HOW DOES HE FEEL NOW? IN HIS ROBOTIC FORM, CAN HE EVEN FEEL?
HE FOUND HER VIDEO DIARY THIS MORNING.
HE COULD WITHHOLD IT FROM THEM.
DENY THEM THEIR FUTILE, EMOTIONAL... HUMAN... NEED TO SAY "GOOD-BYE."
HALLIE TAKAHAMA DIARY DOWNLO
HE COULD DO THAT...

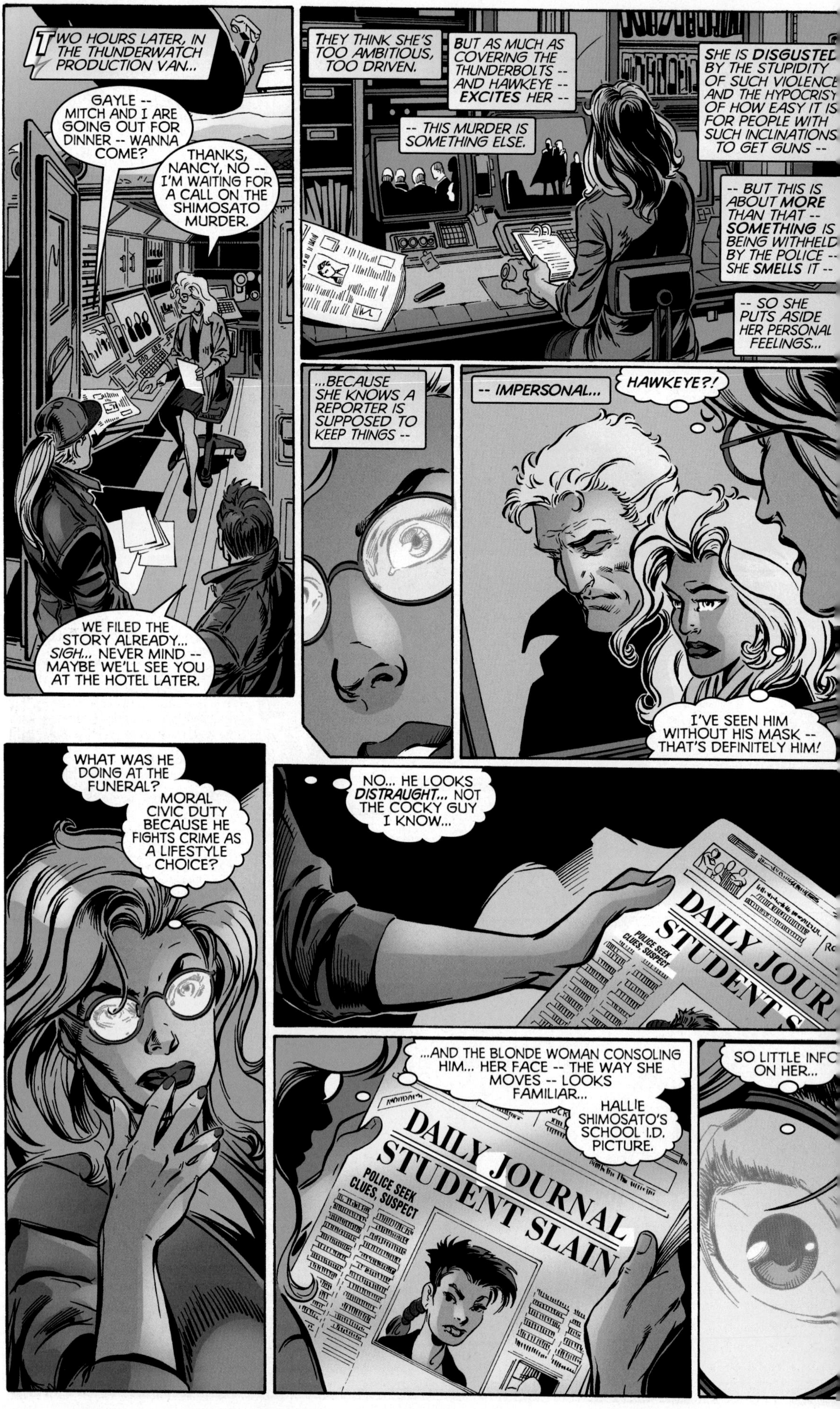
TWO HOURS LATER, IN THE THUNDERWATCH PRODUCTION VAN...
GAYLE -- MITCH AND I ARE GOING OUT FOR DINNER -- WANNA COME?
THANKS, NANCY, NO -- I'M WAITING FOR A CALL ON THE SHIMOSATO MURDER.
WE FILED THE STORY ALREADY... *SIGH*... NEVER MIND -- MAYBE WE'LL SEE YOU AT THE HOTEL LATER.
THEY THINK SHE'S TOO AMBITIOUS, TOO DRIVEN.
BUT AS MUCH AS COVERING THE THUNDERBOLTS -- AND HAWKEYE -- **EXCITES** HER --
-- THIS MURDER IS SOMETHING ELSE.
SHE IS **DISGUSTED** BY THE STUPIDITY OF SUCH VIOLENCE AND THE HYPOCRISY OF HOW EASY IT IS FOR PEOPLE WITH SUCH INCLINATIONS TO GET GUNS --
-- BUT THIS IS ABOUT **MORE** THAN THAT -- **SOMETHING** IS BEING WITHHELD BY THE POLICE -- SHE **SMELLS** IT --
-- SO SHE PUTS ASIDE HER PERSONAL FEELINGS...
...BECAUSE SHE KNOWS A REPORTER IS SUPPOSED TO KEEP THINGS --
-- IMPERSONAL...
HAWKEYE?!
I'VE SEEN HIM WITHOUT HIS MASK -- THAT'S DEFINITELY HIM!
WHAT WAS HE DOING AT THE FUNERAL?
MORAL CIVIC DUTY BECAUSE HE FIGHTS CRIME AS A LIFESTYLE CHOICE?
NO... HE LOOKS *DISTRAUGHT*... NOT THE COCKY GUY I KNOW...
DAILY JOURNAL
STUDENT SLAIN
POLICE SEEK CLUES, SUSPECT
...AND THE BLONDE WOMAN CONSOLING HIM... HER FACE -- THE WAY SHE MOVES -- LOOKS FAMILIAR...
HALLIE SHIMOSATO'S SCHOOL I.D. PICTURE.
DAILY JOURNAL
STUDENT SLAIN
POLICE SEEK CLUES, SUSPECT
SO LITTLE INFO ON HER...

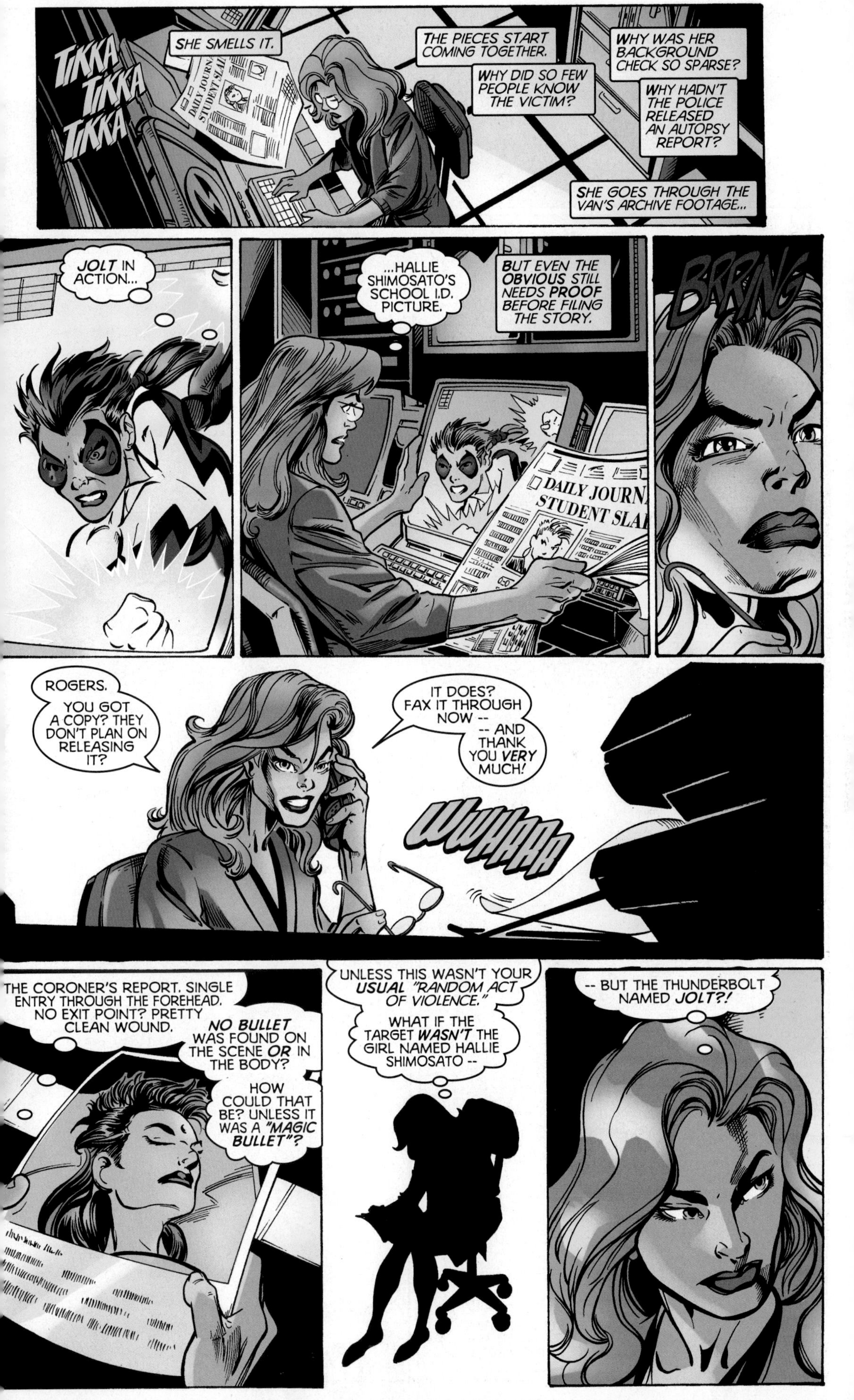
TIKKA TIKKA TIKKA
SHE SMELLS IT.
DAILY JOURNAL STUDENT SLAI
THE PIECES START COMING TOGETHER.
WHY DID SO FEW PEOPLE KNOW THE VICTIM?
WHY WAS HER BACKGROUND CHECK SO SPARSE?
WHY HADN'T THE POLICE RELEASED AN AUTOPSY REPORT?
SHE GOES THROUGH THE VAN'S ARCHIVE FOOTAGE...
JOLT IN ACTION...
...HALLIE SHIMOSATO'S SCHOOL I.D. PICTURE.
BUT EVEN THE OBVIOUS STILL NEEDS PROOF BEFORE FILING THE STORY.
DAILY JOURNA STUDENT SLAI
BRRING
ROGERS.
YOU GOT A COPY? THEY DON'T PLAN ON RELEASING IT?
IT DOES? FAX IT THROUGH NOW --
-- AND THANK YOU VERY MUCH!
WWHRRR
THE CORONER'S REPORT. SINGLE ENTRY THROUGH THE FOREHEAD. NO EXIT POINT? PRETTY CLEAN WOUND.
NO BULLET WAS FOUND ON THE SCENE OR IN THE BODY?
HOW COULD THAT BE? UNLESS IT WAS A "MAGIC BULLET"?
UNLESS THIS WASN'T YOUR USUAL "RANDOM ACT OF VIOLENCE."
WHAT IF THE TARGET WASN'T THE GIRL NAMED HALLIE SHIMOSATO --
-- BUT THE THUNDERBOLT NAMED JOLT?!

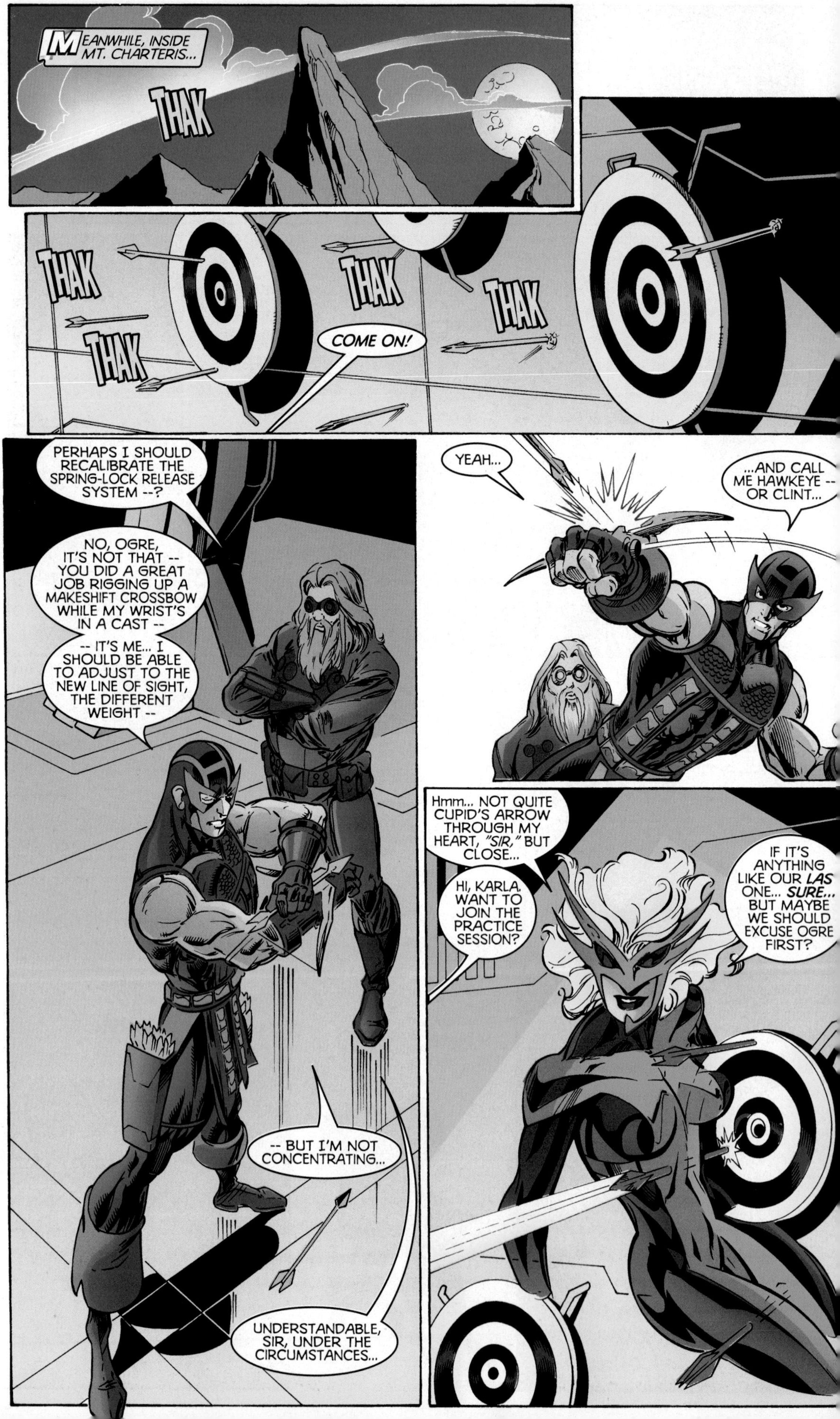
MEANWHILE, INSIDE MT. CHARTERIS...
THAK
THAK
THAK
THAK
THAK
COME ON!
PERHAPS I SHOULD RECALIBRATE THE SPRING-LOCK RELEASE SYSTEM --?
NO, OGRE, IT'S NOT THAT -- YOU DID A GREAT JOB RIGGING UP A MAKESHIFT CROSSBOW WHILE MY WRIST'S IN A CAST --
-- IT'S ME... I SHOULD BE ABLE TO ADJUST TO THE NEW LINE OF SIGHT, THE DIFFERENT WEIGHT --
-- BUT I'M NOT CONCENTRATING...
UNDERSTANDABLE, SIR, UNDER THE CIRCUMSTANCES...
YEAH...
...AND CALL ME HAWKEYE -- OR CLINT...
Hmm... NOT QUITE CUPID'S ARROW THROUGH MY HEART, "SIR," BUT CLOSE...
HI, KARLA. WANT TO JOIN THE PRACTICE SESSION?
IF IT'S ANYTHING LIKE OUR LAS ONE... SURE... BUT MAYBE WE SHOULD EXCUSE OGRE FIRST?

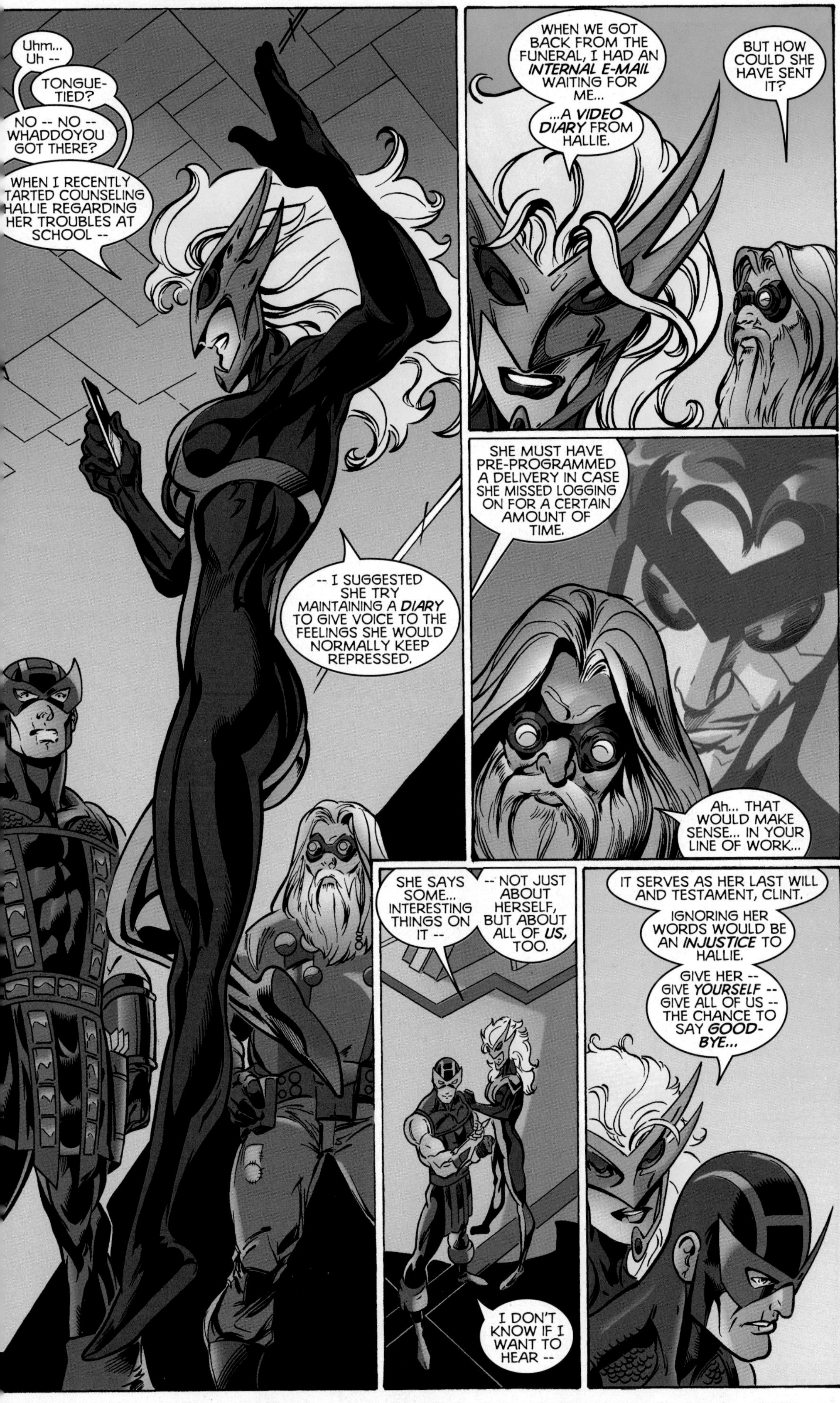
Uhm... Uh --
TONGUE-TIED?
NO -- NO -- WHADDOYOU GOT THERE?
WHEN I RECENTLY TARTED COUNSELING HALLIE REGARDING HER TROUBLES AT SCHOOL --
-- I SUGGESTED SHE TRY MAINTAINING A *DIARY* TO GIVE VOICE TO THE FEELINGS SHE WOULD NORMALLY KEEP REPRESSED.
WHEN WE GOT BACK FROM THE FUNERAL, I HAD AN *INTERNAL E-MAIL* WAITING FOR ME...
...A *VIDEO DIARY* FROM HALLIE.
BUT HOW COULD SHE HAVE SENT IT?
SHE MUST HAVE PRE-PROGRAMMED A DELIVERY IN CASE SHE MISSED LOGGING ON FOR A CERTAIN AMOUNT OF TIME.
Ah... THAT WOULD MAKE SENSE... IN YOUR LINE OF WORK...
SHE SAYS SOME... INTERESTING THINGS ON IT --
-- NOT JUST ABOUT HERSELF, BUT ABOUT ALL OF *US,* TOO.
I DON'T KNOW IF I WANT TO HEAR --
IT SERVES AS HER LAST WILL AND TESTAMENT, CLINT.
IGNORING HER WORDS WOULD BE AN *INJUSTICE* TO HALLIE.
GIVE HER -- GIVE *YOURSELF* -- GIVE ALL OF US -- THE CHANCE TO SAY *GOOD-BYE...*

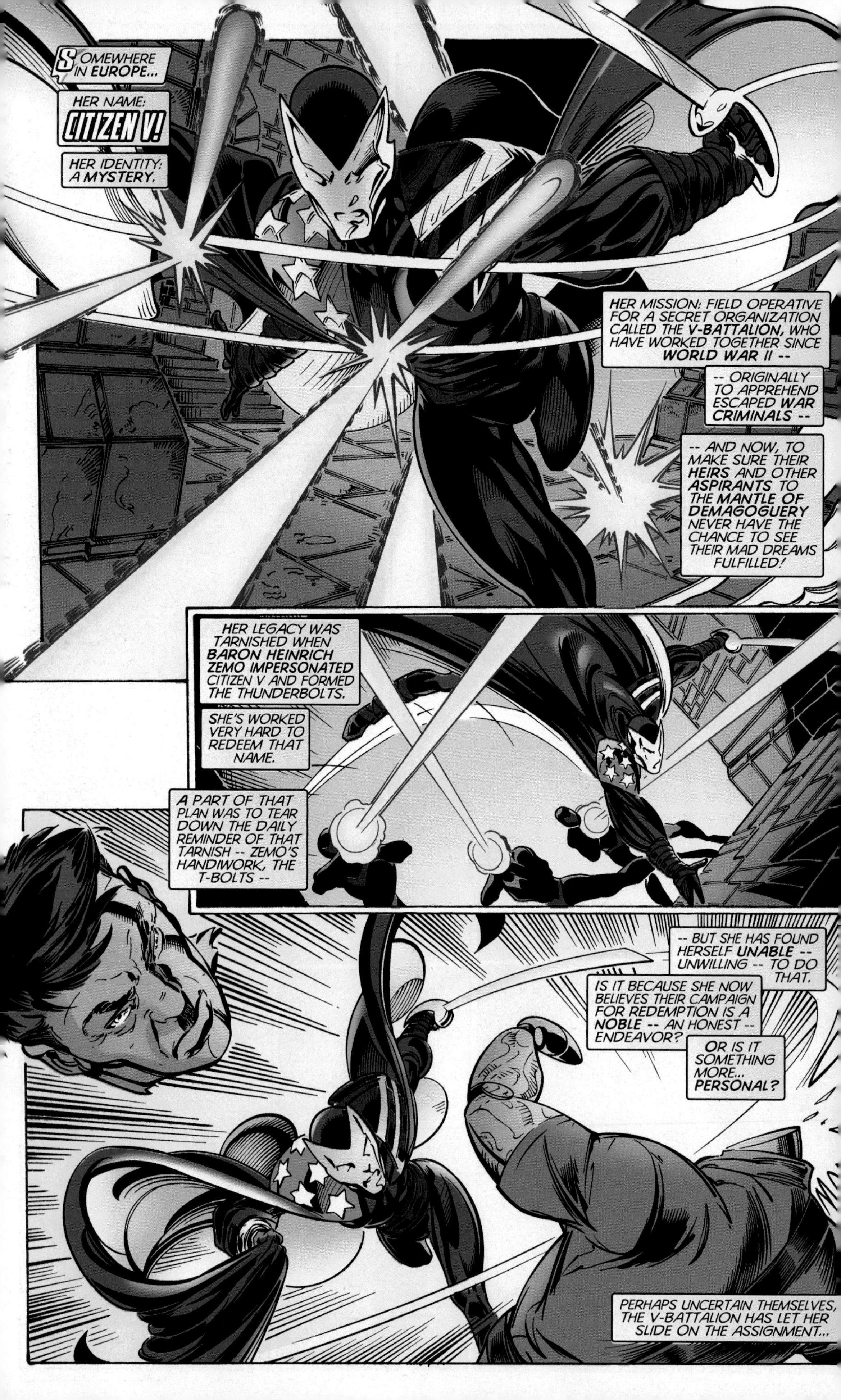
SOMEWHERE IN EUROPE...
HER NAME: CITIZEN V!
HER IDENTITY: A MYSTERY.
HER MISSION: FIELD OPERATIVE FOR A SECRET ORGANIZATION CALLED THE V-BATTALION, WHO HAVE WORKED TOGETHER SINCE WORLD WAR II --
-- ORIGINALLY TO APPREHEND ESCAPED WAR CRIMINALS --
-- AND NOW, TO MAKE SURE THEIR HEIRS AND OTHER ASPIRANTS TO THE MANTLE OF DEMAGOGUERY NEVER HAVE THE CHANCE TO SEE THEIR MAD DREAMS FULFILLED!
HER LEGACY WAS TARNISHED WHEN BARON HEINRICH ZEMO IMPERSONATED CITIZEN V AND FORMED THE THUNDERBOLTS.
SHE'S WORKED VERY HARD TO REDEEM THAT NAME.
A PART OF THAT PLAN WAS TO TEAR DOWN THE DAILY REMINDER OF THAT TARNISH -- ZEMO'S HANDIWORK, THE T-BOLTS --
-- BUT SHE HAS FOUND HERSELF UNABLE -- UNWILLING -- TO DO THAT.
IS IT BECAUSE SHE NOW BELIEVES THEIR CAMPAIGN FOR REDEMPTION IS A NOBLE -- AN HONEST -- ENDEAVOR?
OR IS IT SOMETHING MORE... PERSONAL?
PERHAPS UNCERTAIN THEMSELVES, THE V-BATTALION HAS LET HER SLIDE ON THE ASSIGNMENT...

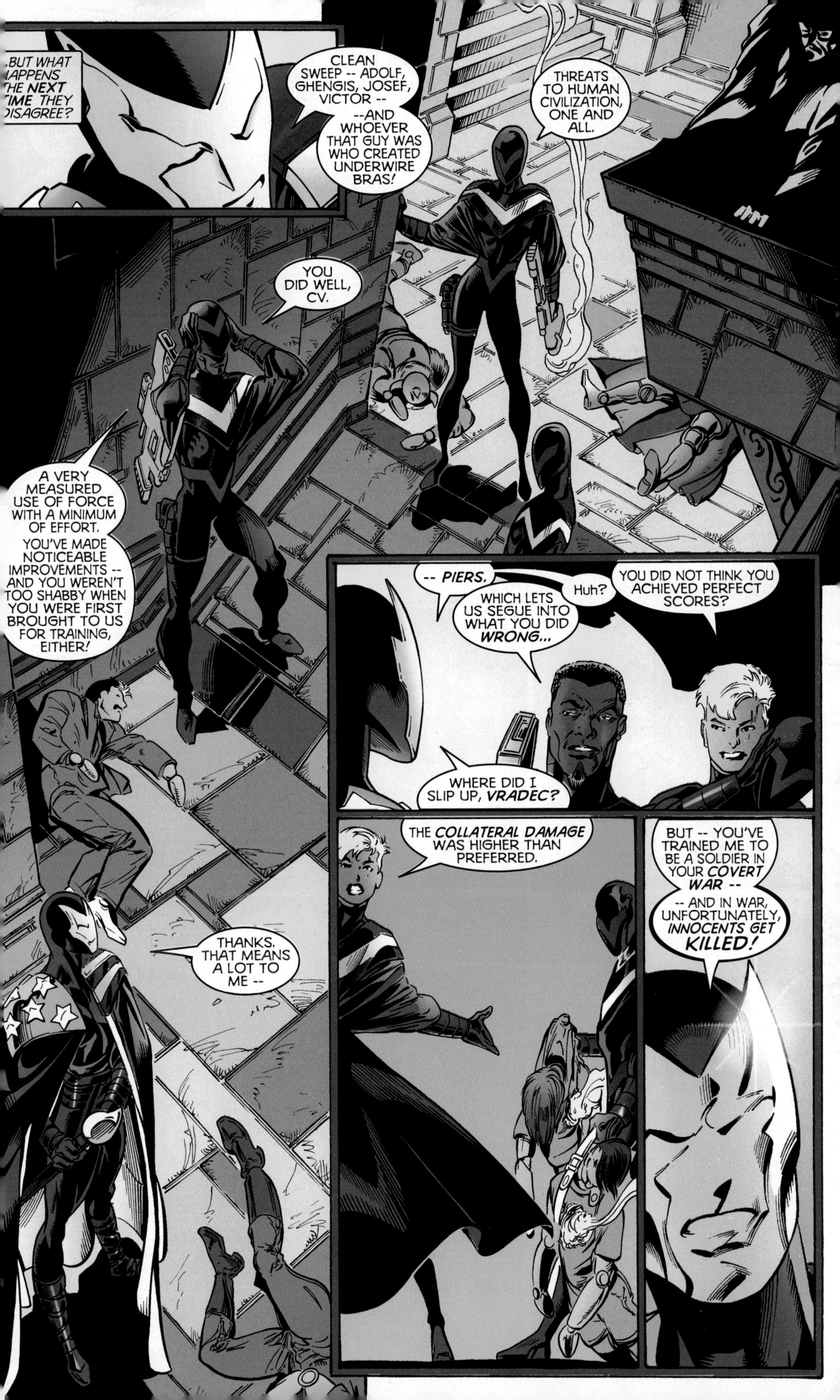
BUT WHAT HAPPENS THE NEXT TIME THEY DISAGREE?
CLEAN SWEEP -- ADOLF, GHENGIS, JOSEF, VICTOR --
--AND WHOEVER THAT GUY WAS WHO CREATED UNDERWIRE BRAS!
THREATS TO HUMAN CIVILIZATION, ONE AND ALL.
YOU DID WELL, CV.
A VERY MEASURED USE OF FORCE WITH A MINIMUM OF EFFORT.
YOU'VE MADE NOTICEABLE IMPROVEMENTS -- AND YOU WEREN'T TOO SHABBY WHEN YOU WERE FIRST BROUGHT TO US FOR TRAINING, EITHER!
THANKS. THAT MEANS A LOT TO ME --
-- PIERS.
Huh?
WHICH LETS US SEGUE INTO WHAT YOU DID WRONG...
YOU DID NOT THINK YOU ACHIEVED PERFECT SCORES?
WHERE DID I SLIP UP, VRADEC?
THE COLLATERAL DAMAGE WAS HIGHER THAN PREFERRED.
BUT -- YOU'VE TRAINED ME TO BE A SOLDIER IN YOUR COVERT WAR --
-- AND IN WAR, UNFORTUNATELY, INNOCENTS GET KILLED!

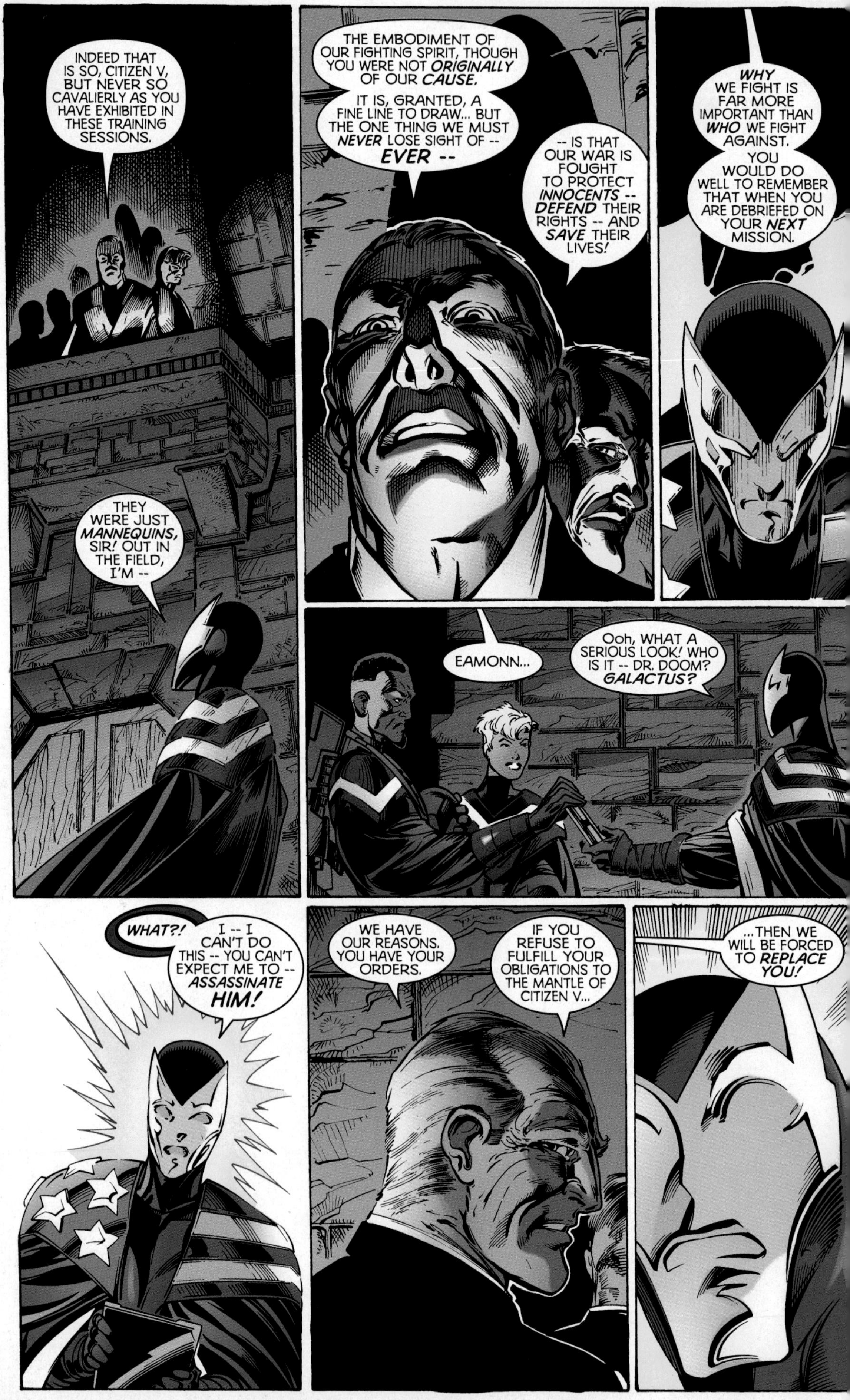
INDEED THAT IS SO, CITIZEN V, BUT NEVER SO CAVALIERLY AS YOU HAVE EXHIBITED IN THESE TRAINING SESSIONS.
THEY WERE JUST MANNEQUINS, SIR! OUT IN THE FIELD, I'M --
THE EMBODIMENT OF OUR FIGHTING SPIRIT, THOUGH YOU WERE NOT ORIGINALLY OF OUR CAUSE.
IT IS, GRANTED, A FINE LINE TO DRAW... BUT THE ONE THING WE MUST NEVER LOSE SIGHT OF -- EVER --
-- IS THAT OUR WAR IS FOUGHT TO PROTECT INNOCENTS -- DEFEND THEIR RIGHTS -- AND SAVE THEIR LIVES!
WHY WE FIGHT IS FAR MORE IMPORTANT THAN WHO WE FIGHT AGAINST.
YOU WOULD DO WELL TO REMEMBER THAT WHEN YOU ARE DEBRIEFED ON YOUR NEXT MISSION.
EAMONN...
Ooh, WHAT A SERIOUS LOOK! WHO IS IT -- DR. DOOM? GALACTUS?
WHAT?!
I -- I CAN'T DO THIS -- YOU CAN'T EXPECT ME TO -- ASSASSINATE HIM!
WE HAVE OUR REASONS. YOU HAVE YOUR ORDERS.
IF YOU REFUSE TO FULFILL YOUR OBLIGATIONS TO THE MANTLE OF CITIZEN V...
...THEN WE WILL BE FORCED TO REPLACE YOU!

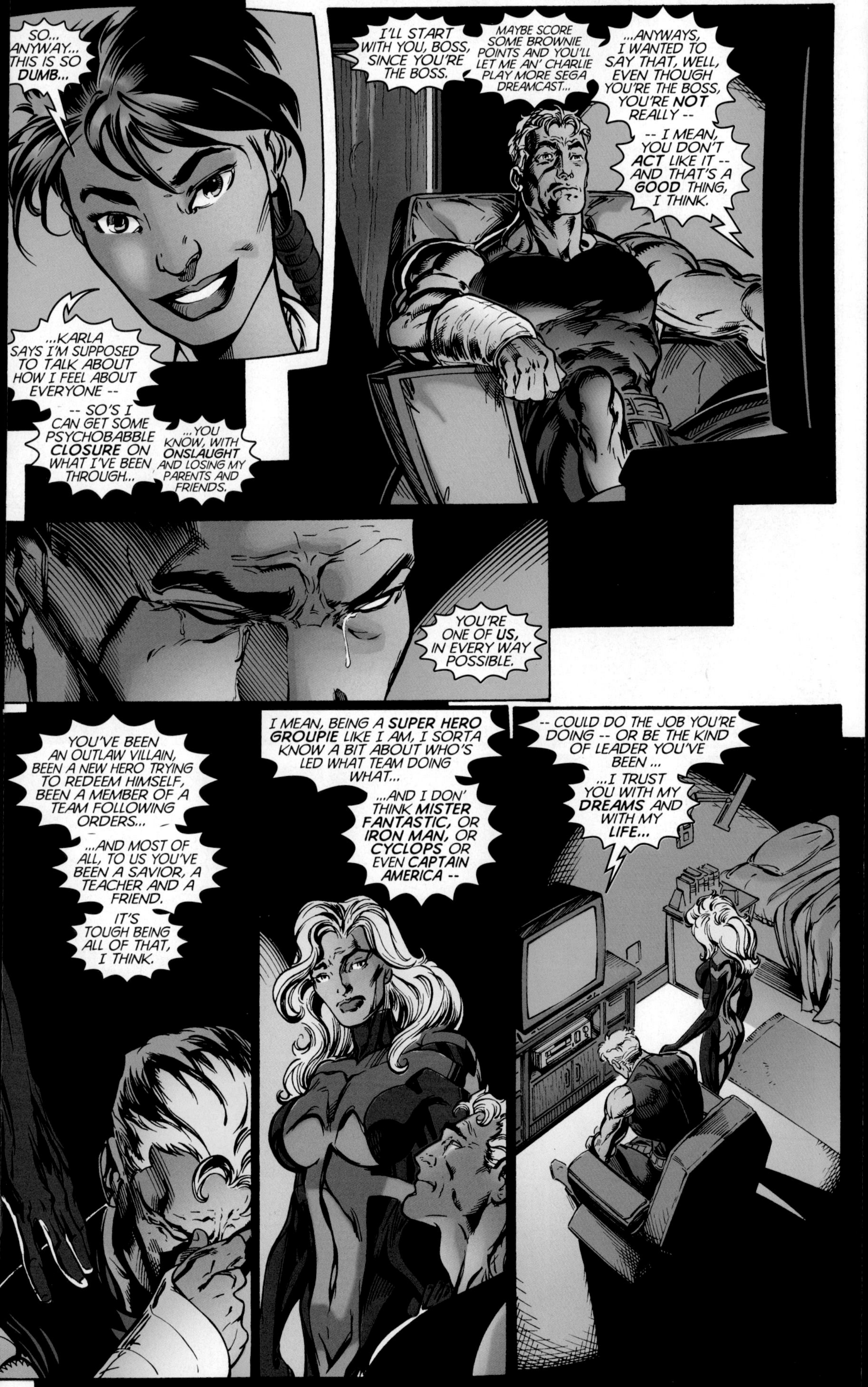
SO... ANYWAY... THIS IS SO **DUMB**...
...KARLA SAYS I'M SUPPOSED TO TALK ABOUT HOW I FEEL ABOUT EVERYONE --
-- SO'S I CAN GET SOME PSYCHOBABBLE **CLOSURE** ON WHAT I'VE BEEN THROUGH...
...YOU KNOW, WITH **ONSLAUGHT** AND LOSING MY PARENTS AND FRIENDS.
I'LL START WITH YOU, BOSS, SINCE YOU'RE THE BOSS.
MAYBE SCORE SOME BROWNIE POINTS AND YOU'LL LET ME AN' CHARLIE PLAY MORE SEGA DREAMCAST...
...ANYWAYS, I WANTED TO SAY THAT, WELL, EVEN THOUGH YOU'RE THE BOSS, YOU'RE **NOT** REALLY --
-- I MEAN, YOU DON'T **ACT** LIKE IT -- AND THAT'S A **GOOD** THING, I THINK.
YOU'RE ONE OF **US**, IN EVERY WAY POSSIBLE.
YOU'VE BEEN AN OUTLAW VILLAIN, BEEN A NEW HERO TRYING TO REDEEM HIMSELF, BEEN A MEMBER OF A TEAM FOLLOWING ORDERS...
...AND MOST OF ALL, TO US YOU'VE BEEN A SAVIOR, A TEACHER AND A FRIEND.
IT'S TOUGH BEING ALL OF THAT, I THINK.
I MEAN, BEING A **SUPER HERO GROUPIE** LIKE I AM, I SORTA KNOW A BIT ABOUT WHO'S LED WHAT TEAM DOING WHAT...
...AND I DON' THINK **MISTER FANTASTIC,** OR **IRON MAN,** OR **CYCLOPS** OR EVEN **CAPTAIN AMERICA** --
-- COULD DO THE JOB YOU'RE DOING -- OR BE THE KIND OF LEADER YOU'VE BEEN ...
...I TRUST YOU WITH MY **DREAMS** AND WITH MY **LIFE...**

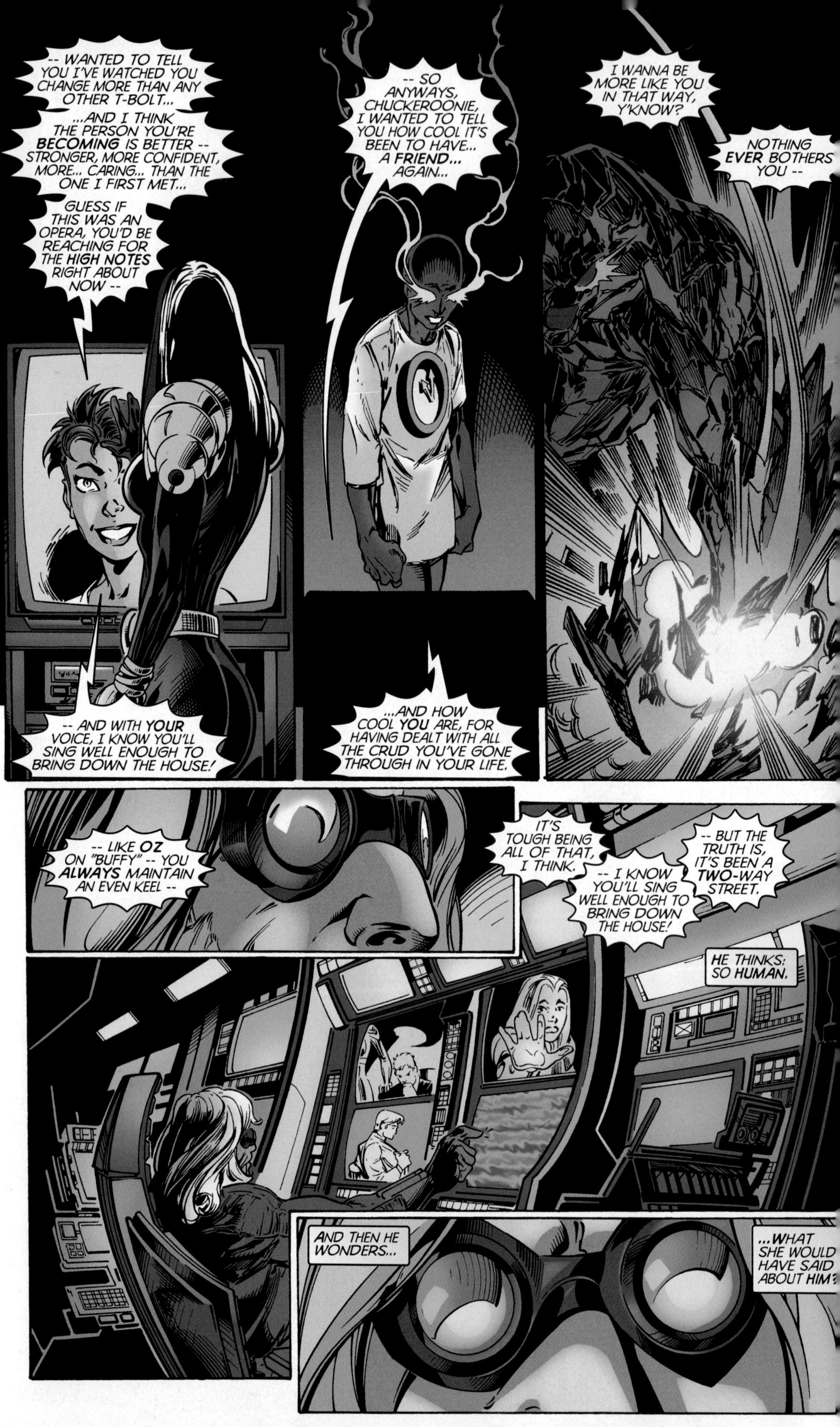
-- WANTED TO TELL YOU I'VE WATCHED YOU CHANGE MORE THAN ANY OTHER T-BOLT...
...AND I THINK THE PERSON YOU'RE BECOMING IS BETTER -- STRONGER, MORE CONFIDENT, MORE... CARING... THAN THE ONE I FIRST MET...
GUESS IF THIS WAS AN OPERA, YOU'D BE REACHING FOR THE HIGH NOTES RIGHT ABOUT NOW --
-- AND WITH YOUR VOICE, I KNOW YOU'LL SING WELL ENOUGH TO BRING DOWN THE HOUSE!
-- SO ANYWAYS, CHUCKEROONIE, I WANTED TO TELL YOU HOW COOL IT'S BEEN TO HAVE... A FRIEND... AGAIN...
...AND HOW COOL YOU ARE, FOR HAVING DEALT WITH ALL THE CRUD YOU'VE GONE THROUGH IN YOUR LIFE.
I WANNA BE MORE LIKE YOU IN THAT WAY, Y'KNOW?
NOTHING EVER BOTHERS YOU --
-- LIKE OZ ON "BUFFY" -- YOU ALWAYS MAINTAIN AN EVEN KEEL --
IT'S TOUGH BEING ALL OF THAT, I THINK.
-- I KNOW YOU'LL SING WELL ENOUGH TO BRING DOWN THE HOUSE!
-- BUT THE TRUTH IS, IT'S BEEN A TWO-WAY STREET.
HE THINKS: SO HUMAN.
AND THEN HE WONDERS...
...WHAT SHE WOULD HAVE SAID ABOUT HIM?

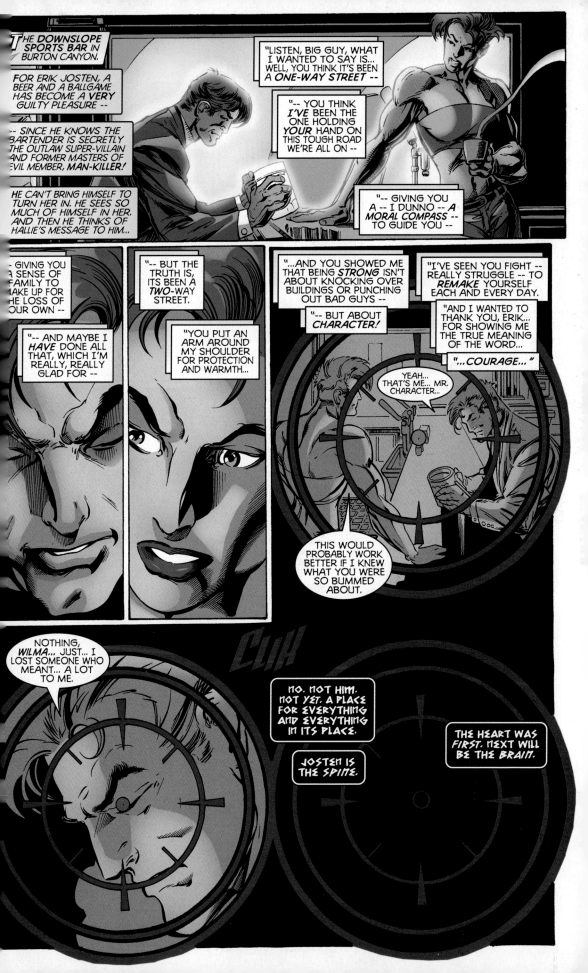

THE *DOWNSLOPE SPORTS BAR* IN BURTON CANYON.

FOR ERIK JOSTEN, A BEER AND A BALLGAME HAS BECOME A *VERY* GUILTY PLEASURE --

-- SINCE HE KNOWS THE BARTENDER IS SECRETLY THE OUTLAW SUPER-VILLAIN AND FORMER MASTERS OF EVIL MEMBER, *MAN-KILLER!*

HE CAN'T BRING HIMSELF TO TURN HER IN. HE SEES SO MUCH OF HIMSELF IN HER. AND THEN HE THINKS OF HALLIE'S MESSAGE TO HIM...

"LISTEN, BIG GUY, WHAT I WANTED TO SAY IS... WELL, YOU THINK IT'S BEEN A *ONE-WAY STREET* --

"-- YOU THINK *I'VE* BEEN THE ONE HOLDING *YOUR* HAND ON THIS TOUGH ROAD WE'RE ALL ON --

"-- GIVING YOU A -- I DUNNO -- *A MORAL COMPASS* -- TO GUIDE YOU --

"-- GIVING YOU A SENSE OF FAMILY TO MAKE UP FOR THE LOSS OF YOUR OWN --

"-- AND MAYBE I *HAVE* DONE ALL THAT, WHICH I'M REALLY, REALLY GLAD FOR --

"-- BUT THE TRUTH IS, ITS BEEN A *TWO*-WAY STREET.

"YOU PUT AN ARM AROUND MY SHOULDER FOR PROTECTION AND WARMTH...

"...AND YOU SHOWED ME THAT BEING *STRONG* ISN'T ABOUT KNOCKING OVER BUILDINGS OR PUNCHING OUT BAD GUYS --

"-- BUT ABOUT *CHARACTER!*

"I'VE SEEN YOU FIGHT -- REALLY STRUGGLE -- TO *REMAKE* YOURSELF EACH AND EVERY DAY.

"AND I WANTED TO THANK YOU, ERIK... FOR SHOWING ME THE TRUE MEANING OF THE WORD...

"...*COURAGE*..."

YEAH... THAT'S ME... MR. CHARACTER...

THIS WOULD PROBABLY WORK BETTER IF I KNEW WHAT YOU WERE SO BUMMED ABOUT.

NOTHING, *WILMA*... JUST... I LOST SOMEONE WHO MEANT... A LOT TO ME.

NO. NOT HIM. NOT *YET*. A PLACE FOR EVERYTHING AND EVERYTHING IN ITS PLACE.

JOSTEN IS THE *SPINE*.

THE HEART WAS *FIRST*. NEXT WILL BE THE *BRAIN*.

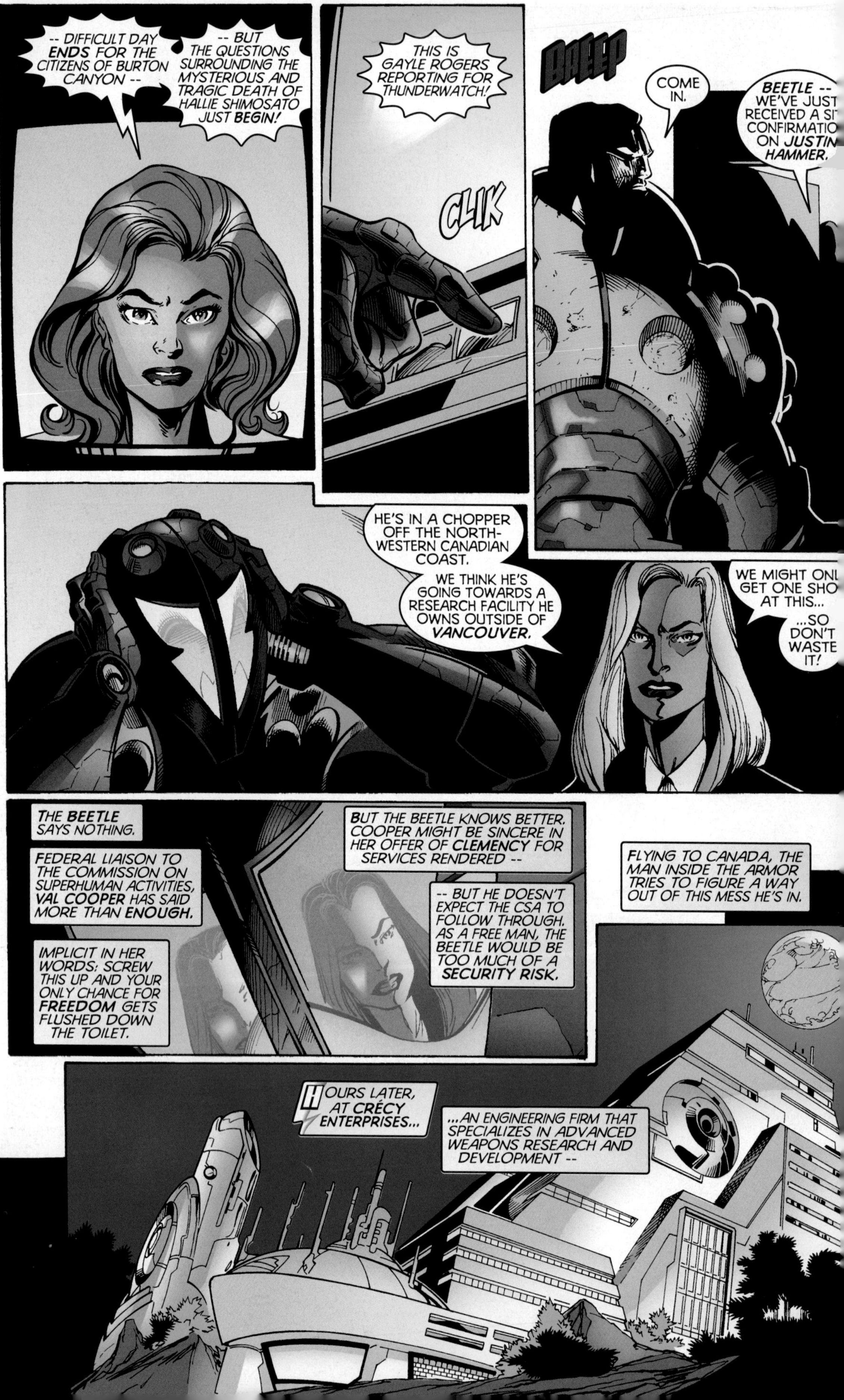
-- DIFFICULT DAY ENDS FOR THE CITIZENS OF BURTON CANYON --
-- BUT THE QUESTIONS SURROUNDING THE MYSTERIOUS AND TRAGIC DEATH OF HALLIE SHIMOSATO JUST BEGIN!
THIS IS GAYLE ROGERS REPORTING FOR THUNDERWATCH!
CLIK
BAEEP
COME IN.
BEETLE -- WE'VE JUST RECEIVED A SI CONFIRMATIO ON JUSTIN HAMMER.
HE'S IN A CHOPPER OFF THE NORTH-WESTERN CANADIAN COAST.
WE THINK HE'S GOING TOWARDS A RESEARCH FACILITY HE OWNS OUTSIDE OF VANCOUVER.
WE MIGHT ONL GET ONE SHO AT THIS...
...SO DON'T WASTE IT!
THE BEETLE SAYS NOTHING.
FEDERAL LIAISON TO THE COMMISSION ON SUPERHUMAN ACTIVITIES, VAL COOPER HAS SAID MORE THAN ENOUGH.
IMPLICIT IN HER WORDS: SCREW THIS UP AND YOUR ONLY CHANCE FOR FREEDOM GETS FLUSHED DOWN THE TOILET.
BUT THE BEETLE KNOWS BETTER. COOPER MIGHT BE SINCERE IN HER OFFER OF CLEMENCY FOR SERVICES RENDERED --
-- BUT HE DOESN'T EXPECT THE CSA TO FOLLOW THROUGH. AS A FREE MAN, THE BEETLE WOULD BE TOO MUCH OF A SECURITY RISK.
FLYING TO CANADA, THE MAN INSIDE THE ARMOR TRIES TO FIGURE A WAY OUT OF THIS MESS HE'S IN.
HOURS LATER, AT CRÉCY ENTERPRISES...
...AN ENGINEERING FIRM THAT SPECIALIZES IN ADVANCED WEAPONS RESEARCH AND DEVELOPMENT --

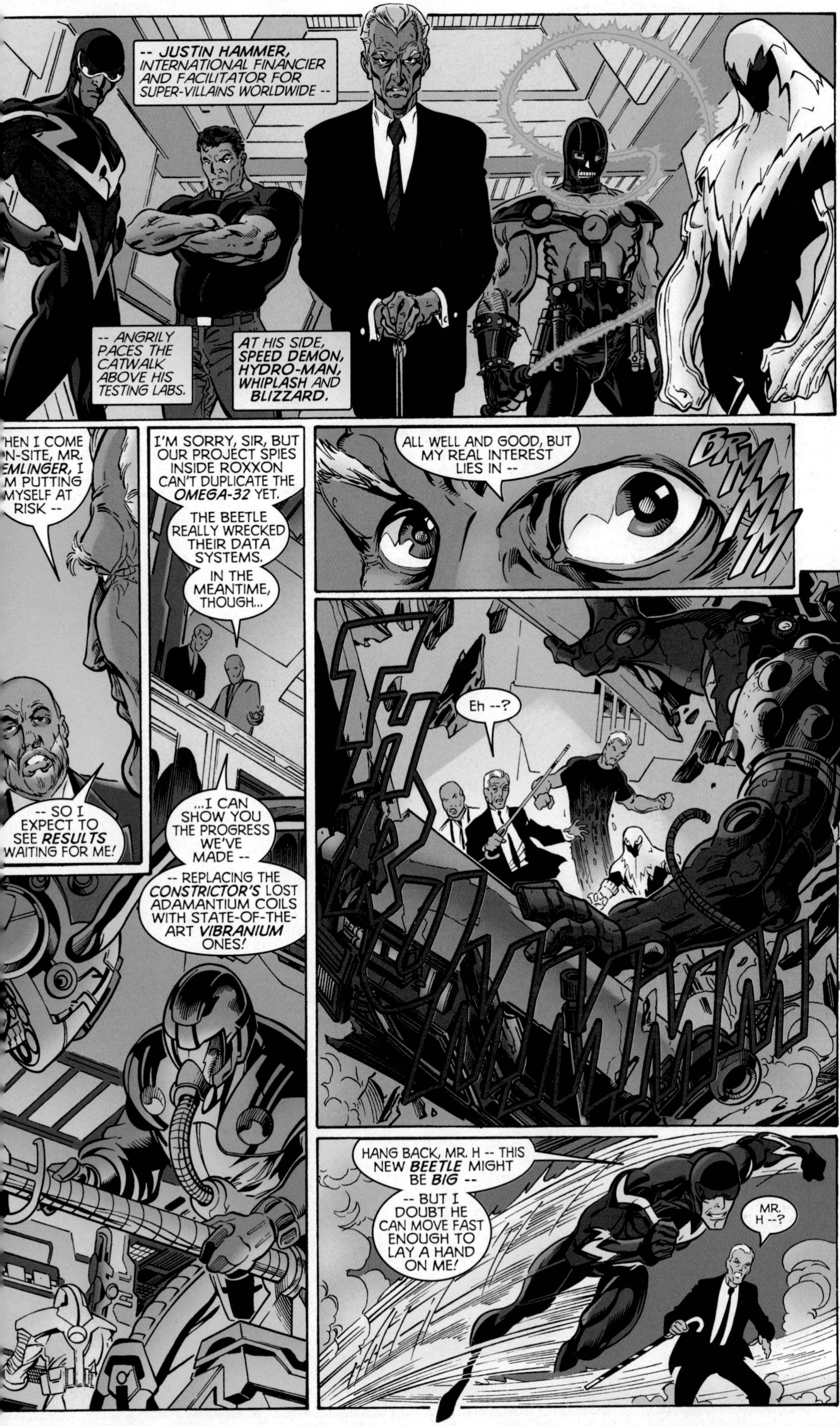

-- JUSTIN HAMMER, INTERNATIONAL FINANCIER AND FACILITATOR FOR SUPER-VILLAINS WORLDWIDE --
-- ANGRILY PACES THE CATWALK ABOVE HIS TESTING LABS.
AT HIS SIDE, SPEED DEMON, HYDRO-MAN, WHIPLASH AND BLIZZARD.
HEN I COME N-SITE, MR. EMLINGER, I M PUTTING MYSELF AT RISK --
-- SO I EXPECT TO SEE RESULTS WAITING FOR ME!
I'M SORRY, SIR, BUT OUR PROJECT SPIES INSIDE ROXXON CAN'T DUPLICATE THE OMEGA-32 YET.
THE BEETLE REALLY WRECKED THEIR DATA SYSTEMS.
IN THE MEANTIME, THOUGH...
...I CAN SHOW YOU THE PROGRESS WE'VE MADE --
-- REPLACING THE CONSTRICTOR'S LOST ADAMANTIUM COILS WITH STATE-OF-THE-ART VIBRANIUM ONES!
ALL WELL AND GOOD, BUT MY REAL INTEREST LIES IN --
BRMMMM
Eh --?
HANG BACK, MR. H -- THIS NEW BEETLE MIGHT BE BIG --
-- BUT I DOUBT HE CAN MOVE FAST ENOUGH TO LAY A HAND ON ME!
MR. H --?

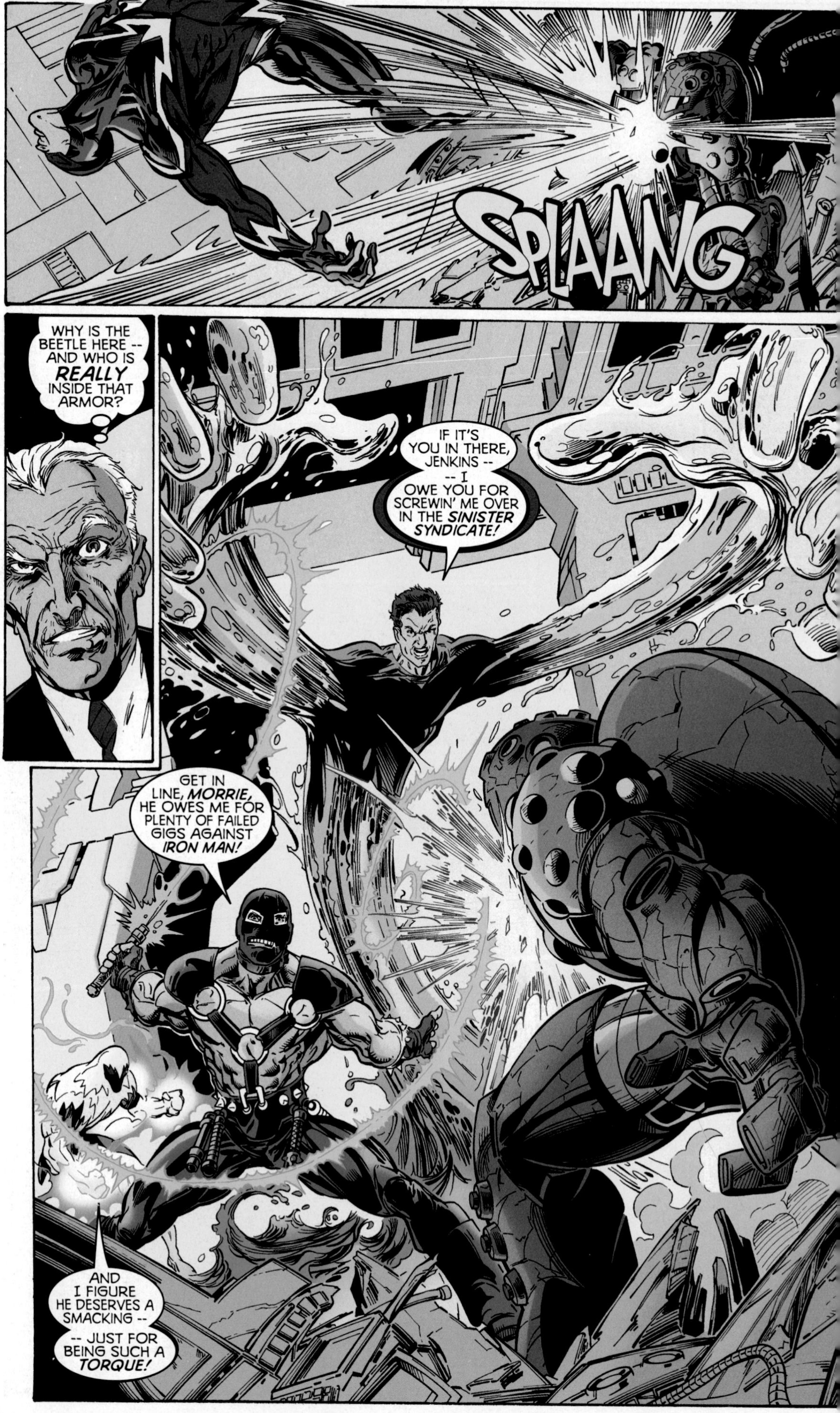
SPLAANG
WHY IS THE BEETLE HERE -- AND WHO IS *REALLY* INSIDE THAT ARMOR?
IF IT'S YOU IN THERE, JENKINS --
-- I OWE YOU FOR SCREWIN' ME OVER IN THE *SINISTER SYNDICATE!*
GET IN LINE, *MORRIE,* HE OWES ME FOR PLENTY OF FAILED GIGS AGAINST *IRON MAN!*
AND I FIGURE HE DESERVES A SMACKING --
-- JUST FOR BEING SUCH A *TORQUE!*

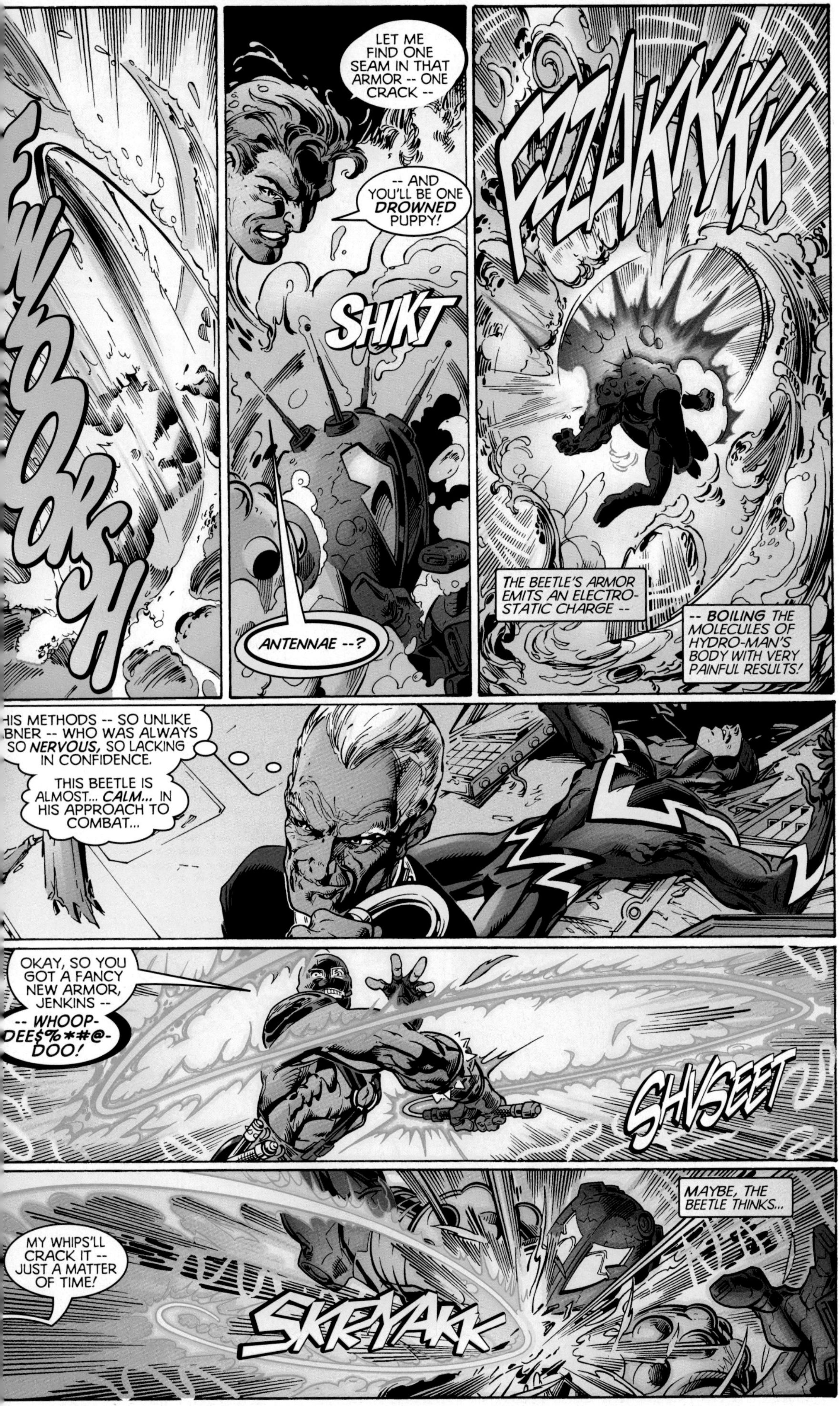
WHOOOOSCH
LET ME FIND ONE SEAM IN THAT ARMOR -- ONE CRACK --
-- AND YOU'LL BE ONE DROWNED PUPPY!
SHIKT
ANTENNAE --?
FZZAKKKK
THE BEETLE'S ARMOR EMITS AN ELECTRO-STATIC CHARGE --
-- BOILING THE MOLECULES OF HYDRO-MAN'S BODY WITH VERY PAINFUL RESULTS!
HIS METHODS -- SO UNLIKE ABNER -- WHO WAS ALWAYS SO NERVOUS, SO LACKING IN CONFIDENCE.
THIS BEETLE IS ALMOST... CALM... IN HIS APPROACH TO COMBAT...
OKAY, SO YOU GOT A FANCY NEW ARMOR, JENKINS --
-- WHOOP-DEE$%*#@-DOO!
SHVSEET
MY WHIPS'LL CRACK IT -- JUST A MATTER OF TIME!
SKRYAKK
MAYBE, THE BEETLE THINKS...

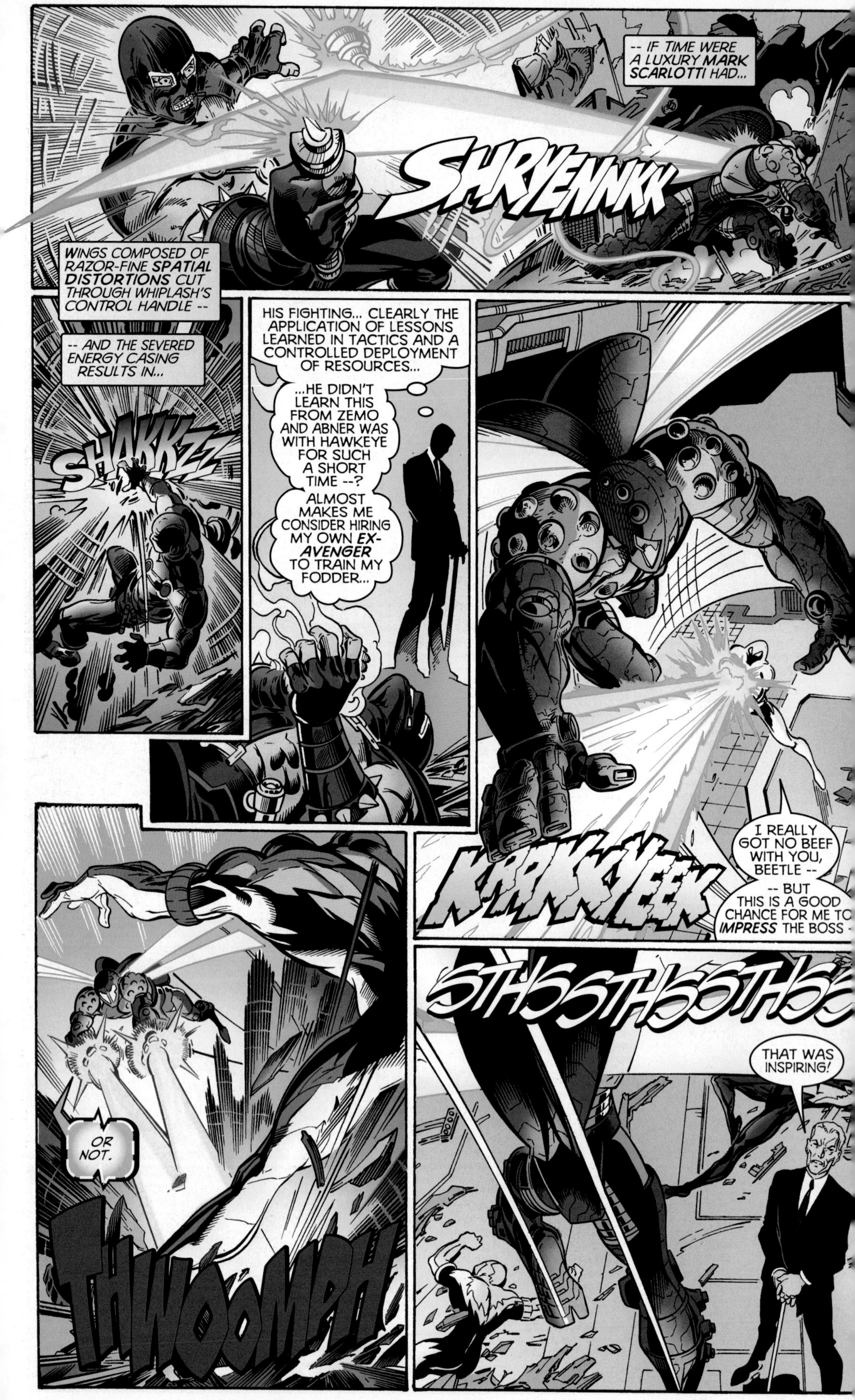

-- IF TIME WERE A LUXURY MARK SCARLOTTI HAD...
SHRYENNKK
WINGS COMPOSED OF RAZOR-FINE SPATIAL DISTORTIONS CUT THROUGH WHIPLASH'S CONTROL HANDLE --
-- AND THE SEVERED ENERGY CASING RESULTS IN...
SHAKKZZ
HIS FIGHTING... CLEARLY THE APPLICATION OF LESSONS LEARNED IN TACTICS AND A CONTROLLED DEPLOYMENT OF RESOURCES...
...HE DIDN'T LEARN THIS FROM ZEMO AND ABNER WAS WITH HAWKEYE FOR SUCH A SHORT TIME --?
ALMOST MAKES ME CONSIDER HIRING MY OWN EX-AVENGER TO TRAIN MY FODDER...
KRAKKEEK
I REALLY GOT NO BEEF WITH YOU, BEETLE --
-- BUT THIS IS A GOOD CHANCE FOR ME TO IMPRESS THE BOSS --
OR NOT.
THWOOMPH
STHSSTHSSTHSS
THAT WAS INSPIRING!

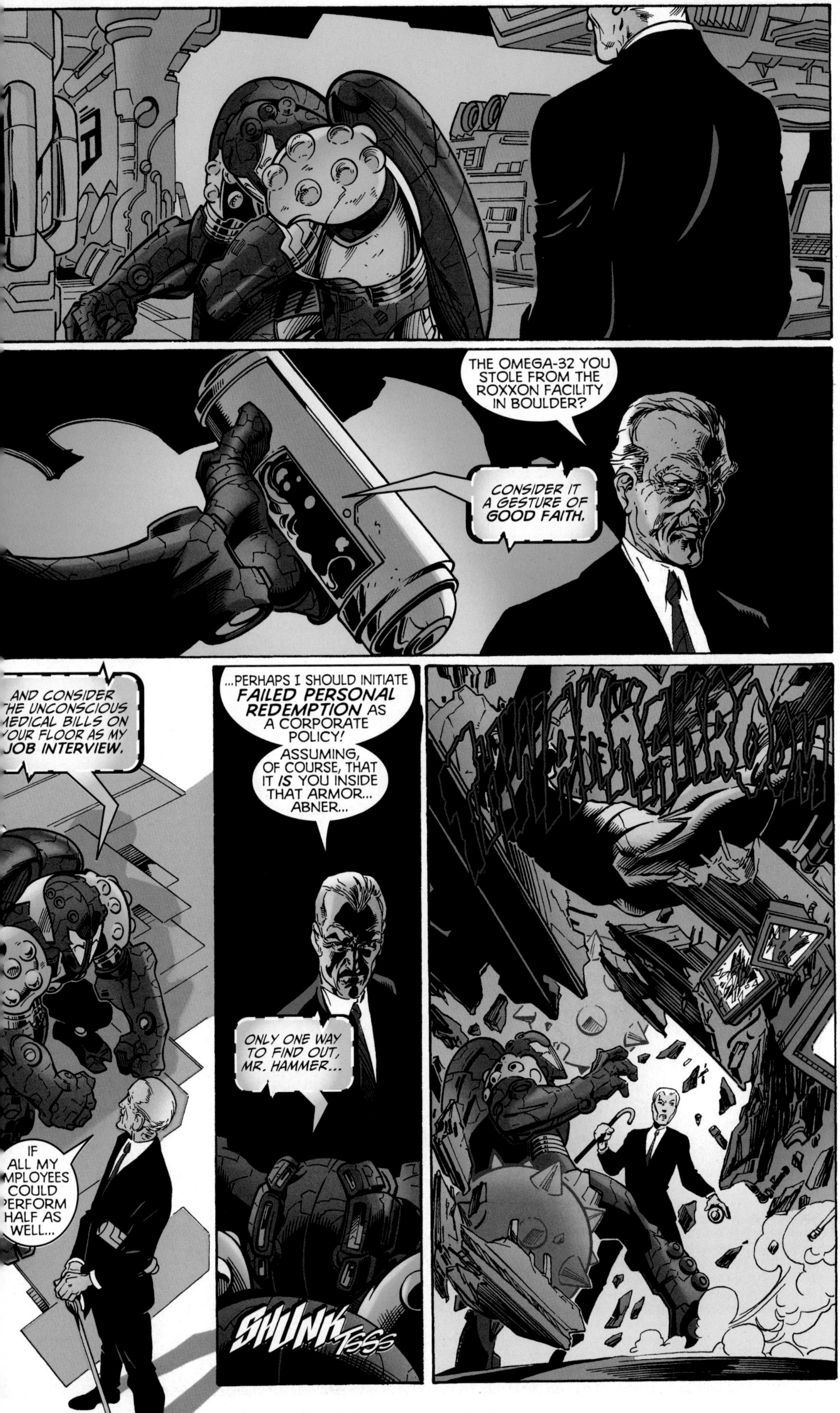
THE OMEGA-32 YOU STOLE FROM THE ROXXON FACILITY IN BOULDER?
CONSIDER IT A GESTURE OF GOOD FAITH.
AND CONSIDER THE UNCONSCIOUS MEDICAL BILLS ON YOUR FLOOR AS MY JOB INTERVIEW.
IF ALL MY EMPLOYEES COULD PERFORM HALF AS WELL...
...PERHAPS I SHOULD INITIATE FAILED PERSONAL REDEMPTION AS A CORPORATE POLICY!
ASSUMING, OF COURSE, THAT IT IS YOU INSIDE THAT ARMOR... ABNER...
ONLY ONE WAY TO FIND OUT, MR. HAMMER...
SHUNK TSSS

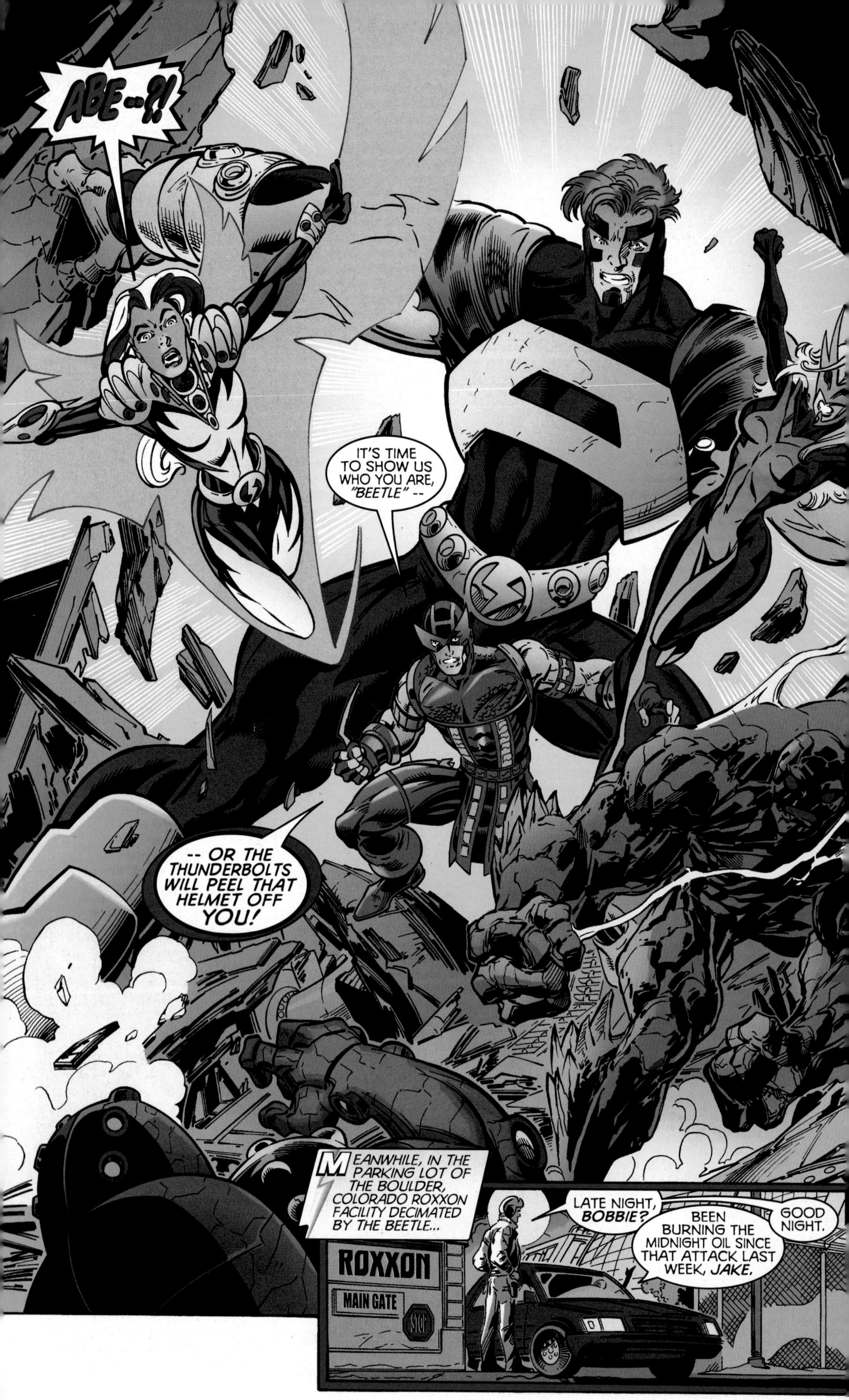
ABE--?!
IT'S TIME TO SHOW US WHO YOU ARE, "BEETLE" --
-- OR THE THUNDERBOLTS WILL PEEL THAT HELMET OFF YOU!
MEANWHILE, IN THE PARKING LOT OF THE BOULDER, COLORADO ROXXON FACILITY DECIMATED BY THE BEETLE...
ROXXON
MAIN GATE
STOP
LATE NIGHT, BOBBIE?
BEEN BURNING THE MIDNIGHT OIL SINCE THAT ATTACK LAST WEEK, JAKE.
GOOD NIGHT.

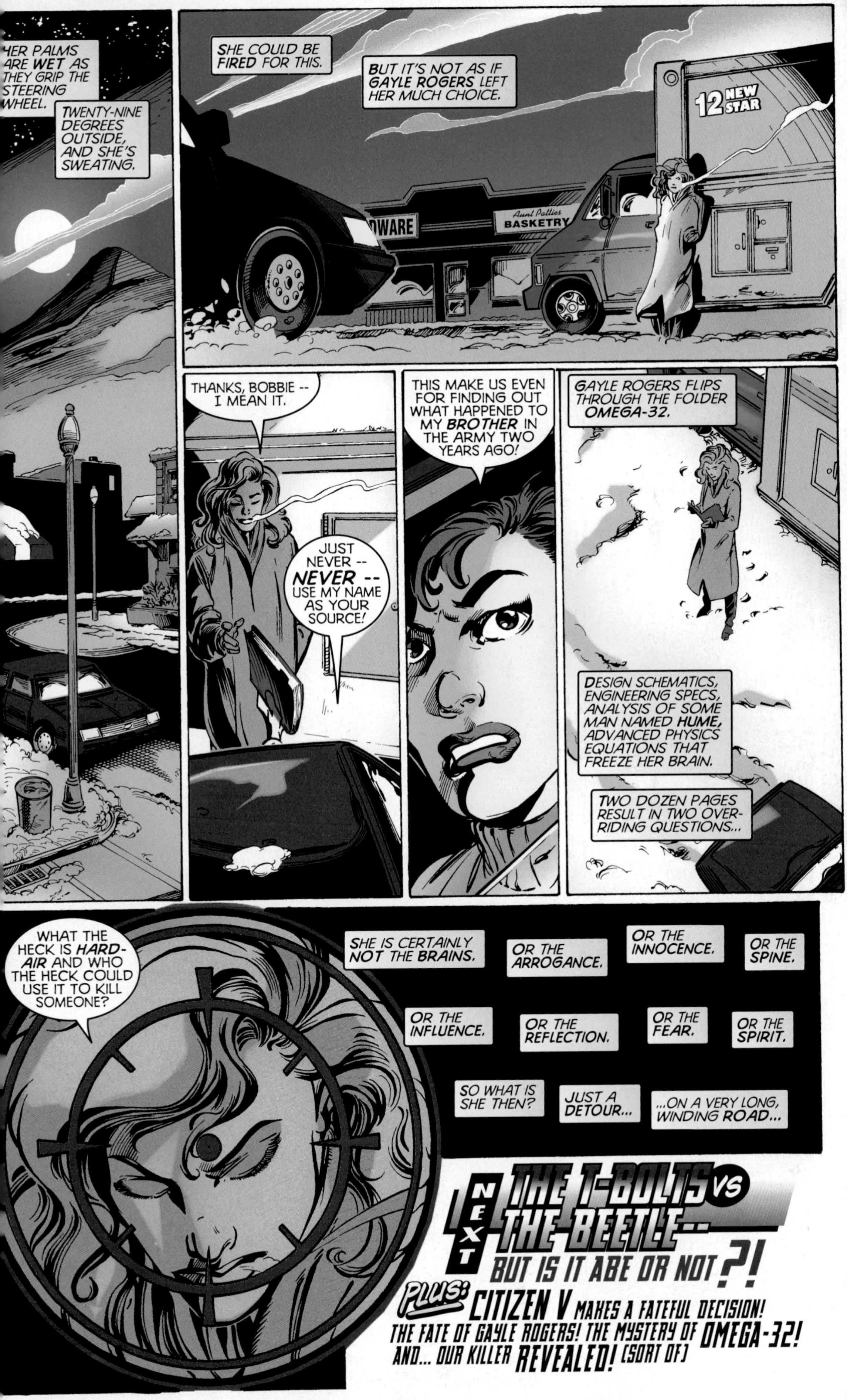

HER PALMS ARE WET AS THEY GRIP THE STEERING WHEEL.
TWENTY-NINE DEGREES OUTSIDE, AND SHE'S SWEATING.
SHE COULD BE FIRED FOR THIS.
BUT IT'S NOT AS IF GAYLE ROGERS LEFT HER MUCH CHOICE.
12 NEW STAR
DWARE
Aunt Patties BASKETRY
THANKS, BOBBIE -- I MEAN IT.
JUST NEVER -- NEVER -- USE MY NAME AS YOUR SOURCE!
THIS MAKE US EVEN FOR FINDING OUT WHAT HAPPENED TO MY BROTHER IN THE ARMY TWO YEARS AGO!
GAYLE ROGERS FLIPS THROUGH THE FOLDER OMEGA-32.
DESIGN SCHEMATICS, ENGINEERING SPECS, ANALYSIS OF SOME MAN NAMED HUME, ADVANCED PHYSICS EQUATIONS THAT FREEZE HER BRAIN.
TWO DOZEN PAGES RESULT IN TWO OVER-RIDING QUESTIONS...
WHAT THE HECK IS HARD-AIR AND WHO THE HECK COULD USE IT TO KILL SOMEONE?
SHE IS CERTAINLY NOT THE BRAINS.
OR THE ARROGANCE.
OR THE INNOCENCE.
OR THE SPINE.
OR THE INFLUENCE.
OR THE REFLECTION.
OR THE FEAR.
OR THE SPIRIT.
SO WHAT IS SHE THEN?
JUST A DETOUR...
...ON A VERY LONG, WINDING ROAD...
NEXT THE T-BOLTS VS THE BEETLE... BUT IS IT ABE OR NOT?!
PLUS: CITIZEN V MAKES A FATEFUL DECISION!
THE FATE OF GAYLE ROGERS! THE MYSTERY OF OMEGA-32!
AND... OUR KILLER REVEALED! (SORT OF)

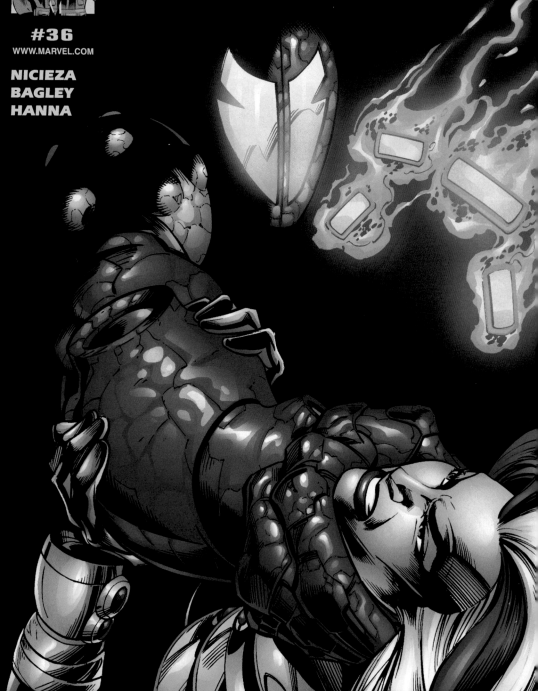

MARVEL COMICS

MARVEL'S MOST WANTED:

THUNDERBOLTS

#36
WWW.MARVEL.COM

NICIEZA
BAGLEY
HANNA

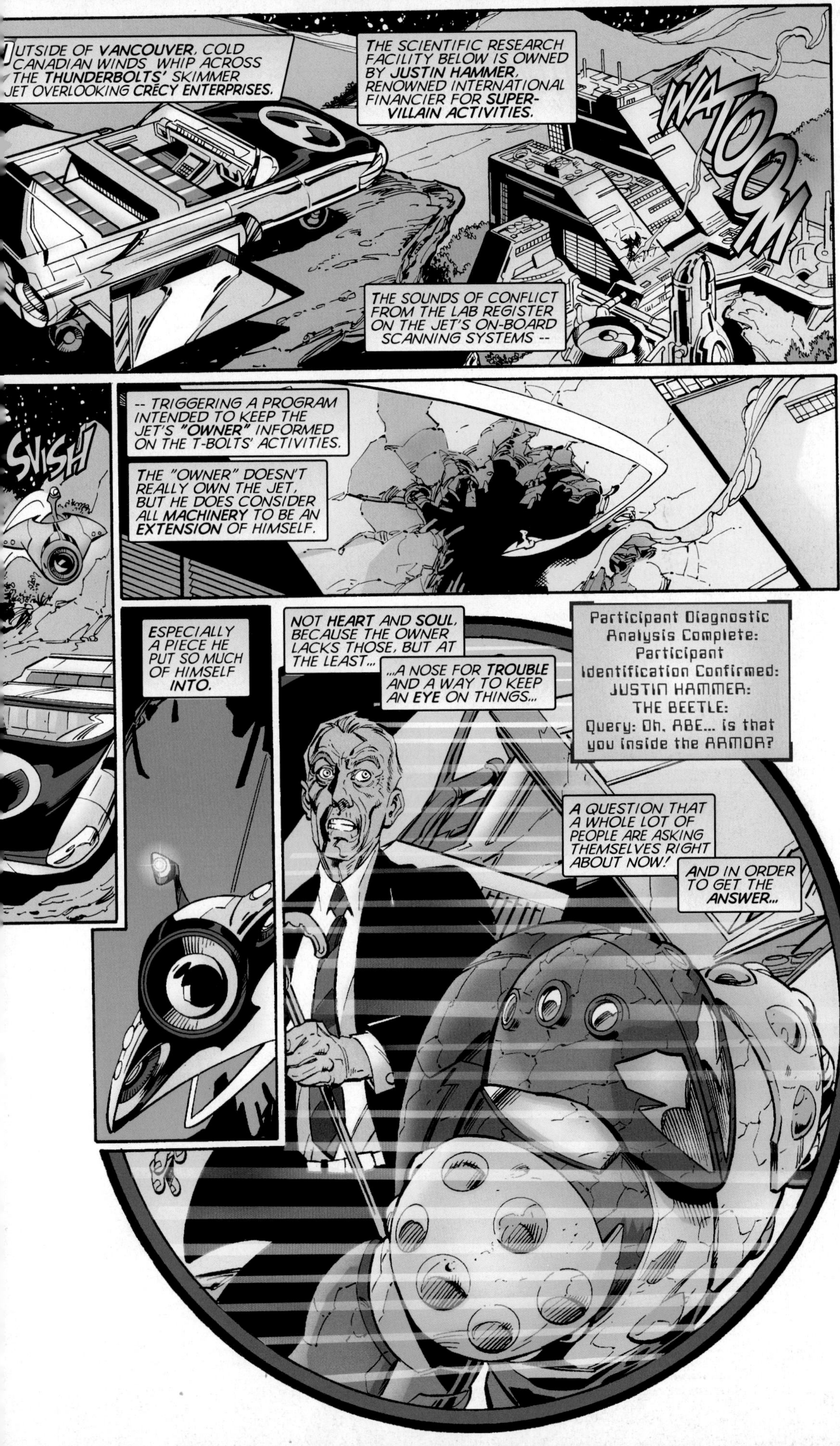
OUTSIDE OF VANCOUVER, COLD CANADIAN WINDS WHIP ACROSS THE THUNDERBOLTS' SKIMMER JET OVERLOOKING CRÉCY ENTERPRISES.
THE SCIENTIFIC RESEARCH FACILITY BELOW IS OWNED BY JUSTIN HAMMER, RENOWNED INTERNATIONAL FINANCIER FOR SUPER-VILLAIN ACTIVITIES.
WATOOM
THE SOUNDS OF CONFLICT FROM THE LAB REGISTER ON THE JET'S ON-BOARD SCANNING SYSTEMS --
SVISH
-- TRIGGERING A PROGRAM INTENDED TO KEEP THE JET'S "OWNER" INFORMED ON THE T-BOLTS' ACTIVITIES.
THE "OWNER" DOESN'T REALLY OWN THE JET, BUT HE DOES CONSIDER ALL MACHINERY TO BE AN EXTENSION OF HIMSELF.
ESPECIALLY A PIECE HE PUT SO MUCH OF HIMSELF INTO.
NOT HEART AND SOUL, BECAUSE THE OWNER LACKS THOSE, BUT AT THE LEAST...
...A NOSE FOR TROUBLE AND A WAY TO KEEP AN EYE ON THINGS...
Participant Diagnostic Analysis Complete: Participant Identification Confirmed: JUSTIN HAMMER: THE BEETLE: Query: Oh, ABE... is that you inside the ARMOR?
A QUESTION THAT A WHOLE LOT OF PEOPLE ARE ASKING THEMSELVES RIGHT ABOUT NOW!
AND IN ORDER TO GET THE ANSWER...

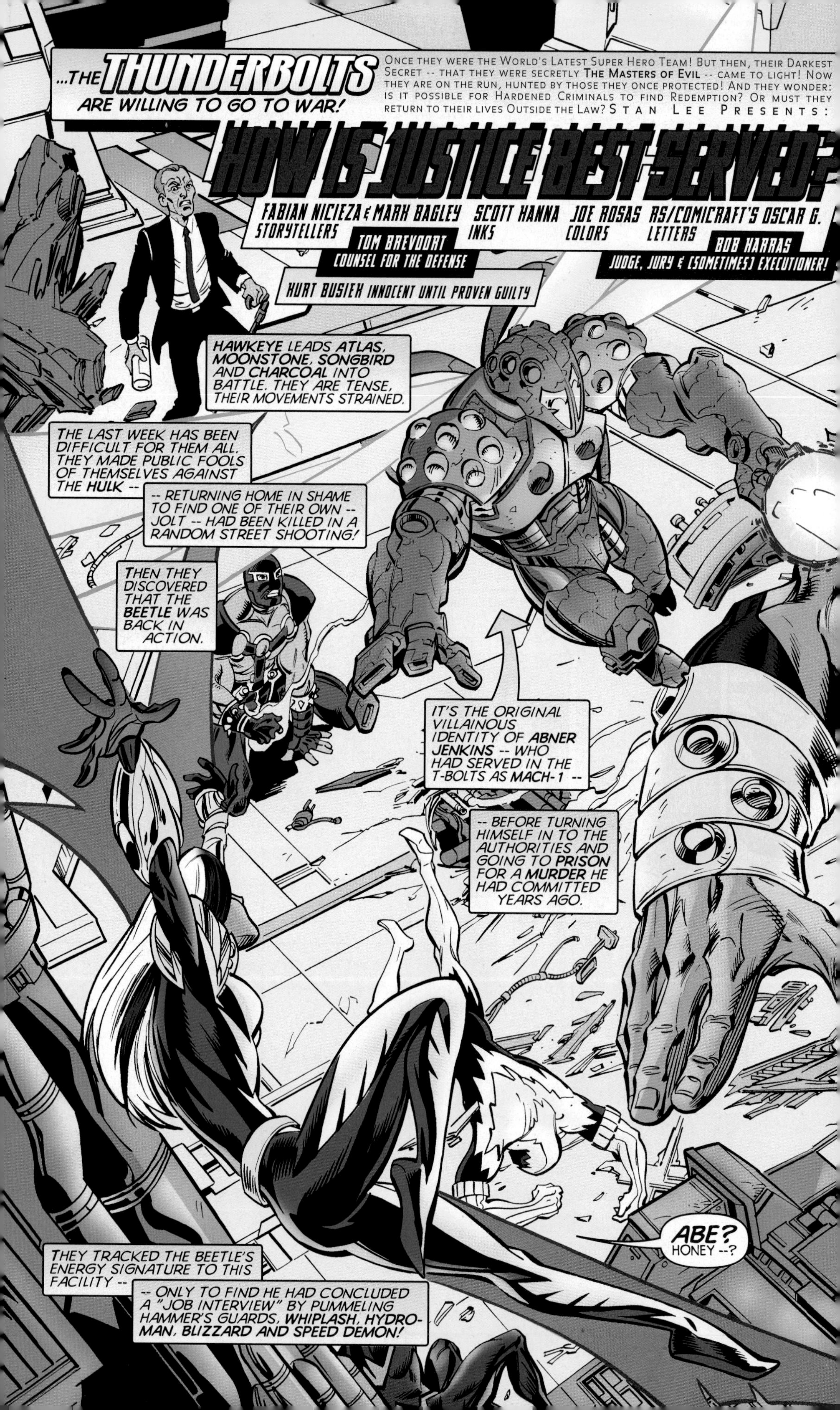
...THE THUNDERBOLTS ARE WILLING TO GO TO WAR!
ONCE THEY WERE THE WORLD'S LATEST SUPER HERO TEAM! BUT THEN, THEIR DARKEST SECRET -- THAT THEY WERE SECRETLY THE MASTERS OF EVIL -- CAME TO LIGHT! NOW THEY ARE ON THE RUN, HUNTED BY THOSE THEY ONCE PROTECTED! AND THEY WONDER: IS IT POSSIBLE FOR HARDENED CRIMINALS TO FIND REDEMPTION? OR MUST THEY RETURN TO THEIR LIVES OUTSIDE THE LAW? STAN LEE PRESENTS:
HOW IS JUSTICE BEST SERVED?
FABIAN NICIEZA & MARK BAGLEY STORYTELLERS
SCOTT HANNA INKS
JOE ROSAS COLORS
RS/COMICRAFT'S OSCAR G. LETTERS
TOM BREVOORT COUNSEL FOR THE DEFENSE
BOB HARRAS JUDGE, JURY & (SOMETIMES) EXECUTIONER!
KURT BUSIEK INNOCENT UNTIL PROVEN GUILTY
HAWKEYE LEADS ATLAS, MOONSTONE, SONGBIRD AND CHARCOAL INTO BATTLE. THEY ARE TENSE, THEIR MOVEMENTS STRAINED.
THE LAST WEEK HAS BEEN DIFFICULT FOR THEM ALL. THEY MADE PUBLIC FOOLS OF THEMSELVES AGAINST THE HULK --
-- RETURNING HOME IN SHAME TO FIND ONE OF THEIR OWN -- JOLT -- HAD BEEN KILLED IN A RANDOM STREET SHOOTING!
THEN THEY DISCOVERED THAT THE BEETLE WAS BACK IN ACTION.
IT'S THE ORIGINAL VILLAINOUS IDENTITY OF ABNER JENKINS -- WHO HAD SERVED IN THE T-BOLTS AS MACH-1 --
-- BEFORE TURNING HIMSELF IN TO THE AUTHORITIES AND GOING TO PRISON FOR A MURDER HE HAD COMMITTED YEARS AGO.
ABE? HONEY --?
THEY TRACKED THE BEETLE'S ENERGY SIGNATURE TO THIS FACILITY --
-- ONLY TO FIND HE HAD CONCLUDED A "JOB INTERVIEW" BY PUMMELING HAMMER'S GUARDS, WHIPLASH, HYDRO-MAN, BLIZZARD AND SPEED DEMON!

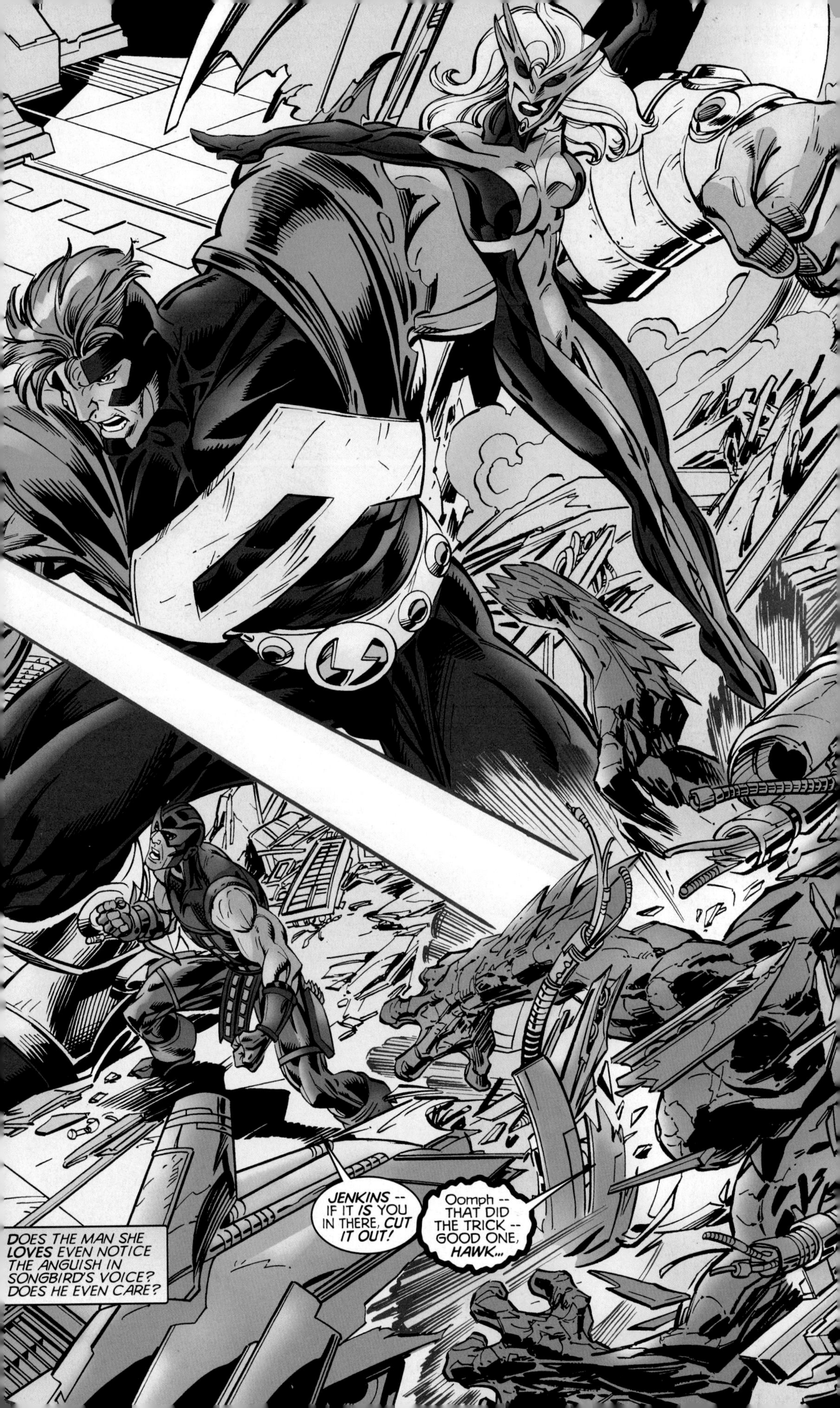

DOES THE MAN SHE LOVES EVEN NOTICE THE ANGUISH IN SONGBIRD'S VOICE? DOES HE EVEN CARE?
JENKINS -- IF IT IS YOU IN THERE, CUT IT OUT!
Oomph -- THAT DID THE TRICK -- GOOD ONE, HAWK...

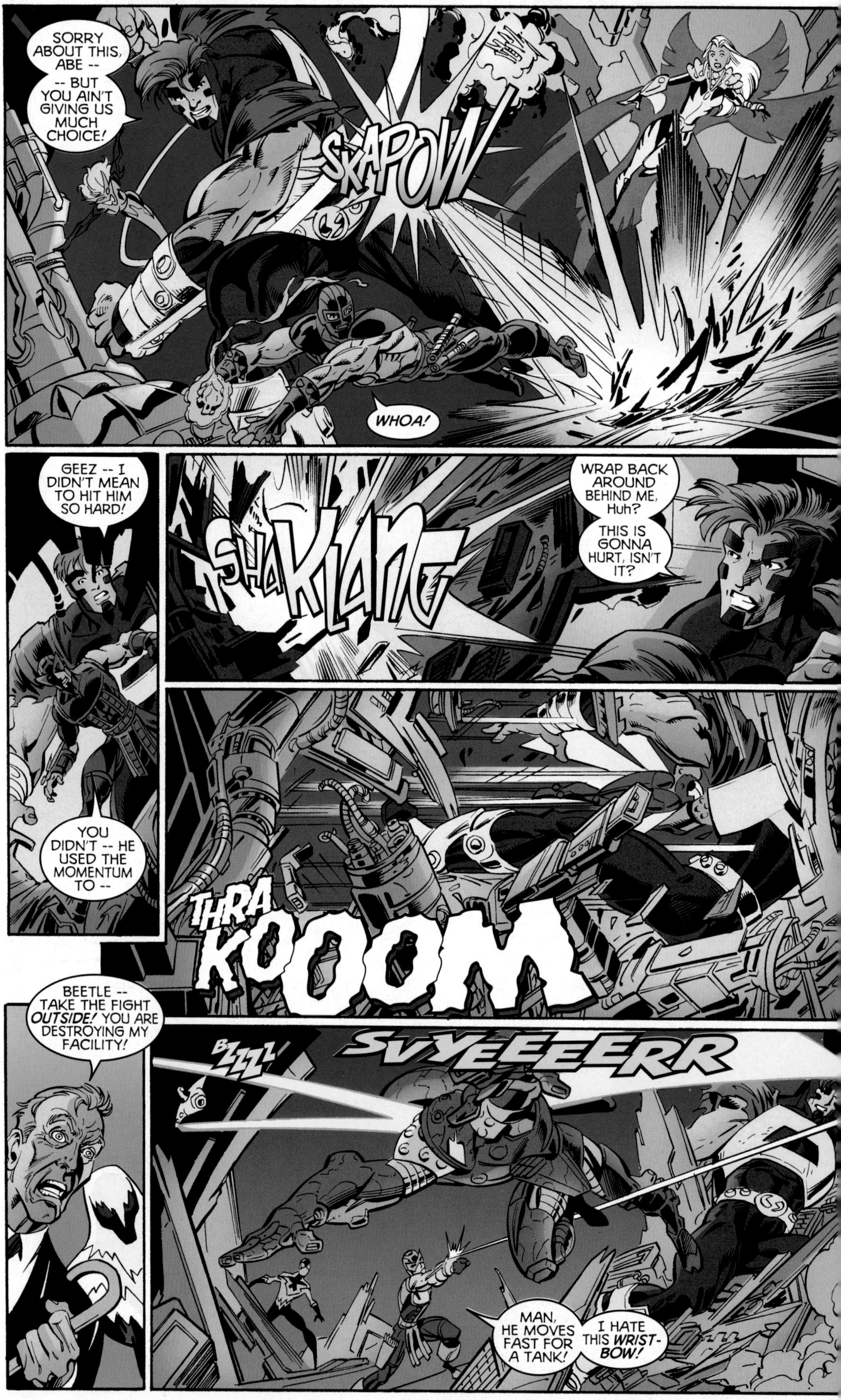
SORRY ABOUT THIS, ABE --
-- BUT YOU AIN'T GIVING US MUCH CHOICE!
SKAPOW
WHOA!
GEEZ -- I DIDN'T MEAN TO HIT HIM SO HARD!
SHAKLANG
WRAP BACK AROUND BEHIND ME, Huh?
THIS IS GONNA HURT, ISN'T IT?
YOU DIDN'T -- HE USED THE MOMENTUM TO --
THRA KOOOM
BEETLE -- TAKE THE FIGHT OUTSIDE! YOU ARE DESTROYING MY FACILITY!
BZZZZ
SVYEEEERR
MAN, HE MOVES FAST FOR A TANK!
I HATE THIS WRIST-BOW!

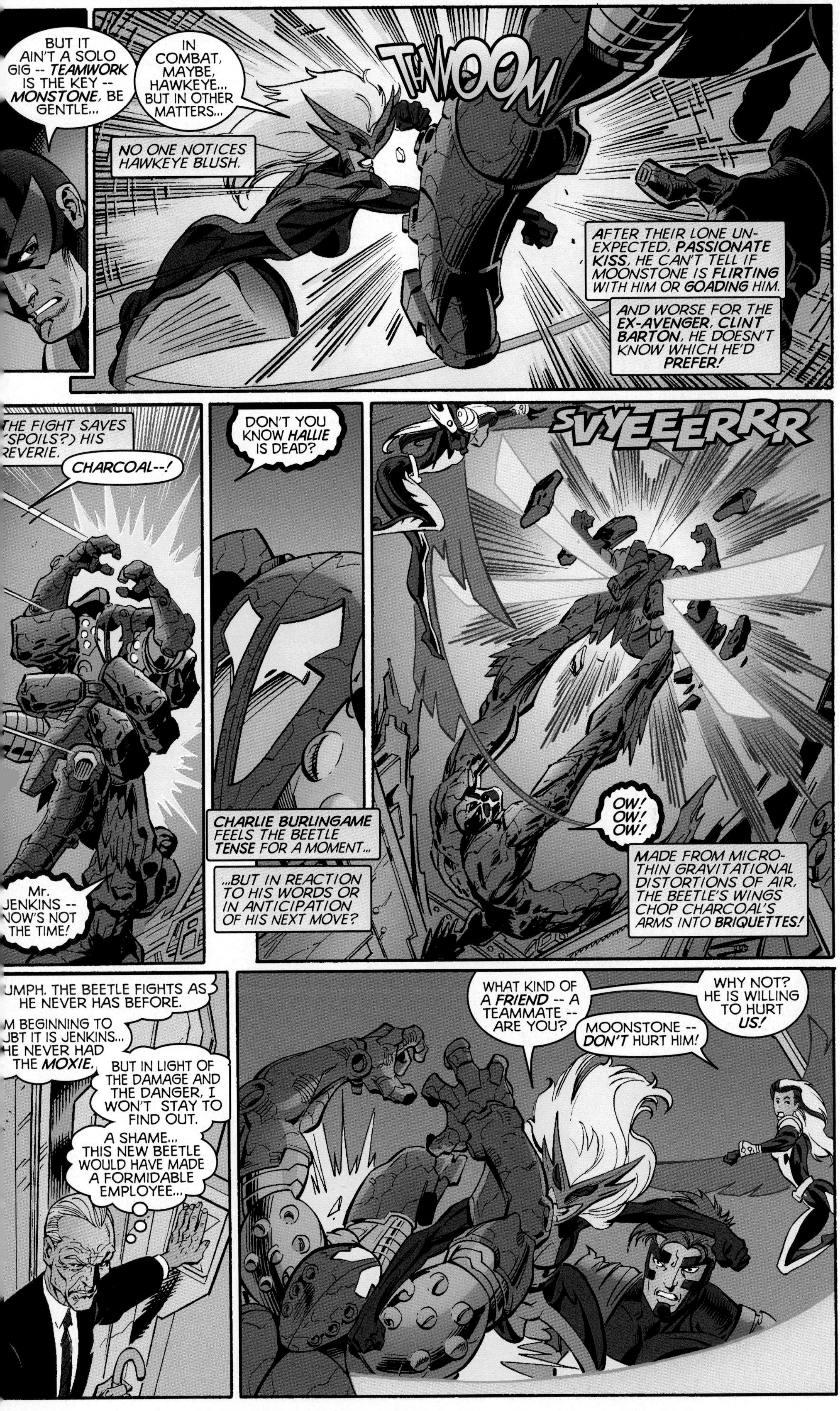

BUT IT AIN'T A SOLO GIG -- TEAMWORK IS THE KEY -- MONSTONE, BE GENTLE...
IN COMBAT, MAYBE, HAWKEYE... BUT IN OTHER MATTERS...
NO ONE NOTICES HAWKEYE BLUSH.
TWOOM
AFTER THEIR LONE UNEXPECTED, PASSIONATE KISS, HE CAN'T TELL IF MOONSTONE IS FLIRTING WITH HIM OR GOADING HIM.
AND WORSE FOR THE EX-AVENGER, CLINT BARTON, HE DOESN'T KNOW WHICH HE'D PREFER!
THE FIGHT SAVES (SPOILS?) HIS REVERIE.
CHARCOAL--!
Mr. JENKINS -- NOW'S NOT THE TIME!
DON'T YOU KNOW HALLIE IS DEAD?
CHARLIE BURLINGAME FEELS THE BEETLE TENSE FOR A MOMENT...
...BUT IN REACTION TO HIS WORDS OR IN ANTICIPATION OF HIS NEXT MOVE?
SVYEEERRR
OW! OW! OW!
MADE FROM MICRO-THIN GRAVITATIONAL DISTORTIONS OF AIR, THE BEETLE'S WINGS CHOP CHARCOAL'S ARMS INTO BRIQUETTES!
UMPH. THE BEETLE FIGHTS AS HE NEVER HAS BEFORE.
M BEGINNING TO UBT IT IS JENKINS... HE NEVER HAD THE MOXIE.
BUT IN LIGHT OF THE DAMAGE AND THE DANGER, I WON'T STAY TO FIND OUT.
A SHAME... THIS NEW BEETLE WOULD HAVE MADE A FORMIDABLE EMPLOYEE...
WHAT KIND OF A FRIEND -- A TEAMMATE -- ARE YOU?
MOONSTONE -- DON'T HURT HIM!
WHY NOT? HE IS WILLING TO HURT US!

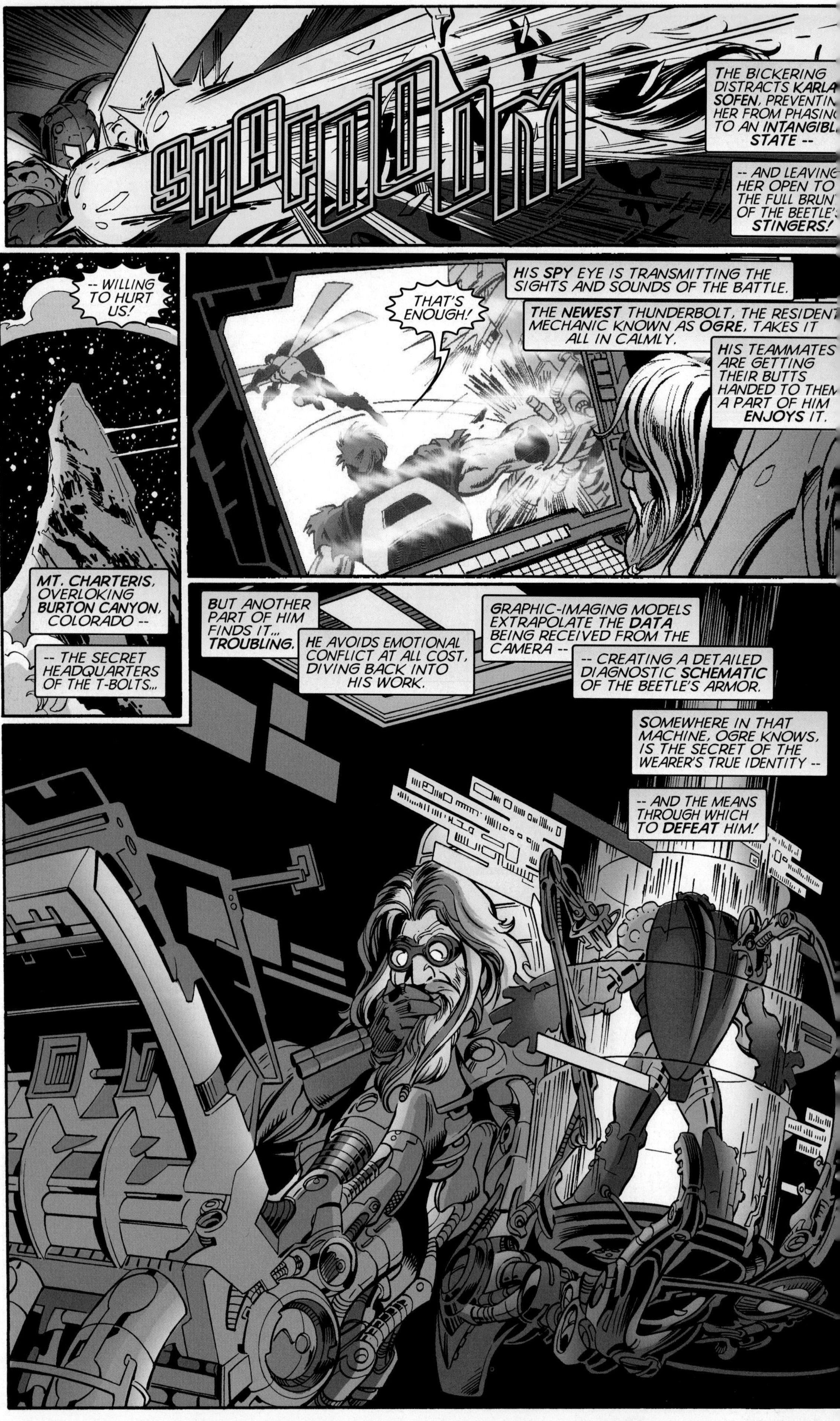
SHAFOOOM
THE BICKERING DISTRACTS KARLA SOFEN, PREVENTIN HER FROM PHASIN TO AN INTANGIBL STATE --
-- AND LEAVING HER OPEN TO THE FULL BRUN OF THE BEETLE' STINGERS!
-- WILLING TO HURT US!
MT. CHARTERIS, OVERLOKING BURTON CANYON, COLORADO --
-- THE SECRET HEADQUARTERS OF THE T-BOLTS...
HIS SPY EYE IS TRANSMITTING THE SIGHTS AND SOUNDS OF THE BATTLE.
THAT'S ENOUGH!
THE NEWEST THUNDERBOLT, THE RESIDENT MECHANIC KNOWN AS OGRE, TAKES IT ALL IN CALMLY.
HIS TEAMMATES ARE GETTING THEIR BUTTS HANDED TO THEM A PART OF HIM ENJOYS IT.
BUT ANOTHER PART OF HIM FINDS IT... TROUBLING.
HE AVOIDS EMOTIONAL CONFLICT AT ALL COST, DIVING BACK INTO HIS WORK.
GRAPHIC-IMAGING MODELS EXTRAPOLATE THE DATA BEING RECEIVED FROM THE CAMERA --
-- CREATING A DETAILED DIAGNOSTIC SCHEMATIC OF THE BEETLE'S ARMOR.
SOMEWHERE IN THAT MACHINE, OGRE KNOWS, IS THE SECRET OF THE WEARER'S TRUE IDENTITY --
-- AND THE MEANS THROUGH WHICH TO DEFEAT HIM!

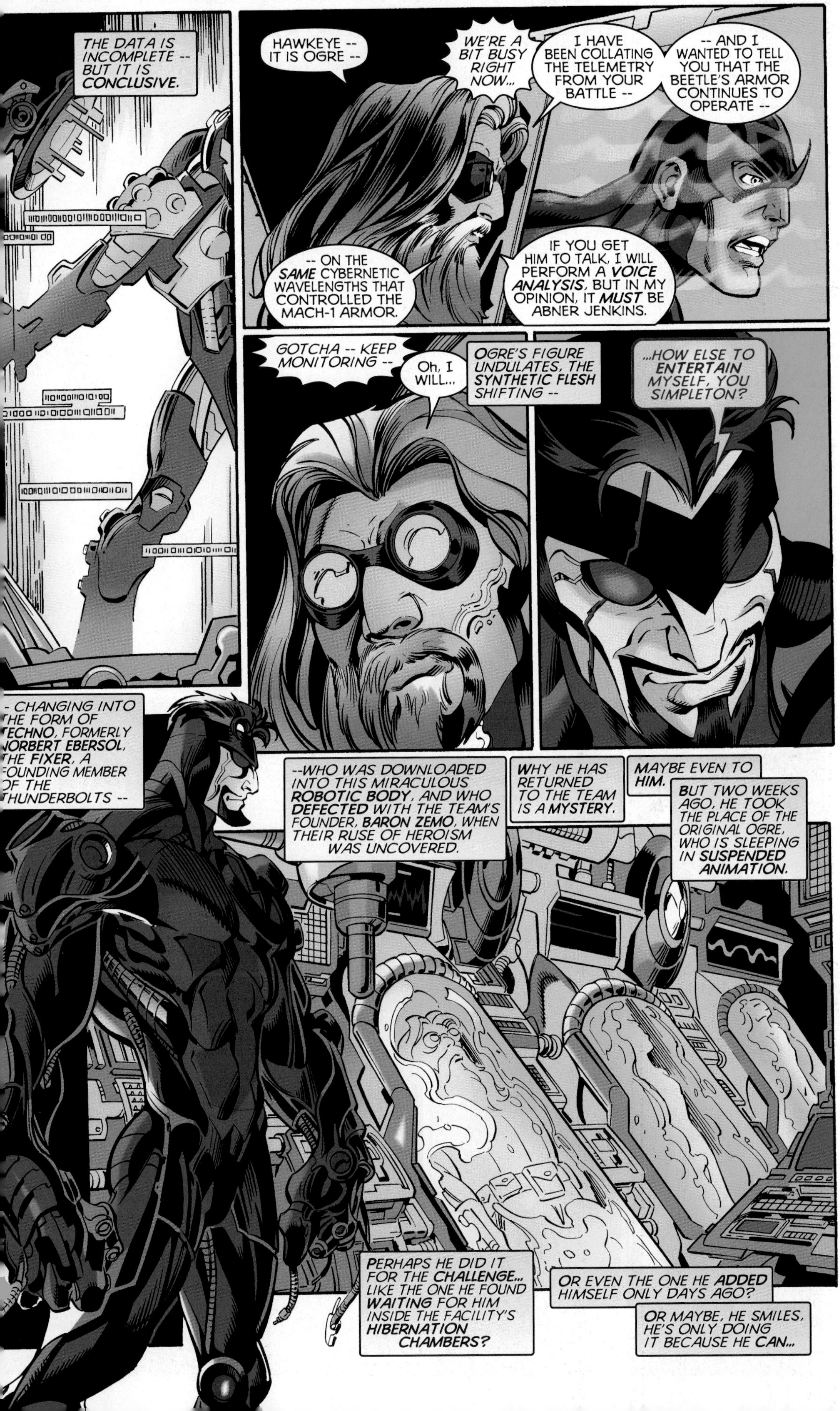

THE DATA IS INCOMPLETE -- BUT IT IS CONCLUSIVE.
HAWKEYE -- IT IS OGRE --
WE'RE A BIT BUSY RIGHT NOW...
I HAVE BEEN COLLATING THE TELEMETRY FROM YOUR BATTLE --
-- AND I WANTED TO TELL YOU THAT THE BEETLE'S ARMOR CONTINUES TO OPERATE --
-- ON THE SAME CYBERNETIC WAVELENGTHS THAT CONTROLLED THE MACH-1 ARMOR.
IF YOU GET HIM TO TALK, I WILL PERFORM A VOICE ANALYSIS, BUT IN MY OPINION, IT MUST BE ABNER JENKINS.
GOTCHA -- KEEP MONITORING --
Oh, I WILL...
OGRE'S FIGURE UNDULATES, THE SYNTHETIC FLESH SHIFTING --
...HOW ELSE TO ENTERTAIN MYSELF, YOU SIMPLETON?
- CHANGING INTO THE FORM OF TECHNO, FORMERLY NORBERT EBERSOL, THE FIXER, A FOUNDING MEMBER OF THE THUNDERBOLTS --
--WHO WAS DOWNLOADED INTO THIS MIRACULOUS ROBOTIC BODY, AND WHO DEFECTED WITH THE TEAM'S FOUNDER, BARON ZEMO, WHEN THEIR RUSE OF HEROISM WAS UNCOVERED.
WHY HE HAS RETURNED TO THE TEAM IS A MYSTERY.
MAYBE EVEN TO HIM.
BUT TWO WEEKS AGO, HE TOOK THE PLACE OF THE ORIGINAL OGRE, WHO IS SLEEPING IN SUSPENDED ANIMATION.
PERHAPS HE DID IT FOR THE CHALLENGE... LIKE THE ONE HE FOUND WAITING FOR HIM INSIDE THE FACILITY'S HIBERNATION CHAMBERS?
OR EVEN THE ONE HE ADDED HIMSELF ONLY DAYS AGO?
OR MAYBE, HE SMILES, HE'S ONLY DOING IT BECAUSE HE CAN...

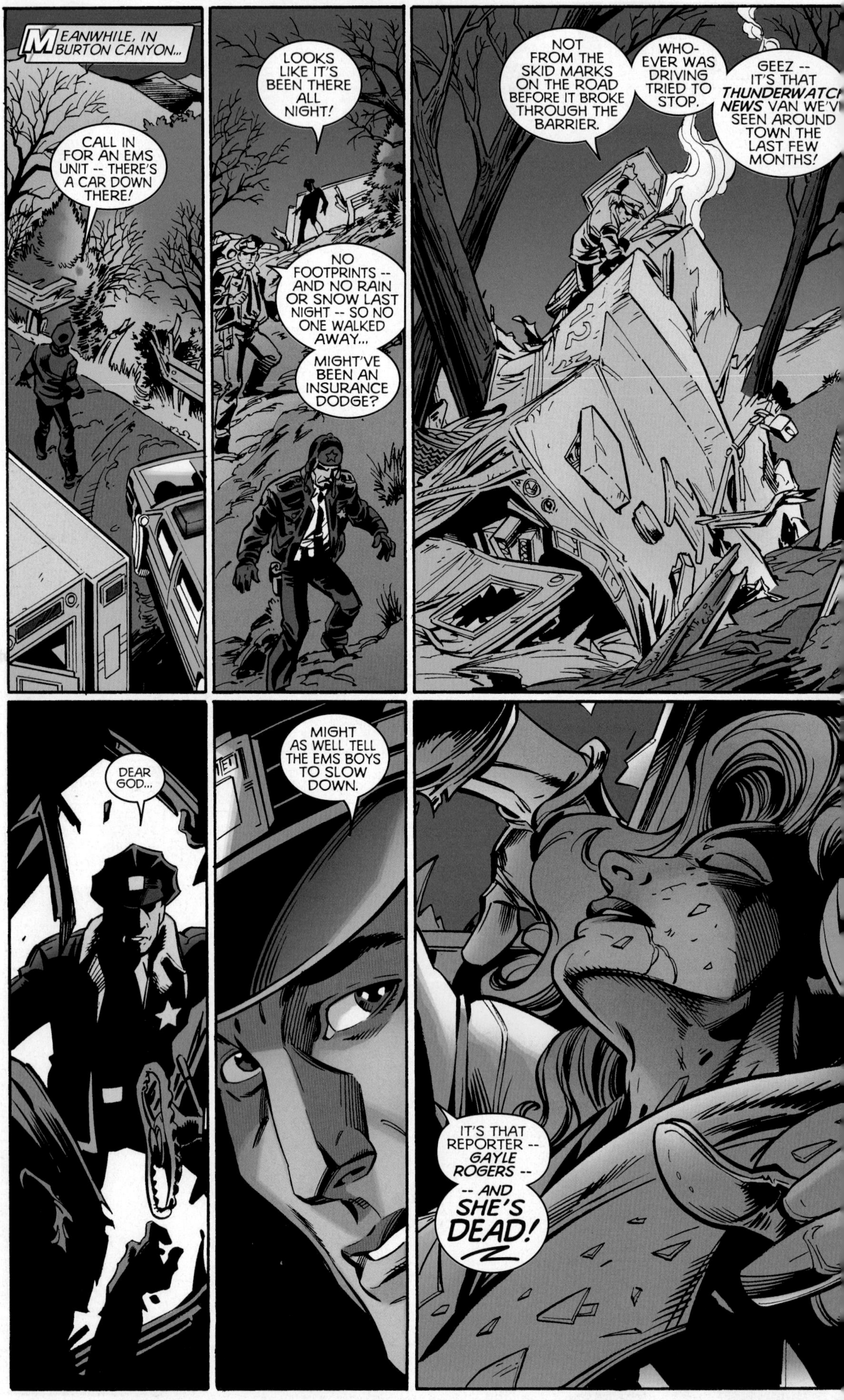
MEANWHILE, IN BURTON CANYON...
CALL IN FOR AN EMS UNIT -- THERE'S A CAR DOWN THERE!
LOOKS LIKE IT'S BEEN THERE ALL NIGHT!
NO FOOTPRINTS -- AND NO RAIN OR SNOW LAST NIGHT -- SO NO ONE WALKED AWAY...
MIGHT'VE BEEN AN INSURANCE DODGE?
NOT FROM THE SKID MARKS ON THE ROAD BEFORE IT BROKE THROUGH THE BARRIER.
WHO-EVER WAS DRIVING TRIED TO STOP.
GEEZ -- IT'S THAT THUNDERWATCH NEWS VAN WE'VE SEEN AROUND TOWN THE LAST FEW MONTHS!
DEAR GOD...
MIGHT AS WELL TELL THE EMS BOYS TO SLOW DOWN.
IT'S THAT REPORTER -- GAYLE ROGERS --
-- AND SHE'S DEAD!

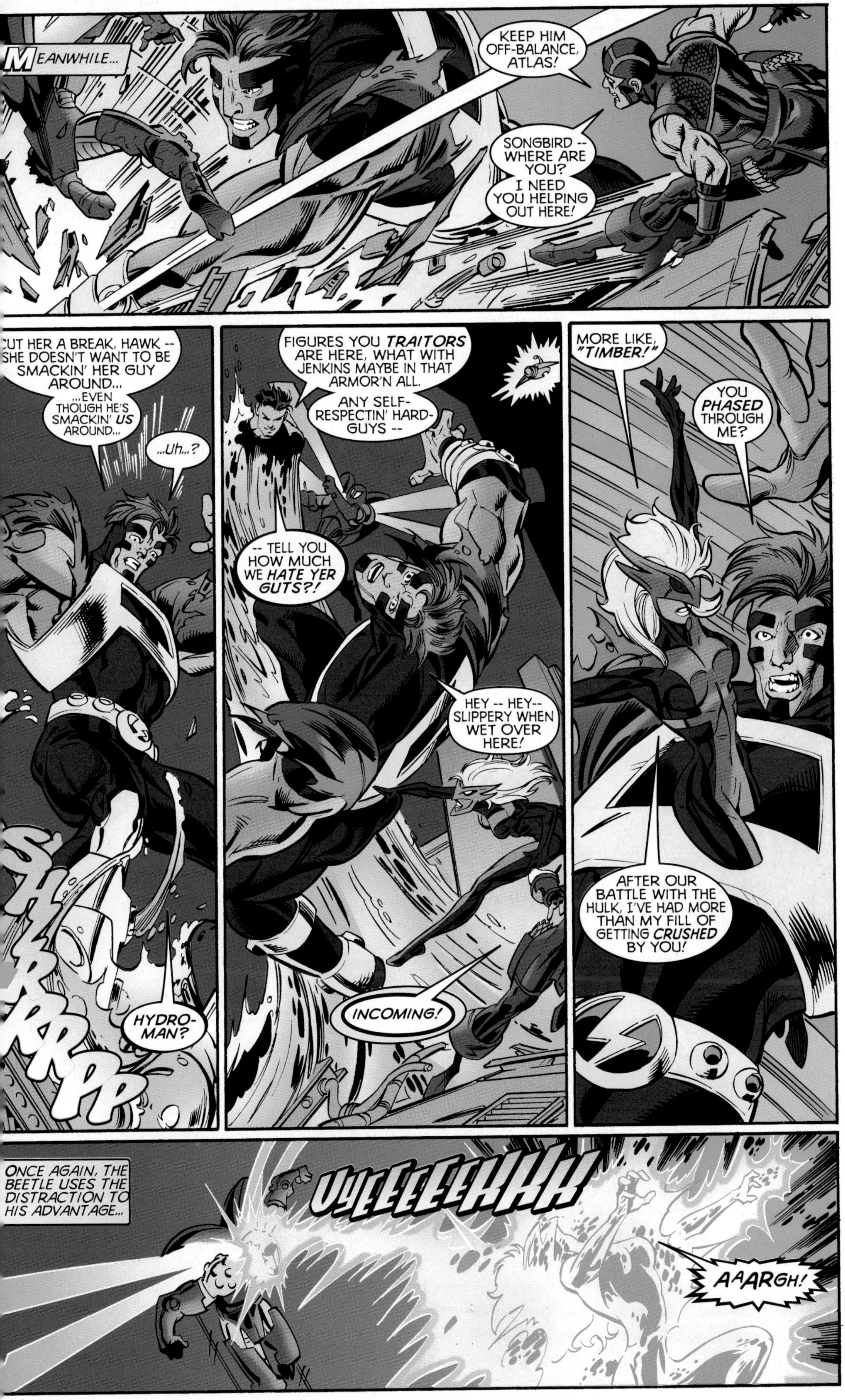
MEANWHILE...
KEEP HIM OFF-BALANCE, ATLAS!
SONGBIRD -- WHERE ARE YOU? I NEED YOU HELPING OUT HERE!
CUT HER A BREAK, HAWK -- SHE DOESN'T WANT TO BE SMACKIN' HER GUY AROUND...
...EVEN THOUGH HE'S SMACKIN' US AROUND...
...Uh...?
SHHRRRPP
HYDRO-MAN?
FIGURES YOU TRAITORS ARE HERE, WHAT WITH JENKINS MAYBE IN THAT ARMOR'N ALL.
ANY SELF-RESPECTIN' HARD-GUYS --
-- TELL YOU HOW MUCH WE HATE YER GUTS?!
HEY -- HEY-- SLIPPERY WHEN WET OVER HERE!
INCOMING!
MORE LIKE, "TIMBER!"
YOU PHASED THROUGH ME?
AFTER OUR BATTLE WITH THE HULK, I'VE HAD MORE THAN MY FILL OF GETTING CRUSHED BY YOU!
ONCE AGAIN, THE BEETLE USES THE DISTRACTION TO HIS ADVANTAGE...
VVEEEEEEKKKK
AAARGH!

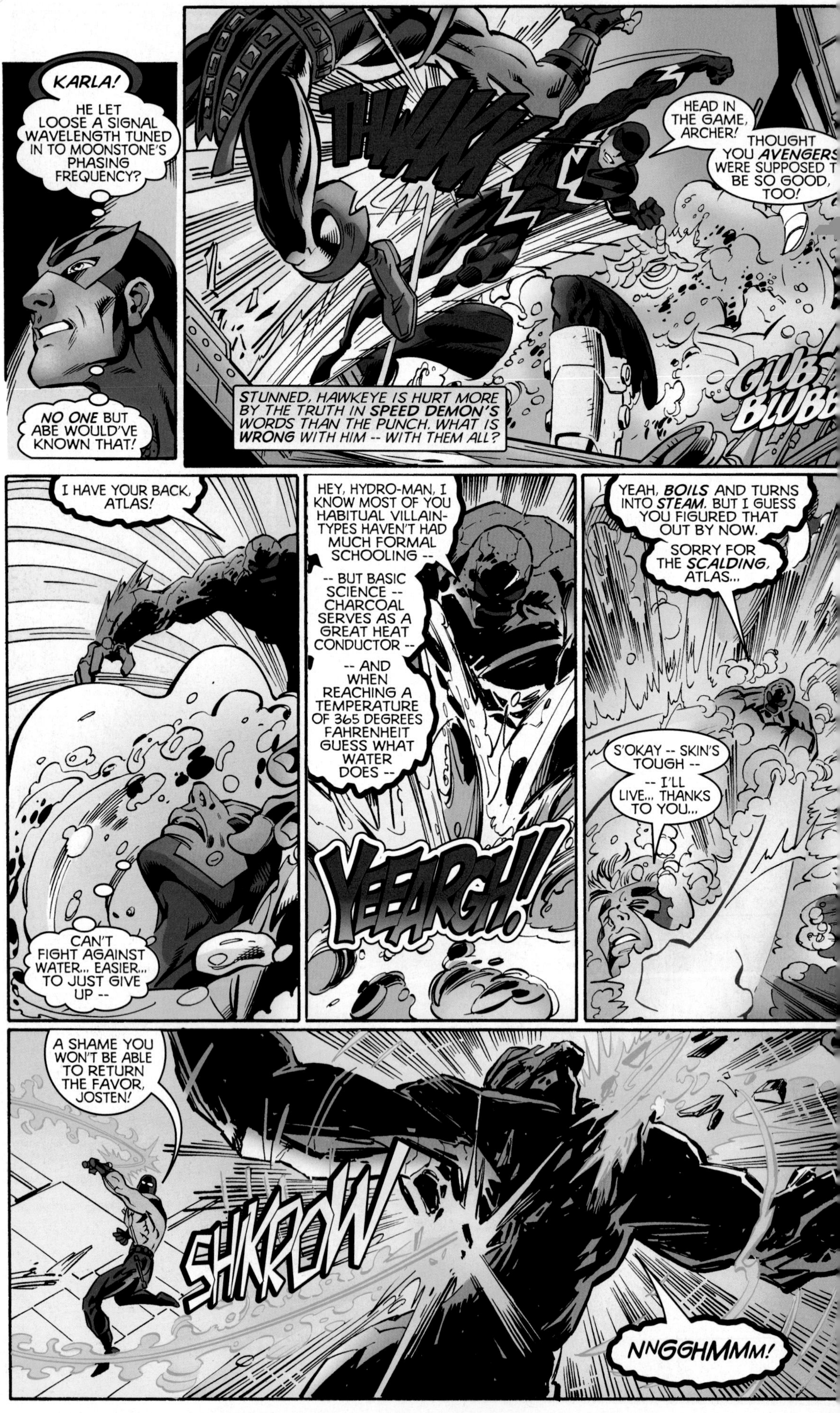
KARLA!
HE LET LOOSE A SIGNAL WAVELENGTH TUNED IN TO MOONSTONE'S PHASING FREQUENCY?
NO ONE BUT ABE WOULD'VE KNOWN THAT!
THWAKK
HEAD IN THE GAME, ARCHER!
THOUGHT YOU AVENGERS WERE SUPPOSED T BE SO GOOD, TOO!
STUNNED, HAWKEYE IS HURT MORE BY THE TRUTH IN SPEED DEMON'S WORDS THAN THE PUNCH. WHAT IS WRONG WITH HIM -- WITH THEM ALL?
GLUB BLUBB
I HAVE YOUR BACK, ATLAS!
CAN'T FIGHT AGAINST WATER... EASIER... TO JUST GIVE UP --
HEY, HYDRO-MAN, I KNOW MOST OF YOU HABITUAL VILLAIN-TYPES HAVEN'T HAD MUCH FORMAL SCHOOLING --
-- BUT BASIC SCIENCE -- CHARCOAL SERVES AS A GREAT HEAT CONDUCTOR --
-- AND WHEN REACHING A TEMPERATURE OF 365 DEGREES FAHRENHEIT GUESS WHAT WATER DOES --
YEEARGH!
YEAH, BOILS AND TURNS INTO STEAM. BUT I GUESS YOU FIGURED THAT OUT BY NOW.
SORRY FOR THE SCALDING, ATLAS...
S'OKAY -- SKIN'S TOUGH --
-- I'LL LIVE... THANKS TO YOU...
A SHAME YOU WON'T BE ABLE TO RETURN THE FAVOR, JOSTEN!
SHKROW
NNGGHMMM!

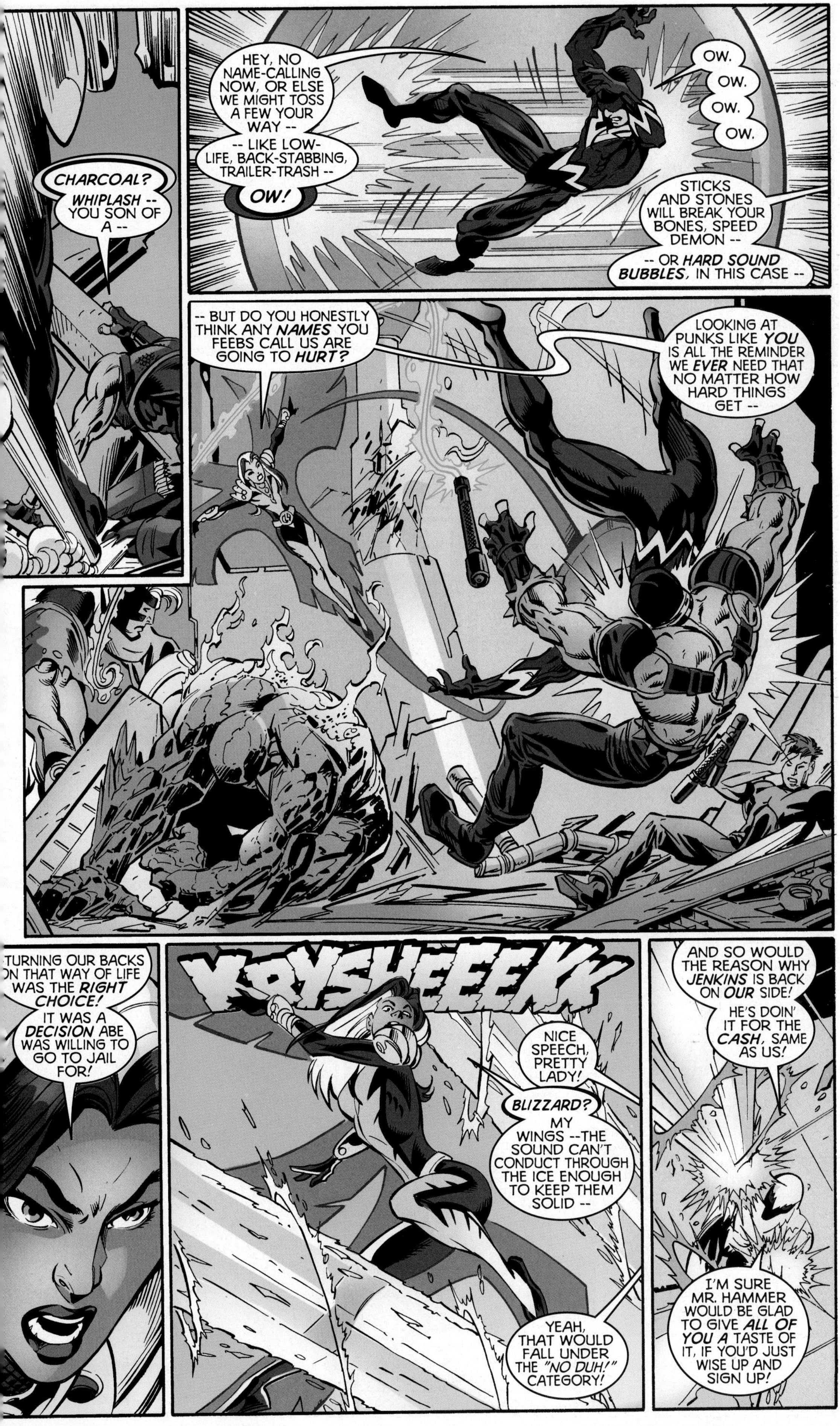
CHARCOAL? WHIPLASH -- YOU SON OF A --
HEY, NO NAME-CALLING NOW, OR ELSE WE MIGHT TOSS A FEW YOUR WAY --
-- LIKE LOW-LIFE, BACK-STABBING, TRAILER-TRASH --
OW!
OW.
OW.
OW.
OW.
STICKS AND STONES WILL BREAK YOUR BONES, SPEED DEMON --
-- OR HARD SOUND BUBBLES, IN THIS CASE --
-- BUT DO YOU HONESTLY THINK ANY NAMES YOU FEEBS CALL US ARE GOING TO HURT?
LOOKING AT PUNKS LIKE YOU IS ALL THE REMINDER WE EVER NEED THAT NO MATTER HOW HARD THINGS GET --
TURNING OUR BACKS ON THAT WAY OF LIFE WAS THE RIGHT CHOICE!
IT WAS A DECISION ABE WAS WILLING TO GO TO JAIL FOR!
KRYSHEEEKK
NICE SPEECH, PRETTY LADY!
BLIZZARD?
MY WINGS --THE SOUND CAN'T CONDUCT THROUGH THE ICE ENOUGH TO KEEP THEM SOLID --
YEAH, THAT WOULD FALL UNDER THE "NO DUH!" CATEGORY!
AND SO WOULD THE REASON WHY JENKINS IS BACK ON OUR SIDE!
HE'S DOIN' IT FOR THE CASH, SAME AS US!
I'M SURE MR. HAMMER WOULD BE GLAD TO GIVE ALL OF YOU A TASTE OF IT, IF YOU'D JUST WISE UP AND SIGN UP!

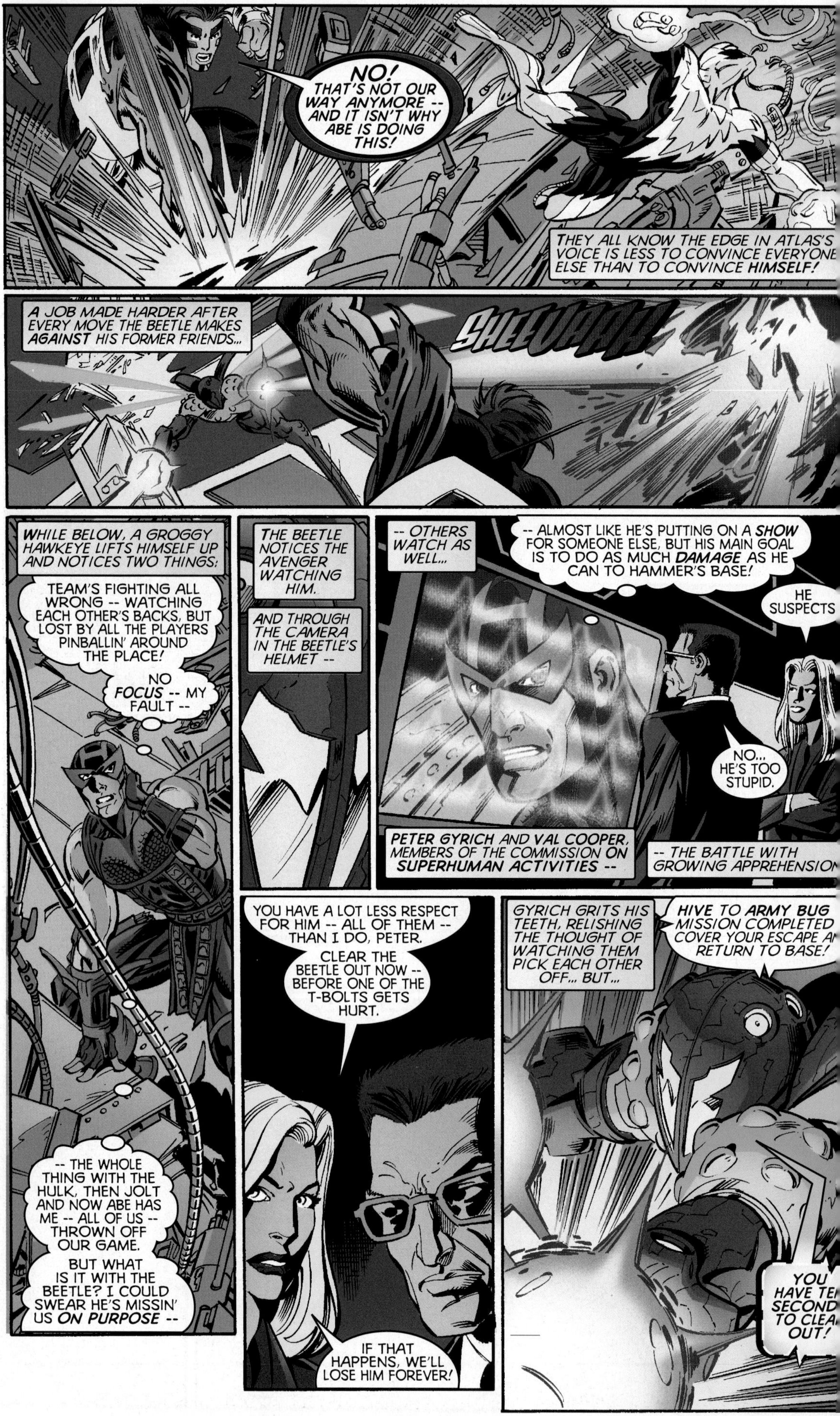
NO! THAT'S NOT OUR WAY ANYMORE -- AND IT ISN'T WHY ABE IS DOING THIS!
THEY ALL KNOW THE EDGE IN ATLAS'S VOICE IS LESS TO CONVINCE EVERYONE ELSE THAN TO CONVINCE HIMSELF!
A JOB MADE HARDER AFTER EVERY MOVE THE BEETLE MAKES AGAINST HIS FORMER FRIENDS...
SHEEUAAA!
WHILE BELOW, A GROGGY HAWKEYE LIFTS HIMSELF UP AND NOTICES TWO THINGS:
TEAM'S FIGHTING ALL WRONG -- WATCHING EACH OTHER'S BACKS, BUT LOST BY ALL THE PLAYERS PINBALLIN' AROUND THE PLACE!
NO FOCUS -- MY FAULT --
-- THE WHOLE THING WITH THE HULK, THEN JOLT AND NOW ABE HAS ME -- ALL OF US -- THROWN OFF OUR GAME.
BUT WHAT IS IT WITH THE BEETLE? I COULD SWEAR HE'S MISSIN' US ON PURPOSE --
THE BEETLE NOTICES THE AVENGER WATCHING HIM.
AND THROUGH THE CAMERA IN THE BEETLE'S HELMET --
-- OTHERS WATCH AS WELL...
-- ALMOST LIKE HE'S PUTTING ON A SHOW FOR SOMEONE ELSE, BUT HIS MAIN GOAL IS TO DO AS MUCH DAMAGE AS HE CAN TO HAMMER'S BASE!
HE SUSPECTS
NO... HE'S TOO STUPID.
PETER GYRICH AND VAL COOPER, MEMBERS OF THE COMMISSION ON SUPERHUMAN ACTIVITIES --
-- THE BATTLE WITH GROWING APPREHENSION
YOU HAVE A LOT LESS RESPECT FOR HIM -- ALL OF THEM -- THAN I DO, PETER.
CLEAR THE BEETLE OUT NOW -- BEFORE ONE OF THE T-BOLTS GETS HURT.
IF THAT HAPPENS, WE'LL LOSE HIM FOREVER!
GYRICH GRITS HIS TEETH, RELISHING THE THOUGHT OF WATCHING THEM PICK EACH OTHER OFF... BUT...
HIVE TO ARMY BUG MISSION COMPLETED COVER YOUR ESCAPE A RETURN TO BASE!
YOU HAVE TE SECOND TO CLEA OUT!

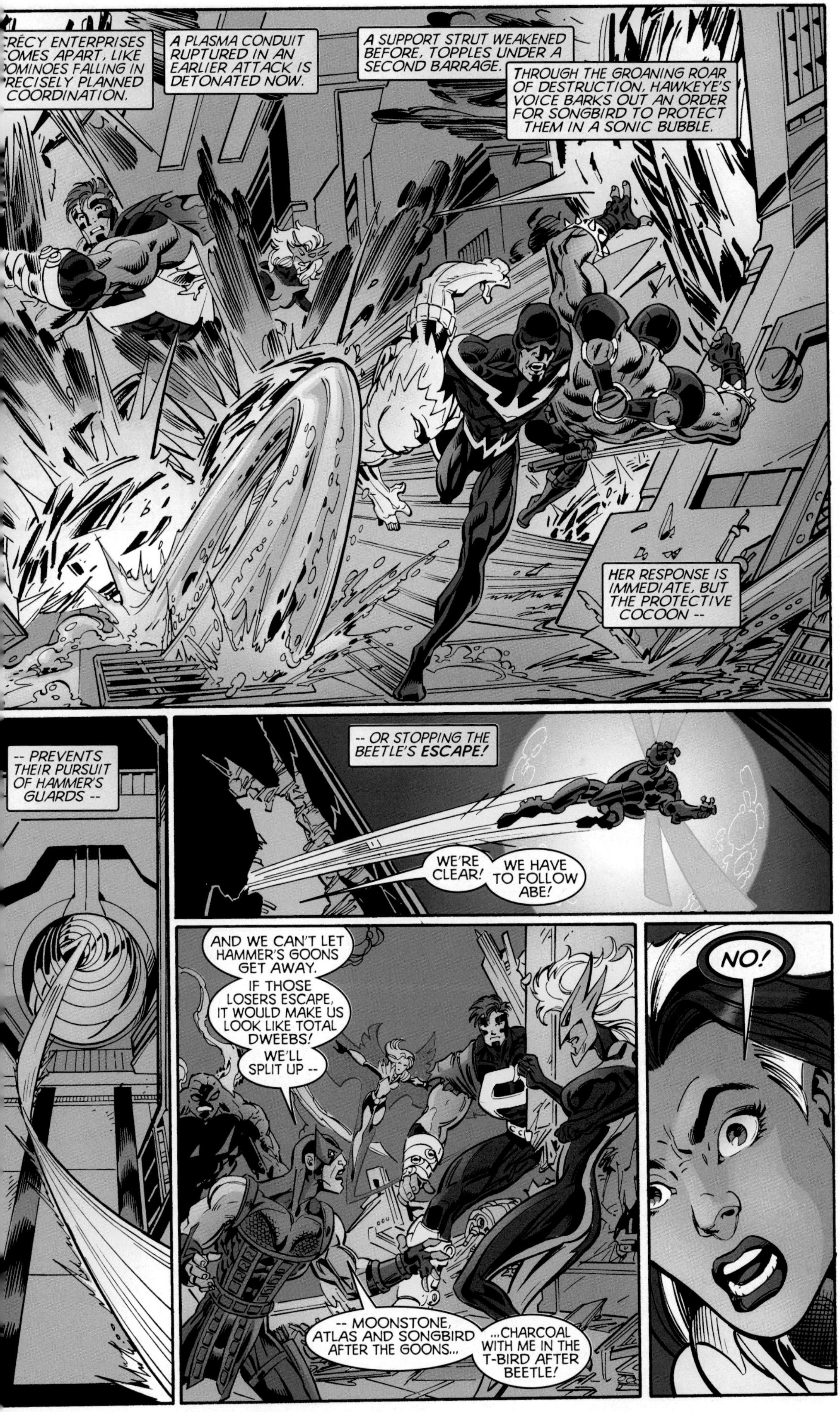
CRÉCY ENTERPRISES COMES APART, LIKE DOMINOES FALLING IN PRECISELY PLANNED COORDINATION.
A PLASMA CONDUIT RUPTURED IN AN EARLIER ATTACK IS DETONATED NOW.
A SUPPORT STRUT WEAKENED BEFORE, TOPPLES UNDER A SECOND BARRAGE.
THROUGH THE GROANING ROAR OF DESTRUCTION, HAWKEYE'S VOICE BARKS OUT AN ORDER FOR SONGBIRD TO PROTECT THEM IN A SONIC BUBBLE.
HER RESPONSE IS IMMEDIATE, BUT THE PROTECTIVE COCOON --
-- PREVENTS THEIR PURSUIT OF HAMMER'S GUARDS --
-- OR STOPPING THE BEETLE'S ESCAPE!
WE'RE CLEAR!
WE HAVE TO FOLLOW ABE!
AND WE CAN'T LET HAMMER'S GOONS GET AWAY.
IF THOSE LOSERS ESCAPE, IT WOULD MAKE US LOOK LIKE TOTAL DWEEBS!
WE'LL SPLIT UP --
-- MOONSTONE, ATLAS AND SONGBIRD AFTER THE GOONS...
...CHARCOAL WITH ME IN THE T-BIRD AFTER BEETLE!
NO!

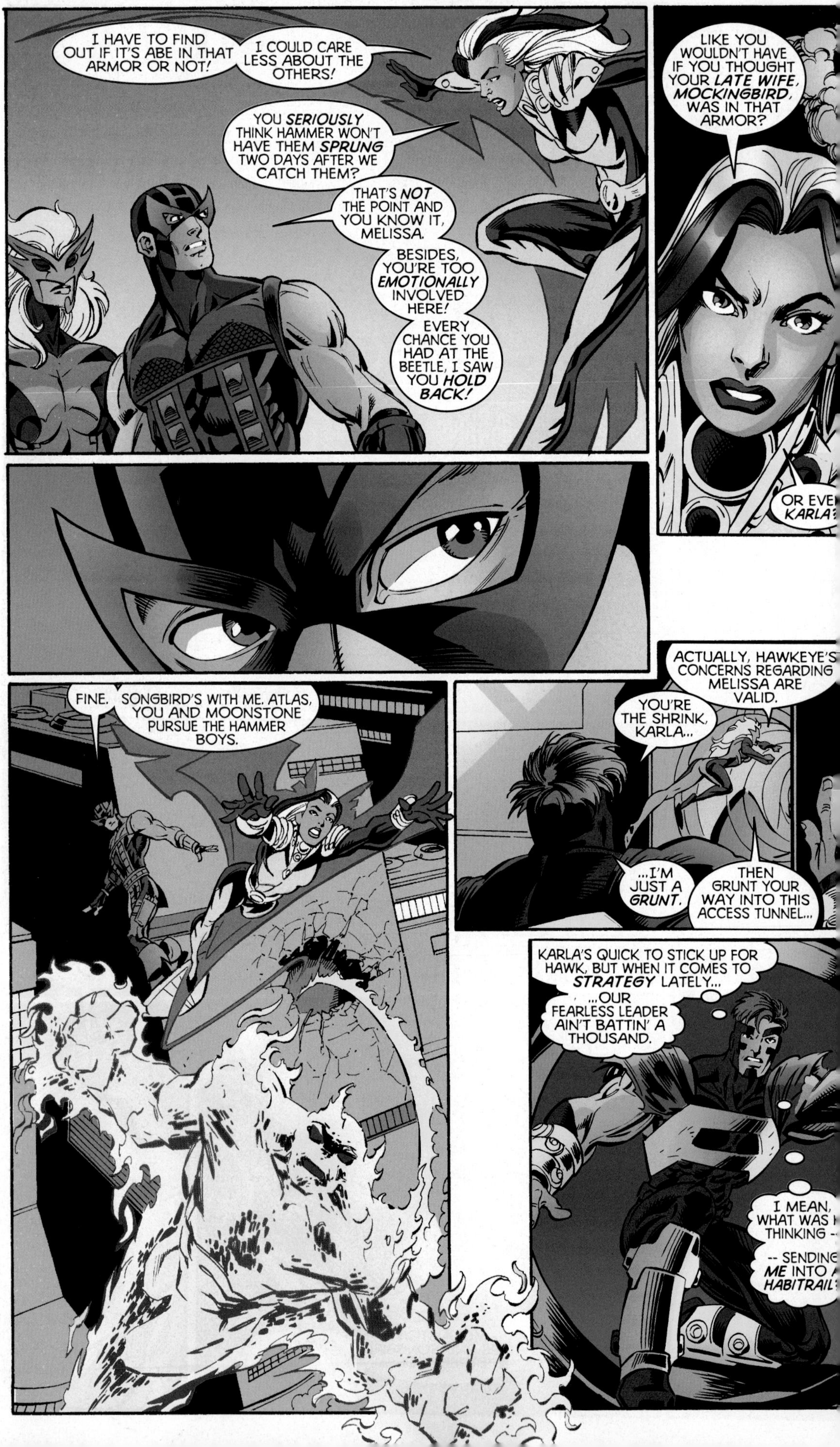
I HAVE TO FIND OUT IF IT'S ABE IN THAT ARMOR OR NOT!
I COULD CARE LESS ABOUT THE OTHERS!
YOU *SERIOUSLY* THINK HAMMER WON'T HAVE THEM *SPRUNG* TWO DAYS AFTER WE CATCH THEM?
THAT'S *NOT* THE POINT AND YOU KNOW IT, MELISSA.
BESIDES, YOU'RE TOO *EMOTIONALLY* INVOLVED HERE!
EVERY CHANCE YOU HAD AT THE BEETLE, I SAW YOU *HOLD BACK!*
LIKE YOU WOULDN'T HAVE IF YOU THOUGHT YOUR *LATE WIFE, MOCKINGBIRD,* WAS IN THAT ARMOR?
FINE.
SONGBIRD'S WITH ME. ATLAS, YOU AND MOONSTONE PURSUE THE HAMMER BOYS.
ACTUALLY, HAWKEYE'S CONCERNS REGARDING MELISSA ARE VALID.
YOU'RE THE SHRINK, KARLA...
...I'M JUST A *GRUNT.*
THEN GRUNT YOUR WAY INTO THIS ACCESS TUNNEL...
KARLA'S QUICK TO STICK UP FOR HAWK, BUT WHEN IT COMES TO *STRATEGY* LATELY...
...OUR FEARLESS LEADER AIN'T BATTIN' A THOUSAND.

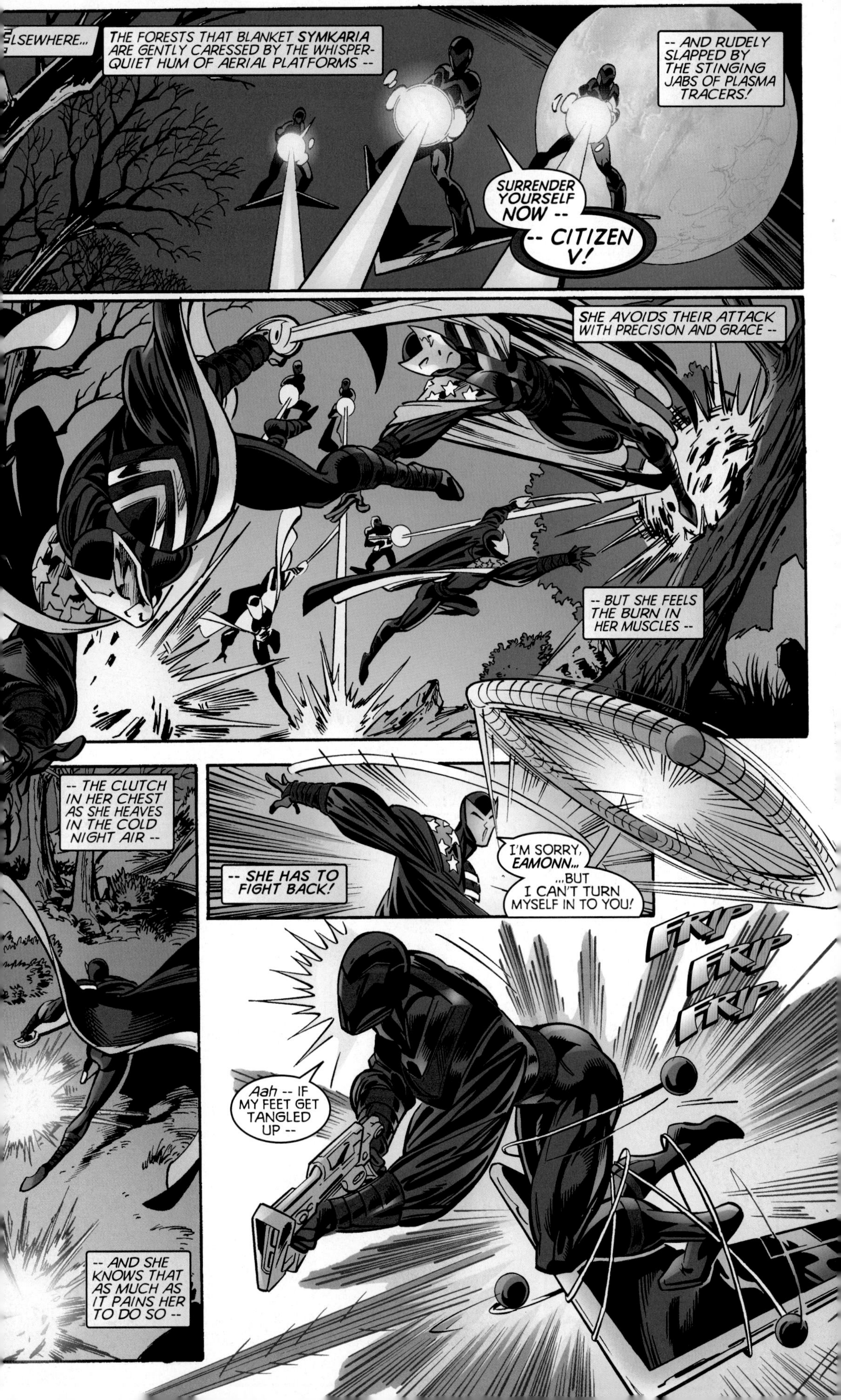
ELSEWHERE...
THE FORESTS THAT BLANKET SYMKARIA ARE GENTLY CARESSED BY THE WHISPER-QUIET HUM OF AERIAL PLATFORMS --
-- AND RUDELY SLAPPED BY THE STINGING JABS OF PLASMA TRACERS!
SURRENDER YOURSELF NOW --
-- CITIZEN V!
SHE AVOIDS THEIR ATTACK WITH PRECISION AND GRACE --
-- BUT SHE FEELS THE BURN IN HER MUSCLES --
-- THE CLUTCH IN HER CHEST AS SHE HEAVES IN THE COLD NIGHT AIR --
-- AND SHE KNOWS THAT AS MUCH AS IT PAINS HER TO DO SO --
-- SHE HAS TO FIGHT BACK!
I'M SORRY, EAMONN...
...BUT I CAN'T TURN MYSELF IN TO YOU!
FRIP FRIP FRIP
Aah -- IF MY FEET GET TANGLED UP --

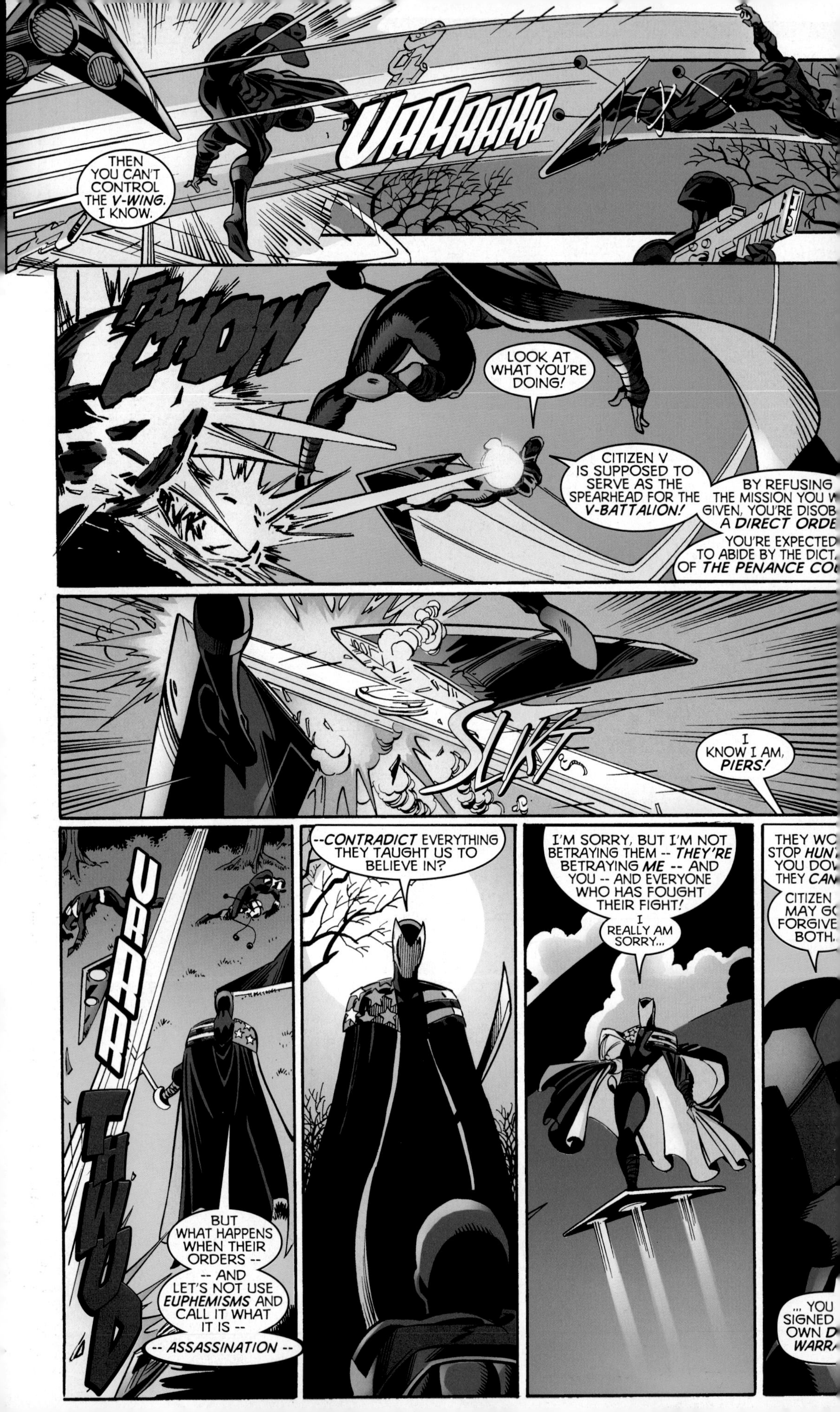

VRRRRRR
THEN YOU CAN'T CONTROL THE *V-WING.* I KNOW.
FA-CHOW
LOOK AT WHAT YOU'RE DOING!
CITIZEN V IS SUPPOSED TO SERVE AS THE SPEARHEAD FOR THE *V-BATTALION!*
BY REFUSING THE MISSION YOU W GIVEN, YOU'RE DISOB *A DIRECT ORDE*
YOU'RE EXPECTED TO ABIDE BY THE DICT. OF *THE PENANCE CO*
SLIKT
I KNOW I AM, *PIERS!*
VRRRR
THWUD
BUT WHAT HAPPENS WHEN THEIR ORDERS --
-- AND LET'S NOT USE *EUPHEMISMS* AND CALL IT WHAT IT IS --
-- *ASSASSINATION* --
--*CONTRADICT* EVERYTHING THEY TAUGHT US TO BELIEVE IN?
I'M SORRY, BUT I'M NOT BETRAYING THEM -- *THEY'RE* BETRAYING *ME* -- AND YOU -- AND EVERYONE WHO HAS FOUGHT THEIR FIGHT!
I REALLY AM SORRY...
THEY WO STOP *HUN* YOU DOW THEY *CAN*
CITIZEN MAY GO FORGIVE BOTH.
... YOU SIGNED OWN *D WARR*

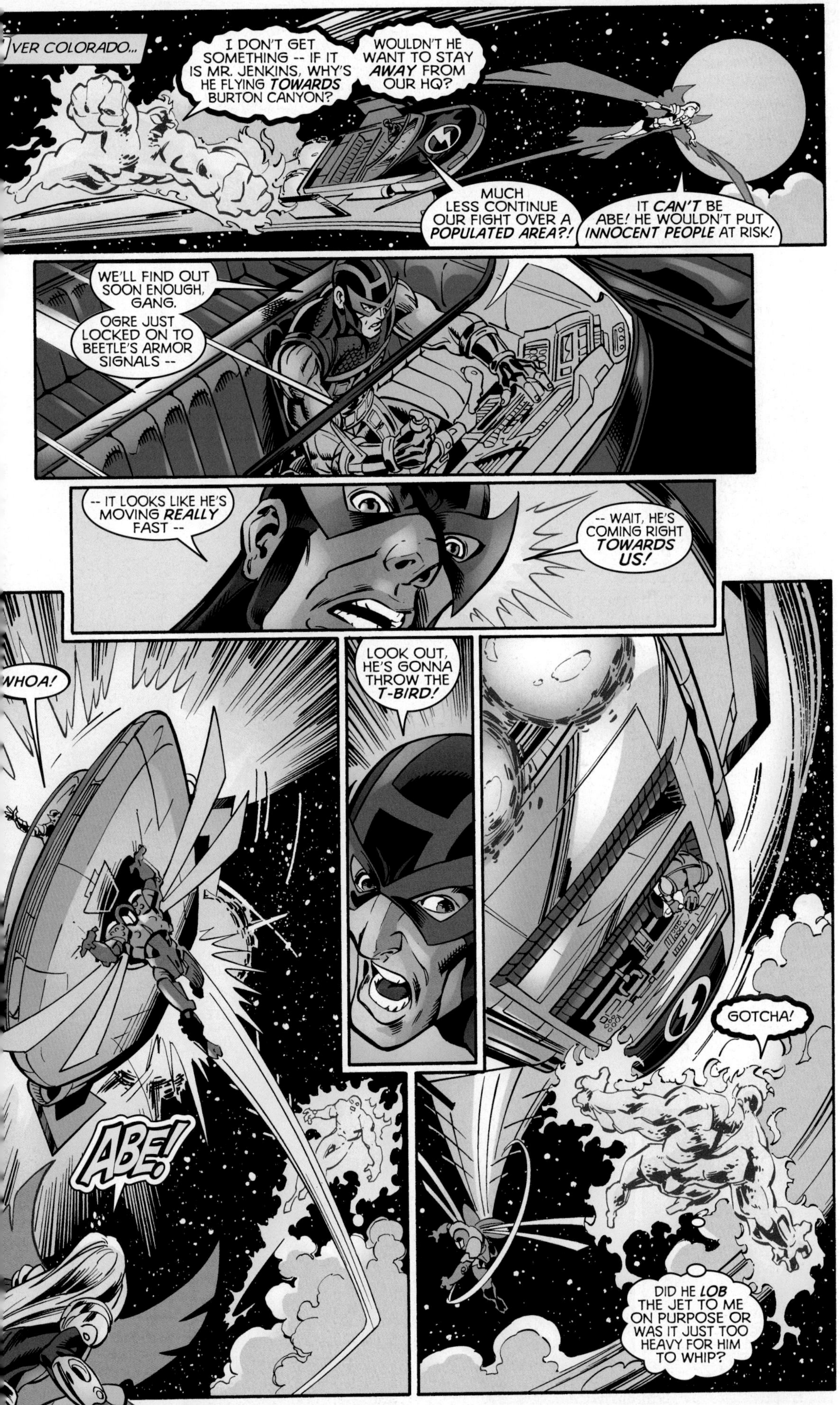
VER COLORADO...
I DON'T GET SOMETHING -- IF IT IS MR. JENKINS, WHY'S HE FLYING TOWARDS BURTON CANYON?
WOULDN'T HE WANT TO STAY AWAY FROM OUR HQ?
MUCH LESS CONTINUE OUR FIGHT OVER A POPULATED AREA?!
IT CAN'T BE ABE! HE WOULDN'T PUT INNOCENT PEOPLE AT RISK!
WE'LL FIND OUT SOON ENOUGH, GANG.
OGRE JUST LOCKED ON TO BEETLE'S ARMOR SIGNALS --
-- IT LOOKS LIKE HE'S MOVING REALLY FAST --
-- WAIT, HE'S COMING RIGHT TOWARDS US!
WHOA!
ABE!
LOOK OUT, HE'S GONNA THROW THE T-BIRD!
GOTCHA!
DID HE LOB THE JET TO ME ON PURPOSE OR WAS IT JUST TOO HEAVY FOR HIM TO WHIP?

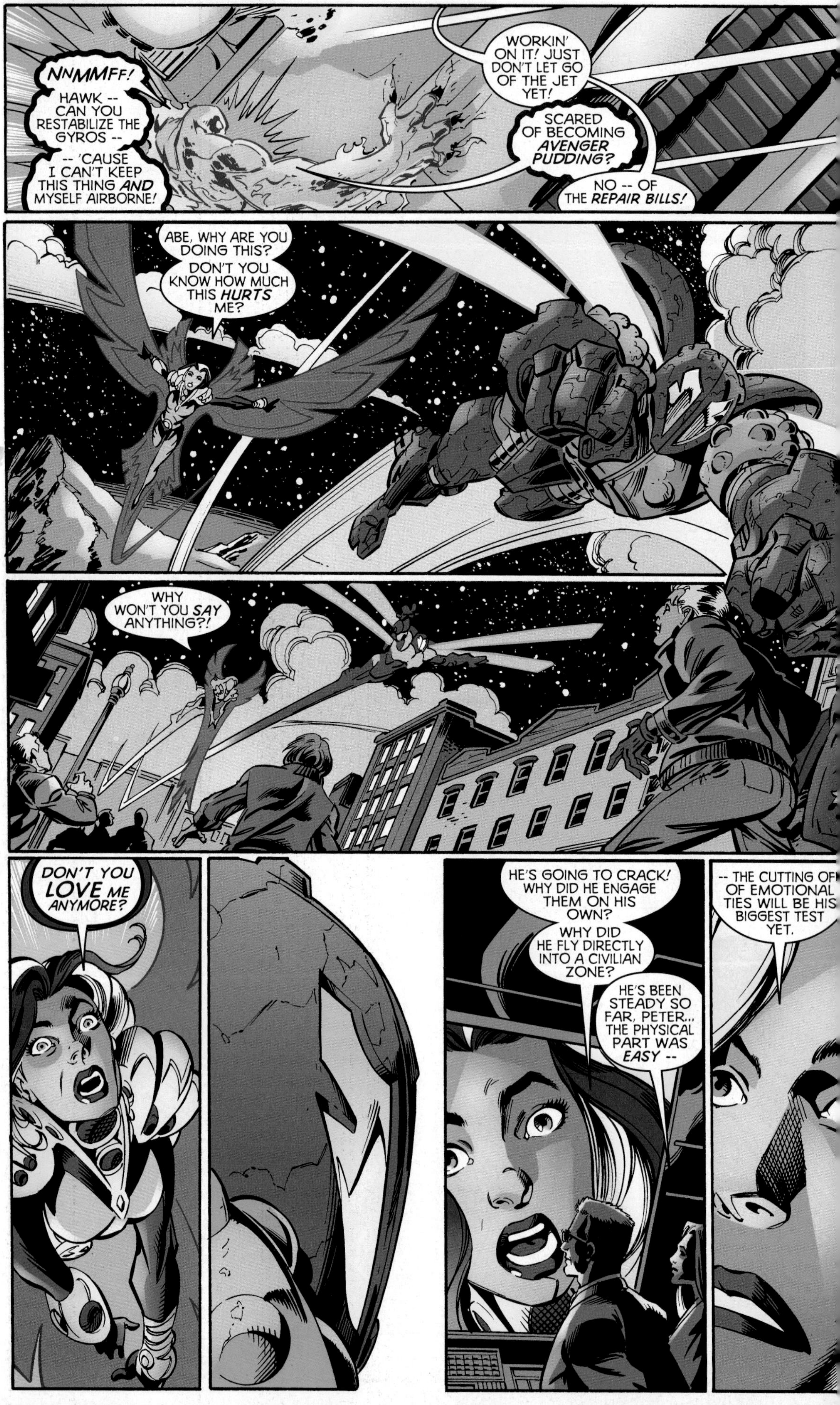
NNMMFF!
HAWK -- CAN YOU RESTABILIZE THE GYROS --
-- 'CAUSE I CAN'T KEEP THIS THING AND MYSELF AIRBORNE!
WORKIN' ON IT! JUST DON'T LET GO OF THE JET YET!
SCARED OF BECOMING AVENGER PUDDING?
NO -- OF THE REPAIR BILLS!
ABE, WHY ARE YOU DOING THIS? DON'T YOU KNOW HOW MUCH THIS HURTS ME?
WHY WON'T YOU SAY ANYTHING?!
DON'T YOU LOVE ME ANYMORE?
HE'S GOING TO CRACK! WHY DID HE ENGAGE THEM ON HIS OWN?
WHY DID HE FLY DIRECTLY INTO A CIVILIAN ZONE?
HE'S BEEN STEADY SO FAR, PETER... THE PHYSICAL PART WAS EASY --
-- THE CUTTING OF OF EMOTIONAL TIES WILL BE HIS BIGGEST TEST YET.

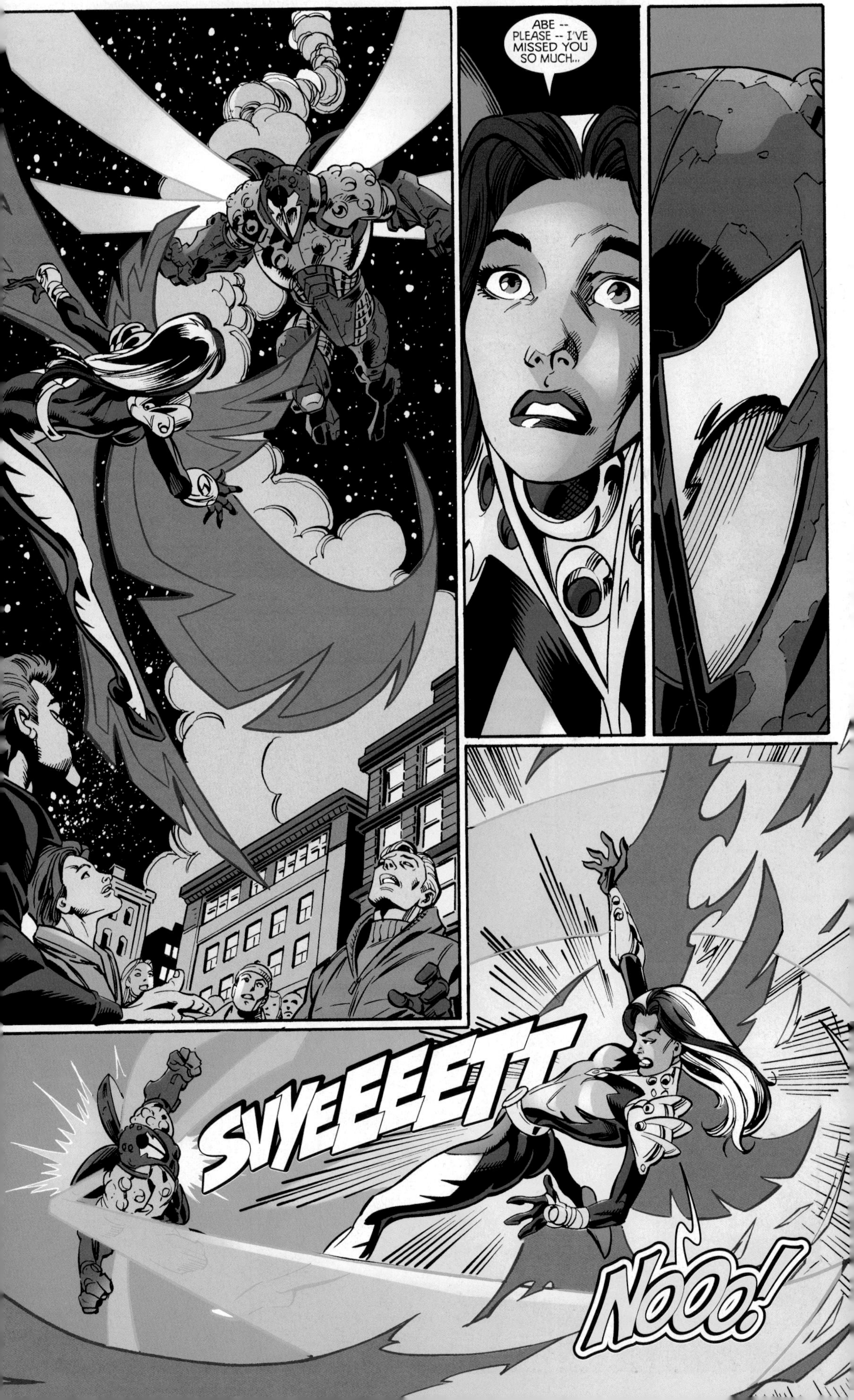
ABE -- PLEASE -- I'VE MISSED YOU SO MUCH...
SVYEEEETT
NOOO!

HOW COULD YOU?

I'M GOING TO START CHARGING BY THE CATCH.

HAWK -- DID OGRE COME THROUGH YET?

THE FREQUENCY'S BEEN TRANSMITTED TO THE ON-BOARD SYSTEMS --

-- AND DOWNLOADED INTO THE INPUT FEED ON MY *SCRAMBLER ARROWHEAD!*

SVIK

"ALL OF WHICH MEANS..."

SKRJ CHAKK

...THE BEETLE IS DOWN FOR THE COUNT!

THKUD

BWAROOM

THERE GOES MY LIFE SAVINGS.

YOU'LL REALLY MISS THOSE TWENTY BUCKS, TOO.

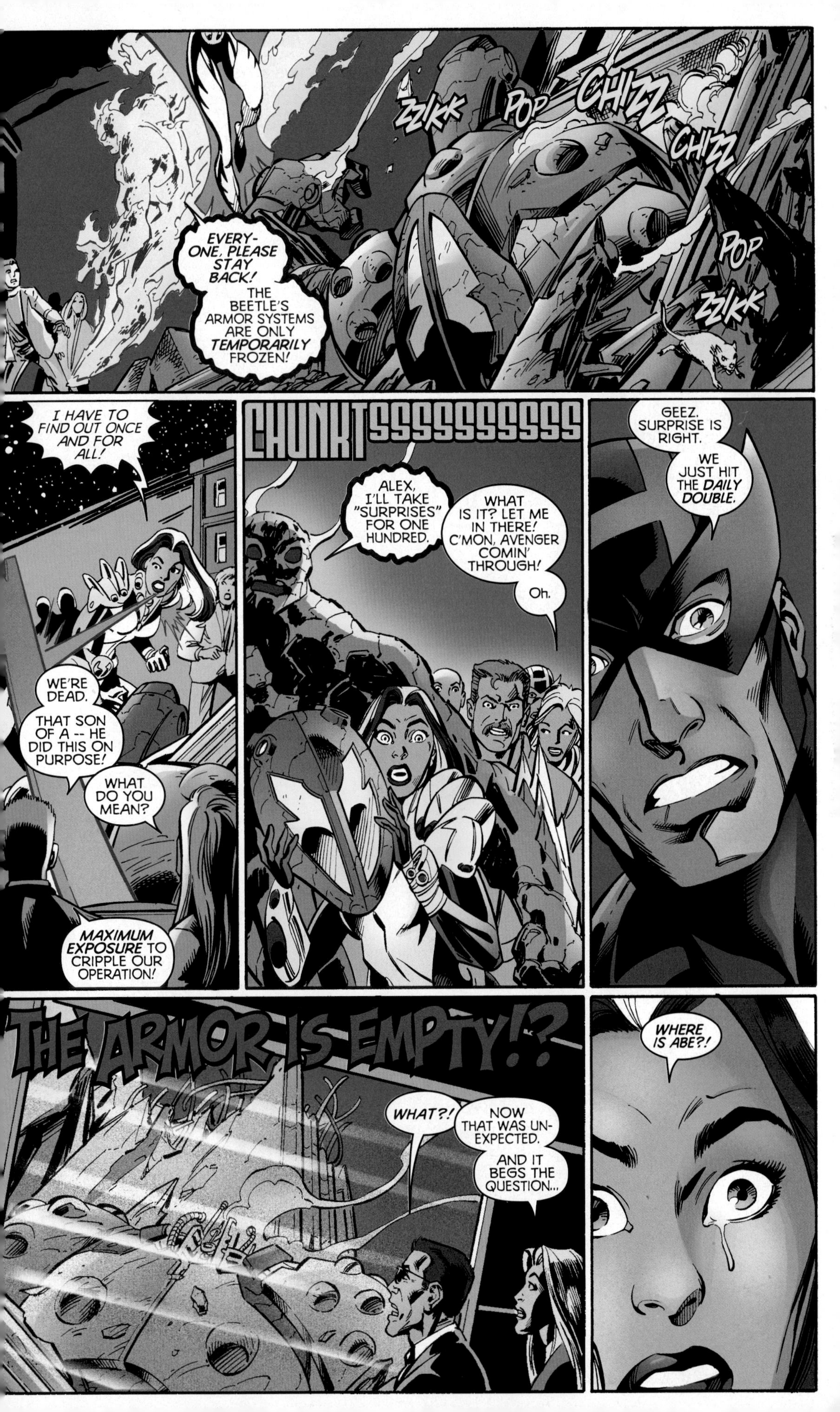
ZZIKK
POP
CHIZZ
CHIZZ
EVERY-ONE, PLEASE STAY BACK!
THE BEETLE'S ARMOR SYSTEMS ARE ONLY TEMPORARILY FROZEN!
POP
ZZIKK
I HAVE TO FIND OUT ONCE AND FOR ALL!
WE'RE DEAD.
THAT SON OF A -- HE DID THIS ON PURPOSE!
WHAT DO YOU MEAN?
MAXIMUM EXPOSURE TO CRIPPLE OUR OPERATION!
CHUNKTSSSSSSSSSS
ALEX, I'LL TAKE "SURPRISES" FOR ONE HUNDRED.
WHAT IS IT? LET ME IN THERE! C'MON, AVENGER COMIN' THROUGH!
Oh.
GEEZ. SURPRISE IS RIGHT.
WE JUST HIT THE DAILY DOUBLE.
THE ARMOR IS EMPTY!?
WHAT?!
NOW THAT WAS UN-EXPECTED.
AND IT BEGS THE QUESTION...
WHERE IS ABE?!

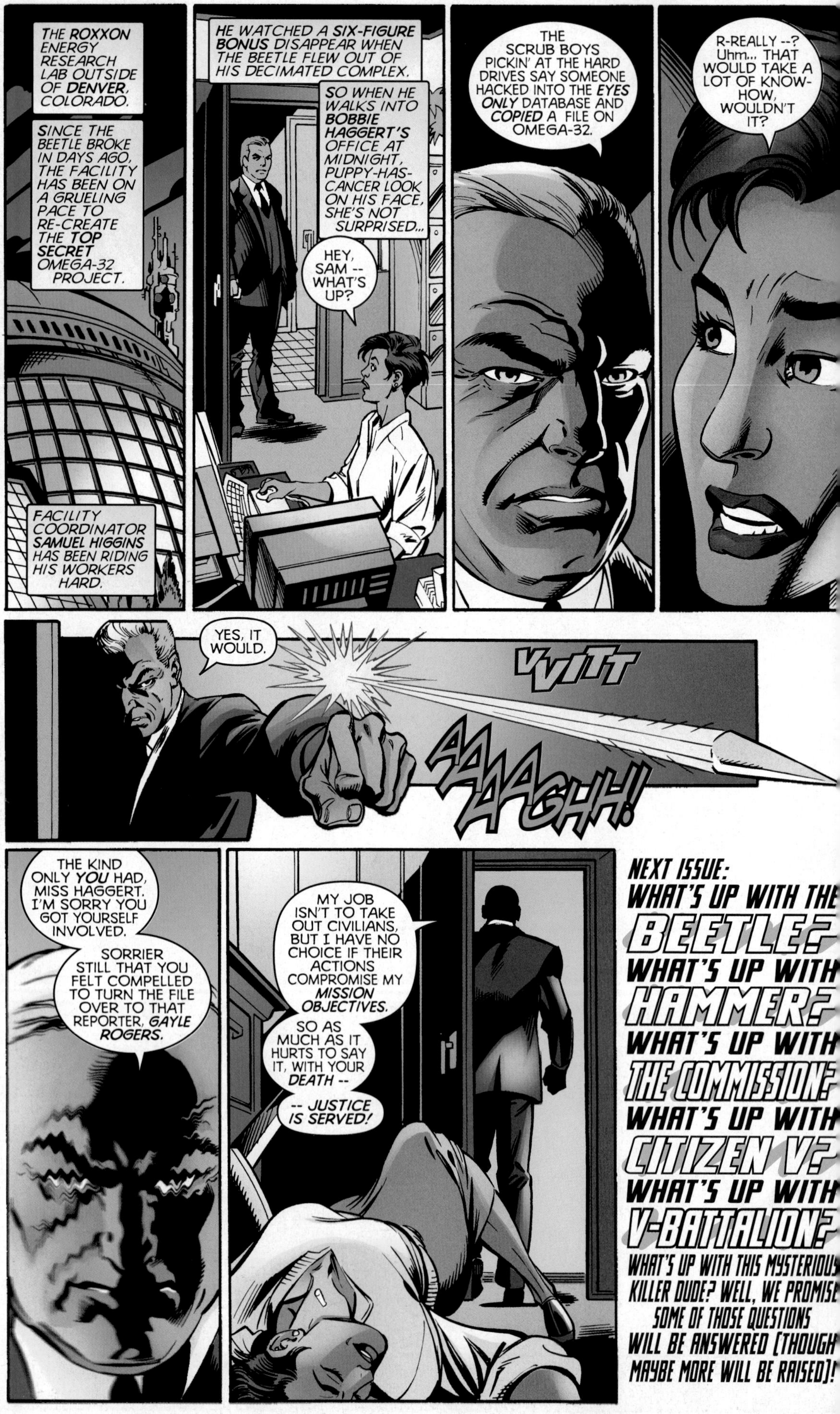
THE ROXXON ENERGY RESEARCH LAB OUTSIDE OF DENVER, COLORADO.
SINCE THE BEETLE BROKE IN DAYS AGO, THE FACILITY HAS BEEN ON A GRUELING PACE TO RE-CREATE THE TOP SECRET OMEGA-32 PROJECT.
FACILITY COORDINATOR SAMUEL HIGGINS HAS BEEN RIDING HIS WORKERS HARD.
HE WATCHED A SIX-FIGURE BONUS DISAPPEAR WHEN THE BEETLE FLEW OUT OF HIS DECIMATED COMPLEX.
SO WHEN HE WALKS INTO BOBBIE HAGGERT'S OFFICE AT MIDNIGHT, PUPPY-HAS-CANCER LOOK ON HIS FACE, SHE'S NOT SURPRISED...
HEY, SAM -- WHAT'S UP?
THE SCRUB BOYS PICKIN' AT THE HARD DRIVES SAY SOMEONE HACKED INTO THE EYES ONLY DATABASE AND COPIED A FILE ON OMEGA-32.
R-REALLY --? Uhm... THAT WOULD TAKE A LOT OF KNOW-HOW, WOULDN'T IT?
YES, IT WOULD.
VVITT
AAAAAAGHH!
THE KIND ONLY YOU HAD, MISS HAGGERT. I'M SORRY YOU GOT YOURSELF INVOLVED.
SORRIER STILL THAT YOU FELT COMPELLED TO TURN THE FILE OVER TO THAT REPORTER, GAYLE ROGERS.
MY JOB ISN'T TO TAKE OUT CIVILIANS, BUT I HAVE NO CHOICE IF THEIR ACTIONS COMPROMISE MY MISSION OBJECTIVES.
SO AS MUCH AS IT HURTS TO SAY IT, WITH YOUR DEATH --
-- JUSTICE IS SERVED!
NEXT ISSUE:
WHAT'S UP WITH THE BEETLE?
WHAT'S UP WITH HAMMER?
WHAT'S UP WITH THE COMMISSION?
WHAT'S UP WITH CITIZEN V?
WHAT'S UP WITH V-BATTALION?
WHAT'S UP WITH THIS MYSTERIOUS KILLER DUDE? WELL, WE PROMISE SOME OF THOSE QUESTIONS WILL BE ANSWERED (THOUGH MAYBE MORE WILL BE RAISED)!

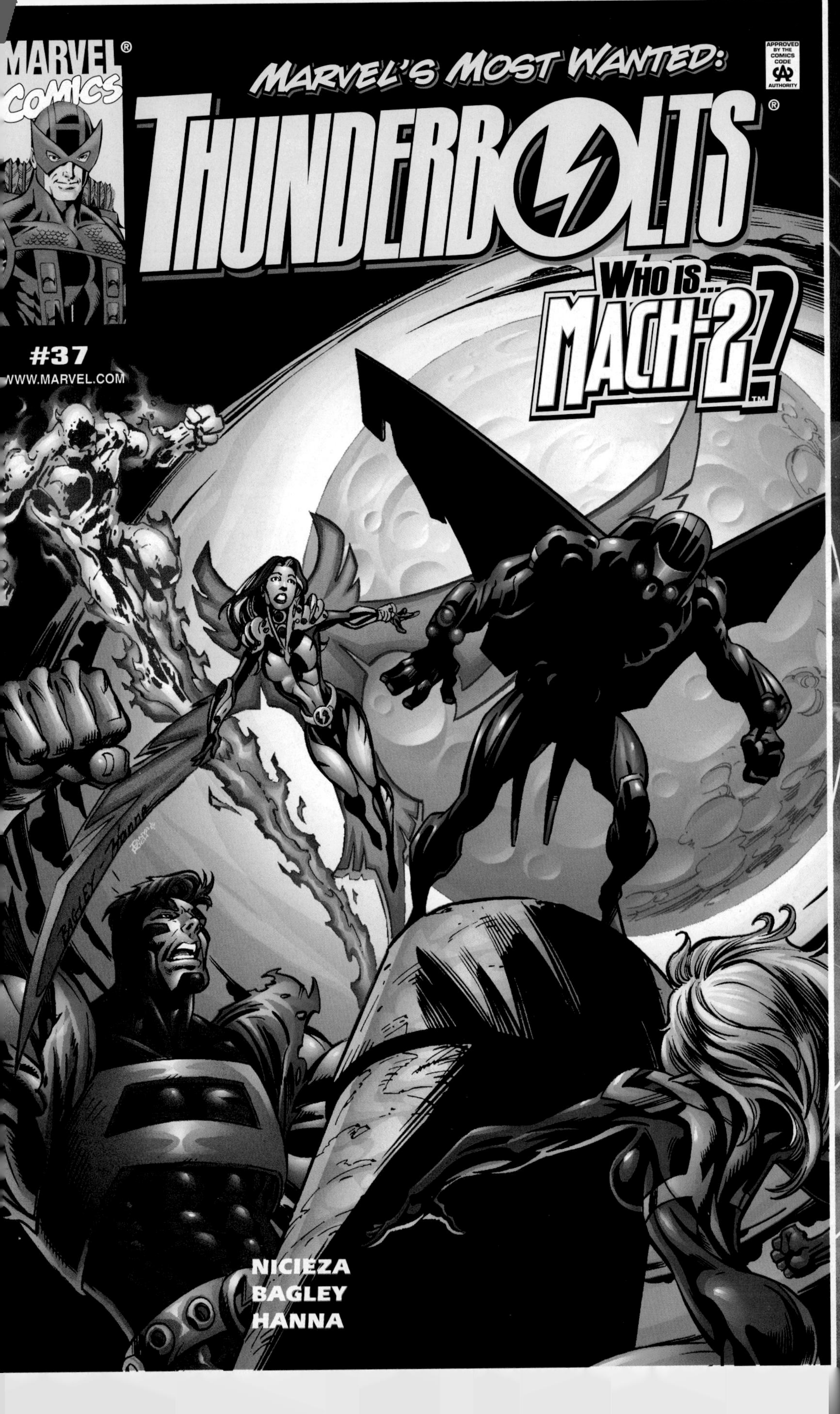
MARVEL COMICS
MARVEL'S MOST WANTED:
THUNDERBOLTS
APPROVED BY THE COMICS CODE AUTHORITY
WHO IS... MACH-2?
#37
WWW.MARVEL.COM
NICIEZA
BAGLEY
HANNA

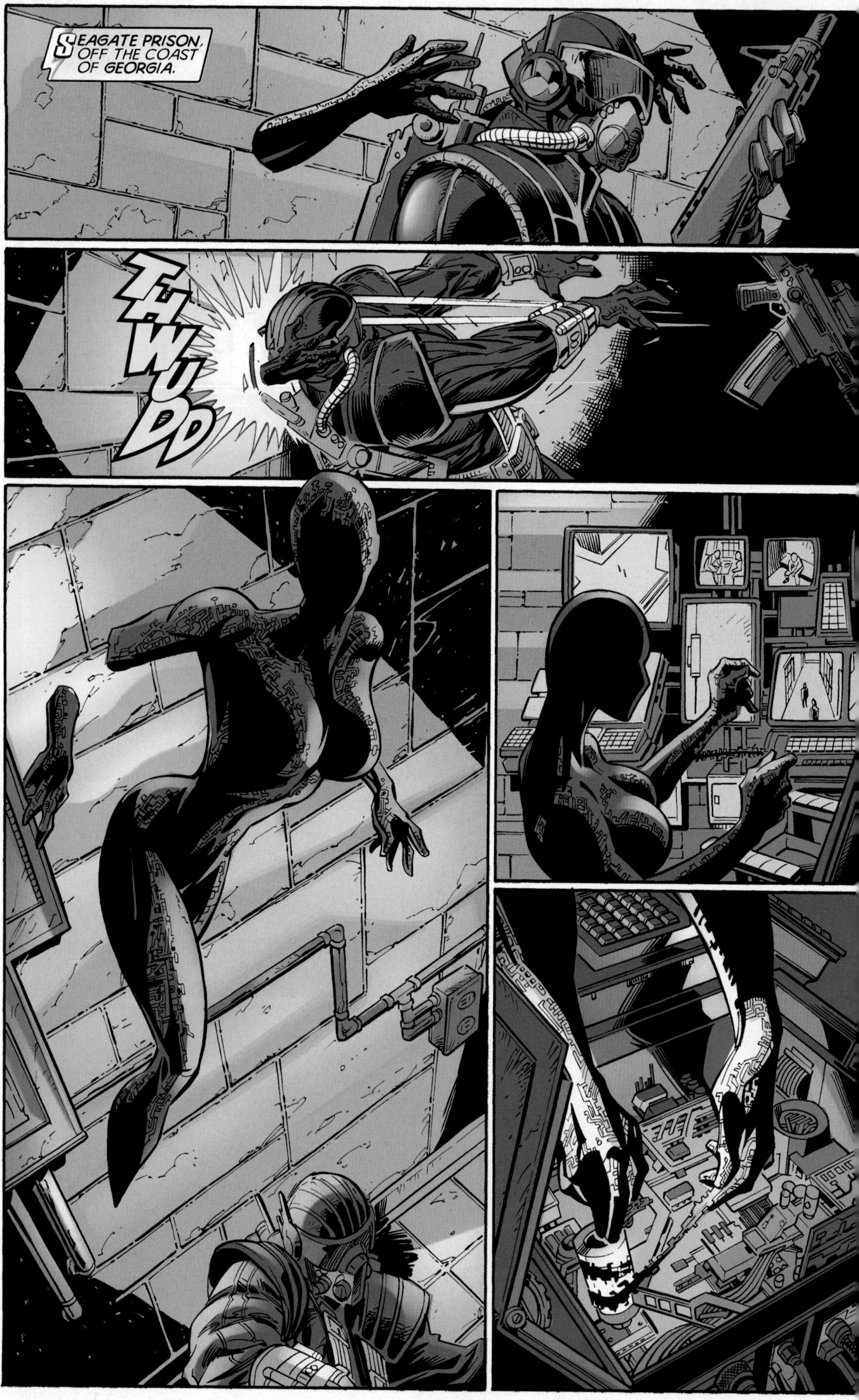

SEAGATE PRISON, OFF THE COAST OF GEORGIA.
THWUDD

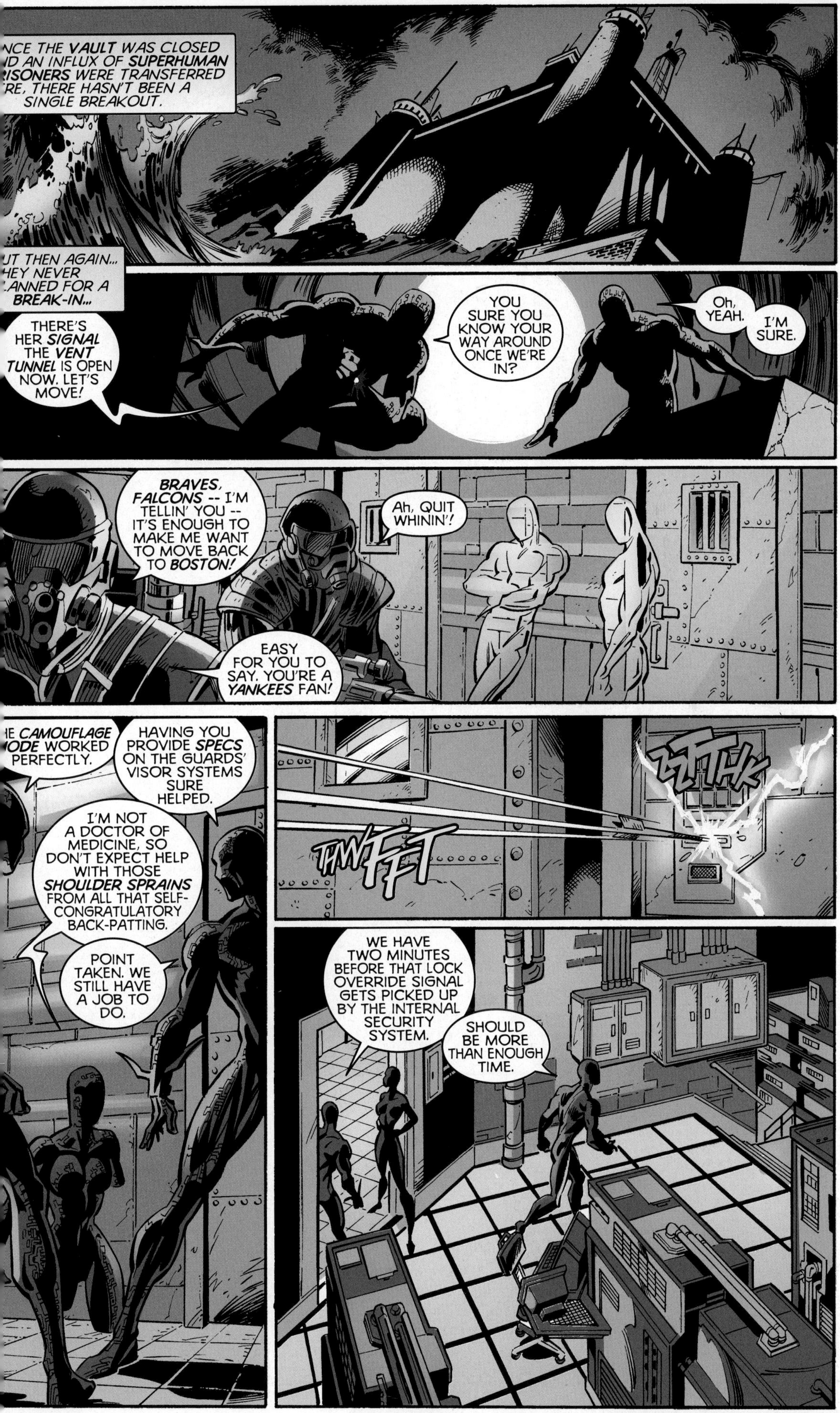
NCE THE VAULT WAS CLOSED ID AN INFLUX OF SUPERHUMAN RISONERS WERE TRANSFERRED RE, THERE HASN'T BEEN A SINGLE BREAKOUT.
UT THEN AGAIN... HEY NEVER ANNED FOR A BREAK-IN...
THERE'S HER SIGNAL THE VENT TUNNEL IS OPEN NOW. LET'S MOVE!
YOU SURE YOU KNOW YOUR WAY AROUND ONCE WE'RE IN?
Oh, YEAH.
I'M SURE.
BRAVES, FALCONS -- I'M TELLIN' YOU -- IT'S ENOUGH TO MAKE ME WANT TO MOVE BACK TO BOSTON!
Ah, QUIT WHININ'!
EASY FOR YOU TO SAY. YOU'RE A YANKEES FAN!
IE CAMOUFLAGE ODE WORKED PERFECTLY.
HAVING YOU PROVIDE SPECS ON THE GUARDS' VISOR SYSTEMS SURE HELPED.
I'M NOT A DOCTOR OF MEDICINE, SO DON'T EXPECT HELP WITH THOSE SHOULDER SPRAINS FROM ALL THAT SELF-CONGRATULATORY BACK-PATTING.
POINT TAKEN. WE STILL HAVE A JOB TO DO.
THWFFT
ZZFTHK
WE HAVE TWO MINUTES BEFORE THAT LOCK OVERRIDE SIGNAL GETS PICKED UP BY THE INTERNAL SECURITY SYSTEM.
SHOULD BE MORE THAN ENOUGH TIME.

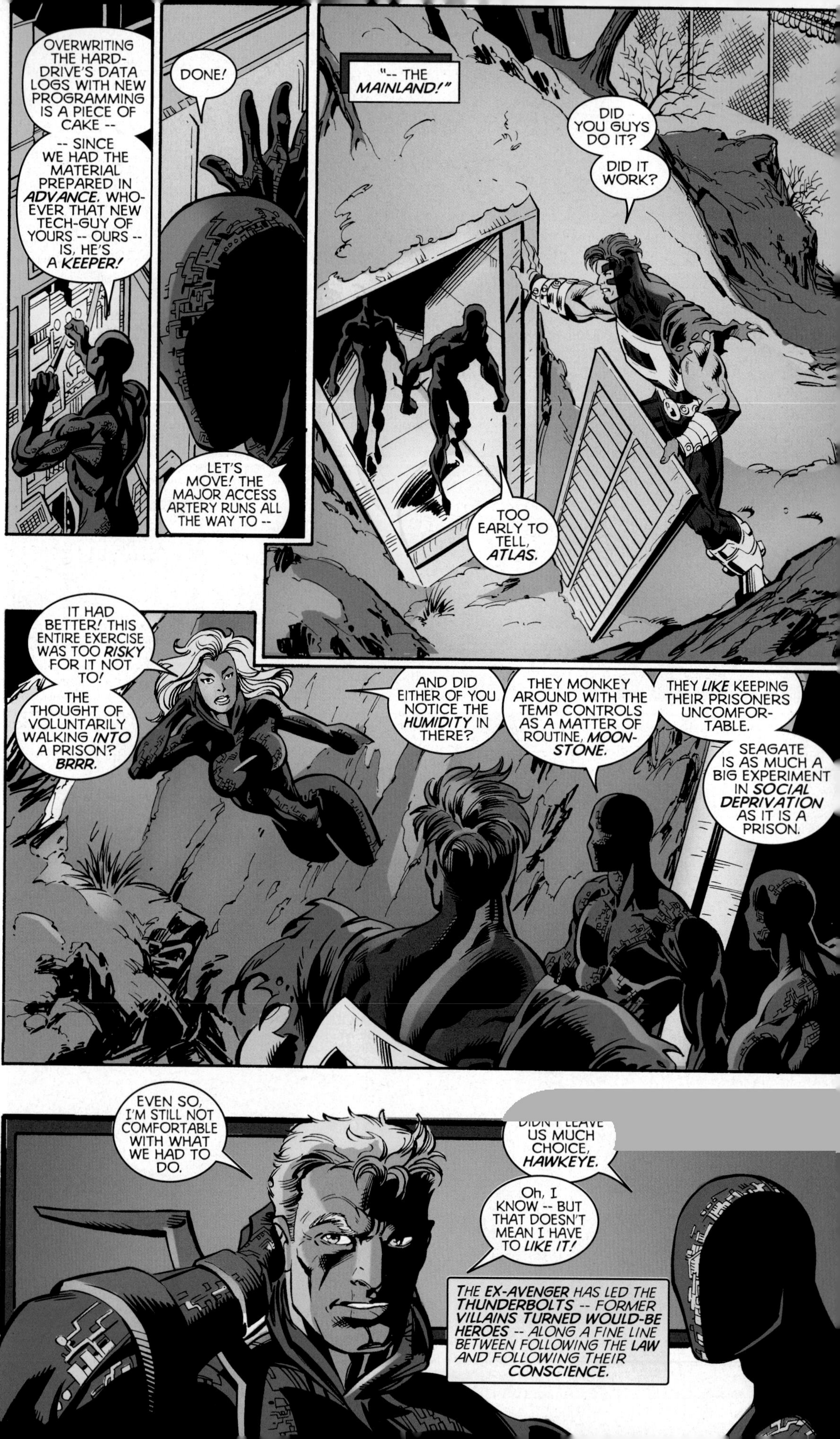
OVERWRITING THE HARD-DRIVE'S DATA LOGS WITH NEW PROGRAMMING IS A PIECE OF CAKE --
-- SINCE WE HAD THE MATERIAL PREPARED IN *ADVANCE.* WHO-EVER THAT NEW TECH-GUY OF YOURS -- OURS -- IS, HE'S A *KEEPER!*
DONE!
LET'S MOVE! THE MAJOR ACCESS ARTERY RUNS ALL THE WAY TO --
"-- THE *MAINLAND!*"
DID YOU GUYS DO IT?
DID IT WORK?
TOO EARLY TO TELL, *ATLAS.*
IT HAD BETTER! THIS ENTIRE EXERCISE WAS TOO *RISKY* FOR IT NOT TO!
THE THOUGHT OF VOLUNTARILY WALKING *INTO* A PRISON? *BRRR.*
AND DID EITHER OF YOU NOTICE THE *HUMIDITY* IN THERE?
THEY MONKEY AROUND WITH THE TEMP CONTROLS AS A MATTER OF ROUTINE, *MOON-STONE.*
THEY *LIKE* KEEPING THEIR PRISONERS UNCOMFOR-TABLE.
SEAGATE IS AS MUCH A BIG EXPERIMENT IN *SOCIAL DEPRIVATION* AS IT IS A PRISON.
EVEN SO, I'M STILL NOT COMFORTABLE WITH WHAT WE HAD TO DO.
US MUCH CHOICE, *HAWKEYE.*
Oh, I KNOW -- BUT THAT DOESN'T MEAN I HAVE TO *LIKE IT!*
THE EX-AVENGER HAS LED THE **THUNDERBOLTS** *-- FORMER* **VILLAINS TURNED WOULD-BE HEROES** *-- ALONG A FINE LINE BETWEEN FOLLOWING THE* **LAW** *AND FOLLOWING THEIR* **CONSCIENCE.**

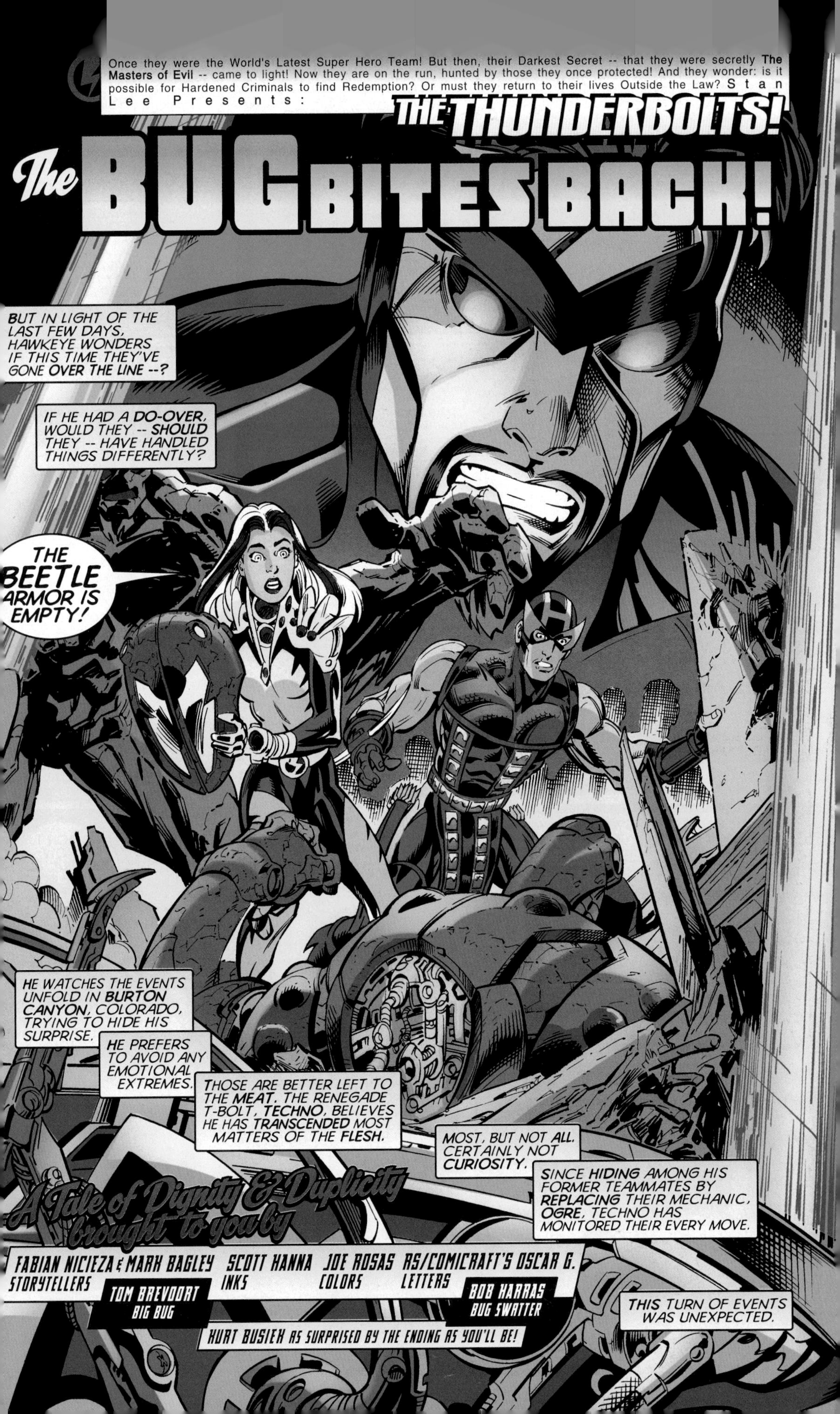
Once they were the World's Latest Super Hero Team! But then, their Darkest Secret -- that they were secretly **The Masters of Evil** -- came to light! Now they are on the run, hunted by those they once protected! And they wonder: is it possible for Hardened Criminals to find Redemption? Or must they return to their lives Outside the Law? Stan Lee Presents:
THE THUNDERBOLTS!
The BUG BITES BACK!
BUT IN LIGHT OF THE LAST FEW DAYS, HAWKEYE WONDERS IF THIS TIME THEY'VE GONE OVER THE LINE --?
IF HE HAD A DO-OVER, WOULD THEY -- SHOULD THEY -- HAVE HANDLED THINGS DIFFERENTLY?
THE BEETLE ARMOR IS EMPTY!
HE WATCHES THE EVENTS UNFOLD IN BURTON CANYON, COLORADO, TRYING TO HIDE HIS SURPRISE.
HE PREFERS TO AVOID ANY EMOTIONAL EXTREMES.
THOSE ARE BETTER LEFT TO THE MEAT. THE RENEGADE T-BOLT, TECHNO, BELIEVES HE HAS TRANSCENDED MOST MATTERS OF THE FLESH.
MOST, BUT NOT ALL. CERTAINLY NOT CURIOSITY.
SINCE HIDING AMONG HIS FORMER TEAMMATES BY REPLACING THEIR MECHANIC, OGRE, TECHNO HAS MONITORED THEIR EVERY MOVE.
A Tale of Dignity & Duplicity brought to you by
FABIAN NICIEZA & MARK BAGLEY STORYTELLERS
SCOTT HANNA INKS
JOE ROSAS COLORS
RS/COMICRAFT'S OSCAR G. LETTERS
TOM BREVOORT BIG BUG
BOB HARRAS BUG SWATTER
KURT BUSIEK AS SURPRISED BY THE ENDING AS YOU'LL BE!
THIS TURN OF EVENTS WAS UNEXPECTED.

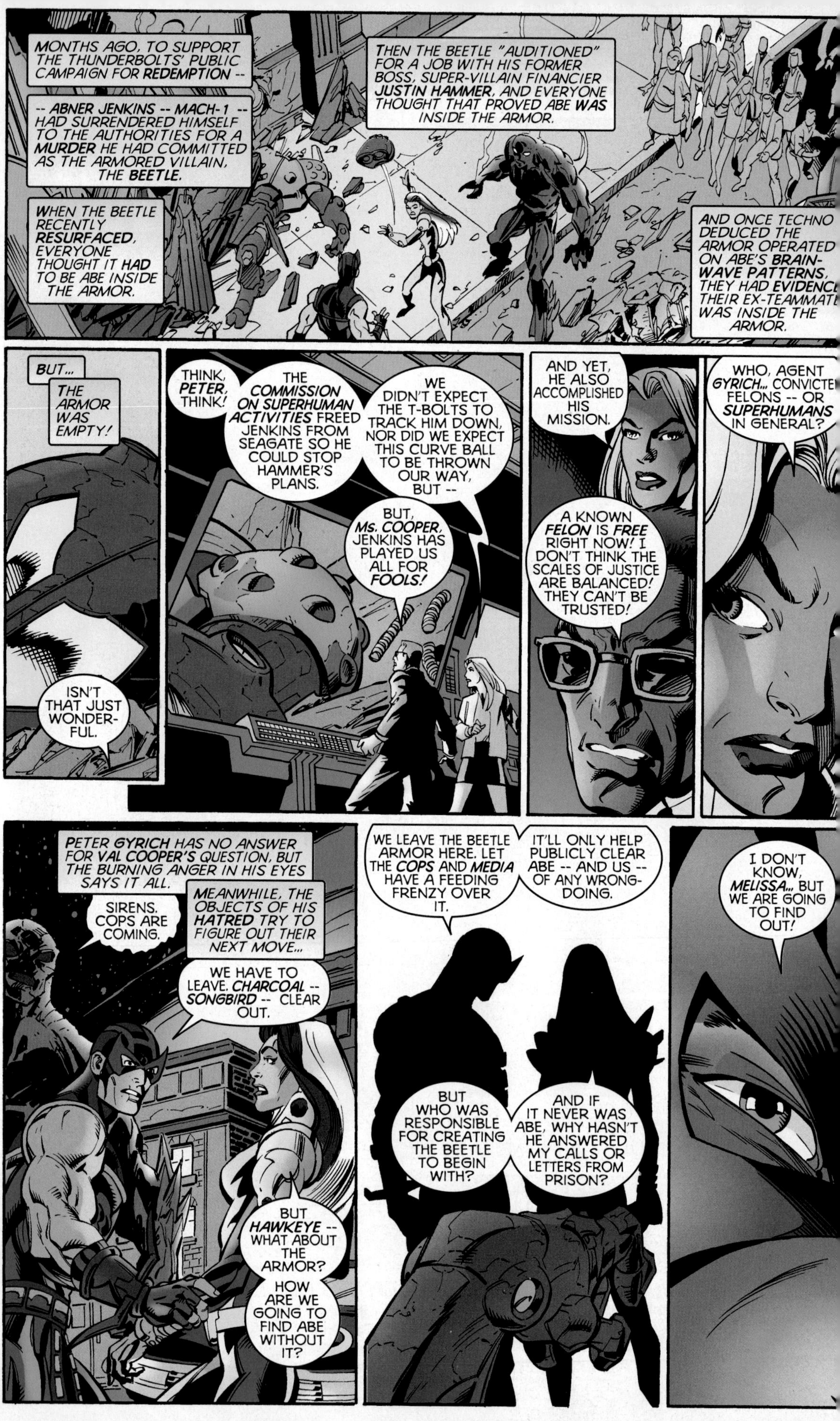
MONTHS AGO, TO SUPPORT THE THUNDERBOLTS' PUBLIC CAMPAIGN FOR REDEMPTION --
-- ABNER JENKINS -- MACH-1 -- HAD SURRENDERED HIMSELF TO THE AUTHORITIES FOR A MURDER HE HAD COMMITTED AS THE ARMORED VILLAIN, THE BEETLE.
WHEN THE BEETLE RECENTLY RESURFACED, EVERYONE THOUGHT IT HAD TO BE ABE INSIDE THE ARMOR.
THEN THE BEETLE "AUDITIONED" FOR A JOB WITH HIS FORMER BOSS, SUPER-VILLAIN FINANCIER JUSTIN HAMMER, AND EVERYONE THOUGHT THAT PROVED ABE WAS INSIDE THE ARMOR.
AND ONCE TECHNO DEDUCED THE ARMOR OPERATED ON ABE'S BRAIN-WAVE PATTERNS, THEY HAD EVIDENCE THEIR EX-TEAMMATE WAS INSIDE THE ARMOR.
BUT...
THE ARMOR WAS EMPTY!
ISN'T THAT JUST WONDER-FUL.
THINK, PETER, THINK!
THE COMMISSION ON SUPERHUMAN ACTIVITIES FREED JENKINS FROM SEAGATE SO HE COULD STOP HAMMER'S PLANS.
WE DIDN'T EXPECT THE T-BOLTS TO TRACK HIM DOWN, NOR DID WE EXPECT THIS CURVE BALL TO BE THROWN OUR WAY, BUT --
BUT, Ms. COOPER, JENKINS HAS PLAYED US ALL FOR FOOLS!
AND YET, HE ALSO ACCOMPLISHED HIS MISSION.
A KNOWN FELON IS FREE RIGHT NOW! I DON'T THINK THE SCALES OF JUSTICE ARE BALANCED! THEY CAN'T BE TRUSTED!
WHO, AGENT GYRICH... CONVICTED FELONS -- OR SUPERHUMANS IN GENERAL?
PETER GYRICH HAS NO ANSWER FOR VAL COOPER'S QUESTION, BUT THE BURNING ANGER IN HIS EYES SAYS IT ALL.
SIRENS. COPS ARE COMING.
MEANWHILE, THE OBJECTS OF HIS HATRED TRY TO FIGURE OUT THEIR NEXT MOVE...
WE HAVE TO LEAVE. CHARCOAL -- SONGBIRD -- CLEAR OUT.
BUT HAWKEYE -- WHAT ABOUT THE ARMOR?
HOW ARE WE GOING TO FIND ABE WITHOUT IT?
WE LEAVE THE BEETLE ARMOR HERE. LET THE COPS AND MEDIA HAVE A FEEDING FRENZY OVER IT.
IT'LL ONLY HELP PUBLICLY CLEAR ABE -- AND US -- OF ANY WRONG-DOING.
BUT WHO WAS RESPONSIBLE FOR CREATING THE BEETLE TO BEGIN WITH?
AND IF IT NEVER WAS ABE, WHY HASN'T HE ANSWERED MY CALLS OR LETTERS FROM PRISON?
I DON'T KNOW, MELISSA... BUT WE ARE GOING TO FIND OUT!

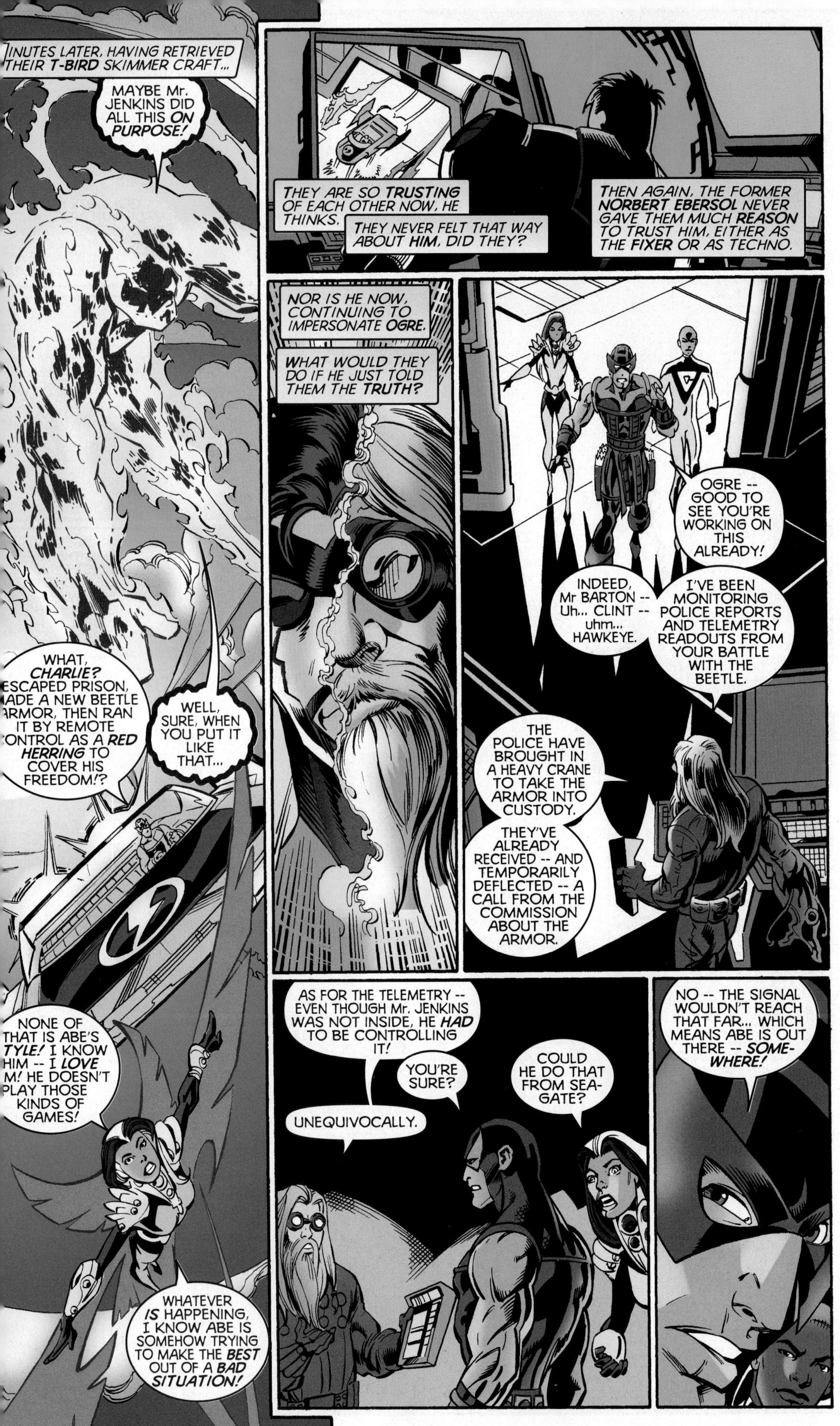
INUTES LATER, HAVING RETRIEVED THEIR T-BIRD SKIMMER CRAFT...
MAYBE Mr. JENKINS DID ALL THIS ON PURPOSE!
WHAT, CHARLIE? ESCAPED PRISON, ADE A NEW BEETLE RMOR, THEN RAN IT BY REMOTE ONTROL AS A RED HERRING TO COVER HIS FREEDOM!?
WELL, SURE, WHEN YOU PUT IT LIKE THAT...
NONE OF THAT IS ABE'S TYLE! I KNOW HIM -- I LOVE M! HE DOESN'T PLAY THOSE KINDS OF GAMES!
WHATEVER IS HAPPENING, I KNOW ABE IS SOMEHOW TRYING TO MAKE THE BEST OUT OF A BAD SITUATION!
THEY ARE SO TRUSTING OF EACH OTHER NOW, HE THINKS.
THEY NEVER FELT THAT WAY ABOUT HIM, DID THEY?
THEN AGAIN, THE FORMER NORBERT EBERSOL NEVER GAVE THEM MUCH REASON TO TRUST HIM, EITHER AS THE FIXER OR AS TECHNO.
NOR IS HE NOW, CONTINUING TO IMPERSONATE OGRE.
WHAT WOULD THEY DO IF HE JUST TOLD THEM THE TRUTH?
OGRE -- GOOD TO SEE YOU'RE WORKING ON THIS ALREADY!
INDEED, Mr BARTON -- Uh... CLINT -- uhm... HAWKEYE.
I'VE BEEN MONITORING POLICE REPORTS AND TELEMETRY READOUTS FROM YOUR BATTLE WITH THE BEETLE.
THE POLICE HAVE BROUGHT IN A HEAVY CRANE TO TAKE THE ARMOR INTO CUSTODY.
THEY'VE ALREADY RECEIVED -- AND TEMPORARILY DEFLECTED -- A CALL FROM THE COMMISSION ABOUT THE ARMOR.
AS FOR THE TELEMETRY -- EVEN THOUGH Mr. JENKINS WAS NOT INSIDE, HE HAD TO BE CONTROLLING IT!
YOU'RE SURE?
UNEQUIVOCALLY.
COULD HE DO THAT FROM SEA-GATE?
NO -- THE SIGNAL WOULDN'T REACH THAT FAR... WHICH MEANS ABE IS OUT THERE -- SOME-WHERE!

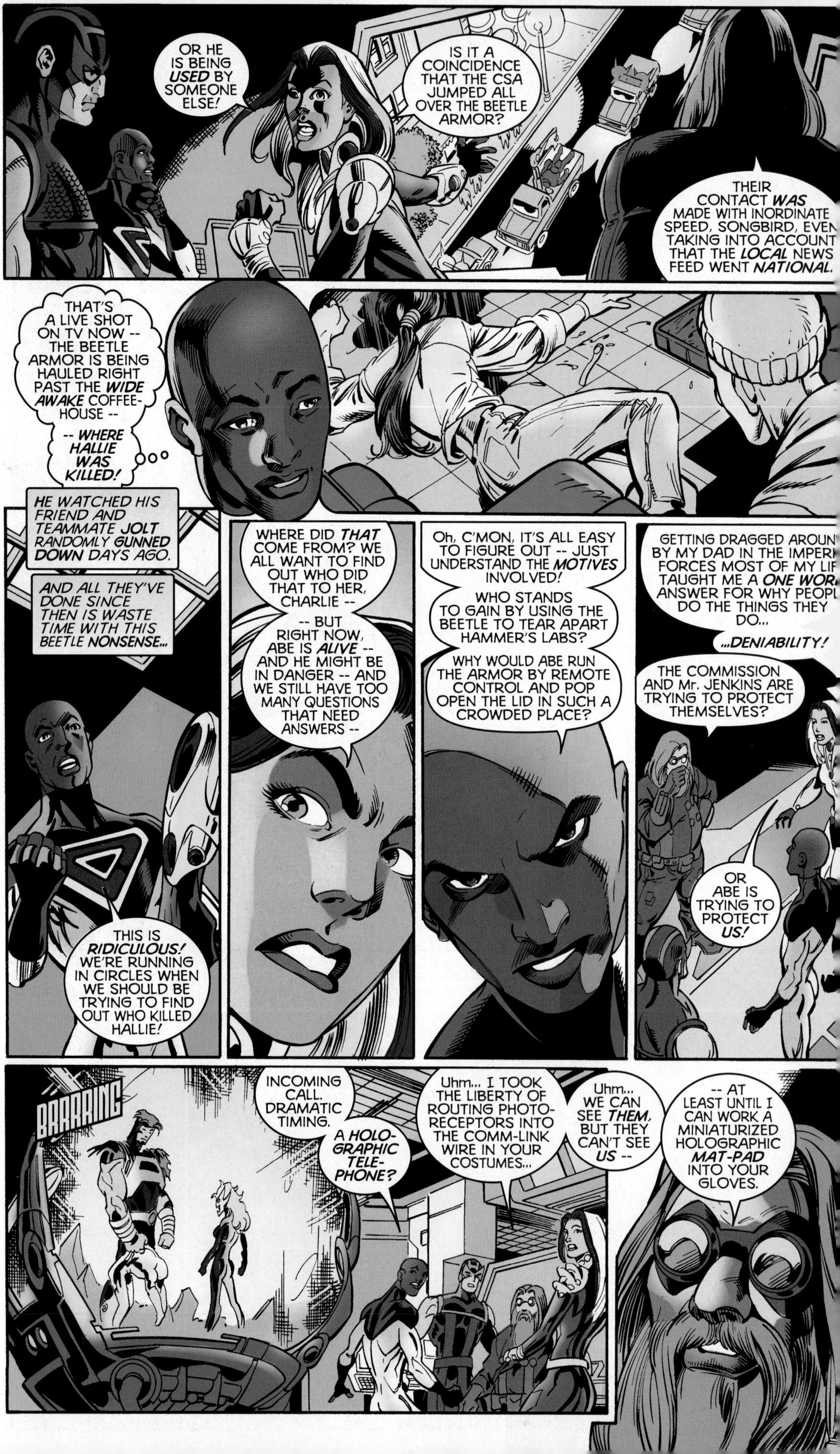
OR HE IS BEING USED BY SOMEONE ELSE!
IS IT A COINCIDENCE THAT THE CSA JUMPED ALL OVER THE BEETLE ARMOR?
THEIR CONTACT WAS MADE WITH INORDINATE SPEED, SONGBIRD, EVEN TAKING INTO ACCOUNT THAT THE LOCAL NEWS FEED WENT NATIONAL.
THAT'S A LIVE SHOT ON TV NOW -- THE BEETLE ARMOR IS BEING HAULED RIGHT PAST THE WIDE AWAKE COFFEE-HOUSE --
-- WHERE HALLIE WAS KILLED!
HE WATCHED HIS FRIEND AND TEAMMATE JOLT RANDOMLY GUNNED DOWN DAYS AGO.
AND ALL THEY'VE DONE SINCE THEN IS WASTE TIME WITH THIS BEETLE NONSENSE...
THIS IS RIDICULOUS! WE'RE RUNNING IN CIRCLES WHEN WE SHOULD BE TRYING TO FIND OUT WHO KILLED HALLIE!
WHERE DID THAT COME FROM? WE ALL WANT TO FIND OUT WHO DID THAT TO HER, CHARLIE --
-- BUT RIGHT NOW, ABE IS ALIVE -- AND HE MIGHT BE IN DANGER -- AND WE STILL HAVE TOO MANY QUESTIONS THAT NEED ANSWERS --
Oh, C'MON, IT'S ALL EASY TO FIGURE OUT -- JUST UNDERSTAND THE MOTIVES INVOLVED!
WHO STANDS TO GAIN BY USING THE BEETLE TO TEAR APART HAMMER'S LABS?
WHY WOULD ABE RUN THE ARMOR BY REMOTE CONTROL AND POP OPEN THE LID IN SUCH A CROWDED PLACE?
GETTING DRAGGED AROUN BY MY DAD IN THE IMPERI FORCES MOST OF MY LIF TAUGHT ME A ONE WOR ANSWER FOR WHY PEOPL DO THE THINGS THEY DO...
...DENIABILITY!
THE COMMISSION AND Mr. JENKINS ARE TRYING TO PROTECT THEMSELVES?
OR ABE IS TRYING TO PROTECT US!
BRRRRING
INCOMING CALL. DRAMATIC TIMING.
A HOLO-GRAPHIC TELE-PHONE?
Uhm... I TOOK THE LIBERTY OF ROUTING PHOTO-RECEPTORS INTO THE COMM-LINK WIRE IN YOUR COSTUMES...
Uhm... WE CAN SEE THEM, BUT THEY CAN'T SEE US --
-- AT LEAST UNTIL I CAN WORK A MINIATURIZED HOLOGRAPHIC MAT-PAD INTO YOUR GLOVES.

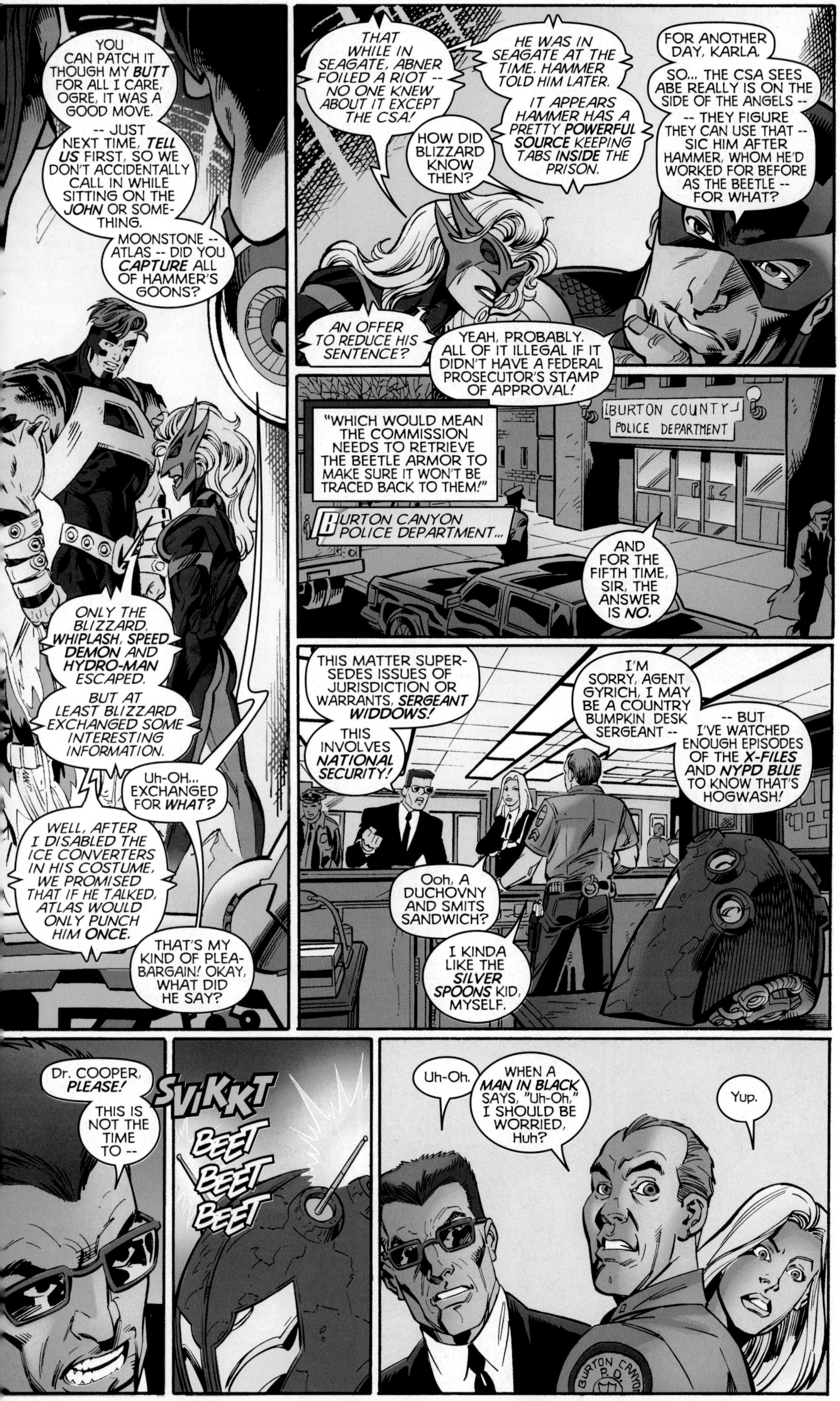
YOU CAN PATCH IT THOUGH MY *BUTT* FOR ALL I CARE, OGRE, IT WAS A GOOD MOVE.
-- JUST NEXT TIME, ***TELL US*** FIRST, SO WE DON'T ACCIDENTALLY CALL IN WHILE SITTING ON THE ***JOHN*** OR SOMETHING.
MOONSTONE -- ATLAS -- DID YOU ***CAPTURE*** ALL OF HAMMER'S GOONS?
ONLY THE BLIZZARD, ***WHIPLASH, SPEED DEMON*** AND ***HYDRO-MAN*** ESCAPED.
BUT AT LEAST BLIZZARD EXCHANGED SOME INTERESTING INFORMATION.
Uh-OH... EXCHANGED FOR ***WHAT?***
WELL, AFTER I DISABLED THE ICE CONVERTERS IN HIS COSTUME, WE PROMISED THAT IF HE TALKED, ATLAS WOULD ONLY PUNCH HIM ***ONCE.***
THAT'S MY KIND OF PLEA-BARGAIN! OKAY, WHAT DID HE SAY?
THAT WHILE IN SEAGATE, ABNER FOILED A RIOT -- NO ONE KNEW ABOUT IT EXCEPT THE CSA!
HOW DID BLIZZARD KNOW THEN?
HE WAS IN SEAGATE AT THE TIME. HAMMER TOLD HIM LATER.
IT APPEARS ***HAMMER*** HAS A PRETTY ***POWERFUL SOURCE*** KEEPING TABS ***INSIDE*** THE PRISON.
FOR ANOTHER DAY, KARLA.
SO..., THE CSA SEES ABE REALLY IS ON THE SIDE OF THE ANGELS --
-- THEY FIGURE THEY CAN USE THAT -- SIC HIM AFTER HAMMER, WHOM HE'D WORKED FOR BEFORE AS THE BEETLE -- FOR WHAT?
AN OFFER TO REDUCE HIS SENTENCE?
YEAH, PROBABLY. ALL OF IT ILLEGAL IF IT DIDN'T HAVE A FEDERAL PROSECUTOR'S STAMP OF APPROVAL!
"WHICH WOULD MEAN THE COMMISSION NEEDS TO RETRIEVE THE BEETLE ARMOR TO MAKE SURE IT WON'T BE TRACED BACK TO THEM!"
BURTON COUNTY POLICE DEPARTMENT
BURTON CANYON POLICE DEPARTMENT...
AND FOR THE FIFTH TIME, SIR, THE ANSWER IS ***NO.***
THIS MATTER SUPERSEDES ISSUES OF JURISDICTION OR WARRANTS, ***SERGEANT WIDDOWS!***
THIS INVOLVES ***NATIONAL SECURITY!***
I'M SORRY, AGENT GYRICH, I MAY BE A COUNTRY BUMPKIN DESK SERGEANT --
-- BUT I'VE WATCHED ENOUGH EPISODES OF THE ***X-FILES*** AND ***NYPD BLUE*** TO KNOW THAT'S HOGWASH!
Ooh, A DUCHOVNY AND SMITS SANDWICH?
I KINDA LIKE THE ***SILVER SPOONS*** KID, MYSELF.
Dr. COOPER, ***PLEASE!***
THIS IS NOT THE TIME TO --
SVIKKKT
BEET BEET BEET
Uh-Oh.
WHEN A ***MAN IN BLACK*** SAYS, "Uh-Oh," I SHOULD BE WORRIED, Huh?
Yup.
BURTON CANYON P.D.

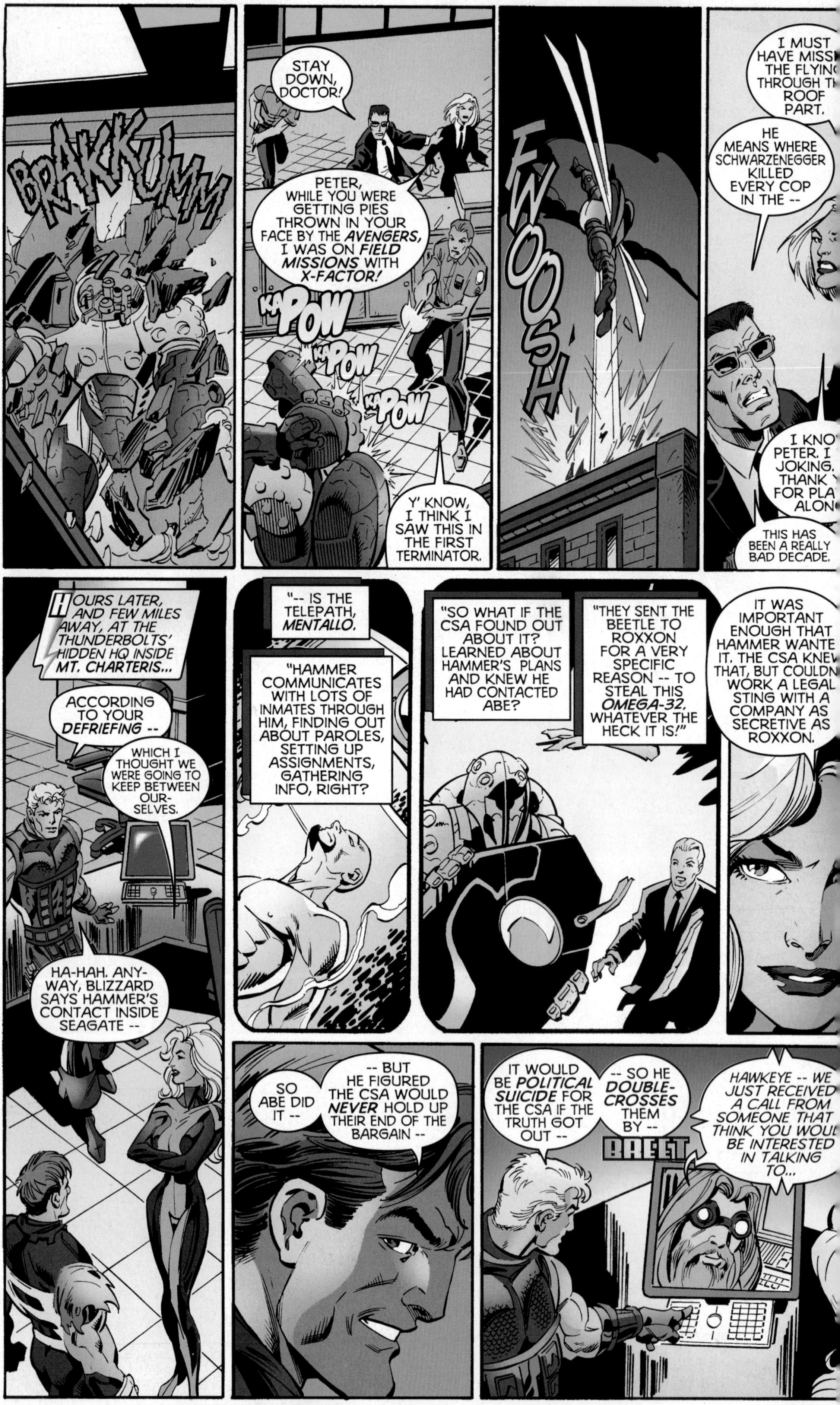

BRAKKUMM
STAY DOWN, DOCTOR!
PETER, WHILE YOU WERE GETTING PIES THROWN IN YOUR FACE BY THE *AVENGERS,* I WAS ON *FIELD MISSIONS* WITH *X-FACTOR!*
KAPOW
KAPOW
KAPOW
Y' KNOW, I THINK I SAW THIS IN THE FIRST TERMINATOR.
FWOOSH
I MUST HAVE MISS THE FLYIN THROUGH T ROOF PART.
HE MEANS WHERE SCHWARZENEGGER KILLED EVERY COP IN THE --
I KNO PETER. I JOKING. THANK FOR PLA ALON
THIS HAS BEEN A REALLY BAD DECADE.
HOURS LATER, AND FEW MILES AWAY, AT THE THUNDERBOLTS' HIDDEN HQ INSIDE *MT. CHARTERIS...*
ACCORDING TO YOUR *DEFRIEFING* --
WHICH I THOUGHT WE WERE GOING TO KEEP BETWEEN OUR-SELVES.
HA-HAH. ANY-WAY, BLIZZARD SAYS HAMMER'S CONTACT INSIDE SEAGATE --
"-- IS THE TELEPATH, *MENTALLO.*
"HAMMER COMMUNICATES WITH LOTS OF INMATES THROUGH HIM, FINDING OUT ABOUT PAROLES, SETTING UP ASSIGNMENTS, GATHERING INFO, RIGHT?
"SO WHAT IF THE CSA FOUND OUT ABOUT IT? LEARNED ABOUT HAMMER'S PLANS AND KNEW HE HAD CONTACTED ABE?
"THEY SENT THE BEETLE TO ROXXON FOR A VERY SPECIFIC REASON -- TO STEAL THIS *OMEGA-32,* WHATEVER THE HECK IT IS!"
IT WAS IMPORTANT ENOUGH THAT HAMMER WANTE IT. THE CSA KNEW THAT, BUT COULDN WORK A LEGAL STING WITH A COMPANY AS SECRETIVE AS ROXXON.
SO ABE DID IT --
-- BUT HE FIGURED THE CSA WOULD *NEVER* HOLD UP THEIR END OF THE BARGAIN --
IT WOULD BE *POLITICAL SUICIDE* FOR THE CSA IF THE TRUTH GOT OUT --
-- SO HE *DOUBLE-CROSSES* THEM BY --
BREET
HAWKEYE -- WE JUST RECEIVED A CALL FROM SOMEONE THAT THINK YOU WOUL BE INTERESTED IN TALKING TO...

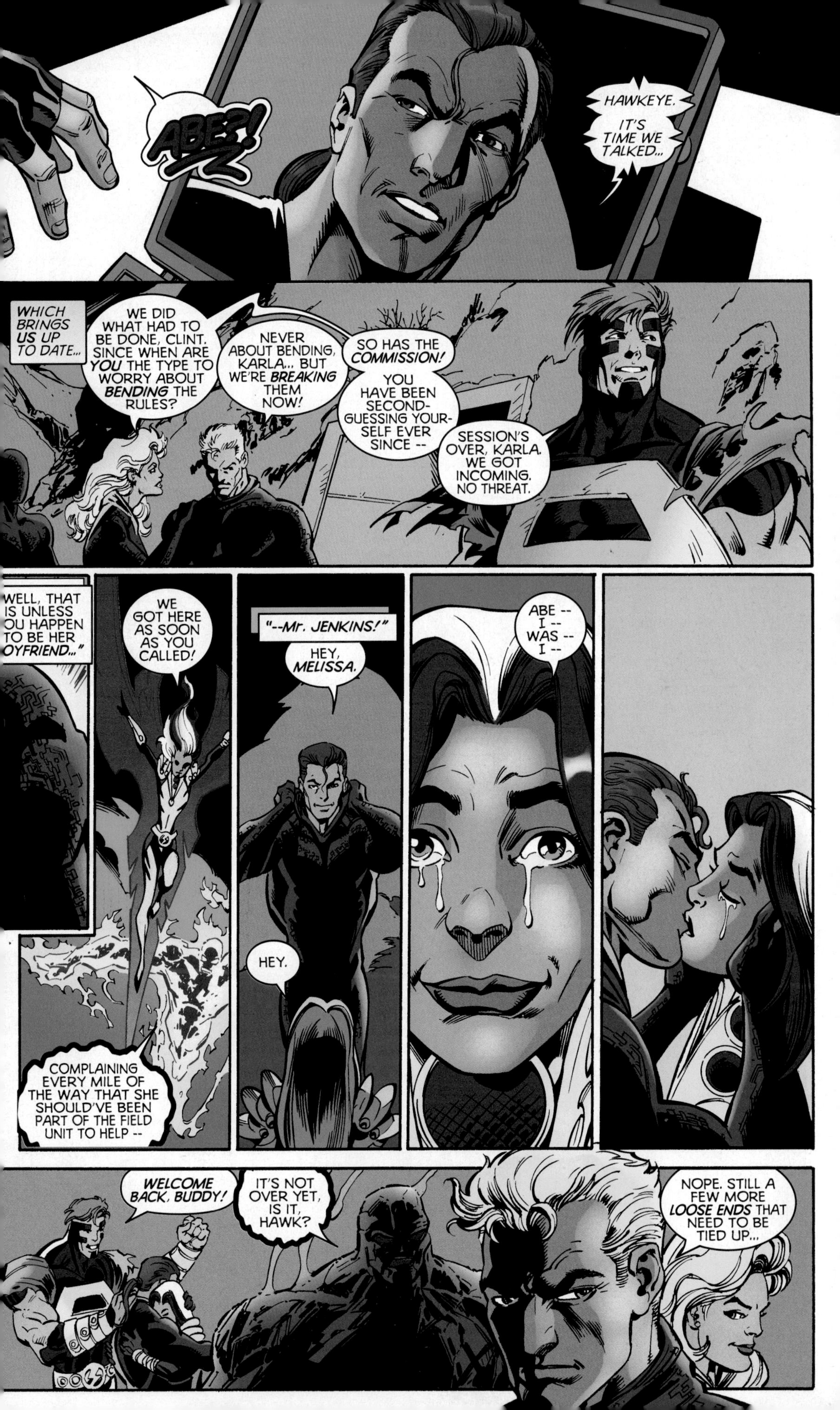

ABE?!
HAWKEYE. IT'S TIME WE TALKED...
WHICH BRINGS US UP TO DATE...
WE DID WHAT HAD TO BE DONE, CLINT. SINCE WHEN ARE YOU THE TYPE TO WORRY ABOUT BENDING THE RULES?
NEVER ABOUT BENDING, KARLA... BUT WE'RE BREAKING THEM NOW!
SO HAS THE COMMISSION!
YOU HAVE BEEN SECOND-GUESSING YOURSELF EVER SINCE --
SESSION'S OVER, KARLA. WE GOT INCOMING. NO THREAT.
WELL, THAT IS UNLESS OU HAPPEN TO BE HER OYFRIEND..."
WE GOT HERE AS SOON AS YOU CALLED!
COMPLAINING EVERY MILE OF THE WAY THAT SHE SHOULD'VE BEEN PART OF THE FIELD UNIT TO HELP --
"--Mr. JENKINS!"
HEY, MELISSA.
HEY.
ABE -- I -- WAS -- I --
WELCOME BACK, BUDDY!
IT'S NOT OVER YET, IS IT, HAWK?
NOPE. STILL A FEW MORE LOOSE ENDS THAT NEED TO BE TIED UP...

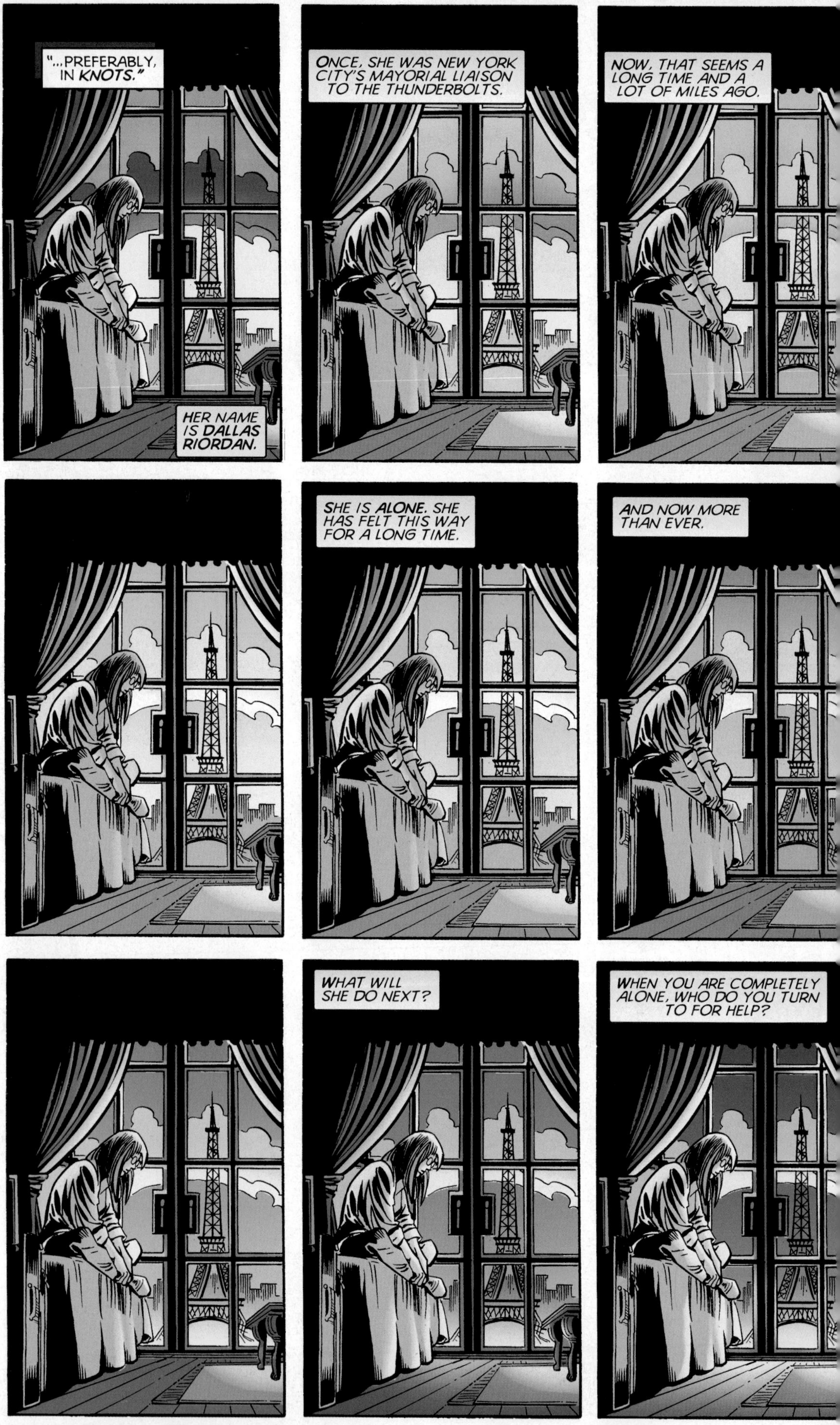
"...PREFERABLY, IN KNOTS."
HER NAME IS DALLAS RIORDAN.
ONCE, SHE WAS NEW YORK CITY'S MAYORIAL LIAISON TO THE THUNDERBOLTS.
NOW, THAT SEEMS A LONG TIME AND A LOT OF MILES AGO.
SHE IS ALONE. SHE HAS FELT THIS WAY FOR A LONG TIME.
AND NOW MORE THAN EVER.
WHAT WILL SHE DO NEXT?
WHEN YOU ARE COMPLETELY ALONE, WHO DO YOU TURN TO FOR HELP?

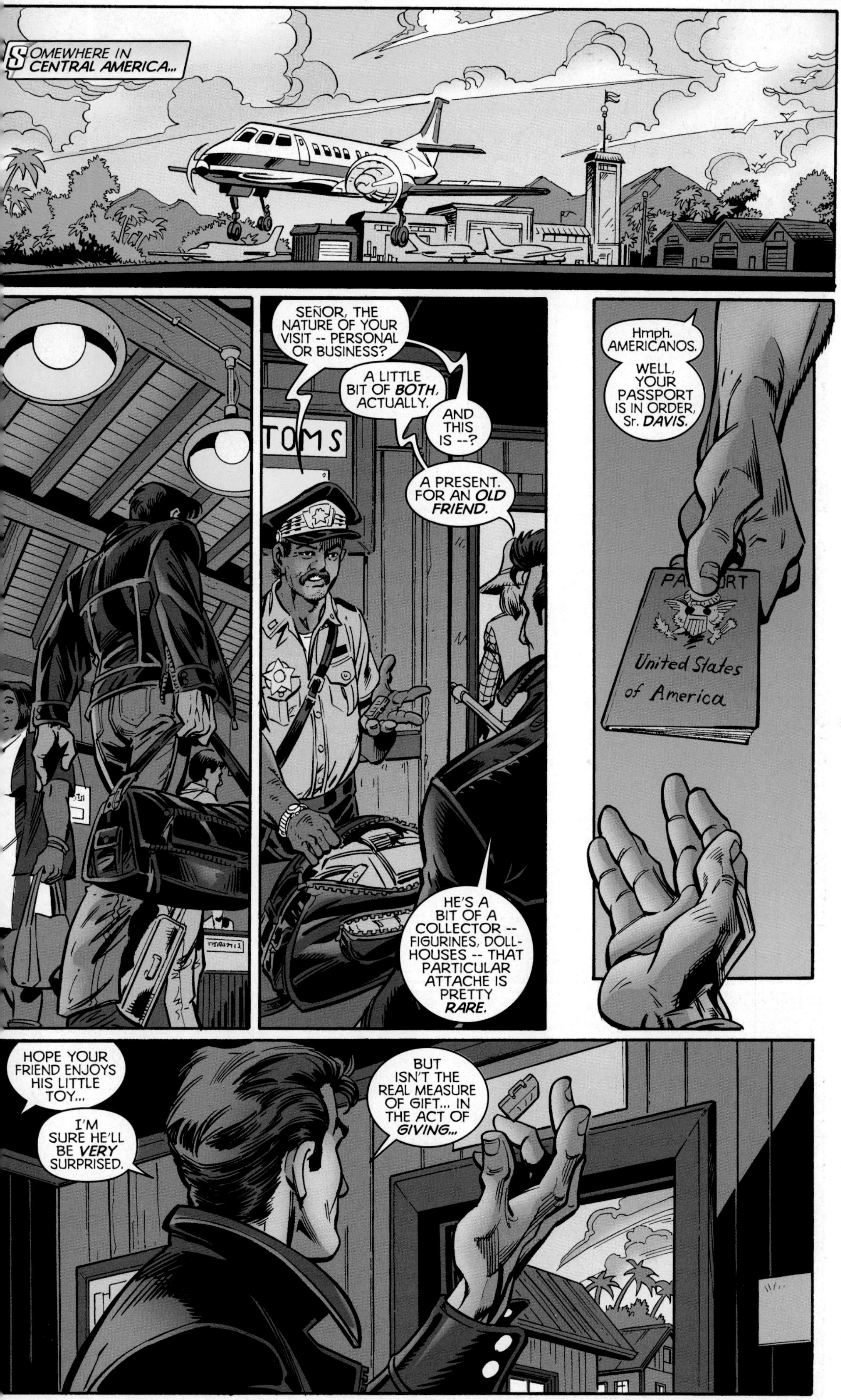
SOMEWHERE IN CENTRAL AMERICA...
SEÑOR, THE NATURE OF YOUR VISIT -- PERSONAL OR BUSINESS?
A LITTLE BIT OF BOTH, ACTUALLY.
AND THIS IS --?
A PRESENT. FOR AN OLD FRIEND.
TOMS
HE'S A BIT OF A COLLECTOR -- FIGURINES, DOLL-HOUSES -- THAT PARTICULAR ATTACHE IS PRETTY RARE.
Hmph. AMERICANOS.
WELL, YOUR PASSPORT IS IN ORDER, Sr. DAVIS.
PASSPORT
United States of America
HOPE YOUR FRIEND ENJOYS HIS LITTLE TOY...
I'M SURE HE'LL BE VERY SURPRISED.
BUT ISN'T THE REAL MEASURE OF GIFT... IN THE ACT OF GIVING...

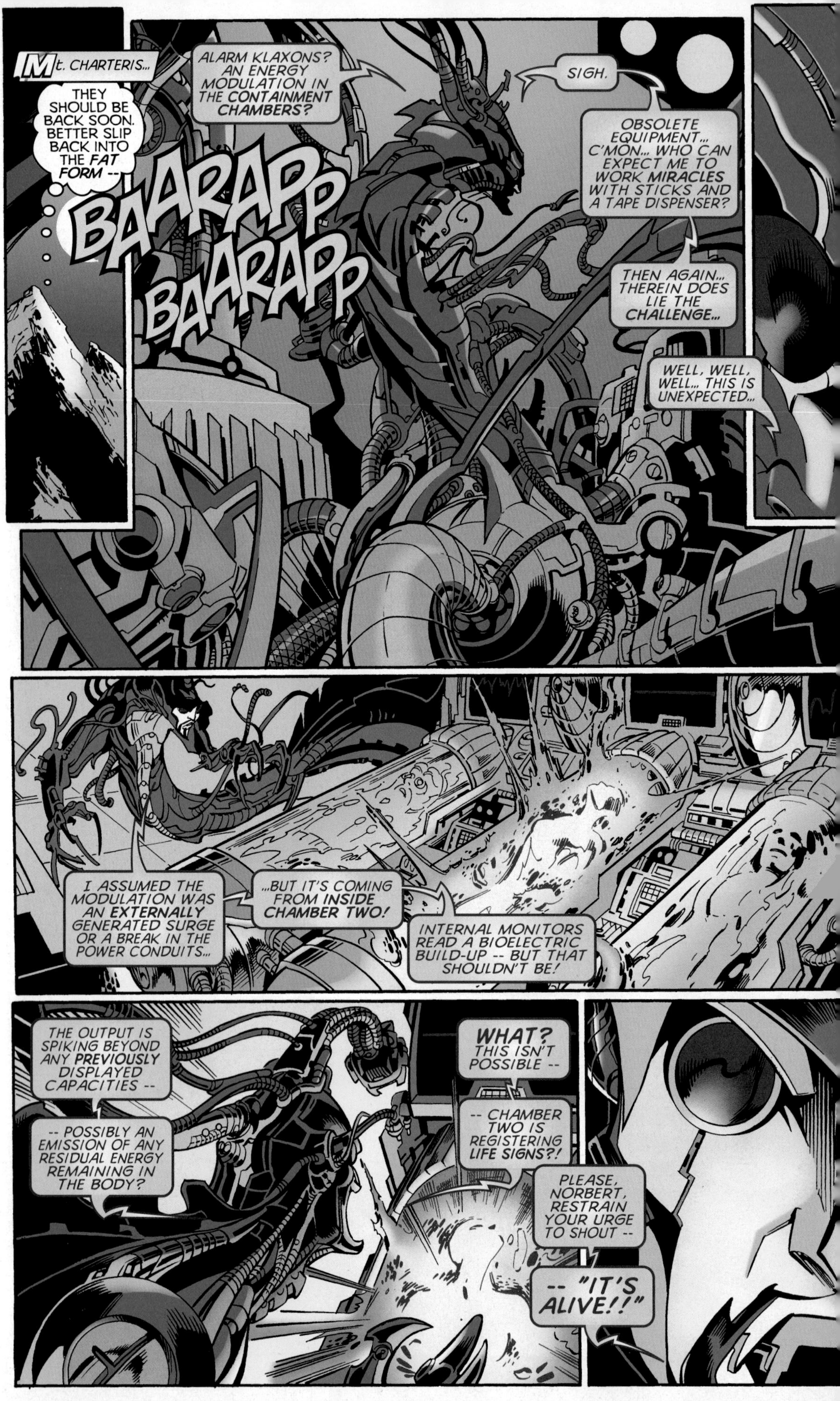

Mt. CHARTERIS...
THEY SHOULD BE BACK SOON. BETTER SLIP BACK INTO THE FAT FORM --
ALARM KLAXONS? AN ENERGY MODULATION IN THE CONTAINMENT CHAMBERS?
BAARAPP BAARAPP
SIGH.
OBSOLETE EQUIPMENT... C'MON... WHO CAN EXPECT ME TO WORK MIRACLES WITH STICKS AND A TAPE DISPENSER?
THEN AGAIN... THEREIN DOES LIE THE CHALLENGE...
WELL, WELL, WELL... THIS IS UNEXPECTED...
I ASSUMED THE MODULATION WAS AN EXTERNALLY GENERATED SURGE OR A BREAK IN THE POWER CONDUITS...
...BUT IT'S COMING FROM INSIDE CHAMBER TWO!
INTERNAL MONITORS READ A BIOELECTRIC BUILD-UP -- BUT THAT SHOULDN'T BE!
THE OUTPUT IS SPIKING BEYOND ANY PREVIOUSLY DISPLAYED CAPACITIES --
-- POSSIBLY AN EMISSION OF ANY RESIDUAL ENERGY REMAINING IN THE BODY?
WHAT? THIS ISN'T POSSIBLE --
-- CHAMBER TWO IS REGISTERING LIFE SIGNS?!
PLEASE, NORBERT, RESTRAIN YOUR URGE TO SHOUT --
-- "IT'S ALIVE!!"

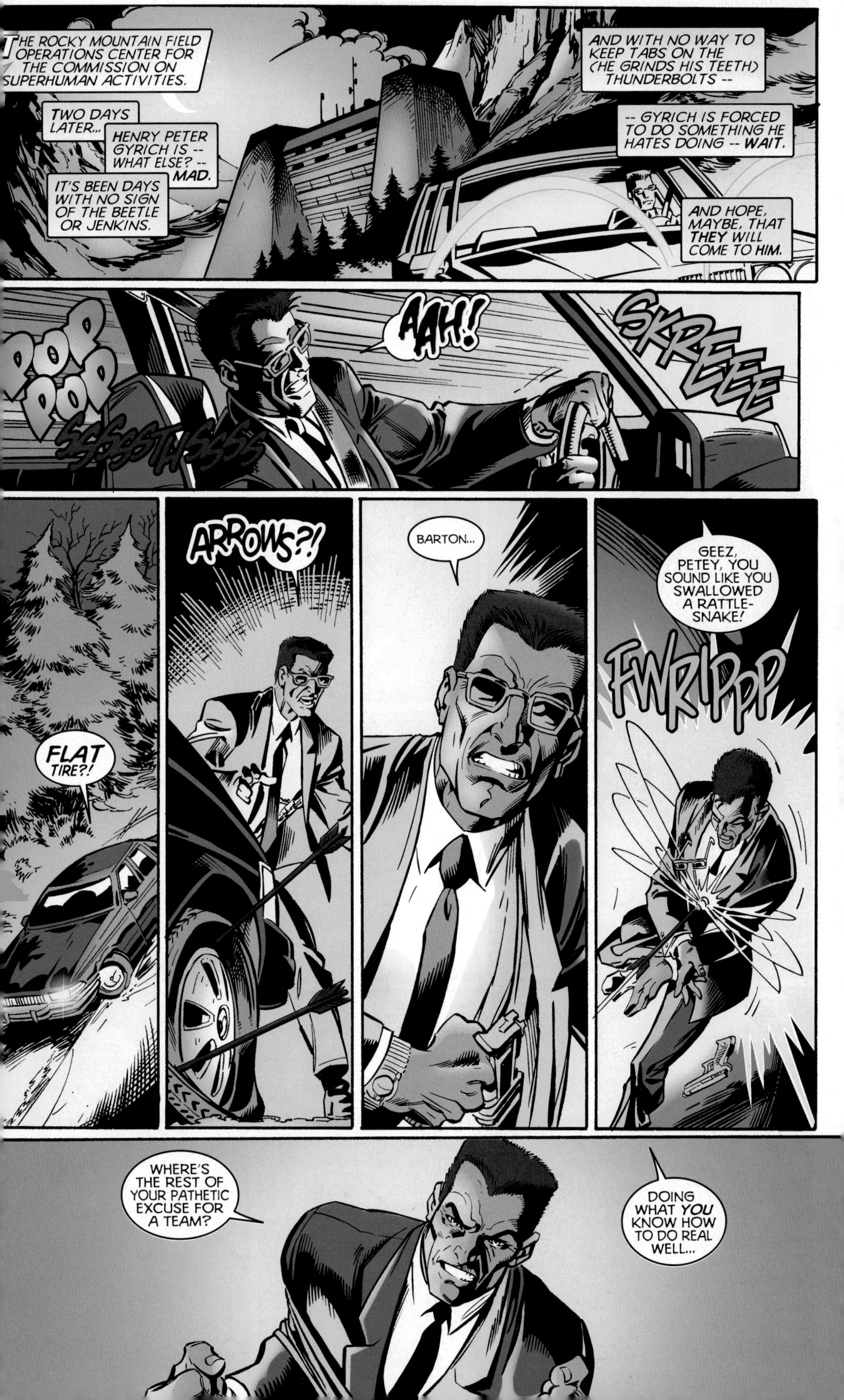
THE ROCKY MOUNTAIN FIELD OPERATIONS CENTER FOR THE COMMISSION ON SUPERHUMAN ACTIVITIES.
TWO DAYS LATER...
HENRY PETER GYRICH IS -- WHAT ELSE? -- MAD.
IT'S BEEN DAYS WITH NO SIGN OF THE BEETLE OR JENKINS.
AND WITH NO WAY TO KEEP TABS ON THE (HE GRINDS HIS TEETH) THUNDERBOLTS --
-- GYRICH IS FORCED TO DO SOMETHING HE HATES DOING -- WAIT.
AND HOPE, MAYBE, THAT THEY WILL COME TO HIM.
POP POP
SSSSSTHSSSS
AAH!
SKREEEE
FLAT TIRE?!
ARROWS?!
BARTON...
GEEZ, PETEY, YOU SOUND LIKE YOU SWALLOWED A RATTLE-SNAKE!
FWRIPPP
WHERE'S THE REST OF YOUR PATHETIC EXCUSE FOR A TEAM?
DOING WHAT YOU KNOW HOW TO DO REAL WELL...

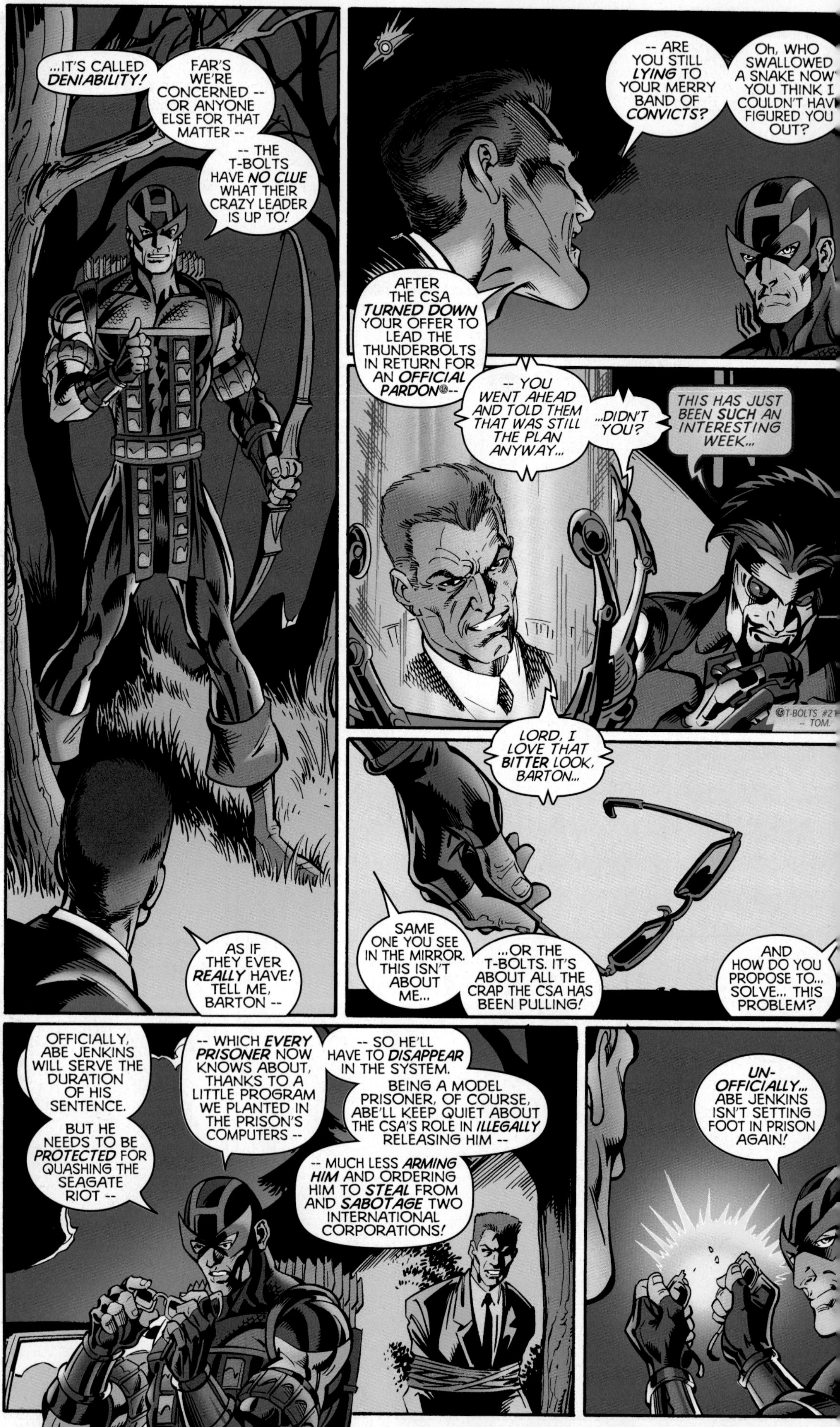

...IT'S CALLED DENIABILITY!
FAR'S WE'RE CONCERNED -- OR ANYONE ELSE FOR THAT MATTER --
-- THE T-BOLTS HAVE NO CLUE WHAT THEIR CRAZY LEADER IS UP TO!
AS IF THEY EVER REALLY HAVE! TELL ME, BARTON --
-- ARE YOU STILL LYING TO YOUR MERRY BAND OF CONVICTS?
Oh, WHO SWALLOWED A SNAKE NOW? YOU THINK I COULDN'T HAV FIGURED YOU OUT?
AFTER THE CSA TURNED DOWN YOUR OFFER TO LEAD THE THUNDERBOLTS IN RETURN FOR AN OFFICIAL PARDON--
-- YOU WENT AHEAD AND TOLD THEM THAT WAS STILL THE PLAN ANYWAY...
...DIDN'T YOU?
THIS HAS JUST BEEN SUCH AN INTERESTING WEEK...
T-BOLTS #21 -- TOM.
LORD, I LOVE THAT BITTER LOOK, BARTON...
SAME ONE YOU SEE IN THE MIRROR. THIS ISN'T ABOUT ME...
...OR THE T-BOLTS. IT'S ABOUT ALL THE CRAP THE CSA HAS BEEN PULLING!
AND HOW DO YOU PROPOSE TO... SOLVE... THIS PROBLEM?
OFFICIALLY, ABE JENKINS WILL SERVE THE DURATION OF HIS SENTENCE.
BUT HE NEEDS TO BE PROTECTED FOR QUASHING THE SEAGATE RIOT --
-- WHICH EVERY PRISONER NOW KNOWS ABOUT, THANKS TO A LITTLE PROGRAM WE PLANTED IN THE PRISON'S COMPUTERS --
-- SO HE'LL HAVE TO DISAPPEAR IN THE SYSTEM.
BEING A MODEL PRISONER, OF COURSE, ABE'LL KEEP QUIET ABOUT THE CSA'S ROLE IN ILLEGALLY RELEASING HIM --
-- MUCH LESS ARMING HIM AND ORDERING HIM TO STEAL FROM AND SABOTAGE TWO INTERNATIONAL CORPORATIONS!
UN-OFFICIALLY... ABE JENKINS ISN'T SETTING FOOT IN PRISON AGAIN!

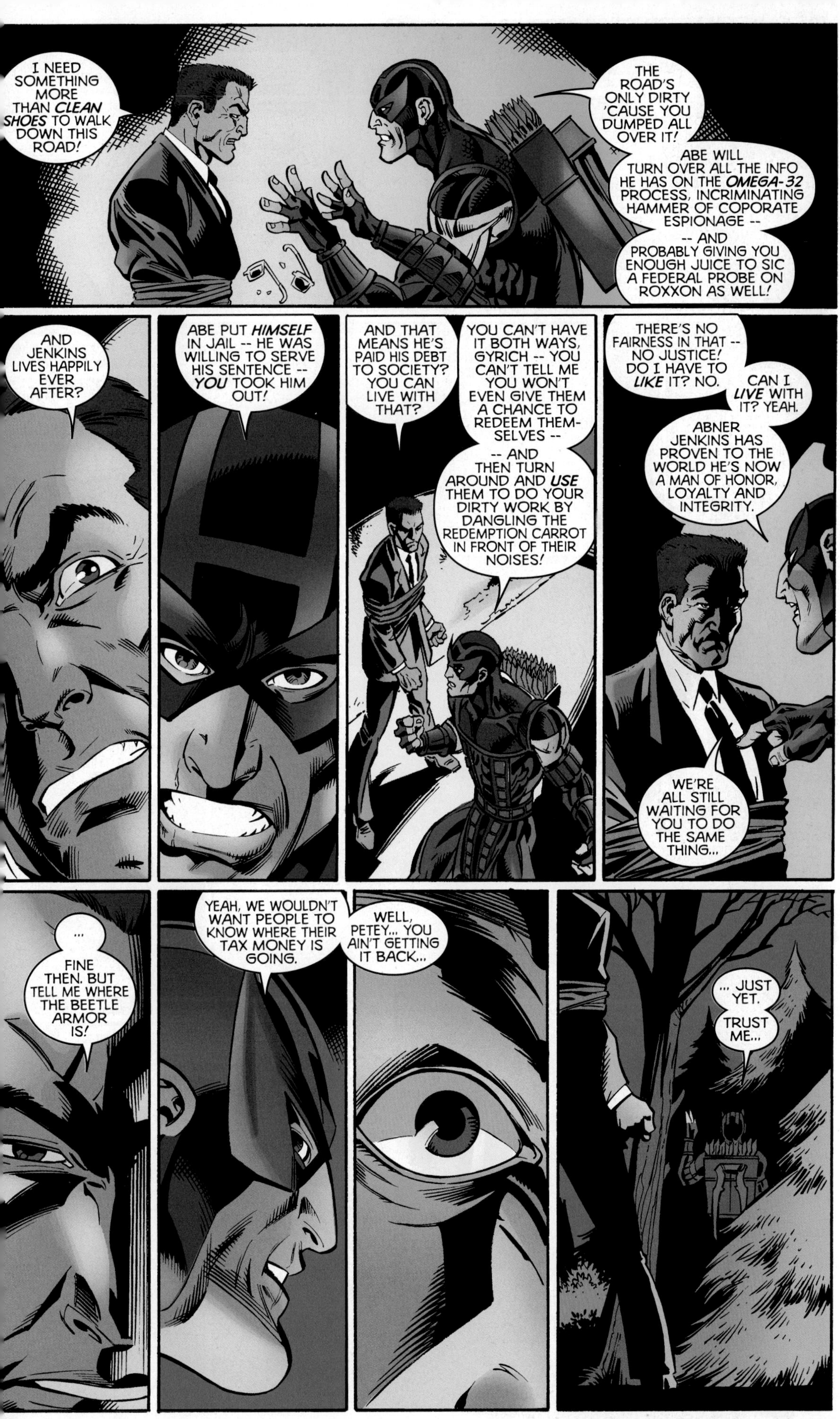
I NEED SOMETHING MORE THAN CLEAN SHOES TO WALK DOWN THIS ROAD!
THE ROAD'S ONLY DIRTY 'CAUSE YOU DUMPED ALL OVER IT!
ABE WILL TURN OVER ALL THE INFO HE HAS ON THE OMEGA-32 PROCESS, INCRIMINATING HAMMER OF COPORATE ESPIONAGE --
-- AND PROBABLY GIVING YOU ENOUGH JUICE TO SIC A FEDERAL PROBE ON ROXXON AS WELL!
AND JENKINS LIVES HAPPILY EVER AFTER?
ABE PUT HIMSELF IN JAIL -- HE WAS WILLING TO SERVE HIS SENTENCE -- YOU TOOK HIM OUT!
AND THAT MEANS HE'S PAID HIS DEBT TO SOCIETY? YOU CAN LIVE WITH THAT?
YOU CAN'T HAVE IT BOTH WAYS, GYRICH -- YOU CAN'T TELL ME YOU WON'T EVEN GIVE THEM A CHANCE TO REDEEM THEM-SELVES --
-- AND THEN TURN AROUND AND USE THEM TO DO YOUR DIRTY WORK BY DANGLING THE REDEMPTION CARROT IN FRONT OF THEIR NOISES!
THERE'S NO FAIRNESS IN THAT -- NO JUSTICE! DO I HAVE TO LIKE IT? NO.
CAN I LIVE WITH IT? YEAH.
ABNER JENKINS HAS PROVEN TO THE WORLD HE'S NOW A MAN OF HONOR, LOYALTY AND INTEGRITY.
WE'RE ALL STILL WAITING FOR YOU TO DO THE SAME THING...
...
FINE THEN. BUT TELL ME WHERE THE BEETLE ARMOR IS!
YEAH, WE WOULDN'T WANT PEOPLE TO KNOW WHERE THEIR TAX MONEY IS GOING.
WELL, PETEY... YOU AIN'T GETTING IT BACK...
... JUST YET.
TRUST ME...

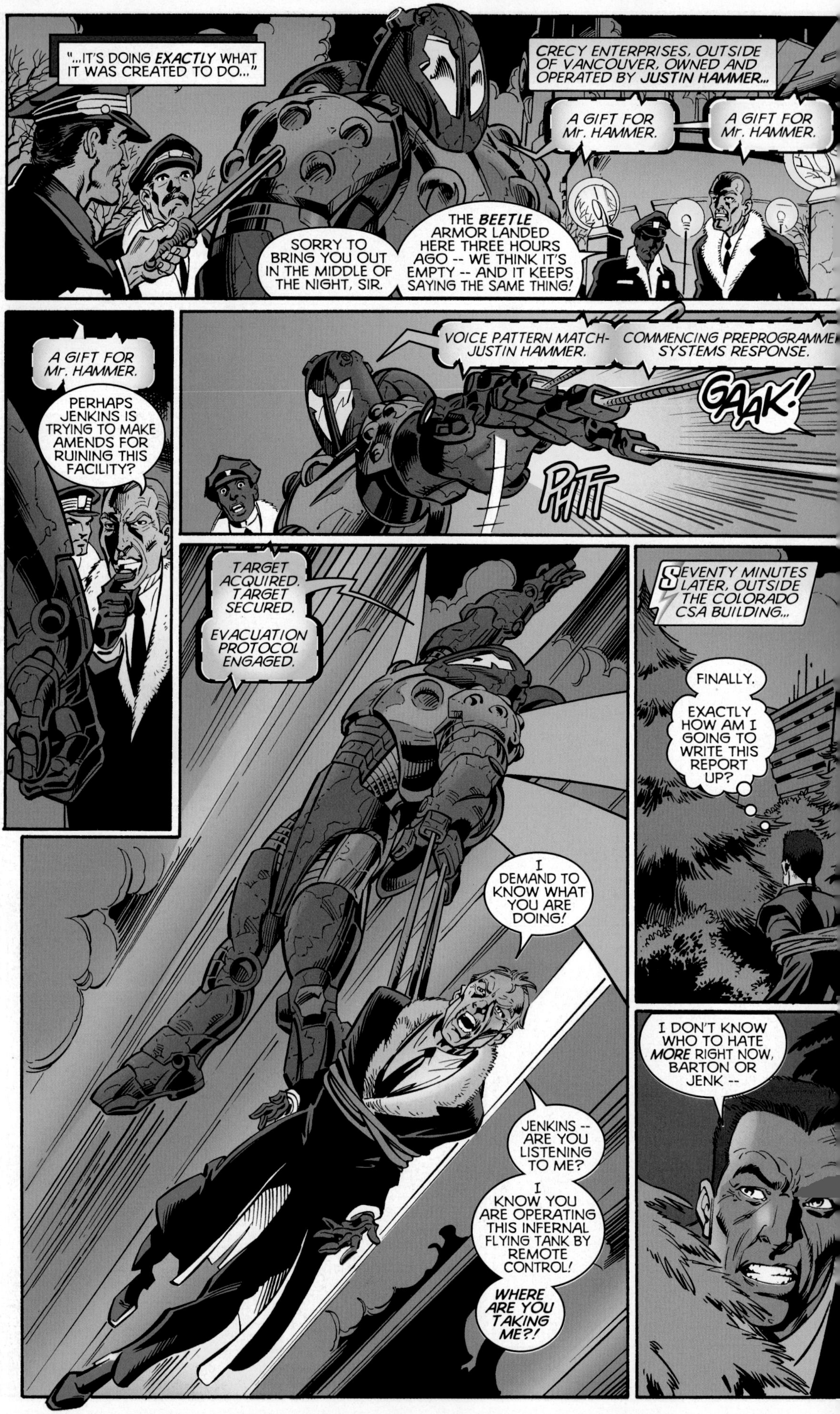
"...IT'S DOING EXACTLY WHAT IT WAS CREATED TO DO..."
CRECY ENTERPRISES, OUTSIDE OF VANCOUVER, OWNED AND OPERATED BY JUSTIN HAMMER...
A GIFT FOR Mr. HAMMER.
A GIFT FOR Mr. HAMMER.
SORRY TO BRING YOU OUT IN THE MIDDLE OF THE NIGHT, SIR.
THE BEETLE ARMOR LANDED HERE THREE HOURS AGO -- WE THINK IT'S EMPTY -- AND IT KEEPS SAYING THE SAME THING!
A GIFT FOR Mr. HAMMER.
PERHAPS JENKINS IS TRYING TO MAKE AMENDS FOR RUINING THIS FACILITY?
VOICE PATTERN MATCH-JUSTIN HAMMER.
COMMENCING PREPROGRAMME SYSTEMS RESPONSE.
GAAK!
PHTT
TARGET ACQUIRED. TARGET SECURED.
EVACUATION PROTOCOL ENGAGED.
I DEMAND TO KNOW WHAT YOU ARE DOING!
JENKINS -- ARE YOU LISTENING TO ME?
I KNOW YOU ARE OPERATING THIS INFERNAL FLYING TANK BY REMOTE CONTROL!
WHERE ARE YOU TAKING ME?!
SEVENTY MINUTES LATER, OUTSIDE THE COLORADO CSA BUILDING...
FINALLY.
EXACTLY HOW AM I GOING TO WRITE THIS REPORT UP?
I DON'T KNOW WHO TO HATE MORE RIGHT NOW, BARTON OR JENK --

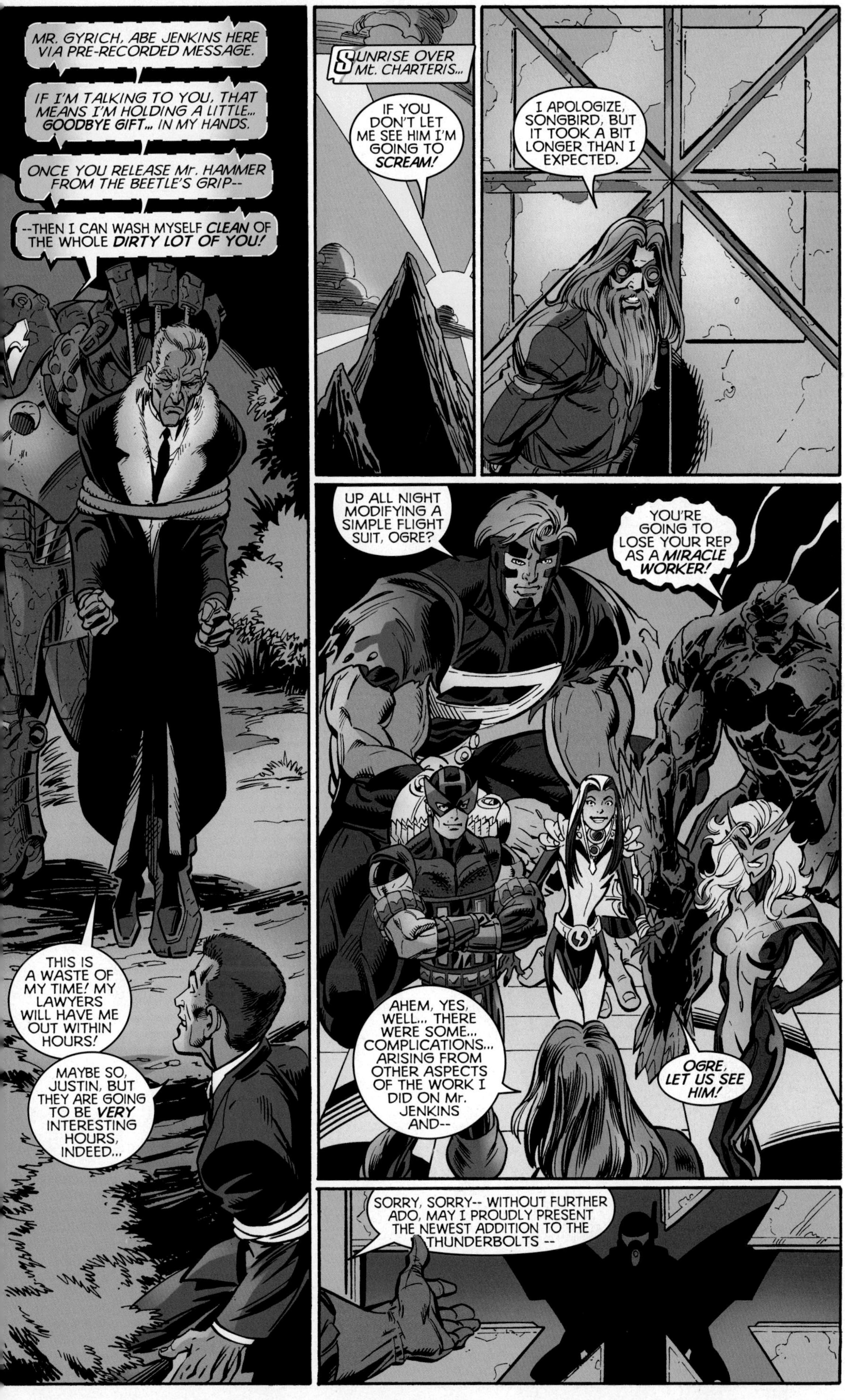
MR. GYRICH, ABE JENKINS HERE VIA PRE-RECORDED MESSAGE.
IF I'M TALKING TO YOU, THAT MEANS I'M HOLDING A LITTLE... GOODBYE GIFT... IN MY HANDS.
ONCE YOU RELEASE Mr. HAMMER FROM THE BEETLE'S GRIP--
--THEN I CAN WASH MYSELF CLEAN OF THE WHOLE DIRTY LOT OF YOU!
THIS IS A WASTE OF MY TIME! MY LAWYERS WILL HAVE ME OUT WITHIN HOURS!
MAYBE SO, JUSTIN, BUT THEY ARE GOING TO BE VERY INTERESTING HOURS, INDEED...
SUNRISE OVER Mt. CHARTERIS...
IF YOU DON'T LET ME SEE HIM I'M GOING TO SCREAM!
I APOLOGIZE, SONGBIRD, BUT IT TOOK A BIT LONGER THAN I EXPECTED.
UP ALL NIGHT MODIFYING A SIMPLE FLIGHT SUIT, OGRE?
YOU'RE GOING TO LOSE YOUR REP AS A MIRACLE WORKER!
AHEM, YES, WELL... THERE WERE SOME... COMPLICATIONS... ARISING FROM OTHER ASPECTS OF THE WORK I DID ON Mr. JENKINS AND--
OGRE, LET US SEE HIM!
SORRY, SORRY-- WITHOUT FURTHER ADO, MAY I PROUDLY PRESENT THE NEWEST ADDITION TO THE THUNDERBOLTS --

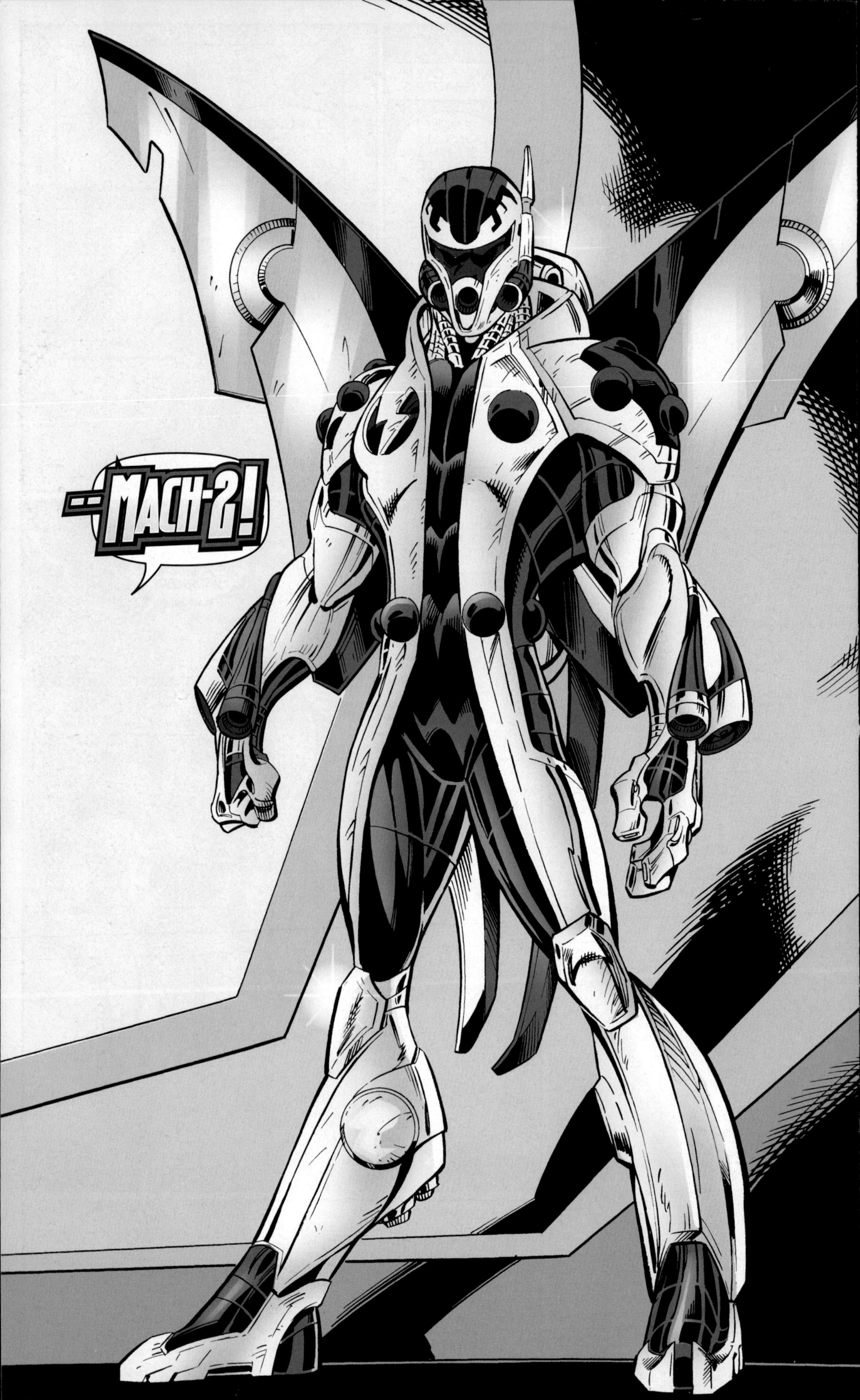
--MACH-2!

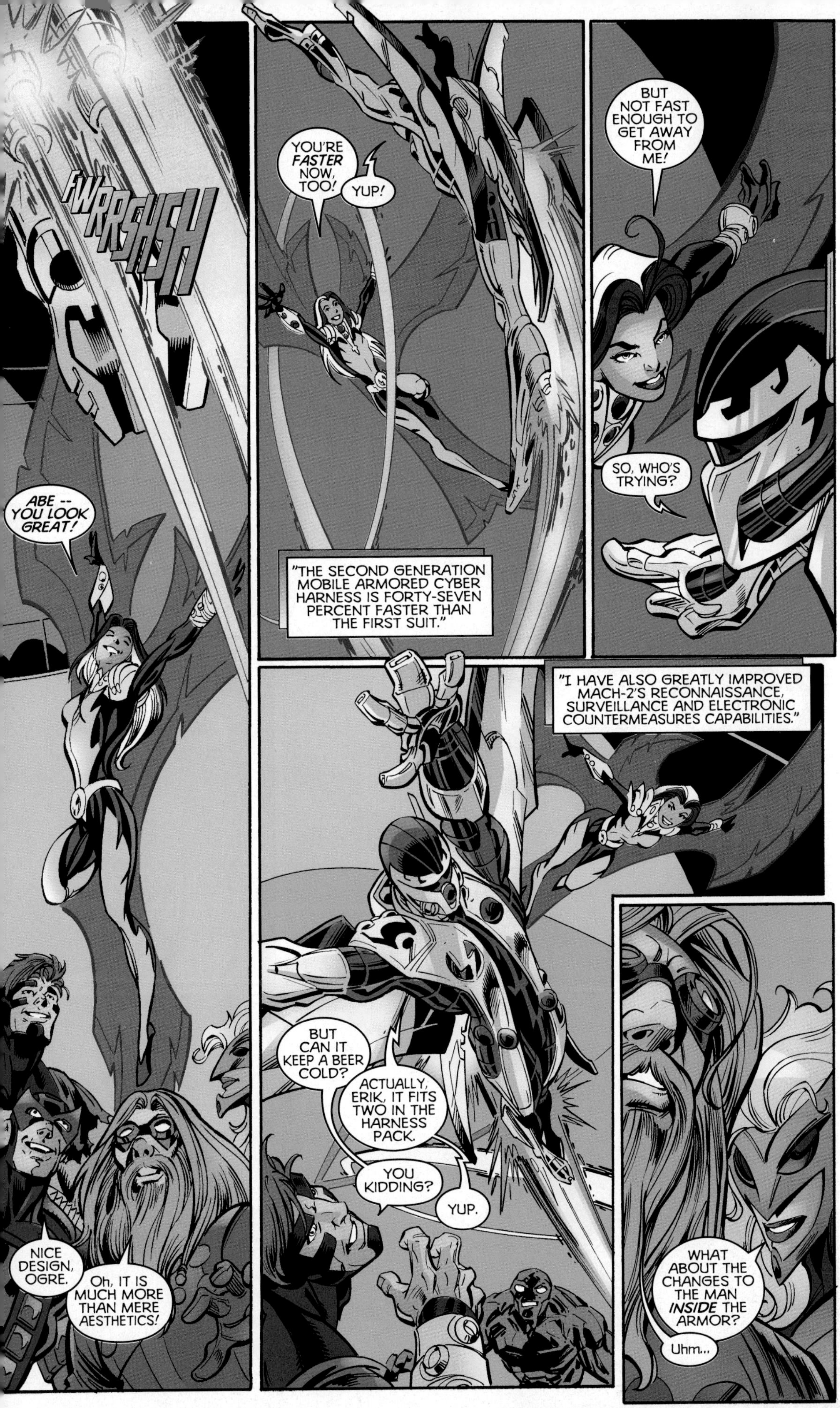
FWRRSHSH
ABE -- YOU LOOK GREAT!
NICE DESIGN, OGRE.
Oh, IT IS MUCH MORE THAN MERE AESTHETICS!
YOU'RE *FASTER* NOW, TOO!
YUP!
"THE SECOND GENERATION MOBILE ARMORED CYBER HARNESS IS FORTY-SEVEN PERCENT FASTER THAN THE FIRST SUIT."
BUT NOT FAST ENOUGH TO GET AWAY FROM ME!
SO, WHO'S TRYING?
"I HAVE ALSO GREATLY IMPROVED MACH-2'S RECONNAISSANCE, SURVEILLANCE AND ELECTRONIC COUNTERMEASURES CAPABILITIES."
BUT CAN IT KEEP A BEER COLD?
ACTUALLY, ERIK, IT FITS TWO IN THE HARNESS PACK.
YOU KIDDING?
YUP.
WHAT ABOUT THE CHANGES TO THE MAN *INSIDE* THE ARMOR?
Uhm...

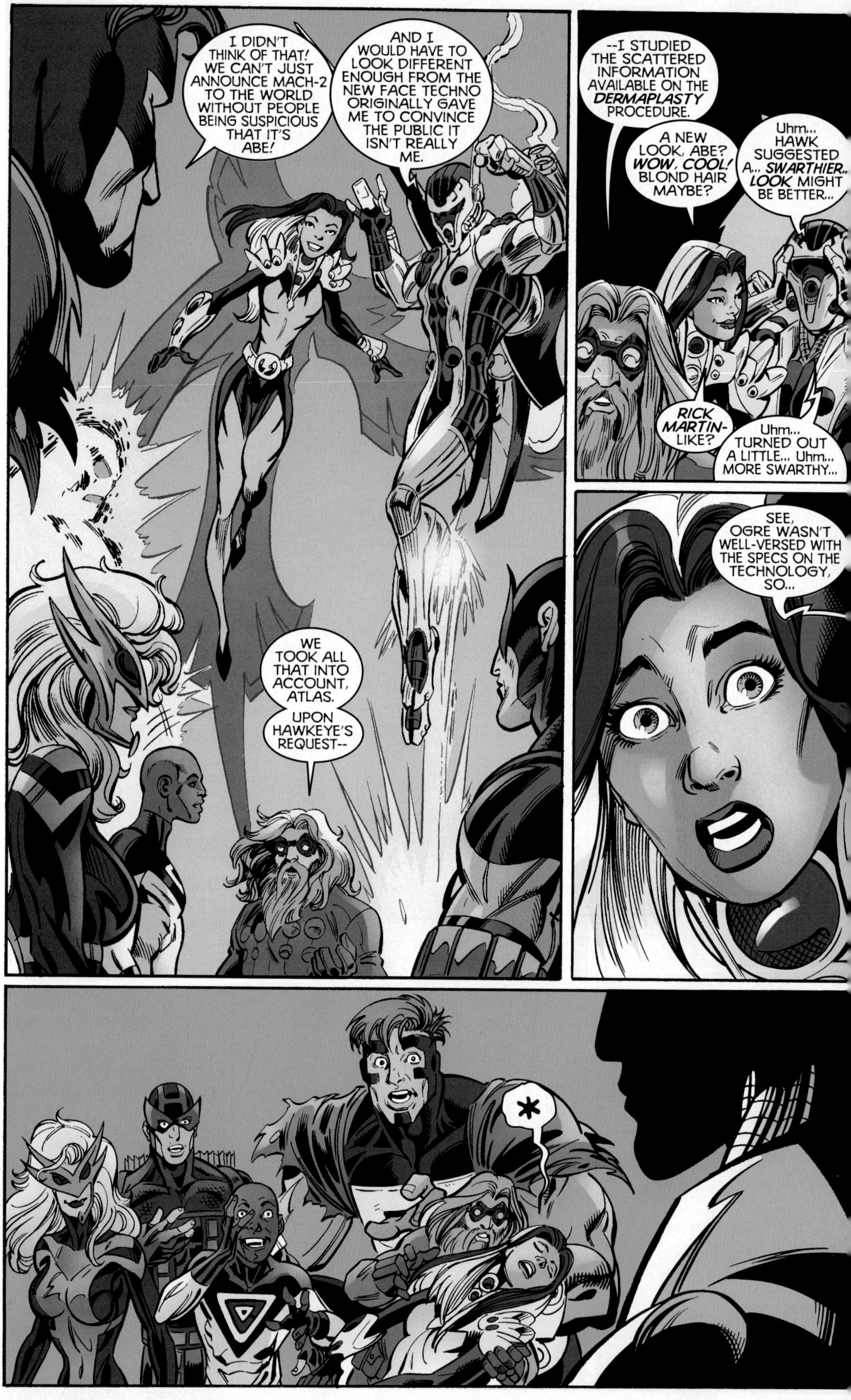
I DIDN'T THINK OF THAT! WE CAN'T JUST ANNOUNCE MACH-2 TO THE WORLD WITHOUT PEOPLE BEING SUSPICIOUS THAT IT'S ABE!
AND I WOULD HAVE TO LOOK DIFFERENT ENOUGH FROM THE NEW FACE TECHNO ORIGINALLY GAVE ME TO CONVINCE THE PUBLIC IT ISN'T REALLY ME.
WE TOOK ALL THAT INTO ACCOUNT, ATLAS.
UPON HAWKEYE'S REQUEST--
--I STUDIED THE SCATTERED INFORMATION AVAILABLE ON THE DERMAPLASTY PROCEDURE.
A NEW LOOK, ABE? WOW, COOL! BLOND HAIR MAYBE?
RICK MARTIN-LIKE?
Uhm... HAWK SUGGESTED A... SWARTHIER... LOOK MIGHT BE BETTER...
Uhm... TURNED OUT A LITTLE... Uhm... MORE SWARTHY...
SEE, OGRE WASN'T WELL-VERSED WITH THE SPECS ON THE TECHNOLOGY, SO...
*

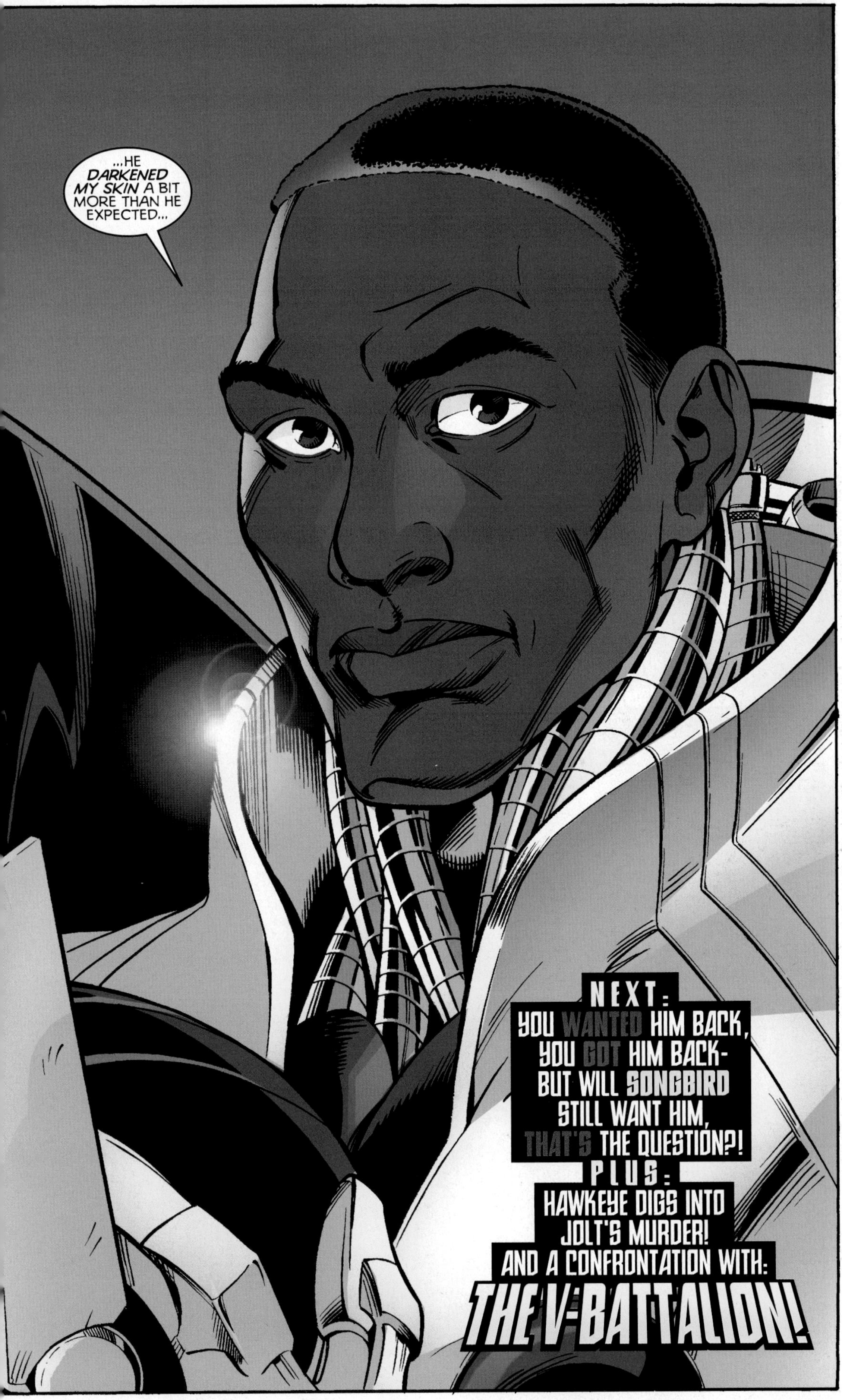
...HE DARKENED MY SKIN A BIT MORE THAN HE EXPECTED...
NEXT:
YOU WANTED HIM BACK, YOU GOT HIM BACK- BUT WILL SONGBIRD STILL WANT HIM, THAT'S THE QUESTION?!
PLUS:
HAWKEYE DIGS INTO JOLT'S MURDER! AND A CONFRONTATION WITH:
THE V-BATTALION!

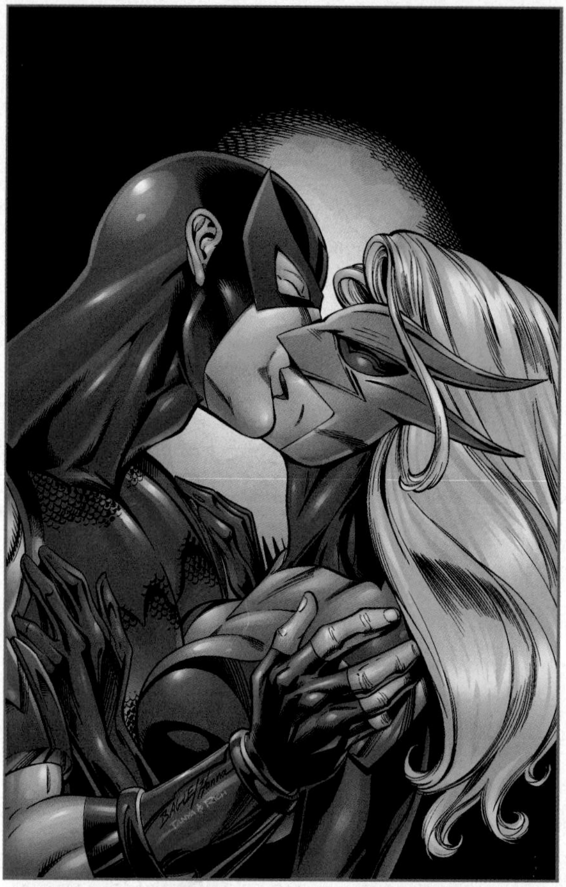
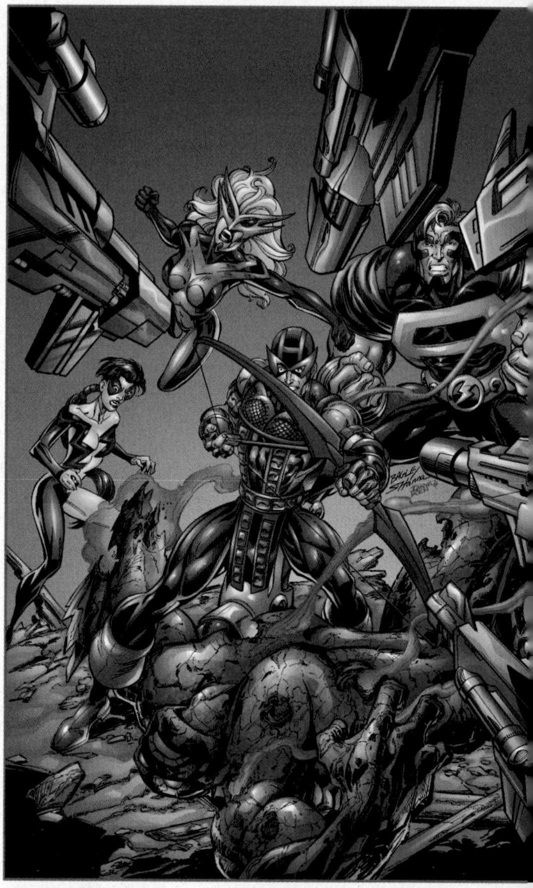
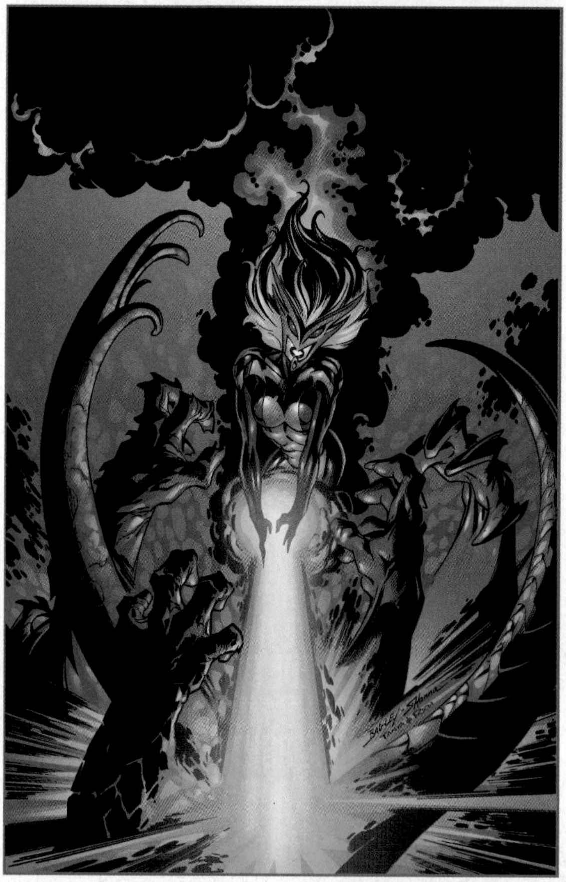
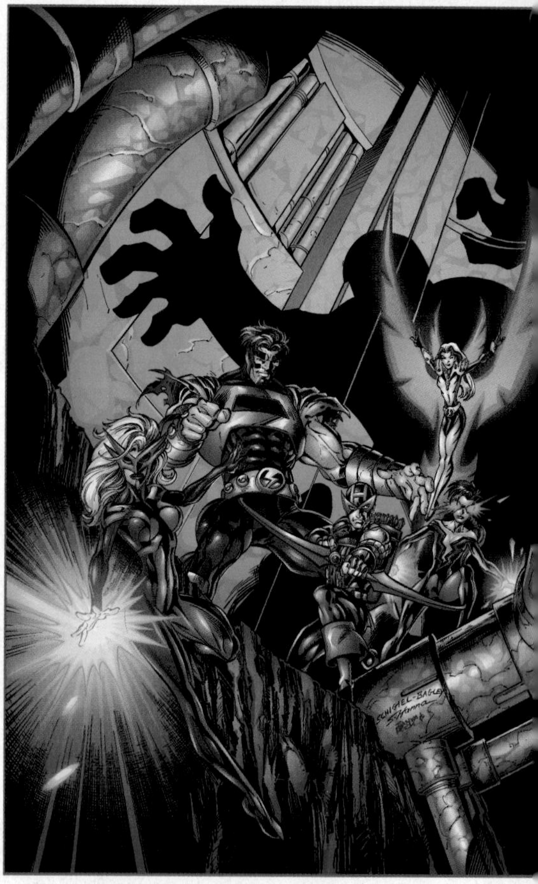

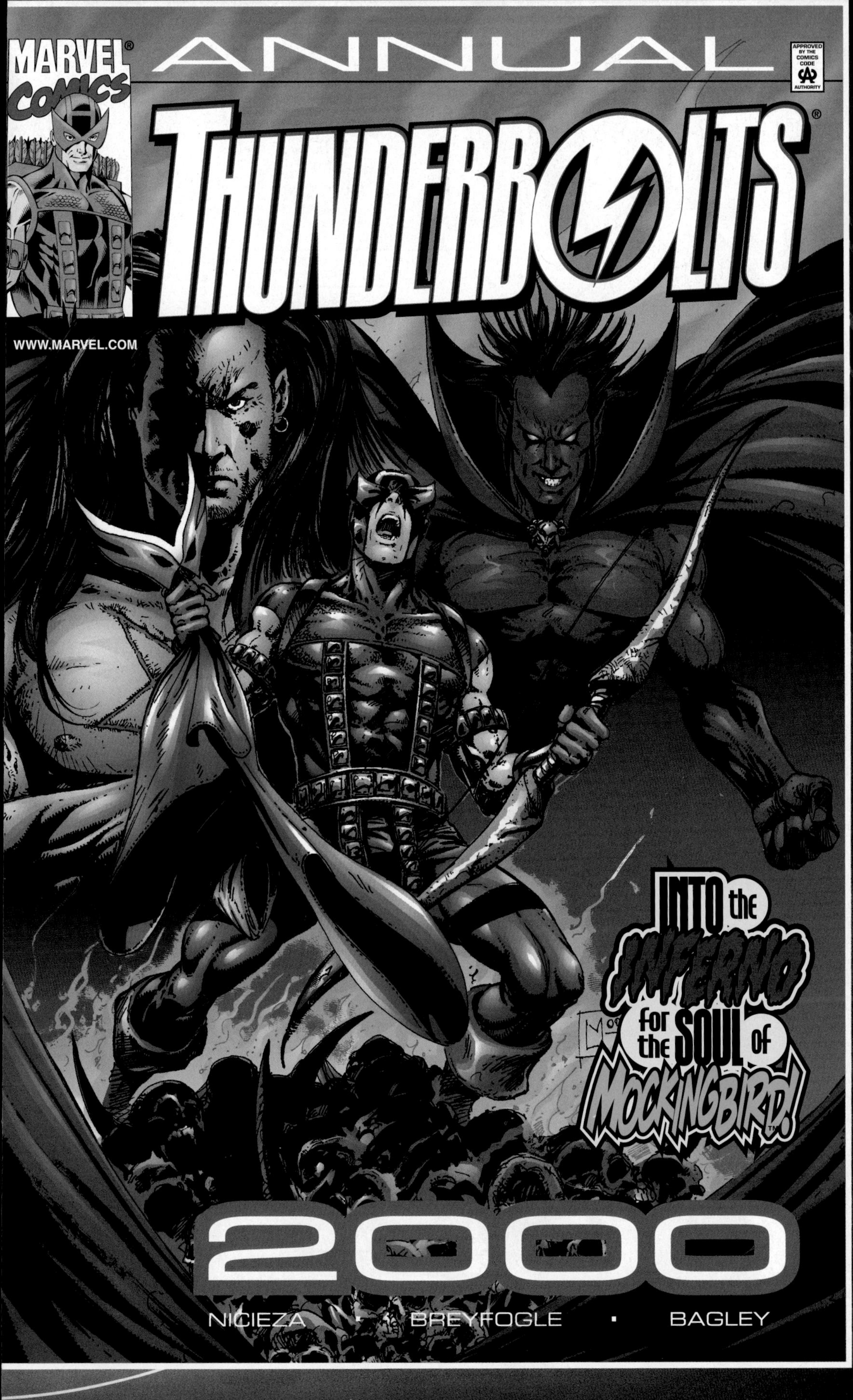
MARVEL COMICS
ANNUAL
APPROVED BY THE COMICS CODE AUTHORITY
THUNDERBOLTS
WWW.MARVEL.COM
INTO the INFERNO for the SOUL of MOCKINGBIRD!
2000
NICIEZA • BREYFOGLE • BAGLEY

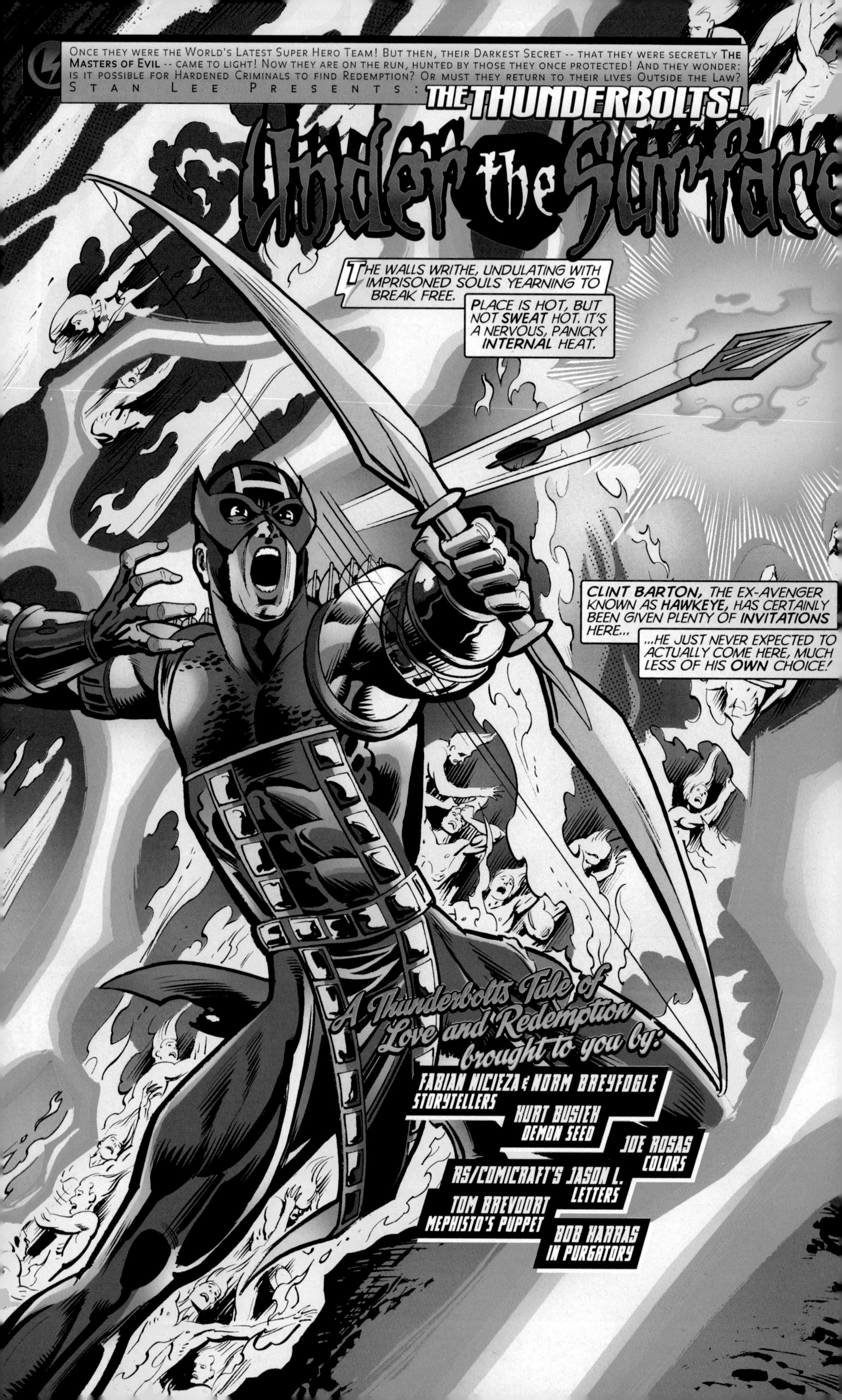
ONCE THEY WERE THE WORLD'S LATEST SUPER HERO TEAM! BUT THEN, THEIR DARKEST SECRET -- THAT THEY WERE SECRETLY THE MASTERS OF EVIL -- CAME TO LIGHT! NOW THEY ARE ON THE RUN, HUNTED BY THOSE THEY ONCE PROTECTED! AND THEY WONDER: IS IT POSSIBLE FOR HARDENED CRIMINALS TO FIND REDEMPTION? OR MUST THEY RETURN TO THEIR LIVES OUTSIDE THE LAW?
STAN LEE PRESENTS: THE THUNDERBOLTS!
Under the Surface
THE WALLS WRITHE, UNDULATING WITH IMPRISONED SOULS YEARNING TO BREAK FREE.
PLACE IS HOT, BUT NOT SWEAT HOT. IT'S A NERVOUS, PANICKY INTERNAL HEAT.
CLINT BARTON, THE EX-AVENGER KNOWN AS HAWKEYE, HAS CERTAINLY BEEN GIVEN PLENTY OF INVITATIONS HERE...
...HE JUST NEVER EXPECTED TO ACTUALLY COME HERE, MUCH LESS OF HIS OWN CHOICE!
A Thunderbolts Tale of Love and Redemption brought to you by:
FABIAN NICIEZA & NORM BREYFOGLE STORYTELLERS
KURT BUSIEK DEMON SEED
JOE ROSAS COLORS
RS/COMICRAFT'S JASON L. LETTERS
TOM BREVOORT MEPHISTO'S PUPPET
BOB HARRAS IN PURGATORY

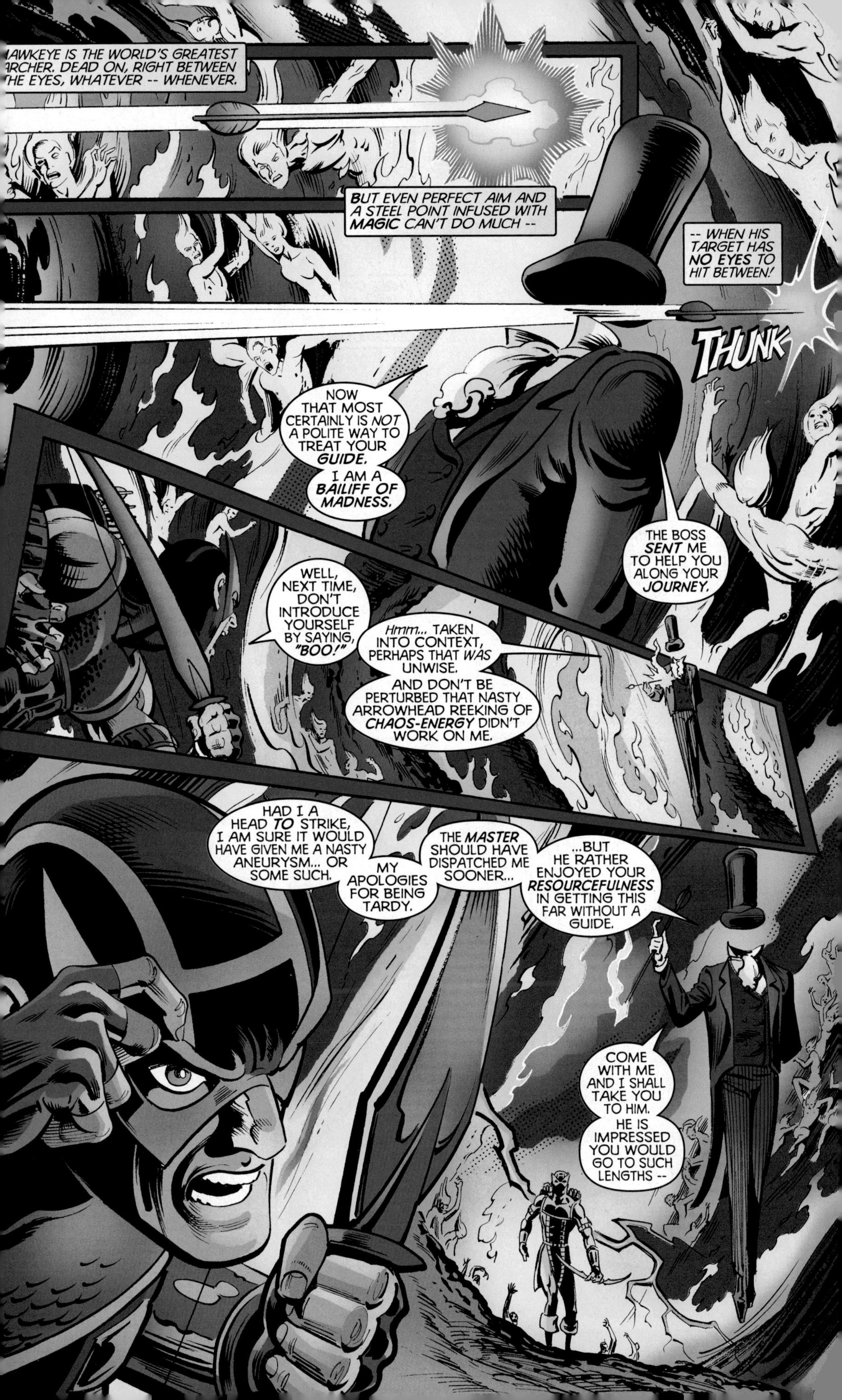
AWKEYE IS THE WORLD'S GREATEST ARCHER. DEAD ON, RIGHT BETWEEN THE EYES, WHATEVER -- WHENEVER.
BUT EVEN PERFECT AIM AND A STEEL POINT INFUSED WITH MAGIC CAN'T DO MUCH --
-- WHEN HIS TARGET HAS NO EYES TO HIT BETWEEN!
THUNK
NOW THAT MOST CERTAINLY IS NOT A POLITE WAY TO TREAT YOUR GUIDE.
I AM A BAILIFF OF MADNESS.
THE BOSS SENT ME TO HELP YOU ALONG YOUR JOURNEY.
WELL, NEXT TIME, DON'T INTRODUCE YOURSELF BY SAYING, "BOO!"
Hmm... TAKEN INTO CONTEXT, PERHAPS THAT WAS UNWISE.
AND DON'T BE PERTURBED THAT NASTY ARROWHEAD REEKING OF CHAOS-ENERGY DIDN'T WORK ON ME.
HAD I A HEAD TO STRIKE, I AM SURE IT WOULD HAVE GIVEN ME A NASTY ANEURYSM... OR SOME SUCH.
MY APOLOGIES FOR BEING TARDY.
THE MASTER SHOULD HAVE DISPATCHED ME SOONER...
...BUT HE RATHER ENJOYED YOUR RESOURCEFULNESS IN GETTING THIS FAR WITHOUT A GUIDE.
COME WITH ME AND I SHALL TAKE YOU TO HIM.
HE IS IMPRESSED YOU WOULD GO TO SUCH LENGTHS --

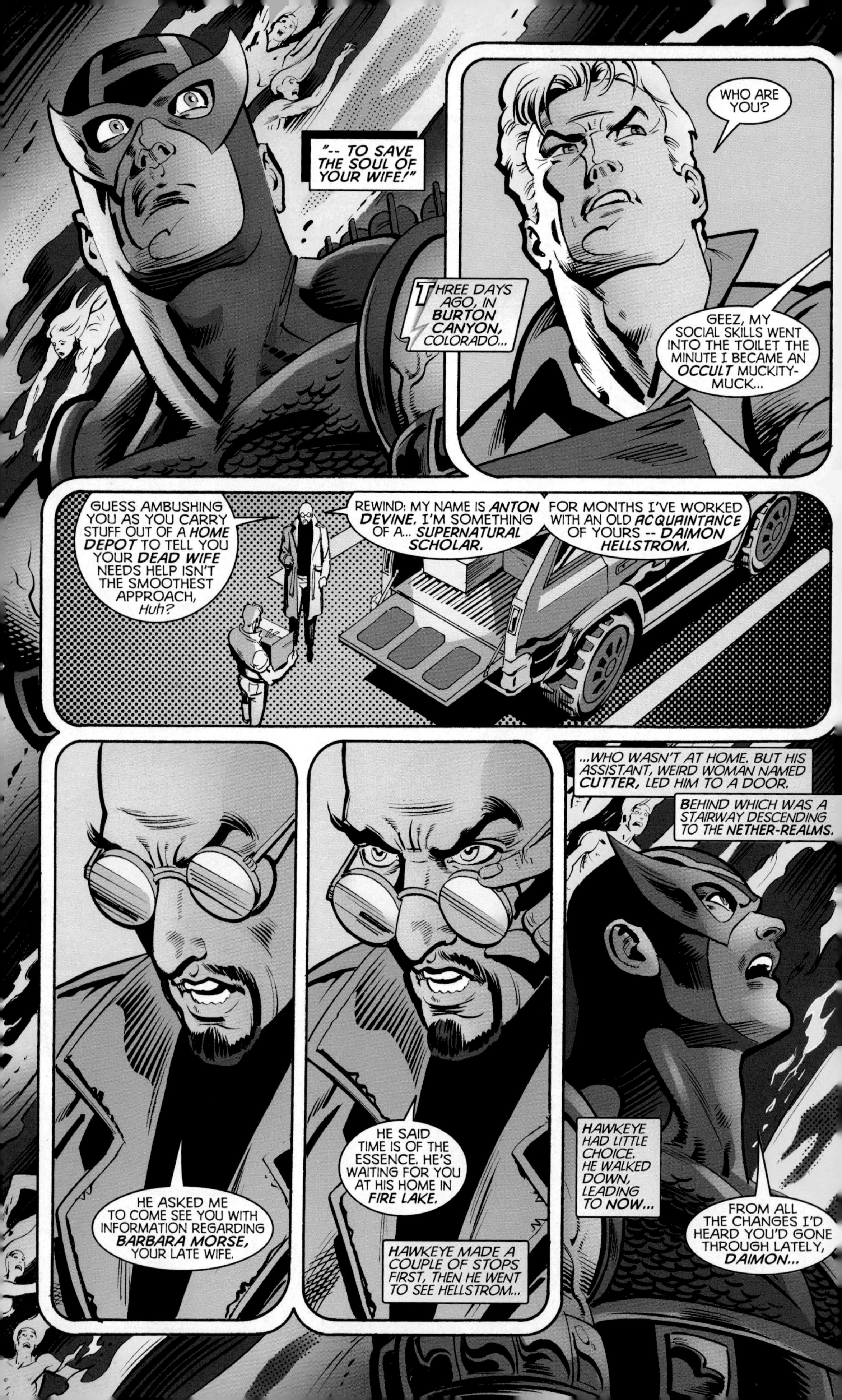
"-- TO SAVE THE SOUL OF YOUR WIFE!"
THREE DAYS AGO, IN BURTON CANYON, COLORADO...
WHO ARE YOU?
GEEZ, MY SOCIAL SKILLS WENT INTO THE TOILET THE MINUTE I BECAME AN OCCULT MUCKITY-MUCK...
GUESS AMBUSHING YOU AS YOU CARRY STUFF OUT OF A HOME DEPOT TO TELL YOU YOUR DEAD WIFE NEEDS HELP ISN'T THE SMOOTHEST APPROACH, Huh?
REWIND: MY NAME IS ANTON DEVINE. I'M SOMETHING OF A... SUPERNATURAL SCHOLAR.
FOR MONTHS I'VE WORKED WITH AN OLD ACQUAINTANCE OF YOURS -- DAIMON HELLSTROM.
HE ASKED ME TO COME SEE YOU WITH INFORMATION REGARDING BARBARA MORSE, YOUR LATE WIFE.
HE SAID TIME IS OF THE ESSENCE. HE'S WAITING FOR YOU AT HIS HOME IN FIRE LAKE.
HAWKEYE MADE A COUPLE OF STOPS FIRST, THEN HE WENT TO SEE HELLSTROM...
...WHO WASN'T AT HOME. BUT HIS ASSISTANT, WEIRD WOMAN NAMED CUTTER, LED HIM TO A DOOR.
BEHIND WHICH WAS A STAIRWAY DESCENDING TO THE NETHER-REALMS.
HAWKEYE HAD LITTLE CHOICE. HE WALKED DOWN, LEADING TO NOW...
FROM ALL THE CHANGES I'D HEARD YOU'D GONE THROUGH LATELY, DAIMON...

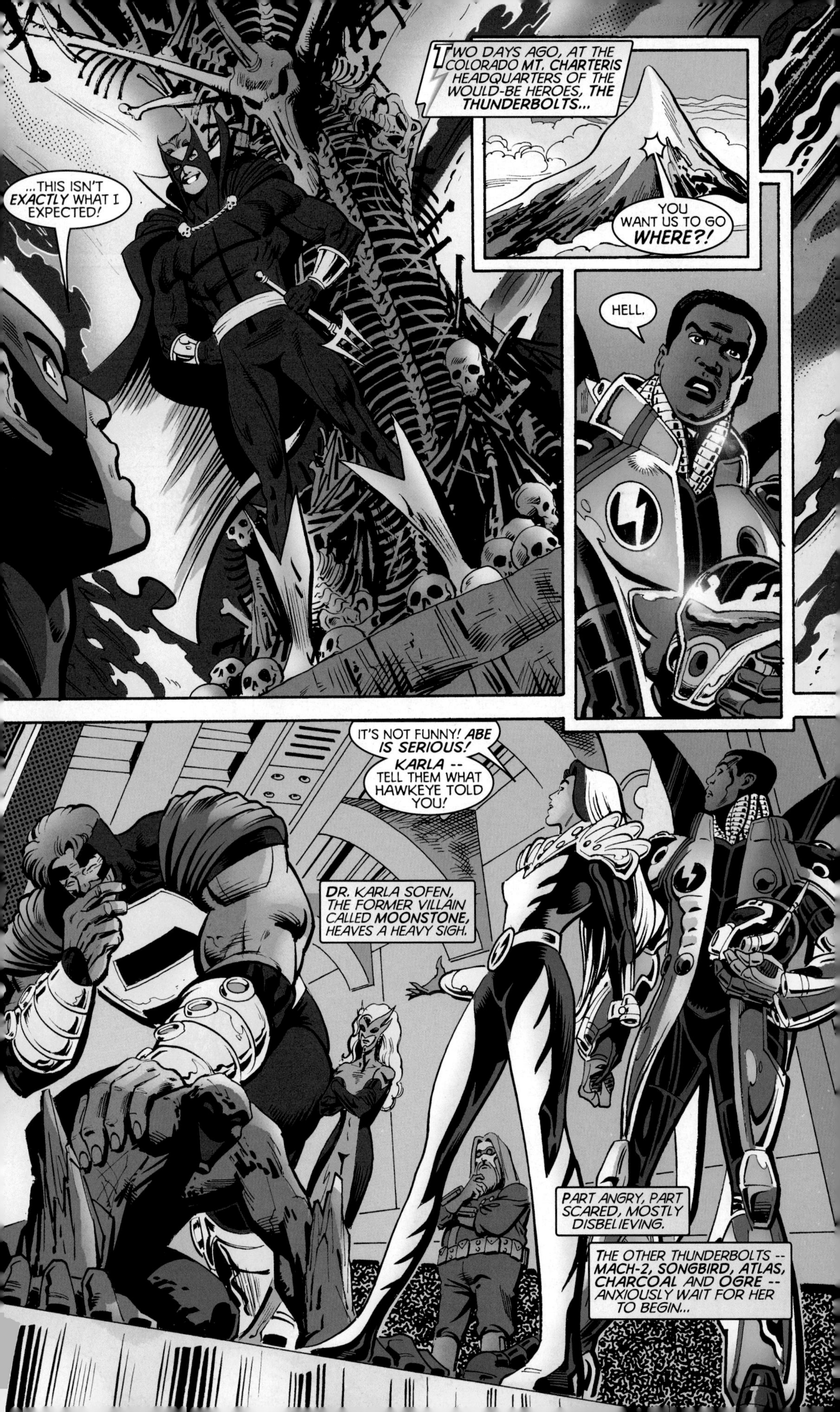
...THIS ISN'T EXACTLY WHAT I EXPECTED!
TWO DAYS AGO, AT THE COLORADO MT. CHARTERIS HEADQUARTERS OF THE WOULD-BE HEROES, THE THUNDERBOLTS...
YOU WANT US TO GO WHERE?!
HELL.
IT'S NOT FUNNY! ABE IS SERIOUS! KARLA -- TELL THEM WHAT HAWKEYE TOLD YOU!
DR. KARLA SOFEN, THE FORMER VILLAIN CALLED MOONSTONE, HEAVES A HEAVY SIGH.
PART ANGRY, PART SCARED, MOSTLY DISBELIEVING.
THE OTHER THUNDERBOLTS -- MACH-2, SONGBIRD, ATLAS, CHARCOAL AND OGRE -- ANXIOUSLY WAIT FOR HER TO BEGIN...

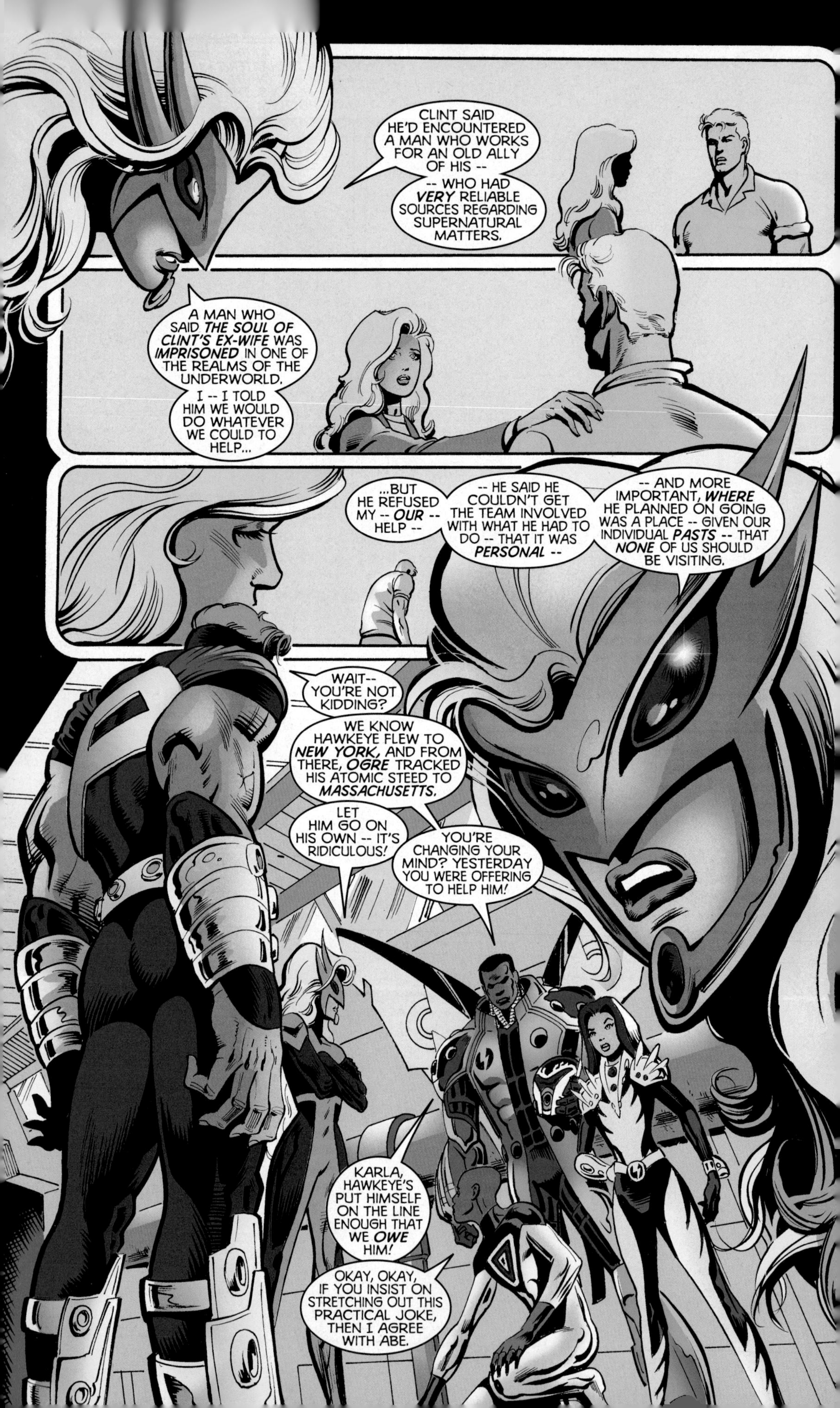

CLINT SAID HE'D ENCOUNTERED A MAN WHO WORKS FOR AN OLD ALLY OF HIS --
-- WHO HAD *VERY* RELIABLE SOURCES REGARDING SUPERNATURAL MATTERS.
A MAN WHO SAID *THE SOUL OF CLINT'S EX-WIFE* WAS *IMPRISONED* IN ONE OF THE REALMS OF THE UNDERWORLD.
I -- I TOLD HIM WE WOULD DO WHATEVER WE COULD TO HELP...
...BUT HE REFUSED MY -- *OUR* -- HELP --
-- HE SAID HE COULDN'T GET THE TEAM INVOLVED WITH WHAT HE HAD TO DO -- THAT IT WAS *PERSONAL* --
-- AND MORE IMPORTANT, *WHERE* HE PLANNED ON GOING WAS A PLACE -- GIVEN OUR INDIVIDUAL *PASTS* -- THAT *NONE* OF US SHOULD BE VISITING.
WAIT-- YOU'RE NOT KIDDING?
WE KNOW HAWKEYE FLEW TO *NEW YORK,* AND FROM THERE, *OGRE* TRACKED HIS ATOMIC STEED TO *MASSACHUSETTS.*
LET HIM GO ON HIS OWN -- IT'S RIDICULOUS!
YOU'RE CHANGING YOUR MIND? YESTERDAY YOU WERE OFFERING TO HELP HIM!
KARLA, HAWKEYE'S PUT HIMSELF ON THE LINE ENOUGH THAT WE *OWE* HIM!
OKAY, OKAY, IF YOU INSIST ON STRETCHING OUT THIS PRACTICAL JOKE, THEN I AGREE WITH ABE.

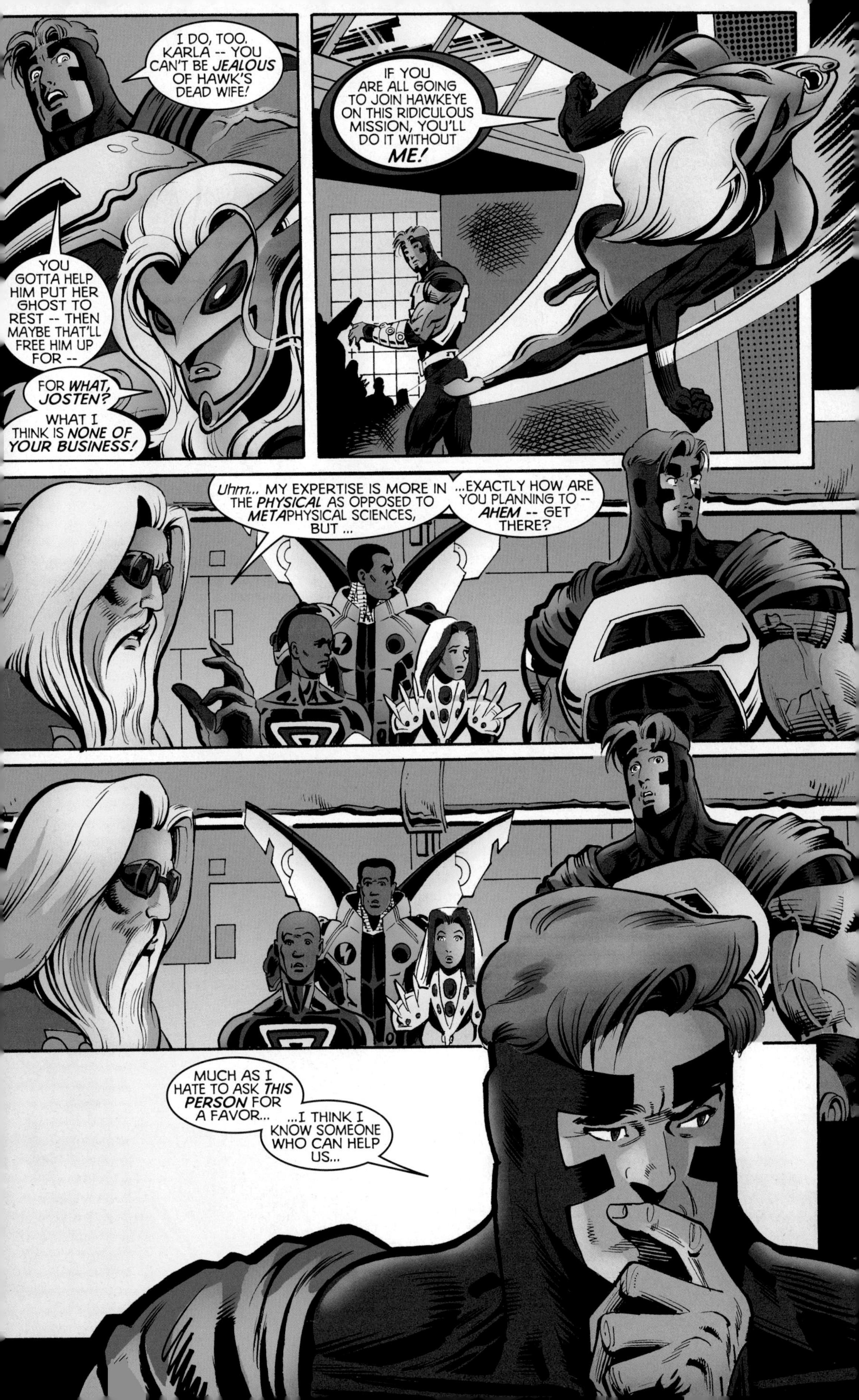
I DO, TOO. KARLA -- YOU CAN'T BE *JEALOUS* OF HAWK'S DEAD WIFE!
YOU GOTTA HELP HIM PUT HER GHOST TO REST -- THEN MAYBE THAT'LL FREE HIM UP FOR --
FOR *WHAT, JOSTEN?* WHAT I THINK IS *NONE OF YOUR BUSINESS!*
IF YOU ARE ALL GOING TO JOIN HAWKEYE ON THIS RIDICULOUS MISSION, YOU'LL DO IT WITHOUT *ME!*
Uhm... MY EXPERTISE IS MORE IN THE *PHYSICAL* AS OPPOSED TO *META*PHYSICAL SCIENCES, BUT ...
...EXACTLY HOW ARE YOU PLANNING TO -- *AHEM* -- GET THERE?
MUCH AS I HATE TO ASK *THIS PERSON* FOR A FAVOR...
...I THINK I KNOW SOMEONE WHO CAN HELP US...

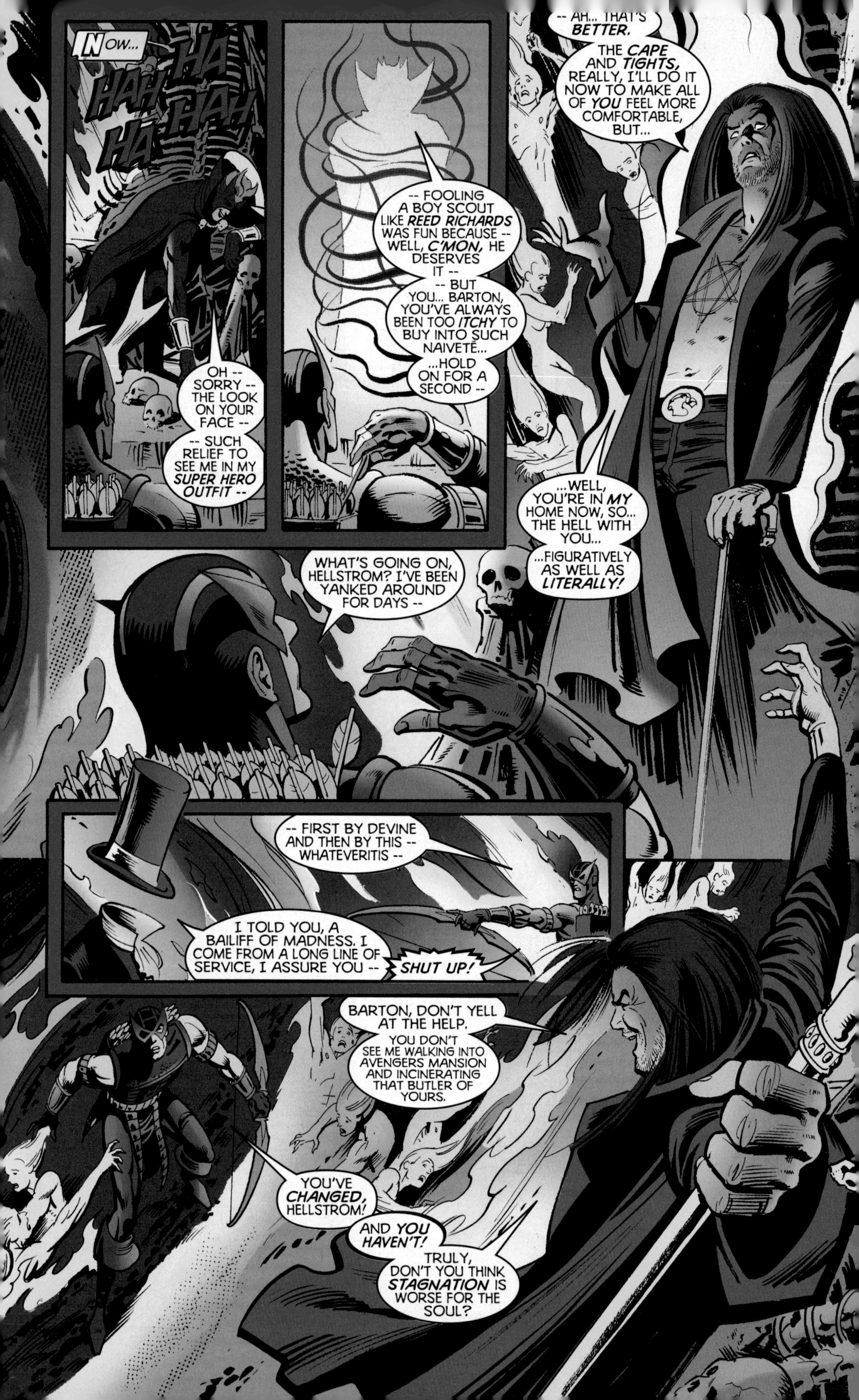
NOW...
HAH HA HAH HA HAH
OH -- SORRY -- THE LOOK ON YOUR FACE --
-- SUCH RELIEF TO SEE ME IN MY SUPER HERO OUTFIT --
-- FOOLING A BOY SCOUT LIKE REED RICHARDS WAS FUN BECAUSE -- WELL, C'MON, HE DESERVES IT --
-- BUT YOU... BARTON, YOU'VE ALWAYS BEEN TOO ITCHY TO BUY INTO SUCH NAIVETÉ...
...HOLD ON FOR A SECOND --
-- AH... THAT'S BETTER.
THE CAPE AND TIGHTS, REALLY, I'LL DO IT NOW TO MAKE ALL OF YOU FEEL MORE COMFORTABLE, BUT...
...WELL, YOU'RE IN MY HOME NOW, SO... THE HELL WITH YOU...
...FIGURATIVELY AS WELL AS LITERALLY!
WHAT'S GOING ON, HELLSTROM? I'VE BEEN YANKED AROUND FOR DAYS --
-- FIRST BY DEVINE AND THEN BY THIS -- WHATEVERITIS --
I TOLD YOU, A BAILIFF OF MADNESS. I COME FROM A LONG LINE OF SERVICE, I ASSURE YOU --
SHUT UP!
BARTON, DON'T YELL AT THE HELP.
YOU DON'T SEE ME WALKING INTO AVENGERS MANSION AND INCINERATING THAT BUTLER OF YOURS.
YOU'VE CHANGED, HELLSTROM!
AND YOU HAVEN'T!
TRULY, DON'T YOU THINK STAGNATION IS WORSE FOR THE SOUL?

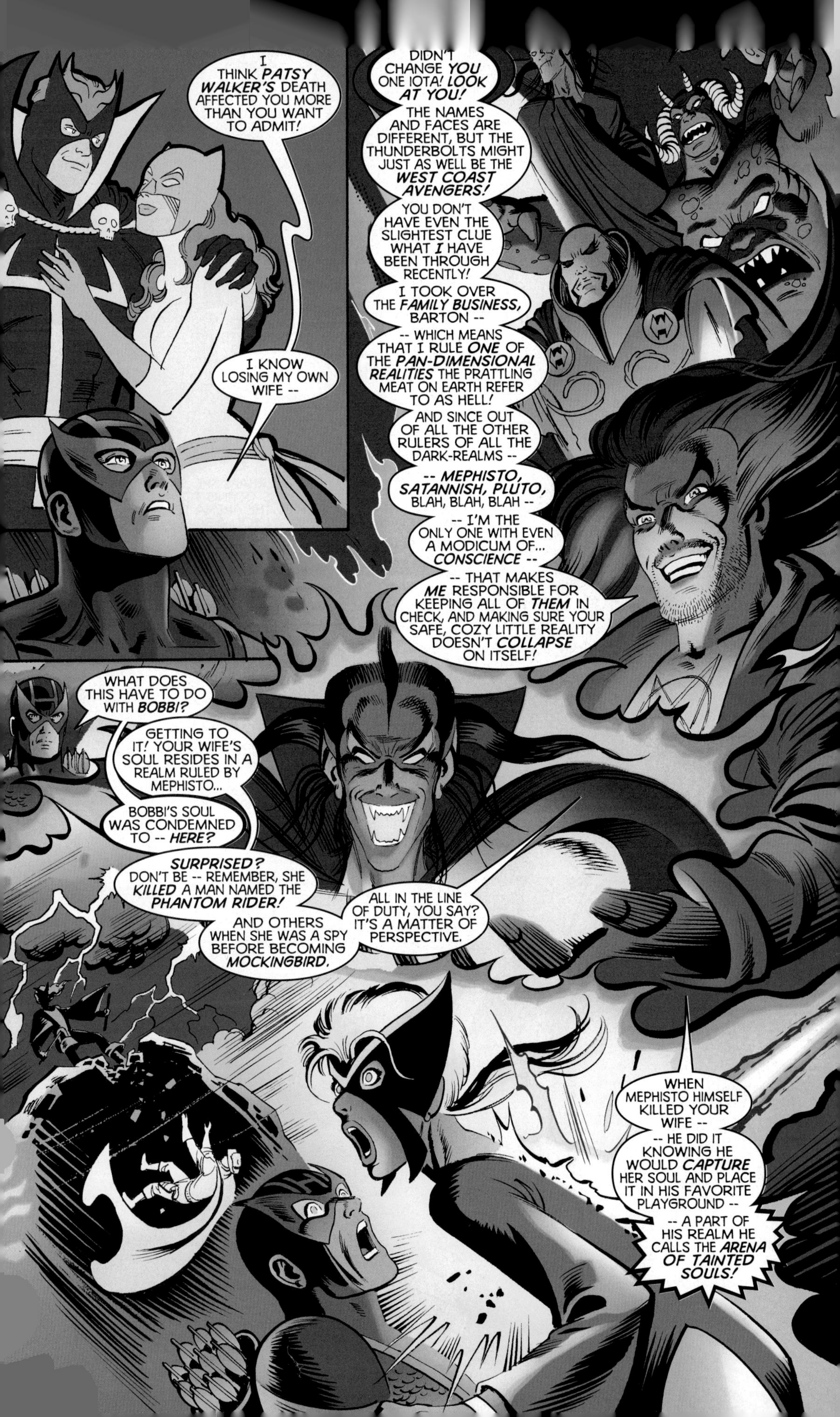
I THINK PATSY WALKER'S DEATH AFFECTED YOU MORE THAN YOU WANT TO ADMIT!
I KNOW LOSING MY OWN WIFE --
DIDN'T CHANGE YOU ONE IOTA! LOOK AT YOU!
THE NAMES AND FACES ARE DIFFERENT, BUT THE THUNDERBOLTS MIGHT JUST AS WELL BE THE WEST COAST AVENGERS!
YOU DON'T HAVE EVEN THE SLIGHTEST CLUE WHAT I HAVE BEEN THROUGH RECENTLY!
I TOOK OVER THE FAMILY BUSINESS, BARTON --
-- WHICH MEANS THAT I RULE ONE OF THE PAN-DIMENSIONAL REALITIES THE PRATTLING MEAT ON EARTH REFER TO AS HELL!
AND SINCE OUT OF ALL THE OTHER RULERS OF ALL THE DARK-REALMS --
-- MEPHISTO, SATANNISH, PLUTO, BLAH, BLAH, BLAH --
-- I'M THE ONLY ONE WITH EVEN A MODICUM OF... CONSCIENCE --
-- THAT MAKES ME RESPONSIBLE FOR KEEPING ALL OF THEM IN CHECK, AND MAKING SURE YOUR SAFE, COZY LITTLE REALITY DOESN'T COLLAPSE ON ITSELF!
WHAT DOES THIS HAVE TO DO WITH BOBBI?
GETTING TO IT! YOUR WIFE'S SOUL RESIDES IN A REALM RULED BY MEPHISTO...
BOBBI'S SOUL WAS CONDEMNED TO -- HERE?
SURPRISED? DON'T BE -- REMEMBER, SHE KILLED A MAN NAMED THE PHANTOM RIDER!
AND OTHERS WHEN SHE WAS A SPY BEFORE BECOMING MOCKINGBIRD.
ALL IN THE LINE OF DUTY, YOU SAY? IT'S A MATTER OF PERSPECTIVE.
WHEN MEPHISTO HIMSELF KILLED YOUR WIFE --
-- HE DID IT KNOWING HE WOULD CAPTURE HER SOUL AND PLACE IT IN HIS FAVORITE PLAYGROUND --
-- A PART OF HIS REALM HE CALLS THE ARENA OF TAINTED SOULS!

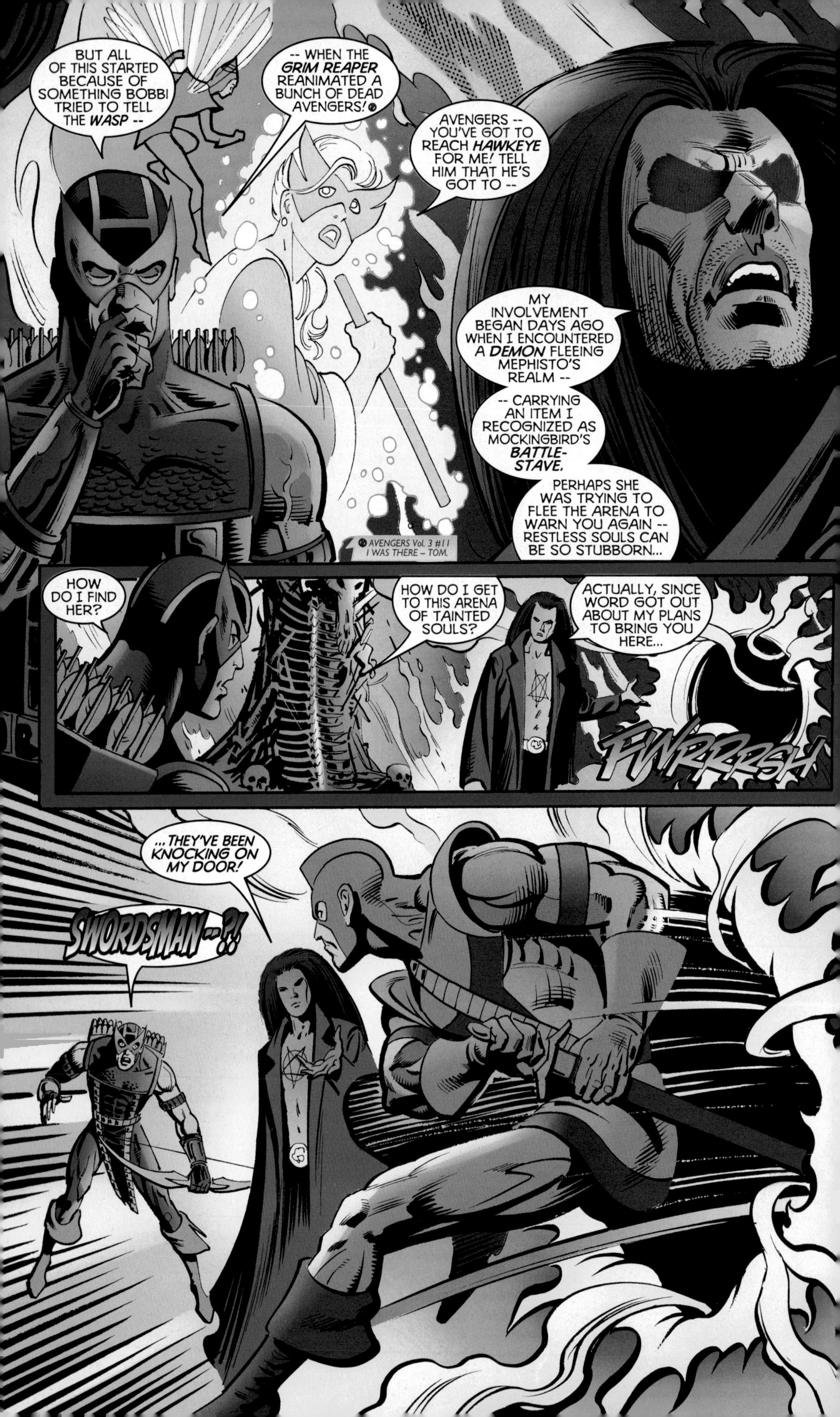
BUT ALL OF THIS STARTED BECAUSE OF SOMETHING BOBBI TRIED TO TELL THE WASP --
-- WHEN THE GRIM REAPER REANIMATED A BUNCH OF DEAD AVENGERS!
AVENGERS -- YOU'VE GOT TO REACH HAWKEYE FOR ME! TELL HIM THAT HE'S GOT TO --
MY INVOLVEMENT BEGAN DAYS AGO WHEN I ENCOUNTERED A DEMON FLEEING MEPHISTO'S REALM --
-- CARRYING AN ITEM I RECOGNIZED AS MOCKINGBIRD'S BATTLE-STAVE.
PERHAPS SHE WAS TRYING TO FLEE THE ARENA TO WARN YOU AGAIN -- RESTLESS SOULS CAN BE SO STUBBORN...
AVENGERS Vol. 3 #11 I WAS THERE – TOM.
HOW DO I FIND HER?
HOW DO I GET TO THIS ARENA OF TAINTED SOULS?
ACTUALLY, SINCE WORD GOT OUT ABOUT MY PLANS TO BRING YOU HERE...
FWRRRSH
...THEY'VE BEEN KNOCKING ON MY DOOR!
SWORDSMAN--?!

MEANWHILE, AT THE POSH ASH HOTEL IN MIDTOWN MANHATTAN --

-- ERIK JOSTEN, THE SIZE-CHANGING ATLAS, GRINDS HIS TEETH --

-- WORRYING ABOUT PULLING OFF A GAME OF MANIPULATION --

-- AGAINST A LITERAL GODDESS OF DECEIT!

DAILY BUC

CLASSIFIEDS

To the AMORA DATING SERVICE: old friend looking for a favor. Am a lot taller now, but just as strong as you made me. Contact ERIK at the Washington Hotel.

Lorem ipsum dolor sit amet, consectetuer adipiscing elit, diam nonummy euismod

Ut wisi enim veniam, qui exerci t suscip aliqui cons

THEY *STILL* HAVEN'T FINISHED REBUILDING *FOUR FREEDOMS PLAZA?*

HOPE WE NEVER RUN INTO THE *FF* -- THEY'RE PROBABLY STILL PEEVED AT US...

MAN, I *NEVER* THOUGHT WE'D BE BACK IN NEW YORK AFTER THE LAST TIME WE WERE HERE!

MUCH LESS MAKING A DEAL WITH THE DEVIL *HERSELF* --

-- IN ORDER TO FIGHT THE DEVIL HIMSELF!

I *REALLY* KNOW HOW TO PICK THE WOMEN, DON'T I?

FIRST *DALLAS RIORDAN,* OUR MAYORAL LIAISON, WHO I BETRAYED --

-- AND WHO TURNED OUT TO BE OUR BIGGEST OPPONENT, THE *CRIMSON COWL* -- WHO RAN THE *MASTERS OF EVIL* --

-- WHICH *MAN-KILLER* WAS A PART OF. 'CEPT NOW SHE'S HIDING OUT IN BURTON CANYON --

-- I HAVEN'T BEEN ABLE TO TELL THE T-BOLTS ABOUT IT. LIKE I SAID... I SURE KNOW HOW TO PICK 'EM!

NOW, OF ALL PEOPLE TO BE ASKING FOR HELP --

-- NOT ONLY IS THIS THE WOMAN WHO ORIGINALLY GAVE ME SUPER-STRENGTH AND MADE ME *POWER MAN* WAY BACK WHEN --

-- BUT SHE'S AN *ASGARDIAN GODDESS,* TOO!

ENCHANTRESS!

ERIK...IT HAS BEEN SO VERY LONG.

AND EXACTLY WHY IS IT YOU ASKED TO SEE ME?

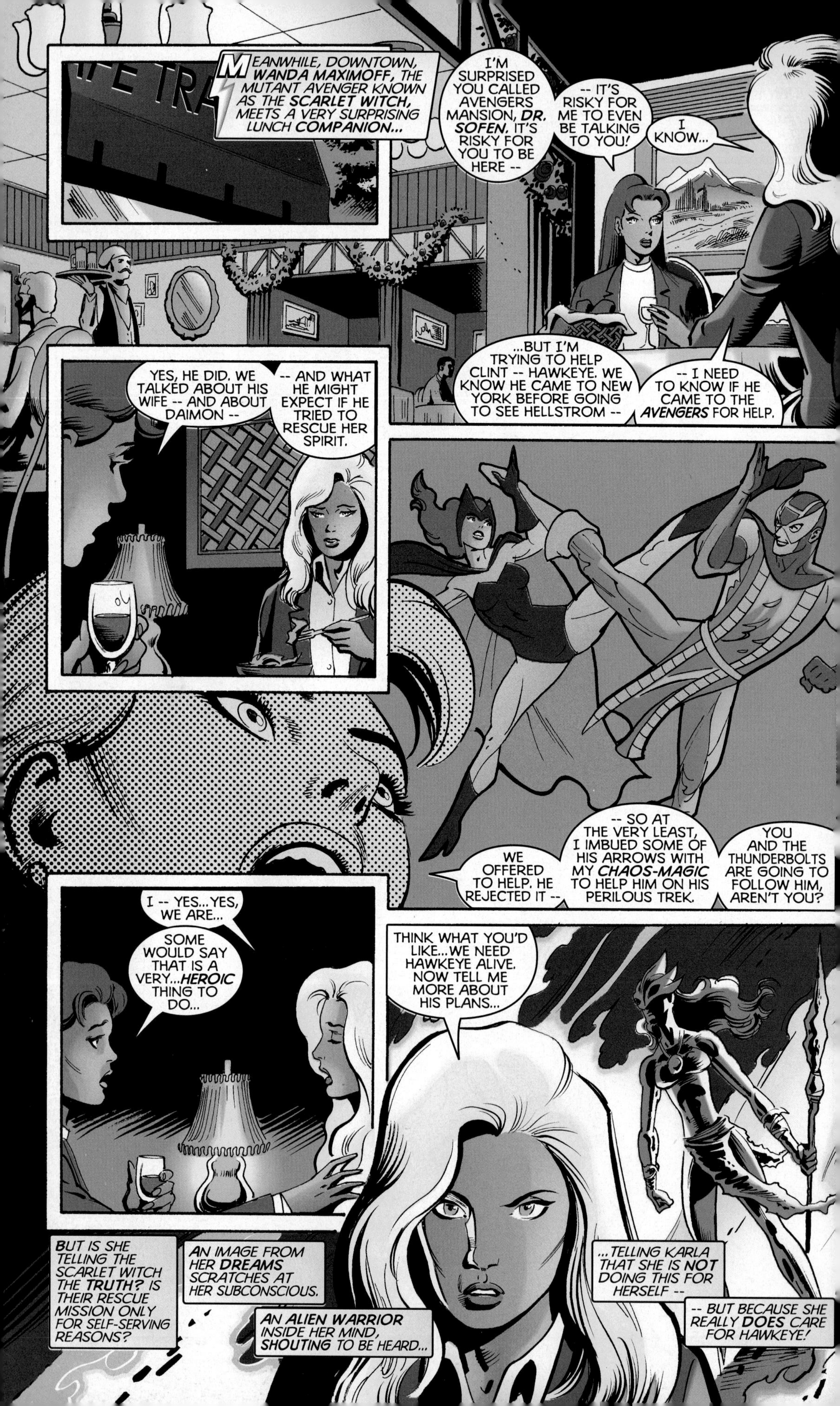
MEANWHILE, DOWNTOWN, WANDA MAXIMOFF, THE MUTANT AVENGER KNOWN AS THE SCARLET WITCH, MEETS A VERY SURPRISING LUNCH COMPANION...
I'M SURPRISED YOU CALLED AVENGERS MANSION, DR. SOFEN. IT'S RISKY FOR YOU TO BE HERE --
-- IT'S RISKY FOR ME TO EVEN BE TALKING TO YOU!
I KNOW...
...BUT I'M TRYING TO HELP CLINT -- HAWKEYE. WE KNOW HE CAME TO NEW YORK BEFORE GOING TO SEE HELLSTROM --
-- I NEED TO KNOW IF HE CAME TO THE AVENGERS FOR HELP.
YES, HE DID. WE TALKED ABOUT HIS WIFE -- AND ABOUT DAIMON --
-- AND WHAT HE MIGHT EXPECT IF HE TRIED TO RESCUE HER SPIRIT.
WE OFFERED TO HELP. HE REJECTED IT --
-- SO AT THE VERY LEAST, I IMBUED SOME OF HIS ARROWS WITH MY CHAOS-MAGIC TO HELP HIM ON HIS PERILOUS TREK.
YOU AND THE THUNDERBOLTS ARE GOING TO FOLLOW HIM, AREN'T YOU?
I -- YES...YES, WE ARE...
SOME WOULD SAY THAT IS A VERY...HEROIC THING TO DO...
THINK WHAT YOU'D LIKE...WE NEED HAWKEYE ALIVE. NOW TELL ME MORE ABOUT HIS PLANS...
BUT IS SHE TELLING THE SCARLET WITCH THE TRUTH? IS THEIR RESCUE MISSION ONLY FOR SELF-SERVING REASONS?
AN IMAGE FROM HER DREAMS SCRATCHES AT HER SUBCONSCIOUS.
AN ALIEN WARRIOR INSIDE HER MIND, SHOUTING TO BE HEARD...
...TELLING KARLA THAT SHE IS NOT DOING THIS FOR HERSELF --
-- BUT BECAUSE SHE REALLY DOES CARE FOR HAWKEYE!

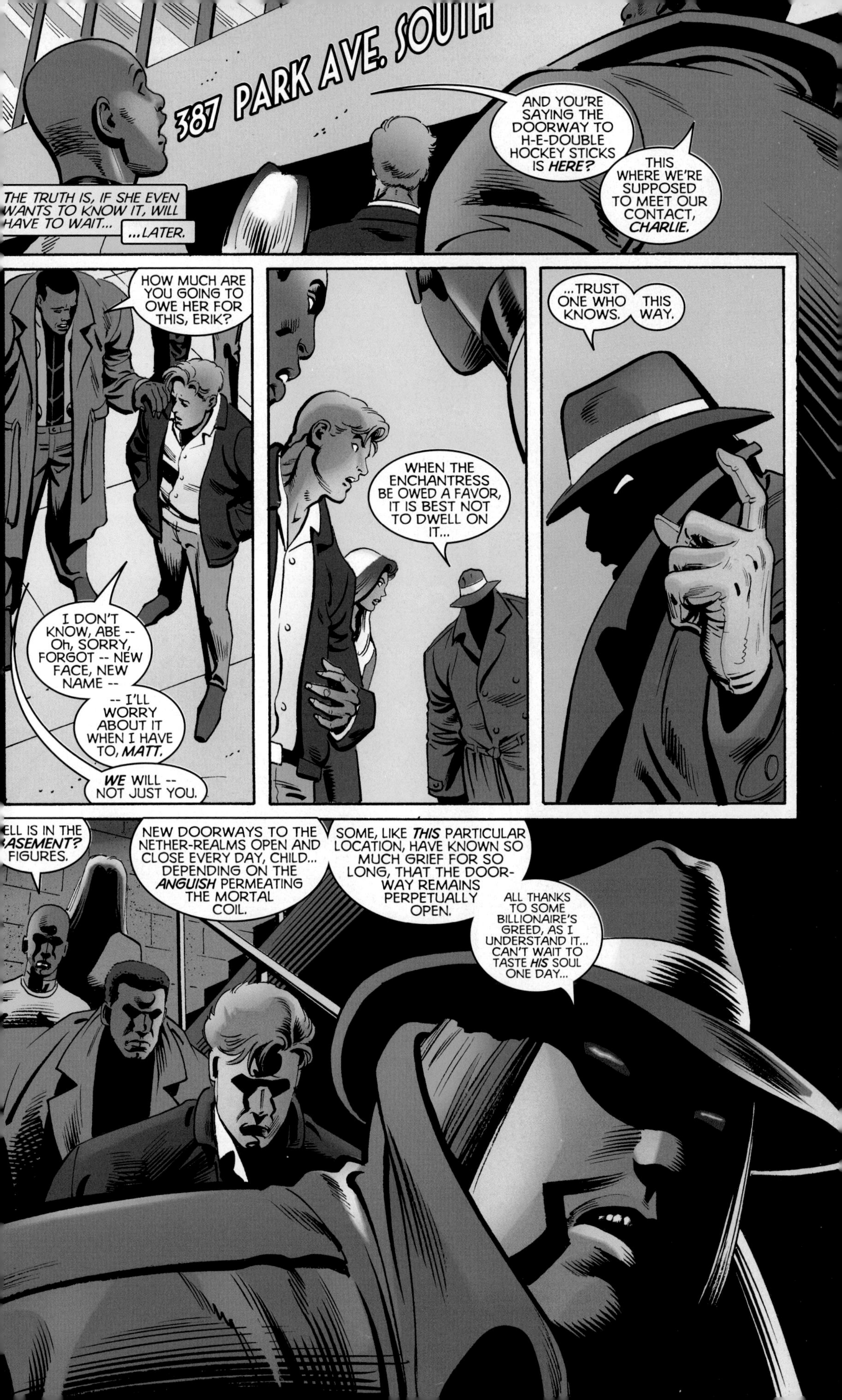
387 PARK AVE. SOUTH
THE TRUTH IS, IF SHE EVEN WANTS TO KNOW IT, WILL HAVE TO WAIT...
...LATER.
AND YOU'RE SAYING THE DOORWAY TO H-E-DOUBLE HOCKEY STICKS IS HERE?
THIS WHERE WE'RE SUPPOSED TO MEET OUR CONTACT, CHARLIE.
HOW MUCH ARE YOU GOING TO OWE HER FOR THIS, ERIK?
I DON'T KNOW, ABE -- Oh, SORRY, FORGOT -- NEW FACE, NEW NAME --
-- I'LL WORRY ABOUT IT WHEN I HAVE TO, MATT.
WE WILL -- NOT JUST YOU.
WHEN THE ENCHANTRESS BE OWED A FAVOR, IT IS BEST NOT TO DWELL ON IT...
...TRUST ONE WHO KNOWS.
THIS WAY.
ELL IS IN THE BASEMENT? FIGURES.
NEW DOORWAYS TO THE NETHER-REALMS OPEN AND CLOSE EVERY DAY, CHILD... DEPENDING ON THE ANGUISH PERMEATING THE MORTAL COIL.
SOME, LIKE THIS PARTICULAR LOCATION, HAVE KNOWN SO MUCH GRIEF FOR SO LONG, THAT THE DOOR-WAY REMAINS PERPETUALLY OPEN.
ALL THANKS TO SOME BILLIONAIRE'S GREED, AS I UNDERSTAND IT... CAN'T WAIT TO TASTE HIS SOUL ONE DAY...

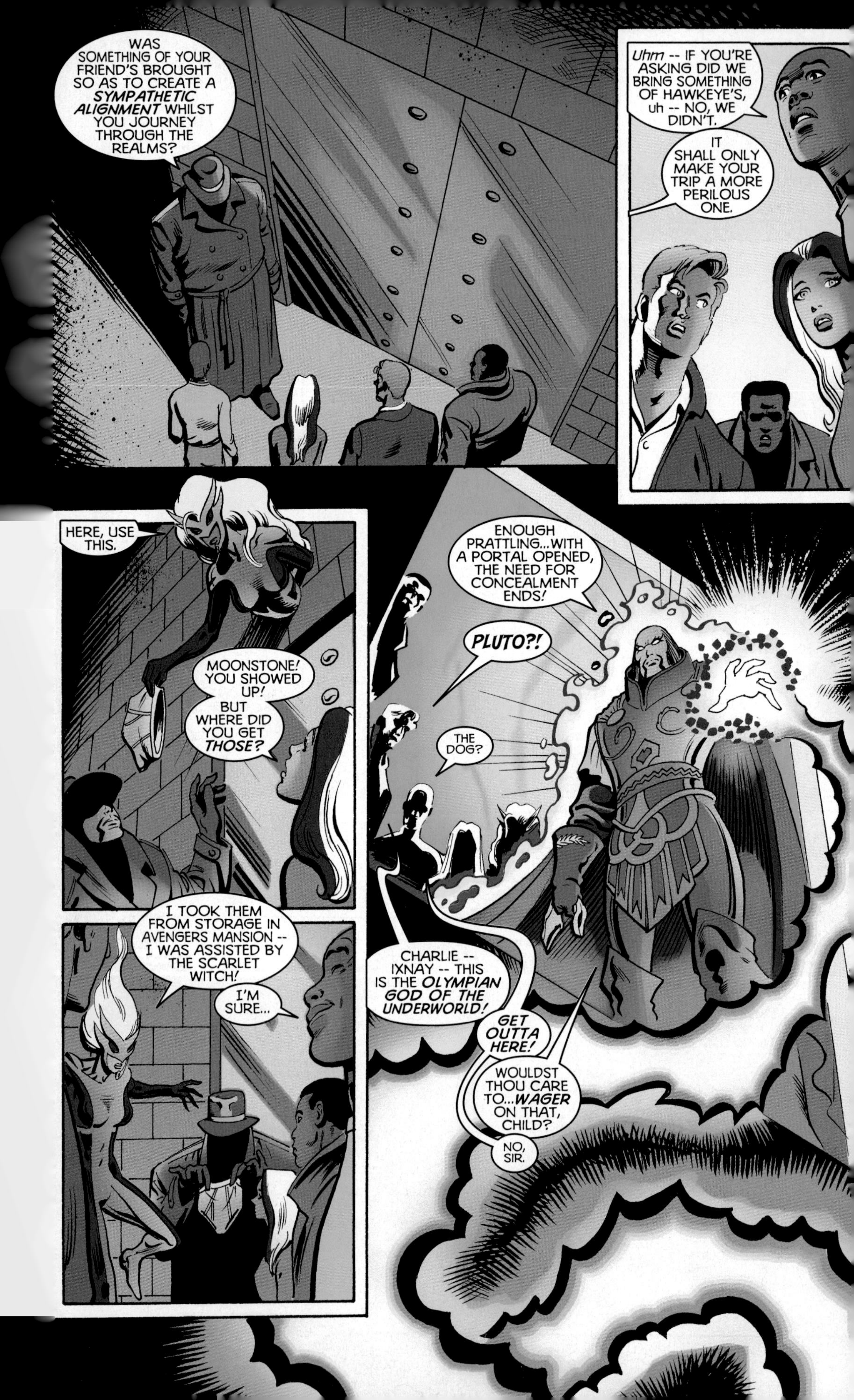

WAS SOMETHING OF YOUR FRIEND'S BROUGHT SO AS TO CREATE A *SYMPATHETIC ALIGNMENT* WHILST YOU JOURNEY THROUGH THE REALMS?
Uhm -- IF YOU'RE ASKING DID WE BRING SOMETHING OF HAWKEYE'S, uh -- NO, WE DIDN'T.
IT SHALL ONLY MAKE YOUR TRIP A MORE PERILOUS ONE.
HERE, USE THIS.
MOONSTONE! YOU SHOWED UP!
BUT WHERE DID YOU GET *THOSE?*
I TOOK THEM FROM STORAGE IN AVENGERS MANSION -- I WAS ASSISTED BY THE SCARLET WITCH!
I'M SURE...
ENOUGH PRATTLING...WITH A PORTAL OPENED, THE NEED FOR CONCEALMENT ENDS!
PLUTO?!
THE DOG?
CHARLIE -- IXNAY -- THIS IS THE *OLYMPIAN GOD OF THE UNDERWORLD!*
GET OUTTA HERE!
WOULDST THOU CARE TO...*WAGER* ON THAT, CHILD?
NO, SIR.

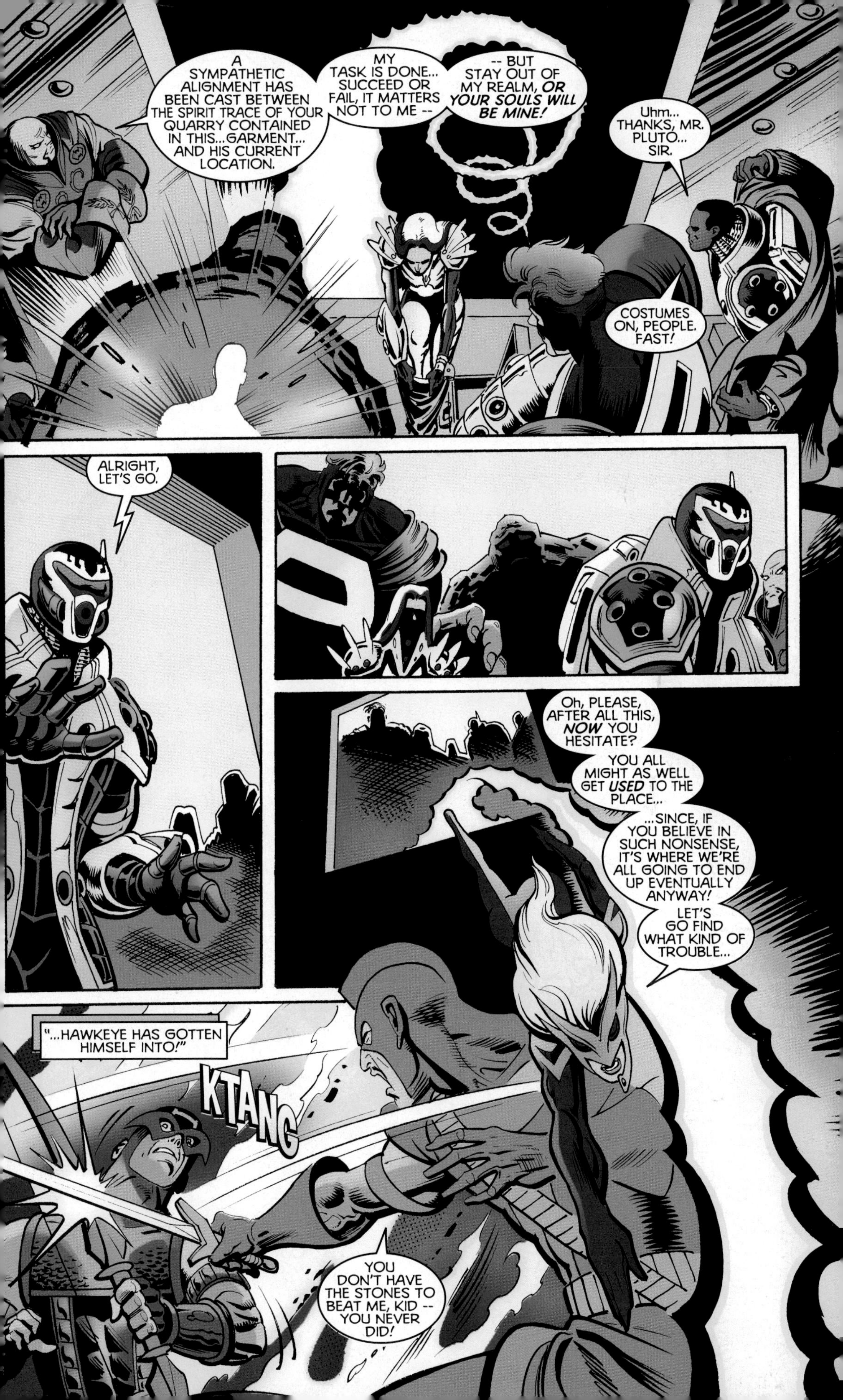

A SYMPATHETIC ALIGNMENT HAS BEEN CAST BETWEEN THE SPIRIT TRACE OF YOUR QUARRY CONTAINED IN THIS...GARMENT... AND HIS CURRENT LOCATION.
MY TASK IS DONE... SUCCEED OR FAIL, IT MATTERS NOT TO ME --
-- BUT STAY OUT OF MY REALM, **OR YOUR SOULS WILL BE MINE!**
Uhm... THANKS, MR. PLUTO... SIR.
COSTUMES ON, PEOPLE. FAST!
ALRIGHT, LET'S GO.
Oh, PLEASE, AFTER ALL THIS, ***NOW*** YOU HESITATE?
YOU ALL MIGHT AS WELL GET ***USED*** TO THE PLACE...
...SINCE, IF YOU BELIEVE IN SUCH NONSENSE, IT'S WHERE WE'RE ALL GOING TO END UP EVENTUALLY ANYWAY!
LET'S GO FIND WHAT KIND OF TROUBLE...
"...HAWKEYE HAS GOTTEN HIMSELF INTO!"
KTANG
YOU DON'T HAVE THE STONES TO BEAT ME, KID -- YOU NEVER DID!

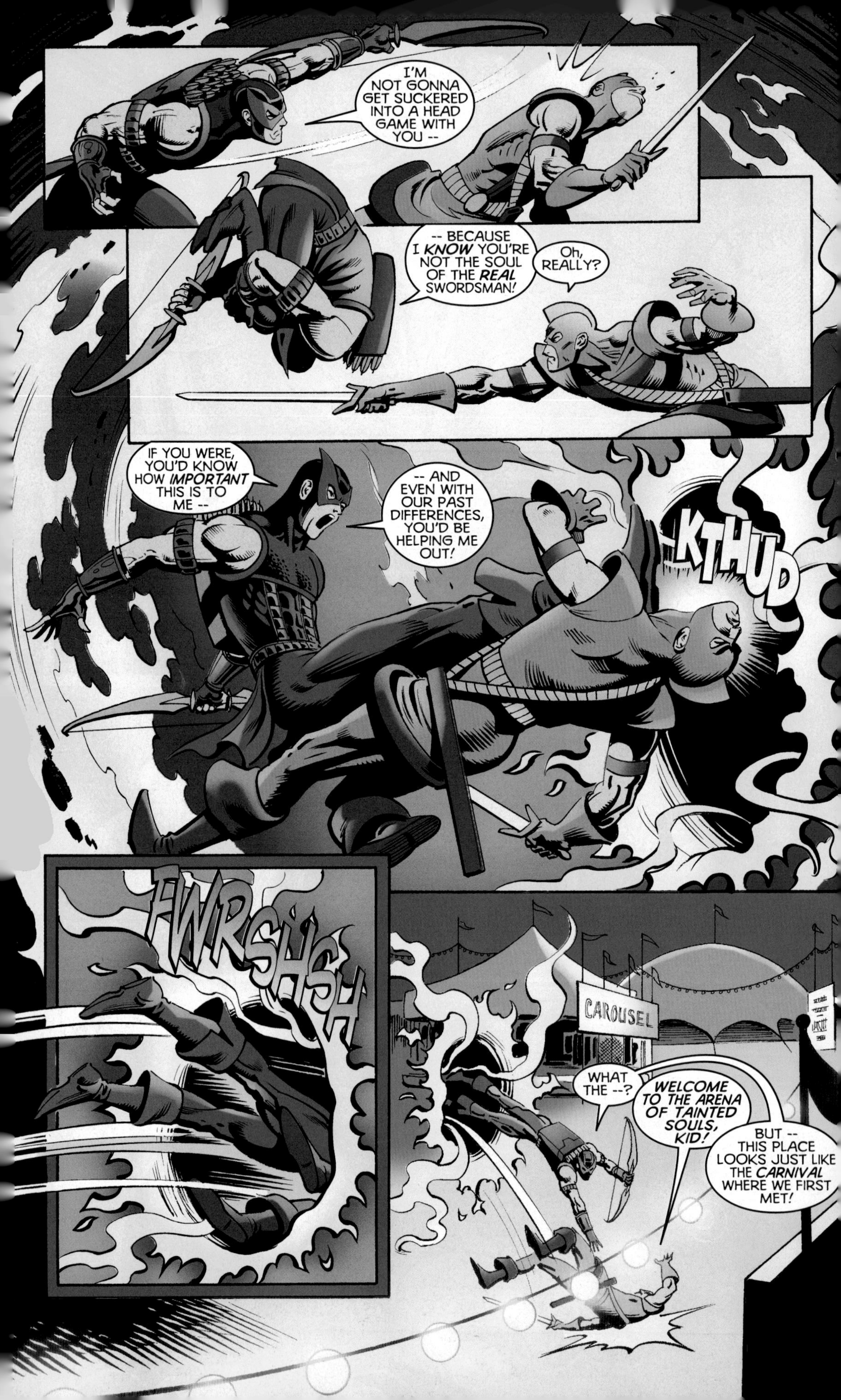

I'M NOT GONNA GET SUCKERED INTO A HEAD GAME WITH YOU --
-- BECAUSE I *KNOW* YOU'RE NOT THE SOUL OF THE *REAL* SWORDSMAN!
Oh, REALLY?
IF YOU WERE, YOU'D KNOW HOW *IMPORTANT* THIS IS TO ME --
-- AND EVEN WITH OUR PAST DIFFERENCES, YOU'D BE HELPING ME OUT!
KTHUD
FWRSHSH
CAROUSEL
WHAT THE --?
WELCOME TO THE ARENA OF TAINTED SOULS, KID!
BUT -- THIS PLACE LOOKS JUST LIKE THE *CARNIVAL* WHERE WE FIRST MET!

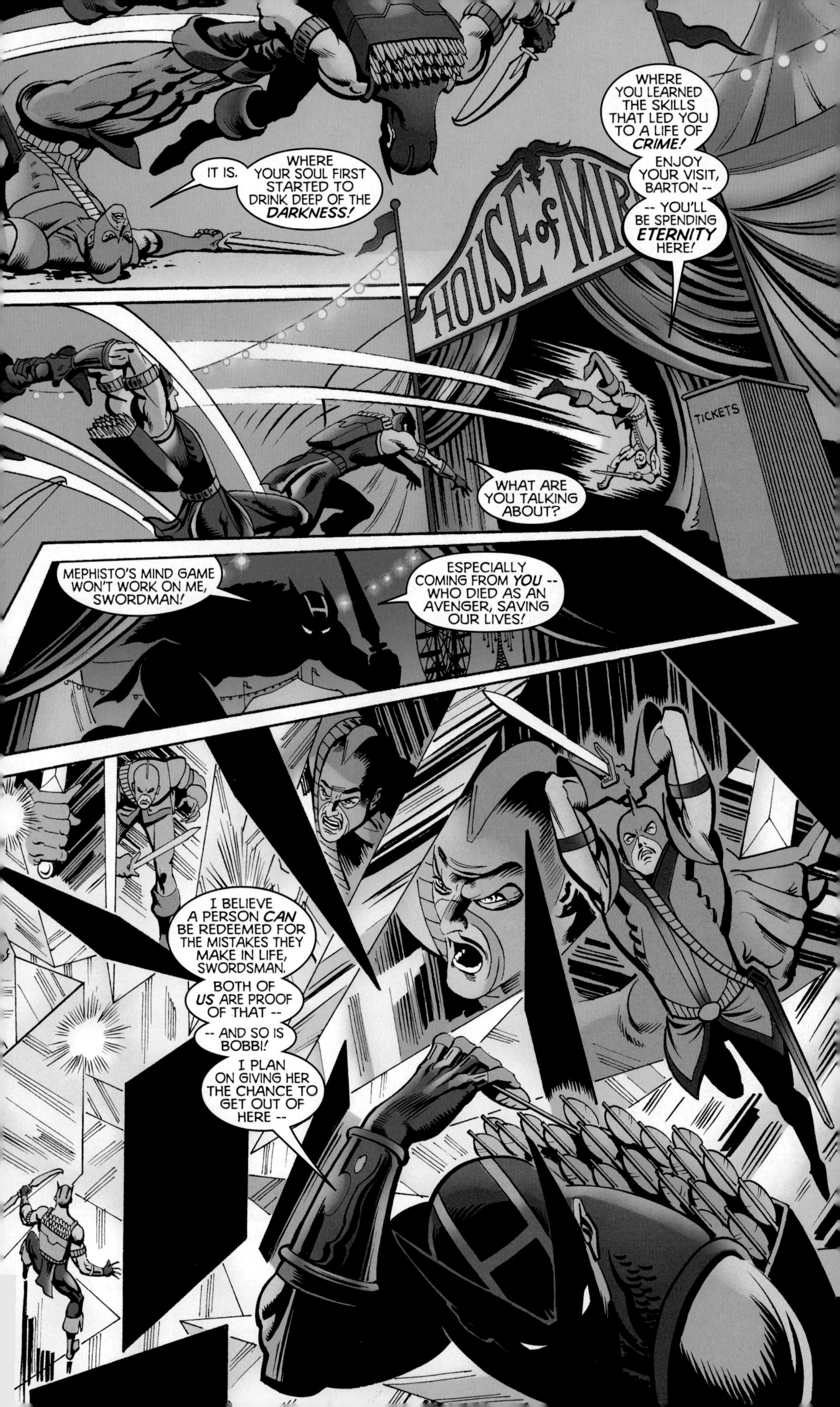

IT IS.
WHERE YOUR SOUL FIRST STARTED TO DRINK DEEP OF THE *DARKNESS!*
WHERE YOU LEARNED THE SKILLS THAT LED YOU TO A LIFE OF *CRIME!*
ENJOY YOUR VISIT, BARTON --
-- YOU'LL BE SPENDING *ETERNITY* HERE!
HOUSE of MIR
TICKETS
WHAT ARE YOU TALKING ABOUT?
MEPHISTO'S MIND GAME WON'T WORK ON ME, SWORDMAN!
ESPECIALLY COMING FROM *YOU* -- WHO DIED AS AN AVENGER, SAVING OUR LIVES!
I BELIEVE A PERSON *CAN* BE REDEEMED FOR THE MISTAKES THEY MAKE IN LIFE, SWORDSMAN.
BOTH OF *US* ARE PROOF OF THAT --
-- AND SO IS BOBBI!
I PLAN ON GIVING HER THE CHANCE TO GET OUT OF HERE --

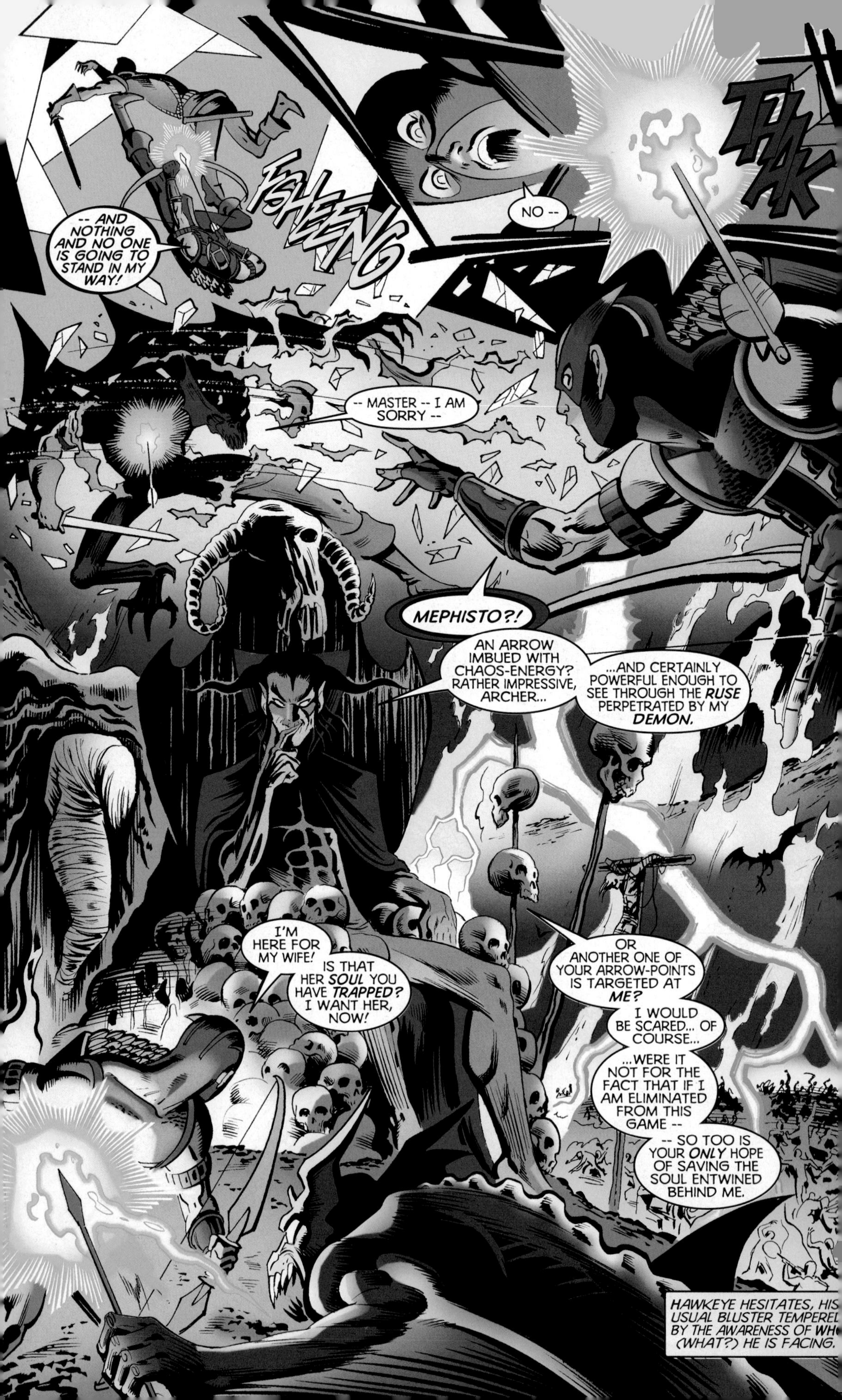
-- AND NOTHING AND NO ONE IS GOING TO STAND IN MY WAY!
FSHEEENG
NO --
THAK
-- MASTER -- I AM SORRY --
MEPHISTO?!
AN ARROW IMBUED WITH CHAOS-ENERGY? RATHER IMPRESSIVE, ARCHER...
...AND CERTAINLY POWERFUL ENOUGH TO SEE THROUGH THE RUSE PERPETRATED BY MY DEMON.
I'M HERE FOR MY WIFE!
IS THAT HER SOUL YOU HAVE TRAPPED? I WANT HER, NOW!
OR ANOTHER ONE OF YOUR ARROW-POINTS IS TARGETED AT ME?
I WOULD BE SCARED... OF COURSE...
...WERE IT NOT FOR THE FACT THAT IF I AM ELIMINATED FROM THIS GAME --
-- SO TOO IS YOUR ONLY HOPE OF SAVING THE SOUL ENTWINED BEHIND ME.
HAWKEYE HESITATES, HIS USUAL BLUSTER TEMPERED BY THE AWARENESS OF WH (WHAT?) HE IS FACING.

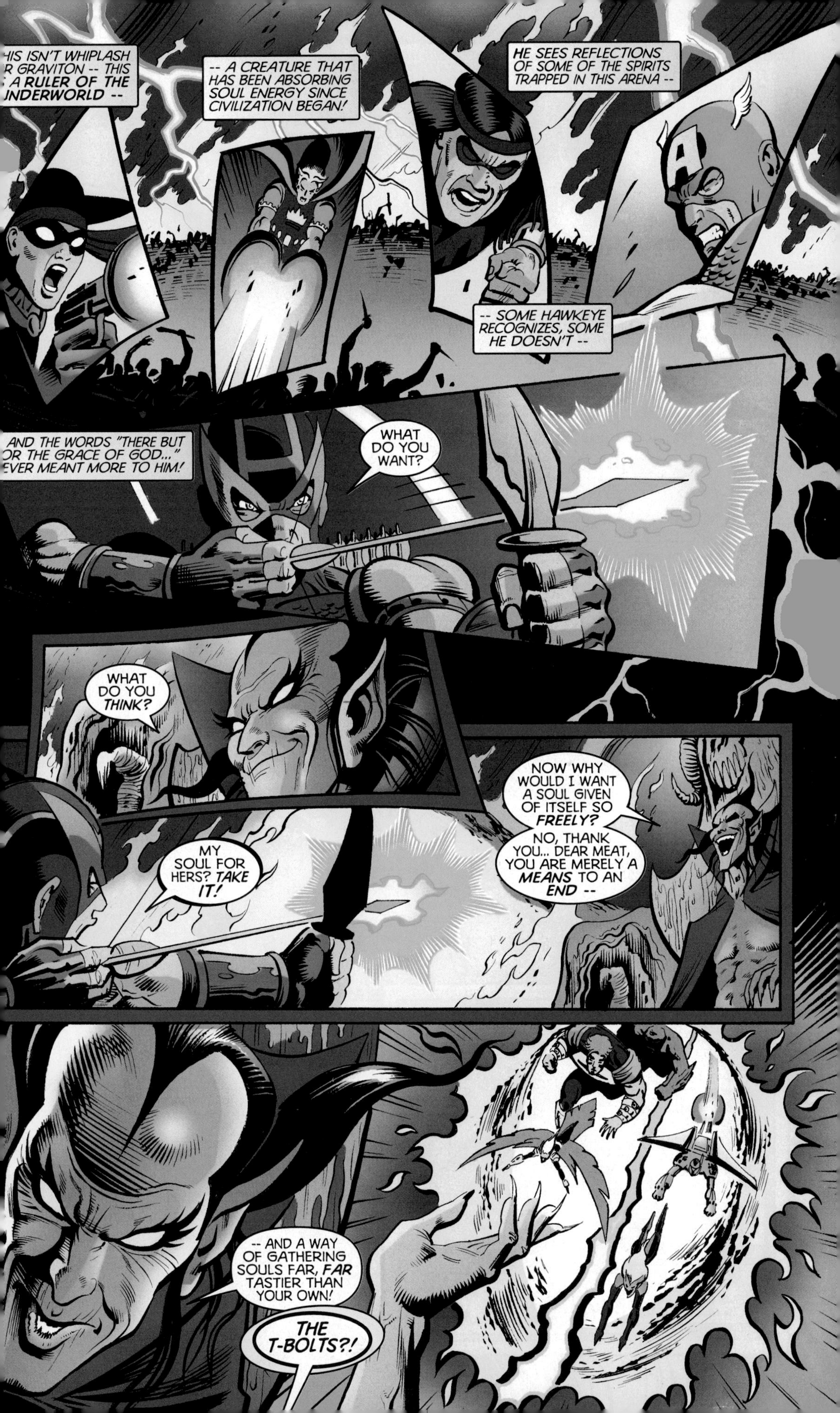

HIS ISN'T WHIPLASH R GRAVITON -- THIS S A RULER OF THE NDERWORLD --
-- A CREATURE THAT HAS BEEN ABSORBING SOUL ENERGY SINCE CIVILIZATION BEGAN!
HE SEES REFLECTIONS OF SOME OF THE SPIRITS TRAPPED IN THIS ARENA --
-- SOME HAWKEYE RECOGNIZES, SOME HE DOESN'T --
AND THE WORDS "THERE BUT OR THE GRACE OF GOD..." EVER MEANT MORE TO HIM!
WHAT DO YOU WANT?
WHAT DO YOU THINK?
MY SOUL FOR HERS? TAKE IT!
NOW WHY WOULD I WANT A SOUL GIVEN OF ITSELF SO FREELY?
NO, THANK YOU... DEAR MEAT, YOU ARE MERELY A MEANS TO AN END --
-- AND A WAY OF GATHERING SOULS FAR, FAR TASTIER THAN YOUR OWN!
THE T-BOLTS?!

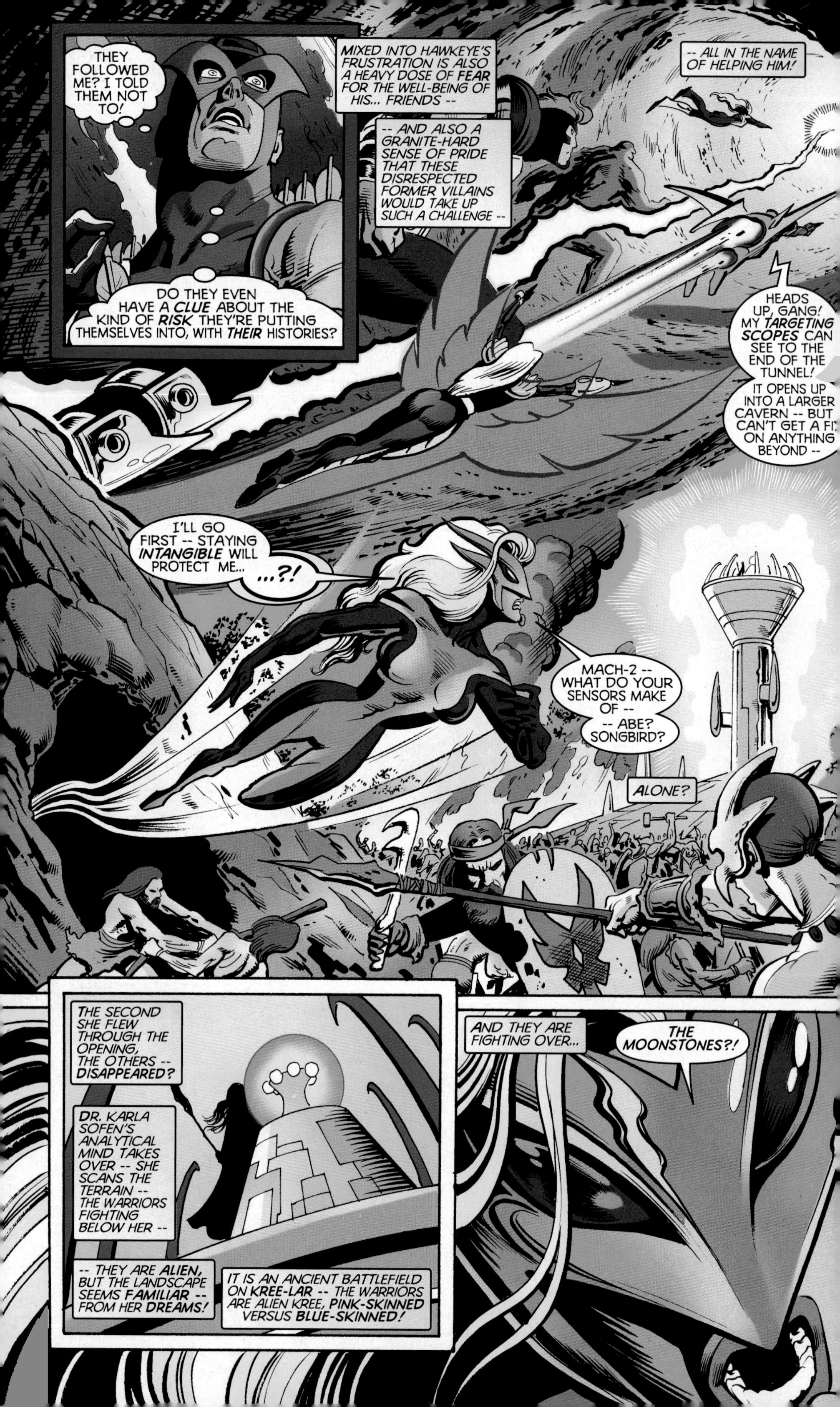
THEY FOLLOWED ME? I TOLD THEM NOT TO!
DO THEY EVEN HAVE A CLUE ABOUT THE KIND OF RISK THEY'RE PUTTING THEMSELVES INTO, WITH THEIR HISTORIES?
MIXED INTO HAWKEYE'S FRUSTRATION IS ALSO A HEAVY DOSE OF FEAR FOR THE WELL-BEING OF HIS... FRIENDS --
-- AND ALSO A GRANITE-HARD SENSE OF PRIDE THAT THESE DISRESPECTED FORMER VILLAINS WOULD TAKE UP SUCH A CHALLENGE --
-- ALL IN THE NAME OF HELPING HIM!
HEADS UP, GANG! MY TARGETING SCOPES CAN SEE TO THE END OF THE TUNNEL!
IT OPENS UP INTO A LARGER CAVERN -- BUT CAN'T GET A FI ON ANYTHING BEYOND --
I'LL GO FIRST -- STAYING INTANGIBLE WILL PROTECT ME...
...?!
MACH-2 -- WHAT DO YOUR SENSORS MAKE OF --
-- ABE? SONGBIRD?
ALONE?
THE SECOND SHE FLEW THROUGH THE OPENING, THE OTHERS -- DISAPPEARED?
DR. KARLA SOFEN'S ANALYTICAL MIND TAKES OVER -- SHE SCANS THE TERRAIN -- THE WARRIORS FIGHTING BELOW HER --
-- THEY ARE ALIEN, BUT THE LANDSCAPE SEEMS FAMILIAR -- FROM HER DREAMS!
IT IS AN ANCIENT BATTLEFIELD ON KREE-LAR -- THE WARRIORS ARE ALIEN KREE, PINK-SKINNED VERSUS BLUE-SKINNED!
AND THEY ARE FIGHTING OVER...
THE MOONSTONES?!

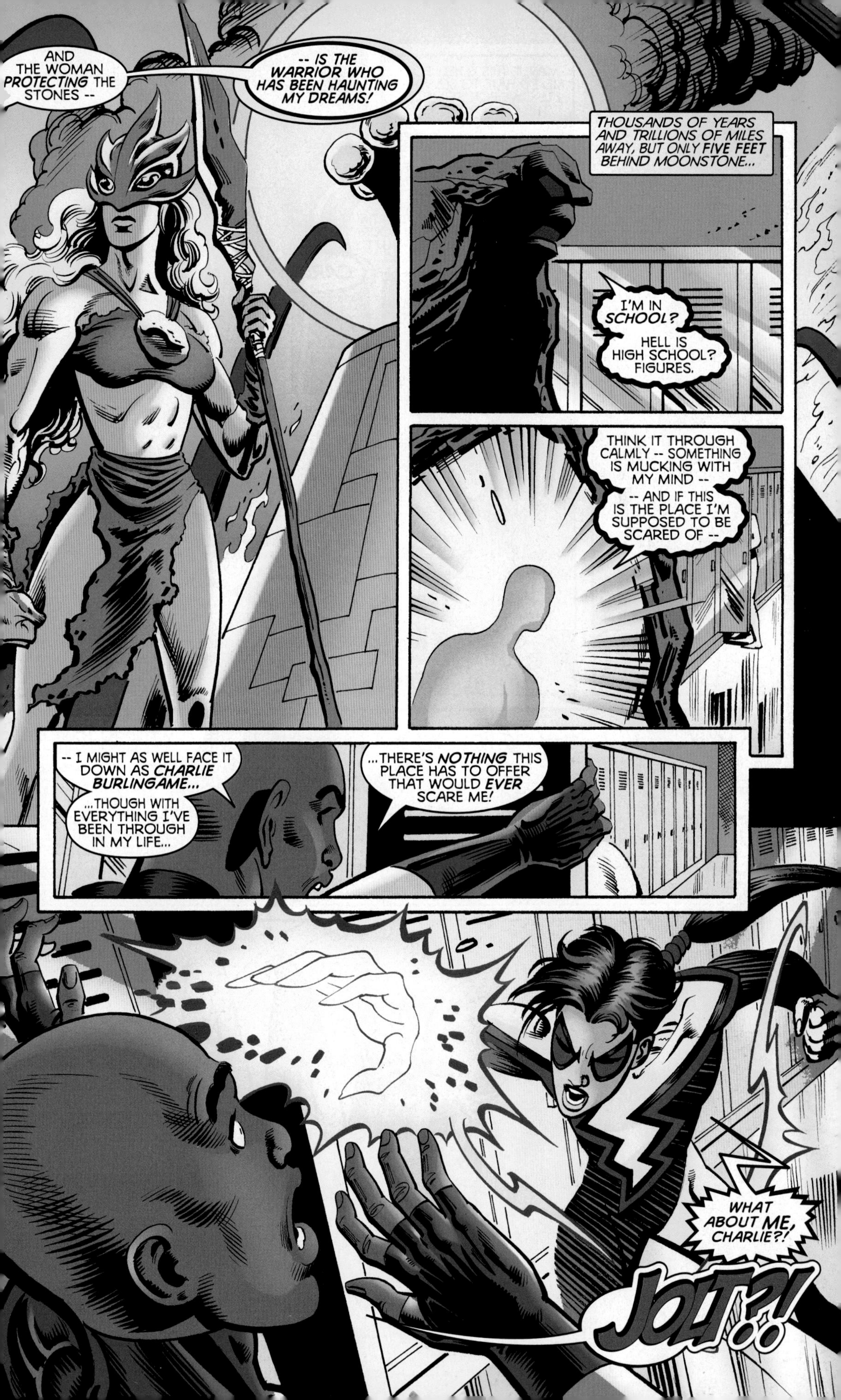
AND THE WOMAN PROTECTING THE STONES --
-- IS THE WARRIOR WHO HAS BEEN HAUNTING MY DREAMS!
THOUSANDS OF YEARS AND TRILLIONS OF MILES AWAY, BUT ONLY FIVE FEET BEHIND MOONSTONE...
I'M IN SCHOOL?
HELL IS HIGH SCHOOL? FIGURES.
THINK IT THROUGH CALMLY -- SOMETHING IS MUCKING WITH MY MIND --
-- AND IF THIS IS THE PLACE I'M SUPPOSED TO BE SCARED OF --
-- I MIGHT AS WELL FACE IT DOWN AS CHARLIE BURLINGAME...
...THOUGH WITH EVERYTHING I'VE BEEN THROUGH IN MY LIFE...
...THERE'S NOTHING THIS PLACE HAS TO OFFER THAT WOULD EVER SCARE ME!
WHAT ABOUT ME, CHARLIE?!
JOLT?!

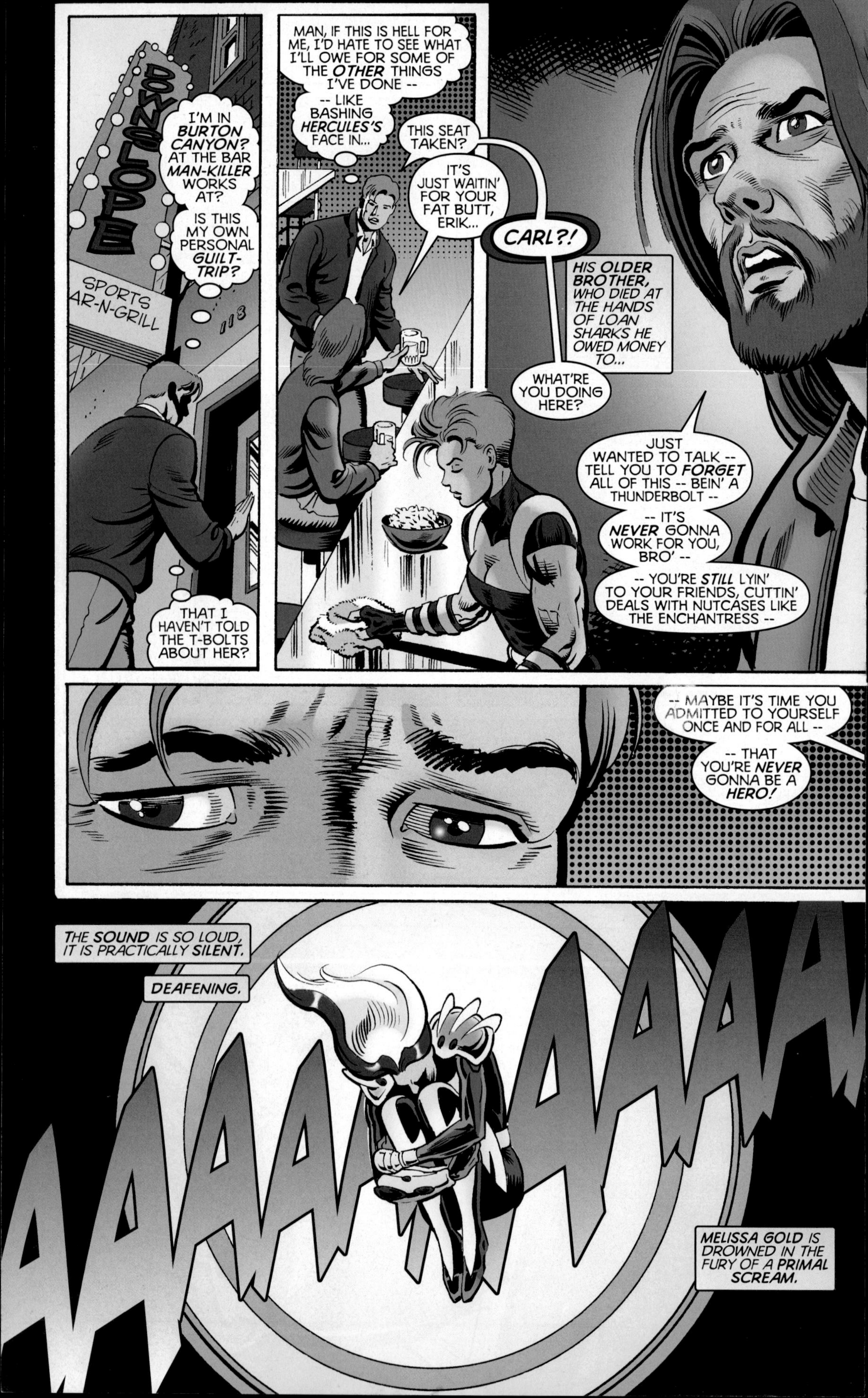
DOWNSLOPE
SPORTS AR-N-GRILL
118
I'M IN BURTON CANYON? AT THE BAR MAN-KILLER WORKS AT?
IS THIS MY OWN PERSONAL GUILT-TRIP?
THAT I HAVEN'T TOLD THE T-BOLTS ABOUT HER?
MAN, IF THIS IS HELL FOR ME, I'D HATE TO SEE WHAT I'LL OWE FOR SOME OF THE OTHER THINGS I'VE DONE --
-- LIKE BASHING HERCULES'S FACE IN...
THIS SEAT TAKEN?
IT'S JUST WAITIN' FOR YOUR FAT BUTT, ERIK...
CARL?!
HIS OLDER BROTHER, WHO DIED AT THE HANDS OF LOAN SHARKS HE OWED MONEY TO...
WHAT'RE YOU DOING HERE?
JUST WANTED TO TALK -- TELL YOU TO FORGET ALL OF THIS -- BEIN' A THUNDERBOLT --
-- IT'S NEVER GONNA WORK FOR YOU, BRO' --
-- YOU'RE STILL LYIN' TO YOUR FRIENDS, CUTTIN' DEALS WITH NUTCASES LIKE THE ENCHANTRESS --
-- MAYBE IT'S TIME YOU ADMITTED TO YOURSELF ONCE AND FOR ALL --
-- THAT YOU'RE NEVER GONNA BE A HERO!
THE SOUND IS SO LOUD, IT IS PRACTICALLY SILENT.
DEAFENING.
AAAAAAAAAA
MELISSA GOLD IS DROWNED IN THE FURY OF A PRIMAL SCREAM.

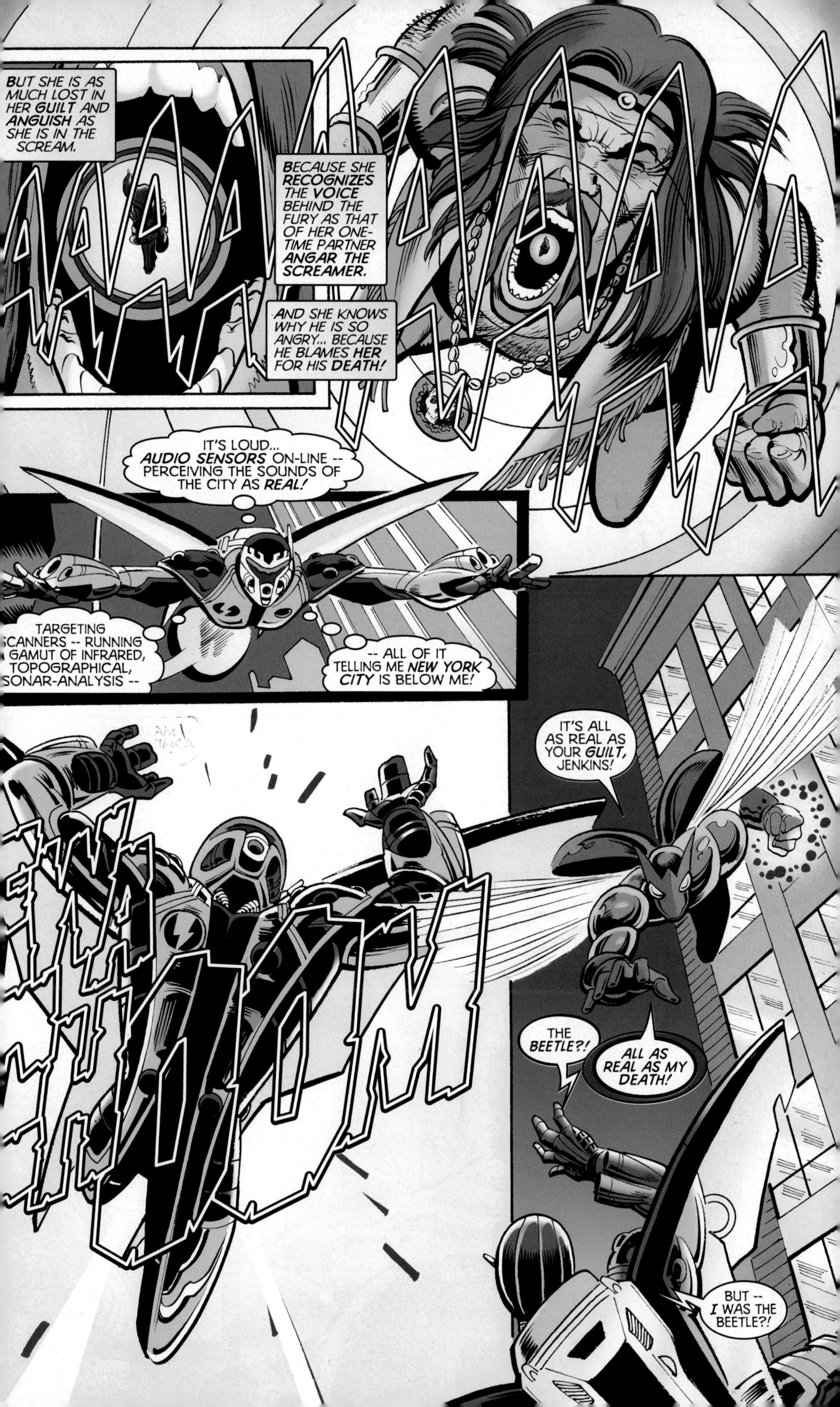

BUT SHE IS AS MUCH LOST IN HER GUILT AND ANGUISH AS SHE IS IN THE SCREAM.
BECAUSE SHE RECOGNIZES THE VOICE BEHIND THE FURY AS THAT OF HER ONE-TIME PARTNER ANGAR THE SCREAMER.
AND SHE KNOWS WHY HE IS SO ANGRY... BECAUSE HE BLAMES HER FOR HIS DEATH!
IT'S LOUD... AUDIO SENSORS ON-LINE -- PERCEIVING THE SOUNDS OF THE CITY AS REAL!
TARGETING CANNERS -- RUNNING GAMUT OF INFRARED, TOPOGRAPHICAL, SONAR-ANALYSIS --
-- ALL OF IT TELLING ME NEW YORK CITY IS BELOW ME!
IT'S ALL AS REAL AS YOUR GUILT, JENKINS!
THE BEETLE?!
ALL AS REAL AS MY DEATH!
BUT -- I WAS THE BEETLE?!

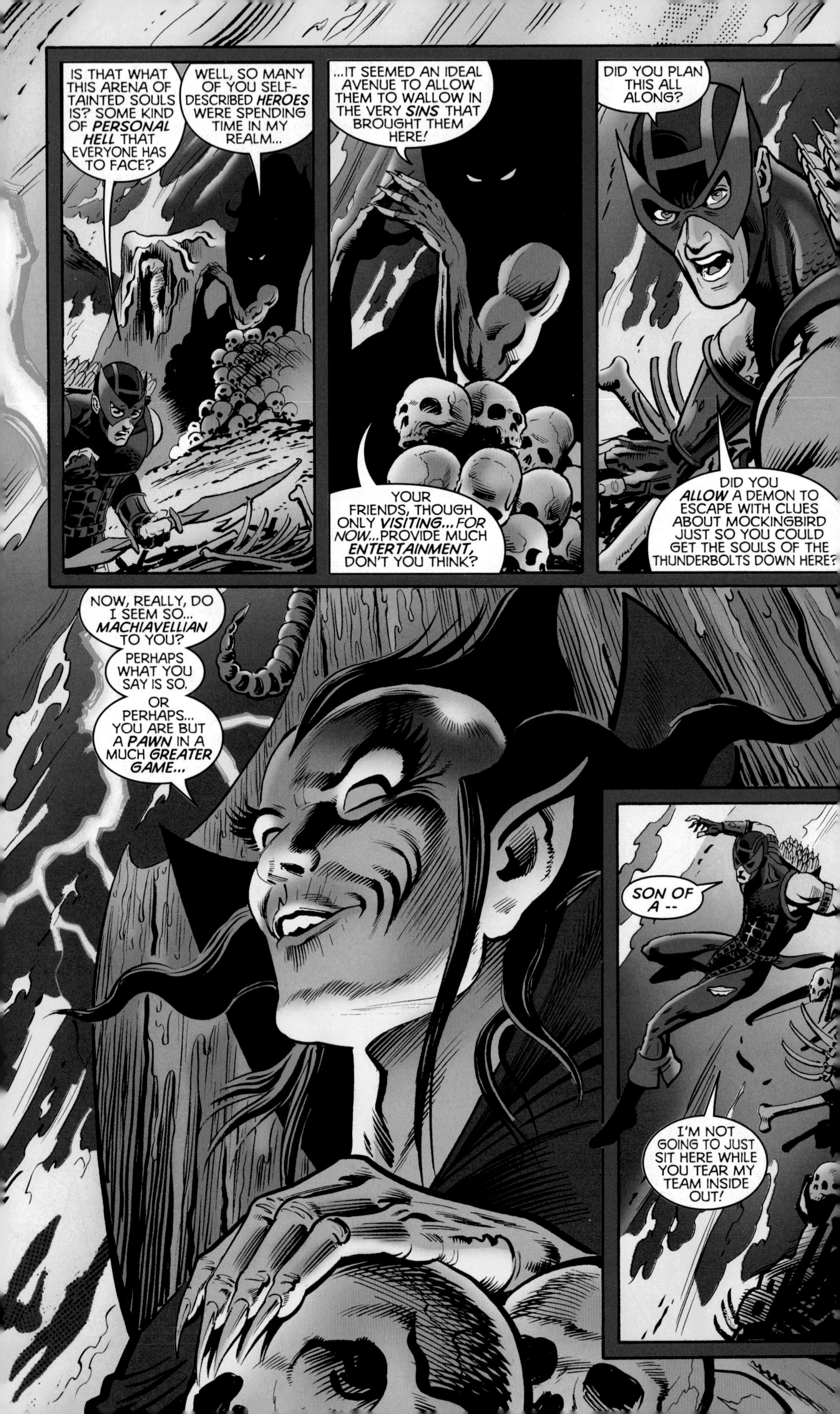
IS THAT WHAT THIS ARENA OF TAINTED SOULS IS? SOME KIND OF PERSONAL HELL THAT EVERYONE HAS TO FACE?
WELL, SO MANY OF YOU SELF-DESCRIBED HEROES WERE SPENDING TIME IN MY REALM...
...IT SEEMED AN IDEAL AVENUE TO ALLOW THEM TO WALLOW IN THE VERY SINS THAT BROUGHT THEM HERE!
YOUR FRIENDS, THOUGH ONLY VISITING... FOR NOW...PROVIDE MUCH ENTERTAINMENT, DON'T YOU THINK?
DID YOU PLAN THIS ALL ALONG?
DID YOU ALLOW A DEMON TO ESCAPE WITH CLUES ABOUT MOCKINGBIRD JUST SO YOU COULD GET THE SOULS OF THE THUNDERBOLTS DOWN HERE?
NOW, REALLY, DO I SEEM SO... MACHIAVELLIAN TO YOU?
PERHAPS WHAT YOU SAY IS SO.
OR PERHAPS... YOU ARE BUT A PAWN IN A MUCH GREATER GAME...
SON OF A --
I'M NOT GOING TO JUST SIT HERE WHILE YOU TEAR MY TEAM INSIDE OUT!

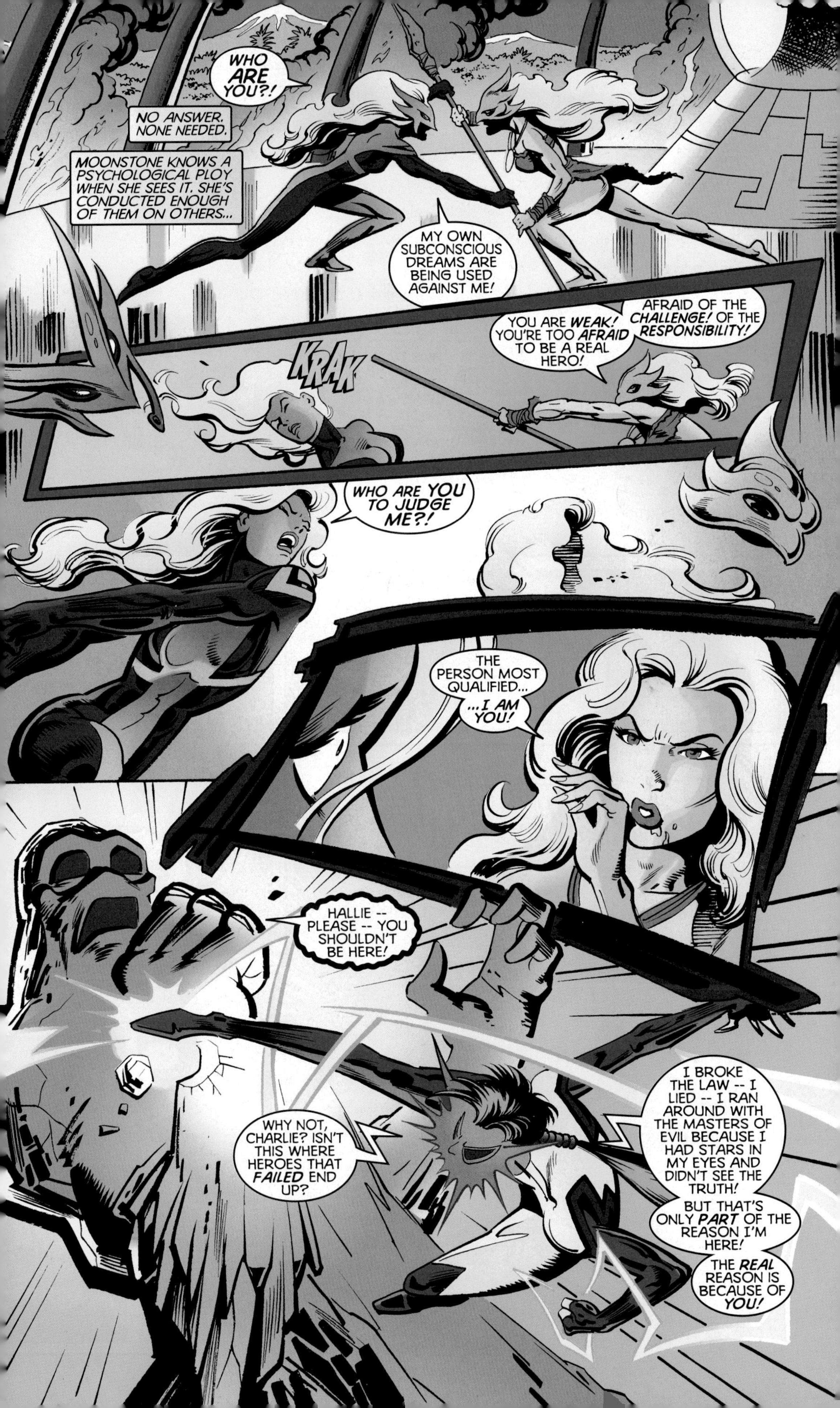

WHO ARE YOU?!
NO ANSWER. NONE NEEDED.
MOONSTONE KNOWS A PSYCHOLOGICAL PLOY WHEN SHE SEES IT. SHE'S CONDUCTED ENOUGH OF THEM ON OTHERS...
MY OWN SUBCONSCIOUS DREAMS ARE BEING USED AGAINST ME!
KRAK
YOU ARE WEAK! YOU'RE TOO AFRAID TO BE A REAL HERO!
AFRAID OF THE CHALLENGE! OF THE RESPONSIBILITY!
WHO ARE YOU TO JUDGE ME?!
THE PERSON MOST QUALIFIED...
...I AM YOU!
HALLIE -- PLEASE -- YOU SHOULDN'T BE HERE!
WHY NOT, CHARLIE? ISN'T THIS WHERE HEROES THAT FAILED END UP?
I BROKE THE LAW -- I LIED -- I RAN AROUND WITH THE MASTERS OF EVIL BECAUSE I HAD STARS IN MY EYES AND DIDN'T SEE THE TRUTH!
BUT THAT'S ONLY PART OF THE REASON I'M HERE!
THE REAL REASON IS BECAUSE OF YOU!

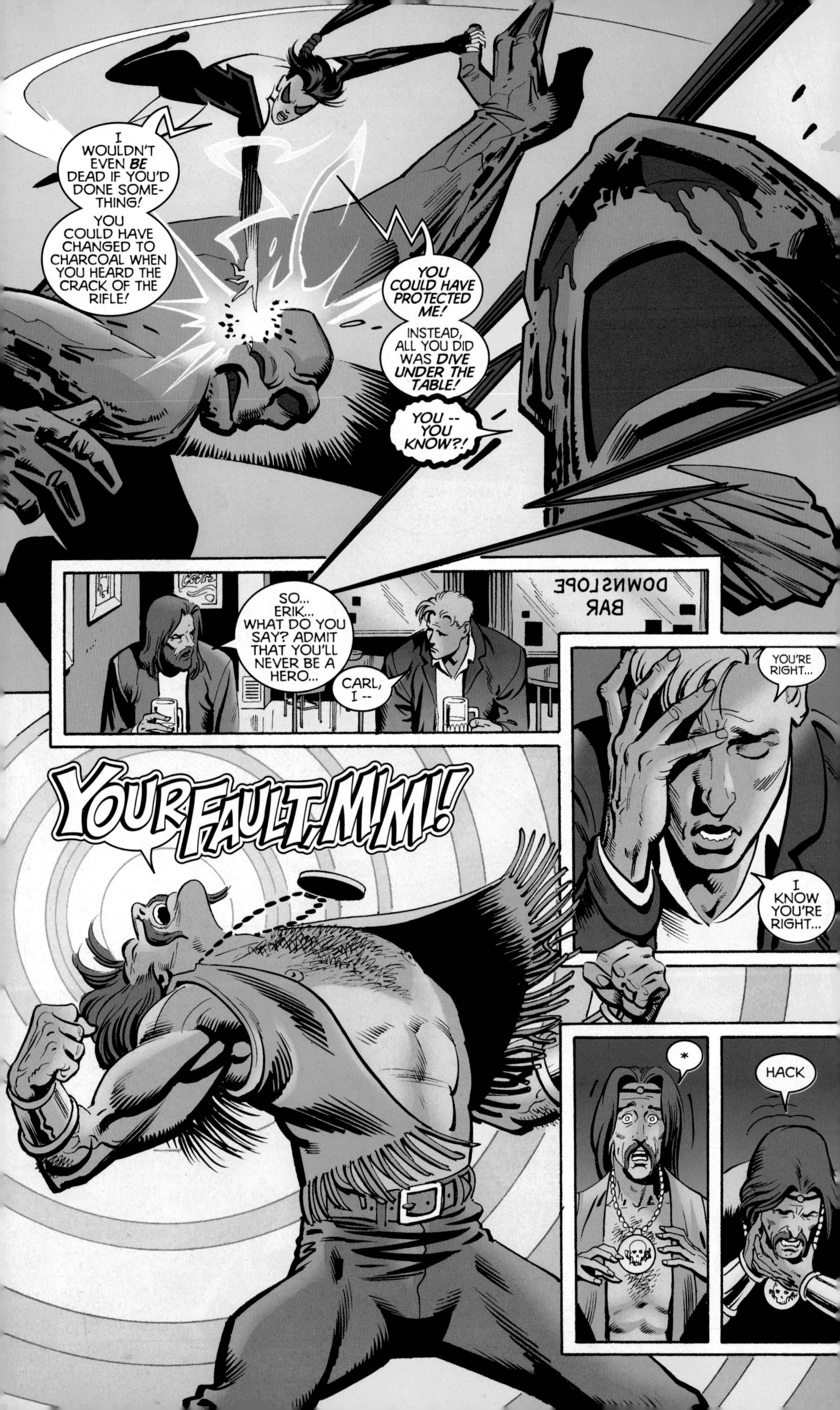
I WOULDN'T EVEN *BE* DEAD IF YOU'D DONE SOME-THING!
YOU COULD HAVE CHANGED TO CHARCOAL WHEN YOU HEARD THE CRACK OF THE RIFLE!
YOU COULD HAVE PROTECTED ME!
INSTEAD, ALL YOU DID WAS *DIVE UNDER THE TABLE!*
YOU -- YOU KNOW?!
DOWNSLOPE BAR
SO... ERIK... WHAT DO YOU SAY? ADMIT THAT YOU'LL NEVER BE A HERO...
CARL, I --
YOU'RE RIGHT...
I KNOW YOU'RE RIGHT...
YOUR FAULT, M!M!
*
HACK

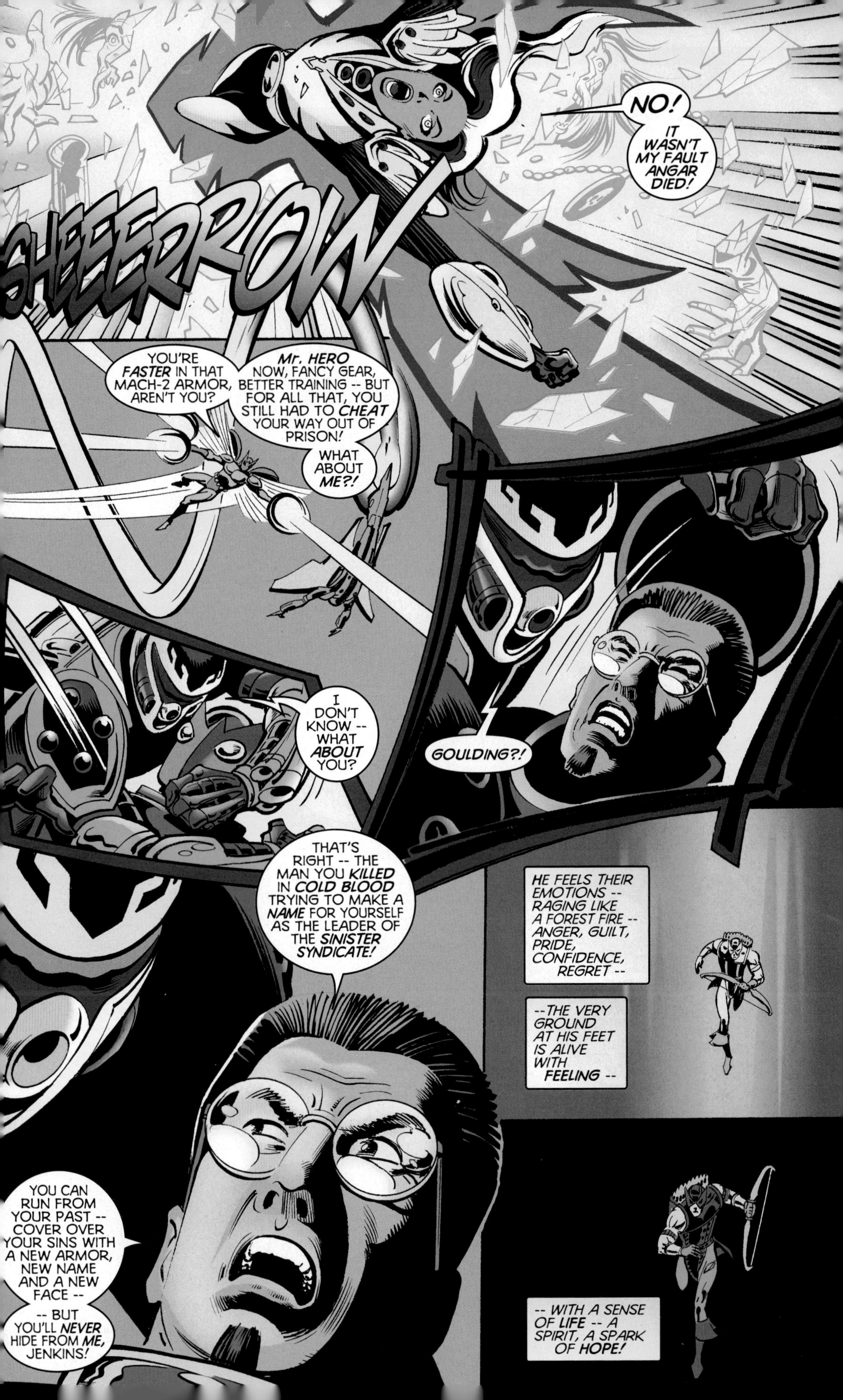
NO! IT WASN'T MY FAULT ANGAR DIED!
SHEEEROW
YOU'RE FASTER IN THAT MACH-2 ARMOR, AREN'T YOU?
Mr. HERO NOW, FANCY GEAR, BETTER TRAINING -- BUT FOR ALL THAT, YOU STILL HAD TO CHEAT YOUR WAY OUT OF PRISON!
WHAT ABOUT ME?!
I DON'T KNOW -- WHAT ABOUT YOU?
GOULDING?!
THAT'S RIGHT -- THE MAN YOU KILLED IN COLD BLOOD TRYING TO MAKE A NAME FOR YOURSELF AS THE LEADER OF THE SINISTER SYNDICATE!
HE FEELS THEIR EMOTIONS -- RAGING LIKE A FOREST FIRE -- ANGER, GUILT, PRIDE, CONFIDENCE, REGRET --
--THE VERY GROUND AT HIS FEET IS ALIVE WITH FEELING --
YOU CAN RUN FROM YOUR PAST -- COVER OVER YOUR SINS WITH A NEW ARMOR, NEW NAME AND A NEW FACE --
-- BUT YOU'LL NEVER HIDE FROM ME, JENKINS!
-- WITH A SENSE OF LIFE -- A SPIRIT, A SPARK OF HOPE!

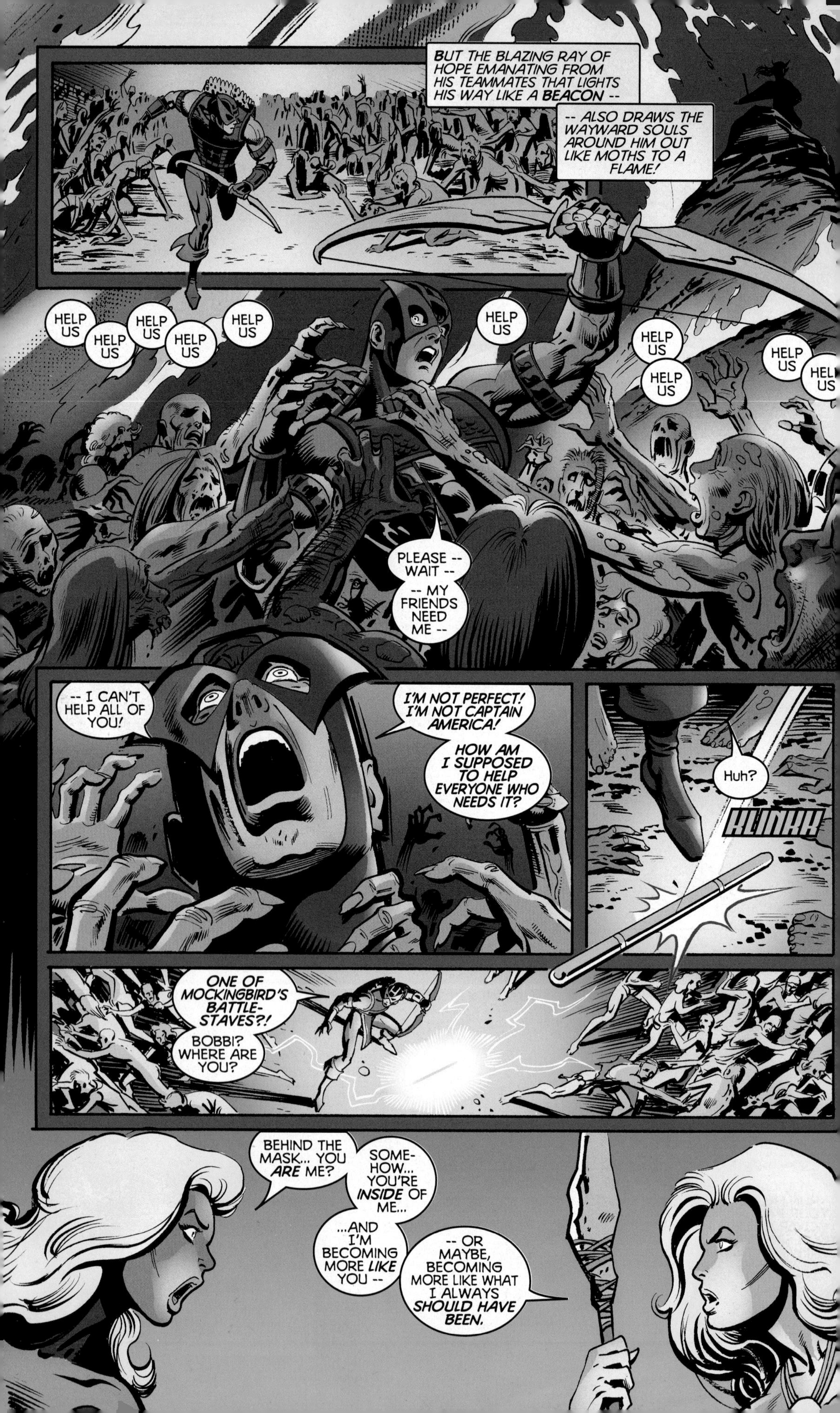
BUT THE BLAZING RAY OF HOPE EMANATING FROM HIS TEAMMATES THAT LIGHTS HIS WAY LIKE A BEACON --
-- ALSO DRAWS THE WAYWARD SOULS AROUND HIM OUT LIKE MOTHS TO A FLAME!
HELP US
HELP US
HELP US
HELP US
HELP US
HELP US
HELP US
HELP US
HELP US
HEL US
PLEASE -- WAIT --
-- MY FRIENDS NEED ME --
-- I CAN'T HELP ALL OF YOU!
I'M NOT PERFECT! I'M NOT CAPTAIN AMERICA!
HOW AM I SUPPOSED TO HELP EVERYONE WHO NEEDS IT?
Huh?
KLINKK
ONE OF MOCKINGBIRD'S BATTLE-STAVES?!
BOBBI? WHERE ARE YOU?
BEHIND THE MASK... YOU ARE ME?
SOME-HOW... YOU'RE INSIDE OF ME...
...AND I'M BECOMING MORE LIKE YOU --
-- OR MAYBE, BECOMING MORE LIKE WHAT I ALWAYS SHOULD HAVE BEEN.

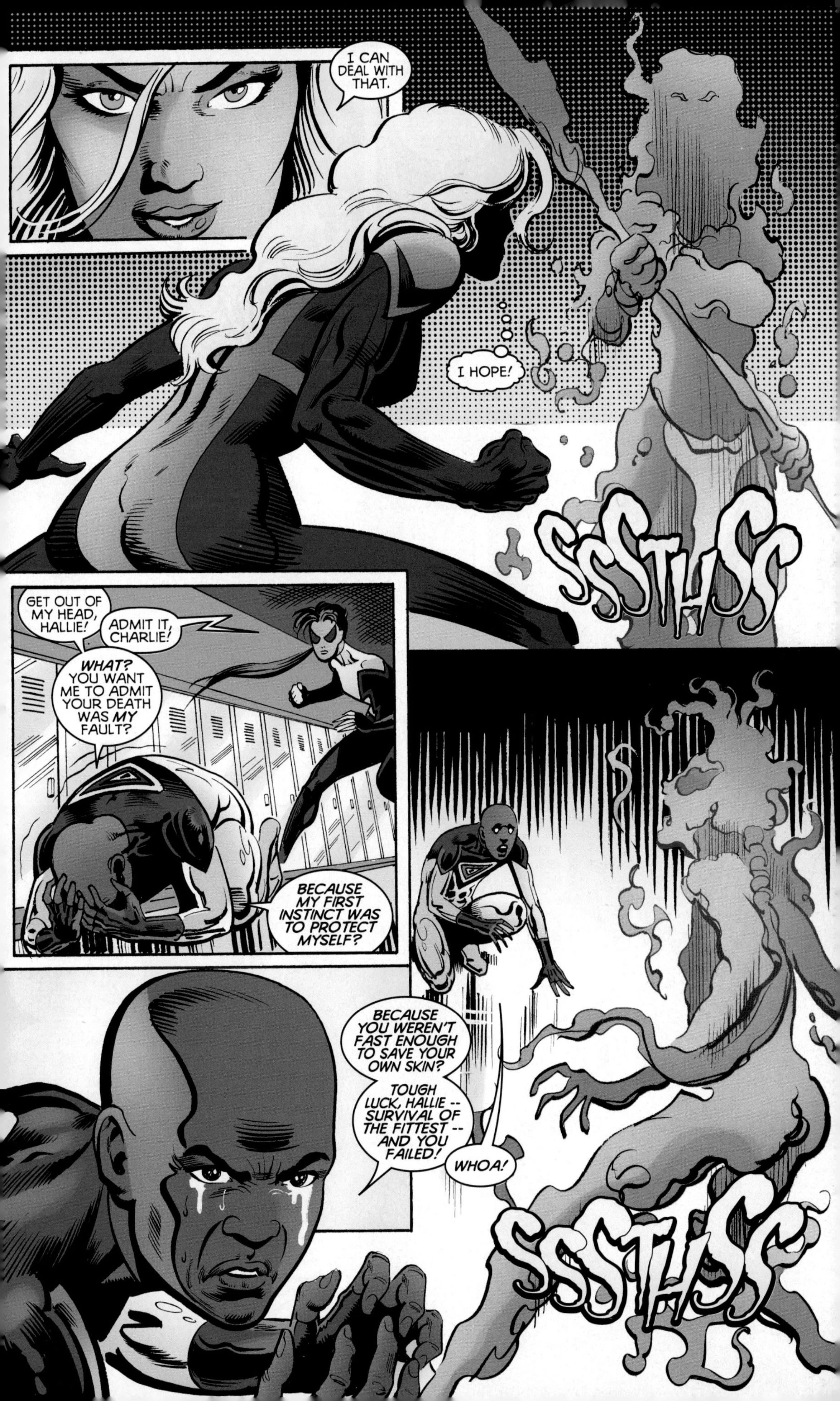
I CAN DEAL WITH THAT.
I HOPE!
SSSTHSS
GET OUT OF MY HEAD, HALLIE!
ADMIT IT, CHARLIE!
WHAT? YOU WANT ME TO ADMIT YOUR DEATH WAS MY FAULT?
BECAUSE MY FIRST INSTINCT WAS TO PROTECT MYSELF?
BECAUSE YOU WEREN'T FAST ENOUGH TO SAVE YOUR OWN SKIN?
TOUGH LUCK, HALLIE -- SURVIVAL OF THE FITTEST -- AND YOU FAILED!
WHOA!
SSSTHSS

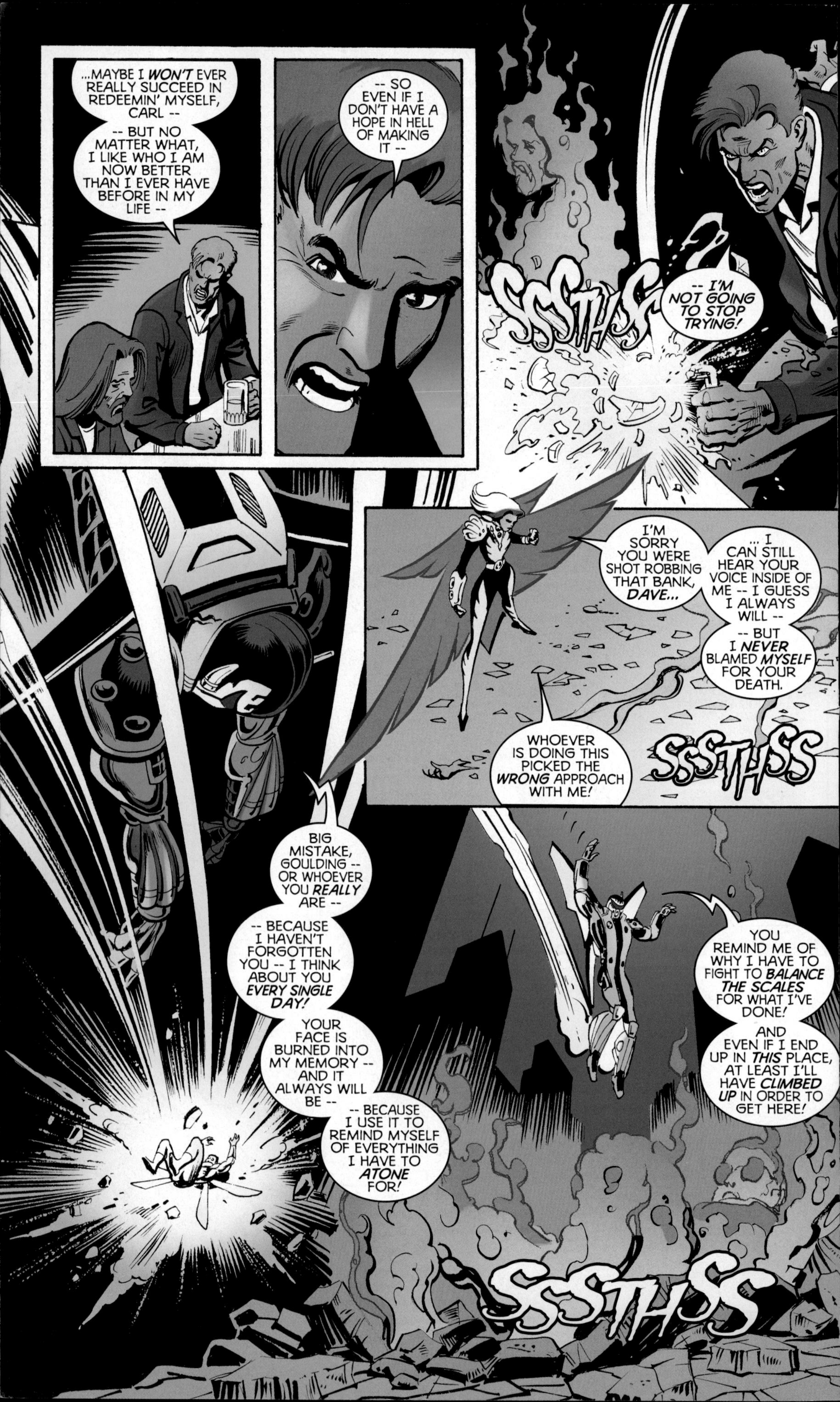

...MAYBE I WON'T EVER REALLY SUCCEED IN REDEEMIN' MYSELF, CARL --
-- BUT NO MATTER WHAT, I LIKE WHO I AM NOW BETTER THAN I EVER HAVE BEFORE IN MY LIFE --
-- SO EVEN IF I DON'T HAVE A HOPE IN HELL OF MAKING IT --
SSSTHSS
-- I'M NOT GOING TO STOP TRYING!
I'M SORRY YOU WERE SHOT ROBBING THAT BANK, DAVE...
... I CAN STILL HEAR YOUR VOICE INSIDE OF ME -- I GUESS I ALWAYS WILL --
-- BUT I NEVER BLAMED MYSELF FOR YOUR DEATH.
WHOEVER IS DOING THIS PICKED THE WRONG APPROACH WITH ME!
SSSTHSS
BIG MISTAKE, GOULDING -- OR WHOEVER YOU REALLY ARE --
-- BECAUSE I HAVEN'T FORGOTTEN YOU -- I THINK ABOUT YOU EVERY SINGLE DAY!
YOUR FACE IS BURNED INTO MY MEMORY -- AND IT ALWAYS WILL BE --
-- BECAUSE I USE IT TO REMIND MYSELF OF EVERYTHING I HAVE TO ATONE FOR!
YOU REMIND ME OF WHY I HAVE TO FIGHT TO BALANCE THE SCALES FOR WHAT I'VE DONE!
AND EVEN IF I END UP IN THIS PLACE, AT LEAST I'LL HAVE CLIMBED UP IN ORDER TO GET HERE!
SSSTHSS

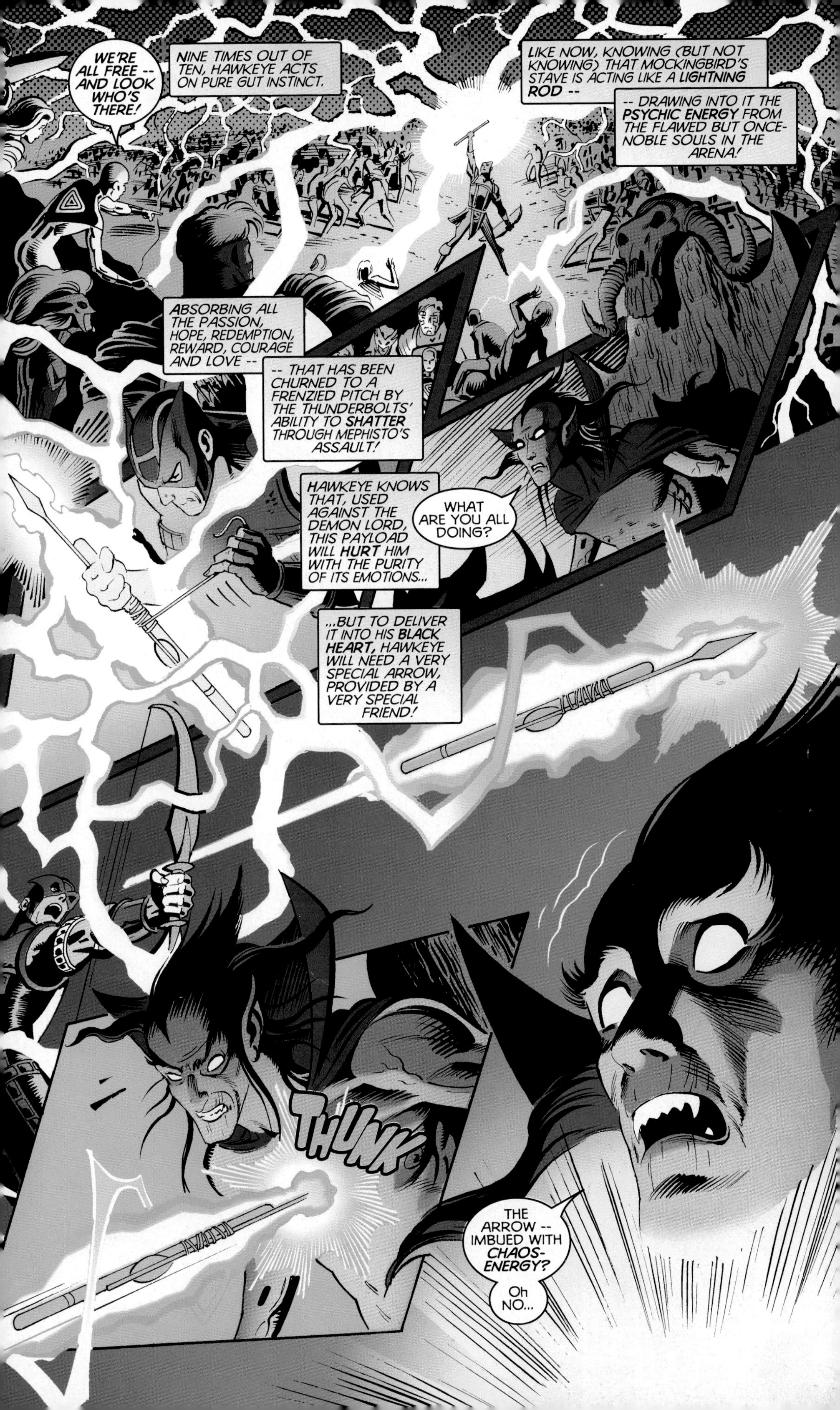
WE'RE ALL FREE -- AND LOOK WHO'S THERE!
NINE TIMES OUT OF TEN, HAWKEYE ACTS ON PURE GUT INSTINCT.
LIKE NOW, KNOWING (BUT NOT KNOWING) THAT MOCKINGBIRD'S STAVE IS ACTING LIKE A LIGHTNING ROD --
-- DRAWING INTO IT THE PSYCHIC ENERGY FROM THE FLAWED BUT ONCE-NOBLE SOULS IN THE ARENA!
ABSORBING ALL THE PASSION, HOPE, REDEMPTION, REWARD, COURAGE AND LOVE --
-- THAT HAS BEEN CHURNED TO A FRENZIED PITCH BY THE THUNDERBOLTS' ABILITY TO SHATTER THROUGH MEPHISTO'S ASSAULT!
HAWKEYE KNOWS THAT, USED AGAINST THE DEMON LORD, THIS PAYLOAD WILL HURT HIM WITH THE PURITY OF ITS EMOTIONS...
WHAT ARE YOU ALL DOING?
...BUT TO DELIVER IT INTO HIS BLACK HEART, HAWKEYE WILL NEED A VERY SPECIAL ARROW, PROVIDED BY A VERY SPECIAL FRIEND!
THUNK
THE ARROW -- IMBUED WITH CHAOS-ENERGY?
Oh NO...

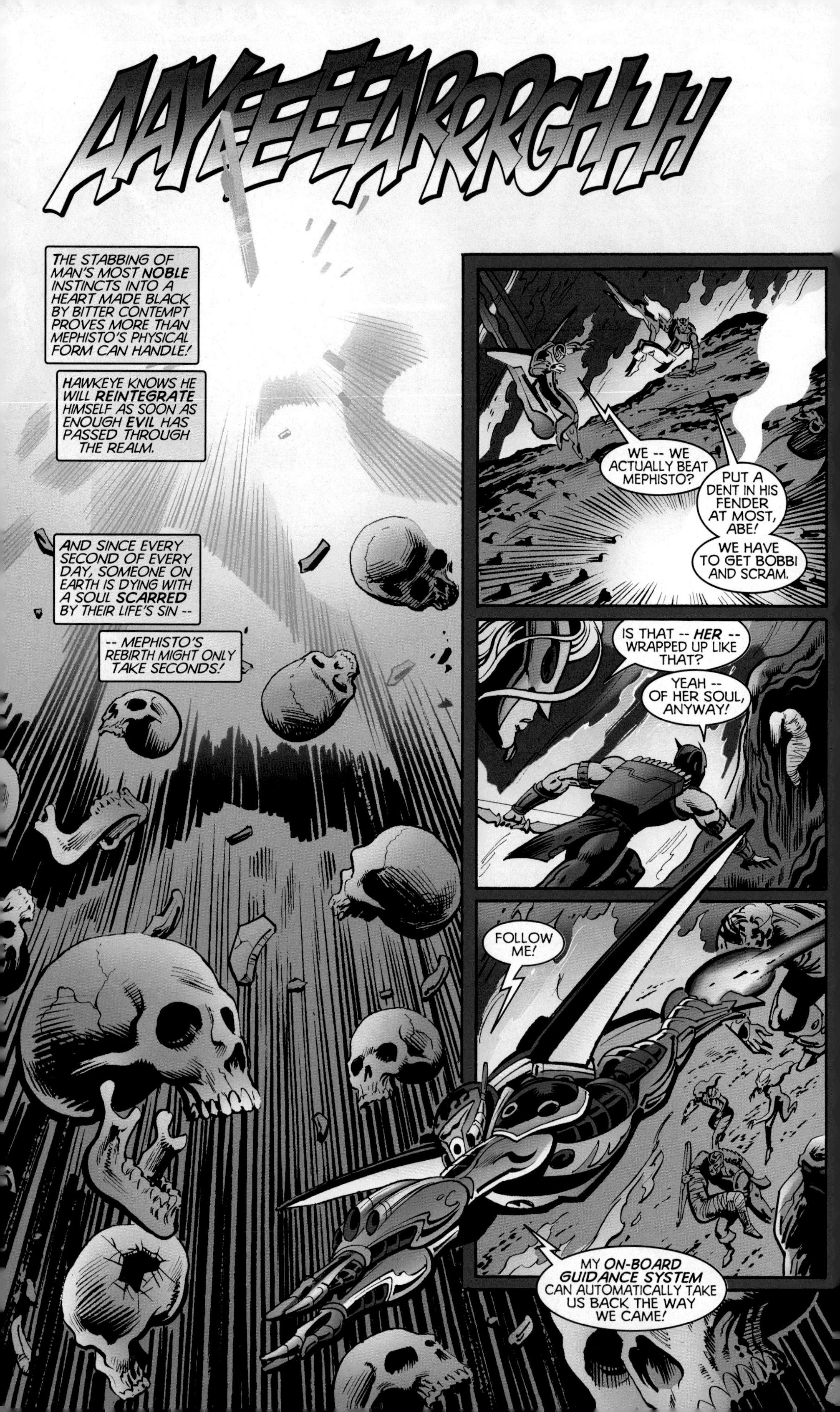

AAYEEEEARRRGHHH
THE STABBING OF MAN'S MOST NOBLE INSTINCTS INTO A HEART MADE BLACK BY BITTER CONTEMPT PROVES MORE THAN MEPHISTO'S PHYSICAL FORM CAN HANDLE!
HAWKEYE KNOWS HE WILL REINTEGRATE HIMSELF AS SOON AS ENOUGH EVIL HAS PASSED THROUGH THE REALM.
AND SINCE EVERY SECOND OF EVERY DAY, SOMEONE ON EARTH IS DYING WITH A SOUL SCARRED BY THEIR LIFE'S SIN --
-- MEPHISTO'S REBIRTH MIGHT ONLY TAKE SECONDS!
WE -- WE ACTUALLY BEAT MEPHISTO?
PUT A DENT IN HIS FENDER AT MOST, ABE!
WE HAVE TO GET BOBBI AND SCRAM.
IS THAT -- HER -- WRAPPED UP LIKE THAT?
YEAH -- OF HER SOUL, ANYWAY!
FOLLOW ME!
MY ON-BOARD GUIDANCE SYSTEM CAN AUTOMATICALLY TAKE US BACK THE WAY WE CAME!

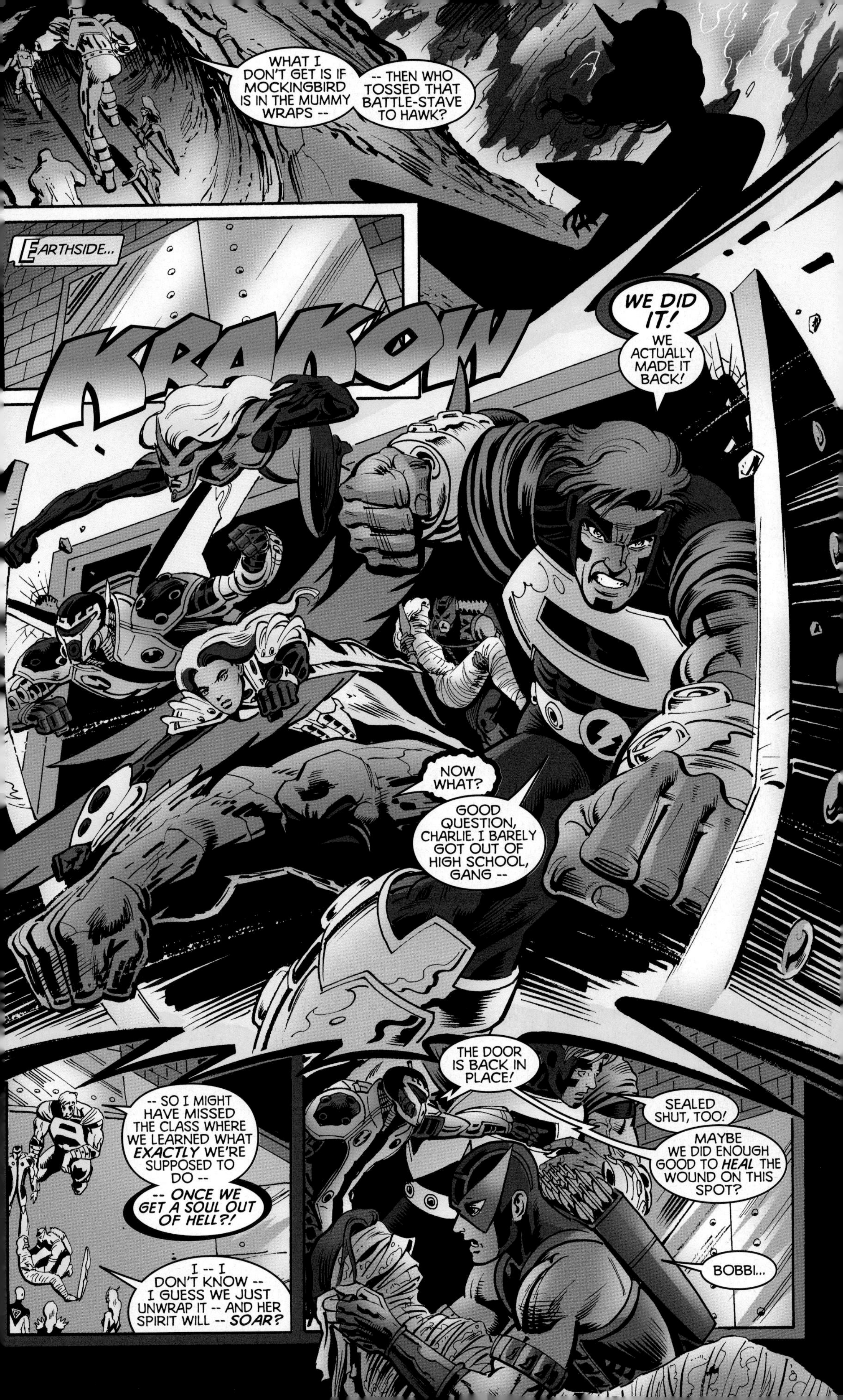
WHAT I DON'T GET IS IF MOCKINGBIRD IS IN THE MUMMY WRAPS --
-- THEN WHO TOSSED THAT BATTLE-STAVE TO HAWK?
EARTHSIDE...
KRAKOW
WE DID IT! WE ACTUALLY MADE IT BACK!
NOW WHAT?
GOOD QUESTION, CHARLIE. I BARELY GOT OUT OF HIGH SCHOOL, GANG --
-- SO I MIGHT HAVE MISSED THE CLASS WHERE WE LEARNED WHAT EXACTLY WE'RE SUPPOSED TO DO --
-- ONCE WE GET A SOUL OUT OF HELL?!
I -- I DON'T KNOW -- I GUESS WE JUST UNWRAP IT -- AND HER SPIRIT WILL -- SOAR?
THE DOOR IS BACK IN PLACE!
SEALED SHUT, TOO!
MAYBE WE DID ENOUGH GOOD TO HEAL THE WOUND ON THIS SPOT?
BOBBI...

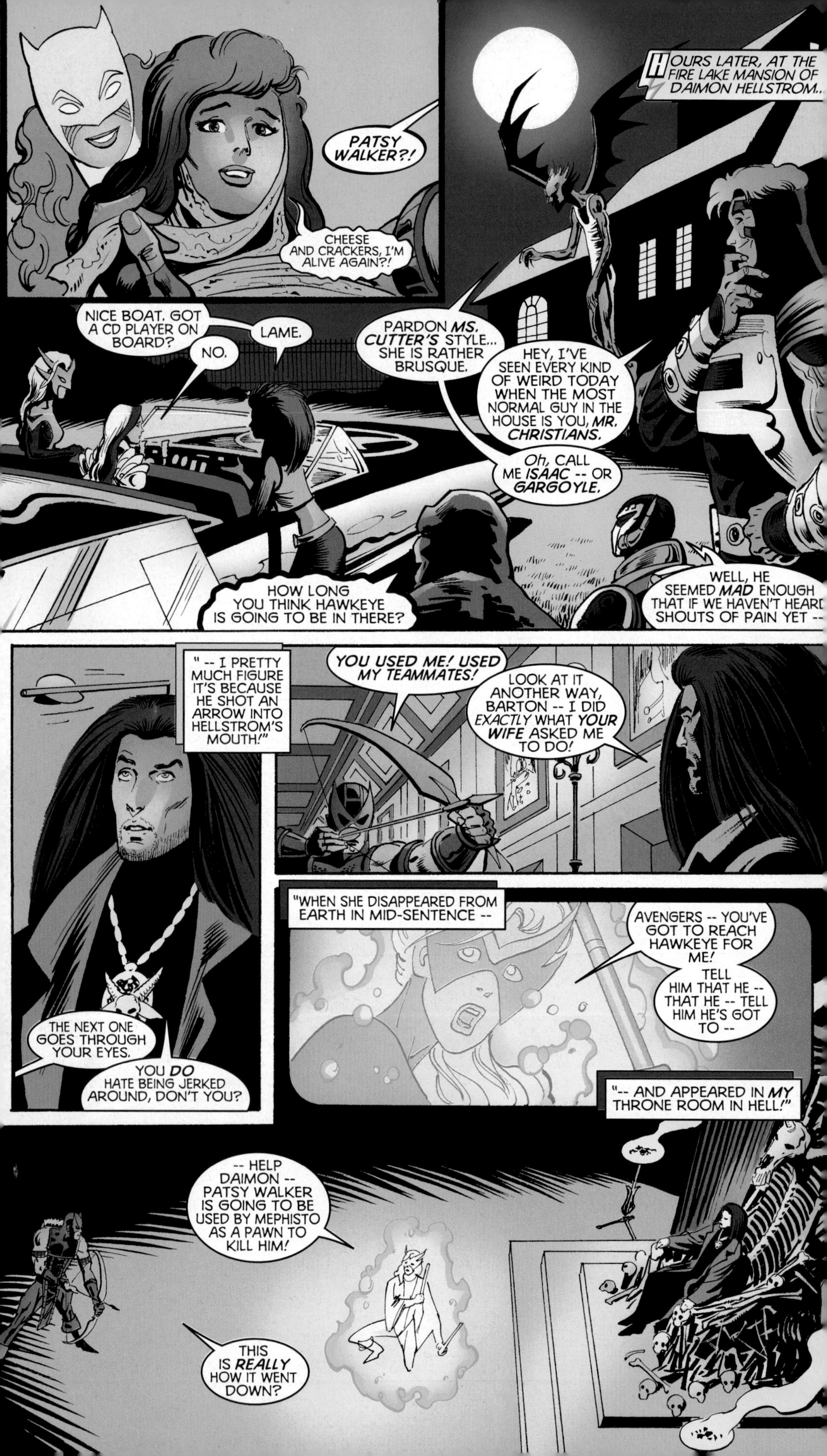
PATSY WALKER?!
CHEESE AND CRACKERS, I'M ALIVE AGAIN?!
HOURS LATER, AT THE FIRE LAKE MANSION OF DAIMON HELLSTROM...
NICE BOAT. GOT A CD PLAYER ON BOARD?
NO.
LAME.
PARDON MS. CUTTER'S STYLE... SHE IS RATHER BRUSQUE.
HEY, I'VE SEEN EVERY KIND OF WEIRD TODAY WHEN THE MOST NORMAL GUY IN THE HOUSE IS YOU, MR. CHRISTIANS.
Oh, CALL ME ISAAC -- OR GARGOYLE.
HOW LONG YOU THINK HAWKEYE IS GOING TO BE IN THERE?
WELL, HE SEEMED MAD ENOUGH THAT IF WE HAVEN'T HEARD SHOUTS OF PAIN YET --
" -- I PRETTY MUCH FIGURE IT'S BECAUSE HE SHOT AN ARROW INTO HELLSTROM'S MOUTH!"
THE NEXT ONE GOES THROUGH YOUR EYES.
YOU DO HATE BEING JERKED AROUND, DON'T YOU?
YOU USED ME! USED MY TEAMMATES!
LOOK AT IT ANOTHER WAY, BARTON -- I DID EXACTLY WHAT YOUR WIFE ASKED ME TO DO!
"WHEN SHE DISAPPEARED FROM EARTH IN MID-SENTENCE --
AVENGERS -- YOU'VE GOT TO REACH HAWKEYE FOR ME!
TELL HIM THAT HE -- THAT HE -- TELL HIM HE'S GOT TO --
"-- AND APPEARED IN MY THRONE ROOM IN HELL!"
-- HELP DAIMON -- PATSY WALKER IS GOING TO BE USED BY MEPHISTO AS A PAWN TO KILL HIM!
THIS IS REALLY HOW IT WENT DOWN?

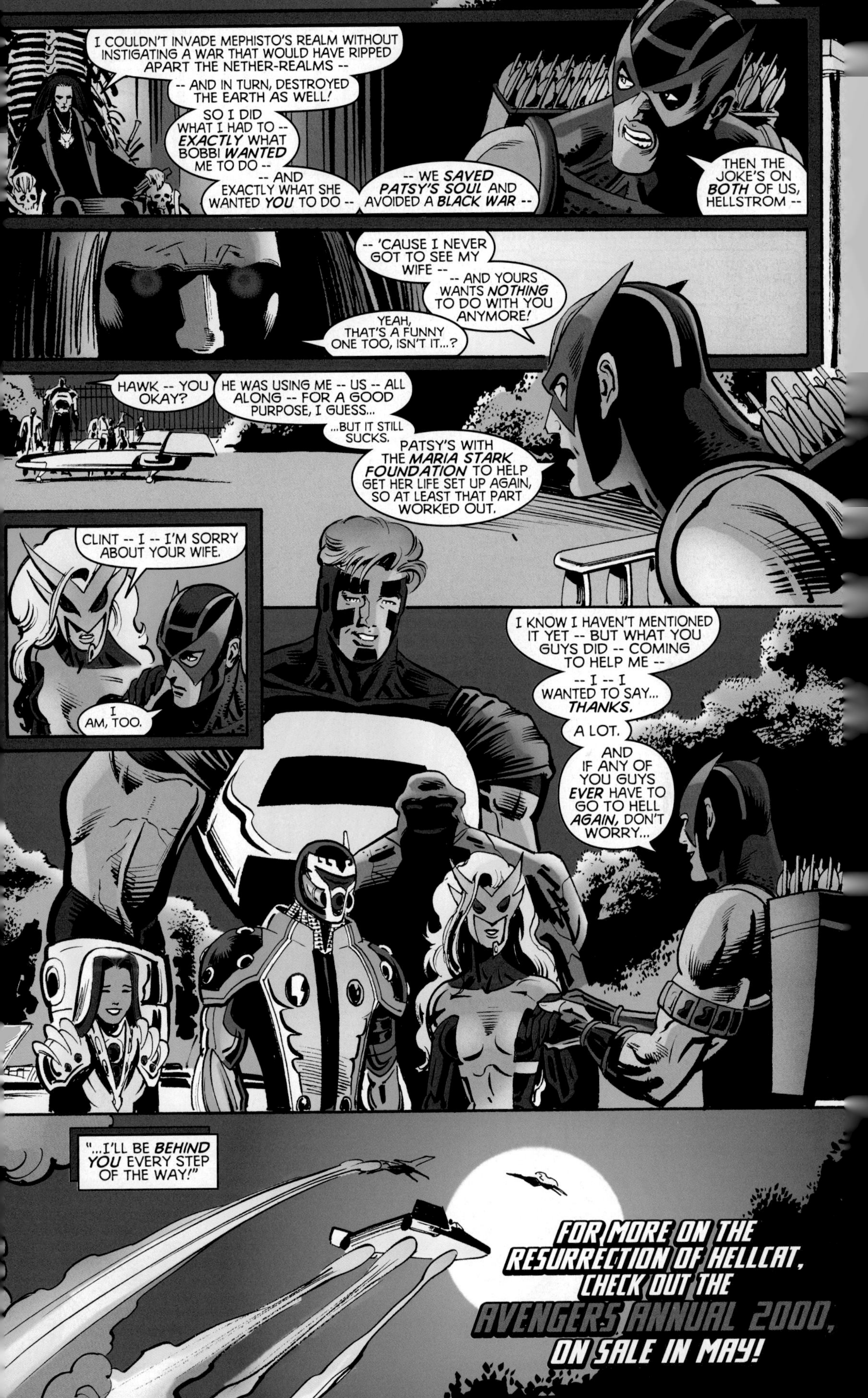
I COULDN'T INVADE MEPHISTO'S REALM WITHOUT INSTIGATING A WAR THAT WOULD HAVE RIPPED APART THE NETHER-REALMS --
-- AND IN TURN, DESTROYED THE EARTH AS WELL!
SO I DID WHAT I HAD TO -- EXACTLY WHAT BOBBI WANTED ME TO DO --
-- AND EXACTLY WHAT SHE WANTED YOU TO DO --
-- WE SAVED PATSY'S SOUL AND AVOIDED A BLACK WAR --
THEN THE JOKE'S ON BOTH OF US, HELLSTROM --
-- 'CAUSE I NEVER GOT TO SEE MY WIFE --
-- AND YOURS WANTS NOTHING TO DO WITH YOU ANYMORE!
YEAH, THAT'S A FUNNY ONE TOO, ISN'T IT...?
HAWK -- YOU OKAY?
HE WAS USING ME -- US -- ALL ALONG -- FOR A GOOD PURPOSE, I GUESS...
...BUT IT STILL SUCKS.
PATSY'S WITH THE MARIA STARK FOUNDATION TO HELP GET HER LIFE SET UP AGAIN, SO AT LEAST THAT PART WORKED OUT.
CLINT -- I -- I'M SORRY ABOUT YOUR WIFE.
I AM, TOO.
I KNOW I HAVEN'T MENTIONED IT YET -- BUT WHAT YOU GUYS DID -- COMING TO HELP ME --
-- I -- I WANTED TO SAY... THANKS.
A LOT.
AND IF ANY OF YOU GUYS EVER HAVE TO GO TO HELL AGAIN, DON'T WORRY...
"...I'LL BE BEHIND YOU EVERY STEP OF THE WAY!"
FOR MORE ON THE RESURRECTION OF HELLCAT, CHECK OUT THE AVENGERS ANNUAL 2000, ON SALE IN MAY!

STAN LEE PRESENTS:

PHYSICIAN, HEAL THYSELF?

by FABIAN NICIEZA & MARK BAGLEY (Kurt Busiek lent us his couch) AL VEY inks
COMICRAFT letters JOE ROSAS colors TOM BREVOORT editor BOB HARRAS editor in chief

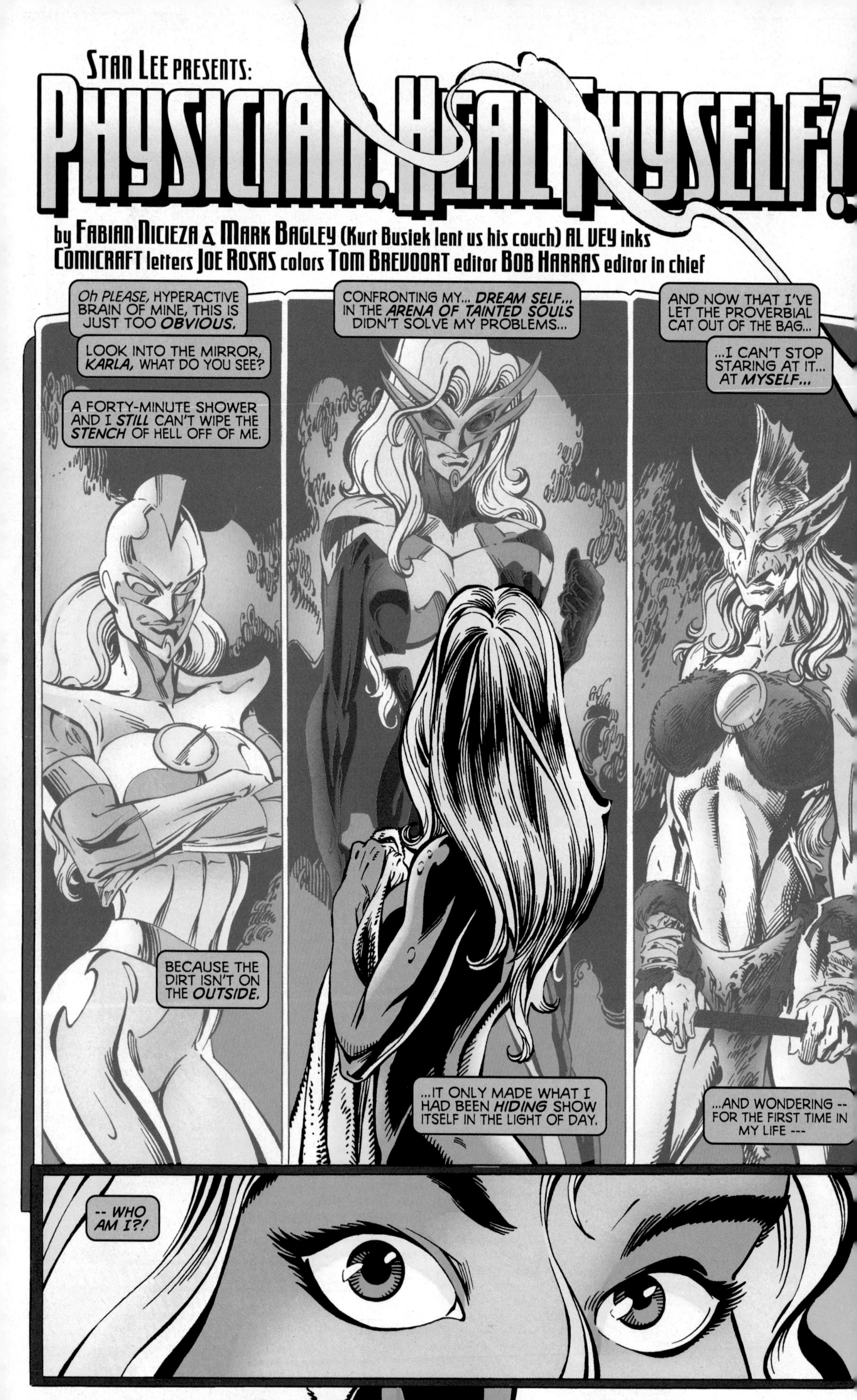

Oh PLEASE, HYPERACTIVE BRAIN OF MINE, THIS IS JUST TOO OBVIOUS.
LOOK INTO THE MIRROR, KARLA, WHAT DO YOU SEE?
A FORTY-MINUTE SHOWER AND I STILL CAN'T WIPE THE STENCH OF HELL OFF OF ME.
BECAUSE THE DIRT ISN'T ON THE OUTSIDE.
CONFRONTING MY... DREAM SELF... IN THE ARENA OF TAINTED SOULS DIDN'T SOLVE MY PROBLEMS...
...IT ONLY MADE WHAT I HAD BEEN HIDING SHOW ITSELF IN THE LIGHT OF DAY.
AND NOW THAT I'VE LET THE PROVERBIAL CAT OUT OF THE BAG...
...I CAN'T STOP STARING AT IT... AT MYSELF...
...AND WONDERING -- FOR THE FIRST TIME IN MY LIFE ---
-- WHO AM I?!

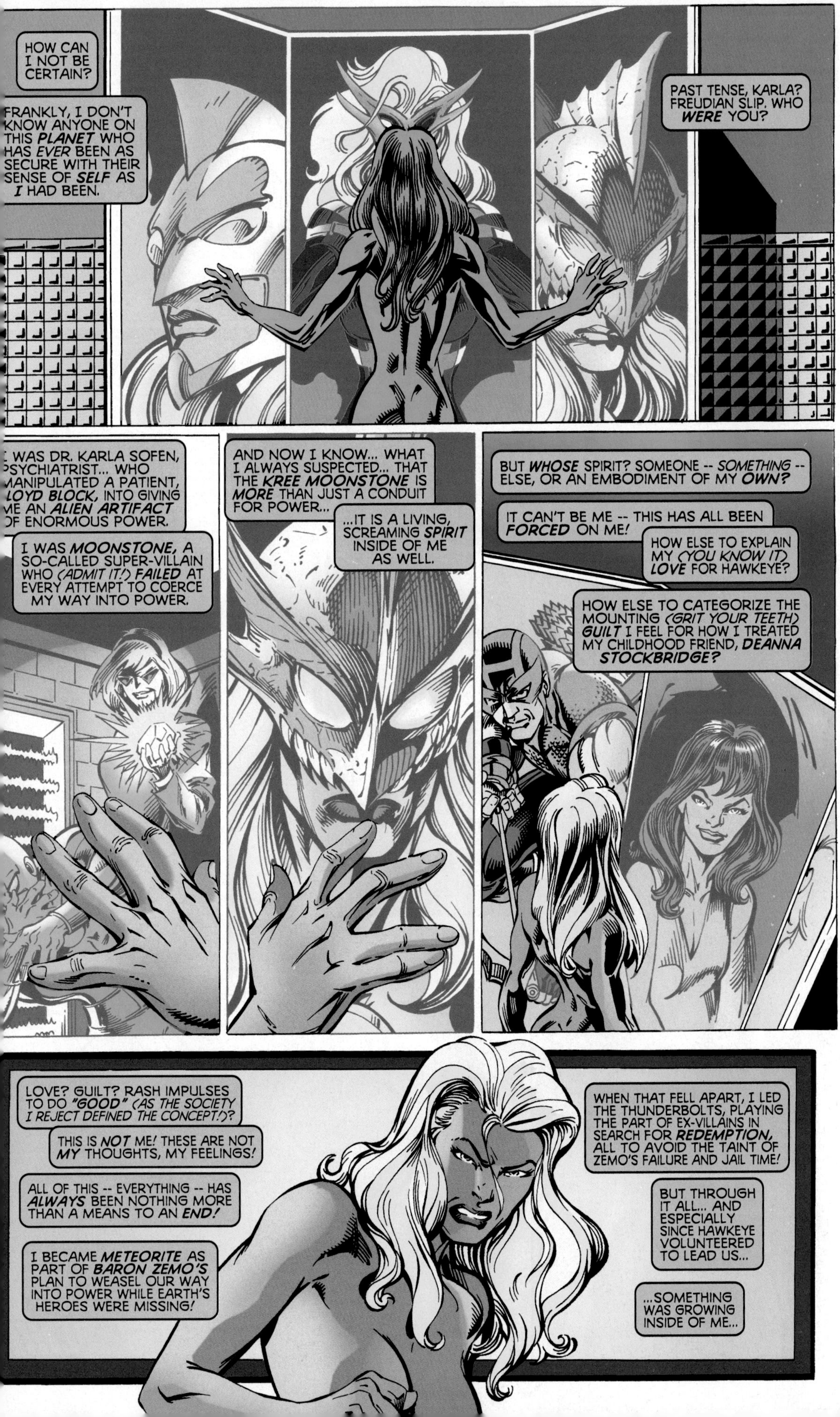
HOW CAN I NOT BE CERTAIN?
FRANKLY, I DON'T KNOW ANYONE ON THIS PLANET WHO HAS EVER BEEN AS SECURE WITH THEIR SENSE OF SELF AS I HAD BEEN.
PAST TENSE, KARLA? FREUDIAN SLIP. WHO WERE YOU?
I WAS DR. KARLA SOFEN, PSYCHIATRIST... WHO MANIPULATED A PATIENT, LLOYD BLOCK, INTO GIVING ME AN ALIEN ARTIFACT OF ENORMOUS POWER.
I WAS MOONSTONE, A SO-CALLED SUPER-VILLAIN WHO (ADMIT IT!) FAILED AT EVERY ATTEMPT TO COERCE MY WAY INTO POWER.
AND NOW I KNOW... WHAT I ALWAYS SUSPECTED... THAT THE KREE MOONSTONE IS MORE THAN JUST A CONDUIT FOR POWER...
...IT IS A LIVING, SCREAMING SPIRIT INSIDE OF ME AS WELL.
BUT WHOSE SPIRIT? SOMEONE -- SOMETHING -- ELSE, OR AN EMBODIMENT OF MY OWN?
IT CAN'T BE ME -- THIS HAS ALL BEEN FORCED ON ME!
HOW ELSE TO EXPLAIN MY (YOU KNOW IT) LOVE FOR HAWKEYE?
HOW ELSE TO CATEGORIZE THE MOUNTING (GRIT YOUR TEETH) GUILT I FEEL FOR HOW I TREATED MY CHILDHOOD FRIEND, DEANNA STOCKBRIDGE?
LOVE? GUILT? RASH IMPULSES TO DO "GOOD" (AS THE SOCIETY I REJECT DEFINED THE CONCEPT!)?
THIS IS NOT ME! THESE ARE NOT MY THOUGHTS, MY FEELINGS!
ALL OF THIS -- EVERYTHING -- HAS ALWAYS BEEN NOTHING MORE THAN A MEANS TO AN END!
I BECAME METEORITE AS PART OF BARON ZEMO'S PLAN TO WEASEL OUR WAY INTO POWER WHILE EARTH'S HEROES WERE MISSING!
WHEN THAT FELL APART, I LED THE THUNDERBOLTS, PLAYING THE PART OF EX-VILLAINS IN SEARCH FOR REDEMPTION, ALL TO AVOID THE TAINT OF ZEMO'S FAILURE AND JAIL TIME!
BUT THROUGH IT ALL... AND ESPECIALLY SINCE HAWKEYE VOLUNTEERED TO LEAD US...
...SOMETHING WAS GROWING INSIDE OF ME...

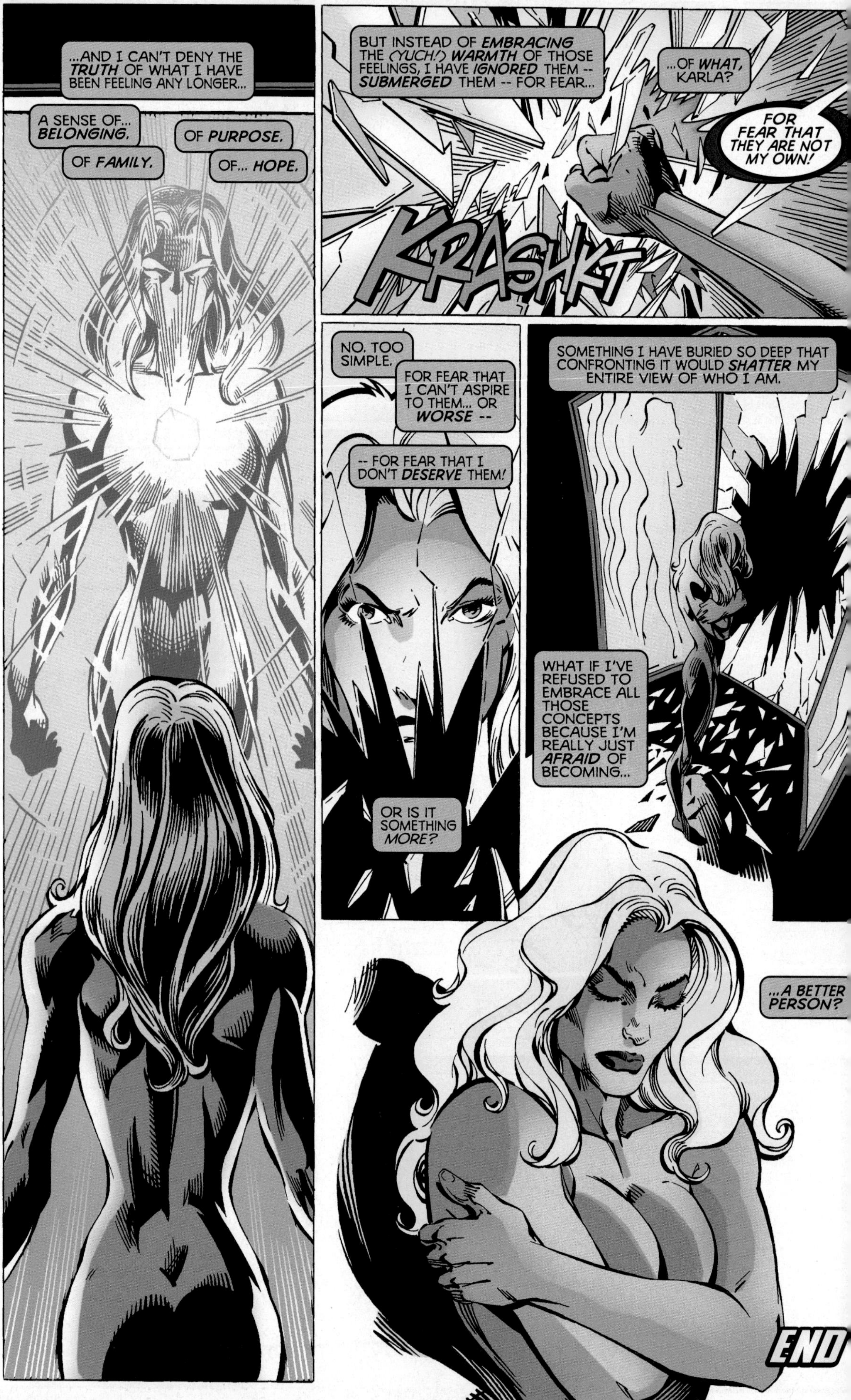

...AND I CAN'T DENY THE TRUTH OF WHAT I HAVE BEEN FEELING ANY LONGER...
A SENSE OF... BELONGING.
OF PURPOSE.
OF FAMILY.
OF... HOPE.
BUT INSTEAD OF EMBRACING THE (YUCH!) WARMTH OF THOSE FEELINGS, I HAVE IGNORED THEM -- SUBMERGED THEM -- FOR FEAR...
...OF WHAT, KARLA?
FOR FEAR THAT THEY ARE NOT MY OWN!
KRASHKT
NO. TOO SIMPLE.
FOR FEAR THAT I CAN'T ASPIRE TO THEM... OR WORSE --
-- FOR FEAR THAT I DON'T DESERVE THEM!
OR IS IT SOMETHING MORE?
SOMETHING I HAVE BURIED SO DEEP THAT CONFRONTING IT WOULD SHATTER MY ENTIRE VIEW OF WHO I AM.
WHAT IF I'VE REFUSED TO EMBRACE ALL THOSE CONCEPTS BECAUSE I'M REALLY JUST AFRAID OF BECOMING...
...A BETTER PERSON?
END

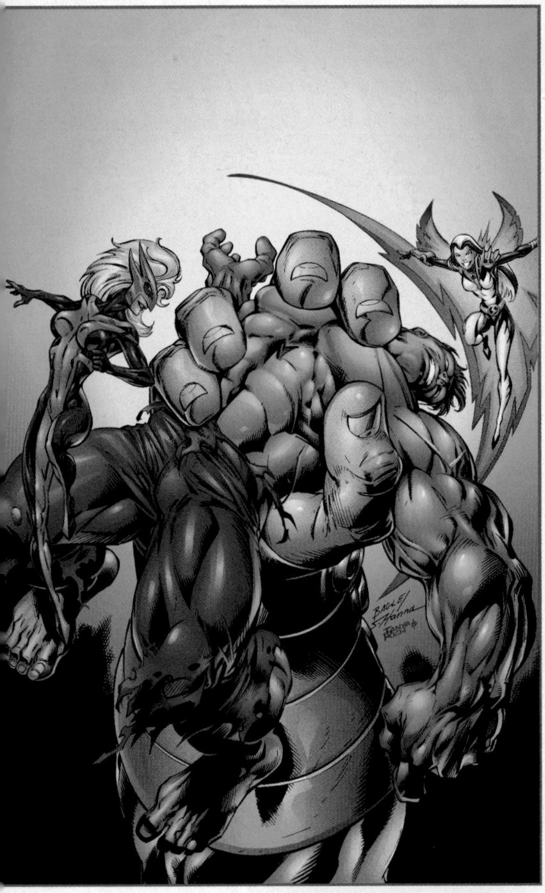

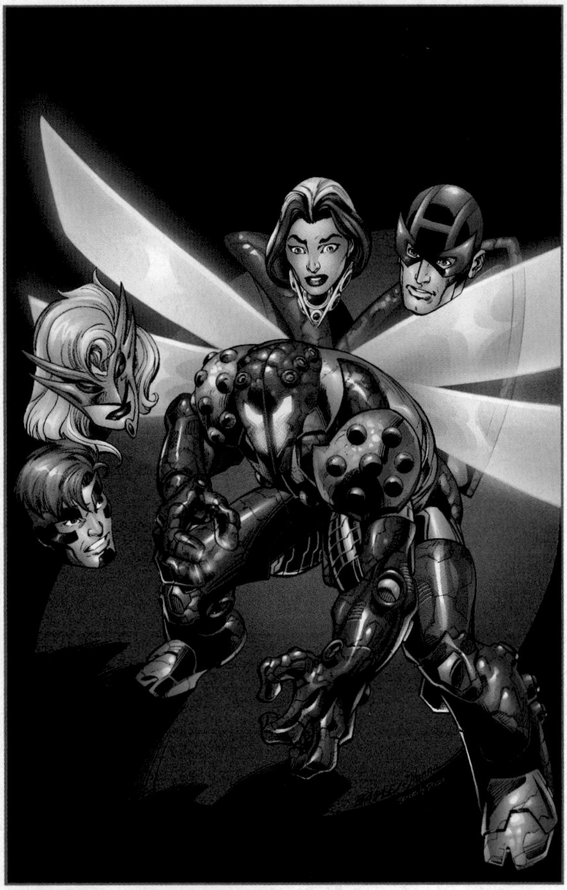

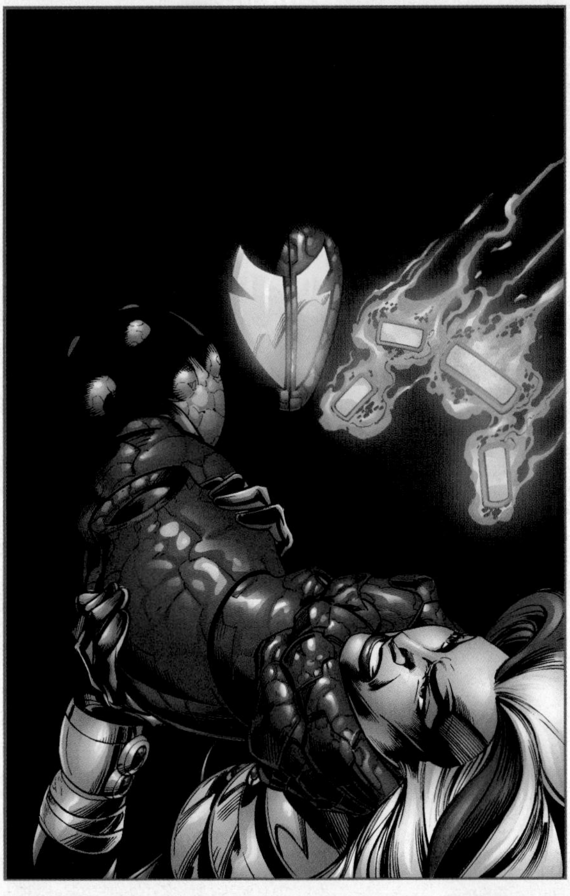

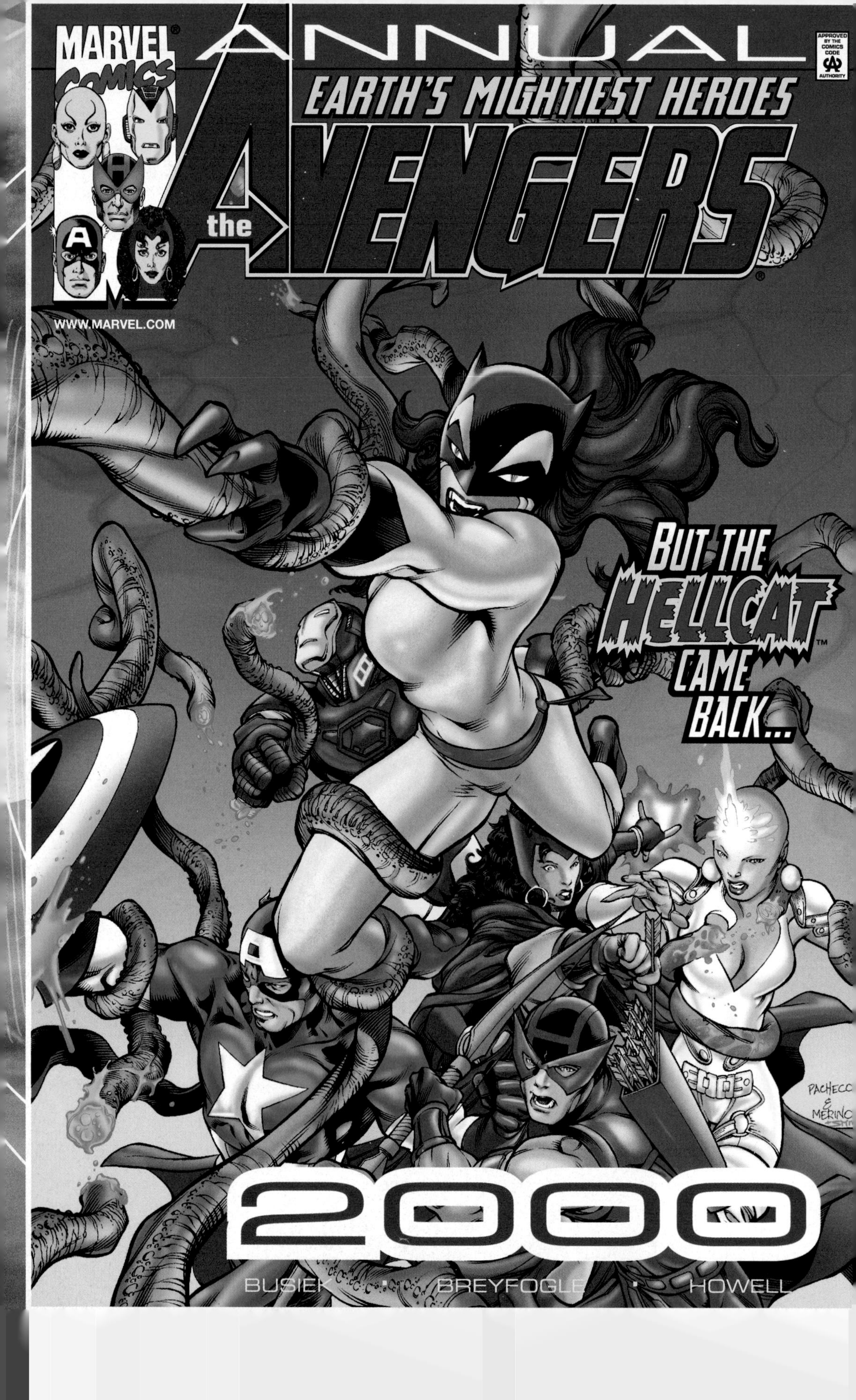
MARVEL COMICS
ANNUAL
APPROVED BY THE COMICS CODE AUTHORITY
EARTH'S MIGHTIEST HEROES
the AVENGERS
WWW.MARVEL.COM
BUT THE HELLCAT CAME BACK...
PACHECO & MERINO
2000
BUSIEK • BREYFOGLE • HOWELL

CHAPTER 1 "...AND WE'RE BACK!"

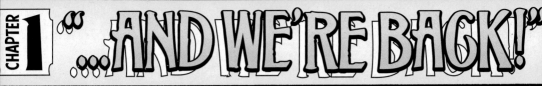

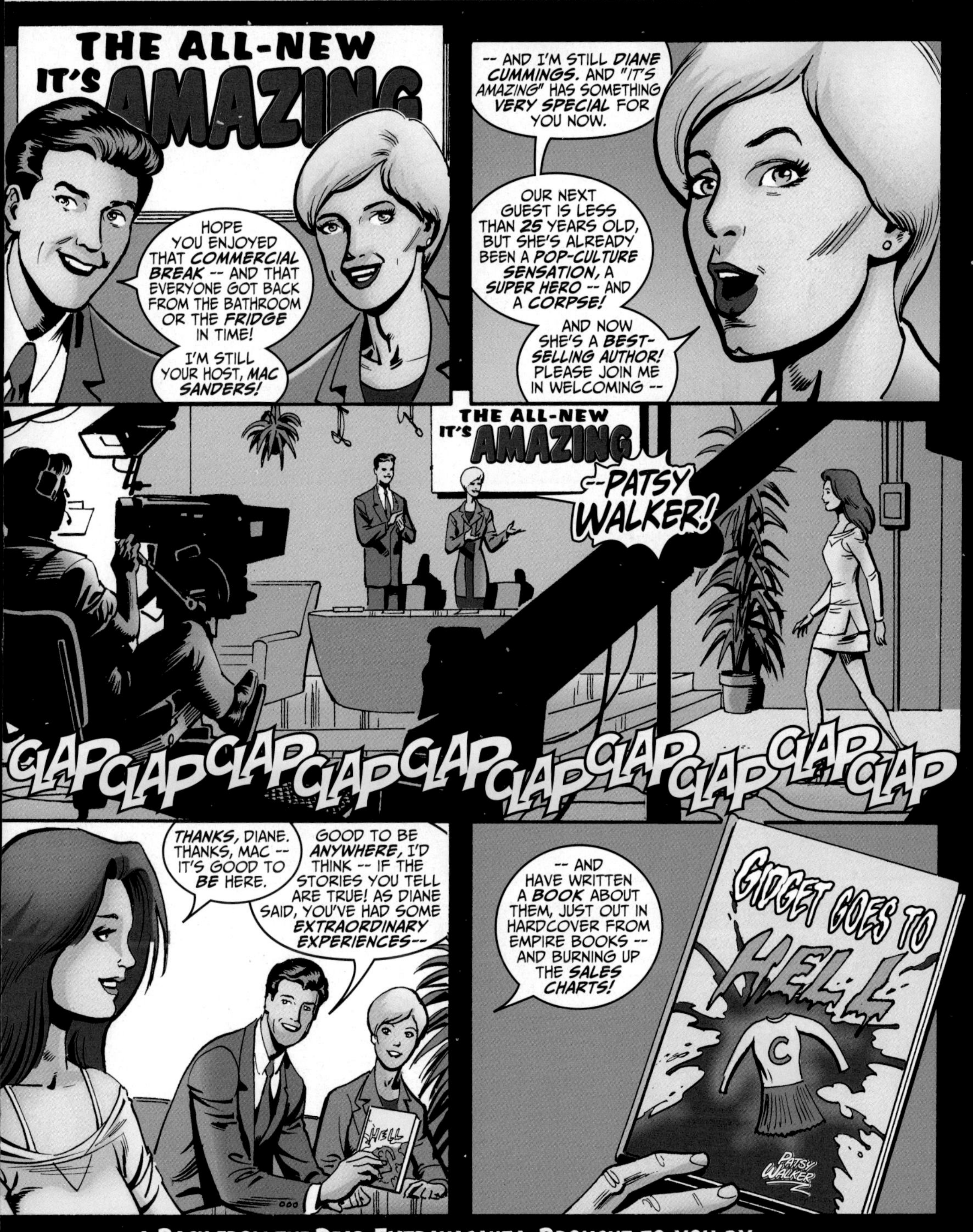
THE ALL-NEW IT'S AMAZING
HOPE YOU ENJOYED THAT COMMERCIAL BREAK -- AND THAT EVERYONE GOT BACK FROM THE BATHROOM OR THE FRIDGE IN TIME!
I'M STILL YOUR HOST, MAC SANDERS!
-- AND I'M STILL DIANE CUMMINGS. AND "IT'S AMAZING" HAS SOMETHING VERY SPECIAL FOR YOU NOW.
OUR NEXT GUEST IS LESS THAN 25 YEARS OLD, BUT SHE'S ALREADY BEEN A POP-CULTURE SENSATION, A SUPER HERO -- AND A CORPSE!
AND NOW SHE'S A BEST-SELLING AUTHOR! PLEASE JOIN ME IN WELCOMING --
THE ALL-NEW IT'S AMAZING
--PATSY WALKER!
CLAP CLAP CLAP CLAP CLAP CLAP CLAP CLAP CLAP CLAP
THANKS, DIANE. THANKS, MAC -- IT'S GOOD TO BE HERE.
GOOD TO BE ANYWHERE, I'D THINK -- IF THE STORIES YOU TELL ARE TRUE! AS DIANE SAID, YOU'VE HAD SOME EXTRAORDINARY EXPERIENCES--
HELL
-- AND HAVE WRITTEN A BOOK ABOUT THEM, JUST OUT IN HARDCOVER FROM EMPIRE BOOKS -- AND BURNING UP THE SALES CHARTS!
GIDGET GOES TO HELL
C
PATSY WALKER

A BACK-FROM-THE-DEAD EXTRAVAGANZA, BROUGHT TO YOU BY
KURT BUSIEK, WRITER... NORM BREYFOGLE, ARTIST... TOM SMITH, COLORIST...
RICHARD STARKINGS & COMICRAFT, LETTERS... TOM BREVOORT, EDITOR... BOB HARRAS, GUARDIAN OF THE GATES!

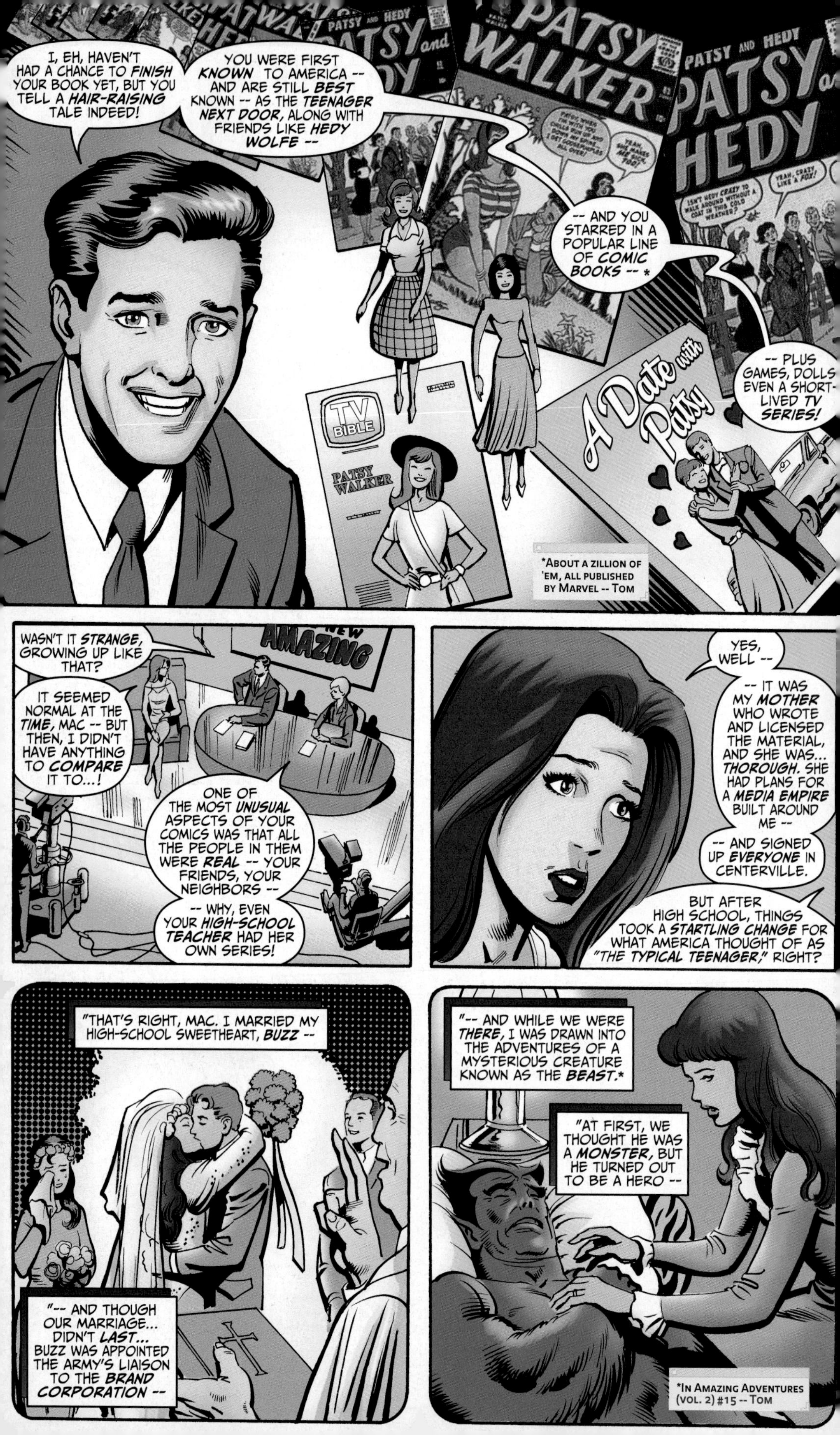
I, EH, HAVEN'T HAD A CHANCE TO FINISH YOUR BOOK YET, BUT YOU TELL A HAIR-RAISING TALE INDEED!
YOU WERE FIRST KNOWN TO AMERICA -- AND ARE STILL BEST KNOWN -- AS THE TEENAGER NEXT DOOR, ALONG WITH FRIENDS LIKE HEDY WOLFE --
PATSY AND HEDY
PATSY WALKER
-- AND YOU STARRED IN A POPULAR LINE OF COMIC BOOKS -- *
-- PLUS GAMES, DOLLS EVEN A SHORT-LIVED TV SERIES!
TV BIBLE
PATSY WALKER
A Date with Patsy
*ABOUT A ZILLION OF 'EM, ALL PUBLISHED BY MARVEL -- TOM
WASN'T IT STRANGE, GROWING UP LIKE THAT?
AMAZING
IT SEEMED NORMAL AT THE TIME, MAC -- BUT THEN, I DIDN'T HAVE ANYTHING TO COMPARE IT TO...!
ONE OF THE MOST UNUSUAL ASPECTS OF YOUR COMICS WAS THAT ALL THE PEOPLE IN THEM WERE REAL -- YOUR FRIENDS, YOUR NEIGHBORS --
-- WHY, EVEN YOUR HIGH-SCHOOL TEACHER HAD HER OWN SERIES!
YES, WELL --
-- IT WAS MY MOTHER WHO WROTE AND LICENSED THE MATERIAL, AND SHE WAS... THOROUGH. SHE HAD PLANS FOR A MEDIA EMPIRE BUILT AROUND ME --
-- AND SIGNED UP EVERYONE IN CENTERVILLE.
BUT AFTER HIGH SCHOOL, THINGS TOOK A STARTLING CHANGE FOR WHAT AMERICA THOUGHT OF AS "THE TYPICAL TEENAGER," RIGHT?
"THAT'S RIGHT, MAC. I MARRIED MY HIGH-SCHOOL SWEETHEART, BUZZ --
"-- AND THOUGH OUR MARRIAGE... DIDN'T LAST... BUZZ WAS APPOINTED THE ARMY'S LIAISON TO THE BRAND CORPORATION --
"-- AND WHILE WE WERE THERE, I WAS DRAWN INTO THE ADVENTURES OF A MYSTERIOUS CREATURE KNOWN AS THE BEAST.*
"AT FIRST, WE THOUGHT HE WAS A MONSTER, BUT HE TURNED OUT TO BE A HERO --
*IN AMAZING ADVENTURES (VOL. 2) #15 -- TOM

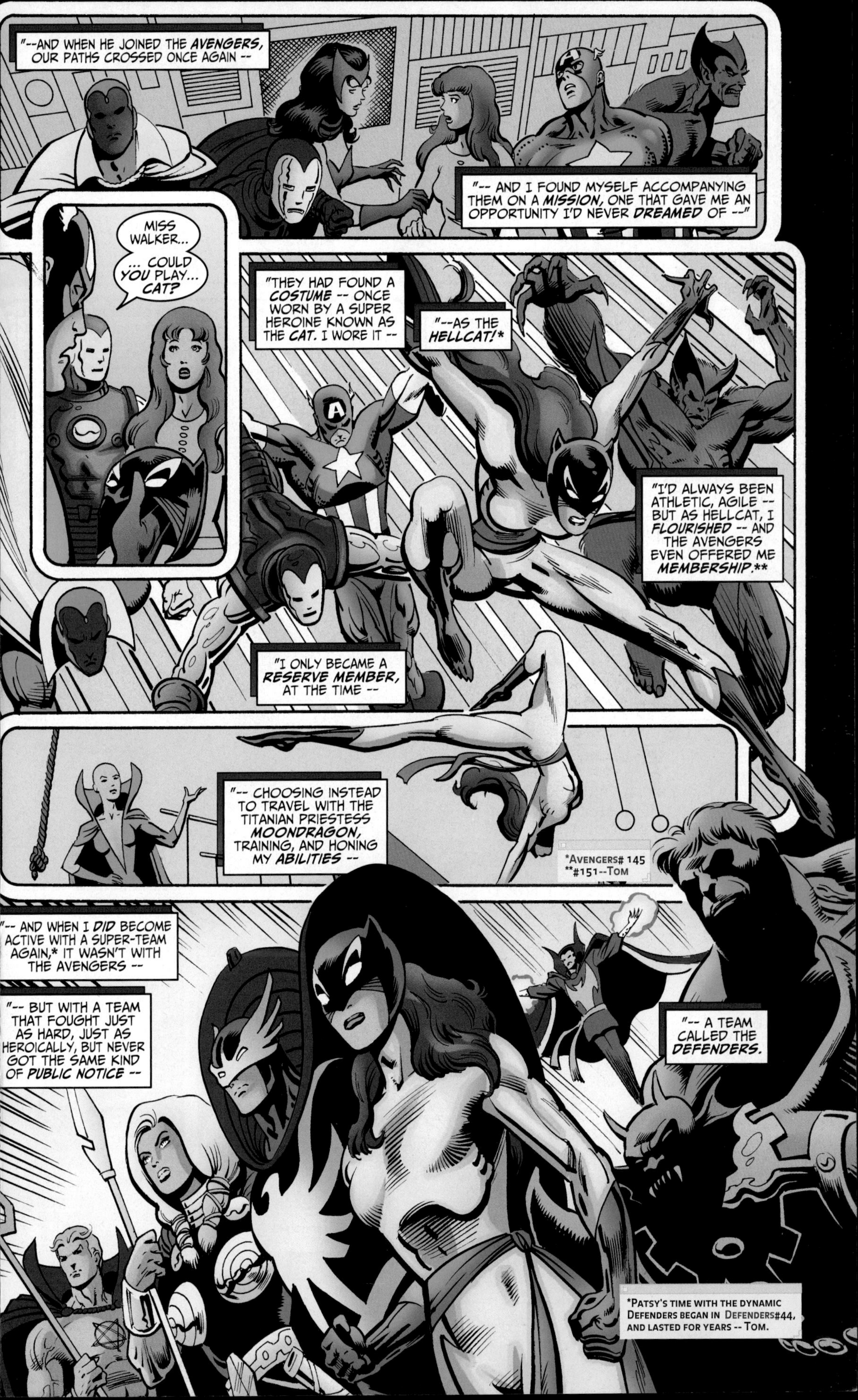
"--AND WHEN HE JOINED THE AVENGERS, OUR PATHS CROSSED ONCE AGAIN --
"-- AND I FOUND MYSELF ACCOMPANYING THEM ON A MISSION, ONE THAT GAVE ME AN OPPORTUNITY I'D NEVER DREAMED OF --"
MISS WALKER... ... COULD YOU PLAY... CAT?
"THEY HAD FOUND A COSTUME -- ONCE WORN BY A SUPER HEROINE KNOWN AS THE CAT. I WORE IT --
"--AS THE HELLCAT!*
"I'D ALWAYS BEEN ATHLETIC, AGILE -- BUT AS HELLCAT, I FLOURISHED -- AND THE AVENGERS EVEN OFFERED ME MEMBERSHIP.**
"I ONLY BECAME A RESERVE MEMBER, AT THE TIME --
"-- CHOOSING INSTEAD TO TRAVEL WITH THE TITANIAN PRIESTESS MOONDRAGON, TRAINING, AND HONING MY ABILITIES --
*AVENGERS# 145
**#151--TOM
"-- AND WHEN I DID BECOME ACTIVE WITH A SUPER-TEAM AGAIN,* IT WASN'T WITH THE AVENGERS --
"-- BUT WITH A TEAM THAT FOUGHT JUST AS HARD, JUST AS HEROICALLY, BUT NEVER GOT THE SAME KIND OF PUBLIC NOTICE --
"-- A TEAM CALLED THE DEFENDERS.
*PATSY'S TIME WITH THE DYNAMIC DEFENDERS BEGAN IN DEFENDERS#44, AND LASTED FOR YEARS -- TOM.

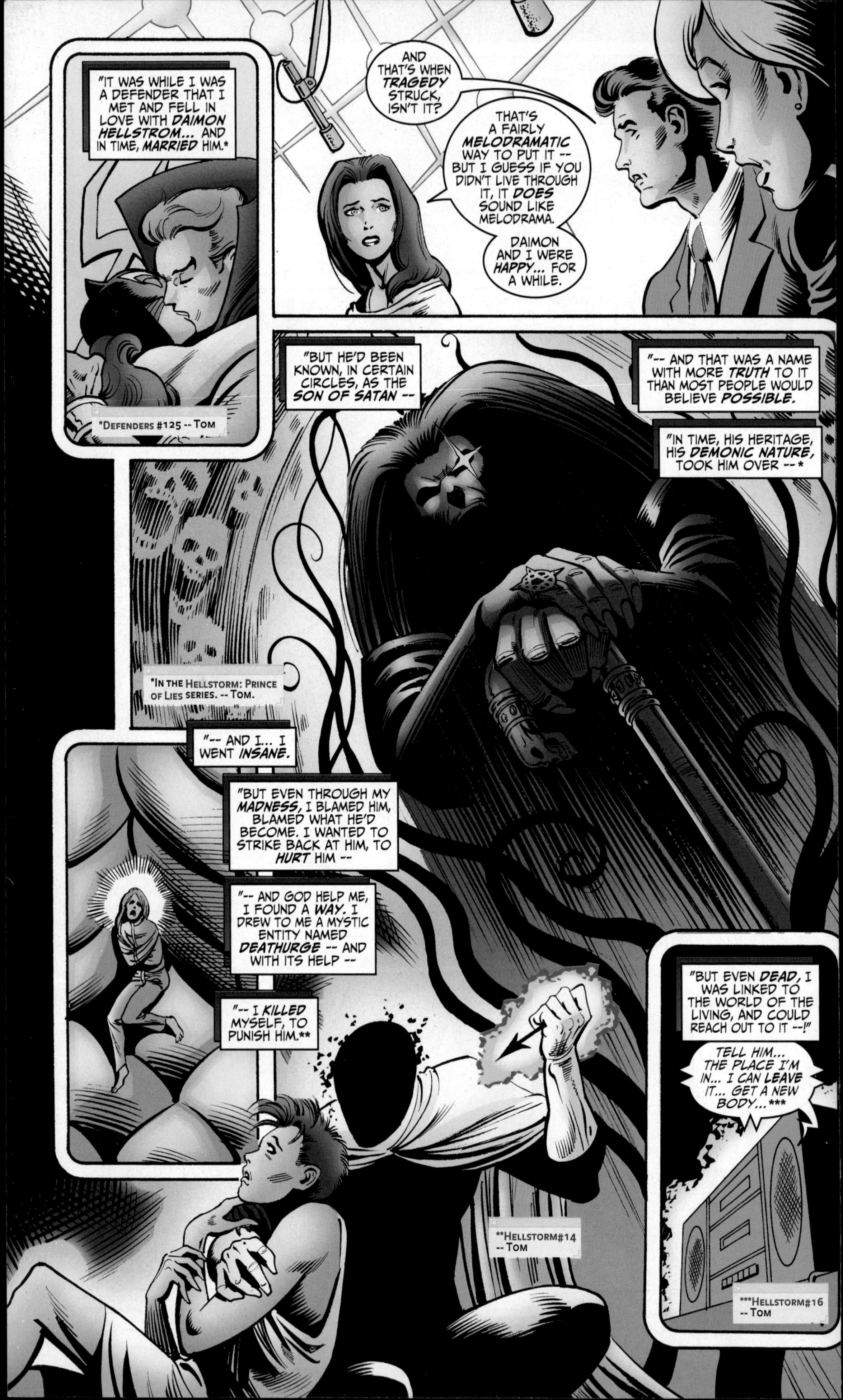
"IT WAS WHILE I WAS A DEFENDER THAT I MET AND FELL IN LOVE WITH DAIMON HELLSTROM... AND IN TIME, MARRIED HIM.*
*DEFENDERS #125 -- TOM
AND THAT'S WHEN TRAGEDY STRUCK, ISN'T IT?
THAT'S A FAIRLY MELODRAMATIC WAY TO PUT IT -- BUT I GUESS IF YOU DIDN'T LIVE THROUGH IT, IT DOES SOUND LIKE MELODRAMA.
DAIMON AND I WERE HAPPY... FOR A WHILE.
"BUT HE'D BEEN KNOWN, IN CERTAIN CIRCLES, AS THE SON OF SATAN --
"-- AND THAT WAS A NAME WITH MORE TRUTH TO IT THAN MOST PEOPLE WOULD BELIEVE POSSIBLE.
"IN TIME, HIS HERITAGE, HIS DEMONIC NATURE, TOOK HIM OVER --*
*IN THE HELLSTORM: PRINCE OF LIES SERIES. -- TOM.
"-- AND I... I WENT INSANE.
"BUT EVEN THROUGH MY MADNESS, I BLAMED HIM, BLAMED WHAT HE'D BECOME. I WANTED TO STRIKE BACK AT HIM, TO HURT HIM --
"-- AND GOD HELP ME, I FOUND A WAY. I DREW TO ME A MYSTIC ENTITY NAMED DEATHURGE -- AND WITH ITS HELP --
"-- I KILLED MYSELF, TO PUNISH HIM.**
**HELLSTORM#14 -- TOM
"BUT EVEN DEAD, I WAS LINKED TO THE WORLD OF THE LIVING, AND COULD REACH OUT TO IT --!"
TELL HIM... THE PLACE I'M IN... I CAN LEAVE IT... GET A NEW BODY...***
***HELLSTORM#16 -- TOM

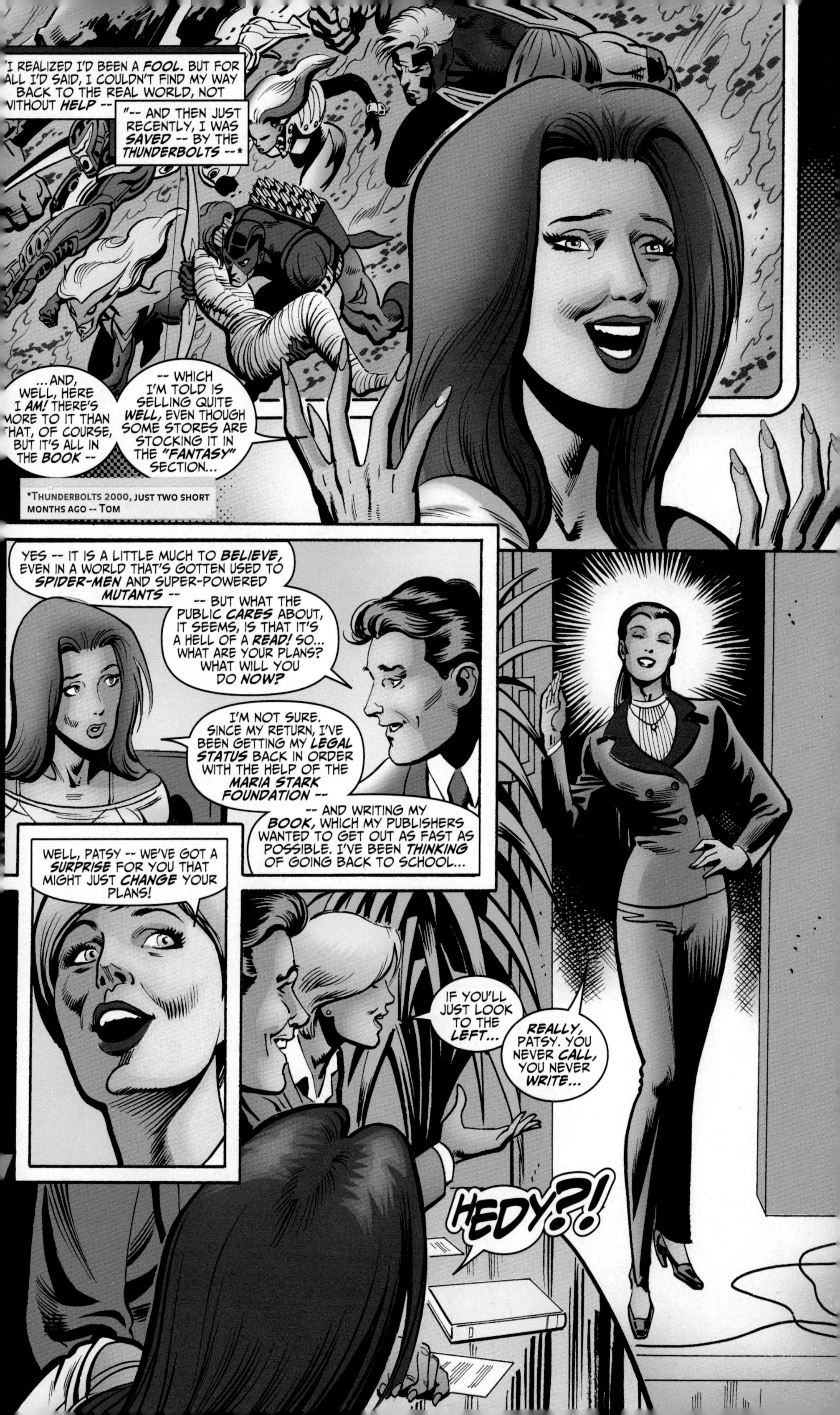
I REALIZED I'D BEEN A FOOL. BUT FOR ALL I'D SAID, I COULDN'T FIND MY WAY BACK TO THE REAL WORLD, NOT WITHOUT HELP --
"-- AND THEN JUST RECENTLY, I WAS SAVED -- BY THE THUNDERBOLTS --*
...AND, WELL, HERE I AM! THERE'S MORE TO IT THAN THAT, OF COURSE, BUT IT'S ALL IN THE BOOK --
-- WHICH I'M TOLD IS SELLING QUITE WELL, EVEN THOUGH SOME STORES ARE STOCKING IT IN THE "FANTASY" SECTION...
*THUNDERBOLTS 2000, JUST TWO SHORT MONTHS AGO -- TOM
YES -- IT IS A LITTLE MUCH TO BELIEVE, EVEN IN A WORLD THAT'S GOTTEN USED TO SPIDER-MEN AND SUPER-POWERED MUTANTS --
-- BUT WHAT THE PUBLIC CARES ABOUT, IT SEEMS, IS THAT IT'S A HELL OF A READ! SO... WHAT ARE YOUR PLANS? WHAT WILL YOU DO NOW?
I'M NOT SURE. SINCE MY RETURN, I'VE BEEN GETTING MY LEGAL STATUS BACK IN ORDER WITH THE HELP OF THE MARIA STARK FOUNDATION --
-- AND WRITING MY BOOK, WHICH MY PUBLISHERS WANTED TO GET OUT AS FAST AS POSSIBLE. I'VE BEEN THINKING OF GOING BACK TO SCHOOL...
WELL, PATSY -- WE'VE GOT A SURPRISE FOR YOU THAT MIGHT JUST CHANGE YOUR PLANS!
IF YOU'LL JUST LOOK TO THE LEFT...
REALLY, PATSY. YOU NEVER CALL, YOU NEVER WRITE...
HEDY?!

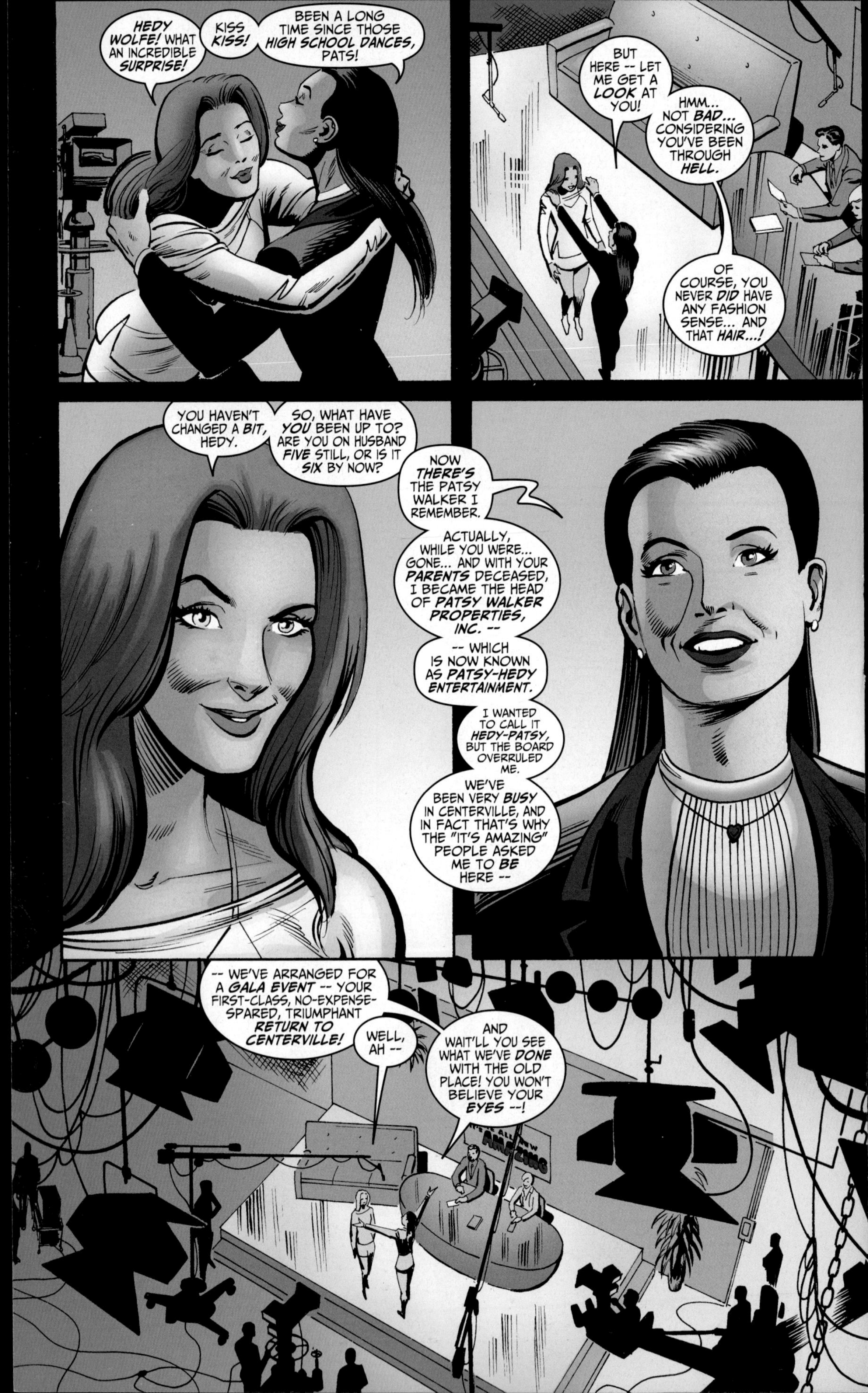
HEDY WOLFE! WHAT AN INCREDIBLE SURPRISE!
KISS KISS!
BEEN A LONG TIME SINCE THOSE HIGH SCHOOL DANCES, PATS!
BUT HERE -- LET ME GET A LOOK AT YOU!
HMM... NOT BAD... CONSIDERING YOU'VE BEEN THROUGH HELL.
OF COURSE, YOU NEVER DID HAVE ANY FASHION SENSE... AND THAT HAIR...!
YOU HAVEN'T CHANGED A BIT, HEDY.
SO, WHAT HAVE YOU BEEN UP TO? ARE YOU ON HUSBAND FIVE STILL, OR IS IT SIX BY NOW?
NOW THERE'S THE PATSY WALKER I REMEMBER.
ACTUALLY, WHILE YOU WERE... GONE... AND WITH YOUR PARENTS DECEASED, I BECAME THE HEAD OF PATSY WALKER PROPERTIES, INC. --
-- WHICH IS NOW KNOWN AS PATSY-HEDY ENTERTAINMENT.
I WANTED TO CALL IT HEDY-PATSY, BUT THE BOARD OVERRULED ME.
WE'VE BEEN VERY BUSY IN CENTERVILLE, AND IN FACT THAT'S WHY THE "IT'S AMAZING" PEOPLE ASKED ME TO BE HERE --
-- WE'VE ARRANGED FOR A GALA EVENT -- YOUR FIRST-CLASS, NO-EXPENSE-SPARED, TRIUMPHANT RETURN TO CENTERVILLE!
WELL, AH --
AND WAIT'LL YOU SEE WHAT WE'VE DONE WITH THE OLD PLACE! YOU WON'T BELIEVE YOUR EYES --!
AMAZING

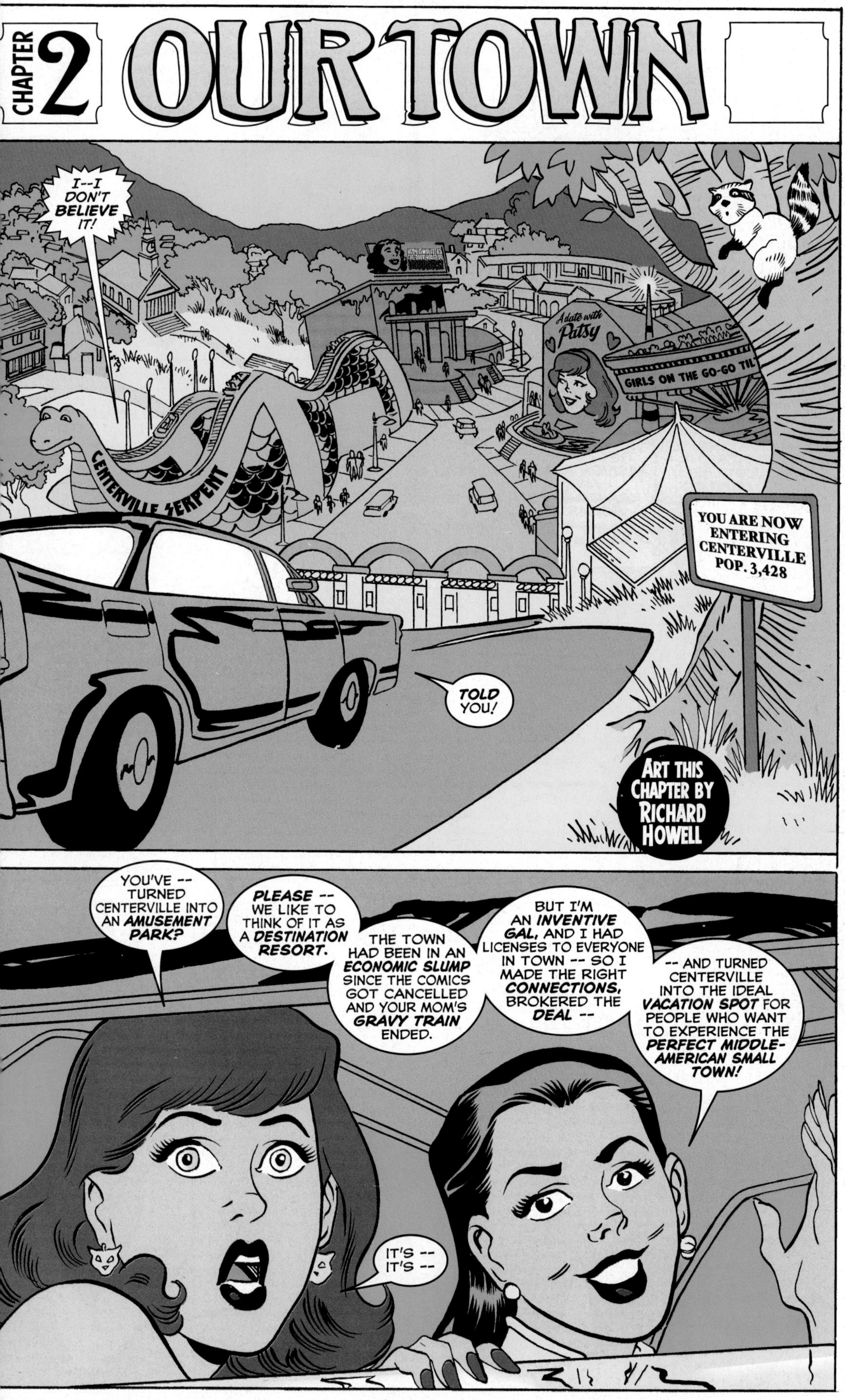
CHAPTER 2 OUR TOWN
I--I DON'T BELIEVE IT!
A date with Patsy
GIRLS ON THE GO-GO TIL
CENTERVILLE SERPENT
YOU ARE NOW ENTERING CENTERVILLE POP. 3,428
TOLD YOU!
ART THIS CHAPTER BY RICHARD HOWELL
YOU'VE -- TURNED CENTERVILLE INTO AN AMUSEMENT PARK?
PLEASE -- WE LIKE TO THINK OF IT AS A DESTINATION RESORT.
THE TOWN HAD BEEN IN AN ECONOMIC SLUMP SINCE THE COMICS GOT CANCELLED AND YOUR MOM'S GRAVY TRAIN ENDED.
BUT I'M AN INVENTIVE GAL, AND I HAD LICENSES TO EVERYONE IN TOWN -- SO I MADE THE RIGHT CONNECTIONS, BROKERED THE DEAL --
-- AND TURNED CENTERVILLE INTO THE IDEAL VACATION SPOT FOR PEOPLE WHO WANT TO EXPERIENCE THE PERFECT MIDDLE-AMERICAN SMALL TOWN!
IT'S -- IT'S --

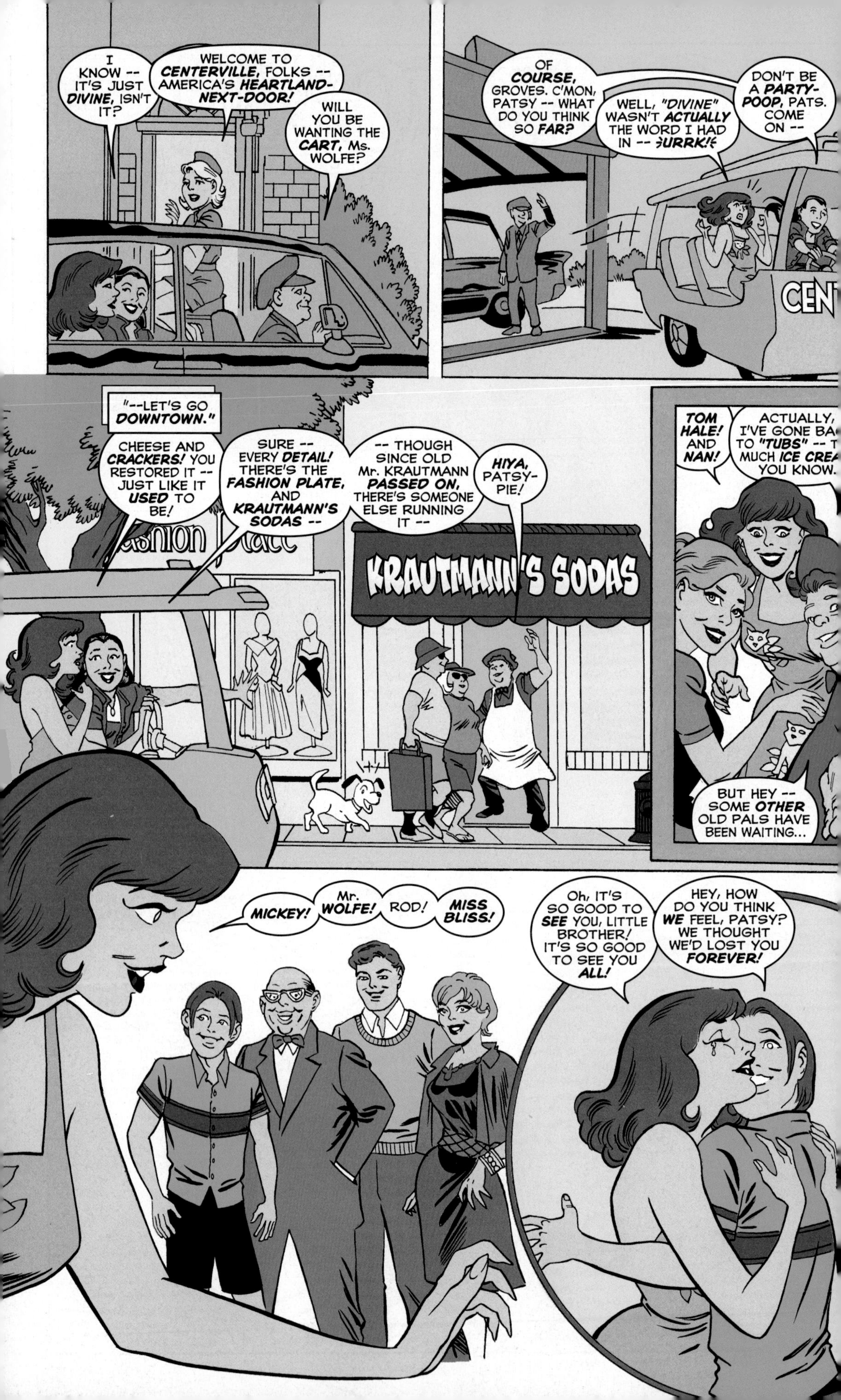

I KNOW -- IT'S JUST DIVINE, ISN'T IT?
WELCOME TO CENTERVILLE, FOLKS -- AMERICA'S HEARTLAND-NEXT-DOOR!
WILL YOU BE WANTING THE CART, Ms. WOLFE?
OF COURSE, GROVES. C'MON, PATSY -- WHAT DO YOU THINK SO FAR?
WELL, "DIVINE" WASN'T ACTUALLY THE WORD I HAD IN -- URRK!!
DON'T BE A PARTY-POOP, PATS. COME ON --
CEN
"--LET'S GO DOWNTOWN."
CHEESE AND CRACKERS! YOU RESTORED IT -- JUST LIKE IT USED TO BE!
SURE -- EVERY DETAIL! THERE'S THE FASHION PLATE, AND KRAUTMANN'S SODAS --
-- THOUGH SINCE OLD Mr. KRAUTMANN PASSED ON, THERE'S SOMEONE ELSE RUNNING IT --
HIYA, PATSY-PIE!
KRAUTMANN'S SODAS
TOM HALE! AND NAN!
ACTUALLY, I'VE GONE BA TO "TUBS" -- T MUCH ICE CREA YOU KNOW.
BUT HEY -- SOME OTHER OLD PALS HAVE BEEN WAITING...
MICKEY!
Mr. WOLFE!
ROD!
MISS BLISS!
Oh, IT'S SO GOOD TO SEE YOU, LITTLE BROTHER! IT'S SO GOOD TO SEE YOU ALL!
HEY, HOW DO YOU THINK WE FEEL, PATSY? WE THOUGHT WE'D LOST YOU FOREVER!

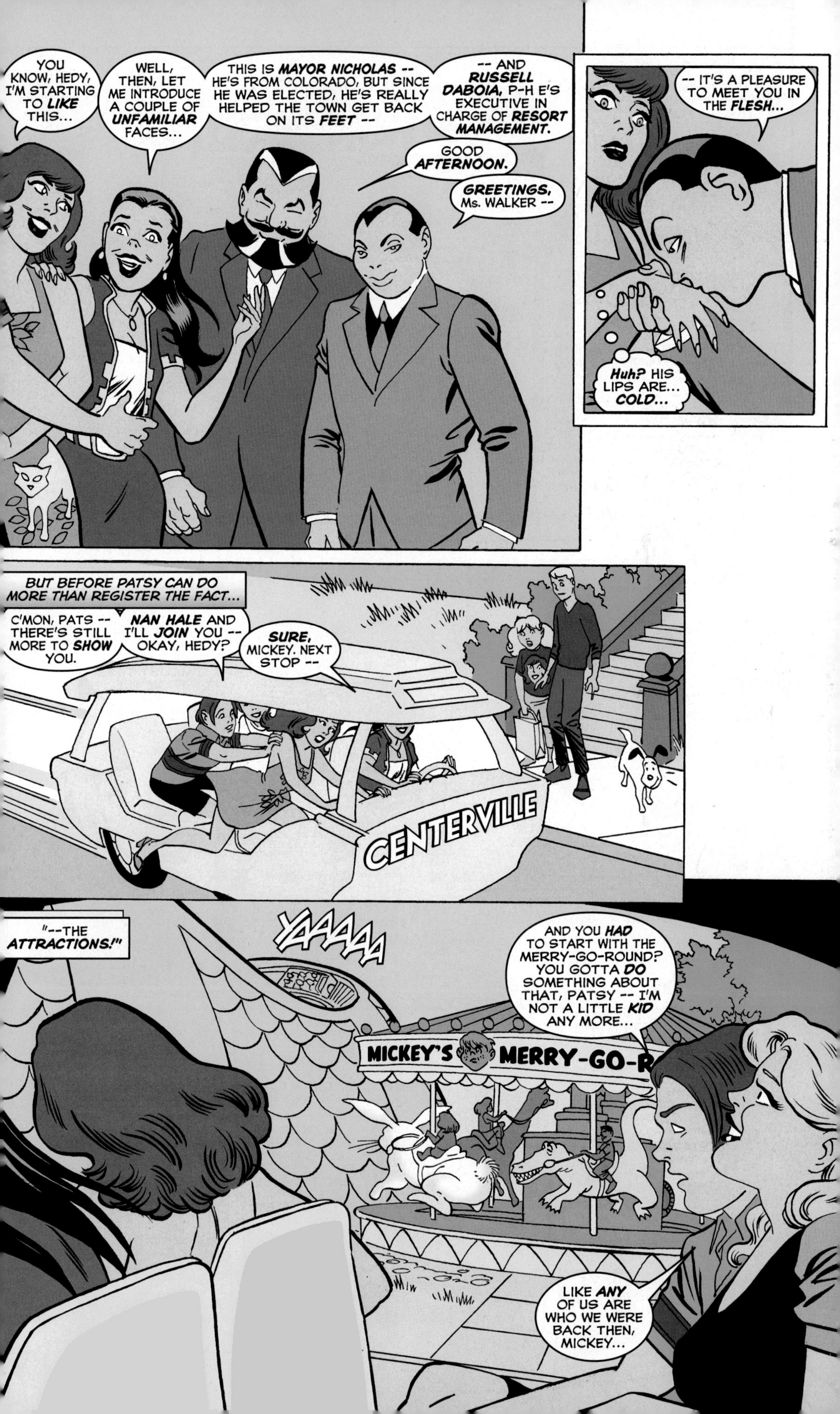

YOU KNOW, HEDY, I'M STARTING TO LIKE THIS...
WELL, THEN, LET ME INTRODUCE A COUPLE OF UNFAMILIAR FACES...
THIS IS MAYOR NICHOLAS -- HE'S FROM COLORADO, BUT SINCE HE WAS ELECTED, HE'S REALLY HELPED THE TOWN GET BACK ON ITS FEET --
-- AND RUSSELL DABOIA, P-H E'S EXECUTIVE IN CHARGE OF RESORT MANAGEMENT.
GOOD AFTERNOON.
GREETINGS, Ms. WALKER --
-- IT'S A PLEASURE TO MEET YOU IN THE FLESH...
Huh? HIS LIPS ARE... COLD...
BUT BEFORE PATSY CAN DO MORE THAN REGISTER THE FACT...
C'MON, PATS -- THERE'S STILL MORE TO SHOW YOU.
NAN HALE AND I'LL JOIN YOU -- OKAY, HEDY?
SURE, MICKEY. NEXT STOP --
CENTERVILLE
"--THE ATTRACTIONS!"
YAAAAA
AND YOU HAD TO START WITH THE MERRY-GO-ROUND? YOU GOTTA DO SOMETHING ABOUT THAT, PATSY -- I'M NOT A LITTLE KID ANY MORE...
MICKEY'S MERRY-GO-R
LIKE ANY OF US ARE WHO WE WERE BACK THEN, MICKEY...

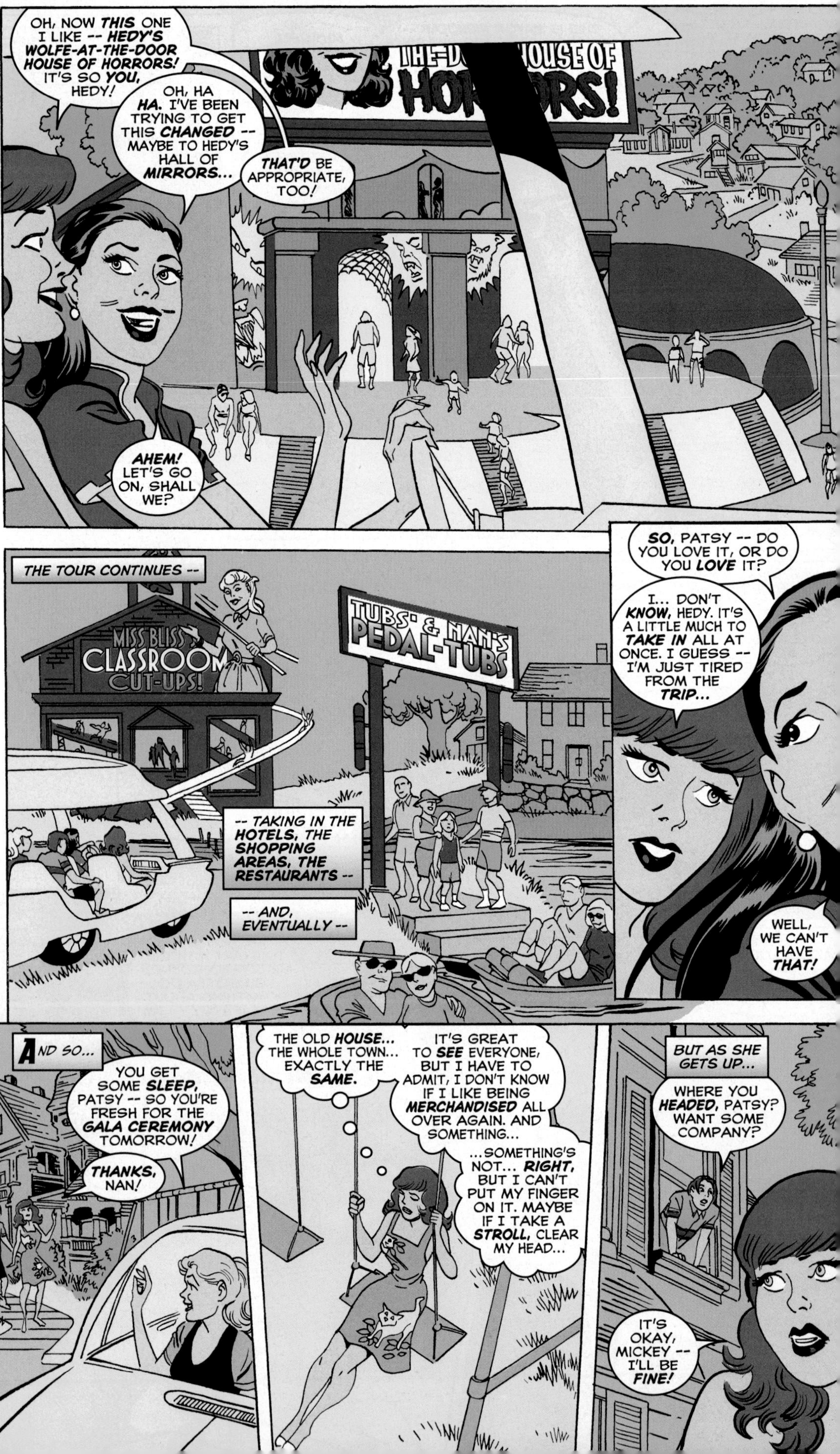
THE-D HOUSE OF HOR ORS!
OH, NOW THIS ONE I LIKE -- HEDY'S WOLFE-AT-THE-DOOR HOUSE OF HORRORS! IT'S SO YOU, HEDY!
OH, HA HA. I'VE BEEN TRYING TO GET THIS CHANGED -- MAYBE TO HEDY'S HALL OF MIRRORS...
THAT'D BE APPROPRIATE, TOO!
AHEM! LET'S GO ON, SHALL WE?
THE TOUR CONTINUES --
MISS BLISS'S CLASSROOM CUT-UPS!
TUBS' & NAN'S PEDAL-TUBS
-- TAKING IN THE HOTELS, THE SHOPPING AREAS, THE RESTAURANTS --
-- AND, EVENTUALLY --
SO, PATSY -- DO YOU LOVE IT, OR DO YOU LOVE IT?
I... DON'T KNOW, HEDY. IT'S A LITTLE MUCH TO TAKE IN ALL AT ONCE. I GUESS -- I'M JUST TIRED FROM THE TRIP...
WELL, WE CAN'T HAVE THAT!
AND SO...
YOU GET SOME SLEEP, PATSY -- SO YOU'RE FRESH FOR THE GALA CEREMONY TOMORROW!
THANKS, NAN!
THE OLD HOUSE... THE WHOLE TOWN... EXACTLY THE SAME.
IT'S GREAT TO SEE EVERYONE, BUT I HAVE TO ADMIT, I DON'T KNOW IF I LIKE BEING MERCHANDISED ALL OVER AGAIN. AND SOMETHING...
...SOMETHING'S NOT... RIGHT, BUT I CAN'T PUT MY FINGER ON IT. MAYBE IF I TAKE A STROLL, CLEAR MY HEAD...
BUT AS SHE GETS UP...
WHERE YOU HEADED, PATSY? WANT SOME COMPANY?
IT'S OKAY, MICKEY -- I'LL BE FINE!

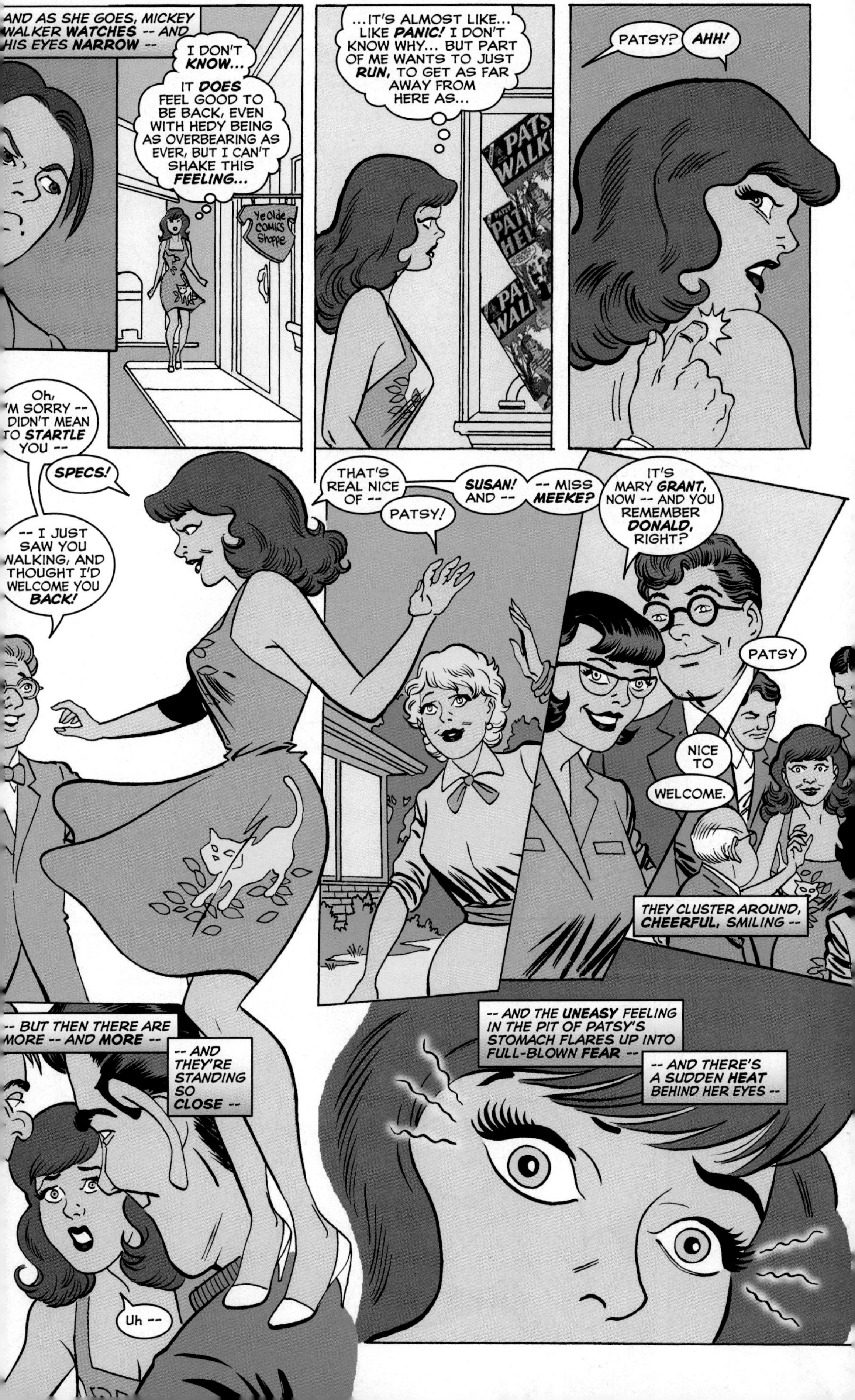
AND AS SHE GOES, MICKEY WALKER WATCHES -- AND HIS EYES NARROW --
I DON'T KNOW...
IT DOES FEEL GOOD TO BE BACK, EVEN WITH HEDY BEING AS OVERBEARING AS EVER, BUT I CAN'T SHAKE THIS FEELING...
Ye Olde COMICS Shoppe
...IT'S ALMOST LIKE... LIKE PANIC! I DON'T KNOW WHY... BUT PART OF ME WANTS TO JUST RUN, TO GET AS FAR AWAY FROM HERE AS...
PATSY?
AHH!
Oh, I'M SORRY -- I DIDN'T MEAN TO STARTLE YOU --
SPECS!
-- I JUST SAW YOU WALKING, AND THOUGHT I'D WELCOME YOU BACK!
THAT'S REAL NICE OF --
PATSY!
SUSAN! AND --
-- MISS MEEKE?
IT'S MARY GRANT, NOW -- AND YOU REMEMBER DONALD, RIGHT?
PATSY
NICE TO
WELCOME.
THEY CLUSTER AROUND, CHEERFUL, SMILING --
-- BUT THEN THERE ARE MORE -- AND MORE --
-- AND THEY'RE STANDING SO CLOSE --
Uh --
-- AND THE UNEASY FEELING IN THE PIT OF PATSY'S STOMACH FLARES UP INTO FULL-BLOWN FEAR --
-- AND THERE'S A SUDDEN HEAT BEHIND HER EYES --

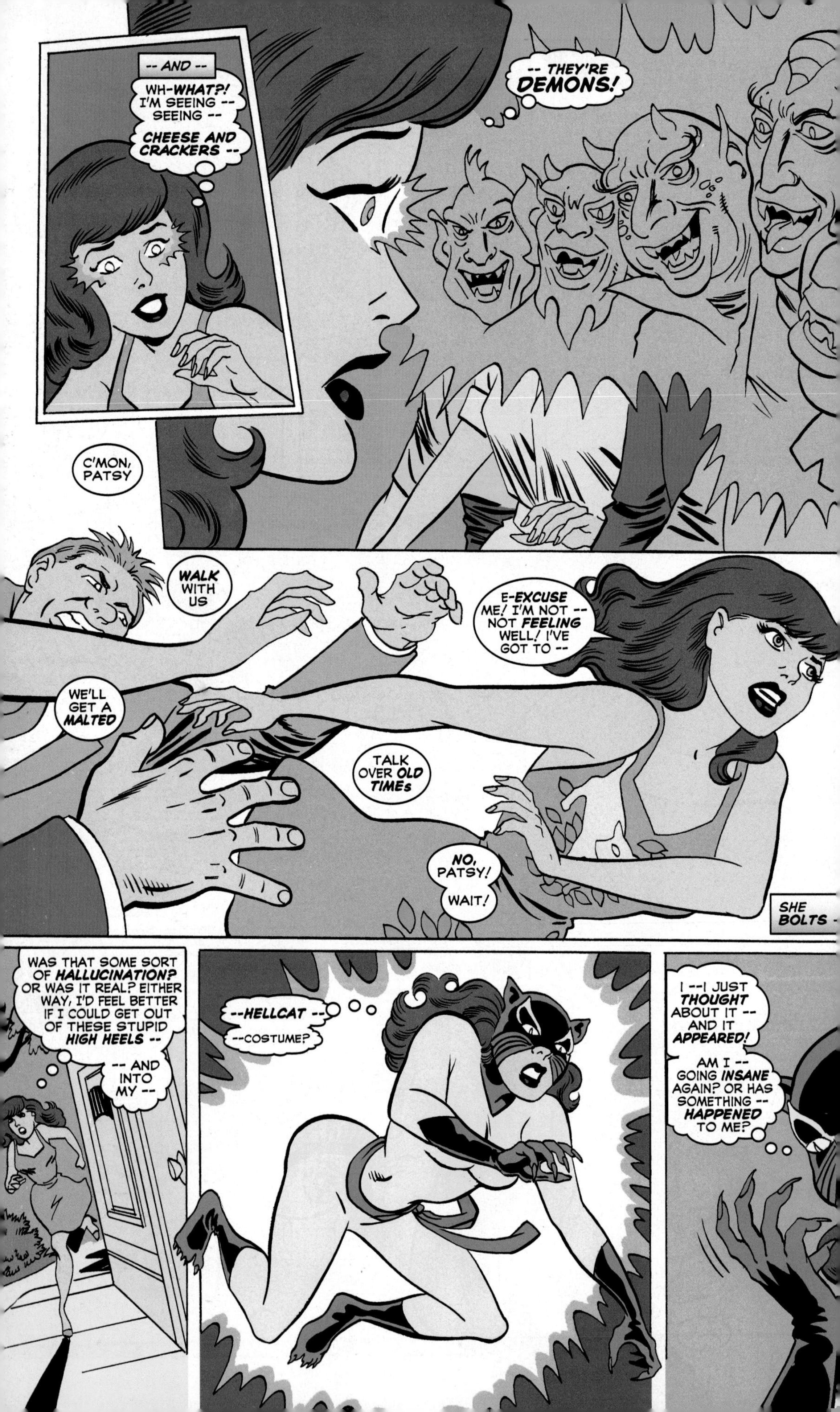

-- AND --
WH-WHAT?! I'M SEEING -- SEEING --
CHEESE AND CRACKERS --
-- THEY'RE DEMONS!
C'MON, PATSY
WALK WITH US
E-EXCUSE ME! I'M NOT -- NOT FEELING WELL! I'VE GOT TO --
WE'LL GET A MALTED
TALK OVER OLD TIMEs
NO, PATSY!
WAIT!
SHE BOLTS -
WAS THAT SOME SORT OF HALLUCINATION? OR WAS IT REAL? EITHER WAY, I'D FEEL BETTER IF I COULD GET OUT OF THESE STUPID HIGH HEELS --
-- AND INTO MY --
--HELLCAT --
--COSTUME?
I --I JUST THOUGHT ABOUT IT -- AND IT APPEARED!
AM I -- GOING INSANE AGAIN? OR HAS SOMETHING -- HAPPENED TO ME?

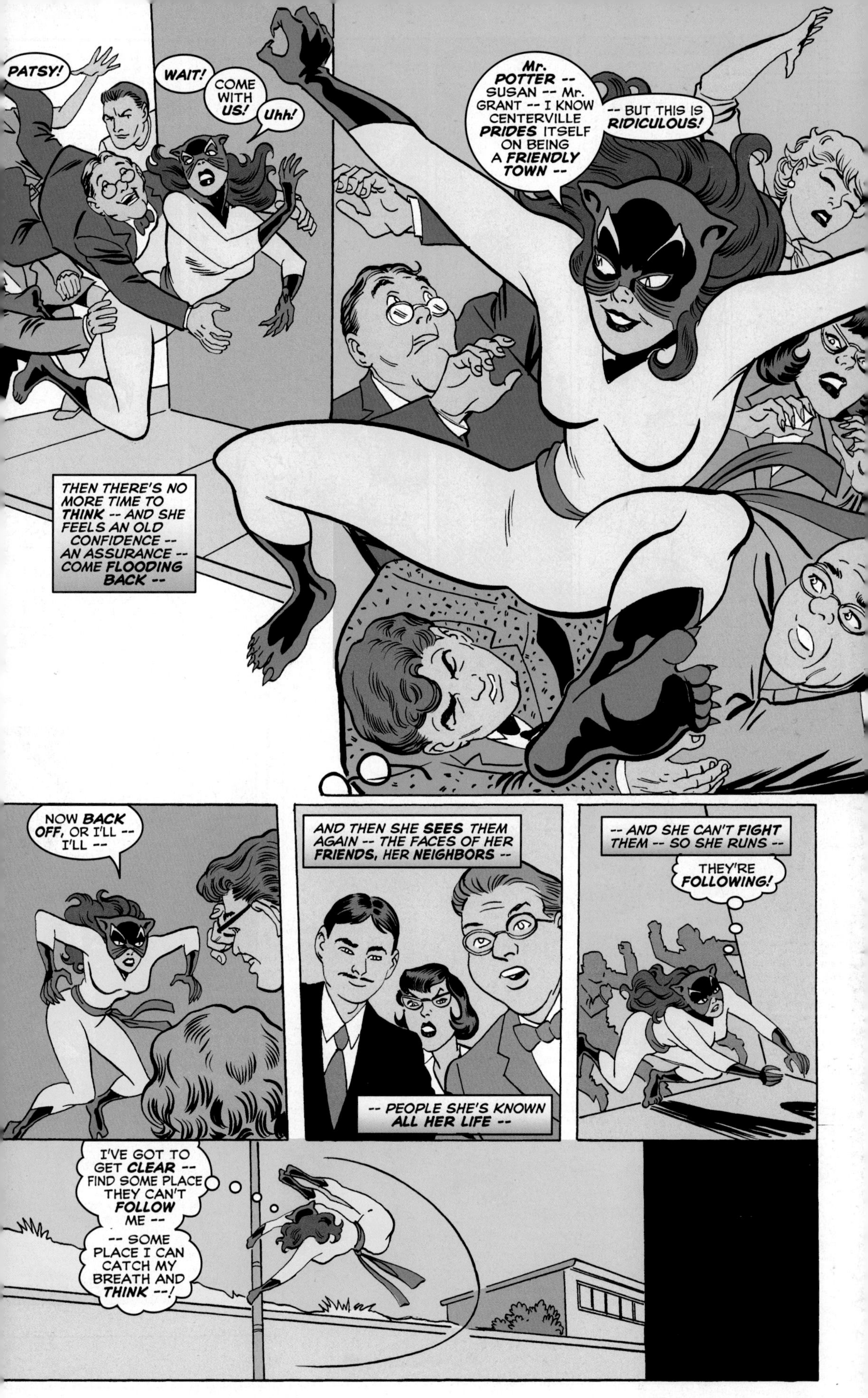

PATSY!
WAIT!
COME WITH US!
Uhh!
Mr. POTTER -- SUSAN -- Mr. GRANT -- I KNOW CENTERVILLE PRIDES ITSELF ON BEING A FRIENDLY TOWN --
-- BUT THIS IS RIDICULOUS!
THEN THERE'S NO MORE TIME TO THINK -- AND SHE FEELS AN OLD CONFIDENCE -- AN ASSURANCE -- COME FLOODING BACK --
NOW BACK OFF, OR I'LL -- I'LL --
AND THEN SHE SEES THEM AGAIN -- THE FACES OF HER FRIENDS, HER NEIGHBORS --
-- PEOPLE SHE'S KNOWN ALL HER LIFE --
-- AND SHE CAN'T FIGHT THEM -- SO SHE RUNS --
THEY'RE FOLLOWING!
I'VE GOT TO GET CLEAR -- FIND SOME PLACE THEY CAN'T FOLLOW ME --
-- SOME PLACE I CAN CATCH MY BREATH AND THINK --!

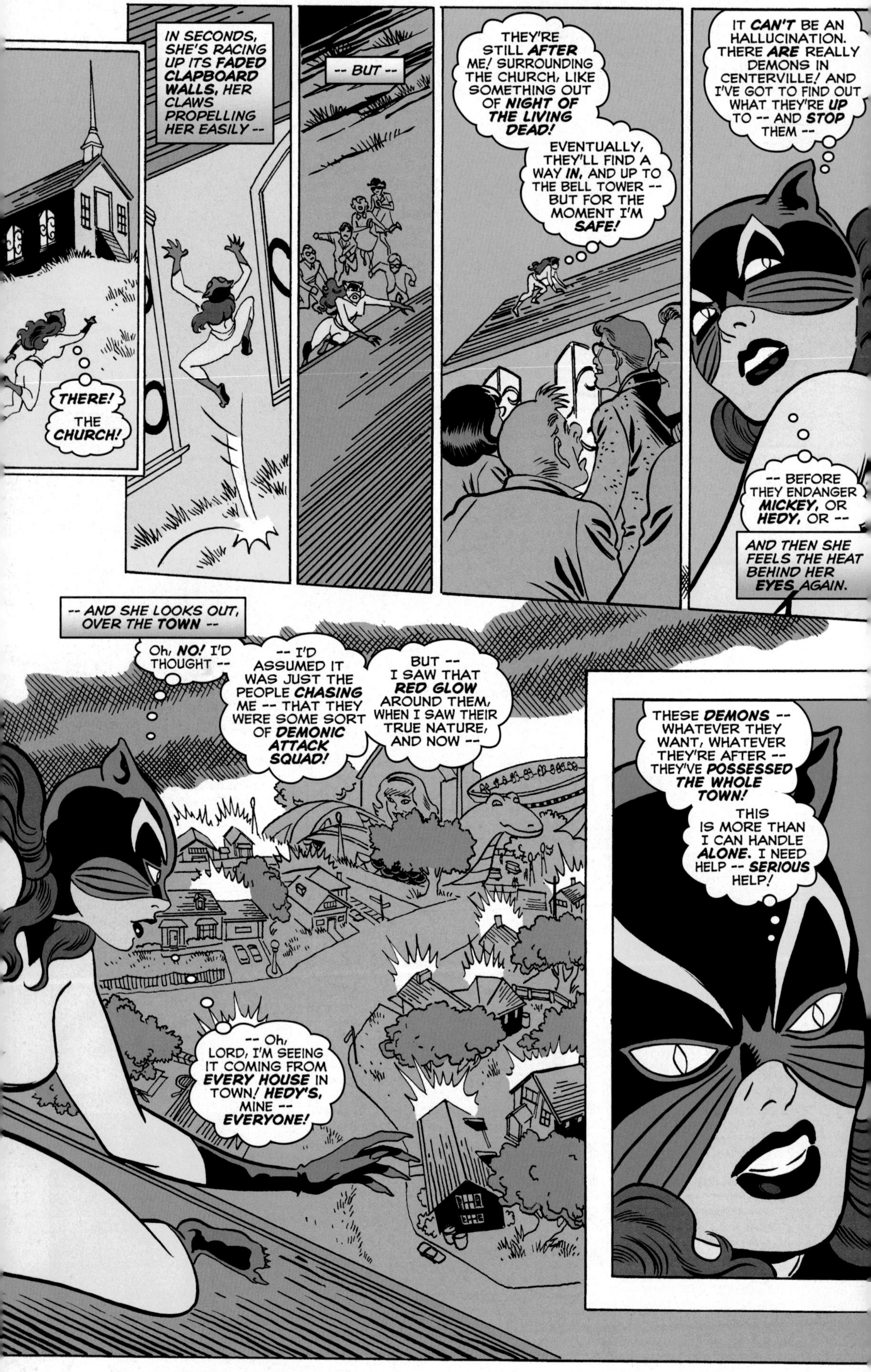
THERE! THE CHURCH!
IN SECONDS, SHE'S RACING UP ITS FADED CLAPBOARD WALLS, HER CLAWS PROPELLING HER EASILY --
-- BUT --
THEY'RE STILL AFTER ME! SURROUNDING THE CHURCH, LIKE SOMETHING OUT OF NIGHT OF THE LIVING DEAD!
EVENTUALLY, THEY'LL FIND A WAY IN, AND UP TO THE BELL TOWER -- BUT FOR THE MOMENT I'M SAFE!
IT CAN'T BE AN HALLUCINATION. THERE ARE REALLY DEMONS IN CENTERVILLE! AND I'VE GOT TO FIND OUT WHAT THEY'RE UP TO -- AND STOP THEM --
-- BEFORE THEY ENDANGER MICKEY, OR HEDY, OR --
AND THEN SHE FEELS THE HEAT BEHIND HER EYES AGAIN.
-- AND SHE LOOKS OUT, OVER THE TOWN --
Oh, NO! I'D THOUGHT --
-- I'D ASSUMED IT WAS JUST THE PEOPLE CHASING ME -- THAT THEY WERE SOME SORT OF DEMONIC ATTACK SQUAD!
BUT -- I SAW THAT RED GLOW AROUND THEM, WHEN I SAW THEIR TRUE NATURE, AND NOW --
-- Oh, LORD, I'M SEEING IT COMING FROM EVERY HOUSE IN TOWN! HEDY'S, MINE -- EVERYONE!
THESE DEMONS -- WHATEVER THEY WANT, WHATEVER THEY'RE AFTER -- THEY'VE POSSESSED THE WHOLE TOWN!
THIS IS MORE THAN I CAN HANDLE ALONE. I NEED HELP -- SERIOUS HELP!

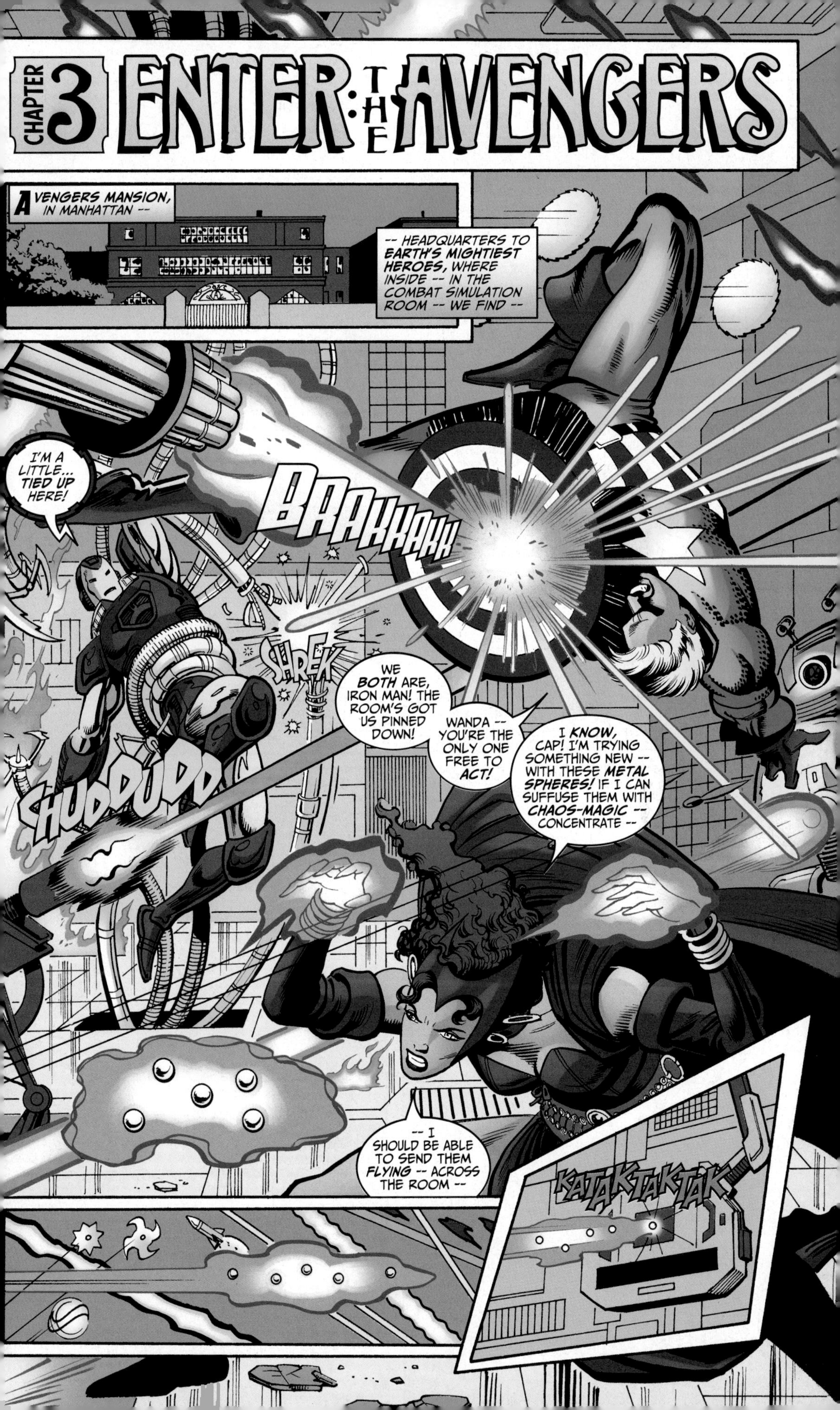
CHAPTER 3 ENTER: THE AVENGERS
AVENGERS MANSION, IN MANHATTAN --
-- HEADQUARTERS TO EARTH'S MIGHTIEST HEROES, WHERE INSIDE -- IN THE COMBAT SIMULATION ROOM -- WE FIND --
I'M A LITTLE... TIED UP HERE!
BRAKKAKK
SHREK
WE BOTH ARE, IRON MAN! THE ROOM'S GOT US PINNED DOWN!
WANDA -- YOU'RE THE ONLY ONE FREE TO ACT!
SHUDUDD
I KNOW, CAP! I'M TRYING SOMETHING NEW -- WITH THESE METAL SPHERES! IF I CAN SUFFUSE THEM WITH CHAOS-MAGIC -- CONCENTRATE --
-- I SHOULD BE ABLE TO SEND THEM FLYING -- ACROSS THE ROOM --
KATAKTAKTAK

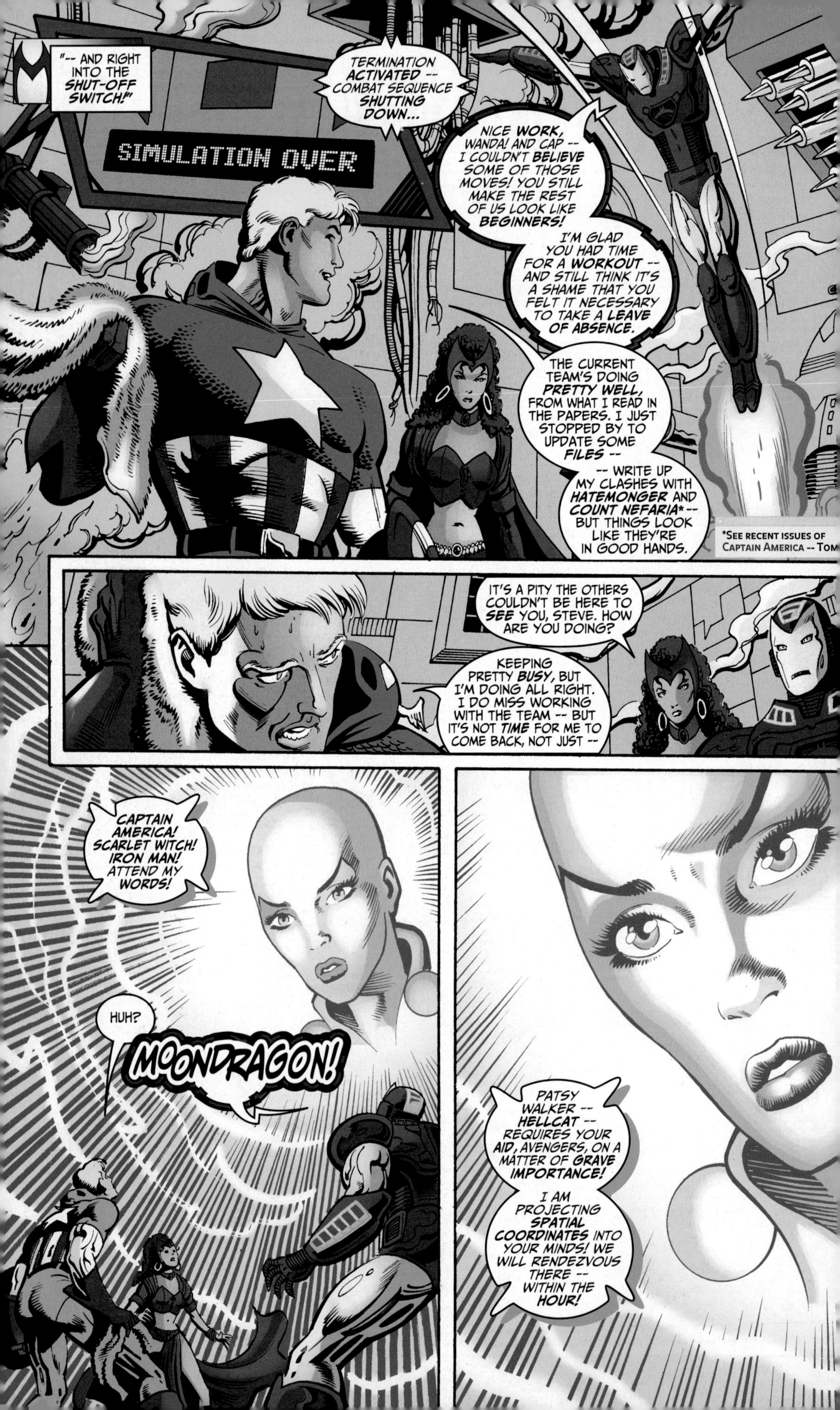
"-- AND RIGHT INTO THE SHUT-OFF SWITCH!"
TERMINATION ACTIVATED -- COMBAT SEQUENCE SHUTTING DOWN...
SIMULATION OVER
NICE WORK, WANDA! AND CAP -- I COULDN'T BELIEVE SOME OF THOSE MOVES! YOU STILL MAKE THE REST OF US LOOK LIKE BEGINNERS!
I'M GLAD YOU HAD TIME FOR A WORKOUT -- AND STILL THINK IT'S A SHAME THAT YOU FELT IT NECESSARY TO TAKE A LEAVE OF ABSENCE.
THE CURRENT TEAM'S DOING PRETTY WELL, FROM WHAT I READ IN THE PAPERS. I JUST STOPPED BY TO UPDATE SOME FILES --
-- WRITE UP MY CLASHES WITH HATEMONGER AND COUNT NEFARIA* -- BUT THINGS LOOK LIKE THEY'RE IN GOOD HANDS.
*SEE RECENT ISSUES OF CAPTAIN AMERICA -- TOM
IT'S A PITY THE OTHERS COULDN'T BE HERE TO SEE YOU, STEVE. HOW ARE YOU DOING?
KEEPING PRETTY BUSY, BUT I'M DOING ALL RIGHT. I DO MISS WORKING WITH THE TEAM -- BUT IT'S NOT TIME FOR ME TO COME BACK, NOT JUST --
CAPTAIN AMERICA! SCARLET WITCH! IRON MAN! ATTEND MY WORDS!
HUH?
MOONDRAGON!
PATSY WALKER -- HELLCAT -- REQUIRES YOUR AID, AVENGERS, ON A MATTER OF GRAVE IMPORTANCE!
I AM PROJECTING SPATIAL COORDINATES INTO YOUR MINDS! WE WILL RENDEZVOUS THERE -- WITHIN THE HOUR!

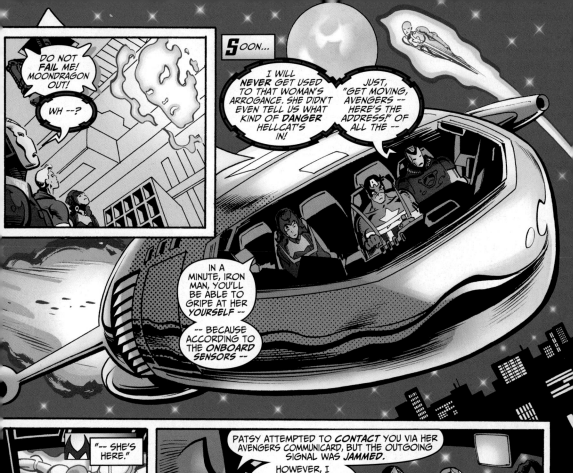

DO NOT *FAIL* ME! MOONDRAGON *OUT!*

WH --?

*S*OON...

I WILL *NEVER* GET USED TO THAT WOMAN'S *ARROGANCE.* SHE DIDN'T EVEN TELL US WHAT KIND OF *DANGER* HELLCAT'S IN!

JUST, *"GET MOVING, AVENGERS -- HERE'S THE ADDRESS!"* OF ALL THE --

IN A MINUTE, IRON MAN, YOU'LL BE ABLE TO GRIPE AT HER *YOURSELF* --

-- BECAUSE ACCORDING TO THE *ONBOARD SENSORS* --

"-- SHE'S HERE."

VERY *GOOD,* AVENGERS. NOW HEAD WEST -- WE MUST REACH *CENTERVILLE* WITH ALL *DUE SPEED.*

NOW WAIT A --

PATSY ATTEMPTED TO *CONTACT* YOU VIA HER AVENGERS COMMUNICARD, BUT THE OUTGOING SIGNAL WAS *JAMMED.*

HOWEVER, I MAINTAIN A *LOW-LEVEL AWARENESS* OF MY FORMER CHARGE, AND *SENSED* HER DISTRESS --

-- SO I CONTACTED HER *TELEPATHICALLY.*

MOONDRAGON, YOU *CAN'T* JUST --

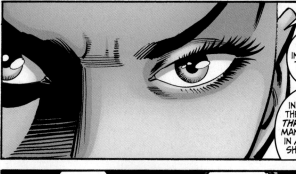

I AM AN *AVENGER,* AM I NOT?

INACTIVE, BUT WITH FULL *PRIVILEGES,* INCLUDING THE RIGHT TO CALL ON THE TEAM IN AN *EMERGENCY?* VERY WELL.

I COULD SENSE IN YOUR MINDS THAT THERE WERE ONLY THE *THREE* OF YOU AT THE MANSION, SO I CALLED IN *ASSISTANCE.* THEY SHOULD BE ARRIVING --

-- *NOW.*

HAWKEYE! AND *SONGBIRD!*

HI, GANG --

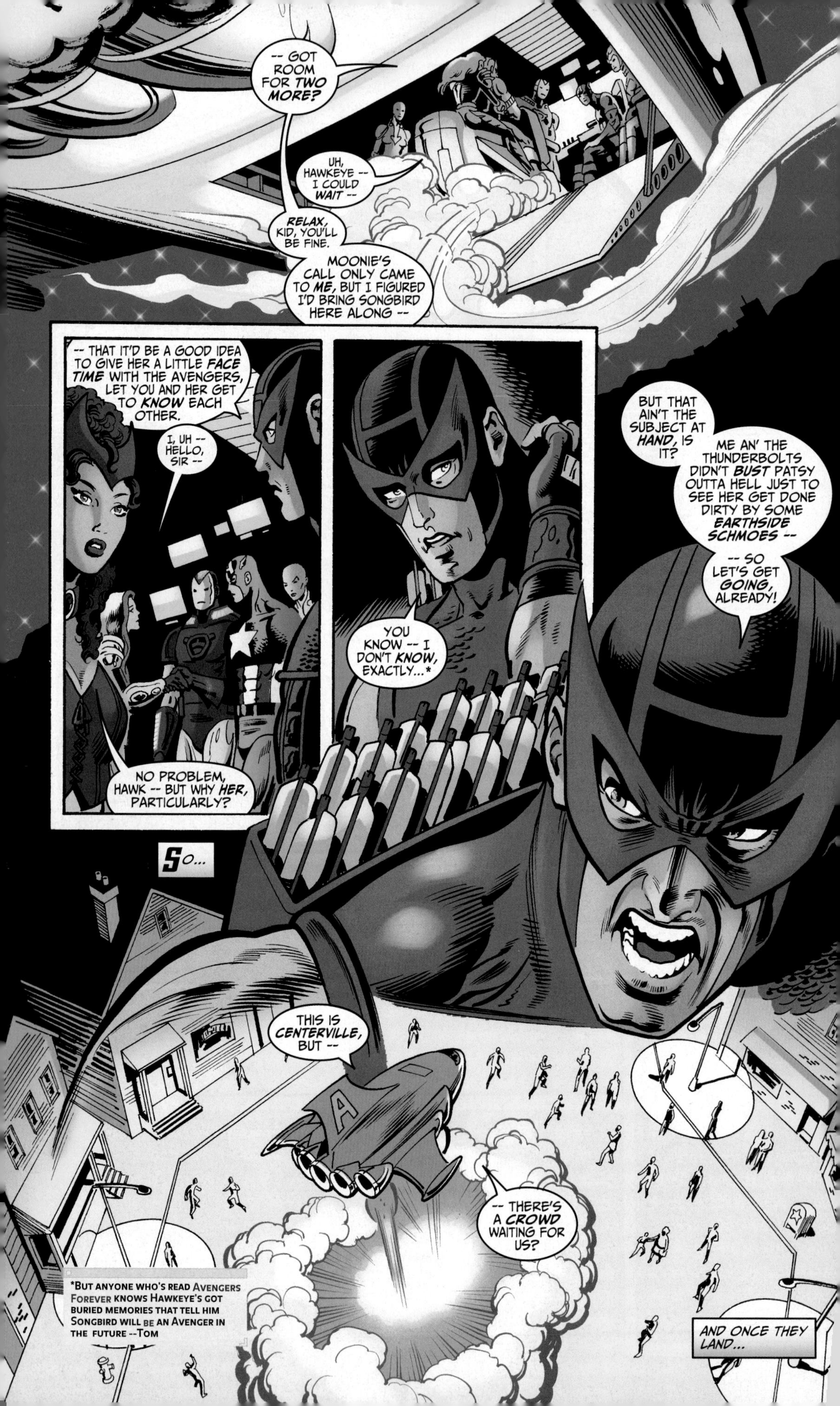
-- GOT ROOM FOR TWO MORE?
UH, HAWKEYE -- I COULD WAIT --
RELAX, KID, YOU'LL BE FINE.
MOONIE'S CALL ONLY CAME TO ME, BUT I FIGURED I'D BRING SONGBIRD HERE ALONG --
-- THAT IT'D BE A GOOD IDEA TO GIVE HER A LITTLE FACE TIME WITH THE AVENGERS, LET YOU AND HER GET TO KNOW EACH OTHER.
I, UH -- HELLO, SIR --
NO PROBLEM, HAWK -- BUT WHY HER, PARTICULARLY?
YOU KNOW -- I DON'T KNOW, EXACTLY...*
BUT THAT AIN'T THE SUBJECT AT HAND, IS IT?
ME AN' THE THUNDERBOLTS DIDN'T BUST PATSY OUTTA HELL JUST TO SEE HER GET DONE DIRTY BY SOME EARTHSIDE SCHMOES --
-- SO LET'S GET GOING, ALREADY!
SO...
THIS IS CENTERVILLE, BUT --
-- THERE'S A CROWD WAITING FOR US?
*BUT ANYONE WHO'S READ AVENGERS FOREVER KNOWS HAWKEYE'S GOT BURIED MEMORIES THAT TELL HIM SONGBIRD WILL BE AN AVENGER IN THE FUTURE --TOM
AND ONCE THEY LAND...

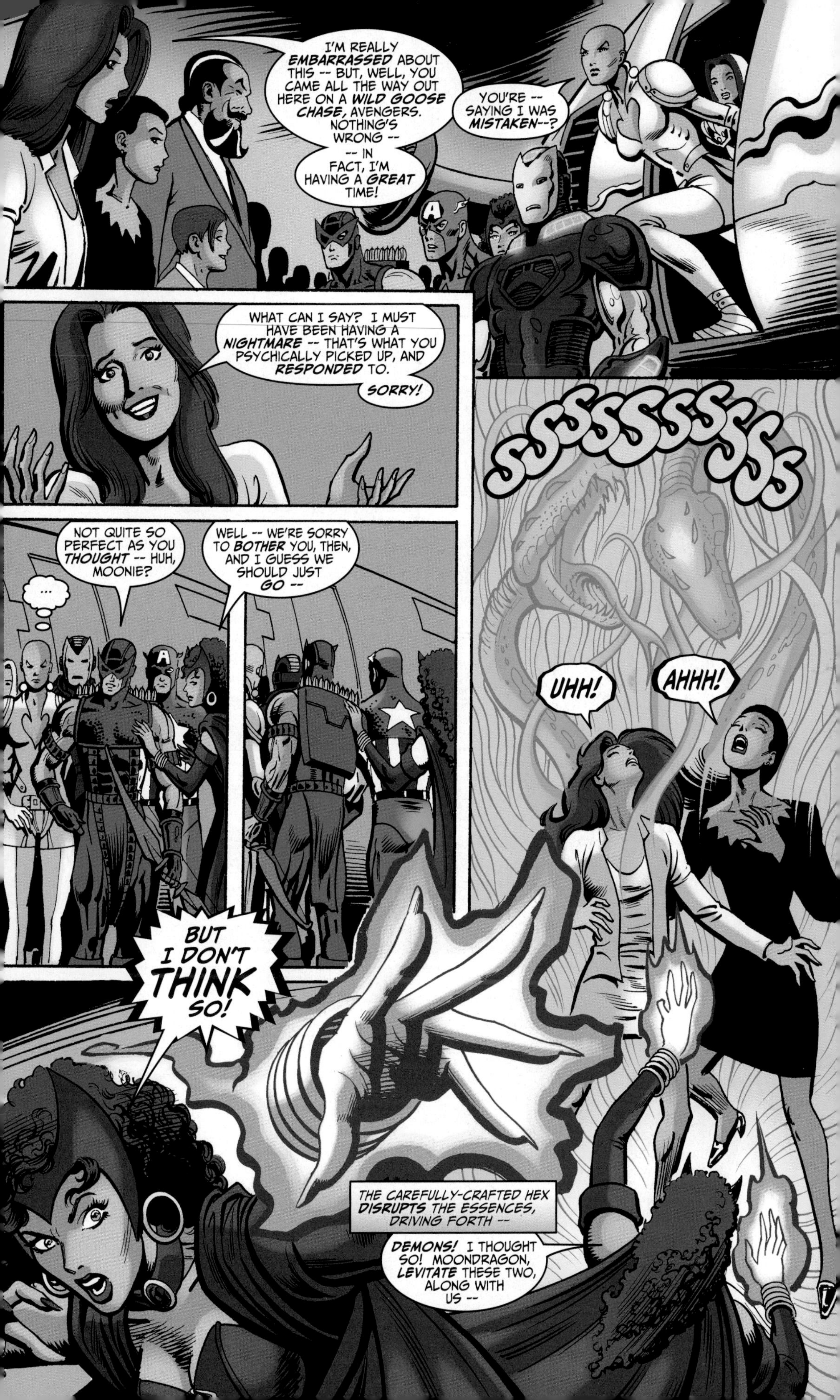
I'M REALLY EMBARRASSED ABOUT THIS -- BUT, WELL, YOU CAME ALL THE WAY OUT HERE ON A WILD GOOSE CHASE, AVENGERS. NOTHING'S WRONG --
-- IN FACT, I'M HAVING A GREAT TIME!
YOU'RE -- SAYING I WAS MISTAKEN--?
WHAT CAN I SAY? I MUST HAVE BEEN HAVING A NIGHTMARE -- THAT'S WHAT YOU PSYCHICALLY PICKED UP, AND RESPONDED TO.
SORRY!
...
NOT QUITE SO PERFECT AS YOU THOUGHT -- HUH, MOONIE?
WELL -- WE'RE SORRY TO BOTHER YOU, THEN, AND I GUESS WE SHOULD JUST GO --
SSSSSSSSSS
UHH!
AHHH!
BUT I DON'T THINK SO!
THE CAREFULLY-CRAFTED HEX DISRUPTS THE ESSENCES, DRIVING FORTH --
DEMONS! I THOUGHT SO! MOONDRAGON, LEVITATE THESE TWO, ALONG WITH US --

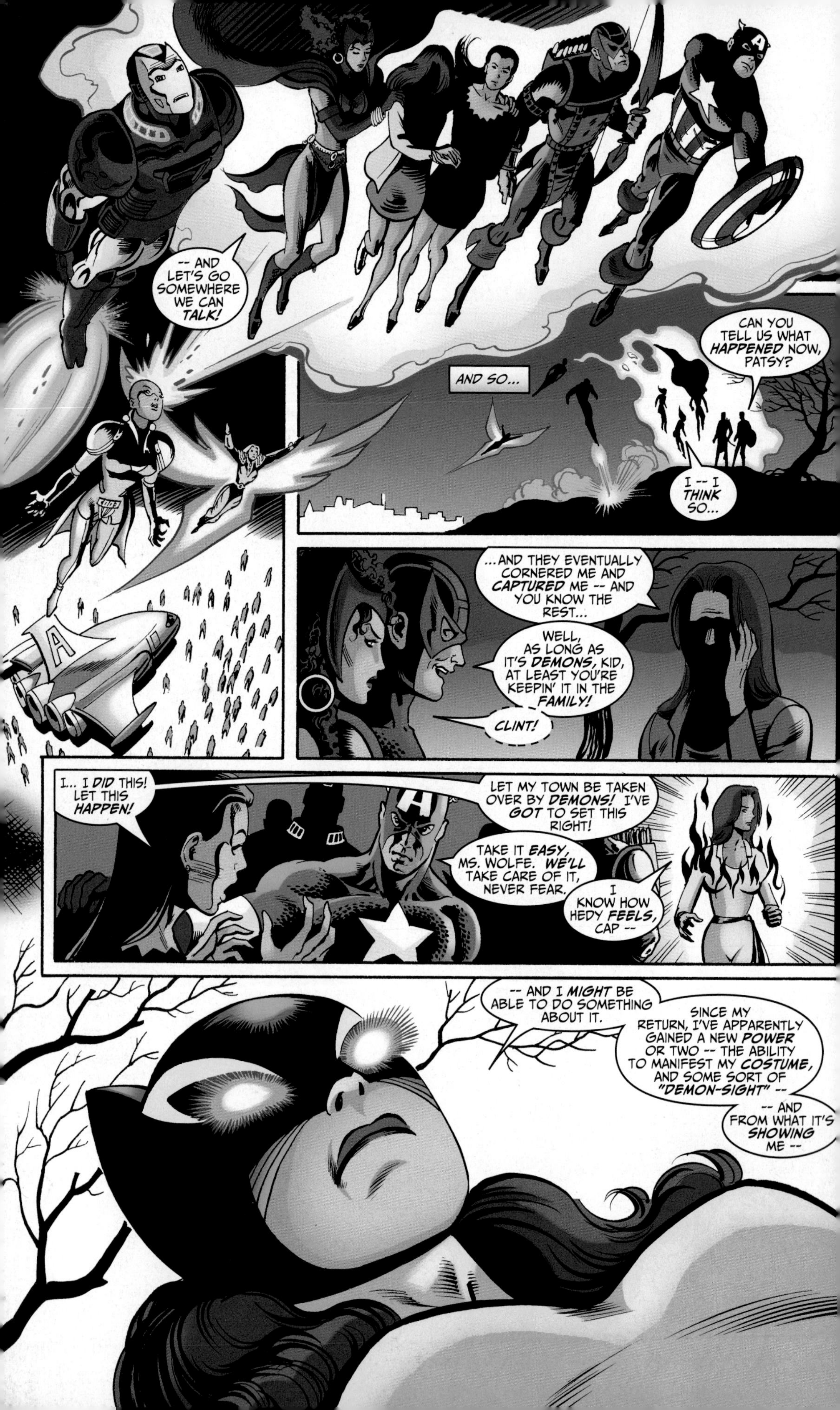

-- AND LET'S GO SOMEWHERE WE CAN TALK!
AND SO...
CAN YOU TELL US WHAT HAPPENED NOW, PATSY?
I -- I THINK SO...
...AND THEY EVENTUALLY CORNERED ME AND CAPTURED ME -- AND YOU KNOW THE REST...
WELL, AS LONG AS IT'S DEMONS, KID, AT LEAST YOU'RE KEEPIN' IT IN THE FAMILY!
CLINT!
I... I DID THIS! LET THIS HAPPEN!
LET MY TOWN BE TAKEN OVER BY DEMONS! I'VE GOT TO SET THIS RIGHT!
TAKE IT EASY, MS. WOLFE. WE'LL TAKE CARE OF IT, NEVER FEAR.
I KNOW HOW HEDY FEELS, CAP --
-- AND I MIGHT BE ABLE TO DO SOMETHING ABOUT IT.
SINCE MY RETURN, I'VE APPARENTLY GAINED A NEW POWER OR TWO -- THE ABILITY TO MANIFEST MY COSTUME, AND SOME SORT OF "DEMON-SIGHT" --
-- AND FROM WHAT IT'S SHOWING ME --

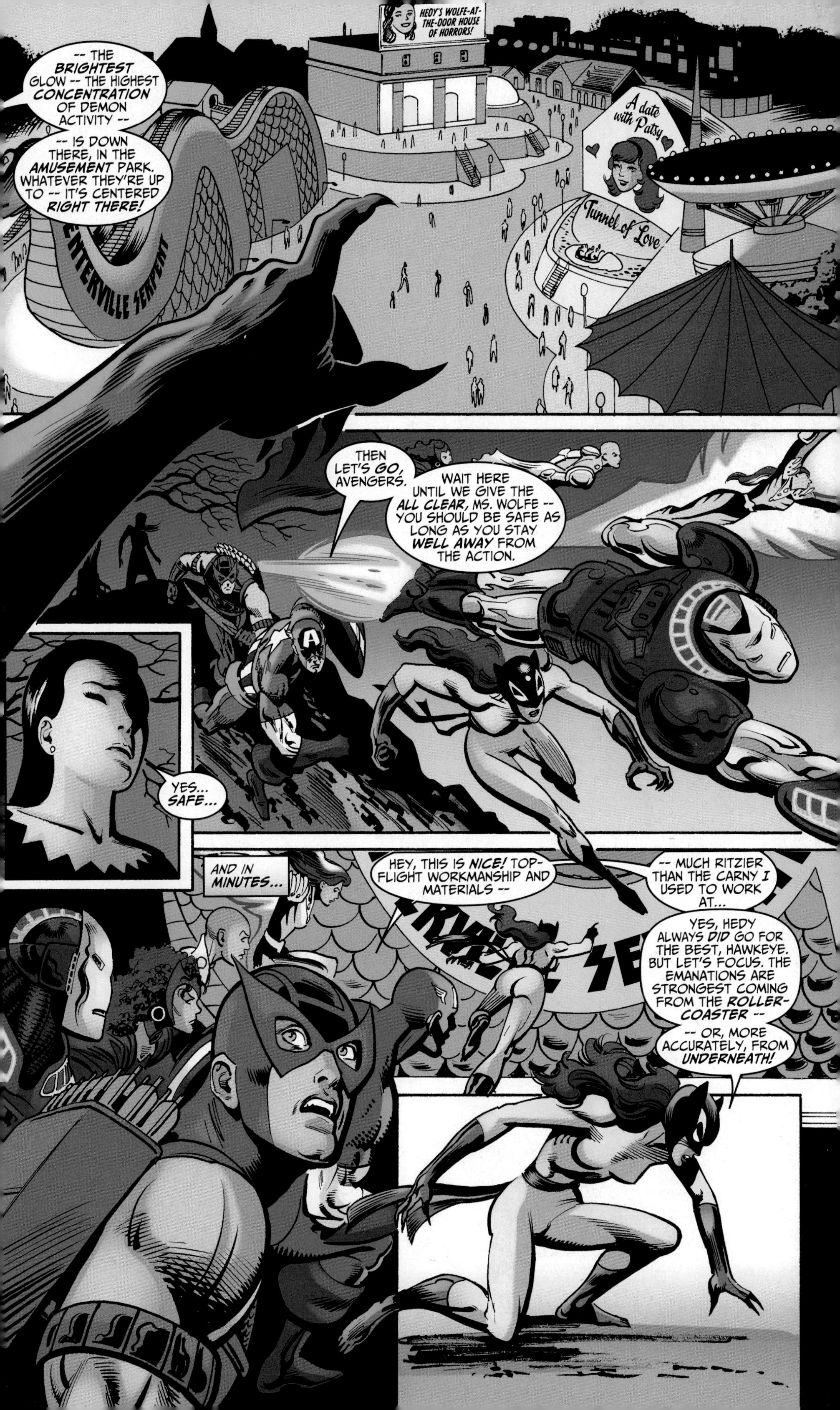
HEDY'S WOLFE-AT-THE-DOOR HOUSE OF HORRORS!
-- THE BRIGHTEST GLOW -- THE HIGHEST CONCENTRATION OF DEMON ACTIVITY --
-- IS DOWN THERE, IN THE AMUSEMENT PARK. WHATEVER THEY'RE UP TO -- IT'S CENTERED RIGHT THERE!
A date with Patsy
Tunnel of Love
THEN LET'S GO, AVENGERS.
WAIT HERE UNTIL WE GIVE THE ALL CLEAR, MS. WOLFE -- YOU SHOULD BE SAFE AS LONG AS YOU STAY WELL AWAY FROM THE ACTION.
YES... SAFE...
AND IN MINUTES...
HEY, THIS IS NICE! TOP-FLIGHT WORKMANSHIP AND MATERIALS --
-- MUCH RITZIER THAN THE CARNY I USED TO WORK AT...
YES, HEDY ALWAYS DID GO FOR THE BEST, HAWKEYE. BUT LET'S FOCUS. THE EMANATIONS ARE STRONGEST COMING FROM THE ROLLER-COASTER --
-- OR, MORE ACCURATELY, FROM UNDERNEATH!

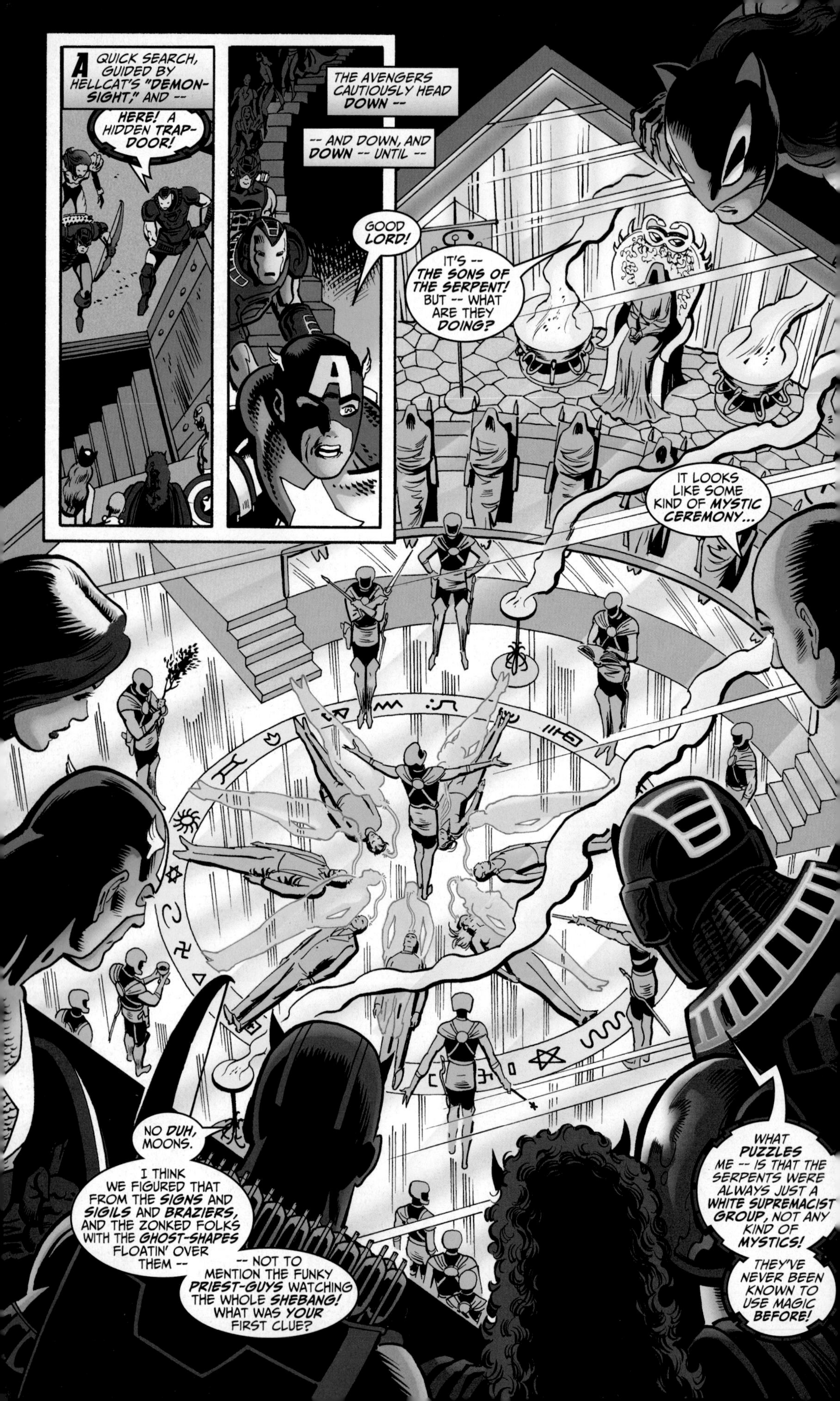
A QUICK SEARCH, GUIDED BY HELLCAT'S "DEMON-SIGHT," AND --
HERE! A HIDDEN TRAP-DOOR!
THE AVENGERS CAUTIOUSLY HEAD DOWN --
-- AND DOWN, AND DOWN -- UNTIL --
GOOD LORD!
IT'S -- THE SONS OF THE SERPENT! BUT -- WHAT ARE THEY DOING?
IT LOOKS LIKE SOME KIND OF MYSTIC CEREMONY...
NO DUH, MOONS.
I THINK WE FIGURED THAT FROM THE SIGNS AND SIGILS AND BRAZIERS, AND THE ZONKED FOLKS WITH THE GHOST-SHAPES FLOATIN' OVER THEM --
-- NOT TO MENTION THE FUNKY PRIEST-GUYS WATCHING THE WHOLE SHEBANG! WHAT WAS YOUR FIRST CLUE?
WHAT PUZZLES ME -- IS THAT THE SERPENTS WERE ALWAYS JUST A WHITE SUPREMACIST GROUP, NOT ANY KIND OF MYSTICS!
THEY'VE NEVER BEEN KNOWN TO USE MAGIC BEFORE!

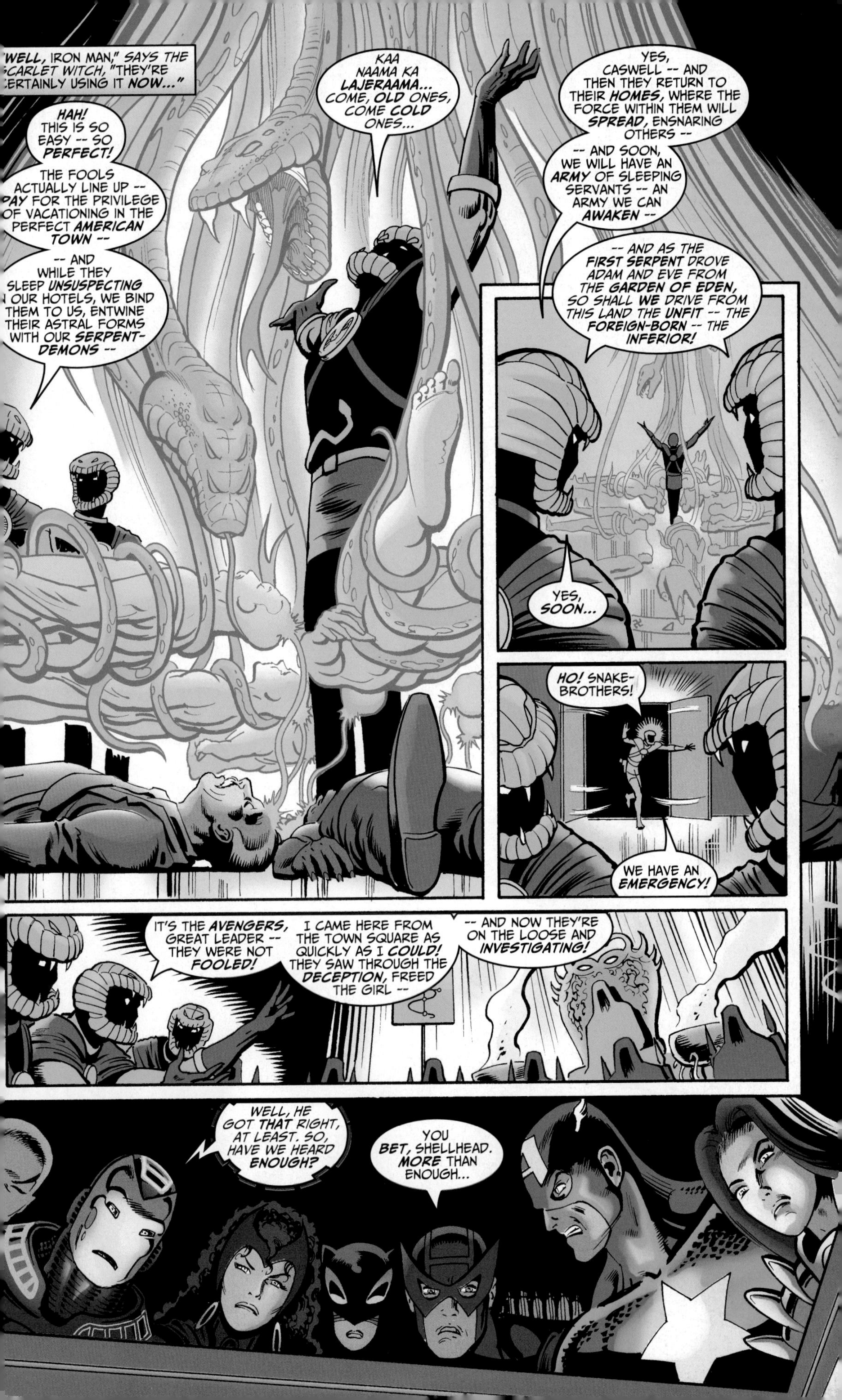
"WELL, IRON MAN," SAYS THE SCARLET WITCH, "THEY'RE CERTAINLY USING IT NOW..."
HAH! THIS IS SO EASY -- SO PERFECT!
THE FOOLS ACTUALLY LINE UP -- PAY FOR THE PRIVILEGE OF VACATIONING IN THE PERFECT AMERICAN TOWN --
-- AND WHILE THEY SLEEP UNSUSPECTING IN OUR HOTELS, WE BIND THEM TO US, ENTWINE THEIR ASTRAL FORMS WITH OUR SERPENT-DEMONS --
KAA NAAMA KA LAJERAAMA... COME, OLD ONES, COME COLD ONES...
YES, CASWELL -- AND THEN THEY RETURN TO THEIR HOMES, WHERE THE FORCE WITHIN THEM WILL SPREAD, ENSNARING OTHERS --
-- AND SOON, WE WILL HAVE AN ARMY OF SLEEPING SERVANTS -- AN ARMY WE CAN AWAKEN --
-- AND AS THE FIRST SERPENT DROVE ADAM AND EVE FROM THE GARDEN OF EDEN, SO SHALL WE DRIVE FROM THIS LAND THE UNFIT -- THE FOREIGN-BORN -- THE INFERIOR!
YES, SOON...
HO! SNAKE-BROTHERS!
WE HAVE AN EMERGENCY!
IT'S THE AVENGERS, GREAT LEADER -- THEY WERE NOT FOOLED!
I CAME HERE FROM THE TOWN SQUARE AS QUICKLY AS I COULD! THEY SAW THROUGH THE DECEPTION, FREED THE GIRL --
-- AND NOW THEY'RE ON THE LOOSE AND INVESTIGATING!
WELL, HE GOT THAT RIGHT, AT LEAST. SO, HAVE WE HEARD ENOUGH?
YOU BET, SHELLHEAD. MORE THAN ENOUGH...

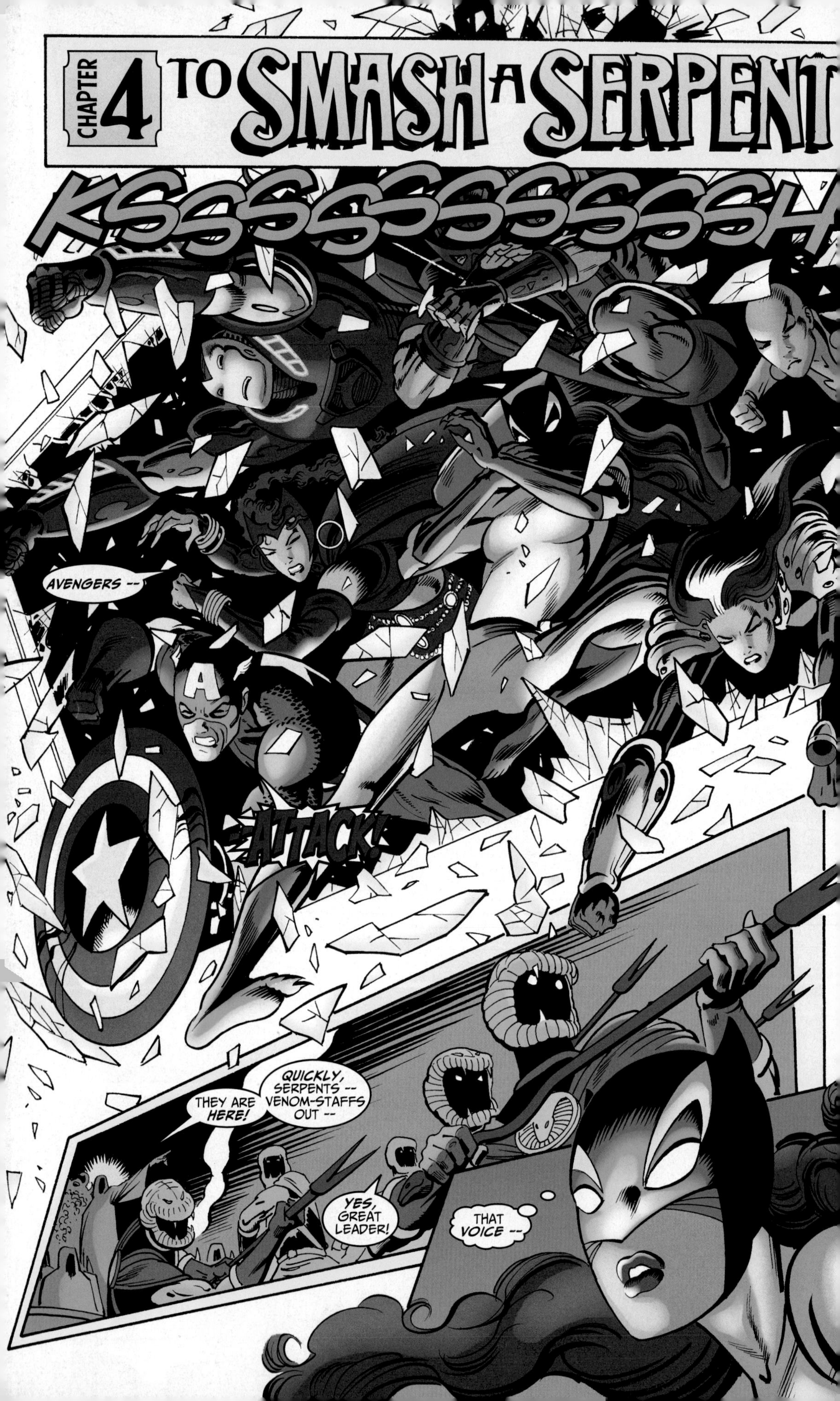
CHAPTER 4 TO SMASH A SERPENT
KSSSSSSSSSSSH
AVENGERS --
-- ATTACK!
THEY ARE HERE!
QUICKLY, SERPENTS -- VENOM-STAFFS OUT --
YES, GREAT LEADER!
THAT VOICE --

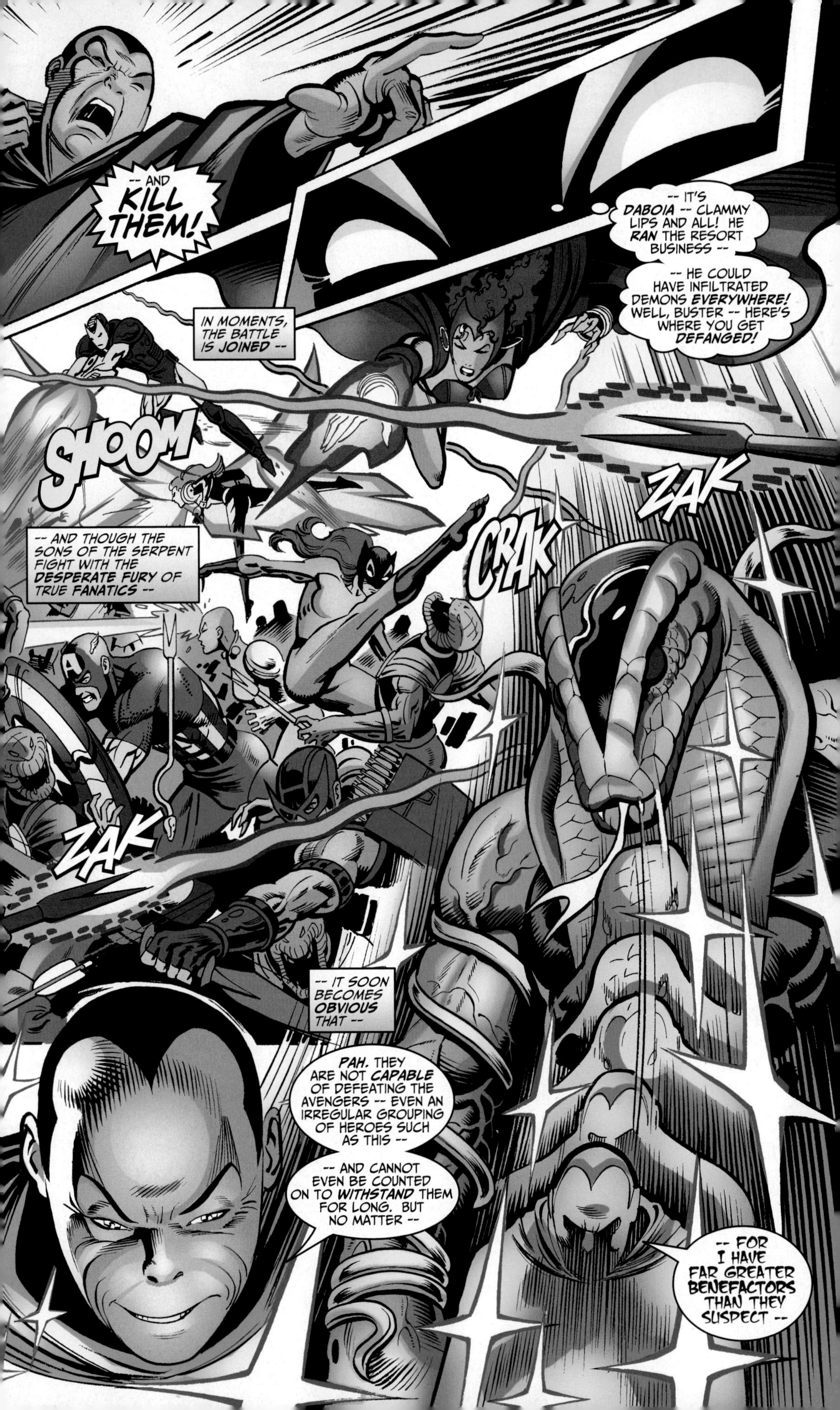
-- AND KILL THEM!
-- IT'S DABOIA -- CLAMMY LIPS AND ALL! HE RAN THE RESORT BUSINESS --
-- HE COULD HAVE INFILTRATED DEMONS EVERYWHERE! WELL, BUSTER -- HERE'S WHERE YOU GET DEFANGED!
IN MOMENTS, THE BATTLE IS JOINED --
SHOOM
-- AND THOUGH THE SONS OF THE SERPENT FIGHT WITH THE DESPERATE FURY OF TRUE FANATICS --
CRAK
ZAK
ZAK
-- IT SOON BECOMES OBVIOUS THAT --
PAH. THEY ARE NOT CAPABLE OF DEFEATING THE AVENGERS -- EVEN AN IRREGULAR GROUPING OF HEROES SUCH AS THIS --
-- AND CANNOT EVEN BE COUNTED ON TO WITHSTAND THEM FOR LONG. BUT NO MATTER --
-- FOR I HAVE FAR GREATER BENEFACTORS THAN THEY SUSPECT --

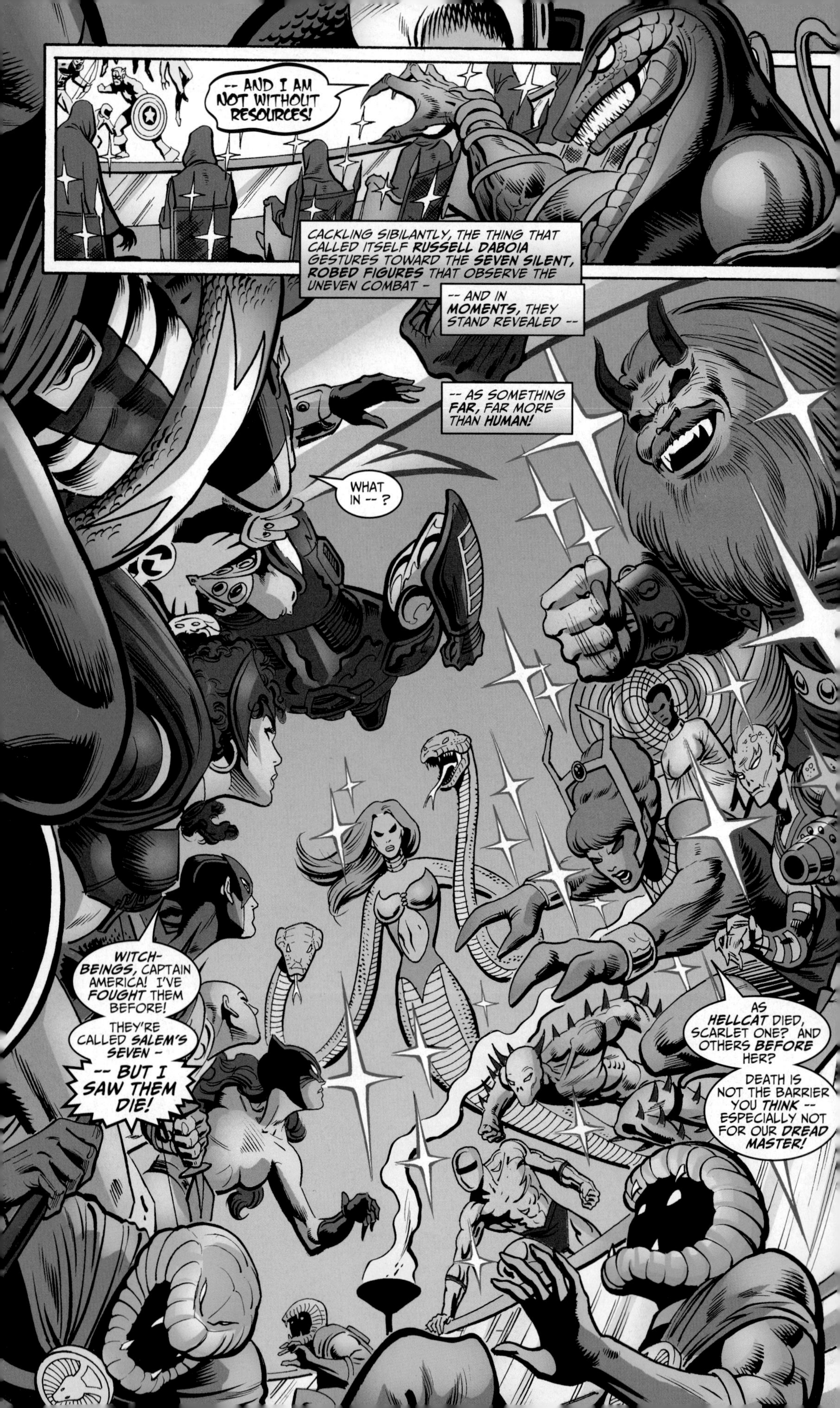
-- AND I AM NOT WITHOUT RESOURCES!
CACKLING SIBILANTLY, THE THING THAT CALLED ITSELF RUSSELL DABOIA GESTURES TOWARD THE SEVEN SILENT, ROBED FIGURES THAT OBSERVE THE UNEVEN COMBAT -
-- AND IN MOMENTS, THEY STAND REVEALED --
-- AS SOMETHING FAR, FAR MORE THAN HUMAN!
WHAT IN -- ?
WITCH-BEINGS, CAPTAIN AMERICA! I'VE FOUGHT THEM BEFORE!
THEY'RE CALLED SALEM'S SEVEN -
-- BUT I SAW THEM DIE!
AS HELLCAT DIED, SCARLET ONE? AND OTHERS BEFORE HER?
DEATH IS NOT THE BARRIER YOU THINK -- ESPECIALLY NOT FOR OUR DREAD MASTER!

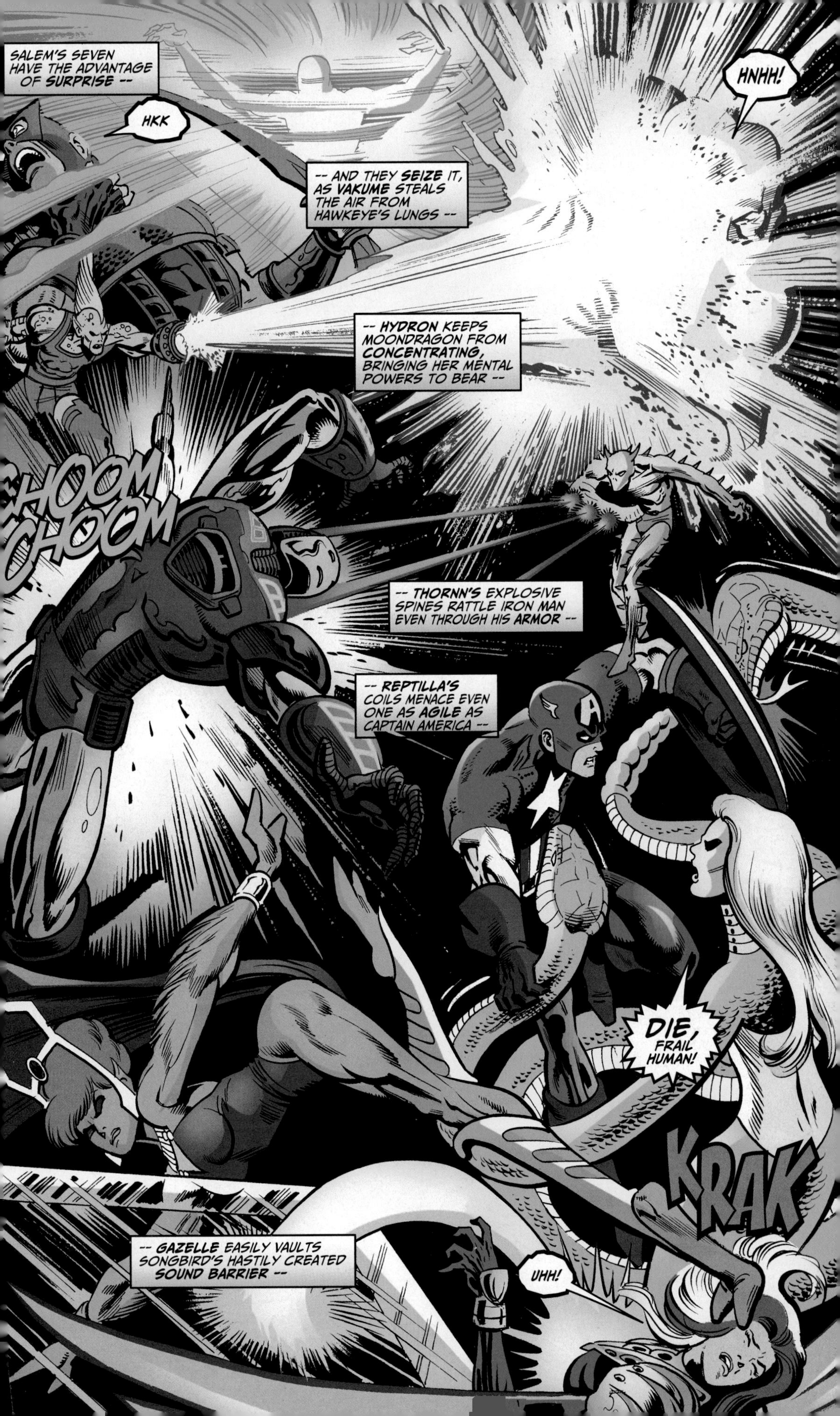
SALEM'S SEVEN HAVE THE ADVANTAGE OF SURPRISE --
HKK
HNHH!
-- AND THEY SEIZE IT, AS VAKUME STEALS THE AIR FROM HAWKEYE'S LUNGS --
-- HYDRON KEEPS MOONDRAGON FROM CONCENTRATING, BRINGING HER MENTAL POWERS TO BEAR --
CHOOM CHOOM
-- THORNN'S EXPLOSIVE SPINES RATTLE IRON MAN EVEN THROUGH HIS ARMOR --
-- REPTILLA'S COILS MENACE EVEN ONE AS AGILE AS CAPTAIN AMERICA --
DIE, FRAIL HUMAN!
KRAK
-- GAZELLE EASILY VAULTS SONGBIRD'S HASTILY CREATED SOUND BARRIER --
UHH!

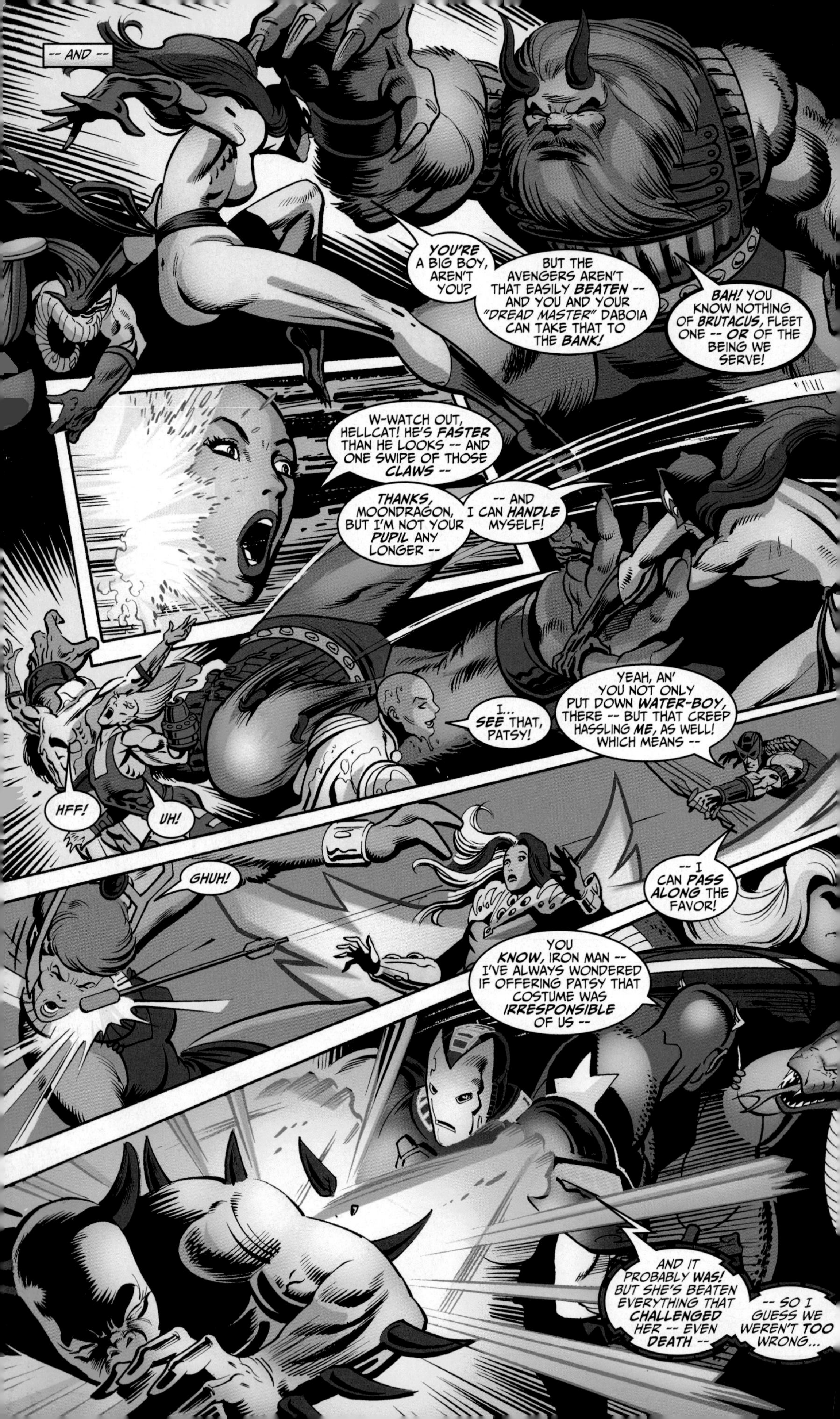
-- AND --
YOU'RE A BIG BOY, AREN'T YOU?
BUT THE AVENGERS AREN'T THAT EASILY BEATEN -- AND YOU AND YOUR "DREAD MASTER" DABOIA CAN TAKE THAT TO THE BANK!
BAH! YOU KNOW NOTHING OF BRUTACUS, FLEET ONE -- OR OF THE BEING WE SERVE!
W-WATCH OUT, HELLCAT! HE'S FASTER THAN HE LOOKS -- AND ONE SWIPE OF THOSE CLAWS --
THANKS, MOONDRAGON, BUT I'M NOT YOUR PUPIL ANY LONGER --
-- AND I CAN HANDLE MYSELF!
HFF!
UH!
I... SEE THAT, PATSY!
YEAH, AN' YOU NOT ONLY PUT DOWN WATER-BOY, THERE -- BUT THAT CREEP HASSLING ME, AS WELL! WHICH MEANS --
GHUH!
-- I CAN PASS ALONG THE FAVOR!
YOU KNOW, IRON MAN -- I'VE ALWAYS WONDERED IF OFFERING PATSY THAT COSTUME WAS IRRESPONSIBLE OF US --
AND IT PROBABLY WAS! BUT SHE'S BEATEN EVERYTHING THAT CHALLENGED HER -- EVEN DEATH --
-- SO I GUESS WE WEREN'T TOO WRONG...

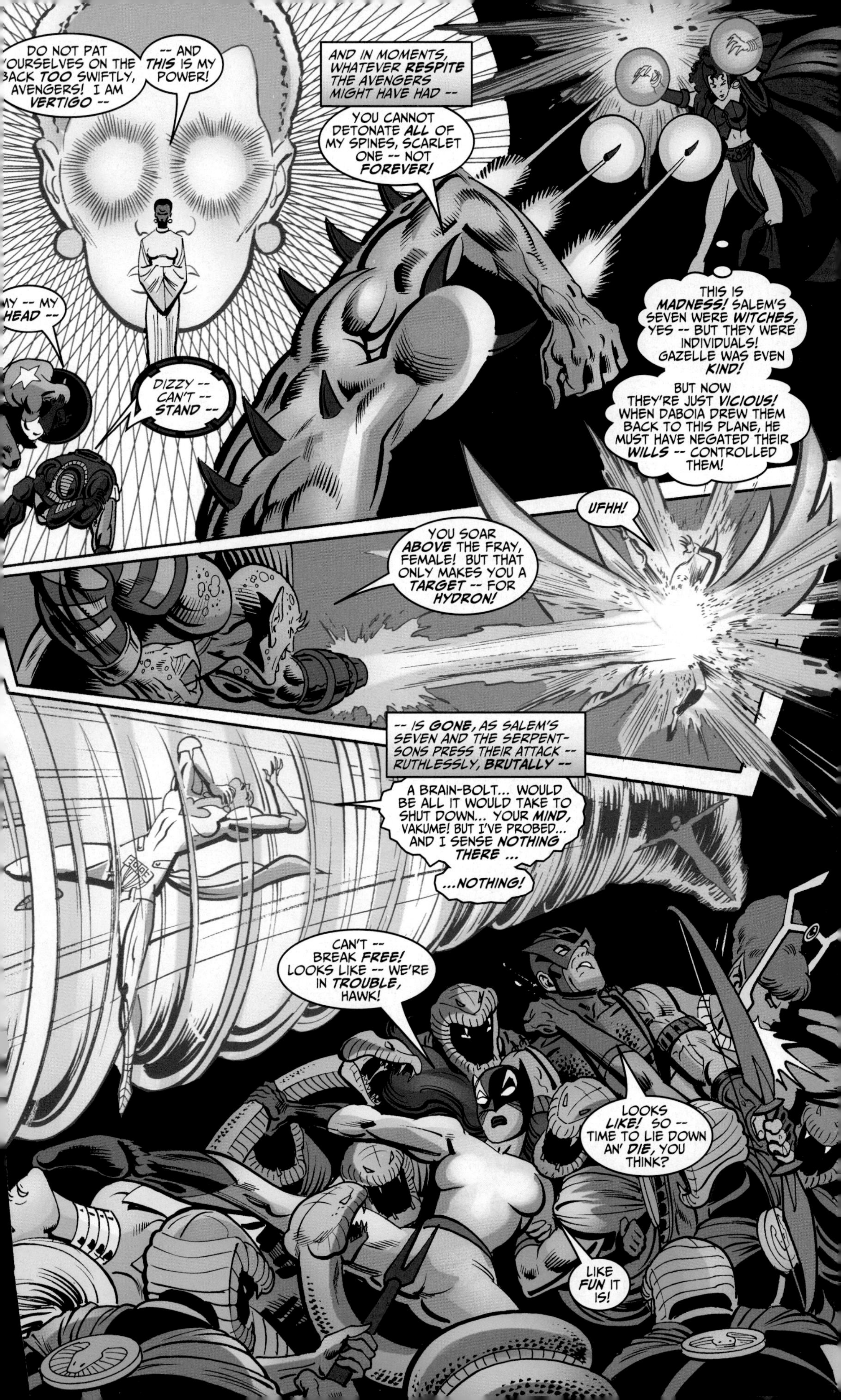
DO NOT PAT YOURSELVES ON THE BACK TOO SWIFTLY, AVENGERS! I AM VERTIGO --
-- AND THIS IS MY POWER!
MY -- MY HEAD --
DIZZY -- CAN'T -- STAND --
AND IN MOMENTS, WHATEVER RESPITE THE AVENGERS MIGHT HAVE HAD --
YOU CANNOT DETONATE ALL OF MY SPINES, SCARLET ONE -- NOT FOREVER!
THIS IS MADNESS! SALEM'S SEVEN WERE WITCHES, YES -- BUT THEY WERE INDIVIDUALS! GAZELLE WAS EVEN KIND!
BUT NOW THEY'RE JUST VICIOUS! WHEN DABOIA DREW THEM BACK TO THIS PLANE, HE MUST HAVE NEGATED THEIR WILLS -- CONTROLLED THEM!
YOU SOAR ABOVE THE FRAY, FEMALE! BUT THAT ONLY MAKES YOU A TARGET -- FOR HYDRON!
UFHH!
-- IS GONE, AS SALEM'S SEVEN AND THE SERPENT-SONS PRESS THEIR ATTACK -- RUTHLESSLY, BRUTALLY --
A BRAIN-BOLT... WOULD BE ALL IT WOULD TAKE TO SHUT DOWN... YOUR MIND, VAKUME! BUT I'VE PROBED... AND I SENSE NOTHING THERE ...
...NOTHING!
CAN'T -- BREAK FREE! LOOKS LIKE -- WE'RE IN TROUBLE, HAWK!
LOOKS LIKE! SO -- TIME TO LIE DOWN AN' DIE, YOU THINK?
LIKE FUN IT IS!

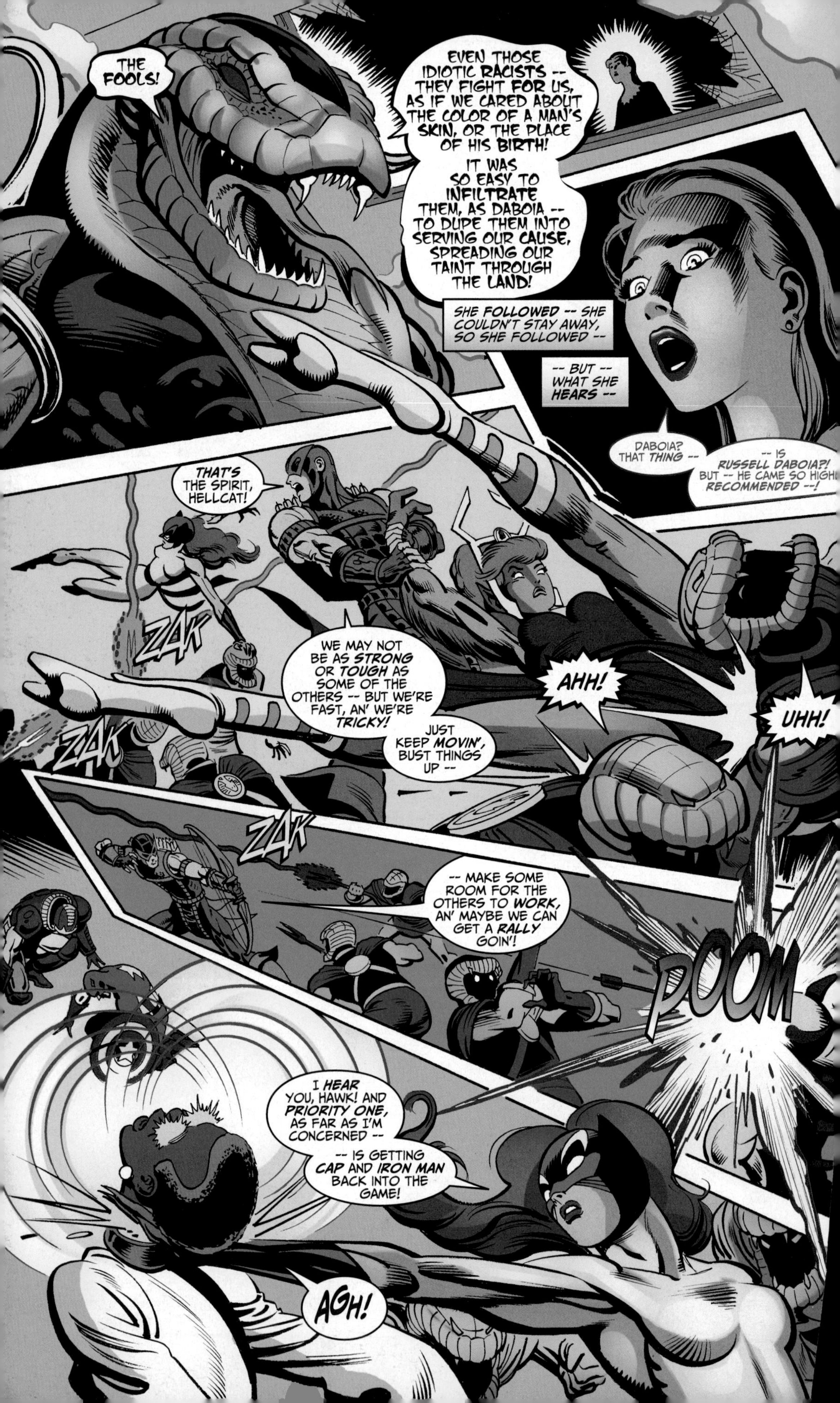
THE FOOLS!
EVEN THOSE IDIOTIC RACISTS -- THEY FIGHT FOR US, AS IF WE CARED ABOUT THE COLOR OF A MAN'S SKIN, OR THE PLACE OF HIS BIRTH!
IT WAS SO EASY TO INFILTRATE THEM, AS DABOIA -- TO DUPE THEM INTO SERVING OUR CAUSE, SPREADING OUR TAINT THROUGH THE LAND!
SHE FOLLOWED -- SHE COULDN'T STAY AWAY, SO SHE FOLLOWED --
-- BUT -- WHAT SHE HEARS --
DABOIA? THAT THING --
-- IS RUSSELL DABOIA?! BUT -- HE CAME SO HIGHLY RECOMMENDED --!
THAT'S THE SPIRIT, HELLCAT!
ZAK
WE MAY NOT BE AS STRONG OR TOUGH AS SOME OF THE OTHERS -- BUT WE'RE FAST, AN' WE'RE TRICKY!
JUST KEEP MOVIN', BUST THINGS UP --
AHH!
UHH!
ZAK
ZAK
-- MAKE SOME ROOM FOR THE OTHERS TO WORK, AN' MAYBE WE CAN GET A RALLY GOIN'!
POOM
I HEAR YOU, HAWK! AND PRIORITY ONE, AS FAR AS I'M CONCERNED --
-- IS GETTING CAP AND IRON MAN BACK INTO THE GAME!
AGH!

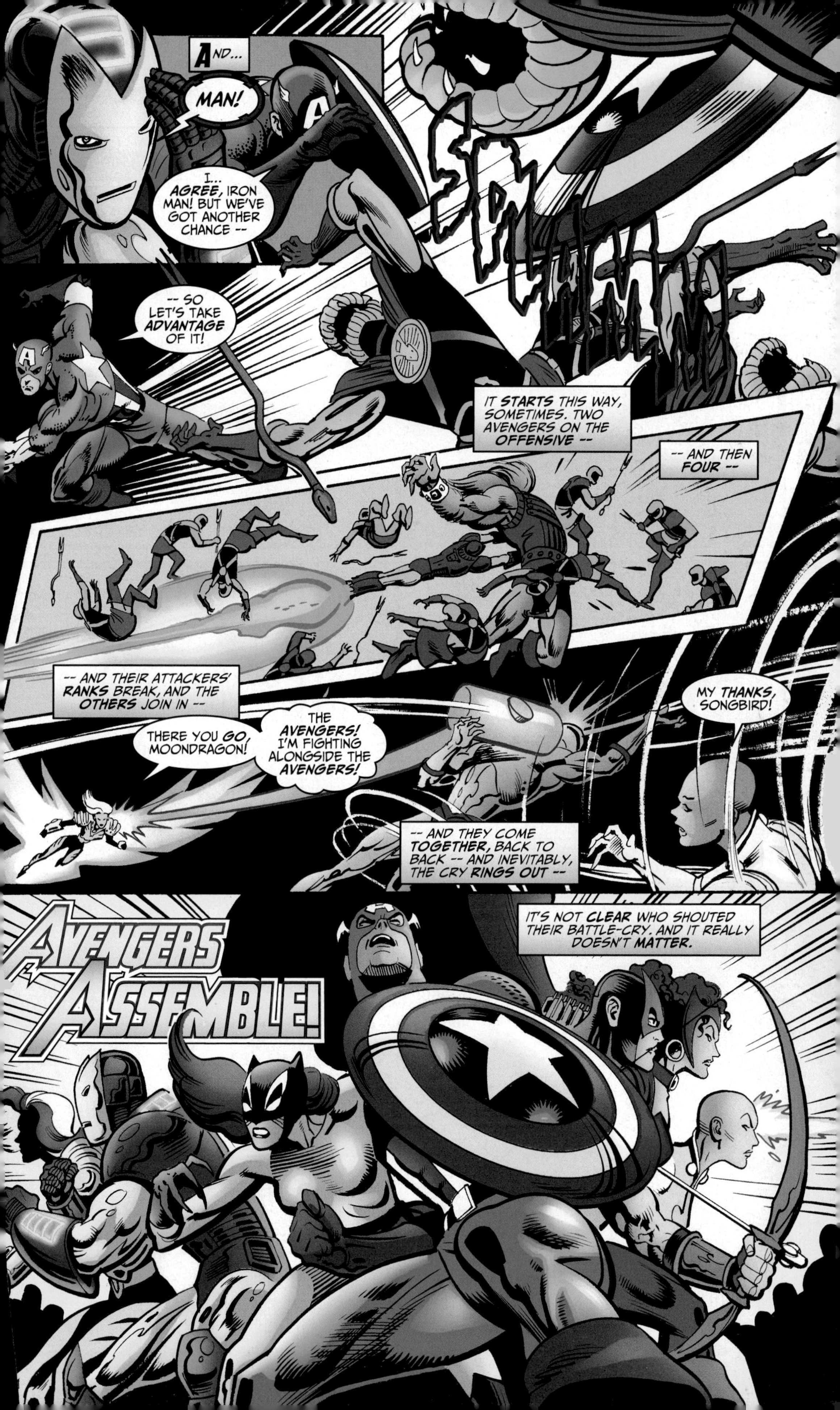
AND...
MAN!
I... AGREE, IRON MAN! BUT WE'VE GOT ANOTHER CHANCE --
-- SO LET'S TAKE ADVANTAGE OF IT!
IT STARTS THIS WAY, SOMETIMES. TWO AVENGERS ON THE OFFENSIVE --
-- AND THEN FOUR --
-- AND THEIR ATTACKERS' RANKS BREAK, AND THE OTHERS JOIN IN --
THERE YOU GO, MOONDRAGON!
THE AVENGERS! I'M FIGHTING ALONGSIDE THE AVENGERS!
MY THANKS, SONGBIRD!
-- AND THEY COME TOGETHER, BACK TO BACK -- AND INEVITABLY, THE CRY RINGS OUT --
AVENGERS ASSEMBLE!
IT'S NOT CLEAR WHO SHOUTED THEIR BATTLE-CRY. AND IT REALLY DOESN'T MATTER.

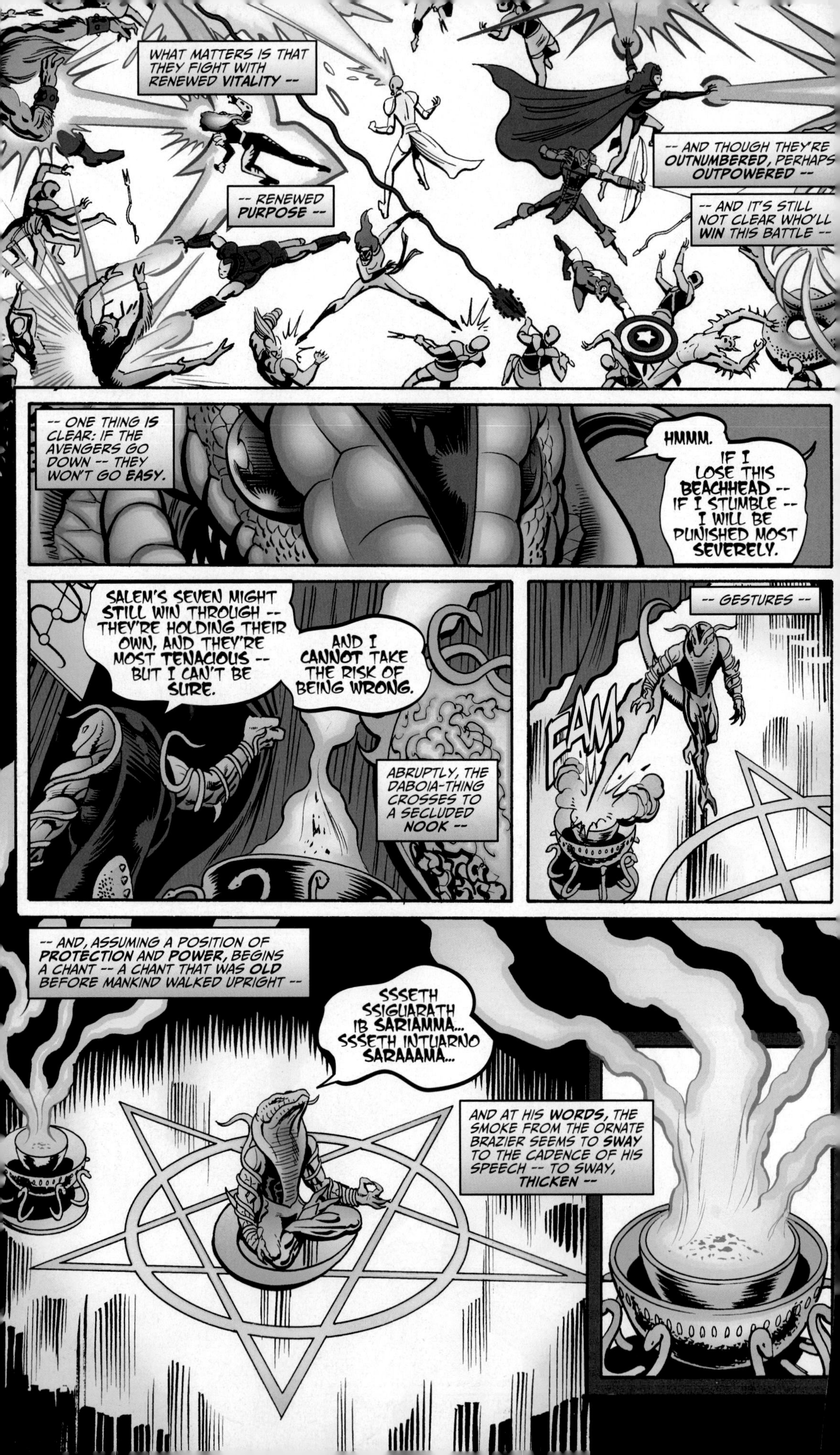

WHAT MATTERS IS THAT THEY FIGHT WITH RENEWED VITALITY --
-- RENEWED PURPOSE --
-- AND THOUGH THEY'RE OUTNUMBERED, PERHAPS OUTPOWERED --
-- AND IT'S STILL NOT CLEAR WHO'LL WIN THIS BATTLE --
-- ONE THING IS CLEAR: IF THE AVENGERS GO DOWN -- THEY WON'T GO EASY.
HMMM.
IF I LOSE THIS BEACHHEAD -- IF I STUMBLE -- I WILL BE PUNISHED MOST SEVERELY.
SALEM'S SEVEN MIGHT STILL WIN THROUGH -- THEY'RE HOLDING THEIR OWN, AND THEY'RE MOST TENACIOUS -- BUT I CAN'T BE SURE.
AND I CANNOT TAKE THE RISK OF BEING WRONG.
ABRUPTLY, THE DABOIA-THING CROSSES TO A SECLUDED NOOK --
-- GESTURES --
FAM
-- AND, ASSUMING A POSITION OF PROTECTION AND POWER, BEGINS A CHANT -- A CHANT THAT WAS OLD BEFORE MANKIND WALKED UPRIGHT --
SSSETH SSIGUARATH IB SARIAMMA... SSSETH INTUARNO SARAAAMA...
AND AT HIS WORDS, THE SMOKE FROM THE ORNATE BRAZIER SEEMS TO SWAY TO THE CADENCE OF HIS SPEECH -- TO SWAY, THICKEN --

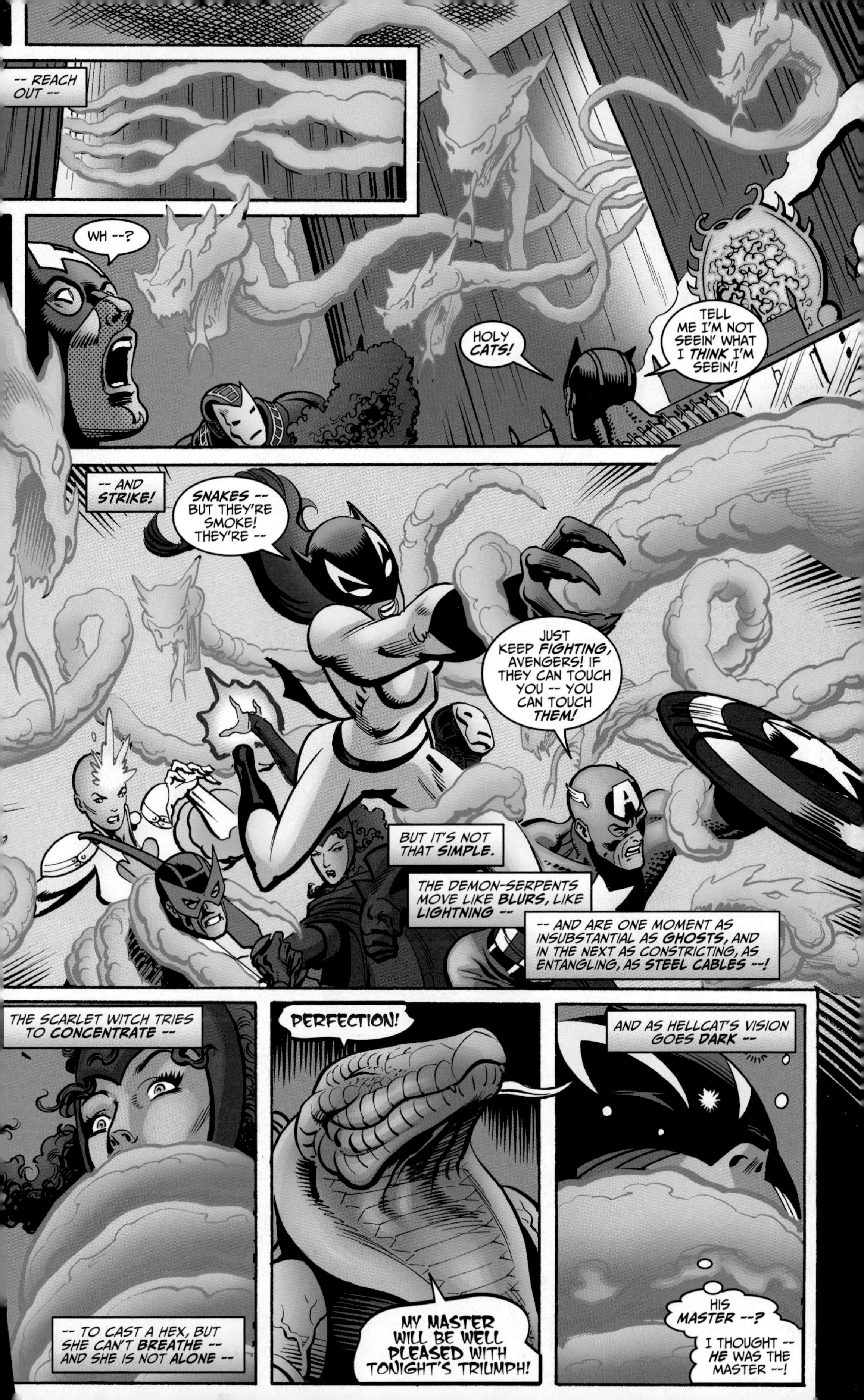

-- REACH OUT --
WH --?
HOLY CATS!
TELL ME I'M NOT SEEIN' WHAT I THINK I'M SEEIN'!
-- AND STRIKE!
SNAKES -- BUT THEY'RE SMOKE! THEY'RE --
JUST KEEP FIGHTING, AVENGERS! IF THEY CAN TOUCH YOU -- YOU CAN TOUCH THEM!
BUT IT'S NOT THAT SIMPLE.
THE DEMON-SERPENTS MOVE LIKE BLURS, LIKE LIGHTNING --
-- AND ARE ONE MOMENT AS INSUBSTANTIAL AS GHOSTS, AND IN THE NEXT AS CONSTRICTING, AS ENTANGLING, AS STEEL CABLES --!
THE SCARLET WITCH TRIES TO CONCENTRATE --
-- TO CAST A HEX, BUT SHE CAN'T BREATHE -- AND SHE IS NOT ALONE --
PERFECTION!
MY MASTER WILL BE WELL PLEASED WITH TONIGHT'S TRIUMPH!
AND AS HELLCAT'S VISION GOES DARK --
HIS MASTER --?
I THOUGHT -- HE WAS THE MASTER --!

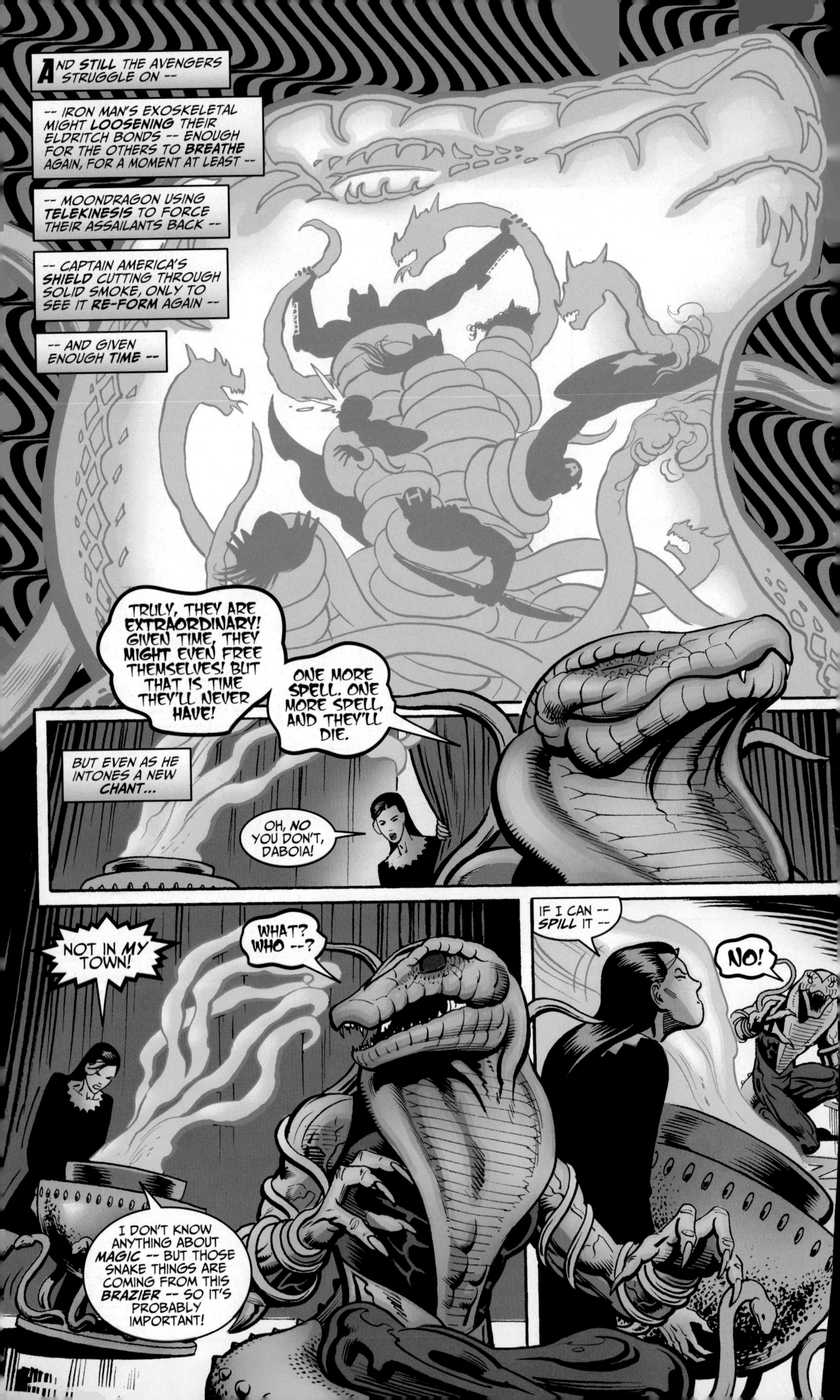
AND STILL THE AVENGERS STRUGGLE ON --
-- IRON MAN'S EXOSKELETAL MIGHT LOOSENING THEIR ELDRITCH BONDS -- ENOUGH FOR THE OTHERS TO BREATHE AGAIN, FOR A MOMENT AT LEAST --
-- MOONDRAGON USING TELEKINESIS TO FORCE THEIR ASSAILANTS BACK --
-- CAPTAIN AMERICA'S SHIELD CUTTING THROUGH SOLID SMOKE, ONLY TO SEE IT RE-FORM AGAIN --
-- AND GIVEN ENOUGH TIME --
TRULY, THEY ARE EXTRAORDINARY! GIVEN TIME, THEY MIGHT EVEN FREE THEMSELVES! BUT THAT IS TIME THEY'LL NEVER HAVE!
ONE MORE SPELL. ONE MORE SPELL, AND THEY'LL DIE.
BUT EVEN AS HE INTONES A NEW CHANT...
OH, NO YOU DON'T, DABOIA!
NOT IN MY TOWN!
WHAT? WHO --?
I DON'T KNOW ANYTHING ABOUT MAGIC -- BUT THOSE SNAKE THINGS ARE COMING FROM THIS BRAZIER -- SO IT'S PROBABLY IMPORTANT!
IF I CAN -- SPILL IT --
NO!

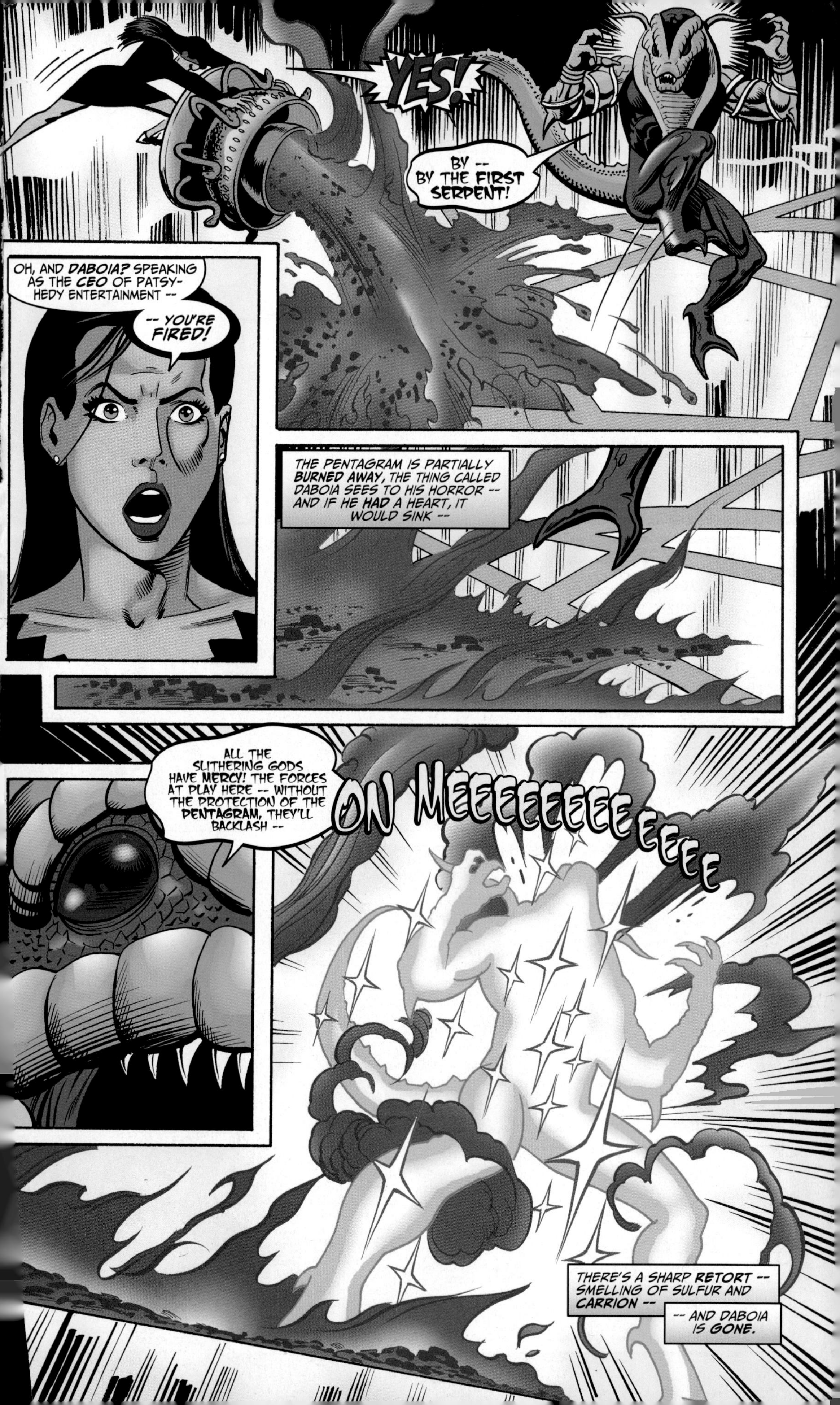
YES!
BY -- BY THE FIRST SERPENT!
OH, AND DABOIA? SPEAKING AS THE CEO OF PATSY-HEDY ENTERTAINMENT --
-- YOU'RE FIRED!
THE PENTAGRAM IS PARTIALLY BURNED AWAY, THE THING CALLED DABOIA SEES TO HIS HORROR -- AND IF HE HAD A HEART, IT WOULD SINK --
ALL THE SLITHERING GODS HAVE MERCY! THE FORCES AT PLAY HERE -- WITHOUT THE PROTECTION OF THE PENTAGRAM, THEY'LL BACKLASH --
ON MEEEEEEEEEEEEE
THERE'S A SHARP RETORT -- SMELLING OF SULFUR AND CARRION --
-- AND DABOIA IS GONE.

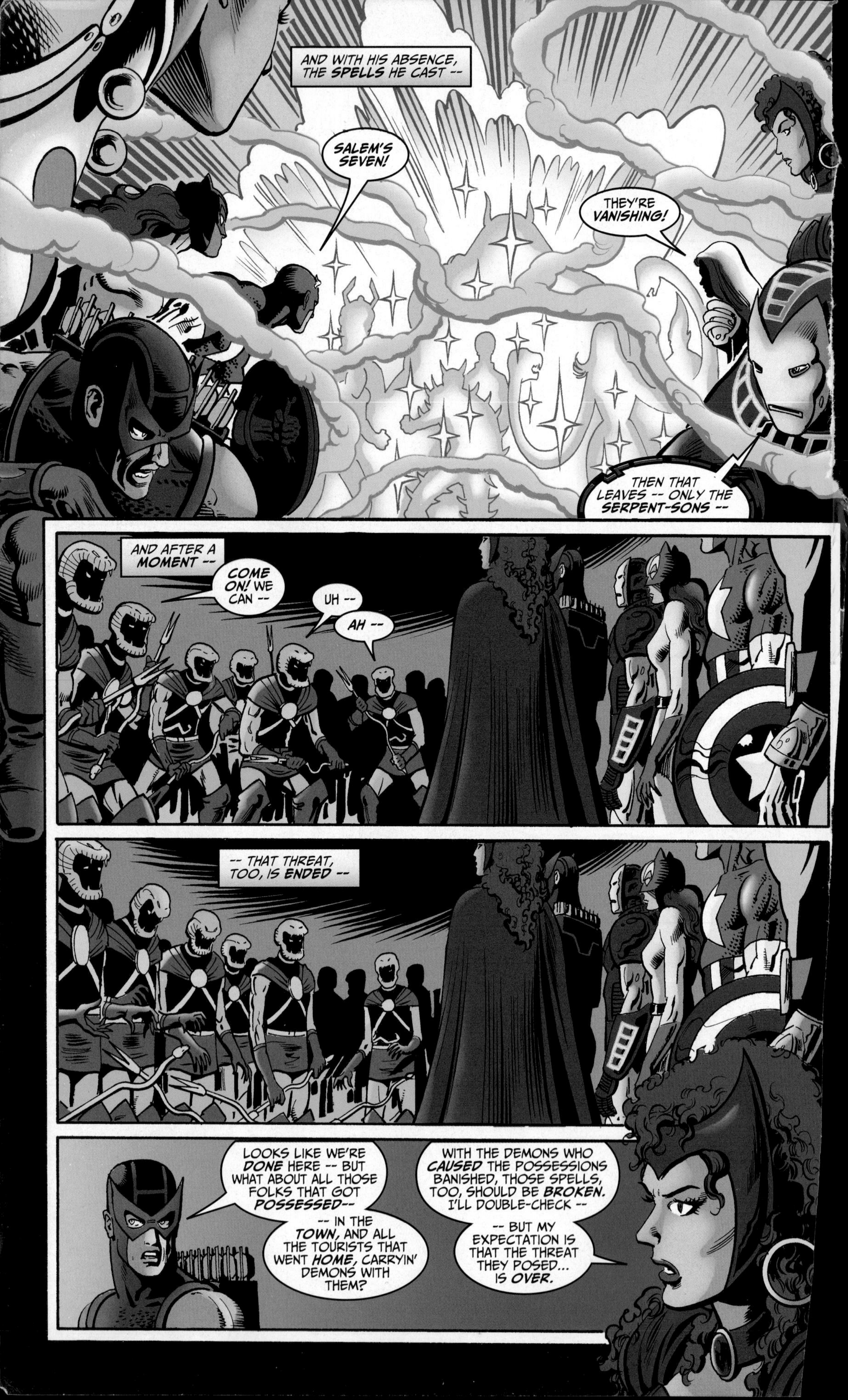
AND WITH HIS ABSENCE, THE SPELLS HE CAST --
SALEM'S SEVEN!
THEY'RE VANISHING!
THEN THAT LEAVES -- ONLY THE SERPENT-SONS --
AND AFTER A MOMENT --
COME ON! WE CAN --
UH --
AH --
-- THAT THREAT, TOO, IS ENDED --
LOOKS LIKE WE'RE DONE HERE -- BUT WHAT ABOUT ALL THOSE FOLKS THAT GOT POSSESSED--
-- IN THE TOWN, AND ALL THE TOURISTS THAT WENT HOME, CARRYIN' DEMONS WITH THEM?
WITH THE DEMONS WHO CAUSED THE POSSESSIONS BANISHED, THOSE SPELLS, TOO, SHOULD BE BROKEN. I'LL DOUBLE-CHECK --
-- BUT MY EXPECTATION IS THAT THE THREAT THEY POSED... IS OVER.

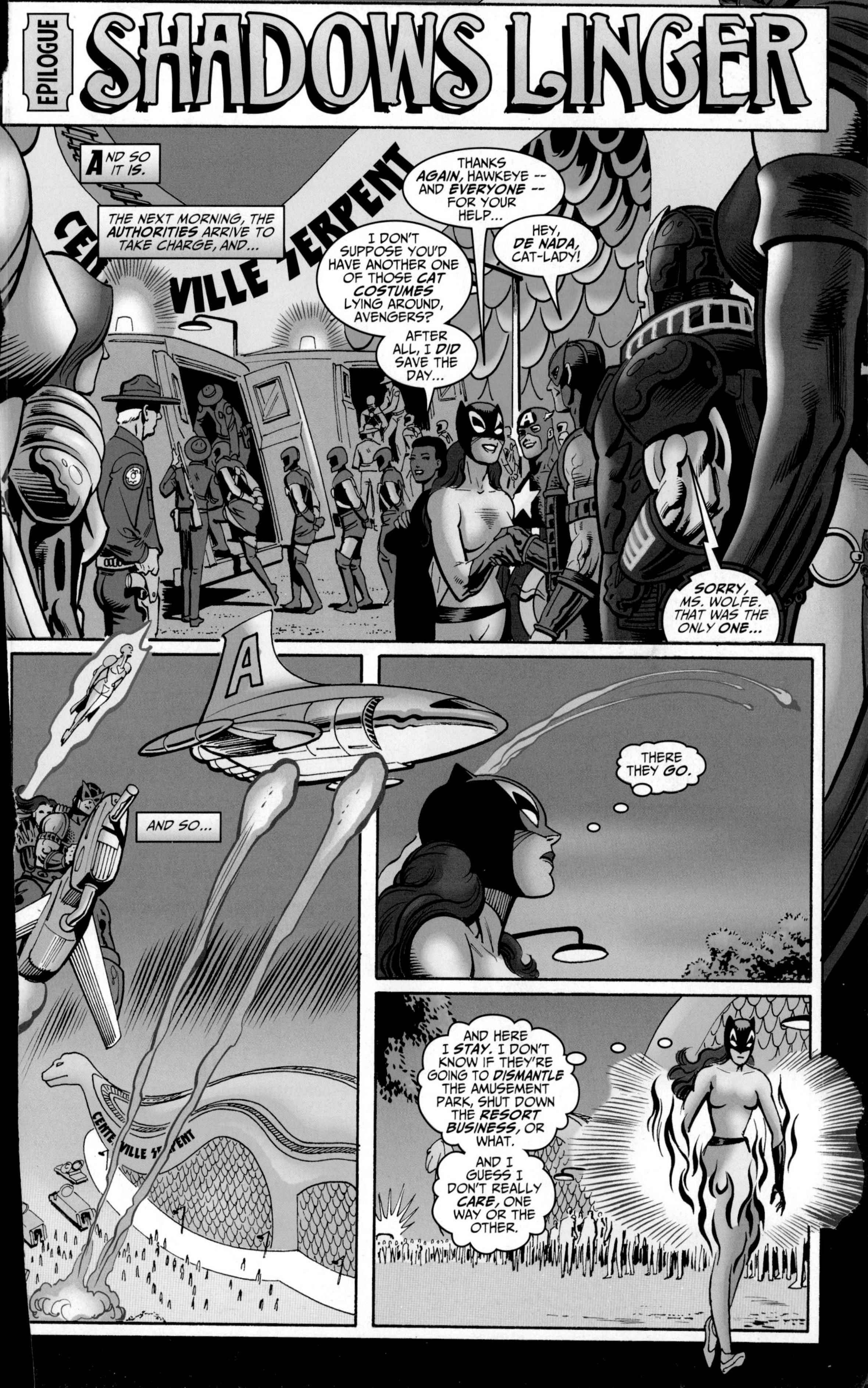
EPILOGUE
SHADOWS LINGER
AND SO IT IS.
THE NEXT MORNING, THE AUTHORITIES ARRIVE TO TAKE CHARGE, AND...
CENTERVILLE SERPENT
THANKS AGAIN, HAWKEYE -- AND EVERYONE -- FOR YOUR HELP...
I DON'T SUPPOSE YOU'D HAVE ANOTHER ONE OF THOSE CAT COSTUMES LYING AROUND, AVENGERS?
AFTER ALL, I DID SAVE THE DAY...
HEY, DE NADA, CAT-LADY!
SORRY, MS. WOLFE. THAT WAS THE ONLY ONE...
A
AND SO...
CENTERVILLE SERPENT
THERE THEY GO.
AND HERE I STAY. I DON'T KNOW IF THEY'RE GOING TO DISMANTLE THE AMUSEMENT PARK, SHUT DOWN THE RESORT BUSINESS, OR WHAT.
AND I GUESS I DON'T REALLY CARE, ONE WAY OR THE OTHER.

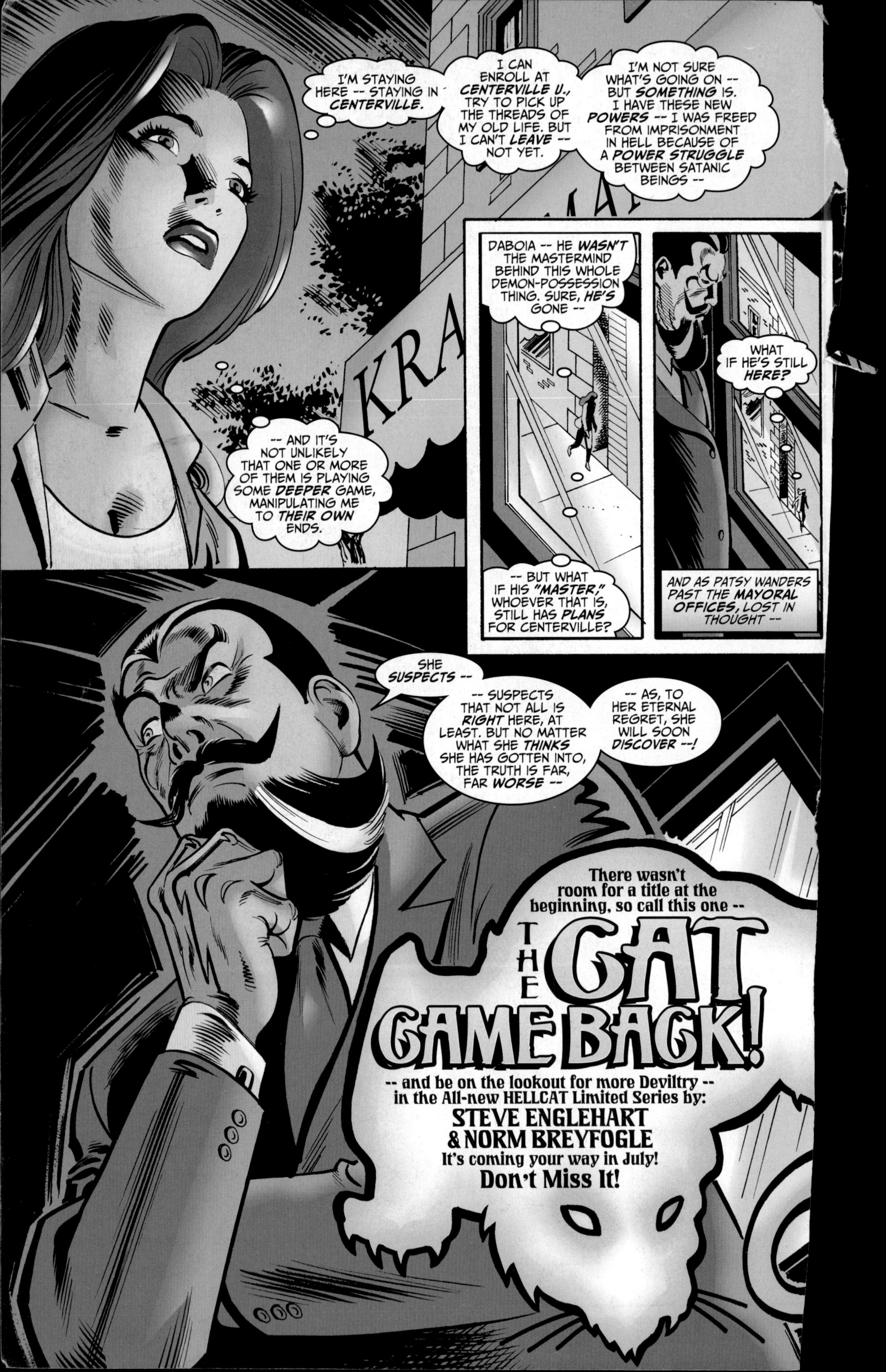
I'M STAYING HERE -- STAYING IN CENTERVILLE.
I CAN ENROLL AT CENTERVILLE U., TRY TO PICK UP THE THREADS OF MY OLD LIFE. BUT I CAN'T LEAVE -- NOT YET.
I'M NOT SURE WHAT'S GOING ON -- BUT SOMETHING IS. I HAVE THESE NEW POWERS -- I WAS FREED FROM IMPRISONMENT IN HELL BECAUSE OF A POWER STRUGGLE BETWEEN SATANIC BEINGS --
KRA
-- AND IT'S NOT UNLIKELY THAT ONE OR MORE OF THEM IS PLAYING SOME DEEPER GAME, MANIPULATING ME TO THEIR OWN ENDS.
DABOIA -- HE WASN'T THE MASTERMIND BEHIND THIS WHOLE DEMON-POSSESSION THING. SURE, HE'S GONE --
-- BUT WHAT IF HIS "MASTER," WHOEVER THAT IS, STILL HAS PLANS FOR CENTERVILLE?
WHAT IF HE'S STILL HERE?
AND AS PATSY WANDERS PAST THE MAYORAL OFFICES, LOST IN THOUGHT --
SHE SUSPECTS --
-- SUSPECTS THAT NOT ALL IS RIGHT HERE, AT LEAST. BUT NO MATTER WHAT SHE THINKS SHE HAS GOTTEN INTO, THE TRUTH IS FAR, FAR WORSE --
-- AS, TO HER ETERNAL REGRET, SHE WILL SOON DISCOVER --!
There wasn't room for a title at the beginning, so call this one --
THE CAT CAME BACK!
-- and be on the lookout for more Deviltry -- in the All-new HELLCAT Limited Series by:
STEVE ENGLEHART & NORM BREYFOGLE
It's coming your way in July!
Don't Miss It!

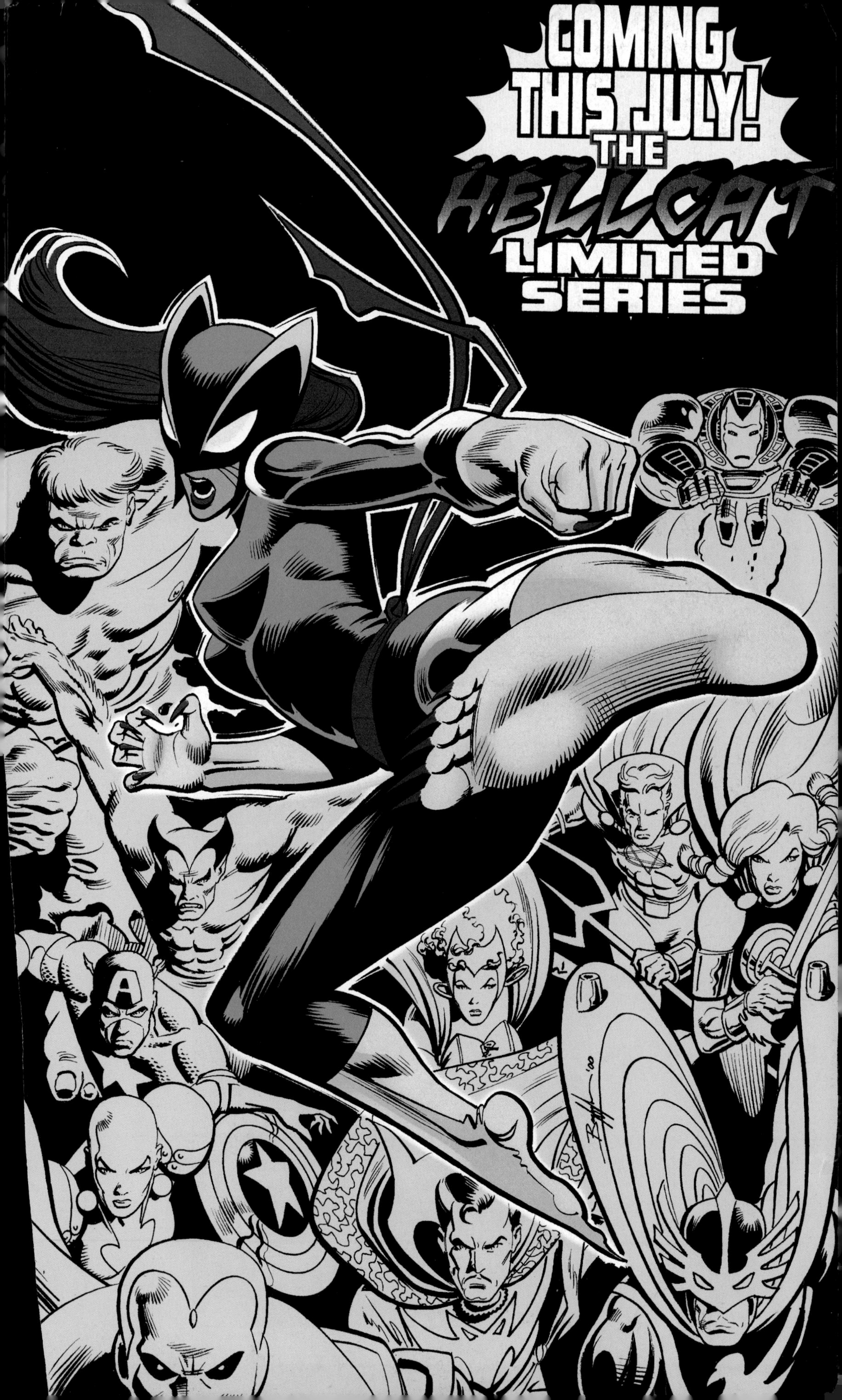
COMING THIS JULY!
THE HELLCAT LIMITED SERIES

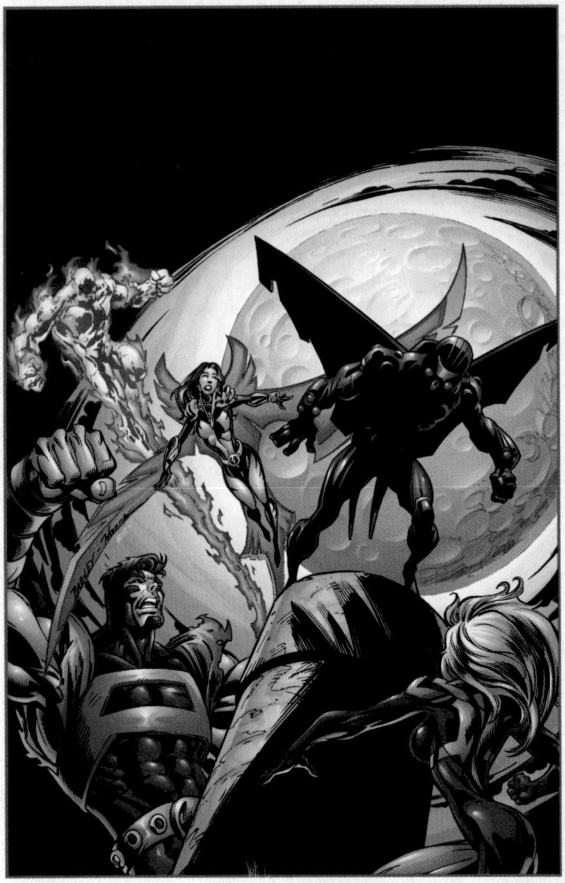

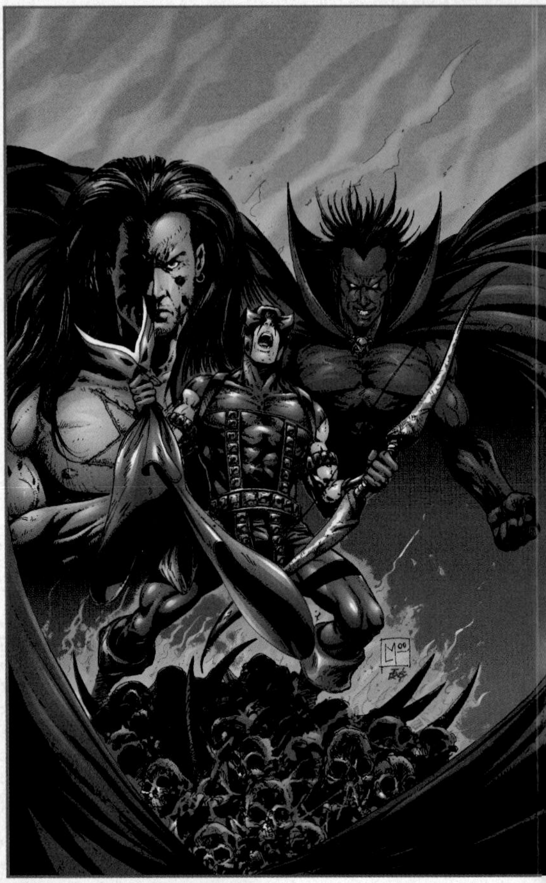

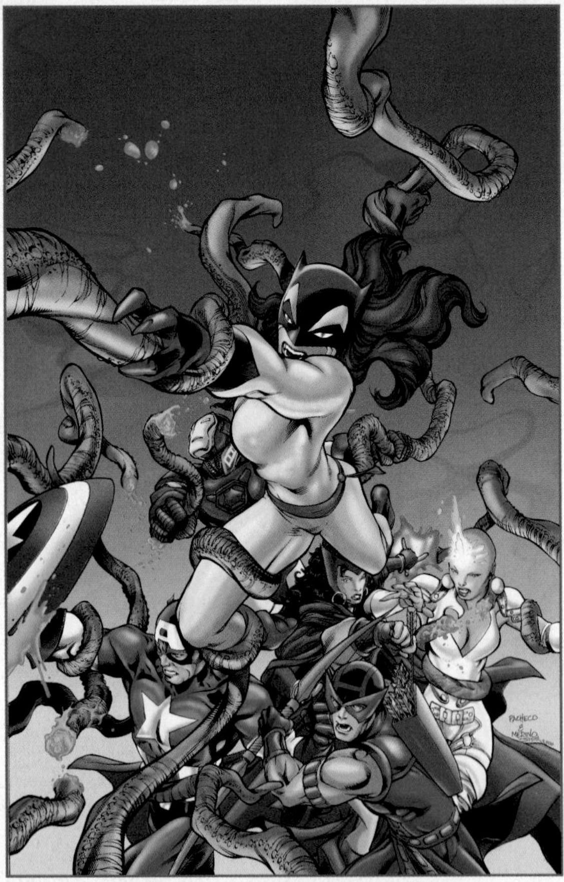

CONTEST · CONTEST

Wanna win a prize? Here's what you gotta do: Check out the double page spread in this issue that introduces the 25 members of the new, deadly Masters of Evil. Then, write down on a piece of paper each villain's name and where he/she made their first comic book appearance (we're talking title of the book and issue number). Easy, right? Not as easy as you think. Mail in your answers to the address at the bottom of this letters page. The first person with ALL the correct answers (based on postmark date on the envelope) will be the winner. What do you win? A slew of stuff, including a copy of the original plot to the issue, signed by Kurt Busiek; a copy of the THUNDERBOLTS: MARVEL'S MOST WANTED TPB, and a copy of this very issue, THUNDERBOLTS #25, autographed by 25 actual Marvel Comics professionals! Clear? Excellent! The game is afoot!

CONTEST · CONTEST

And now, the legal stuff...
No purchase necessary. Contest is open to anyone except employees of Marvel Enterprises, Inc., and their immediate families. Print your name, address, city, state, and zip code on your entry. Enter as many times as you like (although you only need to be right once...and first). Mail each entry separately to "Rap Sheet Contest" c/o Marvel Comics, 387 Park Avenue South, New York, NY 10016. All entries become property of Marvel Enterprises and will not be returned. All taxes (federal, state, and local, if any) will be the responsibility of the prize winner. Prize is awarded in the name of the contest winner and is non-transferable. Offer void where prohibited, regulated or restricted by law in a manner inconsistent with the purposes of the rules hereof. *Contest ends as soon as first correct entry is received.* Marvel is not responsible for lost, late, misdirected, or damaged entries. Winner will be notified within two weeks of receipt of correct entry. If an entrant, having been declared as a winner, does not accept the prize or the prize notification is undeliverable, another entry will be selected. In the event that a prize is not available or it becomes impossible for the sponsor to award the prize which has been designated, the sponsor retains the right to substitute a prize or product of equal value to the winner. Determination of whether a prize or product is of equal value is in the sole discretion of the sponsor. Winner will be announced in a future THUNDERBOLTS letters page.

DO YOU WANT ANSWERS? YOU THINK YOU'RE ENTITLED. DO YOU WANT ANSWERS? YOU WANT THE TRUTH! YOU CAN'T HANDLE THE TRUTH!!

But can you handle the correct answers to the THUNDEREBOLTS #25 contest? Well, here they are, all 25 Masters of Evil and their first appearances:

Aqueduct — Ghost Rider #23 (as Water Wizard)
Bison — Thunderstrike #13
Blackwing — Daredevil #118
Boomerang — Tales to Astonish #81
Cardinal — New Warriors #28
Constrictor — Incredible Hulk #212
Crimson Cowl — Thunderbolts #3
Cyclone — T-Bolts #3
Dragonfly — Uncanny X-Men #94
Eel — Power Man & Iron Fist #92
Flying Tiger — Spider-Woman #40
Icemasater — "Human Torch in Icemaster Cometh", Hostess Fruit Pie Ad, found in Avengers #191 (and other books dated cover month January of 1980)
Joystick — Amazing Scarlet Spider #2
Klaw — Fantastic Four #53
Lodestone — (mentioned) Darkhawk #6, (appears) Darkhawk #7
Man-Ape — Avengers #62
Man-Killer — Marvel Team-Up #8
Quicksand — Thor #392
Scorcher — Untold Tales of Spider-Man #1
Shatterfist — Thor #440
Shockwave — Master of Kung Fu #60
Slyde — Amazing Spider-Man #272
Sunstroke — West Coast Avengers #17
Supercharger — Amazing Fantasy #17
Tiger Shark — Sub-Mariner #5

THUNDERBOLTS #25* CONTEST ANNOUNCEMENT, AND ANSWER KEY FROM *THUNDERBOLTS #30

***MARVEL CATALOG: FEBRUARY 1999* ARTICLE**

T-BOLTS VS. MASTERS OF EVIL: SHOWDOWN!

THUNDERBOLTS readers hoping to catch their breath after the latest hairpin turn on Kurt Busiek's wild ride may have to wait a few more months. Just a stone's throw away from this month's pivotal Avengers face-off in THUNDERBOLTS #22, the team's world gets turned on its ear, again, in the special double-sized T-BOLTS #25, an issue that culminates the title's second big year-long epic storyline.

In typical Busiek-like fashion, the writer isn't giving away much, but he does offer a few hints as what to expect. "The T-Bolts have faced their leadership crisis (and they're not yet 100% sure they like the results) just in time for the big showdown with the Masters of Evil," offered Busiek. "Readers will get to see a global crisis, with catastrophe everywhere — and, we expect, cameos by Marvel heroes around the globe — and the T-Bolts as the only ones in position to do anything about it. But they're outnumbered and outgunned, and unless they manage to come up with a solution, it'll be the world that pays the price. Plus, we'll settle some questions about the team's immediate future, we'll see the Crimson Cowl unmasked, and more!"

For Busiek, celebrating the title's 25th issue is of special importance in times sometimes unkind to new ideas. "It's gratifying to hit #25, especially since some of the books we launched alongside didn't make it this far," explained the writer. "It's a testimony, I think, to the loyalty of the T-BOLTS fans, who've supported a young book far more steadily than we had any right to expect. We're delighted we've been able to inspire such loyalty, and I hope readers will be just as committed to the book over the next 25 issues!"

THUNDERBOLTS #25 is on sale February 17th.

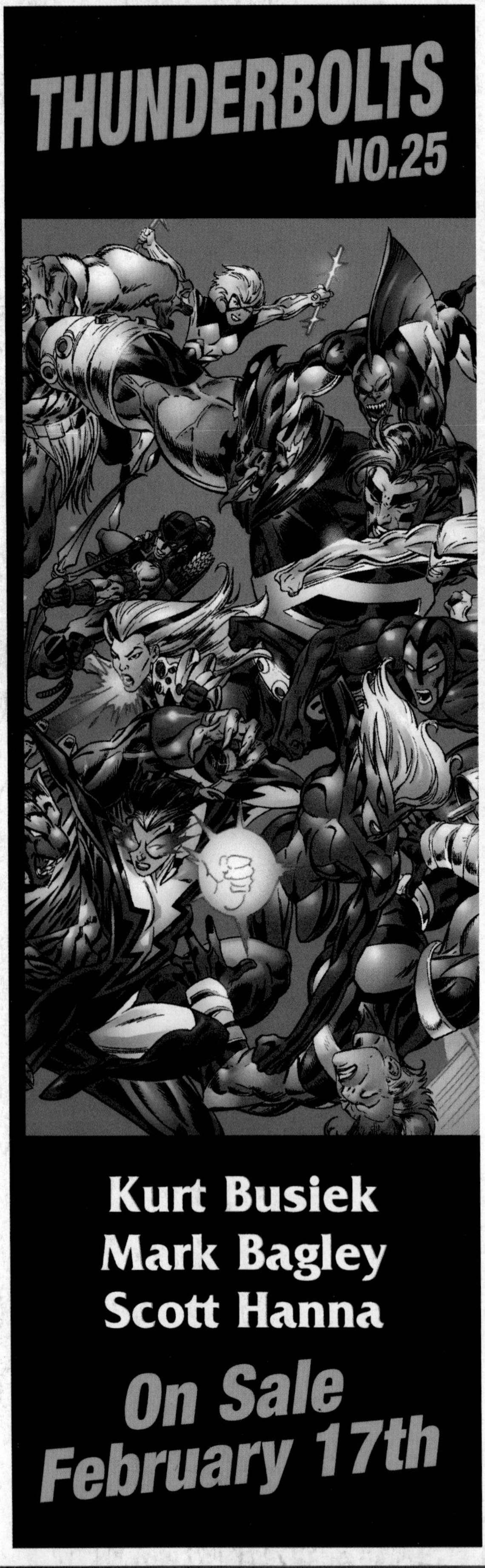
THUNDERBOLTS
NO.25
Kurt Busiek
Mark Bagley
Scott Hanna
On Sale
February 17th

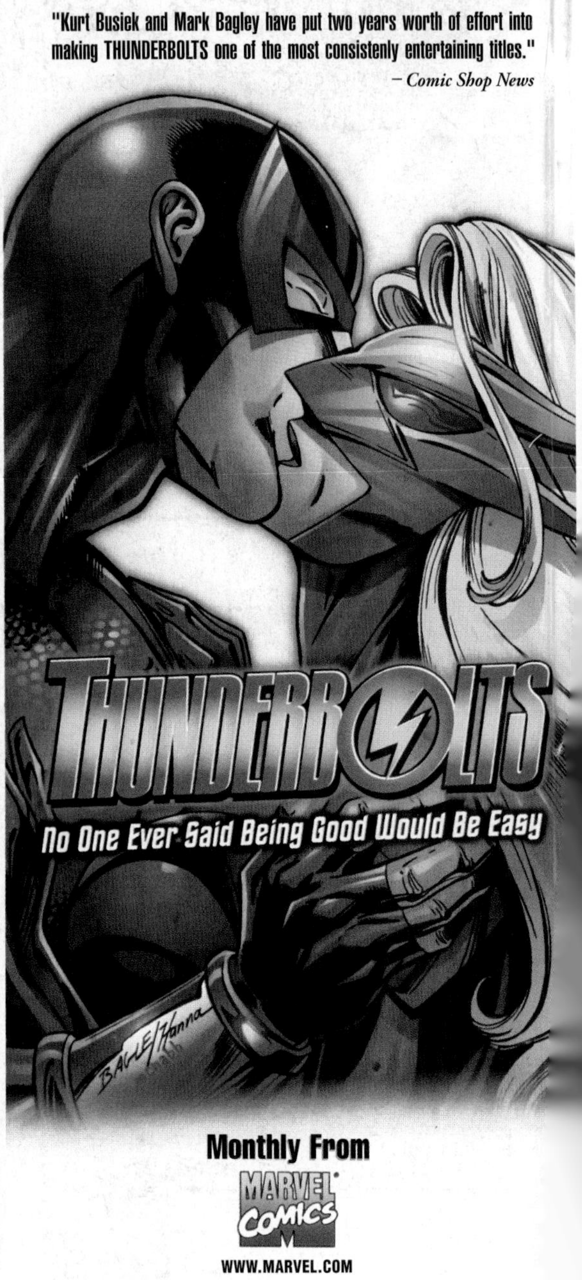
"Kurt Busiek and Mark Bagley have put two years worth of effort into making THUNDERBOLTS one of the most consistenly entertaining titles."
– Comic Shop News
THUNDERBOLTS
No One Ever Said Being Good Would Be Easy
Monthly From
MARVEL COMICS
WWW.MARVEL.COM

▲ *THUNDERBOLTS #30*
HOUSE AD BY
MARK BAGLEY,
SCOTT HANNA
& MARK MCNABB

◀ *THUNDERBOLTS #25*
RETAILER AD BY
MARK BAGLEY

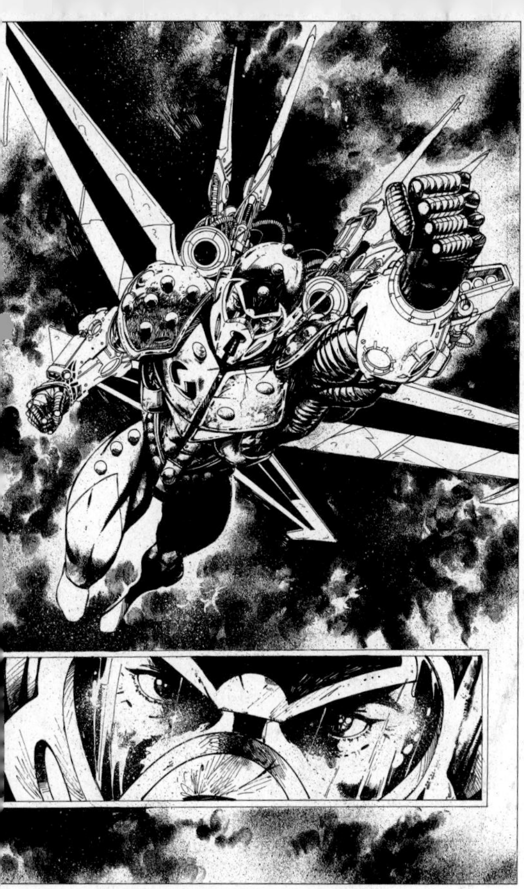

THUNDERBOLTS #26, PAGE 3
ART BY LEONARDO MANCO

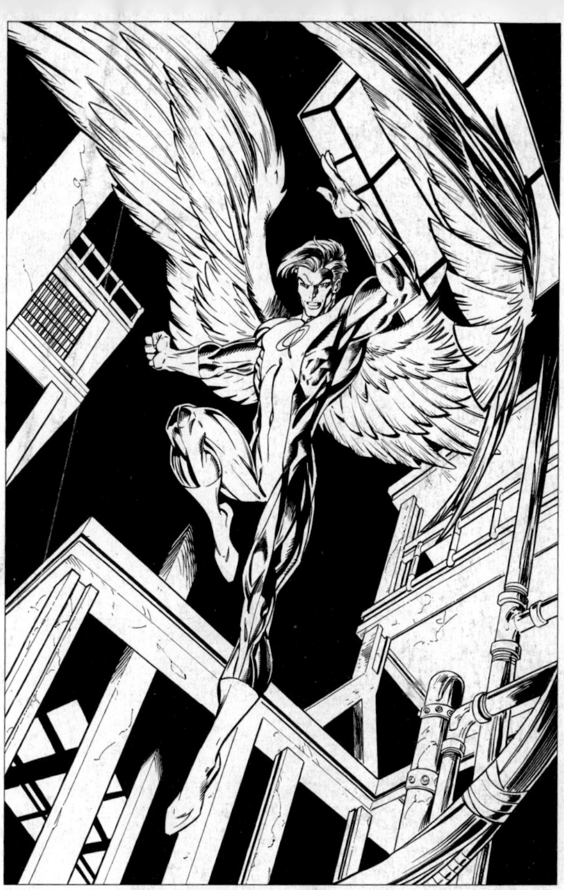

THUNDERBOLTS #27, PAGE 15
ART BY MARK BAGLEY & SCOTT HANNA

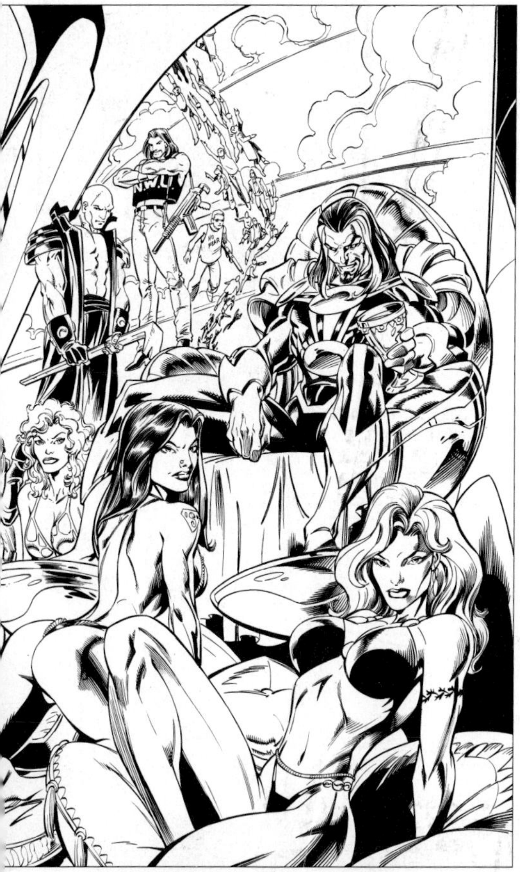

THUNDERBOLTS #27, PAGE 22
ART BY MARK BAGLEY & SCOTT HANNA

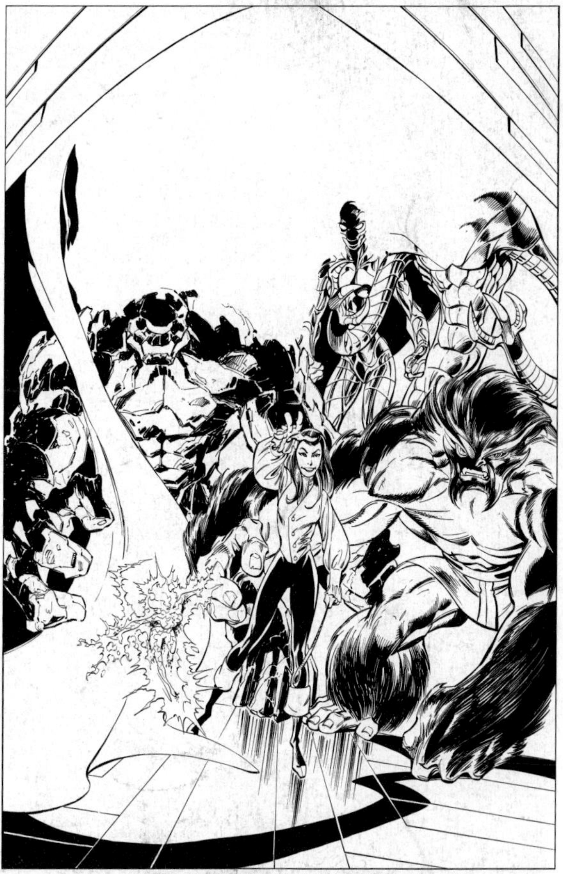

THUNDERBOLTS #31, PAGE 15
ART BY MARK BAGLEY & SCOTT HANNA

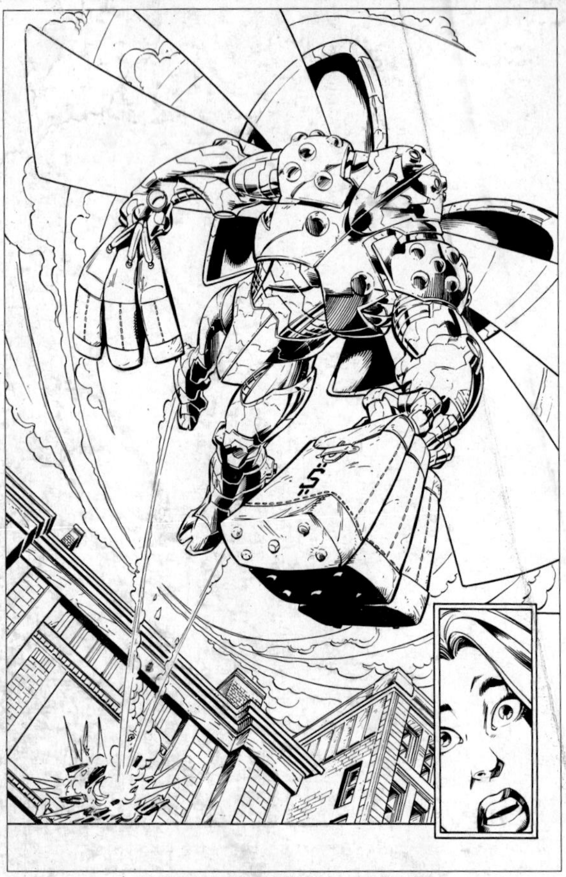

THUNDERBOLTS #33, PAGE 20
ART BY MARK BAGLEY & SCOTT HANNA

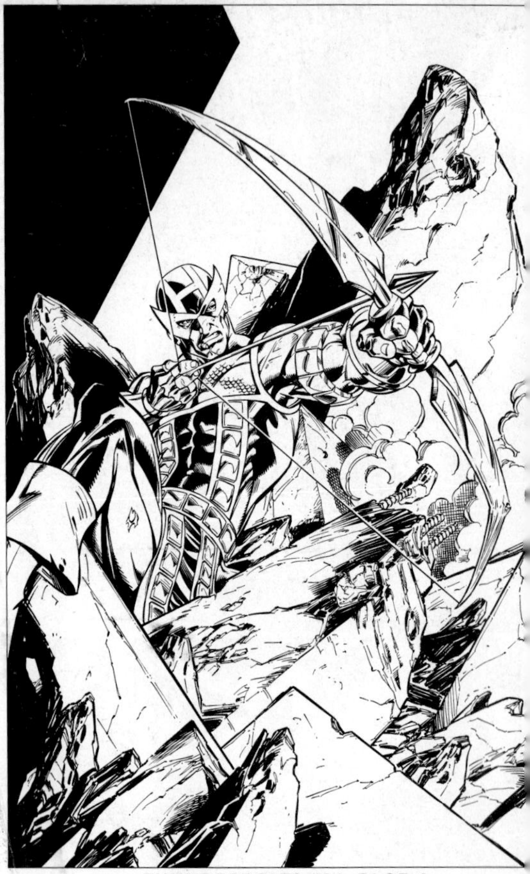

THUNDERBOLTS #34, PAGE 1
ART BY MARK BAGLEY & SCOTT HANNA

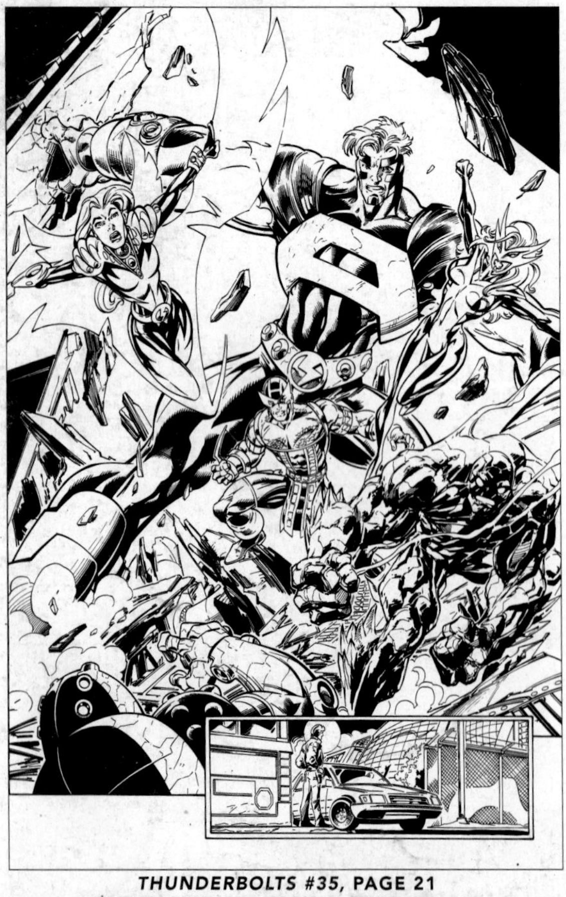

THUNDERBOLTS #35, PAGE 21
ART BY MARK BAGLEY & GREG ADAMS

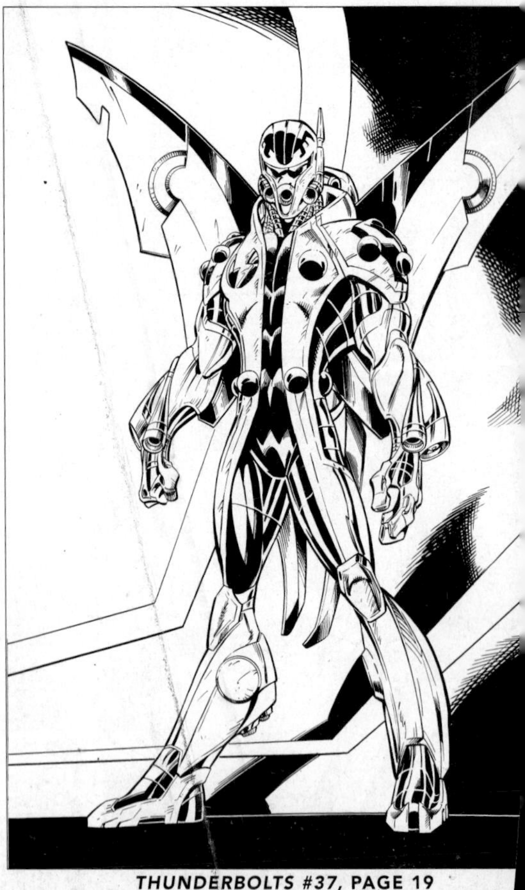

THUNDERBOLTS #37, PAGE 19
ART BY MARK BAGLEY & SCOTT HANNA